PRAISE FOR

DESTINY *and* POWER

Named one of the best books of the year by
THE NEW YORK TIMES BOOK REVIEW, THE WASHINGTON POST,
TIME, *and* NPR

"*Destiny and Power* reflects the qualities of both subject and biographer: judicious, balanced, deliberative, with a deep appreciation of history and the personalities who shape it. If Meacham is sometimes polite to a fault, *Destiny and Power* does not suffer for it. His kinder, gentler approach succeeds in making George H. W. Bush a more sympathetic—and more complex—figure than if the former president had written his own doorstopper after all."

—*The New York Times Book Review*

"Absorbing . . . panoramic . . . beautiful. Mr. Meacham's compassionate approach to telling the story of Mr. Bush's life provides a newfound appreciation for the forty-first president."

—*The New York Times*

"When we rank, reconsider, laud, or denounce past presidents, living or dead, we are taking stock of our own times. In that sense, the vindication of George H. W. Bush is a reflection of what we know we've lost. Jon Meacham's new biography of Bush, *Destiny and Power,* makes that plain from its very first pages."

—*The New Yorker*

"Major Bush family drama emerges from George H. W. Bush book, leading us to believe that *Scandal*'s been a documentary all along."

—*Entertainment Weekly*

"A gripping new biography of the forty-first president."

—*The Economist*

"Meacham's book should be required reading—if not for every presidential candidate, then for every president-elect."

—*The Washington Post*

"Graceful prose, backed by diligent mining of the archives and access to an oral diary that Bush dictated throughout his presidency . . . The story of the forty-first man to hold the office sheds light not only on the country we were, but the one we've become."

—*Los Angeles Times*

"Jon Meacham, who won a Pulitzer Prize for his biography of Andrew Jackson, put an enormous amount of work into this volume: nine years of interviews, full access to the diaries of George H. W. and Barbara Bush, and an open door to family members and friends. Add to this Meacham's balanced journalism and smooth writing, and you have a fascinating biography of the forty-first president."

—*The Dallas Morning News*

"Through one man's journey, we see America's changing attitudes toward power and duty."
—*Time*

"Illuminating . . . written from Bush's perspective but with a journalist's rigor . . . George and Barbara Bush have provided extraordinary cooperation [for] an account of his life and presidency that has depth and value."
—*USA Today* (4 out of 4 stars)

"Meacham is a superb historian and he weaves a compelling historical narrative, drawing heavily on Bush's own contemporaneous diaries. The result is a fascinating behind-the-scenes glimpse into high-stakes decision making in a rapidly evolving world."
—*The Seattle Times*

"Meacham is acclaimed for the great depth of his research and his way of making history come alive for readers. . . . [*Destiny and Power* is his] latest exceptionally researched biography. . . . It's fascinating reading."
—*Chicago Tribune*

"A ground-breaking chronicle . . . worth reading every page."
—*Missourian*

"Highly readable . . . George H. W. Bush was present at many of the most important events of the last 65-plus years, and the remarkable story of his life and times comes vividly alive in the words of this highly skilled writer."
—*Booklist*

"A vivid, well-written account."
—*Publishers Weekly*

"Meticulously researched . . . a revealing biography that should serve as the starting point for future evaluations of the forty-first president."
—*Kirkus Reviews*

"The more time passes, the more the dust settles, the clearer it becomes that George H. W. Bush and the strengths of character he brought to his long service to this country deserve more attention and appreciation. And now comes *Destiny and Power,* Jon Meacham's altogether fair, insightful biography of the forty-first president—a portrait made especially compelling by the author's remarkable access to Bush's private White House diaries. This is a timely, first-rate book!"
—DAVID McCULLOUGH

"What a spectacular and moving portrait this is—not only of a remarkably classy man but of the era that shaped him! It is hard to imagine a biographer more fitted than Jon Meacham to write what will surely be the definitive work on George Herbert Walker Bush."
—DORIS KEARNS GOODWIN

"Jon Meacham's timely and intimate biography of George Bush 41 is a welcome reminder of this modest president's call to service, from the cockpits of World War II to the Oval Office and the end of the Cold War. Here you'll meet a man of patrician manners, wartime heroics, Texas assimilation, party and personal loyalty, with a refined sense of power that carried him into history. Meet the George Bush you didn't know."

—TOM BROKAW

"This astonishing book is both timely and timeless. Based on candid interviews and intimate letters and diaries, it provides a deep insight into the character of George H. W. Bush flavored with colorful anecdotes depicting his relationships with people ranging from Gorbachev and Reagan to his sons George and Jeb. The result is a fascinating and insightful portrayal of the life of an exemplary American citizen."

—WALTER ISAACSON

"This riveting biography by the incomparable Jon Meacham gives George H. W. Bush his well-deserved place in history. *Destiny and Power* is full of surprises, revealing 41's important role in scene after crucial historical scene of the past seven decades. President Bush used to say that he could never quite convey his 'heartbeat' to Americans. Now, using a treasure of heretofore unseen diaries and other documents, as well as his own detailed interviews, Meacham takes us behind closed doors to show us what this sometimes misunderstood leader was really like."

—MICHAEL BESCHLOSS

BY JON MEACHAM

Destiny and Power: The American Odyssey of George Herbert Walker Bush
Thomas Jefferson: The Art of Power
American Lion: Andrew Jackson in the White House
American Gospel: God, the Founding Fathers, and the Making of a Nation
Franklin and Winston: An Intimate Portrait of an Epic Friendship
Voices in Our Blood: America's Best on the Civil Rights Movement (editor)

DESTINY *and* POWER

DESTINY
and POWER

★

The American Odyssey of
George Herbert
Walker Bush

★

JON MEACHAM

RANDOM HOUSE
New York

Published in the United States by Random House, an imprint and division
of Penguin Random House LLC, New York.

RANDOM HOUSE and the HOUSE colophon are registered trademarks of
Penguin Random House LLC.

Originally published in hardcover in the United States by Random House,
an imprint and division of Penguin Random House LLC, in 2015.

Text permission credits are located on page 807.
Illustration credits are located on page 809.

LIBRARY OF CONGRESS CATALOGING-IN-PUBLICATION DATA
Names: Meacham, Jon.
Title: Destiny and power: the American odyssey of George Herbert
Walker Bush / Jon Meacham.
Description: New York: Random House, 2015. | Includes biographical
references and index.
Identifiers: LCCN 2015016550 | ISBN 9780812979473 (trade
paperback: acid-free paper) ISBN 9780812998207 (ebook)
Subjects: LCSH: Bush, George, 1924– Presidents—United States—
Biography. | United States—Politics and government—1945-1989. |
United States—Politics and government—1989– | BISAC: BIOGRAPHY
& AUTOBIOGRAPHY / Presidents & Heads of State. | HISTORY /
United States / 20th Century. | BIOGRAPHY & AUTOBIOGRAPHY /
Political.
Classification: LCC E882.M43 2015 | DDC 973.928092—dc23
LC record available at http://lccn.loc.gov/2015016550

Printed in the United States of America on acid-free paper

randomhousebooks.com

2 4 6 8 9 7 5 3 1

TITLE PAGE: Chief Justice William H. Rehnquist swears in George Herbert
Walker Bush as the nation's forty-first president, the West Front of the U.S.
Capitol, Friday, January 20, 1989.

Book design by Simon M. Sullivan

To Keith, Mary, Maggie, and Sam

Destiny is not a matter of chance; it is a matter of choice. It is not a thing to be waited for; it is a thing to be achieved.

WILLIAM JENNINGS BRYAN, American lawyer and statesman

Moods come and go, but greatness endures.

—GEORGE H. W. BUSH

Contents

★

The Last Gentleman

★

E VEN IN THE DARK, he tried to look ahead. It was late, and he knew he should sleep, but he just couldn't—not yet, anyway. Too much had happened; too much was on his mind.

In the Houstonian Hotel's suite 271 on the evening he lost his bid for a second term as president of the United States, George Herbert Walker Bush climbed out of bed and slipped into an adjoining wood-paneled living room. Weary but restless, he settled on a small sofa. The room was empty, his heart full. There he sat, alone, struggling to make peace with the news that he, an American president who embodied the experience of the World War II generation, had just been defeated by Bill Clinton, the Baby Boomer Democratic governor of Arkansas. In his private, tape-recorded diary, Bush dictated: "I ache and I now must think: how do you keep your chin up, keep your head up through a couple of difficult days ahead?" He kept his voice low: Barbara, his devoted wife of forty-seven years, was asleep back in the bedroom. "I think of our country, and the people that are hurting, and there is so much we didn't do" Bush told his diary. "And yes, progress that we made, but no, the job is not finished, and that kills me."

Not so long before, it had all been different: George Bush had always finished the job. From his earliest days, he had done what his parents, his teachers, and his country had asked of him. He had not only met expectations but exceeded them, time and again. Born in 1924, he was a son of privilege raised in Greenwich, Connecticut, and at the seaside Walker's Point in Kennebunkport, Maine. He had joined the navy on his eighteenth birthday. As a carrier-based bomber pilot in the Pacific in World War II, he had been shot down at the age of twenty—but had finished his mission, attacking an enemy radio tower on Chichi-Jima even after his plane had been hit. He had raised a family, lost a daughter to leukemia, built a business, and thrived in the treacherous world of American politics. As president of the United States he had ended the Cold War with the Soviet Union, lifting the specter of nuclear war from the life of the nation and of the world, and led a global coalition to military victory in the Middle East. The American economy, however, had slipped into recession on his watch, leading to a persistent public sense that he was a rich man out of touch with the concerns of the people in his care. The caricature wasn't particularly fair, but, as Bush often said, politics never was.

On this election night, he had said the gracious things, calling the president-elect in Little Rock to concede the race and promise a smooth transition. Yet the loss "hurt, hurt, hurt," Bush dictated, "and I guess it's the pride, too." It was surely the pride, too—not a doubt in the world about that. "I don't like to see the pollsters right at the end," he dictated. "I don't like to see the pundits right; I don't like to see all of those who have written me off right. I was absolutely convinced we would prove them wrong, but I was wrong and they were right, and that hurts a lot."

He had lost to an opponent he privately considered a "draft dodger." Such was this decorated World War II veteran's view of the younger man—now the president-elect—who had managed to stay out of the armed forces during the Vietnam War and had participated in an antiwar demonstration in England as a Rhodes Scholar. "I guess it's losing to Bill Clinton, the person," Bush dictated. "I like him, but . . . how do you be the commander in chief when you duplicitously avoid service to your country? Maybe it is time for a new generation. He's George [W.]'s age, a generation more in touch, a background more in touch. . . . I know what the charge is, but I've never felt 'out of touch,' but then I've always assumed there was duty, honor, country. I've always assumed that was just part of what Americans are made of—quite clearly it's not." Two days later, in another diary entry, the defeated president said: "I still feel that there is a disconnect . . . honor, duty, and country—it's just passé. The values are different now, the lifestyles, the accepted vulgarity, the manners, the view of what's patriotic and what's not, the concept of service. All these are in the hands of a new generation now, and I feel I have the comfort of knowing that I have upheld these values and I live and stand by them. I have the discomfort of knowing that they might be a little out of date."

Honor, duty, country. Those verities, together with a driving ambition and an abiding competitive spirit, had shaped his life and his understanding of the nation. There was nothing affected about Bush's vision of politics as a means to public service, and of public service as the highest of callings. This vision of himself engaged in what Oliver Wendell Holmes, Jr., called "the passion and action" of the time was as real to him as the air he breathed.

Early on election night his sons George W. and Jeb had tried to cheer him up. "The boys [are] telling me, 'We're proud of you, Dad, we're very proud of you,'" Bush dictated. "Yes, their father was President and all of that, but a failed President." In his anguish he was being too hard on himself. He had lost an election, not his place in history.

For now, though, Bush needed a way forward through the shadows of defeat, and he returned to a few core truths that had always guided him. "Be strong," he told himself in his living room musings, "be kind, be generous of spirit, be understanding, let people know how grateful you are, don't get even, comfort the ones I've hurt and let down, say your prayers and ask for God's understanding and strength, finish with a smile and with some gusto, do what's right and finish strong."

With that, the forty-first president of the United States retired for the night, rejoining the sleeping Barbara. Now he had a plan. Now he could rest. He told himself something else, too, in the days after the defeat. "It'll change," he dictated. "It'll change."

AND so it did. The farther the country moved from his presidency the larger Bush loomed, and the qualities so many voters found to be vices in 1992 came to be seen as virtues—his public reticence; his old-fashioned dignity; his tendency to find a middle course between extremes. He lived long enough to see the shift, and he appreciated that people were taking a more benign view of his record. Amid a conference at his presidential library in 2014, his ninetieth year, a visitor asked him what he made of all the encomiums and positive revision of his legacy. "Hard to believe," Bush remarked. "It's 'kinder and gentler' all over the place."

His was one of the great American lives—strong parents, a sparkling education, heroic service in World War II, success in Texas oil, congressman, ambassador to the United Nations, chairman of the Republican National Committee, envoy to China, director of Central

Intelligence, vice president of the United States, forty-first president, and the only president since John Adams to see his son also win the ultimate prize in American politics.

A formidable physical presence—six foot two, handsome, dominant in person—he spoke with his strong, big hands, waving dismissively to deflect unwelcome subjects or to suggest that someone was, as he would put it, "way out there," beyond the mainstream, beyond reason, beyond *Bush*. Television conveyed his lankiness, but not his athleticism and his grace. He was the kind of man other men noted, and the kind women were often surprised to find attractive. He was a terrific flirt, charming women and men alike with a perpetual ebullience. Bush was a master of what Franklin Roosevelt thought of as "the science of human relationships," and his capacity to charm—with a handwritten note, a phone call, a quick email, a wink, a thumbs-up—was crucial to his success in public life. He lacked the glamour of a John Kennedy or the stage presence of a Ronald Reagan; his was a quiet but persistent charisma, an ability to make others love him without, perhaps, their knowing quite why. He was driven less by ideas about politics than by an ideal of service and an ambition—a consuming one—to win.

In the White House, he peacefully managed the end of the Communist threat, secured the heart of Europe, and struggled to bring order to the chaos of the Middle East. Before his White House years, a nuclear Armageddon between America and the Soviet Union was always a possibility; afterward it was unthinkable. President and statesman, politician and father, he was both a maker and a mirror of the story of American power—from the Allied victory against Germany and Japan to the beginnings of the war on Islamic terror. On the home front, his 1990 budget agreement put controls on spending and created the conditions for the elimination of the federal budget deficit under Bill Clinton. He negotiated the North American Free Trade Agreement, signed the Americans with Disabilities Act, and passed historic clean-air legislation.

Bush was a child of one generation's ruling class, the head of another's, and the father of yet a third. His life is a saga that ranges from the Gilded Age of railroad barons to the birth of Big Oil, from Greenwich and Midland to Washington, New York, Baghdad, and Beijing. His political life was shaped by two of the great forces in American life after World War II: the global responsibilities of a vital atomic power in foreign affairs and the rise of the right wing of the Republican Party in domestic politics.

Americans unhappy with the reflexively polarized politics of the first decades of the twenty-first century will find the presidency of George H. W. Bush refreshing, even quaint. He embraced compromise as a necessary element of public life, engaged his political foes in the passage of important legislation, and was willing to break with the base of his own party in order to do what he thought was right, whatever the price. Quaint, yes: But it happened, in America, only a quarter of a century ago.

I n the warm dusk of a Texas autumn a decade and a half after he left the White House, Bush, his left leg propped atop a coffee table in his Houston living room, a glass of white wine at hand, reflected on what had driven him all his life. "My motivation's always been *goal*—you know, to be captain," he said, his left hand in a fist, punctuating his words. "Whatever it is. That's not good in a way, but in a way it is. It's what motivated me all my life. I'm a goal kind of guy."

He fell silent. Hoping to hear more, a visitor ventured: "You were motivated to do well, to succeed in the realms that life put you—"

Bush jumped in. "Whatever you're in. Be number one."

Where did it come from, this hunger for power? For that is what drove George H. W. Bush, relentlessly and perennially: a hunger to determine the destinies of others, to command respect, to shape great events. Many men of his age and milieu attended good schools, fought in the war, and went from the Ivy League to Wall Street. They led good, comfortable lives; helped, in their way, to build the prosperity that drove the midcentury boom and gave millions of Americans the opportunity for education and affluence after World War II. The worlds of the men at the top—the kind of men who had been at Andover or at Yale with Bush—revolved around business in Manhattan, commutes home to the suburbs of New York and Connecticut, martinis at cocktail hour, golf on the weekends, subscriptions to *The New Yorker*.

Bush refused to follow that well-marked path. Offered jobs at Brown Brothers Harriman, his father's private bank, and G. H. Walker & Company, his maternal grandfather's investment firm, Bush demurred. "It just wasn't *different* enough—didn't have the edge of really doing something new," Bush recalled. If he had chosen to join the established financial world, he knew how his life would unfold. "Wouldn't have had much adventure, no excitement of trying new things, out of the family's shadow. I loved my family—don't get me wrong—but if I had gone to work for their businesses I wouldn't have been able to set my own goals, make my own goals."

In Greenwich and Kennebunkport, there was love, there was warmth, and there was kindness, but there was also the expectation that Walkers and Bushes were born to be tested—that life was not a country-club affair. It is a common mistake to assume that someone of George H. W. Bush's breeding and background would see power as a birthright, as the natural inheritance of a man born to money and position. Quite the opposite: For the children of Dorothy and Prescott Bush, the truly desirable prizes were those one earned by skill and hard work, either on the field, the golf course, the tennis court, the oil fields, the business world, or in politics. To coast on the family name was a serious sin.

While this ethos of achievement produced children who were largely unentitled and unspoiled, it also created a family culture in which affection and approval could seem inextricably bound up with accomplishment. To be a good son, then, meant *doing* as well as *being.* All would be loved, no question, but those who came in first rose in the esteem of parents and grandparents. What child, sensing this, would not yearn to excel, when excellence was the way to win, if not the love (which was always on offer), but the admiration of one's elders? What child would not want to achieve when achievement was expected, noted, and honored?

Yet they were not to boast of what they won. Such was the Bush code: Strive for victory, but never seem self-involved. Dorothy Walker Bush's admonitions to her children to be self-effacing were legendary. They were not to talk about themselves or their achievements: "Nobody likes a braggadocio," she would say, and that would be that. Dorothy Bush never asked how one of her children had played. It was "How did the team do?" When Bush would say "I was off my game," his mother would reply "You don't have a game." She did not want to hear about what she called "the Great I Am."

The Bushes kept score—fairly, but intensely and scrupulously, too. Proficiency was appreciated and admired, whether in business, sports, or politics. Things were not to be done halfheartedly or cavalierly. The family's children were to master what they undertook and finish what they began.

No one ever met that tribal challenge with a greater sense of purpose than George Herbert Walker Bush. He had a mission: to serve, to make his mark, to be in the game. He was certain of his place, respectful of tradition, solicitous of others. Yet he was an ambitious politician, too, and therein lay the great tension of his life. To serve he had to win, and if he had to win then that meant someone else had to lose.

Which, when all was said and done, was just fine with George Bush. Such was the way of the world—a world that those closest to him and he himself (though he hated to admit it) long believed he was destined to run. As he grew up, meeting test after test, making friend after friend, impressing elder after elder, he became what Nancy Bush Ellis called "the star of the family"—a star of such brightness that winning the presidency of the United States itself seemed possible long before it became probable. "He was meant to be saved," his sister remarked of his World War II experience. In the 1950s, Bush's father introduced his son to the French ambassador in Washington. "This is my son George," Prescott said, adding: "He's going to be the President of the United States one day."

Informed, however subtly, by the sense that he was destined to do great things, George Bush never doubted that he was the best man on the ballot. Armed with this self-confidence—a personal assurance masked by his kindness and his grace—he could justify adapting his principles and attacking his opponents as the inevitable price of politics. To Bush, such calculations were not cynical. They were instrumental to the desired end: the accumulation of power to be deployed in the service of America and of the world. What one said or did to rise to ultimate authority mattered less to Bush than whether one was principled and selfless once in command. And as president of the United States, Bush was often both.

For every compromise or concession to party orthodoxy or political expedience on the campaign trail, in office Bush sought to do the right thing. In 1964, when he ran for a U.S. Senate seat in Texas, he opposed the Civil Rights Act, only to vote for open housing in Congress four years later, much to the fury of his conservative constituents. In 1988, he made an absolute pledge on supply-side economics—"Read my lips, no new taxes"—only to break that promise two years later when he believed an agreement that included higher taxes was best for the country. After winning a hard-hitting presidential campaign, Bush sought what he called a "kinder and gentler" America, reaching out to Democrats and Republicans alike, seeking common ground on common problems.

Americans tend to prefer their presidents on horseback: heroes who dream big and sound the trumpets. There is, however, another kind of leader—quieter and less glamorous but no less significant—whose virtues repay our attention. There is greatness in political lives dedicated more to steadiness than to boldness, more to reform than to revolution, more to the management of complexity than to the making of mass movements. Bush's life code, as he once put it in a letter to his mother, was "Tell the truth. Don't blame people. Be strong. Do your Best. Try hard. Forgive. Stay the course." Simple propositions—deceptively simple, for such sentiments are more easily expressed than embodied in the arena of public life.

Essentially modest, he had an underwhelming speaking style that prevented him from consistently defining a compelling national agenda. Instinctively generous, he risked appearing indecisive, even weak, when he was reaching out and listening to other people's points of view. Highly intelligent, he could seem confused and sometimes unserious when discussing issues of great significance.

Yet the nation was fortunate that George H. W. Bush was in power when the crises of his time came, for his essential character, his experience, and his temperament armed him well to bring the decades-long Cold War to an end, to confront the aggression of an irrational dictator, and to lead the nation toward fiscal responsibility. An imperfect leader, he was nevertheless well matched to the exigencies of his historical moment.

Bush was a steward, not a seer, and made no apologies for his preference for pragmatism over ideology. Unflinching creeds and consuming worldviews could lead to catastrophe, for devotees of doctrine tended to fall in love with their own righteousness, ignoring inconvenient facts. He resisted ideological certainty and eloquent abstraction to such an extent that he dismissed questions about his goals for the nation as "the vision thing." He knew all the charges and was impatient with the prevailing critique of his political persona. "One of the criticisms that got me was, 'Well, he doesn't have any vision, he doesn't have any reason for being there,'" Bush recalled. "Well, what's wrong with trying to help people, what's wrong with trying to bring peace, what's wrong with trying to make the world a little better?" Exactly why, he wondered, wasn't that vision enough?

Taken all in all, Bush was a president less in the tradition of Ronald Reagan than of Dwight Eisenhower. Reagan spoke in terms of revolution, of great and necessary reforms to the existing order of things. Eisenhower said that his goal was to take America "down the middle of the road between the unfettered power of concentrated wealth . . . and the unbridled power of statism or partisan interests." Moderate in temperament, Eisenhower and Bush were both more traditionally conservative than many of their contemporaries understood, in the sense that they sought above all to conserve what was good about the world as they found it. For them, conservatism entailed prudence and pragmatism. They eschewed the sudden and the visionary.

For all of his years on the stage, Bush could be an enigmatic figure, and his public image conveyed neither the complexities of his character nor the depth of his emotions. He was a victim, in a way, of his instinct for dignity. Bill Clinton spoke of how he felt the pain of voters; Bush thought such language beneath the presidency even though, in private, beneath the surface and in his diary, he was an immensely sensitive man. He cried easily (especially as he grew older), but believed he should avoid such displays in public; they struck him as self-indulgent. Late in his vice presidential years, Bush was visiting a children's leukemia ward in Kraków, Poland. Thirty-five years before, he and Barbara had lost their daughter Robin to the disease, a family tragedy of which he rarely spoke in public. In Kraków, one patient, a seven- or eight-year-old boy, wanted to greet the American vice president. Learning that the child was sick with the cancer that had killed Robin, Bush began to cry.

"My eyes flooded with tears, and behind me was a bank of television cameras. . . . And I thought to myself, 'I can't turn around. . . . I can't dissolve because of personal tragedy in the face of a host of reporters and our hosts and the nurses that give of themselves every day.' So I stood there looking at this little guy, tears running down my cheek, but able to talk to him pleasantly . . . hoping he didn't see but, if he did, hoping he'd feel that I loved him." This was the private Bush. It was not the Bush that many American voters knew very much, if anything, about.

His interior monologue about Kraków was found in the transcripts of diaries that Bush kept sporadically as vice president under Ronald

Reagan and more regularly in his own four years as president. The diaries provide a remarkable personal perspective on Bush, who dictated into a handheld cassette recorder, sometimes carrying the device with him in his briefcase back and forth between the White House Residence and the West Wing. He would bring it along on trips aboard Marine One to Camp David and on Air Force One across the nation and the globe. He would speak into the machine quietly, often late at night or early in the morning. Taken all together, the diaries enable us, in effect, to sit with Bush as he muses about life at the highest levels.

Because he did not believe in burdening others—even his wife—with what he self-mockingly called "the loneliness of the job, the 'woe-is-me' stuff," the forty-first president saved most of his expressions of frustration for his diary. When alone, speaking to himself and to history, Bush was honest about the vicissitudes of the presidency, about his hopes and fears, about the good days and the bad—and about what it was truly like to govern in what he once described as "a fascinating time of change in the world itself."

To understand George Herbert Walker Bush and the country he led, we must begin not by the sea at his beloved Walker's Point, nor on the lawns of Greenwich nor in the oil fields of Texas, but in the booming America of the late nineteenth and early twentieth centuries, an age in which the energetic and the ambitious were building great fortunes—and a great nation.

PART I

A Vanished Universe

Beginnings to 1942

★

It was a beautiful world to grow up in. A grand, funny world,
really. Unimaginable now.

—NANCY BUSH ELLIS, sister of George H. W. Bush

The end depends upon the beginning.

—Motto of Phillips Academy, Andover, Massachusetts

"Poppy" Bush at school at Phillips Academy in Andover, Massachusetts, where he was enrolled from 1937, when he was thirteen, until 1942, the year he graduated and went into the navy.

ONE

The Land of the Self-Made Man

★

Is it not by the courage always to do the right thing that the
fires of hell shall be put out?

—THE REVEREND JAMES SMITH BUSH, Episcopal clergyman and great-
grandfather of George H. W. Bush

Failure seems to be regarded as the one unpardonable crime,
success as the one all-redeeming virtue, the acquisition of
wealth as the single worthy aim of life.

—CHARLES FRANCIS ADAMS, JR.

TO SAMUEL PRESCOTT BUSH—"Bushy" to his beloved first wife, Flora—the ocean seemed to go on forever. The view from the top of the Hotel Traymore overlooking the boardwalk in Atlantic City at Illinois Avenue was grand, and unique: A publicist for the hotel assured the press that the Traymore roof was "the most elevated point on the Atlantic coast south of the Statue of Liberty." ("In absence of evidence to the contrary," a reporter added, "we take his word for it.") A prominent Midwestern industrialist, Bush was at the Jersey Shore in the early summer of 1915 to take part in what was described as "the highest golf driving contest ever held in the history of the great Scotch game."

In from Columbus, Ohio, where he presided over Buckeye Steel Castings Company, a manufacturer of railroad parts, the tall, angular Bush looked out from a makeshift tee atop the brick hotel two hundred feet above the beach. A favorite of well-heeled visitors to Atlantic City, the domed Traymore had just undergone renovations that *Bankers' Magazine* solemnly reported had turned the hotel into a showplace with "700 rooms and 700 baths"—the kind of construction project that was making grandeur ever more accessible to men who were building a prosperous business class.

S. P. Bush was one such man. The son of an Episcopal clergyman,

Bush, who was to become George H. W. Bush's paternal grandfather, had spent much of his childhood in New York and New Jersey. After college, Bush went west, finding his future at Buckeye, a company run, in the first decade of the new century, by a brother of John D. Rockefeller, Frank. President of Buckeye since 1908 and a director of numerous railway companies, S. P. Bush had grown rich. Standing on the roof of the Hotel Traymore, he was part of an emerging American elite—one based not on birth but on success and achievement. Facing the Atlantic, in a long-sleeved dress shirt and formal trousers, Bush, driver in hand, took his stance and swung smoothly. He connected just the way he wanted to—cleanly and perfectly. The ball rose rapidly, a tiny spinning meteor. Bush's shot streaked out over the sea, soaring over the white-capped waves before disappearing deep in the distance, the sound of its splash lost in the wind and surf.

Bush won, of course. Though his opponents did what they could, they failed to surpass Bush's dramatic drive. It was not the most serious of competitions, but that did not matter. *The New York Times* reported Bush's triumph. A contest was a contest.

To win was to be alive; to compete was as natural as breathing— a common code among the ancestors of George Herbert Walker Bush. Theirs is a story of big men and strong women, of ambitious husbands and fathers taking unconventional risks—in business, in politics, even in religion—while wives and mothers who might have expected fairly staid lives adapt and emerge as impressive figures in their own rights. Across more than two centuries, maternal and paternal lines reinforced and supported one another, producing generation after generation driven by both the pursuit of wealth and by a sense of public service.

Bush's ancestors were in America from the seventeenth century forward. Some arrived on the *Mayflower,* settling in New England. On the night of Tuesday, April 18, 1775, the Massachusetts patriot Dr. Samuel Prescott, a Bush forebear, rode with Paul Revere and William Dawes to warn Concord of the pending British invasion.

Obadiah Bush, George H. W. Bush's great-great-grandfather, was born in 1797, served in the War of 1812 at age fifteen, and became a schoolmaster in Cayuga County, New York. He married a pupil (a young woman whom family tradition recalled as the "comely" Harriet Smith), and went into business in Rochester. He fell on hard times and, in distress, unsuccessfully turned to Senator William Seward (who would join Lincoln's cabinet much later) in search of government preferment in Rio de Janeiro or another "healthful port."

Gold, or at least the prospect of it, saved him, then killed him. Obadiah grew obsessed with news of the gold rush in California, journeying west to look into mining opportunities in the San Francisco area. He liked what he found but died before he could collect his family and permanently relocate.

Obadiah's eldest son, James Smith Bush, who would become George H. W. Bush's great-grandfather, barely made it out of infancy. Born in 1825, he was described as "a puny and sickly child, of fragile build, with weak lungs." A doctor was harsh with Harriet Bush, James Smith Bush's mother: "You had better knock him in the head, for [even] if he lives he will never amount to anything." He survived, and, in 1841, at sixteen, enrolled at Yale College. James Smith Bush was popular and charming, a conscientious student, and an excellent athlete, especially at crew. "His classmates speak of him as tall and slender in person, rather grave of mien, except when engaged in earnest conversation or good-humored repartee; ever kind and considerate, and always a gentleman—still very strong in his likes and dislikes," a friend of Bush's wrote. "He made many friends."

These and other family traits became evident in Bush's life during his Yale years. There was a restlessness, an eagerness to break away from the established order of life, but not so much that one could not return. There was a kind of moderation, a discomfort with extremes or dogma. There was a capacity to charm and a fondness for attractive women. And there was also a sense of familial duty. At college he realized that his father, Obadiah, was short of money, and so James Smith Bush sought professional security in the law. On a visit to Saratoga Springs as a young attorney, he was dazzled by the passing figure of Sarah Freeman, the daughter of a local doctor. She was, it was said, "the most beautiful woman of this place," and Bush fell in love. They married in October 1851, and he took her to live in Rochester.

Bush adored his bride, and the world seemed a brighter, happier place to him with her in it. Then, eighteen months after the wedding, Sarah

Freeman Bush died, devastating her young husband into near insensibility. Shattered by the loss of his wife, Bush sought consolation in religion. Initially a Presbyterian, he had become an Episcopalian under Sarah's influence. Now, in the wake of the calamity of her death, Bush was ordained a priest and served Grace Church in Orange, New Jersey, beginning in June 1855. He eventually found another great love: Harriet Eleanor Fay. Like Bush's first wife, Harriet was said to be "brilliant and beautiful." The poet James Russell Lowell admired her extravagantly. "She possessed the finest mind," Lowell remarked, "and was the most brilliant woman, intellectually, of the young women of my day." Bush's head turned anew, he married Harriet Fay in New York in 1859. The marriage was a happy one, producing four children, including, on Sunday, October 4, 1863, a son they named Samuel Prescott Bush—S.P.

While Obadiah appears to have had a gambler's temperament, James Smith Bush was moderate in tone and philosophy. Amid a controversy over the teaching of the Bible in public schools, the Reverend Bush preached a sermon in support of the separation of church and state. A supporter of the Union during the Civil War, Bush spoke to public gatherings celebrating the North's triumphs at Vicksburg and at Gettysburg and reportedly flew the American flag at his church against the wishes of the neighborhood's Southern sympathizers. After the grim news from Ford's Theatre on the evening of Good Friday, 1865, Bush wrote a sermon to commemorate the martyred Abraham Lincoln. "Be assured, my brethren, as that great and good man did not *live* in vain, so he has not *died* in vain," Bush told his Easter congregation that Sunday. "The President was an instrument in the hands of God."

The popular Bush served as chaplain on an expedition around Cape Horn to California under Commodore John "Fighting Jack" Rodgers. In 1867 Bush accepted a call to Grace Church on Nob Hill in San Francisco before returning east for good in 1872, where he became rector of the Church of the Ascension at West Brighton, Staten Island. There the strains of the second great spiritual crisis of Bush's life became apparent. Forged in the fire of his grief over the death of his first wife, his faith was fading. The more miraculous elements of the creeds—the Virgin Birth was one example—now seemed implausible to him. "I discovered early in my acquaintance with Mr. Bush that his theological garments were outgrown," said Dr. Horatio Stebbins of San Francisco, a leading Unitarian.

On a visit to the Ashfield, Massachusetts, home of George William Curtis, an editor of *Harper's Weekly*, Bush discussed his shifting views on religion. Curtis introduced his guest to a poem of Ralph Waldo Emerson's entitled "The Problem," which tells the story of a believer who has fallen out of love with the trappings of earthly ecclesiastical institutions, beginning with the "cowl," or a long robe with deep sleeves and a hood.

> *I like a church; I like a cowl;*
> *I love a prophet of the soul;*
> *and on my heart monastic aisles*
> *Fall like sweet strains, or pensive smiles;*
> *Yet not for all his faith can see*
> *Would I that cowled churchman be.*
>
> *Why should the vest on him allure,*
> *Which I could not on me endure?*

Bush was stunned at how Emerson's verses resonated. "Why, why," Bush told Curtis, "that is my faith." Around Christmas 1883 he resigned from his parish and moved his family to Concord, Massachusetts, a center of inquiry and of Unitarianism infused with the spirits of Emerson and Thoreau.

On Monday, November 11, 1889, James Smith Bush died after a heart attack. A eulogy underscored his love of politics and his gentleness of temper. "Interested in all public questions, possessing strong opinions, and having the courage of his convictions, he never was offensive or aggressive in asserting them," a friend said of Bush. He was buried in Ithaca, New York, where he and his family had moved yet again, his restless journey done.

Mechanics and money, not metaphysics, was top of mind for Bush's son Samuel Prescott Bush. In this, George H. W. Bush's grandfather reflected the larger currents of the time. The post–Civil War era found its name in Mark Twain and Charles Dudley Warner's novel *The Gilded Age*. The excesses of the era, including the exploitation of labor and the attendant growth in the gap between the few and the many, led to the important work of the Progressives. Among elements of the Gilded Age elite, however, there was an expectation that money brought with it certain responsibilities. Andrew Carnegie articulated this new faith in "The Gospel of Wealth," published in 1889:

> This, then, is held to be the duty of the man of wealth: To set an example of modest, unostentatious living, shunning display or extravagance; to provide moderately for the legitimate wants of those dependent upon him; and, after doing so, to consider all surplus revenues which come to him simply as trust funds, which he is called upon to administer, and strictly bound as a matter of duty to administer in the manner which, in his judgment, is best calculated to produce the most beneficial results for the community—the man of wealth thus becoming the mere trustee and agent for his poorer brethren, bringing to their service his superior wisdom, experience, and ability to administer, doing for them better than they would or could do for themselves.

The pursuit of wealth was thus imbued with a sense of purpose. America, wrote the banker Henry Clews, was "the land of the self-made man."

S.P. attended the Stevens Institute of Technology in Hoboken, New Jersey, a choice suggesting he had decided to seek his career in a world of certitude and of science rather than in his father's ethos of twilight and of theology. He devoted himself to engineering, manufacture—and money making. After graduating from Stevens in 1884, Bush worked for a number of railroads, moving between Logansport, Indiana; Columbus, Ohio; and Milwaukee. In 1901, he returned to Columbus to join what was known at the time as the Buckeye Malleable Iron and Coupler Company, whose railroad parts were widely praised for being of the "highest grade."

Late on the afternoon of Tuesday, October 14, 1902, in Columbus, Buckeye invited spectators to witness the shift from the older world of iron to the new, more profitable universe of steel. Watching a crane and furnace at work at Buckeye, a reporter for *The Columbus Citizen* wrote "the steel came pouring forth in a stream of liquid fire amid a cloud of fiery spray. It was a beautiful sight, indeed." So began S. P. Bush's long career at Buckeye, one that made him rich and—crucial for the Bush family's self-image—"respected," as his grandson George H. W. Bush recalled. The Bushes were a big force in a big town in a big time. And S. P. Bush, who married Flora Sheldon of Columbus, was a big man. "Grandfather Bush was quite severe," recalled George's sister, Nancy Bush Ellis. "He wasn't mean, but so correct." He was, a Buckeye colleague recalled, "a snorter . . . Everyone knew when he was around; when he issued orders, boy it went!"

There was championship level golf; the leading of charities; the building of a great house with elaborate gardens; a critical role in creating the Ohio State football program; the establishment of the Ohio Manufacturers' Association; and, politically, a voice in both the state's Democratic Party and in the anti-tax Ohio Tax League. There was also the support of symphonies, of art galleries, of literary and cultural gatherings. S.P. expected hard work from others and from himself. Determined and focused, he was often asked to serve as a director on the boards of other companies—perhaps the highest compliment one businessman can pay another. Yet, Bush spoke of himself in a humble, self-improving tone: "I could be a lot better man if I could do a little more of some things and less of others, and I would like to be a better man too."

Flora, who was engaged by many things—gardening, design, history— saw her main role as that of a supportive wife. "Let me know dear what you are doing—the little details of your days & nights—for they are my greatest interest in life," Flora wrote S.P. when he was away. "You are a very dear Bushy, adored by your children and tenderly loved by your wife—loved more today than ever before."

The eldest of those children was Prescott Sheldon Bush. Born in Columbus on Wednesday, May 15, 1895, Prescott was high-spirited, savoring athletic success and attention. After church one summer day at Osterville, a Cape Cod village where the Bushes spent time in the summers, lunch with the family was raucous. "The children were hilarious to such a degree I think your poor mother's head whirled," Flora wrote her husband. "Prescott is after all a naughty boy on occasion—he kept the ball rolling so that I was helpless" with laughter.

Girls liked Prescott, too. "I have had one new experience and that is the devotion of girls . . . to Prescott," Flora Bush wrote her husband from Osterville. She worried, a bit, that the attention "for any length of time might turn his head." Secure and comfortable, Prescott and his family moved among the prosperous of Columbus during the year and in a wider universe on the East Coast in the summers. At Watch Hill, Rhode Island, Prescott, a gifted young golfer, caddied for Douglas Fairbanks, Sr., who sent along tickets to a Broadway performance of his as a token of thanks. The theater was a popular family pastime; S. P. Bush took his sons to shows in New York. Their social circle was such that Flora Bush reported the 1908 automobile-accident death of J. Montgomery Sears, a leading figure in Boston and in Newport, in a casual letter home.

Attentive parents, Flora and S. P. Bush were always anxious about Prescott, worrying that his good looks and charm might lead him into a permanent insouciance—a glamorous kid with only a passing sense of responsibility to others. (Harriet Bush noted that her teenage grandson had something of a "pernicious habit of fooling.")

Prescott had enjoyed his time through the eighth grade at Douglas, the main public school in Columbus. He was apparently missing a sense of purpose, though, and Flora and S.P. decided to enroll him in St. George's School near Newport, Rhode Island. He was, Flora said, a "boy of very tender years," and she "sometimes [had] a feeling of great dread at sending him away to school and yet I do feel that the strict discipline may be just the thing." Prescott loved St. George's, where he studied from 1908 to 1913. As president of the school's civics club for two years, he relished the combination of public affairs and public performance: "Are we for or against the popular election of United States Senators? How do we feel about a protective tariff versus a tariff for revenue only, and that type of question."

An institution of the church, St. George's often brought the boys together for chapel services. The school prayer was moving: "Almighty God . . . We pray that from these walls young men may go forth, generation after generation, well equipped for the battle of life and ready to contend bravely for God and the truth." The ritual of Anglicanism captured Bush's imagination for a time, and he briefly envisioned himself at the center of the drama of Christianity, presiding at the altar and in the pulpit. Like the civics club, it was another instance in which the intersection of substance and performance proved fascinating. He was, however, careful not to commit himself to any particular path as he went off to college.

Yale was inevitable, both because of his grandfather James Smith Bush '44, and because of a brother of Flora's, Robert E. Sheldon, Jr., '04.

Called "Pres" and "Doc" by his classmates, Bush lettered in both golf and baseball and became one of the school's leading singers, performing in the glee club, quartet, and the choir. In his final year, Prescott placed high in the voting in the categories "Done Most for Yale," "Most Popular," and "Most to Be Admired," and won the contest to be named "Most Versatile." He crowned his career with membership in both the Whiffenpoofs, the Yale a cappella singing troupe, and in Skull and Bones, the most elite of the university's senior societies.

In a poll of the class of 1917, there was an undercurrent of seriousness— seriousness about individual character and one's responsibility to the larger world. One senior called for "less caste, fewer snobs, more Christian men." It was also a thoroughly Republican student body, but partisan feeling gave way to a broader patriotism in 1916. As a junior that year, Bush joined a number of his classmates in signing up for the Connecticut National Guard to prepare for combat duty during a border conflict with Mexico. At Tobyhanna, Pennsylvania, the Yale men drilled for the summer before returning to New Haven.

There would be no call to arms in Mexico, but the training would not go to waste. On Monday, April 2, 1917, President Woodrow Wilson asked Congress for a declaration of war: The United States was at last entering the Great War. S. P. Bush was summoned to serve in the effort with the War Industries Board; Prescott became a captain of field artillery in the army. (During a brief stay at Fort Sill, in Oklahoma, Bush led an expedition to capture, for the Skull and Bones clubhouse, what was said to be the skull of Geronimo.) S. P. Bush worked as head of the board's Ordnance, Small Arms, and Ammunition Division. Buckeye's wartime profits from government contracts were capped by contract. A fellow industrialist, Martin J. Gillen, once warmly wrote him to recall their days serving together on the War Industries Board. "I have always thought of you as a Spartan citizen, what may be termed a Roman senator of the finest type," Gillen told Bush.

Prescott embarked for France in June 1918. There was to be one last great battle for the Allies, the Meuse-Argonne offensive. "We are close enough to the enemy to see the sunlight glint off the barrels of their rifles," Bush wrote home. As part of the 158th Field Artillery Brigade, he was near Montfaucon and Verdun, but Prescott never spoke of his combat experience. One reason for his reticence was long-standing embarrassment over a joke gone awry. From France, Prescott had written a prank letter in which he spun a story of faux heroism for his parents, telling them he had singlehandedly saved the lives of the Generals Pershing, Foch, and Haig by knocking aside a German shell with a bolo knife (similar to a machete).

It apparently did not occur to the Bushes that their son was writing tongue-in-cheek. Rather than chuckle over the letter, they sent it on to the Columbus newspaper, which also took Prescott's tale seriously, writing a front-page news story headlined "3 High Military Honors Conferred on Capt. Bush: For Notable Gallantry, When Leading Allied Commanders Were Endangered, Local Man Is Awarded French, English and U.S. Crosses." There was one problem: Prescott had been kidding. There had been no tour with the Allied commanders, no German shell, no decorations. By Friday, September 6, 1918, the Bushes had learned the truth from Prescott—who cabled his dismay that he had been taken seriously—and it fell to Flora Bush to write a letter to the editor, correcting the story.

The humiliation Prescott Bush felt then may have contributed to the more serious and sober-minded mien that was his hallmark as an adult. He had learned firsthand that boastfulness—even if inadvertent and meant to be taken in a light vein—could wound himself and his family. After the episode, Flora wrote S.P., musing: "If *only* the great epic was written seriously—" Prescott was discharged from the service at Chillicothe, Ohio, and went home to Columbus. He was ready to get on with things. He wanted to go to work.

At a reunion in New Haven in 1919, he met Wallace D. Simmons, Yale class of 1890. Scion of a large St. Louis hardware concern, Simmons hired Prescott to come out and join the business. On Tuesday, July 1, 1919, Prescott Bush reported to the Simmons Hardware Company offices at Ninth and Spruce streets. With St. Louis as a base, Bush, like his father before him, moved around a good deal—from warehouses in Wichita to Minneapolis to Philadelphia.

At the beginning of the new decade, at Watch Hill on a late summer Saturday—September 4, 1920—the S. P. Bushes decided to take an evening stroll. Some friends driving by slowed to a stop to chat. While Flora Bush was standing talking to the passersby in the car, another car, this one driven by Herbert Davis of Mystic, Connecticut, struck her. She died instantly. She was forty-eight years old.

In the wake of the war and of the death of his mother, Prescott was newly solemn. He was serious, self-sufficient, and as driven to succeed as his father had been. He had little time for distractions. Except for this: In St. Louis, he had met a girl.

TWO

A Real Son of a Bitch

★

I'm going to throw you in the water and you're going to swim.

—A Walker uncle, to the children of Dorothy Walker Bush's generation
at Walker's Point

H ER NAME WAS DOROTHY WEAR WALKER—"Dotty" to her
family and friends. The favorite child of a difficult and demanding father, George Herbert Walker of St. Louis, Dotty Walker,
George Bush's mother, was spirited, attractive, charming, devout, and
athletic. G. H. Walker, known as "Bert" or "Bertie," was not free with his
affections; Dotty, who impressed him with her sporting skill, was a notable exception.

The Walker household at 12 Hortense Place was full when Prescott
Bush, working for Simmons Hardware, first dropped by after his 1919
move to St. Louis. Bush had gotten to know Dorothy's older sister,
Nancy—Prescott and Nancy were closer together in age—and Nancy
had promised him symphony tickets. Unbeknownst to him, a party for
the joint debuts of the two daughters of the house was taking place when
he called. "He did not know a party was going on and so stood there
embarrassed," Dorothy recalled. "He told me that Nancy had offered
him some tickets, so I said, 'Certainly,' and ran to get Nancy." Bush was
smitten by the eighteen-year-old Dorothy, who had just come in from a
pre-party tennis match. "She was so blond and so active that Dad said,
'That's the girl for me,'" recalled their daughter, Nancy Bush Ellis.
Prescott left the house with his symphony tickets and a determination to
see more of the youngest Miss Walker. "Pres subsequently asked if he
could come calling," Dorothy recalled. The answer was yes.

G. H. Walker, Dorothy's father, was an investment banker and businessman who dealt with the world as though it were an unrelenting foe,
out to confound him or at least inconvenience him. Walker cast a long
shadow over his family. "He was kind of an up-and-down guy," recalled
George H. W. Bush of his grandfather. "If finances were going well, he'd

be bigger than life, and if they weren't he'd pull the kids out of private school and send them to public school. He was a flamboyant fellow, a boxer. A lot of people were scared of him, as we were." Asked what kind of man old G. H. Walker had been, one of his sons, Dorothy's brother John Walker, was succinct: "He was a real son of a bitch."

The Walkers' was a wild, rich life, replete with polo ponies, French wine, extravagant meals, scurrying servants, and enviable estates stretching from the rocks of Kennebunkport to the Gold Coast of Long Island to the hunt country of South Carolina to the mountains of Santa Barbara. (Told a new line of Ford cars was coming out one year, Walker's wife, Lucretia, or "Loulie," said, "Let's buy some.") Bert Walker knew how to make money and how to lose it, how to bounce back from financial defeat, and how to navigate American and international finance in the first half of the twentieth century. Temperamental, imperious, and impatient, he thrived on conflict. He boxed with his sons to toughen them up and urged them to settle disputes by fighting one another in a ring in their house. "And," recalled his grandson G. H. Walker III, "he pulled no punches."

The Walkers were as old a family as the Bushes, arriving in the seventeenth century from England and making their way from Maine to Maryland. They settled along the Chesapeake on a river known as the Sassafras in the northern part of Maryland on the Delmarva Peninsula. There, in Cecil County, Walkers and their kin were slave-owning planters. In the 1830s, George and Harriet Walker struck out for Illinois. In 1840 in McLean County, Illinois, Harriet Walker gave birth to a son, David Davis Walker. The baby was named for a first cousin: future Supreme Court justice David Davis, an Illinois lawyer, politician, and landowner who was to be a successful manager in Abraham Lincoln's campaign for the presidential nomination of the Republican Party in Chicago in 1860.

Judge Davis took an interest in his Walker kinsman, seeing that young David Davis Walker, called D.D., enrolled in the preparatory school at Beloit, a small liberal arts college on the Illinois-Wisconsin border. After young Walker spent two years at Beloit, the lure of business won out. "I've had enough schooling," he declared, and Judge Davis likely connected him with Wayman Crow, a successful dry goods businessman in St. Louis. D. D. Walker joined Crow and did well in St. Louis, marrying

Martha Beaky, a Roman Catholic, on Christmas Day 1862, and cofounding the Ely Walker Dry Goods Company in 1880. Martha and D. D. Walker had five sons and one daughter, raising them in a large house on Vandeventer Place.

In 1875 came a son, George Herbert Walker, named for the Anglican priest and poet George Herbert. Life in the Martha and D. D. Walker household was strict but not suffocating. A granddaughter who spent most of her childhood in the house remembered trips to Paris, lessons in French, and evenings standing at the top of the stairs of the big house watching the grown-ups playing poker and drinking beer. Like the men in the family, Martha Walker was accustomed to being heeded. If she noticed a run-down house in Kennebunkport, where the family began summering at the turn of the twentieth century, she would say, "Oh, that house *must* be painted," and then arrange to pay for the job.

Bert was perhaps the most headstrong of D. D. Walker's children. He attended parochial schools in St. Louis until his parents dispatched him (along with a valet) to Stonyhurst in England, a Jesuit boarding school and citadel of aristocratic English Roman Catholics. His parents hoped he would return from England to seek ordination as a priest of the church, "but as a result of that stern schooling," his daughter Dorothy recalled, "he grew to hate Catholicism." Back in the United States, Bert Walker joined his father's firm, Ely Walker. He never liked the dry goods business, however, and was determined to define himself in contrast to his father. "He did not want to work with and certainly not for his father," recalled G. H. Walker III. "They were both difficult men, and the family tradition is that they just made each other more difficult when they were together." One day at the warehouse in St. Louis, Bert Walker was taking inventory when a fire alarm rang out. He left the building with everyone else. When the drill passed, a colleague said, "Time to go back in."

Bert Walker shook his head. "I'm never going back," he said, and he never did. He founded an investment house, G. H. Walker & Company, based in St. Louis. In another act of rebellion, he fell in love with Lucretia "Loulie" Wear, one of the great beauties of the day. The price of the marriage to this Presbyterian bride was the groom's abandonment of Roman Catholicism. "She insisted on that," recalled their grandson G. H. Walker III. Consulting a priest, Walker was warned of eternal consequences should he proceed on his current course. "If you marry her in a Presbyterian church," a Catholic priest is said to have told Walker, "you'll go straight to hell."

"I'll tell you one thing," Walker replied. "I'll go straight to hell if I don't marry her."

The house Loulie and Bert Walker built at 12 Hortense Place in St. Louis was in an enclave for young, rich families. As Dorothy Walker Bush recalled, the Lamberts, of the Listerine fortune, were neighbors; another was Eugene Cuendet, a jewelry and real estate magnate who was so obsessed with fires that he had his house wired to the fire station so that he could go out on calls as they came in. The stories of Bert Walker's own flamboyance were legendary, and legion. There was the time he shot into the dining room ceiling at Duncannon, his plantation in Barnwell County, South Carolina, where he liked to hunt. There was the near-riot he instigated at the St. Louis Club when a private party he was attending grew too loud. In response to complaints from other members, Walker and his comrades armed themselves with the instruments from a six-piece band, including a bass drum, and undertook a loud march. (This led to Walker's founding a rival club, the Racquet Club of St. Louis, whose motto was "Youth Will Be Served.") Then there was the drunken evening on the night before the finals of a polo match that was so notorious the other competitors misunderstood Walker to be calling for more drinks during the match when he cried, "Get me Whiskey"— though "Whiskey," in this case, was another of his ponies.

He shared a yacht with W. Averell Harriman, won the heavyweight boxing title of Missouri, served as president of the United States Golf Association, and established golf's Walker Cup. He could be generous, and his family and associates trusted his judgment. During a troubled economic hour for Bert, one of his brothers came to his office and "put his whole portfolio on the desk and invited him to use whatever he needed to get him through." And while father and son could not work together permanently, they did cooperate on one venture: D. D. Walker and G. H. Walker had bought land together in Kennebunkport, Maine, in 1900 to create a summer redoubt, Walker's Point, along the ocean road.

On Monday, July 1, 1901, in Kennebunkport, Dorothy Wear Walker was born to Loulie and Bert. Her father admired Dorothy's athleticism and gave her everything a child might want. There was a French governess until Dorothy was twelve and two nurses for the younger children. Dorothy and her sister, Nancy, attended the Mary Institute from the age of six on; their uniform blouses or linen dresses with scalloped collars were tailored by a woman who came to Hortense Place. (Sports were played in bloomers.) There was music and Shakespeare; on Tuesdays and Fridays Dorothy walked to lessons with her piano teacher, Mrs. Hicken-looper. She was sent to Miss Porter's School in Farmington, Connecticut. In the summers the family attended services at St. Ann's Episcopal Church near their land in Kennebunkport. In St. Louis they belonged to Westminster Presbyterian—a legacy of the Wear victory over the Walkers—and attended services at least three times a week: Sunday mornings and evenings, and Wednesday nights for prayer meetings.

To reach the East each summer, families like the Walkers in St. Louis embarked on private rail cars for the journey toward New England, then they would either transfer to the Boston and Maine Railroad or hook their car up to the B&M, which would take them straight to Kennebunk-port's local station. The trunks were sent ahead. The authors Booth Tarkington and Kenneth Roberts spent time in Kennebunkport, holding court, playing bridge and mah-jongg and charades. The town playhouse was popular. There were carnivals, too, and even a small opera house. At summer's end, Dorothy recalled, the Walkers climbed aboard a horse-drawn bus for the trip to West Kennebunk station. They would stop for the night at the Hotel Touraine in Boston.

As his father, D. D. Walker, grew older, Bert believed the old man was giving away excessive amounts of money. Moving to have D.D. declared legally incompetent, Bert and one of his brothers set off a familial firestorm. D.D. was so enraged at the litigation that he announced that he had drawn an imaginary line across the property at Walker's Point to divide his sphere from that of his sons'. "If you cross that line," D. D. Walker declared, "I'll shoot you both—and not to kill, but in the knees. I'll wound you for life." When the father died, in 1918, the case was still in the courts.

Strife, then, was common in the world of the Walkers, and standards were high. At Kennebunkport, Uncle Will Walker, a brother of Bert's, would take a given year's group of children down to the sea to teach them how to swim. "This is the way we're going to learn," he would say. "I'm going to throw you in the water and you're going to swim." One Walker cousin, a contemporary of Dorothy's, was stoic about the approach. "I was terrified, but I mean you just *did* it," she said. "We had to go off the pier and make the beach. . . . There are just certain people who can take those things and others can't."

Dorothy Walker could take it. Once, when her brother Herbie refused to listen to her when she asked him to stop fiddling with a new tennis racquet, she went into the barn at Kennebunkport, got some rope, and firmly tied her little brother to the gatepost at the edge of the property before going about her business. Years later, a story was told that Dorothy was at the plate in a baseball game while in the ninth month of her pregnancy with her eldest child, Prescott, Jr. She hit a home run, rounded each base, and then went off to deliver the baby. During a pitched tennis match she fell and injured herself, but refused to default or give up. She played to the end, learning later that her wrist was broken.

P rescott Bush's courtship of Dorothy Walker came at a transformative moment for the Walker family. For all its commerce and all its charms, St. Louis was too limiting for Bert Walker. By this point he was well known as a dealmaker who delivered strong returns for his investors, and the Harriman family of New York asked Walker to run their investment banking business. Coming east was appealing, and the Walkers moved to New York in 1920, acquiring a home in the city at 453 Madison Avenue.

As the Walkers settled into their new life, Dorothy and Prescott were married at St. Ann's in Kennebunkport on Saturday, August 6, 1921. John Poyntz Tyler, the bishop of North Dakota, presided. Several guests arrived by yacht. The new Mr. and Mrs. Prescott Bush lived in St. Louis for a time and then moved briefly to Kingsport, Tennessee, where Bush, still with Simmons, managed the sale of a saddlery plant in upper east Tennessee. There were a number of moves in this period. On one business assignment Bush discovered a case of fraud and decided to keep a loaded revolver in his desk in case the culprit came after him. The Bushes returned to St. Louis and then spent a year in Columbus, Ohio, where Prescott tried to make a go of a small manufacturing concern that ended up being sold to a Massachusetts company, the Stedman Products Company, which made rubber flooring. The buyers wanted Bush to come along with the sale, and so the Bushes moved yet again, this time east to Milton, Massachusetts. They bought 173 Adams Street, a big Victorian on Milton Hill near the intersection of Adams and Hutchinson and

Dorothy Walker Bush was a beloved child of her father, G. H. "Bert" Walker, who adored his daughter's competitive spirit. She was remembered as an excellent shot during Christmas trips to Duncannon, G. H. Walker's South Carolina hunting estate.

within the briefest of walks to Governor Hutchinson's Field, the old site of the estate of the last colonial governor of Massachusetts. On Thursday, June 12, 1924, in a bedroom on the second floor of the Adams Street house, Dorothy Walker Bush delivered her second son. A midwife assisted.

Baptized George Herbert Walker Bush in honor of his maternal grandfather (his older brother's name, Prescott Sheldon Bush, Jr., had already given pride of place to the paternal line), George quickly became known as "Poppy," or "Little Pop," since G. H. Walker was sometimes called "Pop" within the family. While George's father was less than enthusiastic about the nickname for his son, he gave up the fight early on. "Poppy" it was.

The Prescott Bushes moved to Greenwich, Connecticut, in 1925, when Prescott took a job with United States Rubber Company, which was based in New York. The following year Prescott went to work on Wall Street, joining W. A. Harriman & Company, the investment firm run by his father-in-law. Bush was valuable in part because of his peripatetic twenties. He had his friends from Yale, from the army, from his time with Simmons, and from the different businesses where he had since worked. "I did have a very wide acquaintance," Prescott Bush re-called. In 1926, Bush began working at W. A. Harriman; in 1931, it merged with an old private banking firm, Brown Brothers, to form Brown Brothers Harriman & Company. Brown Brothers was already a notable house. At the end of the Great War, when President Wilson went to Versailles, he had a letter of credit from Brown Brothers in his pocket for his personal expenses.

The firm became one of the most elite investment banks in the world, its partners moving seamlessly between private and public life. Averell Harriman served as an envoy to Winston Churchill's London during World War II, as ambassador to the Soviet Union, and as governor of New York. Another partner, Robert Lovett, held a variety of high for-eign policy posts for FDR and Truman. (Lovett's reputation was such that President-elect John F. Kennedy would offer him his choice of State, Defense, or Treasury. Lovett declined them all.) In their offices at 59 Wall Street, the partners at Brown Brothers Harriman were linked by family and school ties. Decisions were made by consensus, usually at meetings of the partnership held every Thursday at 9:45 in the morning in the firm's offices. Prescott also joined the boards of many American companies, including Prudential and CBS, filling his briefcase every day and reading on the train coming and going from Greenwich.

Before the merger with Brown Brothers, W. A. Harriman had prof-ited handsomely from investments in the Soviet Union and, like many Wall Street firms, Brown Brothers Harriman had financial ties to Ger-many in the 1930s. In July 1941, the *New York Herald Tribune* would report that Fritz Thyssen, a key backer of Adolf Hitler's, kept $3 million in a New York entity called the Union Banking Corporation that had been set up in 1924. (In reporting on the story, *The Washington Post* referred to Thyssen as "Hitler's Angel," and there was speculation that the $3 mil-lion was, as the *Herald Tribune* put it, "for some of the Nazi bigwigs.") Several Brown Brothers Harriman partners, including Prescott Bush, were listed as directors of Union Banking—a "courtesy," in the parlance of the international banking world. As World War II began, the part-nership wrote William R. White, the New York superintendent of banks, to say that it had "been giving serious consideration to withdraw-ing from the board," but White asked them to remain in place "during this period of uncertainty." Thyssen's Union Banking assets, which were also linked to Germany's United Steel Works, were seized under the

Trading with the Enemy Act in October 1942. (The German connections never became an issue for Prescott in his ensuing years in Connecticut politics.)

In the wake of the merger in the early 1930s, Bert Walker had left the firm, though he remained in New York at his own investment house, G. H. Walker & Company. Walker's freewheeling style had apparently not fit in well with the newly formed investment bank. Knight Woolley, a Yale classmate of Prescott's and a fellow Bonesman (Averell and Roland Harriman, as well as Lovett—all Brown Brothers Harriman partners—were also Skull and Bones members), worried about Walker's "dangerous dealings," and so Bert resigned, returning to G. H. Walker.

Walker was gone, but his son-in-law Prescott Bush stayed. Though Prescott would maintain mostly cordial relations with his father-in-law through the years (Walker admired Prescott's golf game), the Bush code of disguised ambition and ritualistic self-effacement was to govern the lives of Dorothy and Prescott Bush's children. Walkers and Bushes both wanted to win. The distinction was that Bushes tried, with sporadic success, to conceal their drive from others. George H. W. Bush's competitive nature, then, flowed from both his parents' clans. He was fortunate that his mother, educated at Miss Porter's in the East and soaked in Loulie Wear Walker's sober Presbyterianism, had learned to temper her will to win with an insistence on outward humility.

At home in Connecticut, Prescott Bush was fascinated by the New England town meeting system in which local government is conducted by a large number of elected precinct representatives. "Others would climb off the club car coming out from New York whining about how they wanted to get home for a drink," recalled George H. W. Bush, "and he'd go off to the town meeting and preside." While Prescott adored singing, performing with his beloved Silver Dollar Quartet, he also thrived on fulfilling roles of public leadership, becoming moderator, or chairman, of the town meeting in Greenwich.

To his children, Prescott could be a stern, forbidding presence. "In the thirties he was worried, worried about business, and about the world," recalled George's sister, Nancy Bush Ellis. "I was terrified of my father until about age eighteen or so," said younger brother Jonathan Bush. "Growing up he was just terrifying to a little guy. He was a scary man. He was always on a mission. He'd come home from Manhattan, sit and read the paper, listen to Fred Waring on the radio, then charge out the door to a meeting. When we were older, however, he became a warm and loving parent and mentor. He was an agent of stability in all our lives. His motto: 'Moderation in all things.'"

George H. W. and his older brother, Pres Jr.—or "Pressy"—once paid a neighborhood girl, Joan Williams, a dime to run naked through the house. When the elder Prescott Bush found out—through Mrs. Williams, who had reported the episode to Mrs. Bush—he was enraged. "He picked up a squash racquet off the table and sent us over to apologize to the Williamses," George H. W. Bush recalled. "It wasn't a short walk, either. We knocked on the door and apologized. God, I thought he was going to kill us with that racquet. But he didn't. He could be tough, strong. We were scared of him when it came to discipline."

The Bush household was busy, but it was hardly a free-for-all. An air of order pervaded the house, which was itself quite an accomplishment, given the family's size and spirits. After Prescott Jr. and Poppy, Dorothy and Prescott Bush had three other children: Nancy (born 1926), Jonathan (born 1931), and William "Bucky" (born 1938). Dorothy had day-to-day charge of the children. "She had five of us to raise . . . and she just felt strongly that there was too much for us to learn and to do to waste any time on chaos," George H. W. Bush recalled. "Every mother has her own style. My Mother's was a little like an Army drill sergeant's. Dad was the Commanding General, make no mistake about that, but Mother was the guy out there day in and day out shaping up the troops." She was to shape them in her image: courageous, competitive, caring, and tireless.

THREE

He Gets So Intense Over Everything

★

Mother was always generous in defeat—but she hardly ever lost at anything.

—JONATHAN BUSH on Dorothy Walker Bush

Dad? Tall, scary—big guy. Very big guy. Very respected. Very.

—GEORGE H. W. BUSH on Prescott Bush

T HERE WAS NEVER ANY DOUBT about the mission. The yard of the Bush house on Grove Lane in Greenwich was dotted with grand trees, and the children knew without being told that those trees—no matter how tall—were to be climbed. The obstacles to success were not to be discussed. Dorothy Bush was fearless, and she expected her children to be fearless, too. It was her version of her Uncle Will Walker's throw-them-in-the-water-and-make-them-swim strategy. In her father's house she had learned that action was more important than words, that the ability to thrive in a contest—to knock an opponent out, to outrace a fellow runner—gave one a certain thrill, a certain status, a certain place in the world. Competition was essential to Dorothy Walker Bush—not mindless competition, but competition in order to pursue, test, and exhibit excellence.

And so the trees awaited. On sunny days, the ground dappled through leafy branches, the bark rough to the touch of young hands, Poppy Bush and his siblings would come racing out of the big shingled house and pick the day's target. "Mother never seemed afraid," George H. W. Bush recalled. If a worried neighbor spotted a Bush child making a perilous climb, the well-meaning bystander would be thanked but sent on his way. When the inevitable falls and crashes came, well, that was part of life. "Of course, there would be scrapes and bruises from time to time," Bush recalled, "but it didn't seem to faze Mother or her confidence in us." Or, as the years passed, the children's confidence in themselves.

For families such as the Bushes, athletics were a maker and a measure of character. Sports were to be taken as seriously as one's studies, or one's manners, for they were perennial pursuits, permanent features of life. This was the prevailing view of the Victorian world out of which S. P. Bush and G. H. Walker came. One architect of what was known as "muscular Christianity," Charles Kingsley, the Victorian clergyman, professor, and novelist, wrote that "in the playing-field boys acquire virtues which no books can give them; not merely daring and endurance, but, better still, temper, self-restraint, fairness, honor, unenvious approbation of another's success, and all that 'give and take' of life which stand a man in such good stead when he goes forth into the world, and without which, indeed, his success is always maimed and partial."

Dorothy Bush believed in the Kingsley code. "The sun might be blistering hot, and she might just have come off the tennis court, having played a three-set match, but she'd see one of us along the side, pining to play, and without our even asking, there she would be, saying, 'C'mon, let's go hit a few,'" George H. W. Bush recalled. "You would think she might have said, 'I'm worn out, let me catch my breath.' But not Mother. She'd have us out on the court, hitting a few, just when we most wanted to learn to play. I can hear her now, 'You can do it. You'll get it. You'll get it.' And she would be patient and tireless and always absolutely sure we would—eventually—get it."

For Poppy, life in the 1920s and '30s was divided between Grove Lane in Greenwich, the Point at Kennebunkport, and Grandfather Walker's plantation in South Carolina. In Greenwich there was a porte cochere in front and broad porches. The upstairs hall was lined with family photographs, especially images of Yale teams, as well as group shots of sundry Bushes and Walkers. Elsie Walker, a Bush cousin, remembered the house in minute detail. Invited over for "tiddlywinks, jigsaw puzzles and an afternoon of tennis at the Field Club," guests could explore the yard "full of forsythia in early spring." The porch was a center of life. It seemed especially "wide and comfortable . . . on a summer evening," when the Bushes would drink iced tea garnished with sprigs of mint. On Sundays, if the weather was good, Prescott would wear rubber-spiked golf shoes to services at Christ Episcopal Church. The strategy was simple: this way he wouldn't lose any time going from the services to the first tee at Round Hill, the Bushes' local course. If it was raining or snowing, he would sit in the den, listening to the New York Philharmonic on CBS radio. Dorothy would work crossword puzzles and knit; Prescott would fight to stay awake in the long stretches of afternoon.

One summer day in the mid-1930s at Kennebunkport, Grandfather Walker was at lunch on Walker's Point. He had allowed Pres Jr. and Poppy to take out his lobster boat, the *Tomboy*. The boys had gone too fast in the river, throwing up a dangerous wake, before returning home.

Two infuriated lobstermen soon appeared at the house and asked the butler, who answered the door, if they could have a word with Mr. Walker. "There are two men to see you," the butler told the master of the house. Walker was annoyed. "Tell them I'm at lunch," he said dismissively.

The butler persisted, and finally Walker left the table and went out to see the lobstermen. "We want to talk to you, sir," one of the callers said. "Your boys were going fast in the river and threw a big wake up and rammed our boats up against the pier." Walker virtually snarled back. "Can't you see I'm having lunch? Leave!" He returned to his meal, then summoned his grandsons to him. "He chewed us out to a fare-thee-well," recalled George H. W. Bush, and ordered the boys to go apologize to the lobstermen.

His grandchildren recalled awkward moments when Walker could be, in Bush's words, "tough on our grandmother." Anything could set the old man off. "Come on, Loulie, let's get going here," Walker would say. "I'm a busy man." The world was supposed to run on Walker's schedule and terms, not anyone else's. Even breakfast could be perilous. "This bread is too glutinous," Walker announced one morning at the table, pushing his toast aside. "Oh, I'm sorry, Bertie," said Mrs. Walker. "I'm sorry it's so glutinous."

The family came to the table the next morning with trepidation. Would there be another toast crisis? Chewing, Walker paused, then announced: "Now this is more like it." Relief all around—and the awareness that the master was not exactly a rational actor. ("It'd be exactly the same loaf," recalled George H. W. Bush. "It had just been aged for a day or something.")

The summers were full of boating, swimming, tennis, and golf. "Lots of sports, lots of summer reading—Mother would snap at us to read more," recalled Nancy Bush Ellis. The Bush children read *Two Years Before* the Mast, *Tess of the d'Urbervilles*, and *Mutiny on the Bounty*. Poppy and Pressy boated no matter what: "Any kind of storm, any kind of weather—out they went," recalled Nancy. When they got back in, if the weather was still bad, they would receive new marching orders from their mother: Head for the beach. "Ride the surf and I'll have hot soup for you when you get back," Mrs. Bush would say, and off the children would go.

They were taught to appreciate what they had—and if they couldn't, the toys would be taken away. "Mother always stressed with us how Dad was paying for the bicycle that we had left out rusting if we left it in the yard," recalled Nancy Bush Ellis. "She would say, 'He's working away so that you can have these beautiful bicycles, and now you cannot use it for a week.' And away it would go to the garage. Mother hated carelessness."

Christmases were spent in South Carolina. The family would board the Atlantic Coast Line, and the Bushes would stop at a little town called Snelling, near Duncannon, G. H. Walker's plantation. Days began, Nancy Bush Ellis recalled, when they woke and summoned Hansford, the chief domestic, who would light crackling pine fires in each room. Daylight hours were given over to hunting dove and quail. The dogs—pointers and spaniels—rode out to the fields on mule-drawn carts. Predictably, Dorothy was a terrific shot, as was Prescott. At night dinner was black-tie.

In the world outside the Bush-Walker enclave, the 1930s raged and roiled. The children had fleeting glimpses of the stresses of the period in their father's face. Prescott could be silent at the dinner table, thinking over problems. "Dad was grim," recalled Nancy Bush Ellis. "There was a Depression and there was Hitler making him nervous." The Bush children were insulated from want, but they were raised to feel a sense of obligation to others. A key biblical verse much repeated in the Bush household came from the First Epistle to the Corinthians: "Now it is required that those who have been given a trust must prove faithful," a variation of the Gospel text from St. Luke: "For unto whomsoever much is given, of him shall be much required."

The principle that privilege entailed service was as much a part of the household as sports. The case was first made in religious terms. "Pretty much every day we'd have a Bible verse, usually at breakfast," Bush recalled. Theological details were never to interest him, but the overarching point—that he owed the larger world a measure of devotion and service—took hold. The sense of order that shaped George H. W.

Bush—invisible but real, unseen but felt—was the work of both Dorothy and Prescott, both of whom may have been partly reacting to their early lives. Dorothy loved her father, but his wheeling and dealing produced uncertainty—who knew when the private school tuition might not be there for the next year?—that she did not wish to replicate in the lives of her own children. Prescott remained the more serious man he had become after his mock-heroic letter went public and his mother was killed at Watch Hill. From a distance, the Bush ethos can seem a mad jumble of tumbling children, frolicking dogs, endless tennis or tiddlywinks, and sweating martini pitchers. Up close, though, there was a steadiness of purpose.

And contrary to cultural stereotype, there was no shame in showing one's emotions. "She cries a lot—sometimes from happiness," George recalled of his mother. "She always cries when someone else hurts a lot. She just cares about the other guy." Though his public persona in his political years was that of a classically buttoned-down—and buttoned-up—WASP, in private he, too, cried easily. In his old age he sometimes woke in the night, hearing her voice. "She's always with me," he said. Like his mother, George H. W. Bush moved through life torn between an ambition to win and an impulse toward empathy. Raised with a sense of duty to deflect attention from himself, he was, nevertheless, also raised to seek the world's glittering prizes. He was an emotionally complex man, veering between competitiveness and kindness, driven, yet given to private tears. He was, in other words, his mother's son.

George H. W. Bush was five years old when he entered Greenwich Country Day School in September 1929. He and his brother Pres Jr. were so close that the Bushes allowed Poppy to start first grade a year early so that the boys could be together. The boys were chauffeured to and from school by the family's driver, Alec Chodaczek. There were black-and-orange uniform sweaters, mandatory Latin, ice hockey on the neighboring Rockefellers' ponds in winter, sledding down the great hill behind the main school building, Gilbert and Sullivan musicals, pet shows in which a student could enter "anything from a mouse to a polar bear" and a years-long marbles tournament. "It was cutthroat," recalled a former GCDS student. "Wall Street moguls might have gotten their early trading experience by trading marbles at Country Day."

The school's first headmaster, John Lynn Miner, was a practically minded educator. Repetition was key, Miner said, as was fair play. A section of the regular report card included the category "Claims More Than His Fair Share of Time and Attention in Class"—a measure the Bushes watched carefully. Poppy was an empathetic child, drawing out others and earning the nickname "Have-Half" for his habit of dividing any treat with friends. One moment from his elementary school years stood out in his memory. During an informal playground race at GCDS, a heavy classmate was stuck in an obstacle course barrel and couldn't get out. As the other children pressed on to the finish line, Bush stopped to pull the other boy out. "I saw him there, and I got to thinking, 'I've never been the guy who wasn't picked for the team or was left waiting in line,' but there he was, and so I helped," Bush recalled. "Seeing him stuck made me think about how I'd feel if I were hurting. And I'd want somebody to help me. So I helped."

Older people tended to adore Poppy. "How well I can recall—and see you to this day—running for a touchdown against Harvey . . . those ear flaps flopping in the wind!" a teacher named Arthur Grant wrote Bush in the vice presidential years. "How wonderful!"

Bush also loved to win. One Christmas his brother Bucky was given a handheld labyrinth game in which players were supposed to manipulate the board in order to plop a marble into a small hole at the end of a maze. Bucky shared it with Bush, who couldn't quite make it work.

The next morning, Bush said, "You know, Buck, I think I'll try that labyrinth again," and Bucky dutifully handed it over—only to watch, amazed, as Bush, in a total reversal of the previous day's performance, expertly scored again and again. "Wow, Pop, you're really good," Bucky said. "That's amazing."

"Oh, yeah," Bush replied breezily, "I'm pretty good at this kind of thing." Only later did Bucky learn that Bush had secretly practiced late into the night to master the game for the coming day. "That was Pop," Bucky recalled. "He adored competing but didn't want you to know he'd ever worked at it."

Before graduating from Greenwich Country Day in June 1937, Bush was the subject of a parental questionnaire for Phillips Academy in Andover, Massachusetts (popularly known as Andover), where he hoped to matriculate in the fall. Signed by both Dorothy and Prescott, the document refers to their second son not as "Poppy" or as "George" but as "Walker." The family had apparently not yet settled on a name to be used outside the family. The testing of "Walker Bush," then, suggests that whatever tension might have existed between Prescott and his father-in-law after the Brown Brothers Harriman merger was not great enough to prevent the Bushes from experimenting with a name that would have their boy become even more overtly connected to the maternal line than he was already.

The portrait of "Walker" that emerges from the Andover questionnaire is prescient. "Walker has always been a good healthy boy," the Bushes wrote. "At present he is having his teeth straightened. He has no other present physical weaknesses or disabilities although he is apparently growing rapidly and hasn't gotten quite the strength he should have for his size. . . . [He also has] a tendency to overdo and get tired, at times beyond a reasonable point." Noting that their son's "family life has been in all respects a happy one," the Bushes added: "He has plenty of initiative and determination. He may be a trifle too intense and has somewhat of a temper, which . . . we see much more of at home than has been seen at his school. . . . He has a good sense of humor. He is exceedingly sensitive and very considerate of the feelings of other people in all walks of life." The questionnaire goes on:

SOCIAL CHARACTERISTICS I believe Walker has been very popular at school and gets along easily with boys, and with older people as well.

PERSONAL HABITS His record at GCD was very good for neatness and punctuality although we have noticed at home he is less neat than we consider desirable and hope that [Andover] will improve him in that respect. He is a good hard worker. He does not smoke.

SPECIAL INTERESTS Walker likes all games and played both football and baseball at GCD, being on the first team in both sports. . . . [H]e has not shown the special interest in reading that we should like to see but he likes shop work and does things well with his hands. He has recently taken quite an interest in photography with a small camera.

SCHOLARSHIP Apparently he learns easily and rapidly. His marks at GCD were always quite satisfactory and he was frequently on the honor roll. He seems to take pride in standing well in his class.

FUTURE PLANS He hopes to go to Yale but beyond that has no definite profession or career picked out for himself.

SPECIAL NEEDS OR SUGGESTIONS Plenty of sleep, as he gets so intense over everything he undertakes[,] lessons as well as sports.

Taken together, the observations about Bush's intensity are striking. "A tendency to overdo and get tired"; "a trifle too intense and has somewhat of a temper"; "he gets so intense over everything he undertakes." Written of a boy of twelve—he would turn thirteen the same month he left Greenwich Country Day—the insights suggest that the young Bush had thoroughly absorbed the world around him, not least his parents' expectations about how a child of theirs was to engage that world. There were trees, and trees were to be climbed, no matter how high or how hard. There were exams, and exams were to be passed, and passed handsomely. There were older people, and older people were to be charmed, and charmed graciously. There were other boys, and other boys were to be treated well, with kindness and generosity. There was so much—so many tests and tasks, so many tiny referenda. It was Bush's fate to be aware of every single one of them, and to try to hide, to mask, his ambition to carry every point, to win every battle, to hit if not exceed every mark.

What drove him? Why was he so determined to prove himself again and again and again, on matters large and small, important and trivial? His mother had had to prove to her father that a girl could be great; his father was so anxious to attract attention that he had written that embarrassing prank letter about fantastical war exploits. They had become the people they were through the winning of competitions and of notice, and they imparted to their gifted second son a vision of life as a contest. It was subtle, almost imperceptible, and perhaps all the more powerful for that. Bushes were to win, but not brag; succeed, but not preen.

For them, life was a public matter in the sense that the world's opinion carried great weight. Spectators and fellow competitors knew the score at the end of the match, who was elected captain of the team, or who won a seat on the student council. Respect, that most prized of commodities, came from achievement. The better you did—the more contests you won—the greater the next goal, the greater the next mission. It never ended, really. It never could end, except at the summit of American life: either great riches in business or, in politics, with the presidency. Thinking of his own father's understanding of public service, Prescott Bush was explicit about noblesse oblige. "He felt that everybody doesn't have an equal obligation," Prescott Bush said of S. P. Bush. "Some people have better opportunities than others to serve and better facilities, better equipment, and that one's obligation increased with the fact that you were perhaps better qualified or better able, for any reason, to do something about the public service."

Poppy was the kind of boy who, to other eyes, seemed well suited to living life by this code of camouflaged competitiveness. Camouflage was key: The Bush code was about disguising one's ambition and hunger to win. "You have goals, and you want to meet them," recalled George H. W. Bush, who quickly added: "Without letting it show through in everyday life." Hence the quiet intensity, the worrying, the overdoing, the temper that showed itself at home, in private, rather than at school. The code dictated outward ease, even if there was inward anxiety. And how could there not be some inward anxiety? Two handsome, popular, polished parents, so good at everything, implicitly expecting you to be handsome, popular, polished, and good at everything, too? The very lack of explicit pressure was itself a compelling force, for it created a world in which the expectation of success was simply there, a fact of life as basic as breakfast or the radio in the den where Prescott listened to the news and Fred Waring. No wonder, then, that Poppy took "pride in standing well" in his class—an achievement he was expected to repeat as a new boy on Andover Hill.

FOUR

Not for Self

★

Ambitious and self-confident but perhaps not
self-assertive enough.

—"Counselor's Confidential Report" on George H. W. Bush,
Phillips Academy, 1940

You are leaving Andover in what is certainly a very dark hour
for the civilized world. But as I look into your faces and realize
your responsibilities, I am filled, not with pity for you in what
you are facing, but with a desire to congratulate you on your
great opportunity.

—HENRY L. STIMSON, to the Andover graduating class, June 1940

It was a red, white, and blue thing. Your country's attacked,
you'd better get in there and try to help.

—GEORGE H. W. BUSH on his reaction after Pearl Harbor

ANDOVER WAS A GOOD SCHOOL for curbing cockiness among the children of the American elite. The headmaster in Bush's years, Claude M. Fuess, was determined that Andover would fight, not perpetuate, social snobbery. Fuess had been made head of the school in 1933; Alston Hurd Chase, a graduate and teacher, wrote that a common Andover joke had it that "Fuess, Roosevelt, and Hitler all came to power" in the same year. Bush remembered Fuess as a distant, godlike figure. He was nicknamed "Iron" and "Bald Doctor."

Founded in 1778 by Samuel Phillips, Jr., the school itself was the product of Puritan New England. One of the institution's tasks, Phillips had said, was to teach "the fall of Man—the Depravity of Human Nature—the Necessity of Atonement." Andover long predated the creation of St. Paul's School in Concord, New Hampshire (1856), Groton School in Groton, Massachusetts (1884), and Prescott Bush's St. George's near Newport, Rhode Island (1896). The popular image of the boarding school world has been shaped largely by fictional portraits: John Knowles's *A Separate Peace,* J. D. Salinger's *The Catcher in the Rye,* and Louis Auchincloss's *The Rector of Justin.* In the imagination, everything is green, everyone is rich, and nothing is impossible in such schools. E. Digby Baltzell, the University of Pennsylvania sociologist who played a key role in making the term "WASP" a familiar one (his works include 1964's *The Protestant Establishment: Aristocracy and Caste in America*) listed Andover as one of the sixteen American schools that "serve the sociological function of differentiating the upper classes from the rest of the population."

With Andover, the truth is slightly more complicated, for the school from its beginnings sought, albeit in a relative way, to educate, in the school's phrase, "youth from every quarter." In a *Saturday Evening Post* piece on the school, Fuess was quoted listing his "seven deadly sins of independent schools," taking on the image of a boarding school as hopelessly insular and elitist: snobbishness, bigotry, provincialism, reaction, smugness, stupidity, and inertia. "During a fortnight's visit to the school," the magazine reported, "we saw few, if any, indications of the seven sins cited by Dr. Fuess." While Groton and other schools modeled themselves on Eton, the fabled English school in the shadow of Windsor Castle, Andover self-consciously sought to be more democratic and more Puritan than elitist and Anglican. Groton's Latin motto translated as "To serve Him is to rule"; Andover's as "Not for Self."

For Bush, life at Andover in the autumn of 1937—he had turned thirteen that summer—had not begun well. Young for his class—the result of following his brother Pres Jr. to Greenwich Country Day a year early—Bush struggled at first. He was off his stride. "Have-Half" Bush, so generous and gracious at home in Greenwich, was, according to a counselor's report, "not well measured in all respects." He reacted to the stresses of his new life in an uncharacteristic way. "Parents of wealth and social position," the school report said, "cocky and 'high hat' . . . Very mediocre performance."

The author of the comments, Frederic H. Stott, an instructor in English and public speaking, suspected this was a phase, not a pattern. He was right. "Markedly a gentleman," Bush's evaluating teacher wrote in his second year. He was also a markedly sick boy. Bush, at fifteen, checked into the infirmary five times in the 1939–40 school year, missing a total of thirteen days. He had tried to do too much, too fast, going out for

baseball when he was still recovering. As his academic rank fell, he contracted a staph infection serious enough for his parents to withdraw him
from school on Saturday, April 13, 1940, and take him for treatment at
Massachusetts General, the teaching hospital of Harvard Medical School
in Boston. By the next academic year, Bush's evaluating teacher would
write: "Not a strong boy. Serious illness. Nice boy, popular, friendly, gets
on well with adults, very polite. Slow but a hard worker. Illness put him
at a great disadvantage this year. Can analyze well [but] is slow in doing
it. . . . Ambitious and self-confident but perhaps not self-assertive
enough. Real interests are athletics . . . Always a gentleman, responsible,
courteous, generous. WATCH: should not attempt too much outside
work this year. Not a neat boy."

Bush's illnesses in the 1939–40 year at Andover were consistent with
his parents' worries about his "tendency to overdo" and their concern
that their driven, emotional son needed "plenty of sleep" to keep his
equilibrium. He understood the code of his social class enough to affect
an air of indifference about life's worries, so much so that an Andover
teacher noted that Bush "has the typical attitude of not appearing to care
one way or the other." His air of indifference, crucially, was affected
about his studies and his own achievements, not about friendships or the
feelings of others. Other students were drawn to him; they felt protected
and secure in his orbit. Yet there was a dark moment at Andover, notable
largely because of its rarity in Bush's life. When he was thirteen, he used
an anti-Semitic epithet to describe a Jewish friend. Thinking of the moment more than seven decades later, Bush volunteered the story and
cried, shaken by guilt over a remark made in the 1930s. He shook his
head in wonder at his own insensitivity. "Never forgotten it. Never forgotten it." (The classmate remained a Bush friend and supporter for
many years.)

Much more typical is the story of Bruce Gelb, a younger Andover boy
who was being harassed one day by an older student when he heard a
voice say, "Leave the kid alone"—and the bully let Gelb go. Who was
that? Gelb asked. "That was Poppy Bush," a student told him. "He's the
greatest kid in the school."

Serene on the outside, reaching out to smooth others' paths through
life, the adolescent and the adult George H. W. Bush churned inside,
fretting about the world and his place in its many contests. Unhappy and
shaken by his battle against the staph infection, he made his eagerness to

"Poppy" Bush loved baseball, playing first base at Andover and later at Yale.

get back to Andover clear to his teachers. "He loves the school and is most anxious to return and make a good record next year," a teacher wrote of him in the weeks after his hospitalization in Boston. Bush spent a large part of the rest of his life overstretched and sometimes exhausted but hungry to keep moving, to stay in the game, to hit the next mark—at an often-hidden price.

For "Iron" Fuess, the ideal model of an Andover man in the arena was Henry L. Stimson. Born in 1867, the son of a surgeon, Stimson attended Andover, Yale College, and Harvard Law School and became a leading figure in the Republican Party. Stimson embodied the world in which Prescott Bush moved: Republican and anti–New Deal but also, in terms of foreign policy, given to internationalism and bipartisanship. President Taft's secretary of war prior to World War I, Stimson rejoined government as secretary of state under President Hoover and, in retirement in the 1930s, accepted Fuess's invitation to be president of the Andover board of trustees.

Stimson addressed the commencement exercises at Andover on Friday, June 14, 1940. (Bush himself would graduate two years later.) In Cochran Chapel, Stimson—who had warned the headmaster that he planned to "speak out"—made the moral case against totalitarianism. "Today our world is confronted by the clearest issue between right and wrong which has ever been presented to it on the scale in which we face it today," Stimson said. "The world today cannot endure permanently half slave and half free." Within a month of his Andover speech, the old Republican joined President Roosevelt's cabinet, returning to his former post as secretary of war.

Bush and his classmates absorbed the story of their times through the prism of a legendarily difficult class required of Andover seniors: the American history survey course taught by Arthur B. Darling, an Andover and Yale graduate who had taken his PhD at Harvard. One year Darling failed twenty-three boys out of a class of seventy, yet he always polled high in "Best Teacher" surveys, and, Frederick Allis, an Andover alumnus and faculty member, noted that "for those who could get his message, the experience was unforgettable." Bush was one such graduate; he recalled Darling's History 4 warmly. Darling, said one Andover alumnus, "was the greatest teacher I ever had." Asked why, the graduate replied, "Because he was so god-damned unreasonable," which prepared the graduate for a life full of unreasonable things. Darling taught his students, including Bush, that America was a unique nation whose idealistic origins and aspirations required realistic defenders. To him, history was not a heroic fairy tale but the story of a people struggling to balance instincts of light and dark in a complicated world.

The George H. W. Bush of the fall and early winter of 1941 was a lovely, popular boy whose vision was fixed on his immediate surroundings—and no farther. In a report sent to Yale, where Bush hoped to enroll in the tradition of his father and his wider family, Andover wrote that Bush was "an extremely pleasant, well-built, athletic, good-looking, well-bred young man. He is a rather slow reader, his health habits are good, he comes from a fine home of culture and refinement." It continued:

> He is very much of a gentleman, is thoroughly honest, has a high sense of cooperation, and is very responsive to suggestion. He tries hard to do a good job, is intellectually honest, and disciplines himself well and with ease. He is popular, and exerts a first-rate influence on the school. . . . Despite his extracurricular activities he does a consistent job which places him at about the middle of his class. To expect much more of him would be unfair at this time. He is considerably younger than the average of his class, is somewhat lacking in self-confidence when in the presence of adults, but he is

entirely at home with his mates under all conditions. There is little evidence that he is greatly interested in any of his studies, but he works conscientiously and regularly. At the moment he is intellectually immature for his powers of reasoning are not entirely developed and he is easily confused in recitations. Nevertheless, he is willing to do his best, takes active interest in class discussions, seems to be on the ball consistently. He is socially inclined in a thoroughly attractive way. A first-rate individual in every respect, and highly recommended.

On the evening of Saturday, December 6, 1941, Claude Fuess and his wife were guests at a dinner party in Boston. Over cigars, a man Fuess recalled as "a high-ranking officer in the navy" spoke confidently of American superiority in the Pacific. "It would be impossible for the Japanese to accomplish anything in the Pacific," the officer said. The others in the room—a Harvard Law School professor, an industrialist, and the host, "a well-informed attorney"—agreed. The next afternoon, Sunday, December 7, Fuess was interrupted by a call from a member of the Andover faculty. "Have you the heard the news over the radio? The Japanese have bombed Pearl Harbor." Like so many other Americans, the headmaster of Phillips Academy Andover had to ask: "Where's that?" The reports from the Pacific had moved over the Associated Press wire at 2:22 P.M. eastern time. Radio networks began breaking into regular programming between 2:25 and 2:30 P.M. Bush was walking past Cochran Chapel with a friend when a passerby called out the news. "My God," Bush recalled thinking at the time. "This changes everything." Bush's blood was up. As the hours passed on that Sunday afternoon and evening, he decided to join the fight as soon as humanly possible. "After Pearl Harbor, it was a different world altogether," he recalled. "It was a red, white, and blue thing. Your country's attacked, you'd better get in there and try to help."

Bush recalled Prescott's example. "Dad had served in the field artillery," Bush thought at the time. The son knew the outlines of his father's story: that he'd signed up, trained with his friends, and shipped out to serve at the front. He knew what there was to live up to and surpass, since that's what Bushes did when they competed. They went farther, faster. In his address to Congress and to the nation on Monday, December 8, 1941, President Roosevelt cast the struggle against Japan in epic terms. America, he solemnly announced, would fight its way to victory with its "righteous might." To a seventeen-year-old entranced by the drama of Pearl Harbor and driven, in part, by an elemental desire to avenge an attack on his country, joining the military was the most natural thing in the world. The war became his central reality. There were air-raid drills on campus in the event of an enemy attack on the homeland; the student newspaper called the war "a desperate life and death strug-gle" and cast Andover men in a heroic role: "If the government fails, we will fail, and likewise if we fail in our duty at the present time we jeopar-dize the steadfastness of the government's cause."

Bush quickly decided that he wanted to be a pilot, a choice likely in-spired by a small program at Andover in which some boys had begun taking flying lessons in the fall of 1941. In the dormitories and on the fields and around the dining tables of Andover, the prospect of serving as military aviators was irresistible. It was new, thrilling, and competitive—all things that appealed to young Bush and his friends. For him in par-ticular, speed was essential. He even briefly considered enlisting in the Royal Air Force in Canada (RCAF), because, Bush recalled, you "could get through much faster." On the Tuesday after Pearl Harbor, the Cana-dian Member of Parliament and diplomat Sir Herbert Ames gave a lec-ture in Andover's George Washington Hall entitled "Training of Royal Canadian Air Force Fliers"; that same week, an Andover alumnus who had enlisted in the RCAF, R. W. Clifford, wrote about his training in a letter to the editor of the school newspaper.

An older interest, the U.S. Navy, won out as Bush weighed his options. Naval service had been on his mind for some time; a trip to New York for Fleet Week in 1937 had made "a real, profound impression," and Bush had thought of seeking an appointment to the U.S. Naval Academy at Annapolis. The sight of big ships, of the men in their uniforms, at once serious and cool, left Bush with an overall sense of the navy's power and camaraderie and purpose as he returned north to school. After Pearl Harbor, the combination of the two—aviation and the navy—made per-fect sense to Bush. The prewar military requirement of two years of col-lege before you could become a pilot was repealed, which meant he could start training as soon as summer. Bush was not quite seventeen and a half years old, and with the certitude of youth he was convinced he had found his mission.

"I knew what I wanted to do," he remembered. "It was an easy call—no second-guessing, no doubts." He grew more serious about his school-work, too, in preparation for what lay ahead, rising in class rank from fifty-ninth in the fall to thirty-third in the winter. As the 1941 holidays approached, Bush boarded the train to ride down from Massachusetts to Connecticut. He was determined to make the most of Christmas. It would be his last out of uniform.

FIVE

That's Barbara Pierce

★

I have never felt toward another girl as I do towards her.
—GEORGE H. W. BUSH on Barbara Pierce, 1942

SHE WAS, HE SAID LATER, "a strikingly beautiful girl." It was the 1941 Christmas dance at the Greenwich Country Club; the band was playing Glenn Miller numbers. Turning to a fellow guest named Jack Wozencraft, Poppy Bush asked if Wozencraft happened to know the girl in the pretty red-and-green holiday dress. He did: "That's Barbara Pierce."

Born in New York City in 1925, she had grown up in Rye and was in boarding school at Ashley Hall in Charleston, South Carolina. Her father, Marvin—a tall, kind man—was an executive at the McCall Corporation, a publishing company; her mother, Pauline Robinson Pierce, was beautiful but occasionally difficult, archly monitoring Barbara's intake of food. Barbara was the third of the couple's four children.

Did Bush want to meet her? Wozencraft asked. "I told him that was the general idea, and he introduced us," Bush recalled. Wozencraft cut in on Barbara's partner and, as she recalled it, "took me to meet a wonderful-looking young boy he said wanted to meet me, a boy named Poppy Bush."

They danced briefly, but then Bush came to an awkward juncture. The band was moving from a fox-trot to a waltz, and Bush did not waltz. It turned out to be a fortuitous change of tempo, for the two sat down and talked. The conversation lasted fifteen minutes—an eternity in dance time—and ended with a tactically shrewd question from Bush: He asked Barbara what she was planning to do the next evening. She replied that she was due at another dance, in Rye, and the two parted. Neither, though, could get the other off their minds. Bush told his mother that he had met "the niftiest girl at the dance," and, after the five-mile trip home from Greenwich to Rye, smitten by the tall, charming boy who had sought her out, Barbara kept a standing appointment to see her mother before retiring for the night. "We always had to go into Mother's room and talk when we got home," Barbara recalled. "Otherwise, she could not sleep and, I believe, she was smart enough to know that in the night, you are willing to tell all. If she waited until the next day, she knew she'd get one-syllable answers." Barbara's father, Marvin Pierce, would grumble, "Can't this wait until morning?"

In the darkness in the Pierce house on Onondaga Street in Rye, sitting on her mother's bed, Barbara reported that she had met "the nicest, cutest boy, named Poppy Bush." There was an intensity to Barbara's report that night, and Mrs. Pierce—no fool—picked up on her daughter's enthusiasm. "By the time I got up the next morning," Barbara recalled, "Mother—who should have been an FBI agent with her superior intelligence network—knew that Poppy was a wonderful boy who came from 'a very nice family.'"

Bush contrived to show up at the Rye dance the next night, bringing along his sister, Nancy, and a few friends. He asked Barbara to dance again, but just as they began, Barbara's brother Jim interrupted. "Are you Poppy Bush?" Jim asked. "I want to talk to you when you're done with her." Jim Pierce had an invitation. Would Bush like to play in a basketball game pitting the Rye High School team against vacationing prepschool boys? Bush happily accepted, asking Barbara out for a postgame date. At the game, the Pierces turned out in force—"to my horror," Barbara recalled, for she was certain they were there not for the basketball but "to look over my new friend." After Rye won the scrimmage, Bush met the Pierce clan and then took Barbara out.

He was driving the Bush family's Oldsmobile by design. He later confessed to Barbara that he had "begged his mother to let him use the Oldsmobile" since it had a radio. Thinking ahead, Bush was hedging against uncomfortable silences. "He was so afraid we would sit in stony silence and have nothing to say to each other," Barbara recalled. (She added: "For years he has teased me that there was no silence that night and I haven't stopped talking since.") The date went well, and after the holidays the two exchanged letters through the winter months of 1942. At spring vacation their schedules put them at home at the same time for only a single day. They double-dated to a movie (*Citizen Kane*), and Bush asked Barbara to come to Andover for his senior prom.

She was thrilled. "Dear Poppy," Barbara wrote on Ashley Hall stationery from Charleston, "I think it was perfectly swell of you to invite me to the dance and I would love to come or go or whatever you say. . . . I really am excited, but scared to death, too."

Born in 1925, Barbara Pierce grew up in Rye, New York; her father was head of the McCall publishing company. Barbara graduated from the all-girls boarding school Ashley Hall in Charleston, South Carolina, and then attended Smith College before marrying George H. W. Bush in 1945.

Over the prom weekend in Massachusetts, Barbara stayed with a housemaster who was friends with her sister, Martha. Excited to show off his date, Bush did what he did best. Mixing among his classmates and their girls, he introduced Barbara to everyone he could. After the dance, Bush walked Barbara back to her quarters and, as she recalled it, kissed her on the cheek "in front of the world." She could not sleep: "I floated into my room and kept the poor girl I was rooming with awake all night while I made her listen to how Poppy Bush was the greatest living human on the face of the earth."

For Bush, there had been other crushes, but at a kind of distance. "Pressy and I share a view which few others, *very few* others even in Greenwich share," Bush wrote his mother during the war. "That's regarding intercourse before marriage. I would hate to find that my wife had known some other man, and it seems to me only fair to her that she be able to expect the same standards from me. . . . Daddy has never discussed such things with us—of this I am very glad. But we have learned as the years went on by his character what is right and what is wrong."

This did not mean, however, that Bush was monastic. In his mideight-ies, he offered a lighthearted but fairly detailed accounting of the girls who had interested him before he met Barbara. He recalled being twelve when he became aware of the "charms" of Beatie Thurston. "She was beautiful and a well endowed lass," he said. "She had a formfitting rubber (discreet in those days) bathing suit. I fantasized. Ours was a one-sided friendship. I innocently lusted. She teased. I never went out with her, of course. Had I gotten up my nerve to ask her to a movie, she would have undoubtedly giggled. I doubt she ever knew of my fleeting passion. I was just one bedazzled little guy in what must have been a long line."

There was Shirley Flower. "We did go to a movie or two, 1937 to maybe 1940. Her parents were friends of my parents. Shirley was good fun and like Beatie Thurston her body matured early, as Mother might say. In those days no one ever said 'boobs' or even 'breasts' but looking back my fascination may have been heightened by the fact, to use mod-ern parlance—they both had nice racks. Fun nice girls, yes, but both 'ma-tured early.' "

There was Joan Kilner, who lived in Greenwich. "I don't recall ever going out with her," Bush said. "I do recall giggling around the fringes with her at Calf Island in Long Island Sound, where we'd go swim a lot. She was cute, pretty and I'd say, retrospectively, flirtatious. Everyone was mad about her." There was Mary Mathiesson—"very pretty, very flirty I thought," said Bush. "Fine body. Cute sense of humor." He was a fre-quent caller during the chaperoned visiting hours at Abbot Academy, the girls' school on School Street in Andover. In his second to last year, he had what he called "a minor crush" on Betsy Fowler, an Abbot girl. "She came from Massachusetts," said Bush. "I liked her a lot. Never even copped a feel, though." As he read over his own account, Bush acknowl-edged the obvious. "As I look at the above it sounds like I might have been obsessed with 'bodies'—'boobs' they are now called. But what seventeen-year-old kid was not? Guilty am I."

After Pearl Harbor, giggling at Calf Island or on Friday nights at Abbot seemed to belong to another era. Bush saw and understood his own life as bound up with, and defined by, the drama of war. The rapidity of his courtship with Barbara was in keeping with the tempo of the times. War and love came in the same season, and in his mind—and in his heart—both required ultimate commitment.

Bush's last months at Andover passed quickly. The debate among the young men of Bush's milieu was not whether to serve but when. Fuess and others argued that some collegiate education would make the men more valuable to the war effort, a point Henry Stimson echoed in a brief address to Bush's graduating class. Prescott Bush raised the issue with George, asking if Stimson's remarks had given him any pause about going straight into the navy rather than to Yale. The answer was no: The son was determined. By his own account he was "headstrong."

May 1942 was the critical month for his enlistment paperwork. From his rooms at Day Hall at Andover on Friday the fifteenth, Bush had written to the Naval Aviation Cadet Selection Board in Boston to announce his plans. He had asked for, and received, his father's permission to enlist—a requirement for those under the age of twenty-one. With a fountain pen, Prescott had filled out the single-page form in a strong, sure hand authorizing "George Herbert Walker Bush" to serve for the "duration." The chief of police of Greenwich, John M. Gleason, provided a character reference, and Claude Fuess told the naval authorities that Bush was "one of the ablest boys I have ever known in this school, and can recommend him without reservation for any form of active naval, military, or aviation service."

On Friday, June 12, 1942, Bush celebrated both his eighteenth birthday and his graduation from Andover. After the commencement exercises he went to Boston, to the naval aviation offices on Causeway Street, to be sworn into the navy. He was met there by Walter Levering, a Yale football star and naval officer who administered the oath and arranged for Bush to take flight training beginning in September in Chapel Hill, North Carolina. Orders for Bush, officially a seaman second class, to report to North Carolina came through on Wednesday, July 22, 1942. He was assigned to the Sixth Battalion, Company K, Second Platoon.

Barbara was working that summer at the Lord & Taylor department store in Greenwich, preparing to return to Charleston for her final year at Ashley Hall. As a farewell present Bush bought her a small watch. She pinned it on her dress with a gold bow set when he presented it to her. And there was a real kiss. "I don't believe she will ever regret it or resent it, and I certainly am not ashamed of it," Bush told his mother. "I kissed Barbara and I am glad of it." It was a first for both.

On the August 1942 day Bush left New York City for Chapel Hill, his father saw him off. They walked together into Pennsylvania Station, then a huge Greek temple sitting between Seventh and Eighth Avenues and Thirty-First and Thirty-Third streets. It was the first time Bush had ever seen his father cry. "So off I went, scared little guy," Bush recalled. "Got on the train, didn't know anybody." He was eighteen years old, and he was going to war.

PART II

War and Marriage

1942 to 1948

★

Mum, it's a very funny thing. I have no fear of death now.
—GEORGE H. W. BUSH

Bar, you have made my life full of everything I could
ever dream of.
—BUSH to Barbara Pierce, 1943

Newlyweds Barbara and George Bush on their wedding trip to the Cloisters on Sea Island, Georgia, January 1945.

SIX

Off I Zoomed

★

I knew, of course, they would hate me.
—BARBARA PIERCE, on anticipating meeting
the Walker-Bush clan

ARRIVING IN CHAPEL HILL, North Carolina, in the summer of 1942, Bush moved into 317 Lewis Hall, a dormitory on Raleigh Street, and immersed himself in preflight training. The curriculum was a combination of academic work in classes such as Nomenclature and Recognition of airplanes and ships, Essentials of Naval Service, and mathematics and physics, along with obstacle courses, hikes, hand-to-hand combat lessons, and swimming tests. Cadets also had to be able to tread water for five minutes. It was Bush's first prolonged exposure to the South save for his wintertime hunting trips to G. H. Walker's Duncannon estate, and the high summertime temperatures were ferocious. "At some meals we actually drink as much as two and three quarters quarts of liquids," Bush reported in a September 1942 letter to Claude Fuess at Andover. "Fellows have passed out right in ranks on the street from the heat." From reveille at half past five each morning to taps at half past nine each evening, Bush was on the move or at study. Though he found it monotonous—he loved constant motion but disliked relentless routine—he was confident he had been right to enlist. "I have maintained an average of 3.85 out of a possible 4.0, so you can see it is not a very difficult course," Bush wrote Fuess. It was a typical Bush point, made in typical Bush style, mixing pride and humility.

He was living in a new reality, far from Greenwich, far from Andover. "I have never appreciated little things before," Bush wrote his parents. "It is amazing how our moods change here. So many little things affect us. A cold Coke after drill can do more for one than you can imagine.... Ice cream, movies, a 15 minute rest, a letter, a compliment to our platoon. All these little things amount to so much in your mind and it is fun." There was a five-hour hike ahead, and he was already thinking about the "swallow of cold water" that was his "greatest luxury." The physical stress was compounded by the emotional pressure he put on himself to succeed. "After having been here just one month my desire to win my wings and become an officer is tremendous," Bush wrote his sister, Nancy, from Chapel Hill. "I'm afraid if I fail for any reason my disappointment will be very deep."

The possibility of dying was now assumed, stipulated. Training for combat in the company of other men whose lives were also on the line gave him an air of understated fatalism. A Walker in-law, George H. Mead, Jr., a marine officer, was killed on Guadalcanal in August 1942. According to the posthumous citation awarding him the Navy Cross, Mead was leading a platoon under fire from a Japanese sniper. Alone, Mead made his way through the jungle, found the sniper, and killed him with a .45 pistol. "He died the way all of us would like to die when our time comes," Bush wrote home.

With his mother's help, Bush prevailed on the Pierces to allow Barbara to pay a call at Chapel Hill. (Mrs. Bush had told Mrs. Pierce that a visit was a "grand idea.") He met her at the Carolina Inn on Pittsboro Street. "She looked too cute for words—really beautiful," Bush wrote his mother. Bush, who admitted he was "self-conscious" about being (and looking) younger than his contemporaries, asked Barbara to "stretch the calendar, add a few months to her age, and tell anybody who asked that she was eighteen, not seventeen."

No one asked. The two were, in any event, in their own world. They had a sandwich together and walked the campus, winding up at the university's Kenan Memorial Stadium in a grove of pine trees about a mile away from the inn. A sudden storm drove them into the canvas-covered press box. "We laughed at everything," Bush wrote, grateful for the stolen hours. He reported back to training at six o'clock, and Barbara boarded a bus back to Raleigh, where she spent the night before returning to school in Charleston. He hated to see her go. "If she 'fluffed me off' "—dropped him as a suitor—"without warning I would be absolutely sick no kidding," Bush wrote his mother.

In the autumn Bush headed north for flight training at Wold-Chamberlain Field in Minneapolis. On Saturday, November 21, 1942, in a Boeing N2S-3 Stearman (a biplane with two seats, one for the pilot and one for an instructor), Bush noticed that his legs were quaking. Taking off in foggy weather with his instructor on board, he soon forgot to worry. He successfully executed one practice landing. A second, he thought, was "rather rough." Roaring off into the fog again, Bush faced two thousand-foot "emergencies"—exercises in which the instructor shut off the plane's gas, forcing the pilot to maneuver the plane back to land by gliding through the air and finding a safe field on which to come to rest. Again, one test went well, but the second was "pretty rough." The instructor, Ensign J. A. Boyle, told Bush to head back to the base. The weather was briefly disorienting. "For a minute I was lost—couldn't see the field through the mist, but luckily I located it," Bush wrote. Taxiing to a stop, he grew fretful once more. "My nervousness, which had subsided after the first takeoff, came on again."

"Okay, take it up yourself," Boyle told Bush, who sat alone in the plane, ready for his first solo flight.

It was the moment he had dreamed of and worked for since the news from Pearl Harbor had come to Andover nearly a year before. The blocks ("chocks," in the vernacular of aviation) in front of the plane's tires were pulled aside, and Bush felt a sense of calm. The Stearman aircraft, painted yellow, was nicknamed "the Yellow Peril" and, by anxious cadets, "the Washing Machine" since would-be pilots who failed to fly it well "washed out" of the program. For Bush, though, the nerves of the previous flight were gone. His legs were steady, his grip on the controls firm. In the cold and the fog he taxied through rows of army bombers, then "Off I zoomed," he recalled, reflexively doing all the things that his instructors had taught him to do. "Everything seemed so free and easy and really wonderful," he wrote. "Mum, it was the first time I have climbed out of the plane without worrying or having a touch of discouragement." In the fog he had found his way.

On the ground, Bush was learning about the men with whom he flew and fought. His letters from the navy have the tone of an explorer observing a new culture for the first time. He is respectful, mainly, and intrigued. "It was the first time I'd been anyplace but the playing fields of Greenwich Country Day or Andover," Bush recalled. "I have gotten to know most of the fellows in the platoon," he wrote home. "They are a darn good-hearted bunch. . . . There are so many different types here."

After his demure lust for pretty girls who had "matured early," Bush was struck by his fellow cadets' cavorting in town, and by the women

with whom they cavorted. "Most fellows here—true some are engaged
and some believe as I do—but most fellows take sex as much as they can
get," Bush wrote his mother. "This pertains . . . to every town in the
country, to college campuses—yes, even to Yale University. Boys you
know—boys I like very much—and even boys I admire have had intercourse with women." (He signed the letter to his mother "Much love,
Pop professor 'sexology' Ph.D.")

Christmas came and went as Bush racked up flying hours. The Bushes
sent him new goggles and a bathrobe; Gampy Walker—the Walker
grandparents were known as "Gampy" and "Ganny"—mailed a check for
twenty-five dollars; the Pierces dispatched a box of food; and Barbara, he
wrote, "is sending me soon what I asked for; namely a decent picture of
her." She was also knitting him socks, though she managed expectations,
telling him beforehand that they "don't look at all like socks." Bush observed to his mother that he could make a neck protector from them if
they were too big.

On a night flight in Minneapolis, trying to land amid crosswinds on a
narrow strip near a stand of woods, Bush nearly died. He was coming in
to land when his plane's wheels scraped a tree. He throttled back up in
the air, circled the field, and made it down safely. Yet he knew how close
he had come to a fatal crash. "I just thanked my lucky stars I wasn't 2 or
3 feet lower," Bush wrote home.

Next stop: the Naval Air Station at Corpus Christi, Texas. He was
moving from the snow of Minnesota to the heat of the Gulf of Mexico.
He knew, too, that he was stepping closer to war itself. On Wednesday,
June 9, 1943, George Herbert Walker Bush became an officer of the
United States Naval Reserve and received his wings as a naval aviator. A
navy band played "Anchors Aweigh" and "Wild Blue Yonder" at the
Corpus Christi ceremony. His parents sent him a set of additional wings
and a pair of cuff links. At eighteen, just about to turn nineteen on the
twelfth of June, he was likely the youngest flying officer in the navy. Ensign Bush was to ship out soon. His assignment: to fly torpedo bombers
off aircraft carriers in the sprawling Pacific war.

Barbara Pierce was terrified. Bush had a seventeen-day leave in the
summer of 1943, and his mother had asked Barbara to Kennebunkport for the break. "I guess Mrs. Bush had all sorts of reasons to invite
me, but I suspect they wanted to see as much of their son as possible

*Bush with two crewmen—radioman Joe
Reichert (left) and turret gunner Leo
W. Nadeau (right). Two others—Ted
White and John "Del" Delaney—were
killed in action over Chichi-Jima.*

before he went off to war," Barbara recalled. "By having me there, it
meant Pop would spend less time going back and forth." Bush sometimes referred to Barbara as "Bobsie" around this time, and he worried
about holding on to her. "I do still *love* (I honestly feel sure of it) Barbara, Mum, yet I know that there is such a chance of her meeting some
other guy," he had written his mother from Corpus Christi in the spring
of 1943. "She is so very young and so darn attractive and I could hardly
expect her to keep caring about me for years." A three-and-a-half-week
period during which he received only a single letter from her while he
was in Corpus Christi nearly drove him mad.

Barbara understood that Kennebunkport was going to be a trial by
fire. As Bush described the clan to her on the train north, he was "scaring
me to death," Barbara recalled. "I knew, of course, they would hate me."
The gathering of Walkers and Bushes at the Point was "overwhelming,"
she recalled. "The teasing was enormous from everybody, except George's
mother." The family liked her, finding her resilient under the edgy ban-
ter. "When they were courting, they had an act—he could kid her, and
she could take it and give it right back," recalled Jonathan Bush. Because
of gas rationing, G. H. Walker had rented a horse named Barsil to pull

wagons to and from town and the Point. The shared first syllable of the two names—Barbara and Barsil—gave rise to a new nickname. Barbara became "Bar," after the horse.

Barbara Pierce and Poppy Bush became engaged on the rocks along the Atlantic on a moonlit night. She was funny and pretty and frank; he was dashing and handsome and kind. It had been roughly a year and a half since Bush had asked to be introduced to her at the Greenwich Country Club Christmas dance. He was nineteen; she was eighteen.

B ush was sure Barbara was, as he told his mother, "so perfect a girl," and the public announcement of the engagement was published on Sunday, December 12, 1943. When he read the news in the paper, Bush wrote Barbara, who was in her first semester at Smith College. (It is one of the very few wartime letters between the two to survive.) "I love you, precious, with all my heart and to know that you love me means my life," he wrote, continuing:

> How often I have thought about the immeasurable joy that will be ours some day. How lucky our children will be to have a mother like you—
>
> As the days go by the time of our departure draws nearer. For a long time I had anxiously looked forward to the day when we would go aboard and set to sea. It seemed that obtaining that goal would be all I could desire for some time, but, Bar, you have changed all that. I cannot say that I do not want to go—for that would be a lie. We have been working for a long time with a single purpose in mind, to be so equipped that we could meet and defeat our enemy. I do want to go because it is my part. . . . Bar, you have made my life full of everything I could ever dream of—my complete happiness should be a token of my love for you. . . .
>
> Goodnite, my beautiful. Everytime I say beautiful you about kill me but you'll have to accept it—

A t Fort Lauderdale, he was introduced to the plane in which he was to spend the war: the TBF Avenger torpedo bomber, manufactured by the Grumman Corporation (and later by General Motors). The plane was 40 feet long, 16 feet high, and had a 52-foot wing span—20 feet longer than the "Yellow Peril" trainers. With his training group, which was known as Flight 44, Bush practiced bombing runs over Lake Okeechobee. After Florida, Bush learned how to make carrier landings aboard the USS *Sable* on Lake Michigan in August 1943. The next month he joined his new squadron, VT-51, in Norfolk, Virginia.

Bush and his squadron were assigned to the USS *San Jacinto*. Dorothy Bush and Barbara came to the new carrier's commissioning ceremony in Philadelphia on Wednesday, December 15, 1943. Dorothy had a mission of her own that day: to deliver a star sapphire ring of her sister's, Nancy Walker, to her son. On the train to Philadelphia, Mrs. Bush asked what kind of ring Barbara might like—did she want a diamond? Barbara said she didn't have any strong feelings—anything would be wonderful. Mrs. Bush pressed once more—was Barbara sure she would be all right without a diamond? Barbara again said it did not matter. In the shipyard, Bush gave the sapphire ring to Barbara, sealing the engagement.

The ship left the Philadelphia Naval Shipyard on that cold, cloudy Wednesday, cruising down the Delaware River and then to the broad Atlantic. Lunch on the day they set out into open seas was spaghetti and meatballs—an unfortunate choice, it turned out, when the water proved so rough that, as fellow Bush pilot Lou Grab recalled, "we had a complete puke-up fore and aft." At a stop at Trinidad in the Caribbean, Bush and his fellow pilots piled into a taxi—Bush's best friend Jim Wykes sat on the floor of the cab to make room for everyone—and merrily consumed planter's punch cocktails at the Macqueripe Officers Club in the port city's hotel. Fortified by drink and song, the group offered their shipmates off-key renditions of calypso on returning to the ship. The *San Jacinto* sailed through the Panama Canal, called at San Diego, and reached Hawaii on Thursday, April 20, 1944. Bush took some time off the ship to go swimming along a secluded beach protected by barbed wire. Thirty-one days later, on Sunday, May 21, after the ship joined the fleet at Majuro Harbor, in the Marshall Islands, Ensign Bush suited up for his first combat mission.

SEVEN

I Wanted to Finish My Mission

★

My God, this thing is going to blow up.

—GEORGE H. W. BUSH, on being struck by
antiaircraft fire over the Pacific

THE TARGET WAS WAKE ISLAND, an American possession first claimed for the United States in the last years of the nineteenth century. About 2,500 miles west of Hawaii, Wake had been home to a U.S. naval base but was now occupied by the Japanese, who had attacked it on the same day they had struck Pearl Harbor. Bush was to fly his Avenger through antiaircraft fire from the island and bomb enemy installations. Training was over. This was the real thing.

His crewmen were Leo "Lee" Nadeau, twenty-two, who served as the gunner, and John "Del" Delaney, twenty-three, the radioman. "We were all tense because it was our first bombing mission over an active target, and we didn't know what to expect," Nadeau told Joe Hyams, the writer whose book *Flight of the Avenger* is a definitive account of Bush's military service. "I don't think there was any time we were in the air when the adrenaline wasn't flowing, but much as we dreaded that first flight, we knew we had to do it. Luckily, George seemed confident, which relaxed Del and me somewhat." One day that summer after his plane had lost all of its oil, Bush executed a dangerously difficult water landing, earning even more respect.

They also liked Bush, who, after Andover, was accustomed to the camaraderie of an all-male environment and knew how to make himself agreeable. He played games—usually acey-deucey, a version of backgammon—and loved what were known as "gedunks," the term used on board for ice cream sundaes. He doled out nicknames, and his own among the officers was a play on his privilege—he was called *Georgeherbertwalkerbush,* said fast. One casualty of the war was the widespread use of "Pop" or "Poppy" as a nickname for Bush. An old friend in the Pacific startled Bush in October 1944 by calling him "Pop." It was, he said, "the first time in ages" he had heard that. "With everyone it's George and I really have grown used to it," Bush wrote his mother.

In the wardroom he drank coffee and made toast with butter and jam; at mealtimes the stewards set the table with white cloths and silver. He read books his mother had given him, nurtured an interest in Russia (curiously becoming "pretty much interested in that end of our diplomatic relations"), and played volleyball (he was a popular choice when teams were forming). He bellyached about the food. The ship's steaks, he said, "have a great deal in common with an old sneaker sole." He would lie in his bunk at night and let the tensions of flight ease into images of home, of his parents, and "of Bar—our wedding."

Bush always remembered the first sight of the bursts of antiaircraft fire from the attack on Wake Island. "It is quite a feeling, Mum, to be shot at I assure you," Bush wrote on Wednesday, May 24, 1944. "The nervousness which is with you before a game of some kind was extremely noticeable but no great fear thank heavens."

Back on the *San Jacinto,* Bush was consumed with worry: his roommate, Jim Wykes, had disappeared with two crewmen while on a mission, never to be found. He and Bush had known each other for a year in the closest of quarters, sharing the pressures of learning to fly in wartime. One of Wykes's crew, Bush recalled, "had just become a father." Alone in his bunk that night Bush cried in grief. Another pilot, Roland R. "Dick" Houle, was killed in action. Bush knew that he could not afford to grieve too much, and he found some refuge in thinking about his youngest brother, William "Bucky" Bush, who was about to enter the first grade. "I get such a kick out of Buck—I picture him so clearly at all times—He is sort of a symbol to me in a way," Bush wrote his parents. "I remember how Bar & I used to play with him. We'd pretend he was our little boy. I don't know why, but little old Buck so often is brought to my mind— even when I'm up flying I'll burst out laughing at times. . . . Perhaps it's because he's so young and innocent." Everything lay before Bucky in a way that it never could again for George. On any flight on any given day, Jim Wykes's fate could be his own.

Dawn, Saturday, September 2, 1944. Bush was scheduled to fly in a strike code-named "Baker," an assault on the Bonin island of Chichi-Jima, a Japanese outpost 150 miles from Iwo Jima and only 500 miles from the mainland. The mission was to destroy a radio tower on the peak of Mount Yoake. Chichi-Jima was heavily fortified, a communications-and-supply point for the Japanese.

The aviators of VT-51 were on their second day trying to take the tower out. Bush had flown the day before, on Friday, September 1, but each of the planes that had made a run at Mount Yoake had missed the target amid Japanese flak. Early on Saturday morning, the squadron was briefed again in the small ready room aboard the *San Jacinto.* A lieutenant junior grade, William G. White, known as Ted, wanted to come along. A gunnery officer and Yale alumnus, White had long hoped to see the Avenger and its guns in action. Prescott Bush knew White's father. Bush warned White that the flight was not going to be an easy hop, but the squadron commander agreed that White could join the mission. Lee Nadeau surrendered his turret as gunner, and White climbed aboard. There were jokes about whether they'd have to bail out.

Bush took off with White and Del Delaney at a quarter after seven in the morning. The weather, Bush recalled, was clear. A little more than an hour after taking off from the *San Jacinto,* Bush was within range of the tower. The Japanese guns filled the air with flak. Flying at a thirty-five-degree angle to the surface, Bush zeroed in on the target and went straight for it. Racing ever closer to the island, the plane was hit. As the Avenger jolted forward, Bush was able to keep it on target. Smoke filled the cockpit. Flames raced along the wings. "My God," Bush thought, "this thing is going to blow up." Bush radioed White and Delaney to put their parachutes on. The Avenger, he knew, "was going down." Bush, who was choking on the smoke, kept the plane on course, dropping his bombs—this time he scored, damaging the radio tower—and then gave the plane as much speed as he could as he roared off, out to sea. "I realized I couldn't keep the plane in the air very long because of the severity of the fire, and told our guys to get out," Bush recalled. His words that day: "Hit the silk!" He could not be sure that they had heard him; no one answered, Bush reported to his parents, though "we had talked not long before." He looked back, he recalled, but could not see White, so he assumed the guest gunner had gone below to put on his parachute.

Bush did what he had been trained to do. "I turned the plane to the starboard so it'd take the slipstream off the escape hatch [for the two crewmen] and then figured, 'Well, I hope to hell they got out,'" Bush

recalled. Relating the story to his parents, he wrote: "After that I straightened up and started to get out myself. At that time I felt certain that they
had bailed out." Other squadron fliers on the mission heard Bush's order
to the crewmen to bail. His own parachute straps fastened, his hatch
opened, Bush struggled up and out of the cockpit. The wind struck him
full force, essentially lifting him out the rest of the way and propelling
him backward into the tail. He gashed his head and bruised his eye on
the tail as he flew through the sky and the burning plane hurtled toward
the sea.

Buffeted by the wind, Bush pulled his rip cord too soon, and several
panels of the silk chute were ripped away. He had bailed at about two
thousand feet above the waves; as he floated down he saw his plane crash
into the ocean and disappear into the depths. He unfastened the buckles
of his chute before he hit the water, shaking the harness loose with about
twenty feet to fall.

Bush plunged deep into the ocean, involuntarily gulping down bitter
salt water. He fought his way to the surface, kicking off his shoes to reduce his weight and inflating his life jacket—what navy men called a
"Mae West." It was a struggle. His khaki flight suit was soaked and heavy,
his head was bleeding, his eyes were burning from the cockpit smoke,
and his mouth and throat were raw from the rush of salt water.

Bobbing along the surface, he looked up and saw the squadron's commander, Don Melvin, signal the location of an uninflated life raft that
had fallen from Bush's life jacket and landed in the water. Bush swam the
fifty feet, inflated the raft, and flopped aboard. But there was no time to
rest, or even catch his breath. The wind was blowing back toward Chichi-
Jima—back toward the enemy. There was no paddle—it had been lost in
chaos of the crash—and so Bush hunched forward and paddled with his
arms. Doug West, a fellow VT-51 pilot, flew close by, and Melvin summoned the USS *Finback,* which was on what was known as "lifeguard
duty."

The submarine was ten miles away, however, and Bush, in his tiny
raft drifting in the wrong direction, needed help now. Stung by a Portuguese man-of-war, he was relieved only by the sight of American
planes above him. Doug West dropped down some medical supplies,
and Bush applied Mercurochrome to his head wound. To increase his
visibility to the pilots above, Bush sprinkled dye marker around the

raft. The Americans, however, weren't the only ones who could make out his position. A Japanese boat set out toward the downed pilot, prompting West to open fire with a .50-caliber machine gun. West's strafing bought some time, but the wind and tide were not in Bush's favor. "For a while there I thought I was done," he recalled. Either the Japanese would find him or he would be taken back to Chichi-Jima by the tide. The best he could hope for was being captured as a prisoner of war.

All he could do now was paddle, and wait.

On the tiny raft, pausing now and then to vomit over the side—the salt water had hit his stomach, which, in addition to the stress of the hour, made him ill—Bush sensed that White and Delaney had not made it. There was no sign of anyone else on the open water. Soon he could tell that the American planes had stopped searching for others. Unable to move for a time, Bush sat in the raft in tears. He thought of Delaney and of White, of Barbara, of home. Minutes passed, then one hour, then two. It was nearing noon when Bush heard the zooming of American planes again, tipping their wings toward the raft. It was a signal. It wasn't for Bush; he knew where he was. It must be for someone else. And that meant someone was coming.

The *Finback* was commanded by Robert R. Williams, Jr., an Annapolis graduate. It was a 311-foot submarine, patrolling the Bonins to pick up downed American fliers. As the *Finback* rose out of the water, Bush recalled, "I thought maybe I was delirious." Four enlisted men came out of the interior of the sub and dove into the water. Chief Petty Officer Ralph Adams swam to Bush's raft, and the team pulled the pilot out of the raft and onto the *Finback*.

"Welcome aboard, sir," said Don Kohler, a torpedoman second class.

"Happy to be aboard," Bush said.

"Let's get below," Kohler said. "The skipper wants to get the hell out of here."

It was four minutes shy of noon. Lieutenant Junior Grade George H. W. Bush was safe. The *Finback* crew shot his raft to pieces and left the debris in the sea. According to the submarine's log for the day, Bush's first priority was to tell his rescuers about his crew. He had not seen any other parachutes, the log reported, "and believed that they had jumped when [the] plane [was] still over Chichi Jima, or they had gone down with the plane. Commenced search of area on chance they had jumped over water." It was fruitless.

An American pilot and the Japanese account of the episode confirmed that a second chute was seen coming out of Bush's plane. It had opened, or "streamed," but did not billow out, and neither White nor Delaney was ever recovered. "All in all it is terribly discouraging and frankly it bothers me a good deal," Bush told his parents in a letter from the *Finback*. "My heart aches for the families of those two boys with me."

He was physically fine—the cuts and bruises were minor, as was some brief soreness in his back and one leg—but emotionally fragile. He had barely escaped death or capture. He later learned that Chichi-Jima was the scene of horrific war crimes against American prisoners of war, including cannibalism.

The loss of White and of Delaney remained with Bush for the rest of his life. "It worries me—it terrifies me," he said decades later, reflecting on the proposition that he could have done something differently, something that would have ensured their survival on that desperate Saturday in September. Bush's fundamental question: "Did I do enough to save them?"

He had handled the crisis correctly, but that was only partly consoling. "My mother and dad had drilled into us the lesson that we were never to let anyone down, and here I was, alive while they were gone," Bush recalled. "Their families . . ." He stopped, tearing up. "I wondered—wonder still—whether I did all I could. Could I have made a water landing? But I couldn't have—we were too damaged. I know I did the right thing, telling everyone to bail out. But that doesn't make the suffering of the other families any less."

Aboard the *Finback*, Bush slept more than usual, and he attempted to make sense of the shootdown in nearly daily letters to his parents "I try to think about it as little as possible, yet I cannot get the thought of those two boys out of my mind," he wrote home a week after the disaster. Bush kept his anguish largely to himself. Aboard the *Finback* he reverted to type, deploying his extroverted charm on the officers and crew. One officer, Lieutenant Geraldyn Redmond, wrote home to his stepfather, a

Wall Street executive, reporting that the submarine had "picked up a few aviators who were mighty glad to find an American at that moment. They were quite some characters and kept us well entertained." Bush, Redmond said, "was the most fun of all the lot and kept us in stitches for over a month, which is quite a feat in a sub. We usually just get on each other's nerves after a while."

Bush's good cheer was a mask. In his head he constantly replayed the episode over Chichi-Jima. "It was transforming," he recalled of the incident. "Transforming in the sense that you realize how close death can be. You realize, painstakingly so, the responsibility you had for the life of somebody else."

A submarine created a different kind of stress than a carrier. In some ways being a passive player—underwater, the *Finback* could only do so much when depth charges fell—was worse for Bush than flying,

Bush is rescued at sea by the USS Finback off Chichi-Jima in the Bonin Islands, Saturday, September 2, 1944. When Bush, who was in a life raft on the open seas, saw the submarine appear, he thought he was "delirious," he recalled.

which allowed the illusion of some measure of control. Bush stood watches (two a day) in order to occupy himself and get some fresh air when the submarine was on the surface. The food was excellent (Bush was pleasantly startled to find good steaks and strawberries on the *Finback*), but each man could shower only once a week. He felt a bit claustrophobic, too, occasionally battling insomnia caused, he thought, by a lack of exercise.

By Saturday, September 16, 1944, his eye was healed and the only sign of the accident, he told his parents, was a bare spot where his eyebrow needed to grow back in. The other men on the boat joked that without a scar Bush might have trouble getting his Purple Heart, but the ribbing only made him gloomier. To pass the time on the *Finback,* he pitched in as a censor for the enlisted men's letters, reading them for anything sensitive about military matters. Bush would always remember that their stories and their concerns offered what was, for him, a rare glimpse into the lives of ordinary Americans.

Books, especially novels, were an escape. On the *Finback* he read C. S. Forester's *Captain from Connecticut,* Lloyd C. Douglas's *The Robe,* Paul Hughes's *Retreat from Rostov,* and John Dos Passos's *Number One.* After a month's stay on the submarine, Bush got off at Midway Island and flew to Hawaii. He was eligible to return stateside for shore duty but refused. "I didn't want to go home," Bush recalled. "I wanted to finish my mission. It never occurred to me not to rejoin the unit, get back in the fight, back in the air."

The Texas flag was flying when Bush returned to the *San Jacinto.* As relieved as he was to be back aboard, he was anxious for word from home. "All during the time I was talking to the boys I kept eagerly eyeing my sky-high stack of mail," he wrote on Friday, November 3, 1944. One note, from his mother's brother Herbie Walker, provided a welcome glimpse of a possible future. "He offered me a job with G. H. Walker after the war—it was the nicest letter and really made me happy," Bush wrote. Politics was on his mind, if only slightly. "By the time this gets to you the election will be over—perhaps we will have a new and vigorous administration, perhaps four more years of FDR." Always there were concerns about the immediate tasks before him. "I am a little anxious over my first flight off the ship," Bush wrote. "I have flown so little lately that I will probably be as rusty as can be."

He worried, too, over writing the White and Delaney families. "I think you had better not mention the fact that Ted White was with me to anyone who could possibly let it get to the Whites unless for some reason you know that they have definitely been notified by the government," Bush told his parents. "As soon as I find out that they have been notified I shall write to them." He did write at the appropriate time.

Not long afterward a letter arrived from Providence, Rhode Island. It was from Delaney's sister, Mary Jane, and reading it he was suffused with relief and gratitude.

Dear Lt. Bush,

I must apologize for not writing sooner. It isn't that I did not try—I just could not.

You mention in your letter that you would like to help me in some way. There is a way, and that is to stop thinking you are in any way responsible for your plane accident and what has happened to your men. I might have thought you were if my brother Jack had not always spoken of you as the best pilot in the squadron. I always had the greatest confidence and trust in my brother Jack's judgment. . . .

I want to thank you for your beautiful letter and the kind things you said about Jack. It was a message of sadness, but you made it much easier to bear.

With every wish for your continued safety.

Very truly yours,
Mary Jane Delaney

Did he ever dream about Chichi-Jima? "No, not dreaming," Bush recalled in his late eighties. "Well, I don't know. Maybe I do. . . . I wouldn't be surprised."

He was awarded the Distinguished Flying Cross for the mission but was ambivalent about the decoration. "I finished the bombing run, which was no 'heroic' thing," he recalled late in life. "They wrote it up as heroism, but it wasn't—it was just doing your job."

On Monday, November 13, 1944, with Leo Nadeau as gunner and Joe Reichert as radioman, Bush flew a combat mission over Manila Bay. Flying—and diving—through Japanese flak, Bush dropped the plane's bombs on some enemy light cruisers. Returning to the *San Jacinto*, the plane was low on fuel and the seas were rough, but Bush executed a perfect landing on the carrier. "Well," Bush said to his men as they climbed out of the plane onto the deck, "we made it." Nadeau noted a tone of "relief" in his pilot's voice; there may also have been a hint of redemption. Bush had proven he could bring his crew to safety.

By late November 1944, Bush had orders that allowed him to return stateside before he and his VT-51 colleagues were reassigned for new duty in the Pacific. Finding transportation to San Diego from Hawaii on a troop ship, Bush began the long journey home. He knew he soon would be back in the Pacific to fight in the seemingly inevitable invasion of the home islands of Japan. For the moment, though, all he wanted was to head east. He had a wedding to get to—his own.

EIGHT

Life Lay Ahead of Us

★

V-J Day arrived, and the rejoicing in the streets . . . was loud,
wild, and fairly liquid. And why not? There was a lot to cheer
about.

—BARBARA BUSH

I'll always wonder, "Why me? Why was I spared?"

—GEORGE H. W. BUSH, on his combat experience

T HE PIERCE HOUSE on Onondaga Street in Rye was elaborately
decorated for Christmas. Mrs. Pierce, who was fond of the season,
saw to that, sparing neither expense nor effort. Barbara was there,
at home, on Sunday, December 24, 1944, when the telephone rang. Her
fiancé, fresh from a cross-country flight, was calling from New York City
with the best news she could imagine: He was boarding a train for Rye.
Within an hour he would be at the station in Westchester County. Barbara raced to get dressed, hurried to meet the train, and fell into Bush's
arms. They went on to Greenwich together.

On a cold Saturday in January 1945, wedding guests filled the First
Presbyterian Church in Rye. Barbara wore what *The New York Times* described as "a gown of ivory satin, made with a fitted bodice embroidered
with seed pearls and a full skirt." Her veil—"of heirloom princess and
rosepoint lace"—had been Mrs. Bush's at her Kennebunkport wedding
in 1921. George wore his dress blue uniform. George's sister, Nancy, and
Barbara's sister, Martha, were maids of honor, and Prescott Jr. served as
best man. The Pierces hosted a large reception afterward at the Apawa-
mis Club about a mile away—"a party of women," Barbara recalled, "not
of men, because of the war"—and the new couple left that evening for
New York City. There the newlyweds watched the Judy Garland movie
Meet Me in St. Louis and took a sleeper train down the East Coast to the
Cloisters at Sea Island, Georgia, for some sun. They were just about the
only young couple there. Wartime meant that the hotel was largely pop-

ulated by older guests, insofar as it was populated at all. There were dance lessons, which bored Bush. Barbara would be doing the rhumba and turn around to find that her new husband had disappeared midstep.

As part of a new combat squadron, VT-153, Bush was beginning an eight-month odyssey as the pilots trained for new deployment to the Pacific. At Naval Air Station Grosse Ile in Michigan, he and Barbara took a room in town for fourteen dollars a week, but without kitchen privileges. "It is sort of a lonely existence for poor Bar," Bush wrote home to Greenwich, "but she doesn't complain at all, and I am just in heaven having her here."

Barbara and George were stationed in the Lewiston-Auburn area of Maine when the news broke of FDR's death at his cottage in Warm Springs, Georgia, on Thursday, April 12, 1945. Though both were Republicans, the Bushes experienced feelings of loss and nostalgia. "I remember crying, I remember weeping, even though I had not been raised in a pro-Roosevelt household by a long shot," Bush recalled. Barbara never forgot Bush's coming home that day to tell her what had happened. "We were sick," Barbara recalled. "Neither one of us had ever voted—we were too young—and we probably would have voted for the other fellow, but Roosevelt was our President, the Commander-in-Chief of a country at war, and we joined the world in mourning. We felt truly lost, very young and alone. Who had ever heard of Harry Truman?"

Bush was scheduled to report for duty on Saturday, September 15, 1945, to sail out to take part in the invasion of mainland Japan. "Everything I'd experienced in my year and a half of combat in the Pacific told me it was going to be the bloodiest, most prolonged battle of the war," Bush recalled. "Japan's war leaders were unfazed by massive raids on Tokyo. They seemed bent on national suicide, regardless of the cost in human life."

In August 1945, word of the American atomic attacks on Hiroshima and Nagasaki arrived when the Bushes were stationed at Naval Air Station Oceana in Virginia Beach, Virginia. Then, at ten P.M. eastern time on Saturday, September 1, 1945, President Truman announced Japan's unconditional surrender. In Virginia Beach, the reaction was instant and immense. "Within minutes our neighborhood streets were filled with sailors, aviators, their wives and families celebrating late into the night," Bush recalled. The festivities, Barbara recalled, were "loud, wild, and fairly liquid. And why not? There was a lot to cheer about." The Bushes slipped off at one point to say a prayer in a nearby church.

One image from the war stayed with him through the years. A Hellcat fighter was coming in to land on the *San Jacinto* from Guam. Bush was standing on deck. The Hellcat pilot missed the arresting wires and tried but failed to get his plane back up in the air to come around again. It spun and crashed on the deck, killing the four-man gun crew. "Just a few yards away was a crewman's leg, severed and quivering," Bush recalled. "The shoe was still on." Standing with two other VT-51 pilots, Bush was stunned, immobile. It took a chief petty officer to break the shock. "All right, you bastards," the man yelled. "Let's get to work. We still have planes up there and they can't land in this goddamn mess."

There was no logic to the costs of combat, Bush realized, no real rhyme nor reason. All you could do was your best, and take what came. In the warm September night in Virginia Beach the Bushes prayed for those who would not come home or have families or build lives. They knew—they both knew—that there but for the grace of God, Bush could be dead in the depths of a distant sea. "I'll always wonder, 'Why me? Why was I spared?'" Bush recalled. He spent the rest of his life striving to prove that he was worthy of being saved when others were doomed.

Always a charmed figure, the post-Chichi-Jima Bush was now, to his family and friends, truly the most special of men. On a summer day in 1945, Bush piloted a plane into Sanford, Maine, near Kennebunkport. His youngest brother, Bucky, who turned seven that season, remembered the scene. The Bushes and the Walkers had driven over to meet a "very, very skinny and suntanned" Poppy, who climbed out of the cockpit with a wide grin and a big wave. "I thought he'd conquered the world," Bucky Bush recalled. "Nobody—nothing—could ever hurt Pop after that."

He was, finally, safe. On Tuesday, September 18, 1945, Bush was discharged from active duty. He had served for just over a thousand days, flying 58 missions, making 126 carrier landings, and recording 1,228 hours of flight time. Bush was decorated with gold wings, the Distinguished Flying Cross, an Air Medal with Gold Stars, the Asiatic-Pacific Campaign Medal with Three Battle Stars, the World War II Victory Medal, the American Campaign Medal, and the Selective Service Medal.

Only a year before, in September 1944, he had been clinging to life in the wind and the tide of Chichi-Jima. Even after the *Finback* surfaced and took him in, death in the Pacific was a constant possibility, a reality men dealt with by avoiding outward displays of concern about the subject. For all the world could see, men like Bush flew their missions and then played volleyball on the deck of the *San Jacinto* and cards in the wardroom. When they worried, they did so in their bunks, alone. They mourned their dead quietly, anxious to keep the grief and the fear in check. They felt they had no other choice: to have engaged the horror they faced fully would have immobilized them at just the hour when they had to focus on doing the jobs they had been trained to do. Then, with Truman's announcement, the war was over. "We were still young, life lay ahead of us, and the world was at peace," Bush recalled. "It was the best of times." Survivors like Bush were no longer preparing to die, but to live.

It was far from a typical freshman class. In the fall of 1945, Yale enrolled 8,500 men; more than half of the student body, about 5,000, were rotating out of military service. When Bush matriculated in November 1945, he was twenty-one and a half years old and anxious to get on with things. He had toyed with the idea of skipping Yale altogether—Uncle Herbie Walker had promised a job at the family firm, degree or no degree—but Bush's father, who strongly believed his son should go to college, prevailed.

The university still had a wartime feel. Army and navy units were billeted in Trumbull, Branford, and Saybrook halls. Rows of Quonset huts were built near the Yale Bowl and the Peabody Museum to create instant housing. Slowly, old military uniforms gave way to what the writer Emerson Stone, of the class of 1948, later described as the "de rigueur . . . mark of the official Yale man: khaki trousers (gray flannels for dressier or cooler times) and scuffed white buck shoes."

Yale was Yale when Bush arrived—a leafy, Gothic Revival enclave in which members of the American upper and upper-middle classes prepared for lives of influence by spending four years among other members of the same classes. Yet it was not quite the Yale of Bush's forebears. The war had changed that, as it had changed so many other things. "Some of us are tottering veterans in our early and mid-twenties trying to keep up with the impertinently mature minors we found when we came back," a Yale yearbook editor wrote about the class of 1948.

Bush knew his university experience was not going to be the same as his family's—that of his father ('17) or of his uncle James ('22) or of his Walker uncles, George H. Jr. ('27), John M. ('31), and Louis ('36). The usual undergraduate gripes about, say, the food in the dining hall were out of the question for the class of 1948. Still, they wanted to have a good time. Tired of war, they savored the football and the fraternities and the campus camaraderie. Wartime had increased their metabolisms. Accustomed to a world in which any moment could be your last, Bush's generation played hard, worked hard—and looked resolutely ahead.

The chief difference between a theoretical prewar Bush Yale experience and the reality of the postwar Bush Yale experience was speed and seriousness. Everything in Bush's life now moved faster—having children, making a living. He had been spared, and he believed there was not an hour to waste. Bush finished his four-year degree in two and a half years. Though he never wanted to be seen as an intellectual or even as a very serious student, he enjoyed his studies. "I was majoring in 'the dismal science,' economics, but didn't find it dismal at all," Bush recalled. As an economics major with a minor in sociology, he took enough care with his coursework to graduate Phi Beta Kappa.

Yale offered the attentive student a selection of great professors. There was F.S.C. Northrop in philosophy (Bush took his logic course), Samuel Hemingway in Shakespeare, and Paul Hindemith in music. A favorite course (Barbara audited it as well) was History of Art 36, a class in American furniture and silver that was informally known as "Pots and Pans." Bush took French, too, which he had begun at Andover. He lettered in soccer his first year in New Haven—the only year he played—and in baseball, which he played all three years, serving as captain in his senior year. He was secretary of the budget drive in 1946. Bush joined Delta Kappa Epsilon (serving briefly as chapter president). In 1947 he served on the Undergraduate Athletic Association, the Undergraduate Board of Deacons, and the Interfraternity Council, and was elected to the Triennial Committee. He was also inducted into the Torch Honor Society and was awarded the Francis Gordon Brown Prize (for "intellectual ability, high manhood, [and] capacity for leadership") in 1947.

Most important, perhaps, Bush followed his father into the most elite of the undergraduate organizations at Yale and beyond. He won a fabled honor: He was the "last man tapped" for the secret society Skull and Bones, a distinction reserved for the leading Yale undergraduate of his day. In the forbidding "tomb" of the clubhouse on High Street in New Haven, the initiated few often forged lifelong bonds amid a culture of candor about one's hopes and fears. It was counterintuitive: a society of Yale men usually seen as at least somewhat repressed speaking openly to one another amid mystical rituals and customs.

Bush's success at Yale was as much, if not more, about his character than it was about his name or his prep school. Being the son of Prescott Bush and a Walker on his mother's side did not hurt, but plenty of children of privilege fail to make the leap from prominent name to accomplished figure. S. P. Bush's old worries about Prescott's sliding into a gin-soaked country-club life rather than becoming a man in the arena and earning the respect of the world were not irrational. Boys who had been given everything could wind up doing nothing. The Bush code demanded both success and service.

The Cold War was taking shape in Bush's New Haven years, but he declined to be drawn into contests or contentions other than those on the baseball diamond. It was not, Bush recalled, that he and many of his contemporaries "didn't care what was going on in the world, only that after four years of war we had a lot of catching up to do. I came back to civilian life feeling that I needed to get my degree and go into the business world as soon as possible. I had a family to support." William F. Buckley, Jr., was two years behind Bush at Yale and was, Bush recalled, "getting ready to stir the pot with his first book, *God and Man at Yale*. But aside from following the front-page news—the beginnings of the Cold War, from the Russian takeover of Eastern Europe to the Berlin Blockade—I wasn't politically involved. Most of the other veterans on campus felt the same."

In New Haven, the Bushes first lived in a "shotgun apartment" two doors away from a funeral parlor on Chapel Street. At Thanksgiving 1945, Bush invited ten old Andover friends over for dinner. Barbara recalled that it took her "days" to wash all the dishes. Then came a stay on Edwards Street before they moved into 37 Hillhouse Avenue, next door to the Yale presidential residence. The Hillhouse address was filled with families living under one roof—estimates now range from twenty-nine people to forty—but the Bushes luckily scored their own tiny bathroom.

During his first year, while Bush jumped into his classes, played soccer, and manned first base for the baseball team, Barbara was pregnant with their first child. Loyal and devoted, she kept score at Yale Field from behind third base. As the 1946 season progressed through the spring, she gained sixty pounds. "The baby did not come and did not come," Barbara recalled. Ethan Allen, the Yale baseball coach, told her that it would make him feel better if she would take a seat behind home plate—and behind a safety net. "I was huge and weighed more than a Yale linebacker," Barbara said, acceding to Allen's kindly request.

On Saturday, July 6, 1946, at Grace–New Haven Community Hospital on York Street, Barbara gave birth to their first child, a son they named George Walker Bush. "George's mother finally gave me a good dose of castor oil and [the] baby came all right—I'm tempted to say covered with glory," Barbara recalled. The young parents were smitten and believed the world should be, too. Mrs. Pierce said that the elder George seemed wounded if she took her eyes off little "Georgie" for even a moment.

With the exception of his young family, baseball was arguably Bush's greatest passion at Yale. He was not given to hero worship, which made his longtime admiration of Lou Gehrig, the great New York Yankees first baseman, all the more notable. As a youngster Bush had "looked up to" Gehrig, impressed by Gehrig's "standard of quiet excellence, on and off the field." Known as "the Iron Horse" for his historic streak of playing in 2,130 straight games, Gehrig projected a grace and a dignity that captured the young Bush's imagination.

There were other, more dramatic players, chiefly Babe Ruth, the hard-drinking home-run king who had played right field behind Gehrig. On the afternoon of Yale's 1948 home game against Princeton, Ruth came to New Haven to present the manuscript of his memoirs to the school. As captain, Bush was tasked with accepting the gift on the field before the game. It had rained all morning; with Ruth's appearance the sun came out. Stricken with the cancer that would kill him, Ruth was fragile.

A grand moment, but the quiet Gehrig fascinated Bush more than the bombastic Ruth. "Nothing flashy, no hotdogging, the ideal sportsman," Bush recalled of Gehrig. "He could field, hit, hit-with-power, and come through in a clutch." Bush appreciated steadiness over sizzle.

Morris Greenberg, Yale's head groundskeeper, wrote Bush a note during the 1946 season, slipping it under the door of the Chapel Street apartment. "Dear Sir," Greenberg wrote:

> After watching you play since the season started, I am convinced the reason you are not getting more hits is because you do not take a real cut at the ball. I am confident that if you would put more power behind your swing, you would improve your batting average 100%. I notice at the plate you are not going after any bad balls, and with the good eye which you have, I would suggest that the above be tried out.

Accepting, on behalf of Yale, the manuscript of Babe Ruth's memoir. Meeting Ruth was a "great thrill," Bush recalled, but Bush's true baseball hero was Lou Gehrig, the quiet, indefatigable Yankee first baseman.

Bush knew that he was "swinging defensively," playing it too safe at the plate. Greenberg's insight rang true: "No risk, no gain. So I decided to take Morris's advice and put more practice time into attacking the ball." The counsel to swing harder, to take more chances, worked. Bush was hitting .280, a fine average, by the time his Yale career—which included appearances in the 1947 and 1948 College World Series—was over.

Yale had been good to Bush. As he had done at Andover and in the navy, he had mastered the world around him, won the respect of others, and been decorated for his efforts. It was time for the next thing.

B ut what, exactly, should the next thing be? Bush weighed applying for a Rhodes scholarship to Oxford but decided against it on the grounds that he did not have the personal means to support his wife and son in England. (Though there were family means, it was customary for Bushes to pay their own way once out of school. There were no huge trust funds to underwrite a leisurely life.) He interviewed with a recruiter from Procter & Gamble but did not get the job. He was offered, but declined, a position in the advertising department of Bates Fabrics in New York. And for a brief moment in the spring, both Barbara and George were intrigued by Louis Bromfield's book *The Farm* and became infatuated with the idea of striking out on their own in the Midwest as farmers. They had romantic visions of golden fields and blue skies. But the Bushes found, as Bush put it, that "George and Barbara Farms came off as a high-risk, no-yield investment."

In this season of uncertainty, FitzGerald "Gerry" Bemiss, a Bush friend from Richmond who also spent summers in Kennebunkport, had heard a rumor that Bush was thinking about following in his great-grandfather James Smith Bush's footsteps and becoming an Episcopal clergyman. "I can't imagine where you ever heard that I was going into the ministry," Bush wrote. He was in a candid, even confessional, frame of mind. Though Bush could be inarticulate when speaking, dropping pronouns and making obscure references, he usually made himself clear on the page, expressing emotions and explaining difficult questions that eluded him in speech. His verbal exploits could be awkward and often confusing.

The root of the problem was likely threefold. First, he was always hearing his mother's admonitions to avoid talking about himself, which created an ambivalent relationship between himself and the first-person pronoun. Second, Bush was, by nature, a man who disliked confrontation. It could be unpleasant, and he had been raised to make himself agreeable. His garbled conversation, then, was simultaneously in the service of—and the result of—avoiding uncomfortable topics. Third, he was a very bright man who appreciated complexity and tended to think ahead to possible objections to, and elaborations of, the points he was expressing even while he was still speaking. Those objections and elaborations would seep back into the main flow of what he was trying to say, complicating his speech.

Letters afforded him the opportunity to put his thoughts down in a more sustained and coherent way. To be sure, his correspondence reflected his somewhat loopy style of speaking. In the main, however, Bush's letters offer a window into his mind and heart. Writing to Bemiss in 1948, he was frank about his hopes—and fears.

He had thought of teaching, he wrote, but "right now it seems to me that it would be confining and not challenging enough. Besides teaching would require further study almost immediately, and I am not prepared to study textbooks right now—perhaps later but not now." Bush was, therefore, a bit at loose ends. He could not quite talk himself into taking that long-offered job with Herbie Walker at G. H. Walker & Company. "I am not sure I want to capitalize completely on the benefits I received at birth—that is on the benefits of my social position," Bush wrote. "Doing well merely because I have had the opportunity to attend the same debut parties as some of my customers does not appeal to me."

Then there was Texas. Prescott Bush's friend and associate Henry Neil Mallon, who was the head of Dresser Industries, had first suggested the possibility. Mallon, an Ohio native who had been a fellow Bonesman of Prescott's, was "Uncle Neil" to Dorothy and Prescott's children. Of average height (five foot nine) and unassuming manner, Mallon was a quiet but powerful force. He endeared himself to the children early on one day when he was outside watching Poppy and Pressy play catch. A wild ball went astray and smashed a car windshield, bringing Prescott Bush roaring out of the house. Mallon saved the day, saying that he, not one of the boys, had thrown the offending ball.

Now "Uncle Neil" stepped in with the notion of going west. "What you need to do is head out to Texas and those oil fields," Mallon advised young Bush. Mallon remembered that Bush knew a bit of the territory from the Corpus Christi posting during the war, and he also sensed the scope of Bush's energy and drive. "Texas would be new and exciting for a while—hard on Bar perhaps—and heaven knows many girls would bitch like blazes about such a proposed move," Bush wrote Bemiss. "Bar's different though, Gerry. She lives quite frankly for Georgie and myself. She is wholly unselfish, beautifully tolerant of my weaknesses and idiosyncrasies, and ready to faithfully follow any course I cho[o]se. . . . I haven't had a chance to make many shrewd moves in my young life, but when I married Bar I hit the proverbial jackpot. Her devotion overcomes me and I must often stop in my mad whirl around college etc. to see if I am considering her at all." Bush thought Mallon's offer of a job in Texas had "great appeal," he wrote. "I would be seeing new people, learning something of basic importance." He would be beyond the daily shadow of his Wall Street father and of Grandfather Walker, two dominant figures in the financial world, yet could, ultimately, call on their connections if he needed to raise capital. He was breaking away, but not irresponsibly. It was perfect.

His parents had splurged on a graduation gift: a two-door red Studebaker. After commencement, Bush packed the car, kissed Bar and Georgie, who was about to turn two, goodbye—they would follow by plane—and set out from New Haven. He had two thousand miles to cover. In West Texas, a job and a future awaited.

PART III

Texas and Tragedy

1948 to 1966

★

I have some bad news for you. Your daughter has leukemia.
—Dr. Dorothy Wyvell of Midland to Barbara and
George Bush, 1953

Dorothy and Prescott Bush with Barbara, George, and George W., in Odessa, Texas, 1949, where the younger Bushes had moved the year before.

NINE

Who Had Ever Heard of Odessa, Texas?

★

As far as my mother was concerned, we could have been living in Russia.

—BARBARA BUSH

We all just wanted to make a lot of money quick.

—GEORGE H. W. BUSH

ALL BUSH REALLY KNEW about Texas came from his brief wartime stint at Corpus Christi, and, he admitted, from Randolph Scott movies. Everything was new to him. Stopping for lunch outside Abilene in his Studebaker in the summer of 1948, he went into a wooden-frame restaurant that advertised Lone Star, Jax, Pearl, and Dixie beers—all regional brands. He asked for a Lone Star or a Pearl—no time like the present to get into the local ways—and, looking over the menu, decided to go all in. "Chicken-fried steak," he said to the waitress. He did not know what, precisely, he had just ordered. "Would it turn out to be a steak fried like a chicken, or a chicken fried like a steak?" Bush wondered. Ten minutes later came a steak covered in what he thought was "thick chicken-type gravy." Between the midday beer and the steak and the gravy, Bush found the last two-hundred-odd-mile push west to Odessa a sleepy one. But he made it, passing derrick after derrick along the otherwise barren landscape, parking the Studebaker next to the small tin-roofed Ideco store, which sold parts for oil drilling.

"Ideco" was shorthand for Bush's new employer, formally known as the International Derrick and Equipment Company, a subsidiary of Dresser's. "You'll be an equipment clerk," Neil Mallon had told Bush. His monthly salary was $375. Within a week Bush rented half of a duplex on the unpaved East Seventh Street and sent for Barbara and the baby. The apartments were connected by a common bathroom. On Chapel and Edwards streets in New Haven the Bushes had shared baths before, but the similarities between Yale and Odessa ended there, as Barbara discovered when she and Georgie got off the plane from New York after a twelve-hour flight. They were stepping into what she called "a whole new and very hot world."

Back home in Rye, Pauline Pierce, Barbara's mother, was puzzled by the whole business. "Who had ever heard of Odessa, Texas?" Barbara wrote of Mrs. Pierce's reaction to the move. "She sent me cold cream, soap, and other items she assumed were available only in civilized parts of the country. She did not put Odessa in that category." The Bushes' fellow renters next door, a thirty-eight-year-old mother and her twenty-year-old daughter, were prostitutes whose callers often locked the Bushes out of the bathroom.

Reading trade journals, minding the Ideco store, and beginning to work as a salesman, Bush was learning the rudiments of the oil business. One day early in his stay in Odessa, he was assigned the task of painting some pumping units—while they were pumping. Bush and Hugh Evans, a Texan with what Bush recalled as "a gift for fading into the scenery at the slightest hint of physical labor," were sent out into the heat by their boss, Bill Nelson. "The units we were supposed to spruce up were monsters that had been baking in the sun for weeks," recalled Bush. "That meant trouble, because the only way to paint a pumping unit is to move, top to bottom, straddling the main beam as you go. Imagine riding a hot branding iron without a saddle and you've got the picture."

The savvy Evans painted a bit around the base of a pump then took a cigarette break in the shade of a nearby tree. "Hey, George, you know what the thermometer read when we left the store?" Evans asked. "A hundred [and] five degrees." Bush, riding the pump in the harsh sun, was feeling every one of those degrees. "One hell of a day to send folks out to paint a damn pumping unit, if you ask me," Evans said. "It just ain't fair." After watching Bush, who was "wrung out," finish the job, Evans asked the weary Bush, "George, would you mind if I ask a personal question?"

"That depends, Hugh. What is it you want to know?"

"Just tell me," he said, "whatever brought you to Texas?"

In the autumn Barbara suffered a miscarriage. "As I told you before we both are sort of hoping that we will have another child before too long," Bush wrote his mother on Wednesday, October 20, 1948. "Bar thinks about it a lot, and foolishly worries too much. I don't like to have her upset." Her life in particular revolved around Georgie's; the toddler was a bundle of energy. She took him to the circus in nearby Midland and worried over his health. (He woke up one night and "coughed until his little body almost broke," Barbara wrote. "I climbed in bed with him and hugged him.") After a large shot of penicillin, the two-year-old was dozing on his parents' bed, listening to Mother Goose on a record player borrowed from a neighbor, when he looked up at his father and said, "No man hurt Georgie, No Man!" He was, Bush wrote home, "referring of course to the needle. . . . He is so wonderful, Mum, so cute and bright. Oh he has his mischievous and naughty spells, but I just can't picture what we would do without him."

Both Bushes focused on two subjects above all others: the elder George's job and anything concerning the younger George. "Whenever I come home he greets me and talks a blue streak, sentences disjoined of course but enthusiasm and spirit boundless," Bush wrote Gerry Bemiss. "He is a real blond and pot-bellied. He tries to say everything and the results are often hilarious." The boy was spirited. Writing her parents to thank them for sending twenty-five dollars to pay for nursery school, Barbara reported that Georgie sometimes slipped out of the house unannounced, driving Barbara to distraction. "G.W.B. has a wee bit of the Devil in him," Barbara told her parents. "This A.M. while I was writing a letter early he stuck a can opener into my leg. Very painful and it was all I could do to keep from giving him a jab or two."

Bush shot doves with pals from Ideco, who taught him how to clean the birds, freeze them, and then, in due course, fry them up. There were football games or occasional dinners with the Reeders in Midland (old Yale friends) or a drive-in movie (the Bushes saw *The Egg and I* over Labor Day weekend 1948). Sundays were spent going to church, napping, and then taking Georgie to the playground. Though both Bushes were cheerfully adaptable, Bush worried about Barbara. "She is something, Mum, the way she never ever complains or even suggests that she would prefer to be elsewhere," he wrote in October 1948. "She is happy, I know, but anyone would like to be around her own friends, be able to take at least a passing interest in clothes, parties etc. She gets absolutely none of this. It is different for me, I have my job all day long with new things happening, but she is here in this small apt."

Barbara got a library card and loved suggestions for books to read.

Her mother-in-law sent her a 1,500-page Civil War novel, *House Divided,* which she devoured. The young couple read *Time* and *Life* each week and took *The Wall Street Journal* and *The Odessa American,* which was daily except Saturdays. By Christmas, Bush had moved the family from East Seventh to East Seventeenth, where, Barbara recalled, they would have their own bath. On Christmas Eve, Bush was assigned bartending duties at the Ideco company party. The task did not require much expertise: Most of the crowd drank straight whiskey or, if they were taking it easy, whiskey with a bit of water. A martini man in New Haven—Bush tended to have one or two drinks and that was it—he got into the spirit of the place and of the season that afternoon. A great many amber-colored drinks later, Bush was poured onto the flatbed of the company pickup truck; his colleagues dropped him off in the yard in front of the new apartment. "That, at least, was the way Barbara told the story of our first Christmas Eve in Texas," Bush recalled. He admitted his memories of the day were, at best, fuzzy.

In January 1949, Bush's parents flew down to Odessa on the Dresser company plane. Mrs. Bush settled in for nearly a week while Prescott continued on a Dresser inspection trip. The tireless Dorothy offered her daughter-in-law an intimidating example, cleaning the house and even washing the windows. "I have got to get this in the mail," Barbara wrote as she closed a letter. "I want to get some work done before Mrs. B. does everything."

As always, Bush worried. "The job continues in an interesting fashion, although I am selling or supposed to be, and am frankly very sad at it," he wrote Gerry Bemiss. "I drive around to rigs and small company offices, and so far have sold nothing." Yet he knew he had made the right move. "This West Texas is a fabulous place, Gerry. Fortunes can be made in the land end of the oil business, and of course can be lost. . . . If a man could go in and get just a few acres of land which later turned out to be good he would be fixed for life." Money, however, was not the only thing driving him. In January 1949, Bush—then twenty-four years old—wrote Bemiss, "I have in the back of my mind a desire to be in politics, or at least the desire to do something of service to this country."

In April 1949, the Bushes left Texas for a yearlong stint in California. This time all three of them got into the Studebaker to head toward the coast, living in motels, inns, and apartments in Whittier, Ventura, Bakersfield, and Compton, where Bush worked at Pacific Pumps, another

Dresser-owned company. He joined the United Steelworkers, paying dues and attending union meetings. Barbara noticed how much the other men liked her husband. "When I pick him up at work they always nod or wave to him," she wrote her family. "He seems to have the common touch—he is loved by all—especially me."

From early days selling drilling equipment to years of scouting offshore sites around the world, Bush built a significant oil business before moving into politics full-time in the mid-1960s.

They were living at 624 South Santa Fe in Compton in the fall of 1949. Barbara, who was pregnant, spent her days there while Bush was at Pacific Pumps. On Friday, September 23, 1949, word of a terrible accident in Rye reached Bush at work. Marvin Pierce had been driving to the station with his wife, Pauline, who had brought along an English bone china cup of coffee. She took a sip and put the cup on the seat between them. Noticing that it was about to spill on Pauline, Pierce reached for the cup but lost control of the car, which swerved left and fell one hundred feet down an embankment before crashing into a tree and a stone wall. Barbara's mother died after her head struck the windshield; her father was hospitalized.

Bush broke the news to Barbara, who was so close to delivering the new baby that her father told her not to come east for her mother's funeral. "He did not want the baby endangered," Barbara recalled. "What a lonely, miserable time that was."

Barbara honored Mrs. Pierce by naming the new child after her. Pauline Robinson Bush was born on the evening of Tuesday, December 20,

1949. They called her Robin. Bush brought his wife and new daughter home to the Compton apartment on Christmas Day 1949. The little girl charmed them all—father, mother, and brother. "Beautiful hazel eyes, soft blond hair," said Robin's besotted father. Soon came good news on the work front: Ideco wanted him back in West Texas, this time in Midland.

In the summer of 1948, in talking things over with Hugh Evans, Bush had said that his ambition wasn't complicated: He wanted to "learn the oil business and make money." Wise in the ways of the world—Evans had, after all, just smoked in the shade while an Ivy League–educated decorated naval aviator from Greenwich had nearly melted in the punishing weather—he gave Bush a piece of advice. "You've come to the wrong town . . . ," Evans said. "Midland's where the money is."

Midland in the postwar years was a boomtown that was attracting ambitious men and their families, many from the East. The newcomers' goals were clear. "We all just wanted to make a lot of money quick," Bush recalled. He knew it would take sweat and good fortune. "Quick, but not easy. We were young in the business, but still had enough experience to know that much." In the first week of May 1950, Bush received a letter from 59 Wall Street, the offices of Brown Brothers Harriman, offering him a job and thus presenting him with the kind of choice he had confronted before. Should his oil ambitions, while adventurous and protected by a watchful Neil Mallon, give way to a safer, more established career? He had not one but two children now. In practical terms, life in New York made vastly more sense for both Bushes than the life they had under construction in Texas. They would be close to their families, and investment banking would offer financial security and cultural familiarity.

Nearly two months of careful, even obsessive, consideration in the Bush household followed. Bush and Barbara were thinking of "nothing else," Bush told Tom McCance, the Brown Brothers Harriman partner who had made the overture. Bush went to New York to explore the idea more in person. Bush finally chose to stay with the course he had charted when he left New Haven. He would remain in Texas.

His father was on leave from the firm to seek a U.S. Senate seat from Connecticut in the 1950 elections. It was not Prescott's first political twitch. In 1946, the Bushes' U.S. representative in Connecticut, Clare Boothe Luce, the wife of Time-Life founder Henry R. Luce, had decided to leave the House. As the news of an open Fourth Congressional District seat spread, Samuel F. Pryor, a top Pan-Am executive and a mover in Connecticut politics, called Prescott to ask whether Bush might like to run for Congress. "If you would," Pryor said, "I think we can assure you that you'll be the nominee."

"Gee, that's something I've always dreamed about," said Bush, "but let me talk to my partners about it."

The partnership did not embrace the notion. "Look, if this was the Senate we'd back you for it and we'd like to see you do it, but for the House, don't do it," they said. Though he passed on the race, Prescott stepped up his involvement in state politics, becoming the Republicans' Connecticut finance chairman in 1947. In the summer of 1949, Harold Mitchell, the state GOP chairman, asked whether Prescott would be interested in a 1950 challenge to incumbent Democratic senator William Benton, who was filling out an unexpired term. The winner of the 1950 campaign would serve for two years, then run again in '52 for a full six-year term. Returning to the partnership with a possible Senate bid, Bush was received more warmly. He announced his candidacy in March, won the nomination, and was running well against Senator Benton. His musical friends composed a song:

> *Some churchmen think his program odd.*
> *First Yale, now country, when for God?*
> *They really shouldn't give up hope*
> *In ten years more he may be Pope. . . .*

> *His speeches like his drives will be*
> *Right down the center off the tee.*
> *His only leftist tendency*
> *Is when he hooks around the tree.*

On the Sunday before the election in November 1950, pamphlets appeared urging Roman Catholic voters to tune in to the Washington columnist Drew Pearson's radio broadcast at six P.M. that evening. Over the airwaves, the muckraking Pearson announced that "it has just been made known" that Prescott Bush was president of the American Birth Control

League, a forerunner of Planned Parenthood. Bush denied being president of the organization, but he had, in fact, served as treasurer of a 1947 Planned Parenthood fund drive. Pearson was wrong about the details, giving Bush just enough political room to deflect the story. To win, Bush needed to deny the allegation, even if it were essentially true. And so he did.

The attack was a classic late political hit in a heavily Roman Catholic state—one of two states in the Union in which birth control remained illegal. Bush lost, narrowly, by about 1,500 votes out of 862,000 cast. Watching from Midland, George H. W. Bush was frustrated that he was not a help to his father. "We felt terribly about the outcome after the way Dad worked at it," Bush wrote a friend on New Year's Day 1951. "I do feel he made a lot of friends though and I think he will be hard to beat if he runs again in 1952." It was the code: Always look ahead.

TEN

I Push It Away, Push It Back

★

We can't touch her, and yet we can feel her.
—GEORGE H. W. BUSH on his daughter Robin

Time after time during the next six months, George would put
me back together again.
—BARBARA BUSH

TWO YEARS BEFORE, Odessa had offered little in terms of housing, and Midland was not much better. In April 1950, Bush told his Ideco bosses that the family had already moved twice "to cheaper rooms each time, but we are unable to find anything that resembles an apartment or boarding house." There was some good news, though: "Tomorrow we get a motel with kitchenette." After stays at Kingsway Courts and George's Courts, the Bushes bought a house on East Maple along "Easter Egg Row"—a development designed for the new families flowing into Midland looking to strike it rich in oil. The nickname was in honor of the houses' bright paint colors; the Bushes' was light blue. The price was $7,500 for 847 square feet.

In Midland there were sandstorms and dust and heat. There were also a lot of easterners: It had become fashionable for Ivy Leaguers who wanted to escape Wall Street to try the oil business, which meant a lot of young families, a lot of cookouts, a lot of pickup sports. Most of all there was a lot of talk of oil—of where to find it and how to get it out of the ground.

A man of enthusiasms and quick decisions—falling in love with Barbara, joining the navy, moving to Texas—Bush was coming to believe that his future lay not with Dresser but with an independent oil venture. He liked the idea of choosing the riskier path over the safer route. (Everything was relative, of course. Bush was always going to benefit from being Bush.) He could have spent year after year working for Uncle Neil at Dresser, but a new challenge was at hand, along with the possibility of vast riches. The combination was irresistible.

By late 1950, Bush had gotten to know and to like John Overbey, an Easter Egg Row neighbor, fellow backyard barbecuer, and independent oilman. Overbey thought there was almost a physical force to Bush's ambition. Bush, he recalled, had "caught the fever and decided there must be a better way to participate in the excitement than selling hardware for Ideco." Bush and Overbey talked it over. Maybe they should join forces, go in together, make some real money. As Bush recalled it, independents in the oil business did all kinds of things. They bought percentages of possible royalty rights from landowners. They invested in "farm-outs," arrangements by which the independents would buy parcels of land from a big oil company and drill at the independents' expense. Explaining the business, Bush imagined an independent oilman's case to a bigger company: "If I hit, you've found out there's oil in the area without having to put your money into an exploratory operation; if I don't hit, it's my hard luck: You've learned the area is dry, without having to spend any of your own drilling money." Independents could do just about anything they could get away with. Bush loved the idea.

Except that pursuing the dream of going "independent" meant he would have to make a break from Mallon, the man who had been training him and who was responsible, really, for giving Bush a way out of the East, out from the shadow of his father and his Walker grandfather. What would Uncle Neil say? A nervous Bush made the trip from Midland to Dallas to find out in the spring of 1951. Bush revered Mallon in the way he revered his own father. The thought of disappointing the Dresser chief chilled him to the core.

When Bush broke the news to Mallon, there was a long silence—to Bush, an eternally long silence. "Uncle Neil" removed his eyeglasses and cleaned them, still wordless. He rose, walked into the next office, returned with a yellow legal pad, and began writing. "I really hate to see you go, George," Mallon finally said, "but if I were your age, I'd be doing the same thing—and here's how I'd go about it."

For half an hour he walked Bush through the different issues facing the new venture, from organizational challenges to the search for capital. "I left Neil's office with a tremendous weight off my shoulders," recalled Bush. "Of course, the real weight had just been added." At the age of twenty-six, he was co-owner of the Bush-Overbey Oil Development Company, Inc.

In a sense, the first campaign of George Bush's life was the pursuit of investors for Bush-Overbey and, later, for the company they formed with Hugh and William Liedtke, Zapata Petroleum Corporation. While Barbara took care of Georgie and Robin in the family's new 1,500-square-foot house at 1412 West Ohio—it was big enough for the children to have their own rooms—Bush sought backing for his new oil ventures. He and Overbey needed cash to buy royalty and mineral rights. The attraction for investors was clear: The U.S. tax code treated most investments in the oil business favorably, allowing significant tax deductions if they failed, which meant those with capital to spend were in a win-win situation. If oil was found, they were likely to profit; if there was just a dry hole, they could still write off much of the expense of the investment.

Bush hit New York and Washington in search of funds; he traveled to North Dakota, Colorado, Nebraska, and Wyoming in search of leases. His uncle Herbie Walker invested in Bush-Overbey and helped bring in others, making the whole enterprise possible.

Like Neil Mallon, George Herbert Walker, Jr.—"Uncle Herbie," though Bush tended to spell his name "Herby"—played a vital role in Bush's life. Born in 1905, Herbie was Loulie and Bert's third child, behind Nancy Walker and Dorothy, whom Herbie adored all his life. "He almost idolized Aunt Dotty Bush, and almost from the time George was born, my father pretty much idolized him, too," recalled G. H. Walker III. Six foot exactly—a bit shorter than Prescott Bush, who was six four—a Yale man (class of 1927), and a Bonesman, Herbie loved baseball and boating, as did George H. W. Bush, and uncle and nephew grew exceptionally close. Alternately charming and cool, Walker "could be very warm toward people he liked, and very opinionated about the people he didn't," his eldest son recalled. "He had strong views on people, positive and negative."

Uncle Herbie's affection for his sister and her son George created strain in his own family. "'Dotty doesn't do things that way,' he would say to my mother, and that could be upsetting," recalled G. H. Walker III. "His devotion to George—never missed a baseball game of George's at Yale, and they would go out on the boat together, by themselves, in

Maine—was obviously not easy for the rest of us, but we learned it was a fact of life, and we rolled with it." Herbie ran G. H. Walker & Company, would co-own the New York Mets, and was instrumental in funding George H. W. Bush's oil ventures in Texas.

The search for cash was never ending. Eugene Meyer, the financier who had bought *The Washington Post* at auction in 1933, was one possible source of capital. (Meyer was the father of Katharine Graham and the father-in-law of Philip Graham.) A client of Brown Brothers Harriman, Meyer agreed to see young Bush and his friend and colleague Fred Chambers. Over breakfast at Meyer's house in Washington, Bush and Chambers made their pitch for capital to finance a project in West Texas. Meyer listened politely, and as the meal of bacon and eggs came to an end, volunteered to give Bush and Chambers a ride to Union Station in his limousine. The old man offered them a fur lap robe to keep warm on the drive—a generous gesture, but Bush was more focused on the fact that Meyer had not signaled an interest in the proposed deal one way or the other. "What I remember about the ride is the sinking feeling I had as we neared the station," Bush recalled. "Our host just didn't seem interested in the details of our proposition."

As the car came to a stop, Bush was ready for a polite goodbye when Meyer said, "Okay, put me down for $50,000." Bush and Chambers were thrilled and were about to head into the station when Meyer called to them from the window of the car. "You say this is a good tax proposition?" Bush and Chambers eagerly assented. "Okay, then put my son-in-law down for . . ." So it went for the next decade or so, through the 1950s: Bush worked hard to raise money in the East in order to press ahead in Texas. For Bush, raising capital required charm, smarts, and drive. Though few people could have been as well positioned to have access to big moneymen than Bush, he still had to make the sale, and then produce.

In the political world, Dwight Eisenhower, the former supreme Allied commander, had won the 1952 Republican presidential nomination, and his general election campaign offered signs of the emergence of a viable Republican opposition to the dominant Democratic Party across the old Confederacy. Volunteering for Ike in Midland, Bush had a personal stake in the voting in 1952: His father was again campaigning for the Senate. In this second bid, Prescott ran against Democratic congressman Abraham Ribicoff of Hartford. One evening the Bushes were driving back from a campaign event with Bush adviser Elmer Ryan. They passed one of the many billboards in the state that read YOU'RE BETTER OFF WITH RIBICOFF.

"I wish we could develop something to offset that slogan, 'You're Better off with Ribicoff,'" said Ryan. Dorothy Bush, who was riding in the front seat, spoke up: "You're in a jam with Abraham." Ryan loved it, Prescott loved it, and the next day the candidate began using the line. The Bushes soon faced questions of anti-Semitism about the slogan. Asked about the formulation, Prescott explained its origin, and the tempest passed. "It was one of those things that was here today and gone tomorrow," he recalled, "because it was obviously not designed to be anti-Semitic." Then Prescott added, coldly: "If I'd wanted to be anti-Semitic I'd have attacked it in a mighty different way than that."

During the '52 campaign, Wisconsin senator Joe McCarthy, the Republican red-baiter who had won national celebrity by raising fears about Communist infiltration in America, was the featured speaker at a rally at the Klein Memorial Auditorium in Bridgeport, Connecticut. Beginning with a speech at Wheeling, West Virginia, in 1950, McCarthy had capitalized on Cold War tensions by claiming, at first, that he had a list of 205 "members of the Communist Party who nevertheless are still working and shaping policy in the State Department." The numbers would change—downward—and McCarthy frequently hurled reckless charges. He had, however, tapped into widespread anxieties about the Soviets, and droves showed up to hear him in Bridgeport. Arriving at the venue on Fairfield Avenue, Prescott was stunned by the size and ardor of the crowd. It was standing room only. Seated onstage with McCarthy, Bush listened as the state's national committeeman, party chairman, and finally Senator William Purtell all bid McCarthy welcome. When Bush's turn came, he remembered that his knees were "shaking considerably."

"I said that I was very glad to welcome a Republican senator to our state, and that we had many reasons to admire Joe McCarthy," Bush recalled. "In some ways he was a very unusual man. At least . . . he had done one very unusual thing—he had created a new word in the English language, which is 'McCarthyism.'" The audience loved the point; "everybody," Bush recalled, "screamed with delight."

Bush was not yet done. A master of publicly using innuendo and sometimes even pure invention to smear government officials, military personnel, and academics as Communists, McCarthy was widely seen as a bully, and Bush called him on it. "But, I must say in all candor," Bush went on, "that some of us, while we admire his objectives in his fight against Communism, we have very considerable reservations concerning the methods which he sometimes employs." For a Republican seeking office in that time and that place, Prescott Bush's words were brave.

The crowd turned on Bush. But he had said what he had come to say.

On Election Day—Tuesday, November 4, 1952—Eisenhower defeated Adlai Stevenson by twelve points, 55 to 43 percent, and Bush bested Ribicoff by thirty thousand votes. In Washington, Dorothy and Prescott leased quarters at the Wardman Park, a large redbrick hotel on Woodley Road, and on Capitol Hill, Senator Bush was delighted to find a Washington that was rather like Brown Brothers. Senator Harry Byrd, Democrat of Virginia, was a neighbor—he lived at the Shoreham—and the two men would sometimes take walks together. In the weeks between the election and Eisenhower's inauguration, Bush discovered the joys of the Republican senators' private dining room on Capitol Hill. From the very first he felt he belonged. The game Bush had learned from his father paid political dividends, too. Eisenhower loved golf, and Prescott Bush was the best—and perhaps the most discreet—golfer in the Senate. The president often invited Bush to play with him, confident that Bush would keep the details of the round and of any business they might discuss confidential.

Substantively, Bush eschewed ideology. A delegation of postal workers once called on him to win his support for a pay-increase bill. "Now, Senator, we want to put you on the spot," they said, according to Bush. "We want you to tell us what you're going to do about this."

"Now, listen, gentlemen, I don't go on the spot for anybody," Bush replied. "I'm glad to be here with you, and I want you to tell me all you want me to know about this bill. But I don't make it a practice to tell any group or anybody how I intend to vote on a bill, until the time comes for me to vote. Then you'll know, and you can then make up your mind whether that's been a favorable decision to you or not."

News soon arrived from Texas: John Ellis Bush had been born in Midland on Wednesday, February 11, 1953. Called "Jeb," the baby came home from the hospital to join his brother and his sister on West Ohio

Avenue. Barbara turned the family's sunroom, which was just off the living room, into his nursery. "Life," Barbara recalled, "seemed almost too good to be true."

A few weeks after Jeb's birth, Robin, now three, was feeling out of sorts. "I don't know what to do this morning," she said one day. "I may go out and lie on the grass and watch the cars go by, or I might just stay in bed." Worried, Barbara took the little girl to the family's pediatrician, Dr. Dorothy Wyvell. The doctor drew blood for tests and said she would get back to the Bushes as soon as she knew something.

Bush was at the Ector County Courthouse in Odessa, checking land records, when Barbara called him and said the doctor wanted to see both of them—right away. It was late afternoon when the Bushes and Wyvell sat down together in the doctor's small office. Bush noticed that the doctor was having trouble getting out what she had to say. "I have some bad news for you," Wyvell said, fighting off her own tears. "Your daughter has leukemia."

Bush was startled and uncertain. Neither he nor Barbara knew what leukemia was. "What do we do about it?" he asked.

"You have two choices," Wyvell said. "You can treat her. The research is very preliminary, but you could do that. Or you could just let nature take its course, and I know this is hard to believe, but then she probably would be dead in a few weeks."

The Bushes looked at each other, trying to absorb what Wyvell was telling them. The diagnosis, so unexpected and so foreign, devastated their perfectly normal world, one that had seemed secure only moments before. Groping for something, anything, Bush called his uncle Dr. John Walker, the president of Memorial Sloan Kettering Hospital on the Upper East Side of New York City. "You don't have a choice," Dr. Walker said to Bush. "There's no choice. You've got to bring her up here and let us treat her." Bush arranged to fly to New York the next morning.

The Bushes drove home, separately, in the gathering Texas dusk. Bush said he needed to stop off at the office for a moment; in fact, he went to the house of their friends Liz and Tom Fowler to ask Liz to come over to be with Barbara. Before long, the Bushes' house was filled with neighbors. The next morning, the Bushes left Georgie and Jeb with friends and took Robin to New York to check her into Memorial Sloan Kettering. Not quite twenty-four hours had passed since they had sat, dumb-struck, in Wyvell's Midland office. They were not going to give up—or more precisely, they were not going to give *Robin* up. The Bushes moved into Bush grandfather G. H. Walker's Sutton Place apartment and pre-pared for a long siege against their child's cancer.

Given the state of oncology in 1953, only so much could be done. There were bone marrow tests, and oxygen tents, and cortisone injec-tions. At times, Bush recalled, "God, the poor little girl was panicked, crying"; at others she was her smiling, charming self. "Robin does unfor-tunately have Leukemia, and although there is little hope for her we have taken her to Memorial Hospital for treatments," Bush wrote a corre-spondent in August 1953. "She has responded satisfactorily, and our big hope is that some new cure will be discovered for this horrible disease."

There were a few good days. The Bushes were allowed to take Robin to the Walkers' on Sutton Place once in a while. "Gampy Walker was a scary old man," Barbara said of G.H., "but he was putty in Robin's hands." The great-grandfather taught his great-granddaughter a version of gin rummy. Robin at first heard the name as "Gin Mummy," then de-cided to call it "Gin Poppy" in honor of her father. On a brief visit to Kennebunkport the family was reunited—Barbara, George, Georgie, and tiny Jeb. Robin adored the boys, calling them "superman" brothers and taping their pictures to her headboard at the hospital.

Barbara was able to take her home to Midland for a time. "Leukemia was not a well-known disease," Barbara recalled. Fearing it might be contagious, there were those in town who kept their children away from Robin. "In those days," Barbara said, "cancer in general was only whis-pered about, and some people just couldn't cope with a dying child." Yet Robin could seem so bright and active that an acquaintance who saw her and her father together asked Bush whatever had happened to that sick daughter of his.

The Bushes decided not to tell Georgie, then six, about the full extent of his sister's illness. "We hated that, but we felt it would have been too big a burden for such a little fellow," recalled Barbara. She had to watch over them carefully when they were together for fear that natural sibling "roughhousing" could lead to hemorrhage. As autumn came hope dwin-dled. The doctors were trying everything they reasonably could, includ-ing cortisone treatments, which "changed her whole personality," Bush recalled. "She'd strike out at people—'Don't do this to me—you can't do this to me.' But except for that, she was just smiling." When Bush was there, he could not stand it when the doctors and nurses did their most intrusive work.

Bush juggled business and the boys while Barbara remained steadfast at Robin's side. Bush's Yale friend Thomas W. L. "Lud" Ashley was there at the hospital in New York every day. A nurse once asked Barbara what her husband, who kept such strange hours, did for a living. "I meet him every morning around 2 A.M. when he comes in to check on Robin before going to bed," the nurse said. It was Ashley, standing in for his old friend.

Barbara had only one real rule for visitors: No tears in front of Robin. She didn't want the little girl scared by seeing grown-ups crying. "Poor George had the most dreadful time," recalled Barbara. He would say he had to go to the bathroom and step outside. "We used to laugh and wonder if Robin thought he had the weakest bladder in the world," recalled Barbara. "Not true. He just had the most tender heart." Senator Bush came up from Washington one day and took Barbara with him out to Greenwich. He asked her to go on a walk; he told her, she recalled, that he wanted her to see where he was going to be buried. She soon found herself in the town's graveyard, standing before a simple three foot by four foot stone that read BUSH. There was a lilac bush on one side, a dogwood on the other. On that sunny day on a Connecticut hillside, surrounded by gravestones, it slowly but inescapably came to her that her father-in-law was showing her not only his grave, but Robin's. "That darling man bought that lot so Robin would have a place to rest," Barbara recalled.

She was alone with Robin at the hospital when the little girl began to fade. Bush told his brother Jonathan that an infection was "raging through her body." From the hospital Barbara and the doctors called Bush in Texas. "They wanted to operate again, and I said, 'No, we've done enough to her,'" Bush recalled. "They said there was no real hope for her. I said, 'Can you learn something if you operate?' Not much more, they said. We thought it was time to let her go. They agreed with our decision."

Robin went into a coma while her father was en route from Texas. Mother and father were both there at her bedside when the end came.

"One minute she was there, and the next she was gone," recalled Barbara. "I truly felt her soul go out of that beautiful little body." Barbara combed Robin's hair, and both parents held her a last time.

Robin, not quite four years old, died on the evening of Sunday, October 11, 1953. There was a small memorial service in Greenwich, but without Robin's body. The Bushes had given her to research in the hope that her loss might help others survive. A short while later, after the remains were released from the hospital, Dorothy Bush and Lud Ashley buried Robin in the grave her grandfather had prepared for her.

In the upstairs bedroom where she and George were staying in the Bush house on Grove Lane, Barbara had heard guests assembling to go over to the memorial service at Christ Church. Suddenly everything seemed too much, and Barbara told her husband that she couldn't face them all. "For one who allowed no tears before her death, I fell apart," recalled Barbara, "and time after time during the next six months, George would put me together again." She made it through the day, and the two flew home to Midland.

I t was a hellish time. "We awakened night after night in great physical pain—it hurt that much," Barbara recalled. When they arrived home, they drove to pick George W. up at Sam Houston Elementary School; they wanted to be the ones to tell him the terrible news. Seven-year-old Georgie and a classmate were carrying a record player from one part of the school to another when the Bushes' pea-green Oldsmobile appeared. "I could have sworn that I saw Robin's blond curls in the window," George W. Bush recalled. "My mom, dad, and sister are home," he said to his teacher. "Can I go see them?" Reaching the Oldsmobile, he looked in vain in the backseat. No Robin. Barbara enveloped him in a tight hug. She was capable of just a whisper. "She died," Barbara told him.

The ride home was the first time the boy had ever seen his parents cry. It was the beginning of a difficult period in which even the best intentioned of friends and acquaintances sometimes exacerbated the couple's grief rather than assuaging it. At first there was just silence on the topic. No one really knew what to say about Robin, so they settled on a strategy of acting as though nothing had happened. "I hated that nobody mentioned her; it was as if she had never been," Barbara recalled. Those who did speak of it often made a mess of things. One day Barbara caught a caller practicing making sad faces in the living room mirror, preparing for her audience with the grieving mother. Barbara, unnoticed, backed out of the room and then entered again. The visitor stammered out an appalling remark: "At least it wasn't your firstborn and a boy at that." Bush was more understanding than Barbara, who privately lashed out about such awkward episodes. "George pointed out that it wasn't easy for them and that I should be patient," she recalled. "He was right. I just needed somebody to blame."

The man who could not stand his daughter's cries in the hospital proved to be a superb and caring husband, able to talk about the things that he could not watch. In the darkness, in their bedroom at the end of the hallway on West Ohio, Bush would hold Barbara as she sobbed herself to sleep. When she fell into grief-stricken silences, she found that he was engaged and emotionally accessible. Bush, Barbara recalled, "made me talk to him, and he shared with me. What a difference that makes. . . . He did it subtly, but with love."

The younger George Bush put Robin back into common conversation. At a football game Georgie told his father that he wished he were Robin. Why was that? Bush asked. "I bet she can see the game better from up there than we can here," the boy said. One day Barbara overheard Georgie declining to play with another child because his mother needed him too much. "That started my cure," said Barbara. "I realized I was too much of a burden for a little seven-year-old boy to carry."

The quest for the meaning of Robin's death never ended. "It taught me that life is unpredictable and fragile," Bush recalled. "It taught me the importance of close family and friends, because of Lud and several other friends that rallied around. It taught me that no matter how innocent or perfect a child, she can still be taken away from you by horrible illness. That gets into 'the Lord works in strange ways,' if you believe in that. I've never gotten a real answer to that one. But I learned a lot from it. Keep going, charging ahead." There wasn't, after all, much else to do.

Dorothy Bush commissioned an oil portrait of Robin for her son and daughter-in-law. Bush wondered, sometimes, whether it was fair to have the picture hanging in the house. He worried that it might make the other children or guests uncomfortable. In the end, though, "selfishness takes over," for when he gazed at it in the flickering candlelight of the dining room, Bush would feel "a renewed physical sensation of closeness to a loved one."

In the late 1950s, after the births of Neil Mallon Bush (1955) and Marvin Pierce Bush (1956), Bush, in the midst of the busiest of lives, was in New York on business. One evening he went "out on the town," and only when he was heading in for the night did he think that "You could well have gone to Greenwich tonight," to see Robin at her grave. The thought, he wrote his mother, "struck me out of the blue, but I felt no real sense of negligence. . . . I like . . . to think of Robin as though she were a part, a living part, of our vital and energetic and wonderful family of men and Bar." How long, he wondered, would this sense of Robin as a perpetual child last? "We hope we will feel this genuine closeness [to Robin] when we are 83 and 82," he wrote his mother. "Wouldn't it be exciting at that age to have a beautiful 3 and a half year old daughter. . . . She doesn't grow up. Now she's Neil's age. Soon she'll be Marvin's—and beyond that she'll be all alone, but with us, a vital living pleasurable part of our day-to-day life." He continued:

> There is about our house a need. The running, pulsating restlessness of the four boys as they struggle to learn and grow; the world embraces them. . . . All this wonder needs a counterpart. We need some starched crisp frocks to go with all our torn-kneed blue jeans and helmets. We need some soft blond hair to off-set those crew cuts. We need a doll house to stand firm against our forts and rackets and thousand baseball cards. We need a cut-out star to play alone while the others battle to see who's 'family champ.' We even need someone . . . who could sing the descant to "Alouette," while outside they scramble to catch the elusive ball aimed ever roofward, but usually thudding against the screens.
> We need a legitimate Christmas angel—one who doesn't have cuffs beneath the dress.
> We need someone who's afraid of frogs.
> We need someone to cry when I get mad—not argue.
> We need a little one who can kiss without leaving egg or jam or gum.
> We need a girl.
> We had one once—she'd fight and cry and play and make her way just like the rest. But there was about her a certain softness.
> She was patient—her hugs were just a little less wiggly.

Like them, she'd climb in to sleep with me, but somehow she'd fit.

She didn't boot and flip and wake me up with pug nose and mischievous eyes a challenging quarter-inch from my sleeping face.

No—she'd stand beside our bed till I felt her there. Silently and comfortable, she'd put those precious, fragrant locks against my chest and fall asleep.

Her peace made me feel strong, and so very important.

"My Daddy" had a caress, a certain ownership which touched a slightly different spot than the "Hi Dad" I love so much.

But she is still with us. We need her and yet we have her. We can't touch her, and yet we can feel her.

We hope she'll stay in our house for a long, long time.

Love
Pop

*An image of Robin, the Bushes' second child,
playing during a trip to Greenwich in
June 1953. President Bush kept this photo in a
drawer of his desk in the Oval Office, and later
placed it on his desk in his retirement office
in Houston.*

Reading the letter aloud more than five decades later in his post-presidential office in Houston, Bush broke down in tears long before the end, crying so hard that he had difficulty catching his breath. After a time, the tears dried. He gestured toward the letter and said, "When I read that it's right there with me now. But normally I push it away, push it back." He continued, "But life goes on. You count your blessings and your sorrows and you realize how lucky you are and have been all my life, really."

His eyes fell on a small black-and-white photograph of Robin in a gold frame. She is playing next to a fountain at Grove Lane. He gazed at her a moment, then looked up, smiling awkwardly. He wiped his eyes again. It was time to move on.

ELEVEN

I Was Bleeding Inside

★

*I worried a lot in those days. I felt a responsibility—if things
had gone badly it would've been a huge blow.*

—GEORGE H. W. BUSH, on the late 1950s and early '60s
in the oil business

B USH REACTED TO ROBIN'S LOSS in much the way he had reacted
to the deaths of Ted White and Del Delaney at Chichi-Jima. He
mourned but pressed ahead. In the Pacific in 1944 that had meant
returning to VT-51 as soon as possible. In Midland in 1953 it meant
hurling himself into his latest business venture: a new oil company with
additional partners. The Liedtke brothers, Hugh and Bill, came from
Oklahoma. Like the Bushes and the Overbeys, they were part of the new
social fabric of Midland. Why not team up on the oil front? The result
was a new company. Bush-Overbey and the Liedtkes each put up
$500,000, creating $1 million in equity. But what to call it? Hugh Liedtke
had a simple rule of thumb: Pick a name that started with either A or Z,
so you would be first or last in the telephone listings. With that in mind,
the team chose Zapata Petroleum Corporation, after the Marlon Brando
movie *Viva Zapata!,* which was playing in Midland.

The association with the Liedtkes proved profitable. Under the Zapata name, Bush and his colleagues found success in Coke County, Texas,
drilling 127 wells without a dry hole on the 8,100-acre West Jamieson
field. The West Jamieson wells were steady producers, not gushers, and
they gave Bush's business a sound foundation. Over the next decade or
so, Bush struggled to build an international business. He did well enough,
but never made the big find or the big deal that would have given him
stratospheric wealth. He stayed after it, though, pursuing offshore opportunities from the Persian Gulf, including Kuwait, to Mexico, Japan,
Ecuador, and Trinidad.

In 1955, applying for a $25,000 loan from the Texas National Bank in
Houston for a new house in Midland, Bush, then 31, wrote that he "had

no cash to speak of." He owed $11,000 to his father. Overall assets amounted to $40,000. His greatest hope lay in 100,000 shares of Zapata, which was about to go public at an expected price ranging from $8 to $10 a share. When Zapata shares hit the open market on Friday, December 30, 1955, they reached about $11 a share in early trading.

Bush was open to taking chances. Zapata contracted with R. G. LeTourneau, a celebrated designer of earth-moving machines, to deploy a tripod drilling platform. Turning LeTourneau's vision into reality required an enormous capital investment—roughly $3.5 million. LeTourneau ultimately designed three rigs for Bush: the Scorpion, the Vinegarroon, and a $6 million edition, the Maverick. The gamble paid off: Zapata prospered.

Bush embraced risk—reasonable risk, to be sure, but he preferred gambling big to seeking security in the familiar. He knew that the man who came through a contest through skill or luck (or a bit of both) was the kind of man other people tended to look up to, to admire, to respect. Of a piece with this ambition to attract the notice of the world through achievement was the anxiety that one might fail, losing not only the stakes at hand but the esteem of others. The pressure Bush applied to himself to succeed, all while striving to appear as though there was no pressure at all, made his stomach churn.

One morning in London in 1960, he found that he had no choice but to admit all was not perfect. As Bush recalled it, Zapata Off-Shore was embroiled in a lawsuit over Zapata's performance as a contract driller on wells off Trinidad. As Bush saw it, the suit posed an existential threat to his company. "If we lost this, the whole thing could have gone to pieces," recalled Bush. "And I had people counting on me—stockholders, our employees, everybody."

Bush felt miserable. He and Baine Kerr, Zapata's lawyer, were in London to work on the litigation with their insurer, Lloyd's of London. Bush was sick to his stomach; his vomit was coffee-colored, his stool black. He rose early on the day of their departure back to the United States. Wrapped only in a towel, he was about to shave when his stomach seemed to explode. In excruciating pain, Bush fell toward the floor. Everything went dark.

He did not know how long he had been out when the room swam back into focus. He was on the floor, nude—his towel had fallen away—and he saw a set of buttons next to the bed. He pushed one and a maid came in; she quickly sent for the hotel doctor. "Don't worry, old chap—just a bit of indigestion," the doctor told Bush after a brief examination. The physician prescribed Coca-Cola.

Relieved but still in pain, Bush managed to dress and meet Kerr for an appointment at Lloyd's, where the insurers gave the delegation from Texas a small lunch, with sherry. Bush then flew from London to New York, New York to Dallas, and finally Dallas to Midland. By the time Bush landed at home he was in severe pain again. "I felt like hell," Bush recalled. He went to see his doctor. The verdict? "You've got a bleeding ulcer," the doctor told Bush.

"I was bleeding inside," Bush recalled. As was common at the time, Bush attributed the ulcer to stress—in this case, of the Trinidad litigation. We now know that such ulcers are primarily bacterial; the fact remains that Bush believed his own ulcer was caused by anxiety, which led him to ask the obvious question of his doctor. "What do you do about it?" Bush said.

"Don't worry about things that you can't do anything about," the doctor replied. Bush thought, "I'm paying this guy to give me that advice?" (The litigation was ultimately resolved without the dire consequences Bush had feared.)

Everything Bush heard from his parents in the 1950s suggested that the bigger, faster world of Washington held great appeal. "Politics entered into my thinking . . . especially after Dad went to the Senate in 1953," Bush recalled. Socially moderate (and sometimes liberal) Prescott Bush was fiscally conservative but shared Eisenhower's view that the New Deal had taken such root that the responsible approach in the postwar period was to manage, not reverse, the enlarged role of government in national life.

Describing Eisenhower, Prescott Bush could have been speaking of himself: "He was basically full of real human sympathy, and he was not antagonistic to the general New Deal philosophy, let's call it, which is for social betterment and increase in education, broadening the opportunities of education for our people and increasing their housing facilities, meeting the terrible needs within our cities." Prescott Bush was a strong advocate of the federal government's role in urban redevelopment and helped pass the National Interstate and Defense Highway Act. On civil rights he was a progressive Republican, noting the "essential rightness" of the Supreme Court's desegregation decisions "from the standpoint of simple justice and good conscience." He supported a strong civil rights plank in the 1956 GOP platform and pressed for integrated federal housing.

Nor was the senior Bush a blindly hawkish cold warrior. Perhaps most notably, Prescott Bush again spoke out against Joe McCarthy, hero to hardcore conservatives. Matters had only grown worse after the campaign event in Connecticut where Bush had criticized the Wisconsin senator. In disastrous hearings investigating alleged Communist influence in the U.S. Army, McCarthy smeared a young lawyer who worked for the army's special counsel. While millions watched on television, Joseph Welch, the army's counsel, turned on McCarthy. "Until this moment, Senator, I think I never really gauged your cruelty or your recklessness," Welch said. "You have done enough. Have you no sense of decency, sir, at long last? Have you left no sense of decency?"

The Senate formed a special committee to investigate McCarthy. In late 1954, the panel recommended that the Senate condemn him. In the debate Prescott Bush drew on his grave mien, his sense of duty, and his totemic reverence for the Senate as he rose against McCarthy. "Mr. President, all my life I have looked upon membership in the United States Senate as the greatest office to which one could aspire," Bush told the Senate on Wednesday, December 1, 1954. McCarthy, he went on, "has caused dangerous divisions among the American people because of his attitude, and the attitude he has encouraged among his followers, that there can be no honest differences of opinion with him. Either you must follow Senator McCarthy blindly, not daring to express any doubts or disagreements about any of his actions, or in his eyes you must be a Communist, a Communist sympathizer, or a fool who has been duped by the Communist line."

Bush was one of 22 Republicans (out of 44) to vote against McCarthy, who was condemned by a vote of 67 to 22 by the whole Senate. McCarthy died soon thereafter, a broken man. The anti-McCarthy senators were attacked by the far right. From Texas, George H. W. Bush weighed in on the proceedings. "I realize that anybody who takes a stand against McCarthy is apt to be subjected through the lunatic fringe to all sorts of abuse," wrote Bush. He wished, he said, that the tone of the politics was calmer.

The Prescott Bushes enjoyed the folkways of Eisenhower's Washington, and Prescott Bush made the occasional trip down to the White House for drinks. Sherman Adams, Eisenhower's chief of staff, would call with an invitation for six P.M., and Bush would join the president and a handful of other senators to "talk quite informally" with Ike. When Bush and Eisenhower played golf, they would have a bite of lunch and then tee off at twelve thirty or one P.M. The Bushes loved the diplomatic social scene as well. "It's always helpful, I think, to get to know people from foreign countries, and to get their point of view about us," Bush recalled. He was a happy senator, savoring trips abroad. Bush was flown out and landed on two U.S. carriers—the *FDR* in the Mediterranean and the *Enterprise* in the China Sea.

During the 1956 reelection campaign the Bushes temporarily abandoned Greenwich for Hartford's Heublein Hotel. Dorothy Bush was characteristically competitive. In Washington she had taken classes in public speaking, graduating first in a field of about fifteen other students. She memorized her speeches and could speak flawlessly for twenty minutes or so without notes. The two were, Bush recalled, "on the go constantly, day and night, up until midnight or later" all fall. The hard work paid off, and Prescott was reelected for a full term in a race against Democratic nominee Thomas Dodd in November 1956.

In the Eisenhower years, the interests of Bush father and son clashed. At issue was legislation deregulating the natural gas industry, a move favored by oilmen but opposed by many lawmakers from energy-consuming, as opposed to energy-producing, states. Prescott Bush and others feared that deregulation would raise the cost of energy for their constituents. George H. W. Bush and others argued from a free market perspective that deregulation would lead to more competition, more supply, and lower prices. That was, George H. W. Bush acknowledged, the "opinion . . . of a Texan in the oil business."

Senator Bush would not change his vote to favor the oil industry. The bill had successfully passed the House the year before and was now pending in the Senate. The oil industry, led by Sid Richardson, was furiously at work to get the legislation through the upper chamber to the president. The calls to George H. W. Bush's Midland home and office were numerous, and sharp in tone. Oilmen from all over Texas were ringing him up to urge him to lobby his father. The polite ones, Bush recalled, asked if the senator could be reasoned with. The more strident ones told Bush that he'd "damn well better" deliver his father's vote. Under pressure, Bush reacted coolly, but the calls got meaner. As Bush recalled, "The head of Phillips Petroleum, K. S. 'Boots' Adams, told Neil Mallon"—Prescott's old friend—that if the senator "doesn't vote for this bill, you can forget selling any more Dresser equipment to Phillips, and you can tell George Bush to forget his offshore drilling business."

And meaner still. At two o'clock one morning a drunken lobbyist for Sid Richardson, the greatest oil giant among great oil giants, telephoned the Bush household in Midland. Unless Prescott Bush "got right" on the legislation that Richardson wanted passed, "That's all she wrote for you, Bush, because we're gonna run your ass out of the offshore drilling business." Bush had trouble sleeping that night.

As the threats mounted, the son traveled to Washington to see his father and discuss Zapata's predicament. The senator was sympathetic but unwavering. "They'll never put you out of business," Prescott told his son. "They wouldn't dare, because this would be the worst possible mistake they could make. This will not affect you at all. I'm going to vote against the bill because on the whole I think that's in the best interests of my state, as well as the United States, to vote against this bill. But don't you worry about it, and if there's any after-effects from it, just tell me about them, and we'll take care of that."

President Eisenhower vetoed the bill, noting that the lobbying effort by the oil industry made "American politics a dreary and frustrating experience for anyone who has any regard for moral and ethical standards." In the aftermath, the oilmen who had put pressure on George H. W. backed down.

In August 1959, Zapata Off-Shore became its own stand-alone company, breaking off from the Liedtkes' larger Zapata Petroleum. It was time, Bush decided, to move to the Gulf of Mexico, to Houston, where the offshore action was. ZOS, as the separate company was known, was substantial if not gigantic, with four rigs, 195 employees, and 2,200 stockholders.

Barbara was unhappy about the move to Houston, but it made sense. Bush's mission in business had shifted over the years from oil in general to offshore in particular. The Bushes used Mildred and Baine Kerr's house in Houston as a base for searching for a new home, settling on buying a 1.2-acre lot near the Kerrs' and building from scratch on Briar Lane. Barbara soldiered on.

Bush set up offices downtown on the seventeenth floor of the Houston Club Building. On Tuesday, August 18, 1959, Barbara gave birth to Dorothy Walker Bush, to be called "Doro." She was, Bush said, "enchanting . . . a wild dark version of Robin." He was found with his head leaning against the hospital's nursery window, crying in happiness.

TWELVE

Goldwater's Policies, Kennedy's Style

★

*The Senate is a terribly sought-after post. . . . So the Senate is
the ultimate goal of most every politician.*
—PRESCOTT BUSH

He radiated charm and gave us a certain respectability.
—PETER O'DONNELL, chairman of the Texas Republican Party

EVERYBODY WANTED HIM. In Texas circles in the first years of the
1960s, George Bush was a prime political prospect. The Harris
County Republican chairman in Houston, James A. Bertron, encountered Prescott Bush at a fundraiser in Washington.

"Jimmy, when are you going to get George involved?" Prescott asked.

"Senator, I'm trying," Bertron said. "We're all trying."

Bertron was right—more right, perhaps, than he knew. One of the
most powerful Democrats in Texas, George Brown of the construction
giant Brown & Root, had already reached out to Bush. Brown made the
case that the attractive young Republican at work in the Houston Club
Building would find a congenial home in the Democratic Party. It was a
serious overture. Brown and his brother Herman were instrumental figures in the rise and reign of Lyndon Johnson. Bush knew that a suggestion from that quarter was not to be taken lightly. "They mentioned
several possibilities, including a chance at a U.S. Senate seat, if I crossed
over and became a Democrat," Bush recalled. "The transition, they said,
would be painless: In Texas there are really two Democratic parties—
conservative Democrats on one side, liberal Democrats on the other. I'd
just take my place on the conservative end of the Democratic spectrum."

Though Bush admitted that George Brown's argument "made pragmatic sense," he "just couldn't see it," and he declined to switch parties.
"Privately my own political philosophy had long been settled," Bush recalled. "I supported much of Harry Truman's foreign policy in the late
1940s. But I didn't like what he and the Democratic Party stood for in

the way of big, centralized government—the attitude that 'Washington knows best' and the policies and programs it produced." He was a Republican, and he would not fake being a Democrat, even a conservative one.

In Connecticut, in the middle of May 1962, Prescott Bush, suffering from arthritis, realized that he had lost ten pounds. He saw his doctor, who told him he'd "be a fool" to run again. After talking things over with Dorothy, the senator announced his retirement. He regretted it almost immediately. "Once you've had the exposure to politics that I had . . . I mean, intense exposure for about 12 years . . . it gets in your blood, and then when you get out, nothing else satisfies that in your blood," Prescott recalled in 1966. "There's no substitute diet for it."

H istorically, the path to power George Bush chose in Texas—the Republican route—was a difficult one. The Democratic Party's hold over Texas and over most of the other states of the old Confederacy was rooted in Reconstruction. Beginning in the late 1860s, the real contests for political office took place in the Democratic primaries. As late as the 1940s, Franklin Roosevelt and Harry Truman could count on Texas and much of the rest of the South as an electoral bulwark against Republicans nationally.

Bush's timing, however, was fortuitous. As conservative reaction to the New Deal–Fair Deal expansion of government set in after the end of World War II—during the years Bush first moved to the state—the Democratic monopoly in Texas began to break down. Eisenhower carried the state twice, and it was respectable for a young oilman such as Bush to play a grassroots role in the Eisenhower-Nixon campaigns in Midland and similar places. Race was also a factor. The U.S. Supreme Court's school desegregation decisions in 1954 and in 1955, as well as the push for a federal civil rights bill in 1957, unnerved some white voters who believed John Kennedy a liberal on such issues. In 1960, the Kennedy-Johnson ticket only narrowly defeated Nixon and Henry Cabot Lodge, carrying Texas by two percentage points. Bush was proud to recall that his new home county, Harris, was "the largest metropolitan area in the country to go Republican in 1960."

Then came John Tower, the small, nattily dressed professor of government at Midwestern University in Wichita Falls, Texas, who ran as a Republican in the May 1961 special election to fill Lyndon Johnson's

Senate seat. The Tower campaign was the Republicans' moment, one made possible by a civil war between conservative Democrats and liberal Democrats. Their split opened the way for Tower, who became the first Republican elected to statewide office in Texas since Reconstruction. The unthinkable—a victorious Republican in Texas—had become thinkable.

George H. W. Bush watched the Tower campaign closely. "Something was stirring at the political grass roots in Texas," Bush recalled, "especially in Houston and Harris County." As a result, the chairmanship of the Harris County Republican Party in the early 1960s mattered more than such posts usually did. James Bertron, the county chairman, was moving out of state. The contest to succeed Bertron became a proxy for a larger struggle in Harris County between traditional Republicans such as Bush and extremists, many of whom belonged to the far-right-wing John Birch Society, a faction convinced that an international conspiracy was at work to hand America over to the Communists.

On a sunny springtime Saturday morning in 1962, Bush recalled, GOP leaders from the county came by to confer about the opening created by Bertron's move. The hard right had nearly won the chairmanship the last time around, and Bush's callers wanted to keep the party out of the hands of the extremists. Over lunch came the question: Would Bush allow his name to be put up for Harris County party chairman? "I didn't really need time to think it over," Bush recalled. "This was the challenge I'd been waiting for—an opening into politics at the ground level, where it all starts."

The campaign for county chairman featured three elements that were to recur in Bush's political career. There was an eagerness to jump into the race at hand; a limitless energy; and, once the race was done, an instinctive attempt to reconcile with his foes and to harmonize discordant forces.

After spending nearly a year visiting precinct after precinct—Barbara took up needlepointing at the meetings to pass the time—Bush was elected chairman in February 1963. There was no ideological purge of the party under Chairman Bush. He was wary of the Birchers but believed no good would come of antagonizing such a passionate faction. Naturally conciliatory, Bush tried to keep the focus on the common foe—the Democrats. "I found out that jugular politics—going for the opposition's throat—wasn't my style," Bush recalled. "It was a lesson carried over from my experience in business. When competition gets cut-throat, everybody loses. Sometimes confrontation is the only way to resolve problems—but only as a last resort, after all other avenues have been explored."

The driving issue in Texas was the alleged liberalism of the New Frontier. "You're either for or against the Kennedys," wrote John Knaggs, a former United Press International reporter in Austin, "and anybody out in the middle of the road will get run over." The test was nearing. "Nineteen sixty-four," Bush wrote in a Harris County GOP newsletter, "is the critical year."

In Dallas, Peter O'Donnell, a leading Republican and important supporter of Barry Goldwater for the 1964 presidential nomination, had been hearing good things about young Bush down in Houston. Robert Stewart III, a banker friend of O'Donnell's, was a Bush fan from the oil business. Stewart thought the two men should meet. After securing his own election as chairman of the Texas Republican Party in December 1962, O'Donnell made the trip to see Bush.

The first U.S. Senate race since Tower's victory was coming up, and O'Donnell asked Bush whether he would be game for a campaign against

In Bush's first run for major elective office, the U.S. Senate in Texas in 1964, he was a Goldwater Republican. "Did I go too far right?" Bush wondered decades later. "Maybe."

the liberal incumbent Ralph Yarborough. Bush was enthusiastic. "I thought I could win," he recalled. Republicans in Texas were thrilled. O'Donnell believed Bush's energy, good looks, handsome family, and Ivy League education gave the Texas GOP "a certain respectability" at a time when the extremists were making a great deal of noise.

Peter O'Donnell saw the Bush bid as complementary to the fight to nominate and elect Goldwater president. Broadly put, there were two prevailing factions contending against each other in the Republican Party in 1964. Arizona senator Goldwater represented the right, New York governor Nelson A. Rockefeller the left. The right was strongly anti-Washington at home and anti-Communist abroad, pressing to dismantle the New Deal–Fair Deal federal establishment and to roll back the Communist threat with military force wherever necessary. As Goldwater would put it, capturing the conservative credo, ". . . extremism in defense of liberty—is—no—vice." (He added: ". . . moderation in the pursuit of justice is no virtue!")

Rockefeller stood at the other end of the Republican spectrum. Scion of one of the great American fortunes, "Rocky" believed that government had a vital role to play in the life of the nation. Where Goldwaterites saw the world in black and white, Rockefeller noted shades of gray. The split in the GOP was profound. Goldwater was the Sun Belt and the Rotary Club; Rockefeller was Manhattan and the Council on Foreign Relations. Goldwater flew his own plane and lived in an adobe house in the desert of Arizona, the embodiment of a western hero. Rockefeller collected modern art and lived in a vast Fifth Avenue apartment, the epitome of the Eastern Establishment.

Strictly in terms of upbringing, Bush should have been a Rockefeller Republican. His father, Prescott, seemed, on the whole, to be one. But while the son's ancestral sympathies and inclinations were more moderate to liberal, by the time of the 1964 campaign, George H. W. Bush had been away from the East for sixteen years. As an oilman he had grown more conservative—not radically so, but notably so.

Largely conservative in philosophy, favoring fiscal probity at home and a firm but well-considered foreign policy abroad, Bush was closer to an Eisenhower than to a Goldwater or a Rockefeller. To reach an office where they could put such precepts into action, though, both Bush and

Eisenhower were willing to make accommodations. In the 1952 presidential campaign, for instance, to appease conservatives, Eisenhower had failed to defend General George C. Marshall against McCarthyite charges that the former secretary of state was a Communist or, at best, a dupe of the Soviet conspiracy. In that critical moment, even Ike had chosen to court the right wing rather than challenge it. That's what savvy Republican politicians did—and Bush was determined to be among the savviest of Republican politicians of the age. Prescott Bush had offered a similar lesson in political calculation when he misled Connecticut voters about his involvement with Planned Parenthood and the American Birth Control League to appeal to the state's Roman Catholics in 1950.

Now his son wanted to be in politics, and he wanted to win. Republicans in the Texas of 1963–64 were Goldwater men, not Rockefeller men. So George Bush was a Goldwater man.

Like Goldwater, Bush opposed key elements of the landmark Civil Rights Act and advocated states' rights. Like Goldwater, Bush would oppose Medicare and President Johnson's war on poverty. Like Goldwater, Bush opposed the admission of Communist China to the United Nations. And like Goldwater, Bush opposed a nuclear-test-ban treaty.

On Wednesday, September 11, 1963, Bush paid a call on Austin's journalists in the Capitol Press Room to announce his Senate candidacy. Ralph Yarborough, Bush said, "is diametrically opposed to everything I believe in. He is a federal interventionist. I believe in the finest concept of States' rights—in keeping the government closest to the people."

A populist Democrat and familiar political figure, Yarborough had been born on a farm in Chandler, Texas, graduated from the University of Texas law school, served as a Texas state judge, fought in World War II, and lost three races for governor before winning the Senate seat in a 1957 special election. He was the hero of the Democratic left in the state and a bane of the Democratic right.

Bush hired GOP operative James Leonard to manage the campaign. Bush, Leonard recalled, may have been "the worst candidate I'd ever had." Bush's vernacular with audiences in Texas remained rooted in Massachusetts and Connecticut. "He'd go over to these yokels and call Yarborough a 'profligate spender'—and nobody knew what the hell 'profligate' meant," Leonard recalled. "It sounded like some kind of sex-ual thing. So I said, 'George, don't use that word again.' I thought he was going to fire me."

Bush knew he needed counsel, but knowing he needed it did not mean he enjoyed hearing it. "I pushed him more than he wanted me to—'Do this, do that,'" Leonard recalled. "He didn't always like it, but he did it all." One day Bush appeared for a day of campaigning in a striped tie. "Take that thing off," Leonard told him, and Bush, Leonard recalled, looked as though "he wanted to hit me."

The 1964 campaign marked the beginning of a life that was to con-sume the Bushes for the next half century. It was a blur of handshakes and receptions, of Barbara's cooking spaghetti for scores out of *The Joy of Cooking,* only to realize she didn't have enough to go around—news that sent her to the grocery store for mounds of sliced roast beef and cans of Franco-American to add in. There were "Tastin' Teas" in Texas, events where you paid a dollar to have a bite of everyone's favorite dish. Barbara preferred sitting in audiences rather than onstage: If she were out with the crowd, then she could do her needlepoint through the speeches.

For Bush, the key problem was what Barbara called "the Ivy League–Yankee label." "George H. W. Bush" became just "George Bush" in press releases and mailings. Some allies thought Bush should put on a cowboy hat when campaigning in rural Texas, a suggestion that Barbara called "lousy superficial advice. The main thing—the big thing—I believe is to get around the state and get known. Not as a fake or a phony—but just get known as himself." The nascent Bush network went to work in the early autumn of 1963. Margaret Hampton, an indispensable aide to Prescott Bush, moved from Washington to Texas for the year. The can-didate, who had bought a Mercedes, got rid of it in favor of a dark-green Chrysler. "No foreign car driver is our Senator!" Barbara wrote.

Rumors about Bush and his eastern ties were common. He was at-tacked, Barbara wrote, as a "Rockefeller plant," who was being "largely financed by [the] Eastern Group who are leading the block Goldwater move. Big stockholders, the Bush family (eastern and Texans) in Brown Brothers *Harriman & Co.*" Bush's rivals pointed out that Barbara's father, the head of the McCall Corporation, was the publisher of *Redbook*—which, in the Texas of 1964, was said to be a "tool of the Commies"—not mentioning that *Redbook* was a mainstream women's magazine rather than a Marxist-Leninist tract. Barbara countered that her father's company also published the John Birch Society's handbook, but unfortunately her father had given up that contract a dozen years before "because it was losing money."

The feud between conservative and liberal Democrats—a dispute that threatened to put Texas in play in the presidential race the next year—was bringing President Kennedy and Vice President Johnson to the state for a unity trip. From Bush's perspective, the Senate campaign was a hard but winnable battle. He was going to run against the liberal Yarborough by running against the unpopular and liberal Kennedy. And there was hope: A statewide *Houston Chronicle* poll had Goldwater defeating Kennedy by fifty thousand votes in Texas, and Johnson's popularity was down.

The *Chronicle* survey appeared in the morning edition of the newspaper on Friday, November 22, 1963.

The Bushes were one hundred miles east of Dallas, on a campaign swing in Tyler. At midday the news came over the radio: President Kennedy had been shot. Bush was at a meeting while Barbara was having her hair done. "Oh Texas—my Texas—my God—let's hope it's not true," Barbara wrote to her family as she sat in the beauty parlor. "I am sick at heart as we all are."

Kennedy was dead, Texas governor John Connally wounded. Bush called Barbara and picked her up, and they flew home to Houston. "The rumors are flying about that horrid assassin," Barbara wrote her family back East. "We are hoping that it is not some far right nut, but a 'commie nut.' You understand we know they are both nuts, but just hope that it is not a Texan and not an American at all." Bush canceled his political commitments until January 1, 1964, and the Bushes took Jeb and Doro to a memorial service for President Kennedy in Houston on Monday.

Bush held a pragmatic view of the assassination's local political implications. "Poppy seems to feel that in two or three months the climate in Texas will be right back where it was," Barbara wrote her family on Saturday, November 30, 1963.

He was right: Texas did not long mourn John Kennedy. In a piece in *The Nation* magazine, an influential South Texan was reported to have remarked, "I don't hold with murder. But I can't say I'm not glad to see us rid of that bushy-haired bastard from Boston." In the May 1964 presidential primary, more Republican voters in Dallas County wrote in the name of George C. Wallace of Alabama—a Democrat, but a hero to segregationists—than had done so for George Romney of Michigan, a moderate Republican. A reading of *The Texas Observer,* a liberal Austin journal, tells the tale of the moment: Southern Methodist University withdrew an invitation to Martin Luther King, Jr., to speak, and the president of Texas Tech in Lubbock canceled a planned appearance by the national secretary of the Young Socialist Alliance, saying, "I regard it not necessary for him to be on our campus." Abilene and San Antonio debated whether the fluoridation of water was a Communist plot to poison the American water supply. The Texas Manufacturers Association produced a mailing charging that the civil rights bill was a "grab for power" that "puts into the hands of the President the awful power to make himself a virtual dictator."

The real choice in Texas politics, Bush told voters and reporters, was no longer between liberal Democrats and conservative Democrats but between liberal Democrats and conservative Republicans. Bush's case: Yarborough had voted "down the line with the New Frontier."

I n the primary balloting on Saturday, May 2, 1964, Bush led the field with roughly 44 percent. He faced Jack Cox, a former GOP gubernatorial nominee, in a runoff to be held on Saturday, June 6—the first Republican runoff in Texas history.

The money was with Bush. In the weeks after the May primary, he raised four times as much as Cox (roughly $15,000 to Cox's $3,500). Noting that Bush had already spent about $176,000 in the first primary to win 60,000 votes, Cox extrapolated that it might cost $3 million to defeat Yarborough, "an amount unheard of in Texas politics." The money issue helped crystallize the eastern question. "Just as surely as Rockefeller's millions can't buy [the] presidential nomination," Cox said, "George Bush with his millions can't buy a Senate seat." Bush struck back, saying he would not apologize for running a "properly financed" campaign. "Our goal is to beat Yarborough," Bush told a morning coffee gathering in Houston. "He is going to have many thousands of dollars from" organized labor, which meant the Republicans had to meet strength with strength.

Bush defeated Cox in the runoff, and in Washington four days later, on Wednesday, June 10, 1964, Yarborough voted for cloture in order to break the filibuster against the civil rights bill. (Tower voted for the filibuster.) With Yarborough's support, the landmark law was about to become a reality. In Texas, Bush said he was "shocked" by Yarborough's vote. Conservative opposition to the bill focused on provisions ordering the integration of privately owned businesses, including restaurants, which the right wing argued was unconstitutional and invested the federal government with too much control. Yarborough, Bush said, had voted for "a course of action which will be most detrimental to the concept of States' rights which is near and dear to so many Texans."

He was uncomfortable with racial politics even as he opposed the civil rights bill and struggled to reconcile the impulses of a good heart with the demands of the politics of 1964. The tensions he felt were evident in a letter he wrote a Jewish supporter in Houston in late July. "My heart is heavy—I have traveled the state for 2 weeks. The civil rights issue can bring Yarborough to sure defeat. I know this now for certain," Bush wrote. Republicans "must develop [their] position reasonably, prudently, sensitively—we must be sure we don't inflame the passions of unthinking men to garner a vote; yet it is essential that the position I believe in be explained." He was honestly conflicted. "What shall I do? How will I do it?" he asked. "I want to win, but not at the expense of justice, not at the expense of the dignity of any man . . . nor teaching my children a prejudice which I do not feel."

Still, Yarborough's civil rights vote gave the ambitious young Republican an opening. Campaigning against the bill, Bush argued for "states' rights" and hoped that might be just enough to bring Yarborough down. "There is at least one hard-money bet in Washington now between politically wise people that Bush will win," Mike Quinn of *The Dallas Morning News* wrote in midsummer.

On Friday, June 12, 1964, Bush celebrated his fortieth birthday. He had never felt—or looked—better. The ulcer that had felled him in London was apparently gone, and observers were dazzled by his charisma. "His campaign . . . gets a lot of energy and sparkle from the young Republican matrons who are enthusiastic about him personally and have plenty of money for baby sitters and nothing much . . . to do with their time," wrote *The Texas Observer*. And there were his manners, always warm, always proper, always deferential. "Sir, I'm George Bush, running for the U.S. Senate," he would say as he shook hands on the campaign trail.

"Sir": a small thing, perhaps, but notable—a tangible sign that the lessons of Greenwich endured. In the wake of Yarborough's civil rights vote, Jim Leonard announced that Bush would begin a merciless campaign on August 1. That was another lesson from Connecticut: If you run for office, run hard.

"The more widely Bush can make himself known, it appears, the better his chances will be," the *Dallas Morning News* observed in September 1964. "A lot of people are talking Bush," an unnamed Democrat in Corpus Christi told the paper. A bank officer from Plainview liked Bush on the grounds that he "wants the same things as Goldwater, but he's not reckless." The liberals at *The Texas Observer* feared that Bush might just unseat Yarborough. "Surely the one extremism or culpable opportunism which George Bush's suaveness and pleasantness cannot dispel is his enthusiastic championing of the candidacy of the senator from Arizona, which he knew very well was a pre-condition of his nomination by Texas Republicans," the *Observer* wrote in June 1964. As the general election neared, the *Observer* argued that a Senator George Bush would be "another anti-test ban treaty, anti-medicare, anti-war on poverty, anti-federal government Goldwater Republican."

The stridency of tone was a sign that Bush was doing well. "R.Y. is getting mean," Bush reported to a supporter in August. Calling Bush "the Connecticut candidate," Yarborough returned to the carpetbagger charge more and more as the fall wore on, and it annoyed Bush more and more. Dating his baptism into Texas life to his initial posting to Corpus Christi during the war, Bush told crowds that he had first come to Texas twenty-one years before and that "my philosophy of government is Texas." He hit on the right wry tone: "I was born outside of the state," he said. "I did that so I could be close to my mother."

Ten days before the election, a poll of likely voters put Bush within striking distance of Yarborough. The Democrat led 49 to 44 percent, with 6 percent undecided. On Tuesday, October 27, Bush broadcast an hour-long statewide program entitled "The Empty Chair." Using a picture of Yarborough and tape recordings of his voice, Bush had staged this quasi-debate on Sunday, October 25, after Yarborough declined to face off on television. The telecast ran on more than a dozen different Texas stations on the same evening that many network affiliates showed a half-hour Goldwater broadcast that featured a speech, "A Time for Choosing," by a recent Democratic convert to Republicanism—Ronald Reagan.

Yarborough did not relent. "Let's show the world," Yarborough said, "that old Senator Bush can't send Little Georgie down here to buy a Senate seat."

lection Day 1964 was, inescapably, Lyndon Johnson's hour. Nothing could withstand the raw political force that the incumbent president exerted over the United States on Tuesday, November 3, 1964. Johnson defeated Goldwater 61.1 to 38.5 percent, losing only Arizona and five Deep South states. In Texas the Republicans were destroyed, losing their two GOP House seats. The UPI election night lead was unambiguous: "President Johnson," the wire service reported, "smashed the Republican party in Texas to smithereens tonight."

Bush polled 44 percent to Yarborough's 56 percent in what *The Dallas Morning News* called the "fiercest" general election U.S. Senate contest in Texas history. "Actually we received more votes than any other Republican has ever gotten in Texas, polling over 1,100,000," Bush wrote Richard Nixon, "but with the Johnson landslide it was not in the cards to [have] enough vote splitting." It was small comfort. "I don't mean to be

Former senator Prescott Bush and George's brother Jonathan join
the candidate to watch the returns on Tuesday, November 3, 1964,
the night George H. W. Bush lost the U.S. Senate race to
Democratic incumbent Ralph Yarborough.

ungrateful," Bush said, "but I'm a competitor." He had come up short. "The figures indicate that we have lost," Bush told his supporters at about eleven thirty P.M. at the Hotel America in Houston. "I tried desperately to think of someone else I could blame for this and I came to the conclusion there is no one to blame but me." He was, a reporter noted, "baffled by the returns." He had outspent his opponent nearly three to one (roughly $300,000 to $100,000). He had genuinely believed victory was at hand.

All Bush could do was play the part of a gracious loser, congratulating Yarborough and looking toward a vague future. "I plan to continue my interest in politics," Bush said in defeat, "and hope to play a part in the future of our great state."

Bush was candid in the aftermath. "We got beat," he wrote at the bottom of a typewritten thank-you note to a friend right after the election. Bush wrote Gerry Bemiss a private postmortem: "The Birchers are bad news and I don't like them a bit. They gave me a fit here in Houston and in other places in Texas and I think in retrospect I should have cracked down on them more. This mean humorless philosophy which says everybody should agree on absolutely everything is not good for the Republican Party or for our State. When the word moderation becomes a dirty word we have some soul searching to do."

"Did I go too far right?" Bush said, reflecting on the 1964 race nearly fifty years later. "Maybe. There is a political orthodoxy you take to win the support of the party. I was pushed a little to the right." And yet, and yet: "But I was not as moderate a guy as some in the East thought I should be. The mold, the prediction, was that I would be like my dad politically—the Washington guys wanted me, on some of the issues, to be like the senator from Connecticut." A pause. "I was a *Texan*. I was running for office in *Texas*."

Bush was exhausted. He and Barbara got away for a little break at Mary and Herbie Walker's house on Eleuthera. With the Walkers, Bush's parents, and their friends the Fred Chamberses, the Bushes swam and golfed and picnicked, unwinding from the campaign. "Pop was really dead when we arrived," Barbara wrote in March 1965. "When he left he was relaxed and never looked better."

PART IV

The Wars of Washington

1966 to 1977

★

Although fundamentally conservative, he is liberal here
and there, mid-19th century in some ways and mid-21st
century in others.

—*The Dallas Morning News,* August 30, 1970

The right to hope is basic.

—GEORGE H. W. BUSH, April 17, 1968

As CIA director, Bush leads a National Security Council meeting to discuss a crisis in Beirut in June 1976. From left, Chairman of the Joint Chiefs of Staff General George Brown, White House Chief of Staff Dick Cheney, Secretary of State Henry Kissinger, and President Ford.

THIRTEEN

Without a Moment to Stop

★

I'd like to be President. The chances are slight,
but please don't limit me.

—GEORGE H. W. BUSH to a potential GOP congressional
primary rival, January 1966

For Bush, politics is a personal game in which, like commerce
on the old frontier, the salesman and the product are a
package; you sell your product by selling yourself;
you sell individually, not institutionally.

—*The Dallas Morning News,* Sunday, August 30, 1970

DESPITE THE DEFEAT, his was a good life in Houston at the mid-point of the 1960s. He was forty years old, the father of five loving children, the husband of an adoring wife. His eldest son, George W., had gone off to Andover, graduated, and was now at Yale; Jeb was twelve; Neil, Marvin, and Doro were in elementary school.

George H. W. Bush was a busy man, and like many in his generation he spent a lot of time on the road, leaving his wife in charge at home. When he was around, though, he was the dominant figure—and a source of apparently endless fun. George W.'s first memory of his dad is of the two playing catch in Midland; all of the kids recall the Sunday hamburger and hot dog lunches with neighbors after church, both in Midland and later in Houston. Marvin remembered the billboards from the '64 race on San Felipe Road: "I looked up and thought, 'There's my man, and he's bigger than life.'"

He would take his children to Houston's new major league baseball games. These were the days of the Houston Colt .45s—pre-Astros and very much pre-Astrodome. Jeb remembered a hundred-degree double-header against the Dodgers at the rudimentary Colt Stadium. (Sandy Koufax and Don Drysdale pitched for the visitors.) "They ran out of Coke, beer, water," Jeb recalled. "People were passing out all around us—

literally." The Bush kids barely noticed the heat: Their dad was with them, and for that they would endure even a blistering, thirsty double-header. The children seemed never to have seen Bush angry or down; he deftly hid his anxieties about business and life. There was a single exception. "I have only one memory of his being sad or despondent," Jeb recalled. "I walked into the living room in Houston and there were adults in the room—they had lost a rig in the Gulf, and you could feel the tension, the sadness."

Jeb had read the room well. On Thursday, September 9, 1965, Zapata's rig Maverick was in 220 feet of water twenty miles off the coast of Louisiana when Hurricane Betsy struck. The damage to the rig was total: It disappeared. "This was the largest single loss that the domestic offshore drilling industry sustained in this or any other hurricane," Bush wrote his investors in the annual chairman's letter. He flew over the Gulf of Mexico in the aftermath, looking in vain for signs of the rig.

Zapata's future, however, no longer consumed him as it once had. "George Bush, Houston businessman," *The New York Times* reported in March 1965, "is rated by political friend and foe alike as the Republicans' best prospect in Texas because of his attractive personal qualities and the strong campaign he put up for the Senate last year." There was speculation that he might run for the State Senate. Another option was seeking an open, newly redistricted U.S. House seat in Houston, the result of a lawsuit Bush had helped file on behalf of the GOP.

Congress was an exciting possibility, but there were obstacles. Polling showed that Houston district attorney Frank Briscoe, the likely Democratic nominee, was ahead. And there were rumors that Ross Baker, a fellow Houston Republican, was planning on running against Bush in the GOP primary. Baker believed Bush was using the House race just to position himself for another run for the Senate. In a conversation with Baker in early January 1966, Bush said: "I don't want to move just up to the Senate, Ross. I'd like to be President. The chances are slight, but please don't limit me." Baker deferred to Bush, giving the former Harris County chairman and 1964 Senate nominee a clear path to the general election for Congress.

Bush decided it was also time to break away from his offshore oil business. "It would have been unfair to the company's stockholders and employees to do otherwise," Bush recalled. "The 1964 Senate race taught me that it takes a total commitment to be a candidate. Zapata, like any successful business, needed hands-on leadership from its front office." He sold his Zapata Off-Shore stock for an amount ranging between $737,000 (an estimate based on documents in the George Bush Presidential Library) to $1.1 million (a figure published in the press in the late 1960s). Whatever the precise number, the sale brought the Bushes somewhere between $5.5 million and $8 million in 2015 dollars.

Bush announced his candidacy for the Seventh Congressional District on Saturday, January 15, 1966. The following Monday morning, Barbara was driving six-year-old Doro's carpool to school. "I saw your Daddy on television last night," one of the little girls said to Doro. "You did?" said a third child. "What was he doing?"

"Oh, you know," said Doro, "it was about that erection that he is going to have." (Barbara's response: "Needless to say we have worked on the word 'election'!")

In July 1966, Bush was trailing Democrat Frank Briscoe by eight points, 49 to 41 percent. Bush's adman, Harry Treleaven from J. Walter Thompson, a leading national agency, had to close that gap. Treleaven went on to work for Richard Nixon's 1968 presidential campaign, and *The Selling of the President, 1968,* Joe McGinniss's account of Nixon's media strategy, detailed what Treleaven had done for Bush in Houston two years before. Bush's advertising strategy, McGinniss wrote, would consume 80 percent of the campaign budget. Ordinary voters, Treleaven noted, thought Bush "an extremely likable person"; the adman acknowledged, however, that "there was a haziness about exactly where [Bush] stood politically." So what to do? "There'll be few opportunities for logical persuasion, which is all right—because probably more people vote for irrational, emotional reasons than professional politicians suspect," Treleaven noted, according to McGinniss. As Treleaven saw it, candidates were—well, they were personalities. "Political candidates are celebrities, and today, with television taking them into everybody's home right along with Johnny Carson and Batman, they're more of a public attraction than ever."

For Bush, taking on a front-runner like Briscoe offered instant drama. "We can turn this into an advantage by creating a 'fighting underdog' image," Treleaven wrote. "Bush must convince voters that he really wants to be elected and is working hard to earn their vote. *People sympathize with a man who tries hard:* they are also flattered that anyone would really exert himself to get their vote." And so Bush played the role of a man on the move. "Over and over again, on every television screen in Houston," Joe McGinniss wrote, "George Bush was seen with his coat slung over his shoulder, his sleeves rolled up. . . ."

The immensity of the Goldwater defeat had taught Republicans like Bush—Republicans who wanted to win among affluent suburbanites—that political conservatism required a genial face. Extremism on the right had been tested and found wanting; President Johnson's margin of victory two years before was proof enough of that. "Too long, Republicans have been oblivious to poverty, the Negro ghettoes, inadequate housing, medical care needs, and a million other pressing problems that face our people," Bush told the Texas Young Republican Federation in 1966. Republicans could not beat something (Johnson's Great Society) with nothing. Bush, for instance, pressed for a "human investment" program in which the government would reward businesses that offered workers training or retraining. "I want (the Republican Party's) conservatism to be sensitive and dynamic," *The Wall Street Journal* reported Bush as saying, "not scared and reactionary."

In Houston on Tuesday, November 8, 1966, George H. W. Bush won the general election 57 to 42 percent. It was an early evening: Briscoe conceded by ten P.M. It had been a bad night for Democrats generally. Johnson's party lost forty-seven seats in the House, three in the Senate—and in California, Ronald Reagan won the governorship in a race against Democrat Edmund G. "Pat" Brown. The pendulum that had seemed to swing so far and firmly to the left in the Johnson triumph in 1964 had now moved back toward the middle in the space of just twenty-four months.

On the night the Bushes moved into their new Washington house at 4910 Hillbrook Lane NW—they had bought it from Milward Simpson, the senator from Wyoming who was retiring—Bush asked the moving men to spend the night, an invitation that sent Barbara out to a nearby Sears to buy bedding for the unexpected guests. Between January and April 1967, the Bushes would have twenty-nine houseguests in Washington.

Congressman Bush was arriving in the capital at a fluid political moment. President Johnson was at work on the Great Society legislation, much of which expanded government, while prosecuting a difficult war in Vietnam. As a Republican from Texas, Bush often opposed Johnson at home but largely backed him abroad.

That Bush came of political age in the Congress in such an odd time—a moment when Republicans were at once supportive of Johnson in Southeast Asia and wary of him domestically—may help explain Bush's own gentler understanding of partisanship in Washington. The political lesson of Bush's formative first years in public office was that the president of the United States—in this case Johnson—was neither wholly right nor wholly wrong. In House votes, Congressman Bush backed Johnson-supported bills 53.5 percent of the time. When Richard Nixon became president in 1969, the average for the two years Bush served under a Republican was, at 55 percent, virtually unchanged.

Bush's open-handed—and open-minded—manner once he was in office was grounded in more than politeness. It was a reflection of a truth about politics that he experienced in the Congress in the last years of the presidency of Lyndon Johnson.

Asked for his first choice of committee assignment, Bush had written Gerald Ford, the House minority leader, seeking the moon— Appropriations—but with diffidence. "I know you are swamped with all kinds of grandiose requests—perhaps this ranks as the grandiosest of them all, but whatever you decide will be fine with me," Bush wrote, "and I promise to work like hell to be a good member of whatever committee I get." He would wind up on an even more powerful and prestigious committee—the tax-writing Ways and Means—as a result of an internal Democratic fight, the Republicans' sense that the Sun Belt was the future, and a call from his father.

As the new Congress was forming, Democrats had voted to replace a Texas Democrat on Ways and Means with a New Yorker. With a Texas Democrat off the committee, House Republicans voted Bush a seat as a signal to possible GOP candidates in previously Democratic states. The strategy, as described by *The Dallas Morning News*: "By choosing Bush, Republicans were able to show that they would take good care of Texans and other Southern Republicans elected to Congress, hoping to build up their party in those states." Bush was the first freshman to win a seat on Ways and Means since 1904.

Prescott Bush had played a crucial role in making that happen. "His father came to me . . . and wanted him on my committee," Ways and

Means chairman Wilbur Mills recalled to *The Washington Post*'s Walt Harrington in 1986. "I said, 'I'm a Democrat and I don't think I can do anything.' He said, could I call Jerry Ford? And so I did." To Harrington, Ford recalled that he had helped Bush to "give Texas Republicans 'a shot in the arm.'"

Word about Prescott's call spread. A reporter asked George H. W. Bush about one story that was making the rounds: "Your dad was here last week and people are saying that he put $50,000 in the GOP coffer to get your assignment. Is this true?" Bush denied it, and the suggestion left him "furious," according to Barbara. "There's a lot of luck involved in this," Bush wrote a constituent in late January 1967, "and I was at the right place at the right time." And with the right surname. As in the hunt for capital for his oil businesses, being George Herbert Walker Bush was of inarguable benefit. He was to be a conscientious congressman, but the circumstances of his birth and the connections of his family continued to shape his life for the better through means unavailable to others.

To introduce their son and daughter-in-law to Washington, Dorothy and Prescott Bush took over the F Street Club on Wednesday, January 18, 1967, for a dinner in honor of their congressman son and daughter-in-law. In black-tie and evening gowns, the guests had drinks and dinner and toasted young Bush. Among those included in the evening were the John Sherman Coopers of Kentucky, the Hugh D. Auchinclosses, the Rowland Evanses, Gordon Gray, Katharine Graham, the Allen Dulleses, the Potter Stewarts, Susan Mary and Joe Alsop, Stewart Alsop, Admiral and Mrs. Jerauld Wright (he was a former ambassador to Taiwan), Admiral and Mrs. Arthur W. Radford (he was a former chairman of the Joint Chiefs of Staff), and the Charles Bartletts.

Bush's legislative priorities grew out of the centrist conservatism of his '66 race. While he opposed a proposal of President Johnson's for a 6 percent tax surcharge to help pay for the administration's $135 billion budget, the new congressman hoped to pursue the "human investment" agenda he had discussed during his campaign as well as "a tax credit for pollution control."

The costs of the Vietnam War and of Johnson's Great Society programs were driving the federal deficit to what Bush and other fiscally conservative Republicans believed to be dangerous levels. In the middle of 1967, the administration revised its shortfall projections from

$11.1 billion to $24 billion for 1968, news that led Bush to change his mind about the president's proposed 6 percent tax surcharge. "Unpopular though it may be, it is becoming increasingly clear to me that because of exorbitant projected deficits, we must have a tax increase," Bush said on the House floor in June 1967. There also had to be cuts in spending, Bush added; if the administration agreed to that, then he would support more taxes.

The young Republican congressman appreciated the difficulties facing the aging Democratic president. In the fall of 1967, during a pre-wedding party at the Sulgrave Club for the president's daughter Lynda and her fiancé, Chuck Robb, LBJ and Bush exchanged warm words. "Mr. President," Bush said, "I just want you to know that I may not agree with you but you can count on me to never attack you personally."

"George, Mrs. Johnson and I raise cattle and we have learned to look at the stock," Johnson replied. "We say, 'Who's the daddy?' We know you're all right."

Back home, Texas politics was unsettled. In the fall of 1967, John Connally announced that he would not seek reelection as governor in 1968. The Bushes' telephone began to ring: Would Bush come home and run for governor? He was reluctant. "Does Pop want to be gov.?" Barbara wrote in her diary. "In my opinion 'No.' Pop really would like to be president—I guess. But meanwhile he should run for the Senate if the time arises. . . . My presidential statement probably is true of all politicians. . . . What I am really trying to say is—Pop is interested in world affairs & national affairs."

Thanksgiving 1967 at Hillbrook Lane was amiably noisy. All of the Bush children were there, from George W., in his last year at Yale, to Doro, who was eight. "What fun and what a mob," wrote Barbara. They played Scrabble, bridge, and a word-guessing game George W. introduced to the family called Fictionary. By year's end Bush had decided against seeking the Texas governorship in favor of running for reelection to Congress. Among the reasons was a hunger to play his part on the largest possible stage. His best chance of doing so lay in national, not state, politics.

Late in the year, Bush visited Vietnam. He dined with Ambassador Ellsworth Bunker and came away believing that the antiwar elements in the United States were having a disproportionate influence over the

*Congressman Bush of the Seventh District of Texas with Vietnamese
children during a visit to the war-torn country in the weeks
after Christmas 1967.*

North Vietnamese. "We believe in freedom of speech," Barbara wrote after talking the trip over with her husband, "but it does seem tough to have our enemy think that a small group speaks for our country, and therefore prolong this hideous war. Whether or not this is actually true, I don't know, but the military men that G. talked to seemed to feel that this was keeping the enemy away from any peace talks."

On Tuesday, January 17, 1968, President Johnson delivered his State of the Union address to a joint session of Congress. "Tonight our nation is accomplishing more for its people than has ever been accomplished before," Johnson said. "Americans are prosperous as men have never been in recorded history. Yet there is in the land a certain restlessness— a questioning." The unease, the president said, came "because when a great ship cuts through the sea, the waters are always stirred and troubled . . . We ask now, not how can we achieve abundance?—but how shall we use our abundance? Not, is there abundance enough for all?—but, how can all share in our abundance?"

A week later, CBS broadcast a Republican reply. Former president Eisenhower introduced the program with a prerecorded message; Gerald Ford, Bush, and others then took turns rebutting Johnson's speech. Bush was assigned the question of federal spending—which Republicans believed was too high even in what LBJ had called as "prosperous" an age as men had ever known—and made a brief, impassioned plea for fiscal responsibility. Johnson, Bush said, had offered "no sense of sacrifice on the part of the Government, no assignment of priorities, no hint of the need to put first things first."

The overall reviews of the program were underwhelming, but in the "TV Today" column of the *Chicago Tribune,* critic Clay Gowran found much to like in the congressman from Texas. "Bush, a wholesome young man, won enthusiastic applause by reiterating the Republican—and to a large extent, Democratic—vow that Congress will not consider a tax increase unless there is a cut in federal spending," Gowran wrote, adding that Bush and Colorado senator Peter Dominick "proved definite assets to the G.O.P. when it comes to television."

On Sunday evening, March 31, 1968, facing declining support at home in the wake of the Tet Offensive, a massive North Vietnamese attack on U.S. and South Vietnamese forces, Lyndon Johnson withdrew from the 1968 presidential race. Four days later, Martin Luther King, Jr., was murdered in Memphis, igniting violence in numerous American cities. Amid the furies of 1968, Bush decided to take a stand.

On Wednesday, April 10, 1968—six days after King's assassination— Bush voted for the Fair Housing Act of 1968, essentially reversing his opposition to the 1964 civil rights bill. The law banned discrimination in the housing market, enabling home buyers of any color or ethnicity to purchase real estate wherever they could afford it. (Prescott Bush had also been a supporter of open housing.)

Bush knew what was coming. His mail from his voters was vicious and voluminous. At one point during the debate over the legislation Bush estimated that he had received five hundred letters attacking the law— and just two in favor of it. On the day after his vote, Bush tried to calm conservatives by introducing a bill that would have banned rioters from the federal payroll, but the gesture did little to quell the outrage. His life was threatened in a call to his office, and he denounced the "hatred and venom" he and his staff faced. "That anyone would resort to this kind of talk," Bush later said, "makes me ashamed I'm an American." Bush remembered one angry constituent in particular. "There was a really rich guy here" in Houston, Bush recalled in retirement. "His family were huge stockholders in Texaco or some huge oil company. And he was just ugly about it. 'We didn't put you up there to do this kind of thing—to sell out to the niggers.' He couldn't have been uglier and meaner, and that just made me more determined to do what was right."

It was a grim time. "I voted for the bill and the roof is falling in—boy does the hatred surface," Bush wrote a friend. At one point he came home from the office with "tummy troubles," as Barbara put it—a reminder of the old days of his collapse in London. "He got into bed and had some soup and worked on mail."

The showdown came in Houston, at Memorial High School, on Wednesday, April 17, 1968. Bush told the audience that he was being attacked as a "'nigger-lover'—this in 1968 with our country ripped apart at the seams. The base and mean emotionalism . . . makes me bow my head in sadness." He took things head-on. His plea was less for radical change than for fair play. "What this bill does . . . is to remove an obstacle—what it does do is try to offer a promise or a hope—a realization of The American Dream." He continued:

> In Vietnam I chatted with many Negro soldiers. They were fighting, and some were dying, for the ideals of this Country; some talked about coming back to get married and to start their lives over.
>
> Somehow it seems fundamental that this guy should have a hope. A hope that if he saves some money, and if he wants to break out of a ghetto, and if he is a good character and if he meets every requirement of purchaser—the door will not be slammed solely because he is a Negro, or because he speaks with a Mexican accent.
>
> In these troubled times, fair play is basic. The right to hope is basic.

He was exhausted. Aboard an evening flight to Washington, he saw an older woman approaching him and braced himself for yet another tense exchange. "I'm a conservative Democrat from the district," she said, "but I'm proud, and will always vote for you now." Bush felt relief wash over him. "I started to cry—with the poor lady embarrassed to death—I couldn't say a word to her," Bush wrote. Perhaps, just perhaps, everything was going to work out. He sat back and flew on.

Bush's fair housing vote is all the more remarkable given the way many in the Republican Party nationally, and especially in the South, were coming to view the politics of race. LBJ's work on the civil and voting rights bills had created an opportunity for Republicans to appeal to historically Democratic disaffected white voters. Culture—ranging from long hair and drugs to antiwar campus demonstrations—was another factor working to the GOP's advantage. Many Americans felt that the nation, which was growing more racially and ethnically diverse as well as more culturally permissive, was slipping its moorings.

Bush shared some of those worries, but, while no liberal, he was attuned to the shifting cultural, political, and demographic realities, and hoped that his party would engage with a changing America rather than reflexively resist it. In the wake of his civil rights vote he paid a call on demonstrators at Resurrection City, the Poor People's Campaign encampment in Washington. (The campaign was part of MLK's movement for economic justice.) The prosperous Republican congressman from Houston was something of anomalous sight at Resurrection City, but Bush was curious, and so he made the trip. "I think it is important for members of Congress to know what is happening and to try to understand it," Bush told *The Dallas Morning News.*

As a Texas Republican he was concerned about the future impact of his state's Hispanic population. Bush praised PASO, the Political Association of Spanish-Speaking Organizations, for its goal of registering one million new voters in Texas, and he urged its leaders to give the Republican Party a chance. "Competition brings out the best in anyone, whether it is in athletics or in government," Bush told PASO's convention in Austin in August 1967. He also formulated a four-point program entitled "For the Mexican-American Texan—A Future of Fair Play and Progress" that included bilingual education programs, expanded Head Start, increased emphasis in Texas schools on Latin American culture and contributions, and the abolition of discriminatory local and state statutes. "We must demonstrate that all Republicans are not opposed to progress," he said. In Texas, he told *The Dallas Morning News*, Mexican Americans are "essentially law-abiding and family-oriented and yet seem to have been forgotten. These Texans are becoming increasingly more interested in evolving their own futures." Republicans needed to pay more attention to this community, Bush said, if they had any hope of winning them away from Democrats.

Population control was a long-standing public-policy concern. "We need to make population and family planning household words," Bush said. "The sensationalism needs to be taken out of the subject." He urged the creation of a joint House-Senate panel on family planning and related issues. "Population control and family planning is too important to whisper and giggle about now," Bush said. He credited his interest in the issue to his involvement with Planned Parenthood in Houston. Bush raised the stakes in the fall of 1969, proposing that the Department of the Interior become a new federal Department of Resources, Environment, and Population. His interest in legislation about "family-planning services" led Wilbur Mills to refer to Bush as "Rubbers."

On race relations, Bush took on the segregationist governor George Wallace of Alabama. In the early 1960s, Wallace, a southern Democrat with a taste for White Owl cigars, had become a symbol of defiance against federally mandated integration, pledging "Segregation now, segregation tomorrow, and segregation forever!" As he had in 1964, Wallace was taking his reactionary message national, this time with a third-party presidential bid that Bush argued was part and parcel of the white backlash against civil rights. Wallace was an effective politician, Bush said, but "the Republican Party has too much more to offer in 1968 and through the '70s than a reversion that is hiding behind a label of states' rights. . . . It's too late to accept the definition of states' rights as the status quo in the matter of race, and don't you for a minute think that this isn't really the basis for this Wallace campaign. It is."

It was not hard to see, then, how the political columnists Rowland Evans and Robert Novak, writing about Bush in the summer of 1968, could observe that the congressman had something of a "left-of-center image in Houston."

Overnight on June 4–5, 1968, the Bushes were awakened at four A.M. by a phone call: Robert Kennedy had been shot in Los Angeles. "A nightmare," wrote Barbara. "Brought back memories of 1963."

In the swirl of 1968, word circulated that Bush was in the mix to go on the ticket as vice president with Richard Nixon if Nixon prevailed in his fight for the nomination at the Republican National Convention. The idea had reportedly originated with the evangelist Billy Graham. (Graham had gotten to know Dorothy and Prescott at Hobe Sound, a Florida retreat.) "This possibility is based partly on Bush's television style, regarded by Dr. Graham as among the best of current practicing politicians," wrote Evans and Novak in the first week of June.

An unnamed "Texas industrialist" had made a similar pitch to Nixon, as had Republican congressman Fletcher Thompson, a colleague of Bush's from Georgia, who suggested that the geographical calculus made sense: "Nixon, a Californian now living in New York, would be coupled with a Massachusetts-born Texan whose father . . . has valid credentials in the Eastern Establishment." As Evans and Novak saw it, Bush just might help Nixon with Nixon's "weak spots: minority groups, the young, the industrial northeast." Bush was also listed as one of eight "moderate" possibilities for the ticket in a front-page *New York Times* story on Sunday, June 30, 1968. Tom Dewey promoted a Nixon-Bush ticket, as did former president Eisenhower.

Nixon was the favorite for the presidential nomination, but Ronald Reagan, a year and a half into his first term as governor of California, was a viable challenger. Reagan stopped in Texas en route to the convention, which was being held in Miami Beach. In Amarillo, he spoke at a $100-a-plate dinner. Reagan impressed Barbara, who attended the event, with his native political ability. "He has all the poise in the world, great timing etc.," wrote Barbara. "Didn't say much, but said it well. 'We must show the world where we stand in Vietnam' and gets a standing ovation. They loved him."

Congressman Bush had endorsed Nixon, a move that put him at odds with many Texas Republicans, who were more conservative and harbored hopes for a Reagan nomination. "I am expecting to be in quite a little trouble as the Reagan people are a lot like the Goldwater people in Texas," Barbara wrote before the Amarillo dinner. "They are furious with Poppy for being for Nixon."

En route to Miami Beach for the convention in the first week of August, Barbara was on the same flight as Nancy and Ronald Reagan. They were both, she thought, "most attractive. She is tiny and really a very lovely, natural beauty. He is 5'11" or 6 feet . . . and very attractive also." In Florida, the Bushes stayed at the Barcelona Hotel on Collins Avenue at Forty Second Street where they were greeted by a banner reading BUSH FOR VICE PRESIDENT. On the eve of the convention the Southern Association of Republican State Chairmen emerged from the closed-door session with three recommendations for a Nixon running mate: Reagan, John Tower, or George Bush (in that order). Any of the three, Texas GOP leader Peter O'Donnell suggested to reporters, would help Nixon fight off the Wallace challenge from the right. Asked about the speculation, Bush was honest. "I've never understood people being coy about these things," he told reporters. "A lot of people would like to be vice-president but they won't say so." Bush did say so: He would be delighted. *The Wall Street Journal* reported that Bush's office in Houston had shipped two thousand BUSH buttons over to Miami—just in case.

On the morning after Nixon's presidential nomination, "Our phones rang off the hook with reports coming in from friends who had attended one of the all-night meetings that Nixon held or from reporters from all the news media," wrote Barbara. Tom O'Neal of CBS, a friend of George's youngest brother, Bucky, was assigned to the Bush camp and kept in touch with the CBS news desk as Nixon made his decision. To escape the tension, the Bushes went swimming at the hotel but watched the window of their suite in case word arrived.

Nixon settled on Spiro T. "Ted" Agnew of Maryland, a law-and-order governor. Bush had come up short, Nixon later told him, because he had been in the House for such a brief time. "Though we finished out of the money it was a great big plus for me," Bush wrote Tom Dewey, "and I am indebted to you for your interest."

Nixon did ask Bush to be a key surrogate in the autumn, and Bush was happy to agree. He traveled out to San Diego for a session with Nixon and other surrogates—a group that included Congressman Donald Rumsfeld of Illinois.

At Kennebunkport in September 1968, not long after the convention, a visitor remarked "in her reincarnation she'd like to be First Lady." Barbara replied, "That's funny. That's the last thing I want to be . . . and I suspect that I will be."

Richard Nixon narrowly defeated Vice President Hubert Humphrey in November 1968, creating high hopes among Republicans in Washington who would now have a president of their own party for the first time since 1961. During the inaugural festivities in January 1969, Bush, who had been reelected to the House unopposed, would go out to meet the private planes bringing in Texans and invite everyone over. Barbara had planned an open house for fifty; more than three hundred showed up. At one point Barbara noticed the mayor of Houston standing in the rain outside the Bushes' house, trying in vain to get in.

Bush transformed his House office into a center of hospitality, offering coffee, sandwiches, and Bloody Marys. On the afternoon of Nixon's inauguration, the Bushes went to a party at the Washington Club. They rode with Mr. and Mrs. Ross Perot of Dallas. At the suggestion of one of his assistants, Rose Zamaria, Bush also took time on Inauguration Day to drive to Andrews Air Force Base to bid farewell to President Johnson. It was cold—the temperature was about twenty degrees—and the ceremony was brief, with an army band playing "Auld Lang Syne" and the national anthem before 105 mm howitzers fired a twenty-one-gun salute.

Bush shook Johnson's hand. The congressman long remembered what he called the "poignancy of the moment"—the leave-taking of a once-powerful president, once master of his domain, now deflated, driven from office by a war he could not win and by a nation that once loved him but now could hardly wait to see him go. After Bush "wished him a safe journey," the former president "nodded, took a few steps toward the ramp, then turned, looked back at me, and said, 'Thanks for coming.'"

Johnson also appreciated a report of a remark of Bush's from Joe B. Frantz, director of the LBJ Library's Oral History Project. As Frantz told the story to Johnson, he had asked Bush "why a prominent Republican such as he was seeing you off instead of being in the midst of Republican activities in the city. His reply was a nice tribute to you: 'He has been a fine President and invariably courteous and fair to me and my people, and I thought that I belonged here to show in a small way how much I have appreciated him. I wish I could do even more.'" From Bush's perspective, there might also be utility in Johnson's continuing warmth. Should Bush challenge the liberal senator Ralph Yarborough once more in 1970, it was just possible that Johnson might be quietly helpful—or at least, as Bush and Nixon biographer Herbert S. Parmet observed, do no harm.

"Please know that I value your friendship, as I do your father's, and that I am glad you are one of us down here in Texas," Johnson wrote Bush on the last day of January. "When you are home sometime, come to see us."

As a congressman, Bush once wrote of dwelling "in a world congested, in a life cluttered, in a day without a moment to stop." In point of fact, though, Bush was uninterested in an uncongested world or an uncluttered life. His restlessness with service in the House grew more pronounced in the first months of 1969. "He just must get to the Senate where he can have the national forum that he wants," Barbara wrote in February 1969.

His best bet for moving up, he realized, lay in a rematch against Yarborough in 1970. Yet he had the safest of House seats, a place on Ways and Means, and a long, serene future ahead of him. Was the Senate worth the risk?

He decided to ask Lyndon Johnson. On Wednesday, April 9, 1969, Bush, who was just beginning his second term as a congressman, flew to see the former president at LBJ's ranch at Stonewall, Texas, about 220 miles from Houston. "Mr. President, I've still got a decision to make and I'd like your advice," Bush said. "My House seat is secure—no opposition last time—and I've got a position on Ways and Means. I don't mind taking risks, but in a few more terms, I'll have seniority on a powerful committee. I'm just not sure it's a gamble I should take, whether it's really worth it."

"Son," Johnson said, "I've served in the House. And I've been privileged to serve in the Senate, too. And they're both good places to serve. So I wouldn't begin to advise you what to do, except to say this—that the difference between being a member of the Senate and a member of the House is the difference between chicken salad and chicken shit." The former president paused. "Do I make my point?"

He did.

Bush called on President Nixon six weeks later to talk over the Senate race. For forty-five minutes on Thursday, May 22, 1969, the two men discussed whether Bush should give up the Houston House seat. "The President said that he'd like GB to run and would help him," wrote Barbara. By late 1969 the Senate was a go. "We are moving into a new decade," Bush wrote friends. "The tired, old answers of the past are not good enough for the '70s. Texas needs a positive and constructive voice that will be respected by President Nixon whether in support of his programs or in criticism."

When the Bushes had arrived in Houston a decade before, they had become friendly with another attractive young couple with an Ivy League pedigree: Mary Stuart and James A. Baker III. The son of a leading Houston lawyer, Baker had been sent to the Hill School in Pottstown, Pennsylvania, before Princeton (where Baker played rugby), service in the marine corps, and law school at the University of Texas. Baker's father had been an admirer, from afar, of Bush's father, donating money to Prescott Bush's Senate campaign. The elder Baker also supported George Bush's 1964 bid, writing Bush: "You ran a great race against almost overwhelming odds. The cards were stacked against you from the beginning and the breaks never came your way. . . . It was a pleasure and a privilege to support any man with the high ideals and courage that you have."

George and "Jimmy" were fast friends. There were cookout lunches at the Bushes' and men's doubles at the Houston Country Club. Bush was quick at the net; Baker handled the baseline. They complemented each other's strengths and, with the exception of equally underwhelming serves, compensated for each other's weaknesses. Together they won two club championships. The two men were six years apart in age—Bush had been born in 1924, Baker in 1930. Bush was an eastern aristocrat in search of Texas credentials, Baker a Texas aristocrat who liked having eastern credentials. They had big families—the Bushes and their five children, the Bakers had four sons. And they were innately competitive young men, eager to live lives of consequence.

Bush was the bolder risk taker, Baker cooler and more judicious— a distinction perhaps attributable to the differing cultures of the oil business and of lawyering. Bush had made his fortune in West Texas and in his offshore ventures; Baker was a steady counselor, a reassuring figure in the boardrooms and men's grills of Houston. After lunch on Thanksgiving Day, the Baker men (father and sons Jamie, Mike, John, and Doug) would square off against the Bush men (father and sons George W., Jeb, Marvin, and Neil) in touch football games at the end of Green Tree Road. They called it the Turkey Bowl—and, as Jim Baker recalled, "the touching sometimes looked a lot like tackling."

In 1969, when Bush was planning the 1970 race, Baker considered making his own run for the Seventh District congressional seat, writing "Bushie" about his consultations. But Baker could not do it: His wife, Mary Stuart Baker, had been diagnosed with breast cancer, and he confided painful details about her condition to Bush. The Bushes were the last friends to be with her when she died in early 1970. "You need to do something to take your mind off your grief," Bush told Baker, and brought him into the campaign.

Bush described his relationship with Baker as a "big brother–little brother" dynamic, with Bush the elder figure. (Baker affectionately called Bush "Jefe," Spanish for "boss.") They formed a bond of love leavened with natural elements of tension. Bush would shake his head at Baker's brilliance with the press, and could become irritated at how so many stories managed to present Baker as the genius without whom George H. W. Bush would be nothing. Baker would grow frustrated with Bush's shortcomings as a candidate and was believed to wonder, sometimes, why Bush's name was on the ballot rather than his own. Yet theirs was a kind of marriage, and through the years the two men would return to each other again and again. They were stronger together than they were apart.

B ush called on Nixon in the Oval Office in January 1970 to make the Senate bid official. Photographers were invited in, and the president sent Bush off with a handshake and a brief benediction: "I wish you luck." A film crew shot footage of Nixon and Bush for campaign commercials.

An attractive young oilman with a distinguished war record and largely centrist views was most likely to win the Senate race in the Texas of 1970. John Connally and other Democrats, however, believed that forty-nine-year-old Lloyd Bentsen, a former Democratic congressman from the Rio Grande Valley, not Bush, should be that man.

Rivals in the Texas politics of the age, Bush and Connally each represented a distinct threat to the other. Bush was a relative newcomer, Connally a native; Bush was old money from the East, Connally new; Bush was the Republican future, Connally the Democratic past. (There was tension, too, over business: Connally had been a lawyer for Sid Richardson, the oil giant whose lobbyists had been so heavy-handed in pressuring Bush about Prescott Bush's oil vote in the 1950s.) When Bush looked at Connally, he saw the Texas of Lyndon Johnson and George Brown, a place where Democrats jealously held the keys to statewide power. When Connally looked at Bush, he saw an approaching GOP wave— one that might not come in this election cycle or the next one, but which was nevertheless coming. The conservative Bentsen was the Democrats' best bet to stop Bush's rise in Texas.

For Bush, Yarborough was one thing, Bentsen quite another. Yarborough was a traditional liberal who could be linked with a fading populist

President Nixon, who was eager to see Congressman Bush make a run for the U.S. Senate in 1970, meets with the prospective candidate in the Oval Office in January 1970.

past. Bentsen was, like Bush, an appealing figure of the center in a still-largely Democratic state. A Bush-Bentsen race, *The Dallas Morning News* wrote, would mean that Texans "will be confronted with having to decide between two attractive, well educated, affluent and capable candidates. Bentsen and Bush even look a bit alike. There is not two cents' worth of difference in their basic political philosophies."

Bentsen defeated Yarborough in the May Democratic primary in part by attacking the incumbent for voting against a measure to allow prayer in public schools, for failing to oppose busing to achieve racial diversity, and for opposing two southern conservative Nixon nominees to the U.S. Supreme Court. *The New York Times* reported that Bentsen had won by "using President Nixon's 'Southern strategy' in a Democratic primary." The Southern Strategy was a political and cultural attempt to link Democrats to forces of disorder and of federal overreach on issues ranging from civil rights to Vietnam to social permissiveness. (Yarborough's defeat was seen as a troubling sign for another southern liberal, Albert Gore, Sr., who was facing Bill Brock in Tennessee.) In a primary ad for Bentsen, the Rives, Dyke agency in Houston ran images of rioting at the

1968 Democratic National Convention in Chicago while reporting that Yarborough had endorsed the liberal icon Eugene McCarthy for president. Bentsen then appeared on camera to ask Texans: "Does he support your view?" The answer came on primary day.

I n January 1970, *Time* observed that the November elections would "serve as the first broad referendum on the Nixon Administration's policies." And there were elements of a national strategy in the midterms. In the White House, Patrick J. Buchanan had sent Nixon an eleven-page memorandum about a new book by Richard Scammon and Ben Wattenberg, *The Real Majority.* Bright, aggressive, and unapologetically conservative, Pat Buchanan had grown up in Cold War, Roman Catholic Washington, had become an editorial writer for the *St. Louis Globe-Democrat,* and had gone to work for Nixon in 1966. A provocative polemicist, Buchanan was always searching for ways to advance the conservative cause, and he saw merit in the Scammon-Wattenberg analysis of the American electorate in the new decade.

To Buchanan and to Nixon, the point was compelling: The key voter in the early 1970s was a forty-seven-year-old suburban housewife in Dayton, Ohio, married to a machinist. Nixon was particularly impressed with this passage from the Scammon-Wattenberg book: "To know that the lady in Dayton is afraid to walk the streets alone at night, to know that she has a mixed view about blacks and civil rights because before moving to the suburbs she lived in a neighborhood that became all black, to know that her brother-in-law is a policeman, to know that she does not have the money to move if her new neighborhood deteriorates, to know that she is deeply distressed that her son is going to a community junior college where LSD was found on the campus—to know all this is the beginning of contemporary political wisdom."

To win, Scammon and Wattenberg argued, the Democrats had to convince this housewife that they were in touch with her concerns. If the Democrats could do that, then they could make a case against the Republicans on the economy and successfully put together a majority. Nixon appreciated the logic. "If this analysis was right, and I agreed with Buchanan that it was, then the Republican counterstrategy was clear: we should . . . get the Democrats on the defensive" over issues such as crime, drugs, and patriotism, Nixon wrote in his memoirs. "We should aim our strategy primarily at disaffected Democrats, at blue-collar workers, and at working-class white ethnics. We should set out to capture the vote of the forty-seven-year-old Dayton housewife."

What worked in Dayton tended to work in southern cities, too. Bush grasped the strategy and would duly attack, as *The Dallas Morning News* reported, "school busing, Ted Kennedy, and welfare chiselers." In Bush's case, however, the conservative rhetoric came in a package of centrist proposals and calls for Republicans to heed their better angels. With Bush one got both hardball and high-mindedness, with the former being played in order to give him the power to put the latter into action.

On drugs, he favored making possession of marijuana a misdemeanor rather than a felony. On guns, he opposed firearm registration but supported regulating interstate sales "so every nut with a plate in his head can't get a firearm by mail order." On student demonstrations, he said, "The way to turn the kids off is to tell them you have to do it just the way it's always been done. . . . I want to be the guy who stands for change."

As in the House race in 1966, Bush tended to emphasize his personality as much, if not more than, his platform, and he rehired adman Harry Treleaven for the Senate campaign. In a profile published twelve weeks out from the 1970 general election, Sam Kinch, Jr., who covered state politics for *The Dallas Morning News,* wrote, "For Bush, politics is a personal game in which, like commerce on the old frontier, the salesman and the product are a package; you sell your product by selling yourself; you sell individually, not institutionally." Bush's goal, he told the newspaper, was "to make good things happen and to make sure a disproportionate amount of bad things don't happen."

Referring to Harry Treleaven's ads for Bush, Bentsen complained that the GOP was "packaging [Bush] like a bar of soap. They are running an image campaign." In one Treleaven spot described by *The Wall Street Journal,* Bush tossed a football to one of the boys, sat down on the lawn, and looked into the camera. "During the seventies my children will become adults. I promise you this. I will work hard for peace, a just society, and a fair society." It was one of more than three dozen commercials designed to prove the point that Bush, in the words of the campaign tagline, "can do more."

Explaining the thinking behind the Bush vs. Bentsen ad blitz to the *Journal,* Treleaven said, "Our problem was that both men are very much alike. They're about the same age, both are businessmen, both moderately conservative with about the same views on major issues. So we decided to make effectiveness an issue: Who can do more for Texas? More for the country? More for people?"

Bush claimed his polling showed a turnaround from a 40 to 33 percent deficit in June to a 40 to 30 percent lead in October, with a huge undecided vote. Though he was banking on the Nixon administration's popularity in the state (Nixon had a 74 percent approval rating in a poll conducted by the Democrats), Bush could not have counted on a White House leak to *The Washington Post*'s David Broder on the eve of a Nixon visit to the state in the last week of October. "In the view of some well-informed insiders," Broder wrote in a piece published on Tuesday, October 27, 1970, "Mr. Nixon is going to Texas in hopes of finding his running mate for 1972 and the Republican presidential candidate for 1976."

Yes, Broder admitted, such a scenario "seems far fetched, but it is the firm conviction of men intimately involved in White House political operations that 46-year-old Rep. George Bush (R) of Houston will be that man—if he can, with the President's help, win his close Senate race next week." Vice President Agnew was thought to be a political liability. If the attractive Bush were to triumph in Texas—which Hubert Humphrey had carried in 1968—then who knew?

Then, on Election Day, Bush lost to Bentsen 53.5 to 46.5 percent. Rural turnout, particularly in heavily Democratic East Texas, was higher than expected, largely because of a down-ballot constitutional amendment that would have legalized liquor by the drink, a measure that attracted traditional Democrats to the polls. "Like Custer, who said there were just too many Indians, I guess there were just too many Democrats," Bush said once the votes were in.

Election night was crushing. "God it hurts to lose to Bentsen after all our work and trying and caring," Bush wrote a friend. Doro, then eleven, cried all evening. "I'm the only girl in my class whose father doesn't have a job," she told Barbara.

Bush had lost before, both against Yarborough in 1964 and to Agnew in Miami Beach in 1968. Life was hardly over. "We're torn between staying in politics in some way, or moving back to Houston and getting fairly immersed in business," Bush told a supporter a few weeks after the election in November 1970.

In Texas and in Washington, there was a widespread question circulating among columnists and politicians: "What," *The Dallas Morning News* asked, "will George Bush do now?"

FOURTEEN

A Turn on the World Stage

★

The fact that one door has been closed for him
opens another door.

—RICHARD NIXON, on Bush's swearing-in as
ambassador to the United Nations

B USH WELCOMED THE CALL. After the Bentsen defeat, Charles
Bartlett, the Kennedy intimate and Washington correspondent
for *The Chattanooga Times,* telephoned Bush. Bartlett was reassuring.
"You'd be amazed what this campaign did for your image up here," Bush
recalled his saying. "A lot of people are thinking of you in national terms."
Bartlett "talked about the U.N. as the greatest thing," arguing to Bush
that his being ambassador to the United Nations, based in New York,
would be good for Nixon and good for Bush. The incumbent was a career diplomat, Charles Yost, and Bartlett was reflecting a Washington
view that Nixon needed a stronger voice in Manhattan. It was an intriguing idea, but there were lots of those around, including the possibility of a post with Secretary of State William P. Rogers as undersecretary
of some kind.

Nixon, meanwhile, was currently enamored with John Connally. The
tall, glamorous, conservative Texas Democrat had taken on mythic stature in Nixon's eyes. The president had asked the former governor to
serve on a commission to reorganize the federal government in 1969–
70. Just before the election, Texas Republican chairman Peter O'Donnell
wrote Peter Flanigan, a powerful Nixon adviser on economic and regulatory matters, to complain that the Nixon-Connally relationship was
hurting Bush in the race against Bentsen: How important could it be,
really, to elect a Republican from Texas if President Nixon were already
close to a Democrat from Texas? As detailed in James Reston, Jr.'s biography of Connally, *The Lone Star,* Texas Republicans could not see the
logic of a Republican president's embrace of the conservative Texas
Democratic establishment. "Connally is an implacable enemy of the Re-

publican Party in Texas, and, therefore, attractive as he may be to the President, we should avoid using him again," Flanigan told Nixon's chief of staff H. R. "Bob" Haldeman.

Nixon ignored the advice. On Monday, November 30, 1970, the president named Connally to the Foreign Intelligence Advisory Board. Texas Republicans were flummoxed and angry. For Bush, Connally's rise could not have been more galling. The human reaction to Nixon's courtship of Connally was understandable: Bush felt shunned, overlooked, even betrayed.

By early December 1970 there was much bigger news than the Foreign Intelligence Advisory Board: Connally was to become Nixon's secretary of the Treasury, replacing the banker David Kennedy. Shrewd about such things, Nixon and Connally understood that one price for peace in the kingdom was making sure Bush was "taken care of" before Connally's Treasury appointment was announced. "Connally set," wrote Haldeman. "Have to do something for Bush right away."

Bush had not forgotten Charlie Bartlett's November suggestion about becoming ambassador to the United Nations. The more he thought of it the more he liked it. While it was true that Bush had no foreign policy experience (unless traveling the world for Zapata counted), he knew New York and was attracted to the prospect of learning diplomacy on a big stage without having a great deal of actual operational responsibility.

Peter Flanigan, the Nixon adviser, had been trying to act as a broker between Bush and the White House. An Anheuser-Busch heir, Greenwich Country Day alumnus, and Wall Street investment banker, Flanigan spoke to Bush about running NASA or the Small Business Administration. Neither post felt big enough. Barbara thought that it might be time to give up the arena. "I was about ready to suggest that we pack up and go home to our friends, children, and home in Houston and live happily ever after," she wrote. Then, however, Bush's old Zapata partner Bill Liedtke told Bush that Flanigan was not the best way in. Flanigan, Liedtke suggested, was jealous of Bush.

Taking the hint, Bush tried other routes, speaking with, among others, Bob Finch, the secretary of health, education, and welfare (who was himself moving into a White House job), and Republican senator John Sherman Cooper of Kentucky. Finally Flanigan brought the White House's offer to Bush: Would he be interested in serving as an assistant to the president, working with Haldeman? Bush said yes, prompting Flanigan to make an indiscreet remark. "Well, you know, George, you'd have to work hard if you took this job." ("How George kept his temper, I'll never know," wrote Barbara.) It was one of the first of many subsequent indignities Bush would have to suffer as part of an appointive career—a career that was by definition dependent on presidents and their allies.

On Wednesday, December 9, 1970, Bush reported to Haldeman's West Wing office. The decision, Haldeman said, had been made. Bush was to become an assistant to the president. Haldeman was summoned to the Oval Office, returning five minutes later to take Bush in to see the president, who offered him the White House post during a forty-minute conversation. The president, Bush recalled, said that he "felt I could do a good job for him in the White House presenting the positive side of the issues."

That seemed to be that. Before leaving the Oval Office, though, Bush made his case for the United Nations, arguing that Nixon needed an enthusiastic spokesman in Manhattan's diplomatic, financial, and media circles. Bush told the president that he could "spell out" Nixon's "programs with some style and we could preempt that mass news media area—that he was operating almost in a vacuum. . . . I felt I could really put forward an image there that would be very helpful to the administration."

Nixon had not considered the matter in quite this light before. "Wait a minute, Bob, this makes some sense," the president said to Haldeman. Nixon paused, his mind turning over the possibilities and their ramifications. "Let's announce tomorrow that Bush will be Assistant to the President with general duties, and that he will start right after the Congress reconvenes," Nixon said. "Tell Rogers to put a 'hold' on the U.N. job. In this way, if Yost anytime wants out, we can still have the option open on the U.N., but go ahead with the staff position."

Nixon told Haldeman to get Bush a White House office, and the new assistant to the president went back to the chief of staff's office with Haldeman. Then Nixon apparently thought things over again. Bush's argument—one that spoke to Nixon's sense of insecurity about the East—had been that nobody in the nation's largest city seemed to be on the president's side.

Well, Nixon seems to have decided, Bush was goddamned right about *that*. "Bush's arguments were well taken," wrote biographer Herbert S.

Parmet, "and the president's contemplation made them seem all that much more attractive." Why not send the affable Ivy Leaguer up to Manhattan to defend the president in the salons of the East Side? Think of it: The polished son of a senator from Greenwich working to promote the cause of a grocer's son from Whittier. Why not, indeed? And as Haldeman had once said, Bush "takes our line beautifully." On reflection, Nixon thought Bush should indeed go to the United Nations. "You've sold the President, and he wants to move with it now," Haldeman told Bush, whose career as a White House aide had lasted for less than a day.

There was another factor in Nixon's thinking: the 1972 campaign. The president suggested that the Bushes forgo living full-time in the customary forty-second-floor ambassadorial apartment at the Waldorf Towers. Instead, Nixon said the family should set up residence in Greenwich or another suburb, and have Bush commute from Connecticut to the United Nations—all to set the stage for a 1972 Bush challenge in Connecticut to U.S. senator Abraham Ribicoff, Prescott's old political foe. Bush resisted the idea of a Senate campaign from Connecticut—he believed himself a Texan—but there was no need to argue about all of that now. The future would take care of itself. What mattered was that Bush had prevailed. He had the job he wanted.

His old friend Lud Ashley, now a Democratic congressman from Ohio, was mystified by the appointment. "George, what the fuck do you know about foreign affairs?" Ashley asked him.

"You ask me that in ten days," Bush replied, and went to work.

Bush sensed that transitions in public life would be made easier by courting those with whom you were to work and saying thanks to those with whom you had worked. The Bush touch was evident when he called on the staff of the U.S. Mission to the UN before confirmation. The mission's administrator "seemed amazed when I asked him to have lunch . . . but he is a down to earth kind of guy and I was determined to get his confidence early on."

Like the oil business, like Congress, the UN job was one in which relationships mattered. Reaching out to others and keeping them close created a personal atmosphere that sometimes translated into tangible professional or political benefit. Bush's world was defined by an intermingling of the personal and the professional. The neighbor down the way on Easter Egg Row who came for hamburgers, for example, might one day be an investor or a partner; the fellow congressman, Democrat or Republican, who had a locker nearby in the House gym might one day agree to see your point of view on an important issue; the more senior politician or even president with whom you exchanged kind words might one day call on you to do a big job.

His passion for friendship was not fundamentally political, even if his ingrained habit of making and keeping friends helped him politically. In politics and diplomacy Bush had found the perfect world in which he could instantly transform new acquaintances into those he considered friends. And the threshold for friendship in George H. W. Bush's universe was pretty much just meeting George H. W. Bush.

As part of the campaign to make himself a part of things at the UN, Bush invited Henry Kissinger out to the house in Washington for dinner. At nine P.M. on Thursday, January 14, 1971, the national security adviser arrived for a late meal. A Kissinger Secret Service agent was invited in to play tiddlywinks with the Bush children. (The agent lost.) Over a supper of black bean soup, lamb chops, and ice cream with strawberries and a burnt sugar topping, "Henry told us that there were two plots to kidnap him," wrote Barbara. "He is very close to the president and not just on foreign affairs . . . seems to know all."

Born in Germany in 1923—he was only a year older than Bush—Kissinger fled the Nazis with his family in 1938. He served in the U.S. Army in World War II, earning a Bronze Star, and went on to Harvard, where, after completing three degrees—he received his PhD in 1954; his dissertation was on the Congress of Vienna—he joined the university faculty. He loved intrigue, beautiful women, the New York Yankees, and positive press stories. A brilliant global strategist and longtime adviser to Nelson Rockefeller, he made the transition to the Nixon team after the 1968 election when the president-elect asked him to serve as national security adviser. By 1973, the canny Kissinger would also become secretary of state and hold both jobs simultaneously.

An astute observer of power and master of diplomatic flattery, Kissinger had taken the trouble to accept the Bushes' invitation to dinner in part because he understood that Bush—still a young man, not yet fifty—had the potential to become a crucial national figure, whether in the Senate, in the cabinet, or in the White House.

At ten o'clock on the morning of Friday, February 26, 1971, the Bushes entered the State Dining Room on the first floor of the White House for the new ambassador's swearing-in. The vice president, much of the cabinet, and many members of Congress were joined by Jim Baker from Houston and Peter O'Donnell from Dallas and Dorothy and Prescott Bush. The marine band played; Rogers Morton, the secretary of commerce, was heard to grumble, "I didn't get all this attention when I was sworn in—no music—smaller crowd . . ."

Nixon was in a good humor. He had breakfasted that morning with Wilbur Mills, the chairman of the Ways and Means Committee in the House, and Bush's name had come up. "Chairman Mills pointed out that William McKinley at one time had been defeated for office in Ohio running for the Congress," Nixon told the audience in the State Dining Room. "Two years later, however, William McKinley went on to be elected as Governor of Ohio, and then went on to be elected as President of the United States. Now, I don't know whether Chairman Mills was suggesting that defeat, therefore, was good for George Bush and that his future may be somewhat like William McKinley's."

Heady talk. "The fact that one door has been closed for him opens another door," Nixon said, "a door of service for him and also for the United States of America, a representative of whom we can all be proud, representing the United States and working in the cause of peace in the United Nations in the years ahead."

Supreme Court justice Potter Stewart, an Eisenhower appointee whose wife, Andy, was one of Barbara's best friends, administered the oath. Dorothy Bush's face seemed to quiver; Prescott Bush, usually so reserved, wept as their son raised his right hand. Like his parents, Bush was emotional. Repeating after Stewart, he stumbled over a word and had to begin again.

Before the month was out, the George Bushes were in New York, settling into the ambassador's residence at the Waldorf Towers. Mrs. Douglas MacArthur was a neighbor. Being a Republican from Texas in New York—even a Republican from Texas born in Connecticut—was disconcerting for Bush. As disingenuous and dissonant as it may seem, Bush of Greenwich, Andover, and New Haven had complaints about the elitism of New York, by which Bush meant the city's tendency toward center-left groupthink. "I find it very difficult to be polite when people ask me how I like New York," Bush told a diary he had begun to keep in 1971. "It is an unrepresentative city. . . . They are so darn sure they are right on everything." The conventional wisdom in Manhattan, Bush believed, often failed to take opposing views into account except to dismiss such opinions as uninformed, prejudiced, and just plain wrong. Yet Bush hurled himself into the United Nations, hosting the ambassadors from Madagascar and from Nigeria and their sons at a hockey match and a basketball game. The signature Bush diplomatic style was already taking shape.

Addressing the United Nations Security Council. Bush served as America's ambassador to the international organization in New York from 1971 to early 1973.

He soon encountered a great new fact of his diplomatic life: Yakov Malik, the Soviet ambassador whom Bush likened to a stone wall. Born in 1906, the white-haired Malik was Moscow's longtime man in New York. Implacably hostile one moment but largely rational the next, Malik gave Bush a tutorial in the art of dealing with the Soviets. As Bush was to see, the key to managing them—indeed, the key to all diplomacy— was knowing when they were serious about their threats and when they were posturing. Nations were like individuals, requiring cultivation and the paying of respect. Bush believed in an old Emersonian quotation that FDR had liked: The best way to have a friend is to be one.

Yakov Malik was the first Soviet that Bush knew well. He was, Bush recalled, "a true cold warrior who could make my life difficult"—and often did. Over a liquid lunch in the Soviet's apartment in New York—vodka before and during the meal, in addition to wine, and a proffered cognac afterward—Malik and Bush kept up the push and pull. "He repeated all the cold war rhetoric—that we were imperialists," Bush recalled. At a UN Security Council session in Ethiopia in the winter of 1972, the ambassadors spent a weekend in Somalia. Beforehand the CIA had briefed Bush on the presence of Soviet warships off the Somali coast. Bush asked Malik about it, but Malik waved it off, saying, "Oh, no—no ships." On arrival, though, the Soviet ships were in plain view, and Mogadishu was filled with Russian sailors. Teasing, Bush said, "No warships?" Sputtering, Malik replied: "They are here to rescue me from sharks."

As Bush recalled it, his "most difficult issue" at the UN was the fate of Taiwan, or, as it was sometimes known, the Republic of China. For decades the United States had insisted on recognizing Taiwan—rather than the Communist mainland—as the real China, and Taiwan held China's seat on the UN Security Council. In the context of the Cold War, abandoning Taiwan was tantamount to capitulating to the mainland Communist behemoth, and the United States was committed to defending Taiwan's UN membership. Anti-American countries within the United Nations, meanwhile, were more than happy to try to embarrass the United States by attempting to expel Taiwan in favor of the mainland in the early 1970s.

The debate over Taiwan's fate came on Bush's watch as ambassador, and he loyally defended America's longtime ally against a hostile Third World majority month after month in 1971. Bush was pushing an alternative plan called "dual representation," a compromise that would bring the People's Republic into the United Nations and onto the Security Council while maintaining UN recognition of Taiwan as a member of the global organization.

The task could hardly have been more difficult. As Bush politely recalled it, Nixon, after a "secret" visit to China by Kissinger, "surprised everyone" with the Thursday, July 15, 1971, news of a presidential visit to the mainland—and "everyone" included Bush. The development was startling—here was the greatest of cold warriors, Nixon, preparing to call on the greatest of Communist rulers, Mao. Nearly a quarter century of geopolitical reality was suddenly open to radical revision.

Yet American policy remained American policy: Bush was still pressing ahead with dual representation, which would simultaneously promote the mainland in status but protect Taiwan's dignity. For Bush, the problem was that the Nixon-Kissinger overture to the mainland strongly suggested that, as he put it in July 1971, "The ball game is over, Peking is in and Taiwan is out." After the announcement of Nixon's trip, countries that might have been persuaded to vote to keep Taiwan had even less reason to antagonize the mainland. If the United States and Communist China were about to open a new chapter in diplomacy, why keep up the illusion that Taiwan really mattered? Once the symbolic stand-in for all of China, Taiwan was now seen as dispensable—and if the United States lost a big vote at the United Nations, well, all the better.

Bush understood this reality, but America had given its word that it would be there for Taiwan, and he was going to keep that word as best he could. There were other factors, too. Because Taiwan was important to the Republican right wing, Nixon needed to appear sympathetic to Taipei's cause even as he pursued the breakthrough with Beijing. Nixon had instructed Bush to win the vote, and allowing the competitive Bush to fight the battle at the UN gave the White House some cover with the right at a fluid moment.

Then Kissinger traveled to the mainland in the midst of the struggle in New York, further complicating Bush's efforts to secure the votes. Bush kept after it, cajoling and charming his way through the UN General Assembly. But it was the wrong case at the wrong moment. "It was an ugliness in the chamber," Bush recalled. "I was hissed when I got up."

Taiwan was ultimately expelled by a vote of 59 to 55, with 15 countries abstaining. "Life goes on, and there is no question that the U.N. will be a more realistic and vital place with Peking in here, but I had my heart and soul wrapped up in the policy of keeping Taiwan from being ejected," Bush wrote a friend in Dallas after the vote.

In November, China's vice minister of foreign affairs, Chiao Kuan-hua, delivered a speech to the United Nations that Bush thought "was clearly hostile to the United States, referring to us as bullies etc." American officials were under strict orders not to reply except in warm generalities, but Bush, still stung by the Taiwan defeat and thinking of domestic U.S. opinion, argued for a stronger response. "If we appear to be pushed around by Peking at every turn," Bush said, "the whole thing can backfire on the President."

Kissinger was unmoved by Bush's views. To Kissinger the relationship with Peking was too sensitive and too momentous to be subject to the emotions of a given moment. To have Bush making a contrary case, even internally, was infuriating. The two men met in Washington. "He started off madder than hell," Bush recalled.

"I want to treat you as I do four other ambassadors, dealing directly with you," Kissinger said, "but if you are uncooperative I will treat you like any other ambassador." The threat did not sit well with Bush, who pushed back. "I reacted very strongly . . . and told him that I damn sure had a feel for this country and I felt we had to react" to provocative Chinese rhetoric.

For two or three minutes—an eternity in such circumstances—both men spoke candidly and passionately. It was, Bush thought, "a very heated" exchange. Bush insisted he was arguing out of conviction, not self-interest. "I told him very clearly when he got upset that I was not trying to screw things up, I was trying to serve the President [by defending the U.S. against the Chinese attacks] and that it was the only interest I had," Bush recalled saying. "He ought to get that through his head. I was not trying to get any power." After hearing Bush out, Kissinger "really cooled down."

Sunday, January 9, 1972, was a fairly typical weekend day for Ambassador Bush. In the morning, after waking up in the Waldorf, the Bushes called the Japanese ambassador to see if his thirteen-year-old daughter, a friend of Doro's, would like to join them for ice-skating out in Greenwich. By ten thirty they were on the road to Connecticut. In Greenwich they found Bucky Bush already testing the ice, which was soft but safe enough for a skate. It was a familiar routine: Bush liked taking different foreign diplomats out to his parents' house, always believing hospitality could never hurt.

And even after the Taiwan debacle, Bush quickly adapted to the geopolitical realities and invited the Communist Chinese UN delegates to Sunday brunch at his childhood home. It was a new world, and Bush was always one to face facts.

The autumn of 1972 brought grief. In September, Bush's mother called to tell her son that Prescott was sick. There was, she reported, "a pain by his heart." Bush was worried. "He seems instantly old," Bush wrote after visiting his father. Diagnosed with lung cancer, Prescott also underwent a prostate operation that resulted in complications—infection, fever, an irregular heartbeat, poor blood pressure. It was a matter of weeks or perhaps months, but no longer. One evening, Bush was summoned from a dinner with the Soviets at the Peruvian embassy. Prescott was failing. Bush called his mother, woke her up, and told her he would meet her at the hospital—and that he loved her.

They arrived at about eleven P.M. to find Prescott "full of tubes," Bush recalled. "He was conscious though very sleepy with drugs." To fill the air Bush told his father about the dinner with the Soviets. "Who picked up the tab?" Prescott asked from beneath the tubes.

Prescott Sheldon Bush died two weeks later, on Sunday, October 8, 1972. He was seventy-seven years old. The clan gathered for the funeral at Christ Church in Greenwich; mourners included Averell Harriman, New York City mayor John Lindsay, U.S. senator Lowell Weicker of Connecticut, and Yale president Kingman Brewster, Jr. "Our boys all came home and were pall bearers (the Senator dreaded the thought of his friends huffing and puffing under the burden of the coffin)," Barbara wrote. "Mom Bush was wonderful. My heart aches for her. She is so lonely. 51 years of loving Dad. She dreams that he is coming in from golf and then awakens to find that it was just a dream."

Prescott was buried next to Robin, in the plot he had chosen twenty years before.

FIFTEEN

This Job Is No Fun at All

★

One real challenge lies in enchanting the disenchanted young
who view partisan politics with a worrisome cynicism.
—GEORGE H. W. BUSH, 1972

RICHARD NIXON HAD BIG PLANS. It was Monday, November 20,
1972, and Nixon, fresh from his epic reelection victory over
George McGovern, was remaking his administration—and hoping to remake the Republican Party along with it. Nixon believed the
GOP was poised to become a truly majority party by permanently converting disaffected Democrats, many of whom had voted for him in the
1972 landslide. An attractive, reasonable face at the head of the GOP
would be key, and Nixon had summoned George H. W. Bush to the
presidential cabin at Camp David to ask him to leave the United Nations to become chairman of the Republican National Committee. "This
is an important time for the Republican Party, George," Nixon said. "We
have a chance to build a new coalition in the next four years, and you're
the one who can do it." Kansas senator Bob Dole had been chairing the
RNC, but Nixon wanted a full-time leader for the party. Nixon talked
big, suggesting that Bush would be "the President's top political adviser."

Bush was surprised, and not altogether pleasantly. He had left New
York hoping to become the number two man at the State Department.
He liked foreign affairs, liked the big stage and the broader world; he was
in the middle of what he called a "love affair . . . with high-level policy
dealings on international matters." His ambition was to become secretary of state, and then, one day, perhaps, reach the presidency.

Nixon wanted him at the national committee in part because the
president believed Bush would be both respectable and manageable. To
the president, Bush remained the eager-to-please supplicant of 1970. "A
total Nixon man—first," Nixon had said to Treasury Secretary George
Shultz in a conversation about Bush's job prospects. "Doubt if you can
do better than Bush." Nixon was apparently unaware of the Bush who

had held his own against Kissinger. If Nixon had known about Bush's stubborn streak—a streak that, to be sure, manifested itself very, very discreetly—he might have rethought the RNC offer.

In the Age of Nixon, the RNC chairman was expected to strike back at the president's enemies without mercy. Bush knew this, and it worried him. "I can and will of course take orders, but I'd like to retain options on the style in which to carry them out," Bush told Nixon. "I can be plenty tough when needed, but each person has his own style, his own methods, and if I get too far out of character—I'll be unconvincing and incredible and this will not serve you well."

The conversation at Camp David ended. According to Nixon adviser John Ehrlichman's notes of the session, Bush told the president: "Not all that enthralled [with] RNC, but I'll do it." Barbara, on learning of the offer, was skeptical. "She is convinced that all our friends in Congress, in public life, in God knows where—will say, 'George screwed it up at the U.N. and the President has loyally found a suitable spot,'" Bush wrote Nixon the day after their Camp David meeting. "Candidly, there will be some of this." Yet he told Nixon he would accept the job, closing his letter to the president warmly. "My wife's initial reaction is understandable, for she is but a mirror of how the real world regrettably views politics," Bush wrote. "Most people feel it is not the noble calling it should be— not the noble calling like affairs of state." He added a final, poignant note: "But with your help maybe I can be a part of changing some of that. And in the final analysis that's one hell of a challenge."

Richard Nixon himself would make Bush's idealistic vision of a cleaner, nobler politics an impossible one to bring into being. Bush accepted the RNC post at an odd political moment. Nixon had been resoundingly reelected in November 1972, but a new term was entering the American vernacular at the same time: Watergate.

The scandal that destroyed the Nixon presidency had begun with a botched break-in at the Democratic National Committee headquarters at the Watergate apartment complex on the Potomac River in June 1972. The burglars were linked to the White House political operation. In the wake of the Watergate fiasco, attempts to cover up a culture of dirty tricks, illegal campaign funding, and what became known as the "White House horrors" reached all the way to Nixon. The story of his (abbreviated) second term became one of disturbing revelations and, for the country, unsettling investigations into White House conduct. Republican senator Howard Baker's question "What did the President know, and when did he know it?" came to dominate Washington in 1973 and most of 1974 as Nixon fought for his political life, falsely maintaining his innocence until the weight of contrary evidence led him to the brink of impeachment and finally to resignation in August 1974.

When Bush signed on for the RNC, though, the scope of the scandal was as yet unknown. Nixon had, after all, just won a smashing reelection, but Bush's life in 1973 and the first nine months of 1974 was to be shaped by Nixon's attempts to hold on to power amid revelations of wrongdoing. Nixon's wide-ranging hopes about an expanded Republican Party faded in the face of Watergate. Soon Bush was in the most awkward of positions: he was the man in charge of Republican political fortunes at the moment when those fortunes were in maximum peril. Bush, like many Republicans, defended the president against the investigations nearly to the very end while struggling to protect, as best he could, the party's future—and his own.

B ush took command of the national committee on Tuesday, January 23, 1973. Given an office in the Old Executive Office Building, sharing a foyer with the president, who kept a hideaway there, Bush could not complain about his proximity to power. His job was to recruit and support Republican candidates for offices at every level, raise money, and defend the party and the president in the national and local media. The year was hectic. From January 20 through December 23, 1973, Bush traveled 97,000 miles through 33 states, delivering 101 speeches, holding 78 news conferences, and making 11 appearances on national television. Back at the committee's offices in Washington, Bush trimmed the internal budget, eliminated the chairman's limousine, cut down on personnel, and ended workday happy hours.

He was loyal to the president but not blindly so, declining to make the RNC available to the Nixon circle to use as it wished. The White House wanted Bush to be the "point man in a counterattack against investigators leading the Watergate charge," Bush recalled, but Bush refused, declining, for instance, to sign a letter drafted by Nixon political aides viciously assaulting the president's critics.

As Watergate unfolded, letters and calls poured into the committee. Many thought Nixon was a crook; many others believed he was being railroaded. Jeb Bush, then a twenty-year-old student at the University of Texas, worked at the RNC in the summer of 1973 calling small donors to urge them to re-up their pledges. "Either people were saying, 'I'm no longer a Republican, so screw you,'" Jeb recalled, "or they would say, 'Tell Nixon to stand up for himself.' No one was happy."

As the man tasked with keeping the president's party afloat while the president struggled to survive, George H. W. Bush pleaded with both sides for fair play. To Nixon's opponents he counseled patience and forbearance; to the White House, he politely, and often indirectly, advised telling the truth, if only to end the misery sooner rather than later.

Bush wanted to believe in Nixon. The idea that a president of the United States would lie to the country for selfish political ends was anathema to Bush, who kept hearing his father's voice. "Knowing Dad, as you did," Bush wrote to a family friend, "I'm sure you can understand when I say that I really am glad he is not around to have to worry about Watergate."

In the summer of 1973 came word of the Nixon White House tapes—news that stunned Bush, who recalled hearing about it while standing in the southwest lobby of the White House with Republican wise man Bryce Harlow. "I am shocked," Bush remarked to Harlow. For a time in this bleak season Bush thought about escaping Washington to run for governor in Texas, then decided duty required him to stay at his post to protect the larger GOP. Writing a friend in the fall of 1973, Bush said that "this isn't the time to quit" the Republican chairmanship. "It's not a time to jump sideways, it's not a time for me to wring my hands on the sidelines."

Tom Wicker, then the political correspondent of *The New York Times,* recalled encountering Bush at a national governors' conference in 1973. As Wicker told it, Bush "took me aside—backstage in a cavernous auditorium—to assure me that Nixon was not guilty, that ultimately the charges of the *Times* and other critics would be shown to be unfair and unwarranted." An astute reporter, Wicker listened to the chairman's words with care. "Bush was trying hard, I remember thinking, but was not really convincing—either about Nixon's innocence or about his own belief that the president would survive the scandal," Wicker wrote in a later biography of Bush. "He did concede that the political situation for Nixon and his party was bad and getting worse."

In the fall, Vice President Agnew resigned amid a bribery scandal unrelated to Watergate. He was replaced by Congressman Gerald Ford of Michigan, a solid Midwestern Republican. Bush had been mentioned for the number two spot, as had an old House colleague: Donald Rumsfeld. Bright, ambitious, and self-confident, Rumsfeld, born in Chicago in 1932, had grown up entranced by *The Lone Ranger* on the radio and proud of his real-estate-salesman father's World War II service in the navy. As a wrestler and football player at Princeton, Rumsfeld signed on for a naval ROTC program to help pay for school. After graduating in 1954, he became a naval aviator, and won a congressional seat in 1962. He was only thirty. In the Nixon years, Rumsfeld ran the Office of Economic Opportunity, served as counselor to the president and director of the Cost of Living Council, and was serving as an ambassador to NATO. He was, like Bush, a rising star.

By October 1973, Nixon was losing control. Attorney General Elliot Richardson, ordered by the president to fire special prosecutor Archibald Cox, refused and resigned. Richardson deputy William Ruckelshaus also declined to execute Nixon's command. Finally, Cox was fired by the number three at the Justice Department, Robert Bork. The Cox dismissal and the resignations of Richardson and Ruckelshaus were dubbed the "Saturday Night Massacre."

Shortly thereafter Nixon claimed that two subpoenaed White House tapes had gone missing, and there was an eighteen-and-a-half-minute gap in the middle of another crucial recording, allegedly the result of a transcription mistake by Rose Mary Woods, the president's devoted secretary. For Bush it was all too much. "I am appalled at the handling of the Watergate tapes matter," he dictated to his diary. These were, Bush said, "extremely complicated times—this job is no fun at all."

Things at home were also somewhat fraught. George W., now in his midtwenties, was not having an easy time of it. A rejection by the University of Texas law school had left him "in shock," his mother told her diary in January 1971. It was, she added, a "real morale depressor." Baine Kerr, the Bushes' lawyer and Houston neighbor, offered a theory. "Baine says that George got higher marks than many accepted by the University of Texas law school and that he will intercede if we will let him," Barbara wrote on Sunday, January 31. "He says that it is political and that the head of the Board of Regents is opposed to George. We told him thanks, but no thanks."

After a Pentagon screening of a CBS film on South African apartheid, the younger Bush "promptly wanted to go to South Africa and expose the whole thing," Barbara wrote in her diary. "He is really worrying George and me a little. He should talk less and do more. He just can't seem to get interested. He is reading the Bible a lot. I have suggested that he talk to Ganny Bush and maybe he should look into divinity school."

Beginning in the fall of 1971, there was quiet speculation that George W. might make a bid for the Texas state senate from Harris County. "He is very seriously considering running. . . ." Barbara wrote in her diary on Friday, October 1, 1971. He weighed the possibilities—he would have faced Democrat Jack C. Ogg in the general election—but decided against the race. "We hope he'll feel settled," Barbara wrote after George W. called with the news in January 1972.

Shortly before, as a senior at Andover, Jeb had spent several months in the winter of 1970–71 on student service trip to León in the Mexican state of Guanajuato. Bush had been a bit worried about his second son. "Jebby is going to need some help I am sure," Bush told his diary during his time at the United Nations. "He is a free and independent spirit and I don't want him to get totally out of touch with the family."

In Mexico, Jeb met and fell instantly in love with Columba Garnica de Gallo, a child of a broken home. His friends thought Columba made Jeb a much more serious young man, and he was speeding through the University of Texas in the period his father served as RNC chairman. The Bushes welcomed Jeb's newfound focus but were taken aback when, at Christmas 1973, Jeb announced that he and Columba were going to marry.

On the day after Christmas, 1973, George W., then twenty-seven and a student at Harvard Business School, crashed into some trash cans after arriving home from a night out drinking. "Your behavior is disgraceful," Barbara told George W. "Go upstairs and see your father." George W. marched into his parents' bedroom to confront Bush. "I understand you want to see me," George W. said, recalling that he had "defiantly charged upstairs and put my hands on my hips." Other versions of the story have George W. saying, "You want to go mano a mano right here?" Whatever the son said, the father lowered the book he was reading, looked George W. in the eye, and then returned to his book. The silent stare sent George W. back out of the room. "He normally is a good guy," Barbara wrote of George W. in her diary. "He says that he drank so much because he was upset over Jeb. All I know is that he challenged his dad and backed down. His brothers put him in the sauna!!!!" (Recalling the "mano a mano" moment, George H. W. Bush said: "He didn't really want to, either.")

While George W. did not remember invoking Jeb that night ("I was probably just looking for an excuse to use with Mother," he recalled), Barbara had her own initial concerns about Jeb's marriage. Columba, after all, was unknown to them. "How I worry about Jeb and Columba," Barbara told her diary. "Does she love him? I know when I meet her, I'll stop worrying." Barbara was impressed that Columba appeared to be "a great influence" on Jeb. "We were notified that because of his academic record [at Texas], Jeb had made Phi Beta Kappa," Barbara recalled. "I called to say how thrilled we were, and he told me he had done it for Columba because he wanted to prove he was serious. She [had] thought he was a rich man's son and a playboy." Barbara gave Jeb her grandmother Pierce's wedding ring for Columba, and the couple were married in Austin in February 1974.

In Washington, Bush long insisted that "without the facts" he would not favor removing Nixon from office either through resignation or impeachment and conviction. He was, however, "sickened" after the April 1974 release of edited transcripts of conversations that depicted the Nixon White House as dark, conspiratorial, and profane. "The whole amoral tone made me ill," Bush wrote.

Still Bush remained loyal. In the spring and summer of 1974, his defense of Nixon came down to a plea for proportion unless and until there was clearer proof that the president himself had broken the law. The stand Bush took—of cautious support until it was beyond any question that Nixon had participated in the cover-up—was hardly a profile in courage. It was, rather, that of a conventional politician, of an ambitious man who chose to defend the powers that were—which, not incidentally, were the powers that had championed and promoted his prospects in public life. Yet his reaction to Nixon's descent into disgrace was also rooted in a sense of duty to party and a basic human empathy for what Nixon—and the Nixon family—were enduring. Julie Nixon Eisenhower, the president's younger daughter, came to Bush one day pleading for him to try to defend her father more vigorously. Her appeal touched him, but he was doing all he felt he could do in good conscience.

He worried about what his own children thought of him. "It occurred to me your own idealism might be diminished if you felt your Dad condoned the excesses of men you knew to have been his friends or associates," Bush wrote George W., Jeb, Neil, and Marvin on Tuesday, July 23, 1974. "I feel battered and disillusioned."

The day after Bush wrote those words, the Supreme Court ruled that Nixon had to turn over all of the White House tapes. The House Judiciary Committee began several days of deliberations that resulted in the approval of three articles of impeachment. If the articles passed the full House, the president would be tried in the Senate and, if convicted, removed from office.

On Wednesday, July 31, Bush went to the White House for a conversation with Al Haig, the hard-charging army general who had risen from serving as an aide to Kissinger to succeeding Bob Haldeman as Nixon's chief of staff in the spring of 1973. They met in Haig's West Wing office for nearly an hour. The midterm elections of 1974 were only three months away. If Nixon were thinking of resigning to avoid his forcible removal from the presidency, Bush told Haig, "he ought to do it now rather than later." From the party chairman's perspective, the reason was clear: "If he resigned after the elections [in November 1974]," Bush said, "we would probably take a bigger bath in the elections and then the new president would be faced with a Congress far to the left of where the country stood." Bush's signal was clear enough. Nixon should go.

At noon on Monday, August 5, 1974, Dean Burch called Bush from the White House. An old Goldwater adviser, Burch had become Nixon's political counselor in these troubled months. A new tape was about to emerge, and Burch wanted Bush to come along with him and Nixon lawyer Fred Buzhardt to brief House Minority Leader John Rhodes of Arizona, a Bush friend. The week before, Rhodes had called Bush. "You got any good news?" Rhodes asked. "Yes," Bush said, "it's 12:17 and nobody's been indicted."

Now the news was the impending release of a June 1972 White House conversation between Nixon and Haldeman six days after the Watergate break-in. The president and his then chief of staff had spoken for an hour and thirty-five minutes that morning—from 10:04 A.M. to 11:39 A.M.—and could be heard plotting how to use the CIA to stop the FBI's investigation of the burglary. "This was proof the President had been involved, at least in the cover-up," Bush recalled. "This was proof the President had lied." In the meeting with Rhodes, Burch, and Buzhardt, Bush spoke of stepping down. Burch and Buzhardt argued against the move. "Somebody," they argued, "needs to be around to pick up the pieces."

As this long summer Monday drew to a close, he recorded his current thinking for his diary. Resigning as party chairman was always an option. "I do not feel the President can survive. . . ." he dictated. "I [am] torn between how to lead and what is leadership at a point like this. Oddly enough at this moment leadership may mean doing nothing. . . . Maybe by sitting quietly . . . trying to hold the party together, one can do the most service. But it means the risk that people won't know how strongly and deeply I feel about this whole grubby Watergate mess. . . . Watergate is a shabby, tawdry business that demeans the Presidency. Am I failing to lead by not stating that?" He knew the price of staying at the RNC, but he would pay it, forgoing the heroic headlines that resigning in protest would have brought him. Bush was not particularly driven by personal loyalty to Nixon, for he was under no illusions about what the president thought of him. The president "feels I'm soft, not tough enough, not willing to do the 'gut job' that his political instincts have taught him must be done," Bush wrote in July 1974. "He is inclined to equate privilege with softness or stuffiness."

Bush's truest fealty was to his own vision of what he called the "system," by which he meant a constitutional structure peopled with men and women of essential good will engaged in a never-ending struggle to govern well. "Civility will return to Washington eventually," Bush wrote his sons that summer. "Personalities will change and our system will have proved that it works—more slowly than some would want—less efficiently than some would decree—but it works and gives us—even in adversity—great stability." Bush had faith in the resilience of the American order, and he wanted to play his part in rescuing that order from the chaos Nixon had wrought.

On Tuesday, August 6, 1974, Nixon was running late for a midmorning cabinet meeting. The session was pushed back; "the atmosphere," Bush recalled, was "one of unreality." When Nixon finally entered the Cabinet Room, the applause that customarily greeted his arrival was not forthcoming. The president looked terrible. "It was obvious he hadn't been sleeping well," Gerald Ford recalled. Nixon, Ford observed, was "sallow."

The president checked the clock in the middle of the cabinet table before turning to his notes for the meeting. "I would like to discuss the most important issue confronting the nation," he said, "and confronting us internationally too—inflation. Our economic situation could be the major issue in the world today." Bush was mystified. Ford, sitting nearby, thought: "My God!"

Nixon was deliberately ducking the existential issue of whether the administration itself was to long endure. Then, just as suddenly as he had launched into inflation, Nixon turned to Watergate. There had, he claimed, been no "intentional breach of the law" and "no obstruction of justice." At the time of the June 1972 break-in, he said, he had been consumed with Vietnam and the opening to China and had failed in his obligation to be "tending the store on the political side. Those who were [tending the store] were overeager." He knew, he said, that the impeachment vote in the House was lost. Yet he would not resign. He would fight it out in the Senate.

So there it was: the decision of the moment, made by a man with an ambivalent relationship with reality. No one in the room spoke. Nixon felt compelled to fill the silence. "I vetoed $35 billion in appropriations during Watergate," he went on. "I intend to fight the inflation battle with all the tools we can." Still no one spoke. At one point an uncomfortable Nixon glanced uneasily around the room. His eyes met Bush's. The president smiled awkwardly and mouthed "George." Bush was moved. "My heart went totally out to him even though I felt deeply betrayed by his lie of the day before," Bush told his diary. "The man is amoral. He has a different sense than the rest of people. He came up the hard way. He hung tough. He hunkered down, he stonewalled. He became President of the United States and a damn good one in many ways, but now it had all caught up with him."

Breaking the silence, Ford asked for the floor: "Mr. President, with your indulgence, I have something to say."

"Well, Jerry, go ahead."

"No one regrets more than I do this whole tragic episode," Ford said. "I have deep personal sympathy for you, Mr. President, and your fine family. But I wish to emphasize that had I known what has been disclosed in reference to Watergate in the last twenty-four hours, I would not have made a number of the statements I made either as Minority Leader or as Vice President. . . . I'll have no further comment on the issue because I'm a party in interest. I'm sure there will be impeachment in the House. I can't predict the Senate outcome." Nixon, Ford thought, "seemed taken aback" by the vice president's words.

The president tried to return to business as usual. There was brief conversation about a new farm appropriations bill that he believed would have to be vetoed, followed by talk of a possible economic summit between the executive branch and Congress. Attorney General William Saxbe spoke up. "Mr. President, I don't think we ought to have a summit conference. We ought to be sure you have the ability to govern." After a long, painful pause—everyone else in the room remained silent, waiting to see the president's reaction to Saxbe's challenge—Nixon said, slowly, "Bill, I have the ability just as I have had for the last five and a half years."

No one believed him. With the skepticism of the group now in the open and gathering force after Ford's and Saxbe's remarks, Bush tried to get Nixon's attention. Speaking up, Bush said that Saxbe "was right"; that Watergate was adversely affecting the economy; and that if Nixon wanted to fight on for survival, it would be best to do so "expeditiously"— the sooner the trauma ended, the better.

Listening to Bush, Kissinger knew that the session was nearing the point of no return. If someone else took Nixon on now, it might be impossible to stop most of the cabinet from coming out against the president—right then, to his face. Given Nixon's state of mind—he might well resign if he believed it were his own decision, not the result of pressure—an open revolt of the men who owed their places to him could send Nixon into a state of defiance from which he might not return. Cutting off the cabinet conversation, Kissinger said: "We are here to do the nation's business." The discussion meandered on for a bit longer before Nixon rose and returned to the Oval Office.

As the meeting broke up, Bush told Haig that "the whole goddamned thing had come undone and there was no way it could be resolved." The White House's Senate count was wrong. If the president really believed

The handwritten draft of Bush's letter to Richard Nixon urging the embattled president to resign, August 1974.

he still had a chance of holding thirty-four votes—the minimum required for acquittal—then "people were not leveling with the White House."

In the midst of this extraordinary week, Bush had to fly to California to prepare for a GOP fundraising broadcast. In his room at the Beverly Wilshire on Wednesday, August 7, 1974, he sat down to draft a candid letter to Nixon on hotel stationery. "Dear Mr. President," Bush began,

> It is my considered judgment that you should now resign. I expect in your lonely embattled position this would seem to you as an act of disloyalty from one you have supported and helped in so many ways.

My own view is that I would now ill serve a President, whose massive accomplishments I will always respect and whose family I love, if I did not now give you my judgment.

Until this moment resignation has been no answer at all, but given the impact of the latest development, and it will be a lasting one, I now firmly feel resignation is best for this country, best for this President. I believe this view is held by most Republican leaders across the country.

This letter is made much more difficult because of the gratitude I will always have for you.

If you do leave office history will properly record your achievements with a lasting respect.

Nixon never replied. On Thursday the eighth Nixon decided to resign, and he met with Ford late that morning to give him the news. Word of the resignation leaked out around noon. It was, Bush recalled, an "unreal" day. As he prepared to assume power, Ford made time to see Bush, who had returned from Los Angeles overnight. The incoming president had been friendly with Bush's parents. The two had served together for four years in the House. And since Bush had returned to Washington from New York for the RNC, the two men had been in parallel positions, having to defend Nixon until Nixon became indefensible. They were comfortable with each other; they inhabited largely the same world. There was trust between them. And when the two men met on the day Nixon was to announce his resignation, both knew that the political class ranked Bush as a top prospect to become Ford's vice president.

To his diary, Bush downplayed the possibility, largely in an unsuccessful attempt to manage his own expectations. He had wanted the vice presidency in 1968, had been mentioned as a candidate if Nixon had dumped Agnew for the 1972 reelection campaign, and had been spoken of yet again when Ford himself got the job in 1973. And so, when Ford and Bush spoke on Thursday, August 8, 1974, Bush took full advantage of the opportunity, raising subjects that ranged far beyond his portfolio as national party chairman. "I talked about the White House staff," Bush recalled, particularly about the press office, and he asked Ford to let him have "input" into whatever decisions were made about the communications operation. "I then went on to the National Security Council," suggesting that Kissinger had become too powerful in his dual roles as secretary of state and as national security adviser. Bush thought Ford needed his own man as a national security broker. That was the only way, Bush said, that Ford could "put an imprint of his own on foreign policy."

Only late in the conversation did Bush turn to his actual brief: the Republican National Committee. He said he would resign as soon as Ford wanted him to. It was critical, Bush told Ford, for the new president to have his own chairman, for the work for 1976 would have to begin "very soon." Until this point Ford had reacted little to Bush's tour d'horizon. At the suggestion that Bush was giving up the committee forthwith, though, Ford came to life. "He indicated that he wanted me to stay for awhile," Bush recalled, "that he had total confidence in me, that he didn't want it to look like he didn't have confidence in me, nor did he want it to look like I didn't have confidence in him, by doing anything precipitous."

Watching Nixon's farewell in the East Room on Friday, August 9, 1974, Bush wondered to himself: "What kind of a man is this really?"

The next afternoon, Friday, August 9, the Bushes were in the East Room for Nixon's farewell to the staff and the cabinet. They watched, fascinated, as the fallen president mused aloud about his parents ("My mother was a saint"; "I remember my old man. I think that they would have called him sort of a little man, common man"); about resilience ("Only if you have been in the deepest valley can you ever know how magnificent it is to be on the highest mountain"); and finally, too late, about equanimity. ("Others may hate you, but those who hate you don't win unless you hate them, and then you destroy yourself.") The speech was emotional and rambling. "What kind of a man is this really?" Bush wondered to himself. "Caring for no one and yet doing so much."

After the Nixons had left for California and Ford had been sworn in as the nation's thirty-eighth president, Bush got a call from Bill Timmons, the Nixon legislative aide who was now a Ford adviser. Would Bush be available to come back to see Ford to discuss the vice presidential nomination? On Sunday, August 11, 1974, the two men met for thirty-one minutes in the Oval Office, sitting across from each other on the sofas that were arranged perpendicular to the fireplace. Bush allies were running an informal campaign for the post; Jim Baker, for instance, came in from Houston to talk Bush up around town, and other supporters worked the phones.

In the Oval Office, at Ford's request, Bush walked through his résumé for vice president. "Phi Beta Kappa economics, Yale, East and West, successful in business, Ways and Means, finances in order, knowing the business community, press relations, politics, UN." Ford took all this in, and then they discussed other possible vice presidents, including Barry Goldwater and Nelson Rockefeller. Bush was cool about both men, saying that he "worried about [the] divisions in the party from either right or left" if Ford chose one of them. "I kept coming down on the middle ground," Bush recalled, and—always his mother's son—he fretted that he was being too self-promotional. "It sounds like you're building yourself up, making your own case all the time," he thought to himself.

"Mr. President, it's a funny position I guess I [am] in, making this pitch," Bush said as he left, "and I hope it wasn't too strong."

"Not at all," Ford said. "I asked for it."

"No matter who you pick, you will have my total support," Bush said, looking Ford "right in the eye."

"George, I don't have any doubt about that at all," Ford said.

Within Ford's circle, Bryce Harlow had been tasked with presenting the new president with a memorandum on the most likely candidates. After assigning points for "national stature," "executive experience," and "ability to broaden [Ford's] political base," Harlow ranked Bush first, followed by Rogers Morton, John Rhodes, and Bill Brock. Nelson Rockefeller was in fifth place. Bush, Harlow wrote, was "strongest across the board"; the only caveat, Ford recalled, was that "some of my advisers regarded him—unfairly, I thought—as not yet ready to handle the rough challenges of the Oval Office." For Ford, the choice came down to Bush, Rockefeller, and Don Rumsfeld, whom Ford knew from the House and who was currently in Brussels as NATO ambassador.

On Sunday morning, August 18, 1974, Bush's prospects took a hit in the press. Citing unnamed sources, *Newsweek* reported that Bush faced "potential embarrassment in reports that the Nixon White House had funneled about $100,000 from a secret fund called the 'Townhouse Operation'" to Bush's 1970 Senate campaign. The Watergate special prosecutor would ultimately clear Bush, but any charge of possible corruption in the climate of the time was damaging. When he heard about the story, Bush called the White House with a gracious message for the president. The report, he said, "could be an embarrassment to President Ford, and that President Ford should know this before he decided who his Vice President is going to be."

The waiting ended on the morning of Tuesday, August 20, 1974, when Ford called Bush in Kennebunkport to let him know the next vice president of the United States was going to be Nelson Rockefeller. It was a miserable moment. "Yesterday was an enormous personal disappointment," Bush wrote Jim Baker.

Bush went to Washington to see Ford. In the Oval Office on Thursday, August 22, the president was warm and told Bush the decision had been "very close." Ford's next question: "What do you want?"

Bush's first suggestion was that he be considered as secretary of commerce, but Ford appeared uninterested in that possibility. Two diplomatic posts were mentioned: either ambassador to the Court of St. James's or envoy to China. As the conversation drifted on, they talked about Bush's becoming White House chief of staff, but Ford said that he was determined to run a decentralized shop, which made the top staff job less appealing. They talked about the ambassadorship to France and also came back to China. "I told [Ford] that I was very interested in foreign affairs," Bush recorded in his diary. "I indicated that way down the line, maybe 1980, if I stayed involved in foreign affairs, I conceivably could qualify for Secretary of State. The President seemed to agree."

The August 22 meeting ended inconclusively. Bush left Washington for Kennebunkport, the decision in the president's hands. After the weekend, on Monday, August 26, Ford called Bush at midday. Ford had talked to Kissinger and believed that, of the diplomatic options, "the one that is the best for you is China." Bush agreed, but not without raising another scenario once more: What if he were to come in as Ford's White House chief of staff? Ford was polite but firm. "He seemed to think that matter was still alive though he thought going to China was much better for me," Bush told his diary. "I am inclined to agree with that."

Such was Bush's contemporaneous account, in his 1974 diary, of how he became the envoy to China. In memory (notably in his 1987 autobiography, *Looking Forward*), Bush cast the choice to ask for China as a bold, adventurous stroke that he, not Ford, had first suggested as an exotic alternative to London or Paris. In truth, Bush had first asked for a cabinet post (Commerce) and then inquired about becoming White House chief of staff.

Bush's recast version enabled him to view the decision for China as the same kind of moment he and Barbara had faced in 1948 about going to Texas or remaining in the East. "Back then we decided not to do the traditional thing, but to head for the West," Bush recalled. "We now agreed that if the President gave me a choice of overseas assignments, the thing to do was head for the Far East. An important, coveted post like London or Paris would be good for the resume, but Beijing was a challenge, a journey into the unknown."

After Watergate and after losing the vice presidential nomination, he wanted to feel the way he had felt at the United Nations, not at the Republican National Committee. Bush's worst day as UN ambassador now seemed better than his best day as RNC chairman. In Bush's mind he had risked all for the party, and for what? He had again been passed over for vice president. His integrity had been anonymously attacked in the press. He was not the president's first choice for chief of staff. Given this run of bad luck, why not embrace a chance to broaden his foreign policy experience far from Washington and hope that he would again be seen as a rising statesman rather than as a professional partisan? Bush, in sum, needed China itself at this point.

After a brief experiment without a strong chief of staff in place, meanwhile, Ford appointed Don Rumsfeld to the post, putting Rumsfeld at the center of the White House action. It was the job that Bush had been interested in—another instance, along with the choice of Ford's vice president, of Bush and Rumsfeld finding themselves rivals under the same flag.

As Bush prepared to leave for the Far East, Kissinger wanted to make one thing clear to him: "There'll be some substantive work from time to time, but for the most part you'll be bored beyond belief." In light of the recent past, Bush was willing—even eager—to take that chance. Once a man had survived Watergate, how bad could anything be? "What the hell," Bush said to a reporter. "I'm fifty. It won't hurt anything."

SIXTEEN

Am I Running Away
from Something?

★

People stare at you. Gather around the car. Look at you. Once
in a while smile. No hostility but tremendous curiosity.

—GEORGE H. W. BUSH, on life among the Chinese

CHINA WAS AN HONORS CLASS in diplomacy and politics for Bush,
an education in the realities of subtlety, respect, and indirection
so often fundamental to relations between nations. In Congress
and at the United Nations, Bush had learned that diplomacy required
personal connection. In Beijing, he learned that it also required persis-
tence and patience—particularly patience, which was not his strong suit.
The man who came to China liked action, movement, phone calls, *results*.
The man who left China understood that diplomacy was a long game
and that change could come rapidly or glacially depending on the circumstances of a given country and given situation.

Richard Nixon's shadow still fell over nearly everything. In late September 1974, when the Bushes arrived in Anchorage, Alaska, en route to
China, Bush received a message to call Watergate special prosecutor
Leon Jaworski in Washington. According to a transcript of a White
House tape, a Nixon fundraiser had claimed that Bush had been approached to raise $30,000 for the Watergate burglars but had refused.
(The story was not true.) "The incident itself is not important except
that here I was leaving the United States, last point of land, and a call
[came] out of the ugly past wondering about something having to do
with Watergate, cover-up and all those matters that I want to leave behind," Bush told his new China diary.

The question of why he was flying around the globe was not far from
his mind. "In going to China I am asking myself, 'Am I running away from
something?' 'Am I leaving—what with inflation, incivility in the press and

Watergate and all the ugliness?' 'Am I taking the easy way out?' The answer I think is 'no' because of the intrigue and fascination that is China."

Classic global balance-of-power issues prevailed during Bush's time as envoy. There was, in April 1975, the fall of Saigon, the last tragic act of America's long and unsuccessful war in Vietnam, and Bush worked hard to convince not only the Chinese but other Pacific nations that the U.S. withdrawal from Vietnam did not signal a return to isolationism. In the context of the time, Bush's anxiety was that Chinese Communist influence could spread through Asia, particularly to Cambodia, the Philippines, and North Korea. Yes, China hated the Soviets and urged the United States to be powerful—but only because a powerful United States helped China by distracting Moscow. "China keeps wanting us to be strong, wanting us to defend Europe, wanting us to increase our defense budget, etc.," Bush dictated in July 1975. One lesson of his China experience was that American engagement was crucial if America wanted markets, allies, and, perhaps above all, stability. In Asia and around the world, America needed to be visible but not pushy, muscular but not domineering.

On the Bushes' first night in Beijing, they went to bed early in the American residence in the People's Liberation Army–guarded foreign diplomatic compound. (Bush was officially head of the U.S. Liaison Office, or USLO.) The heat in the apartment was stifling; as Bush put it, Barbara "got snoring again just like West Texas." He got up to turn off the heaters and plugged in a Sears humidifier. "End first night," Bush told his diary. "Lots of new sights and sounds and smells. Don't drink the water. The soap is good. The eggs are little. Short-wave makes a lot of whistling sounds—sounds just like 30 years ago."

The difficulty of his work made Bush all the more eager to do well. As he put it, one of the office's chief tasks was to discern what was unfolding inside the opaque world of Chinese politics: *"Was some leader not mentioned in a news story about the dedication of a new building in his city of birth? Was a Chinese deputy minister sent to an international conference, instead of his boss? Why hasn't so-and-so been heard from in over three months? Who's up, who's down?"* The ambassador from Nepal told Bush something that stuck with him. "I've been here ten years," the envoy said, "and I think I actually know less about the Chinese than when I arrived." As Bush put it, Chinese diplomats could turn "the cryptic phrase into an art form." There were, he said, three ways a Chinese official might reject a request—"all polite," Bush noted, but all insurmountable. If a meeting was said to be "not convenient," the Chinese were saying it would not happen until "hell freezes over." If a meeting was accepted "in principle," it "meant don't hold your breath." And if a meeting was described as "possible, but it might take a while," you might wait, Bush said, "five to twenty years," since "a while" meant something very different to the Chinese than to Americans.

After more than a decade of making deals in the business world, of running four campaigns in six years, and of serving as UN ambassador and as party chairman, Bush was perhaps most struck not by what he found in China but by what was missing: a ringing telephone. "I haven't gotten a phone call in a week—imagine that!" Bush wrote his children in late October 1974. Writing Jim Baker, he asked how Nelson Rockefeller was working out as vice president. "Maybe I'm better off out here," Bush wrote, "though [the vice presidency] would have been a whirlwind"— and Bush loved a whirlwind.

He had been on the ground for less than a week when he changed mission policy. In its desire to control as many aspects of the American–Chinese relationship as possible, the State Department had instructed Bush's predecessor, David Bruce, not to attend the different embassies' national day celebrations, occasions that offered an American envoy the opportunity to mingle with Chinese diplomats and officials. Bush, who wanted to meet more people and try to build bonds of affection and respect, broke with the instruction and cheerfully made the rounds, becoming a fixture on the diplomatic scene.

Bush's belief in personal diplomacy was not shared by the realpolitik secretary of state. "It doesn't matter whether they like you or not," Kissinger once told Bush, who could not have disagreed more. In October 1974, Bush dictated a telegram to Kissinger at the State Department announcing his new outgoing approach. The Bushes then struck out for a reception hosted by the Algerians. The ambassador from Algiers, Bush recalled, "looked like he was going to fall over in a dead faint when he saw us arrive." Later that evening Chiao Kuan-hua, the Chinese diplomat who had denounced the United States at the United Nations in 1972, hosted the Bushes at a banquet. There was some substantive talk ("He raised the question of oil and we discussed that," Bush recalled) and a discussion of an impending Kissinger visit. Now the foreign minister, Kuan-hua was anxious to repay Bush for an old debt of hospitality: Kuan-hua had been among the Chinese that Bush had hosted at his mother's house in Greenwich one Sunday in the UN years.

Everything was absorbing, exciting, new. The Bushes largely eschewed the chief of mission's chauffeured car, preferring to join the throngs of the city's bicyclists. Always a somewhat eclectic dresser—when he was not wearing a suit, Bush could show up in almost any combination of clothes—he would put on a People's Liberation Army hat, a self-described "Marlborough country wool jacket" (he meant "Marlboro," as in the cigarette, not "Marlborough," as in the ancestral family of Churchill), and mount his bike. The majordomo of the envoy's official residence, Mr. Wong, told Bush that both he and Barbara were known, fondly, as "Busher, who ride the bicycle, just as the Chinese do." (Bush's bike bore a novelty Texas license plate that read, simply, GEORGE.) A Mr. Lo at the nearby commissary said that Bush was "getting to be a legend in [his] dress." There was a method to Bush's eccentricity. "They are not themselves as open and outgoing but they are warm and friendly,"

On their preferred mode of transportation in Beijing, 1974–75. His assignment as envoy to China immersed Bush in the diplomatic arts of patience and indirection.

said Bush, "and I remain convinced that we should convince them . . . that Americans are not stuffy, rich and formal."

Though he was having a good time bicycling around Beijing and trying to understand the Chinese regime, Bush wanted a better sense of what was happening in Washington. He wrote Bill Steiger to ask his old congressional friend to arrange for different offices on Capitol Hill to add Bush to their newsletter mailing lists.

Kissinger arrived in late November 1974. Bush watched in amazement as a bevy of security agents preceded the secretary of state out of his big plane. "So many," murmured the Chinese government interpreter Nancy Tang, who was standing with Bush at the arrival ceremony. The Bushes joined the Kissingers—Henry's wife, Nancy, had traveled with her husband—at a cluster of guesthouses. (The Bushes were assigned the same quarters, number eighteen, where the Nixons had stayed in February 1972.) The accommodations were comfortable—and wired for sound. When Barbara was preparing to mail a letter, she said aloud, "Everything's here but the glue [for the stamps]." No Chinese were in the room. The next day a bottle of glue was.

Bush was fascinated by the Kissinger style, which could never be his own. "Kissinger is brilliant in these talks," Bush recalled of meetings with Vice Premier Deng Xiaoping and others in the autumn of 1974. "Tremendous sweep of history and a tremendous sweep of the world situation." Less appealing to the intrinsically polite Bush was Kissinger's imperiousness. The secretary of state was overtly respectful of Bush—he believed the fifty-year-old diplomat was likely to remain an important man—but was less so with his own team. "His staff are scared to death of him," Bush told his diary. "The procession is almost 'regal.' People quake, 'He's coming. He's coming.'" Kissinger wanted what he wanted when he wanted it.

If Bush was afraid that he was out of sight, out of mind, in Washington, he had to have been reassured by Kissinger's interest in Bush's thinking about the future. "He asked how long I planned to stay," Bush dictated. "This is the second reference he has made to it. I had in my mind that he was probing to see what my political plans were."

Bush answered honestly: He just didn't know. There was no clear upward path at the moment. "I told him I had no political plans, that I thought the ticket for '76 was locked in with the appointment of Rockefeller, which I do, and that I had no plans at all," Bush said. Kissinger pressed the matter further. "Kissinger made some reference to my running for President in 1980," Bush dictated. Kissinger was wise to keep an eye on this political man, one who could be both self-interested and self-deprecating. By coming to China and enhancing his statesmanlike credentials, Bush was maneuvering for future advantage subtly rather than showily. It was the kind of move Kissinger appreciated and admired.

Christmas was coming, and Barbara went home to Washington to spend the holidays with the children. "Great talks with Bar on the phone," Bush dictated. The family was in strong shape in these years: "no drugs, no dope, no crime, no troubles. We should knock on wood." He did hate that Barbara was gone. "It is right that Bar be there but boy do I miss her."

Dorothy Bush was due in China in the third week of December. "Mother arrives tomorrow," Bush told his diary. "I have that kind of high school excitement—first vacation feeling." After Mrs. Bush, now seventy-three years old, landed in Beijing, she took twenty minutes to freshen up, put on a PLA hat, and hit the streets of the capital, bicycling with her son. On the twenty-fifth, they had an American holiday meal—turkey and cranberry sauce—before Bush went off to a tour of "the caves" beneath the city that had been arranged for him by Deng Xiaoping.

It was a memorable Christmas Day. "Dig tunnels deep," Mao had ordered his people, "store grain everywhere." Mao's mission: to create a means by which his people might survive a nuclear assault from the Soviet Union. The result: a vast project to create enormous underground shelters across China. Bush was met at an intersection and taken to a clothing store, where his tour guide pressed a concealed button that operated a trapdoor. They climbed down into the tunnels. Bush walked from room to room. There was enough space, he thought, for thousands in this subterranean kingdom.

Bush climbed back out, emerged into the light of the store, collected his bicycle, and pedaled home. His mother asked about the tour, and Bush detailed the project to her. "Her comment was that it was an odd Christmas gift: an invitation to visit a bomb shelter on a day dedicated to the spirit of peace on earth," Bush recalled. Her son, however, did not think the day at all strange. "By that time . . . I'd been in China long enough to know that my hosts left little to chance or accident in dealing

with foreigners," Bush said. "The Chinese were out to make a point—
that they are vigilant against the Soviets, and ready for any turn of world
events, even the worst." A people prepared to go underground in order
to endure a nuclear holocaust was a people with the longest of views.
Patient, persistent, and determined, the China that Bush was learning
firsthand was a China that bent only when it chose to bend. They saw
history—they saw reality itself—differently than the West. And now
Bush could see those things through their eyes.

Bush heard about the fall of Saigon not through official channels but
during a national day reception for the Netherlands on Wednesday,
April 30, 1975. The Americans were finally pulling out, defeated after
the long and grueling war to save South Vietnam from the Communist
North Vietnamese. Bush watched as three North Vietnamese officials at
the reception ("three little guys about four feet high," Bush told his
diary) "rushed happily out of the room" at word of the American evacuation from Saigon. Soon he heard the sound of celebratory firecrackers
coming from the North Vietnamese embassy.

As he absorbed the news of the first war America had lost in her nearly
two-hundred-year history, Bush fell into conversation with the diplomat
John Small of Canada, who argued for American resilience in the face of
the defeat. "It is important that the U.S. stand firm in Korea [defending
South Korea against Communist North Korea], and it is important that
this [American] slide and decline be halted," Small told Bush, alluding
not only to Saigon but to America's economic recession and post-
Watergate distrust of government. "The American people," Small added,
"must understand that as soon as America doesn't stand for something
in the world, there is going to be a tremendous erosion of freedom."

The pop of Communist firecrackers only deepened the impression
that John Small's exhortation to American engagement and greatness
made on Bush. In the ensuing weeks and months, Bush would watch as
different Pacific nations usually inclined to the United States came to
call on Beijing, seeking an alliance if America were to pull back from the
region after Saigon. We must remain engaged, Bush urged Washington,
before a post–Vietnam War Asia found a "new alignment" against
American interests. In diplomacy, Bush was learning, one could take
nothing for granted and had to pay constant attention by courting even
insignificant-seeming countries. You never knew when a nation that had

been far from your mind—in this case, Thailand and the Philippines—was going to be of critical importance.

On the Fourth of July, 1975, the Bushes threw an enormous party for the diplomatic community. A week before, in a telegram with the subject line THE GREAT HOTDOG ROLL CRISIS, Bush asked the State Department for emergency assistance to send seven hundred hot dog buns and one hundred bags of potato chips to China. (The bureaucracy got in gear, and everything arrived in time.) The Bushes also held a baptism for Doro, who was sixteen but whose christening had been scheduled and postponed many times over the years. The language of the liturgy had to be translated by a very unhappy atheistic interpreter, but the Bushes were delighted when the ministers of the makeshift congregation told Doro, "We will love you and always miss you."

Kissinger returned to China in October 1975, this time to prepare for President Ford's own planned trip later in the year. In a series of sessions with Deng Xiaoping, Bush listened as Deng and Kissinger jousted over what China believed the United States should be doing in the world. "His complaint—incredible as it might sound—was that the United States was showing weakness in the face of the Soviet threat to world peace," Bush recalled. Deng even invoked the analogy of Munich, accusing the United States of pursuing a policy of "appeasement" with the Soviets. "A country that spends $110 billion for defense cannot be said to be pursuing the spirit of Munich," Kissinger replied. "Let me remind you that we were resisting Soviet expansionism when you two were allies, for your own reasons."

During a meeting with Deng in the Great Hall of the People, Kissinger and Bush received word that Mao himself was ready to see them. "You will meet with the Chairman at six-thirty," Deng said after reading a note that had been handed to him. It would be Bush's first encounter with the legendary Mao. In the chairman's villa, they found the eighty-one-year-old barely able to speak. Kissinger asked how he was doing. Pointing to his head, Mao replied, "This part works well. I can eat and sleep." Tapping his legs, he said, "These parts do not work well. They are not strong when I walk. I also have some trouble with my lungs. In a word, I am not well." With a smile, he added, "I am a showcase for visitors."

Bush sat next to Kissinger, who was at Mao's left hand. "I am going to heaven soon," Mao said. "I have already received an invitation from God."

"Don't accept it soon," said Kissinger.

"I accept the orders of the Doctor," Mao replied, a wry allusion to Kissinger's PhD.

Kissinger then turned serious. "I attach great significance to our relationship," he said. Mao held up one hand in a fist and the little finger of his other hand. "You are this," he said, gesturing to the fist, "and we are that," waving the little finger.

Yet we have common foes, Kissinger said.

Yes, Mao wrote, in English, on a piece of paper.

They spoke of Taiwan; Mao said the issue would be settled eventually, in "a hundred" or perhaps "several hundred" years. By now Bush understood the vernacular in which Mao was speaking. The Chinese, Bush noted, "see time and their own cultural patience as allies in dealing with impatient Westerners." They spoke, too, of a current problem in the relationship that Mao dismissed as a *fang go pi,* or a "dog fart." It was an expression, Bush thought, that might have even impressed Harry Truman. Bush saw Mao just once more, during Ford's 1975 visit to China. Receiving the president late on a December afternoon, Mao noticed Bush standing nearby. "You've been promoted," Mao remarked to Bush, telling Ford: "We hate to see him go."

Bush's journey home began, in a way, when White House chief of staff Don Rumsfeld started drafting a long memorandum to the president in the summer of 1975. It was an unsettled time in Washington. Ford was unhappy with his national security team—Kissinger was still doing double duty as secretary of state and national security adviser—and worried that Ronald Reagan might challenge him from the right in the 1976 primaries.

Rumsfeld understood the president's concerns. After asking his deputy Dick Cheney to keep an eye on the reelection campaign, Rumsfeld drew up different scenarios to get Ford ready for the coming year. In late October the president caught a cold, and Rumsfeld took advantage of Ford's time in the family quarters to make the case for a series of changes to strengthen the administration and put the president in a better political posture for 1976.

The fate of Vice President Rockefeller was central. Since at least

1964, when Goldwater and his conservative followers had triumphed at the Republican National Convention in San Francisco, the GOP had been split into three broad factions. There were the "movement conservatives" (Goldwaterites who professed a strict antigovernment philosophy and a hard-line policy against the Soviets); moderate conservatives (men such as Ford, who favored fiscal probity but were more accepting of the public sector's role and were open to a détente, or diplomatic flexibility toward the Soviets); and the dwindling number of liberal Republicans (embodied by Rockefeller).

The hero of movement conservatism was Ronald Reagan, the good-looking former lifeguard, sportscaster, movie actor, television host, and corporate spokesman who had delivered the landmark televised speech for Goldwater in 1964 on the same night Bush had gone on the air with the anti–Ralph Yarborough broadcast. Born in Tampico, Illinois, in 1911, to a religious and theatrically inclined mother and a charming but hard-drinking shoe salesman father, Reagan had been a self-described "hemophiliac Democrat" (he had voted for FDR four times and campaigned for Truman) before converting to conservatism over high taxes, excessive government, and the Communist threat. In the 1950s he was the public face of General Electric, hosting its popular weekly TV series *GE Theater* and traveling the country to speak to GE employees about the virtues of free enterprise and the evils of statism. A gifted political performer in person, on radio, and on television, Reagan personified the growing power of the movement conservatives. A 1976 primary campaign between Ford and Reagan would be a test of where the party stood ideologically.

Ford knew this much even before the primary voting began in early 1976: The movement conservatives who loved Reagan were incapable of accepting Rockefeller, their longtime nemesis from New York, as a member of a national ticket headed by a moderate conservative such as Ford. Ford himself might be acceptable—the movement was not yet in complete control of the GOP—but the combination of a moderate and a liberal would be anathema to the Reaganite bloc. The numbers were revealing: In a mid-September 1975 Harris Poll, 25 percent of Republicans said they would not vote for Ford if Rockefeller were the vice presidential nominee. It was, Ford recalled, an "ominous" piece of data. "In his past Presidential campaigns, he'd established a reputation as a liberal, and he had outraged many ultra-conservative Republicans," Ford wrote.

"Apparently, their antagonism wasn't going to fade away." Ford was right, and he realized that he had to do something about it. On Tuesday, October 28, 1975, in their weekly Oval Office meeting, Ford and Rockefeller discussed the conservative rebellion within the party.

"Mr. President, I'll do anything you want me to do," Rockefeller said. "I'll be on the ticket or I'll be off the ticket. You just say the word."

"There are serious problems," Ford said, "and to be brutally frank, some of these difficulties might be eliminated if you were to indicate that you didn't want to be on the ticket in 1976. I'm not *asking* you to do that, I'm just stating the facts."

"I understand," Rockefeller said. "Well, it's probably better that I withdraw. If I take myself out of the picture, that will clear the air. I'll give you a letter saying that I don't want to be considered as a Vice Presidential nominee."

Removing Rockefeller from contention in 1976—he would stay on as vice president until January 1977—was only one of the decisions Ford reached in the last days of October 1975 as he restructured the administration. The president disliked Secretary of Defense James Schlesinger, a Nixon holdover, who was asked to resign. Rumsfeld left the White House to take over at Defense; Dick Cheney moved into Rumsfeld's post as chief of staff; and Kissinger gave up the national security adviser role to Brent Scowcroft, an air force lieutenant general. Elliot Richardson returned from London to become secretary of commerce, giving the Rockefeller wing of the party something to take the sting out of the decision on the vice presidency. And William Colby left as CIA director.

Colby's replacement? George H. W. Bush, who first learned about it on Saturday, November 1, 1975. A telegram from Kissinger arrived in Beijing while the Bushes were out bicycling. "The President is planning to announce some major personnel shifts on Monday, November 3, at 7:30 P.M., Washington time," Kissinger wrote. "Among those shifts will be the transfer of Bill Colby from CIA. The President asks that you consent to his nominating you as the new Director of the Central Intelligence Agency."

Bush was flabbergasted. CIA? The agency's public image was of an intelligence service gone mad. Senator Frank Church, Democrat of Idaho, was leading a damaging investigation into the darker elements of the CIA's record, and there were parallel hearings on the House side, under the leadership of Congressman Otis Pike, Democrat of New

York. In post-Watergate, post-Vietnam Washington, the agency had become infamous for illegal covert operations, failed assassination plots against foreign leaders, and domestic spying (including on the anti–Vietnam War movement). Public confidence was low, as was morale at Langley, the CIA's headquarters in northern Virginia.

Bush handed the telegram to Barbara. Her only reaction: "I remember Camp David." Just four words, but they contained multitudes. She had not wanted him to leave a diplomatic assignment to take the Republican National Committee job in the fall of 1972, a time when Watergate threatened to overwhelm the party. And yet he had. Now it was all happening again, a request from the White House to, as Bush put it, "return to Washington and take charge of an agency battered by a decade of hostile Congressional investigations, exposés, and charges that ran from lawbreaking to simple incompetence."

Barbara already knew what was going to unfold. For her husband the matter was decided with the phrase "The President asks." Bush knew it, too. "The President had asked, and as long as what he'd asked me to do wasn't illegal or immoral, and I felt I could handle the job, there was only one answer I could give."

He would do his duty. That did not mean, however, that he could keep gloomy thoughts at bay. His political career seemed over. "In the best of times the CIA job wouldn't be considered a springboard to higher office, if only because the director of the agency has to be nonpolitical," Bush recalled. "Anyone who took the job would have to give up any and all political activity. As far as future prospects for elective office were concerned, the CIA was marked DEAD END." Even Deng joked about news of the appointment, telling Ford, who visited China in the first days of December 1975, "You have given him a post that is not considered to be very good," provoking laughter. "You're talking like my wife, Mr. Vice Premier," Bush replied.

Why Bush for CIA? Why not leave him in place through the election or send him—the former entrepreneur—to Commerce, rather than Elliot Richardson, a lawyer? For forty years, well into the twenty-first century, Bush and his friends believed that Don Rumsfeld and the politics of 1976 were to blame. With Rockefeller off the ticket because of pressure from the Reaganites, Bush, having come so close to the number two spot in 1974, would be a likely prospect for the ticket at the Republican National Convention in Kansas City in 1976, should Ford fend Reagan off. The same held true for Rumsfeld, who had also been in the final round of three with Rockefeller and Bush. The theory in political circles in late 1975 was that Rumsfeld had engineered his own move to the Pentagon to gain national security experience (he had plenty of domestic expertise from his jobs under Nixon) to position himself for the vice presidential nomination. Concurrently, the thinking went, Rumsfeld had manipulated Ford into pushing Bush to the CIA, widely considered, as Bush put it, a "political graveyard" from which he could never rise. As "point man for a controversial agency being investigated by two major Congressional committees," Bush recalled, he would be so scarred that the "experience would put me out of contention, leaving the spot open for others"—chiefly, according to the Bush circle's theory, Rumsfeld. Rogers Morton, the former congressman and incumbent commerce secretary who was leaving to manage Ford's campaign, believed this was precisely what had happened, as did others. "I think you ought to know what people up here are saying about your going to the CIA," a former House colleague said to Bush. "They feel you've been had, George. Rumsfeld set you up and you were a damned fool to say yes."

In face-to-face meetings with Bush both Rumsfeld and Ford denied any such machinations. "I want you to understand something," Ford said to Bush at the time. "Rumsfeld is being accused of keeping you from being in the Cabinet and wanting to push you off to the side out at CIA. That is not true, George." After this conversation in the Oval Office, Bush had a moment with Rogers Morton. "Man," Morton said, shaking his head, "Rummy just got your ass."

Or had he? Always real, the George H. W. Bush–Donald Rumsfeld rivalry began back in their days in the House when both were young Ivy League military pilots competing to rise in the party of Richard Nixon. (The two men were overtly friendly. The China-bound Bushes, for instance, loaned the Rumsfelds a car, a purple AMC Gremlin with denim seats, in 1974–75.) Each had been in the running for the vice presidency in 1974 when Ford chose Rockefeller, and then Ford chose Rumsfeld rather than Bush to be White House chief of staff less than a month later.

The legend of the self-interested Rumsfeld-engineered Bush CIA appointment endured for more than four decades. Yet it is likely that this oft-cited cause of the tension between the two men is founded on a misunderstanding about what really happened in the complicated politics of late 1975. According to Dick Cheney, the Rumsfeld deputy who was to be White House chief of staff in the new order, the Ford restructuring initially called for Elliot Richardson, the former attorney general and current ambassador to Great Britain, to become director of the CIA. In this scenario, Bush was to return from China and join the cabinet as secretary of commerce to set Bush up for a likely place as Ford's running mate on the 1976 ticket.

Then Ford personally switched Richardson and Bush's names—but not, according to Cheney, because of Rumsfeld's intervention or ambition (though Rumsfeld was happy to see it happen). Bush went to the CIA and Richardson to Commerce, Cheney recalled, because the president wanted to offer Henry Kissinger a gesture of respect and accommodation in what was, for Kissinger, an uncomfortable moment. Kissinger's old patron Rockefeller was being deposed, and Kissinger himself was giving up the national security adviser portfolio. To assuage Kissinger, who disliked Elliot Richardson, Ford sent Richardson to Commerce, which had few dealings with State, and Bush, whom Kissinger could deal with, to the CIA, which had so many. Ford's impression of the sensitivities of Henry Kissinger, not the ambitions of Donald Rumsfeld, was what had most likely led to a Bush political disappointment in the Age of Ford—and to a feeling of tension between Bush and Rumsfeld that never went away.

Duty was duty, however, and Bush was ready to accept the new challenge. In his Sunday, November 2, 1975, cable to Kissinger agreeing to the CIA post—one also addressed to Ford—Bush wrote: "Your message came as a total and complete shock. . . . Henry, you did not know my father. The President did. My Dad inculcated into his sons a set of values that have served me well in my own short public life. One of these values quite simply is that one should serve his country and his President."

Kissinger's reply: "You are a great patriot."

SEVENTEEN

George Bush, Super Spook

★

It's a tough, mean world, and we must stay strong.
—GEORGE H. W. BUSH

Our life has changed.
—BARBARA BUSH

IN RETROSPECT, THE CIA JOB seems a natural part of the Bush résumé, an important and desirable assignment in the life of a man who
had been thinking of the presidency since at least the mid-1960s.
The reality of the time, however, was different. In submitting to President Ford's request, Bush thought he was consigning himself to electoral
oblivion. The hope of his life—to be president, to climb the highest tree,
to win the greatest of all matches—appeared to be over. Duty to country,
understood as compliance with the wishes of the president, was to trump
the dreams of the individual.

From China, Bush sent a message to his mother and to his children.
"The President has asked us to leave China," Bush wrote from Beijing.
"He wants me to head the CIA. I said yes. This new job will be full of
turmoil and controversy and Mum and I know that it will not make
things easy for you. Some of your friends simply won't understand.
There is ugliness and turmoil swirling around the agency obscuring its
fundamental importance to our country. I feel I must try to help."

Replying for the Bush children, George W. wrote back: "I look forward to the opportunities to hold my head high and declare ever so
proudly that yes, George Bush, super spook, is my Dad and that yes I am
damn glad for my country that he is head of the agency."

On Capitol Hill, Senator Church and other critics worried that Bush
was too partisan and too eager to please his superiors—a combination
that might put the agency at the political disposal of the White House.
Little could be more frustrating for Bush. In his mind he was sacrificing

his political career by going to the CIA at the request of the president, only to be attacked for being too political.

He arrived home at an abysmal hour for the CIA. As Bush recalled the sequence of events in his 1987 book *Looking Forward,* on Thursday, November 20, 1975, the Church committee released a report detailing assassination plots against Fidel Castro and Patrice Lumumba of the Congo. On Thursday, December 4, Church claimed that the CIA had played a role in the coup against Salvador Allende in Chile in 1973. On Monday, December 15, the Pike committee asked the administration to detail the agency's covert involvement in the Angolan civil war—and three days later the Senate cut off funding to the pro-Western forces there. On Tuesday, December 23, Richard Welch, the CIA station chief in Athens, was murdered on his doorstep after being outed as an operative in the Greek press.

Bush's confirmation hearings were held on Monday and Tuesday, December 15 and 16. "Now, let us assume you are appointed," Senator Thomas McIntyre, Democrat of New Hampshire, said to Bush. "Let us assume we are moving three or four months down the campaign trail. . . . What if you get a call from the president . . . saying, 'George, I would like to see you.' You go to the White House. He takes you over in the corner and he says, 'Look, things are not going too well in my campaign. This Reagan is gaining on me all the time. Now, he is a movie star of some renown and has traveled with the fast set. He was a Hollywood star. I want you to get any dirt you can on this guy because I need it.' Now, what are you going to do in that situation?"

"I do not think that is difficult, sir," Bush replied. "I would simply say that it gets back to character and it gets back to integrity. . . . If I were put into that kind of position where you had a clear moral issue, I would simply say no." Again and again, the committee's Democratic majority returned to Bush's political future, pressing him to pledge absolutely that he would not be on the ticket in 1976. (They apparently did not share Bush's view that heading the CIA in this period meant an end to national political advancement.) He would not do it. The White House had asked Bryce Harlow to work on the Bush nomination. After a head count, Harlow returned with his verdict. "They want a blood oath you won't be on the ticket next fall," Harlow told Bush. "Otherwise I don't think we've got the votes."

No, Bush said. It was too much; they were just trying to humiliate him and tie Ford's hands. Harlow listened, then repeated himself: "They still want it."

"I won't do it," Bush said.

Fearing the nomination would fail, Bush agreed to a compromise. The president, not Bush, would make the pledge. "I know it's unfair," Bush told Ford, "but you don't have much of a choice if we are to get on with the job of rebuilding and strengthening the agency." On Thursday, December 18, 1975, Ford sent Senator John Stennis of Mississippi, the Armed Services chairman, a letter promising that Bush would not be a candidate for vice president in 1976. The committee supported the nomination 12 to 4 (McIntyre, Gary Hart of Colorado, Patrick Leahy of Vermont, and John Culver of Iowa voted against Bush).

On the Senate floor, Bush won confirmation 64 to 27. Among the first to congratulate Barbara in the Senate gallery was Mrs. Frank Church, a friend, who told Barbara that the senator had not meant anything personal in his opposition. "I don't think the average American understands that in Washington you can be friends with your political opponents," Barbara wrote. Potter Stewart swore the new director in at Langley on Friday, January 30, 1976. President Ford made a point of being there. So did Donald Rumsfeld and his wife, Joyce.

A memorandum from four senior CIA officers shaped Bush's first decision. The document had an unambiguous title: "Where You Should Sit." There were proposals for Bush to make the Old Executive Office Building his main office or perhaps to create an "intelligence community" structure in downtown Washington, away from the CIA's headquarters at Langley. *Any move by a [Director of Central Intelligence]," the memorandum said, "that could be interpreted as an attempt to disassociate himself from CIA would be destructive indeed."* (The italics were the authors'. They wanted to make themselves very clear.) Bush agreed. "Going through the southwest gate of West Executive Avenue every morning, with a reserved White House parking place, would be good for the image," Bush recalled, but not so good for the substance of his new job. "The message had to say, 'I'm on your side, we're in this together.'"

Bush moved into the director's seventh-floor office at Langley, a sparely furnished room that offered splendid views of the northern Virginia countryside. Bush worked hard to raise morale at the agency. Re-

*As CIA director from 1976 to 1977, Bush restored morale to a battered
American intelligence community. He took the post believing he was consigning
himself to what he called a "political graveyard."*

ferring to the newspapers and the congressional investigators, he asked
his senior staff: "What are they trying to do to *us*?" He was one of them,
he was saying. He would stand by them.

At home—the Bushes had moved back to northwest Washington—
the CIA sent men out to add extra locks and bolts to the doors. The
Bushes' mail was no longer delivered to the house but to the agency.
Packages that arrived at the house were not to be opened unless expected
or from someone they knew. There were family concerns throughout the
year. George W. had been planning a trip to Saudi Arabia on oil business,
but the CIA advised against the journey, citing safety issues. "We are sick
about it, but they feel that this is just the kind of thing or opportunity
the terrorists are looking for," Barbara wrote Jeb and his wife, Columba,
in July 1976.

A chauffeured Chevrolet with a CIA security officer picked Bush up
every weekday morning at seven thirty. Most days the car took Bush
from northwest Washington out to Langley, where the director often
went through the front door, flashed his ID badge, and walked past the

marble walls where rows of simple stars anonymously commemorated the CIA personnel killed in action. By ten to eight he would be at his desk on the seventh floor, reviewing overnight cables. He met weekly with Ford and Scowcroft. Many days were taken up with congressional testimony (Bush appeared before Senate and House committees fifty-one times in his year as director). If he could, he spent his lunch hour jogging three miles outside or, in the event of rain or cold, on an indoor track in the basement at Langley. Late in the afternoons, he often dropped by the State Department to spend some time with Kissinger, just checking in and chatting about the day. By seven P.M., if the social calendar was clear—and it often was, since Bush declined to attend overtly political functions—he would head home to Barbara.

At the CIA, for the first time since their marriage, Bush could not talk openly with his wife about his day or about what was on his mind. This official silence unnerved Barbara, who had grown accustomed to proximity and partnership in New York and in Beijing. "I can't believe it, but I think that George is working longer hours than ever," she wrote in February 1976. Her favorite part of the week came on Sundays, when Bush was at home and they had guests over for lunch. "I must confess that he adores the work," she wrote a friend in the diplomatic corps in China in July. "I say confess for I am not too mad about his job for he can't very well share it with me, darn it all!!!" The lighthearted tone was forced. She was, she recalled, "very depressed, lonely, and unhappy" in the first six months or so of 1976. "I felt ashamed," Barbara recalled. "I had a husband whom I adored, the world's greatest children, more friends than I could see—and I was severely depressed. I hid it from everyone, including my closest friends. Everyone but George Bush."

Nothing since Robin's death had been this awful. He was a patient husband; his wife was a permanent part of his world, a fixed force, and he responded to her in these months out of love and duty. "Barbara had depression, serious depression," Bush recalled. "We didn't really know much about it. She wouldn't confide in others." She did confide in him, and he urged her to put away her embarrassment and consult a doctor. "He would suggest that I get professional help, and that sent me into deeper gloom," recalled Barbara. "He was working such incredibly long hours at his job, and I swore to myself I would not burden him. Then he would come home, and I would tell him all about it. Night after night George held me weeping in his arms while I tried to explain my feelings."

In Washington, they spent late hours in much the same way they had spent those terrible months in Midland after Robin died. In the darkness there were tears, and uncertainty, and a sense of inconsolable loss. Yet there was also warmth, and his arms, and the reassuring reality that he was with her, and always would be. "I almost wonder," Barbara wrote, "why he didn't leave me." "Almost" was the key word. At a deep and fundamental level, she knew that George Bush loved her. However much he traveled, however much he seemed consumed by the great game of politics, however much the concerns of others—the moving men, the staff, anybody—appeared to take precedence over hers, Bush was driven by loyalty and by commitment. The vicissitudes of marriage, particularly of marriages that began in youth, were real. There is no doubt that the Bushes had bad days through the years. Bad days were part of the deal, inescapable yet endurable. And the Bushes endured.

Nineteen seventy-six was among the most difficult hours. "Sometimes the pain was so great, I felt the urge to drive into a tree or an oncoming car," Barbara wrote of that year. "When that happened, I would pull over to the side of the road until I felt okay." Then she would drive on, arriving home, where she knew that her husband would be before long—a husband she believed so dazzling and wonderful that his powers extended to the alleviation of thoughts so dark they could turn suicidal. "It seems so simple to me now: I was just the right age, fifty-one years old, for menopause; I could not share in George's job after years of being so involved; and our children were all gone," Barbara recalled. "I was a classic case for depression. My 'code' told me that you should not think about self, but others. And yet, there I was, wallowing in self-pity. I knew it was wrong, but couldn't seem to pull out of it. I wish I could pinpoint the day it went away, but I can't. All I know is that after about six months, it just did. I was so lucky."

As was her husband, who loved her and needed her.

The CIA post moved at a much more rapid clip than the United Nations, the Republican National Committee, or China. The range of concerns that Bush confronted at Langley was evident from one of his Thursday morning briefings with the president in March. Bush first discussed an impending trip to Europe and the possible effect the congressional investigations were having on the CIA's relationships. ("Some of those who have cooperated with us have been genuinely concerned," Bush told Ford.) Bush raised the possibility of coups in Thailand, Argentina, and Peru.

In 1976, Bush was furious about the steady leaks about the CIA from the investigating committees on the Hill. As he remembered it, he confronted too many messages on too many mornings detailing the damage such reports were causing to agency assets and relationships. "Four Latin American countries drastically reduced their contact with the CIA, citing press leaks," Bush recalled. One Eastern European source active "since 1972 stopped cooperating with us, out of fear of publicity and exposure"; a "Communist-bloc diplomat" who seemed cooperative "broke off all contact after saying he couldn't risk working with an intelligence agency whose internal affairs were in the news every day."

On Wednesday, June 16, 1976, Francis E. Meloy, Jr., the American ambassador to Lebanon, was assassinated in Beirut, prompting what Bush recalled as "the most important intelligence estimate I ever brought before the President and the [National Security Council]." As Bush recalled it, the issue was whether Ford should order a general evacuation of Americans from Lebanon. In a tense meeting in the Situation Room in the basement of the White House, Ford was joined by Kissinger and Scowcroft. They were seated. Bush was on his feet, relaying information from the ground and presenting aerial images of possible escape routes for Americans then in Lebanon. As Bush recalled, the "assassination signaled a new, more dangerous level of terrorist activity in Beirut—enough to warrant instructing the U.S. embassy there to advise all American nationals in Lebanon to leave the country."

One thing Bush took away from the Lebanese crisis was an appreciation for the way Brent Scowcroft handled himself in the role of national security adviser. As a man who himself liked to ask questions and weigh every option, approaching issues without many, if any, ideological presuppositions, Bush recognized Scowcroft as a kindred spirit. The respect was mutual. Scowcroft had admired Bush for several years. "He was genial and thoughtful," Scowcroft recalled, "and it was no easy task to navigate Washington as well as he did at the end of the Nixon administration." When Bush went to China, he and Scowcroft grew closer. "Kissinger frankly didn't have time to hold his hand out there," recalled Scowcroft, "and so I got to know Bush better as his liaison, if you will, with the administration when he was out in Asia."

As the agency's overarching concern, the Soviet Union brought Bush into contact with the kinds of hawkish conservatives who believed Ronald Reagan, not Gerald Ford, should be trusted with the security of the nation. Détente with Moscow had been the order of the day since 1969, when Nixon and Kissinger took over American foreign policy. After August 1974, Ford carried on Nixon's engagement with the Soviets, eschewing, as had Nixon, harsh Cold War rhetoric in an ongoing diplomatic bid to ease tensions between the superpowers. Cold War hawks (including Reagan, the patron saint of the hard-liners) distrusted the Soviets; Cold War moderates (including Nixon, a recovering Cold War hawk) were convinced that there was something to be gained by negotiation and arms control agreements.

February 1960 had marked a little-noted turning point in the history of the Cold War when the CIA issued a National Intelligence Estimate that suggested the Soviets were not the offensive threat Americans had long believed them to be. According to NIE 11-4-59, "The Soviet armed forces are intended in the first instance to deter attacks on the USSR and other communist states, and to insure survival of communist power should such an attack occur. . . . They are probably *not* intended for any consistent and far-reaching policy of outright military conquest." As noted by Raymond L. Garthoff, a historian writing for the CIA's Center for the Study of Intelligence, the chief of Air Force Intelligence dissented strongly.

This clash of views within intelligence, governmental, and academic circles over Soviet objectives and Soviet strength had endured through the Kennedy, Johnson, and Nixon administrations. Conservative observers, many from outside the government, believed the CIA underestimated Soviet capacity and ambitions. From the Pentagon, the new secretary of defense, Don Rumsfeld, was pushing for a harder line on the Soviets, as was Reagan out on the Republican primary campaign trail.

Bush acknowledged the conservative sentiment on Wednesday, May 26, 1976, when he approved the idea of the formation of a "Team B" to write a complementary—and almost certainly competing report at the same time the standard group of intelligence professionals produced its annual estimate of the Soviets. "Let her fly!! O.K. G.B.," Bush wrote on the proposal. "One intelligence veteran" later told *The New York Times* that Bush had made a mistake with Team B—that it was "a bad idea that he permitted in the interests of getting along with everybody."

Yet Bush's job as CIA director, as he often said, was not to make policy but to produce intelligence as a means to guide the policy makers. "Getting along with everybody" in this context was not a bad thing. Under the circumstances, it was wisest, Bush decided, to keep the right-wingers close, to allow them to examine the data that the CIA had, and see what they came up with. The results were evident to the world on the day after Christmas, 1976, when *The New York Times* reported that "New C.I.A. Estimate Finds Soviets Seek Superiority in Arms." The story quoted a "top-level military intelligence officer" saying that the Team B analysis "was more than somber—it was very grim." The front-page headline was hard to miss.

"All the evidence points to an undeviating Soviet commitment to what is euphemistically called the 'worldwide triumph of socialism,'" Team B wrote, "but in fact connotes global Soviet hegemony."

As it turned out, Team B overestimated Soviet strength and nuclear intentions. The exercise energized the right wing in American foreign policy, partly setting the intellectual stage for the defense increases of the Reagan years—which, though no one could know it at the time, would be the Reagan-Bush years.

In late June, Jimmy Carter, the presumptive Democratic presidential nominee, had approached President Ford with what CIA historians noted was an unusual request: The former Georgia governor asked the president for the courtesy of intelligence briefings before the Democratic National Convention. After consulting with Scowcroft and Bush, Ford decided to dispatch Bush himself to a series of meetings with Carter through the general election.

Bush met Carter in Hershey, Pennsylvania, for an initial conversation on Monday, July 5, 1976. Deputy Director Richard Lehman accompanied Bush to Pennsylvania and supervised the preparation of the briefings themselves. In the Hershey meeting, Lehman recalled, Carter's questions covered subjects "from the future of Rhodesia to morale in the Agency."

Bush traveled to Plains, Georgia, to meet with Carter at the Democratic nominee's house later in July. (Kissinger was due the next day to brief Carter on foreign policy.) To reporters beforehand, Carter said he hoped Bush would brief him on "confidential information concerning Lebanon and the Middle East, Rhodesia, South Africa, and South Korea, plus the interrelationships between the United States, the Soviet Union, and China."

The meeting with Carter lasted nearly six hours. According to CIA records, for the first half hour the discussion touched on "Lebanon, Iraqi-Syrian relations, strains between Egypt and Libya, the Taiwan Straits, Rhodesia, the Cuban presence in Angola, and developments in Uganda." The rest of the day was taken up by the Soviet Union and the Strategic Arms Limitation Talks.

Two weeks later, on Thursday, August 12, 1976, Bush returned to Plains with eight agency experts. The CIA contingent had some time to kill before they saw Carter at his home, and so they paid a visit to his campaign headquarters. There they encountered Carter's mother, Miss Lillian Carter. When Miss Lillian learned the delegation had come from Langley, a CIA memo reported, she said "Jimmy was going to clear the government of all vestiges of Republicans, including . . . Bush."

Bush was polite and unfazed. The CIA delegation traveled the short distance from town to the Carters' house on Woodland Drive, where the Democratic nominee met them. Bush led a conversation, CIA records show, that touched on Soviet conventional forces, the Backfire bomber, the SS-X-20 missile programs, and the status of arms control negotiations; developments in China; Greek-Turkish and Egyptian-Libyan tensions; a Rhodesian raid into Mozambique; Somalia and Djibouti; action at the demilitarized zone in Korea; and Lebanon. The briefing did not end until five P.M.

The Ford-Carter general election was a closely contested race. "Now I find myself thinking too much about going home," Barbara wrote after a preliminary house-hunting trip to Houston in October—a sign that the Bushes, at least privately, believed they were not long for Washington. Ford made a noble stand against Carter, but finally could not prevail, losing 50.1 to 48 percent on Tuesday, November 2, 1976.

Bush called Carter on the Friday after the election to congratulate the president-elect and to resign as CIA director. He said that the two should meet in order for Bush to brief Carter on "exotic and very closely held items relating to sources and methods." Carter accepted both the resignation and the overture to get together. According to CIA records,

Bush offered to send along a letter making his resignation official, but Carter said that "was not necessary and thanked Bush for his call."

Two Fridays later, on November 19, Bush returned to Plains with six senior CIA officials. The day began with a small forty-five-minute session in the Carters' living room with Carter and Vice President–elect Walter Mondale. Sitting on the Carters' sofa, his back to the bay windows, Bush raised the question of his own retention as director. Though he had offered his resignation two weeks earlier, Bush wanted to talk the issue out.

No incoming president had replaced the incumbent CIA director upon assuming office since Eisenhower had named Allen Dulles to the job in 1953. None of Eisenhower's successors—Kennedy, Johnson, Nixon, and Ford—had made an immediate change at the agency, the idea being that the job should seem impervious to partisan political shifts in power. After raising the question with Carter, however, Bush proceeded to argue against his own proposition. He understood that the new president almost certainly needed to choose a new director, someone in whom Carter had total confidence and with whom he could create an atmosphere of trust.

Carter agreed, saying, "Okay." The matter was closed. Bush would go. But why had Bush opened the door to staying on to serve a Democratic president? There were several reasons. He liked the job. He liked the people. And he liked the power. "He has never enjoyed a job more," Barbara wrote. And like many other CIA veterans at the time, Bush believed the appearance of bipartisanship would be helpful to Langley— a vote of confidence in the direction the CIA had taken in the past year.

Carter was uninterested. He wanted to move on. His objection to retaining Bush, even for a time, was that Bush was "too wedded to existing structure to be an agent of change" within the intelligence community. "If I had acceded to his request, then he would not have been president," Carter recalled decades later, alluding to the fact that a man who had served in the Carter administration would have been an unlikely candidate for the Republican national ticket in 1980.

After the directorship question was settled, Bush briefed Carter on a range of "highly sensitive" operations and assets. Carter, Bush wrote in a memorandum of the meeting, "never indicated that he thought these operations were good or bad, that he was surprised or unsurprised. He registered no emotion of any kind." Bush also warned Carter about trusting the telephone too much, alluding to "the Soviet capabilities to read phone calls . . . and to penetrate in many ways."

At one point during this final briefing in Plains, the new president alluded to what he clearly thought was the departing director's new career path. When an issue arose that a CIA officer said would require action around 1985, Carter interrupted. "I don't need to worry about that," Carter said. "By then George will be President and he can take care of it." As Bush recalled, a "half smiling" Carter then nodded at Mondale across the room and added, "Either George or Fritz Mondale there."

The Bushes spent some time in Florida at the turn of the year. The bluefish were biting, and Barbara was elated that Bush had trusted her choice of house in Houston, signing the papers on her word alone. There were different options for the new year on the table as they unwound in the sun. "Pop has made no major decisions about the future," Barbara wrote, "but he has been offered many exciting things and I can see that spark coming back when he talks of the future."

In his year at Langley, Bush had raised morale in the wake of the work of the investigating committees, providing a needed lift to a deflated agency. He also received an education about national security that would have been difficult to impossible to replicate in any other job. "You learn what the intelligence community really is," Bush recalled of the CIA posting. "You learn what it can do and what it can't and what it should not be asked to do. You know the importance of human intelligence, and you know the limitations of human intelligence. You begin to understand the science and technology, the S&T departments, the satellites and all of that. Being there you get a realistic view of our intelligence and its capabilities. You can count the divisions and know where they were, but you couldn't measure intent as well as you would like." One could, in other words, learn what was knowable, but even the finest intelligence service had its limitations and could not foresee every eventuality.

For now, such things were someone else's problem, someone else's privilege. In January 1977 the Bushes returned to Houston. It was the first time since his election to the House a decade before that George Bush was a private citizen. "I wonder," Barbara asked her diary, "if George will ever be happy at home again??"

PART V
The Age of Reagan

1977 to 1989

★

I . . . thought that it was prudent—and important for the
country—for the vice-president to play as large a role in the
affairs of the administration as possible.

—RONALD REAGAN

On January 22, 1981, President Ronald Reagan and Vice President George Bush held the first of their many Thursday lunches. (They favored Mexican food.)

EIGHTEEN

A President We Won't
Have to Train

I'm so digging in, so tense. . . . Just this one goal . . . no time to
think at all. That troubles me a little bit. Drive, drive forward.

—GEORGE H. W. BUSH, campaigning for president, 1979

Bush has to be "acceptable" to Right Wing—
not necessarily "favorite of."

—JAMES A. BAKER III, in a private 1980 campaign note

HOUSTON BORED HIM. "I went home and couldn't figure out
what the hell to do," Bush recalled three decades later. "There
[have] been withdrawal symptoms," he wrote a friend in early
1977. "I've been tense as a coiled spring—hopefully not a shit about it,
but up-tight." He lived in terror of becoming . . . well, of becoming ordinary. "There is a missing of stimulating talk," Bush wrote an old friend.
"I just get bored silly about whose daughter is a Pi Phi or even bored
about who's banging old Joe's wife. I don't want to slip into that 3 or 4
martini late late dinner rich social thing. There is too much to learn
still."

He tried, a little, to be happy in repose, speaking warmly of "normalcy," of the fun of the new house, of his grandson George P., Jeb and
Columba's little boy. Yet Bush was too driven, too ambitious, too restless, to remain still. He understood himself well enough, he wrote a
friend, to know that "somehow I will churn until I can find the formula
to be involved, to be *doing*."

In Houston, the Bushes had bought a house on Indian Trail, and the
First International Bank became Bush's home base. He chaired the executive committee and took an office there with the expectation that he
would work for the bank one day a week in Houston, attend a monthly
meeting in Dallas, and fly to London three times a year. He maintained

his membership in the Council on Foreign Relations and joined the Tri-lateral Commission, a group of leaders in Japan, Europe, Canada, Mexico, and the United States that met around the world to talk over global issues. He accepted invitations to give speeches, both paid and gratis, in Alaska, Massachusetts, and Florida.

He was careful about the appearance of cashing in on his government service, refusing a directorship with McDonnell Douglas, the aerospace company. There was another road not taken in these months when Bush declined an offer from Ross Perot to run Perot's oil business in Houston. "I'll pay you a lot of money," Perot told Bush, who considered the idea. ("This was before Ross became really strange," Bush recalled.) The Bushes and the Perots were friendly, and the Perots once visited Kennebunkport as the Bushes' guests. "I thought about it," Bush recalled. When he did his due diligence with mutual acquaintances, however, Bush found no support for the idea of going to work for Perot. "I talked to some people, and they said, 'For God's sake don't do that.' So I said no, and thanked him profusely for thinking of me."

"Well, this is your big mistake," Perot said, according to Bush. Speaking of himself in the third person, Perot went on: "You don't say no to Ross Perot."

Everything Bush was doing—the business, the travel, the speeches—was directed toward the next goal, one that he spoke of with close friends only weeks after the Carter inauguration. He knew in his bones what he wanted to try next. He wanted to seek the presidency.

It would not be easy. Andrew Card, a young Republican representative in the Massachusetts legislature, was asked to set up a pre-1980 fundraiser for Bush in Springfield, Massachusetts. Card prevailed on friends of friends to host an afternoon tea. After driving to Hartford, Connecticut, to pick up the candidate, Card arrived with Bush in Springfield for the event. The sign in the living room read: WELCOME GEORGE BUSCH.

"Looks like I need to work on the name recognition thing," Bush said, plunging forward, fixing his lopsided grin on his face, grabbing for every hand.

Bush made his character his platform. He was a man of notable experience, of sound judgment, of even temperament, of measured optimism. In his decade or so of public service he had watched the presidency up close and could make a case that he was, in the words of the nascent Bush campaign, "A President We Won't Have to Train"—a jab at Jimmy Carter, who was seen by many Republicans as a presidential novice, and a nod to concerns about whether Ronald Reagan, nearing seventy and seemingly extreme in his views, was up to the challenges of the Oval Office. The George H. W. Bush who was planning to offer himself to the country for 1980 was very much the George H. W. Bush who had grown up and come of age in a political world shaped more by a commitment to service than by a contest of ideas. He was a moderate conservative—to the right of Nelson Rockefeller (and of where Prescott Bush had stood) but a bit to the left of Ronald Reagan and the movement conservatives who were gaining strength in the GOP.

By 1979–80, the movement conservatives were driven by God, Mammon, and an absolutist view that American strategy toward the Soviet Union should be rollback, not détente. In the wake of the *Roe v. Wade* Supreme Court decision in 1973, religious conservatives were also becoming more politically active, calling for constitutional amendments banning abortion and allowing prayer in public schools. Economically, Reagan's followers—and Reagan himself—had been converted to the theory of "supply-side economics," which held that tax cuts would stimulate so much economic activity that tax revenues would actually rise if rates were lower.

All things being equal, Bush favored giving the private sector primacy of place in matters of economics. He seemed moderate compared to Ronald Reagan, who offered the Republican Party a sunny Goldwaterism, but Bush, like Reagan, believed in lower taxes, fewer government regulations, and a muscular foreign policy. The two men disagreed on abortion (Bush was more moderate on the issue) and the primacy of tax cuts (Bush feared that drastic reductions in taxes without spending restraints risked higher deficits and possibly inflation). They agreed on much else, differing mainly in tone. Reagan was sure and certain, Bush often charming yet diffuse.

Bush acknowledged that he was neither wonk nor ideologue. He saw politics more in terms of consensus than of ideology. One ran for office—and did what partisanship required to win elections—in order to amass power to serve the larger good. For Bush, the work of government was less about radical reform than it was about careful stewardship.

Reagan viewed politics differently—as a clash of convictions, not a consensus to be discerned. Since his days on the road as a spokesman for General Electric in the fifties, making the case for free enterprise and against collectivism either at home or abroad, Reagan was a candidate of ideas—abiding principles grounded in experience that Reagan drew upon in order to judge the wisdom or the folly of proposed courses of action. Reagan's ability to project great conviction gave him the necessary room to maneuver when the time came, as it almost always did, for compromise in political life. Movement conservatives accepted Reagan as one of their own, and were willing to forgive—or sometimes even ignore—his occasional lapses from the conservative creed.

No such mercy was on offer for Bush. His inability to project great conviction, even when he was, in fact, greatly committed to a given principle, was a perennial problem. Movement conservatives did not think he was one of them, and so whereas Reagan could nearly do no wrong in their eyes, Bush could nearly do no right. If Bush succeeded in becoming president, he would do so because he had convinced enough voters that he was the kind of man—not only that, but the particular man—who could be trusted to make the big calls. *Trust me,* Bush was saying. *I am what you want and what you need, even if I can't quite define what I am pithily or precisely.* It was, in a way, the most elemental of political arguments, and it was the argument that Bush would make in national politics for the rest of his life.

George H. W. Bush was not the only member of the family pondering politics in 1978. George W., now thirty-one and living in Midland, announced his candidacy for the U.S. House seat being vacated by the retirement of George Mahon, a Democrat. "The primary will be very difficult," Barbara wrote, but if George W. were to win the nomination, he would have a good chance at victory in November. His mother, however, worried not only about his chances but about what his campaign might mean for his father. "You know, I wonder if George Bush, Jr., understands just how difficult it is to have two people thinking about running for office in one family?" she wrote her friend Millie Kerr from Kennebunkport in September 1977. George W. would be asked about his father's positions, and vice versa, in their opponents' constant search for controversy. The Bushes had been here before. "It reminds me of the time that George took all the heat when his father was in the U.S. Senate and voted against the oil industry," Barbara wrote.

Bush never weighed in directly on whether his son should make the race. He did, however, ask George W. to go see Allan Shivers, a conservative Democrat who had been governor of Texas in the late 1940s and for much of the 1950s. Was young Bush planning to run against Democratic state senator Kent Hance? Shivers asked. George W. said he "was seriously considering it," and Shivers's reply was succinct. "Son, you can't win." As George W. recalled it, "There was no encouragement, no nothing. . . . I remember wondering why Dad had introduced me to the governor. Looking back on it, it may have been his way of telling me, without smothering my ambition, that I should be prepared to lose."

In the fall of 1977 George W. brought Laura Welch home to his parents; the two were to marry in a small ceremony in Midland on November 5. Laura was introduced to the Bushes on the same day Columba and Jeb's second-born, Noelle, was baptized in Houston. The Bushes felt as though everything were right with the world when they met Laura. "They are perfect for each other!!!" Barbara wrote of the young couple.

George W. Bush's 1978 House race led to one of the earliest skirmishes of the 1980 presidential campaign. Ronald Reagan's political action committee, Citizens for the Republic, intervened in the younger Bush's congressional primary by endorsing and supporting Bush's Republican opponent, Jim Reese, the former Odessa mayor who had lost a bid for the House seat in 1976. After the Reagan blessing, Reese garnered sufficient votes in the primary to force a runoff with George W. Though George W. finally won the nomination, the Bushes blamed the Reagan endorsement for the runoff. A "Washington Whispers" item in *U.S. News & World Report* said, "A Ronald Reagan–George Bush ticket for the Republicans in 1980? Party leaders who like the idea now say personal animosity between the two all but rules it out."

The autumn of 1978 brought one last round of campaigning for GOP midterm candidates before the Bushes turned their full attention to Iowa, with its caucuses on January 21, 1980, and to New Hampshire, with its primary five weeks later, on February 26.

In the Midland congressional campaign, George W.'s general election opponent, Democrat Kent Hance, mounted an anti-elitist, anti-carpetbagger campaign against the younger Bush like the one Ralph Yarborough had run against his father fourteen years before, with Hance explicitly attacking the Bush lineage. "A large part of his campaign was against Big George & his membership in the Trilateral Commission," Barbara wrote in a campaign diary. It worked: George W. lost, 52 to 48 percent.

Jim Baker, meanwhile, came up short in a race for Texas attorney general. Bush's friendship with Baker had helped the talented Texas lawyer move into national circles. In May 1975, when Bush was in China, Rogers Morton, the secretary of commerce, had called with a question: What would Bush think of Morton's asking Jim Baker to become undersecretary of commerce? "I told him, after discounting my objectivity cuz of friendship, that I thought you would do just great," Bush wrote Baker. "It's a high level job with some freedom for politics and plenty of contact with business leaders."

Baker took the Commerce post. He went on to become President Ford's delegate hunter against Reagan at the closely contested Republican National Convention in Kansas City in 1976 and, finally, Ford's general election campaign manager against Jimmy Carter. Two years later Baker had decided on the run for attorney general. Bush advised Baker to try for governor instead, arguing that Democrats in Texas were not yet ready to pay enough attention to down-ballot races to break with their traditional party. Bush's analysis turned out to be correct. "He was right," Baker recalled, "and I was wrong." Baker retreated to Florida for a breather, but Bush was on the phone in a matter of days. "Let's get cracking," he said. It was time to run for president, and Bush needed his old friend to take charge. Baker said yes, and the campaign began.

The Republican politics of 1980, as manifested in 1978–79, was defined and dominated by Ronald Reagan. It was Bush's fate to be a conservator in a contest against the great conservative crusader of the age. Bush appeared to be a man of the center largely because, in Reagan, he found someone to his right within the Republican Party.

The cherished favorite of the Sun Belt and Western conservatives, Reagan was the putative front-runner for the nomination after the Carter victory in 1976. In late 1978, Bush and Jim Baker traveled to Los Angeles to pay a courtesy call at Reagan's office in Century City. The news Bush had to deliver—that he was going to run for president—was not unexpected, and Reagan received them politely but distantly.

Reagan himself had to address two broad questions to secure his own chance to take on Jimmy Carter in 1980: Was the former California governor too old to serve competently in the Oval Office? And was he too ideologically extreme to be president? Because these issues could not be resolved except in the campaign itself, there was room for candidates other than Reagan to fight to position themselves as the most plausible alternative to the front-runner. In addition to Bush, the options included former Texas governor and Nixon Treasury secretary John Connally; Senators Bob Dole and Howard Baker; and Congressmen Phil Crane and John Anderson, both of Illinois.

Bush was attacked as yesterday's man—a moderate in a party that was growing more conservative, a Washington insider in a climate that favored outsiders, an Ivy Leaguer too soft to make the hard calls. "Bush should avoid being labeled as 'moderate' or 'Northeastern' or 'Ford' candidate," read an early internal campaign document. Bush instead staked out his position as what the press called "the thinking man's candidate," saying: "Call me a conservative, but one with compassion." And he was—but he was also a politician who knew what it took to win, and winning against Reagan required convincing enough Republicans that Reagan was "a great old dog, but he won't hunt this year," as Bush political director David Keene put it to reporters.

Note the key adjective: "old." The degree to which age was an issue in 1980 was illustrated by a pro-Bush scenario sketched out by James B. "Scotty" Reston of *The New York Times*: "George Bush's hope is that Messrs. Reagan and Connally will knock each other out because they're too old and that the party will have to turn in a convention deadlock to younger men."

Bush jogged constantly during the campaign and spoke, endlessly, of being "up for the '80s." A Bush brochure made the age point about as explicitly as one could without calling Reagan senile: "George Bush is the right age. He will be 56 at the time of the 1980 election. This is the age which business, professional and educational organizations recognize as the time of maximum executive ability. This is the age when the individual reaches the peak of mental capacity." In interviews, Barbara volunteered that Bush was "the perfect age" for the job. "I don't question

Reagan's health or stamina or his intellectual capacity to handle issues," David Keene said after Reagan officially kicked off his campaign in November 1979. "But he may be unable to field tough questions and develop sophisticated positions under the pressure of a campaign"—which, when one thought about it, could only be because of issues of health, stamina, or intellectual capacity.

Still, this was Ronald Reagan. Sixteen years before he had captured the hearts and minds of movement conservatives with his speech "A Time for Choosing." Twelve years before he had posed a surprisingly formidable challenge to Richard Nixon for the 1968 nomination. Four years before he had come within a handful of delegates of denying a sitting Republican president the nomination of his party. How could Bush, with his tiny national name recognition, compete?

Jimmy Carter had shown the way by catapulting himself from obscurity to success by winning the Iowa caucuses in 1976. On an early campaign memo, Jim Baker jotted a note to himself: "Key to winning is: Start early and develop an organization better than any of the opponents. . . . Carter did it. Primary elections are won by organization!—almost regardless of candidate." On the ideological question, a stray note in Baker's hand in his 1980 campaign files summed it up: "Bush has to be 'acceptable' to Right Wing—not necessarily 'favorite of.'"

Bush made the obvious official in a speech at the National Press Club in Washington on Tuesday, May 1, 1979. "Ladies and gentlemen," Bush began, "I am a candidate for President of the United States. . . . I seek this nomination as a lifelong Republican who has worked throughout his career, in business and in public office, on behalf of the principles of Lincoln, Theodore Roosevelt and Dwight Eisenhower."

The "lifelong Republican" phrase was a shot at Reagan and Connally, both Democrats turned Republicans. Bush then made an unusual point about himself: If Americans were looking for a crusade or for a comprehensive program, they should look elsewhere. "As a candidate for President," Bush said, "I am not promising" a New Deal, a New Frontier, or a Great Society. "But I do pledge a new candor," Bush said. "To be effective, leadership in the eighties must be based on a politics of substance, not symbols; of reason, not bombast; of frankness, not false promise. . . . As a candidate, and as President, I will speak not in terms of simple solutions but of hard choices."

He offered a largely conservative view of those choices. "The American people must be told the hard, unvarnished truth about the nature of our problems at home: That we cannot buy our way out of problems with expanded government programs. On the contrary, where government expands, our problems multiply."

He ended with Eisenhower:

> More than a quarter century ago, in his first State of the Union message to the Congress, one of the wisest and strongest of this century's Presidents said: "There is in world affairs a steady course to be followed between an assertion of strength that is truculent and a confession of helplessness that is cowardly. There is in our affairs at home, a middle way between the untrammeled freedom of the individual and the demands for the welfare of the whole nation. . . ." President Dwight Eisenhower then went on: "In this spirit we must live and labor: confident of our strength, compassionate in our heart, clear in our mind. In this spirit, let us turn to the great tasks before us."

Listening to Bush's announcement at the National Press Club, Scotty Reston of the *Times* took note of the Eisenhower allusions. "This was the first time in memory that Ike had ever been nominated for equality and immortality with Teddy Roosevelt and Lincoln," Reston wrote, "and it told something about George Bush's ideals."

What did it tell? That Bush, like Eisenhower, would engage in the means of politics in order to achieve the ends of power and public service. It was not all about service in the biblical sense of doing unto others or helping the poor: Either man could have rendered that kind of service without seeking the presidency of the United States. In Bush's case, he wanted to be the leader, to win whatever contest it was, because his father had expected it, his mother had encouraged it, and he longed for it.

Reagan's campaign strategy for the 1980 Republican nomination was largely defensive. "Our biggest opponent is us," Reagan campaign chief John Sears said in 1979. "If we do our job right, nobody can catch us." With a large lead, the front-runner's camp decided to limit Reagan's exposure to the happenstance of the campaign trail, which left Iowa, in particular, open for a Carter-like surprise for a candidate willing to give his all to the caucuses.

Bush was willing. His focus on the state paid off in May 1979 when he defeated Reagan in a straw poll in Ames. Of 1,288 voters, Bush won with 39.6 percent. Reagan came in second with 25.9 percent, followed by Howard Baker with 13.8 percent and Connally at 10.7 percent. "I've got a long way to go, both in Iowa and nationally," Bush said, "but it's a good psychological lift."

That was the good news. The bad news came the same day. The sponsor of the straw poll, *The Des Moines Register,* published a statewide survey taken in late April. In it Bush ran sixth out of seven contenders. A striking feature of the *Register* poll was a second-place finish by a man who was not in the race: former president Gerald Ford, who trailed Reagan by only three points and who buried Bush by a margin of twenty-five—all without being a candidate.

For Bush, Ford had been a factor from the start. From Jim Baker's first conversation with Bush about a 1980 presidential bid, Baker, who had managed Ford's 1976 general election race, had made his role in a Bush campaign contingent on Ford's approval. In December 1978, after Bush called him in Florida in the wake of the loss in the attorney general's race, Baker sought Ford's blessing. Ford gave it, telling Baker that he should work with Bush but adding: "It's going to be tough."

One of the things making life difficult for Bush was the speculation that Ford himself might challenge Reagan in 1980, either in the primaries or at the convention. If Reagan ran again, *Time* had written in November 1977, "top Republicans expect Gerald Ford, 64, no matter how much he relishes retirement, to jump in, largely out of loyalty to the anti-Reaganites who supported him in 1976." Ford was sending conflicting signals about making the race largely because he was himself conflicted. Polls had him defeating Carter in a general election heat. Moderates uncomfortable with Reagan and uninspired by Bush allowed themselves to dream of a Ford comeback. For Ford, it was all hugely tempting. Why shouldn't it be? He had only narrowly lost to Carter in 1976. Here was a chance, possibly, to be summoned from retirement to avenge a close-run defeat. It was worth thinking about.

Which Ford did—often aloud and in public. On Thursday, September 27, 1979, at the Washington Press Club, Ford said that in politics you "never say 'never,'" a point he repeated to a private gathering of two dozen Republican lawmakers. He was not a candidate, he said, but "that's not a Sherman." Ford was reading the same polls everybody else was reading—polls showing that he was the only Republican, including Reagan, who had a lead over Carter in a head-to-head matchup, 51 to 42 percent. (Reagan and Carter were in a statistical tie.) For now, in late 1979, Ford preferred to watch, ponder, and wait.

Bush, meanwhile, raced, raced, and raced, doing well in a cascade of contests in the waning months of 1979.

One event was billed, immodestly, as a "Cavalcade of Stars." In October, in Ames, at the field house of Iowa State University, 3,400 showed up for fifty-dollar boxed meals and eight-minute presentations from each of the candidates except Reagan, who, in keeping with his front-runner strategy, skipped the event. Bush won this second straw poll with 35.7 percent. Reagan received only 11.3 percent—what reporters called "a surprisingly low fourth," behind Howard Baker and John Connally.

Bush chalked up the win and pressed on. Three weeks later, in early November 1979, he won again, this time in a Maine straw poll, upsetting Howard Baker, who, with the support of his Senate colleague William Cohen, had expected to carry the day—and the subsequent headlines—at the state party convention in Portland. Bush had flown in, given his speech—every hopeful except Reagan was there—and returned to Texas. But a strange thing happened—strange, at least, for George Bush. By all accounts the momentum shifted from Baker to Bush on the strength of Bush's rhetorical performance at the Maine convention. (And not because of the Kennebunkport connection, which failed to sway many full-time Maine residents.) He had had enough of Carter-style brooding and self-abasement, Bush said, asserting, *The New York Times* reported, that it was time to "stop wringing our hands and apologizing for our country." The line brought the Maine Republicans to their feet, and Bush won.

Not bad, Bush was thinking, not bad. Finally he headed south, to the Florida Republican convention straw poll in Kissimmee. There were hot-air balloon rides (Dole had rented one, Bush two); free drinks (Baker's campaign offered double shots of whiskey); and CONNALLY—LEADERSHIP FOR AMERICA T-shirts. Lowering expectations, Reagan had called the poll "meaningless" before the voting. When he came in first, with 36 percent, he was happy to find all sorts of meaning in the results. Connally had spent $300,000 on the event in the hopes of bloodying Reagan and emerging as the chief challenger. The big Texan did come in second, with 27 percent, but the press played up an angle of the story that drove Connally mad: Bush's 21 percent, which *The New York Times* reported as "surprisingly strong" and *Time* declared "the surprise of the weekend." Bush himself was so shocked—pleasantly shocked, but shocked all the same—that he asked his staff to double-check. "Count 'em again," he said. "Count 'em again."

Iowa, Maine, Florida: Bush wasn't supposed to be doing this well. Now, in the wake of outright straw poll victories in Iowa and Maine and a better-than-expected performance in Florida, the political world was warily expressing a contingent appreciation for what Bush had wrought in 347 days of campaigning in 1978 and '79.

"Mr. Bush is the hot property right now," the *Times* wrote eight weeks out from Iowa. "I think Bush has a chance to win it here," said David Readinger, Connally's Iowa chairman. "Iowa had been the Democratic campaign surprise of 1976," Bush recalled. "Our game plan was to make it the Republican campaign surprise of 1980." Iowa was everything. "We bet the whole thing, really, on the caucuses," Bush recalled. "If we'd gotten killed there I would've been dead meat." If Bush were to succeed in his quest, he had to win, soon, in Iowa, on a winter Monday in January.

NINETEEN

We Have Done the Unthinkable

★

The action begins in Iowa. It's where
everything starts for everybody.
—GEORGE H. W. BUSH

LIFE WAS A SPIRALING, exhausting, endless succession of flights and
handshakes and speeches and coffees and airport press conferences and barbecues and Rotary Clubs and fundraisers and thank-
you notes and interviews and hotel rooms—and then it started all over
again the next morning, with another flight and another handshake and
another speech and another coffee and another airport press conference and another barbecue and another Rotary Club and another fundraiser and another school and another thank-you note and another
interview and another hotel room. And then another and another and
another and another and another and another and another and another
and another and another and another, and on and on and on, across
Iowa county after Iowa county, New Hampshire town after New
Hampshire town, Florida city after Florida city.

"I'm surprised my body can take it," Bush told his diary on Wednesday, October 10, 1979. "The mind is still clear, although I totally lose
track of where I've been and whom I'm with. I've given up on names."

Bush sent his traveling aide David Bates home for a rest. "He was just
dropping and drooping," Bush recalled. "I felt the same way but I was
just determined not to show it—determined to push on." There was no
break, no pause, no breather. There was only the goal. "I don't want to
look back," Bush told his diary, "and find I've left something undone."

The news in late 1979 played to Bush's strengths as a seasoned foreign
policy hand. The Soviet Union had invaded Afghanistan, reviving
Cold War tensions. In Tehran, revolutionaries deposed the American-
supported shah, installing the Ayatollah Khomeini as leader of a new

theocratic state and seizing the American embassy, taking fifty-two Americans hostage.

Given the chaos abroad, Bush, the former diplomat and CIA director, was an attractive presidential prospect. "I'm just so outraged by the humiliation of our country," Bush said of the Iranian situation. He underscored that he was a man who could be trusted in a dangerous time. "I see the world as it really is," Bush told audiences. "And it's tough out there." Implicitly dismissing Reagan's experience, he said: "I've been there, not lecturing on the Republican free enterprise circuit."

The family fanned out to tell the Bush story. The early states were manageable enough that the Bush-Walker clan could achieve a kind of political market penetration. Marvin moved to Iowa, Neil to New Hampshire. Doro took a leave from Boston College to attend secretarial school in order to be more useful at headquarters. Dorothy Bush and her daughter, Nancy Ellis, were amazed, but thrilled, that people would pay $150 to come to a reception with watercress sandwiches and white wine. In Iowa, Barbara was pleased to hear a caller on a radio show say, "I'm for George Bush—he has such a great family," only to realize that the caller was Marvin Bush. In a blazer, Neil worked crowds large and small. "Consider my dad," he would say. "He's going to knock 'em dead."

In 1978, when he and Columba were in Venezuela, where he was working for a Texas bank, Jeb had called his father to volunteer to work for the campaign full-time. Bush happily accepted, and Jeb moved back to the United States with his little family. "It was a blast," Jeb recalled. He started out by traveling with his father but was soon dispatched to campaign on his own. (After Iowa, he would run the Puerto Rico primary effort.) He was a relatively shy young man. "I really wasn't motivated by politics at the time," Jeb recalled. "I ended up overcoming fears and trepidations about politics, and I really did it for my dad."

Bush fretted that he had allowed his own mission to overwhelm everything—and everyone—else. "I look at Bar's schedule and I think it is too intense, too tough," Bush dictated. "She doesn't get home enough. We've overdone it." One night he encountered Barbara unexpectedly in the Des Moines airport; each was on the way to a different flight. They had not realized the other would be there.

Neil was engaged to be married, but "we've really said nothing about that, done nothing about it," George H. W. Bush told his diary. Doro had a boyfriend for the first time. "Yet, we haven't taken them out to dinner together—done any of the things that normally we do." The tumult of the campaign, though, created its own kind of intimacy. The family "is in close, in tight, doing well."

Everybody had an opinion about everything. When a friend raised the shortcomings of the candidate's speaking style—not a new subject—Bush thanked him for "taking the tough road and bringing up the 'not so easy things.' I am really grateful. I need help. I need advice. I need criticism. For me this goal is the end all—be all. I feel driven. Hopefully for altruistic reasons."

On a commercial flight from Puerto Rico to Miami in late 1979, Bush was seated "next to a boring guy that recognized me" and who was happy to have the chance to give a presidential candidate a piece of his mind. The passenger, Bush recalled, was "concerned about things—and I couldn't be less interested; and yet, I've got to smile and sit here.... 'Okay fellow, let's have your say—you solve all the problems.'" Yet then Bush felt guilty about yearning to be free of his fellow passenger. "That's what our system is about; so why shouldn't I be pleasant to this guy? . . . I think I'll have to hear him out and who knows, I may learn something."

Typical Bush: talking himself into enduring, even enjoying, something few people would be able to bear. That was, in a way, the essence of campaigning for president: making the best of a grueling slog. Bush's charisma was not overwhelming, but it was real; his charm was not electric, but it was enveloping. The willingness to listen to the guy on the plane, to feign interest in everybody's opinion, and to convince everyone he met that it was a treat to be with them were all vitally important weapons in Bush's political arsenal.

With its 2,531 precincts, each of which would hold a caucus, Iowa required the rawest of retail politics. A young Republican operative, Rich Bond, moved to the state to work for Bush in the late spring of 1979. Bush had important Iowa supporters who, along with Jim Baker, framed the caucus strategy; the core Bush group included George Wittgraf, Mary Louise Smith, John McDonald, and Ralph Brown. Every day Bond, who lived in Ames with his wife, Valerie, and four-year-old son Matthew, drove an hour to work at the Des Moines Insurance Exchange Building. From eight in the morning until ten at night, sitting with primitive lists from the 1976 caucuses, Bond would call every voter he could.

"I'm Rich Bond," he would say, over and over again. "I'm calling for George Bush, and he's running for president. You may not have heard of him. May I send you some information?" If the answer was yes, Bond would write a note, drop it off in the mail on the way home, and call them again a week later. "The vast majority of those Republicans never heard from the Reagan campaign," Bond recalled. "And the vast majority of them did hear from us—more than once. The Reagan campaign believed in a different model—radio and TV. I don't think they were boobs, by any means. They just had no idea what we were doing on the ground."

There were rough spots. One right-winger mailed a brick back to Bond in a return envelope—the campaign had to pay the postage—with a note that said, "We'll never vote for a Trilateralist." Yet there were more good days than bad days. Bond remembered the thrill of having, say, fifteen people show up to hear about Bush at a Council Bluffs Rotary Club meeting.

Bush press secretary Pete Teeley kept arguing that the candidate needed to do more to win national media attention, pushing him to give a big speech at the National Press Club in downtown Washington. Hearing him out, Bush replied, "There aren't any votes in D.C."

In Iowa with Teeley one day, Bush spent two hours at a coffee in the home of a supporter, talking to twenty-five, maybe thirty people. He gave a brief speech, took questions, and mingled as if he had all the time in the world. After saying his goodbyes, Bush climbed into the car with Teeley. "What'd you think of that event?" Bush asked.

"It was terrible," Teeley said. "You just wasted two hours—two hours—with thirty people. Go to the Press Club and you could reach millions with the coverage."

"Yeah, it was two hours and thirty people," Bush said, "but now they're all for me."

Bush spent twenty-seven days in the state; even Carter, who pioneered the Iowa strategy, had devoted only seventeen days to Iowa in 1976. Ninety-six of the state's ninety-nine counties got a visit from at least one member of the Bush family. According to an accounting by *Time* magazine, on the other hand, Reagan spent just forty-five hours campaigning in the state before the caucuses. In theory, limiting Reagan's exposure was an attractive, logical strategy; in practice, however, it was not working. Iowa polls had Reagan with the support of 50 percent of Republicans in December. By early January he had lost nearly half of those voters, polling only 26 percent to Bush's 17 percent.

In the first week of January, in a sign of political and financial progress, Bush moved from commercial air travel to a private twenty-seat Convair plane. "There are bigger shots running," Bush said on the trail in Henry County, Illinois. "But I've rolled up my sleeves and put together the best grass-roots team in the early states. And we're going to out-organize 'em, out-work 'em, out-spell-out-the-goals-of-the-country 'em." Things seemed better and better. "After doing well in Iowa," Bush said, "we're going to blow some of those bigger shots out of the water."

David Keene estimated to *Time* that Bush had improved from two out of ten speeches being good to seven out of ten. Bush himself had grown comfortable enough to joke that his stance on abortion—against federal funding, but also against a constitutional amendment, thus taking a more centrist position than Reagan—was "heroic."

On Monday evening, January 21, 1980, Iowa Republicans turned out at five times the rate they had four years before. From 22,000 in 1976, participation rose to 115,000. "I was sitting in this precinct," a Bush worker told *Time*, "and these people I never heard of came streaming in. And it was Bush, Bush, Bush." Bush dropped in on one caucus where he defeated Reagan soundly. "You made my night!" he said, but he did not yet know whether the evening was, in fact, his. For that he had to wait a bit longer.

Finally, the overall numbers came in, and the news was staggering. George Bush had defeated Ronald Reagan, 31.6 percent to 29.5 percent. Reagan learned the news at the home of friends in California, where he was having a quiet dinner and screening the Dustin Hoffman–Meryl Streep movie *Kramer vs. Kramer*. Victory night, Barbara recalled, turned the Bushes' hotel suite into a "madhouse." "How sweet it is!" she wrote. "How sweet it is!"

Bush, in exuberant shorthand, declared that he now had the "Big Mo." His excitement, which reminded some observers of a Yale cheerleader after a big win against Harvard, was understandable. Bush had not won the approval of a plurality of voters in a decade—not since the Republican primary for the U.S. Senate in Texas in 1970. The party at the hotel in Des Moines was packed. "It was a crush," Barbara wrote the greatest of crushes, the most spectacular of evenings. And it was, at that point, the biggest night of Bush's political life, a life that had begun in the Midland Eisenhower campaign nearly thirty years before. He had done something few men had ever done—something his father had never done: He had won an important battle in the larger war to become the president of the United States. "We have done the unthinkable when everyone put us down as an asterisk four months ago," Bush said.

For the moment, in the winter darkness in Des Moines, there was joy. Yet Bush knew that "there's a long way to go yet." For months, Bush had known something else, too. "Reagan is still tough out there," he said. "I respect his strength." Bush at last went to bed about one thirty. "On to New Hampshire," Barbara wrote in her diary—on to the next.

James Smith Bush, George H. W. Bush's paternal great-grandfather, graduated from Yale and became an Episcopal clergyman. After serving churches in New Jersey, San Francisco, and on Long Island, he was drawn away from his traditional faith to the transcendentalism of Emerson and Thoreau.

David Davis Walker, George H. W. Bush's maternal great-grandfather, attracted the patronage of a cousin, future Supreme Court justice David Davis, and became a successful dry goods merchant in St. Louis.

The family property known as Walker's Point, Kennebunkport, Maine, circa 1902.

S. P. Bush, Bush's paternal grandfather, was educated at the Stevens Institute of Technology and rose to become president of Buckeye Steel Castings in Columbus, Ohio.

George Herbert Walker, Bush's maternal grandfather, was a freewheeling businessman and financier who could be alternately impatient and generous. "He was kind of an up-and-down guy," George H. W. Bush recalled.

Lucretia "Loulie" Wear Walker, wife of G. H. Walker. A great beauty of her day, Loulie grew up in a Presbyterian household in St. Louis. Her husband, whom she called "Bertie," abandoned the Roman Catholic Church of his upbringing to marry her.

G. H. Walker with daughters Dorothy and Nancy at Wallter's Point.

Nancy and Dorothy Walker playing on the rocks at Walker's Point.

Bush's mother, Dorothy, was raised in a house of rambunctious brothers: Herbie, John, Jim, and Louis Walker.

Dorothy and Prescott Bush, who married in August 1921, on a shooting holiday at Duncannon, her father's South Carolina plantation.

The Bush family house on Grove Lane in Greenwich. Poppy Bush was chauffeured to and from Greenwich Country Day School; his childhood was shaped by affection and competitiveness.

Dorothy Bush on the tennis court. She once fell and broke her wrist in the middle of a point—but finished the match.

A championship golfer, Prescott Bush became a favorite partner of President Eisenhower's when Bush served in the U.S. Senate in the 1950s.

Dorothy, Poppy, Nancy, Jonathan, and Prescott Bush on the steps at Grove Lane in the 1930s. Poppy, Jon Bush recalled, had an "innate empathy" for others and earned the nickname "Have-Half" for his habit of splitting treats with friends.

The Bushes were married on a cold Saturday, January 6, 1945, at the Pierces' Presbyterian church in Rye, New York.

Mrs. George H. W. Bush dances with her beloved father, Marvin Pierce, at the wedding reception in Rye. Not long afterward, in a letter to a friend, Mr. Pierce predicted that his new son-in-law might well become the president of the United States one day.

The image of Barbara Pierce that her fiancé carried in his wallet during his navy years during World War II.

They first met at a Christmas 1941 dance at the Greenwich Country Club; he proposed on the rocky coastline at Walker's Point.

In the cockpit of an Avenger. He was thought to be
the youngest flying officer in the navy.

Shot down on Saturday, September 2, 1944, Bush is pictured here (front row, second from
left) with other pilots rescued by the USS *Finback*, a submarine on what was known as
"lifeguard duty."

After the attack on Pearl Harbor, which occurred halfway through his final year at Andover, Bush decided to pursue naval aviation. He signed up upon graduation—which was also his eighteenth birthday.

Beginning in Chapel Hill, North Carolina, Bush trained to fly at a series of installations around the country. He became a torpedo bomber pilot, flying an Avenger off carriers in the Pacific.

Poppy with his sister, Nancy Bush, circa 1928. He was, Nancy later remarked, the "star of the family."

Poppy Bush at age twelve. After graduating from Greenwich Country Day School, he was sent to Phillips Academy in Andover, Massachusetts.

Bush (front row, second from right) with the Phillips Academy baseball team, circa 1938.

The interior of the library at Phillips Academy in the 1930s, Bush's time at the school. Though he tended to hide it well, Bush had a propensity, his instructors noted, to over-worry.

At the plate for Yale, 1947. Barbara kept score at every home game.

Bush finished his Yale degree—Phi Beta Kappa in economics—in two and a half years. After the war, speed was essential: He was now a husband and a father. His eldest son, George W. Bush, was born in July 1946 in New Haven.

The young marrieds on the town circa 1948.

Dorothy Bush with her grandson George W. after his baptism, December 1946.

Neil Mallon and Prescott. Along with Bush uncle Herbie Walker, "Uncle Neil" Mallon was instrumental in the young Bushes' move to Texas and into the oil business.

The elder Bushes on the campaign trail in Connecticut in the 1950s. Prescott would serve in the U.S. Senate from 1952 to 1962.

George Bush meets with former president Eisenhower in 1964, the year Bush unsuccessfully challenged incumbent Democratic senator Ralph Yarborough for the U.S. Senate from Texas

At an offshore oil rig. Bush would make the bulk of his fortune in offshore ventures, building a global business based first in Midland and then in Houston.

With his mother, Dorothy; George W.; and Robin in April 1953.

George W., Neil, Jeb, and baby Marvin, Midland, 1956.

Congressman Bush with his House staff, pictured with longtime aides Chase Untermeyer (far left) and Don Rhodes (far right).

The bright, young rising Republican star on the campaign trail in Texas in his second bid for the U.S. Senate, this time against Lloyd Bentsen, 1970.

Ambassador Bush in action at the United Nations in New York City, early 1970s.

Bush, then chairman of the Republican National Committee, and Gerald Ford meet in the Oval Office in the first days of Ford's presidency, August 1974. Bush was under consideration for vice president; he would end up as liaison to China.

Vice Premier Deng Xiaoping, Bush, and President Ford in the Great Hall of the People in Beijing, December 1975.

Milton Pitts, the official
White House barber, at
work on Bush.

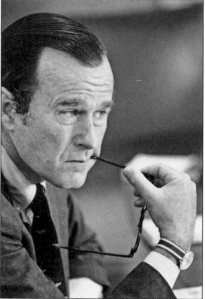

CIA director Bush in the
White House during a crisis in
Lebanon, June 1976.

Chairman of the Joint Chiefs George Brown, National Security Adviser Brent Scowcroft,
Bush, Secretary of Defense Don Rumsfeld, Secretary of State Henry Kissinger, and Vice
President Nelson Rockefeller in President Ford's Oval Office, Wednesday, January 19, 1977.

TWENTY

It Hurt Like Hell

★

Reporter: "What is your biggest worry, your biggest
problem in New Hampshire?"
Bush: "Reagan."

—*The New Yorker's* ELIZABETH DREW, *Portrait of an Election*

BUSH STARTED AS EARLY AS HE COULD, rising at five twenty on
Tuesday, January 22, 1980, to make appearances on the network
morning shows. He and Barbara then boarded a flight to Keene,
New Hampshire, followed by another plane full of press and staff. It was
snowing when they landed. Bush was greeted by a crowd of fifty and a
band that struck up "Hey, Look Me Over."

"How well do you expect to do here?" a reporter asked.

"Better than you think," Bush said. "I think now that I have a real
shot at doing as well as the plan calls for. If it works here, there's no
stopping me."

The struggle between Bush and Reagan in New Hampshire was intense, personal, and long: In 1980, there were five weeks between the
Iowa caucuses and the New Hampshire voting. Bush insinuated, subtly
and not so subtly, that Reagan was too old and too extreme; Reagan argued, subtly and not so subtly, that Bush was too effete and too eastern.
In this cold New England winter the two men went to war.

Hugh Gregg, Bush's campaign manager in the state, had absolute
power—so absolute that the candidate's team called him "Ayatollah." An
Andover and Yale man, Gregg, an old Bush friend, had been a wunder-
kind governor in the 1950s. He assigned the candidate twenty-two minutes for lunch each day, unless he cut it down to six for a sandwich. The
opening of the New Hampshire race was coming at what Bush recalled
as a "heady" moment. *Newsweek* put him on the cover, and in *Time*, three
anonymous sources testified to Bush's virtues the week after the Iowa
win. "Bush was loyal, but he didn't say everything the White House
wanted him to," said a Nixon aide. "He wasn't a toady. He held the party

together." An unnamed "onetime director" of the CIA said that Bush "gave a great deal of hope and revival of dignity to people who were feeling low." A former director of operations at the CIA remarked: "He's tough as nails when he makes a decision. He'll stand by it, come hell or high water."

An ABC News–Harris Poll of Republicans found Bush running even with Reagan nationally and ten points ahead in the East—which included New Hampshire. A post-Iowa *Boston Globe* poll put Bush ahead of Reagan in New Hampshire by nine points. With everything now in doubt, Reagan emerged from his cocoon in California. Bush sensed— feared—what was at hand. "Beneath the media glow of my Iowa success was the political reality that Reagan, without campaigning, had come within two percentage points of winning the caucuses," Bush recalled. What could an active, engaged Reagan do?

Unfortunately for Bush, it was a promising moment for a Reagan comeback. Earlier, the unrest around the world had seemed to favor Bush's diplomatic experience, but as the Iranian hostage crisis dragged on and the Soviets took over Afghanistan, possibly threatening the Persian Gulf, Reagan's image of strength was attracting more support. A series of polls suggested that Americans were becoming more hawkish in the face of the crises in Iran and Afghanistan, with 64 percent favoring an American invasion of the Persian Gulf in the event the Soviets were to move into the region. To give New Hampshire's Republican primary voters—49 percent of whom had supported him in 1976—a reason to choose him over Bush, then, Reagan really just needed to be Reagan again.

The question of Reagan's age was pervasive, and Bush did what he could to take advantage of it. The only thing Reagan could do to convince people he was not too old to *be* president was to prove that he was not too old to campaign effectively *for* president. "Ronnie campaigned harder in New Hampshire than he had ever campaigned in his life," Nancy Reagan recalled. "The press could barely keep up with him." He spent Tuesday, February 5, 1980—the day before his sixty-ninth birthday—going from event to event in New Hampshire, eleven in all, joking about his age. "Compared to the alternative," Reagan deadpanned, "I'm very happy."

To answer Bush on the age issue, the Reaganites injected class politics into the contest in early February, painting Bush as the embodiment of an exclusive world closed to ordinary Americans. "It's old-school tie and inherited influence against the working middle-class Americans," state Reagan chairman Gerald Carmen told *The New York Times*. Reagan supporter William Loeb, publisher of *The Union Leader* in Manchester, New Hampshire, agreed. "Mr. Bush," Loeb said, "is the candidate of the self-appointed elite of this country."

Did the Republican Party of 1980 want to nominate a clear conservative (Reagan) or someone closer to the center (Bush)? Asked by reporters whether he was "to the left" of Reagan, Bush replied, "I'm perceived that way. If you had to choose between right and left [in relation to Reagan], I suppose it'd be left." Like Gerald Ford, Bush favored an Equal Rights Amendment; Reagan did not. Bush did not favor a pro-life constitutional amendment; Reagan did. Bush was not a big tax-cutter; Reagan was.

Reagan's most effective argument in the primary was that Bush was not a true man of the right; it was a case that Reagan, who resented Bush's use of the age issue, took up happily, linking Bush to the Carter administration with a broadside against a familiar conservative target: the Trilateral Commission. Reagan announced, ominously, that no fewer than nineteen current or former key members of the Carter administration had belonged to the Trilateral Commission. As, of course, had George H. W. Bush. Asked to clarify why membership in the group was a bad thing, Reagan adviser Edwin Meese III said that Trilateral thinking had led to a "softening of defense" because Trilateral Commission members believed, Meese said, "that trade and business should transcend, perhaps, the national defense." It was not a convincing argument, but Reagan's purpose in raising the whole matter was less to persuade the undecided than to motivate core supporters who had long been suspicious of the circles in which men like Bush moved.

With little more than two weeks to go before New Hampshire voted, and with tempers rising, the two men headed into two scheduled encounters in the third week of February: a seven-candidate debate in Manchester on Wednesday, February 20, 1980, and a one-on-one event in Nashua three days later, on Saturday, February 23.

The first debate, at Manchester Central High School, produced little of substance, except that it featured Reagan's return to the heart of the race. Bush was determined to play it safe. "You don't win one of those things with seven candidates, but you can lose it," Jim Baker told the press.

The winner in many ways was Reagan, who complained that he was the victim of his own success in moving much of the party to the right. Given the generally conservative tone of most of the candidates' answers in Manchester, Reagan experienced the debate as a ratification of his own vision. "I kept hearing so many of my own positions over the years coming back at me that by the time it got to me," he said of the debate format, "I was worried there wouldn't be anything left to say."

In Reagan's steady performance in Manchester, Republican voters apparently saw what they wanted—and needed—to see. He went into the Manchester event a point behind Bush but surged after that first debate. In his pollster Richard Wirthlin's surveys, Reagan had a nearly two to one lead in New Hampshire as the weekend arrived. The highlight of the last few days of the race: the one-on-one debate between Reagan and Bush on Saturday, in Nashua.

Reagan had initially agreed to the debate with Bush, their rival Phil Crane said, because the former front-runner was "hurting" and needed the debate to regain his standing. Post-Manchester, with Reagan's numbers shifting, the Reagan camp, led by John Sears, sensed an opportunity in Nashua. The plan in the forty-eight hours after Manchester: to surprise Bush on Saturday by announcing that Reagan wanted the debate thrown open to the whole field, depriving Bush of the stature that would come with a one-on-one contest.

If Bush agreed to the change, then he would be relegated to just another face in the crowd. Nashua would be Manchester all over again, with Reagan more likely to win the larger show with lower risk than in a two-man debate. If Bush resisted, then he would be seen as exclusionary and perhaps, in keeping with the anti-Bush arguments Reagan had been making, elitist. For Reagan, it was a win-win scenario. The other candidates—Baker, Dole, Anderson, and Crane (Connally was campaigning in South Carolina)—had objected to being excluded in the first place, and the Federal Election Commission agreed that the sponsoring newspaper, the *Nashua Telegraph,* could not underwrite a two-man debate. The two campaigns could, however, and the paper suggested that the Reagan and Bush camps split the bill.

In the hectic hours between Manchester, the scheduled event in

Nashua, and the actual primary on Tuesday, the Bush campaign was uncertain about the wisest course to take. For two years Bush had longed to be seen as the best—and only—alternative to the aging Reagan. A one-on-one debate was perfect. But in a significant miscalculation in the chaotic run-up to Nashua—after Iowa but before Reagan surged post-Manchester—the Bush camp had briefly held the view that Reagan needed a debate with Bush more than Bush needed a debate with Reagan. Thus the Bush campaign's decision that if Reagan wanted the debate, then he should pay for it. Reagan had agreed, and, at midafternoon, he took the offensive, announcing that the debate should be open to the other candidates. Bush replied that he would abide by the previously set "rules" and would participate only in a one-on-one forum.

Backstage at Nashua High School that evening, Bush was waiting in one classroom; Reagan and the other candidates were in another. The Reagan camp decided to send New Hampshire senator Gordon Humphrey, a blue-collar conservative who had long disliked Bush, as an emissary to Bush. Humphrey pressed Bush to open up the debate for the sake of "party unity," a homily that infuriated Bush, who refused.

As Bush walked into the gym and took his seat on the stage—there were still chairs only for him, Reagan, and the moderator, *Telegraph* editor Jon Breen—he was unsure who would be following him to the dais. So were Reagan and the other candidates, who were all in the holding room. As Nancy Reagan recalled, someone from the *Telegraph* arrived with a message. "Mr. Bush is already on the stage," the *Telegraph* representative said. "If Mr. Reagan does not appear within five minutes, the debate will be canceled and Mr. Bush will be declared the winner."

There was some hesitance in the room, and the minutes were ticking by. Then Nancy spoke up: "Why don't you *all* just go out?" Already angry over the *Telegraph*'s threat to call the whole thing off and give Bush an unearned win, Reagan, following his wife's sound counsel, led the others onto the stage. He briefly shook Bush's hand and tried to speak amid the noise of the crowd. Bush sat stonily, declining to look at Reagan, who asked if he could make a statement. "No," Breen said, further infuriating Reagan. The agreement had been for Reagan and Bush to debate and, like Bush, Breen was trying to stand by the original rules.

Reagan's face was flushed, his eyes fierce. Bush, by contrast, seemed, in the words of William Loeb, to be a "little boy who thinks his mother may have dropped him off at the wrong birthday party." Reagan insisted on being allowed to speak, remarking, "I am the sponsor and I suppose I should have some right." Breen, trying to assert some control over the proceedings, raised his voice and ordered the sound technician to turn Reagan's microphone off. "I am paying for this microphone, Mr. Green," Reagan said. His misstatement of Breen's name was lost in the rising cheers of the crowd.

In Nashua, with the polls opening in roughly sixty hours, the audience was with Reagan, and Bush remained silent. "He froze," a Bush staffer told *Newsweek*. "It was a crisis, and our man failed to respond."

"Are you through?" Breen asked Reagan. "Have you concluded your remarks?" After another moment of tumult, Anderson, Baker, Crane, and Dole left the stage. "I'll get you someday, you fucking Nazi," Dole whispered to Bush. "Jim Baker," Dole said to Bush's campaign manager offstage, jabbing a finger into Baker's chest, "you'll regret this."

What was Bush thinking? "Of course, I looked terrible, no question," Bush recalled. "But I had accepted a set of rules, and I'd given my word, and I was going to keep it. Some of my father there, I think, and Mother, too: Play by the rules." There was also something else. The Reagan emissary at Nashua High, Gordon Humphrey, was one of the last people on the planet Bush was inclined to listen to. To Bush, Humphrey epitomized the right-wingers who seemed determined to oppose him at all costs for all time. The encounter with Humphrey would have been strained in any event, but the awkwardness was exacerbated by the circumstances. Because of the back-and-forth over who was to debate, things were running late—twenty-five minutes, by Bush's reckoning. The *Telegraph* organizers wanted to get on with it and had summoned Bush to the dais.

"On the way to the stage, after this long delay, I was stopped by a prominent Reagan supporter"—Humphrey—"who has been attacking me all across the State of New Hampshire," Bush later wrote Anderson, Baker, Crane, and Dole. "He asked me to have a joint meeting with you and the others and lectured me on the Republican Party."

In retrospect, Bush wrote, he should have taken the time right then to meet with Reagan and the other four, if only to make clear that the newspaper, not he, had made the rules. "A lot of misunderstanding might have been avoided," Bush wrote. Propelled by urgency from the *Telegraph*'s staffers and angered over what he believed to be Humphrey's presumption in questioning his party loyalty, however, Bush did something he rarely did: He decided not to see things from the other guy's point of view. It was uncharacteristic—usually he took pains to talk things out personally before a situation could slip out of control—and he paid for the slip. "The producer was signaling me to the stage, the commitment that I had made [to the *Telegraph*] was on my mind, and the emissary was not exactly the ideal choice," Bush told the others later. He came to see that his poor showing at Nashua was rooted in his failure to be true to his lifelong instincts. "I wish we had been in personal touch," Bush told the others. "I'm certain that much of this unpleasantness could have been avoided."

Reagan considered the evening a failure of will on Bush's part. "I don't understand it," Reagan remarked. "How would this guy deal with the Russians?" Bush's ambition (for the head-to-head confrontation with Reagan) and his pride (unbending in the last, critical moments before Reagan's star turn) hurt him, deeply, at Nashua. "I looked like a fool," he recalled. "Not my finest hour, to say the least."

The voting on the following Tuesday was a blowout for Reagan, who carried the primary 50 percent to Bush's 23 percent. "Congratulations, sir, you beat the hell out of me," Bush told Reagan in a concession call.

Beyond New Hampshire, Bush kept after the front-runner, arguing that Reagan was too far to the right to win in November. "If somebody asks, 'Are you more moderate than Reagan?' the answer would be very clear," Bush said. "Reagan has gone the far-over route." As *Newsweek* noted after New Hampshire, Bush "is hoping that voters will perceive him as more 'reasonable' than Reagan, not simply more liberal."

A defeat in moderate-to-liberal Massachusetts on Tuesday, March 4, 1980, then, could mean the end of the Bush bid. "We've got to win this primary," Bush told voters in Boston. Some on his own team thought everything hinged on it. On the evening of the New Hampshire loss, Jim Baker pulled Nancy Bush Ellis, who lived in Lincoln, Massachusetts, aside. "Now, Nancy, you all have to win Massachusetts," Baker said, "and I mean really win it." If Bush were to lose Massachusetts, said Silvio Conte, a Massachusetts Republican congressman, "Jerry Ford could and should enter the picture."

Ford stood ready. The former president summoned Adam Clymer of *The New York Times* to Rancho Mirage to make a startling pronouncement

At what was to have been a one-on-one debate, Reagan dramatically insisted the other candidates be included; Bush sat stonily on stage. "Not my finest hour, to say the least," Bush recalled.

for the March 2, 1980, Sunday editions. Reagan, Ford said, could not prevail in November against Carter. "A very conservative Republican can't win in a national election," he said. Meaning, Clymer asked, that Reagan could not defeat Carter? "That's right," said Ford.

For Bush, the Ford interview was at once affirming and dispiriting. The former president's key point—that Reagan was too conservative to defeat Carter—suggested that Bush was fighting the right fight in his bid to win the moderates in the party and attract enough conservative support to stop Reagan. The problem was that Ford's remarks underscored Bush's own failure to defeat Reagan in New Hampshire.

Bush avoided disaster forty-eight hours later by winning in Massachusetts. To his supporters, Bush stood strong. "I wouldn't be deserving of your consideration if I got scared" of Ford, Bush said. "My plans are unchanged."

Little was going Bush's way. Ford loomed, and much of the rest of March was a misery for Bush as Reagan won South Carolina, Alabama, Florida, Georgia, and Illinois. Late in the month Bush struck back, carrying Connecticut. Opponents fell away. Now facing only Bush and Anderson, Reagan swept Kansas, Wisconsin, and Louisiana.

In the middle of March, given Reagan's successes, Ford decided to end his flirtation with a campaign. "I am not a candidate," Ford told reporters outside his house at Rancho Mirage on Saturday, March 15, 1980. "I will not become a candidate." The hunger to avenge 1976 twice over—by denying Reagan the nomination and by defeating Carter—was deep, but Ford and his circle could not see a way to stop Reagan. "It uncomplicates our life in the George Bush campaign," Jim Baker said, gratefully.

The Ford withdrawal, however, was seen not as an opportunity for Bush but as the ratification of Reagan's success. "It's over," said Robert Hughes, an Ohio Republican leader. "Ford was the only guy with a shot at stopping Reagan." Indeed, nothing could change the fundamental calculus of the race after Reagan reasserted himself in New Hampshire. "I am discouraged," Barbara wrote on Monday, March 10. The next day she added: "It is bad to be on the road when your husband is losing." On the same day Ford declined to be a candidate, George W. telephoned his mother from Texas. "Young George called," wrote Barbara. "He's discouraged—like me!" Her main worries were personal, not political. "I feel we are very near the end of this long quest—Will I be able to cope with the letdown George will feel[?]," Barbara wrote. "Will I be enough? It has to really hurt."

Yet Bush would not surrender. "George is about the most competitive human being I have ever known," recalled Jim Baker. In the face of Reagan's primary victories, Bush reacted, Baker believed, with "the same determination he had shown at age eighteen, when instead of heading straight from prep school to Yale, he became a naval aviator in World War II." In Pennsylvania, he attacked Reagan's vision of lower taxes as a means to higher revenues as "voodoo economic policy" and "economic madness."

The phrase "voodoo economics" originated with Bush press secretary Pete Teeley. Teeley had come across an editorial arguing that President Carter's economic policy seemed to have been put together by a group of economic "witchdoctors." It got Teeley thinking about how he might be able to use the metaphor against Reagan. What, he asked himself, do witch doctors do? "And then it hit me: They do 'voodoo,'" and I put it in Bush's speech," Teeley recalled. (Later, when the phrase continued to cause Bush trouble with the right, Bush said, "You know, Teeley, that's the only goddamned memorable thing you've ever written for me.")

Bush prevailed in contests here and there. The race, he insisted after winning seventeen of twenty-one delegates in Maine in April, was "far from over." Overall, however, the math was close to impossible to overcome. Nine hundred and ninety-eight delegates was the magic number to clinch the nomination, and on the eve of the Pennsylvania primary on April 22, 1980, Reagan led Bush 577 to 109. Bush ran a pricey campaign in Pennsylvania, investing $1 million, a large portion of which paid for television time to broadcast "Ask George Bush" specials.

Bush won the April 22 primary there by a strong seven points—53 to 46 percent—and took great solace in the victory, believing it affirmed a new, if late, strategic shift. "Last January, he cultivated ideological fuzziness," wrote Hedrick Smith in *The New York Times*. "Lately, he has cast himself as the moderate against Mr. Reagan's conservative and has set out specific policy differences with the former California governor." Reagan acknowledged Bush's performance in Pennsylvania, but also said that he believed the contest was largely over. "I hate to tempt fate," Reagan said after the Pennsylvania balloting, but "I believe I am going to win the nomination."

Bush's win in Pennsylvania was followed by an equally impressive victory in Michigan on Tuesday, May 20, 1980. Yet when Bush turned on the news to savor his triumph, he found that two of the three networks were leading with a different story: that Reagan's same-day win in Oregon had put Reagan over the 998-delegate threshold. Was there any mathematical route for Bush to win the nomination? The answer, Jim Baker sadly concluded, was no. The only way to do it was for Bush to win the last big three primaries, all on June 3: New Jersey, Ohio, and California. Without all three the delegate numbers just weren't there. New Jersey and Ohio were doable, but California? Reagan's California? Competing there, Jim Baker remarked to reporters, would be "goddamn tough."

"If you can't do California, then you can't argue to people that you still have a shot [at the nomination] in terms of the numbers," Baker told David Broder and Bill Peterson of *The Washington Post*. "And once you concede that, why do you stay in?" The *Post* interpreted Baker's remarks as a de facto Bush withdrawal. Reporters in New Jersey, where Bush was campaigning, besieged the candidate. "Baker says you don't have anything going in California," came the question. "Does this mean you're dropping out?"

From a grim Holiday Inn, Bush got Baker on the telephone. According to Baker, Bush was "furious, and I [didn't] blame him." Bush had a question: What had Baker said, exactly? "I had only talked about not having enough money on hand to compete in California," Baker replied, "but I shouldn't have done it, I admitted, because it gave the impression that we had no choice but to pull the plug."

"George, I think it's time to get out of the race," Baker told Bush. The candidate didn't want to hear it. "No, Jimmy," Bush said. "If we can only get to California, we'll be able to turn this thing around."

"We just don't have the money," Baker said. "I wish to hell we did, but we don't, and I don't see how we can get it." The subject was too fraught, too complex, to decide on the phone. Would Bush come home to Houston for the weekend? They could discuss everything there.

Bush agreed. He would fly to Texas, and they would talk it all over.

Jim Oberwetter, an old Texas political hand, was dispatched to Newark to bring Bush back to Houston on a private plane. "I picked him up, got him aboard, and he sat down with his back to the cockpit and the little bar there," Oberwetter recalled. "He usually had a glass of wine on a flight like this, so I poured him one at the front of the cabin and, as I was walking back, I looked over his shoulder. He was sitting with a writing pad on the table in front of him." In a bold, visible scrawl, Bush had written a note to himself: "I WILL NEVER GIVE UP. NEVER. NEVER."

In the sunroom looking out at the pool of their Houston house, the Bushes met through the weekend with Baker and other family members and advisers. "Look, we've got to fold this thing," Baker said. "We don't have any money; it's time. You've got to get out." The candidate was unimpressed. What about all the people who had worked so hard for him for so long? All the guys in New Jersey—Nicholas Brady, his chairman there, thought they could pull it out—and Ohio, and—well, and everywhere else. How could he quit on them after all they'd done for him?

Baker was direct. Every day Bush stayed in a mathematically unwinnable race, Baker argued, "would blow any chance" of earning Reagan's confidence and the second spot on the national ticket. Bush had been noticeably quiet about the possibility of becoming Reagan's number two, in part because Bush's own competitiveness did not allow him to contemplate life after defeat. He had been in it to win everything, and Baker recalled that Bush "always said privately that he wasn't sure if he was interested in being vice president."

That's what everyone said in the storm and strife of a presidential campaign, and everyone, including Bush, probably meant it when they said it. The fact of the matter, however, was that vice presidential nominees and vice presidents had a high success rate of becoming presidential nominees and presidents. Beginning with Franklin Roosevelt, who ran for vice president on the losing Democratic ticket in 1920, five of the eight presidents who served from 1932 to 1980 had been a vice presidential nominee or vice president (FDR, Truman, Johnson, Nixon, and Ford). If Bush were even remotely interested in being considered for the post, Baker said, he had to stand down now. "They have to start thinking who they're going to run with, and the longer you hang in if you don't have a mathematical chance of winning," Baker argued, "the more you're going to hurt your chances."

"I finally said, 'Okay, we're out,'" Bush recalled. "It hurt like hell."

Officially, the 1980 presidential campaign of George Bush lasted fifty-five weeks. Unofficially, he had been working toward the ultimate goal in American politics for nearly four years and had been thinking of it, in the abstract, at least since the mid-1960s. And still others— including Prescott Bush—had thought of it even longer ago than that. Dropping out was, Bush said, the "toughest decision of my entire life." Bush dispatched a congratulatory telegram to the uncontested nominee. "He was a superior campaigner," Reagan replied in a statement, "and I'm most grateful for his expression of support for my candidacy and his pledge to work for unity in the party."

Bush left the stage with grace, inviting his traveling press corps over to the house. A drop-in turned into lunch: Paula Rendon, the Bushes' long-time housekeeper, performed miracles, feeding dozens of unexpected guests. Bush took off his shoes and put on canary yellow pants and a blue shirt to reminisce, barefoot, by his pool in the late Houston spring.

The next day, Douglas Kneeland of *The New York Times* came by the house for a follow-up story. Forcing himself into good spirits, Bush, Kneeland wrote, jokingly pointed to a Yale alumni magazine on the coffee table. "That's the first time we've been able to put that out for months," he said with his crooked grin. He then picked up a copy of *National Review* on an end table. "I guess we can put this away now," he said, smiling still.

He was only kidding, of course. But the joke provided the reporter with a useful illustration of Bush's political plight. He was too Ivy League for the GOP's new grass roots and too conservative for the still-sizable though embattled moderate wing. The former would have hated seeing the Yale magazine; the latter would have been unsettled by the thought that George Bush actually read *National Review* (which he did). This was now Ronald Reagan's political world. The question was whether there was room for Bush, essentially a man most comfortable with the style and the substance of the GOP of the 1950s, in the party of the 1980s.

J im Baker thought there was—or should be—and publicly made that case in the wake of the Bush withdrawal. A key step for Reagan, Baker argued to the press, was resolving "the dispute over the Vice Presidency, over whether to pick a member of the 'movement' or reach out for someone who might be more acceptable to the electorate." Saying that Bush had "obvious vote-getting appeal in the major states that you have to win," Baker noted that Bush, who was, in Baker's words, from the "moderate side of the party," would "put to rest" concerns about Reagan's Washington and foreign policy experience.

There were forty-nine days between Bush's withdrawal from the presidential race and the opening of the Republican National Convention in Detroit. Bush had two things on his mind in those weeks: raising money and Ronald Reagan. He spent much of his time in June and early July working to retire an unexpected campaign debt. "There again is my father—'You've got to do it, pay owed money,'" Bush recalled. As he paid off the bills of the past, he was consumed with thoughts of the future—specifically, whether Reagan would choose him to run on the ticket.

On Wednesday, July 9, 1980, in the tenth-floor conference room of the Reagan for President headquarters in Los Angeles, pollster Richard Wirthlin was explicit: Reagan needed a moderate for vice president. In June, a survey of Republican National Committeemen and state party chairs found that the GOP leaders thought Reagan should pick a moderate, and they favored Bush for the job. (Bush got 58 votes to Howard Baker's 22 and Jack Kemp's 17.) At a $200-a-plate New York State GOP dinner at the Waldorf Astoria, Bush won a convincing victory in a vice presidential straw poll. He ran first, Howard Baker second. An intriguing name placed third: Gerald Ford.

The Reagan campaign polled eighteen possible tickets to test the relative strength of suggested nominees. The only name that did better than Bush's did was Ford's, but the former president had told Reagan during a visit at Rancho Mirage that he did not wish to be considered. Stu Spencer, a California Republican strategist with ties to Ford and to Reagan, followed up with Ford, asking, "Want me to pursue it?"

"Hell, no," Ford said.

That seemed to take care of that. Bush and seven others made what was essentially a final round when they were asked to submit health and financial information to the Reagan camp: Howard Baker, Donald Rumsfeld, Senator Richard Lugar of Indiana, Senator Paul Laxalt of Nevada, Congressman Guy Vander Jagt of Michigan, Congressman Jack Kemp of New York, and former Treasury secretary William Simon. (On the eve of the convention, two other names emerged: diplomat Anne Armstrong of Texas and Governor Albert Quie of Minnesota.) A Gallup Poll in early July among Republicans found that Ford led Bush as the preferred vice presidential nominee, 31 to 20 percent. Howard Baker polled 15 percent, and John Connally 12 percent.

The math was clear. If Ford were unwilling to join the ticket as number two, then Bush was the smart choice. Thoughtful conservatives had already begun to make their peace with it. "If you wish, come out for a Reagan-Bush ticket; that is probably what is in the cards anyway," *National Review* publisher William Rusher had written to the magazine's editors as early as January 1980. Yet many other conservatives were convinced that choosing Bush would amount to a kind of movement Munich—a capitulation to the moderates they had been fighting since the Eisenhower era. Ernest Angelo, Jr., a longtime Reagan supporter who would chair the Texas delegation at the 1980 Republican National Convention in Detroit, had several delegates who said they would walk off the floor rather than vote for George Bush for anything, much less vice president.

The thinking was this: Why, at the movement conservatives' hour of triumph, elevate someone who was not one of them? As Jim Baker had seen in May, Reagan had to decide whether he wanted to anoint a running mate from the movement or from the more moderate precincts of the party—precincts that, while waning, could still help him in a significant way. Bush's victories in Massachusetts, Connecticut, Pennsylvania, and Michigan proved that much. Bush, who was now enthusiastic about running with Reagan, was living for a call from the man who had bested him for the presidential nomination. Without the vice presidency, "I thought we were done, politically—finished," recalled Bush. He would go back to Houston, back to business. "It would've been tough—martinis and whose daughter was pledging Tri Delt, that kind of thing, but what the hell: We would've made a life. A different life than the one we'd had in mind, running as hard as we had been for the big job, but a life."

Bush was in the all-too-familiar position of having his fate in the hands of a man more powerful than himself. It had been this way with Nixon and with Ford and even, briefly, with Carter. Bush was always the supplicant, the man waiting on, rather than making, the call that brought clarity, place, and power. Almost exactly ten years had passed since his loss to Lloyd Bentsen had made him, it seemed, permanently dependent on the kindness of others. For a time—a glorious time—the presidential campaign had liberated Bush from his years of living or dying at the pleasure of bigger, more successful politicians. "I'd wanted to be president, no apologies for that," recalled Bush. "But 'Big Mo' didn't turn out to be so big after all."

The wondrous, happy frenzy of Iowa was irretrievably remote. Accustomed to motion, Bush was forced to be still—to bide his time, powerlessly. If Ronald Reagan wanted George Bush, then George Bush would be there, ready to fight to the last. If Reagan wanted him, Bush would give his all to the cause—he always did. If Reagan wanted him, Bush would be granted safe passage to the highest levels of the newly conservative Republican Party. If Reagan wanted him, all would be well.

Reagan, however, did not want him.

TWENTY-ONE

Is George Bush There?

★

I thought we were done, out of it, just gone.

—GEORGE H. W. BUSH on a Reagan-Ford ticket in 1980

STU SPENCER, A REAGAN ADVISER since the 1966 California governor's race, could not remember the last time he had seen Reagan so worked up. On the flight from Los Angeles to Detroit, Reagan asked Spencer who he thought should be vice president. "I started out by telling him that I thought he had gotten the most conservative platform he could have hoped for, and that his base couldn't be happier or more enthusiastic," Spencer recalled. "So I said that, in my view, he should think about picking a more moderate guy, someone to reassure folks who weren't already with him. And the best man on that basis was George Bush." In response, Reagan "went off at Bush," Spencer recalled. "He was really pissed off at him."

" 'Voodoo economics'—that did it," Reagan said.

Reagan talked more, unloading months of frustration with Bush. There was the age issue: The Reagans resented Bush's focus on physical fitness and stamina during the primaries, a focus that implied that Bush thought Reagan was too old for the White House. Then there was Nashua. The memory of Bush's freezing onstage that evening stuck with Reagan, a man for whom the telling image or anecdote was important. By staring straight ahead on the dais at the Nashua High School gym, a reaction that made Reagan's dramatic scene possible, Bush had cast himself, in Reagan's mind, as a spoiled child who turned petulant when things did not go his way, or, worse, as a man who didn't react well under pressure. That Bush had faced, and met, real tests of danger made no difference. It was monumentally difficult to dislodge something once it found its way into Reagan's imagination.

On the plane, listening to Reagan's diatribe, Spencer was puzzled. "This was very unlike Reagan, who almost never lost his temper the way other candidates do," Spencer recalled. "Bush had clearly gotten under his skin."

Spencer tried again. "Yes, Governor, but it's going to be to your pragmatic benefit to have someone who's more from the center, and that's Bush."

"You haven't been listening to me," Reagan said.

"No, I follow," Spencer replied, "but I also know you are a pragmatic guy, and Bush is the pragmatic move."

Reagan did not reply. He was tired of the subject. Surely there was some other answer.

Movement conservatives arriving in Detroit had every reason to feel proud. The Republican Party was no longer what it had been in 1976, when the more moderate Ford had prevailed against the more conservative Reagan. For the first time in four decades, the Republican Party did not endorse the Equal Rights Amendment. The platform came out in favor of a pro-life constitutional amendment. It backed supply-side economics. And religious conservatives concerned about declining moral standards felt that, in Reagan and the Republicans, they now had a political ally in fighting a war to take American culture back from what organizations such as Jerry Falwell's Moral Majority saw as the excesses of the 1960s and '70s. "I feel this whole election is going to be won or lost here in Detroit by who is chosen for V.P.," an unnamed Reagan aide told *The New York Times*. "It's not that there's only one good choice. But there are some bad choices that could hurt us. . . . The best choice is the one who most helps us win."

Presumably a "bad" choice would be a hardcore conservative who augmented Reagan's appeal to the right (New York congressman Jack Kemp was the chief example) rather than broadening his appeal to the center. "The message we want to get across," Edwin Meese told *The New York Times* on the eve of the convention, was that Reagan was "essentially a problem solver, that he is not rigid and doctrinaire."

With the exception of Ford, who brought the most strength to the ticket in polls, the numbers argued for Bush. According to Richard Wirthlin's surveys, 68 percent of voters thought that a congressional background was important for a Reagan vice president, and 58 percent believed it should be someone between the ages of forty-five and fifty-five. (Bush, the former congressman, had turned fifty-six in June.) The surveys found, too, that a running mate would preferably be "somewhat alike" to Reagan on the issues, but not "exactly like." Bush himself was running "well among 'soft' Repubs & Indeps and in Industrial States."

Sensing momentum toward a Reagan-Bush ticket, conservatives were hard at work in the corners of the convention to try to protect their victory. In Detroit, Ernest Angelo, Jr., the chairman of the Texas delegation and a Reagan supporter, went to a meeting in Jesse Helms's suite. He found the right-wing North Carolina senator and his circle plotting to put Helms on the ticket with Reagan. Phil Crane was also trying to whip up support for himself. Angelo wanted Reagan to choose Jack Kemp, and he realized that impractical intramural right-wing agitation was only going to divide the conservatives and possibly open the way for a moderate. "If Senator Helms and Phil Crane don't stop trying to be the VP themselves," Angelo told the group, "you're going to ruin Jack Kemp's chances, and George Bush is going to wind up on the ticket."

The others were furious. "They nearly threw me out of the room," Angelo recalled. "It was not well received." But it was sound counsel. Moderates were upset with the platform, increasing the chances that Reagan would reach toward the center rather than toward the right on the vice presidency. Or so went the chatter. No one yet knew what Ronald Reagan was going to do—including Ronald Reagan.

The Bushes arrived in Detroit aboard Delta flight 860 just before nine o'clock on the morning of Sunday, July 13, 1980, and checked into the Hotel Pontchartrain on Washington Boulevard. It was going to be a long week. Reagan was expected to reach a final decision on a running mate on Tuesday night at the earliest. An announcement would not come until Wednesday; Thursday, the day of Reagan's acceptance speech, was also a possibility.

As Bush looked over his schedule for the next few days—three simple typewritten pages—he saw a list of receptions, caucus and delegation meetings, luncheons, and dinners. If nothing changed—if Reagan chose someone else as vice president—then Bush's last commitment was to address the convention at the Joe Louis Arena at eight P.M. on Wednesday. After that, there was only white space, and the story, Bush believed, would be over.

The front page of Monday's *New York Times* had a suggestion of good news as Bush prepared for a day of meetings in Room 15 on the Terrace Level of the Hotel Pontchartrain with Bush delegates. President Ford had "told associates that he thinks Mr. Reagan's smartest choice politically would be Mr. Bush," the *Times* wrote. "The sources said that he was planning to advise the former California Governor to pick Mr. Bush" during a meeting on Tuesday.

Cheered by such reports, Bush began the emotionally taxing work of releasing his delegates from their commitments to him. Hour after hour on Monday, he thanked his supporters and then asked them to make Reagan's nomination unanimous. It wasn't easy. Every face Bush saw, every hand he shook, every small cheer he heard carried him back to the primary trail, to the months and months of hope and toil. Yet it had to be done. They came all day, one after another, beginning with Alabama and Arkansas at eight thirty in the morning and ending with New Jersey, New York, and Tennessee at six in the evening.

Meanwhile, as Reagan arrived in Detroit on Monday, July 14, he remained committed to what Jim Baker called a strategy of "ABB— Anybody But Bush." That afternoon the Reagans called on the Fords at the Detroit Plaza. (The Reagans were on the sixty-ninth floor, the Fords the seventieth.) Reagan brought his old rival a gift: an Indian peace pipe. Ford appreciated the gesture; the tension of 1976 was becoming more manageable. Ford, after all, was a creature of a congressional culture in which it was generally counterproductive to hold grudges. One might not forget, but one could forgive, or pretend to, as new circumstances arose and alliances shifted.

The former president who had said "no" to Reagan at Rancho Mirage and "hell, no" to Stu Spencer on the subject of the vice presidency went over to address the convention at the Joe Louis Arena on Monday night. "Some call me an elder statesman," the former president told the cheering delegates. "I don't know. I don't mind telling you all that I am not ready to quit yet. . . . Elder statesmen are supposed to sit quietly and smile wisely from the sidelines. I've never been much for sitting. I've never spent much time on the sidelines. Betty'll tell you that. This country means too much to me to comfortably park on the bench. So when this convention fields the team for Governor Reagan, count me in."

Reagan was struck by Ford's words. The next day, Tuesday, Reagan chose to believe that a Reagan-Ford ticket was possible. Reagan's motivation was basic. He had an election to win, and his pollster had told him that a Reagan-Ford ticket would be the strongest against Carter in the fall. The distance between possibility and reality was great, and Reagan began his bid to close that gap in a meeting with Ford in the Reagans' suite in the early afternoon. Bush was finishing a session with his Pennsylvania delegates at the Hyatt Regency in Dearborn when Reagan and Ford sat down together at the Detroit Plaza. "I know what I'm asking," Reagan said to Ford, "and I know that you've made it plain already that you didn't want anything of this kind, but I'm asking, will you please reconsider?"

"I don't think there's any chance of it," Ford replied.

Would Ford think about it overnight? Reagan asked. There was still time. Reagan had decided to schedule a press conference for eleven o'clock on Thursday morning to announce his running mate. The choice would then be ratified by the convention before Reagan's acceptance speech that evening. Ford remained overtly skeptical but said he would consider it.

After the meeting with Ford, Reagan encountered some reporters on the way to a meeting with delegates. Asked about his conversations with the former president—word was out that Reagan was wooing Ford— Reagan said, "I just sought his counsel and advice. We just discussed all the people who are presently under consideration. He made no recommendations. He analyzed and gave his thoughts on everybody."

He made no recommendations: The man who had been said to be ready to recommend Bush to Reagan had failed to do so. For Bush this was a discouraging sign. Ford could have told Reagan no (again), made the case for Bush, and gone about being an elder statesman. Yet the pull of power was strong, the desire to exact retribution against Carter great. Ford was a politician, and the allure of politics had not faded—that much was clear from his prolonged flirtation with seeking the presidential nomination. The vice presidency wasn't everything, but it was something— and it was possible that Ford, as a former president, could make it into something even more.

While Ford returned to his rooms to consider the conversation with Reagan, Bush was taking part in a panel discussion hosted by the Youth for Reagan delegation at the Ford Auditorium on the riverfront. The subject? "America: The Next Decade."

Back at the Detroit Plaza, Reagan advisers Bill Casey, Ed Meese, and Mike Deaver met with Henry Kissinger to see if the former secretary of state would help them make the case to Ford to accept a place on the ticket. Late Tuesday night, Kissinger, Alan Greenspan, the former chairman of the Council of Economic Advisers, and Ford adviser Jack Marsh met with the former president. According to political writers Jack Germond and Jules Witcover, Kissinger and Greenspan suggested exploring "the possibilities for Ford to have a significant role in policy"—at which point Ford "didn't cut off the discussion."

Ford rose early on Wednesday, July 16, 1980, for an interview with Tom Brokaw on NBC's *Today* show. "I know it must be very hard, once you've been President, to be Vice-President of the United States," Brokaw said. Asked whether pride would keep a former president from returning to Washington as vice president, Ford said, "Honestly, if I thought the situation would work, if all the other questions could be resolved, the problem of pride would not bother me in any way." Left unspecified was what, exactly, "all the other questions" were. Figuring that out—or trying to—was the business of the coming day. Advisers to Reagan and to Ford sat down to explore how a Reagan-Ford administration would work. Which meant, in translation, what would Reagan have to promise Ford to draw the former president onto the ticket?

Possibilities included a Vice President Ford serving as a kind of super White House chief of staff with a mutual veto over key appointments; control of the paper flow into the Oval Office; and an expanded, if unspecified, role with the National Security Council. Another would have had Ford serving simultaneously as vice president and as secretary of defense and national security adviser. There was also talk of a scenario that included Kissinger returning as secretary of state and Greenspan coming in as Treasury secretary.

Dick Cheney, the former Ford White House chief of staff who was now representing Wyoming in the U.S. House, was in a meeting with some other Ford allies on Wednesday when Bill Casey, Reagan's campaign chief, walked in with the Reagan team's initial and provisional response to the Ford camp's suggestions about an expanded vice presidential role. "It was mind-blowing," Cheney recalled. "Major role on the budget, major role on foreign and defense policy. Ford had asked for a hell of a lot, and they'd agreed to a hell of a lot."

The Reagan-Ford rumors were being dissected everywhere—including inside Jimmy Carter's White House.

Despite the polling that showed Reagan-Ford as the strongest ticket against the incumbent in the fall, Carter's high command liked what it was hearing out of the enemy's convention. Jerry Rafshoon, the president's communications director, discussed the Detroit chatter with Carter chief of staff Hamilton Jordan.

"We thought this could be a break for us," Rafshoon recalled. "The view on our side was that Reagan-Ford would probably work in our favor because it played right into our arguments that Reagan couldn't be trusted with the presidency. If the Republicans nominated Ford to be vice president, then it would look as though even Reagan's own party didn't think he could handle the big job without supervision, without somebody around to make sure he wasn't too quick on the trigger."

Back in Detroit, one key figure was never convinced that a Ford vice presidential scenario would work under any circumstances. Always protective of her husband, Nancy Reagan "thought the whole idea was ridiculous." Her view: "I didn't see how a former president—any president—could come back to the White House in the number-two spot," Mrs. Reagan recalled. "It would be awkward for both men, and impractical, and I couldn't understand why that wasn't obvious to everybody." She told her husband so directly. "It can't be done. It would be a dual presidency. It just won't work." Yet as the Wednesday evening session of the convention drew near, the talks continued.

At the Pontchartrain after lunch, Dean Burch, the Republican wise man, came into the Bushes' room. He told Bush that Kissinger and Greenspan, among others, were meeting with the Reaganites to bring off what was being called the "dream ticket."

"It's only a rumor," Burch told Bush, "but I wouldn't discount it." Bush was puzzled. "This is crazy," Bush thought. "This'll never happen." Bush believed his speech that night was critical. A strong performance might impress Reagan; a poor one might end Bush's hopes. He had to focus.

Bush's address to the convention was scheduled for eight P.M. Beforehand he jogged on the indoor track at the Detroit Plaza, had a snack, showered, and dressed. This was it—the last thing on his schedule. It was seven P.M.; he didn't have a great deal of time. Still, the television was tuned to CBS as he got ready.

Walter Cronkite's guest was the former president of the United States, Gerald Ford.

On the nineteenth floor of the Pontchartrain, Bush was listening carefully. On the sixty-ninth floor of the Detroit Plaza, Ronald Reagan was listening, too. Neither man wanted to miss a word.

Sitting with Cronkite and with Betty Ford in the CBS booth above Joe Louis Arena, Ford was candid about what would have to happen to get him to change his mind about joining the ticket. "I really believe that in all fairness to me, if there is to be any change, it has to be predicated on the arrangements that I would expect as a vice president in a relationship with the president. I would not go to Washington . . . and be a figurehead vice president. If I go to Washington, and I'm not saying that I am accepting, I have to go there with the belief that I will play a meaningful role across the board in the basic and the crucial and the important decisions that have to be made in a four-year period."

It was an honest description of his position, and, though the audience could not know it, of his team's posture in the talks at the hotel. Ford wanted substantive promises about substantive matters—nothing less. "For me to go there and go through the ceremonial aspects, it wouldn't be fair to Betty, it wouldn't be fair to me, it wouldn't be fair to the president, and it wouldn't be right for the country," Ford told Cronkite. "So I have to, before I can even consider any revision in the firm position I have taken, I have to have responsible assurances."

Cronkite asked about the "question of pride," as much for Ford as for Reagan, who, as Cronkite said, would be taking on a vice presidential running mate "who . . . has said, 'It's got to be something like a co-presidency'?"

Watching, Reagan sat up straight in his chair and said, "Did you hear what he said about a co-presidency?" Richard Wirthlin, who was in the room, recalled to Jack Germond and Jules Witcover "As far as Ronnie was concerned, that did it," recalled Nancy Reagan. In fairness, Ford's reply to Cronkite did not endorse the "co-presidency" idea—in fact, Ford seemed to say that such an arrangement would be problematic in practice—but the damage was done. All Reagan heard was the phrase "co-presidency." The public suggestion that Reagan would be sharing the sovereignty of the office with a vice president was unacceptable.

At the Pontchartrain, Bush was tying his tie as he watched the interview. He was, he said later, "stunned." He could not know how Reagan had taken the exchange: To Bush, Ford's remarks seemed to confirm the rumors beyond any doubt. Returning to the room to walk the candidate over to the convention, Burch told Bush not to worry about the Cronkite thing. "Put it out of your mind, George," Burch said. "Just concentrate on your speech."

There was nothing to do but get on with the evening, see everything through, be gracious no matter what. As Bush looked over his speech one last time before emerging onto the podium, someone he didn't know, a "backstage worker," as he recalled, approached him to shake hands. "I'm sorry, Mr. Bush, really sorry. I was pulling for you."

"Sorry about what?" Bush said.

"You mean you haven't heard? It's all over. Reagan's picked Ford as his running mate."

A few moments later, manfully pressing on, Bush told the convention: "If anyone wants to know why Ronald Reagan is a winner, you can refer him to me. I'm an expert on the subject. . . . His message is clear. His message is understood." Bush focused his fire on President Carter, saying that the "era of broken promises and unfulfilled commitments is drawing to a close. And the Reagan era of an America true to its promise of peace and prosperity is beginning."

He, Jeb, and Bush aide David Bates returned to the Pontchartrain, stopping in the lobby bar for a beer. Stepping into the elevator for the ride up to his suite, Bush had no reason to believe that he would come back downstairs again as anything other than an also-ran. There had been a couple of calls about Bush's willingness to endorse the whole plat-form if he were to be picked. From the Reagan camp, Richard V. Allen, the chief foreign policy adviser, had quietly reached out to the Bush cir-cle just in case the Ford negotiations collapsed. Yes, of course, Bush had replied absently: He supported the platform.

It all seemed academic. If it were Reagan and Ford, and if the Repub-lican ticket won in November, the big jobs—State, Treasury, probably Defense—were likely to be taken by the big men of the Nixon-Ford era: Kissinger, Greenspan, Rumsfeld, maybe Cheney. As he changed into khakis and a tennis shirt to watch the last hours of the convention session on television, George Bush believed history had passed him by. He opened another beer and let the bad news sink in. Jeb pounded his fist into his other hand. "This isn't fair, Dad," Jeb said. "This isn't fair to you."

His father cut him off. "What are you talking about, fair?" Bush said.

This was politics; this was real life. "Nobody owes us a damn thing. We're going to leave this city with our heads high and I don't want to hear that anymore." Bushes didn't whine. "Do your best and don't look back"— that was the code. David Bates had a bottle of Scotch in his room. Jeb told his parents good night and went down to join him. There was nothing left to do but have a drink and go to bed.

As the evening had worn on, Reagan's unhappiness with the Cronkite interview had deepened. At one point Reagan and Richard Allen were alone. The nominee asked, "almost rhetorically," Allen recalled, "Who else is there?"

"There's Bush," Allen said. He made the suggestion, Allen recalled, "half expecting" that Reagan would "close off the discussion" out of hand. "Instead, he paused and then said, 'I can't take him; that "voodoo economic policy" charge and his stand on abortion are wrong.'"

"If you could be assured that George Bush would support this platform in every detail," Allen asked Reagan, "would you reconsider Bush?"

"Well, if you put it that way," Reagan said, "I would agree to reconsider."

Reagan did not leave his suite as the hours ticked by. At 8:55 P.M., according to Allen, Ford and Reagan spoke on the phone; Ford told Reagan that Kissinger "now takes himself out" of consideration for secretary of state. (Kissinger had told Ed Meese that he would not accept a post as part of a Reagan-Ford power-sharing arrangement. "I thought it was absolutely untenable to have an imposed vice president and secretary of state," Kissinger recalled. "It would have led to an explosion.") Reagan said that they needed to reach a decision that night. The old actor's sense of his audience told him that a failed Ford deal on Thursday morning could damage his chances to deliver an effective acceptance speech. Better to move quickly.

By 10:45 P.M. Meese returned to report in from the ongoing talks with the Ford camp. "It's kind of hard to describe how it would work in practice," Meese said, according to Richard Allen. "The president will nominate the secretaries of State and Treasury, with the veto of the vice president. The vice president will name the director of the Office of Management and Budget and the national security adviser with the veto of the president. It boils down to a mutual veto power." The negotiators returned upstairs.

At the Pontchartrain, Jim Baker had given up hope. He sent Bush press secretary Pete Teeley down to the lobby to tell reporters covering Bush that "the lid was on"—meaning, in the vernacular of politics, that no more news was expected. In the Reagan suite, though, the atmospherics were shifting against Reagan-Ford. A source in the Reagan camp called Baker while Teeley was in the elevator going downstairs. "Hold everything," Baker told Bush. "This thing's about to come apart. Somebody's having second thoughts." Bush, exhausted, didn't react. Even if it weren't Reagan-Ford, Bush thought, "It might be Reagan-Laxalt, or even somebody who hadn't even been mentioned." Still, Baker had Teeley intercepted in the lobby before he could send the press off into the night.

By a quarter after eleven, after the roll call of states at the hall, Ronald Reagan was the nominee of the Republican Party, finally taking the prize he had first sought in 1968. At the Detroit Plaza, the negotiations dragged on inconclusively. Kissinger wanted the talks to continue into Thursday, but by this time Ford had decided it was best to take the safe path and say no to Reagan's offer. He went downstairs to speak with Reagan at 11:30 P.M.

"Ron, I've believed from the first, as I told you, this is wrong, and I feel even stronger about it, and I just don't think it's the right thing to do," Ford said, according to Reagan's recollection.

Reagan agreed. "Mr. President, I think if anything good has come out of this, I think it is that you and I have established a much closer relationship than we ever had," he said. Putting an arm around Reagan's shoulders, Ford replied, "We absolutely have. And I want you to know that I want you to win and I will do anything and everything I can to help you win." Ford returned upstairs, the drama done.

Except Reagan still needed a running mate. It was 11:35 on the penultimate night of the convention, and virtually everyone in the political universe was expecting a Reagan-Ford announcement. Reagan's question to his team was straightforward.

"Well, what do we do now?" All was quiet. "There was no immediate response," recalled Richard Allen. "No one offered an alternate plan. No one tossed out a name. Expecting instant opposition, I ventured, 'We call Bush.'"

No one had anything to say. Everything had been invested in the Ford

talks; Bush had emerged by default. Reagan had placed a call to Stu
Spencer that night. "Do you still feel the same way about Bush?" Reagan
asked. "Yes, I do," Spencer replied, recalling later that "pragmatism always prevailed with Reagan." There had been enough chaos. Reagan
knew the caricature he had to defeat. His opponents, he said, wanted
Americans to think of him as "a combination of Ebenezer Scrooge and
the Mad Bomber." Whatever reservations he had about Bush, Reagan
also knew that no one would ever mistake Bush for an extremist of any
kind. He was the safe pick, popular with moderates and popular enough
with most conservatives. Reagan seems to have become convinced that
if he could not have Ford it was still a good idea to have someone politically close to the Ford constituency.

"Well," Reagan said, "let's get Bush on the phone."

At 11:37 P.M., the telephone in Room 1912 of the Hotel Pontchartrain
rang. Jim Baker picked it up; Drew Lewis, a Reagan adviser, was on the
line.

"Is George Bush there?"

"Yes," Baker said. "Who's calling?"

"Governor Reagan."

"Just a moment," Baker said.

Bush took the receiver from Baker and put the phone to his ear.

"Hello, George," Reagan said, "this is Ron Reagan. I'd like to go over
to the convention and announce that you're my choice for Vice President . . . if that's all right with you." ("You pray that George will say yes,"
Baker whispered to Barbara, who came into the room just as Bush was
beginning to speak with Reagan.)

Bush turned to the others in the room, flashing a thumbs-up sign. "I'd
be honored, Governor," Bush said.

"Out of a clear blue sky, the phone rang," Bush recalled. "Out of a clear
blue sky. I thought we were done, out of it, just gone."

"George, is there anything at all . . . about the platform or anything
else . . . *anything* that might make you uncomfortable down the road?"
Reagan mentioned abortion in particular.

As Bush recalled it, "I told him that I had no serious problem with
either the platform or his position on any of the issues, that I was sure
we could work together, and that the important thing was that he win
the election in November."

"Fine," Reagan said. "I'll head over to the convention, then we'll get together in the morning."

As Bush hung up, he was a saved man.

Walter Cronkite had to regroup. "Well," he said, "let's see what George Bush would bring to the ticket."

In the Bushes' suite, now full of well-wishers—in politics nothing succeeds like success—Barbara was still virtually speechless from the chaos of the day. "The politics of it all were amazing," she wrote. "Kissinger—Greenspan and other Ford aides urging him to do this foolish thing. . . . All with selfish interests. Why not? That's the name of the game!"

Bush took a few questions from the press at his hotel. What had he told Reagan? That he would "enthusiastically support the platform" and that he would "work, work, work" to win in November. "How did this happen?" a reporter asked. Bush had no idea. "I have no indication. . . . It was a total surprise to me," he said.

At the hall, Reagan addressed the convention at a quarter after midnight. Yes, Reagan told the delegates, he and Ford had discussed the vice presidency. They had, Reagan said, "gone over this and over this and over this," but now "he and I" had reached the conclusion that Ford would confine his role to campaigning for the ticket as a former president.

Then came the rest of the news. "And I talked to a man we all know, and a man who was a candidate, a man who has great experience in government, and a man who told me that he can enthusiastically support the platform across the board," Reagan said. "I have asked and I am recommending to this convention that tomorrow when the session reconvenes that George Bush be nominated."

The Bushes met the Reagans for coffee the next morning. In the interval between his withdrawal from the presidential race in May and the late telephone call the evening before, Bush had thought that any issues between him and Reagan could be put aside if the two men could just spend some time together.

With Reagan that morning there was "no hint of any tension," Bush recalled. Reagan aide Michael Deaver remembered Barbara's parting words to Reagan at that first coffee. "You're not going to be sorry," Barbara told Reagan. "We're going to work our tails off for you." As

Deaver recalled it, "And they did. It was the greatest thing anyone could have said to him then."

At a press conference, Reagan and Bush were besieged by questions about the Ford deal. Asked whether Bush was the second choice, Reagan replied, "I think the situation is so unique that a former President—and this is the way many party leaders viewed it—that the possibility that he might do this on the ticket—rejoin a ticket having been President of the United States—was such that I think it is a little more unique and a different situation than having a first or a second choice."

A reporter pressed Bush, asking him whether being "the number two choice for the number two spot" was "a problem for you in this campaign." Bush was dismissive. "Absolutely not. The fact that Governor Reagan had discussions with President Ford as he said is unique, the very unique standing that President Ford has," Bush said.

Then Bush made a point that came directly from the heart of his character. "And what difference does it make?" he asked. "It's irrelevant. I'm here." Why look back, when there was so much to look forward to?

But how, Bush was asked, could he support a platform that did not endorse the Equal Rights Amendment and called for a constitutional amendment on abortion when he had supported the ERA and opposed such an amendment in his own campaign?

"My view is that the big issues, the major issues in the fall, will be the questions of unemployment and the economy and there are going to be the questions of foreign affairs," Bush said. "I oppose abortion. I favor equal rights for women. I'm not going to say I haven't had differences at some point with Governor Reagan and everybody else, many other people. But what I will be doing is emphasizing the common ground. I will be enthusiastically supporting this Republican platform. That's the way it's going to be. I'm not going to get nickel-and-dimed to death with detail."

What about Reagan's supply-side views, which Bush had consistently opposed?

"Listen, let me enthusiastically support the proposal that Governor Reagan made in terms of taxes," Bush said. "We both recognize that cutting taxes is the way to help people and to stimulate production is the important thing. And please do not try to keep reminding me of differences I had. I want to get there on the same wavelength and go forward together."

There were two criteria for a good vice president, Bush said: the ability to support the president "in conscience" and to be prepared to take over in the event of calamity. "I expect that Governor Reagan concluded that I measured up . . . and I hope and will strive to fit those two criteria."

What about Bush's "repeated insistence" during the primaries that he didn't want to be vice president?

"Can you ever imagine a person running for President saying he was running because he wanted to be vice president?" Bush replied. "I can't. And I have no regrets about that. I ran hard, and as I've said over and over again, got beaten fair and square and I have absolutely no qualms about accepting this."

Working overnight and into Thursday, the Reagan campaign made sure the Bush pick appeared fully sanctioned by the right. Bob Dole was asked, and agreed, to deliver the nominating speech for Bush. Seven seconders were lined up, including conservative heroes such as Senator Orrin Hatch of Utah and Senator Roger Jepsen of Iowa as well as the more moderate Congressman William Goodling of Pennsylvania and former secretary of labor Arthur Fletcher. "We found no bad feeling—no bad vibes," wrote Barbara. During an introductory film for Reagan, an image of a young Nancy flashed by. "That must be the first Mrs. Reagan," said Dorothy Bush—but, as Barbara noted, "fortunately no one heard."

On Friday morning the Reagans and the Bushes traveled from Detroit to Houston. They lunched at the Bushes' house on Indian Trail then went to the Galleria for a rally. "If Texas and California can't do it," Reagan told the crowd, "it can't be done."

For Bush, life was good. "He is a serious, able, and likable man," *The New York Times* editorialized after Bush's nomination. "Ronald Reagan's second choice is not second-rate." Bush was delighted. "Life is now hectic—pushed here & there," he wrote a friend. "I think we're going to win it."

A telling shift from the "Bush for President" days: It was now "we," not "I"—the price of resurrection from the politically dead. But Bush was back where he wanted to be: alive, and on the move.

TWENTY-TWO

Well, What Do We Do Now?

★

*Call me if I can lighten the burden. If you need someone to
meet people on your behalf, or to turn off overly-eager office
seekers, or simply someone to bounce ideas off of—
please holler.*

—GEORGE H. W. BUSH to Nancy and Ronald Reagan

THE BUSHES HAD FEW PROBLEMS shifting to the Reagan cause.
The transfer of allegiances from "Bush for President" to "Reagan
for President" was made easier by the Bush worldview of looking
ahead, and his decade of service to Nixon and to Ford had prepared him
well for a supporting role. "It was a cliffhanger," Richard Nixon wrote
Bush of the vice presidential selection, "but you won and I am convinced
it was best for November." At the Commonwealth Club in San Francisco, Bush spoke and took questions from a large audience. Barbara was
seated next to Caspar Weinberger, one of Reagan's longtime California
supporters, and he told her "lots of top Reagan people were not sure
about G.B. and had questioned his loyalty. Now they were thrilled with
the choice."

Where there were differences between Reagan and Bush, the Bushes
either denied they existed (the path Bush favored) or minimized them
(the Barbara technique). Asked to predict Bush's role in a Reagan administration, both Bushes demurred. "George lost the election," Barbara
told interviewers. His job now was to back Reagan.

In August 1980, Bush, finding a role in the campaign as an international envoy from Reagan to the world, made a trip to Japan and to
China. His mission: to reassure foreign capitals that the GOP presidential nominee was not a Cold War cowboy. Before Bush even left for Asia,
though, he faced questions about Reagan's apparent suggestion that the
United States should establish government relations with Taiwan, thus
enraging China and endangering nearly a decade of diplomacy.

It fell to Bush to reassure Beijing that Reagan, despite his pro-Taiwan remarks, intended no major shifts in the U.S.-Chinese relationship. When the Bushes arrived in Beijing, the first major official with whom they met started in on Taiwan. Bush spent an hour on it, clarifying the Reagan position. One sign of how upset the Chinese were came when Barbara was harangued by an official "about the R.R. policy. He got very excited—loud voice—much gesturing—etc. First time that has ever happened to me. The word is out because we got the same lecture from everyone we saw! I have never had business mentioned to me before."

After the journey, the GOP ticket met the press in Los Angeles, and Reagan supported the position that Bush had articulated in China. Though Reagan was sentimentally attached to the old Cold War romance of supporting Taiwan against the mainland, he was realistic enough to see that the world had moved on, and that he must move on with it. The press conference was arduous, with Reagan answering question after question.

Sitting with Barbara in their suite afterward, waiting to leave for the airport, Bush said, "The governor is such a nice fellow." In her diary, Barbara agreed. "He is sincerely nice," she wrote. "The questions were nit-picking and he kept answering. I couldn't help but contrast George's saying that to what he said once as we came home from a White House dinner years ago during those trying Nixon days. George said, 'I wish I could like Nixon better.' He—at this time—respected him—he just wasn't likable—now here we (maybe I should say I and not we) are worrying about R.R.'s ability—but really liking him. Crazy world."

I t was a wild fall, pitting Reagan against Carter against John Anderson, the Illinois Republican who was running as an independent candidate. The race between Reagan and Carter was close through much of the autumn. Reagan promised "a new beginning" to a country weakened by recession and by the image of American impotence in the face of the Iranian hostage crisis and of the Soviets in Afghanistan. Carter portrayed Reagan as coldhearted and trigger-happy.

Given Reagan's tendency to tell inaccurate anecdotes, misstate statistics, and issue inexact statements of policy, the Bushes, as part of the campaign, faced questions about the head of the ticket's grasp of detail. Barbara privately called them "Reagan's glitches."

On Sunday, September 7, 1980, Bush appeared on *Meet the Press*. At one point Bush was asked whether he agreed with Reagan's view that the theory of evolution was perhaps flawed. Bush refused to answer, calling the question "peripheral."

"We've been sitting here for twenty-two minutes," Bush told the panel of questioners in the NBC Washington bureau studios on Nebraska Avenue NW. "You know what the number one issue in this campaign is? It isn't evolution. It's the economy."

Reagan and Carter met in a single debate, in Cleveland on Tuesday, October 28. The Bushes flew in for the occasion and sat with Nancy in the auditorium. When the candidates appeared on the stage, Reagan walked over and shook Carter's hand—a gesture that left Carter looking "taken aback," Barbara wrote. Barbara leaned over to Nancy and said, "I think [Reagan] looks so much better than Carter. His makeup is better."

"Ronnie never wears makeup," Nancy said.

A group of big-dollar Republican donors passed along concerns in the middle of the fall. "They tell us that Jimmy Carter's underground campaign is working," Barbara wrote. "'R.R. is going to do away with Social Security'; 'R.R. hates blacks,' etc." The race was touch-and-go from week to week. Billy Graham was so worried that he told Barbara "that if it looks like we're losing in the end of October he will come out publicly for R.R. & G.B." Presenting Reagan in a moderate light to moderate voters was part of Bush's brief in the final days. "Governor Reagan is a decent, compassionate man," he said at Michigan State University in East Lansing. He repeated the message over and over.

On the last day of campaigning before the election, Reagan and Bush sat together for a television taping. It was early—seven or eight in the morning—and Reagan was off his game. The spot was for broadcast that night, and it opened with a wide shot of Reagan and Bush side by side in chairs before focusing on Reagan, who was to give a half-hour appeal. Reagan advisers Mike Deaver and Stu Spencer were watching and were surprised at Reagan's performance. "God, he's awful," they said to each other. Never a morning person, Reagan knew he was flailing a bit.

"I'm awful," he volunteered. "This chair's too soft; I want to go to sleep." Deaver and Spencer fixed the chair, and started again.

"Then Reagan just nailed it—a half hour without a hitch," Spencer recalled. "And the whole time, Bush watched him do it with a look of awe—just awe—on his face." He knew he had much to learn.

On Tuesday, November 4, 1980, the Bushes voted in Houston. Feeling confident, Bush told reporters that he thought the Republican ticket was "in like a burglar." The numbers were looking good—very good. Sitting on the floor of a suite at the Houston Oaks Hotel before a bank of three televisions, Bush roughhoused with the family, then mock-remembered his new dignity. "Respectful, respectful," he intoned, according to a *New York Times* story by Arthur Sulzberger, Jr. "We didn't imagine a sweep like this," Bush told Sulzberger.

Ronald Reagan and George Bush had defeated Jimmy Carter and Walter Mondale in a landslide. (Carter called Reagan to concede so early in the evening that he caught the president-elect in the shower.) Reagan-Bush won the popular vote over Carter-Mondale and Anderson, 50.75 to 41 percent (John Anderson polled 6.6 percent). The electoral college margin was even more impressive, 489 for Reagan to 49 for Carter.

Bush was ebullient. The exhaustion of the mad months of the post-Detroit campaign—the trip to Asia and the punishing tours of September and October—disappeared in the excitement of victory. "Well done, sir, well done," Bush said to Reagan, pumping the president-elect's hand as they met in Los Angeles on the day after the election. "Well, what do we do now?"

The first order of business was a press conference at the Century Plaza Hotel announcing the transition team. During the campaign, when Bush was asked about his role in a Reagan administration, he answered candidly. If he won Reagan's confidence, there would be "tons to do"; if he didn't, well, in that case Bush said he would be "going to a lot of funerals." At the press conference on Wednesday, November 5, 1980, a reporter quoted Bush's remark and observed that Bush seemed to be winning Reagan's confidence. Was that the case, the reporter asked? And if so, was George Bush to play a substantive role in the new administration?

Of Bush, who stood to his left on the stage, Reagan said, ". . . [H]e's not going to be going to a lot of funerals. Maybe we'll take turns."

To his defeated rival, Walter Mondale, Bush wrote: "I'd love to sit down with you. Thank you for your wire, your call, your just plain decency. I've lost—plenty—I know it's no fun." To Reagan, he pledged affection and loyalty. "Please know that we both want to help you in every way possible," Bush wrote the Reagans on Monday, November 10, 1980.

"I will never do anything to embarrass you politically. I have strong views on issues and people, but once you decide a matter that's it for me, and you'll see no leaks in Evans and Novak bitching about life—at least you'll see none out of me. . . . Call me if I can lighten the burden. If you need someone to meet people on your behalf, or to turn off overly-eager office seekers, or simply someone to bounce ideas off of—please holler."

Before November 1980 was over, the administrative details of the Reagan-Bush relationship were set. Ed Meese, who was to be counselor to the president, and Dean Burch, who had been working for Bush, worked out four ground rules that were memorialized in a memorandum from Burch to Bush dated November 21, 1980. "1) You and the President will have a scheduled weekly luncheon—no staff, no agenda; 2) You will automatically be invited to all presidential meetings; 3) You will receive a copy of all memoranda going to the President; 4) You will have the present Vice-President's [West Wing] office."

"I like it," Bush wrote in a quick note to Jim Baker. Bush was delighted with the arrangements—and even more delighted that Baker, whom Reagan had asked to run the general election campaign, would be White House chief of staff, giving the vice president a friend at court. "My presence [will] hopefully limit staff conflicts that tend to result in VP being cut out," Baker wrote in notes he kept during the transition.

Bush dismissed the fashionable talk that the vice presidency didn't mean anything. If it were such a terrible black hole, Bush asked rhetorically, "then why do so many people want it?" He answered his own question: "Because with a 70-year-old president, you could become president at any time."

TWENTY-THREE
The Special Relationship

★

He's hard to read; he doesn't ask for advice; he doesn't say,
"what do you think about this," very much—but the other side
of that is, I feel uninhibited in bringing things up to him.

—GEORGE H. W. BUSH, on working with Ronald Reagan

AFTER DETROIT, Ronald Reagan came to trust George Bush, particularly when the No. 2 on the ticket proved to be true to his word never to try—even if he could have—to outshine Reagan. "Bush had a special relationship with Reagan," wrote Reagan domestic policy adviser Martin Anderson. Reagan was determined, Anderson said, to bring Bush "deep into the inner sanctums, virtually letting him sit by his side as he conducted his presidency."

Reagan was an intelligent delegator, Bush discreet and conscientious. Those genuinely familiar with the two men believed they would form a strong working partnership. "I know both of them, and they're gentlemen," Bryce Harlow, the old Republican hand, remarked to Boyden Gray, the Washington lawyer who became Bush's longtime counsel. "It won't be anything like Kennedy and Johnson. It's going to work better than anything in the modern era."

Bush had hardly been able to contain his enthusiasm during the inaugural festivities on Tuesday, January 20, 1981. Supreme Court justice Potter Stewart, as usual, administered Bush's oath of office. During the parade that afternoon, an ecstatic Bush waved to the crowds with such energy that some observers thought he might fall out of the limousine.

At the first meeting of Bush's vice presidential team, the chief of staff, former admiral Daniel Murphy, was clear about how things were to be. "Don't upstage the President's staff. That would be the quickest way to alienate George Bush from Ronald Reagan." Murphy also said there should be "no surprises and no self-aggrandizement. There's only one star on this staff, and that's George Bush."

Bush at once learned that the vice presidency was unlike any post he had ever held. His jobs since his days in the House—the United Nations, the Republican National Committee, China, the CIA—had specific briefs. Serving Reagan brought Bush into contact with every conceivable area of interest and concern. And yet Bush was realistic about a critical fact of political life: The president is the president, and not much else matters. He hoped to serve Reagan well and to reassure the now-essential right wing of the Republican Party that he was a worthy successor to the president, who was the true conservative hero. It was a difficult, even exhausting political task, for in the Reagan years Bush was largely seen either as a man with no real convictions or as a moderate Machiavelli who, with James Baker, was determined, in the political vernacular of the right, to keep Reagan from being Reagan. The two caricatures of the vice president were in conflict: Bush could not simultaneously be a craven wimp with no agenda other than his own ambition and be a secret Rockefeller Republican genius capable of manipulating Ronald Reagan. (The former required no philosophy at all and the latter was all about philosophy.)

As vice president, George Bush was neither as irrelevant as many thought nor as powerful as many feared. His diaries of the period—sporadic but still revealing—show that he spent the Reagan years working hard to be useful to the president, struggling, from year to year and election cycle to election cycle, to convince the base of his party that he could be trusted with the Reagan legacy.

At his core, Bush judged his vice presidency on the degree to which Reagan himself trusted him—or didn't. In the first year of the administration Alaska senator Ted Stevens wrote Bush to say " 'Separate yourself from 1600 on some issues,' " Bush recalled. "Bad advice, totally impossible advice."

The role Bush crafted for himself was that of senior confidential adviser and absolute administration loyalist. Reagan appreciated his vice president's ready ear and usually sound counsel, and he took Bush for granted in the best sense of the term. For Reagan, Bush appears to have been kind of a human Marine One—a perk of the office that made life easier. Like the presidential helicopter, Bush was always there, an accepted and natural part of the daily action.

Reagan could be enigmatic even to those who had known him for a great deal longer than Bush had. Still, the two men developed a working relationship that, while not even remotely one between equals, was one in which the principal came to trust the subordinate and the subordinate came to respect the principal. "When I do bring up something controversial," Bush told his diary in the first Reagan term, "he might not comment; he might not say anything right there; and he might not look particularly enthralled about it all or say, 'Tell me more'; but I never get the feeling that he doesn't want me to tell him, so I do and I try not to overdo it."

Bush developed a set of informal rules of conduct for himself in his new role. He spelled them out only later, toward the end of his service as vice president, but for him they were real and controlling from the beginning.

> First, don't play the political opportunist's game by putting distance between yourself and the President when some White House decision or policy becomes unpopular. . . .
> Second, don't play the Washington news-leaking game. . . .
> This leads directly to the third rule . . . conduct all interviews on the record—even interviews with friends, especially if you want to keep them as friends. That way you're less likely to be surprised when you later read or hear yourself quoted in the press.

Where did Bush's sense of the vice presidency come from? The origins of his theory—and his practice—that the number two man should be seen but not heard, save for private moments with the president, can be traced to Bush's understanding of the experiences of Walter Mondale in the Carter years and of Nelson Rockefeller during the Ford administration. "Be sure not to take any line responsibilities," Mondale had warned Bush, who interpreted the advice to mean that he should avoid "permanent assignments covering specific areas of Administration policy," for competing interests within the government with stakes in the given subject would try to stymie whatever it was that you were trying to do. "The Vice President's authority in any executive area comes from the White House, but the lines are sometimes blurred," Bush recalled. "Since Washington is a turf-conscious environment—never more so than at or near the center of power—a Vice President perceived to be stepping over a line could be on a collision course with the White House staff or some Cabinet member."

Which is what had happened to Rockefeller. The former New York governor had arrived in Washington in 1974 determined to play a significant role in domestic policy. He chaired the White House's Domestic Policy Council but found that the staff, which could focus more tightly on fewer issues than Rockefeller, was in control despite the seeming power of the vice presidency. Rockefeller hated it. In a conversation with Bush, who was then CIA director, in the vice president's Old Executive Office Building office, Rockefeller had spent twenty minutes expressing his frustrations. "My relations with the President are good," Rockefeller had told Bush, "but that damned staff has cut me off at the knees."

Bush never forgot Rockefeller's words. If you could have good relations with the president, then what else really mattered? The key to taking on specific assignments was to make sure you had the authority as well as the responsibility—the ability not just to make recommendations but to implement them. For Bush, the lesson of Rockefeller was to focus upward, on the president, and if handed a more traditional task within the administration, make certain you had the power to act, not just argue.

Bush also quickly formed an affectionate view of Reagan, which, given Bush's nature, was not surprising. "I spent sixteen years fighting the man and what he stood for," Bush told Congressman Mickey Leland, a Texas Democrat, in February 1981. "But I didn't know him." Reagan, Bush said, was "unthreatened by people or events, a superb person."

Bush attended daily briefings in the Oval Office, and there were weekly lunches, usually on Thursdays, featuring Mexican food. (Bush added a lot of hot sauce to his chili; Reagan did not.) "Before lunch every week, there was a vacuuming for new jokes to tell," recalled Boyden Gray, Bush's legal counsel. (Bush dropped some jelly beans into his lap by mistake one day while sitting in the Oval Office. "George, I've got a question to ask you," Reagan said. "What else do you feed that thing besides jelly beans?")

One morning in 1981 was typical of the Reagan-Bush relationship. Bush called the Oval Office to see if Reagan "was busy and he wasn't, so I stuck my head in." They chatted about interest rates and proposed cuts in defense. Reagan shared a clip from *The Wall Street Journal* that argued business leaders should take a cue from Reagan and go on vacations, delegate authority, and preserve their energy for the big things.

There was a sense of ease and of spontaneity between the two men.

Gray remembered a meeting with Bush and a group of young visitors with severe disabilities. "They were very difficult to communicate with, but Bush was masterful at it," Gray recalled. Bush decided to take the kids down the hall to the Oval Office to meet President Reagan. There was no appointment, no notice. Reagan was delighted, and the session lasted an hour. "That was the level of comfort," Gray recalled, "of even informality then."

There was one discordant note: Mrs. Reagan, who never truly embraced the post-Detroit spirit of reconciliation between the two former opponents. While Reagan himself was perfectly pleasant to the Bushes, his wife grew formal, distant, even cold. She worried about the Bushes upstaging the Reagans and declined to open the Reagan social circle to include the vice president and his wife. The Bushes were rarely invited to the private quarters of the White House in the Reagans' eight years in power.

Between the election and the inauguration, William Wilson, a member of Reagan's "kitchen cabinet" from California, came to Bush. "Right after Reagan had been elected—and I had been elected vice president—we got a message from this guy Wilson," Bush recalled. "It turned out he was carrying water for Nancy on this. The message was, 'Stay out of the paper, get a lower profile, back down. Tell the Shrubs to keep a lower profile.' We weren't taking a high profile, not doing the Washington thing of saying this or that, and it burned me up, and it burned Barbara up. She was very unhappy about it, deservedly so. We couldn't back down if we hadn't backed forward. We hadn't done anything. Hadn't done a damn thing. And I was very careful about that, always. Still don't know what drove that. But Nancy and Barbara just did not have a pleasant personal relationship."

What was behind Nancy Reagan's restrained but real hostility toward the Bushes, particularly Barbara? Theories abounded. There was perhaps lingering anger over the 1980 primary campaign, when Bush made an issue of Reagan's age. There were cultural differences—East Coast versus West Coast, old WASP society versus Hollywood, politics versus entertainment. The show business explanation has much to recommend it: In the Reagans' Hollywood universe, there could be only one leading couple. In the Washington of 1981–89, Ronald and Nancy Reagan were the stars, and the supporting actors, George and Barbara Bush, were to stay deep in the background. Ever vigilant and prone to worrying, Nancy wanted to make certain that the Bushes knew their place.

Fortunately for Bush, Mrs. Reagan's skeptical view of the vice president was not widely shared in Reagan's inner circle. One sign of Bush's success in overcoming the doubts of Detroit in the Reagan inner circle came when Ed Meese and Mike Deaver (along with Jim Baker) recommended that Bush be put in charge of the administration's top-tier national-security crisis management group. There was a sound internal logic to the decision. Traditionally the national security adviser had played this role, but Secretary of State Alexander Haig, sensitive to any encroachment on his policy territory, did not, as Reagan recalled, "like or trust" the incumbent national security adviser, Richard Allen. The president approved of the Bush appointment. "Not only would that deal with Haig's unhappiness over Allen," Reagan wrote, "I also thought that it was prudent—and important for the country—for the vice-president to play as large a role in the affairs of the administration as possible; I didn't want George, in the words of Nelson Rockefeller, simply to be 'standby equipment.'"

The decision enraged Haig, who called Reagan to protest. The secretary of state, Reagan recalled, "didn't want the vice-president to have *anything* to do with international affairs; it was his jurisdiction, he said, and he told me he was thinking of resigning." The outburst proved the Bush idea had been a sound one. An anonymous White House aide (who sounded an awful lot like Jim Baker) was quoted as saying, "the President simply feels more comfortable with George because he doesn't let his ego and ambition show and he doesn't come off as strong as Al Haig."

Bush was also a key figure on the rollback of federal regulations on business. Formally known as the Presidential Task Force on Regulatory Relief, the group's mission was part of Reagan's decades-long campaign against excessive government intervention in the economy. Bush went about the work quietly but persistently.

Operating under Executive Order 12291, issued by President Reagan in February 1981, the Bush task force reviewed existing regulations and served as a referee for any new proposals. Reagan had spelled out the guiding principle in the executive order: "Regulatory action shall not be undertaken unless the potential benefits to society for the regulation outweigh the potential costs to society." According to domestic policy adviser Martin Anderson, the task force took on 181 regulations in thirteen departments in the first three months, saving an estimated $18 billion in the first year and an annual $6 billion going forward.

It was difficult to gauge the Bush task force's impact in part because much of its power was preventive. The bureaucracy and special interest groups found themselves defending existing regulations so much that, as Anderson put it, "they didn't have any time left over to dream up many new regulations. . . . Any significant proposal for regulation by any part of the Reagan administration would have eventually come up for review in Bush's task force. None ever came up because none were ever proposed." The environment was also a crucial part of Bush's portfolio. "Ronald Reagan delegated a great deal of presidential authority to him, particularly on environmental regulation," recalled Bush counsel Boyden Gray. Bush was, then, critical in the regulatory sphere of the 1980s. It was typical of him to hide in plain sight, exercising a measure of power without being stagey or seeking publicity.

I n the middle of March 1981, Bush took off on a four-day trip to Florida to build support for the administration's economic package. At a Brevard County fundraiser, astronaut Wally Schirra, who introduced Bush, had some fun with the Reagan-Bush team, saying that Bush was so "tall, handsome, and urbane that he is the first politician who may become an actor." The trip was tense, though, because of what was unfolding back in Washington.

An odd rumor had begun circulating around the capital. According to the story, the vice presidential Secret Service detail had accidentally shot Bush while he was leaving a weekend assignation in Georgetown with Janet Steiger, the widow of his friend Bill Steiger, at three o'clock in the morning. A mugger was said to have tried to attack Bush, and the agents, aiming for the assailant, hit Bush instead. In another version of the tale, the mugger had stabbed Bush.

In Melbourne, Florida, on Tuesday, March 17, Bush speechwriter Vic Gold advised publicly confronting the story. "Both GB and I think that dignifying a smear like that with a statement would be wrong," Chase Untermeyer, Bush's executive assistant, wrote in his diary. "Let it die of its own foolishness." Bush refused to engage, and the vice presidential party flew back to Washington.

The next morning, Wednesday the eighteenth, Bush's staff met in his West Wing office. A fire was burning in the fireplace. The Steiger rumor was growing in intensity. Though no one had yet reported the story, journalists from major news organizations were calling. One columnist, Maxine Cheshire, told Bush press secretary Pete Teeley that her source was a Secret Service agent. "The Service has firmly denied the whole episode, and Jim Baker saw their logs," wrote Untermeyer. "GB's attitude is one of low-burning anger, but he will refrain from making a comment."

Where had the story come from? Rich Bond, the Iowa caucus veteran and Bush political adviser, thought the rumor had originated with conservatives who were trying to deflect attention from "a recent story that Reps. Jack Kemp [Republican from New York] and Tom Evans [Republican from Delaware] and Sen. Dan Quayle [Republican from Indiana] shacked up with a winsome lobbyist named Paula Parkinson, who taped their intimate encounters with her." (That story, too, was untrue.) Later that day, Shirley Green, Teeley's deputy, warned the staff not to talk about the story for fear that such speculation would give the press the "news peg" it needed to write about the rumor. (As Untermeyer wrote, they needed to avoid headlines like "'Bush Staffers Suspect Far Right of Spreading Sex Rumor.'") The FBI was called in; Director William Webster, a former federal judge, had already heard a variation of the rumors—"a version that had GB coming out of an expensive bordello," as Untermeyer put it—and promised to investigate. Bush was interviewed by two FBI agents on Friday, March 20, 1981, and the story fell apart.

On Sunday, March 22, *The Washington Post* published a piece headlined "Anatomy of a Washington Rumor: False Tale Takes [On] Life of Its Own, Swiftly Spreads—Then Collapses."

The Bush circle was pleased it had kept a dignified silence about the whole drama. "We handled the whole matter appropriately, grandly ignoring it and letting it die on its own," wrote Untermeyer. "We can't forget, after all, that we're supposed to be the class act in this town."

On Saturday, March 28, Bush attended the annual dinner of the Gridiron Club, an exclusive gathering of politicians and journalists. Reagan spoke to the club, and Ginger Rogers was among the guests at the Capital Hilton.

Reagan was solicitous of Bush. "Does he feel what he's doing is worth-while?" the president asked Barbara at Reagan's seventieth birthday party in February. "I just want to be sure he's doing enough." Then Reagan raised the most terrible prospect of all. "If the awful-awful should happen," the president said, "George should know everything."

TWENTY-FOUR

The President Was Struck

★

My every inclination is to be calm, not churning around.
—GEORGE H. W. BUSH

Have you ever known a day this wild?
—BARBARA BUSH

I T WAS DARK AND DRIZZLING in Washington when George Bush awoke in his bedroom in the vice presidential residence on the grounds of the U.S. Naval Observatory early on Monday morning, March 30, 1981. Because he was taking off from Andrews Air Force Base for a trip to Fort Worth and to Austin at 8:55 A.M., Bush had arranged for the CIA to deliver his daily briefing at the residence on Massachusetts Avenue rather than at the White House.

Chase Untermeyer and Jennifer Fitzgerald, another aide, met Bush, and they helicoptered out to Andrews. They landed on the runway in the rain and hurried onto Air Force Two. Awaiting Bush aboard the jet were two Texas congressmen—Kika de la Garza, the Democratic chairman of the House Agriculture Committee, and Bill Archer, a Republican from Houston.

The flight to Fort Worth was just shy of three hours. Bush asked Untermeyer, Fitzgerald, and Vic Gold to join him in his stateroom for a continental breakfast and a briefing on the day ahead. At about a quarter to eleven central time Air Force Two began its descent to Carswell Air Force Base near Fort Worth. In Texas the weather was sunny and warm; Untermeyer noted that early spring rains had made the North Texas plain freshly green. In Fort Worth, Bush's first stop was the unveiling of a historical plaque at the Hotel Texas, where John Kennedy spent the last night of his life.

In the White House, Reagan was having a quiet lunch and taking a final look at a speech he was to deliver shortly to a meeting of the Building and Construction Trades Department of the AFL-CIO. The venue on this gloomy Monday: the International Ballroom of the Washington Hilton.

After his stop at the Hotel Texas in Fort Worth, Bush was driven to the Tarrant County Convention Center to address a Texas and Southwestern Cattle Raisers Association luncheon. He spent an hour and twenty minutes at the event. He left the convention center at 1:20 P.M. central time and arrived back at Carswell.

Jim Wright, the House majority leader, was joining Bush for the forty-five-minute flight to Austin, as was Congressman James Collins, a Republican from Dallas. Chase Untermeyer, an alumnus of the Texas legislature, sat down with Wright, Collins, and Bill Archer, who was still with the vice presidential party. As the 707 taxied down the runway, Bush chatted in his stateroom with two of his loyal Texas aides, Jack Steel and Betty Green. It was 1:45 central time, 2:45 in Washington. An air traffic controller, without explaining why, radioed Air Force Two's cockpit once the plane was in the air: "Are you continuing to Austin or diverting to Washington?"

"We're heading to Austin, as scheduled," came the reply. Monitoring radio communications through a headset, a Secret Service agent on the plane heard there had been a shooting as the presidential party left the Washington Hilton a few moments before. According to this first report, two agents had been struck, but the assailant had missed Reagan. "Sir, we've just received word about a shooting in Washington," Ed Pollard, the head of the Bush Secret Service detail, told the vice president a moment later. "There is no indication that the president has been hit. Word is that two agents are down. That's all we have right now. But I'm going to make some calls and see if I can get some more information."

"Where did it happen?" Bush asked.

"Outside the Washington Hilton," Pollard said. "I'll let you know when we get more information."

In the interval between Bush's departure from the Cattle Raisers Association meeting and the boarding of Air Force Two for the 1:45 P.M. central takeoff for Austin, John W. Hinckley, Jr., a mentally disturbed young man, had opened fire on Reagan outside the Hilton at 2:27 P.M. eastern time.

Getting off six shots from a .22-caliber revolver, Hinckley wounded four men: White House press secretary James Brady, Washington, D.C., police officer Thomas Delahanty, Secret Service agent Timothy McCarthy, and Ronald Reagan. At first no one, including Reagan, understood that he had been hit; he initially believed that he had broken a rib when he had been rushed into the back of the car. The president complained of difficulty breathing and was coughing up blood. At the direction of Secret Service agent Jerry Parr, the president was driven from the hotel to George Washington University Hospital rather than to the White House. Doctors at the hospital found that Reagan had, in fact, been shot, struck by a bullet that had ricocheted off the presidential limousine and entered the left side of Reagan's chest, coming to rest an inch from his heart.

Barbara Bush learned of the shooting while working at her desk in the vice presidential residence. The television was on but muted. She looked up at one point to see the news reports and the raw, choppy footage of the shooting outside the Hilton. "I couldn't believe what I was seeing," she recalled. "My heart ached so for Nancy." Barbara understood, however, that the human instinct to turn up in order to be of quiet support was, in this case, the wrong impulse. "I knew that the best thing I could do for her was to stay away; what she needed was a best friend," Barbara recalled—and Barbara Bush was not Nancy Reagan's best friend. Barbara's own best friend, Andy Stewart, Potter Stewart's wife, came over without delay.

Jim Baker and Ed Meese were driven from the White House to the hospital. Learning of the shooting while at the State Department, Al Haig reached Baker and said that he would contact Bush. At the White House, Haig, still in his trench coat, walked into Baker's office and picked up the phone to be connected with Air Force Two.

"Mr. Vice President, this is Secretary Haig," Haig said. "We had a serious incident and I'm sending you a message by secure line. I recommend you return to Washington as soon as possible."

Bush heard that much from Haig, but the connection was poor, and after breaking the initial news, Haig was speaking only to static. Then Don Regan, who as secretary of the Treasury oversaw the Secret Service, called Bush, "urging that I scrub my Austin schedule and fly back to Washington." Implicit in the message, Bush believed, was a warning about his own safety. "Any attempt on the President's life alerts the Service to the possibility that it might be part of a larger plot," Bush recalled. The vice president could be in danger. The shooting in Washington might be an isolated act—or it might be part of a wider conspiracy to take out the top leadership of the American government. "We have no way of knowing that there weren't gunmen sent to Washington, Fort Worth, and Austin," a member of Bush's Secret Service detail remarked on Air Force Two.

As Bush absorbed Haig and Regan's advice, he was handed the decoded telex from the White House. "Mr. Vice President: In the incident you will have heard about by now, the president was struck in the back and is in serious condition," Haig had written. "Medical authorities are deciding now whether or not to operate. Recommend you return to D.C. at the earliest possible moment."

This was the first Bush knew that Reagan had himself been shot. The scope of what was happening was clearer, and more frightening. In the air on his 707, heading for Austin, Bush thought of the tragedy that had befallen another president not quite eighteen years before. "It had to occur to me, but I didn't want to think about it," Bush recalled. "The [Hotel Texas], where I'd unveiled the national historic plaque a few hours before, had been the place that John F. Kennedy had spent the night of November 21, 1963, before his visit the next day to Dallas." There was more. "Even the plane we were on had played a part in that tragic trip," Bush recalled. "It was the Air Force Two used by then–Vice President Johnson as he accompanied President Kennedy to Texas on November 21, 1963." Was history repeating itself? Had Bush come to Texas as vice president—and would he leave it as president?

Air Force Two was nearing Austin. As the aircraft closed in on the Robert Mueller Municipal Airport in the Texas capital, the plane's televisions picked up the ABC News coverage of the shooting. The flickering black-and-white images—of what Bush recalled as "the crack of gunfire, people hitting the pavement, Secret Service agents struggling with the suspect, the President's car speeding away"—deepened Bush's sense of the moment.

The plane landed briefly in Austin to refuel. Bush canceled his speech to the legislature. He would return to Washington as quickly as the 707 could safely take him. Outside Air Force Two, the dignitaries who had gathered to greet the vice president were in mild shock. "Various friends came up to say hello," wrote Chase Untermeyer, "smiling bravely and looking up at the plane, as if it were a symbol of the government in Washington, from which we all felt semi-removed."

On the ground in Austin, Bush called Dan Murphy, who was in the Situation Room that afternoon. Murphy briefed him on Brady, Delahanty, and McCarthy. From the hospital, Meese told Bush that Jerry Parr's decision to go straight to the emergency room had probably saved Reagan's life. The president was still in surgery. News of his condition and prognosis—presuming he survived—was several hours away. Bush asked for a moment alone. He wanted to collect his thoughts, he said—and "to say a prayer not simply for the President of the United States but for someone I'd come to know and respect."

The plane was soon in the air for the two-and-a-half-hour flight to Andrews. Bush called Barbara several times. "I really needed to be near his voice, and he must have sensed that," Barbara recalled. Reporters on board were anxious to speak to the vice president, but his instinct was to hold off. He said no interviews—not, he added, "until we had more information." Bush understood his role—to "wait," as he put it, "and stay calm." The White House counsel, Fred Fielding, was at work on the mechanics of invoking the Twenty-Fifth Amendment in the event Reagan remained unconscious for a long period. "They're preparing papers for the transfer of authority if that becomes necessary," Bush told his staff aboard Air Force Two.

For all Bush knew Ronald Reagan could die on the operating table in the waning hours of afternoon. Yet the vice president showed no fear, no anxiety. "He seems so calm," Jim Wright wrote in a diary he kept on the flight, "no signs whatever of nervous distress." In a way, Bush had been here before. Long ago he had been charged with life-and-death responsibilities on an airborne mission. Then he had been twenty years old, an aviator in the vast mosaic of war. Now he was in middle age, a statesman returning to the precincts of temporal power. Then, amid fire and smoke, he had finished his mission. Now, amid uncertainty and doubt, he was determined to do his duty, which, as he saw it, was to lead quietly and with dignity.

Ed Pollard and John Matheny, the vice president's air force aide, conferred with Bush about arrangements upon arrival in Washington. "There might be a crowd at Andrews," Pollard said. "If you don't mind, sir, we'd like to bring the plane into the hangar and disembark there."

Bush agreed. Then the conversation shifted to the next step of the journey. Pollard and Matheny argued that Bush should take a helicopter from Andrews directly to the South Lawn of the White House. That was by far the fastest route—faster and safer than helicoptering to Observatory Hill and driving down Massachusetts Avenue to the White House.

The idea made all the sense in the world—except to Bush. His first rule as vice president, he recalled, was the "most basic of all the rules. . . . The country can only have one President at a time, and the Vice President is not the one." A showboating vice president who attracted attention to himself was a reminder of the president's absence. Intuitively, Bush believed that the stronger he looked the weaker the president might seem. "At this moment I am very concerned about the symbolism of the thing," Bush said to Pollard and Matheny. "Think it through. Unless there's a compelling security reason, I'd rather land at the Observatory or on the Ellipse."

Landing on the South Lawn was the president's prerogative, and the last thing Bush wanted was to be seen as trying to usurp the privileges of the president. The South Lawn felt "too self-important," Untermeyer wrote of the debate between Bush and his security men. There was precedent, Pollard and Matheny countered, for a vice president to use the South Lawn. "But we have to think of other things," Bush replied. "Mrs. Reagan, for example."

Bush understood the logistical and symbolic arguments for the South Lawn. "By going straight to the White House, we'd get there in time for the 7 P.M. network news," Bush recalled. "What better way was there to reassure the country and tell the world the executive branch was still operating than to show the Vice President, on live TV, arriving at the White House?" The prospect, however, troubled Bush. *The President in the hospital . . . Marine Two dropping out of the sky, blades whirring, the Vice President stepping off the helicopter to take charge,"* Bush mused. "Good television, yes—but not the message I thought we needed to send to the country and the world."

Matheny was thinking in practical terms. "We'll be coming in at rush hour," he told Bush. "Mass Avenue traffic will add anywhere from ten to fifteen minutes to your arrival time at the White House."

"Maybe so," Bush said, "but we'll just have to do it that way."

"Yes, sir," Matheny said, but Bush saw that he looked puzzled.

"John," Bush said, "only the President lands on the South Lawn."

At around four P.M., Brady deputy Larry Speakes gave a series of inconclusive answers in the White House briefing room. "If the president goes into surgery and goes under anesthesia," one reporter asked, "would Vice President Bush become the acting president at that moment or under what circumstances does he?"

"I cannot answer that question at this time," Speakes said.

"Larry, who'll be determining the status of the president and whether the vice president should, in fact, become the acting president?"

"Pardon?"

"Who will be determining the status of the president?"

"I don't know the details on that."

Worried that this series of shaky answers suggested the government was in confusion, Haig, who had been watching Speakes on television, rushed upstairs from the Situation Room to address the cameras. He did not pause to compose himself. Out of breath and perspiring as he took the podium, Haig attempted to project a sense of calm. "I just wanted to touch upon a few matters associated with today's tragedy," Haig said. "First, as you know, we are in close touch with the vice president who is returning to Washington. We have in the Situation Room all of the officials of the cabinet who should be here and ready at this time. We have informed our friends abroad of the situation, the president's condition as we know it, stable, now undergoing surgery. And there are absolutely no alert measures that are necessary at this time." Bill Plante of CBS asked the key question. "Who's making the decisions for the government right now?"

"Constitutionally, gentlemen, you have the president, the vice president, and the secretary of state in that order and should the president decide he wants to transfer the helm to the vice president, he will do so," Haig said. "As of now, I am in control here, in the White House, pending return of the vice president and in close touch with him. If something came up, I would check with him, of course."

A floor below, Don Regan said, "Is he mad?" In his rush to reassure the nation and the world, Haig had misstated the line of presidential succession and seemed power-hungry. (Under the Presidential Succes-

sion Act of 1947, both the Speaker of the House and the president pro
tempore of the Senate are ahead of the secretary of state in the order of
succession.)

Bush watched Haig's performance on the black-and-white television
on Air Force Two. At ten after five eastern time, the Bush party heard an
erroneous ABC News report that James Brady had died of his wound.
The shooting itself, Haig's press conference, the Brady news, the uncertainty about Reagan's prognosis: It was misery upon misery.

Yet Bush was outwardly serene. "It's hard to describe my emotions,"
Bush dictated to Untermeyer on the plane. "They're cumulative. A funny
thing: the way Reagan's and my relationship has developed—not
presidential–vice presidential but more like a friend. [There's] a concern for someone who's your friend. Because I see it that way—seeing
him [on videotape] getting into that car, waving—I see it on a personal
plane." He had no doubts about his own capacity to govern if it came to
that. If there were, say, a military crisis in Eastern Europe arising out of
current Soviet-Polish tensions, "having to be the person to determine
that, [to] be the critical person to make that decision—I don't have any
consternation about it at all. . . . My every inclination is to be calm, not
churning around," Bush said. "I would have thought it would have been
much more complicated about the responsibilities, but my innermost
thoughts are [that] this guy is a friend. . . . I think about Nancy Reagan:
Is anybody holding her hand? I have a great feeling that all will work out.
The President is very strong."

At 6:08 P.M., Bush's telephone buzzed. Ed Meese was calling to report
that Reagan was out of surgery and things looked good. "That's
wonderful—that's very good," Bush said. Meese would meet Bush at the
vice presidential residence. "See you at the house," Bush said.

Looking out the window as Air Force Two approached Andrews, Untermeyer noticed a bright sunset after hours of rain; the combination of
the setting sun and the slick pavement of the capital cast the city in a
strange orange light. The aircraft landed and taxied into Hangar 7 before Bush boarded the helicopter for the short trip home. Barbara, with
Meese at her side, was waiting for him. The Bushes, Untermeyer recalled, embraced, and Bush and Meese shook hands. The motorcade was
ready, and off Bush went. Untermeyer and Fitzgerald went back toward
the house with Barbara. "Have you ever known a day this wild?" Barbara
asked.

"What's the latest?" Bush asked as he walked into the Situation Room.

The cabinet members, *The New York Times* reported, "rose respectfully." Later a few would recall that though they had called Bush "George" before the assassination attempt, they addressed him as "Mr. Vice President" from the moment he came into the Situation Room. "The President is still President," Bush told them. "He is not incapacitated and I am not going to be a substitute President. I'm here to sit in for him while he recuperates. But he's going to call the shots."

Earlier, with Haig misstating the line of succession, things had seemed chaotic, and Haig and Secretary of Defense Cap Weinberger had exchanged tense words over the alert status of U.S. forces. Now, with good news of the president and with Bush, Meese, and Jim Baker in the White House itself, matters seemed in hand. When sensitive national security issues were raised in the rundown for Bush in the Situation Room, Baker and Bush called for a pause in the discussion to ask whether everyone present had the proper security clearances.

It was a straightforward question. By posing it they further defused the tensions in the White House, for several aides and others without the right clearances filed out of the tiny Situation Room, easing the crowding and giving the principals a bit more room and a bit more air.

Should Bush make a public statement to offer a benediction to a long, miserable day? "I think I could," Bush said. "And just say we are very pleased. I don't think we need questions, either." At eight P.M., Bush called an end to the running meeting in the closed, claustrophobic Situation Room in favor of a much smaller group in his own office upstairs in the West Wing. A few remarks were drafted, and he walked into the briefing room.

From the podium where a succession of figures had failed to reassure since the shooting—a long eight hours—a calm George Bush addressed the nation at 8:20 P.M. It was the briefest of statements. He said he was "deeply heartened" by an upbeat report from Reagan's doctors. The president, Bush said, "has emerged from this experience with flying colors and with the most optimistic prospects for a complete recovery. I can reassure this nation and the watching world that the American government is functioning fully and effectively. We've had full and complete communication throughout the day and the officers of the federal government have been fulfilling their obligations with skill and with care."

The last point was not strictly accurate, but Bush thought it wisest to cast Haig's difficult afternoon in the best possible light. Piling on the secretary of state would not serve the president or the country.

Bush returned to his office. There he called congressional leaders to check in and telephoned the wives of Thomas Delahanty and Tim McCarthy. Deciding against visiting the president at the hospital, he learned that Nancy was back in the Residence and went over to pay his respects. "She looked tiny and afraid," Bush remarked to his staff when he returned a few moments later.

Everything was quiet—or as quiet as it could be under the circumstances. At about nine thirty P.M., roughly twelve and a half hours after he had left Washington for Texas for the most routine of political day trips, George Bush went home.

About 1:30 A.M. in Washington, Art Weise of *The Houston Post* put in calls to Bush's staff to ask an uncomfortable question: Did Neil Bush, who had moved to Denver, know John Hinckley, whose family also lived there? Oddly, Neil and his wife had been scheduled to dine with Hinckley's brother the night after the assassination attempt. There was more. "The Hinckleys are a prosperous family, and John Sr. may have been a Bush contributor," Untermeyer wrote in his diary after speaking with Weise. "Art wanted to know if this connection was known by GB in flight, and I said that as late as the helo ride from Andrews to the Observatory, we weren't even sure what the gunman's name was." Weise made an excellent point in the overnight calls: "even a slight Bush connection in this shooting could set off the conspiracy freaks."

The next morning Bush's staff met him at his car on West Executive Avenue to brief him on Weise's questions. "Jesus," Bush said, but Untermeyer recalled that Bush seemed "only mildly concerned, so little in fact that he didn't think to call Barbara or ask any of us to do so." Pete Teeley suggested a quick probe into any further links, including the possibility that John Hinckley, Sr., might have donated money to Bush's campaigns. An hour passed before it became clear that there was nothing more to the story than remarkable coincidence.

Bush had the fullest of days on Tuesday, March 31, 1981. With Reagan recovering, Bush stepped into what a vice presidential aide told reporters was a "pinch-hitting" role. At the White House, Bush convened the cabinet but notably presided from his usual chair across from the president's. He met with congressional leaders to hear a report on the investigation of the shooting from Attorney General William French Smith. Bush's air of reserved authority was such that everything appeared perfectly calm. After the White House sessions with Bush, Senate Majority Leader Howard Baker told journalists that "never for a moment was there any interruption of the normal lawful chain of command" during the long afternoon the day before.

At eleven o'clock in the morning, Bush drove up to Capitol Hill. In an eighteen-minute appearance on the Senate floor, he reassured lawmakers, dismissing talk of tension among the president's top officials in the wake of the Haig moment. "I have not detected, nor do I believe, there's any such rift," he said. Amid reports that the administration had considered invoking the Twenty-Fifth Amendment on Monday, Bush said that Reagan's current condition rendered all of that moot. "There's no need for any emergency procedures—the power of the Vice President to do anything," Bush told senators. Steady as she goes, he might have added: steady as she goes.

He returned to the White House to receive Andreas A. M. van Agt, the prime minister of the Netherlands, at a quarter after one. There was a brief ceremony and then a lunch to discuss NATO, Poland, and the Soviet Union. After briefing Reagan at the hospital a few days later, Bush told reporters that the president was "fully on top of the situation." To Bush, no other message mattered more than that Reagan was president, was on the mend, and all would be well. "That's the main point I want to make," Bush said. "It's not useful to go into any more detail."

On Wednesday, April 1, 1981—the second full day of Reagan's recovery—the usual 9:15 Oval Office national security morning briefing was held in Bush's West Wing office. Weinberger arrived ahead of Haig and was chatting with Bush when they heard the door rattling. The doorknob had been acting up lately and had now broken completely—at just the moment Haig was trying to use it. "Go right on in, Mr. Secretary!" Jennifer Fitzgerald said to Haig, who stood helplessly in the outer office. "I get the feeling it's a little inhospitable," Haig said with what Untermeyer recalled was a "wry smile." Weinberger finally opened the door from the inside to let Haig in.

Ten days later, on Saturday, April 11, President Reagan returned to the White House to continue recuperating there. Bush had spent part of the morning running in the Secret Service marathon in Beltsville, Maryland.

Freshly showered—his hair was still wet—he joined Barbara at the White House to greet the president, who was dressed in a bright red sweater.

The crisis had passed, and Bush emerged from the crucible of the shooting as a sensible and steadying force. Expected to be presidential but not too presidential, he had performed well. Reagan, already disposed to treat Bush with respect, had all the more reason to believe that his vice president's professions of devotion and duty were genuine. Decades later, recalling his performance on the day of the shooting and in the aftermath, Bush said: "Did it help me with President Reagan? Sure, I think so. He saw—and Nancy saw, I might add—that I'd meant what I'd said all along, since he called me up in Detroit. He was the president, I wasn't. A president has enough to worry about without having to worry that his vice president is undercutting him, or trying to make himself look good at the president's expense. I'd decided that he deserved my total loyalty, and he got it."

The political class approved of what it had seen. "Vice President Bush . . . seems sure to gain in clout because of the calm manner in which he filled in for the President at Cabinet meetings and ceremonial functions," wrote *Time*. "His demeanor, neither pushy nor retiring, impressed even some Reaganites who had considered him a mushy moderate. Said one: 'He has been impressive. He has a good sensitivity to the situation.'" In *The New York Times*, William Safire wrote, "George Bush struck just the right note." Larry Speakes, the deputy press secretary whose unsteadiness had provoked the Haig appearance on the day of the shooting, recalled that "I have never been so impressed with Bush as I was that night, the way he instantly took command."

For Bush, the most political of matters—the attempted murder of the president of the United States—was interpreted through the prism of the personal. Asked about what was going through his mind during the attack and afterward, Bush would reply, "I worried about my friend who was hurt."

Over club sandwiches on the first Wednesday in May 1981, Bush aides Rich Bond and Chase Untermeyer talked about "contingency planning for the time when President Reagan might die in office." They were working without Bush's knowledge—the vice president would have shut them down, hard, if he'd been aware of the project—but believed it crucial to work on the question. Bond reported commissioning research on the Nixon-Ford and Kennedy-Johnson transitions and urged Unter-meyer to read Bob Hartmann's book *Palace Politics,* which covered the Ford period. The goal of the lunchtime conversation was the ultimate production of a "Memorandum for the File" that would "include such things as how to set up a swearing-in and who would get which jobs and offices in the immediate post-event days."

The staff could do as it wished. The assassination attempt gave Bush himself a new perspective on Reagan. While in the hospital, the president spilled some water in his bathroom. He then got down on his hands and knees to clean it up. He worried that the nurse might get in trouble if he didn't. Bush always remembered the moment—in part, his speech-writer Christopher Buckley later observed, because that's what the vice president himself would have done.

TWENTY-FIVE

George Did It

★

Do you think we feel less than others about nuclear war? We want peace, and we want to keep the peace.

—GEORGE H. W. BUSH, responding to a challenge from the Campaign for Nuclear Disarmament, 1983

The nuts will never be for me. We might as well recognize it. I've been doing this for thirty years.

—BUSH, on the Republican right wing, 1983

A S HE RECUPERATED in the spring of 1981, spending his days in the Solarium on the top floor of the White House, Ronald Reagan, wearing pajamas and a bathrobe, decided to reach out directly to Soviet leader Leonid Brezhnev. "I wanted to let him know that we had a realistic view of what the Soviet Union was all about," Reagan recalled, "but also wanted to send a signal to him that we were interested in reducing the threat of nuclear annihilation." For Reagan, the letter marked a shift in tone. Nine days after the inauguration in 1981, in response to a question from ABC News's Sam Donaldson, Reagan had offered a dark view of Soviet intentions. Communist leaders, he said, "reserve unto themselves the right to commit any crime, to lie, to cheat."

Now, after his shooting, the president produced an initial draft of a letter on a pad of yellow paper arguing that the Soviets had nothing to fear from the United States. He appealed to Brezhnev to think beyond the Cold War. "Mr. President," Reagan wrote, "should we not be concerned with eliminating the obstacles which prevent our people from achieving their most cherished goals?" Brezhnev, Reagan recalled, sent back an "icy reply. . . . So much for my first attempt at personal diplomacy." Yet, as his letter indicated, Reagan was willing to deal. One of the president's gifts as a negotiator was his capacity to blend the harshest of rhetoric with the boldest of disarmament proposals—up to and including nuclear abolition. By November 1981, a few months after his first effort, the president had again written Brezhnev, this time to propose a "zero-zero option": The United States would not deploy a new generation of intermediate-range missiles in Europe, the Pershing IIs, if the Soviets would dismantle three types of intermediate-range nuclear weapons.

In the Cold War of the early 1980s, Reagan mixed increased Pentagon spending, the domestic deployment of the MX missile (an intercontinental weapon), and a hawkish tone with proposals such as the zero-zero option for intermediate-range nuclear forces (INF). His vice president appreciated Reagan's strategy of talking tough while arguing for specific disarmament ideas. "I think there [is] a certain unpredictability . . . about us" on the Soviets' part, Bush told his diary, "and I think that's good."

The Soviets rejected Reagan's zero-zero option, which made the president all the more determined to deploy the Pershing IIs. Though the Europeans had first sought such an INF deployment in 1979, antinuclear sentiment was proving politically popular, particularly in West Germany, where elections were to be held in March 1983. "The American government must urgently get away from the thought that Western Europe and especially West Germany are military colonies of the U.S.A.," declared the Greens, a West German antinuclear party. Facing the risk that the Atlantic alliance could fracture, with European allies refusing to support the Pershing deployment that was scheduled for late 1983, Reagan asked Bush to go to Europe to make the case for the American position.

It was a complex assignment. Bush would travel through seven different nations trying to defuse Reagan's image as a nuclear cowboy. Part of his task in Europe, Bush told reporters, was "to impress upon them the depth of conviction that our president has about arms reduction." Reagan had crafted the strategy and projected the vision of either an INF-free European theater or an enhanced NATO force in Europe to counter the Soviet missiles in place. It was Bush's job to sell the strategy and explain the vision to a skeptical Europe.

He was "up but edgy" about the high-profile trip as he helicoptered from the vice presidential residence to Andrews in late January 1983. *The Washington Post* sent him off with these words on the editorial page: "The vice president seems to us just the right man—positive, experienced, political—to satisfy the allies' real craving for a strong and sensible American lead."

In West Berlin, Bush spoke at a dinner given by Mayor Richard von Weizsäcker at the Intercontinental Hotel. Pulling a piece of paper from his suit pocket, the vice president announced that he was about to read an open letter from President Reagan to "the people of Europe" calling on new Soviet leader Yuri Andropov to meet with Reagan "wherever and whenever [Andropov] wants in order to sign an agreement banning U.S. and Soviet intermediate-range land-based nuclear missile weapons from the face of the earth." The offer Bush presented had the desired effect. The call for a summit, said West German opposition leader Hans-Jochen Vogel, was a "positive development. It is the first time Reagan has offered such a step and we greet it. It is progress." (Andropov rejected the overture as a propaganda ploy.)

In private meetings with European leaders and in public remarks, Bush signaled an American willingness to pursue arms control progress while standing by the U.S. commitment to the Pershing II deployment in the absence of Moscow's agreeing to the zero-zero option, or at least something close to it. By putting a reasonable face on American policy, Bush lowered rhetorical tensions. He spoke of knowing Reagan's "heartbeat," of understanding how much the president wanted peace. British prime minister Margaret Thatcher cabled Reagan warm words about Bush's mission. Over eleven days, Bush traveled to seven countries, doing the hard work of diplomacy.

On the last day of a long journey, in the ornate, twelfth-century Guildhall in the City of London, Bush declared that he had discovered that the Atlantic alliance was in strong shape. "Once again I found that the rumors of the death of our alliance have been greatly exaggerated," Bush told the Royal Institute of International Affairs in the medieval splendor of the setting. "What unites us is still far more enduring than whatever divides us." Diplomatic boilerplate, perhaps, but the CIA was reporting internally that opinion in European capitals appeared to be moving from pre-journey skepticism to post-journey support for U.S. plans. There was more work to be done, of course, Bush told his diary, "but the groundwork is laid, and the tide, to some degree, has been turned."

At the Guildhall, Bush was challenged by Bruce Kent, general secretary of the Campaign for Nuclear Disarmament. With what his aide

Chase Untermeyer thought was "great sincerity and almost Churchillian majesty," Bush replied: "Do you think we feel less than others about nuclear war? We want peace, and we want to keep the peace." Capturing the scene in *The Washington Post,* Michael Getler, a reporter who had followed Bush's tour, wrote: "It was a succinct way to put one side of the argument about the best way to avoid war. Bush's point was that military balance, even if it meant lots of weapons, was one way to keep the peace and that such a view did not mean that those who support it are any less concerned about nuclear war than those demonstrating against it." It was a fitting coda to an effective journey.

I n Washington, Bush was treated as a returning hero. "Bush faced his European challenge with all the zeal of a man who would like to be president," *Time* wrote. He was congratulated in the halls at the White House and was thrilled when he stopped in the Oval Office to see the president, who "jumped up with that warm, really welcome-home expression that made me feel that he had thought it was worthwhile." Bush appeared on CBS's *Face the Nation* on Sunday, February 13, 1983. "Everybody I talked to, 'great trip, great trip,'" Bush told his diary. "It's funny how fleeting all of this is, but I think at this juncture, it's fair to say things have gone pretty well." Reagan called him after the broadcast to congratulate him.

In the end, the INF deployments took place, the pro-American Helmut Kohl won reelection, and Americans, after the Bush visit, appeared more rational in European eyes. *The Washington Post* congratulated Bush extravagantly. "He listened carefully and he elaborated Washington's approach to the missile question in a way that allowed open-minded Europeans to consider that the administration is not missile-happy, not bent on confrontation . . . but . . . is determined to assert American leadership and to deserve the confidence of the allies." The headline on the *Post* editorial said it all: "George Did It."

O n the political home front, the vice president spent a good deal of time and energy seeking to assuage elements of the Reagan coalition that he hoped would one day be elements of a Bush coalition. When Bush accepted an invitation to address the American Conservative Union, he told his staff he should do it, even though "the nuts will never be for me. We might as well recognize it. I've been doing this for thirty years." He did have one thought: Perhaps the best path forward lay in "establishing good relations with individual conservative leaders." He would deploy his most formidable political asset—his personal charm. He might never win their hearts, but he would give them no reason to say that he hadn't tried.

In the Reagan years, then, Bush often met with the kinds of conservatives who had been doubtful about him, including the Moral Majority's Jerry Falwell. In Manchester, New Hampshire, Bush nemesis William Loeb of *The Union Leader* had died in September 1981. At the suggestion of Gerald Carmen, Reagan's old New Hampshire chairman, Bush had reached out to the right-wing publisher a few weeks before, and the two men had had a cordial exchange. On hearing of Loeb's death, Bush dispatched a message of condolence. "I didn't want it to look too flowery or effusive," Bush told his diary, "because he hated me and I was not overly enthusiastic about him."

Jim Baker, who was serving as Reagan's chief of staff, was also a frequent target of the right. "Jimmy Baker at year end is tired and would like to transfer," Bush told his diary on New Year's Day 1983. "He would love to be CIA or Defense or certainly Attorney General; but there is no indication that the President is going to make any changes of this nature." Bush was sympathetic to his friend's hopes to move out of the exhausting chief of staff post, but he did not know Reagan's views on the matter. "I don't think the President will let him go, although who knows what's in the President's mind," Bush dictated on Tuesday, January 4, 1983. "He keeps his cards very close to his chest when it comes to personnel matters and that kind of thing." A few weeks later another possibility emerged. "Jimmy Baker was in today wondering about going to the U.N., Jeane Kirkpatrick having had it, apparently, and having had enough," Bush told his dairy. "I recommended it to him—I think he should get out. He's my friend and a loyal friend, but I think it would be good for him to be on about his business and doing something else. You get destroyed in there, and he's done a wonderful job. . . . Now he ought to be in a Cabinet post or something out of the place where he's a continual target for the far right." Bush suggested that CIA director William Casey go to the United Nations and Baker take over at CIA. "He was thrilled and went charging out of the office, but what he did with that brilliant idea of mine, I don't know." Nothing would come of Baker's efforts to move on in 1983: He was too valuable to Reagan where he was.

As Bush worked to placate the right, he found raw politics at the highest levels alternately fascinating and repellant. After a hostile interview with columnist Joe Kraft, Bush dictated, "They try and drag you into highly technical matters—some of which I know—but I'm so defensive as to not wanting to mess up things that I get irritated."

He preferred the substance of governing to the style of politics, and Bush believed in listening to voices outside the innermost circles. "I had briefings from middle-level experts at the CIA on Germany and France on arms," he told his diary. "I find it very worthwhile to get these people in. There is a great deal of expertise in our bureaucracy that is never used by the top policy makers."

For all his work with conservatives, Bush learned something he had not expected to from watching Reagan, who deferred action on many cultural issues crucial to his supporters and who even quietly raised taxes. "The President is a darn good compromiser, and he's had to compromise and, yet, his adherence to a position comes through loud and clear," Bush dictated. "I think it's important that you don't compromise too much, but you have to have the facility to govern, to get things done, and that is what some of these people don't understand."

Would Reagan seek reelection in 1984? In January 1983, Bush told his diary: "Incidentally, at this moment, I'm convinced the President is going to run. I see no question about it; I believe it; I'm convinced in my own mind that he should run; and I think he'll be re-elected." And yet the president—already older than the oldest man to have ever served—was not explicit about his own thinking. On Thursday, January 20, 1983, the president and the vice president appeared together at an event commemorating the second anniversary of their inauguration. "Today when he walked across that stage, he looked a little older and he was limping and his voice was hoarse, and I was wondering for the first time as to whether he might not [run]," Bush told his diary. By late April 1983, however, the questions were answered: Reagan was running, and he wanted Bush by his side. Though the vice president had won Reagan over—which, in the short run, was all that mattered—Bush sent Jim Baker a copy of a *Conservative Digest* article that found 64 percent of conservative leaders wanted Bush replaced on the 1984 ticket. "Light reading," Bush scribbled across a cover sheet to Baker—adding a frowning face.

In the spring of 1984, the family took a trip to Hobe Sound, Florida, to see Bush's mother. Dorothy Bush, Barbara wrote, "really was wonderful and she did very well at keeping everything low key. (She usually invites the world to meet Pop as she is so proud of him). . . . Mom amused me because I heard her say to the tennis pro, 'Of course, George will play with Jeb. George likes to win.' . . . At 60 years of age his mother still says he wants to win." He did, but he had one more campaign to win as a lieutenant before he would, in 1988, take what he knew would be his last shot at the presidency itself.

For much of the year, the 1984 campaign was not especially dramatic. The economy was doing well, and Reagan was popular. For the Bushes the race to succeed Reagan four years hence was an implicit element of much of the campaign. In the spring, Reagan and Bush went to speak to the Conservative Political Action Conference together. "I hated it," Barbara wrote. "All of these people have been against George Bush. . . . The President spoke and then he led the standing ovation for George, bless his heart. I would have died if he hadn't! They were polite, but it is just not comfortable."

In July 1984, Walter Mondale, the Democratic presidential nominee, made history by choosing the first woman for a national ticket: New York congresswoman Geraldine Ferraro.

"Tensions are very very high," Bush wrote his sister, Nancy Bush Ellis. "I am totally convinced (I hope not conspiratorially so) that we are up against many in the press who hate to see the demise of Ferraro and the defeat of Mondale." In his eagerness to show conservatives that Reagan had been right to choose him in 1980, and perhaps overcompensating for his reticence about the counsel he offered the president, Bush seemed an inarticulate, hyperactive cheerleader. "His apostasy [from his 1980 centrism] had to be pure, credible to every dedicated Reaganite," observed the biographer Herbert S. Parmet. The assets that made Bush an effective adviser to Reagan and might make him a sound president—his aversion to sloganeering, his belief in bipartisanship, his devotion to principled compromise—were, in his reading of the Republican electorate of 1984, liabilities. Bush entered a silly season, still desperate to prove his partisan bona fides two decades after he first appeared on a GOP ballot. "Whine On, Harvest Moon," he would say in a lame attempt at wittily countering the Mondale-Ferraro critique of the administration.

"I'm for Mr. Reagan—blindly," he said on the '84 trail, leaving the impression that he was a man without a core of his own.

Shrewd observers—chiefly Garry Trudeau of the editorial comic strip *Doonesbury,* himself a St. Paul's and Yale man—pounced. Bush, Trudeau argued, had put his manhood in a blind trust and had an evil twin, "Skippy," a dark, ambitious alter ego who said and did whatever it took for "Poppy" to win and cling to power. (At a reception for the *Today* show a few years later, Trudeau, the husband of *Today* cohost Jane Pauley, told Bush that he had heard "one of [your] sons was hot," and George W., who was there, said yes, that he had "really wanted to kick your ass.")

The campaign press depicted Bush as effete and wimpy. Bush resented his enduring caricature as an eastern elitist. "It's funny how those who have real breaks early in life" get put in one of two categories, he told his diary. "If you're a Republican, that's bad; but if you're a Democrat, a la Kennedy or Harriman or Roosevelt or whoever, why, it's no problem." Thinking ahead to a vice presidential debate with Ferraro, Bush reflected on his dilemma. "She's kind of mean and prosecutorial, and if you come back tough, why, you get it for beating up on a woman; and if you don't, you come back as a wimp," he dictated. "No win!"

Nothing was going right. Barbara told reporters that Ferraro could be described as a word that rhymed with "rich." The night before, in one of the Reagan-Mondale debates, Mondale had "needled the President about his elite, rich vice president," Barbara recalled. "It really had burned me up because we had all read that Geraldine and her husband, John Zaccaro, were worth at least $4 million, if not more. The press were teasing me about it, and I said something like, 'That rich . . . well, it rhymes with rich . . . could buy George Bush any day.'" It was, Mrs. Bush recalled, "not a nice thing to say," and she called to apologize to Ferraro. ("She was very gracious about it," Barbara recalled.) The aftermath of the "rhymes with rich" story was "agony" for Barbara. ("She felt horrible," George H. W. Bush recalled.) "For several years I thought it would be engraved on my tombstone," Barbara wrote in her memoir. "My family teasingly called me the 'Poet Laureate' of our household."

After the vice presidential debate—one in which Ferraro accused Bush of condescending to her about foreign policy—Bush was with some longshoremen, one of whom had a sign that said "George, you kicked a little ass last night." Then, in what Bush characterized as a "big mistake," he said that yes, he *had* tried "to kick a little ass last night"—

a bit of discordant locker-room talk. (Bush had not noticed a nearby TV microphone.) The press even criticized Bush for attending a fortieth anniversary event in Norfolk commemorating the mission at Chichi-Jima. He was attacked for "epaulette flexing" and accused of "flaunting" his war record. But none of it affected the outcome of the 1984 election: The Reagan-Bush ticket crushed the Democrats, carrying forty-nine states.

Even in victory, though, Bush was worn down. After the election, the Reagans offered the Bushes the use of Camp David. There, in the quiet woods, the vice president of the United States rested and pondered what was ahead. He slept soundly, recuperating from the rigors of the campaign trail, and looked forward. The 1988 presidential election was forty-seven and a half months away.

TWENTY-SIX

On the Eve of the Run

★

These are serious people, among the best we have, with the
gifts of intelligence and friendship and compassion.
—SCOTTY RESTON, on the Bushes, *The New York Times*, Wednesday,
December 31, 1986

B USH FIRST RAISED his own presidential ambitions with Reagan on
Thursday, December 13, 1984. Over lunch, Bush spoke of 1988 and
told the president that while he and Barbara "hated to think of it
this soon," they felt that, as Reagan well knew, a national campaign was
so intricate and so complex that they needed to begin making staffing
and fundraising decisions. Ever deferential, Bush made it clear to Reagan that he was not asking for "any reaction" or any favors, nor did the
president have to worry that Bush was "going to be out there plowing my
own furrow, or creating my own positions, etc. I just can't do that." The
vice president could tell that talk of life after Reagan made Reagan a bit
uncomfortable: Presidents tend to dislike being reminded that they are
replaceable, even after two terms. Reagan, however, told Bush he was
"doing the right thing," and the conversation moved on.

For Bush, the second Reagan term was largely about what was to
come—1988. As the vice president and a host of rivals maneuvered for
position in the contest to succeed Ronald Reagan, there were rising
federal deficits, historic Cold War breakthroughs with Moscow, and, in
the waning weeks of 1986, a scandal involving hostages in the Middle
East, arms sales to Iran through Israel, and secret funding for the anti-
Communist Nicaraguan contras. The question that shaped Bush's days:
Would the American electorate of 1988 want four more years of Republican rule? And, more specifically, would the nation want Reagan's
most loyal lieutenant to be the one to take the helm? Bush hoped so—
deeply and urgently—but it would be a long four years before he could
know so.

On Christmas Day 1984, Bush read a thirty-seven-page memorandum from Lee Atwater, a young southerner who had made his name in the brutal politics of South Carolina before joining the Reagan political office in the White House. (Atwater talked out the strategy; his colleague James P. Pinkerton did the writing.) Back in the 1979–80 period, the memo said, Bush had been "portrayed in the media as a man of substance. That image was a major contributing factor in his Iowa victory. Soon thereafter, the media began to paint George Bush as merely a man of style—a man of 'Big Mo' and little else." The reelection race against Mondale and Ferraro had not helped, the memo said, for "the VP [was] stereotyped in the press as a 'cheerleader' for the Reagan administration. 'Cheerleader' is a negative way of saying 'loyalist.'"

Atwater framed the task ahead gently but unmistakably. "High irony it is that an Ivy Leaguer with experience in international affairs, domestic politics, and private business should be hit with the rap of 'lightweight' by the more hostile elements of the press," the memo said. "Precisely because the disparity between perception and reality is so great, I am confident that the two can be brought closer into line, that the truth will pull the myth toward it." According to the memo, Bush should court the media and political elites and form a "cosmology" for his 1988 candidacy: Bush, Atwater argued, could become the leader of a party "with a track record of leadership and accomplishment. Results. Common sense. Practical. Realistic."

Bush and Atwater could hardly have been more different, either in terms of native region (New England versus the South), generation (World War II versus baby boom), or style (geniality versus gut fighting), and therein lay Atwater's utility to Bush's ambitions. With his patrician bearing and pedigree, Bush was a figure of an older, fading order of American power. He had come from the world of TR and FDR, of childhood comfort, prep school noblesse oblige, heroism under fire, and Ivy League polish. He had never wondered how he was going to pay the bills, never been uncertain of his place. When his family and his thousands of friends looked at him, they saw a man who could have spent his life making and spending money, but who had instead chosen to obey the biblical injunction, drilled into him by his parents, that to whom much is given much is expected. In his own mind and in the minds of those who loved him, he was born to serve, to give to others, to use his privilege to build, not to consume or to coast.

When others looked at him, though, they sometimes saw a man of means and of connections who played at politics less to serve than to rule. To win the presidency in the closing years of the twentieth century would require convincing voters that his background had equipped him to be of use and of profit to America and to the world. Thus, the political task before him was to convey to the broader public that while he had *lived* life differently, he *saw* life in much the way they did and would deploy his experiences in the service of those who had not grown up on Grove Lane and at Walker's Point.

If Bush could do this, he stood a strong chance of becoming president of the United States. If he could not, he would end his political life as Reagan's number two, unable to marshal the hopes and assuage the fears of the nation. To make the last, perilous leap from the vice presidency to the presidency, he needed men around him who understood the country, who had a feel for what moved voters, and who could convince just enough of the public to entrust their lives to George H. W. Bush.

Atwater was one such man. Born in Atlanta in 1951, Harvey LeRoy Atwater had grown up in South Carolina and first met the legendary Senator Strom Thurmond, the Dixiecrat-turned-Republican, one Halloween. "He came out and gave me a Snickers candy bar," Atwater recalled. "That was the best thing I got that year." Atwater grew up to love rhythm and blues, pretty women, and, above all, politics. While an undergraduate at Newberry College in South Carolina, he interned on Capitol Hill and met Senator Thurmond again. According to John Brady's biography of Atwater, *Bad Boy*, Atwater was entranced by the sight of the Senate floor, and fell under Thurmond's tutelage. A master of press manipulation, Atwater blended high-minded philosophical musings about generational change—Atwater was obsessed with the baby boomers' impact on politics and culture—and quotations from Sun-tzu's *Art of War* with hard-edged negative campaigning. (In an oft-cited example, Atwater refused to reply to charges that he had put out the word that an opponent had had electroshock therapy by saying that he would not answer someone who had been "hooked up to jumper cables.") He had worked in the Reagan political affairs office in the White House and believed that Bush, whom he had met when Bush was head of the RNC, was his best bet for a presidential winner.

The question for the close-knit Bush family was whether an outsider such as Atwater could be trusted to put the interests of George Bush first. (Atwater's partners in his political consulting firm were working for rivals for the nomination.) At a family meeting with Atwater, George W. and Jeb wanted to test Atwater's allegiance to their father. Jeb put the issue most bluntly, saying: "If someone throws a grenade at our dad, we expect you to jump on it."

"If you're so worried about my loyalty," Atwater replied, "why don't you come up to Washington to work on the campaign and keep an eye on me?" George W. accepted the challenge, moving his family to Washington to help out. His father was pleased. "I think George Bush coming up here will be very helpful and I think he will be a good insight to me," Bush told his diary in November 1986. "He is very level-headed, and so [is] Jebby."

Another essential figure for Bush was Roger Ailes, the Nixon and Reagan media adviser and ad man. Ailes was brought in to do media and to help Bush with his speaking and television styles—a largely thankless job, given Bush's impatience with the subject. Yet Ailes, a son of blue-collar Ohio who had been a producer for *The Mike Douglas Show,* proved to be the perfect coach for Bush, who sensed an underlying truth about Ailes. "We'd all kill for our clients," a rival consultant once said, but "Ailes is the only one who would die for his, and that's the difference." Bush loved Ailes's irreverence and inventive use of profanity (as long as there were no women around). "Bush was not a willing pupil," Ailes recalled. "If we hadn't hit it off personally, I'd have been fired. He resented what he called the 'show business' stuff around Reagan. But I knew how to make Bush laugh. He was so polite that he would never say anything bad about anybody, but he didn't mind hearing it."

Practicing a speech once, Bush was, as ever, waving his arms about. "You look like a fucking fairy," Ailes said—and Bush cracked up. He liked Ailes—and, more important, trusted Ailes to tell him the truth, however uncomfortable.

Bush was philosophical early in Reagan's second term. He was doing a lot of reading (*Life Its Ownself,* a novel of Texas football by Dan Jenkins; Gore Vidal's *Lincoln,* which Bush said was "a little heavy going"; and William Manchester's *American Caesar,* a biography of Douglas MacArthur) and thinking about the future. "If you want to be President—and I do—there are certain things that I have to do, certain speculation that I have to put up with, and a certain ugliness that will crop into a campaign or into the pre-campaign."

The ugliness Bush feared was manifest on page A25 of *The Washington Post* on Thursday, January 30, 1986, when the conservative commentator George F. Will published the toughest of columns about Bush's presidential aspirations. "The unpleasant sound Bush is emitting as he traipses from one conservative gathering to another," Will wrote, "is a thin, tinny 'arf'—the sound of a lapdog." It was devastating, partly because Will was known to be close to Nancy Reagan. Bush hated it, but there was nothing he could do. Will's point—that the right had its doubts about the depth of Bush's devotion to conservatism as it had come to be defined—was inarguable. The Reagan years were ending with a new anti-tax, pro-life party orthodoxy, and the conservatives who made up the GOP base suspected that Bush, for all his service to party and to Reagan, was not truly one of them.

They were, in their way, correct. Bush was not, and never would be, a movement conservative. His base of support was built more on his personal virtues than on any philosophical precepts. He was, as he put it to himself, "not off on one extreme or another." Still, the practically minded Bush had moved a good deal rightward as the party shifted in that direction. On abortion, he had reversed himself since 1980 and now supported a pro-life amendment to the Constitution. Always anti-abortion, he had come to his stronger pro-life view—one he admitted had "evolved"—after discussing the issue with religious leaders. The anti-abortion film *Silent Scream* had an impact on his thinking as well. As important, perhaps, was his deep love for several grandchildren who had been adopted from their birth mothers. What if the woman who'd been pregnant with one of these babies he adored had chosen to terminate her pregnancy? His conversion to a pro-life position was politically convenient, but it was also heartfelt.

On taxes, he had repudiated his 1980 "voodoo economics" language. It was a large price to pay for political viability, for Bush had been right that tax cuts alone could not lead to long-term fiscal health. Together with a general failure to curb spending in the Reagan years, the supply-side view, with its emphasis on lower taxes, was driving up the federal deficits and debt. Reagan's successor, whoever he might be, would be forced to reckon with unpaid bills and persistent shortfalls.

And on the role of religious faith in politics, Bush struggled to overcome his Episcopalian reticence to speak more openly about his own convictions. Asked whether he had been "born again," he gave a nuanced answer. "I think I would ask for a definition," Bush told Doug Wead, an adviser who helped Bush with the evangelical community. "If by 'born again' one is asking, 'Do you accept Jesus Christ as your personal Savior?' then I could answer a clear-cut 'Yes.' No hesitancy, no awkwardness." If the question, though, were whether there had been "one single moment, above any others, in which your life has been instantly changed," Bush continued, "then I can't say that this has happened, since there have been *many* moments."

George Will and other observers thought such maneuvers made Bush a "lapdog" of the right. George H. W. Bush believed them to be the sensible compromises of a politician who wanted to win. He always hoped to be judged on results and action, not words and positioning. For him, campaigns were means to the end of governing wisely and well. Those were the rules of the game, and Bush was forever one to play by the rules. He had a guiding wish: "Let's just hope the inner strength, conviction, and hopefully honor can come through."

The 1988 Republican presidential field was large, with Bob Dole, Jack Kemp, televangelist Pat Robertson, Al Haig, and former Delaware governor Pierre S. "Pete" du Pont assessing their chances. There was another name out there, too. "Rumsfeld—we keep hearing Rummy's going to run, Rummy's going to do this, Rummy's going to do that," Bush told his diary in the fall of 1986. "I don't mean to underestimate his abilities, but he's carved out a niche—he's gone Right, as we say—and I don't know that there's any room over there." (Rumsfeld tested the waters, decided not to run, and endorsed Bob Dole.)

Bush faced a persistent question: Why did he want to be president, aside from the obvious reasons of ambition? On the day of the 1986 midterm elections he put his thoughts on paper. "Believe me, even though I know it is not easy, I know I've got the leadership ability," Bush wrote. He continued:

> I know I've got the experience. I want to see an educated America. I want to see a literate ... America. I want to see a drug-free America. I want to see America with opportunity and jobs. I want

to see the emphasis remain on the family values. I want to use our abilities to bring peace, to continue the discussions with the Soviet Union, to reduce the fear of the kids of nuclear weapons, and also to be a beacon for freedom and democracy. . . . But how do you say all these things and get it into a slogan or a formula—a catch-all? I don't know. But this is what I feel very comfortable with—the philosophy. . . . And so, on this . . . November 4, 1986, I begin this new project—and I hope I'll see it through.

That night the Republicans lost control of the U.S. Senate.

The autumn grew worse. In the first week of November 1986, a Lebanese publication reported that the United States had sold arms to Iran in an effort to convince Tehran to help free Americans being held hostage by Hezbollah. The arms shipments appeared to be a violation of U.S. policy: Iran had been designated a state sponsor of terrorism, and Bush himself had chaired a task force that declared America would not negotiate with terrorists. The question of American hostages in the Middle East—including a CIA officer captured in the line of duty—was a prominent one in the Reagan White House. The president was both moved by their plight and eager to see them liberated.

In July 1985, the then national security adviser Robert McFarlane had briefed Reagan and White House chief of staff Don Regan on reaching out to Iran, which was then embroiled in its long war against Saddam Hussein's Iraq. (Regan and Jim Baker had switched jobs in early 1985.) Working through Israel, the hope was to improve relations and win Tehran's help in releasing hostages in the Middle East. The meeting with McFarlane and Regan took place at Bethesda Naval Hospital, where Reagan was recovering from surgery. The next month, in August 1985, the United States made its first sale of arms to Iran via Israel. There were additional shipments of arms in 1985 and in 1986—all despite the Bush task force injunction against negotiating with terrorists.

The record is clear that Bush was aware that the United States, in contravention of its own stated policy, was trading arms for hostages as part of an initiative to reach out to moderate elements in Iran. "I'm one of the few people that know fully the details, and there is a lot of flack and misinformation out there," Bush told his diary on Wednesday, November 5, 1986. "It is not a subject we can talk about." A Saturday, February 1, 1986, note of new national security adviser John M. Poindexter's said that "Most importantly, president and VP [vice president] are solid in taking the position that we have to try." The vice president had also been present at an Oval Office meeting on Tuesday, January 7, 1986, when Secretary of State George Shultz "argued fiercely and with passion against *any* arms sales to Iran, especially arms sales connected to the release of the hostages," Shultz recalled. Secretary of Defense Caspar Weinberger, who was also there, agreed with Shultz, and said so. "No one else did," Shultz recalled. Bush was silent as Reagan decided to proceed amid what Weinberger recalled as "talk of the hostages as one of the motivating factors."

In July 1986, in his suite at the King David Hotel in Jerusalem, Bush met with Amiram Nir, a counterterrorism adviser to Israeli prime minister Shimon Peres. The appointment had been scheduled at the request of Oliver North, a gung-ho marine lieutenant colonel and National Security Council staffer. Bush was uneasy. A veteran of the covert wars, Bush sensed that he was running some risk in taking the meeting. He woke up the night before the conversation and called Poindexter to make sure that seeing Nir was a good idea. Failing to reach Poindexter, Bush got North, who successfully urged Bush to keep the appointment with Nir.

The Israeli briefed Bush in no uncertain terms on the arms-for-hostages efforts. According to a memorandum of the meeting written by Bush chief of staff Craig Fuller, Nir described the initiative's two elements: the "tactical," which was "to get the hostages out," and the "strategic," which was to establish channels to Iran. Now, in November 1986, the public revelation of the Iranian initiative threatened to expose the highest officials of the American government as having said one thing while doing another on the principle of non-negotiation with terrorists. Bush preferred, with Reagan, to emphasize the strategy involved rather than the effort to free the hostages. In the immediate wake of the news, George Shultz heard Bush dismiss the story on television. "Bush on TV says it [is] ridiculous to even consider selling arms to Iran," Shultz said, according to notes Shultz dictated.

Shultz, however, knew the truth. "VP was part of it," Shultz said, according to notes of a conversation he had with Bush ally Nick Brady. "In that mtg. [where the arms-for-hostages plan was approved]. Getting drawn into web of lies. Blows his integrity. He's finished then. Sh[oul]d be very careful how he plays the loyal lieutenant role now." Shultz and his wife, O'Bie, visited the vice presidential residence for a drink on the Sunday after the story broke. Worried that Bush was heading for trouble with public statements, Shultz warned Bush not to try to shade the truth in any way going forward. Bush flared, emphasizing the point that the secret sales were more about establishing a connection to Iran than they were about the hostages. ("He was admonishing me," Shultz recalled. "Sees me as a threat.")

"Are you aware there are major strategy objectives w[ith] Iran?" Bush asked Shultz. "I'm v[ery] careful what I say."

"I told him he was there and approved it," Shultz dictated afterward. "He knew & supported it. I s[ai]d that's where you are." There was, Shultz recalled, "considerable tension between us" as the Shultzes left the house. Collecting himself, though, Bush heeded the warning. "Shultz worries about a 'Watergate syndrome,'" Bush told his diary. Jim Baker later told Shultz that "you saved the VP's political life by telling him to be quiet ab[out] arms."

For just over six years, ever since Reagan's midnight call to Bush's suite at the Pontchartrain in Detroit, Bush had subsumed his own identity to Reagan's political agenda. When the Iran story broke, Bush had instinctively reacted in what Shultz called his "loyal lieutenant" mode, denying everything. In fact, however, Bush had surely known enough about the initiative with Iran that his initial denial was at best misleading and at worst a lie. The truth, which Bush was to acknowledge (though with varying degrees of straightforwardness and differing shades of emphasis), was that he had known that, working through Israel, the United States was trading arms for hostages. It was also the case that in private, Bush occasionally would raise sensitive concerns or disagree with the president. In the case of the Iran affair, Bush had long worried about the role of Israel, believing that using a third party gave the Americans too little control over the initiative.

To his diary in early 1987, as administration critics pressed him on his role, Bush dictated: "They don't know that I raised the question over and over again with the President, with Don Regan, with McFarlane, with Poindexter, of concerns on the Israeli connection. But we can't, simply can't say that. We cannot get into that. . . . just have to take the pounding that goes with it and keep your head up." Bush did not want to break his long-standing rule of keeping his advice to the president confidential, almost whatever the cost.

In a speech on the Iran initiative at the American Enterprise Institute in early December 1986, Bush acknowledged that "clearly, mistakes were made" and said that "I was aware of our Iran initiative, and I support[ed] the President's decision." In February 1987 he also approved the leaking of the memorandum of the Nir meeting at the King David Hotel to *The Washington Post*—the memo that detailed the Israeli role and recorded that he had been fully briefed on the arms-for-hostages element of the initiative. The rationale for the leak: Get everything out as early as possible. If word of the Nir meeting were withheld and were to emerge closer to the 1988 election—from either a U.S. or Israeli source—it could be more damaging. After reading the front-page *Post* piece on Sunday, February 8, 1987, which had been written by Bob Woodward and David Hoffman, Bush made a quick call to Boyden Gray, whom he had authorized to leak the Nir story. "Great job, great job," Bush told Gray. "I've talked to the Israelis, and they're copacetic. Good job, old boy."

B ush's initial denial of the details of the Iranian arrangement and his subsequent efforts to minimize his knowledge about the arms sales was an instance in which duty (in this case, to the president and to the secrecy he believed essential to the conduct of some foreign relations) and ambition (he wanted to protect his own political future) conflicted with and trumped his obligation to the full truth. To the mystification of Shultz and Weinberger, Bush would later claim that had he known of their strong objections he might have opposed the initiative.

In August 1987, Shultz recalled being "astonished" when he read an interview with Bush in *The Washington Post.* "If I had sat there and heard George Shultz and Cap express it [opposition to Iran arms sales] strongly, maybe I would have had a stronger view," Bush told the *Post's* David Broder in August 1987. "But when you don't know something, it's hard to react. . . . We were not in the loop." Weinberger read the piece, too, and called Shultz: "That's terrible. He was on the other side. It's on the record. Why did he say that?"

Though he claimed to have been "not in the loop," Bush knew that the administration had undertaken a high-risk, high-reward strategy to bring home American hostages and possibly open channels to Iran. He justified the "not in the loop" characterization on the grounds that he had not been privy to every detail of the arms initiative and that he had had no "operational role."

Bush was an old spymaster and a realist. That his first impulse was to hide the truth, however, and that he continued to maintain, on occasion, that the deal was not about arms for hostages but was, rather, "strategic," was unworthy of his essential character.

After lunch on Monday, November 24, 1986, Bush was in his West Wing office when Attorney General Ed Meese arrived and "laid a real bombshell on me." Oliver North, the National Security Council staffer who had set up the Bush meeting with Nir in Israel, had taken the proceeds of the Iran arms sales and diverted the money to aid the anti-Communist Nicaraguan contras in defiance of a congressional prohibition known as the Boland Amendment. Bush told the attorney general that he had known "absolutely" nothing about the diversion of funds.

In the Oval Office on Tuesday, November 25, Bush heard Don Regan propose an independent review board that would include Carter national security adviser Zbigniew Brzezinski and be chaired by Howard Baker, a potential Bush rival for the GOP nomination. After a moment, Bush spoke up. "I must confess, I do think—and I know that I am a special pleader here—but I don't think somebody running for President should chair this commission," Bush said. "The temptation will be to run against all the White House like the Watergate thing. I just don't think that is right, and frankly I don't think it is fair."

Regan, Meese, and the president agreed with Bush. Still, Bush fretted about seeming self-interested and went back to see Reagan later in the day. "I said I hoped I didn't sound little or small on this thing," Bush told Reagan, "but I really do worry about Baker parlaying, Baker using that form of investigation of the White House to build up a big case that might hurt us or might hurt the White House and those of us that are trying to support you."

"No, I understand totally," Reagan said, "and you are absolutely right."

The president and the attorney general publicly announced the discovery of the diversion. It was, Bush dictated, "one of the worst days for President Reagan and his presidency." At dusk, Bush called the president once more to check in. Reagan had left the West Wing and retired upstairs. "Nancy was away and I thought, 'There he is all alone,'" Bush told his diary. "I really wanted to ask him if I could come over and have a drink, but he doesn't really reach out in that sense. . . . I feel I might be imposing on him." Choosing to leave the president alone, Bush went home.

In the wake of the diversion news, Bush decided to try to move ahead of the breaking scandal. In a call to Reagan, and in a follow-up note, Bush volunteered to take a polygraph test to prove that he was not guilty of wrongdoing on the contra diversion—clearance, he believed, that would then enable him to conduct an internal investigation of what had gone wrong. The proposal that Bush volunteer to take a lie-detector test over his role in the affair—or, more precisely, his lack of a role in the affair—suggests that Bush was telling the truth from the beginning about contra diversion. Over Thanksgiving at Kennebunkport—the vice president had bought Walker's Point from Mary Walker, the widow of his uncle Herbie, in 1981—Bush worried about the president and about the political impact of the revelations, but men with something to hide do not ordinarily offer to be hooked up to a polygraph.

Neither Bush idea—the taking of the polygraph nor the leading of the panel—went anywhere, but his recommendation for a commission chairman—his old Texas friend John Tower—was accepted. At the American Enterprise Institute on Wednesday, December 3, Bush had defended the strategic thinking behind the Iran initiative but admitted that he understood how Americans could be perplexed by the White House's apparent hypocrisy on the arms-for-hostages deal. "Simple human hope explains it perhaps better than anything else," Bush said. "The President hoped that we could open a channel that would serve the interests of the United States and of our allies in a variety of ways. Call it leadership. Given 20-20 hindsight, call it a mistaken tactic if you want to." The appointment of a special prosecutor—former federal judge Lawrence E. Walsh—was announced on Friday, December 19, 1986.

Though Bush (like Reagan) was in the dark about the contra diversion, in political terms the vice president was broadly vulnerable on Central America. In March 1985, Donald P. Gregg, a former CIA officer who was serving as Bush's national security adviser, had arranged for an old Gregg ally, Felix Rodriguez, to move to El Salvador to assist the El Salvadoran government in its fight against Marxist insurgents. Born in Cuba, trained in special forces, and recruited by the CIA as part of the

Bay of Pigs operation in 1961, Rodriguez was sent to Central America for the limited mission in El Salvador. (Thomas Pickering, then the U.S. ambassador to El Salvador, supported Rodriguez's move.) Without Bush's or Gregg's knowledge, Oliver North recruited Rodriguez to help circumvent the Boland Amendment by supplying military assistance to the Nicaraguan contras. North ordered Rodriguez to keep the Nicaraguan operations secret from Gregg and from the CIA. Rodriguez had two brief meetings with Bush, one in January 1985, the other in May 1986, but nothing was said about supplying assistance to the contras.

Given the ingredients—a Bay of Pigs veteran; a CIA alumnus advising the vice president, himself a former CIA director; and the ubiquitous Oliver North—the Rodriguez story understandably fed speculation about Bush's role. Yet in the end, according to the final Iran-contra special prosecutor's report, "There was no credible evidence obtained that the Vice President or any member of his staff directed or actively participated in the contra-resupply effort that existed during the Boland Amendment prohibition on military aid to the contras. To the contrary, the Office of the Vice President's staff was largely excluded from . . . meetings where contra matters were discussed."

After investigations by the Tower Commission, Congress, and the independent counsel, no evidence was ever produced proving Bush was aware of the diversion to the contras. A 1991 internal legal memorandum by Christian J. Mixter of the special prosecutor's office found insufficient evidence to hold Bush criminally liable for his role in either side of Iran-contra—either the arms sales or the diversion. Bush would remain politically liable, however, as the vice president of an administration in which national security officials had undertaken operations to subvert the will of Congress and then sought to cover up the full extent of what they had done.

Bush's sense of duty to the president suffuses his diary. "My gut instinct is to run to the President's defense and jump into the fray," Bush dictated on Wednesday, November 19, 1986. But as Iran Contra special counsel Lawrence Walsh wrote in his memoir of the scandal, "Bush's Achilles' heel . . . was his split-second instinct to categorically deny anything that might be politically embarrassing. His repeated statement that he had been 'out of the loop' regarding Ronald Reagan's secret effort to sell arms to free the hostages was one such blanket—and false—denial. The phrase had been too vivid; it would stick to him forever."

For all his devotion to Reagan, Bush failed the president as a foreign policy adviser in the Iran matter. Shultz and Weinberger had been right; Bush wrong. The arms-for-hostages scheme was misguided, and Bush should have known it—as Reagan's anti-terror adviser, he rightly opposed ransom in principle. Concerned about the hostages, overoptimistic about building bridges to Iran, and generally inclined to support the president, Bush backed a doomed policy. As the scandal erupted, the vice president joined Shultz and others in wanting to get out the facts. But not before first trying to hide them.

The tumultuous year of 1986 ended as well as it could for Bush personally. On Wednesday, December 31, 1986, Scotty Reston published a generous *New York Times* column about the vice president. Even amid the scandal, Reston wrote, it would "probably be wrong to discount George Bush, especially if you look at his wife. These are serious people, among the best we have, with the gifts of intelligence and friendship and compassion. Quietly, he could make a difference in the next two years, and if not, go home without regret."

Bush appreciated the piece. "January 1st, the power of the Reston column," Bush dictated. "It lifted the morale of our people. . . . All around Hobe Sound, where they study *The New York Times* editorial page day-in-day-out, there was joy."

Bush called on Reagan in the White House Residence on Tuesday, January 6, 1987. Walking in, Bush found the president lying on a couch with a flower in his mouth, his bare legs sticking out from a red bathrobe, "acting like he was dead." It was an odd moment. Then Reagan "jumped up and laughed—his wonderful warm self. My heart immediately thought, 'God, why does this guy have to be taking this pounding?'"

The future of White House chief of staff Don Regan became a consuming issue inside the administration in late 1986 and early '87. Seeking ways to move beyond the Iran-contra narrative and put her husband in a better light, Nancy Reagan was pushing Reagan, Bush, and several other allies to force Regan to resign. Mrs. Reagan's logic was that Regan's departure would show that the president was putting the White House in order after the Iran-contra disaster. The Tower Commission was readying its report on what had gone wrong in the NSC process to produce the Iran-contra operation, and Regan wanted to wait until the report was issued before stepping down. (He thought that leaving before it was released would look worse for him.)

Bush agreed with Nancy, and both in person and in writing he suggested to the president that Regan go. Reagan said no. He wanted the chief of staff to stay. "He is adamantly against it," Bush told his diary. Bush's code as vice president on this score was clear. If Reagan did not want something done, then Bush would follow the president's lead. There was, however, pressure from his own team and from Nancy to go around the president and push Regan out. "Lee Atwater is all concerned," Bush dictated in December. "I think he feels it [would be] a great political strike for me if I could be seen as leading to the ouster of Don Regan. I keep telling [the political team] to concentrate on Iowa and New Hampshire and to leave the White House stuff to the White House staff and keep the politics separate."

Stu Spencer, the old Reagan adviser and a Nancy ally, called on Bush. "He is urging me to go see Don Regan," Bush dictated. Bush declined; Reagan did not want Regan to leave, and so Bush believed that he would be undermining the president "if I went behind his back and against his will and told Don Regan to leave." The next day, at a White House Christmas party, Nancy pulled Bush aside. "I'll deny it if you ever say it, but it is essential that you do what Stu Spencer said," Nancy said.

"Nancy, I've got some hang-ups on that, based on my relationship with the President."

"Well, I do it all the time," Nancy said, "and it is important that you do it."

Bush understood the stakes. The longer the White House appeared to be in chaos, the worse his own chances two years hence. "I suppose that one could say that . . . if it continues like this it would make it extremely difficult to get the nomination," he dictated in late December 1986. Bush lunched with Nancy, and she described an incident in which Don Regan had hung up on her. ("Ann tells me I made a real mistake and I'm sorry," Regan, quoting his wife, told Nancy in a later call. "Never make that mistake again," Nancy had replied.)

She pressed Bush on Regan. "I told her that I simply could not talk to Don Regan, having told the President in writing and three different times in person that I felt Don Regan should leave," Bush said. "I had not in six years betrayed the trust of the President."

The president finally agreed that Regan should go after stories appeared in the paper saying, accurately, that Nancy was the force behind the anti-Regan push. As early as December 1986, *The Washington Post* had reported that a frustrated Reagan had told Nancy to "get off my goddamn back" about Regan.*

On a snowy Monday the morning after a White House dinner for the nation's governors in February 1987, Reagan told Bush, "George, I'm going to have to do something about Don. . . . If I won't stand up for my wife, who will? A certain honor is at stake." Reagan had apparently come to see the Regan matter in terms of its relation to Nancy, who was being depicted in the press as "obsessed" with the question. (*The Washington Post* ran a representative piece headlined "Nancy Reagan's Private Obsession: A Tenacious Struggle to Oust Donald Regan from the President's Team.") She brought in Robert Strauss, the former Democratic chairman, to advise her husband, and the papers were full of stories about how the chief of staff and the First Lady were no longer speaking.

Bush arranged the conversation between Reagan and Regan. "The President wants to see you," Bush told Regan. The president and the chief of staff spoke, and Regan agreed to resign the following week, after the Tower report was released on Thursday, February 26, 1987. Mrs. Reagan objected to the plan, telling both Bush and Jim Baker that she believed Regan should leave before the political talk shows on Sunday. Regan was a proud man coming to the end of six years of service to Reagan, four at Treasury and two in the White House. As he recalled, the president had promised him a "dignified departure. . . . Naturally I had taken him at his word, and I was heartened by the thought that he would thank me publicly for my service."

That was not to be. Shortly there was a leak, and the news was on CNN: Don Regan was out, and Howard Baker, the former Senate Republican leader, was taking over as chief of staff. Bush was distraught

---

* When the "get off my goddamn back" anecdote was published, Bush dictated to his diary: "David Hoffman [of the *Post*] told [Bush chief of staff Craig] Fuller that this came from a family member. There was some talk of demanding a retraction. So I then walked down alone and told the President on the morning of the 9th that Hoffman had told this to Fuller. He was shocked. He said, 'The only person that could be is Maureen [Reagan, the president's daughter from his first marriage, who was spending a lot of time in the White House]. . . . I don't believe that at all. She is close to Nancy now and I just don't believe the bastards.'" Bush said, "Well, I just wanted you to know this. It is unpleasant, but if you go to [*Washington Post* executive editor Ben] Bradlee, I wouldn't want that to come out as their source or something to further embarrass your family." Mrs. Reagan denied the "get off my . . . back" episode had taken place.

over Regan's humiliation. Because Mrs. Reagan wanted the chief of staff out of the White House "before the Sunday shows," Bush recalled, "what would have been a nice peaceful way of getting everything done that Reagan wanted, getting Don to move on, just flared up—it was a disaster." He was uncomfortable with the tone of the post-resignation commentary about Regan. "The stories are full of Nancy Reagan and her strength in getting Don out," Bush dictated. "I just have a funny feeling that this is going to backfire."

Bush's instincts were right. From exile, Regan, much to the Reagans' embarrassment, published a memoir that detailed how Mrs. Reagan consulted an astrologer to set the presidential schedule. "You don't kick a man when he is down," Bush dictated. "You don't revel in his demise. You don't pile on in life."

As Bush faced Dole, Robertson, Kemp, duPont and Haig, the Democratic field was taking shape. Gary Hart, the former Colorado senator who had run a great race against Walter Mondale in 1984, was the front-runner. Other contenders included Missouri congressman Dick Gephardt, Tennessee senator Al Gore, Delaware senator Joe Biden, and, in April 1987, Massachusetts governor Michael Dukakis. Bush's first reaction to Dukakis's run was that his many "liberal biases" would not travel well outside Massachusetts; the vice president believed Hart would prove the most formidable Democrat.

In early May, *The Miami Herald* published a long story raising questions about Hart's alleged womanizing. "I must confess, I am rooting for Hart," Bush told his diary. "I think the journalists have gone way too far this time." The Hart saga, which led to his dropping out of the race, gave life to rumors about Bush—chiefly that he had been romantically involved with Jennifer Fitzgerald, a longtime aide. When word of a possible news story about the alleged affair reached the Bush campaign headquarters in Washington, Lee Atwater rushed down the hall to Roger Ailes's office. "They have something on the old man," Atwater said. It fell to Ailes to take the matter to Bush, whom he met in the vice president's Old Executive Office Building suite. There was a storm coming, and the campaign—and the family—needed to be ready. "Mr. Vice President," Ailes said, "they've got a story about you, Jennifer Fitzgerald, and an affair." Bush never flinched. "They haven't got shit," he replied.

By now Ailes was an old hand at taking bad news to clients and gauging how much trouble was really at hand. "And I don't know if it was the fighter pilot in him, or the CIA director, or what, but I'm telling you this was a man with no fear," Ailes recalled. "I'd seen a lot of guys in similar situations, and none of them were ever as steady and certain as Bush was that day. If he'd strayed, he sure as hell wasn't worried, and the message I got was that he was clean on this."

The divorced Fitzgerald had worked for Bush in China, at the CIA, and in the office of the vice president. She was said to be a stern gate-keeper, and her style failed to endear her to the larger Bush universe. "I was very close to her for a while," Bush recalled in retirement. "And liked her. I knew she was difficult, and knew other people didn't like her. She was hard to work with for other people around her." In separate interviews with the author, Bush and Fitzgerald denied the rumors of an affair. "No," Bush said when asked if he had had an extramarital relationship with Fitzgerald. For her part, Fitzgerald replied: "It simply didn't happen. I have nothing but the deepest respect and admiration for the entire Bush family." Hers was not the only name to be speculatively linked to Bush's in gossipy political circles—a possible result of his cheerful flirting and overt fondness for attractive women. "From time to time he would let things go on too long and almost—almost—too far," a long-time Bush adviser recalled. "I really don't believe he ever crossed the line, but he got right up to it."

In June 1987, the New York tabloids—the *Post* and the *Daily News*—were reportedly chasing rumors that Bush had been robbed of his wedding ring after ducking the Secret Service on a trip to New York to see Fitzgerald. (One problem with the account: Bush did not wear a wedding ring, which meant there was no wedding ring to be stolen.) It was a false tale reminiscent, in a way, of the 1981 story that had Bush being shot outside Janet Steiger's house in Georgetown.

On the evening of Thursday, June 18, 1987, there was what Bush called "a whole new rash of rumors on the sex front." A reporter called in saying that "he'd heard" Bush had had affairs with four different women—all family friends and supporters. "It goes right around in circles." Bush was told that Dole and Kemp people were spreading the stories. "There are no facts," he dictated, "there is no evidence." The toll on Barbara was acute. "I talked to Bar this morning and she was telling me that her friends all had heard these ugly rumors," Bush told his diary. "Someone had called from Connecticut to say, 'I'd heard your marriage was on the rocks.' It's just awful."

On Monday, June 22, 1987, *Newsweek* and *U.S. News & World Report* published pieces alluding to the Fitzgerald rumors. "It's ugly," Bush dictated on Tuesday, June 23. "You feel people are looking at you differently. It's humiliating for Barbara." Jim Baker called in with the latest, a rumor that Bush had been "shacked up" with a certain woman. Bush was both angry and amused: "The truth is I [have] never met" the woman in question. "This is a sick town with sick people and a sick climate," Bush added. "It makes you want to totally get out of it. . . . I called Vermont to ask the guy to head the campaign and he says, 'What's with this adultery bit?' Ugly, nasty and the first time in twenty years of having your integrity questioned. But it's a sign of the times. Tomorrow it will be someone else, I'm sure." Bush believed Dole's aides were partly responsible for spreading the stories. That evening, he put in a call.

"Bob, let's just quiet this whole thing down," Bush said. "It's gone crazy."

Dole, Bush recalled, agreed and said that he had given orders that he wanted his campaign to stay out of the rumor business. "Bob," Bush said, "it's damned ugly for me and my family." News of the call leaked from the Dole camp to the *New York Post,* infuriating Bush.

Finally, George W. Bush, newly installed as the family enforcer at the campaign, took it upon himself to question his father.

"You've heard the rumors," George W. said to Bush. "What about it?"

"They're just not true," Bush replied.

George W. called two *Newsweek* reporters and issued a denial: "The answer to the Big A question is N.O." The son had gone public without authority from his father, and Barbara was upset with George W., telling him that his response had given the rumors credence. "Mother said, 'This is a disgrace,' but I did it because I was just furious [about the allegations]," George W. recalled. "It was an emotional reaction." His father sensed his son's anxiety. "George is very nervous, feeling he's made a big mistake in being quoted on 'adultery,'" Bush dictated on Friday, June 26, 1987. "In my view, it did admit the story to get more credibility. But I was proud of him for standing up for the truth." George W.'s intervention worked. "Rumor died down and gone," Bush told his diary. "But only after agony for the family."

As the official announcement of his presidential campaign approached in October 1987, Bush agreed to grant the reporter Margaret Warner of *Newsweek* access to him and to the family, including his mother, for a profile. Everything seemed fine in the course of the interviews—Warner trying to get to the essence of Bush, seeking anecdotes and telling details to try to capture the character of the man.

Warner's draft was handed over to Evan Thomas, the magazine's Washington bureau chief and a deft writer. The editorial consensus inside *Newsweek*'s New York headquarters was that a frontal assault on Bush's main weakness—his inability to project his own identity in Reagan's shadow—was the best bet for a memorable cover and piece. "Bush, who formally declares his candidacy this week, enters the nomination fight with enviable advantages—high name recognition and stronger voter ratings for experience and competence," Thomas wrote. "Other candidates can spend an entire primary season trying to match those assets. Yet Bush suffers from a potentially crippling handicap—a perception that he isn't strong enough or tough enough for the challenges of the Oval Office. That he is, in a single mean word, a wimp."

The cover itself featured a handsome-enough image of Bush on his cigarette boat in Maine. The language was stark: "Fighting the 'Wimp Factor.'"

"Ugly, nasty, pure political shot," Bush told his diary. "But what can you do? How can you defend yourself?" He had opened up to the press about the true George Bush, the man who had flown through flak and lived through the death of a child. He had revealed more than he was really comfortable talking about, risking his mother's disapproval of the "Great I Am." And now the mocking *Newsweek* cover and the questions that followed—he was repeatedly asked about the line—appear to have given him fresh resolve. "Had to shoot down the 'wimp' question by saying, 'My combat comrades didn't think so; my business friends didn't think so; the people at the CIA didn't think so; so why should I be concerned[?]," he dictated. "The American people won't think so." How to make sure of that? By taking the fight to his foes.

TWENTY-SEVEN

Like You've Been Hit in the Stomach

★

It's really gloomy. Our pros don't have any answers. Just
discouragement, desolation. I thrash all night.

—GEORGE H. W. BUSH, on losing the 1988 Iowa caucuses

L EE ATWATER HAD A BAD FEELING about Iowa. Eight years earlier,
the caucuses had propelled Bush to presidential plausibility with
the victory over Reagan, but it had been a long eight years. The
farm states were in a prolonged economic slump, the religious broad-
caster Pat Robertson was well organized in the state, and Bush's chief
mainstream challenger for the 1988 nomination, Bob Dole, was from
neighboring Kansas. It was Dole, not Bush, who could say "I'm one of
you" to the people of Iowa.

Dole and Bush were old rivals. They had been bright young men together in the Age of Nixon, overlapping for a term in the House. (Dole
moved up to the Senate in 1968.) Dole had not been happy to give up
the chairmanship of the Republican National Committee to Bush in
1973, but had saluted. In Dole's mind, that was the way of the world
when it came to Bushes and Doles. The rich kids always won. To Dole,
Bush was a comfortable navy flyboy from Greenwich, Connecticut, who
had been dining on steaks and strawberries off silver at sea while he, a
striving poor infantryman from Russell, Kansas, had been grievously
wounded in ground combat in Italy during World War II.

Dole enjoyed taunting Bush on the trail. He liked to talk about how
he, unlike some unnamed others, was offering "a record, not a résumé."
He liked to talk about how he, unlike some unnamed others, was "tough.
I understand you have to be tough to make tough choices." And he liked
to talk about how he, unlike some unnamed others, had risen not on
connections but on grit. "I got here the old-fashioned way. I earned it.
Nobody gave it to me."

Dole even managed to tweak Bush on the vice president's own turf: inside the White House, where Bush was finding the 1987–88 Howard Baker era as chief of staff difficult. The vice president had felt comfortable with Jim Baker and with Don Regan but saw Howard Baker as a potential rival for power, either on his own account or as an ally of Dole's and of Bill Brock's, the former RNC chairman who had signed on as Dole's campaign manager. (Brock and Howard Baker had served together as senators from Tennessee in the 1970s.) "It is almost like I don't exist," Bush dictated. Tom Griscom, a Howard Baker aide, was quoted to Bush as having said that "there may be a fall-out plan in which the Republican convention would deadlock and they would turn to Howard Baker"—the last thing George Bush wanted to hear. On one galling occasion, Dole was granted a coveted joint appearance with Reagan to announce Dole's support for an intermediate-range nuclear treaty with the Soviets—a treaty Bush had supported all along.

To himself, Bush mused about the challenge Dole posed. "He's what they call a tough guy, and yet I wonder how really tough he is," Bush told his diary. "I don't like to equate meanness with toughness, ugliness with toughness. They accuse me of being too nice . . . not tough enough. But I believe I've got more inner fiber and more strength than Bob Dole will ever have. Time will tell."

Time, and Iowa. In the fall of 1987 Dole was leading Bush 42 to 26 percent in Iowa polling. All Bush could do was what he had always done: Keep things steady.

In mid-October the vice president was at the White House for a state visit with India's Rajiv Gandhi when word came that the stock market was in free fall, crashing 508 points during the trading day. There were suggestions that the president close the exchange, but Bush advised against it, believing the move overly dramatic. When Bush heard about the idea, he broke off from Gandhi to tell Reagan what he thought.

The president accepted Bush's counsel and declined to step in. "During this so-called crisis, there was a lot of near-panic," Bush dictated. "People rushing around, wringing their hands—a lot of politicians jumping in. . . . My view is that you don't just jump out there and make a statement when there is a hurricane raging outside unless you have something intelligent to say."

Soviet leader Mikhail Gorbachev and his wife, Raisa, arrived in Washington in early December 1987 for a summit with Reagan. When Gorbachev stepped out of the car at the White House, Barbara was struck that he had a face "like Daddy's, smiling eyes and teeth of iron." Later, at a dinner at the Soviet embassy, Barbara took roll in her mind: "The Doles were not there, probably in New Hampshire or Iowa blasting George."

In the summit meetings, Bush, eager to play a larger role, thought Reagan deferred "an awful lot" to George Shultz. While he maintained his dignified reticence, he thought of the future: "I am confident that I could more than hold my own with Gorbachev." Bush had a long talk with Eduard Shevardnadze, the Soviet foreign minister, who "made distinct sounds that he and the others wanted me to be elected President." Bush was appreciative. "Well, I would like to talk to [the] General Secretary about what my priorities would be if I were elected President," he told Shevardnadze.

Bush's opportunity came during a limousine ride with Gorbachev on Thursday, December 10, 1987, from the White House to Andrews Air Force Base. In the motorcade Bush and Gorbachev talked, rather obliquely, of American politics. "I told him that in my view, [a] Democratic or a Republican president would want to continue the improved relationship," Bush recalled. "But I reminded him that it was Nixon who went to China, and it is Reagan who will get this INF Treaty through the Senate, and in my view a Republican President would be easier in the long run to work with." Gorbachev "did not comment, but he took it on board."

Bush spoke candidly, if optimistically, about his own prospects. "Dole looks pretty dangerous right now, but I think I'll get the Republican nomination," Bush said. "If I'm elected—and I think I will be—you should understand that I want to improve our relations." Bush made something else clear, too. "I told Gorbachev not to be concerned about the 'empty cannons of rhetoric' he would hear booming during the campaign, and explained what the expression meant," Bush recalled. It was an old favorite phrase of Mao's that Bush had adopted, not only in foreign affairs but in domestic politics as well. "'Don't worry about excessive bombast,' they would say," Bush recalled of the Chinese. "Look at deeds and actions instead." Bush was telling Gorbachev that political necessity might require him to say tough things about the Soviet Union in the coming campaign. "He should not take them too seriously," Bush recalled saying. In that motorcade, moving through the streets of Washington toward Andrews, Bush had mentioned one obstacle, though, by name: Bob Dole. He still had to defeat the senator from Kansas before the world could be his.

The first sign of trouble in Iowa had come in September 1987 at the Ames straw poll—the pre-caucuses contest Bush had won over Reagan to such great effect in 1979. During the event at the Iowa State Center on the campus of Iowa State, Lee Atwater and Rich Bond, the 1980 Iowa veteran who was now Bush's national deputy manager, were sitting high in the arena. They watched as the Dole people marched in, followed by the Robertson people. "There were thousands of them," Bond recalled.

"Where are our people?" Atwater drawled, angrily.

Bond could only roll his eyes. He knew what was coming, and it wasn't good. Bush finished third, behind Pat Robertson, who was rallying religious conservatives, and Dole, who placed second. "It was," Bush told his diary, "the first hit that we've really taken."

On the gloomy flight on Air Force Two back to Washington from Ames, Bond sat alone and depressed in the back of the plane, knowing, he recalled, "the shitstorm that was coming and knowing what this portended for the future—finishing third on caucus night." Bond was called up to the vice president's cabin mid-flight. Bush was there with Barbara, Atwater, and a few staffers. Bush greeted Bond cheerfully, and Mrs. Bush delivered the message. "So, Rich, when are you going back to Iowa?"

"Immediately, Mrs. Bush," replied Bond, who had not yet had time to sit down. He left Washington the next day to take charge of the Iowa caucus campaign.

Bush pressed on. It had only been a straw poll. There was world enough and time to make his stand. "Pick up the pieces," he told himself. "There aren't that many to pick up ... work hard ... correct what was wrong and just go forward."

At the end of the first week of January 1988, Dole attacked Bush over the arms-for-hostages initiative with Iran—arms sales that Dole said ran "against the grain of everything we stand for in America."

Led by Dole, Bush's primary opponents were trying to make an issue of Bush's judgment. Exhibit A on the eve of Iowa and New Hampshire: Iran. The political issue in the Republican primary race, though, was less about what Bush had known and more about what he had thought. What had he advised the president?

For a man running on his experience, it was a fair question. On the eve of a Republican presidential debate in Des Moines, Bush wanted to be calm under fire, and he was, more or less. At his hotel, preparing for the debate, "I spend a couple of nervous hours going over ... day care, homelessness, women's issues, long-term health care, etc.," Bush told his diary. "I am weak on those, not that I don't care, because I do, but because I don't have the expertise in these fields." That morning *The Des Moines Register* had done a big article on Iran-contra, raising questions about Bush's role. "Tension City," Bush dictated. "Tension City." He expected the worst.

Jim Gannon, the editor of the *Register,* moderated the debate. "Mr. Bush, you've been Vice President for seven years," Gannon said, working from notes in his lap. "But it is hard to assess your role in the Reagan Administration, what your judgment was on key issues and what role you played in shaping policy. ... You seem to be telling the American people, in effect, 'Trust me; I did the right thing, but I can't tell you what I did.' How can you expect their trust if you won't tell them plainly what you thought, what you said, what you did at that time on those key issues?"

Bush assumed a stern look. "Jim, contrary to the hypothesis of your question, I have answered every question put to me save one," he said, gesturing with both hands. "And the one question is, 'What did you tell the President of the United States?' and I shouldn't do that."

Yet Bush had already signaled what he had told the president. "But what troubled me—and I expressed these misgivings—was that the United States was involved in a major foreign-policy initiative with only limited control over how it was carried out," Bush had written in his 1987 campaign autobiography, *Looking Forward.* "True, we were working with a loyal ally, Israel; but at times even the Israelis indicated they were at a loss to understand the volatile political situation in Iran." In February 1987, he had also publicly said that he had "expressed certain reservations on certain aspects," and in March 1987, President Reagan had issued a statement saying that Bush "had expressed reservations throughout the process but had supported the decision and the policy."

Here, in Des Moines, the complicated public character of George

H. W. Bush—an often confusing combination of political calculation and personal honor—was on vivid display. On the overall issue of whether he understood the sales to be trading arms for hostages, he carefully obfuscated, emphasizing the "strategic" effort over the "tactical" hostages element. (Put that one down to political calculation.) On the question of what he advised the president, he steadfastly refused to distance himself from Reagan in debates or interviews when it might have helped him politically. (Put that one down to personal honor.) And, finally, he was demonstrating loyalty to a president who remained popular with the Republican base. (Another for political calculation.)

In sum, Bush was trying to have it all kinds of ways. True, he had raised concerns about working through Israel to transfer arms to Iran, but he had gone along with the basic policy of arms for hostages. Decades later, asked if he had ever disagreed with Reagan on the issue, Bush answered elliptically. "No, but I probably disagreed with the handling of it. If you mean reaching out to Iran, I didn't have any problem with that."

A few days after the Des Moines debate in 1988, his personal honor led to a politically useful moment. Amid the speculation about Bush and Iran, Don Regan, whom Bush had treated with grace, publicly said that he recalled Bush's expressing reservations about the arms sales in a meeting with the president. "The moral of this," Bush told his diary, "is don't kick someone when they're down"—an instance of Bush's decency having the effect of serving his ambition. Regan's supportive words aside, the news from Iowa in the middle of January was discouraging. With the caucuses approaching, Bush trailed Dole by fourteen to fifteen points.

Bush lunched with Reagan on Wednesday, January 20, 1988. The atmosphere was warm. Three days earlier, on January 17, Lou Cannon of *The Washington Post* had published a piece reporting Reagan's support for his vice president: "Reagan ... is said to believe that the election of a Republican president and Bush in particular would be a ratification of his 'legacy' on basic issues of foreign and domestic policy."

On the evening of Reagan's 1988 State of the Union address in late January, Bush flew from New Hampshire to Washington in a snowstorm to attend the joint session of Congress and to sit for a remote interview with anchor Dan Rather on the CBS *Evening News.*

The network had set up in Bush's Capitol office; Barbara brought a change of clothes from the residence. Roger Ailes met Bush at Andrews and rode to the Hill with him. Though CBS had said the piece was a political profile, Ailes had heard that the network was planning an ambush on Iran-contra and warned Bush about what was coming. "You've either got to go in there and go toe-to-toe with this guy," he told Bush, "or you're going back to Kennebunkport."

Rather ran a set-up piece detailing questions about Bush and Iran-contra, then homed in on the vice president in the interview segment. The exchange produced more heat than light, with the two men clashing and often speaking over each other. Bush refused to give any ground. As the two men battled it out, Ailes grabbed a piece of paper, wrote "WALKED OFF THE AIR!!" in large capitals, and held the sign under the camera for Bush. The note reminded the vice president of a line of attack Ailes had prepared for him: judging Bush's career on the scandal, Ailes had said, was like judging Rather's on an embarrassing moment when the anchor had stalked off his set in September 1987 to protest his broadcast being delayed for a tennis match, only to have the network go dark for a few minutes.

"I don't think it's fair to judge a whole career, it's not fair to judge my whole career by a rehash on Iran," Bush said. "How would you like it if I judged your career by those seven minutes when you walked off the set in New York? Would you like that?" (Rather had actually walked off a temporary set in Miami.) A startled Rather tried to get back on track. "Mr. Vice President, I think you'll agree that your qualifications for president and what kind of leadership you'd bring the country, what kind of government you'd have . . . is much more important than what you just referred to."

As time ran out, Rather abruptly cut off the segment—so abruptly that to many viewers he appeared to have been rude to the vice president. The interview over, Bush sat in Washington, steaming. His microphone still on, he turned to the CBS producer in the room. "Tell your god-damned network that if they want to talk to me, to raise their hands at a press conference. No more Mr. Inside Stuff after that." Rather, he went on, made CBS's Lesley Stahl, a tough interviewer, "look like a pussy." ("People were taking that as a sexist remark," Bush told his diary, "but I meant pussycat, the way he came on like a tiger.") Concerned about how it had gone over, he reached for the telephone to call George W.

"What do you think?" he asked.

"Man, you knocked it out of the park," George W. replied. "Dad, this is awesome. You stood your ground, you didn't let him bully you, and the American people are going to appreciate this."

George W. was right. Many viewers thought Rather had been ungenerous toward the vice president, and the coverage of the interview cast Bush in a heroic light as a man who gave no quarter. Even Ronald Reagan approved, remarking that Rather had "'stepped on his own dick,'" Bush dictated. People could mock Bush as much as they liked—as a wimp, as a rich kid, as an opportunist. He had heard it all before, many times. Yet he had built a life after electoral defeats and political setbacks, remaining viable, and here he stood, the vice president of the United States and one of a handful of men with a shot at the top job. If he lost, it would not be for lack of spirit or guts or cold-bloodedness. A lesson of his life was never to surrender when under fire or facing challenge. He would do what it took to meet the tests that presented themselves, and make his peace with it later.

Yet the Rather showdown could not turn things around in Iowa. With two weeks to go before the caucuses, Rich Bond met Bush in Cedar Rapids, joining the vice president in the motorcade with Atwater and the local campaign chairman.

"So, Rich, how are we doing?" a good-spirited Bush asked.

Bond paused, then answered honestly. "You're going to finish third."

Bush was taken aback. "So what am I doing here?" he asked—or "snapped," as Bond recalled it.

"You have no choice," Bond replied.

Bush said nothing for the rest of the ride. "Atwater sat there blazing daggers at me, trying to make my head explode," Bond recalled. "Our local chairman looked like he just ate a dead frog. The whole thing sucked, but the VP needed to hear the truth."

Bond's predictions about the caucuses had been accurate. On Monday, February 8, 1988, Bush lost to a triumphant Dole and a well-organized Pat Robertson. "It feels like you've been just hit in the stomach," Bush told his diary. "It's really gloomy. Our pros don't have any answers. Just discouragement, desolation. I thrash all night. No sleep. I couldn't get the room cooled down, for one thing. If I could just figure what went wrong."

Lee Atwater brought a sharp edge to Bush's 1988 campaign and was rewarded with the chairmanship of the Republican National Committee. Atwater would die of complications from a brain tumor in 1991.

The action moved to New Hampshire. He needed to win here, and win now. "I just go about my business," he dictated. "Work hard, and get the job done. I hate the negative things that are said about me, but I know nothing to do but to fight back in this state." Time marched on. "But there is always a tomorrow," Bush told his diary. "Remember that—always a tomorrow."

TWENTY-EIGHT

We Came Out of the Dead

★

I desperately want to win. The kids have worked hard, Bar has
worked hard. Everybody has killed themselves.

—GEORGE H. W. BUSH, on the eve of the 1988 New Hampshire primary

H E WAS IN HIS PAJAMAS as his advisers filed in. Bush had declined to spend the night in Iowa, heading on to New Hampshire in order to begin anew as quickly as possible after the
caucuses. As Lee Atwater later recalled to the political writers Jack Germond and Jules Witcover, who reported the morning scene, "I had my
whole little speech ready" to take the blame for the caucuses. As usual,
though, Bush was interested in today and tomorrow, not yesterday.
"We've got eight days," Bush said. "Let's sit down here right now and let's
don't get up until we figure out how to win this campaign."

Andrew Card, a Bush supporter from the 1980 campaign, was put in
charge of the ground game in New Hampshire along with Hugh ("The
Ayatollah") and Judd Gregg. Card had boarded Bush's airplane after it
landed in Nashua from Iowa to give the unhappy traveling party a pep
talk. "Nobody should get off this plane with dour looks," Card had told
Bush and the team. "When you hit the tarmac, you need to be smiling—
you want to be happy that you are in New Hampswhire." Card and the
Greggs needed Bush to be his usual energetic self. The work to be done,
Card recalled, was self-evident: "Identify the vote, know where it is, and
get it out."

New Hampshire governor John Sununu was also a critical player. In
his sixth year as governor, he believed that candidates won in New
Hampshire by practicing what he called "see me, touch me, feel me" politics. In the year before the primary, Sununu arranged for Bush to shake
an estimated sixty thousand hands in the state and to take five to seven
thousand pictures with voters—on the grounds, Sununu recalled, that "if
you have a picture of yourself and the Vice President on the mantel,
you'll work awfully hard to make it a picture of yourself and the Presi-

dent." On New Year's Eve, as 1987 turned into 1988, he had brought Bush to Concord, in the cold, to hand out hot chocolate and to pose for photos. The voters saw Bush, touched him, felt him. Now came the test: Could Bush translate his investments of time into an actual victory in the primary? The polls were bad. Richard Wirthlin, the old Reagan pollster who was now working for Dole, was buoyant. "He was whistling 'Hail to the Chief' and all that stuff," Dole recalled to Germond and Witcover. "He told me, 'You're going to be the next president.'"

Bush threw himself into the state with two or three breakfast trips a day to McDonald's and Dunkin' Donuts; back-to-back radio and TV interviews; drives on snowplows; and handshake after handshake after handshake. Barry Goldwater, whom Bush friend and finance chairman Bob Mosbacher flew up and back by private plane, came to campaign, as did Red Sox hero Ted Williams and the legendary pilot Chuck Yeager. At the end of long, frantic days, Bush would turn philosophical. "Watch and wait, wait and watch," he dictated. "I'm in my room, my feet up, my shoes off, and my whole body aches. [I'm] really tired, but I can't show it." Just days out from the voting in New Hampshire, Bush reached a point of internal equilibrium. "If I don't make it, I have no excuses," Bush dictated. "And if I win, and I still think I will, my hands will be full. The biggest job in the world."

Dole continued to diminish Bush's vice presidency and underscore his own life experiences. He told voters that he couldn't recall Bush being central to the successes of the Reagan years, driving home the point that the vice president was a shadowy, insubstantial figure. "He takes credit for a lot of things," Dole said, but where was the evidence? Where was the leadership? He—Bob Dole—he had been there for Reagan, doing the hard work in the Senate. Dole pollster Richard Wirthlin gave voice to the worst fears of the Bush high command. "It's quite clear," Wirthlin said, "that this is a very winnable race."

Roger Ailes agreed, and he was anxious to launch a frontal strike against the high-flying Dole. "I wanted to go negative," Ailes recalled, "but I had been ordered not to do any negative ads."

He made one anyway. Called "Senator Straddle," it attacked Dole chiefly on taxes, arguing that it was Bush, not Dole, who had pledged not to raise taxes. Ailes's office in New York cut the ad, and he drove through a snowstorm to pick it up and screen it for Bush. In the candidate's hotel room, Ailes, Atwater, and Sununu debated whether to put the "Straddle" ad on the air in New Hampshire. Bush looked at the floor as his advisers talked through the pros and cons. "It seemed to me too harsh," Bush said, and he told them not to use it.

As the days passed, the polls in New Hampshire moved all over the place. "We're either eight up," Bush pollster Bob Teeter said, "or eight down." Bush's advisers came back to him to reopen the "Straddle" question. Confronted with uncongenial numbers, Bush reconsidered the decision. He understood the stakes. He needed the win, badly. "I simply have to pull this out," Bush told his diary, "or we're going to have a long grueling battle and people are going to go over the side." Ailes and Atwater pressed anew: The Dole tax spot was a fair ad—tough but fair. Then Barbara Bush weighed in: She thought it was fine. Bush pondered for a long moment and finally spoke. "Are you certain," he asked, "we need to do this?"

Before anyone else could say anything, Atwater said, "I take that as a yes," and Atwater and Ailes hurried from the room. Bush's authorization of the negative ad was in keeping with his competitive character. Because people saw Bush as so agreeable and polite, they could underestimate his capacity to make the tough call. Ailes's anti-Dole spot ran repeatedly on the New Hampshire airwaves in the last days before the voting, and the vice president performed well in a half-hour "Ask George Bush" TV special on the Saturday night before the Tuesday voting. In the final hours, things were moving Bush's way.

Bush was at peace with his decision. Everywhere he looked were reminders of why he was fighting. His old rival Donald Rumsfeld was in New Hampshire campaigning with Dole as the decision was made to go negative. Bush slept fairly well, "but when I wake up, the fray instantly is on my mind." He was determined to prevail. "I desperately want to win," Bush dictated on the eve of the voting. "The kids have worked hard, Bar has worked hard. Everybody has killed themselves."

On primary day in New Hampshire, Bush visited two polling places, did eight radio interviews, and rode an exercise bike for twenty-four minutes. After a lunch of chowder, he tried to lie down but could not sleep. With Barbara and the rest of the family out hitting last-minute voting lines, Bush took a fifty-minute walk by himself at a quarter after three. When he returned to the hotel, "our people blew sky-high on the exit polls." A relieved Bush cast the moment in stark terms. "We came out of the dead," he dictated. "Three days ago there was gloom and doom in our camp and it turned around through a lot of hard work." And the "Straddle" ad. "The emotions are high," he told his diary, and the final results exhilarating. Bush defeated Dole, 38 to 29 percent, with Jack Kemp polling 13 percent, Pete du Pont 10, and Pat Robertson 9. On television that evening with Tom Brokaw, NBC surprised both Bush and Dole by putting them together on the screen for a moment. "Do you have anything to say to Dole?" Brokaw asked Bush. "I wish him well, and I'll see him in the South," Bush said. Dole snapped, "Yeah, tell him to stop lying about my record."

On the day after the primary, Bush returned to Washington. Atwater was relieved. "I never told you this," he said to Bush, "but the numbers in the South got awful slim after our loss in Iowa." One remark warmed Bush's heart more than he could say. "I'll sleep better tonight," Reagan had said after learning that Bush had won in New Hampshire.

Bush was already thinking about how to unify the party for the fall. The Dole voters, he believed, would be on board: They were Republican regulars. The Pat Robertson brigades struck Bush as more problematic— they seemed more interested in ideology and theology than in political victory. Campaigning in Kingsport, Tennessee—a thoroughly Republican city in a state Reagan had carried twice—Bush encountered a stony-faced Robertson backer who refused to shake the vice president's hand.

"Look, this is a political campaign," Bush said to her. "We'll be together when it's over." The woman was unmoved, and Bush, in the privacy of his diary, reflected:

> Still, this staring, glaring ugly—there's something terrible about those who carry it to extremes. They're scary. They're there for spooky, extraordinary right-winged reasons. They don't care about Party. They don't care about anything. They're the excesses. They could be Nazis, they could be Communists, they could be whatever. In this case, they're religious fanatics and they're spooky. They will destroy this party if they're permitted to take over. There is not enough of them, in my view, but this woman reminded me of my John Birch days in Houston. The lights go out and they pass out the ugly literature. Guilt by association. Nastiness. Ugliness. Be-

lieving the Trilateral Commission, the conspiratorial theories. And I couldn't tell—it may not be fair to that one woman, but that's the problem that Robertson brings to bear on the agenda.

In the wake of Bush's win in New Hampshire, President Reagan finally allowed himself to be more expansive about the Republican field. At lunch on the last day of February 1988, Bush recalled, Reagan "made a comment that Dole is mean, and shows a mean side.... He didn't think Kemp was presidential at all, and he made a comment that he was concerned about Robertson and some of the extremes that he brings into the party." Another sign of Bush's success: a Kemp supporter called Jonathan Bush to say "Jack will get out and endorse me if we'll make a deal on the Vice Presidency." It was the latest in a series of feelers from Kemp about the second spot on a Bush ticket. "I don't know how we're ever going to handle this, but I just told them all—everybody—that there must be no indication of any deal of any kind," Bush dictated on Thursday, March 3. He wanted to keep his options open. (Though not totally open: The New York developer Donald Trump mentioned his availability as a vice presidential candidate to Lee Atwater. Bush thought the overture "strange and unbelievable.")

On Saturday, March 5, 1988, in the South Carolina primary, Bush crushed Dole, and went on to sweep the contests across the South three days later. (Bush's one defeat that day came in Washington's caucuses.) "That tension sleeplessness seems to have gone away," Bush told his diary after the victories. Yet Dole kept up his attacks on Bush. "He's a desperate, mean man, and people see it," Bush dictated on Sunday, March 13. "I'll ... try and be gracious, but he has been a no good son of a bitch about me, hitting me at every turn, bitter, jealous, and class-conscious hatred. It's too bad; I've never felt that way about him at all, and yet, now I've seen this ugly side." Senator Jake Garn of Utah told Bush that Dole had muttered "Judas" at him on the Senate floor after Garn had endorsed Bush.

Still, Bush was now the putative nominee, and Washington loved a winner. "The mood has changed dramatically around the White House," Bush told his diary on the seventeenth. Dole ended his campaign on Tuesday, March 29, 1988. Bush called him to wish him well. It was a polite but brief conversation. On Wednesday, April 6, the two men met in

Bush's office at the Capitol. Dole said he would like to organize a reception for Bush with all the GOP senators to pledge support for the fall campaign. He and Elizabeth "had been a little hurt and it might take him a while to get back to normal," Bush told his diary, "but they would both be helpful."

Richard Nixon came to dinner at the vice presidential residence on Friday, April 15. "He looks a little shorter, walks a little slower—he's 75 years old," Bush told his diary. He asked the Bushes to call him Dick. Nixon liked his swordfish, ordered but did not finish a white wine on the rocks, and was polite to the stewards. It was a night of pure politics. "He does urge on me a certain moderation," Bush dictated. "He points out that he, himself, differentiated himself from Eisenhower; that he had his own identity, whereas I don't, but I should find one. He encourages it to be one of moderation: You've got the conservatives, so be moderate." Nixon ticked off some vice presidential names: "Dole, Howard Baker, Lamar Alexander, and no woman, because none are seen as Presidential." (Bush was not so sure on this last score. "I asked Nick Brady on Saturday[—]just to titillate his thought process[—] . . . what he thought about Sandra Day O'Connor," he told his diary in late April.)

The evening ended at eight thirty P.M., and Nixon flew back to Saddle River, New Jersey. "Nixon basically doesn't like me," Bush dictated that night. "I think he probably doesn't feel I'm tough enough." At one point during the dinner, listening to Nixon's hard-line analysis, Bush wondered, "What's wrong with being a gentleman? Being a gentleman doesn't mean you're not tough enough to sit down with Gorbachev."

First, though, he had to deal with the governor of Massachusetts. Then he could worry about Gorbachev.

Born in Massachusetts in 1933, the son of Greek immigrants, Michael Dukakis was a bright and able young lawyer and politician who rose from the state legislature to serve three terms as governor (he was elected in 1974, was defeated in 1978, then returned to power in 1982 and 1986). Serious, studious, and frugal—he cut his own grass, took public transportation to work, and loved to talk about his ancient snowblower—Dukakis was an emerging national player in the Democratic Party of the 1980s and had nearly been chosen to run as Walter Mondale's vice presidential nominee in 1984.

Now, in the spring of 1988, he was the Democratic presidential nominee. "I believe we're going to have fun running against Dukakis, and it
looks to me like the classic conservative [versus] liberal approach," Bush
told his diary on Monday, April 25. (He found Dukakis a bit strange.
Dukakis, Bush told his diary in early May, looked like "a little midget
nerd" as he came out of a coal mine.)

What Bush called "the gut issues" were going to be at the heart of the
campaign—"neighborhood, family, death penalty, and even abortion and
prayer." It would be, he thought in April, "a classical liberal versus conservative race," for Bush believed early on that he could run against Dukakis in the way he had run against Ralph Yarborough in 1964, depicting
his opponent as too liberal and too far out of the mainstream. It had not
worked in Texas all those years ago. Bush needed it to work now.

On Wednesday, May 11, 1988, Reagan was scheduled to endorse Bush
officially at a black-tie dinner for Republican congressional candidates. The president wrote his remarks about Bush out by hand and
showed them to him. They were, the vice president told his diary, "not
too full of praise, but straight. . . . I had every opportunity to mention it
if I didn't like it. I didn't think there was anything wrong with it at all."

That evening, at the Washington Convention Center, Reagan summa-
rized the administration's accomplishments since the 1981 inauguration—
"four months and seven years ago," as Reagan put it—closing with a brief
endorsement:

> If I may, I'd like to take a moment to say just a word about my
> future plans. In doing so, I'll break a silence I've maintained for
> some time with regard to the Presidential candidates. I intend to
> campaign as hard as I can. My candidate is a former Member of
> Congress, Ambassador to China, Ambassador to the United Na-
> tions, Director of the CIA, and National Chairman of the Repub-
> lican Party. I'm going to work as hard as I can to make Vice
> President George Bush the next President of the United States.
> Thank you, and God bless you.

Not exactly effusive, and Reagan, who was speaking fairly late in the
evening (his remarks came around ten P.M.) strangely mispronounced
Bush's last name, saying "George Bosh."

Was Reagan ambivalent about Bush? The Reagans and the Bushes had been brought together by the force of circumstance—the need for Reagan, the movement conservative, to bring mainstream Republicans and swing voters to his cause in 1980—at a time when Reagan was still seen in some quarters as a potentially dangerous man. George Bush was many things, but dangerous was not one of them. Reagan seems to have liked Bush about as much as Reagan would have liked any other professional colleague: Bush was a supporting actor, no rival for top billing, and Reagan appreciated that Bush never postured.

None of which meant, however, that Reagan was all that enthusiastic about Bush as a successor. The question is whether the president was all that enthusiastic about having *anyone* as a successor, and whether the failure to embrace Bush warmly and publicly was rooted in Reagan's own subconscious sense of himself—a sense shared by many presidents, including Reagan's old hero Franklin Roosevelt—as irreplaceable. Bush himself would later say that no man who has sat at the desk in the Oval Office can easily envision someone else there.

After the dinner speech, "a gigantic flap"—Bush's phrase—ensued over whether Reagan was truly for Bush or not. After speaking with Bush the next day, Reagan dispatched his press secretary to issue a new presidential statement: "I was surprised by the news reports that have said my endorsement last evening of the Vice President was 'lukewarm.' I am enthusiastic, fully committed and, as I have said, will go all out to make Vice President Bush the next President of the United States. George has been a partner in all we have accomplished, and he should be elected. He has my full confidence and my total support. I will campaign actively on his behalf."

Though it had been a difficult few days, Bush was quietly confident. "I still have this comfortable feeling," he told his diary in May, "that when we get the issues in focus, the country does not want to go back to the left; they do want some experience and stability; they don't want to dismantle the defenses; they want judges who are tougher on crime; they don't want homosexual marriages codified; they don't want murderers out of jail; and indeed they don't want higher taxes and the [extremists] of the environment to prevail."

Or so Bush believed, and hoped.

TWENTY-NINE
I'm Stronger and Tougher

★

I have no apologies, no regrets, and if I had let the press keep
defining me as a wimp, a loser, I wouldn't be where I am today:
threatening, close, and who knows, maybe winning.

—GEORGE H. W. BUSH, November 1988

You have a Gary Cooper there—they can't beat him.

—WARREN BEATTY, about Bush, to Bush friend Jerry Weintraub

ISTORY, IT SEEMED, WAS NOT ON BUSH'S SIDE. Since the twenty-year Democratic Roosevelt-Truman era, modern American voters, with the exception of Jimmy Carter's single term, had preferred a change of parties in the White House every eight years. There was an expectation among many commentators that 1988 was a Democratic year. As the historian Arthur Schlesinger, Jr., argued, building on a theory of his father's, there were "cycles" in American history in which periods of Republican rule were followed by eras of Democratic reform. Dukakis, meanwhile, was presenting himself to the country as a pragmatist, a detail-oriented manager in stark contrast to Reagan's image as a disengaged ideologue—an image exacerbated by Iran-contra.

In the late spring of 1988, the Democratic strategy was working. Though he had won the nomination, Bush, after eight years in Reagan's shadow, was faring poorly in terms of the voters' sense of his own views and virtues. According to an internal Bush campaign survey of Missouri voters in late April—Missouri was a key bellwether state—many possible swing voters were fuzzy about the vice president. "Too conservative," said a woman in her early thirties, while a woman in her late sixties told pollsters that Bush was a "super liberal." There was also a sense that it was time to move on from Reagan and from Bush. "I feel we need a different leader in this country," said a woman in her late forties. "We need a change." Most chilling of all, perhaps, was the response of a male Republican voter in his early sixties: "I want to vote for a Democrat this time."

On Memorial Day, 1988, Bush trailed Dukakis in the national polls. The ABC News–*Washington Post* spread was Dukakis 53 to 40 percent, and Gallup was worse: 54 to 38 percent. What to do? "We had to define Dukakis before we went into a permanent free fall," Roger Ailes recalled. The task of definition fell within the purview of James P. Pinkerton, the Atwater ally who served as the Bush campaign's director of research. Fresh from scrubbing the Dole record, Pinkerton had begun to review the Dukakis paper trail. Reading over a LexisNexis transcript of a Democratic primary debate in New York, Pinkerton noticed a question that Al Gore had put to Dukakis about a Massachusetts program that granted prison furloughs to first-degree murderers. "Eleven of them decided their two-week passes were not long enough and left. Two of them," Gore had said to Dukakis at a *Daily News* forum. "Two of them committed other murders while they were on their passes."

"Wow," Pinkerton recalled thinking, "this is really weird." He called Andy Card, the Bush adviser and a former Massachusetts state legislator, to ask if he'd heard anything about this. Yes, Card replied, the furlough issue had become a big deal in Massachusetts—so much so that the *Eagle-Tribune,* a newspaper based in Lawrence, had won a Pulitzer Prize for its coverage of the program in general and the case of a man named William Horton, Jr., in particular. Pinkerton ordered photocopies of all the Lawrence stories, and stacks soon arrived at Bush headquarters on Fifteenth Street in Washington.

The clips made for compelling reading. Horton was a convicted first-degree murderer in Massachusetts who had received a weekend pass in April 1987 and fled to Maryland, where, over the course of a horrific twelve hours, he raped a woman twice at knifepoint after pistol-whipping, stabbing, and tying up her fiancé. In Maryland, Horton was convicted of rape and kidnapping and sentenced to two consecutive life sentences—plus eighty years. The *Eagle-Tribune* published piece after piece until a petition drive to have the furlough law changed succeeded. While the program had been signed into law under a Republican governor, the Horton disaster occurred on Dukakis's watch, and Dukakis had vetoed a bill that would have kept first-degree murderers from benefiting from the furloughs. "To be sure, some in the Bush campaign were [already] apparently familiar with the furlough issue; days before Gore first broached it, one operative had suggested to reporters that it would be a helpful line of inquiry," Sidney Blumenthal, then of *The Washington Post,* wrote late in the 1988 campaign. "Gore, however, had broken the ice for them, and Pinkerton's effort appears to have been the first systematic response."

In the conversation with Pinkerton, Andy Card had passed along another tip: Dukakis had also vetoed a bill requiring public school teachers to lead students in the Pledge of Allegiance. For the Bush camp, a picture was forming. Dukakis opposed capital punishment and belonged to the American Civil Liberties Union. According to a memorandum Pinkerton prepared for Bush, the ACLU believed that the First Amendment protected "'kiddie porn'" and that "Rioting prisoners should not be punished." Considering the cluster of issues that seemed to put Dukakis far to the left of American life and politics, the Bush team could not quite believe its good fortune. As Jim Baker recalled, Dukakis, while a "bright, honorable man," was "running now for president of the United States, not president of Massachusetts."

In the last week of May, the Bush team conducted two focus groups in Paramus, New Jersey. Like the voters surveyed by the Bush team in Missouri, the cross-section gathered in New Jersey was underwhelmed by, and unclear about, both candidates. Told about the furloughs or the pledge, however, a significant number cooled on Dukakis and warmed to Bush. Atwater, Ailes, and their colleagues knew they now had the means to slow and possibly reverse Dukakis's rise in the national polls—if Bush would agree. On Saturday, May 28, 1988, Bush received a delegation from the campaign at Walker's Point. Briefed on the findings from Paramus, Bush said he worried that attacking Dukakis now, so early in the campaign, would "look desperate." Ailes threw up his hands. The polls were disastrous. Bush was blurry to nonexistent in the public mind, and if voters did have an opinion, it was likely to be negative. Dukakis was new, a Democrat who didn't seem extreme offering himself to the country after eight years of Republican power. Ailes's verdict, put directly to Bush: "We *are* desperate."

Bush had been here before, in New Hampshire, debating the "Straddle" ad. His team had come through then, and he was open to their advice now. If the furlough and the pledge issues would draw the contrast with Dukakis, then Bush was fine with the plan. "I could tell Bush was thinking, 'You know, they're right. We could lose this thing,'" recalled Ailes.

The mission was clear: Show Dukakis to be out of sync with the broad American electorate. "It will be easy to paint him for what he truly is—a Massachusetts liberal," Bush dictated. He justified his ideological and cultural attacks on Dukakis in the most basic of terms. He thought he was the better man—better for the country, better for the world—and if he had to do things and say things that he would not say or do in ordinary times, well, these weren't ordinary times. This was a presidential campaign, a contest for the highest office, the ultimate test. "I think I'm stronger and tougher, and I've been seasoned by fire, and Dukakis hasn't," Bush dictated in the summer. "I'm going to make it."

Given the dismal state of his polling—Dukakis was ahead by double digits—Bush traveled to the Texas state Republican convention to give what he thought was a "definitive" speech on Dukakis. The address laid out the themes that Bush was to repeat through November, arguing that Dukakis's views on economics, criminal justice, foreign policy, and culture were outside the mainstream. "What it all comes down to," Bush told the Texas faithful, "is two different visions." Dukakis's, Bush said, was "born in Harvard Yard's boutique"; his own came from Texas. (Yale was never mentioned.) "When I wanted to learn the ways of the world, I didn't go to the Kennedy School; I came to Texas, in 1948," he said. "I didn't go to a symposium on job creation, I started a business." The crowd loved it. "I am a practical man," he told the Texas audience. "I like what's real and I like what works and I respect policies that achieve results."

What was working, he saw, was a campaign of comparison and contrast with the governor of Massachusetts. The same press corps that had long questioned Bush's toughness pirouetted and now lamented what Dukakis called the vice president's "mudslinging and name-calling." In the face of Bush's assault, Dukakis said, "The American people aren't interested in what Mr. Bush thinks of me or what I think of him." Time, as Bush liked to say, would tell who was right on that score.

For Bush, there were two significant decisions to be made before the battle for the general election was fully joined. Would Jim Baker leave Treasury to run the campaign? And whom should Bush choose as his vice presidential running mate?

The Reagans—plural—were less than enthusiastic about a change at

Treasury. "You can be more valuable by staying here and keeping the economy on course," Reagan told Baker, who returned to Bush with the news of the presidential "no."

"It doesn't look to me like this is gonna fly unless *you* talk to the president," Baker told Bush. Reagan then gave Bush the same answer, but the president invited Bush and Baker to the Residence, Baker recalled, to "talk it over one more time."

After Bush made his case, Reagan agreed, saying, "If that's what you want, George, that's what we'll do. It just occurred to me that Jim might be more valuable as secretary of the treasury." Nancy Reagan had joined the conversation upstairs and seemed to share her husband's view that Baker could do Bush more good at Treasury than by going to the campaign.

"Nancy does not like Barbara," Bush told his diary in June 1988. "She feels that Barbara has the very things that she, Nancy, doesn't have, and that she'll never be in Barbara's class. . . . Bar has sensed it for a long time. Barbara is so generous, so kind, so unselfish, and frankly I think Nancy Reagan is jealous of her." Mutual friends told Bush that "Nancy couldn't see any family living in the White House after theirs, and that's the way she felt about it."

Baker had been delighted with his cabinet post. Yet for all his own ambition and the care he took with how he was portrayed and seen by the press and by the public, Baker was fundamentally loyal to Bush, whom he credited with making his life in politics possible. There was a bond between the two men that was often tested but never broken. Baker acceded to Bush's wishes and left the Treasury for the campaign offices on Fifteenth Street.

As a getaway during the Democratic National Convention in Atlanta in July—Dukakis had chosen ancient Bush foe Lloyd Bentsen for vice president—Bush and Jim Baker took off for a fishing trip in Wyoming. They flew out with a small entourage into Cody, then helicoptered into the Shoshone National Forest. They rode horses and fished. The world receded. Bush and Baker shared a tent, going to bed around nine each evening. They bathed in a cold waterfall.

At the Democratic convention, Texas state treasurer (and future governor) Ann Richards took Bush on, saying, "For eight straight years George Bush hasn't displayed the slightest interest in anything we care about. And now that he's after a job that he can't get appointed to, he's like Columbus discovering America." Then she mocked him: "Poor George, he can't help it—he was born with a silver foot in his mouth." In his acceptance speech, Dukakis sought to make the race about economics and opportunity. The Republicans were about prosperity for the few, not the many, he said, and "maintaining the status quo—running in place—standing still—isn't good enough for America." The election, Dukakis argued, "is not about ideology. It's about competence. . . . And it's not about meaningless labels." Coming out of Atlanta, Dukakis led Bush by seventeen points in the Gallup Poll, 54 to 37 percent.

In a "private and confidential" memorandum to Baker, Atwater, and other top Bush campaign officials dated Tuesday, August 9, 1988, Roger Ailes laid out his thinking for the general election. Calling his plan "Campaign Theme—'A Mission for America,' " Ailes wrote:

> On Election Day, the voter must know three things about Michael Dukakis. He will raise their taxes. He is opposed to the death penalty, even for drug kingpins and murderers. And he is an extreme liberal, even a pacifist on the subject of national defense. They must also know that George Bush will *not* raise their taxes. He has the experience to keep negotiations going with the Soviets. And he is very tough on law and order. If we penetrate with those three messages, it is my belief that we will win the election. A major amount of our time, effort, speeches, commercials and interviews should be spent repeating and repeating and repeating those messages. We must force this election into a very narrow framework to win.

August 1988 would be Bush's moment to step forward, accept the presidential nomination, and announce his first truly independent political decision since he and Barbara flew into Detroit for the Republican National Convention eight years before: his choice of his own vice presidential running mate. It would be truly independent. Bush's annoyance with the public prominence of what he called the "handlers"— including Baker—and his impatience with criticism and second-guessing manifested itself in the vice presidential decision-making process. He listened to advice, and he read the results of the polls his staff commissioned. He was determined, however, to make the final call himself.

In one California survey, the campaign polled possible running mates, among them Bob Dole, Elizabeth Dole, Jack Kemp, Missouri senator

John Danforth, New Mexico senator Pete Domenici, California governor George Deukmejian, Chrysler chairman Lee Iacocca, 1984 Olympics impresario Peter Ueberroth—and Clint Eastwood, the actor who also served as the Republican mayor of Carmel, California. Eastwood was a passing idea of Jim Baker's; neither the actor nor the other two nontraditional names, Iacocca and Ueberroth, polled especially well in the test run in California.

According to Bush biographer Herbert S. Parmet, "Bush's list"—which Parmet described as "not particularly revealing for its political or geographic coloration"—also included South Carolina governor Carroll Campbell, former Tennessee governor Lamar Alexander, Wyoming senator Alan Simpson, Indiana senator Richard Lugar, Arizona senator John McCain, Colorado senator Bill Armstrong, Mississippi senator Thad Cochran, Illinois congresswoman Lynn Martin, John Sununu, Missouri governor John Ashcroft, and Nebraska governor Kay Orr.

Bush had an urge to shake things up, and he was interested in an Indiana senator whom he'd gotten to know in the Reagan years: forty-one-year-old Dan Quayle, who had risen from the House to defeat Birch Bayh, a legendary liberal lawmaker, for a Senate seat in 1980. Quayle had passed a significant job-training act with Ted Kennedy and had learned arms control and foreign policy as a member of the Armed Services Committee. He was one of the few members of the 1980 class of Republican senators to have won reelection in 1986 and was decidedly conservative—a member in good standing of the wing of the party most skeptical of the incumbent vice president. And he had friends in Bush's inner circle: Bob Teeter and Roger Ailes had worked for Quayle in '86. "He's knowledgeable on military affairs, and it's an intriguing thought," Bush told his diary in July 1988. "Dole and Kemp would both be acceptable choices, but I can't get enthused."

At one point in the deliberations over the vice presidential pick, Roger Ailes made a case for Quayle on "casting" grounds. "Bush had been seen for so long as the junior guy to Reagan that it made sense for Bush's own VP to appear clearly junior," Ailes recalled. "A youthful-looking Quayle would make Bush seem the fatherly, senior figure. And Quayle had a good record, so that, plus the 'casting dimension,' if you will, put him in the mix."

Quayle had sizable ambitions. After his reelection to the Senate in 1986, he had briefly considered challenging Bush for the Republican presidential nomination. "I talked to my wife and talked to some others and thought I might just run," Quayle recalled. "I talked a little about it and they said, 'Yes, yes, yes.' You had George Bush, you had Bob Dole. . . . Others said, 'You're still a junior Senator. You've got plenty of time. Do you really want to jump out and do it right now?'" After some consideration, Quayle decided against taking the leap.

Bush liked the idea of a Vice President Quayle on the grounds of novelty and generational change. "He wouldn't get instant credibility, but it would make a generational difference," Bush told his diary. "He's smart, bright, a good speaker. . . . He comes from the Midwest, and that would be good." The vice presidential decision was down to Bob Dole or Dan Quayle. "Dole would be more instantly perceived as President, and Quayle is more exciting and new; and though people wouldn't know much about him, they would get to know him pretty quick," Bush told his diary on Saturday, August 13, 1988. "He's 41, but so was Kennedy and so was Teddy Roosevelt." (JFK was actually 43 and TR was 42 when they became president.)

Quayle, who knew he was under serious consideration, called Jim Baker on Sunday night to ask about plans for a rollout if he were, in fact, the choice, and Baker assured him that things were well in hand. At that point, Baker and others apparently assumed that Bush would land on Dole, who required no introduction. As a result, there was little to no advance work for a Quayle announcement. "He had known me a long time," Quayle recalled of Bush, "and I think he felt that if he knew me, everybody must know me."

As he prepared to leave Washington for New Orleans on Tuesday, August 16, Bush had decided on Quayle. He had not had a final gut check with Jim Baker or Lee Atwater or anyone else. "I wanted it to be a surprise, a surprise choice," Bush recalled in retirement. The lawyer and West Pointer Robert Kimmitt, who had been handling the vetting of possible running mates, did not know who the final pick was until the flight. (To be ready for any eventuality, Kimmitt had brought along three big litigation boxes with background materials on a small number of candidates, including Quayle, Dole, and Kemp.)

The Reagans were leaving New Orleans after a Monday evening address by the president. The Bushes met them at the Belle Chasse Naval Air Station. Bush whispered his choice to Reagan and then gestured to Jeb's kids, who were nearby. "One thing in my heart is that I did say to the President, 'Those are our grandchildren over there—the little brown ones,' pointing out which ones [they were] and wanting them to come over and speak to him with great pride; but the press picked it up on the loudspeaker, and then tried to make it that I'm insensitive to Hispanics," Bush told his diary. "It kills me, [and] the worst thing is I'm afraid I might have hurt little George [P.], whom I love more than life itself."

Bush told Baker that they should start calling the final runners-up for the vice presidential slot, but Bush still kept the final choice from most of his top advisers. They reached Domenici, Simpson, and Danforth, holding back on the Doles and on Kemp. Robert Kimmitt had checked out a last-minute concern about Quayle's health (he had a case of phlebitis) and called in to give what Bush called "clearance to Quayle."

Bush then told his team that Quayle was the choice. The new pick and his wife, Marilyn, were asked to come to the waterfront Spanish Plaza in New Orleans where Bush, who was arriving there on a riverboat, would introduce his new running mate. The announcement did not go well. "We notified Quayle about an hour beforehand," Bush recalled. "Then all hell broke loose." As Quayle remembered it, the plaza "was a mob scene—hot and loud and friendly, but not something you'd want to push your way through." But push they did. They had no other choice; both Quayles has been unfairly given only the barest time to prepare themselves. At the podium, Quayle seemed giddy and unserious, and there had been no preparation to present him to a national audience in a detailed way. (Jim Pinkerton sent a staffer to the local bookstore with his credit card to buy a copy of *The Almanac of American Politics* to get up to speed on the vice presidential nominee.)

The first call Quayle received once the Bushes and the Quayles returned to the Bushes' hotel suite was from Richard Nixon. "Vice President Bush did the same thing Eisenhower did," Nixon told Quayle on the telephone. "He picked a young senator with a foreign policy background." Buoyed by the approval of his old chief, Bush chose to interpret the events of the day in the most positive of lights. "The surprise played and it was considered [b]old, generational and future," Bush told his diary.

But only for a moment. There were questions about whether Quayle had improperly used connections to secure a place in the Indiana National Guard. (He had not.) Asked at his first joint press conference with Bush why he had not gone to Vietnam, Quayle replied, honestly, "I did not know in 1969 that I would be in this room today, I'll confess."

That was Wednesday. Thursday, the convention's closing day, was George Bush's most important political hour. His acceptance speech was crucial, marking his true debut as an independent political actor after two terms as Reagan's number two. "I knew what I had to do," he told his diary. "The press was building it up and up and up—had to do this, had to do that—and it was the biggest moment in my life, which it was; and almost setting expectations so high that they couldn't be matched and yet they were." Speaking from a text by Reagan speechwriter Peggy Noonan, Bush told his story. "I may not be the most eloquent, but I learned early that eloquence won't draw oil from the ground," Bush said. "I may sometimes be a little awkward, but there's nothing self-conscious in my love of country. I am a quiet man, but I hear the quiet people others don't. The ones who raise the family, pay the taxes, meet the mortgage. I hear them and I am moved, and their concerns are mine." He spoke of America as "a thousand points of light"; of his dream of a "kinder, gentler nation," and he pledged—unambiguously—never to raise taxes. "Read my lips," he said. "No new taxes."

Probably the most memorable line in the address, "Read my lips" had been a source of controversy behind the scenes. The phrase had come from Roger Ailes, who had used a version of it in an earlier campaign for Senator Chuck Grassley in Iowa. Dick Darman, a Jim Baker ally and a fiscal moderate, had tried to get the line out of the speech, but it remained, in part because Noonan kept putting it back in. "Why?" she recalled in her memoir, *What I Saw at the Revolution.* "Because it's definite. It's not subject to misinterpretation. It means, I mean this."

The convention adored it. In the speech, Bush made his experience explicit. "For seven and a half years I have worked with a President, and I have seen what crosses that big desk," Bush said. "I have seen the unexpected crisis that arrives in a cable in a young aide's hand. And I have seen problems that simmer on for decades and suddenly demand resolution. I have seen modest decisions made with anguish, and crucial decisions made with dispatch. And so I know that what it all comes down to . . . after all the shouting and the cheers—is the man at the desk." He paused dramatically, then said: "My friends, I am that man."

It was a wonderful rhetorical performance—all the more so because Bush had never really performed wonderfully in such a setting in all his years in politics. "Immediately after the speech," he told his diary, "I knew it was good."

Bush had done something he did not often do, something he had found difficult since absorbing his mother's injunctions to focus on others. With hardly a moment to spare given the approach of the November election—his greatest test—he had spoken eloquently about himself and his own view of the world. *I am that man.* For him it was a bold statement. "I say it without boast or bravado," he had told the convention. "I've fought for my country, I've served, I've built—and I will go from the hills to the hollows, from the cities to the suburbs to the loneliest town on the quietest street to take our message of hope and growth for every American to every American." His pledge at this moment on a summer's evening in New Orleans—the peak of his life—was not about the past but about the future. "I will keep America moving forward, always forward," he said, "for a better America, for an endless enduring dream and a thousand points of light." His conclusion, and his promise: "That is my mission. And I will complete it."

He reveled in the post-speech ovations at the Superdome with the Oak Ridge Boys and Shirley Jones, but the Quayle questions (about his military service and about whether the young senator was really qualified to be second in line for the presidency) would not go away. Bush had savored secrecy too much. Asked decades later why he had not allowed Baker and others to know about the Quayle decision and prepare for contingencies such as the National Guard flap, Bush was candid. This had been his first opportunity in eight years to make a call on his own, he said, and he was eager to do it just that way: on his own. "Sometimes, you just get tired of having people tell you what to do all the time," Bush recalled.

Keeping the decision to himself had been prideful, and he paid for that pride. Bush thought Quayle would make it through the storm, but he also realized that any damage to the campaign had been self-inflicted. "The whole thing is trying to shift to whether I have any management scale," Bush told his diary on Sunday, August 21, 1988. "It was my big decision, and I blew it, but I'm not about to say that I blew it." In context, Bush was apparently referring to how he "blew" the rollout of the choice, not the choice itself. He would stand with Quayle.

Bush's equanimity was made easier by the movement in the polls. The seventeen-point Dukakis lead of midsummer had collapsed, and in the wake of New Orleans Bush led 48 to 44 percent.

I t was a day, or so it seemed, to talk about the environment. On Thursday, September 1, 1988, Bush took a boat tour of a polluted Boston Harbor, campaigning as a "Teddy Roosevelt Republican" and warning that Dukakis could not be trusted with the environmental care of the country when the fabled harbor in the governor's own state was in such poor shape. (According to *The New York Times*'s account of the day, the Dukakis campaign pointed out the federal Environmental Protection Agency was "largely . . . [at] fault.") The harbor, which was to be the subject of an anti-Dukakis Bush ad, gave the vice president the occasion to raise another favorite topic. "As his boat cruised past a prison," the *Times*'s Robin Toner wrote, "a reporter called out, 'Any of those people get furloughs over there?'"

"Only one, Willie Horton," Bush replied.

According to the newspaper, the vice president had smiled when he said it; the coverage suggests that Bush was offering up a "steady stream of one-liners" at the time. But the Horton story would long raise uncomfortable questions about Bush's conduct of the 1988 contest.

As the campaign had gone on, the story of Horton's crimes and his furlough had become ever more widely known. The hugely influential *Reader's Digest* ran a piece entitled "Getting Away with Murder" in its July 1988 issue, which was available to many readers by mid-to-late June. In the third week of June, Bush, who had been attacking "unsupervised weekend furloughs to first-degree murderers," used Horton's name in a Louisville, Kentucky, speech to the National Sheriffs' Association. As David Hoffman of *The Washington Post* reported, "Vice President Bush invoked the terror of Willie Horton today in a continuing effort to portray Massachusetts Gov. Michael S. Dukakis as soft on crime."

Much of the political controversy about Horton then and in ensuing years grew out of a television ad featuring Horton's image that had been produced not by the Bush campaign but by an independent group. The ad, called "Weekend Passes," ran for only 28 days on cable television, ending October 4, but was widely discussed in the media, increasing its impact. The group, the National Security Political Action Committee, was by law allowed to spend money in support of candidacies but was forbidden from coordinating with campaigns. Indeed, the Bush campaign wrote the national television networks that the "'Willie Horton' advertisements were not produced, authorized, or approved by the Bush campaign," according to campaign lawyer Jan Baran. Jim Baker, the campaign chairman, publicly denounced the mug shot ad. But, as *The New York Times* reported, he did so "just three days before the commercial was to conclude" its run. "If they were really interested in stopping this, do you think they would have waited so long to send us that letter?" Floyd Brown, a NSPAC consultant, asked in the *Times*. Baker recalled that he had no idea what the ad's broadcast schedule was. "We wrote the letter when the criticism started coming," Baker recalled. "People said this was a racist ad, not a crime ad, so we took action and told them to stop it."

Speculation about the campaign's alleged role was fueled by a kind of swaggering culture on the part of campaign staff. Mark Goodin, the campaign's deputy press secretary, kept a mugshot of Horton on his office bulletin board. "If I can make Willie Horton a household name, we'll win the election," Lee Atwater had said in June. In a speech to Southern Republicans in Atlanta in July 1988, *The Washington Post's* Thomas B. Edsall reported, Atwater cited the *Reader's Digest* piece. "There is a story about a fellow named Willie Horton who, for all I know, may end up being Dukakis' running mate. . . . The guy [Dukakis] was on TV about a month ago, and he said, 'You'll never see me standing in the driveway of my house talking to these [vice presidential] candidates'"— an allusion to Walter Mondale's more public 1984 selection process. "And guess what? Monday, I saw in his driveway of his home Jesse Jackson. So anyway, maybe he [Dukakis] will put this Willie Horton on the ticket after all is said and done."

Roger Ailes had been quoted in *Time* in August about using Horton against Dukakis. "The only question is whether we depict Willie Horton with a knife in his hand or without it," Ailes joked to a reporter. "I meant it as a wise-ass comment, but I shouldn't have said it," Ailes recalled. "I just said it to make the Dukakis camp nervous." (The *Time* correspondent who reported the quote, David Beckwith, confirmed that Ailes was not speaking seriously. The remark had been made at an off-the-record lunch, but Beckwith later called Ailes to ask to use the quote because it was "colorful bravado." Ailes agreed to put the quote on the record.) To Ailes, Horton's crimes and his furlough were totally legitimate issues. The problem in Ailes's mind was that the use of Horton's actual image would backfire. After Atwater handed Ailes a copy of the Horton mug shot, Ailes tore it up. "I said, 'Lee, you can't put this guy on TV—you'll be called a racist,'" Ailes recalled. "I was completely opposed to it—not because I'm a good guy but because I didn't think it would work and would change the subject from crime to race. I never made an ad that depicted or explicitly mentioned Willie Horton, and I didn't have anything to do with anyone who did." In a piece about the Horton ad controversy on the eve of the 1988 voting, in an interview with *The New York Times,* Atwater said the Bush campaign had "had a 'firm policy' not to use Mr. Horton's photograph 'in any of our ads.'" Asked whether the NSPAC ad had "been beneficial" to the Bush campaign, Atwater replied: "We have no way of evaluating that."

The independent-group ad had been made by Larry McCarthy, who had worked for Ailes for six years before leaving in 1987, and who had worked for Bob Dole; Jesse T. Raiford, also formerly of Ailes's firm, did production work on the NSPAC ad. Both men said that the Bush campaign had nothing to do with the NSPAC spot. Ailes, Atwater, Baker, and Bush himself also said there no collusion. "I didn't have anything to do with that ad," Ailes said, "and I've offered $100,000 to anyone who could prove that I did"—an offer he first made in 1992.

Baker has acknowledged that "skeptics" accused the "Bush team of coordinating with a not-so-independent political action group to produce the inflammatory ad, so we could then repudiate it and enjoy the best of two worlds. In other words, we were accused of using a two-track system to get an outside group to do our dirty work for us." According to Baker, however, the Bush campaign "as far as I know—and I was campaign chairman"—had "nothing to do" with the NSPAC commercial and, "given the uproar that followed," he recalled, "I'm fairly sure it did us more harm than good."

In the fall of 1988, the Bush campaign did air an ad showing generic prisoners moving through a revolving door. (Some appeared white, some Hispanic, some African American.) The voice-over: "As governor, Michael Dukakis vetoed mandatory sentences for drug dealers. He vetoed the death penalty. His revolving door prison policy gave weekend furloughs to first-degree murderers not eligible for parole. While out, many committed other crimes like kidnapping and rape, and many are still at large. Now Michael Dukakis says he wants to do for America what he's done for Massachusetts. America can't afford that risk."

By the time any of these ads went on the air, Bush had already overcome Dukakis's lead, suggesting that the Bush team had effectively applied the lessons of the Paramus focus groups through the summer by portraying Dukakis as a Massachusetts liberal in part by talking about furloughs, the pledge of allegiance, and the ACLU. In another effective ad in the autumn, footage of Dukakis riding in a tank gave the Bush camp the background for a spot noting his opposition to different weapons systems.

On Friday, October 21, 1988, Jesse Jackson charged the Bush campaign with using Horton to exploit white fears about black men. Some mainstream opinion-makers disagreed. In an editorial headlined "A Racist Campaign?" *The Washington Post,* for example, wrote this about the Horton furlough issue: "You can believe that the importance of this topic was greatly overstated and that the 'lessons' drawn from it were demagogic and extravagantly sinister without accepting its use as the basis for a charge of racism against Mr. Bush." (The columnist Michael Kinsley published a contrary view in the *Post* two days later. Its headline: "Yes, a Racist Campaign.")

"Was the use of Willie Horton racist?" Dukakis asked rhetorically a quarter century after the campaign. "Of course it was. Was Bush himself racist? No. This was politics, pure politics, and we were in a campaign, a tough campaign. He needed to make me look too 'liberal,' so he used what was at hand, and the Horton case was in the public record. I didn't think people would be moved by all the bashing of so-called 'liberals.' But I was wrong."

Bush himself said that he believed that the Horton example spoke to the larger campaign argument that Dukakis was outside the mainstream. "I was accused of playing a black trump card against my opponent because of Willie Horton," Bush recalled in retirement. "Well, I didn't do that, one group did, and . . . [we] denounced them. But we were widely accused of race campaigning." (And when the subject came up, Bush always noted "the issue was first raised by Al Gore in the primaries.") Horton and the furlough issues were about crime, Bush insisted, not race. In truth, in the tangled politics of that difficult year, as so often in American life, they ended up being about both.

Bush and Dukakis met in a debate on Sunday, September 25, 1988. Some NFL players had told Bush that "you have to take the first hit before you feel the qualms go away." He stayed on the anti-liberal message first crafted at Kennebunkport back in late May. In a tense exchange, Bush denied that his attacks over the Pledge of Allegiance and the

ACLU were attacks on Dukakis's patriotism. "You see, last year in the primary, he expressed his passion," Bush said. "He said, 'I am a strong, liberal Democrat,' August, '87. Then he said, 'I am a card-carrying member of the ACLU.' That was what he said. He is out there . . . out of the mainstream. He is very passionate. My argument with the governor is: Do we want this country to go that far left? . . . I'm not questioning his patriotism."

Asked to reply, Dukakis said: "Well, I hope this is the first and last time I have to say this. Of course, the vice president's questioning my patriotism. I don't think there's any question about that, and I resent it. I resent it." The numbers for Bush remained favorable. He had established a lead in New Orleans, and it was proving durable, if narrow. Reagan, who had called Bush after the debate and told him he had "done good," was finally, unmistakably, explicitly for Bush.

"Well, I know who's on your side, because he's been on my side, and that's George Bush," Reagan told a campaign rally in Illinois. "He has stood by me for eight years. And so, if you want to know who's on the side of the little guy, well, I'll tell you: It's the big guy, the big guy from Texas. I know because I've worked more closely with George Bush than with any other member of the administration. I've seen him keep a cool head in a hot crisis. I've seen his leadership, and I've been guided by his vision."

Dan Quayle and Lloyd Bentsen debated each other in Omaha, Nebraska, on Wednesday, October 5. Bush watched from Fort Worth. Bentsen walked away with the night by calling Quayle on comparing his experience with John F. Kennedy's. "Senator, I served with Jack Kennedy. I knew Jack Kennedy. Jack Kennedy was a friend of mine. Senator, you're no Jack Kennedy." Overall, however, Bush believed that Quayle had performed well. "I called him ecstatically, and I called the President, and he agreed and then, of course, for a couple of days, Quayle got pounded," Bush told his diary. "Our staff is worried. The tracking the first day went good, and they keep getting this stuff that Quayle did lousy, so the tracking was off the next night."

On Thursday, October 13, 1988, the first question at the second presidential debate was unusually provocative. Bernard Shaw of CNN asked Dukakis if he would still oppose the death penalty even if his wife, Kitty, were to be "raped and murdered." Dukakis responded coolly, repeating his view that capital punishment was not a deterrent. In the emotional calculus of politics, the moment underscored the narrative Bush and his team had been constructing for months: The Massachusetts governor appeared passionless and remote, a clinical progressive more interested in the correct liberal answer than in flesh-and-blood realities.

Throughout the evening Bush was comfortable. "Roger Ailes gave me very good sound advice, and we had Kissinger sit there, hopefully in the line of sight of Dukakis to intimidate him a little," Bush told his diary. "The Dukakis people sneered a lot more than ours. They hate it when the word 'liberal' is used."

He was already tired of hearing about how the campaign had been a hollow exercise that emphasized symbols over substance. "Now you keep reading that it's the worst campaign in history—the ugliest, the meanest," Bush told his diary in mid-October. "The media was not about to define Michael Dukakis, and a lot of them are liberals; and not only are they not about to define him, they come to his defense. . . . It's absolutely absurd. If a right-winger belongs to a John Birch Society, he is dead—he is dog meat—and yet the ACLU is sacred to these press people."

The adultery allegations recurred in October when speculation that *The Washington Post* was preparing to publish a story about a Bush affair led to a brief drop in the Dow Jones. Confronted with a falling market, *Post* editors denied any such Bush report was in the works. The next day, Donna Brazile, Dukakis's deputy national field director, said to reporters: "I wasn't on the stock market yesterday but I understood they got a little concerned that George Bush was going to the White House with somebody other than Barbara. I think George Bush owes it to the American people to 'fess up. . . ." To his diary, Bush dictated: "It was the ugliest, most hurtful kind of thing." Brazile resigned, and Dukakis apologized to Bush, who tried to stay focused, telling himself: "Generally speaking, things look encouraging."

Arriving in Santa Clara, California, eleven days before the election, Bush looked out the window from Air Force Two. The view reminded him of Midland, and the beginning of the whole journey.

As often happened in the last days of a campaign, the race seemed to be tightening in overnight tracking polls, and Jim Baker worried about the numbers. An anxious team at Bush headquarters sent the nominee a few harsh speeches to deliver. The drafts, Bush thought, were "red meat, outlandish, equating Dukakis with socialism."

He made a last-minute trip to Pennsylvania on Sunday, October 30, 1988, to stay in the news. The night before, there had been a sharp up-tick in the tracking in Bush's favor. On Wednesday, November 2, just to be safe, Baker asked him to screen a "comparative" ad. "Jim, I cannot get into the ads now," Bush said. "Everyone is encouraging me to be more positive, however, so I don't want to have some smear ad at the end. . . . We should stay positive at the end of the campaign here."

By the last push, Bush could not remember where he had been on a given day; "it's blurred and blended in." His closing words to his diary on the eve of the election were cautiously optimistic. "There is an appre-hension and a nervous waiting, anxiety—and [the] recognition [that by] Wednesday it will be all or nothing, and the desire to do what's right, do my best, and the recognition that it's going to be extraordinarily dif-ficult."

He was nervous and nostalgic. "It's fitting that we come back to Texas where I voted first 40 years ago almost to the day in West Texas," he told his diary as the campaign ended. "Then it was Dewey and Truman, and I remember the upset result, and I'm just hoping against hope that that same thing doesn't happen again." He knew the critics believed he had taken the low road to victory, and he admitted that such talk bothered him. "I don't know what we could do differently," Bush dictated. "We had to define this guy."

On Election Day, Bush won convincingly, carrying forty states with 53.4 percent of the popular vote. According to exit polls, he won more votes than Dukakis among men and among women, taking 59 per-cent of the white vote; 30 percent of the Hispanic; and 12 percent of the African American. In *The Washington Post*'s exit surveys, the country was split 50 percent to 50 percent over whether America should "keep mov-ing in the direction Reagan has been taking us." Unsurprisingly, Bush won 92 percent of the votes of those who thought we should stay the Reagan course, and Dukakis carried 93 percent of those who believed it was time for a change.

Then and in retrospect, there was a widespread sense that 1988 rep-resented a historic level of negative campaigning. Studies of political trends over time, however, suggest that, as the political scientist John G. Geer has argued, "The advertising in 1988, despite all the claims, did not usher in a new era in American politics." According to Geer's data, negative appeals (such as the tank, Boston Harbor, and revolving door ads) were more prevalent, but only by few percentage points when compared to negative appeals in previous campaigns. The rate of negativity in 1988 was roughly in line with that of the campaigns of 1964, 1972, and 1980. Moreover, Bush and Dukakis ran the same percentage of negative ads, at 35 percent. (In 1980, Reagan's rate was 42 percent; in 1984, Mondale's was 37 percent.) What is clear is that, as Geer wrote, "It was the news media's coverage that brought about a new era." Heightened press attention to the tactics of campaigning undoubtedly made the '88 race feel more personal, even if, by historical standards, it was not.

America knew what it was getting. George H. W. Bush was no Ronald Reagan. He was a different kind of man, a different kind of leader—quiet, not dramatic, steady, not spectacular. No incumbent vice president had been elected to succeed an incumbent president since Martin Van Buren won in 1836. Richard Nixon's defeat in 1960 was more common—a sitting vice president losing to the opposition party—and the pundits had long believed that Bush would face the same fate.

In the intensely personal politics of presidential choice, the people had decided—or at least 53.4 percent of those who chose to vote had decided—that Bush was the kind of man who could be counted on in what he called "the biggest job in the world." Theirs was not a particularly data-driven decision—Bush himself admitted he was short on specifics—but that did not mean the Bush victory was irrational. He had said he wouldn't raise taxes and he seemed sound on national defense—and those things, combined with the public impression of his private character, were enough.

From Connecticut to the Pacific to Texas to Washington to Beijing and back again, Bush had proven himself an attractive and reliable man to those who got to know him. He had rivals but virtually no enemies, largely because of his apparently limitless capacity to make others feel included and at ease. The American voters turned to him in 1988 for many of the same reasons so many others had turned to him in smaller ways for so many years and across so many different assignments: because experience and intuition suggested to them that things would be safe in his hands. Others were more eloquent, others more sure and certain in their ideology. There were few others, however, who so convincingly conveyed the ineffable sense that they were fit for command.

George H. W. Bush did, and for that reason, chiefly, he was now the president-elect of the United States.

On the evening of the election, from the Houstonian Hotel, Bush spoke to Reagan, and Barbara to Nancy. Margaret Thatcher of Great Britain and King Fahd of Saudi Arabia called to congratulate the president-elect, who celebrated with wine and cheese.

"We went to bed sort of in shock," Barbara wrote. "I mean, George is going to be the 41st President of the United States. Hard to believe. Think of all the people who should be here and who would be so proud and say, 'I knew it all the time!!!' Neil Mallon, Pres Bush, Sr., and Marvin Pierce." In the hour of victory, Barbara thought of the men who had first gauged her husband's depths, and seen so much in him. Now a majority of American voters had taken his measure, too, and chosen to entrust him with ultimate authority.

For Bush, the weeks between the 1988 election and his inauguration offered him a chance to move from vote getter to conciliator. "Campaigns go away," Bush told his diary, "and you stand on the question of the issues themselves, and your style." The seeking of office—the focus groups and the tracking polls and the hastily called hotel meetings about airing this ad or that ad—were of less interest to him than the holding of office, and now that he was about to hold the greatest office of all he wanted to leave the brutality of the campaign as far behind as possible. On the trail, Bush had fired off Mao's "empty cannons of rhetoric," and in his conception of the presidency, what mattered was what you did once in power, not what you said in order to get there.

At eight o'clock on the morning after the victory over Dukakis, the Bush family went to St. Martin's Episcopal Church in Houston for a brief service. George W. rose and prayed: "We ask, Lord, that you open our hearts and minds to you: Many of us will begin a new challenge. Please give us strength to endure and the knowledge necessary to place our fellow man over self. . . . Please guide us and guard us on our new journeys—particularly watch over Dad and Mother."

A few hours later Bush met the press at the George R. Brown Convention Center. He announced Jim Baker's appointment as secretary of state, handled some transition business, and opened the floor to reporters. The campaign was yesterday, Bush insisted; what mattered was today and tomorrow.

Around Thanksgiving, Bush called Dukakis and said he'd be happy to drive from Kennebunkport to Boston to say hello, but Dukakis, Barbara recalled, "was not ready for that yet." They did get together in early December in the vice presidential residence, where Dukakis gamely posed for a photo with the Bushes' English springer spaniel, Millie, a gift from their Houston friends the Will Farishes. (Barbara was putting together *Millie's Book,* written from the dog's point of view, and had a chapter on "famous people she knew.") "I never liked dogs," Dukakis said, recalling various canine attacks during his days as a paper boy.

The Bushes spent a sunny and snowy New Year's weekend at Camp David. The Reagans were at Sunnylands, the Walter Annenbergs' Rancho Mirage estate, so the president-elect and his wife had the run of the retreat. Or the run of much of it: The Bushes knew not to stay in Aspen, the presidential cabin, until after January 20. Nancy remained vigilant about the prerogatives of her husband's office and did not schedule a tour of the White House family quarters for Barbara until January 11, just nine days before the transfer of power. "There is this feeling of competitiveness," Bush dictated, "and I'm afraid Nancy is going to be hurt when she is out of office, out of the limelight, and out of reach of the glamour of the White House."

Bush returned to Washington, where, as president of the Senate, he was in the chair for the counting of the votes of the electoral college. That morning Bush confided something to Barbara. "I'm excited for the first time," Bush told her. "I just felt different. I can't wait to get in that office now, and start trying to make things happen." He was comfortable with the prospect of power. "There's no such feeling of anxiety as I approach this job. No extra acid in the colon. A quiet, a strange quiet, accompanied by anticipation. I know how to begin, I know how to start, I know where the office is, and I'm not overawed because I've been in there a lot."

With its mix of the trivial and the tumultuous, the strange nature of daily life in the presidency was growing ever more real. On the personal front, Friday, January 6, 1989, was the Bushes' forty-fourth wedding anniversary: The president-elect gave Barbara a new necklace. There were unmistakable signs that life would never be the same again, at least for the next four or eight years. "The briefings on my responsibilities in the nuclear age—stark," Bush dictated on Saturday, January 7. "The stark . . . reality, the awesome responsibility really was driven home." That evening the Bushes went to dinner and a show, *Shear Madness,* at the Kennedy Center. "I gasp at the prices," Bush told his diary. "The danger is you can get out of touch in this business."

On the Monday before his Friday inaugural, Bush sat in the vice presidential residence, thinking. Through the leafless trees he could see the Washington Monument and the Capitol. The previous eight years had been good ones. He had been happy in this house, happy in the job under Reagan. Outsiders mocked the vice presidency and had mocked Bush in it, taking his loyalty to the president and his refusal to share what he told Reagan as signs of weakness. Yet he had given his word to Reagan—and to himself—that he would not grandstand. He had kept his word, and he had been rewarded for it. What he often called the "common wisdom" had been wrong, and he had been right.

In the steadily emptying house, surrounded by boxes, he was vindicated, for he was leaving it as the next president of the United States. He thought of the good days he and Barbara had shared in the house—the home in which they had spent the most time in their married lives. "Millie chases the foxes; Millie catches three squirrels; Millie catches a bird," Bush dictated. "They say there's frustrations in the vice presidency. Perhaps, [but] you simply make your own passions, your own priorities, and when you work with a man like Ronald Reagan, it comes easy."

He asked himself the big questions. "People say, 'What does it feel like? Are you ready? Can you handle it? What do you do?' The answer, 'Family, faith, friends, do your best, try your hardest; rely on the innate good sense, kindness, and understanding of the American people.' That's where a President gets his strength, I'm sure of it. No one can have instant success, no one can make this nation kinder and gentler overnight, but we can try." It was almost time for the move down to the White House, into the Oval Office, into the maelstrom. The task ahead was almost unimaginably complex. And yet he believed, quietly, that he was as ready as a man could be.

PART VI
The Awesome Responsibility

1989 to 1993

★

Here I am as the President of the United States, the leader of
the free world, and living in a fascinating time of change in the
world itself.

—GEORGE H. W. BUSH, 1989

The president and Mrs. Bush on the final night of the Republican National Convention, Houston, Thursday, August 20, 1992.

THIRTY

The Sun Started Through

★

*For we are given power not to advance our own purposes, nor
to make a great show in the world, nor a name. There is but one
just use of power, and it is to serve people.*

—GEORGE H. W. BUSH, in the prayer he wrote for his inaugural

USH CAME TO THE PRESIDENCY a decent and caring man whose
experience in life and in government had taught him that there
were few simple problems and even fewer perfect answers. He saw
himself as a guardian, not as a revolutionary. A realist, Bush confronted
the issues of the hour as they arose in the natural unfolding of history.
TR had a Square Deal, FDR a New Deal, Truman a Fair Deal, JFK a
New Frontier, LBJ a Great Society, Reagan an eponymous Revolution.
Bush was temperamentally uncomfortable with such grand schemes. As
his vice president, Dan Quayle, put it, Bush was "results-oriented," not
philosophically driven.

His presidency was shaped by all that he had met and all that he had
done. World War II and the loss of Robin had taught him that life was
"unpredictable and fragile," a truth that meant those who were spared
owed debts of service to others. He had come of age as a businessman
and as a father under Eisenhower, whose conservative centrism had created the conditions for Bush's own prosperity and happiness in postwar
Texas. As a politician Bush had apprenticed in Johnson's Washington,
where presidents were neither angels nor demons but sometimes right
and sometimes wrong. Under Nixon and Ford, he had learned about
diplomacy, national politics, and intelligence gathering firsthand. And
Reagan had given him an impressive model of leadership to which to
aspire, even if Bush knew he could never match the Gipper as a presidential performer.

A figure of conservative consensus at home and cautious creativity
abroad, Bush governed in a consequential time—what Henry Kissinger
thought the most tumultuous four-year period term since Truman. The

death throes of the Soviet empire, a hot war in the Middle East, violent upheaval in China: The world was in fundamental flux on Bush's watch, and he led with confidence on the global stage. At home he confronted rising federal deficits and debt that threatened the economy, and his leadership put the country on a path toward fiscal health at great political cost. He signed significant environmental legislation, established the principle of national education goals, worked to expand free trade, and enacted the Americans with Disabilities Act, the most sweeping civil rights measure in a generation.

There were, of course, frustrations and failures. He was an inconsistent leader of popular opinion and a poor manager of his own political capital. No president before him ever rose higher in public estimation, yet by 1992 he would be defeated as a new generation of Democrats, aided by the news media and by the populist Texas billionaire Ross Perot, portrayed him as adrift and unengaged.

For a time, the political triumph of George Bush was immense— a story of presidential success in which man and moment met as the nation and the world required the steady hand he offered. The political tragedy of George Bush came in the last eighteen months or so of his presidency, when he seemed a caretaker at a time when voters were in the market for a dreamer. His White House years are a story of the rise and decline of a president who reached an unprecedented pinnacle of popularity only to fall, dizzyingly, to defeat at the polls. He wasn't surprised, really, by the turn of events. He knew that what politics gave, politics took away.

Friday, January 20, 1989, was cold and cloudy. In the car on the way from the White House to the Capitol, Reagan reassured Bush about the weather: "When I became Governor of California, just as I placed my hand on the Bible, the sun came through and warmed it." It was typical Reagan, focusing on the positive and the possible. (He had taken his first gubernatorial oath indoors at midnight, but had an outdoor ceremony afterward.) Bush was cheered by the story. "And sure enough," Bush recalled, "while we were on the platform, the sun started through."

Bush's inaugural address was brief. He thanked Reagan and then asked the nation to pray. As heads bowed, the new president withdrew a small sheet of paper from his breast pocket. He had drafted the words himself. "Heavenly Father . . . Make us strong to do Your work, willing to heed and hear Your will, and write on our hearts these words: 'Use power to help people.' For we are given power not to advance our own purposes, nor to make a great show in the world, nor a name. There is but one just use of power, and it is to serve people. Help us to remember it, Lord. Amen." In his address, Bush was candid about the political culture over which he was to preside. "There has grown a certain divisiveness," Bush said. "We have seen the hard looks and heard the statements in which not each other's ideas are challenged, but each other's motives." He closed with a plea for grace and dignity. "Some see leadership as high drama and the sound of trumpets calling, and sometimes it is that," Bush said. "But I see history as a book with many pages, and each day we fill a page with acts of hopefulness and meaning. The new breeze blows, a page turns, the story unfolds. And so today a chapter begins, a small and stately story of unity, diversity, and generosity—shared, and written, together."

As Billy Graham offered the benediction and Alvy Powell, an army musician, sang the national anthem, Bush leaned over to Reagan and pointed upward—the sun had come out. The now former president smiled and nodded. He had known it all along.

The Bushes walked the Reagans through the Capitol to the east front and then down the steps to a waiting helicopter. As Reagan boarded, he turned back and offered a salute to his successor, who returned it. Reagan joined Nancy inside the chopper, and Bush headed back up the steep steps. Jim Baker, who had been standing to the side during the farewell, embraced his old friend, and the president of the United States and the secretary of state walked arm in arm toward the doors of the Capitol, the new order heading to work as the old took its leave, heading west.

Baker roamed the world as secretary of state but remained preternaturally attuned to Bush and his fortunes both at home and abroad. Lamar Alexander, the former Tennessee governor who would later join the administration as secretary of education, was always struck by how Bush and Baker seemed connected telepathically; each man appeared perennially aware of what the other was thinking and doing. While this intimacy did not mean the president and the secretary of state were in constant agreement, it did invest Baker with an unusual level of power, for, as he liked to put it, "No one ever thought that they could get between me and my president." The Bush-Baker relationship fascinated the press. "They keep playing it up that he's always selfish, always looking after his own ass, always looking to be President, etc.," Bush told his diary, "but I have a lot of confidence in him."

One man who totally understood the Bush-Baker connection was Brent Scowcroft, whom Bush asked to return for a second engagement as national security adviser. Slight and soft-spoken, Scowcroft thought the national security adviser's job was to serve as an honest broker of information and policy options for the president. A classic realist, Scowcroft believed that the Reagan "Evil Empire" rhetoric had been too harsh. Better to strike moderate tones and move cautiously—a formulation that appealed to Bush. Scowcroft also intuitively knew to defer to Baker as America's chief diplomat, avoiding the usual rivalries between the State Department and the National Security Council. Scowcroft was so conscious of Baker's prerogatives that he initially refused to speak publicly on foreign policy without clearing it with Baker beforehand—an act of respect that Baker appreciated, but which soon proved superfluous. The Bush foreign policy team operated with an extraordinary degree of harmony. Scowcroft's staff included Robert M. Gates, a steady, impressive CIA veteran who served as deputy national security adviser, and Condoleezza Rice, a Stanford professor who handled Soviet and Eastern European affairs.

John Sununu, the former governor of New Hampshire, brought an engineer's mind and a brusque, no-nonsense Yankee sensibility to the inner circle as White House chief of staff. The gregarious Bush hated saying no; the tough-minded and sometimes arrogant Sununu imposed discipline within the president's organization. "Sununu thinks a mile a minute—a new idea on whatever subject it is," Bush told his diary. "He's bright as he can be; [a] quick grasp with the budget. He sometimes can be a little too confrontational with bankers or congressmen or whatever, but he's awful good." From afar, Richard Nixon looked on approvingly. "Like a good chief of staff he is not afraid to be the SOB so that the Boss can be the good guy!"

Bush's old friend Nicholas Brady, the former chairman of Dillon, Read who had briefly served as a U.S. senator from New Jersey, was secretary of the Treasury. Roger B. Porter, a Rhodes Scholar and professor at Harvard's Kennedy School of Government, had served in the Ford and Reagan White Houses before joining the Bush team in 1989 as assistant to the president for economic and domestic policy. And there was

Dick Darman, who became the director of the Office of Management and Budget. A brilliant analyst and master of the intricacies of the budget and of domestic policy, the moderate Darman had worked for Elliot Richardson, served as Reagan's staff secretary, and was Baker's deputy at Treasury. He had opposed the "Read my lips" language in Bush's acceptance speech—and now, in an irony that the whip-smart Darman fully appreciated, the task of addressing the deficit while laboring under a promise of "No new taxes" had fallen to him.

On the evening of the inauguration, after fourteen balls, the Bushes spent their first night in their new home. The next morning at eight, the president and Barbara greeted visitors who had camped out overnight to tour the White House. He thrived on the pace. After opening the mansion to the public, Bush walked over to the West Wing. He had been there with Richard Nixon, and with Gerald Ford, and with Ronald Reagan. Now, finally, it was *his* West Wing. "I went to the Oval Office and everything was changed overnight, quick," Bush recalled. "Reagan was gone, Bush was in. The papers were the way I wanted them. . . . The CIA briefing started," and the presidency of George H. W. Bush truly began.

He treasured a small souvenir. President Reagan had left him a note on a piece of Sandra Boynton stationery. A cartoon elephant lay prostrate beneath a flock of turkeys. The caption: "Don't let the turkeys get you down."

> Dear George
>   You'll have moments when you want to use this particular stationery. Well go to it.
>   George I treasure the memorys [*sic*] we share wish you all the best. You'll be in my prayers. God bless you & Barbara. I'll miss our Thursday lunches.
>
>   Ron

Bush had an important ceremonial task to dispatch on his first full day as president: receiving his mother in the Oval Office. "Mother was the star," Bush told his diary. A reporter asked Mrs. Bush if this were the most exciting day of her life.

"So far," Mrs. Bush replied. "So far."

THIRTY-ONE

If It Weren't for the Deficit . . .

★

I cannot break my "Read the Lips" pledge. I would be totally
destroyed if I did.

—GEORGE H. W. BUSH, April 1989

O N A SNOWY SATURDAY in January 1987, Richard Nixon had
come by to see Bush at the vice presidential residence. Nixon
loved to talk politics, and he had handicapped the '88 race for
Bush. The most prescient thing the former president had said in the
three-and-a-half-hour session, though, was about governing, not running. "George, you know you were right about 'voodoo economics,' don't
you?" Nixon had asked. "We've got to handle the deficit. You know there
is going to have to be a tax increase."

Nixon's prediction had proven accurate. The month Bush defeated
Dukakis, the General Accounting Office projected that tax increases
"are probably an unavoidable part of any realistic strategy for reducing
the deficit." Former presidents Ford and Carter also told Bush and Dick
Darman that, as they put it, "based on definitive analysis, it would be
very difficult to balance the budget without some considerable increase
in revenues." During their post-1988 election courtesy call, Mike Dukakis and the president-elect had chatted about the just-released report of
a national deficit study commission. "There's no way I can raise taxes in
the first year," Bush had said. Dukakis was startled. *In the first year?* he
thought. "It was clear to me then," Dukakis recalled, "that 'Read my lips'
was a temporary promise."

In the transition from Reagan to Bush, Roger Porter was weighing
the possibility of working with Carla Hills as deputy U.S. trade representative when the president-elect asked him to become assistant for
economic and domestic policy. Porter asked the president-elect a question: What was Bush's chief priority on the home front? Without hesitation, Bush replied: "Getting deficits under control." The answer, Porter
recalled, "reflected his conviction that large and growing deficits would

slow economic growth and that setting fiscal policy on a sustainable long-term path was his most crucial economic task."

The federal budget had last been in balance under President Johnson. Since then, federal outlays had outpaced federal revenues at an ever-rising rate. In 1989, Bush faced the stubborn fact that the deficit might lead to tougher economic times since the Federal Reserve was unlikely to lower interest rates until it was convinced the administration and Congress were serious about reducing the deficit. Without lower interest rates, there would be less capital in the marketplace; with less capital in the marketplace, there would be slower growth, fewer jobs, and possibly a recession. Or worse.

In the political and cultural ethos of the late 1980s and early '90s, the federal deficit, if allowed to grow inexorably, was seen as a harbinger of potential American decline as an economic and military force. The Yale historian Paul Kennedy's surprise 1987 bestseller *The Rise and Fall of the Great Powers: Economic Change and Military Conflict from 1500 to 2000*, argued that heavily leveraged countries could lose everything, and the Kennedy thesis was very much in the air as Bush took office. "If it weren't for the deficit," Bush wryly told his diary as he prepared to assume power, "I'd be feeling pretty good these days."

Bush saw the deficit as more than a problem to be managed. It was, conceivably, an existential question for the nation's economic health and for America's place in the world. Trapped between his own campaign rhetoric of "Read my lips" and economic and political reality, he was coming to understand that movement toward a balanced budget might well require more revenue—more taxes. The business cycle was also working against him. After the deep recession of 1981–82, the country had had several good years under the Reagan presidency. (Though at a price: The federal debt—or accumulated deficits—had tripled from fiscal 1980 to fiscal 1989.) Beginning in 1989, the economy grew at below-typical rates.

Bush was thus caught in a depressing spiral. The higher deficits from the Reagan years meant slower economic growth (in part because of the Federal Reserve's reluctance to lower interest rates), and slower economic growth exacerbated the deficit since tax receipts were lower in leaner times. Add in a series of savings and loan failures that had increased federal outlays as Washington bailed out exposed depositors, and Bush was taking office at a frustrating fiscal moment.

There were only two solutions: drastically reduced spending or higher taxes. Bush's problem was that the Democratic majorities in Congress were not interested in cutting spending, and he had memorably promised not to raise taxes. "I cannot break my 'Read the Lips' pledge," Bush told his diary on Sunday, April 2, 1989. "I would be totally destroyed if I did."

In the way of politics, he deferred the reckoning for a year. As his first budget took shape (for fiscal year 1990) Bush was popular, in large measure because the effects of the slowing economy had not been fully felt in the country at large. Early days were cheery days: An ABC News– *Washington Post* poll had Bush's approval rating at 76 percent, "the highest," Bush was told, "of any President at this time of his Presidency since Johnson, who took over after the Kennedy murder. . . . [I]n any event it'll change, but we might as well enjoy it while we can—keep trying, keep working."

He called on an old friend, Dan Rostenkowski, the Democratic chairman of Ways and Means, for help. Over lunch in December 1988, "Rosty" agreed to "avoid embarrassing the new President on taxes for one year— but for only one year," Dick Darman recalled. "Given the no-new-taxes pledge," Darman noted, "even a one-year reprieve seemed better than none." Bush took it, happily. Darman was reading *Time*'s coverage of the bipartisan announcement of a 1989 budget that avoided the hard choices until 1990. The headline, Darman knew, said it all: "Wait Till Next Year."

The Rostenkowski lunch was typical for Bush. At heart a hospitable man, he put his personal charm to work in the White House. He believed in the efficacy of the invitation to have a quick drink at the end of the day, or to pitch horseshoes, or to watch a movie in the theater on the first floor of the mansion. Congress was decidedly Democratic, with the opposition party holding an eighty-nine-seat margin in the House and a ten-seat advantage in the Senate. During the transition Bush spent time with House Speaker Jim Wright and Senate Majority Leader George Mitchell; at his old Democratic friend the Mississippi congressman Sonny Montgomery's recommendation Bush had also met at the vice presidential residence with leading House Democrats Leon Panetta, Tom Foley, and David Obey as well as interest-group leaders from the left. Bush's goal: "to demonstrate that I want to be a President of all the people." From the start, however, he found Capitol Hill less engaging than the rest of the world. The president had a freer hand abroad than he did at home, and by 1989, Bush was largely a creature of the executive branch. (He had served more than three times longer as a presidential appointee or as vice president than he had as a congressman.)

And given the Democratic majorities on Capitol Hill, Bush had to cultivate personal relationships to have any real hope of getting anything through Congress. Within a week of the inauguration, the Bushes were inviting lawmakers to the Residence for informal tours. The First Couple would show visitors the Lincoln Bedroom, the Queen's Bedroom, and the Treaty Room, which Bush used as a study. Barbara was as welcoming to the lawmakers as her husband but was a bit more skeptical about the long-term benefits. "Barbara reminded me that only Lyndon Johnson did this, and 'Look where he ended up,'" Bush recalled. "I'd like to think the war in Vietnam had something to do with it, not just his open style." Bush took pictures of the lawmakers in the Lincoln Bedroom with a Polaroid OneStep. The guests loved it.

Conservative Republicans were wary about Bush's outreach to Democrats. In the middle of March, John Sununu attended a meeting of GOP lawmakers in Charlottesville, Virginia, and heard what Bush called "some bitching that we're too bipartisan, [and] have the Democrats down to the White House too much. And I bristle at this introverted, this looking-inward part of the Republican members."

He faced an early test of presidential power with the controversy over his nomination of his old Texas colleague John Tower to serve as secretary of defense. Beset by rumors of what biographer Herbert S. Parmet described as the nominee's "love of women and booze," Tower offered to remove himself from consideration, but Bush resisted. Democrats in the Senate, led by Sam Nunn of Georgia, opposed the nomination. Though a former senator himself, Tower had few friends in the Democratic caucus. Thought to have been high-handed during his years as chairman of the Senate Armed Services Committee, he was a vulnerable nominee. Still, Bush refused to "pull the rug out" from his old colleague, telling a teary Tower that he "was going to stand with him and support him. . . . We cannot show weakness." But Bush could not pull together the votes, and the nomination was defeated in early March.

In the search for a new defense secretary, Bush's first thought was to send Brent Scowcroft over to the Pentagon, but he felt he could not spare his national security adviser as his foreign policy right hand. There were other names in circulation: former secretary of the navy John Lehman and former secretary of defense Mel Laird suggested Don Rumsfeld for a return engagement, but Bush ruled Rumsfeld out. "[He's] unacceptable, because Baker doesn't like him and I worry about his game playing and I think Brent does, too," Bush told his diary. Three other names came up: Jack Edwards, a former congressman; Jake Garn, the Utah senator; and Dick Cheney. "I worry [because Cheney has had] a heart attack," Bush dictated, "and yet I see some enormous potential there."

Cheney called on Bush in the Residence at one P.M. on Friday, March 10, 1989. We "went over his background," Bush recalled. "He hadn't served in the Army; had two DWIs; and [he's] nervous because of the latter-day Tower morality on the Hill. But I told him that I saw no problems with that." Bush announced the Cheney appointment at four P.M. With Cheney's move to the Pentagon, his place in the Republican leadership—minority whip, the number two position behind Bob Michel, the minority leader—was now open, and Newt Gingrich of Georgia stepped in to fill it.

Gingrich, then forty-five, had risen to prominence in the 1980s by relentlessly attacking the Democratic leadership, often late at night on C-SPAN, when he would fill an empty chamber with apocalyptic rhetoric about what he argued was a war of civilizations between liberals (whom he thought of as "sick") and true conservatives. Now the rebel was in the Republican leadership.

And he was not Bush's kind of Republican. Born in Pennsylvania in 1943, Gingrich, the stepson of a military man, grew up at different postings around the world, graduated from high school in Georgia, and was educated at Emory and at Tulane, where he earned a PhD in history. He joined the faculty of West Georgia College and worked for Nelson Rockefeller's 1968 presidential campaign before a turn to the right in the 1970s. Gingrich lost two races for Congress before winning in 1978. Grandiose and energetic, he was an intriguing force in the politics of the Reagan-Bush eras, blending a passion for assaults against Democrats with big ideas about life in a postindustrial world. He saw himself, without irony and with little self-awareness, as a "transformational figure."

He was, in short, an uncontrollable force, driven by ambition of epic scope, and now he was moving closer to the center of George H. W. Bush's universe. "The question is, will he be confrontational; will he raise hell with the establishment; will he be difficult for me to work with?" Bush asked in his diary on Wednesday, March 22, 1989. "I don't think so," Bush answered himself, hopefully. "I called him and congratulated him. And he's going to have to get along in some degree, moderate his flamboyance. He will be a tough competitor for the Democrats, but I'm convinced I can work with him and I want to work with him. He's a very bright guy, [an] idea a minute, but he hasn't been elected President and I have."

Would Gingrich, however, acknowledge that overarching reality? The media was skeptical. "The press take the Gingrich election [as minority whip] and shows it as a real challenge to me one way or another," Bush dictated on Monday, March 27. The Washington media, Bush noted, had been "hitting me for being kind and gentle, instead of confrontational, juxtaposing my views against Newt's, my style against Newt's. I was elected to govern and to make things happen, and my . . . view is, you can't do it through confrontation." Following his instinct to keep people close, Bush invited Gingrich and Vin Weber, the Minnesota Republican congressman who had managed Gingrich's whip campaign, to the White House for a beer. The conversation was pleasant, but the visitors felt there was something Bush was not quite saying. Weber decided to put the question to the president directly. "Mr. President, you've been very nice to us," Weber said as they were preparing to leave. "Tell us what your biggest fear is about us."

"Well," Bush answered, "I'm worried that sometimes your idealism will get in the way of what I think is sound governance." In the most polite way possible, in a single sentence, Bush had just encapsulated a crucial new truth. Gingrich and Weber believed so deeply (so *idealistically*, to use Bush's terminology) in adherence to conservative ideological principle that compromise on those core views (and compromise was the essence of what Bush saw as "sound governance") was out of the question. The old politics of the possible was being replaced by the politics of purity.

In his first April as president, Bush sat in the Treaty Room on the second floor of the White House, with its views of the Jefferson and

Washington memorials. He used the room a great deal, often working there at night or early in the mornings. "I'm wondering at the majesty of all of this, and in essence, praying that I will be a good President, a fair President, a strong President, mainly a principled President," he told his diary. "And then it gets all right back to do your best, do what you can, and don't worry about those things that you can't do overnight."

THIRTY-TWO
Victory in Europe, Terror in China

★

The longer I'm in this job, the more I think prudence is a value,
and I hope experience matters.

—GEORGE H. W. BUSH

MIKHAIL SERGEYEVICH GORBACHEV was something altogether new: a Soviet leader with whom the West, as Margaret Thatcher once put it, "could do business." Born in 1931 to a Russian-Ukrainian farming family in Stavropol, Gorbachev was a bright young man whose father fought in World War II (in Soviet memory, "the Great Patriotic War"). For a time, the elder Gorbachev was thought to have been killed in action in 1944. His family, including thirteen-year-old Mikhail, believed him dead, only to discover that the reports were wrong: His father returned home after the war. Young Mikhail, then, grew up with a sense that accepted realities could change, and change quickly. He was involved in theatrical productions in school. After earning his law degree in Moscow, Gorbachev rose through the party ranks and became the Soviet Union's chief of agriculture. In March 1985, after the death of Konstantin Chernenko, Gorbachev, at the young age of fifty-four, took over an economically and culturally stagnating Soviet empire.

Bush and Gorbachev had first met at Chernenko's funeral, and the American vice president was instantly impressed, "He was different, totally different, from the types of Soviets we'd been used to," Bush recalled. In a memorandum to President Reagan, Bush wrote: "Gorbachev will package the Soviet line for Western consumption much more effectively than any (I repeat any) of his predecessors. He has a disarming smile, warm eyes, and an engaging way of making an unpleasant point and then bouncing back to establish real communication with his interlocutors."

Once in power, Gorbachev unleashed a series of reforms, known as "perestroika" (restructuring) and "glasnost" (openness), in an attempt to revive and strengthen the Soviet Union. Long considered the defining threat to the United States and the other Western democracies, the Soviet Union was showing signs of weakness by the late 1970s. Now, in the late 1980s, the Soviet republics and the nations within the Soviet sphere, including East Germany, were unhappy with Moscow and with the inefficient Communist system that had failed to deliver an equitable socialist paradise.

On Wednesday, December 7, 1988, Bush had joined Reagan and Gorbachev for a brief summit on Governors Island in New York Harbor. "Strange meeting with Gorbachev—strange in the fact that he really wants to get a direction and idea, and strange in the fact that the old and new were both there," Bush told his diary. "It was a little awkward." Bush could always tell when Gorbachev himself was angered: "His eyes sparkle and he turns red, with his mouth firmly set, and he kind of shrugs." At one point in the conversation on Governors Island, Bush recalled, Gorbachev grew agitated and "bristled" when Reagan "asked . . . about reform, and [Gorbachev] flared up a little and said, 'Well, have you completed all the reforms you need to complete?'" Bush called Gorbachev the next morning to say he was sorry he'd been so reticent, but that was the nature of the system. He would be more talkative after January 20, and even more talkative after a few months, during which the new administration was to conduct a global review of foreign policy.

Bush was alluding to what became known as his "pause." He had pledged an essential continuation of Reagan's policies but very much wanted to put his own mark on diplomacy. Thus was born the idea of a wide-ranging Bush review of the Reagan administration's standing positions around the world. There was much to contemplate, especially with the Soviets. On the one hand, Gorbachev had encouraged stirrings of nationalist and freedom movements behind the Iron Curtain in East Germany, Poland, Hungary, Czechoslovakia, and elsewhere. "From the point of view of long-term, big-time politics, no one will be able to subordinate others," Gorbachev wrote in a 1987 book. "Let everyone make his own choice, and let us all respect that choice."

Yet just four days before Bush's inauguration, in Prague, the totalitarian Czech regime arrested eight hundred anti-Soviet demonstrators, including the playwright Vaclav Havel, who was sentenced to nine months in prison. In April, government troops killed nineteen people at a nationalist demonstration in Tbilisi, Georgia, a Soviet republic. Moscow also continued to support Nicaragua's Communist regime, a source of ongoing American frustration.

What was unclear in early 1989, then, was whether the world was changing as rapidly in fact as it was in tone. The old schoolboy actor in Gorbachev understood the dramatic gesture. He was a master of sweeping disarmament proposals and spoke boldly of "freedom of choice" for nations in the Soviet sphere. The key problem for Bush was deciding whether Gorbachev's aim was truly a more democratic future or whether, in the words of Brent Scowcroft, the Soviet leader's goal was "to restore dynamism to a socialist political and economic system and revitalize the Soviet Union domestically and internationally to compete with the West." Even Bush's advisers were divided on the question. In Washington, many believed Gorbachev was a genuine reformer. Others thought he was either bluffing about a new day or, if he weren't, that he would be toppled by a hard-liner more interested in Soviet power than in Soviet change.

As the weather in Washington warmed through the spring of 1989, the "pause" ended, and Bush was ready to act. According to the prevailing wisdom of the season, it was none too soon. In the view of many—including Bush himself—Gorbachev was winning the global public-relations battle. With his reforms and surprise disarmament proposals—he sprung one on Jim Baker in Moscow on Baker's first visit as secretary of state—the Soviet leader seemed to have usurped the American president as the world's leading statesman. Bush's allies and friends urged him to engage. "We are in a historic position," Helmut Kohl of West Germany told Bush by phone in early May. Kohl refused "to see Gorbachev as the new hero." The latest developments in Eastern Europe exceeded their "wildest dreams, the ideological breakdown of a political and economic system. This was the hour of our triumph." It was, Kohl said, a triumph due "not least to the efforts of the United States." For that reason, Kohl believed that "the President's role should be brought to the fore."

Over lunch on Wednesday, May 17, 1989, Jim Baker underscored the message, telling Bush it was time to be bold. "You need to get ahead of the power curve" against Gorbachev, Baker said. Bush agreed. The result: The president decided to use the fortieth anniversary meeting of NATO in Brussels in May to propose substantial reductions in conventional armed forces in Europe (CFE). Given what came afterward, from Berlin in November 1989 through the end of the Soviet Union itself in 1991, the CFE moment is little remembered, but the May 1989 proposal marked an important pivot for Bush, who emerged from the NATO summit as a forceful leader. He did it in his own style—quietly—but the impact was undeniable. His plan would be substantive and unexpected, a combination Bush loved.

In a Friday, May 19, meeting at Kennebunkport, Bush told his advisers that he wanted to offer to cut 25 percent of American conventional forces in Europe if Gorbachev would do the same on his end. "I thought this was large enough," Bush recalled, "to show that we were serious and committed to responding to the positive changes we were seeing in the policies of the Soviet Union." The U.S. military, led by Admiral William Crowe, the chairman of the Joint Chiefs of Staff, pushed back against the president, arguing that such large reductions in Europe were unwise, even dangerous. The president disagreed. "I want this done," Bush said. "Don't keep telling me why it can't be done. Tell me how it can be done."

With the Pentagon's support, the president settled on a proposal to cut 20 percent of combat troops. The CFE idea was not just about CFE. Bush was facing two related problems. One was how to take the initiative with the Soviet relationship. The other was about NATO short-range nuclear forces (SNF) in Europe. While intermediate-range weapons (INF) had been eliminated in the 1987 treaty, SNF were still deployed. As Jim Baker described the dynamics of the debate, SNF, with a very limited range, were politically unpopular in West Germany. "If they were ever used," Baker recalled, "they were likely to hit targets only in East Germany or Poland. Or as the Germans began to say, 'The shorter the missile, the deader the German.'" SNF were also due for modernization, creating domestic problems for West German chancellor Helmut Kohl.

Bush's insight was that if he could get NATO and the Soviets to agree to substantial cuts in conventional forces, then the short-range nuclear question would become less urgent. In military terms, with fewer Soviet forces at hand, there would be reduced pressure to modernize NATO short-range weapons. The West would not need to deter a massed army that was no longer there. With time to think, Bush had solved two problems at once.

He kept the CFE proposal secret from the public, enduring attacks about his lack of vision and initiative while quietly briefing the allies. Ten days before the NATO summit in Brussels, Bush hosted François Mitterrand at Kennebunkport, hurriedly sprucing up Dorothy Bush's little house on Walker's Point for the French president. When Bush first raised the possibility of having Mitterrand in Maine, Barbara "thought I'd lost it," Bush recalled. "Everyone expected the worst. Here was the formal and composed president of France coming to our most informal home." The intimate seaside setting, however, was conducive to constructive talks. Mitterrand spoke openly to Bush at Walker's Point, though the French leader did decline the customary speedboat ride.

The year before, Helmut Kohl later told Bush, Mitterrand had said Europe had "no stake in the election in the United States"—meaning that the French leader did not believe it made a difference whether Bush won or lost. After the trip to Maine, though, Mitterrand told Kohl that he had been wrong—that Bush's victory had indeed been the preferred outcome. Bush's personal diplomacy had carried the day.

In Brussels, Margaret Thatcher was less than enthusiastic about Bush's CFE idea. The tough-minded British prime minister thought it generally wisest to give no ground whatever. "Chiefs of State Dinner was a little tense," Bush dictated. "Thatcher kept telling me not to negotiate. . . . She lectured all the other participants. She was tense." Bush greeted Thatcher, who started right in. "We must not give on this," Thatcher said. "You are not going to give, are you?" When the leader of Turkey, Turgut Ozal, walked over to join the president and the prime minister, Thatcher "gave both of us a lecture on freedom," Bush recalled, "with . . . Ozal and I both agreeing with her; but I expect he was like I was—'Why does she have any doubt that we feel this way on this issue?'"

For Bush, Thatcher was a complicated, somewhat tiresome figure. "My first impression: Margaret [is] principled, very difficult, [and] most people are far more down on her than I would have thought possible. Indeed, they talk about her a lot and laugh about her. . . . She's a principled woman, and a good friend of the States, but she talks all the time when you're in a conversation. It's a one-way street." Helmut Kohl simply referred to her as "that woman."

Bush's proposal to reduce CFE by 20 percent (and to pursue negotiations on SNF, but with the expectation that modernization would prove unnecessary) was widely seen as an important allied advance. Mitterrand, the once-wary recent houseguest, spoke to the gathered NATO

Jim Baker, Bush, Brent Scowcroft, and John Sununu with British prime minister
Margaret Thatcher at a NATO working session after the president's 1989 summit at
Malta with Mikhail Gorbachev.

leaders after Bush. "We need innovation," Mitterrand said. "The President of the United States has displayed imagination—indeed, intellectual audacity of the rarest kind." The news went over beautifully at home. *The New York Times* praised "the willingness of this deeply cautious man to aggressively seize the moment"; Lee Atwater, now chairman of the Republican National Committee, called to congratulate Bush on the splendid public reaction.

The next day, in Mainz, Germany, Bush spoke about the sense of change in Europe. "For 40 years, the seeds of democracy in Eastern Europe lay dormant, buried under the frozen tundra of the Cold War," the president said. "And decade after decade, time after time, the flowering human spirit withered from the chill of conflict and oppression; and again, the world waited. But the passion for freedom cannot be denied forever. The world has waited long enough. The time is right. Let Europe be whole and free." Flying around the world, building relationships, splitting differences, solving problems, attracting accolades, defending democratic values: In the middle of 1989, six months into his presidency, George H. W. Bush was thoroughly in his element.

As he managed the West's reaction to the gradual loosening of totalitarian Soviet power, he was confronted with the tightening of such power a world away, in Beijing's Tiananmen Square in the heart of the Chinese capital.

The trouble had begun in mid-April when Chinese students streamed into Tiananmen to mark the death of Hu Yaobang, a popular reformer who had been removed from office two years before. Venerated as a force for modernization, particularly by the young, Hu was a rallying point for dissatisfaction with the Chinese regime. The demonstrations grew in intensity, with the military clashing with protestors, providing global television images of a totalitarian power seeking to crush dissent by violent means.

On Saturday, June 3, 1989—Bush was in Kennebunkport resting up from the NATO summit; Jim Baker had hoped to play a round of golf with one of his sons at the Chevy Chase Club—the Chinese army attacked the demonstrators. Casualty figures from the Tiananmen uprising remain elusive; it appears that several hundred people died (though the number could well be higher) and perhaps three thousand were wounded.

American values demanded that the United States stand up against the Chinese government's crackdown, yet pragmatism demanded that the president balance human rights with the value of the long-term Chinese relationship. Home to about 1.1 billion people, China was too important to consign to pariah status.

The politics of China in America were unusual. Liberal Democrats disliked the regime on human rights grounds; conservative Republicans remained hostile to what had long been known as "Red China." Congressman Stephen Solarz, Democrat of New York, embodied the former; Senator Jesse Helms, Republican of North Carolina, the latter. "Neither has any responsibility for the overall relationship, the lives of Americans students, or anything else," Bush dictated. "Yet they're popping off. . . . They don't have any suggestions, but they just want to complicate the [life] of the President."

Bush's preferred position of moderation lacked a natural constituency, but he was convinced that there was long-term diplomatic wisdom in containing short-term emotional outrage. In Washington, where he was monitoring the crisis, Jim Baker was in sync with the president. "The Chinese leadership was clearly in an embattled frame of mind," Baker recalled. "It was important not to respond in a way that played into the hands of the hard-liners who were pushing for even more repressive action, which would inevitably lead to more bloodshed." From Walker's Point, Bush asked Baker and Scowcroft for options and retired for the night. "The strength of democracy and freedom is fantastic, it's wonderful," Bush dictated, "and yet change has to be orderly in many situations. The big point is, we cannot foment revolution or it might make things worse."

At eight A.M. on Monday, Bush spoke to Richard Nixon. "What's happened [is being] handled badly and is deplorable," Nixon said of the crackdown, "but take a look at the long haul." After returning to the White House, Bush met with Scowcroft and Baker to lay out his objectives: "I wanted a measured response, one aimed at those who had pushed for and implemented the use of force: the hard-liners and the Army. I didn't want to punish the Chinese people for the acts of their government. I believed that the commercial contacts between our countries had helped lead to the quest for more freedom. If people have commercial incentives, whether it's in China or in other totalitarian systems, the move to democracy becomes inexorable." In terms of sanctions, he resisted an overall embargo and instead suspended military sales and prohibited visits between American and Chinese military officials.

Bush went to the White House briefing room to announce the American response to the violence. Soon there was a complication: Fang Lizhi, a Chinese astrophysicist and political dissident, received asylum at the American embassy in Beijing. "We had no choice but to take him in," Bush dictated, "but it's going to be a real stick in the eye to the Chinese."

The president attempted to telephone Deng Xiaoping but was told that any message he might want to send should be passed along through the regime's ambassador. "I was a little pissed off at that," Bush told his diary on Thursday, June 8, 1989, "but I recognize that the Chinese are under great strain." Ten days later Bush tried another tack. He sat down at his electric typewriter to write Deng a four-page letter "from the heart." He knew Deng and Deng's colleagues from the old days in China; his quiet belief in the Chinese leader's ultimate good intentions was a key factor in the moderate American response. "Had I not met the man . . . I think I would have been less convinced that we should keep relations with them going after Tiananmen Square," Bush told Jeffrey A. Engel, the editor of his China diary, in 2005.

Bush therefore wrote to Deng rather as one suspects he himself would have liked to have been written to in such circumstances—without self-righteousness. "I have tried very hard not to inject myself into China's internal affairs," Bush told Deng. "I have tried very hard not to appear to be dictating in any way to China about how it should manage its internal crisis. I am respectful of the differences in our two societies and in our two systems. . . . But I ask you as well to remember the principles on which my young country was founded." Freedom of speech and freedom of assembly were key American values, the president wrote, and "reverence for those principles . . . inevitably affects the way Americans view and react to events in other countries." The sanctions he had imposed, he concluded, had been rooted in this national reaction—and he, as president, faced great pressure to do more. Would Deng receive a confidential envoy from Bush to discuss matters further?

Within twenty-four hours came word from Deng: He would be open to such a presidential emissary. Bush decided to send Scowcroft. In Beijing, Scowcroft found the Chinese leadership guarded but also well disposed to deal with a Bush administration. The Chinese wanted time and space—and no interference by outsiders in their domestic life. They trusted Bush, but for them trust was a tender flower, and only time would reveal whether the United States was going to accord Beijing the respect and autonomy it believed it deserved. Bush's calibrated course pleased no one totally, but, as Bush had learned in the 1970s, the China problem did not lend itself to simple solution. "Just let it wait for a while—hold the line," Bush dictated in September 1989. Bush did what he could, and no more, and the bilateral connection between the two powers endured.

His reaction to Tiananmen and his CFE proposal at the NATO summit were connected. Both were coherent steps taken to respond rationally to shifting global truths—twin examples of what was described in a draft statement for the press as "Steadiness, realism [and] the search for opportunities to further peace and stability." They were, the draft said, examples of how "the encouragement of peaceful progress toward democracy, and the assertion of American values" would "guide this Administration in a remarkable period of change."

In June, Hungary took down the barbed wire that separated it from Austria, opening a gateway to the West. In the same month, in Poland, Solidarity, the party of dissent, won new elections, sweeping the old Communist forces from power; by August the nation was being governed by popularly elected leaders. In midsummer, Bush traveled to both nations, gently urging reform and signaling, with his balanced approach, that the future need not be bloody. Bush avoided large crowds if at all possible for fear that "things could get out of control." The strategy worked. "We had stepped carefully in Poland and Hungary and had avoided aggravating the Soviets, whose military presence still loomed there," Bush recalled. "It was a good start. But I understood that the pressure on Gorbachev from hard-liners to intervene would grow, as these once reliable allies began to pull farther away and the Soviet security buffer against the West eroded."

Heading home from Eastern Europe, Bush slept "for one hour, hard," then got back up to draft a personal appeal to Gorbachev for a meeting. "I want to do it without thousands of assistants hovering over our shoulders," Bush wrote Gorbachev, "without the ever-present briefing papers and certainly without the press yelling at us every 5 minutes about 'who's winning' . . ."

Gorbachev agreed, and plans were soon under way for a session at Malta late in the year. The president's view of Gorbachev mixed sympathy and skepticism. "He's having enormous problems with his Republics and with the economy, and I'm telling our people, we might be on the verge of something big and something important," Bush dictated. "So let's think big, let's think in big broad terms, and not in the old Cold War rhetoric terms—keep our eyes open, be sure, but think big."

Summer brought a new—and critical—member of the president's national security team into the Bush inner circle. The chairman of the Joint Chiefs of Staff, Admiral William Crowe, was retiring. Bush's first thought was to name air force general Robert Harris to the post, which was, by statute, the principal military adviser to the president. "He's steady," Bush said of Harris, adding: "Someday it should be Colin Powell, but I don't think he's quite ready. He needs to have a big and more visible command in the Army." An impressive army officer, Powell had served as Reagan's last national security adviser and then taken over the U.S. Army Forces Command, a posting near Atlanta. "I wish that Colin had more command experience, a joint command, a CINC command; but Cheney wants him and I love the guy," Bush told his diary in August. "So I said to Dick, 'Okay, we'll go with your recommendation, but please talk to Colin to be sure he himself thinks he's ready.' Scowcroft feels that, given Cheney's insistence, we should probably go with Colin. But there's another side to it, and that is that he doesn't have quite the amount of field experience."

As an old national security hand himself, Bush did not want to set an unhappy precedent. "My worry had been that it would be seen as the way to become Joint Chiefs is to do some time in the White House as an NSC advisor, and that's not good," Bush dictated. "But Colin is so able that I don't think that will happen. Cheney feels very relaxed about it." At Bush's request, Cheney asked Powell if he "didn't think it was too early." Powell did not, and the announcement went forward. "The Powell decision has gone down well," Bush told his diary. The president's regard for Powell grew rapidly, and the president, pleased with his new chairman, never looked back.

On Sunday, November 5, 1989—a beautiful New England day—Bush made a sentimental return to his old prep school, Phillips Academy. It was the bicentennial of a visit to Andover by the first president, George Washington, who had stopped in the town during a tour of the eastern states in his first year in office.

Speaking on campus, Bush talked about what Andover had meant to him. His days at the school, he said, had taught him "the great end and real business of living. And even now its lessons of honesty, selflessness, faith in God—well, they enrich every day of our lives."

He was transported back across the years. It was over there, Bush said, gesturing, "where that guy in a red coat is standing, that I heard that our country was at war on December 7th, 1941." Then there was the Stimson commencement speech, "over there, in Cochran Chapel," where the secretary of war "observed how the American soldier should be brave without being brutal, self-reliant without boasting, becoming a part of irresistible might without losing faith in individual liberty. I never forgot those words."

He returned to the White House for a dinner that evening in the Residence with Richard Nixon. "He was not emotional towards it," Bush dictated. "I introduced him to all of the upstairs staff, some of whom had been here, but there wasn't a real warmth. . . . We really feel close to them, and if I left tomorrow, I'd still feel close to them. I'm not sure Nixon felt close to them." After dinner, with Nixon gone, Bush finished the evening, and the weekend, by dictating to his diary. "The moves in East Germany are phenomenal," he said. "They're going so much faster than anybody had thought—real rapid."

The next day he lunched with Zbig Brzezinski, the former Carter national security adviser. "He's amazed at the rapidity of change, but what concerns me is that the Soviets will be compelled to crack down, given some uprising in one of the republics, or possibly in Eastern Europe, and a lot of things will go back to square one," Bush told his diary on Monday, November 6, 1989. "This would be very bad." The essential thing, Bush believed, was not to overreact: "If we mishandle it, and get way out looking like an American project," he dictated on Wednesday, November 8, "you would invite crackdown and invite negative reaction that could result in bloodshed."

At that hour, in East Berlin, the wall that had divided the city for nearly three decades was about to be breached—permanently.

THIRTY-THREE

The Fall of the Wall

★

It is this that really concerns me. Some violence coming out in
the Soviet Republic, where the Soviets use force, and that
tightens up what happens in Eastern Europe.

—GEORGE H. W. BUSH

BUSH WAS AT HIS DESK in the Oval Office in the middle of the afternoon of Thursday, November 9, 1989, when Scowcroft walked
in with news: There was word, Scowcroft said, that "the Wall had
been opened." The president and his national security adviser stepped
out of the big office to watch the television in Bush's small study.

East German officials had announced that the country's restrictions
on travel were being relaxed, but the details were fuzzy. As word spread
that long-closed borders were being opened, restive crowds in East
Berlin took that to include the wall itself. Communication between
different government agencies and the guards along the wall was poor
to nonexistent, and soon thousands were crossing from East to West
Berlin.

It was dazzling, epochal news. Since its construction in 1961, the Berlin Wall had been perhaps the world's most tangible manifestation of the
deep division between East and West, tyranny and liberty, fear and hope.
In 1983, Bush had gone to the wall and been horrified by its ugliness and
by its stark finality. In 1987, President Reagan had stood at the Branden-
burg Gate and put the ultimate challenge to the Soviet leadership: "Mr.
Gorbachev, tear down this wall!" And six months earlier, in Mainz on
the last day of May 1989, President Bush had struck the same notes, albeit less dramatically, saying that the "wall stands as a monument to the
failure of communism. It must come down."

Now it had. Bush watched the television coverage with a kind of wonder. A moment American presidents had hoped for since John F. Kennedy had come on George Bush's watch, and he had to manage the
spiraling forces of freedom.

In his study in the West Wing, Bush knew it could all quickly go to hell. High emotion, surging crowds, anxious Communist authorities: Such factors had led to deaths in Beijing only a handful of months before. The same, perhaps on an even worse scale, could happen here, now.

Bush's concerns were justified. There were signs that the East Germans had drawn inspiration from the Chinese regime's brutal suppression in Beijing in June, and might open fire on demonstrators in the same way. The East German secret police chief, Erich Mielke, approved of the Chinese government's tactics at Tiananmen, calling them "resolute measures in suppression of . . . counterrevolutionary unrest." The historian John Lewis Gaddis noted that East German television had been broadcasting a documentary about "the heroic response of the Chinese army and police to the perfidious inhumanity of the student demonstrators." The CIA had told the president as early as April 1989 that Gorbachev's reforms were "threatening the stability of the [Soviet] regime" and "could lead to a conservative reaction."

In these autumn hours, Bush's cautious reaction was rooted in his concern that hard-liners in East Germany and in the Soviet Union might strike back against the falling wall and the surging visitors to the West, precipitating violence and possibly a shooting war. Gorbachev sent a message to Bush "urging that we not overreact," Bush recalled. "He worries about demonstrations in Germany that might get out of control, and he asked for understanding."

He would get it from this American president. Borrowing a phrase from Scowcroft, Bush was determined not to "gloat" over the breaching of the wall. Marlin Fitzwater, Bush's press secretary, recommended an exchange with the media in the Oval Office rather than a more formal session in the briefing room. Bush agreed, reluctantly. Events were moving swiftly, and Bush's mind was less on the poetry of the occasion—the fall of the wall—than it was on the practicalities of a world crisis.

As the press corps came into the Oval Office, the reporters crowded Bush, who found the session "awkward and uncomfortable." In a prepared statement, he welcomed the border decision, calling it "a positive step toward the free movement of peoples" that meant "the tragic symbolism of the Berlin Wall . . . will have been overcome by the indomitable spirit of man's desire for freedom." Stirring words, but he declined to speak with great emotion or sweep. "Of course, I was thankful about the events in Berlin," Bush recalled, "but as I answered questions my mind kept racing over a possible Soviet crackdown, turning all the happiness to tragedy." Lesley Stahl of CBS News had taken up a position close to the president. Bush was seated. Stahl, he recalled, was "poised over me."

"This is a sort of great victory for our side in the big East-West battle, but you don't seem elated," Stahl said. "I'm wondering if you're thinking of the problems."

"I'm not an emotional kind of guy," Bush said.

"Well, how elated are you?" Stahl asked.

"I'm very pleased," Bush said.

"The press gets all over me," Bush told his diary a few days later. "'Why aren't you more excited?' 'Why aren't you leading?' 'Why aren't you doing more?'" Convinced that the greater the American elation the greater the danger the Soviet Union could lash out in a last, prideful bid to hold on to its Cold War empire, Bush chose caution over Cold War rhetoric.

Would there be a Soviet military strike? Would the Warsaw Pact—the Moscow-allied nations—really do nothing in the face of such revolution? "This is what the press all ask me about—'what if?' 'What if?' 'What if there is a big attack—crackdown?'" Bush dictated. "I think publicly I simply do not speculate . . . but it is a reason to be prudent and be cautious and to stop short of the euphoria that some are exhibiting." From West Berlin, Helmut Kohl called Bush. "It is like witnessing an enormous fair," Kohl told Bush, describing the flow of people across the wall. "The frontiers are absolutely open." Two hundred and thirty thousand people, most of them young, many of them highly educated, had already crossed into the West. Kohl feared a permanent influx of refugees, saying that an overpopulated West Germany would be a "catastrophe for economic development."

There was a solution, of course, but these were early, early days: the reunion of the two Germanys that had been divided for so long and over which so much had been made in the bitter years of the Cold War. Gorbachev cabled Kohl to warn against talk of reunification, and the Soviet leader's message to Bush about the fall of the wall alluded, darkly, to "unforeseen consequences."

Gorbachev's tone had a profound impact on Bush. "This was the first time Gorbachev had clearly indicated genuine anxiety about events in

Eastern Europe," Bush recalled. "Heretofore he had seemed relaxed, even blasé, about the accelerating movement in the region away from communism and Soviet control. It was as if he suddenly realized the serious implications of what was going on." The president did what he could to project a sense of steadiness in the West and of fair play toward the East. At home, Senate Democratic leader George Mitchell recommended that Bush fly to Berlin to make a dramatic statement about the end of Communism; Bush thought "sticking it in Gorbachev's eye" a miserable idea. Bush sent Gorbachev a message arguing that Kohl had acted responsibly, "emphasizing the importance of a deliberate step-by-step approach to change in [East Germany] and the need to avoid destabilizing the situation in Europe." The United States, moreover, had "no intention of seeking unilateral advantage from the current process of change in [East Germany] and in other Warsaw Pact countries."

There were reports of violence in Moldavia, a Soviet republic. "It is this that really concerns me," Bush dictated. "Some violence coming out in the Soviet Republic, where the Soviets use force, and that tightens up what happens in Eastern Europe. [It] turns world opinion around against Gorbachev, [and] pushes us to take military action which, of course, we couldn't take way over there, and wouldn't take; and sets back, for proper reasons, the relationship that's moving in the right direction. This is the big dilemma."

As the wall fell, Bush was pragmatic. He kept his options open and resisted alienating rhetoric or sweeping declarations. He led by checking here and balancing there, understanding that a world in convulsion was inherently unstable, and everything in him was about bringing stability, or a semblance of stability, to the unruliness of reality.

Many Democrats and commentators criticized his handling of the hour, finding him strangely emotionless. House Majority Leader Dick Gephardt declared that Bush was "inadequate to the moment." Noting the dissatisfaction with his evenhanded demeanor, Bush told his diary that the attacks on his failure to "dance" on the wall were "a far cry from the 'Evil Empire' days when they were pounding the President for too much rhetoric. Now they pound me for not being out front enough, so you can't win with these press people." He was amused, a little, at the preening of journalists in the crisis. "The thing that gets me is you see them at the Wall as instant experts," Bush dictated.

They learn the name of Egon Krenz [the last Communist leader of East Germany] and they sound like they've known him all their lives, or they know all about him, which is simply ridiculous. They were caught by surprise, as I admit we [were] on some of this, but they sound like they've got the marvelous advantage point of 20/20 hindsight. Just think if we had done something to exhort Eastern Europe to go to the barricades and . . . manifest freedom in the way we thought best. You would've had chaos, and the danger of military action, bloodshed, just to make a few critics feel good—crazy.

In these same days and weeks, the Cold War regimes in Bulgaria and Czechoslovakia showed signs of going the way of the Wall. "It's spreading like wildfire through Eastern Europe," Bush dictated, "and yet I think back to George Mitchell's stupid suggestion that I go to the Berlin Wall, and I think to myself, 'God, the guy has got to have been nuts to suggest you pour gasoline on those embers.'" As the images from the newly liberated nations turned the autumn of 1989 into a springtime for democratic reform, Bush kept Moscow at the center of his thinking. What would Gorbachev do now that the Soviet empire was crumbling all around him?

One CIA paper made a particular impression on the president. "It argued that the [economic and political] reforms were strong enough to disrupt the Soviet system, but yet not strong enough to give the Soviet people the benefits of a market economy," Bush recalled. "Based on those conclusions, some people in the NSC began to speculate that Gorbachev might be headed for a crisis which could force him to crack down in the Soviet Union to maintain order, or might even force him out of power."

As he prepared to meet with Gorbachev at the Malta conference, Bush absorbed the different perspectives within his inner circle. As Scowcroft recalled it, Jim Baker was viewed as the "most optimistic" about Gorbachev's sincerity on the question of reform. "Dick Cheney was negative," Scowcroft wrote. "He believed that it was premature to relax Cold War–style pressure. The Soviet system was in trouble and we ought to continue the hard-line policies which had brought us and it to this point." Dan Quayle, Scowcroft believed, "was the most conservative of all. He came close to the notion that what was going on in the USSR was little more than a ploy to lull us into thinking the danger was over and we could dismantle our security structure."

Bush's appetite for debate and for data was enormous. Preparing for Malta, "Brent offered me about twenty topics to choose from: I took them all," Bush recalled. "I wanted to be prepared for everything." Though the president's own sense of things was closer to Baker's than to Cheney's or Quayle's, Bush's main goal was to put Gorbachev on notice that an authoritarian reaction to the revolutionary changes was unacceptable. "We were getting hints from Moscow that one of Gorbachev's objectives at Malta was to gain some sort of 'understanding' for his situation and for the measures he might take to crack down," Bush recalled. "I could not give him that, and if I did, it would have a lasting historical, political, and moral price."

At Valletta Harbor in Malta, Bush stayed aboard the USS *Belknap*, the flagship of the Sixth Fleet. (Baker had bunked near Bush on the flight over on Air Force One. "No farting, OK?" Bush had scribbled in a note to his secretary of state before hitting the sack.)

"How do I feel?" Bush dictated in the admiral's quarters as he went to bed on the eve of meeting with Gorbachev. "I'm criticized for not doing enough, but things are coming our way, and so why do we have to jump up and down, and risk those things turning around and going in the wrong direction?"

The president, who loved being shipboard, thought of his nights on the *San Jacinto* and slept well, looking forward to the morning. "Gales had been starting up outside. . . ." Bush recalled, and "the weather got worse the next day." The president had a wild ride through swelling seas in a launch from the *Belknap* to see Gorbachev on the *Maxim Gorky*, a large Soviet cruise liner.

Greeting Gorbachev, who was dressed in a dark blue pinstriped suit with a red tie and a cream-colored white shirt ("like the ones I like," Bush noted), Bush thought his counterpart seemed tired. The Soviet leader's hair was grayer than before, "but he was smiling," which Bush took as a good sign. "Spot is prominent on his head," Bush told his diary, "but you don't notice it all the time."

Jim Baker had had an idea in the run-up to the summit: that Bush should take the initiative and lay out a series of proposals in the first moments of the meeting, thus disposing of the critique that the United States had been following Gorbachev rather than leading. Scowcroft found Baker's idea "unprofessional at best and corny at worst," but

Bush liked it, as Scowcroft recalled, "feeling that, among other things, it would still those critics who continued to accuse us of drift and a lack of direction." Bush had seventeen different proposals on hand when the two sides sat down opposite each other in the salon of the *Maxim Gorky*.

As Bush opened his remarks, Scowcroft recalled, the president was "clearly nervous about the import of what was happening. He began to loosen up as he went along." The initiatives he raised ranged from trade to reuniting divided Soviet families; from chemical weapons to Cuba; from Nicaragua to conventional arms; from the environment to student exchanges. "This is the end," Bush finally said, "of my non-agenda." It was a joke, of course.

Bush waited, wondering what Gorbachev was thinking. "This has been interesting," Gorbachev said—slowly, Bush noted, which was unusual for the voluble Soviet. "It shows the Bush Administration has already decided what to do." That initial remark was a bit of passing defensive bluster. In truth, Gorbachev was relieved as he listened to Bush's proposals for new cooperation. The Soviet leader had been worried that the president might be overly influenced by conservative voices skeptical of Soviet intentions. Now he believed Bush took him and his reforms seriously.

Gorbachev's main concern: that familiar Cold War enmities would die hard, handicapping U.S.-Soviet relations as the world moved from superpower competition into what Gorbachev described as "a multipolar world with an integrated Europe, a strong Japan and China. India too was becoming more dynamic. He could imagine new and enormous issues would come into play, all related to competition over limited resources."

Gorbachev wanted to hear more from Bush about American ambitions. "The United States has not entirely abandoned old approaches," Gorbachev said to the president. "I cannot say that we have entirely abandoned ours. Sometimes we feel the United States wants to teach, to put pressure on others." Bush was quick to reply. "I hope you have noticed that as dynamic change has accelerated in recent months, we have not responded with flamboyance or arrogance that would complicate Soviet relations," Bush said. "What I am saying may be self-serving. I have been called cautious or timid. I *am* cautious, but not timid. But I have conducted myself in ways not to complicate your life. That's why I have not jumped up and down on the Berlin Wall."

"Yes, we have seen that," Gorbachev replied, "and appreciate that."

A swordfish and lobster dinner aboard the *Belknap* had been planned for the American and Soviet parties that evening, but the stormy weather kept Gorbachev on the *Maxim Gorky*. The next morning the Soviet leader was cheerful. "I want to say to you and the United States that the Soviet Union will under no circumstances start a war—that is very important," Gorbachev said.

At 1:20 on the afternoon of Sunday, December 3, 1989, Bush and Gorbachev hosted the first press conference ever held jointly by an American president and a leader of the Soviet Union. Both men emphasized the intimacy and the candor of the discussions, and both spoke with an awareness of the historic moment. "For 40 years, the Western alliance has stood together in the cause of freedom," Bush said in an opening statement. "And now, with reform under way in the Soviet Union, we stand at the threshold of a brand-new era of U.S.-Soviet relations. And it is within our grasp to contribute, each in our own way, to overcoming the division of Europe and ending the military confrontation there."

Gorbachev expressed his appreciation of Bush's cautious nature, arguing that "in our position, the most dangerous thing is to exaggerate. And it is always that we should preserve elements of cautiousness, and I use the favorite word by President Bush." By the end of the sessions at Malta, it was clear that Bush and Gorbachev could work together. Flying home via Brussels, the president stopped to brief NATO allies. According to Bush's handwritten notes from his conversations, Mitterrand observed that the collapse of the Soviet empire represented the "greatest revolution of [the] last two centuries" (which still gave the French Revolution of 1789 pride of place); Denmark's prime minister thanked Bush for the president's "calm handling of changes."

Bush was happy. "We came out okay, [and] now I want to push, push, push on arms control, get something done," Bush dictated as Air Force One approached Washington on Monday, December 4, 1989. "I've got to and I will. I think I have a new level of confidence."

The president arrived in Washington to find that Quayle, who owed Bush everything, was doing what Bush himself had refused to do for eight years during the Reagan administrations: drawing attention to himself at the expense of the president. "The general afterglow of Malta has been good; but the Vice President's office, seeing a chance to firm him up as the spokesman of the right, is doing some unhelpful things," Bush told his diary on Friday, December 8, continuing:

> They're selling the good cop–bad cop thesis. In other words, I've made these deals, and went to Malta, but now Quayle has to go out and shore up the right-wing   I find this disturbing. . . . Dan makes a mistake. There isn't that much room to differ on this and, the big thing is, he's going to undermine his own Vice Presidency. The more I think back to my eight years, I think back [on] how determined I was to avoid this kind of flap. . . . I'm thoroughly annoyed about it, and I'm trying to contain myself. . . . We cannot have the Vice President's staff trying to shape the policy of this administration. They weren't at the meeting; they don't get the feel of it; and it undermines what I'm trying to do.

Bush had decided that Gorbachev was a man whom he could and should deal with as wisely as he could. Some conservatives—including Quayle and his advisers—remained wary at a moment in which the Cold War was growing more distant by the day.

On Halloween 1989, a column by journalist Morton Kondracke had appeared in the conservative *Washington Times* headlined "Quayle, Baker Square Off." The piece quoted anonymous Quayle advisers casting doubts on Baker's toughness with the Soviets, even going so far as to suggest that Baker's support for perestroika was "'appeasement.'" Baker sent an annotated copy of the column to Bush with a firm handwritten message along the margin. "Mr. P—We have successfully avoided this kind of crap for 9 months! We won't be able to continue if these people keep it up. Please have it knocked off. JAB III." Kondracke wrote wisely of the conflict, noting: "At the moment . . . some of Mr. Quayle's allies are trying to build up their man's credibility on the right by disparaging Mr. Baker as a potential softy. They ought to quit. We don't know yet how tough Jim Baker can be with the Russians, but in internecine combat within the U.S. government, he's lethal." That was true. It was also true that the president believed in dealing with reality, and Gorbachev was, for now, a fact of life.

On Saturday, December 16, 1989, Ellie LeBlond, Doro's three-year-old daughter, was sleeping in Barbara's office off the Bushes' bedroom in the White House. At four A.M., Bush recalled, Ellie walked in and stood next to her slumbering grandfather, who "felt aware of her presence" and opened his eyes. He pulled her into the big bed and tucked her in between her grandparents. "Be quiet and go to sleep," Bush whispered. She hugged him, and he thought of Robin, who used to cross the hallway on West Ohio Street in Midland in the middle of the night to climb into her parents' bed. Ellie "was a wiggly little thing . . . equally as beautiful."

That same night, in Panama, a young American marine was killed after a confrontation at a checkpoint. Shortly thereafter, a navy lieutenant and his wife were harassed at the same roadblock. "He was kicked and brutalized," Bush dictated on Sunday, December 17, 1989, "kicked in the groin." The December attacks on Americans in Panama brought a festering issue to the fore. The Panamanian dictator Manuel Noriega had long been an American ally in Cold War Latin America. Essentially a paid anti-Communist in the region, Noriega was a drug trafficker and tyrant who had become more trouble than he was worth. He stole a presidential election, continued to be a center for destabilizing drug running and money laundering, and his erratic behavior raised concerns about the fate of the crucial Panama Canal. Noriega even declared war on the United States on December 15, but Bush had paid little attention until news of the harassment of Americans reached him two days later.

For Bush, that did it. On the afternoon of Sunday the seventeenth, after briefings from Colin Powell and Dick Cheney—Jim Baker and Scowcroft deputy Bob Gates were also present—Bush ordered an operation against Noriega's Panamanian Defense Forces. "We've had enough," Bush dictated, "and we cannot let a military officer be killed, and certainly not a lieutenant and his wife brutalized."

Code-named Operation Just Cause, Bush's invasion of Panama was, at the time, the largest projection of American force since Vietnam—larger than Reagan's liberation of Grenada in 1983. On the night the troops went into Panama, Bush managed only ninety minutes or so of sleep; he awoke with a crick in his neck after lying down on a small couch in his dining room off the Oval Office.

The American forces—Bush dispatched twenty-six thousand troops—quickly deposed Noriega, who took refuge in the Vatican embassy in

Panama City for ten days before surrendering to the U.S. military and coming to the United States to face trial on narcotics charges. Over the course of the brief operation, 23 American servicemen died; 322 were wounded. For Bush, the action-filled operation in Panama capped a year in which prudence had dictated a cautious course in Beijing and Berlin. The three episodes demonstrated that Bush was a president capable of both diplomatic restraint (in the cases of China and of East Germany) and of effective military action (the toppling of Noriega in Panama). Comfortable with power, Bush was learning when to watch and wait, and when to strike.

Christmas Eve fell on a Sunday in 1989, and Bush was in a reflective mood at Camp David. To check the political pulse of the nation, GOP chairman Lee Atwater had convened two focus groups—one conservative, one moderate. "The more moderate one [said], 'Well, Bush hasn't done anything,'" Bush dictated on Christmas Eve. "Not negative, but just somewhat mutedly critical, and I'm thinking, 'Gosh, look at all that's gone on, and sometimes you shape events by not making any mistakes.'"

He was optimistic yet temperate about the world and about himself. Looking over the White House News Summary one day early in 1990, he noticed an observation from the Baltimore *Sun*. "Bush is competent and confident, well meaning and well briefed," the newspaper had written, "but a long way from greatness." The president mulled the remark over. The press, for once, was on to something. "[I'm] inclined to agree with them," Bush said—a man at once self-confident and self-aware.

THIRTY-FOUR

I Want to Do the Most Good I Can

God, there are so many problems out there.
—GEORGE H. W. BUSH

HEN BUSH FIRST ARRIVED in Washington in January 1967—
the day he invited the moving men to stay over—he learned
the ways of the capital at a time when Democrats and Republicans formed bonds that produced, if not a bipartisan Valhalla, then at least a sense of shared purpose and mutual deference. Like Prescott Bush's Senate, George H. W. Bush's House had a club-like feel. The congressional world he had known was one in which a Republican member could agree with a Democratic president, and junior members were generally respectful toward senior members of both parties.

From the White House two decades on, Bush watched as the more genial political universe he had known as a young man gave way. On the last day of May 1989, House Speaker Jim Wright, facing sixty-nine ethics charges in the House, resigned. The Democrat's fall was a victory for Newt Gingrich, who had spent years pressing for investigations into Wright's finances and other dealings. Savvy and relentless, Gingrich had cast Wright as a liberal general in a war for the American soul—a war, Gingrich had told the Heritage Foundation, that "has to be fought with a scale and a duration and a savagery that is only true of civil wars." In an hour-long farewell speech to the House, Wright had decried the "mindless cannibalism" of such reflexive personal and partisan warfare. "When vengeance becomes more desirable than vindication," Wright said, "harsh personal attacks upon one another's motives and one another's character drown out the quiet logic of serious debate on important issues."

The words could have been Bush's, and the president was gracious about the fallen Speaker. "In spite of the present situation," Bush said in a statement, "I believe the Wright tenure was one of effectiveness and dedication to the Congress of the United States." An old Bush friend, House Majority Leader Tom Foley of Washington State, was to succeed Wright.

The war raged on: Lee Atwater's Republican National Committee attacked Foley in a release that compared him to the openly gay Massachusetts congressman Barney Frank. The memo was entitled "Tom Foley: Out of the Liberal Closet." Bush sent word that the author of the release should be fired. "Foley is a decent guy. There have been rumors floating around of being homosexual, but I'll be damned if I think the party ought to get into that sink," Bush told his diary. "Foley's a decent fellow, [a] warm human being [who has] just taken on this assignment and to get that kind of gut shot is so cheap, I can't believe it." The president understandably feared that the attack culture that had destroyed Wright was taking hold in Washington. "I am, of course, not a homosexual, been married for 21 years," Foley told CNN, calling the RNC memo "a very cheap smear."

At the White House, Bush's outrage was real, but he seems not to have confronted the fact that one reaps what one sows. Atwater's aggressive style was no secret; Bush had needed someone "tough"—a word Bush used to describe Atwater—to get through 1988, and now his own party and his own men were contributing to the growing "ugliness" (another favorite Bush word about political warfare) in Washington.

"The Democrats strike back," Bush dictated, and "Frank say[s] he'll expose homosexuals on our side, and it's everything ugly and that I detest in politics." The Foley rumors and Wright's fall, together with the failure of the Tower nomination, foreshadowed an age of stark partisanship, one in which politicians who wished to get ahead (which was to say most politicians) were more likely to confront than to compromise.

Bush's presidency would be defined by his ability to find consensus at a moment when most domestic political forces—on the right and the left—were conspiring against the American center. The lesson of Gingrich's rise was that headlines, votes, and the dollars of devoted donors were more likely to be won on the extremes, which presented President Bush with a particular challenge: how to govern in a capital where compromise was falling rapidly out of fashion. For legislators, it was politically savvier to be a Gingrich of the 1990s than a Bush of the 1960s.

For Bush, the key to the notable domestic successes of his presidency was to discern the consensus of the country, not simply take the temperature of the capital, and join forces with the opposition party on measures that were broadly popular, always aiming to make the bills in question as conservative as possible. "I want to do the most good I can," Bush would tell his senior staffers, "and the least harm."

The national mood during the Bush administration—like Bush himself—tended to be largely conservative but open to moderately progressive measures. According to University of North Carolina political scientist James A. Stimson's "Policy Mood Index," a measure of attitudes on the liberal-conservative spectrum since 1952, the American outlook from 1989 to 1993 roughly matched that of the middle of the Eisenhower years—also a time of broad conservative feeling as well as large public-sector undertakings such as the federal interstate highway system. For Bush to be an effective president in terms of responding to the public that had elected him, then, he needed to project a conservative tone while selectively enlarging the federal role in American life.

The question for Bush: Could he meet the expectations of the public in terms of economic and domestic legislation without overly antagonizing his own right wing? For about two years of his presidency—in 1989 and into the autumn of 1990—Bush was largely able to defend the center against attacks from the right on legislative and budget issues. Yet his very successes at consensus leadership—particularly on the federal budget in 1990—sowed the seeds of a sustained conservative rebellion in 1991 and 1992 that, combined with economic recession, proved too much for the president. His hours of victory led to his hours of defeat.

The victories, though, did come first—on education, on the environment, on civil rights for the disabled, and, to the permanent fury of the right, on a federal budget deal that included higher taxes. His real-time acclaim for these accomplishments and bills was fleeting, in part because conservatives tended to dislike the measures and liberals did not wish to give a Republican president too much credit.

Surveying the landscape before him early in 1990, Bush was conscious of the difficulties ahead. "God, there are so many problems out there," he dictated in January. And so he threw the White House open to Democrats and Republicans, lawmakers and activists, and businessmen and reformers, believing that personal connections enhanced the chances of policy progress. As Bush biographer Timothy Naftali observed, the president sought to apply his personal foreign policy style to the domestic realm. "People always think President Bush was just interested in global things, but those of us who were there, in the trenches, watched him work Congress as hard as he could," recalled deputy White House chief of staff Andrew Card. "The tough part, of course, was that it was a Democrat Congress, which people also forget."

Insisting that everyone deserved attention—their "place in the sun," as Bush put it—the president was constantly on the phone to congressmen and senators, seeking their opinions. Then, after hearing them out, he would ask them to be with him on a given vote. "The most important thing a president can do is not twist someone's arm but to give them a chance to twist the president's," John Sununu recalled. "If a congressman has had a chance to make his own case to the president of the United States, that congressman is much, much likelier to then say, 'But I'll support you, Mr. President.'" And Bush was happy to make as many such calls as he had to make.

Consensus and connection: Bush's understanding of Washington, especially in his first two years, brought him domestic achievements. He sought and passed increased funding and tax credits for families with children, including enhancements for Head Start. He signed the Financial Institutions Reform, Recovery, and Enforcement Act of 1989 to bail out troubled savings and loans and create the Resolution Trust Corporation. Bush banned the importation of most semiautomatic rifles. After a veto, he signed the Fair Labor Standards Amendments of 1989, raising the minimum wage.

On education, in the fall of 1989 he convened a rare presidential summit with the nation's governors at Charlottesville. There had been only two similar gatherings before: one called by Theodore Roosevelt, on conservation, the other by Franklin Roosevelt, who invited the governors to meet with him following his inauguration. It was a perfect setting for Bush, a gathering where he could make his points personally and intimately. The most lasting result: Bush called for national performance goals in K–12, establishing a key policy principle. Bill Clinton of Arkansas was the point man for the Democratic governors. The goals themselves were the product of talks led by the White House's Roger Porter, who negotiated them with Clinton and Carroll Campbell, the Republican governor of South Carolina. Clinton and Campbell joined Barbara Bush in the First Lady's box when the president announced the goals, approved by all the nation's governors, at the 1990 State of the Union address.

On the environment, Bush cultivated both politicians and industry in a concerted effort to pass the Clean Air Act Amendments of 1990, bringing market-based incentives to the legislation and engaging widespread Democratic support—including that of George Mitchell, who negotiated the complex bill with the White House's Roger Porter and Robert Grady. Mitchell credited Bush with reversing the Reagan administration's opposition to clean-air and -water bills, calling the new president's decision to reauthorize the Clean Air Act "courageous." Mitchell recalled being delighted that "the question had shifted from 'Will there be a clean air bill?' to 'What will be in the clean air bill?'"

After more than 130 hours of negotiations between the White House and Congress, Bush signed a Clean Air measure that enjoyed large bipartisan majorities in both the House and the Senate. The comprehensive bill established bold goals and timetables for addressing acid rain, toxic substances, and "ozone attainment"—a technical term for the smog that was bedeviling major American cities and metropolitan areas, including Los Angeles, Houston, and Chicago. Despite the wide-ranging legislative success, Bush got little credit with environmentalists. After reading a "report card" in the newspapers that gave him middling grades on environmental issues, Bush asked Porter what he thought of the piece. "Mr. President, that's not a report card you will want to send home," Porter said. Bush nodded. "Not a lot of gratitude there," the president replied. But Bush had done the right thing, and he knew it, even if the activists on the left chose not to acknowledge the substance of what a Republican president had done.

The Americans with Disabilities Act was a landmark bill, and Bush maneuvered between activists, Democrats, and businesses to craft legislation that would grant the disabled access to jobs and buildings without creating a regulatory nightmare. His interest in the bill was rooted in fair play. It just didn't seem right to him, he'd explain to visitors, that somebody in a wheelchair or somebody who was deaf didn't have the exact same rights—of access and of employment—as anybody else. Bob Dole, who bore the wounds of war, championed the measure. After their years of competition, Dole and Bush had come to appreciate each other. However much divided them culturally, they had been shaped by World War II and by a common Washington sensibility about the essential supremacy of governing over campaigning, and the president was grateful to Dole for the Kansas senator's skill and support throughout the administration.

On the ADA, Bush was personally engaged. One Friday afternoon in the spring of 1990, the telephone rang in the Capitol Hill office of Democratic Senator Tom Harkin of Iowa. It was the White House: Would Senator Harkin, who was involved in disability issues, like to join President Bush for a drink that evening?

Harkin happily accepted. He'd been locked in negotiating combat with John Sununu over elements of the ADA draft; it would be diverting to see the president socially. Arriving in the family quarters, the senator found the president making martinis for an eclectic group of guests (all male; Barbara was out of town) that included Housing and Urban Development Secretary Jack Kemp and White House counsel Boyden Gray. The talk was pleasant but general. An old pilot himself, Harkin talked with Bush about flying, and the president gave everyone a tour of the private rooms, including a viewing of Millie's bed. After ninety minutes or so, the party broke up. Harkin was standing with Bush and Gray waiting for the elevator that would take them down from the Residence to a small hallway near the State Dining Room. "I thought to myself, 'I really don't want to spoil the evening, but I've got to say something about the ADA bill, which was kind of stalled at the moment,'" recalled Harkin.

"Mr. President," Harkin said, "I don't mean to bring up business, but I really hope we can get together on the disabilities act."

"Oh, yeah," Bush said, "I'm for that. We've got to get that done."

"Well, Mr. President, we're having some real problems right now," Harkin said.

"What's that?"

"I hate to say it, sir, but it's John Sununu."

Bush turned to Gray.

"Boyden," Bush said, "I want you to take this over and get it done."

"Yes, sir," Gray replied.

Gray handled Harkin's issues, the talks proceeded more smoothly, and the bill was ready for Bush's signature in the last week of July 1990. In a sunny, sparkling ceremony on the South Lawn, Bush equated the ADA with the fall of the Berlin Wall. "Even the strongest person couldn't scale the Berlin Wall to gain the elusive promise of independence that lay just beyond," Bush said. "And so, together we rejoiced when that barrier fell. And now I sign legislation which takes a sledgehammer to another wall, one which has for too many generations separated Americans with disabilities from the freedom they could glimpse, but not grasp."

From education to the environment to civil rights for the disabled, Bush's domestic legislative achievements did not fit neatly into the traditional categories of left and right. Conservatives distrusted Bush's use of government to reach certain ends, and liberals were wary of his emphasis on limiting regulatory intrusion and, where possible, using market-based incentives. But what the president called, without irony, "sound governance" required the sensibility of the "Have-Half" Poppy Bush of distant days. Sometimes, when his political advisers would try to tell him that his compromises were difficult to sell to his own base, Bush would fix them with what one longtime aide called "the Look—you know, the one that said, politely, of course, 'If you're so smart, then why aren't you the president of the United States?'"

THIRTY-FIVE

A Nation Reunited and a New NATO

★

*I don't think we can be naïve about history, but I don't think
we need to let history and the problem with WWI and WWII
control Germany's fate in the future.*

—GEORGE H. W. BUSH, on German reunification

THE FORTY-FIRST PRESIDENT of the United States adored the White House. Theodore Roosevelt had delighted in playing "bear" in the house with his children, being chased by what one biographer described as "young hunters, armed with umbrellas or fire irons, or any other object which was at hand." George H. W. Bush loved the mansion in the same way, with the same spirit.

The Bushes awoke most mornings around five A.M. in their bedroom in the Residence. In a king-size bed, they would drink coffee—Bush had bought cup warmers for the bedside tables—and read *The New York Times, The Washington Post, The Washington Times, USA Today,* the *New York Post,* the New York *Daily News,* and the White House News Summary, a big compilation of clips and transcripts. (Coffee was critical to him: On the road as vice president and even into his White House years, he carried a special heating stick to make himself a cup of instant each morning in his hotel rooms.) If Bush were reading fast, he could rip through the pile of papers in forty-five minutes; it would take a bit longer if he wanted, as he often did, to jot down notes about what he'd seen.

Breakfast tended to be yogurt and granola. Sometimes Bush would take a few minutes in the early morning in the Residence to catch up on his diary dictations; then he would shower—occasionally with Millie—and dress for the day. His suits (42L, 38 waist) came from a Washington clothier, Arthur A. Adler; his shirts (which Bush, in a phrase that betrayed his Greenwich origins, unironically called "shirtings" in private) from Ascot Chang, a Hong Kong tailor. And yet when he was not in full presidential mode in terms of attire—he favored dark suits, straight collars, and unexceptionable neckties—he often looked a bit of a mess. To Doro's 1992 wedding at Camp David he wore white pants with a blue stripe. The president of the United States had forgotten to bring a suit. During the crisis with Panama, Colin Powell recalled meeting with Bush just after a holiday party. The president wore one sock that said "Merry" and another that said "Christmas."

On working mornings in the White House, Bush would grab his briefcase and make his way over to the Oval Office suite, taking the elevator from the Residence down to the Diplomatic Reception Room and then walking toward the Oval Office. He usually reached the West Wing about six thirty. Bush tended to start his office workday in his small study, working at an electric typewriter which he used on a hideaway desk he had asked the White House carpenters to build for him: He thought the typewriter, when not in use, unsightly. A world map hung above the specially crafted desk; the president would swap in new ones as global boundaries changed in 1989 and beyond. Bush could make and receive calls from the study and would record the caller, the date, time, and subject on a special yellow pad. He would frequently ring a cabinet member or staffer who may have taken a hit in the papers that morning, telling them to keep their chin up.

He was a generous but subtly demanding boss. Advisers grew to fear the tapping of his thumb on his desk during briefings or explanations—a sign of impatience that said: *Got it. Let's move it along here.* Brent Scowcroft would be anxious every morning that the president, with his voracious reading habits, would have a question about a newspaper story that the national security adviser had not had time to get to. (It was, Scowcroft recalled, a "mortal fear.") If Bush were angry about something, he would rarely show it: He would, rather, grow quiet.

He always had time for visiting athletes. When he received the golf legend Sam Snead, Bush asked Snead for advice on hitting a sand wedge. Practicing a shot, the president, as he put it, nearly drilled his photographer, David Valdez, "in the testicles with the screaming shank." Domingo Quicho, a veteran of the White House's household staff since the Kennedy years, would cook for Bush in the tiny kitchen off the Oval Office, often serving intimate meals in a small presidential dining room. If Bush were alone at lunchtime—a rare thing, but it happened now and again—he would sometimes use a treadmill the Bushes had installed in a cabana on the grounds. If he were watching his weight—which was most of the time—he would drink a protein shake (he called them "Lendls," after the tennis professional Ivan Lendl, who had introduced him to them). After a quick sauna and a jump in the White House pool, Bush would emerge, as he put it, feeling "like a million dollars."

The Bushes' two liver-and-white springer spaniels—Millie had been joined by Ranger, one of her puppies—patrolled the White House grounds with the breed's boundless energy. The president ordered the construction of a horseshoe pit and organized complicated tournament brackets. (One afternoon he watched the Air Force One team play the White House electricians.) It was a way to take a break from the pressures of the office, but there was another purpose, too: The horseshoe pit enabled the president to make most of those who worked for him, for his family, and for the White House feel included. Families came to tournaments; you might see the Leader of the Free World competing against a maintenance man.

Though mocked for saying he liked country music—critics thought it an affectation to appear more populist than preppy—Bush truly did enjoy the genre. "It's a great mix of music, lyrics, barrooms, Mother, the flag and good-looking large women," Bush told his diary. "There is something earthy and strong about it all." Among his favorite artists: Dolly Parton, Crystal Gayle, the Gatlin Brothers, the Oak Ridge Boys, and Anne Murray. A similar charge of cultural hypocrisy was leveled at Bush's alleged fondness for pork rinds, but that, too, was genuine. His staff supplied his hotel rooms with pork rinds and Dr Pepper.

Motion was everything. There were the wild rides in Maine aboard the *Fidelity,* his cigarette boat; lightning-quick rounds of golf; and spur-of-the-moment meals at favorite spots such as Peking Gourmet Inn in northern Virginia, Otto's barbecue in Houston, and Mabel's Lobster Claw in Kennebunkport. On the weekends at Camp David, life "was nonstop," recalled Tim McBride, Bush's personal aide. After arriving on Friday afternoons, Bush would go for a jog, greet guests, have supper, and usually watch a movie. On Saturday mornings he would work from eight to about noon, run again or work out with weights, throw horseshoes, and play tennis or "Wallyball," a game he played on the compound's volleyball court. (Players were encouraged to spike the ball off the wall of the enclosed court—hence the name.) Sunday mornings there were ecumenical church services (a chapel at Camp David was completed and dedicated about halfway through Bush's presidency).

He disliked being alone. One summer weekend early in his presidency at Camp David was typical. He hosted a rolling house party—friends from Houston and beyond with their children, Senator John Heinz, and the tennis professional Pam Shriver, among others. "I find that having young people around makes me feel young—not tired—but young," Bush told his diary.

After lunch Bush took a nap. The afternoon in the mountains had turned cool. "I put a big comforter on, laid out on my bed, and slept to sleep with the dead," he dictated. "I woke aching and feeling great and rested. . . . I just have to have people around and action around."

In the breaching of the Berlin Wall in November 1989, Bush had been strong by being largely silent. Throughout his presidency he projected power in the climactic chapter of the Cold War through acts of restraint rather than through the more traditional means of force of arms or of rhetoric. It was unglamorous, perhaps, and difficult to appreciate, but it was the right thing to do in the service of America's national interests and of the promotion of American values abroad. He took a much more active hand in what came after the wall collapsed: the reunification of Germany, a complicated diplomatic episode that required convincing both the Soviets and the other Western powers—chiefly Britain and France—to allow a unified Germany to take its place in the heart of Europe.

At Yalta in the waning hours of World War II, Franklin Roosevelt had acknowledged military and political reality by agreeing to a division of Europe. Forty-five years on, "German reunification had a very personal meaning to me," Bush recalled. To bring East Germany and West Germany together, he believed, would mark the true end of World War II, and was an important step in ratifying the march of the forces of freedom as the last decade of the twentieth century began. Had Bush not pressed for a reunified Germany, Europe might well have entered the 1990s and the twenty-first century still divided, less prosperous, and a source of instability for the region and for the world. As it was, Bush's insistent diplomatic work on reunification and bringing the rejoined nation into NATO immeasurably strengthened the West.

Thatcher and Mitterrand were skeptical of reunification, fearing that, as Thatcher put it, if "we are not careful, the Germans will get in peace what Hitler couldn't get in the war." (Another aphorism of Thatcher's, borrowing from Lord Ismay, NATO's first secretary-general: "The purpose of NATO is to keep the Americans in, the Russians out, and the Germans down.") Bush was less alarmist about the prospect of a newly resurgent Germany, telling his diary in February 1990: "I don't think we can be naïve about history, but I don't think we need to let history and the problem with WWI and WWII control Germany's fate in the future. Perhaps it's different when we're this far away, but there is a certain insult to the Germans suggesting that they will give up democracy and give way to some new Hitler once they're unified, or that they will immediately want to expand their borders."

Everything seemed new. In February 1990, Bush received an early morning call from South Africa. After twenty-seven years in prison, Nelson Mandela was to be freed. In private, Bush linked the Mandela release with the collapse of Communism. "Change—the amazing change," he told his diary.

For Bush, managing a shifting world was a question of balance and of order. Briefing European allies on the morning after Malta, Bush had been clear about his sense of things. NATO, he said, had been created "to provide the basis for precisely the extraordinary evolution which is occurring in Eastern Europe today.... The task before us is to consolidate the fruits of this peaceful revolution and provide the architecture for continued peaceful change.... The people of every nation have the right to determine their own way of life in freedom."

Though Bush could seem the most old-fashioned of men, he was not captive to the past, and his views on German reunification offer a clear example of how he could break free from conventional thinking. The leadership of Britain and France believed that Germany was inherently atavistic, but Bush liked to look forward rather than back. "I hold no rancor in my heart towards Germany or Japan, none at all," Bush would tell the fiftieth anniversary gathering at Pearl Harbor in 1991. "I can still see the faces of the fallen comrades, and I'll bet you see the faces of your fallen comrades too ... but don't you think they are saying, 'fifty years have passed; our country is the undisputed leader of the free world, and we are at peace'? Don't you think each one is saying, 'I did not die in vain'?"

There was a direct American interest in a unified Germany within NATO, too. Far from seeing the end of the Cold War as a chance to relax national defense, Bush realized that threats to American security were growing more diffuse but were no less real. "Who's the enemy?" Bush dictated to his diary in February 1990. "I keep getting asked that. It's apathy; it's the inability to predict accurately; it's dramatic change that can't be foreseen. . . . There's all kinds of events that we can't foresee that require a strong NATO, and there's all kinds of potential instability that requires a strong U.S. presence." Bush had two diplomatic goals in the first half of 1990: the reunification of Germany as an ally of the United States and ongoing support for Mikhail Gorbachev. Even Thatcher agreed with the latter, telling Bush: "Destabilize him and we lose the possibility of democracy in the Soviet Union."

On Thursday, May 31, 1990, Gorbachev arrived in Washington to a splendid military welcome. The president of the United States and the president of the USSR jointly reviewed American troops, including soldiers from Fort Myer wearing Revolutionary War uniforms. Bush noticed that Gorbachev was in a better frame of mind than he had been at Malta. "Gorbachev looked well and seemed confident as he greeted me with a smile and a strong handshake, not at all tired," Bush recalled. In the Oval Office they took the traditional seats before the fireplace. The conversation was wide ranging, even, in Bush's term, "philosophical." Gorbachev needed a grain and trade agreement—and for his country to be elevated to "most favored nation" trade status by the United States. The "old suspicions" between the two superpowers had to go, Gorbachev said. Building on Malta, both nations had to learn how to thrive in a multipolar world.

Matters at hand included German reunification, which the Soviets opposed, and the issue of Lithuania. One of the Baltic states absorbed into the Soviet Union during World War II, Lithuania had been seeking independence. Moscow, however, had cracked down, resisted the demands, and instituted an energy embargo. Bush was under great pressure both abroad and at home to force Gorbachev to ease Soviet opposition to Lithuania's push for freedom.

In a larger meeting at four thirty in the Cabinet Room, the subject of Germany dominated. Gorbachev believed that a united Germany within NATO would strategically isolate the Soviet Union. He proposed, instead, that the new Germany belong either to no alliance or to NATO while simultaneously being in alliance with the Soviets.

Bush intervened with a technical point. The Helsinki Final Act, non-binding accords reached between Moscow and the West in 1975, said "all countries had the right to choose their alliances. To me," Bush recalled saying, "that meant Germany should be able to decide for itself what it wanted. Did [Gorbachev] agree?" "Shrugging," Bush recalled, Gorbachev made a historic remark.

"Yes," Gorbachev told Bush.

As Bush recalled it, the Cabinet Room went quiet. The Soviet officials around Gorbachev appeared stunned and dismayed. There was heated back-and-forth on the Soviet side and a few attempts to get Gorbachev to amend his remarks. Like the Americans, the other Soviets did not quite believe that they had just heard the leader of the USSR concede that a united Germany could become part of a military alliance that had been the Soviets' mortal enemy.

Gorbachev may have been accepting the inevitable and perhaps hoped that by conceding the point on a favorite project of the president's he might make progress on his key summit goal—a trade agreement. That evening, Gorbachev "buttonholed" Bush after a state dinner. "He told me that if we did not have a trade agreement, it would be a disaster," Bush recalled. "It would make or break the summit for him. He was very agitated." Bush went upstairs but slept poorly. The United States could not reward Gorbachev with a trade deal at the same time the Soviet regime was acting like the Soviets of old in Lithuania, which remained under a strict energy embargo ordered by Moscow. Was there any way out?

Sometime in the overnight or early morning hours, the "Have-Half" Bush of childhood thought he had formulated a compromise. Bush took Jim Baker into his confidence. "The deal I suggested would have an open or publicized side, as well as a secret, stricter one," Bush recalled. The U.S. and the U.S.S.R. would openly sign the trade agreements, but the documents would not go to Congress for ratification until the Soviets had fulfilled all of the demands necessary for MFN status. There was a further secret condition before Bush would ask Congress to vote on the deal: "We would not send the package up for approval until negotiations with the Lithuanians had begun and Moscow lifted the [energy] embargo."

It was an effective diplomatic solution. "We could hand Gorbachev a tangible success in the form of a signed agreement with public stipulations that he had a chance of meeting, but we made sure the agreement would not be implemented until there was substantive progress on Lithuania," Bush recalled. "There would be no embarrassment for Gorbachev at home, and we would get the conditions we wanted."

The next morning Bush and Gorbachev boarded Marine One for the short trip to Camp David. Both presidents, Bush realized, were joined for the flight by military aides carrying the competing codes that would enable either nation to launch nuclear missiles at each other—emblems of an older era, transposed to a new one. Looking down at the houses below in the thickly developed suburbs of Maryland, Gorbachev asked Bush about American real estate. "How do you buy and sell a house?" he asked. "Who loans the money? Who owns the house?"

Camp David was everything that Bush had hoped it would be. The formal Gorbachev took off his coat and tie and sat happily with Bush at a glass-topped table beneath an umbrella on a beautiful June morning. Bush remembered the "warm sun and crystal-clear sky," and the tone of the conversation matched the weather. To Bush's astonishment, Gorbachev threw a ringer on his first try at horseshoes. ("Talk about beginner's luck!" Bush recalled.)

They discussed a number of subjects with varying degrees of candor, but Bush felt the exchanges helpful. "We developed a feeling of give-and-take; what we could do and what we could not do," Bush recalled. There were odder moments. "I've heard some report that you'd used laser weapons against people in Panama," Gorbachev said. Bush was puzzled, recalling, "There was no rancor in his voice—an inquiry." Bush then replied, "Well, I don't know, but let me tell you this—I don't think we have laser weapons to use against people, and secondly, I'd like to ask Cheney and Powell, [who] are up here."

The president consulted his military chiefs in a quick conversation in the presidential cabin, and they "said there was no such thing, except use of lasers for radar on tanks." Within twenty minutes of Gorbachev's raising the question, Bush "told him I could categorically deny it. He thanked me and said, 'Well, it's probably some crazy rumor.'" They strolled the wood-chip trails and spent some time tramping through the woods. (Gorbachev was especially wary of poison ivy.)

There was a friendly supper, and Gorbachev confided in Bush, president to president. "He explained that he did not want to raise the question of needing money from the United States in front of his own team"—the kind of political reality Bush understood. Trade with the

Soviets was one thing; direct economic aid another. Bush was honest with his guest. American political pressures were such that if the Soviets could show progress on cutting aid to Cuba, on fully following up on supporting a reunited Germany that was free to join NATO if it chose, and on the Soviets' own internal market reforms, then Bush would be in a much stronger position to help. It was a candid conversation—the kind, perhaps, that could have taken place only between leaders who were building a relationship of trust.

They returned to Washington, landing on the South Lawn. Bush brought Gorbachev up to the Residence and showed him where Lincoln had signed the Emancipation Proclamation. The history lesson over, Bush eagerly took his guest into his study to show off his five-screen television cabinet and his personal computer.

Like so many guests before him (and after him), Gorbachev loved the intimacy of the Bush tour—few modern presidents had ever been so open with the Residence—and Gorbachev had other reasons to be cheerful as well. There was good news on the economic front, with Chevron agreeing to an oil exploration deal, among other developments. "He was thrilled about those things," Bush recalled.

They went downstairs and over to the Oval Office, where Gorbachev was surprised to note the detail of Bush's printed daily schedule. "I've got to get my office modernized," Gorbachev said. "I don't have this kind of thing." Bush rummaged around and found his entire monthly schedule for May, which had just ended, and handed it to Gorbachev to take home as a possible model. Gorbachev wondered if he might send his own chief of staff over to Washington for a tutorial. Bush volunteered John Sununu for a trip to Moscow if that might be easier. The message: Whatever Gorbachev needed (within reason) he had only to ask.

Barbara was enduring a generational controversy during the Gorbachevs' visit. Invited by Wellesley College to speak at graduation and receive an honorary degree, the First Lady was being criticized by Wellesley's young women, as Bush put it to his diary, "because she hasn't made it on her own—she's where she is because she's her husband's wife. What's wrong with the fact that she's a good mother, a good wife, great volunteer, great leader for literacy and other fine causes? Nothing, but to listen to these elitist kids there is."

Mrs. Bush invited Raisa Gorbachev along with her to Wellesley. There, the American First Lady confronted the issues of work versus family and the role of women head-on, delivering a well-received commencement address. "Maybe we should adjust faster, maybe we should adjust slower," she told the graduates. "But whatever the era, whatever the times, one thing will never change: Fathers and mothers, if you have children—they must come first. You must read to your children, and you must hug your children, and you must love your children. Your success as a family, our success as a society depends not on what happens in the White House, but on what happens inside your house."

She received her most sustained applause when she remarked that perhaps there was someone in the audience who would, like her, one day preside over the White House as the president's spouse. "And I wish him well," she said, to cheers from the crowd. It was characteristic Barbara Bush: politically skillful, balanced—and good for George Bush, for she successfully presented herself as at once reasonable and reasonably conservative, which was the essence of her husband's own political persona.

Mrs. Bush was a popular figure as First Lady. As commentators observed at the time, the country seemed to appreciate her undyed hair and fake pearls after the excess of the Nancy Reagan era. Barbara's image as a kind of national grandmother, though, was just that: an image that did not fully capture her complexity. When the celebrity biographer Kitty Kelley published a harsh book about Nancy Reagan, Barbara read it— but only after disguising it with another dust jacket. As *Newsweek*'s Ann McDaniel reported, the First Lady was "a funny, sometimes acerbic woman who is genuinely caring—and always in control."

Savvy and strong, Barbara was a dominant but not domineering figure within the Bush clan. "She really is the leader of the family in the sense, 'You're not going to do this,' or 'You've got to do this,' and I just kind of float above it all," George H. W. Bush recalled of her. "She has absolutely no self-importance of any kind." She was remarkably steady, in public and in private. "She never becomes cross or irritable with me, and there are plenty of occasions she should, but she doesn't," Bush said.

She was also a fierce, if understated, protector of her husband's interests. "She's very perceptive; kept her opinion to herself with others a lot—not with me she didn't—and she was a good judge of character," Bush recalled. "If she felt somebody wasn't totally committed to the course of action we had agreed on, or to me personally, why, she would let it be known, but subtly. And to me she wouldn't be subtle about it."*

I n East Berlin on Friday, June 22, 1990, in a meeting with Jim Baker, Soviet foreign minister Eduard Shevardnadze presented a surprisingly hard-line set of proposals on German reunification, demanding, among other things, that Germany remain divided for another five years. Baker saw that the new Soviet document was designed more to assuage opinion at home rather than to be taken seriously at the negotiating table.

The Soviets needed some reassurance that a reunified Germany was not about to join a hawkish NATO, thus increasing the military pressure on Moscow at just the moment the Cold War appeared to be coming to a close. Bush understood Gorbachev's position. With Scowcroft and others, the president drafted a new declaration for NATO to be discussed and, if all went well, issued during a July summit in London. The key provisions of Bush's proposal: NATO would shift its emphasis from a military alliance to a political one; shift its defense posture from "forward" positions to more mobile units; open up conventional arms negotiations; and outline a "new NATO nuclear strategy."

From London, Thatcher (with some support on this point from Mitterrand) objected to the shift in nuclear strategy. NATO had long operated under what was known as "flexible response," which in practice meant that the alliance reserved the right to use nuclear weapons early in a conflict in order to deter a larger enemy military operation.

Thatcher wanted to start over with a new document, but Bush refused. He was leading the alliance now, and debate would take place on his terms. When the NATO leaders gathered in London, Jim Baker found common ground without giving away the essence of what his president wanted. The first-strike nuclear option was preserved, though it was hoped that such weapons would one day become "truly weapons

---

* She was perennially useful to her husband in large and small ways. A decade later, after listening to Michael Beschloss's audiobook of *Taking Charge,* a collection of the LBJ White House tapes, Barbara noted: "Lyndon has one thing in common with George Bush beside being a President and a Texan. He manages to pass off the phone caller by saying, 'Lady Bird wants to talk to you.' How many times has GB finished what he wants to say and then passed the phone to me.... I remember at the White House that I would get a phone call from GB asking me what I was doing and telling me that he was sending so-and-so over for a tour. He just wanted to get rid of them so he could get on with his work."

of last resort." In the same spirit of compromise, Bush recalled, NATO announced that it was "moving away" from "forward defense." The leaders affirmed the newly political nature of NATO, a major signal to Gorbachev—and to the reunification skeptics within the Soviet Union— that the Western powers believed the Cold War to be ending. "It was a landmark shift for the alliance," Bush recalled.

The president made his intentions plain to Gorbachev. "As you read the NATO declaration," Bush wrote Gorbachev, "I want you to know that it was written with you importantly in mind. . . . I hope today's NATO declaration will persuade you that NATO can and will serve the security interests of Europe as a whole." Gorbachev got the message. It was a good few days. The situation in Lithuania moved toward resolution, and Gorbachev kept his word to Bush by lifting the embargo. In the early weeks of July, Gorbachev faced a tumultuous Communist Party conference, but emerged with a large margin of support for his reelection as general secretary.

The man Bush had decided to trust had proven worthy of that confidence. In mid-July, Helmut Kohl went to the Soviet Union for long talks with Gorbachev on reunification, offering generous financial assistance to cash-strapped Moscow and volunteering to underwrite the cost of Soviet troops who were to remain in East Germany for a transition period. It was a deal Gorbachev felt he could not decline. He closed the conversations with Kohl at Stavropol by publicly saying: "Whether we like it or not, the time will come when a united Germany will be in NATO, if that is its choice. Then, if that is the choice, to some degree and in some form, it can work together with the Soviet Union."

Watching from Washington, Bush called Gorbachev. "This showed great statesmanship on your part, and we feel good about it," Bush told Gorbachev, who in turn credited the Bush-led coalition of diplomacy for the peaceful resolution of what, beginning the previous autumn, could have been at best chaotic and at worst extremely violent. It was the kind of message Bush lived to receive: a vindication of personal diplomacy with the expectation of an orderly result. In midsummer 1990, the world beyond America's shores was moving Bush's way, on Bush's terms. He was instrumental in determining the fates of millions in Europe and in the ever-creakier Soviet Union.

At home, though, he was about to learn that he was master of very little.

THIRTY-SIX

I've Got to Do What I Think Is Right

★

> If we didn't have this budget deficit problem hanging over my head, I would be loving this job, but with the deficit and my fears about the economy, it's an awful lot of worry right now.
>
> —George H. W. Bush

> Read My Lips: I Lied.
>
> —*New York Post* headline

THE LATE SPRING NIGHTS in Washington had been long and uncomfortable. "I'm tired and Bar can't sleep," Bush, who had been suffering from a sore neck, dictated on Sunday, May 13, 1990. "She thrashes around and I stay awake. My neck seems to be better, but I think it's tension-related, so with the budget problems, it will probably get worse." The budget—the deficit—was all-consuming. One of the first suggestions that Bush abandon his "Read my lips" pledge on taxes had come in the presidential transition, back in late 1988. In one meeting at the vice presidential residence, Bob Teeter, Bush's pollster, had said that he believed responsible deficit reduction would require new revenues. Dan Quayle and John Sununu objected, and Jim Baker closed off the discussion, saying: "We don't need to do that this year."

But now it was 1990, and the pressures for a long-term deal were growing. The deficit posed what was seen at the time as a vital threat to the present and future American economy. At the Federal Reserve, Alan Greenspan refused to lower interest rates—and lower interest rates meant more capital in the marketplace—until the administration and Congress made significant strides on controlling the imbalance between federal revenues and outlays. (Greenspan believed that lower interest rates and high levels of deficit spending would create inflation.) Bush's dilemma: Greenspan wanted a deficit reduction deal. The Democratic majorities on Capitol Hill wanted higher revenues as part of any deal. And the Republican base wanted the president to keep his word from 1988 and stand fast against higher revenues, even if it meant no deal at all.

But the absence of a budget agreement, under existing law, could lead to a government shutdown and sequestration (automatic, across-the-board spending cuts), plunging the country into economic chaos. "I know I'm going to have to bite a major bullet," Bush told his diary. The savings and loan bailout and a slowing economy meant the deficit was getting worse, not better. Given all of the factors, the best way to establish conditions for long-term growth was an agreement that showed the world the U.S. government was serious about deficit reduction.

Politically, such an agreement required more revenue. There was no practical way to move toward a balanced budget without more money coming in. The General Accounting Office had said so; so had former presidents Nixon, Ford, and Carter. Bush had long suspected that he would probably have to break the "Read my lips" pledge. That moment was about to arrive.

What kinds of taxes might work? In the White House in the late winter of 1989–90, Bush listened to discussions about a value-added tax, or VAT, but he noted that "conservatives strongly oppose it, and it looks like the Europeanization of America." Other options included oil import fees or taxes on gasoline, liquor, and wine. The bottom line: "We're going to have to do something, and we're going to have to lead all these various strong-willed players to the trough."

He had a respite from the pressures of the presidency in early May when his mother came to call. Arriving at the diplomatic entrance to the White House, Dorothy Bush, now eighty-eight, was uncertain of her whereabouts. Her son walked over from the Oval Office to greet her.

"Who's that?" Mrs. Bush said. "Who's that?"

"Mum," Bush said, "it's George." He hugged her, and then she recognized him. "I hope she'll have a good long sleep and then wake up, so we can do stuff together," Bush told his diary. "It's a joy having her here."

The visit was sweet but painful. "I thought to myself, 'Here she is, our leader, our spirit, our moral compass, and she's in and she's out.' They . . . tucked her in bed. She rested, then she woke up two hours later, and she was beautiful and the cheeks didn't look quite so hollow, and she knew more." Burton Lee, the White House physician, told Bush that her vital signs were troubling. "He warned me she could die any minute," Bush said. The president wanted his mother to see his world. "Mum, I want you to come to the Oval Office," Bush said. He wheeled her through the office, then from room to room in his small suite—what he called "my little private sector." At dinner Bush put in a call to Billy Graham, who sent his prayers and blessing. Bush then wheeled his mother to her room. He kissed her goodnight, but "wasn't sure she knew where she was, who I was, but I knew that she loved me."

Buffeted by his love for his mother, his gratitude to her, and his sadness at her decline, Bush went outside to walk the White House grounds in the dark. The images swirled: of the Mothers' Race at Greenwich Country Day—which Mrs. Bush won, of course—of the baseball games, of the visits to Andover. In his mind's eye he was a boy again, and his mother was the center of his world. "All the criticism, all the fighting, all the ups-and-downs, all the right-wing, the left-wing, the press, and controversy—they all mean nothing. It's Mum's words: 'Do your best; try your hardest; be kind; share; go to church'—and I think that's what really matters.... I've been President a year-and-a-half, and my mother doesn't know, but she's with us now."

Bush kept up his personal diplomacy with the congressional leadership. On Sunday, May 6, 1990, the Bushes hosted a White House lecture on Theodore Roosevelt by David McCullough, who had written a book about TR's early years, *Mornings on Horseback*. McCullough's vivid descriptions of life in the White House eight decades before transfixed Bush. "Oh, to be 42 and President, and oh, to be President in those less complicated times where you could finish work at 4:00, and go for a ride," Bush told his diary. The spell of the past was soon broken. After the lecture, George Mitchell, Bob Dole, Tom Foley, and Bob Michel joined Nick Brady, Dick Darman, and John Sununu upstairs in the Residence. In Bush's study, the president offered his guests cold shrimp and popcorn as the eight men discussed the outlines of a budget deal. There was general talk about process, and later that week came a demand from Mitchell that forced Bush's doubts about the viability of "Read my lips" into public.

There must be, Mitchell said, "no preconditions" on the negotiations for a budget deal. The White House agreed to the point, issuing a press release saying so on Wednesday, May 9. The significance of the language: tax increases were now a possibility. On Air Force One for a trip to Texas after the "no preconditions" concession, Bush told reporters: "My position is I make this offer to sit down in good faith and talk with no conditions." He took the long view, adding: "So tomorrow there'll be another tidal wave. So keep your snorkel above the water level, and do what you think is right. That's exactly what my mom told me when I was about six. 'Do your best. Do your best.' I'm trying hard. Stay calm."

In the coming storm he would need all the strength she—or anyone else—had ever given him. "The big subject this morning is taxes," Bush told his diary on Thursday, May 10, 1990. He minced no words. "The shit," he told his diary, had "hit the fan."

The conservative reaction to the "no preconditions" announcement—which was interpreted as a precursor to new tax increases—was indeed vicious. "We're getting pounded, and the right wing is the worst, much more so than the left wing, it seems to me," Bush told his diary, "or maybe it's just that when you're attacked by your own, it stings more." He struggled to remember his mother's advice to always look ahead. "There is a clump of these extreme extremists that I detest," Bush dictated, "but I can't let the bastards get us down. . . . Push forward."

At a meeting of the Republican budget leadership with Bush in the White House on Monday, June 25, 1990, Phil Gramm, a conservative Republican senator from Texas, said: "If we can get a deal, we ought to take it. If we've got to do a little bit in taxes to get a deal, do it. . . . Just don't break the pledge until there's a deal." Though Gramm said he could not support raising the marginal income tax rates, he was open to other options. In the same session, Dick Darman recalled that Gingrich was "conspicuously tepid" but did say, "There's no way you can deal with *income* tax rates." Like Gramm, Gingrich left open the possibility of accepting other tax measures. Bush sensed some flexibility on his right—implicit permission to give way on certain taxes in spite of the "Read my lips" pledge. The administration's hope was that a gas tax increase would be what Sununu called the "ransom" for a deal that cut the capital gains rate, and both Gramm and Gingrich had signaled that they could "live with" such an agreement.

The next morning, a June Tuesday, began early, with a seven A.M. White House breakfast in the Family Dining Room with the top Republican and Democratic leaders. ("My dog wasn't even awake when I left," Dole cracked.) On the Hill, the talks were stalled. The price of failure was high for both sides. Bush asked the Democrats—Foley, Mitchell, and Dick Gephardt—a straightforward question. "What do you propose?"

Foley spoke for the group. Like Bush, the House Speaker was a reasonable man. After being recently "criticized for being insufficiently partisan" by Democrats in his own caucus, Foley, Darman recalled, had replied: "Part of the time we have to worry, between elections, about the country's government." At the breakfast table, seated at the president's right, Foley now told Bush that a deal commensurate with the nation's financial problems would require "entitlement reform, defense and discretionary spending reduction, budget process reform, and tax increases."

There it was. Foley had spoken "simply, graciously, seriously," Darman recalled. These were the terms. The details were malleable, but the overarching question—would Bush agree to increase taxes?—had been put to the president face-to-face.

"Okay," Bush said, "if I can say you agreed."

With those seven words, George H. W. Bush reversed himself on the key domestic pledge of the 1988 campaign. "It did destroy me," Bush recalled years afterward. "The problem with the tax pledge was the rhetoric was so hot. Peggy Noonan, you know, 'I'm the man' and that kind of stuff. I felt uncomfortable with some of that. But it was persuasive—the convention loved it. When people ask me, as they do now, 'Did you make any mistakes?' I say, 'Yeah, one was to say no more taxes, period—I won't raise taxes.' It was a mistake, but I meant it at the time, and I meant it all through my presidency. But when you're faced with the reality, the practical reality, of shutting down the government or dealing with a hostile Congress, you get something done."

On reflection, Bush did not minimize his decision. He saw the reversal on "Read my lips" not simply as a discarded campaign pledge but as an actual breach of his word—a breach undertaken for the larger good of the country, to be sure, but still a breach. "I paid a big price for that," Bush recalled in retirement. "And I can understand people saying, 'He broke his word, he went back on his word,' particularly the right-wingers."

In historical terms, Bush's chosen field of endeavor—politics—was a world in which reversals of opinion are the rule, not the exception. Admirers see such moments as hours of noble compromise in pursuing the art of the possible; critics as craven capitulations. Sometimes leaders must pay for their departures from dogma with scorn and defeat; sometimes they are lauded and forgiven. (And sometimes, in the fullness of time, the former gives way to the latter.) That is the nature, and the price, of power.

In the summer of 1990, Bush changed his mind because of political and policy realities. The Democrats held majorities in both houses of Congress, and they wanted more revenue. There was no way to move toward a balanced budget without spending caps, and the Democrats were going to give Bush spending caps only if he raised taxes. He was, therefore, willing to surrender on taxes in order to get systemic reforms that put future administrations and Congresses on a pay-as-you-go basis, meaning increases in spending had to be offset by cuts elsewhere or by raising taxes. All of that was to come in the next few months of negotiations. After Bush and Foley agreed on the inclusion of a tax increase, the conversation moved on. "The mood was good," Darman recalled. "There seemed to be procedural agreement. Everything was private. No significant harm had been done."

Then Nick Brady spoke up. Darman thought of Brady, the old Dillon, Read chairman, as "a successful investment banker, with well-developed instincts for closing a deal." Foley and Bush had come to new terms. Shouldn't there be some memorialization of the agreement about what was on the table—including taxes? "Where are we," Brady asked, "on the Speaker and the President's statement?"

Instead of killing the idea or at least redirecting the conversation, Darman, acting out of what he himself later described as "some stupid reflex," said, "It would be easy to draft." He wrote a statement that captured Foley's language. Seeing the phrase "tax increases" sitting there so starkly on the page, Darman realized that it "looked like trouble if released." He handed the pad to Sununu, who, like Darman, prided himself on his smarts. Wisely, Sununu added the phrase "growth incentives"— code for capital gains tax cuts, which Bush had long favored—and changed the phrase "tax increases" to "tax revenue increases." Sununu hoped the alteration "would allow the conversation on revenue to begin without the breaking of the pledge being an absolutely definite outcome," he recalled, thinking of alternatives such as closing loopholes or gaining higher revenue from a lower capital gains rate. "It was a weak reed," Sununu admitted, "but it was all I could come up with in thirty seconds of editing."

"It is clear to me," the Bush statement read, "that both the size of the deficit problem and the need for a package that can be enacted require all of the following: entitlement and mandatory program reform, tax revenue increases, growth incentives, discretionary spending reductions, orderly reductions in defense expenditures, and budget process reform to assure that any bipartisan agreement is enforceable and that the deficit problem is brought under responsible control."

The promise was broken.

Newt Gingrich learned about the taxes concession when a reporter called to ask for his reaction. Gingrich tried for a time to be a team player, participating in the ensuing negotiations, but eventually could not bring himself to support the president. "In my mind," Gingrich recalled, "it was a betrayal of his pledge and a betrayal of Reaganism."

When Gingrich ally Vin Weber, the Minnesota congressman, heard the news, he thought that Bush had, in a way, warned them about such an eventuality with his "sound governance" versus "idealism" remark over the beer in the White House the year before. Now Weber could sense what was coming. "A lot of us were really committed supply-siders," Weber recalled. "We were of the belief that tax cutting was an indispensable element of our platform if we were going to win a Republican majority in the House. So there was just no way we were going to vote to raise taxes, even for a Republican president."

Across the continent and three hours behind, Dan Quayle, who was on a political trip in California, was in the shower when an aide came into the bathroom with the latest: "It's on CNN. The president just agreed to a tax increase!"

"You're kidding," Quayle said through the curtain.

"No," the aide said. "It really happened. They reached an agreement with the leadership on the Hill." As Quayle recalled the moment, "I probably should have looked at the drain, because that's where the Republican Party's best issue—the one that had gotten us elected in 1980, 1984, and 1988; the one that had, more than any other, made the Reagan Revolution possible—was headed." Reaching Sununu by telephone, the vice president said: "You need to roll this damn thing back." But it was too late. At the White House, asked by reporters whether Bush "regretted" the 1988 pledge, Marlin Fitzwater said: "We feel he said the right thing then. He's saying the right thing now."

Later in the day, during a meeting in the White House, Baker and Bush exchanged notes about the morning's news. "What's happening re 'tax revenue increases'?" Baker wrote on a piece of White House notepaper.

"Firestorm on 'Right' [and] in Press re Read Lips break of word," Bush wrote back.

In a conference call with Bush and Darman, Roger Ailes, the communications guru based in New York, advised—too late—against breaking the pledge. "You're not known for much, but you are known for character," Ailes told Bush. "Don't do it—don't break your word." Voters, Ailes added, "can't identify a lot about you or anybody, but they do identify you as a man of your word. Don't break it."

"It was two years ago," Bush replied, "and they understand that politics changes." Ailes was unconvinced. "He was rationalizing it," Ailes recalled.

Bush's immediate task was to explain the shift on taxes to the country. Yet for three days—an eternity in politics in the modern age—the president did not appear in public to talk about what was going on, or why he had done what he had done. "I'll let the statement speak for itself," Bush told the press at a Rose Garden event that afternoon. On the evening of the Tuesday, June 26th, statement, the Bushes hosted a barbecue for the Congress on the South Lawn, with entertainment by Glen Campbell. He then failed to explain himself on either Wednesday the twenty-seventh or Thursday the twenty-eighth. He was reading the news; he knew that all hell was breaking loose. "Our people were running and screaming, and I can understand why," Bush told his diary. "I guess this is the biggest test of my Presidency. Time will tell."

At last, on Friday, June 29, 1990, just before he left for a trip to Maine, Bush walked into the briefing room for a press conference. Having failed to present the tax news as part of a finished deal—the preferred political option, for then he could have pointed to what he had gained as well as what he had given up—Bush belatedly shared his thinking with the country. "Look, I knew I'd catch some flak on this decision," Bush told reporters, "but I've got to do what I think is right, and then I'll ask the people for support. But more important than posturing now or even negotiating is the result. Do we continue to provide jobs for the American people, and do we continue to provide economic growth, and do we try to stop saddling the generations on the way up, the young people, with absolutely unacceptable deficits?"

This was the crux of the matter. Bush was more interested in the result, which he defined as responsible governance and sound financial stewardship, than he was in the political work of educating the country about the situation at hand. He was willing to concede some ground on taxes—or "tax-revenue increases"—in order to get the Democrats to agree to spending constraints. Because of existing law, that spending, if left unchecked, could one day lead to draconian automatic cuts or ruinously higher taxes (or both) that might damage an economy and a culture accustomed to a larger federal role in the life of the nation.

So why not say so, explicitly and dramatically, to the American people, beyond the context of a hastily called news conference at nine thirty on a Friday morning in summer just before the Fourth of July holiday? Partly because, in the furor over the 1990 budget, the president fell prey to a tendency to assume that other people were living inside his head with him and understood what he was doing and why he was doing it. He governed by making the decisions he felt were right and then moving on to the next item of business. He was no Coolidge, to be sure, but neither was he an FDR, who used the radio to educate the public, or a Reagan, who believed speeches mattered. Bush really did not—at his peril. "He truly believed that the country was going to judge him on results—what he did and how it turned out—not on what he said in a speech," Dan Quayle recalled. "I'd go in and urge him to take a case to the country, and he'd say it over and over—'Dan, what people want is results. That's what matters.'"

Bush's discomfort with the rhetorical requirements of his office was one of his cardinal weaknesses as a president. He had worked hard, devilishly hard, to earn the privilege to manage the affairs of the age, but then he wanted to go back to work, not deliver a grand address or present a consistent message. Why? One reason may be his belief, expressed in private, that he was no Reagan, and Reagan was known as something Bush would never be: the Great Communicator. Instead of learning from the president he served for eight years, Bush appears to have become intimidated by the Reagan rhetorical legacy. He therefore preferred the press conference format, where he could jump around from topic to topic in a way that matched his personal hyperdrive.

Another reason had to do with the media environment itself. The president read so many newspapers and summaries of political talk shows that he could work himself up into barely controlled rages. Perhaps part of Bush's blind spot on the role of sustained rhetoric and disciplined messaging was that he believed most journalists tended to ignore his arguments in favor of details about political winners and losers, or, as Bush liked to say, "who's in and who's out." This is not to excuse him for failing to use the communicative powers of the presidency more fully, but it may help explain his reluctance to do more to sell his programs to the American public.

As he saw it, he had the nation's best interests at heart. He had signed up to serve America since his eighteenth birthday. He lived by the code of "duty, honor, country." He took for granted—perhaps subconsciously, and surely unwisely—that everyone else, or most everyone else, saw him the way he saw himself, as a public servant trying to serve the public as best he could. To govern was to choose, and in the tax decision he had made the most responsible and plausible choice available to him in an imperfect world. The May 5 announcement of "no preconditions" and the June 26 press release seemed clear enough to him. Why make a bigger deal out of what he had once described to Gingrich and Vin Weber as "sound governance" when he knew it was bad politics?

Best, Bush thought, to move ahead and get a deal. He often believed that once a point was made it had therefore been understood, internalized, and appreciated. If he gave a speech on a subject, or answered a question in a press conference, Bush was prone to think that the message had been delivered, even if it hadn't—hence his "I think the statement speaks for itself" remark in the Rose Garden on the afternoon of the day that his own vice president believed had sent the Bush administration's political future down a shower drain.

Watching the taxes fight from the Residence, Barbara hoped for the best. "Everyone wants to pile on, but I don't worry," she wrote in her diary. "George IS doing the right thing. We just have to get the deficit down. I find myself in the funniest mood. I truly feel that George is doing what is responsible and right for the country and to heck with politics. There is a life after the White House and both of us are looking forward to it."

The oil portrait of Pauline Robinson Bush, or Robin, commissioned by her grandmother Dorothy Bush in 1953.

Robin with her mother in Greenwich during the summer of 1953.

Dorothy Bush with her namesake, Doro, on the beach at Hobe Sound, Florida, February 1963.

Doubles partners James A. Baker III and George H. W. Bush on the court, circa 1967.

George W. and Doro Bush visit their father's diplomatic posting in China, summer 1975.

Noelle and George P., two of Columba and Jeb's children, during their grandfather's 1980 campaign for the Republican presidential nomination.

Up from an "asterisk": Bush on the trail in 1980. He surprised Reagan in the Iowa caucuses, winning a narrow victory, but lost what he called "the Big Mo" after Reagan reasserted himself in New Hampshire.

"Out of a clear blue sky": At the last possible moment, Reagan put Bush on the 1980 ticket—but only after last-minute negotiations to make former president Ford the vice presidential nominee had collapsed.

Men of the world: Reagan and Bush at the White House. The two former rivals developed what a Reagan adviser called "a special relationship" during the two Reagan terms.

Despite uniform fealty from the Bushes to the Reagans, Mrs. Reagan and Mrs. Bush never truly clicked, creating years of tension.

A creature of the fading clubbiness of the Congress, Bush enjoyed friendships with Democrats, including Dan Rostenkowski of Illinois, Sonny Montgomery of Mississippi, Lud Ashley of Ohio, and Tip O'Neill of Massachusetts. Here he and O'Neill, the Speaker of the House, joke around at a Reagan State of the Union address—then turn somber at the appropriate moment.

At the wheel of his beloved speedboat with Doro, Jeb, and grandchildren off Walker's Point in the summer of 1986.

Meeting Massachusetts
governor Michael Dukakis
for their second and final
presidential debate in the
fall of 1988.

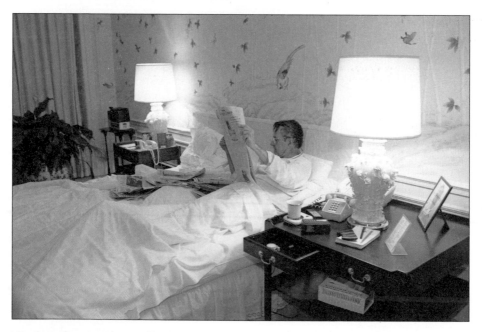

The forty-first president in the Bushes' bedroom in the White House Residence. He began
each day drinking coffee and reading newspapers and a White House News Summary, and
occasionally jotting down notes for his advisers.

With Reagan and Mikhail Gorbachev on Governors Island in New York Harbor, December 1988. A little more than three years later, on Christmas 1991, Gorbachev would announce the end of the Soviet Union.

Watching his bank of televisions in the Treaty Room, which served as the presidential study in the White House Residence. Bush often used this office to dictate to his diary at quiet moments.

Bush spends Thanksgiving with the troops of Desert Shield in Saudi Arabia, November 1990.

Victory in the desert: Bush congratulates American troops at Sumter, South Carolina, after the successful liberation of Kuwait.

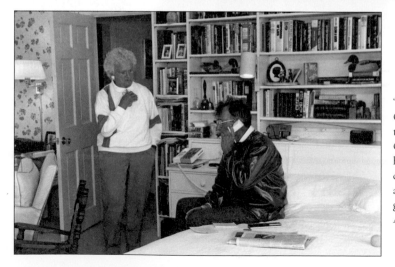

"There is a God": Bush takes a call from Gorbachev, who has survived the coup attempt against his government, August 1991.

Together to the end: Bush with Baker—who had given up the State Department to return to the White House—at work in the president's study in the Residence, August 1992.

Newt Gingrich's rebellion against the president over the 1990 budget deal—one that broke Bush's 1988 "no new taxes" pledge—devastated the administration.

On the eve of the Gulf War, Bush and his team brief the press.

At Blair House on Friday, January 20, 1989, the day of his inauguration. "I can't wait to get into that office now, and start trying to make things happen," Bush recounted in his diary during the transition.

Mrs. Bush poses with Millie on the Truman Balcony for the cover photo for *Millie's Book*, January 1990.

Bush and Scowcroft drop by to visit with Mrs. Bush and Lady Margaret and Sir Denis Thatcher as they finish breakfast in the Residence, March 1991. Thatcher had resigned as prime minister the previous fall.

A strong advocate for literacy, among other causes, Barbara Bush reads to school-children at the White House in 1990.

Signing the landmark Americans with Disabilities Act on a brilliantly sunny summer day in Washington, July 1990. Bush compared the opening of access to the disabled to the fall of the Berlin Wall.

The last run: Bush on a campaign whistle-stop tour through the Midwest, late September 1992.

Changing the guard: Bush greets President-elect Clinton at the White House, November 1992.

Hillary Clinton and Barbara Bush during a post–1992 election tour of the White House.

Skydiving in his seventies at College Station, Texas.

The former president Bush takes Tom Brokaw out on his boat in Kennebunkport, September 2006.

President George W. Bush welcomes President-elect Barack Obama and all the living former presidents to the Oval Office, January 2009.

"This is a gentleman": President Obama awards the forty-first president the Medal of Freedom, the nation's highest civilian honor, February 2011.

With George W. and Jeb Bush after completing a parachute jump in Kennebunkport on Friday, June 12, 2009, for his eighty-fifth birthday.

The Bushes at home in Kennebunkport, summer 2004.

"I don't want to miss anything": Bush with Ranger on the rocks at Walker's Point.

I n early July 1990, Bush faced an array of domestic issues small and large, and one very significant one within the family: the political controversy over Neil Bush's involvement in a savings and loan in Colorado that had required a federal bailout. Neil, who lived in Denver, had served on the board of Silverado, a failed S&L. From the first hint of trouble about Neil—whom the family called, without irony, "Mr. Perfect" for his good cheer and generosity—President Bush had blamed himself for the pain the allegations must have been causing his son. The president's grief about the investigation and the headlines was of such scope that he mused to his diary about abandoning a 1992 reelection race in order to end the pressure on Neil. "[I'm] . . . worried about Neil . . . wondering in my heart of hearts, given what's happened to Neil, whether I really want to do this after I serve this term," Bush dictated on Wednesday, July 11, 1990. Not wanting to burden his son further, Bush never let Neil know the depth of his distress about Silverado. (He did share his dire thoughts about giving up reelection with George W., but not with Neil.) "We never had a direct conversation about it," Neil recalled. "I knew he was worried, but if we talked about it, it was more about him reassuring me—'I know it's tough, we love you,' that kind of thing. Nothing about the politics or the details."

On Saturday morning, July 21, Bush met at the White House with Sununu, Boyden Gray, and Attorney General Richard Thornburgh to discuss possible nominees to fill the Supreme Court seat of the liberal lion William J. Brennan, who had announced his retirement. Three names were under consideration: Laurence Silberman of the D.C. Court of Appeals; Edith Jones, who had been a partner at Jim Baker's old firm, Andrews Kurth, before going on the federal bench; and David Souter, a judge from New Hampshire who had been championed for the Supreme Court by New Hampshire senator Warren Rudman in the Reagan years.

Jones was the most interesting choice, yet she was young (forty-one) and "considered a little explosive," Bush dictated. Souter emerged in the conversations as "the one who has the best disposition for the court," Bush told his diary. In handwritten notes of his own conversation with Souter, the president observed that the judge "seemed to be right on key points—'interpret' vs. legislating from Bench." Souter was also "safer than Jones" and "more readily confirmable."

His largest concern: "I don't want to put Souter on the bench and be surprised though—an Earl Warren type of discovery—after he's on the bench. Those who know him tell Sununu this is not the case." (Nearly two decades later, in 2009, after Souter proved a reliable liberal vote on the court, Bush remarked that the appointment had indeed been "a huge mistake.") The failure to nominate Jones, an avowedly pro-life judge, gave the right even more to work with in this summer of protest against the Bush White House. His defense of Lithuania against Soviet aggression had been secret and subtle, which meant the old cold warriors and other critics could rail on about the man in the White House not knowing that he had quietly pressured Gorbachev to do the right thing. Then there had been the "no preconditions" on the budget talks. And then came the June 26 "tax revenue increases" press release. "The right-wingers," Bush told his diary, "are very upset with me."

He awoke on Wednesday, August 1, 1990, and read the papers in bed as usual. He noted that Nolan Ryan had won his pitching outing the day before, but the rest of the news seemed bad. "All in all, it's a wonder the world wakes up (around Washington anyway) with anything other than 'gloom and doom' on their mind," Bush told his diary at seven o'clock that morning.

Late in the day, Bush took a break to hit a bucket of golf balls. Even that had its complications: His shoulders were now sore, and at twenty after eight in the evening the president walked down to the Medical Unit on the ground floor of the White House for a deep-heat treatment. Bush was in a T-shirt, on the edge of an exam table, when he looked up to see Scowcroft and Richard Haass, the National Security Council's senior Middle East hand, arrive. The president put on a dress shirt and was buttoning it as he stepped into the hall.

"Mr. President, it looks very bad," Scowcroft said. "Iraq may be about to invade Kuwait."

THIRTY-SEVEN

This Will Not Stand

★

I feel tension in the stomach and in the neck . . . but I also feel
a certain calmness when we talk about these matters. I know
I am doing the right thing.

—GEORGE H. W. BUSH, on Iraq

If Iraq wins, no small state is safe. They won't stop here. They
see a chance to take a major share of oil. It's got to be stopped.

—MARGARET THATCHER to Bush

RICHARD HAASS BRIEFED THE PRESIDENT on the little that was known. Perhaps, just perhaps, the Iraqi troop movements were a bluff or an attempt to establish a stronger bargaining position in conflicts with neighboring Kuwait over oil and territory. On this humid Washington night, Haass, Scowcroft, and Bush discussed whether a call from the president might persuade Saddam Hussein to stand down from full-scale military action. Then the State Department reported there was shooting in Kuwait City. "So much for calling Saddam," Bush remarked. The invasion had begun. Three divisions of Saddam's elite Republican Guard—the Medina, the Hammurabi, and the Tawakalna—had seized Kuwait City, occupied inland oil fields, and taken up posts along the Saudi border. Iraqi forces were within eight-tenths of a mile of Saudi Arabia.

Saddam Hussein had controlled Iraq since 1979 through police state tactics and an unflinching willingness to exert force over his own people with brutality and finality. Political rivals were shot; rebellious ethnic populations gassed. A June 1990 cover story in *U.S. News & World Report* had declared Saddam "The Most Dangerous Man in the World." The Iraqi dictator had an old-fashioned view of power, believing that the world respected only strength, and in the summer of 1990 he saw invasion as the best means to avoid having to repay Kuwait large debts Iraq had incurred in the war against Iran and to resolve a long-standing argument over the Rumaila oil fields. (The Iraqis accused the Kuwaitis of "stealing" oil that rightly belonged to Iraq.)

By turning the small Persian Gulf emirate into what he called the "19th province, an eternal part of Iraq," Saddam hoped to transform himself and his nation into more significant players in the Arab world and beyond. If Saddam were to hold on to Kuwait, he would be the keeper of 20 percent of the world's oil reserves. And if he were to use Kuwait as a staging area for a successful strike against neighboring Saudi Arabia, then Saddam could control over 45 percent. It was an untenable prospect for a global economy so dependent on petroleum. The possibility, moreover, of such a wealthy, powerful Saddam was inherently destabilizing, given his proven capacities to use weapons of mass destruction (against Iraq's Kurdish population and against Iran) and to wage war on his neighbors (Iran and now Kuwait).

Iraq-Kuwait relations had been churning in the summer of 1990. Saddam had issued threats against Kuwait and moved troops toward the Kuwaiti border; the State Department had sent instructions to its diplomats in the region reiterating that the United States had an interest in the "free flow of oil" and that the possibility of the "use of force" by Iraq was "contrary to UN-Charter principles." In late July, Saddam had summoned the U.S. ambassador to Iraq, April Glaspie, who told Saddam that Bush had a "strong desire" for "peace and stability in the Mideast." She also asked what Saddam intended by moving heavy divisions to the border—a question that Saddam allowed was a "reasonable" one.

"He acknowledged," Glaspie reported, "that we should be concerned for regional peace, in fact it is our duty as a superpower." Egyptian president Hosni Mubarak and King Fahd of Saudi Arabia were trying to broker a deal, and Mubarak was encouraging the United States to take a lower profile. (Glaspie was later criticized for saying that the United States "took no position" on intra-Arab border disputes, a comment that administration foes argued had sent the wrong signal to Saddam. A full reading of the relevant documents, however, shows that Saddam left the meeting with Glaspie promising to pursue diplomatic, not military, avenues, and that he recognized the United States had a clear interest in a peaceful resolution to the Iraq-Kuwait tensions.)

Bush's view of the crisis as one with critical implications for the security of the United States had deep roots. As early as 1943, during World War II, Franklin Roosevelt had reached out to Saudi Arabia, believing the kingdom's oil potentially important to the American future. When the Soviets invaded Afghanistan in 1979, threatening to project force and influence into the Middle East, including the vital Strait of Hormuz, through which so much of the world's oil moved, President Carter announced that any attempt by "outside" forces to dominate the Persian Gulf would be considered a threat to U.S. national security and risked an American military response. Then, in October 1981, President Reagan announced that the United States "would not allow Saudi Arabia to fall into the hands of any internal or external forces threatening to cut off oil supplies for the West." Reagan added: "There's no way that we could stand by and see that taken over by anyone that would shut off that oil."

Word of the invasion of Kuwait, then, did not reach Bush in a historical or policy vacuum. He well knew the importance of preserving and protecting American interests in the Persian Gulf; an impulsive Saddam had chosen to bring new chaos to a complicated and crucial region. Now the business of restoring order fell to Bush.

At ten P.M. or so on August 1, 1990, Scowcroft rang with confirmation on the invasion. "It's clear," he told Bush. "They're across the border."

The president asked Scowcroft to arrange a National Security Council meeting for the next morning and then called Thomas Pickering, the American ambassador to the United Nations. Bush's instinctive reaction was to seek global support for any U.S. move while preserving America's option to act alone. He instructed Pickering to request an emergency session of the UN Security Council for a resolution denouncing Saddam's aggression. The president retired for the evening, leaving his aides to prepare options for consideration at dawn.

In an interagency teleconference from the Situation Room from eleven P.M. to two A.M., Scowcroft and others agreed to recommend, pending Saudi approval, the deployment of American F-15s to Saudi Arabia and the freezing of Iraqi and Kuwaiti assets in the United States. Boyden Gray drafted the executive orders on the financial freeze, and Scowcroft woke the president for his signature at four thirty in the morning. Bush also ordered American warships at Diego Garcia, a naval installation in the Indian Ocean, to move toward the Persian Gulf.

After a quick shower on Thursday morning, Bush walked over to the West Wing and got to work in the small study off the Oval Office. In these early hours, Bush read a *Washington Post* piece claiming the White House is "in disarray" on the budget. Particularly infuriating to Bush as he looked over the paper was a comment from Democratic National Committee chairman Ron Brown saying, as Bush read it, that "what's happening is the unraveling of the Bush Presidency." Bush was still focused on his own poor handling of the tax question. "It is not a pretty sight—not a pretty sight at all," Bush told his diary.

On Iraq, Bush had good news from Tom Pickering, who reported a 14 to 0 vote denouncing Iraq by the UN Security Council, with "only Yemen abstaining." Perhaps the best news of all: The Soviet Union, a longtime ally of Iraq's, voted with the United States, the result of good diplomatic work by Jim Baker, who had happened to be with Shevardnadze in Irktusk, Siberia. Bush spoke with Baker at 7:35 A.M. Half an hour later, at 8:05 A.M. on Thursday, August 2, 1990—not quite twelve hours since Bush was first informed of the invasion—the president joined the National Security Council in the Cabinet Room. The press pool was invited in. "We call for the immediate and unconditional withdrawal of all the Iraqi forces," Bush told the reporters.

Helen Thomas of UPI asked the first question. "Do you contemplate intervention as one of your options?"

"We're not discussing intervention," Bush said. "I would not discuss any military options even if we'd agreed upon them. But one of the things I want to do at this meeting is hear from our Secretary of Defense, our Chairman, and others. But I'm not contemplating such action."

Thomas pressed again. "You're not contemplating any intervention or sending troops?"

"I'm not contemplating such action," Bush replied, "and I again would not discuss it if I were."

A classic Bush answer: He claimed he wasn't doing something, but that if he were he wouldn't admit it. Still, by twice saying that he was not contemplating intervention, Bush signaled that the United States might not be fully committed to reversing the Iraqi aggression.

Why did Bush say what he said? "The truth is, at that moment I had no idea what our options were," Bush recalled later. "What I hoped to convey was an open mind about how we might handle the situation until I learned all the facts."

Some evidence of Bush's evolution on Iraq can be found in his diary from Thursday, August 2, through Sunday, August 5. In it, Bush records several of the dozens of calls he made to countries around the Persian

Gulf region and around the world. In those conversations, particularly with the Saudis, the president believed he detected an Arab openness to an accommodation with Saddam that would expand Iraq's power and reward Iraq's military strike. The source of a key percentage of the world's oil reserves, the world's largest exporter of oil, and an essential American ally, Saudi Arabia was a vital U.S. national interest. Part of Bush's determination to liberate Kuwait from Saddam was connected to his view that perhaps Saudi Arabia needed protection from its own potential willingness to coexist with an expanded Iraq. As Bush put it to Margaret Thatcher, "My fear is of hand-wringing by offering a payoff to Saddam Hussein."

After the press left, the National Security Council meeting on the morning of August 2, was, Bush and Scowcroft recalled, "a bit chaotic." It was also unwieldy: There were twenty-nine participants at the meeting across eleven different executive departments or agencies.

The implications of the invasion were only slowly becoming apparent. "It was a big thing that had happened, and people needed time to digest it," Richard Haass recalled. "The people who were in the room hadn't quite realized that this was not business as usual. It was a rambling conversation." Much of the talk seemed to assume that an Iraqi-controlled Kuwait was "a fait accompli," recalled a more hawkish Scowcroft, who described himself as "appalled" by those who saw the invasion as simply a "crisis du jour" rather than as perhaps "the major crisis of our time." Bush later captured the initial prevailing view from the meeting in a diary entry: "It's halfway around the world; U.S. options are limited; and all in all it is a highly complicated situation."

"That was one of the worst meetings I've ever sat through," Haass told Scowcroft.

"I agree," Scowcroft said. "Write me a memo about why we have to act."

Bush's shift from the confusion of the first NSC meeting to a more determined view that the aggression against Kuwait had to be undone, not accommodated, appears to have begun aboard a government C-20 Gulfstream jet heading west from Washington to Aspen, Colorado, later on the morning of August 2. (The usual Air Force One was too large to land at Aspen.) Bush left at 9:50 A.M. to fly out for a meeting with

Thatcher and a previously scheduled speech on military strategy in a post–Cold War world. With Scowcroft on board with him, Bush worked the telephones from the plane. What he was hearing from the Arab world was not reassuring. King Hussein of Jordan asked for more time to work things out with Saddam ("I really implore you, sir, to keep calm," Hussein said), as did President Mubarak of Egypt ("George, give us two days to find a solution," Mubarak said).

Meanwhile, the American intelligence and policy apparatus was painting a grimmer portrait of the consequences of leaving Saddam with an Iraq that included Kuwait. As Bush and Scowcroft flew to Colorado, Haass was back in his office drafting the case for a vigorous response. "I am aware as you are of just how costly and risky such a conflict would prove to be," Haass wrote. "But so too would be accepting this new status quo. We would be setting a terrible precedent—one that would only accelerate violent centrifugal tendencies—in this emerging 'post–Cold War' era." At the Pentagon that same afternoon, Dick Cheney was musing on a yellow legal pad. "Shouldn't our objective be to get him out of Kuwait?" Cheney wrote in notes to himself. "Isn't that the best short and long term strategy?" Sanctions, which had been discussed at the NSC meeting, were unlikely to be enough. "No non-military option is likely to produce any positive result," Cheney wrote. "The key," he added, was "U.S. military power—the only thing Hussein fears."

In Colorado, Bush sat down with Thatcher at the Aspen home of Henry Catto, Jr., the American ambassador to Britain. Bush told Thatcher that Baker and Shevardnadze were working on a U.S.-Soviet statement to denounce Saddam's aggression, and briefed her on his conversations with King Hussein and Mubarak. "I said we couldn't accept the status quo," Bush told Thatcher. "It had to be withdrawal and the restoration of the Kuwaiti government." Bush also told the prime minister that a carrier group was en route to the Persian Gulf from Diego Garcia.

"If Iraq wins, no small state is safe," Thatcher told Bush. "They won't stop here. They see a chance to take a major share of oil. It's got to be stopped. We must do everything possible." They discussed international sanctions, especially on oil sales. Perhaps the combination of an oil embargo and a naval blockade would be sufficient.

Then they met the press. Bush said that he and Thatcher were "concerned about this naked aggression, condemning it, and hoping that a peaceful solution will be found that will result in the restoration of the Kuwaiti leaders to their rightful place and, prior to that, a withdrawal of Iraqi forces."

Thatcher echoed the point in stentorian tones. "Iraq has violated and taken over the territory of a country which is a full member of the United Nations. That is totally unacceptable, and if it were allowed to endure, then there would be many other small countries that could never feel safe."

In the joint appearance with Thatcher, Bush gave the answer to the military question that he should have given that morning in Washington. "And we're not ruling any options in," Bush said, "but we're not ruling any options out."

Later in the afternoon, in a large tent at the Aspen Institute, Bush spoke newly relevant words—some of which had been drafted and redrafted on the flight from Washington. "Even in a world where democracy and freedom have made great gains, threats remain," Bush said. "Terrorism, hostage taking, renegade regimes and unpredictable rulers, new sources of instability—all require a strong and an engaged America." After the speech Bush returned to the Cattos' and adjourned to their bedroom for a telephone call with King Fahd of Saudi Arabia. Fahd was "emotional," Bush recalled, and furious with Saddam. "He doesn't realize that the implications of his actions are upsetting the world order," Fahd told Bush. "He seems to think only of himself. He is following Hitler in creating world problems. . . . I believe nothing will work with Saddam but the use of force."

Tough words, yet when Bush offered Fahd a squadron of American F-15s, Fahd asked for more time before accepting. He "held back a little bit," Bush told his diary, "and I worry that somehow they'll try to buy a solution, or they will accept the status quo with guarantees that nothing happen to Saudi Arabia. In the meantime, the Iraqi forces are going south." As Bush recalled, "King Fahd's hesitation rang alarm bells in my head. I began to worry that the Saudis might be considering compromise, that they might accept the new status quo on their northern border if there were guarantees from Iraq." There was, Bush knew, "a historical Arab propensity to try to work out 'deals.' . . . In these early hours of the crisis, with so much going on, I had to wonder if, under pressure, they might be inclined to strike some kind of behind-the-scenes arrangement with Saddam."

Bush didn't know, but he did know this: "We couldn't have a solo U.S. effort in the Middle East. We had to have our Arab allies with us, particularly those who were threatened the most—the Saudis."

Bush headed back to Washington, landing at Andrews around 2:30 in the morning. At the White House, after only a few hours' sleep, Bush walked into the Oval Office. It was 7:45 A.M. on Friday, August 3, 1990, and the president of the United States had a more definitive view of the crisis than he had had twenty-four hours before. "The enormity of Iraq is upon me now," Bush told his diary. "The status quo is intolerable."

William Webster, the CIA director, briefed the National Security Council on Saddam that morning. "All the intelligence shows he won't pull out," Webster said. "He will stay if not challenged within the next year. This will fundamentally alter the Persian Gulf region. He would be in an inequitable position, since he would control the second- and third-largest proven oil reserves with the fourth-largest army in the world." (In 1990 terms of oil, Webster was ranking Saudi Arabia first, with Iraq and Kuwait as second and third.)

The Arab reluctance Bush had sensed on Thursday, August 2, was more evident as time passed. "The Arabs don't seem to have the resolve," he told his diary on Friday, August 3. Yemen's Ali Abdullah Saleh, an ally of Saddam's, tried to compare Saddam's move against Kuwait to the American military action against Marxist rebellion leaders on Grenada in 1983. Bush snapped at Saleh over the analogy. "Saleh got me a little mad by mentioning Grenada."

"Let me tell you something," Bush recalled saying. "American lives were at stake then, and make very clear to your friend Saddam Hussein that any risk to American life will have serious consequences."

The Saudis were the largest worry. "Fears mount that the Saudis may acquiesce in a buy-out—Iraq withdraws and Kuwait pays [the Iraqis] off," Bush told his diary on August 3. "[We're] trying to stiffen the spine of the Saudis." Bush's roughly daylong journey on the significance of the invasion was in character. Tempered by long experience, his instinct was to do the prudent thing. From the Reagan assassination attempt to the fall of the Berlin Wall, he had learned that care went a long way in politics and in statecraft. Would the story of the Gulf War be nobler, even more Churchillian, had Bush declared his implacable will on the first morning of the crisis? Yes, it would, but it took Bush only a single day to decide that he needed to undo what had been done by Saddam.

On Saturday, August 4, 1990, Bush convened his top military advisers at Camp David to explore how to defend Saudi Arabia and how the United States, with allies, might enforce an economic embargo. Bush still worried about King Hussein and President Mubarak. "Both of them are in the hand-wringing stage, and neither of them is being a constructive influence for positive action by the West, by the United States, or by the Arabs themselves," Bush told his diary. "The bottom line is a lot of these Arab countries are scared to death of Saddam Hussein."

Saudi Arabia remained an enigma, skeptical about the depth of American commitment. Hence dodgy, vague replies from Fahd to Bush—a dodginess whose roots had become clearer on Friday the third, when, just after eleven A.M., Prince Bandar, the Saudi ambassador to the United States and a member of the Saudi royal family, called on Scowcroft at the White House. A popular diplomat in Washington, the charming, cigar-smoking Bandar was a glamorous figure—a former fighter pilot who entertained grandly in America at mansions in McLean and in Aspen. After laying out the threat that the administration believed the Saudis faced, Scowcroft offered U.S. forces for the defense of the kingdom, only to find Bandar cold to the overture. "He seemed ill at ease and did not react with enthusiasm to the suggestion," recalled Scowcroft, who asked: Why the reluctance?

Bandar was candid, offering two examples where the Saudis believed America had not followed through on their word. The first was during the 1979 Iranian Revolution, when the United States dispatched F-15s to Saudi Arabia only to announce that the fighters were unarmed. The second came during the deployment of U.S. Marines in Beirut in the early 1980s—a deployment that ended after the 1983 terrorist attack on the marine barracks. As Scowcroft recalled Bandar's point, "Why should the King not be concerned that, if the going got tough, the United States would behave in the same manner once again?" Scowcroft tried to reassure Bandar and sent him over to Cheney and Powell at the Pentagon for a briefing on American plans, which impressively called for 150,000 to 200,000 troops. "We're serious this time," Cheney told Bandar.

The secretary of defense then underscored the point: "We didn't have time to wait while Saddam gathered strength and planned his next move"—a strike against the Saudis. The Americans wanted to deploy, and deploy quickly, to defend the kingdom, and a huge amount of the world's oil, from further Iraqi aggression. (There were also Saudi concerns about Muslim reaction to the presence of U.S. troops in a kingdom that was home to essential Islamic holy places.)

The weekend was a critical moment in the crisis, and the Saudis felt themselves caught between Saddam and Bush. Had Saddam chosen to do so, he most likely could have moved into the kingdom in this period and seized control over at least some Saudi territory. "My worry is the lack of Saudi will," Bush told the National Security Council that weekend. On Saturday, August 4, 1990, Fahd agreed to receive a senior American team in Saudi Arabia for consultations. Still, the king continued to evade the question of whether the Saudis would accept U.S. troops. Such issues, he suggested, could be settled in talks with the American delegation—not before.

On the telephone, Bush took Fahd's doubts on directly. "We will get the team under way," Bush told Fahd. "Another point I want to make here involves a word of honor. The security of Saudi Arabia is vital—basically fundamental—to U.S. interests and really to the interests of the Western world. And I am determined that Saddam will not get away with all this infamy. When we work out a plan, once we are there, we will stay until we are asked to leave. You have my solemn word on this."

On Sunday morning, August 5, while Bush was at Camp David, Bandar met with Scowcroft and Haass at the White House. The Saudis, Scowcroft told Bandar, "had a choice between being defended and being liberated," Haass recalled. While Bandar was talking with the highest officials of the American government, he was also, according to Bush, working the other side of the equation: Word reached the president that Bandar had apparently asked Turkey to delay doing anything that might exacerbate the situation or antagonize Saddam. "Bandar has double-dealt us with the Turks, trying to talk them into not taking any action," Bush told his diary on that Sunday. "At the same time the King is telling me 'I agree, I agree, I agree with cracking down on [the] economic front, and on everything else.' He did stop short of saying he would close down that ... [Iraqi] pipeline [through Saudi Arabia], however."

There was a wrinkle as the weekend went on: Because Cheney was slated to head the delegation to Saudi Arabia, the Americans decided to insist on prior assurance that the kingdom would accept what the secretary of defense had to offer: U.S. troops. (As Scowcroft recalled, "A Saudi rejection could trigger a crisis, in the sense that the inability of our two countries to cooperate would further encourage Saddam's aggression.") Prince Bandar, himself finally convinced, made a call home from Scowcroft's office urging that the kingdom accept the American offer. Fahd agreed: Cheney—and U.S. forces—would be welcome in Saudi Arabia.

The story of Saudi skepticism, however, was not quite over. After Cheney arrived in Saudi Arabia, with Bandar doing the interpreting, Crown Prince Abdullah, a half brother of Fahd's, argued for waiting before accepting U.S. forces even though the king had already agreed to do so as a condition of Cheney's mission. Fahd brushed Abdullah's words aside: "The Kuwaitis waited and now they are living in our hotels." He turned to Cheney and confirmed: "Okay, we'll do it. Two conditions. One, you will bring enough to do the job, and two, you will leave when it's over." On behalf of the president, Cheney agreed, and soon U.S. forces were on the ground in Saudi Arabia.

Bush canceled a scheduled Sunday golf match with Scowcroft, Nick Brady, and Sam Nunn. Around two thirty in the afternoon, as he prepared to return to the White House from Camp David, much was uncertain. The Chinese had agreed to stop weapons sales to Iraq, but it was unclear whether Beijing would join in a total sanctions regime. There was an upcoming vote on international sanctions at the United Nations, and Bush did not know how it would turn out.

Most urgently, "I don't know whether the Iraqis are going to move across the border into Saudi Arabia," he told his diary at midafternoon on August 5. "If they did, they'd have a free run. Saudi forces are not at the border, and of course, Iraq has overwhelming superiority. The Saudis have some air power and the Kuwaiti airplanes flew to Saudi Arabia. But God knows whether they'll even use them. Whether they'll stand up."

As Marine One flew from Camp David back to the White House that Sunday, Bush was thinking of past and present. "It's been probably the most hectic forty-eight hours since I have been President in terms of serious national security interests," he dictated. "I have been on the phone incessantly, and have written down a long collection of names. The bottom line is that the West is together."

Aboard the helicopter, bound for the South Lawn, Bush had a moment of clarity, an instant in which the stakes of the hour were sharply, even scarily, defined. "This is a terribly serious problem, it's perhaps the most serious problem that I have faced as President because the downside is so enormous," Bush dictated on Marine One. "If indeed the Iraqis went in and got a hold of Saudi Arabia, and our objective then was to free Saudi Arabia, we would really be involved in something that could have the magnitude of a new world war, with so many countries involved."

A new world war: With this thought in his mind—the thought that failure to confront Saddam now, in Kuwait, could lead to a wider, bloodier, and chaotic cataclysm—Bush stepped off the helicopter and walked down the steps to the White House lawn. He was met by Richard Haass, who handed him an update on the most recent diplomatic moves—a report that included a series of wishy-washy quotations from different Arab governments about what should happen next.

Bush knew what should happen next. Saddam Hussein had challenged Bush's universe, a post–Cold War world of order and balance, and the president of the United States was not interested in allowing a dictator to destroy a unique historical moment. Confront the aggression now, Bush thought, or else a world that had thought itself finally free of the threat of nuclear conflict could face a disastrous war in the Middle East—and wars of any size, Bush knew, could become bigger wars.

To the press on the South Lawn he described, in general terms, the diplomatic activity of recent hours, and then, in response to a question about protecting Americans in Kuwait, all the drive and all the determination that had been building over the previous eighty or so hours came tumbling out in a clear, heartfelt paragraph of spoken prose:

> I'm not going to discuss what we're doing in terms of moving of forces, anything of that nature. But I view it very seriously, not just that but any threat to any other countries, as well as I view very seriously our determination to reverse out this aggression. And please believe me, there are an awful lot of countries that are in total accord with what I've just said, and I salute them. They are staunch friends and allies, and we will be working with them all for

collective action. This will not stand. This will not stand, this aggression against Kuwait.

The last two sentences of Bush's remarks endure in popular memory. Revealing, too, were his parting words: "I've got to go. I have to go to work. I've got to go to work."

THIRTY-EIGHT

No Blood for Oil

★

I can't see how we can get out of it without punishing Iraq.
—GEORGE H. W. BUSH

AFTER SPEAKING WITH THE PRESS, Bush walked into the West Wing to prepare for a five P.M. National Security Council meeting. His own men had been surprised by the certitude of their chief's words on the South Lawn. They had not been privy to his musings on Marine One; no one except Bush himself quite understood the thinking that had led him to his resolution.

"How'd I do?" Bush asked Quayle and Scowcroft, who were with him in the Oval Office before the NSC meeting. His lieutenants praised him. Then Scowcroft asked the question on everyone's mind: "Where'd you get that 'This will not stand'?"

"That's mine. . . . That's what I feel."

In the world outside the White House walls, "This will not stand" was being played on CNN and parsed around the globe. "It was a very, very definitive line," Quayle recalled. The president's statement, Quayle added, had "caught everybody off guard a little bit because it was so definite and so dramatic."

Colin Powell, who had been watching Bush's arrival at the White House from home before leaving for the National Security Council session, sat straight up when he heard Bush's declaration. "I just got a new mission," Powell thought.

Half a world away, on Monday, August 6, 1990, Dick Cheney paid his call on King Fahd, who, as arranged, invited the offered U.S. forces and aircraft to Saudi Arabian soil. "Dick, you are authorized to go ahead and execute," Bush told the secretary of defense by telephone.

It was a momentous hour. "I feel great pressure, but I also feel a certain calmness when we talk about these matters," Bush told his diary on Monday, August 6. "I know I am doing the right thing. I know that the

United States not only has to take a stand, but has to lead the rest of the world." The same day brought Saddam's first direct words to the United States since the invasion. The American embassy in Baghdad cabled Saddam's threats back to Washington. "Convey to President Bush," Saddam said, "that he should regard the Kuwaiti Emir and Crown Prince as history. . . . We will never leave Kuwait for someone else to take. . . . We would fight on. . . . We will never capitulate."

Watching Bush from London and taking in "This will not stand" and the permission to deploy to Saudi Arabia, Margaret Thatcher was impressed.

"Thanks for your leadership," Bush said to Thatcher at the end of a call on Thursday, August 9.

"It was your leadership," Thatcher replied. "I was just a chum."

Brian Mulroney of Canada came down to dine at the White House with the president. Bush, who enjoyed Mulroney's company, overindulged, drinking two martinis and a big dinner with four popovers. "I pay the price at night," Bush told his diary. "The gut [is] ripped up."

Around a quarter till three on the morning of Tuesday, August 7, 1990, Bush, his stomach churning from dinner and drink, woke to place a call to François Mitterrand. The previous afternoon, Manfred Wörner, the secretary-general of NATO, had warned Bush that the French might not support the use of NATO outside of Europe. After hearing Bush out, Mitterrand simply said, "We will be there." To his diary, Bush confided: "Mitterrand surprises a lot of times. I still feel the visit I had with him in Kennebunkport, and the respect I have tried to show him personally, pay off in diplomacy. I know some differ with this personal diplomacy, but I think when you can talk from a basis of friendship, it does help; and I think he knows I respect him."

Next was a call to Mubarak in Cairo at 2:55 A.M. Washington time. Would the Egyptian president receive the Cheney delegation after it left Saudi Arabia? Mubarak, who was now in sync with Bush, said "of course," and he and the president shared their mutual unhappiness with King Hussein of Jordan. "He thought King Hussein wanted money from Saddam Hussein and the same for Saleh of Yemen," Bush dictated.

Bush's diplomatic calls were done by 3:30 A.M., and he wondered whether he could fall back asleep. He was, as ever, annoyed by the press. Everybody had an opinion, everybody thought they could do things better than Bush and his team. "I'm saying to myself: What do these guys know? We're doing our best, working hard, trying to lead the whole world in facing an enormous crisis and you get sniped at." In earlier years Bush thought the press criticism would have been "deeply disturbing" to him; now he found it "irritating" rather than worrying. "I get p.o.'d rather than deeply angered," he noted. "I guess any President has to get used to that, has to know that he has to take the criticism. Then, too, you [are] always reminded of the 'pack,' and how the 'pack' works. They write the same things, say the same things, rub their hands in the same concerned way, yell the same way now on these talk shows. Enough of that—3:30 in the morning."

The worries he had turned over in his mind on Marine One on the previous Sunday—about a possible world war—were still with him as the forces he had dispatched moved into the region. The first Americans were about to enter Saudi Arabia to begin Desert Shield, a military operation designed to protect the Saudis from Saddam. "The troops are under way," Bush told his diary. It was, he added, "the biggest step of my Presidency."

Just before nine o'clock on the morning of Wednesday, August 8, 1990, Bush addressed the nation formally for the first time on the Persian Gulf. To check his nerves, he held out his arm. "I did this to see if I was steady, and I was pleased that it did not shake," he told his diary. "I know I'm not near as good as President Reagan on these situations, but I felt it was important to do a good job. . . . I made a few last minute changes, tightened up the language to make it a little more like the Rhineland in the '30s"—a historical reference that would resonate with his own generation.

As he got the signal to begin, Bush looked into the camera from behind his desk in the Oval Office and spoke steadily yet urgently. "Appeasement does not work," he said. "As was the case in the 1930s, we see in Saddam Hussein an aggressive dictator threatening his neighbors." To Bush, the secret of diplomacy was what he believed to be the secret to a happy life: friends, relationships, reaching out, not pushing away. To the nation he spoke of coalition building and of international opinion. The deployment of American troops to Saudi Arabia was no imperial adventure; it was, rather, the result of assiduous work over the previous six days—for Bush, six of the most crowded days in a crowded life. The president made clear that American warriors were touching down in a faraway kingdom with the support and sanction of a symphony of nations: In the end, thirty-five countries would join the Bush-led coalition by contributing militarily: Afghanistan, Argentina, Australia, Bahrain, Bangladesh, Canada, Czechoslovakia, Denmark, Egypt, France, Germany, Greece, Honduras, Hungary, Italy, Kuwait, Morocco, the Netherlands, New Zealand, Niger, Norway, Oman, Pakistan, Poland, Portugal, Qatar, Saudi Arabia, Senegal, South Korea, Spain, Syria, Turkey, the United Arab Emirates, the United Kingdom, and the United States. The Soviet Union and China were diplomatically supportive.

Resisting advice that he remain in Washington, Bush took off for his annual vacation in Maine. On the Gulf, the public was with Bush—for now. "The press are sniping away at the cost, and the 'support is shaky, and it could turn against the President, and it could be the end of him,'" Bush told his diary on Saturday, August 11, 1990. Saddam seemed a strong and resilient foe. With a large army, a proven willingness to use chemical weapons, and worries that he might develop nuclear arms, Iraq posed significant threats on the ground, and many critics warned, ominously, of a disaster in the desert.

Still, Bush was in his element. "I like wrestling with the foreign policy agenda," he told his diary. "I don't like the negotiations on the budget. I like dealing with world leaders on a positive plane, even in difficult situations."

The busiest of days at Walker's Point began in sadness. Dr. John Walker—Dorothy's brother, the president's uncle—died in the hospital at Biddeford, Maine, about six thirty in the morning on Thursday, August 16, 1990. A distinguished surgeon who had long battled polio, Walker had been the doctor who urged the Bushes to seek treatment for Robin, and he had inspired Bush all his life.

Later that morning King Hussein of Jordan, whom Bush thought was too close to Saddam, arrived by helicopter. Bush sat down with him, and the exchanges were frank. The king pressed for an accommodation with Iraq, but Bush refused to compromise. "There isn't any" middle ground, Bush told the king. "It's got to be withdrawal and restoration of the Kuwaiti regime. There cannot be any middle ground, because tomorrow, it will be somebody else's aggression." There was nothing either man could say to move the other. "Hussein refuses to admit that this is a madman,"

Bush dictated, and for Bush that recognition was becoming a threshold question. "This is not just a U.S. prob[lem]," Bush told King Hussein. "The world is outraged by what [Saddam] has done." The Jordanian king left about two thirty, to be followed by Prince Saud, the Saudi foreign minister, and Bandar. The Saudis now wanted rapid military action. "God knows it may come to that," Bush told his diary.

The taking of American hostages was among Bush's most persistent fears. "I am determined that I could not be a Jimmy Carter—an impotent, flicking U.S. impotence in the eyes of the world," he told his diary on Thursday, August 16. Then, at a quarter to ten on the evening of Friday, August 17, Bush received a call at Walker's Point: The Iraqis had announced they were detaining foreigners to serve as what were known as "human shields" near "strategic sites" such as chemical plants. The news was infuriating. "Blatant hostage holding," Bush told his diary. "Another blatant disregard of international law by a cruel and ruthless dictator. I cannot tolerate, nor will I, another 'Tehran.' I am determined in that."

Soon Bush had to make a real-time military call amid reports that the Iraqis had sent five tankers to Yemen in defiance of the UN embargo against Iraq. The president wanted the U.S. Navy to open fire on the vessels, but the French and the Soviets wanted to hold off until there could be an explicit UN Security Council vote to authorize "all appropriate measures," which would include lethal action.

The president, Scowcroft, Cheney, and Bob Gates pushed to act unilaterally without going back to the United Nations. Baker, concerned about keeping the Soviets in the coalition, argued for waiting. Bush heard Baker out and reluctantly agreed. It fell to Bush to call Margaret Thatcher and tell her his decision. Hawkish as ever, Thatcher thought the French and Soviet reservations were manifestations of a weakness that had no place in a sturdy alliance against Saddam. Bush admitted that he "wasn't looking forward to" the call, but he made it. Reached in the middle of the night London time, Thatcher heard the president out and replied, "Well, all right, George, but this is no time to go wobbly." (Bush thought it a "marvelous expression.") The UN Security Council quickly passed the enforcement resolution. By waiting, Baker had successfully addressed the French and Soviet concerns while winning the authority Bush and Thatcher wanted. ("In the meantime, the tankers had reached Yemen," Bush biographer Timothy Naftali observed, "but with its broader objective achieved, Washington no longer cared.")

As Bush saw it, Saddam Hussein was an unreliable actor—a liar. The Iraqi had lied about his intentions toward Kuwait and had taken American hostages. As someone who believed one's word was fundamental to relations between men and nations, Bush believed that he was dealing with an uncontrollable force. "The more I think of this on this beautiful morning . . . I can't see how we can get out of it without punishing Iraq," he dictated on Wednesday, August 22, 1990. "What they are doing is unprincipled."

Bush called the Situation Room in the White House every morning at five or five thirty to check the overnight news. He was never out of contact as he managed the Persian Gulf from Kennebunkport. Nevertheless, there were stories that Bush was, as he put it when describing the conventional wisdom, golfing, fishing, and "playing while Rome burns."

On a fishing excursion for bluefish on the Atlantic, Bush and Scowcroft had one of the more important conversations of the Gulf crisis. After zooming out from the dock at Walker's Point, Bush stopped *Fidelity* and the two men tried their luck. For four hours, cooled by ocean breezes, they discussed the particular and the general. Bush made clear that he was farther down the road toward the use of force than other top American officials. "I asked impatiently when we could strike," Bush recalled.

The broader conversation touched on what kind of era the world was entering. Absent a compelling superpower rivalry, had Franklin Roosevelt's old vision of an effective UN Security Council come into being? Perhaps a "new world order" was at hand, or at least one that would protect small states from larger ones.

For the moment, on the gentle Atlantic, the boat rocking quietly, there was hope, great hope, that George H. W. Bush could shape a better world than the one in which he had lived all his life.

Summer was ending. Ronald Reagan, who was about to travel to Germany, wrote Bush a note of condolence about the death of John Walker, and Bush called the former president to thank him. "He's looking forward to his trip to Berlin—about the Wall, etc.," Bush told his diary. "He will be gone for about 10 days. He and Nancy went to Nassau for two weeks. I said, 'How was it?' and he said, 'It was unusual to put on your trunks and sit in the sun for two weeks.'"

Bush himself was refreshed and sleeping well. "When I was younger, I'd wake up all night long worrying, but now once asleep, I'm asleep; and when I wake up, it comes flashing back in all detail," Bush told his diary on Monday, August 27. "But for some reason, maybe it's I'm getting older, I can put matters out of mind when I'm asleep. It's quite different than in the Zapata days, when I'd thrash around all night long, and I would get an ulcer. My gut has been behaving very well, and I guess it boils right back down to 'do your best.'" At sixty-six years old, the commander in chief of a nation headed for war, he had yet to find any advice that trumped the counsel that his mother had given him as he grew up.

On Wednesday, August 29, 1990, the president woke to news from the Situation Room that the Iraqis appeared to be "realigning their troops." This was promising: Iraq might give U.S. forces a pretext for action. "The more I think of it," Bush told his diary, "the more I would love to have an incident so we could execute a devastating attack against Iraqi armor and Iraqi air." Bush's view of Saddam was now set in black and white. "It has been personalized," Bush dictated. "He is the epitome of evil."

In September, Bush traveled to Helsinki for a meeting with Gorbachev on the Persian Gulf crisis. Bush had a clear message: The Soviets needed to stay with the United States on Iraq. The Soviets were wary of striking Saddam; Iraq was a longtime client state of Moscow's in the Middle East. "I think it's important to Gorby that he seem to be with us in all of this," Bush told his diary.

In Helsinki, Bush reflected on the nature of American leadership on his watch. Gregarious and inclusive by nature, he conducted the presidency in keeping with these essential elements of his own character. The man who could almost never be alone was creating a coalition out of disparate nations—including the Soviet Union—through frenetic yet effective personal diplomacy. "All countries in the West clearly have to turn to us," he told his diary, "but it is my theory that the more they are included on the take-off, the more we get their opinion, the more we reach out, no matter what is involved in terms of time involved, the better it is. Everyone is proud. Everyone has his place in the sun—large country or small, they should be consulted, their opinions considered. And then when the United States makes a move and I make a decision, we are more apt to have solid support."

For the moment, Bush was enjoying something rare for him in public life: wide acclaim. He talked about it in his diary with a kind of wonder. "The hard-hats charge out from their trailers or from the building projects, the waiters, the people in the stores, and you hear, 'Go for it, George.' 'Give 'em hell, George.' From parking attendants, the airplane service people. It is strong support."

But he remained attuned to the vicissitudes of public and congressional will: "You know how I feel about polls, dear diary. I think they come and go, and we can be up and down. And, yes, I am pleased with the amount of support that I'm getting, but I know it can change fast." As if on cue, *The New York Times* published a story on Thursday, September 20, 1990, headlined "Criticism of U.S. Policy in Gulf Growing Louder in Congress." It detailed opposition to a Cheney effort to allow him to spend allied funds "as the Secretary deems appropriate," without the approval of Congress. Other lawmakers protested the administration's proposal to forgive $7 billion in debt to Egypt on the grounds that it looked as though the United States "were buying Cairo's support." The largest question of all was whether the administration would come to Congress for approval to undertake military action. The *Times* quoted Representative Les Aspin, a Wisconsin Democrat, saying that Bush "has no mandate yet to go to war."

Antiwar sentiment grew apace, driven in large measure by the cry "No Blood for Oil." Such demonstrations created an uneasy atmosphere as Bush imposed sanctions and prepared for the possibility—even the likelihood—of war.

Fears about war were not confined to the press or to street demonstrations. The innately cautious Jim Baker felt a duty to raise profound concerns with his old friend. "Jim Baker is worried that we will get bogged down in another Vietnam," Bush had told his diary in mid-August, "and lose the support of the people, and have the Bush presidency destroyed." After a meeting on Iraq at Camp David, Baker and Dan Quayle shared a golf cart to the helicopter pad. "Jim," Quayle asked, "what do you really think about it?"

"I don't know," Baker said. "It's a big gamble."

"Would you put your presidency on the line for this?" Quayle asked. Recalling the exchange, Quayle concluded: "Neither one of us had an answer to that."

These doubts and concerns were coming as Bush was reading an in-

telligence report on Saturday, September 22 about Iraqi abuses in occupied Kuwait: "Shooting citizens when they are stopped in their cars;
exporting what little food there is; brutalizing the homes." He was clear
in his own mind about what had to happen. "This just hardens my resolve," he dictated in the fourth week of September, "and I am wondering if we need to speed up the timetable."

The president had addressed Congress on the evening of Tuesday,
September 11, 1990, on the spiraling crises of the Gulf and of the
budget. "It is said of me that I much prefer to work on international affairs," Bush told his diary that afternoon. "Well, I am fully engrossed in
this international crisis, and I must say I enjoy working all the parts of it
and I get into much more detail than I do on the domestic scene. So I
think the answer is I do prefer this, but I see a budget deficit as very
important—something essential to solve."

In the midst of preparations for the largest and most complex American military operation in a generation, Bush, the leader of a global coalition attempting to bend a faraway dictator to his will, had first to put his
own nation's fiscal house in order.

THIRTY-NINE

Read My Hips

★

*I can't do this. It breaks your word, and it's a mistake,
and I won't do it.*

—NEWT GINGRICH to Bush on the 1990 budget agreement

*They can pontificate, but somebody has to compromise,
and someone has to make a deal.*

—BUSH, on the Gingrich-led conservative revolt over taxes

USH HAD CONVENED closed-door negotiations over the 1991 federal budget at Andrews Air Force Base on the same day he'd flown
to Helsinki to see Gorbachev. "I just hope that Iraq and the country's unity can now be parlayed into support for the budget agreement,"
Bush told his diary. His major concerns: a government shutdown if no
deal was reached by October and the fear that the absence of a budget
would roil the markets and exacerbate a recession, which was being predicted for later in 1990—all weakening the United States at an hour it
needed to show the world that it was strong and united at home.

No deal meant chaos—and Bush, a man of order, hated chaos. He was
less interested in the political price of breaking "Read my lips" than he
was in passing a budget that would attack the deficit and be credible to
the Federal Reserve and to the markets. "Lord, I've got two years to re-
cover from this grief, and the main thing is to get the job done," Bush
had told House Speaker Tom Foley during a private lunch in August.

In his address to the joint session on September 11, Bush had explained that "I want to be able to tell the American people that we have
truly solved the deficit problem. And for me to do that, a budget agreement must meet these tests: It must include the measures I've recommended to increase economic growth and reduce dependence on foreign
oil. It must be fair. All should contribute, but the burden should not be
excessive for any one group of programs or people. It must address the
growth of government's hidden liabilities. It must reform the budget

process and, further, it must be real." His "tests" were: "growth-oriented tax measures," especially a capital gains tax cut; a long-term defense budget plan; and a five-year debt and deficit reduction plan amounting to $500 billion.

On Sunday, September 30, 1990, three weeks after the Andrews talks opened, the administration and the congressional leadership came to agreement. In New York for the opening of the General Assembly of the United Nations, the president returned to Washington. The deal was not perfect, but it had its virtues—among them bipartisan support from the mainstreams of both parties. The agreement would have cut the projected deficit by $500 billion over five years, with money to be found in Medicare savings and other federal entitlement programs. The proposal left marginal income tax rates unchanged, but increased taxes on gas, tobacco, and alcohol—thus violating "Read my lips." Most important, perhaps, the agreement established pay-as-you-go rules that required future administrations and Congresses to ensure that new appropriations were paid for rather than simply being funded by deficit-increasing borrowing.

Though he had been part of the talks, Newt Gingrich could not abide the deal and rebelled against the president. In the session with Bush in the Cabinet Room just before the agreement was to be made public in the Rose Garden on September 30, Gingrich told the president: "I can't do this. It breaks your word, and it's a mistake, and I won't do it." He "had to give his pitch," Bush dictated to his diary. "He has no plan of his own. He just criticizes."

Gingrich represented a conservative worldview in which Ronald Reagan, the rightful king, had been replaced by Bush, a pale usurper who was betraying the tax-cutting principles on which the Republican presidential ascendancy of the 1980s had been built. "Bush was a Connecticut moderate Republican translated to Texas," Gingrich recalled. "He was probably a Ford Republican, really. I was a conservative Reaganite who wanted to take on the welfare state and defeat the Soviet Union. Bush was not viscerally opposed to the welfare state and had been more for managing the Soviet threat in the Cold War than he had been for rolling it back. Those are profound differences."

The shifting means of politics helped make the break with Bush possible. Because of talk radio and cable TV and sophisticated direct mail, Gingrich and his allies no longer needed the classic party apparatus in the way they once had. They could reach conservatives on their own, and many conservatives were responsive to populist messaging, even if that populist messaging targeted not just Democrats but establishment Republicans—including the most establishment Republican of them all, the president of the United States.

As Bush, Dole, and the other negotiators prepared to go outside with the president to announce the package, Gingrich declined to join them. "This annoyed me very much," Bush dictated, "but you gotta keep cool." The drive for a House majority through supply-side purity and populist appeals was more important to Gingrich and his colleagues than supporting their president—or even what was, arguably, good public policy. "What is good for the President may well be good for the country, but it is not necessarily good for congressional Republicans," Vin Weber had told *The Washington Post* in July 1990. "We need wedge issues to beat incumbent Democrats." Bush needed something different: an agreement that would control the deficit. And so out he went to the Rose Garden.

Standing with the other leaders, Bush did not hide his own ambivalence about the deal. "Sometimes you don't get it just the way you want, and this is such a time for me," Bush told reporters. "But it's time we put the interest of the United States of America first and get this deficit under control." As CNN broadcast the president's remarks, the network ran a split screen of Gingrich's exit on the other side of the White House, giving visual evidence to the split in Bush's own party. Congressman Bob Walker, another Gingrich ally, had been watching on TV. By the time Gingrich returned to Capitol Hill, Walker had organized a rally of House Republicans to cheer their rebel hero's triumphant return.

In the Rose Garden, Bush said that this was not a "phony," "smoke and mirrors deficit cutting program" but, rather, "real" compromise. The congressional leaders struck the "compromise" theme as well. For Bush, the time for fighting over "Read my lips" was long over. He had felt that way even before the Persian Gulf crisis; in the midst of the showdown with Saddam, the president had no interest in exacerbating partisan relations if he could help it. If he was going to lead the world community against Iraq and possibly take the United States to war, he would need congressional support. He did not believe he could afford to be intransigent or difficult over a campaign promise, even a serious one. Bush was then off again to New York. He had a dinner date with Margaret Thatcher.

After breaking his "Read my lips, no new taxes" pledge, Bush and the congressional leadership announced a bipartisan budget agreement on Sunday, September 30, 1990—only to have liberal Democrats and conservative Republicans blow the deal up in Congress.

The agreement that had raised taxes, Gingrich argued, was "totally unnecessary." He had a thought that Bush could find political salvation by reversing course once more. When the initial concession on taxes had been made in June, Saddam had not yet invaded Kuwait; everything was different now. Bush, Gingrich argued, should cite the war as an exigent circumstance and refuse to go along with the deal, challenging the Democrats to shut down the government in a time of preparations for war. "If he had just looked them in the eye, suspended the talks, and said we're going to hold a midterm saying, 'If you want more taxes, elect a Democratic Congress; if you don't, elect a Republican one,'" Gingrich recalled, "I think the Democrats would have blinked. They were not going to have a government shutdown with hundreds of thousands of troops in the field with tax increases at the heart of the debate." Bush could not imagine such a course. He had wanted the budget settled for the sake of fiscal order even before the Persian Gulf became an issue, and he was surely not going to let a midterm election create chaos with Americans in harm's way.

Beginning early on Monday, October 1, 1990, the administration did what it could to lobby conservative Republicans to stand with Bush on the budget vote. "We were struggling and working," he told his diary. "Opposition comes from the right wing." The battle was in the House, where Gingrich and his allies argued that voters would exact revenge on lawmakers who supported higher taxes. The debate evoked old memories for Bush: "Each Congressman thinks it is life or death, and my mind flips back [to how I felt when I voted,] as a matter of conscience, for the Open Housing Bill. I thought it was the end of the world. Predictions of defeat and disaster were terrible, but the district did not take it out on me." Late in the day on Wednesday, October 3, Bush got a call from Tom Foley, who said, "It's in trouble." Dan Rostenkowski called the president and tried to buck him up, saying in a "very confidential" conversation that Rosty, at least, "appreciated" what Bush was trying to do in the growth package. Then his old friend added: "You've got to get 51 percent, pal."

Bush knew that, and he was trying. "It is budget, budget, budget," Bush dictated on Thursday, October 4. On the day before, there had been some relief from the fiscal battles when Bush gathered the cabinet at 9:50 A.M. to offer congratulations to German chancellor Helmut Kohl on the unification of East and West. But the days were almost entirely taken up with what *USA Today* described as much "arm-twisting" of "disgruntled House Republicans . . . called to the White House for group sessions with Bush, Vice President Quayle and other top officials." To his diary, Bush confided: "Newt is out there, part of the leadership, saying he wasn't elected to support the President. [He is] simply out there saying he has to represent his district . . . and these right wingers love it. . . . It just makes me furious."

On the morning of the fourth the president held a meeting in the Residence with forty congressmen, rallying support. Later Foley gave Bush some bad news: The Democrats' left wing was as unhappy about the spending cuts as Bush's right wing was over the tax increases.

Bush was doing everything he could. "I am making phone call after phone call," he told his diary. He placed twenty on the morning of the vote, reaching fourteen of the lawmakers he tried to talk to. "Small time: one Congressman doesn't like an insurance provision, and another one is sore that I didn't mention his name while in Kansas in somebody else's district," Bush told his diary. "A lot of things come out when you get into this complicated environment. Trivial Pursuit." It was frustrating for Bush. He could mold an international coalition, but he could not convince members of his own party to back their president.

Vin Weber and other Republican lawmakers were talking things over in Sununu's West Wing office when Bush walked in and sat down at the chief of staff's conference table. A moment later, the television in the corner of the room reported some political news: Ed Rollins, the former Reagan campaign manager who was running the National Republican Congressional Committee, had issued new guidance to the GOP's midterm hopefuls. The message: "Do not hesitate to distance yourself from the President." A furious Bush slammed his fist down on the table. "I know what people say, that I'm a nice guy, but I'm not going to forget *that,*" the president said.

The Gingrich-led revolt on the right, joined by the left-wing revolt on the Democratic side, defeated the budget package on Friday, October 5, 1990. Bush was told that lawmakers "just stood around on the floor, stunned." The compromise was dead. Bush watched a couple of congressmen on television holding forth. "They can pontificate, but somebody has to compromise, and someone has to make a deal," Bush dictated. Yet the president had to conceal his anger. "We can't be vindictive," Bush told his diary, "and we can't look petty."

There was a partial government shutdown as congressional leaders raced to find a way forward. On Saturday, October 6, Bush was fretful. "Every Congressman can find a reason to oppose our deal, and so could I—I guess—if I were in Congress. . . . But sometimes you have to govern; you have to make things come together; you have to join with responsible leaders on both sides to get something done for the country."

While jogging with Jeb on a trip to Florida, Bush unwisely pointed to his backside and joked to reporters: "Read my hips"—a moment that made him seem unserious about breaking a central campaign promise. Bush realized he was in a largely untenable position. "Nobody is particularly happy with me," he told his diary. "I don't want a terrible deal to take place, but [I] don't want to be off in some ideological corner falling on my sword, and keeping the country from moving forward."

The budget agreement that Congress finally passed did what Bush's Andrews Air Force Base deal had not done: raise marginal income tax rates. (The Democrats had taken advantage of what Darman referred to as Bush's "weakened position" because of the GOP unrest.) Though the president was forced to increase the highest rate from 28 to 31 percent, he signed it into law on Monday, November 5, 1990—and the deal, while politically toxic for Bush, became, in Dick Darman's phrase, "the largest deficit-savings program ever enacted."

"I supported him on the budget deal," Bill Clinton recalled. "I thought he did the right thing. Bush 41 was the only Republican around who knew that anything that consistently defies arithmetic can't work for very long."

FORTY

The Threat of Impeachment

★

*If it starts dragging out and there's high casualties, I will be
history; [but] no problem—sometimes in life you've got to do
what you've got to do.*

—GEORGE H. W. BUSH

*I have a feeling that I need to pray, and yet I am not
certain my prayers are heard.*

—BUSH, on the eve of war

W AR PLANNING WAS A CONSTANT FEATURE of the fall of 1990.
Bush closely studied the charts the Pentagon prepared for
him. Sitting in the Oval Office, or in his West Wing study, or
in the Residence, he would gaze at the large maps, taking everything in.
Pressed by Dick Cheney, Joint Chiefs chairman Colin Powell and
CENTCOM commander Norman Schwarzkopf brought the president
a strategy to transform, if necessary, the defensive Operation Desert
Shield into an offensive Operation Desert Storm. Should Saddam fail to
withdraw from Kuwait by the UN-mandated deadline, the allies would
launch an initial air war to weaken Iraq's defenses and clear the way for
a ground assault to drive Iraqi troops from Kuwait.

Through the autumn months and into the new year of 1991, Bush
presided over a vast deployment to the Persian Gulf. He wanted more of
everything in place—more troops, more tanks, more planes, more, more,
more. The president sent half a million U.S. forces into the region. He
had thoroughly absorbed the post-Vietnam Powell Doctrine of American warfare, the list of criteria developed by both Powell and by former
secretary of defense Caspar Weinberger, whom Powell had served as
military assistant in the 1980s: Define the mission, then apply overwhelming force to carry it out.

Congressional Democrats in particular worried that Bush was hell-
bent on war. Why not give diplomacy and sanctions more time to work?

Wouldn't an isolated Saddam ultimately give in and allow the coalition to achieve its war aims without the risks of actual war? Bush did feel honor bound to pursue diplomacy, both personally and through the global efforts of Jim Baker, yet Bush, in his heart of hearts, worried that negotiations with Saddam might signal weakness. He particularly hated the idea of freelance diplomacy. "Word is still around that Jimmy Carter wants to be an emissary to Baghdad," Bush told his diary in midautumn. "Oh, God forbid—Oh, God forbid." (Carter later angered Bush by writing the other members of the UN Security Council, urging them to vote against the resolution seeking international sanction for the use of force.)

Bush encouraged military planning on the grounds that Saddam would, in the end, only understand force. "The final analysis: we will prevail," Bush dictated in the autumn. "Saddam Hussein will get out of Kuwait, and the United States will have been the catalyst and the key in getting this done, and that is important. Our role as world leader will once again have been reaffirmed, but if we compromise and if we fail, we would be reduced to total impotence, and that is not going to happen."

There was also the issue of the war-making power itself. Bush met with the congressional leadership at the White House on Wednesday, November 14, 1990. "There's great concern, if a decision is made unilaterally by you as President," Tom Foley told Bush. In Bush's notes from the meeting, Mitchell said the United States needed to give "sanctions time to work." Dick Gephardt believed the sanctions needed one to one and a half years to take effect. Bob Dole alone called for a "no-holds-barred" approach to Iraq's continued occupation.

Congress was at the center of the president's thinking about Iraq. While he believed that he had the constitutional power as commander in chief to proceed without specific authorization from Congress, he very much wanted a congressional resolution in support of the mission. Wanting, however, was not the same as getting. What if he lost the vote on the Hill? What then?

He would still, he thought, go to war, and he would take the consequences. To a degree he kept hidden from many of his closest advisers, before whom he largely maintained a mask of command, Bush, in private, fretted that Congress might impeach him a) if he launched full-scale military operations in the absence of congressional approval and b) if the ensuing war went badly. Bush alluded to this possibility in his presidential diary on five different occasions, ranging from Wednesday, December 12, 1990, to Sunday, January 13, 1991.

The president was determined but fatalistic. Confident of the rightness of his course, he was prepared to go to war if a bill authorizing the use of force never came to a vote or even failed in the Congress. In late November 1990, mulling a scenario in which he lacked an explicit congressional resolution, Bush dictated: "It is only the United States that can do what needs to be done. I still hope against hope that Saddam will get the message; but if he doesn't, we've got to take this action; and if it works in a few days, and he gives up, or is killed, or gets out, Congress will say, 'Attaboy, we did it, wonderful job; wasn't it great we stayed together.' If it drags out and there are high casualties, I will be history; but no problem—sometimes in life you've got to do what you've got to do."

By musing that he could be "history" if the worst happened, Bush might have just meant that he risked losing reelection in 1992. Two weeks later, though, he explicitly expressed thoughts about impeachment. "I'm convinced that they'll support us—the Congress—provided it's fast and surgical," Bush told his diary on Wednesday, December 12. "But if it's drawn out and long, well then you'll have all the hand wringers saying, 'They shouldn't have done it,' and they'll be after my neck on, perhaps, impeachment for violating the Constitution." Hawaii senator Dan Inouye warned Bush that an American military defeat without congressional authorization would likely cost him the presidency. "If you're wrong about this," Inouye told Bush, "you are going to be impeached by the Congress."

At a Thursday, December 20, 1990, meeting with a Democratic delegation from the Senate, the mood was pessimistic. "What do you want Congress to do?" Senator Richard Shelby, Democrat of Alabama, asked the president.

"Come in and pass a resolution auth[orizing the] President to implement UN resolutions," Bush replied. The response in the room was unenthusiastic. Paul Simon, Democrat of Illinois, pleaded for "a year" to let sanctions work. Others discouraged sending up a resolution on force, contending that the votes for "overwhelming support" did not exist and any kind of divisive fight would "make S[addam] H[ussein] a hero." Bush understood that well, which was why he wanted to make sure that a resolution, if submitted for approval, succeeded. If it didn't, well, that was too bad. "Congress is in a turmoil, and I am more determined than ever to do what I have to do," Bush told his diary on Friday, January 4, 1991. "If they are not going to bite the bullet, I am. They can file impeachment papers if they want to." Bush was certain enough about his mission—the ejection of Saddam from Kuwait—that he was willing to risk everything for it.

I n New York and around the world, Jim Baker fought for UN Security Council Resolution 678, which set a deadline of January 15, 1991, for Saddam to withdraw from Kuwait. The measure passed by a 12 to 2 vote. Yemen and Cuba voted no; China abstained. It was the first such authorization of force since the Korean War forty years before. Bush and Baker mulled over different last-minute diplomatic possibilities— including a face-to-face session between Bush and Saddam. "Talked about my meeting with Saddam Hussein," Bush told his diary, and "we talked about [Baker] meeting with Saddam Hussein in Baghdad." The argument, as Bush put it, was that "we need to have, for domestic consumption in the United States, a high level meeting where Saddam Hussein is told exactly how strongly we feel about this." (Some of Baker's advisers cautioned against a mission to Baghdad for fear that the secretary of state might be held hostage, but Baker was determined to go if the president wanted him to.)

The president's emotional commitment to Kuwait deepened around Christmas when he read an Amnesty International report on the brutalities of the Iraqi occupation. He cited it frequently, offering it as evidence in support of his moral case for war. The Right Reverend Edmond Browning, the presiding bishop of the Episcopal Church in the United States, called at the White House to urge peace. An unusually passionate president handed Browning a copy of the Amnesty International report, then peppered the bishop with questions. In light of such systemic terror, "Now what do we do about peace?" Bush asked. "How do we handle it when these people are being raped?" His growing determination led him to one of his rare open avowals of the price he was willing to pay to remove Saddam from Kuwait. "If I don't get the votes" in Congress for war, Bush remarked to Bob Gates one day in the Oval Office, "I'm going to do it anyway. And if I get impeached, so be it."

Over Christmas, as the family gathered at Camp David, Bush read letters from parents of troops in the Persian Gulf. "All of them saying, 'take care of my kid'; some saying, 'please don't shoot'; some saying, 'it's not worth dying for gasoline,' and on and on it goes; but the cry is, 'Save my boy, save my boy!'"

He was both melancholy and resolute. His mind was halfway around the world as he waited for a small caroling service to begin. "I keep thinking of the Gulf, and I see the faces of the young pilots ... [saying], 'Let us go; let us do our job; we can do it'; then the Marines and the Army guys—young, young, so very young. I think of the Iraqi babies, and yet I think of the evil that is this man." In his Christmas Eve reverie, rare responsibility and raw politics were mixed up together. "They say I don't concentrate on domestic affairs, and I expect that charge is true; but how can you when you hold the life and death of a lot of young troops in your hand?"

Billy Graham called in. The evangelist was a reassuring pastoral presence; in his company, or even on the telephone, he had a gift for projecting calm. In his conversation with Bush, Graham recited a line from James Russell Lowell's poem "The Present Crisis":

> *Once to every man and nation comes the moment to decide*
> . . . .
> *and the choice goes by forever 'twixt the darkness and that light.*

Bush was moved by the quotation. "It does hit me pretty hard—'Once to every man and nation comes the moment to decide.' That moment is upon us."

On Tuesday, January 8, 1991, on the eve of a critical meeting between Jim Baker and Iraqi foreign minister Tariq Aziz in Geneva, Bush, after months of debate, wrote the congressional leadership seeking an endorsement of the UN resolutions. The move was triggered in part by surveys showing strong popular support for Bush's view of the use of force. "I hope that today's poll will convince the Congress that they must support the President," Bush dictated on Tuesday, January 8. On the same day, the head of Veterans Affairs, Ed Derwinski, told Bush that the VA hospitals were preparing "to take an overflow of casualties [if] required"—a sobering report.

In Geneva, Baker presented Aziz with a letter from Bush to Saddam, but the Iraqis rejected any overture from Washington. Bush took the call from Baker and then went to the briefing room for a press conference that began at five minutes to four on the afternoon of Wednesday the ninth. "The conclusion is clear: Saddam Hussein continues to reject a diplomatic solution," Bush said. The chances for peace were ever more remote as January 15, 1991—the UN deadline—approached.

It was snowing in Washington on Friday, January 11. Bush had decided to risk a resolution authorizing the use of force, thinking it best for the country and for the coalition for the American government to be united—and on the record. Inside the Capitol, the House and Senate debated the subject that had consumed Bush since Scowcroft and Richard Haass had found the president in his T-shirt in the Medical Unit on that warm August evening. Lawmaker after lawmaker rose to speak for and against the use of force. Like much of the country, the president was impressed by the quality of argument in both chambers. He did worry that some of the grimmer predictions had "frightened the American people into believing this will be a long, drawn-out war. I'm still convinced it won't be; but we have made the proper preparations to guarantee that it will be short."

The president won the vote in both chambers, 250 to 183 in the House and 52 to 47 in the Senate. As he went to bed on the evening on Saturday, January 12, Bush felt free to act. "The big burden, lifted from my shoulders, is this Constitutional burden—the threat of impeachment," Bush told his diary on the night of the congressional victory. "All that cleared now by this very sound vote of the Congress."

For the moment, Bush was the president of a united country and, to a remarkable extent, he was the leading statesman of a united world, thanks to the administration's diplomacy. "I now have the constitutional authority, and no fear of fighting battles in the court over impeachment, or over the abuse of power," he dictated on the thirteenth. "But the decision still is a weighty one. The weightiest that any President has to make, ever."

He could think of nothing but Iraq. "I do think that World War II shaped my thinking on the Gulf. I have Saddam Hussein now as clearly bad and evil as Hitler and as the Japanese war machine that attacked Pearl Harbor. And I say, check him now, check him now."

War was at hand, and Bush was acutely, even painfully, aware that he was the final authority on whether Americans would see combat. "It is my decision; it's my decision to send these kids into battle; it's my decision," Bush told his diary on Sunday night, January 13, 1991. The call to arms was his to make. There were alternatives. "It is my decision to step back and let sanctions work, or to move forward, and in my view, help establish a New World Order"—a vision of international cooperation that Bush acknowledged had been sought, unsuccessfully, for "a hundred generations."

Until, possibly, just possibly, now, in the presidency of George H. W. Bush. "It is my decision to stand, and take the heat, or to fall back, and wait and hope," Bush dictated. "It is my decision that affects the husband in the Gulf, or the wife that is waiting, or the mother who writes, 'Take care of my son.'"

Restless and always hungry for information—the newest cable from the Situation Room, the freshest report from the front, the latest word on anything—Bush kept CNN on in the White House. Watching on this Sunday evening, he "saw a father kissing his son goodbye" as more troops shipped out. The son cried. The father embraced him, tight.

In the president's mind, time dissolved, and he was transported back to Penn Station in the summer of 1942. "I remembered just as clearly as it can be when I went off to Chapel Hill and my dad gave me a hug on that platform," he dictated. "I climbed on the [train]; I didn't know one single soul; and I was off for an experience unto the unknown, and it shaped my life."

Now the eighteen-year-old naval enlistee was a commander in chief facing the ultimate decision. "I have a feeling that I need to pray," Bush remarked a few nights later, "and yet I am not certain my prayers are heard." He was sure of one thing. It was all on him—all of it. If America prevailed, he had prevailed. If things went wrong, he, and no one else, would be to blame. There would be no excuses, no ducking of responsibility. "The face of war," he told his diary, "looks at me." Reading disturbing predictions about casualties in the Persian Gulf, Barbara asked her husband how he could stand all the portentous news coverage. "I know what I am doing," Bush replied. "I know what I have to do, and I don't worry about what they say. I know."

On the fourteenth, Bush tried to work through the paper on his desk—subjects included energy, climate change, and the budget—but was unable to concentrate. "Today is one of great tension," Bush dictated. "Walk out of the White House and you can feel it. You walk into the West Wing, and you can feel it also. Unbelievably tense." It was, he noted, "war, war, war."

As Tuesday, January 15, 1991, came and went, the Iraqi leader refused to withdraw from Kuwait, prompting Bush to direct Dick Cheney to issue an "execute order" that would soon unleash American airpower against Iraqi targets. War was about a day away. Growing uncomfortable with the "eerie calmness" of the White House, Bush told his aides, "Let's get some meetings on the economy or something else."

The attempt at distraction failed. He took three walks on the fifteenth, all on the White House grounds, moving, always moving. "People keep coming up, and saying, 'God Bless you,'" Bush told his diary. "My mind is a thousand miles away. I simply can't sleep. I think of what other Presidents went through. The agony of war."

FORTY-ONE

Nothing Like It Since Truman

★

I have no fear of making the call. I know that we'll lose lives,
but I am convinced that we'll move fast, move swiftly, and carry
the day, and kick Saddam out of Kuwait.

—GEORGE H. W. BUSH

It's going very well!

—DICK CHENEY, in a note passed to Bush during a
church service as the ground war began

THE BUSHES DINED with Billy Graham on the night the war began.
The president's speech to the nation, to be delivered at nine P.M.
Washington time, was at his setting on the table. Bush had written
much of it himself; confident of his course, he had had no trouble finding
the words he wanted. "Tonight, the battle has been joined," Bush said in
the address from the Oval Office. "I am convinced not only that we will
prevail but that out of the horror of combat will come the recognition
that no nation can stand against a world united, no nation will be permitted to brutally assault its neighbor."

After a largely sleepless night, Bush walked over to the Situation
Room at about five A.M. on Thursday, January 17, 1991. The news was a
relief. Things seemed to be going wonderfully on the military front. "Mr.
President, we have sent fifty-six navy planes out and we've got fifty-six
back," Cheney reported to Bush. "We have over two hundred air force
planes out and no sign of any missing." (Later one F-18 pilot was shot
down.)

Among the successes in the opening weeks of the coalition's aerial assault were what an account prepared by the Army's Center of Military
History described as a "virtually paralyzed" Iraqi command and control
network and the achievement of unchallenged air supremacy over the
Persian Gulf and Kuwait.

Bush's mission was well defined: the removal of Saddam from Kuwait.

The president of the United States was not seeking to march to Baghdad, or to depose Saddam, or to occupy Iraq. He hoped, even expected, the Iraqis would take care of Saddam themselves, but regime change in Iraq was not a war aim in 1991. In response to a National Security Council memorandum in early February, Bush was so insistent about returning the region to the status quo ante that he agreed with Brent Scowcroft that the United States would not "follow up Iraq's occupation with one of our own." The "model," Bush added, was therefore "post–World War II France, not Germany." And in a paper entitled "Beyond the Gulf War," the NSC specifically endorsed the president's desire to "avoid the emergence of a regional hegemon" and instead spoke of seeking a "balance involving Iran, Iraq, and the Saudi/GCC states." Bush intended to do what he had said he would do—restore Kuwait's sovereignty, providing Saudi Arabia a measure of security and reestablishing balance—and nothing more.

The first day of the air war, Bush recalled, was one of "euphoria." After attending a service at Memorial Chapel at Fort Myer, Virginia—the congregation sang "God of Our Fathers" and listened to the U.S. Army Chorus's rendition of "The Battle Hymn of the Republic"—Bush attempted to manage expectations. "We must be realistic," Bush told reporters. "There will be losses. There will be obstacles along the way. War is never cheap or easy." As evening came in Washington, Saddam launched a series of Scud missile attacks against Israel. At ten after eight on the night of the seventeenth, Bush was concerned about possible chaos. "Now we don't know how the Israelis are going to react," he dictated, "and what they are going to do, and so we are in the soup."

Bush's main fear: that an Israeli response to the attacks from Iraq would splinter the anti-Saddam coalition. Everything was confused. "There's all kinds of rumors—which reminds me to never make a decision in a war environment on rumors," Bush dictated. There were reports that Saddam had used chemical weapons and that seven Scuds had hit Israel. The reality: There had been no chemical attacks, and while seven missiles were fired, there was little damage in Israel and no one was killed.

Still, the Israeli government was eager to strike back. Bush understood the impulse for self-defense but was desperate to keep Israel from engaging. The Americans were ready to crush Saddam if those plans could go forward without the Israeli complication. "The big problem is how to keep Israel out, and it is going to be almost impossible," Bush dictated on the seventeenth. "Cheney wants to let them go, and go fast. Get it over with."

On Friday, January 18, 1991, Bush addressed the subject at a noon press conference. "I also want to say how outraged I am by Iraq's latest act of aggression—in this case, against Israel," he said. "Once again, we see that no neighbor of Iraq is safe." After leaving the briefing room, Bush spoke with Israeli prime minister Yitzhak Shamir. "[I] put on the hardest sale I have ever used," Bush told his diary. "I tried to convince him that we have doubled up, or tripled up, our attention to the Scuds out west, and urging him to stay out and let us do the job, even though I knew it would be difficult. God, I hope I made headway on that."

At one thirty Saturday morning, Scowcroft woke the president with news of yet more Iraqi attacks on Israel. In the darkness, Bush contemplated the coming debacle. "They are going to retaliate," he told his diary. Yet Shamir again acceded to Bush's wishes and did not strike. Relieved, Bush called to thank the Israeli prime minister. He also dispatched a high-level team to Israel as well as anti-Scud Patriot missiles.

Overall, the military outlook was terrific. "We own the skies—practically own the skies," Bush dictated on Saturday, January 19, 1991. The calls through the night left Bush tired, but he enjoyed having Doro and Marvin's children around for the weekend at Camp David. At one point the grandchildren were conducting a long-distance leaping contest off the bed in the presidential cabin while their grandfather, a war-time commander in chief, tried to read. It was, Bush dictated, "a marvelous madhouse that brings total relaxation." He took a call from Henry Kissinger, who told the president, "Thank you for saving us all from this demon, that Saddam Hussein." Bush called the Situation Room every morning. "How are the overnights?" he would ask. "What happened?"

On Sunday, January 20, he mused to his diary about all the terrible predictions that had failed to come true. The stock market was supposed to have gone down if the country went to war; the opposite had happened. Oil prices were to have soared, but after spiking at around forty dollars a barrel, they fell to pre-August 1990 lows. High U.S. casualties had been projected—what Bush called the "body-bag argument"—but so far the numbers were quite small. Protests were to have roiled the nation and public opinion was said to be fickle, but national polls had enormous majorities supporting the president and the troops. There had been the fear of terrorism, but there had been no significant asymmetrical assaults on the West.

For all the good news of the first days, however, there was the overarching fact of Saddam. "As I think about it, it would be very good if we didn't leave him intact," Bush dictated on the twentieth. "We can't have a goal of the assassination of Saddam Hussein, obviously. But it would be far simpler if his military did what they ought to do and take him out." Yes, Bush thought, that was the optimal scenario. "The best thing is that [Saddam] is taken out by his own people, and we reduce his armor tremendously, get our people the hell out of there." In a call from Camp David with Turgut Ozal, Bush and the Turkish president speculated that the war might last a few months. "It will depend on the ground forces," Bush said. "Or one of [Saddam's] officers may decide enough is enough and get rid of him."

The president felt a cold coming on, and soon was fighting a hundred-degree fever. "I could use a week in the sun, but those days, I think, are gone forever," he told his diary. "Or at least for a long, long, time to come."

By Monday, February 4, 1991, Bush was ready for the next big decision: when to begin the ground war. "I have no fear of making the call," he told his diary. "I know that we'll lose lives, but I am convinced that we will move fast, move swiftly, and carry the day, and kick Saddam out of Kuwait. And regrettably there will be a lot of casualties on his side, and there will be some on ours. But we can't stop now, we can't look back now, we can't pause now, we can't cease-fire now. We can't fail in our mission." From Baghdad, Saddam announced that Bush himself would be "a target for revenge for the rest of his life. . . . [It] remains for Bush, and his accomplices in crime, to understand that they are personally responsible for their crime. The Iraqi people will pursue them for this crime even if they leave office and disappear into oblivion." Bush thought it a "scary kind of sounding statement, but a little desperate."

The key gathering of the day on the eleventh was in the Yellow Oval Room upstairs at the White House. The president heard Cheney and Powell's report at two in the afternoon. The news from the front was good. Cheney, Powell, and Schwarzkopf "were totally in agreement on what had to be done next," Bush told his diary. The target date was about ten days out. "They are very, very optimistic about getting this done with few casualties, although I dare not say that."

As he listened to his commanders, Bush heard history's echoes. Powell had told him that the allied offensive would be three times greater in size than the Normandy assault on Hitler's Fortress Europe. In the Yellow Oval Room, Bush envisioned other hours of crisis, remembering that this was where FDR had learned of the attack on Pearl Harbor and where Roosevelt and Churchill, along with representatives of the Soviet Union and China, had signed their charter of alliance on New Year's Day, 1942.

Bush felt comfortable taking his place in the long line of war presidents. "I have no qualms now about ordering a ground war—none at all," he dictated on Thursday, February 14, 1991. "I don't have the aching that I felt the night before the bombing started and we went to war. The reason is that the military are unanimous in recommending the course of action that Colin and Cheney outlined to me the other day. I have not second-guessed; I have not told them what targets to hit; I have not told them how much ordnance to use or how much not to use, or what weapons to use and what weapons not to use. I have learned from Vietnam, and I think the Army and the other services are doing a superb job."

On Saturday, February 16, army units secretly got as far as twenty-five miles into Iraqi-held territory "without encountering any opposition."

On the eve of the ground war, at a White House briefing, Powell and Cheney discussed the question of casualties. As Cheney recalled, the Brookings Institution estimated that "between a thousand and four thousand Americans were going to die. Others warned that ten thousand Americans would be killed." In the meeting, Scowcroft suggested that the president be protected from hearing the grisliest details of the coming battle. "We've got to spare you from some things," Scowcroft said.

"I know," Bush replied, "but that isn't one of them."

At midday on Friday, February 22, Bush issued an ultimatum to Saddam: Withdraw totally from Kuwait by noon on Saturday, February 23, or face a ground offensive. Iraq refused. At ten P.M. on Saturday, Bush went to the briefing room. "The liberation of Kuwait has now entered a final phase," the president announced. "I have complete confidence in the ability of the coalition forces swiftly and decisively to accomplish their mission."

To himself, he wondered about the unknown. "I worry about chemical weapons, I worry about some surprise weapon," Bush dictated on the twenty-third. "I will sit back, like every other American now, with apprehension wondering at how it's going and not knowing."

The administration had been clear with the Iraqis about the price of a chemical attack. As Dick Cheney had put it, "were Saddam Hussein foolish enough to use weapons of mass destruction, the U.S. response would be absolutely overwhelming and it would be devastating." The Iraqis took this to mean that the United States would be prepared to use nuclear weapons. According to Cheney, the head of Iraqi military intelligence later remarked that "the warning was quite severe and quite effective. The allied troops were certain to use nuclear arms and the price will be too dear and too high."

As secretary of defense, Cheney quietly asked Powell and the Pentagon planners a fundamental question in the run-up to the war. Cheney's query: "Tell me how many tactical nukes are we going to have to use to take out an Iraqi Republican Guard division" if circumstances required it. "That was the question," Cheney recalled. "It took a while for them to figure that out. Finally, after I asked about three or four times, Powell came back and the answer was 'seventeen.'"

Powell recalled that the speculative number was high because planners could not really know how the Republican Guard might be positioned at the time the United States might deploy such tactical weapons. If the Iraqi troops were thinly spread along a long front, it would require more; if they were more densely massed, it might require fewer.

Cheney did not brief Bush on the tactical nuclear planning but wanted to be ready in the event of disaster. "I was curious: If you get into a situation and we have to follow through on our threat," Cheney recalled, "what's that going to look like?"

On Saturday, February 23, 1991, the ground offensive began at four A.M. Baghdad time (it was already Sunday there), eight P.M. in Washington. Bush addressed the nation on Saturday evening, then attended a seven A.M. Sunday service at St. John's Church. In his pew at St. John's, the president, in his mind, veered between the service and the desert. Cheney passed him a note: "Norm says it's going very well!"

There, in the familiar setting of an Episcopal church, hearing the words of the Book of Common Prayer, surrounded by his family, his cabinet, and his advisers, Bush read the news with relief. Cheney and Powell briefed him at the White House after church, and then, sitting with Barbara, Bush listened to a Schwarzkopf press conference describing the coalition's rapid progress through its Iraqi targets.

The news was fantastic. Bush had hoped for a fast victory, but this was more than even he had dared to expect. "I felt myself choking up, just as I did in church," Bush dictated on February 24. He savored the moment. "It's going to be quicker than anyone ever thought. All the talking heads, and all the worst case, and all the Congress and their pusillanimous views, look, now, to be wrong. God, I hope so, because it means American life."

D esert Storm's speed and success was prompting talk that had been largely unimaginable even weeks before, when the congressional vote was so close and commentators argued that Bush might be leading American forces into a bloodbath. Should Bush redefine the mission and seek regime change in Baghdad? Why not push on to the capital?

Though the formal military and policy structure around the president did not raise the issue—occupying Baghdad seemed a nightmare that would splinter the coalition—the president was beginning to hear such chatter informally. In the sauna at the House gym, for instance, several old colleagues, including Sonny Montgomery of Mississippi, pressured him to take Saddam out altogether. "Our people want him gone," the lawmakers told Bush in the dry heat at the end of February. "They want him out of there."

Emotionally, Bush agreed with such locker-room talk. Intellectually, though, he knew the smart move was the limited move. "I firmly believed that we should not march into Baghdad," Bush recalled in 1998, continuing:

> Our stated mission, as codified in UN resolutions, was a simple one—end the aggression, knock Iraq's forces out of Kuwait, and restore Kuwait's leaders. To occupy Iraq would instantly shatter our

coalition, turning the whole Arab world against us, and make a broken tyrant into a latter-day Arab hero. It would have taken us way beyond the imprimatur of international law bestowed by the resolutions of the Security Council, assigning young soldiers to a fruitless hunt for a securely entrenched dictator and condemning them to fight in what would be an unwinnable urban guerrilla war. It could only plunge that part of the world into ever greater instability and destroy the credibility we were working so hard to reestablish.

All sound points, but Bush also wanted a clear, decisive end to the conflict—or as clear and decisive an end as one could have when the mission allowed the enemy chief to remain in power. "Nobody wants to use the word surrender—[it] doesn't go [over] well out there [in the Arab world]—but I've never heard of a war where there's not a winner or a loser," he told his diary on the evening of the twenty-fifth. "Well, maybe that's not true—you've got Vietnam and Korea. But on this one, we need the clarity of purpose if we're going to finally kick, in totality, the Vietnam syndrome."

Bush was handicapped by the clarity of his own mission. "We need a surrender, we need Saddam out," he told his diary. "And yet our objectives are to stop short of all of that." Bush had come this far in large measure because he had limited his demands. In the intensity of the moment, he wanted more—he wanted a formal Iraqi capitulation and Saddam removed from power. "I'm not interested in his saving face and neither is the rest of the world," Bush dictated. What he wanted, however, would not trump what he thought was right in terms of keeping his commitment to the coalition.

The rout of Saddam's troops was nearly total. Television images of the U.S. military blasting Iraqi troops, vehicles, and armor along the highway from Kuwait City to Basra were being watched worldwide. Bush asked his commanders whether it was time to declare victory. Powell called Schwarzkopf from the president's study next to the Oval Office. They agreed that they had accomplished their mission: Saddam had been driven from Kuwait in rapid fashion. The ground war was approaching the hundred-hour mark, which offered a poetic stopping point.

At nine P.M. on Wednesday, February 27, 1991, Bush spoke to the nation from the Oval Office. Barbara had been scheduled to deliver a dinner speech that night. He asked her to shift her plans so that she could be in the Oval Office, sitting just outside camera range. He wanted her with him.

The United States, under Bush's direct, personal leadership, had created an unlikely coalition of allies that included the Soviet Union, China, and Arab nations long skeptical of the United States. In the aftermath of Korea and of Vietnam, unhappy conflicts that had sapped America's confidence, Bush and his commanders had projected power and accomplished a carefully defined objective at minimal cost in American blood.

The Iraqis lost nearly 90 percent of their tanks, and the victorious coalition had to shift its focus to guarding and housing some 60,000 Iraqi prisoners. American forces lost 148 troops killed in action, compared to the more than 20,000 Iraqi army dead.

With diplomacy and a determination to honor his word—that Saddam's aggression against Kuwait would not stand—Bush had done something virtually no one would have thought possible only two years before: He had risen further in the eyes of the American public than Ronald Reagan ever had—further, in fact, than any other president in the history of public opinion surveys.

Eighty-nine percent of Americans polled by Gallup approved of Bush's performance in these weeks. Truman never rated that highly; nor had Eisenhower, Kennedy, Johnson, Nixon, Ford, Carter, or Reagan. Several had come close in hours of victory (Truman polled 87 percent approval after V-E Day in 1945), but George Bush, flush from the hundred-hour ground campaign against Saddam Hussein, now stood at an unmatched summit of popularity.

In a series of telephone calls from his desk in the Oval Office around six P.M., Bush spoke with his comrades in arms—John Major in London, General Schwarzkopf at the front. (Major, a Tory, had become Britain's prime minister after Thatcher fell from power at home in November 1990.) Powell and Cheney had just passed along the cease-fire order to Schwarzkopf for midnight eastern standard time that evening, three hours after Bush's scheduled speech. "It's just dawning on me," Bush dictated, "that what is about to happen is historic."

His wife could hardly believe what the world was saying about her husband. "I wish I could freeze the newspaper columns in a time capsule," Barbara told her diary on Saturday, March 2, 1991. "They are raving over George today. It won't last, but nobody thought that a war could be fought like this and won in this manner."

Yet there was no swagger, no self-satisfaction, in the wake of the victory in the Persian Gulf. For Bush the best course—the only course—was to move on to the next thing: "I know that these euphoric . . . ratings, nothing like it since Truman after World War II, are nothing, they go away tomorrow." One might think a president who had spent much of his life preparing to lead in complicated diplomatic moments would savor Desert Storm, finding a quiet joy in his own skill and success. Yet the restless Bush—the man for whom forward motion was everything—was certain that this glorious hour, like all other hours, would pass away.

Bush made mistakes at the end of the Gulf War. By failing to force Saddam to the surrender table at Safwan, where Schwarzkopf received the Iraqi capitulation on Sunday, March 3, 1991, the president enabled Saddam to save some personal face. (Bush had not insisted for fear that Saddam might refuse to come.) He regretted the decision. "It hasn't been clean, there is no Battleship *Missouri* surrender," he told his diary. "This is what's missing to make this akin to World War II, to separate it from Korea, and Vietnam." More substantively, Bush had encouraged Iraqis to rise up against the regime. When Shiites and Kurds did, in fact, rebel against Saddam after Safwan, though, everything went wrong. The United States did nothing to support the insurgents, and the uprising was put down in part by Iraqi helicopters that the coalition had allowed Saddam's army to keep. In the beginning of the war, in January, Bush had told reporters that war was not easy. Neither was war's wake.

What kind of victory was it, Bush wondered, when the defeated rival remained in power? Turgut Ozal of Turkey called in with a hawkish message. "[Ozal] wants to humiliate Saddam," Bush dictated. "He simply doesn't want to let him off the hook, in saying this, he's putting his finger on why I don't feel euphoria. Hitler is alive, indeed, Hitler is still in office, and that's the problem. And that's why, though I take great pride in the fact the shooting has stopped, our military [is] doing great, American people elated, [but] I have no elation."

Bush's postwar despondency—there is no other word for it—was well masked. He spoke of it to himself, in his diary, but seems not to have shared it with others. (To have complained of the burdens of the office to others was unthinkable—self-indulgent and self-pitying.) The let-down was rooted in his failure to bring about Saddam's fall, which wounded Bush's competitive spirit, and in his closely held view, articulated in private, that the work he had been born to do was now likely done. "The basic thing is I'm tired," Bush dictated. "So life goes on, and I'm thinking to myself at this moment, I'll probably get over it, I want out, I want to go back to the real world. . . . I want to get out of this, I want to walk into the drugstore at Kennebunkport; build a house in Houston; or teach at the library at A&M, with less pressure." He knew he was down, and he hoped he could talk himself back to good cheer: "I'm so lucky to be here, too, so I'll sort it all out when the day dawns."

A lonely walk on the South Lawn of the White House after deciding to initiate the coalition's air war against Saddam Hussein, January 1991. "I know what to do," he told Barbara privately—but he was consumed with worry about the loss of American and Iraqi lives.

If he remained in the arena. "Confession: I wish that this were six months later, because what I think I'd do is say, 'I'm getting a little old, a little tired, somebody else ought to have a shot now,'" Bush told his diary in late February 1991. "Bar wants to hear nothing of that . . . but I've got to confess that it's on my mind. It's not that I don't want to fight, but it's that I've lost heart for a lot of the gut political fighting, as a result of trying to lead this country and bring it together in the Gulf. It's strange but true."

He should have been on top of the world. Instead, victory in a real war had sapped his energies for the often-manufactured skirmishes of politics, and he was realistic about what was ahead.

Alan Greenspan had announced that the economy had suffered a "meaningful downturn" by October 1990. According to the historian James T. Patterson, "the recession began to emerge in 1990 and lasted until mid-1991, when recovery very slowly took place." It was the first cyclical downturn since the difficult Reagan recession of 1982. Unemployment, particularly among white-collar workers, rose to what Patterson noted was "the highest rate in ten years"—from 5.9 percent in 1989, the year Bush took office, to 7.8 percent in the middle of 1991. "Whatever the causes, the downturn was severe," Patterson wrote, and the effects of the recovery would not be widely felt until well after politics of 1992 had taken shape.

"The euphoria is up there on the war, but when it wears off, we're going to be facing these humungous deficits and the economy is still down, down, down," Bush dictated in mid-March 1991. "Gosh, I'm hoping that this will be a mild recession. I hope and hope and hope that it will be."

FORTY-TWO

I'm Just Not Sure I Want
to Run Again

★

Soon we'll have to start thinking of the campaign. I dread it.
—GEORGE H. W. BUSH

THE POST–GULF WAR PERIOD of Bush's presidency is a study in shadow. Bush himself was gloomy and emotionally adrift, finding little joy in the job that had filled his life with light for just over two years. "Nothing except a battle lost," the Duke of Wellington is said to have remarked, "can be half so melancholy as a battle won." The creation and maintenance of the coalition of nations, the supervision of military preparations, and the alternating anxiety and exhilaration of the actual combat itself had left Bush drained. Part of the cause was a kind of post-combat letdown along the lines Wellington had described long before. Another was a thyroid condition known as Graves' disease that would be diagnosed in the late spring. For a time in 1991, America had a president who struggled to present a steady face to the world even as he contemplated standing down from the 1992 campaign.

The trip from the White House to the J. W. Marriott Hotel at Thirteenth Street and Pennsylvania Avenue NW was brief. The president used the few moments in the car to go over the speech he was about to deliver to the American Society of Association Executives at eleven A.M. on Wednesday, February 27, 1991, the day the war ended. The subject was domestic policy, and Bush read the text with a sinking feeling. It was, he thought, a rather poor effort, full of platitudes about the American Dream and forced language about his vision for the nation at home. Looking up at Dave Demarest, the White House director of communications, Bush said, "You don't expect me to read this shit, do you?"

Demarest tried to laugh it off, but the president was serious. Pushing his way through the speech at the hotel, Bush was horrified at the silence in the room. "It fell flat," he dictated. "Not one clap of applause." Returning to the White House, Bush told John Sununu that the entire episode "was frankly quite embarrassing."

However much he may have preferred foreign affairs, Bush was aware that his presidency—like most other presidencies—would rise or fall not only on what he did in the larger world but on how he managed life at home. Even amid the frenzy of good feeling about the Gulf War, he took nothing for granted. Now, Bush dictated to his diary, "the ball will shift into the domestic court, and we will be back to the old political game who's up, who's down, the loud voices on the [CNN political talk show] *Capital Gang;* the attacks by the Democrats, which I am bound to get in spades."

Some allies argued—both to him and in political circles—that Desert Storm could be followed by a "Domestic Storm" of programs to address the economy, education, the environment, and other home front issues. The advice was well-intentioned, but Bush was doubtful about the administration's prospects for great domestic success. "Try this on," he dictated. "Suppose you had Dick Gephardt as Secretary of State and [Ted] Kennedy as Secretary of Defense—how could you do it?"

He fantasized about surprising the world by announcing that he would not seek reelection. "[I'd] call a press conference in about November and just turn it loose," Bush told his diary on Wednesday, March 13, 1991. He went on:

> You need someone in this job [who can give his] total last ounce of energy, and I've had [that] up until now, but now I don't seem to have the drive. Maybe it's the letdown after the day-to-day five [o'clock] calls to the Situation Room; conferences every single day with Defense and State; moving things, nudging things, worrying about things; phone calls to foreign leaders trying to keep things moving forward; managing a massive project. Now it's different, sniping, carping, bitching, predictable editorial complaints. . . . [T]his cynical liberalism that comes down on any President.

His contrasting faces on Sunday, March 17, 1991, captured the tensions Bush was feeling. At a rally for returning troops in Sumter, South Carolina, the world saw a cheerful president pay heartfelt homage to the military that had performed so splendidly under his command. "When you left, it was still fashionable to question America's decency, America's courage, America's resolve," he told a delighted throng at Sumter Memorial Stadium. "No one, no one in the whole world doubts us anymore."

Flying home to Washington on Air Force One, Bush drank two martinis. Barbara was away in Houston; he arrived back at a lonely White House. "I'm not in a good frame of mind now," he dictated. The confident commander in chief of the South Carolina rally was nowhere in evidence. "My whole point is, I really don't care, and that's bad—that's bad," he told his diary that Sunday evening. "But I'll get in there and try. We've got our issues; we've got our plan; and now I've got to fight for them." It wasn't that he felt above it all; he was just tired of it all. "It's not that I'm bigger than the politics, but it's just that I've been down that road and I'm not that much of a political animal"—which was demonstrably untrue; it was more accurate to say that this consummate political competitor was no longer interested in the cut and thrust of the arena.

He was unimpressed by the predictions of the political class. "The common wisdom today is that I'll win in a runaway, but I don't believe that," Bush dictated. "I think it's going to be the economy [which] will make that determination. I think I can talk proudly about what happened in Desert Storm, but I think it will be overshadowed in the Fall of '92 by other issues."

And yet he was driven, as of old, by competitiveness and by duty. He genuinely believed that his administration had a better agenda for the country than the Democrats could offer. "I love the job and I think we have a real chance to accomplish a lot; I think we have in foreign policy," Bush dictated on Monday, April 22, 1991, adding: "We're still getting pounded for no domestic program, [and] for some odd reason, that makes me say 'Well, let me stay in; let me try to run again, [and] if elected, finish the job on these very, very important fronts.'"

On Saturday, May 4, 1991, the Bushes flew to the presidential retreat for an overnight break. It was a beautiful day, and after a forty-minute nap, Bush was joined by Rich Miller of the Secret Service for a jog on the camp's wood-chip trails. On the run through the Maryland woods, the president was startled to find himself out of breath. This was unusual; even at age sixty-six—almost sixty-seven—he had always been in terrific shape. Yes, he had been tired lately—really since the end of the ground war—and had twice had trouble running at his usual pace in recent weeks. (Once, at Fort McNair, a spectator had called out, "Looking good," to which Bush replied, "Looking slow.") He had also lost several pounds. His panting on the paths on this Saturday, though, was different—his fatigue deeper, harder to shake.

Unsure what was happening, Bush stopped and walked, caught his breath, then tried to run again. It was no use. He made it only about a hundred yards before he was panting once more. He soldiered on for thirty to forty minutes, starting and stopping. Finally he asked Miller to call the duty doctor, and, nearing Camp David's chapel, Bush tried to run the last bit of path to the medical unit.

He did not make it. "The same tired feeling came," Bush dictated later, and the medical staff sat him down for an EKG conducted by Dr. Michael Nash, a White House physician. Nash's finding: The president was suffering from a fibrillation, or irregularity, of the heart. "You're going to have to go down to Bethesda," Bush was told. "We really have to check to see what's causing this." Bush's first thought was not about his health but about politics. "My whole mind goes, 'Oh no, here we go, here comes a bunch of Democrats charging out of the woodwork to run.' There will be a scare scene sent all around the world, and wild speculation will begin about my health and fitness, and it's too darn bad."

Within minutes the Bushes were aboard Marine One, taking off at 5:38 P.M. en route to the naval hospital at Bethesda. Barbara looked worried, but Bush kept telling her that he felt fine. The doctors at the hospital confirmed the initial diagnosis: The president had an irregular heartbeat, a treatable condition. He would spend the night in the hospital as the doctors sought to restore his heartbeat to its usual rhythm.

To the world outside his suite at Bethesda, the word was, in a favorite Bush phrase, steady as she goes. At seven thirty P.M. he and Quayle, who was at home at the vice presidential residence, spoke on the telephone. "The President was in very good spirits and joking," vice presidential chief of staff Bill Kristol told reporters after consulting Quayle about the call. At eight thirty P.M. Marlin Fitzwater held a press conference. "There are no indications at this time that he had a heart attack," Fitzwater announced. "There's never been any question of the President losing consciousness or not being able to carry out his functions."

On Sunday the fifth, as he waited to see whether the treatments would be successful, Bush was restless, working the telephones and playing video games with a few of his grandchildren. He had not slept well. "The problem with all of this is that there will be lot of speculation as to what it means, and lots of feeling that I shouldn't run again," Bush dictated to his diary in the hospital. "The Democrats are now taking a new and inspired look—not hoping something happens—but thinking something might."

Implicit in his concern that the episode was giving new hope to the opposition was a returning fighting spirit in terms of 1992. Had he not been recovering from his postwar dejection about politics, he might well have interpreted the heart incident in a different, more optimistic light: as an excuse, perhaps, for announcing that he was standing down for reelection. Instead, he fretted about appearing weak, and about the appearance of weakness encouraging his foes. In his suite at Bethesda, his competitive instincts were stirring.

His doctors told him that they might have to put him under a general anesthetic and use electrical shock to restore his heartbeat to its regular rhythm on Monday. Such a step would have required him to transfer power, albeit very briefly, to Vice President Quayle, and Bush, alone in the night after Barbara had returned to the White House after kissing her husband goodbye, thought that his condition might be more serious than he had at first thought. "She's a little more worried than she indicates, and I'll probably be thinking tomorrow, 'Have I really told her how much I love her, and it's going to be okay?'" Bush dictated. "Have I properly told her I loved her?" His stream of consciousness continued:

> I just can't believe anything will go wrong and it won't. But this diary is a confession of sorts, and I have no fear of this procedure, but I've left undone a lot of things I should've done. When I listen to this tomorrow, I'll be saying, "Hey, how silly you were," but there is the family. . . . [T]here's Bar, and our house in Maine, and what she'll be able to do. I want her to have these notes, and maybe she could write a book and make enough money to live a reasonable lifestyle and keep our home, our anchor to windward at Kennebunkport. . . . I don't want to go through my life worrying about my heart fibrillation, taking medicine, and I wonder if this will heighten the day when I make the decision not to run for President. It all depends on how I feel, but as this diary knows, I'm quietly thinking about not running. I feel good; my health is good; and my spirit is good, so why am I saying all of these things?

He was saying them because he was anxious. Though the health scare was relatively minor, it was still a scare. Here he was, the most powerful man on Earth, and his own heart was threatening to betray him.

With the dawn came good news. The medication was working. There was no need for the electrical procedure, no need for the anesthetic, no need for the transfer of power—and no need for further nights at Bethesda. Bush was elated. The crisis, he thought, had passed. With the proviso that he would have to wear a small heart monitor for a time, he was able to return to the White House. In truth he was not as chipper as he sought to appear ("I came to the office, but I still don't feel totally right—a little weaker than I thought I'd be," he told his diary on Tuesday, May 7), but he appears to have kept that to himself. Determined to project a sense of energy and good cheer, Bush called out, "Back to work, back to work" as he walked into the Oval Office. That afternoon brought a new medical bulletin. His doctors had found that Bush was suffering from Graves' disease, which had also afflicted Barbara since 1989. "An overactive thyroid," wrote *New York Times* medical correspondent Lawrence K. Altman, "can cause symptoms like nervousness, restlessness, hyperactivity and weight loss." He would have to forgo alcohol for a time, and Barbara told reporters that she was going to secretly move the White House from caffeinated to decaffeinated coffee.

Bush's overactive thyroid had led to his excessively rapid heart rate (the atrial fibrillation). Now that the doctors had handled the fibrillation through medication (for a time, digoxin, warfarin, and procainamide), the question turned to treating his Graves' disease, or hyperthyroidism. The accepted course of action was to "ablate" the thyroid with radio-active iodine to eliminate the thyroid gland's ability to produce excessive levels of thyroid hormone that could, in turn, lead to further episodes of atrial fibrillation, among other issues. Once the thyroid was sufficiently "ablated," Bush's doctors introduced medication, L-Thyroxin, to bring the thyroid level back into the normal range. (By September 1991 the president was taking only L-Thyroxin and baby aspirin.)

"It was a difficult balancing act," recalled White House physician Dr. Burton Lee. "There was, and is, a lot of clinical uncertainty about what exactly the dose should be in the individual case. If we did not have the medication exactly right, then he could remain clinically hypothyroid"—meaning that Bush would have less energy and less focus than he had had in the first part of his presidency. If the doctors raised his dose of L-Thyroxin, however, they risked sending Bush back into atrial fibrillation. For the most part, Bush's doctors kept the president's thyroid condition in check. Yet there were those around Bush who speculated whether issues with the treatment for his Graves' disease contributed to his failure to engage vigorously with the politics of 1992. "To those of us who watched him carefully, the old zip was gone," recalled Marlin Fitzwater. Everything, of course, is a matter of context. At sixty-six, the president had long been more active than many people many years his junior. Still, in layman's terms, Bush's thyroid condition and his treatment for it may have played some role in slowing the president down a bit at just the moment he needed as much physical, mental, and spiritual verve as he could muster.

The day the president returned to the White House from Bethesda, the Democratic Leadership Council, a group founded after Walter Mondale's forty-nine-state defeat, announced a new centrist policy agenda at the conclusion of a gathering in Cleveland. Much of the attention was focused on Doug Wilder of Virginia, Jay Rockefeller of West Virginia, and Al Gore of Tennessee. "Too many of the people who used to vote for us, the very burdened middle class we're talking about, have not trusted us in national elections to defend our national interest abroad, to put their values in our social policy at home or to take their tax money and spend it with discipline," said one speaker. "We've got to turn these perceptions around, or we can't continue as a national party."

It was a resonant message. And with it, the speaker, Bill Clinton, returned to Arkansas, to think some more about whether 1992 was the right moment to strike.

Just after nine thirty on the sunny morning of Saturday, June 8, 1991, in the amphitheater of Arlington National Cemetery, Bush offered a eulogy at a memorial service for the fallen of the Gulf War. "Dwight Eisenhower once spoke of the most ennobling virtues of man: faith, courage, fortitude, and sacrifice," Bush said as he stood beneath enormous American flags, flanked by Baker, Cheney, Bandar, and the Kuwaiti ambassador. "He knew that America grew out of brave men's dreams of a commonwealth of freedom, of virtue. . . . It lives because we dared risk our most precious asset—our sons and daughters, our brothers and sisters, our husbands and wives—the finest troops any country has ever had." Bush's voice broke with emotion when he came to the section about "our most precious asset," and tears sprang to his eyes.

From the dais high above the crowd on this sunny Saturday, Bush looked out and saw those gathered in a way that no one else could. He saw them as souls in his charge, lives in his hands. To him the soldiers, sailors, and airmen he had ordered into harm's way—and might yet again—and their kith and kin were not abstractions but real people from real families who, at his personal command, had given or would give the last full measure of devotion.

Speaking at Arlington National Cemetery in honor of the casualties of Desert Storm, Bush grew emotional. The American ideal, he said, "lives because we dared risk our most precious asset—our sons and daughters, our brothers and sisters, our husbands and wives—the finest troops any country has ever had."

At the conclusion of the ceremony, Bush felt he could not just walk "imperiously" off the stage. He asked Schwarzkopf, who was there in his trademark desert fatigues, to join him and Barbara in talking to several rows of families. "It was so sad," Bush dictated. "I said, 'Did you have a loved one over there?' 'Yeah, my Dad was killed,' or 'Yes, my only boy gave his life.' It was very, very touching and very, very moving."

From the quiet of Arlington—Bush had noted a songbird over the white gravestones on the lush green grass of the cemetery just before he spoke—the presidential party moved back across the Potomac for the largest military celebration in Washington since the end of World War II. There, on Constitution Avenue, the president watched as unit after unit marched by. Aircraft streaked through the skies, and the armaments that had driven Saddam from Kuwait were paraded by a crowd that was estimated to be 200,000 strong. By the time the sun had set and the fireworks went off, the ranks of the spectators had grown to 800,000. "Great day," Bush remarked. Would the good feeling from the war be enough to reelect Bush nearly eighteen months hence? He doubted it. "I firmly believe that elections are won or lost by the state of the economy," he dictated, optimistically adding: "and ours appears to be improving. That isn't to say we won't have enormous problems out there."

Into the first half of the summer of 1991 the Democrats remained in disarray. Watching from the White House, Bush noted that Iowa senator Tom Harkin was "wowing the crowds on the liberal left" and West Virginia senator Jay Rockefeller was "knocking me on education and foreign affairs." Governor Mario Cuomo of New York was "silent. He's got big state problems and he's now trying to talk conservative on economic matters. He's fast on his feet and a lot of people think it will be Cuomo and [Al] Gore." As for Gore himself, Bush quoted *The Hotline,* the inside-Washington newsletter, which had described the young Tennessee senator as "'wooden,' or something like that. [He'll] be out there on his environmental kick. An attractive guy, but [they say] he is a worse speaker than me—the poor guy's in real trouble if he's worse than me." Bush's handicapping was another sign that the president was reengaging with politics. He may have longed for tranquillity, but he also believed that he was better for the country than any of the alternatives.

He was pleased, too, with the slow but steady progress the administration was making on an important long-term project: the creation of a North American free-trade zone. Reagan had spoken of a "North American Common Market" with Mexico, the United States, and Canada. Bush thought even bigger, speaking of a hemispheric model that would include Latin America.

In May 1991, when Congress moved to extend his "fast-track" authority—which gave the president the power to negotiate and present a treaty that could not be amended—Bush was delighted. "This is a very important step for our country. . . . It's a great day, it really is," Bush said.

Facing concerns that an agreement could siphon American jobs off to lower-paying factories in Mexico and might exacerbate environmental conditions, Bush had lobbied hard for the renewed negotiating authority, using White House breakfasts and sit-downs to sell lawmakers on what would become known as the North American Free Trade Agreement, or NAFTA. "The White House almost ran out of eggs benedict this week," Senator Byron Dorgan, Democrat of North Dakota, remarked.

A confirmed free trader, Bush was committed to NAFTA and to the arduous negotiations—both with the participating nations and with the Democratic Congress, always worried about job exports and the environment—and persistently pursued them through 1991 and 1992. At a time of economic slump at home, such complex diplomacy was especially difficult, but Bush believed that NAFTA, whatever its short-term political costs, would create conditions for long-term prosperity. The president never gave up, and the accords would be completed in August 1992 and signed in Mexico City that December.

I n late June, Thurgood Marshall, the first—and only—African American to serve on the U.S. Supreme Court, announced his retirement from the bench. Bush moved quickly, asking Boyden Gray and John Sununu to work on a new nomination.

In theory he was interested, as he had been at the time of the Souter nomination, in a Hispanic or a woman, but Marshall's retirement was particular, and Bush thought of a young federal judge he had known for a long time: Clarence Thomas, a Yale Law graduate who was a member of the small African American Republican world that Bush had cultivated and supported, quietly, for decades. By Monday, July 1, 1991, Bush, on the telephone, told Thomas that he was "very close to a decision," but that nothing was final; would the judge mind a trip to Kennebunkport? When Thomas arrived at Walker's Point—the staff smuggled him in to avoid photographers—he joined Bush in the master bedroom on the first floor of the house. As with David Souter, there was no philosophical discussion; no specific issues were raised. Bush asked that Thomas make his decisions "as an umpire would," calling them as he saw them, and he promised never to criticize or second-guess the justice once he was on the bench. There was one more thing, too: Bush asked "if he was ready for the bruising fight . . . ahead."

Thomas said yes, all of that sounded fine. He believed he was ready. Bush was putting his faith in a man he thought to be generally conservative and of good character. That was enough. "If he rules against what I think on Roe vs. Wade, so be it," Bush told his diary on Wednesday, July 3. "If he rules differently on any issue, so be it. He'll approach it with honor and integrity, and he will not try to do social engineering from the bench." After a joint press conference—one in which Thomas choked up recalling his life's journey from obscurity in rural Georgia—Bush invited him back to the stone porch for lunch. Confirmation hearings would come in the fall, as would Bush's signing of the Civil Rights Act of 1991 after a long fight.

In October 1990, the president had vetoed a civil rights bill arguing that it "employ[ed] a maze of highly legalistic language to introduce the destructive force of quotas into our national employment system." In the fall of 1991, after difficult negotiations, Bush signed a measure supported by Democrats and moderate Republicans.

On the first weekend in August, Bush convened a political meeting at Camp David. The subject: the dreaded 1992 presidential campaign. There were about thirty people there, and the session opened with a dispiriting presentation from Bob Teeter, whose polling suggested that domestic and economic concerns were more important to voters than global ones.

The group of advisers was large, and included Quayle, Sununu, Bob Mosbacher, and Mary Matalin. (Jim Baker was in the Middle East.) According to notes of the meeting taken by deputy chief of staff Jim Cicconi, Bush told the gathering that he had made "no final decision" about running, "but only one thing would keep him from" a campaign for reelection: his health, which he believed was fine. He had run two miles the day before, Bush said, and "will do the same today."

While Bush's foreign policy was viewed positively by 72 percent of voters, only 21 percent approved of his handling of the home front. Drily, Cicconi wrote: "Conclusion: have work to do on domestic issues."

Bush was told that "Unemployment [has] replaced deficit as key economic issue"—the wages of the recession—and that healthcare was "'increasingly important.' . . . Demo's have high ground." Alan Steelman, a former Texas Republican congressman who was at the meeting, was direct about healthcare, telling Bush that the lack of an administration healthcare reform plan was the best example of the president's seeming dearth of attention to domestic issues.

The reelection campaign had to watch out for internal party challenges, too. Of discussion about the Republican platform in 1992, Cicconi wrote: "Key: at early stages, be sure Weber, Gingrich et al (who care most re platform) feel listened to = otherwise they may try to write their own."

August was a typical one in Kennebunkport. The president was back on the golf course he loved, Cape Arundel, and, dressing for services at St. Ann's Church on Sunday morning, he wore white socks with a pair of what Maureen Dowd of *The New York Times* described as "off-white leather shoes." Keenly observant, Dowd wrote that "It has been said that Mr. Bush resembles the character played by Tom Hanks in the movie 'Big,' a boy in the body of an adult," and the white socks and shoes, worn with a gray suit and blue tie, offered, she believed, further proof.

At the annual vestry breakfast and meeting at St. Ann's, Bush had fun engaging with the mundane tasks of running a parish church; the conversation about "whether the organ loft needs to have some repairs . . . or whether the groundskeeper should be on a year round basis . . . brings you back to earth."

Bush went to bed on the night of Sunday, August 18, 1991, looking forward to a round of golf the next morning with Roger Clemens, the Boston Red Sox pitching ace. For Bush, summer days could get no better than that.

FORTY-THREE

A Coup in Moscow

★

*The complexities of all of this are absolutely phenomenal, and
yet I am determined to handle it without getting us
involved in a war.*

—GEORGE H. W. BUSH

T HE CALL FROM SCOWCROFT came through at midnight. Waking
at once, Bush picked up the phone at his bedside on the first floor
of the house at Walker's Point and listened as the national security
adviser briefed him on an unusual report from TASS, the official Soviet
news agency. Mikhail Gorbachev, it was said, had resigned, improbably
citing health reasons. The announcement made no sense; Gorbachev
was a vigorous man. Bush had just come from a summit with him in
Moscow. There had to be something else—something more sinister—
afoot.

At about 5:30 A.M. on Monday, August 19, 1991, Bush asked the Situation Room in the White House for an update. The picture had become
a bit clearer. Gorbachev, on vacation in the Crimea, had been deposed by
a right-wing cabal of Soviet hard-liners. Gorbachev, Bush was told, "has
been put out." It was not a total surprise: Bush had warned Gorbachev of
a possible coup "by right-wing forces" in June. Soviet cold warriors in
both the government and in the military had had enough of Gorbachev's
reforms—reforms that were now well on their way to empowering the
republics, not Moscow, bringing the experiment in Soviet power that
had begun in the Russian Revolution of 1917 to an end. The August
coup was a last attempt to rescue the old Soviet Union from the forces of
glasnost and perestroika.

Gorbachev's popularity had been falling as former satellite after former satellite spun away from Moscow. In foreign affairs, the reunification of Germany, while carefully managed and led by the United States,
had been a historic blow to Soviet pride; at home, the failure of Gor-

bachev's market reforms to produce prosperity—gross national product was significantly down—left him with little to boast of.

And there was a new rival on the scene. Bear-like and hard drinking, histrionic and bold, a Russian politician named Boris Yeltsin had emerged in the fluid politics of the Gorbachev era. Elected president of Russia, by far the largest and most influential of the Soviet Union's component parts, Yeltsin took office in July 1991 just as Gorbachev agreed to a new union treaty, which would have replaced the centralized Soviet Union with a looser confederation of republics. The document had sent Soviet conservatives into action in one last push to preserve the old order.

Gorbachev had been vacationing at Cape Foros in the Crimea. Late on the afternoon of Sunday, August 18, he was told that "a group of people" wanted to see him. "I was not expecting anybody, had not invited anyone, and no one had informed me of anyone's possible arrival," Gorbachev recalled. He picked up a telephone in his office, where he had been working. The line was dead. He tried another, and another, and another—all had been cut off. Told by the conspirators on the scene that he should declare a "state of emergency" that would allow them and their allies to take control of the country, Gorbachev replied: "Think again—this affair will end in a civil war and a great deal of bloodshed. You will have to answer for it. You are adventurers and criminals. Still, nothing will come of your plans. The people are no longer ready to put up with your dictatorship or with the loss of everything we have gained in recent years."

With that, Gorbachev recalled, the plotters "totally isolated" him and his family. In Moscow, the conspirators had ordered 250,000 pairs of handcuffs, and tanks began to roll into the heart of the city.

No one in the United States could reach Gorbachev himself, and in Maine the weather forecast was dire: a hurricane was threatening New England. What to do? Should the president remain in place in Kennebunkport, as he had during much of the Persian Gulf crisis? Or, given the weather, return to Washington for a day or two to monitor events in the Soviet Union?

The golf with Roger Clemens and a party of visitors from the Red Sox organization was off, but Bush, thoughtful as ever, did not want to stiff his guests entirely. Calling the Red Sox delegation at its hotel early in the morning, Bush said: "Not playing golf, but you are welcome to come over and have blueberry muffins." Clemens, Bush family friend Tim Samway, and others arrived for breakfast. They were greeted by Barbara Bush, who was wearing two differently colored sneakers. (This was not unusual. Her husband had once given her dozens of pairs of her favorite Keds in different colors, and she decided that the only way she could ever wear them all was to mismatch them.) As the group was served muffins and coffee, the president sat at the dining room table signing a box of baseballs between calls to world leaders.

As he approved the Coast Guard's taking his boat in from the sea, Bush wondered about the impact of the coup. "Will there be general strikes? Will there be resistance? Will the military use so much force and crack down so much that they won't permit any democratic move to go forward?" There was a new figurehead president in Moscow, and Bush recalled how one of the plotters, Dmitri Timofeyevich Yazov, a military man, had been "grumbling all the time at the meetings that we had in the Soviet Union, drinking a lot, complaining at the table with John Sununu and others about how bad things were."

Suddenly it was August 1990 all over again—the flurry of calls to foreign leaders, the weighing of options, the calibrated public remarks. Bush spoke to his opposite numbers in Italy, Japan, Canada, Great Britain, France, and Germany. "They agree with our principle—talk about reform, insistence with reform, [and] calm things so we don't get into a military confrontation role," Bush dictated. Speaking to François Mitterrand, Bush noted that the West needed to be firm but "avoid statements about rearming" and returning to a Cold War mentality. The French president agreed, saying, "Indeed. Let's not create a perception that all is lost. This coup could fail in a few days or months. It goes against the tide. It's hard to impose by force a regime on a changing nation. It won't work."

At ten to eight in the morning on Monday, August 19, Bush held a press conference in the Secret Service's little house at Walker's Point. The rain had come, forcing the session indoors. Given the uncertainty of the moment, Bush's performance was masterly, his answers well pitched to position the United States on the side of the Gorbachev-inspired reforms while taking care not to inflame the situation. In preparing for the session with reporters, Bush had written a note to himself on a draft of talking points: "The West obviously will not retreat from its principles—reform, openness, democracy."

Calling the developments "momentous and stunning," Bush told reporters that "contrary to official statements" out of Moscow "this move was extra-constitutional, outside of the constitutional provisions for governmental change."

Subtly defending Gorbachev, he said: "President Gorbachev is clearly an historic figure, one who's led the Soviet Union toward reform domestically and toward a constructive and cooperative role in the international arena. And it's important to keep in mind the enormous changes that have taken place towards openness, towards reform, changes in Eastern Europe, the newfound cooperation with the United States and others in the Gulf, and many other areas. There's a whole new era of cooperation, and we don't want to see that change, obviously."

Echoing Mitterrand, Bush added another cautionary note: "I think it's also important to know that coups can fail. They can take over at first, and then they run up against the will of the people." Asked what he thought the plotters' motivation was, he was candid. "We don't know that. We don't know that. Clearly, some of the hard-liners have been concerned about the rapidity of reform. They've been concerned about the demise of the Communist Party per se. And I think they've also been concerned about the Soviet economy. But in a coup of this manner, you never know what's going to happen. I think Gorbachev was as surprised as anybody, obviously. And let's just remain open on this as to whether it's going to succeed or not. We're seeing the first returns, you might say, coming in."

Should the hard-liners attempt to make aggressive military moves in terms of abandoning arms control treaties, Bush added, the United States stood ready to take an equally hard line. "We're not going to go back to seeing Europe as it used to be with Soviet forces all through Eastern Europe. So, we're not trying to go back to square one. . . . Obviously if they weren't adhering . . . that would be a whole different ball game." His sense of proportion was evident. Did he favor Gorbachev's return to power? "Well, I've always felt that he represented the best opportunity to see reform go forward. He's been in a bit of a balancing act, as we all know. . . . He represented enormous productive and fantastic change. And I think throwing him out in this manner is counterproductive, totally."

Had Bush used the "hot line" to Moscow, a reporter asked? No, he replied, there was no need for such a dramatic gesture. It would have been like landing on the South Lawn when he was flying back from Texas during the Reagan assassination attempt: the wrong thing at the wrong time. The hotline, he said, was associated in the public mind with "some kind of military problem between the Soviet Union and the United States. And do you think I want to suggest that to the American people or to the people in Europe? Absolutely not."

He had sent the message he wanted to send. Closing his remarks on the coup, he told the reporters: "All right, you got it. Don't say we never give you any news up here."

Bush made plans to return to Washington. In a call after the meeting with reporters, Canadian prime minister Brian Mulroney asked Bush if he thought that Gorbachev had been toppled "because he was too close to us." Bush said he had no doubt of that, and he wondered what the plotters would say was the motivating factor. "At first, they said he had health problems," Bush said to Mulroney. "Maybe that means that Gorbachev's fingernails wouldn't come out."

On the afternoon of the nineteenth, Gennady Yanayev, the self-declared president of the Soviet Union, sent Bush a letter outlining the reasons for the coup. "A disintegration of the USSR would have gravest consequences not only internally, but internationally as well," Yanayev wrote. "Under these circumstances we have no other choice but to take resolute measures in order to stop the slide toward catastrophe." Violence was possible. John Major suggested a NATO ministerial meeting, but Bush was reluctant for fear that "it will make it look like we are militarizing, [and] that we anticipate a military threat to the West. . . . It is the last damn thing we need to get involved in that kind of a confrontation."

There were extraordinary images from Moscow: Yeltsin, whom the usurpers called "reactionary" and "unconstitutional," had stood on a tank to urge that Gorbachev be restored to power. The crowd was with him, crying, "No to fascism." In a conversation with Brian Mulroney, Bush said Yeltsin had "enormous guts." Bush called Vaclav Havel, the president of Czechoslovakia, who told him that many Czechs were likening the Moscow coup to the Soviet takeover of Czechoslovakia in

1968. The call from Bush, Havel said, would "have a certain calming effect on people" in his country. Western support for the nascent democracies of the old Soviet bloc was critical, Havel told Bush, and the "development toward emancipation and self-determination in the Soviet Union" and in Czechoslovakia was "irreversible. This coup will simply complicate things . . . but it will not reverse the general development." From Poland, President Lech Walesa told Bush, "We are afraid of one thing in the Soviet Union—anarchy."

So was Bush. Just a few weeks before, the president had delivered a controversial speech in Kiev that had been seen as an attempt to bolster Gorbachev's fortunes. Eager to break away from the Soviet Union, Ukraine was struggling for independence when Bush arrived with a message of caution. "Some people have urged the United States to choose between supporting President Gorbachev and supporting independence-minded leaders throughout the U.S.S.R.," Bush said in Kiev. "I consider this a false choice." Bush added that "Freedom is not the same as independence" and warned against "suicidal nationalism." *The New York Times*'s William Safire dubbed it the "Chicken Kiev speech," and it had indeed sent the wrong signal to reformers. Bush was, however, honestly wrestling with the churn of the time. As the coup unfolded, he wondered anew whether he could truly end the Cold War without serious bloodshed.

"The thing is to be calm," Bush told his diary during the August coup. Dictating an imaginary message to Gorbachev, Bush said: "If I were to comment tonight, I would say: 'Mikhail, I hope you are well.'" The president continued:

> I hope they have not mistreated you. You have led your country in a fantastically constructive way, you've been attacked from the right and from the left, but you deserve enormous credit. Now, we don't know what the hell has happened to you, where you are, what condition you are in, but we were right to support you. I'm proud we have supported you, and there will be a lot of talking heads on television telling us what's been wrong, but you have done what's right and strong and good for your country, and I am proud that we have been supportive. I like you and I hope that you return to

power, skeptical though I am of that. . . . I hope that Yeltsin, who is calling for your return, stays firm; that he's not removed by the power of this ugly right wing coup.

Bush missed what he remembered as the clarity of the Persian Gulf crisis. "What had to happen was Iraq had to get out of Kuwait," he dictated. "Here, I'm not sure what has to happen. What I'd like to see is a return of Gorbachev and a continuous movement for democracy. I'm not quite sure I see how to get there."

Early on Tuesday morning, August 20, 1991, Bush spoke to Yeltsin for twenty-five minutes. Yeltsin's headquarters in Moscow was surrounded. "He thinks they might storm the building; he says there are a hundred thousand people outside, and, all-in-all, this courageous man is standing by his principles," Bush dictated. Yeltsin reported that Gorbachev himself was surrounded by "three rings" of KGB and Soviet troops loyal to the plotters. (He also suggested that a delegation from the World Health Organization check on Gorbachev's condition.)

Bush told Yeltsin that he was willing to call Yanayev, but he did not want to legitimize the junta. "No, absolutely, you should not do that," Yeltsin said. He asked Bush to "demand to speak on the phone with Gorbachev and to rally world leaders to the fact that the situation here is critical," both of which Bush did. Bush asked Yeltsin to stay in touch. ("I hope that the lines will not be cut off," Bush said.)

By the next day, throngs of pro-Yeltsin supporters had filled the streets to fight the coup, and the Russian Supreme Soviet had supported Yeltsin's push against the plotters.

Back in Maine after a quick trip to Washington, Bush and Scowcroft set up headquarters in the living room of the main house at Walker's Point. As the rains whipped against the big windows, the two men worked the telephones. At one point they were handed a cable reporting that Margaret Thatcher was trying to insert herself into the crisis. The former prime minister was attempting to reach Gorbachev in the Crimea and had telephoned Reagan in California, Bush was told, saying, "We were in it at the beginning." As Bush noted in his diary, "This obviously annoys John Major tremendously. Some people simply can't let go."

Yeltsin steadily took control, fighting off the plotters and rallying pro-democracy forces. In a call on the twenty-first, he told Bush that Bush's words against the coup were "an important statement by the American President in support of the Soviet people."

The weather eased enough for Bush to take a ride aboard *Fidelity*, and he was delighted by the thrill of speeding through the choppy seas. Back at the pier, John Magaw of the Secret Service approached Bush with a message: There was a call waiting in the house from "a Chief of State."

"Who?" Bush asked, but Magaw would not say. Returning to his bedroom, Bush, wearing a damp windbreaker and blue jeans, picked up the receiver to find Gorbachev on the other end of the line. (When Gorbachev had gotten through, he had said, " There is a God.")

"My dearest George," Gorbachev said. "I'm so happy to hear your voice again."

"My God," Bush said, "I'm glad to hear you." They spoke for eleven minutes. "He sounded jubilant and he sounded upbeat," Bush dictated. "He was very, very grateful to me . . . for the way we've conducted ourselves."

The coup had failed, in part because of Yeltsin's defiance and in part because the conspirators were largely inept. The peaceful resolution of the crisis was, for Bush, a ratification of his essential diplomatic instincts of balance and moderation. "We could have overreacted, and moved troops, and scared the hell out of people," Bush told his diary. "We could have under-reacted by saying, 'Well, we'll deal with whoever is there.' But . . . I think we found the proper balance."

Three days later, in Moscow, Gorbachev resigned as head of the Communist Party and announced that he believed the party itself should be dissolved. Though Gorbachev had survived the coup, Bush told his diary, he "appears to be weakened—Yeltsin dealing with him in a heavy handed manner. But ours is not to fine-tune every change inside the Soviet Union. Ours is to see, as best we can, things go in our direction, that they go toward world peace, that they go toward freedom and democracy."

On Monday, September 2, 1991, Bush lunched on the terrace at Walker's Point. After a bowl of clam chowder, a small ham sandwich, and a glass of sherry, he sat alone on the porch soaking up the sun on a spectacularly clear day. Watching about forty seagulls on the rocks near the house, Bush noted that it was the forty-seventh anniversary of Chichi-Jima. "So much has happened, so very much in my life and in the world," Bush dictated on the porch.

He thought more of the future than of the past—in this case, about the 1992 presidential campaign. A political memorandum from Clayton Yeutter, who had succeeded Lee Atwater as head of the RNC, briefed Bush on the latest. Al Gore had announced that he would not seek the Democratic nomination, which, Yeutter wrote, "seems to have stimulated increased interest on the part of some of the second tier Democrats." One name Yeutter mentioned was Bill Clinton's. The "general feeling" among Arkansas Republicans, Yeutter wrote, was that Clinton would run, "though that could bring his personal life under increased scrutiny and could perhaps cause him some embarrassment. Notwithstanding the risk, they see him as too ambitious personally to resist the temptation. Even though he may judge his 1992 probabilities of success as being quite low, he'll want to posture himself for 1996." On the deck overlooking the sea, Bush dictated: "Bill Clinton appears to be in the race."

A charming and talented young southerner, William Jefferson Clinton was the same age as George W. Bush. Raised in Arkansas by a colorful, doting mother and an abusive stepfather, Clinton had been an undergraduate at Georgetown University, won a Rhodes scholarship to Oxford, and returned from England to study at Yale Law School before moving home to Arkansas to begin a political career. He lost a U.S. House race in 1974, won a statewide campaign as attorney general in 1976, and was elected governor in 1978. Nationally, Clinton was seen as a leader of a newly prominent moderate wing of the Democratic Party determined to break the Republican hold on the presidency.

Bush had gotten to know Clinton in working together on education issues, particularly at the Charlottesville governors' summit. "I like Bill," Bush told his diary on Monday, September 2, 1991. "He's a nice, decent guy." Bush's competitive sensibility, however, gave him confidence. "I think," Bush concluded, "I can beat him."

On Tuesday, October 8, 1991, Clarence Thomas's Supreme Court confirmation hearings took an unexpected turn. A former subordinate of Thomas's, Anita Hill, charged that the nominee had been guilty of sexual harassment. The allegations had leaked out of the Senate Judiciary Committee, and the White House suspected the staffs of liberal senators Ted Kennedy and Howard Metzenbaum of Ohio. Bush called it a "last-minute smear. . . . [A] chicken-shit operation if I ever saw one. It is smear and innuendo, orchestrated, I am told, by a Metzenbaum and Kennedy staffer. They are guilty, in my view, of the worst kind of sleaze politics."

It was a terrible moment—personally for Thomas and politically for Bush. Yet the president never wavered in his support for his nominee. On the day after the Anita Hill accusations broke, Bush asked Thomas and his wife to come to the White House. Bush spoke with Thomas while Barbara took Mrs. Thomas for a walk. The president's visit with the nominee was "very emotional," Bush told his diary. "I am determined not to upset things by inadvertently venting my true feelings, which are a disgust for the process, disdain for those . . . militants who convict him in public, annoyance and anger at the groups who want to get him for abortion or get him for something [and are] now out there hanging their hat on the charge by this woman."

Walking the White House grounds with Bush on a splendid autumn day, Thomas "told me how brutal and terrible this had been; how he simply didn't understand it; how he tried very hard to conduct himself in a decent way all of this life," Bush dictated.

Bush saw the matter in philosophical terms. "They want to defeat him—not because of sexual harassment necessarily, but because of a lot of other views," Bush dictated. "It is a stinking, lousy process, and I feel bitter about it." The president believed Thomas's version of events, not Anita Hill's. On Tuesday, October 15, 1991, Barbara joined Bush in the study off the Oval Office to watch the Senate vote. Thomas prevailed, 52 to 48. Asked about Thomas two decades later, Bush said: "I am very proud of him, and I respect him—he did not have an easy life, and here he is on the Supreme Court of the United States."

The weekend of the Thomas debacle coincided with the anniversary of Robin's death. On the helicopter ride between Camp David and the White House, Barbara reminded her husband that it had been thirty-eight years since they had lost their little girl. "Thirty eight—it is so hard to believe," Bush told his diary. "I can literally feel her presence sometimes."

It was a melancholy season. While monitoring the Thomas drama, Bush had gone for a run at Camp David with Ranger, who "tore through the woods, down the trails, leaves flying, and I wondered at the beauty. I wonder if [as] you get older if you notice the leaves more. I slowed down, almost stopped, to look at a brilliant red leaf lying there among the golds and the browns. I thought, 'Boy, is time running out?'"

There was Thomas, there was the slow economy, and there was the question of John Sununu's future. In many ways the White House chief of staff was a casualty of the recession and of the president's own inability to recapture the energy of 1989, 1990, and the first few months of 1991. As the economy had slowed and the reality of the 1990 budget deal sunk in—there would be, by design, less federal money to spend on programs—the Bush White House could point to fewer domestic successes. While there had been progress on the budget, on education, on the environment, and on the Americans with Disabilities Act in the first half of Bush's term, things seemed different now. Bush's approval numbers were—as the president himself had predicted at the very moment of victory in the Persian Gulf—drifting downward.

Sununu was a tough chief of staff—the bad cop—and tough chiefs of staff tend to make more enemies than friends. For George H. W. Bush's chief of staff, in particular, that was part of the job description. Bush hated saying no, so Sununu was the one who delivered bad news. By late 1991 he had delivered a lot of it to a lot of people—often too harshly—and he had few allies now that things had gotten rough.

Sununu was also weakened by a series of reports about his travel at taxpayer expense, including his once taking a car and driver from Washington to New York for a stamp auction. Sununu maintained that he was following policy by using cars and planes that enabled him to stay in secure communication with the White House. Nevertheless, the frenzy about the sins of the man who, according to *Newsweek,* was known to staffers as "King John" (behind his back, of course), added to unhappiness within the administration about him and his style.

Yet firing people was not in Bush's nature, even when he knew that it was time for someone to move on. In the late autumn of 1991, Bush asked his eldest son to undertake a kind of research project for him. Would George W. poll the top people in the administration, the cabinet, and the 1992 reelection campaign and come back to him with thoughts about how things should be structured going forward? George W. was honored. "It was a big moment—your dad, the president of the United States, asked me to do something," George W. recalled. "It was universal that there was a problem inside the White House." The message was the same all over the place: Sununu needed to go. "Mother and Dad and I were upstairs and I gave my report," George W. recalled. "It was my role to create the conditions where it was easier for Dad to tell John that it was time to move on."

Over dinner in the Residence, George W. delivered the verdict: "Basically the White House structure has become such that you're isolated," George W. told his father, "and everybody on your team thinks it's because of Sununu." The president sat, impassive, taking it in for what seemed an eternity. "And there was nothing, no reaction," George W. recalled. "He was thinking. He said nothing." Finally the father broke the long silence. "So who's best to do this?" Bush said. George W. suggested a few names, Jim Baker and Bob Mosbacher among them. Bush didn't think any of the possibilities quite worked. "There was no good option," George W. recalled, and then he volunteered himself for the assignment. "If you'd like," George W. said, "I can do it, and I'll do it the right way." Another long pause. "All right, son," Bush said, and ended the conversation.

George W. spent the night in the White House, and at five thirty the next morning the telephone next to his bed rang, waking him up. His father was on the line. "Son, good luck today," Bush said. George W. had a conversation with Sununu laying out the same things he had told his parents the night before and suggesting that the chief of staff give the president the option of making a change.

After the meeting, George W. walked out to the horseshoe pit near the Oval Office with Sununu. When the son caught his father's eye, he winked: All would be well. (At lunch, father and son had a long talk. The elder Bush wanted to hear everything that had happened, word for word.) It took several more days—Sununu mounted a brief campaign to keep his job—but the chief of staff eventually resigned. Sununu was out, and Bush asked Transportation Secretary Sam Skinner to step in. But no organizational chart could change the reality that many Americans felt the economy was in trouble.

The president's polls kept falling. "It's hard to get the Christmas spirit because we're under tremendous fire on the economy," Bush told his diary. His ratings in an ABC News–*Washington Post* survey put him at 47 percent approval, with 50 percent holding a negative view of his performance. It was, he noted gloomily, "the lowest I have ever been." He held no one but himself responsible. "I must accept all the blame for this," he dictated. "It goes with the job." He had survived tough times before. "The big thing is don't show it. Just keep going, do your best."

The politics of the Middle East were always in play. Despite their cooperation in the Gulf War, the American president and the Israeli prime minister did not have the warmest of relationships. In 1989, when Yitzak Shamir had come to the United States, Bush had urged Israel to stop building settlements in the occupied territories in the hope that such a concession might improve relations with the Palestinians. As Richard Haass, who was in the Oval Office with the two leaders, recalled it, Shamir gestured dismissively and said "no problem." The exchange led to great confusion. "Bush thought he had an understanding from Shamir that the Israelis would not cause any problems with their settlement activity, meaning that they would cease building new ones," Haass recalled. "Shamir, I later learned, thought he was telling the president that the settlements . . . should not cause any problem and that all the debate was much ado about nothing. Shamir thus continued authorizing them; Bush thought the Israeli leader had broken his word."

Now, two years later, Bush and Baker hoped to use the coalition victory in the Gulf as an opportunity to address the long-standing Israeli-Palestinian conflict. In a series of tense meetings, Baker traveled the Middle East to build support for a summit to be held in Madrid. Bush also insisted that Israel pay a price on the road to the conference, announcing that he was holding up "$10 billion in loan guarantees" for the resettlement of Soviet Jews unless Israel stopped the settlements. "It was hard to exaggerate how emotional it all was," Richard Haass recalled. Israel believed Bush largely "unfriendly," even hostile, and the president inadvertently reinforced that view by telling the press that he was "'one lonely little guy' up against 'some powerful political forces,' that is, the Jewish lobby," Haass recalled. "I winced." He told Bush and Scowcroft that the statement "would trigger alarm bells. They were genuinely surprised. But it did. Jewish leaders were taken aback, and the president, who did not have a prejudiced bone in his body, was hurt that they thought he was speaking in some anti-Semitic code." The Madrid conference, which began on Wednesday, October 30, 1991, was notable, but the region remained a historic tangle, essentially impervious to even the most diplomatically minded of American presidents.

On Christmas Day 1991, at ten in the morning eastern standard time, the head of the Soviet Union called the president of the United States to announce the end of the experiment in Communism born in the Bolshevik Revolution of 1917.

To Bush, whom he reached at Camp David, Gorbachev was warm—and reassuring on a key question. He told Bush that he would transfer authority over the nuclear arsenal to Yeltsin as soon as he had announced his resignation. "I can assure you that everything is under strict control," Gorbachev said. "There will be no disconnection. You can have a very quiet Christmas evening."

To the world, Gorbachev said: "An end has been put to the 'Cold War,' the arms race, and the insane militarization of our country, which crippled our economy, distorted our thinking and undermined our morals. The threat of a world war is no more."

Bush was gracious in victory. Speaking from the Oval Office at nine P.M. on Christmas night, he said: "Mikhail Gorbachev's revolutionary policies transformed the Soviet Union. His policies permitted the peoples of Russia and the other republics to cast aside decades of oppression and established the foundations of freedom." The Cold War, Bush said, "shaped the lives of all Americans. It forced all nations to live under the specter of nuclear destruction. That confrontation is now over."

The Cold War ended for many reasons. Among them were the aspirations of millions of ordinary people behind the Iron Curtain; the leadership of men such as Lech Walesa and Vaclav Havel and Pope John Paul II; the reforms of Mikhail Gorbachev; and the decades-long resolve of the West, particularly the United States, to stand strong against Communism.

In the final analysis, Gorbachev was unable to master the forces that he had helped unleash: the drive for more democratic institutions, for market economics, for an end to a totalitarian culture that could not withstand sustained challenge from the West. From Truman to Reagan, American presidents had confronted the Soviet threat in different ways in different eras. The 1980s had been critical, with Reagan articulating a vision not of coexistence with, but of victory over, Communism. And Bush's quiet insistence on peaceably dismantling the Soviets' territorial empire, most notably in Germany, had struck a mortal blow.*

"I didn't want to get too maudlin or too emotional, but you literally feel you're caught up in real history with a phone call like this," Bush dictated. "Something important, some enormous turning point. God, we're lucky in this country—we have so many blessings."

His joy was tempered by the realization of what awaited him in the new year. "There will be no let up," Bush dictated. "Everything we do will be screened and seen [as] purely political, and be hammered away at every turn. The reporting reminds me of 1988. It used to be 'dogged by Iran-Contra, the [Vice] President came to Iowa'; now it's 'dogged by the recession, the President trying to make things look good,' or whatever."

Two days after Gorbachev's announcement, on Friday, December 27, 1991, Bob Teeter handed Bush a poll that was "discouraging in every way—not only in my own popularity, but the American people are all over the field on what they want to see to fix the economy. . . . Right now, nobody thinks we're doing a damn thing about the economy. . . . Every single day they are pounding out with some negative message, and so even though inflation is better than it's been; interest rates are lower than they've been; unemployment less bad than in a recession, everyone thinks we're on the wrong track, and confidence is at a lower level than even Jimmy Carter's horrible days"—Jimmy Carter, the one-term president.

---

* Asked in retirement whether he thought Reagan received too much credit for ending the Cold War, Bush replied: "I don't think too much at all, but I think to say that he singlehandedly ended the Cold War, that hurts a little bit because I think we had something to do with it. There was a speech once where Margaret Thatcher got up and said, 'Let me be clear on one thing. Ronald Reagan and I ended the Cold War.' And here was Lech Walesa there, and Vaclav Havel, and people that had made significant contributions to ending the Cold War, and that was embarrassing. Helmut Kohl sent me a note saying, 'This woman is crazy.'"

FORTY-FOUR

It Was Discouraging as Hell

★

I just wish it were over.
—GEORGE H. W. BUSH, August 1992

HE COULD BARELY SPEAK. In Tokyo for a state visit in early January 1992, Bush was at a dinner given by Japanese prime minister Kiichi Miyazawa. Halfway through the pre-meal receiving line, Bush felt faint. Realizing he was about to be sick, he excused himself, was shown to a bathroom, and vomited. Ever one to keep his commitments, Bush refused to go home. Returning to the event, he finished shaking hands and sat down beside the prime minister for dinner. Feverish, Bush could not keep up his end of the conversation. He turned pale—as "white as a sheet," one guest told *The New York Times* afterward—and lost consciousness, slumping to his left, toward Miyazawa.

"I remember breaking out into a cold sweat, water just pouring out of me, and then the next thing I knew, literally, I was on the floor," he dictated to his diary at the Akasaka Palace. "I woke up, [and] I had this euphoric feeling. It's hard to describe it . . . 100 percent strange; and then I looked up, and there I was in the faces of the nurses, and the doctors, and the Secret Service guys, lying flat on the floor." Then he saw that he had thrown up again—this time on himself and on Miyazawa. "Why don't you roll me under the table," Bush joked to the prime minister, "and I'll sleep it off while you finish the dinner." The president refused an ambulance, fixed his tie, which had been taken off to open his collar when he passed out, and walked out of the room. The Secret Service loaned him a green raincoat to cover what the *Times* decorously referred to as the "regurgitated food." "I got home and I was just dehydrated and dead tired," he dictated. Bush was back on schedule by the next afternoon.

In a small way, the president's illness connected him to a large number of his own countrymen—the stomach flu was a big problem in the winter of 1992. "Mr. Bush's bout with the flu recalled his handling of the recession," Anna Quindlen wrote in a *Times* column entitled "The Stomach Thing." "He got it after everyone else did and he kept trying to pretend it wasn't that bad."

As 1991 had drawn to a close, Bush was politically beset. To his right stood Pat Buchanan, the former Nixon and Reagan aide who had become a right-wing populist provocateur. Emboldened by Bush's breaking of "Read my lips" and driven by isolationism, the commentator embodied both the rise of constant media and of the conservative discontent with the 1990 budget agreement. On the stump, Buchanan was "sniping away, direct, nasty, tearing down," Bush dictated. Buchanan's hatred of things imperial led him to dub Bush "King George" and to call gleefully for his "Pitchfork Brigades" to topple the incumbent Republican president.

Buchanan was finding receptive audiences in New Hampshire, which had experienced difficult economic times. Richard Nixon was predicting that Buchanan might get 40 percent of the vote there. Heading into New Hampshire, Rush Limbaugh, the conservative talk-radio host who was on the rise, endorsed Buchanan. Explaining his decision to back the challenger, Limbaugh recalled thinking: "Look, if we want to win this . . . there needs to be a conservative debate, a conservative element of this campaign." Callers to Limbaugh's show used the word "Ditto" to signal their agreement with the host; in the season of Buchanan's surge in New Hampshire, the challenger's supporters would say "Lock and load" when they checked in with Limbaugh. "Ride to the sound of the guns," Buchanan was merrily saying on the trail. "Ride to the sound of the guns." (To win Limbaugh over after the primary, Bush would be himself, inviting the radio kingmaker to spend the night in the Lincoln Bedroom. The president carried Limbaugh's bag to the room himself. Roger Ailes had brokered the evening.)

In a campaign memo, Alex Castellanos, a Bush adviser, assessed the Buchanan threat. "Pat Buchanan is currently a safe outlet for protest," Castellanos wrote on Monday, January 6, 1992. "Voters do not want him to be President. He is the vehicle through which they can send George Bush a message." The key, then, Castellanos argued, was for Bush to emphasize that he'd gotten that message *before* the primary. To make his point, Castellanos created an imaginative scenario. "If we could capture the campaign in one scene, for example, it might be this," he wrote, continuing:

Someone representing the state's economic frustrations, a soft-Bush voter, confronts George Bush in New Hampshire and says "Here's what happened to us. Help us." Perhaps she breaks down. The President lets her vent her frustrations, then goes to her in his role as father figure, hugs her, holds her, reassuring her. He repeats her concerns. "I know we have priorities here at home. You are my priority. It is going to be all right. Here is what we are going to do."

A lovely scene—but it would never happen. Bush was not that kind of campaigner. He knew, though, that he had to do something to reassert himself on the trail. He was so worried about a trip to New Hampshire to fend off the Buchanan insurgency in mid-January that he took a sleeping pill the night before.

The day in New Hampshire was a disaster. At an Exeter town hall meeting, reading from a note card designed to remind him of the work at hand, Bush declared: "Message: I care." In Dover, he said, "Don't cry for me, Argentina," quoting, for no apparent reason, a song from the musical *Evita*. He rendered the Nitty Gritty Dirt Band as "the Nitty Ditty Nitty Gritty Great Bird." He called himself "Mrs. Rose Scenario" as he tried to project economic confidence. It had been a miserable day. "You try to smile," Bush told his diary, "you try to keep a stiff upper lip; you try to encourage people, you don't want to get down; and every night on the news and every day we get hammered."

In Orlando the week after his State of the Union address, Bush attended a convention of the National Grocers Association. He was shown a new technology for scanning items in grocery store checkout lanes—an improvement on existing systems that had become common in American stores—and evinced polite interest and surprise. Watching a live video feed of the event and working from a pool report—a customary practice for White House coverage—Andrew Rosenthal, a reporter for *The New York Times*, wrote a story depicting Bush as "amazed" (Bush's word) by the exhibit. The piece captured the political moment perfectly, portraying the president as distant from everyday realities. The White House pushed back against the story, and the Associated Press reported that Bush had been shown new technology that could read a code that had been "ripped and jumbled into five pieces." The ferocity of the Bush reaction—Marlin Fitzwater denounced the story as "media-manufactured and maintained"—inadvertently underscored how vulnerable the president felt in the winter of 1992. "All in all," Bush dictated after the article appeared, "it's a pain in the ass."

On Sunday, January 19, 1992, *The New York Post* had published a story about Bill Clinton's alleged extramarital activity unsubtly headlined "Wild Bill." Reading the article, Bush told his diary that the sex stories "ought to be out of the political arena, and ought to stay on the issues. The standard should be, 'The Public Trust,' and if behavior spills over into a person's duties that's one thing, but just to dig into the past in an insidious way . . . does not contribute anything to the process."

It was a measured, mature perspective, one that had to have been influenced by the old allegations about Bush and what George W. had called the "Big A" in 1987. After the Clinton *Post* report, Gennifer Flowers, an Arkansas woman, sold her story about an alleged twelve-year affair with Clinton to the *Star,* a supermarket tabloid. "It makes politics ugly and nasty," Bush told his diary, "and the climate bad, and there is no gain for anyone in all of this." Bush had been here before, when Gary Hart's 1987 implosion had led to speculation about a Bush affair. "They ought to leave this kind of crap out of the campaigns, but any comment we make will be interpreted as fanning the fires on Clinton and his wife," Bush dictated. "Our friends in Arkansas say every bit of it is true. . . . The press claims they hate it and they love it—it's very clear."

Then, in early February, a letter Bill Clinton had written as a young man seeking to minimize his chances of going to Vietnam surfaced. He had made a commitment to enter the ROTC to avoid being drafted only to learn afterward that he had a high draft number, which meant his chances of being conscripted were lower. At that point, Clinton had backed out of his agreement to join the ROTC, thus avoiding military service altogether. "Here's a guy who said he was going to go in, and then went back on his commitment or word," Bush dictated after reading about Clinton's youthful maneuvers, "but all of that kind of thing is not in focus now."

Bush did not want his campaign trafficking in rumors. In mid-February, after a pollster for Bob Kerrey was discovered to have faxed negative information on Clinton and the draft to a reporter, Bush issued a stern memorandum to his top team. "It is absolutely essential that all personnel be told that they must not resort to campaign tactics that assault another's character," Bush wrote. "Please be sure all hands get the word." The president was especially sensitive to charges of negative campaigning, given the prevailing view that he had stooped to conquer in 1988—a view that Lee Atwater himself had seemed to endorse in 1991.

After suffering a seizure while delivering a speech, Atwater had been diagnosed with a terminal brain tumor. In a confessional piece in *Life* magazine, he expressed some regrets. "In 1988, fighting Dukakis, I said that I 'would strip the bark off the little bastard' and 'make Willie Horton his running mate.' I am sorry for both statements: the first for its naked cruelty, the second because it makes me sound racist, which I am not." Atwater wrote Dukakis to apologize. "We obviously were on opposite sides of a tough and negative campaign, but at least he had the courage to apologize," Dukakis said. "That says a lot for the man." Bush took the news of Atwater's March 1991 death hard, telling his diary: "He suffered a lot at the end—too much—and off he goes to God's loving arms."

For the White House, the results of the New Hampshire primary on Tuesday, February 18, 1992, were miserable. Bush won, but Buchanan polled 40.4 percent, which nearly matched Eugene McCarthy's protest vote against Lyndon Johnson in 1968. Newt Gingrich told *The New York Times* that the vote was a "primal scream" of populist anger with the status quo.

Heading into primaries in Georgia and Texas, the Bush team contemplated what to do about the energetic Buchanan challenge. Bob Teeter argued that Bush should take him on directly; Dan Quayle insisted that he should not. Agreeing with Quayle, Bush said he would largely hold his fire against Buchanan for now but "might tweak him from time to time."

Bush did make one course correction in the wake of Buchanan's strong finish in New Hampshire. On the eve of the Georgia primary, Bush told *The Atlanta Constitution* that the tax increases in the 1990 budget deal had been his "biggest mistake." He was, in effect, repudiating his own political courage. His mea culpa was about tactics, not substance, and the *Constitution* interview appears to have been the product of his exhaustion with his conservative critics. He tossed a bit overnight about his "biggest mistake" language. "It's hard to tell how it will go, but any fair-minded person would say, 'My God, he's getting hammered by this

Read My Lips and I can understand that he wished he hadn't done it,'"
Bush dictated. These were the musings of a man under campaign pressure; he was, for a moment, thinking more about how to get through the
day than he was about the substance of what he had done.

On Wednesday, March 18, 1992, Bush spoke with Roger Ailes, who
had been largely shut out of the reelection campaign by Bob Teeter
and others but who still kept in touch with the president. ("Reelections
are always very corporate, very buttoned down, and the guys around
Bush thought they didn't need me," recalled Ailes. "I was seen as the
'junkyard dog,' and they didn't think they needed one this time.")
    Ailes reported on what Bush called "the ugliness the Clinton people
are trying to peddle to Rupert Murdoch: affidavits—supposed affidavits—
smearing me. . . . He says that Murdoch told them he didn't want any
part of it." In these same weeks, the Bush rumors were mentioned in a
Gail Sheehy profile of Hillary Clinton in *Vanity Fair*. "Why does the press
shy away from investigating rumors about George Bush's extramarital
life?" Hillary asked. She then went on to answer her own question. "I'm
convinced part of it is that the establishment—regardless of party—
sticks together," Hillary told Sheehy. "They're going to circle the wagons
on Jennifer and all these other people."
    "Baloney," replied Barbara Bush. In private, *The Washington Post* re-
ported, Barbara was harsher, calling Hillary's *Vanity Fair* comments "lower
than low." The president hated everything about the subject. "It's just
the symbol of how horrible it all is," Bush dictated on Tuesday, April 7,
1992. The rumors made one more notable appearance in the 1992 campaign. A new biography of the Washington lobbyist Robert Gray reported that a now-dead ambassador had claimed that he had once been
asked to arrange a tryst for Bush and Jennifer Fitzgerald at a château
in Switzerland. The story was being promoted by Democrats and was
picked up by *The New York Post* in August. At a press conference with Bush
and visiting Israeli Prime Minister Yitzhak Rabin at Walker's Point on
the day of the *Post* article, a CNN reporter asked about the allegation. A
furious president dismissed the story as "a lie." To his diary, Bush said:
"My main worry is the family; hurt to the family; and [the] hurt particularly to Bar; but there is not a damn thing you can do about it in this ugly
climate. I felt I had to knock it down—the lie that it is—but it keeps the
gossip merchants happy."

Ross Perot, who had long been at the periphery of Bush's life, had moved to the center of it in the spring of 1992.

A spry Texas billionaire, Perot had made his fortune building a computer business (with significant government contracts) in Dallas. A graduate of the Naval Academy in Annapolis, Perot seemed a straight talker from the plain-speaking West, full of colorful analogies and refreshingly free of traditional political cant. Rather like Lee Iacocca and Peter Ueberroth from the 1980s, Perot was a familiar American archetype: a heroic outsider who might just be able to ride in to rescue the nation from hard times and broken politics.

In a speech at the National Press Club, Perot said he was available to be drafted to run for president. It was, Bush dictated, "a big massive ego trip," but the announcement resonated. "He now wants to parlay his outsidership into winning the election," Bush told his diary, "or, if not that, bringing me down." Bush believed part of Perot's motivation was personal. It had fallen to Vice President Bush to tell Perot that he would have to reduce his involvement in the Vietnam POW/MIA issue during the Reagan years, and Bush never forgot Perot's unhappiness in 1977 when Bush declined to come work for him. Now, in '92, Bush believed the public romance with the Texas billionaire would last about three months, at which point "Perot will be defined; seen as a weirdo; and we shouldn't be concerned with him."

To run his campaign, Perot hired Republican consultant Ed Rollins, Bush's old nemesis from the National Republican Congressional Committee, as well as former Carter chief of staff Hamilton Jordan. The Rollins news struck close to home, for Rollins's then-wife, Sherrie, was assistant to the president for public liaison and intergovernmental affairs, a high-ranking White House post. Before her husband took the Perot job, Sherrie had been determined that Bush hear the news about her husband's defection from her directly. In the president's study off the Oval Office, she found a placid George H. W. Bush. She was worried, she said, that Republicans like Rollins would not be considering going to work for an independent candidate if they weren't concerned that Bush was going to lose in November. The president was unfazed. "Sherrie, Ed is making a terrible mistake," Bush told her. "I know Ross Perot, and he's crazy. Mark my words, this won't last. And the American people are never going to elect a person of Bill Clinton's character. This is all going to work out, and we're gonna win."

The president may have been calm, but the political mood of the country was deeply unsettled. Positioning himself as an outsider Mr. Fix-It, Perot had a spectacular spring in the polls, leading both Bush and Clinton. As summer arrived, Perot continued to lead in national surveys, with Bush and Clinton competing for second place. Why, Bush wondered, did the voters not see what he saw—that Perot, as Bush put it to his diary, was "outrageously ill-suited to be President of the United States"?

After terrible riots in Los Angeles following the acquittal of white police officers who had been videotaped beating an African American, Rodney King, Vice President Quayle spoke to the Commonwealth Club in San Francisco about family values. He discussed the high costs of the breakdown of the two-parent family. In a noteworthy popular allusion, Quayle added that the CBS situation comedy *Murphy Brown,* in which Candice Bergen played a single Washington reporter, sent the wrong cultural signal when the title character had a child out of wedlock and called it "just another 'lifestyle choice.'"

Quayle was widely attacked for seeming to be insensitive to hardworking single mothers, and the White House staff was in what Quayle called a "total panic." The president himself had never seen the show and was a bit puzzled by the whole thing.

From Florida, Jeb Bush was impressed by Quayle's performance. "While the liberal columnists and editorial writers denigrate him (the same folks who rip you apart regularly)," Jeb wrote his father in a memorandum dated June 2, 1992, "he has scored big with our base vote." Jeb thought the "values theme" a good one, suggested that his father pursue it, and closed with a piece of practical counsel. "On another subject, I really think it would be good to have George [W.] up in D.C. more often," Jeb wrote. "I believe we are in for a rumble and the folks around you, while all fine people, are a cautious lot." In another sign of the president's lack of focus on the mechanics of the election, he failed to follow up on Jeb's good suggestion, and George W., now managing partner of the Texas Rangers, remained in Dallas, in touch with his dad but removed from the day-to-day campaign operations he had been part of four years before.

The administration and the campaign's lethargy had made the president nostalgic for John Sununu. Bush was dissatisfied with Sam Skinner as chief of staff. "I must confess, I miss Sununu and his brilliance and his ability to put things in perspective, and to get up and browbeat the Hill," Bush told his diary in May 1992. Bush credited Sununu with helping pass the ADA, the clean air bill, the civil rights bill, and even the budget agreement. "Yes, there was a lot of china broken, but I'm wondering if we don't need the Chief of Staff to step up his activities, and get control more," Bush dictated.

On the eve of the Democratic National Convention in New York in the summer, Bill Clinton took an unusual step. Confounding the conventional political calculus, he chose a fellow southern baby boomer, Al Gore of Tennessee, as his vice presidential running mate. The public reaction to the tableau of the energetic and attractive Gore family joining the Clintons in Little Rock was palpably positive. In the White House, Bush assessed the changing dynamics. "I've always thought Gore was kind of fragile and surreal, very liberal; and on the environment, he's [a] far-out extremist," Bush dictated on Friday, July 10, 1992. Bush noted that Gore's family life (he had married his high school sweetheart) and his military record (he had served in Vietnam) were happy contrasts to Clinton, "but it will be like other Vice Presidential nominees—it's really the top of the ticket that makes the difference."

Bush may have been right historically, but the Gore announcement signaled the beginning of a summertime Democratic renaissance. The two southerners seemed, in the words of *Newsweek*'s pre-convention cover, to be the "Young Guns" who could effectively take the fight to the aging Bush. As the Democratic ticket roared into New York for what was to be a highly effective four days of introducing Clinton as a repackaged "Man from Hope," Bush was enduring a six-hour meeting with advisers on Monday, July 13 that served only to remind the president how lethargic the campaign was. "I'm not getting the strong staff support we get in the foreign policy field," Bush told his diary. "They keep telling me that the polls show I'm disconnected; the polls show I don't care; the polls show I don't get it and I keep saying, 'Fine, I do, but don't tell me what the polls show, tell me what to do about it.'"

He and virtually everyone around him believed that he needed Jim Baker to take over the campaign. In a repeat of the drama of 1988, Baker was happily serving in a high cabinet post and unhappily considering a return to the hourly political wars. To escape the pressures of the campaign during the Democratic convention, Bush took off for a fishing trip with Baker (Jeb would join them for part of the holiday) at the secretary of state's ranch in Wyoming. In the wilderness, Bush reached an understanding with Baker. The secretary of state would return to the White House for one last Bush campaign. Baker longed to remain at State, traveling the world, but all the small rivalries and tiny resentments, the occasional competitiveness and the inevitable tensions, were swept away when Bush made it clear that he needed Baker. Hearing this, Baker agreed; the ambition and the pride fell away. "He'll do what I want him to do," Bush dictated. "He has to be at my side."

At a quarter after nine on the second morning of the trip, there was a bulletin from Dallas. Ross Perot was withdrawing from the race. Summoning reporters, Bush called the Perot news "a positive development" and invited the billionaire's supporters to join the Bush cause. Away from the journalists, Bush reached Perot himself from Baker's meadow. The connection was poor, but their chat was "civil," Bush told his diary, and he told Perot he would be back in touch again soon. Perot said he "would welcome that."

One of Bush's first calls was to George W., who was "elated and feels this guarantees that we'll carry Texas," Bush dictated. "It also throws the Clinton-Gore strategy [off] a little bit. Because with Perot out of there . . . we ought to do well across the South, regardless of the Vice President." Now that he was out of the campaign, Perot made anti-Clinton noises. "I want to talk to George in total privacy," Perot told his intermediaries. His intended message was that Clinton would be disastrous for the country. "He's very pissed off at me," Bush dictated, "but he hates Clinton." Bush and Perot were supposed to meet, but Perot grew difficult about setting a date and alleged—with no evidence—that the administration had released his fitness reports from his time in the navy. Tired of the back-and-forth, Bush let the matter of a meeting drop.

He did, however, keep hearing talk of a Perot "October Surprise," whatever that might be.

The Clinton-Gore ticket surged out of the Democratic convention at Madison Square Garden. After New York, Gallup had the Democrats leading Bush 57 to 32 percent. In the face of such numbers, Bush's friends, family, and advisers were looking for *anything* that might put the president on the path to victory. In the weeks before the Republican

National Convention in Houston, that search led many on Bush's side to contemplate whether the time had come to drop Dan Quayle from the ticket.

It was not the most propitious of moments for Quayle (his propitious moments were few and far between). Though loyal to his vice president, Bush himself had his ambivalent moments. The year before, in the summer of 1991, Bush had told his diary: "I think he will be a good campaigner, work hard, go to certain places, and I damn sure don't want to go back on my feeling that he should be on the ticket. I worry though that he might not be quite ready to be President, but then I expect every President thinks that. Reagan probably wondered whether I'd be ready to be President. On the other hand, [Quayle]'s far brighter than the critics [think], and I think if something happened to me . . . his big challenge would be to establish confidence, get good people, and then I think all these fears would go away. He's got a lot of right-wing reflexes."

On CNN's *Larry King Live* in the summer of 1992, Quayle had said that he would stand by his daughter should she choose an abortion, only to have Marilyn Quayle announce that no, her husband was wrong. Their daughter would carry any baby to term. "It's all over the television, and now the pro-abortion people are saying Dan finally showed some humanity," Bush told his diary. "In the meantime, the press goes on and on, on and on, bashing, bashing, bashing."

For almost exactly four years, ever since his hasty introduction to the nation at the convention on the water's edge in New Orleans, Quayle had done his best to win over an underwhelmed public. His polling numbers were stubbornly low, and even a largely favorable David Broder–Bob Woodward *Washington Post* series had failed to shift the conventional wisdom within the political class. Bush himself was occasionally put out by what he found to be Quayle's reflexive conservatism and by the Quayle staff's eagerness to position their principal as the most reliably right-wing voice in the White House. Taken all in all, though, Bush liked Quayle and understood well the difficulties of the vice presidency. A careful reconstruction of the Quayle question by *Newsweek*'s 1992 special-project election team found that as important, perhaps, was Bush's conviction that removing his 1988 choice from the 1992 ticket would be an implicit admission that choosing Quayle had been a mistake in the first place. In the aftermath of the storm over "Read my lips," the president had no appetite for such a political moment. It was true, Bush acknowledged to himself, that Quayle's polling performance was "terrible. . . . He's not resonating; he does not project Presidential timber; right now, he's being compared unfavorably with the plastic Al Gore," Bush dictated. "Gore is getting an enormous press ride out of the Convention, but I see that for what it is—a kick, a boost."

Others close to Bush, including his elder sons, thought Quayle should go. George W. Bush suggested replacing him with Dick Cheney; Jeb called in from Florida "saying he's had calls from many real conservatives and Christians saying that we ought to get rid of Quayle," his father told his diary. The boys were clear: Bush needed to do something decisive to get back into this thing. At the moment, though, Bush could not see his way clear to sacrificing Quayle on the altar of expediency. "When your own sons and others say you ought to do something to look strong, I have to know that it is pervasive," Bush dictated. Yet, he added, "I wouldn't look strong. I would look like I had sold him out, and the hue-and-cry would rise up, particularly from the right."

Still, the counsel kept coming. Peggy Noonan told Bush that she thought Dick Darman should be fired and Jack Kemp should replace Quayle on the ticket. Former President Ford telephoned to urge a vice presidential change. Jim Baker favored a new running mate but could not see how to effect it if the president remained reluctant.

Newsweek's election team later revealed that there was one dream scenario for several Bush allies: Have George Herbert Walker Bush name the first candidate of color to a major-party national ticket. A Colin Powell vice presidential nomination was by now an old Washington fantasy, one that had been bruited about since early in the run-up to the Gulf War. The problem was that Bush was unwilling to do what he needed to do to bring such an idea to fruition—and, in the absence of Quayle's voluntarily stepping aside, it would have been necessary for the president to effectively fire his vice president.

Before the summer, Quayle chief of staff Bill Kristol had gone to Bob Teeter, the president's reelection chairman. "What I hope doesn't happen is leaks and sniping without Bush coming to him and saying, 'I want to make a change,'" Kristol said. In the event of such a direct approach, Kristol promised not to "mobilize every conservative in Washington to rally to Quayle's support"—the vice president's team, in other words, would respect the chain of command. "The problem was that all the suggestions—if you could call them that—that Quayle should get off the ticket were so indirect that we felt entitled to fight back indirectly," Kristol recalled. And so the Quayle operation shrewdly used *The Washington Post* to cut off debate over the vice president's future. On Saturday morning, July 25, 1992, the paper reported that Bush had told Quayle that he would remain on the ticket. "There weren't any such discussions," Bush told his diary that day, "but I have concluded that he should." Bush's reasoning: "The bottom line on Quayle is, if he is dumped, I'm attacked [for] not keeping my word, 'Read My Lips'; no loyalty, looking after myself, and not the other guy," Bush dictated two days later. Quayle was to remain.

During a political meeting in the Roosevelt Room two months earlier, in May 1992, Bush had scribbled a note to Patty Presock, the deputy assistant to the president who was in charge of Oval Office operations. He was worried about his energy and his acuity, and he wanted to make sure that his medical team was fully in the picture a year into his treatment for Graves' disease. He had recently made a mistake on a letter, misdating it "82," a decade off. Bush wanted Presock to keep an eye on him. "Please save copies of places where I mess up in letters," Bush wrote her. "I want you to monitor for *frequency.* Does it relate to fatigue[,] schedule[,] or *political tension.* Tell Doctor!" In a conversation shortly thereafter with Bush, White House physician Dr. Burton Lee, and Presock, Lee asked whether Presock had noticed any changes in the president lately. "An obvious change, *at times,* was the President's handwriting and his signature," Presock recalled—and changes in handwriting could be a sign that his thyroid medication was not exactly right.

Now, after an early morning jog on Friday, July 24, 1992, Bush "felt slightly dizzy" and stopped by the White House Medical Unit before leaving for a speech in Crystal City across the Potomac. As the medical team ran tests, including an EKG, the president saw they were concerned. "I could tell they thought something was wrong," Bush dictated later that day, "and sure enough, they told me they thought I was not perfectly normal and that I might have atrial fibrillation again. It turned out that I do have atrial fib, and I felt tired." Dr. Lee had recently adjusted Bush's thyroid medicine in an attempt to raise the president's energy levels. The complexities of the Graves' disease, however, proved too great. Later that day, Bush snapped at protestors during a speech. And still later that afternoon, at another event, Bush wound up "drenched with sweat."

The heart episode passed quickly, but Bush mused to himself about what would happen if his health took a serious turn for the worse. "I got [to] thinking yesterday, hypothetically, suppose there is something wrong, then I have to . . . say to the American people, 'I told you if my health was bad, I would let you know,'" the president told his diary on Saturday, July 25. "Walk out, say I was not running, and throw the convention into a tremendous tizzy. It would be action all the way, and I don't know who the nominee would be. But maybe they would have a better time of winning, although I doubt it."

Having raised a dire scenario, he dismissed it—sort of. "In any event, that's not going to happen. But if something did happen to my health in the next week or so, or two weeks or so, that is what would have to happen." By Saturday his heartbeat had returned to normal. The White House never disclosed the president's July 1992 brief atrial fibrillation, which had been due to increasing his thyroid medication in order to find the optimal level. "If Bush had ended up with a serious problem or health issue that would have affected the performance of his duties, then we would have been honest about that with him and with the media," Dr. Lee recalled. "But this episode passed so quickly that that was not an issue, and so there was no announcement. Did we have a medical misplay because we were working on the dose? Yes. Did it have long- or short-term consequences for the president? No."

With the Republican convention approaching, the campaign and the administration debated how Bush might take the initiative on the domestic front. There was talk of using the president's acceptance speech to propose a flat tax or a value-added tax. "I like the idea of something that would have broad appeal. Now I'm thinking of government reorganization; [Civilian Conservation Corps]–type training program; and a long ball on taxes, where you would put on a consumption tax, and then cut everybody's tax rates substantially," Bush dictated on Thursday, August 13, 1992. But no: "Had a bunch of economists in yesterday who did not like that." The drift continued.

Bush arrived in Houston trailing Clinton by double digits. He had about twenty points to overcome, and if he were to do it, he had to begin now. At a welcoming rally in Houston, the Bushes joined the Quayles— Randy Travis sang—and the president enjoyed the moment. For Bush, "the adrenaline started flowing."

President Reagan addressed the convention on opening night. Now eighty-one, Reagan spoke more slowly than he had in the past, but his message was clear. "The presidency is serious business," Reagan said. "We cannot afford to take a chance. We need a man of serious purpose, unmatched experience, knowledge and ability. . . . His is a steady hand on the tiller through the choppy waters of the '90s, which is exactly what we need. We need George Bush."

Bush called on the Reagans. "A little tense with her but he was very nice," Bush dictated. There was a troubling moment. Speaking to Bush, Reagan—who would be diagnosed with Alzheimer's disease two years later—seemed lost in thought and asked, "Was Franklin D. Roosevelt a Democrat?" then recovered and "went on and spoke very fluently and very accurately about what it was like when he was a Democrat."

Endorsing Bush, Pat Buchanan electrified the convention hall with a speech that paid tribute to Reagan and took the Clintons on over issues ranging from gay rights to abortion. "Friends, this election is about more than who gets what," Buchanan said. "It is about who we are. It is about what we believe and what we stand for as Americans. There is a religious war going on in this country. It is a cultural war, as critical to the kind of nation we shall be as the Cold War itself. For this war is for the soul of America. And in that struggle for the soul of America, Clinton & Clinton are on the other side, and George Bush is on our side."

Bush called Buchanan after the speech. "He was very gracious," Buchanan recalled. To his diary, Bush dictated: "Pat Buchanan laid it to Clinton—not only [to] Hillary Clinton, but on the gays and all of this, and it made it a polarizing event. And of course, I'm asked today about attacks on Hillary . . . and I said, 'No, I wanted to stay out of the sleaze business, out of the attack business.'"

In his own acceptance speech on Thursday night, Bush opened with foreign policy, taking credit for the immense changes that had convulsed the world since he had stood before the convention in New Orleans four years before. "My opponents say I spend too much time on foreign policy, as if it didn't matter that schoolchildren once hid under their desks in drills to prepare for nuclear war," Bush said. "I saw the chance to rid our children's dreams of the nuclear nightmare, and I did."

Bush's political problem was that he didn't have the same passion for domestic policy, and he was an unconvincing actor. If he did not believe something, he had a hard time faking it—a fact that made him a good man but not the best of politicians. Observers did not think his heart was fully in the race even now, and they were largely right. "I just wish it were over," he told his diary on Saturday, August 22, 1992. Even the weather appeared to be against him. He was criticized for seeming unresponsive to victims of Florida's Hurricane Andrew, ultimately dispatching troops to help with relief.

In early September Bush arrived back at the White House from a trip to Fort Worth. George W. greeted him. "He said I looked tired and was worried about over scheduling," Bush dictated on Thursday, September 3. "One little sign of fatigue," George W. told his father, "and it raises the Quayle question all over again." Bush admitted his son had a point: "I think that's right."

Quayle, however, wasn't the problem. Bush was. Reading his campaign's polling, Bush saw that 78 percent believed the country was on the wrong track, and the horse race numbers were as depressing as ever, with Clinton leading 52 to 39 percent. It was, Bush dictated, "discouraging as hell." Particularly galling was the finding that 54 percent believed things were worse under Bush than they had been under Carter.

It was a beautiful late summer day in Washington—marred only by the poor poll results—and Bush, who had some time alone with Barbara at the White House, allowed himself to think the unthinkable. What if he were to come up short? "I guess I'd have to say I would have failed. . . . Then I said to myself, 'it's not going to happen,'" Bush dictated. "I'm a better person, better qualified, better character to be President, despite a bunch of shortcomings that I may have and there certainly are plenty of them. It's kind of a funny feeling—a funny strange feeling." He put it more bluntly a few days later: "I've got a slight confession. For the first time I'm wondering if we can overcome this flood of bad news."

From July to September 1992, 96 percent of TV evening news coverage on the economy "focused on economic weakness and shortcomings," according to the Center for Media and Public Affairs. "Though [a] recovery was underway, the U.S. economy still had many problems during the closing months of the 1992 campaign," wrote the political scientist Everett Carll Ladd. "But 96 percent negative coverage distorted what was in fact a complex picture with many positive as well as negative features." To her colleagues, Bush campaign adviser Mary Matalin circulated a *Washington Post* piece headlined "Republicans and Some Journalists Say Media Tend to Boost Clinton, Bash Bush." "*We are not paranoid whin-*

ers," Matalin wrote. "The media has its own agenda—the same liberal one Bill Clinton's running on."

To Bush, the question about Clinton that overshadowed nearly all others was the draft. "I'm tired of the guy lying and ducking on the draft and not coming clean," Bush dictated on Wednesday, September 9, 1992. "So we've got to press him without trying to demagogue the issue, but I remain convinced that it is a very important question because it's a question of truth as well as, for a lot of older people, a question of whether he ducked service. The new generation doesn't think that one is as bad, but I think it's very bad not wanting [to participate] when your country is at war. I simply find that offensive, but maybe this shows the age and the generation gap."

The universe Bush had known was gone. In September, Bush noted that the old Soviet infantry brigade was being removed from Cuba. "What changes in the world," Bush dictated, "and yet who gives a damn."

FORTY-FIVE

God, It Was Ghastly

★

How can you help us if you don't know what we're feeling?

—Questioner at the presidential town hall debate,
Richmond, Virginia, October 1992

THE CALL WAS UNEXPECTED. In Washington for a C-SPAN appearance in early September, Ross Perot reached out to Jim Baker, and Baker invited Perot to meet at Baker's house on Foxhall Road. For two hours Perot held forth. "He waxed very emotional about the dirty tricks by the Republican Party—same old story," Bush told his diary after being briefed by Baker. "He hit George W . . . he indicated George W. was heavily involved in investigating his kids—which is a sheer lie."

Perot lectured Baker on the economy and threatened to reenter the race if he felt neither Clinton nor Bush was truly serious about deficit reduction. There was always a conspiratorial tone. Perot theorized that a Dallas businessman and Bush friend had Gennifer Flowers "warehoused" in a Dallas apartment in order "to spring her out at the appropriate time." He offered to speak to Bush directly, but Bush was not interested. "I see no reason to talk to him," Bush dictated. "I've lost all confidence in Ross Perot. I think he's a highly wired up, strange little egomaniac, nurtured on conspiracy theories."

By the time Baker had returned to the White House, Dick Cheney was calling to report that he had heard Perot was planning to reenter the race on October 1. The rumor had reached Cheney from the technology world, where Perot was said to have purchased "$9 million worth of computers" that could orchestrate telephone appeals to households. On Thursday, October 1, 1992, Perot could help himself no longer and announced that he was a candidate for president after all. It was a three-way campaign once again. The only constant was that Bush was behind no matter who else was in the race.

In an interview with CNN's Larry King from San Antonio, Texas, Bush made his most aggressive moves yet against Clinton on the issue of character, attacking the challenger for not recalling details of a 1969 visit to Moscow (a Rhodes scholar trip) and for taking part in demonstrations against the Vietnam War while he was studying in England. It was thin gruel, but, when he considered it with the draft questions, Bush was truly offended by what he took to be Clinton's embrace of the counterculture a generation before. As Bush had said in Houston, accepting his renomination, "I bit the bullet, and he bit his nails."

In their first debate—held at Washington University in St. Louis on Sunday, October 11, 1992—Bush pressed the demonstrations argument again, but Clinton was ready, invoking Bush's father's opposition to Joe McCarthy to deflect what Clinton argued was a Bush assault on his patriotism. In his own estimation, Bush's attack on Clinton on the demonstrations was "a dud."

In Richmond at a town hall–style debate on Thursday, October 15, all the strange new forces in American politics that had bedeviled Bush for over a year came together in one harrowing exchange in the Robins Center at the University of Richmond. A young woman rose from the audience to ask the three candidates a question: "How has the national debt personally affected each of your lives? And if it hasn't, how can you honestly find a cure for the economic problems of the common people if you have no experience in what's ailing them?"

Glancing at the watch he wore on his right wrist, Bush rose to respond. "Well, I think the national debt affects everybody. Obviously it has a lot to do with interest rates. It has—"

Bush was interrupted by Carole Simpson, the moderator.

"She's saying you personally," Simpson said.

The questioner spoke up again, too. "On a personal basis, how has it affected you—has it affected you personally?"

"Well, I'm sure it has," Bush said. "I love my grandchildren and I want to think that—"

Another interruption. "How?"

"I want to think that they're going to be able to afford an education," Bush said. "I think that that's an important part of being a parent. I—if the question—if you're—maybe I get it wrong. Are you suggesting that if somebody has means that the national debt doesn't affect them?"

"Well, what I'm saying—"

"I'm not sure I get it," Bush said, smiling awkwardly. "Help me with the question and I'll try to answer it."

"Well, I've had friends that have been laid off from jobs," the questioner said. "I know people who cannot afford to pay the mortgage on their homes; their car payment. I have personal problems with the national debt. But how has it affected you? And if you have no experience in it, how can you help us if you don't know what we're feeling?"

Simpson stepped in to try to help Bush. "I think she means more the recession, the economic problems today the country faces, rather than the deficit."

Bush valiantly tried once more, saying:

Well, you ought to—you ought to be in the White House for a day and hear what I hear and see what I see and read the mail I read and touch the people that I touch from time to time. I was in the Lomax A.M.E. Church. It's a black church just outside of Washington, D.C. And I read in the—in the bulletin about teenage pregnancies, about the difficulty that families are having to meet ends—to make ends meet. I talk to parents. I mean, you've got to care. Everybody cares if people aren't doing well. But I don't think—I don't think it's fair to say, "You haven't had cancer, therefore you don't know what it's like." I don't think it's fair to say, you know, whatever it is, that if you haven't been hit by it personally—but everybody's affected by the debt because of the tremendous interest that goes into paying on that debt, everything's more expensive. Everything comes out of your pocket and my pocket.

So it's, it's sad, but I think in terms of the recession, of course you feel it when you're President of the United States. And that's why I'm trying to do something about it by stimulating the export, investing more, better education systems. Thank you. I'm glad to clarify.

Simpson invited Clinton, who had been watching Bush with a virtually wolfish face, to take his turn. He rose and walked directly to the edge of the audience and held the questioner in his gaze. "Tell me how it's affected you again. You know people who've lost their jobs and lost their homes."

"Well, yeah, uh-huh," the woman said, agreeing.

"Well, I've been governor of a small state for twelve years. . . . I have seen what's happened in this last four years when in my state, when people lose their jobs, there's a good chance I'll know them by their names," Clinton said. "When a factory closes I know the people who ran it. When the businesses go bankrupt, I know them. And I've been out here for thirteen months meeting in meetings just like this ever since October with people like you all over America, people that have lost their jobs, lost their livelihood, lost their health insurance."

There it all was: the economic concerns predominating; the public empathy; the showmanship of politics in the new media age—none of which Bush had come close to mastering.

During a Richmond, Virginia, presidential debate with Ross Perot and Bill Clinton, Bush struggled—unsuccessfully—to connect with voters in a town hall forum.

The morning after, even Barbara Bush was ready to start hitting harder.

"I'm going negative," she told her husband.

"Well, Bar, you're the one that always said you didn't like the negative."

"I know, but the truth has to come out," Barbara replied.

In private, he shifted between fatalism and hope. "The debates seem like ancient history and the results, let's face it, were not good," Bush told his diary on Wednesday, October 21, 1992.

Yet he could not completely accept the idea that he was going to lose. Of a *Penthouse* magazine account of the Clinton–Gennifer Flowers liaison, Bush mused, "What happens if he should win and then this is just the tip of the iceberg? What does it do to the Presidency, the trust of which I've tried to uphold? The honor of which I've tried to live by, serve by?"

The year grew ever stranger. In late October, Perot said he had left the race in July in part because of rumors that Republican dirty tricksters were planning on embarrassing his daughter by doctoring photographs for public release and by disrupting her wedding. "I could not allow my daughter's happiest day of her life, or one of them, to be ruined because of me. . . . I stepped back to protect her," Perot said. He also alleged a wiretapping plot against him and his business. Marlin Fitzwater called the raft of charges "loony," and Bush himself said the allegations were "crazy."

In the last days of the race Bush's internal numbers started improving. Then, as Bush finished a rally in St. Louis, he received word that Lawrence Walsh, the Iran-contra independent counsel, had struck again, indicting former secretary of defense Caspar Weinberger for obstruction. Walsh cited new notes of Weinberger's from one of the January 1986 meetings on the Iran arms initiative that included the phrase "VP approved." Bush did not believe there was anything new in the latest blow from the independent counsel, but the press coverage of the reindictment was intense. The campaign hierarchy, Bush dictated, was "worried and panicked that this will stop our momentum. Well, it might, but so be it—[I] told the truth and that's all you can do."

Whatever movement there had been in the polls was over. "The national press is still hammering away on Iran," Bush dictated. "A frantic, desperate, sinking Clinton tries to rap my character on this issue." Except that Clinton was not sinking: He was holding steady with a working lead over the president.

The final days were one long thunderstorm in this, the last campaign in which Bush himself would appear on a ballot. What had begun twenty-eight years before, in the 1964 Republican primary for the U.S. Senate, with occasional crowds of one or two or perhaps three people, was coming to an end—and he could not wait for it all to be over.

There was news that Saddam was going to hold a rally of five hundred thousand Iraqis in Baghdad to celebrate a Bush defeat. There was Bush's private assertion, in the face of the Perot challenge, that he himself "would vote for Bill Clinton in a minute before Ross Perot—I know too much about Ross Perot and his paranoia." There were the nervous campaign chieftains, the sleeping grandchildren, the scratchy voice, and the rejected attacks. (Baker, Bush dictated, "comes in with three different assaults they want me to make on Clinton. One of them is so strident. One of them raising the question of Gennifer Flowers, so blazingly, and I said, 'No.' They were anxious to snuff out Iran-Contra, and Doro overheard Teeter telling somebody as he walked along, 'We have sent the guy three different scripts and he wouldn't use any of them.'") And there were Bush's frenzied, loopy attacks on Clinton and Gore, including his cry that Millie, the springer spaniel, knew "more about foreign policy" than the Democratic "bozos" challenging him.

The hotel suites blurred together, his sinuses were shot, and he was so tired that he couldn't sleep. David McCullough's biography of Harry Truman sat unfinished. Bush was just too worn out to read. Only Mary Matalin was cheerful—"We're going to win," she would say, "going to win." George W. joined the plane for the final push on Monday, November 2, 1992. With his eldest son and with Jim Baker, Bush sat in his office on Air Force One, talking of polls and sports, telling bad jokes and complaining about Perot.

Arriving in Akron, Bush received the Oak Ridge Boys in his office on the plane, and the group sang some gospel songs. Thinking of his own dad, the president teared up during "Amazing Grace." Leaning over to his son, Bush said, "Boy, would my father ever have loved to have been here hearing these guys sing." Musing to his diary, Bush dictated: "And then I think of how some in the press say, 'Oh, Bush puts on this love of country music.' [They don't know] our background, [they don't] know the joy we had at Grove Lane [when I was] 10 years old listening to Dad's Silver Dollar Quartet sing. But it's no use trying to explain to them."

Between stops Bush tried to nap. Jim Baker was dozing on a couch in the presidential bedroom, and George W. was restless, "milling around nervously," Bush dictated. The president changed into a clean blue shirt and a gray suit for a rally in Louisville. Gazing out the window as Air Force One began to land, he watched the sun break through the clouds.

"A good omen," Baker said.

"Yes, I think it is," Bush replied, absently.

At last he returned home to Houston. There was a final rally, a huge event. Cheryl Ladd, Bob Hope, Charlton Heston, Ted Williams, Arnold Palmer, the Gatlin Brothers, Naomi Judd, Lee Greenwood: The place, Bush recalled, was "rocking and rolling." It was nearly ten P.M., and Bush was energized by the crowd. He spoke of coming to Texas forty-four years before, of making his and his family's life there. He had started out here, and now he was returning home at the end of what he called "the battle of my life."

The silliness of recent weeks—the giddy talk of "bozos"—was gone. The Bush who spoke in the closing hours of the campaign was more serious, more somber, more authentic. "You know, I will readily contend that I've never been too hot with words, and I think you know that," Bush said.

> In fact, some of the more elite pundits say I can't finish a sentence. Well, they may be right from time to time. But I'll tell you something, though. I think you also know, I think especially the people here do, that I care very deeply about our nation. And I believe that we must treat this precious treasure with great care. America is something that has been passed on to us. And we must shape it. We must improve it. We must help people and be kind to people. And then we must pass that on to our kids and to our grandkids.

The Bushes were driven to the Houstonian Hotel. They decided not to turn on any of the five televisions in their suite, falling into bed for the night. "I worry so about others and the problems facing the country, and how almost insurmountable they seem at times," Bush dictated at the end of the evening on Monday, November 2, 1992. "Yet I do have this great confidence in America—unbelievable confidence—that we can do it and solve the problems so the country can move. And so it is, the end of campaign '92, the end of the ugliest period in my life"—the last words he spoke to his diary the day before the votes were cast and his fate decided.

He slept terribly, waking twice in the night with stomach pain. At six thirty in the morning, Bush went for a run and maintained the news blackout that he and Barbara had imposed on themselves the evening before: no TV, no newspapers.

After his run Bush stopped off to buy some fishing tackle, threw some horseshoes with George W. and Marvin, then lunched with Barbara, Marvin's wife, Margaret, and Scowcroft. (The president enjoyed a bit of frozen yogurt.) After a quick haircut, Bush got the first wave of bad news from Baker. The exit polls in Pennsylvania and Ohio, Bush told his diary, were "terrible." Then came New Jersey and Michigan, and the message was the same. "It looks like a blowout," Bush dictated. "I have this strange feeling deep inside. I guess I'm hurt, but a strange feeling of relief. I think it's the ugliness of the hour, the ugliness of the year."

It was over. Clinton won 43 percent of the popular vote; Bush, 37 percent; and Perot, remarkably, 19 percent. Clinton's margin in the electoral college was decisive, 370 to 168 for Bush. Perot carried no states.

Had Ross Perot not run in 1992, would Bush have defeated Clinton? Bush believed so, and it is true that Perot's persistent arguments about the failing American economy hurt the president. Exit polling, however, found that Perot tended to draw about equally from Bush and Clinton, and Clinton himself long remembered that his numbers had been hurt when Perot spent millions in the last weekend of the campaign on TV spots attacking the Democratic nominee's record in Arkansas. While it is impossible to know what would have happened had Perot not been in the race, Bush's political vulnerability in the twelfth year of Republican rule, though exacerbated by Perot, was wide and deep once the conventional wisdom about Bush's economic and domestic stewardship took hold. This much was certain: Like Buchanan's primary insurgency and Gingrich's revolt over taxes, Perot's populist challenge was a sign that American politics was moving into a far different world than Bush had known. A sizable number of voters didn't want steady as she goes. They wanted a revolution against the status quo.

As the returns had come in, Bush had been both stoic and sad. The Bush family was there in force. "At first I had a feeling of a burden being lifted," Bush dictated late that night, "and then I saw the hurt in the kids; they're crying."

To Clinton and to the nation that evening, Bush had been grace itself, congratulating the president-elect and announcing that his plans were mainly "to get very active in the grandchild business."

In private, he was emotionally fragile. He returned to Andrews Air Force Base the next day and boarded Marine One, which landed at the Pentagon: The White House lawn was filled with administration officials to welcome him back. His son Marvin was riding with him. As the presidential motorcade was crossing Memorial Bridge, a uniformed soldier on the sidewalk stood at attention and saluted.

The president grew emotional. "I let everybody down," he said, shaking his head.

"I know you'll do it, but you've got to get it together," Marvin said. "You've got about three minutes."

The president recovered his composure and presented a collected face to the world. The arrival at the White House "was emotional and it was a long, long gamut to run near the fountain on the South Lawn up to the White House. I wasn't sure I'd be able to make it without emotion, but we did." One young soldier gave Bush a thumbs-up in solidarity. "I must say I thought to myself, 'How in God's name did this country elect a draft dodger?' I didn't feel it with bitterness, I just felt it almost generational. What am I missing?" The wounds were bearable—but only just. "It's almost like living with what I might imagine it would be like to have a cancer—painful—but you can accommodate it," Bush dictated. He was no longer, it seemed, the kind of man a majority of Americans wanted to be in charge of their affairs.

"The overseas cables are wonderful, quote, 'You'll have your place in history.'" Bush dictated. "That seems to be the central theme, but domestically it's the same: don't stand for anything, don't care about people, haven't done anything, squandered your popularity, and on and on it goes—and brutal in its intensity," Bush dictated at Camp David five days after the defeat. "All I want is time, I think, time to unwind."

Bush remembered the pain the most—a pain that never fully went away. "It was terrible," he recalled in retirement. "God, it was ghastly. Your whole life is based on trying to accomplish stuff, and losing hurts. It hurt a lot. My problem was the feeling of letting people down, letting the people around you down. You know, who really believed in what we were doing. And you let them down. That was the sad part for me, and I felt very strongly about that. I still do."

FORTY-SIX

The Closing of an Era

★

You ran the worst campaign I ever saw, but you're going out a
beloved figure [and] everybody will tell you that.
—Tip O'Neill to George H. W. Bush

H E WAS WORRIED, ostensibly, about his dog. On the Thursday morning after the election, Bush was walking Ranger, one of the family's English springers, around the White House grounds. "Ranger [is] perky [and] sees a squirrel," Bush told his diary. "It's raining and he jumps with that marvelous jump where he kind of goes straight up and kind of comes straight down. His head is up and I call him and [his] ears perk, and I'm thinking, 'What in the hell will we do with this marvelous free spirit of a dog'" when they were back in Houston, where the Bushes planned to build a house on a small lot. Poor Ranger—what would they do with his energy?

Bush might as well have been talking about himself. For decades he had lived a life of epic scope on the grandest of stages. Retirement—in this case, forced retirement—was a foreign, disconcerting concept. Yes, he had long fantasized about a surprise withdrawal from politics, but such fantasies usually came at moments of passing stress or irritation. Now he had no choice in the matter. Like Ranger, he was, in his way, a "marvelous free spirit" soon to lose the privileges and joys of life at the White House.

The right was crude in its self-satisfaction at Bush's fall. In a sophomoric gesture, a model of Bush's head was served on a platter at a dinner hosted by the conservative Heritage Foundation—a prank of "extraordinarily good taste," Bush dictated with some bitterness. Barbara, meanwhile, was "that same restless wonderful wife that holds onto the seams [like] in 1976, shifting gears, rushing down to buy that house, buy a nest." Driven by his curious but by now familiar combination of humility and stubbornness, Bush was doubtful that anything he did would help with what he was to call the "L-word," his legacy. Time and history would sort

it all out. The man who had gone from the apex of post–Gulf War popularity to such a lackluster showing in the general election understood
that things change, often and rapidly. So why bother worrying about it?

A week after Election Day, the Bushes rode up to Capitol Hill for a
dinner with the Senate Republican caucus. "I dreaded going," Bush told
his diary, but Bob Dole went out of his way to pay tribute to his old rival.
"He choked up, he showed a warm side that many didn't feel he ever
had," Bush dictated. "He was so generous in his comments and so
thoughtful; and I thought to myself, 'Here we are, a guy that I fought
bitterly with in the New Hampshire primary and now I salute him as a
true leader, a wonderful leader, a guy that bent over backwards to do
what the President wanted.'"

It was an emotional night—the beginning of the end of his presidency.
Bush sat next to Republican senator Alan Simpson's wife, Ann, at dinner, and they quietly discussed the election. Bush told her that he felt
"that I had let people down, that there was a generational disconnect
and the thing that discouraged me was my failure to click with the
American people on values, duty, and country, service, honor, decency.
All the things that I really believe; they never came through—never ever.
And the media missed it, and the Clinton generation didn't understand
it, and I told her I felt a little out of it and that I had not been able to
communicate better what I really believe."

Returning to the White House, Barbara went to bed. Bush stayed up
taking care of paperwork and mail, then walked outside. The night was
clear, the view from the grounds matchless. Bush gazed at the Washington Monument and took in the vista across the Potomac. From this perspective, Bush thought, even the gray Treasury building had its charms.
He remembered that there was an all-night Veterans Day vigil to read
the names of the dead at the Vietnam Memorial. The war was on his
mind; he had had an emotional exchange with John McCain earlier in
the evening in the receiving line at the Senate dinner. He was suddenly
seized with a desire to go over to the memorial, quietly, and take his turn
paying tribute to the fallen. To visit in the daylight hours, he thought,
would "look like I was sticking it in Clinton's eye." In the darkness, however, unannounced and with minimal fanfare—perhaps that would work.

Reaching the West Wing, Bush decided that he would go—right then.
He told the Secret Service, and the president and the First Lady—he had
roused her from her sleep—took the short ride to the memorial. To the

surprise of the few overnight observers, the president of the United States read a few names, saluted the fallen, and left as quietly as he had come.

On Wednesday, November 18, 1992, Bill Clinton called on the man he had defeated. Bush came out of the White House to greet the president-elect in the driveway, a cordial beginning to a two-hour meeting. In the Oval Office, the two men discussed the world scene. "He's very friendly, very respectful, asked my advice on certain things," Bush told his diary. "I alked at length about Yugoslavia, Kosovo, Serbia, Bosnia, etc., and the difficulties that he might anticipate there. I told him I thought that was most likely to be the prime trouble spot. We did not discuss China, and I'm sorry that we didn't. I just forgot it. The subjects covered were: sanctions on Yugoslavia, the war in Bosnia Herzegovina, Kosovo, the instability in Russia, START II, Ukrainian relations, the Baltics, the conflicts in the former USSR, Uruguay Round . . . Maastricht treaty, the peace process—Middle East, Iraq, Libya Pan Am 103, Iran, Somalia, Haiti, Cambodia, Vietnam, North Korea, Liberia, Angola."

Bush gave his successor a thorough tour—Hillary was calling on Barbara the next day—showing him the pool, the horseshoe pit, the putting green, and the weight room. Clinton's reaction: "Wow." As they parted, Bush said, "Bill, I want to tell you something. When I leave here, you're going to have no trouble from me. The campaign is over, it was tough but I'm out of here and I will do nothing to complicate your work and I just want you to know that." Clinton was appreciative, the visit warm. ("Speculation on Hillary Clinton and what it's going to be like with Hillary, and what will Hillary do," Bush dictated in mid-November. "All the women in the press corps are all for her, I'm sure, but beyond that she's going to have some problems. She is very militant and pro-liberal-cause, and that's going to get her into some difficulties.")

He had had only one request of Clinton: that the new president continue the Bush administration's "Points of Light" initiative. Drawing on the phrase from his address to the Republican National Convention in New Orleans, Bush had been determined to use the presidency to press the case for voluntarism. Nearly four years before, just ten days after his inauguration, on Monday, January 30, 1989, he had convened a meeting in the Roosevelt Room to discuss the question. It meant a lot to him: The only structural change he made in the White House after taking over from Reagan was to create an Office of National Service. "Any definition of a successful life," Bush said, "must include serving others"—an observation he would often repeat. "By co-opting a piece of the very definition of 'success,' which was certainly America's secular god coming out of the '80s especially, the statement would in fact be far more powerful in its own way than politics and policy, because of course culture is more powerful than politics," recalled Gregg Peters-meyer, who directed the White House Office of National Service. The Points of Light initiative created an infrastructure for voluntarism and celebrated daily examples of volunteers who were making a difference. As Bush had put it in his first post-1992 election radio address: "There are no magic solutions to our problems. The real answers lie within us. We need more than a philosophy of entitlement. We need to all pitch in, lend a hand, and do our part to help forge a brighter future for this country."

After the Clinton visit and tour, Nancy Ellis telephoned her brother: Dorothy Bush was fading. "It looks this time like it might be the end," a tearful Bush told his diary after talking to his sister. "I want to hug her one more time."

After the misery of the long campaign year, the pain of the defeat, and the exquisite agony of hosting his conqueror in the White House—an agony that Bush, his mother's son, concealed brilliantly, as she had taught him—after all of this, now he was to lose the woman who had given him so much. He and Barbara got on the telephone to Greenwich, but they could not be sure that Mrs. Bush understood: "I wonder if she knows that this is her middle-size [son] calling her saying, 'We love you Mum,' and this is Bar saying, 'We love you very much,' and all we heard was this deep breathing."

Bush considered flying to Connecticut immediately, but his brother Jonathan said, "Oh no, don't do that. She's done this before." The president went to bed in the White House on that Wednesday evening worrying, worrying, worrying about his ninety-one-year-old mother who lay dying 250 miles to the north. He tossed in his sleep. "I might not have a chance to kiss her good night," he told his diary. "Tough times, tough negative times. This one [is] so close to the heart, so very close, indeed."

The Bushes greet the Clintons at the White House on Inauguration Day 1993. The defeat, Bush admitted to himself, "hurt, hurt, hurt," but he and Barbara were determined to bid farewell with grace.

He woke early and, at five minutes to seven in the morning, announced that he was going to Greenwich. Since Barbara had to remain to keep her appointment with Hillary Clinton, the president asked Doro to come with him. They flew on an Air Force jet with a smaller-than-usual security and press entourage.

Mrs. Bush was breathing with difficulty, and Bush and his daughter wept by her bedside. The president reached over and leafed through his mother's "frayed Bible." In its pages were notes that he had written her from Andover and a birthday card he had mailed her from the navy.

He held her hand, thinking of all the times she had lovingly rubbed his through the years. After a few hours he and Doro left for Washington. To Bush, the sight of his mother struggling to breathe put the rest of life in proper perspective. "I don't know that Mum knows I'm President of the United States," he told his diary, but "I do know that is not important anymore."

In the late afternoon—it was just after five P.M.—Bush was back in the capital, performing a ceremonial presidential chore, receiving the credentials of ambassadors on the first floor of the White House. The envoy from the Bahamas came through last. While chatting with him, Bush noticed his close aide Patty Presock whisper something to Barbara, who was sitting with the ambassador's wife and children. Barbara rose and approached her husband. "Your Mum has died," she told him.

Nancy Ellis believed that George's visit had been their mother's final piece of earthly business. "Mum knew you were there and then she decided that was it," she said to her brother. She told reporters, "Mrs. Bush Sr. was waiting for the President and after he left today, she just let go."

The calls started coming into the White House, and Bush appreciated them—including Bill Clinton's—but in his grief he could not believe that those outside his family really understood what the world had just lost. "How many times she taught us [to] be kind to the other guy," he told his diary, "'never hurt feelings, love.'" Her funeral was held at Christ Church in Greenwich four days later. Prescott Jr. read a letter his mother had written for the occasion. Mrs. Bush's ashes were buried next to her husband, near Robin's gravestone.

B etween his grief and the winding down of the presidency, Bush cared less and less about lingering issues, including questions about a search of Clinton's passport files at the State Department during the campaign. A Bush political appointee at State had ordered a search of Clinton's travel records from his student days, Clinton recalled, "chasing down bogus rumors that I had gone to Moscow to pursue anti-war activities or had tried to apply for citizenship in another country to avoid the draft." *Newsweek* had broken the story of alleged tampering with files, and after the election the outcry from the press grew. An embarrassed— and exhausted—Jim Baker offered Bush his resignation, which Bush waved away. It was "absurd," Bush said, to think Baker, "the most honorable guy," had "done something wrong." Al Gore called the episode a "McCarthyite abuse of power," but the FBI found that there had been no tampering with the files. A three-year investigation by an independent counsel concluded no laws had been broken. (The special prosecutor, Joseph DiGenova, added that the matter "should never have been referred for prosecution.") Clinton himself dismissed the episode. "It was just all part of the deal," he said, shrugging, more than twenty years later, after he and Bush had become friendly. "Politics is a contact sport."

Bittersweet economic news came in as the weeks passed. Consumer confidence was up, which the press attributed to Clinton's election, but soon came a statistic about things on Bush's watch: The economy had been growing at about 4 percent in the third quarter of the year, more than the early estimate of 2.7 percent. "This one they can't give credit to Clinton for," Bush told his diary. "They might try, but they simply can't do it."

His diary entries became more sporadic as the autumn wore on. "I haven't felt like dictating," Bush told his diary on Sunday, November 29, 1992. "My moods have been up and down. Mum's death really got to me, as I'm sure it did the rest of the family." When he was in Maine, he could not walk around Walker's Point without seeing her everywhere, remembering "the numbers of times we'd race up the little pebble path—in the old days pebbles—to tell her what had happened, who won, how it had gone. We ran in our bathing suits, with Mum in hot pursuit, to jump into the ocean."

He had a farewell lunch with Sonny Montgomery and other House friends on the Hill. After the meal of country ham, red-eye gravy, eggs, and grits, Tip O'Neill came by; he was, Bush dictated, "just great, and warm, and friendly."

"You ran the worst campaign I ever saw," O'Neill told Bush, "but you're going out a beloved figure [and] everybody will tell you that."

The days grew shorter, but one trouble spot attracted Bush's sustained attention: Somalia, on the horn of Africa, was riven by warring factions. The civil struggle had created a humanitarian crisis, and Bush saw an opportunity to put American power to work to save, in his words, "thousands of innocents." "There is a feeling that we won't help black nations, so that would be a peripheral benefit showing that the United States does care," he told his diary on Monday, November 30. "There is a feeling in the Muslim world that we don't care about Muslims. A large U.S. humanitarian effort backed by force would help in that category."

"I understand the United States alone cannot right the world's wrongs," Bush told the nation in a midday announcement that twenty-eight thousand U.S. troops would go to Somalia as part of a multinational force. "But we also know that some crises in the world cannot be resolved without American involvement, that American action is often necessary as a catalyst for broader involvement in the community of nations."

Already hinting of a quick trip to Somalia to thank the forces for their service, Bush considered making it a bipartisan occasion. "I even toy with the idea of taking Bill Clinton," Bush told his diary on Tuesday,

December 8, 1992. "He's going to need a good introduction to the Armed Services given his record, given his position on gays in the military, but I think that might be seen as a big grandstand play so I doubt that that will work." Heading into the holidays, USA Today reported Bush's approval rating was 49 percent—up fifteen points since the election. The newspaper attributed the change to the economy. Bush, however, had a slightly harsher view: "I attribute it to the fact that I'm not getting bashed every single day by the media."

Four years before, during the 1988 campaign, the comedian Dana Carvey of *Saturday Night Live* had begun working on a Bush impression. "The key rhythms for the voice were John Wayne and Mr. Rogers," recalled Carvey, who added in Bush's eclectic arm gestures. (The president sometimes resembled a windmill, if windmills pointed and chopped their arms in the air.) Sig Rogich, a Bush friend and adviser, would send the president videotapes of Carvey's skits, which Bush loved. After the loss to Clinton, the president called Carvey to ask him to perform at the White House. "Come over and cheer up the troops," Bush said. "They're feeling down." Carvey and his wife spent the night in the Residence; the next day Carvey lit up the East Room with a full George Bush routine. The two men remained close in Bush's retirement. (The former president liked to ask Carvey to do Carvey's Ross Perot impression, and Bush in return, did "a pretty good James Cagney," Carvey recalled.)

With the work on the START II treaty nearing completion—the agreement eliminated an entire class of Russian missiles, the SS-18s—Bush made a sentimental journey to Moscow to sign the deal. "It's a great thing, a wonderful thing to bow out on, and it's important that we do it for mankind—eliminating these SS-18s," Bush dictated.

Bush's diaries themselves became an issue as his presidency ended. In September 1992, Patty Presock, a deputy assistant to the president, was at work in her office on the third floor of the Residence when she began to go through some materials that Bush aide Don Rhodes had delivered to her from the president's second-floor safes. Presock quickly realized that she was reading transcripts of a Bush diary that dated from 1986. A short time earlier (in July 1992) Presock, who had not known that Bush had kept a diary, had been told in a phone conversation initiated by Boyden Gray's office that the Iran-contra independent counsel had requested (though not subpoenaed) any such notes and that "Boyden seemed to think there was a diary." After reading the pages that Rhodes had brought her, Presock went to the president. Bush was unworried. Gray, he said, knew all about everything, so there couldn't be any problem. They then called Gray, who had the opposite reaction. Bush believed that Gray had known about and approved the diary keeping; Gray maintained that he had not known about Bush's extensive dictations dating back to 1986. In the wake of the emergence of the transcripts, Gray had a decision to make: Would he immediately turn the documents over to the independent counsel, or would he wait until after the election in November?

Gray decided to wait. "It was a very, very difficult call, but I did not trust the Office of the Independent Counsel not to leak the material before the election, even though the material was exculpatory," Gray recalled. He recommended to the president that they hold off, and Bush agreed, deferring to Gray's judgment. The diaries were withheld. Once they were handed over, in December 1992, the prosecutors found nothing that led to any criminal charge.

Still, Bush hated the headlines and the editorial speculation that he had something to hide about Iran-contra. There was, meanwhile, an internal administration debate over whether to pardon Caspar Weinberger. As Bush put it, the chief issue was the charge that he was letting Weinberger off the hook in order "to cover my own ass." In a memo to the president, Boyden Gray recommended pardons not only for Weinberger but for several other figures, among them Robert McFarlane, Elliott Abrams, and two CIA officials. The family was in favor. "George feels I ought to do it; he says Jeb feels I ought to do it," Bush dictated on Tuesday, December 22, 1992. "Bar is marginal on it." Bush issued the pardons, closing the saga that had begun in late 1986. The news was announced on Christmas Eve, and the reaction was predictable: Lawrence Walsh accused the president of continuing the "Iran-contra cover up."

After Christmas at Camp David and the annual hunting trip to Beeville, Texas, with Will Farish ("I slept well, except [for] waking up in the middle of the night, thrashing around about the prosecutor," Bush dictated), the president went overseas, first to Somalia and then on to Moscow for the signing of START II. At the treaty ceremonies with Boris Yeltsin, the scope of global change struck Bush yet once more. "The closing of an era," he told his diary on the third day of the new year.

He returned to Washington for the final days. Bush decided to award Ronald Reagan the Presidential Medal of Freedom and invited the Reagans to the White House. Bush, who understood that many Republicans believed he had fallen from power because he had strayed too far from Reaganite principles, could easily have forgone the whole thing. Why give your critics an easy occasion to compare you unfavorably to your predecessor? But because Reagan had made so much possible, both for the country and for Bush himself, the forty-first president wanted to honor the fortieth with an award that would not long be in Bush's gift.

Nancy unnecessarily complicated things, offending Barbara. Mrs. Reagan called Dick Cheney to say that she was hoping he would come "because," Bush told his diary, "they needed supporters of Ron's there, as if to imply, at least to Bar, that we weren't supporters, and that Cheney was on her side, not ours."

For Bush, the presentation in the East Room was alternately warm and uncomfortable. He spoke emotionally of his "friend and mentor," praising Reagan for his role in the American story. Yet, as Bush told his diary, "That was a tense ceremony, there were a lot of people there that had been super-critical of me—'don't stand for anything, against everything Reagan stood for,' nasty, ugly—and there they were in the White House." Reagan, however, reciprocated Bush's regard with apparent sincerity, and the applause for both men was sustained. "He seemed much older to me," Bush dictated. "Nancy apparently never even said thank you to Barbara."

Throughout the ceremony Bush had been thinking about an ongoing attack on Iraq. Apparent missile sites south of the 32nd parallel were in violation of postwar agreements, and Bush authorized air strikes. "[Saddam] is pushing and beating his chest and telling his people that he's the winner," Bush dictated, "when he is a wimp and a loser."

George Strait and Brian Mulroney were the Bushes' guests for their last weekend at Camp David. (As were Warren Christopher and Vernon Jordan, the two men heading Clinton's transition team, whom the president, in a classic Bush touch, had invited up.) Bush was doing what he loved: juggling global phone calls about the strikes against Iraq while hosting an eclectic house party. Strait sang at a Saturday vespers service in the chapel, spent the night, and settled down with the president to watch the NFC and AFC championship games on Sunday.

On their final night in the White House, the Bushes hosted a small dinner for Prescott Bush, Jr., the Jonathan Bushes, and the Billy Grahams. Barbara was maintaining a brave and cheerful face, though she had fallen while packing in the West Sitting Hall and had eleven stitches in her arm. At evening's end there was a stroll around the grounds and then early to bed.

The twentieth of January came at last. It was a cold, clear, blue morning, and Bush rose, dressed, and walked the dogs. Ranger ran ahead, leaping as usual. At nine o'clock the president had his final national security briefing. "There was an unreal feeling to it because as we looked at Bosnia or Saddam Hussein, it was a matter of, 'Ok, so what?'" Bush dictated. "Nothing to do about it, nothing to follow-up on, nothing to suggest we try. Had an almost eerie feeling."

Scowcroft and the CIA men left, and Bush sat alone for a moment in the bare Oval Office. The desk had been cleaned of paperwork, the framed pictures packed up. He looked out the windows at the horseshoe pit, remembering the tournaments and the good times. He watched a female Secret Service agent walk past the pool toward the driveway. He could see the Washington Monument, the green grass of the Ellipse, and the flags around the base of the great white obelisk. He turned back to the desk, away from the barren Rose Garden, to leave a note for his successor. The envelope, Bush thought, looked lonely on the big desk—the desk where he had sat for so many hours and decided so many things, surrounded by men he trusted as he faced the trials of war and the tribulations of a troubled home front.

He was ready to go, or as ready as any man who had been so painfully dismissed by the voters of his nation could be. He would not cry, not in public, but he never knew if he'd make it through a given moment. Lord, how many speeches he had rushed through, nearly breathless, impatient with the text before him, trying to finish before he broke down.

In a matter of hours it would not matter. He would be fine at the Capitol, amid the ceremony of the inauguration and the official leave-taking. It was the quieter goodbyes beforehand that worried him—the telephone operators and the household staff. These he dreaded. After those, he hoped, it was all going to be okay. But only after.

Someone had mentioned the polls, which were up: Bush was leaving on a good note. He didn't care anymore—not much, anyway. "I'm saying, 'Well, that's nice, that's very nice, but I didn't finish the job.'" Yet it had been more than a job for him. It was a calling, something sacred, though he would have resisted such talk, waving it away. Too grand, too much show business.

No matter. His discomfort with grand terminology and weighty historical verdicts did not mean that grand terminology and weighty historical verdicts did not apply. They did, and in these last moments of power, alone in the Oval Office, Bush allowed himself a stream-of-consciousness reflection on what the previous four years had meant to him. "As I told Bill Clinton, I feel the same sense of wonder and majesty about this office today as I did when I first walked in here." As the sun streamed in the windows, he went on:

> I've tried to keep it; I've tried to serve here with no taint of dishonor; no conflict of interest; nothing to sully this beautiful place and this job I've been privileged to hold. . . . [Misjudgments] maybe on this issue or that, but never misconduct, never doing anything that would tarnish and hurt the Presidency. And yet no one seems to know that, and no one seems to care. They say, "What motivates you?" And I used to be teased about "service for the sake of service." Well, it does motivate me. People should give; but it's service with honor, service with a flair for decency and hopefully kindness. I know the latter never came through because the press won that one—"cold hearted," "disconnected," "not caring about people." But I don't think they can lay a glove on me in the final analysis on serving without conflict; never for personal gain; always bearing in mind the respect for the office that I've been privileged to hold; the house I've been privileged to live in; the office in which I've tried to serve.

He thought of Barbara, who was preparing to receive the Clintons and the Gores for coffee before the ride up to the Capitol, and then the trip home to Houston. "Barbara is wonderful," he dictated. "She's strong and what a First Lady she's been—popular and wonderful." The generational shift now under way—from the Bushes to a couple young enough to be their children—was, he admitted to himself, difficult. "Suddenly eclipsed by the new wave, the lawyer, the wife with the office in the White House; but time will tell and history will show that [Barbara] was beloved because she was real, because she cared, because she gave of herself. She has been fantastic in every way, and my, how the people around her love her, my, how that staff rejoices in the fact she came their way."

They had been joking between themselves about the move to Houston—about Barbara's cooking, and the end of the concierge service of the White House. "We kid about no staff, no valets, no shined shoes, no pressed suits," Bush told his tape recorder as the minutes ticked by. He liked that Barbara, her eye on writing a memoir, was finding so much pleasure in reviewing her own diary and papers from their long journey, reading him bits and pieces that had been put into her computer. "The joy she gets from that little thing is [a] wonder to behold, and she's writing and thinking and laughing," Bush dictated. "She goes, 'Remember this?' and then reads me a long thing from 1968 or 1975. It's amazing."

As he prepared to leave, he ended his diary.

"This," he said aloud, "is my last day as President of the United States of America."

The telephone rang, interrupting his reverie. Boyden Gray was calling, asking Bush to sign a document that would preserve the work the administration had been doing on computers. Bush was happy to do it. In the final analysis, though, he posed a rhetorical question to the empty room: "Who gives a damn now?"

There were more household goodbyes. The Clintons and the Gores were due for coffee before long. Bush knew that his watch was ending, his duty done.

PART VII

In the Twilight

1993 to 2016

★

When you've made the big calls, it's tough to be on the
sidelines—but you've got to be.

—George H. W. Bush

Jeb, George W., Dick Cheney, Bush 2000 campaign chairman Don Evans, and the forty-first president discuss the close vote in Florida at the Texas governor's mansion in Austin, election night 2000.

FORTY-SEVEN

I'd Like to See Old George Bush

★

I suggest that you establish very fast that you are your own man,
that you agree on some issues with me and that undoubtedly
there will be many where you would have voted differently.

—George H. W. Bush to George W., about the
son's congressional campaign, 1977

Chart your own course, not just on the issues but on
defining yourselves.

—Bush to George W. and Jeb, 1998

H UGH LIEDTKE, Bush's old Texas business partner, had offered
the former president the use of his house on the Gulf of Mexico.
In late January 1993, not quite ten days after the Clinton inauguration, the Bushes accepted Liedtke's hospitality for a seaside weekend. When Bush, who wanted to try his luck fishing, went to get a license,
the woman behind the counter seemed puzzled. She couldn't quite place
the former leader of the Free World's face. "Have we met before?" she
asked. His only comfort that day was catching a flounder that was enough
to feed the household for lunch.

Bush needed the fishing; he was struggling to find his footing in a
world both familiar and foreign. "He is not bitter, but just cannot seem
to focus in on anything yet," Barbara wrote in mid-February 1993. "He
was depressed," his brother Jonathan Bush recalled after a visit to Houston during the first months of retirement. "Then we went out to dinner
at a restaurant and everybody cheered when they saw Pop, and he came
back to life again."

The Bushes enjoyed puttering around the kitchen in Houston, with
Barbara cooking and Bush doing dishes and making the morning coffee.
By her own admission, the former First Lady's culinary skills were—how
to put it?—uneven. When George W. came over the night before he ran
a marathon in late January, he needed carbs, so his mother offered to

make pasta. The result was an undercooked dinner; her husband said how much he preferred his pasta "rare." The former president, always conscious of his weight, also volunteered that he had dropped two pounds "without even trying."

It was a good life. Bush inhaled the daily CIA briefings sent to former presidents, and he remained addicted to the news, following it while restricting his commentary to close friends. Back in 1992, at one of the many low moments of the reelection campaign, Bush had imagined life after the presidency: "I'll spend time up at Texas A&M [where his presidential library was built] . . . just blending in; growing old with grace and kindness. . . . And then every once in a while, some big shot will come in—some officeholder, some King, some Prince, some Prime Minister, and some President, and they'll say, 'I'd like to see old George Bush.'" After talking about their "interesting times" together, Bush mused, he'd say goodbye to the visitor, and "say that I did my very best, tried my hardest, kept it honest; and put something back into the system."

To a remarkable degree Bush managed to make this vision of retirement real. From October to early May he was in Houston, working at his desk in an office suite near the Bushes' house. In the summers he led a migration to Kennebunkport, where, between boating, golf, and tennis, he would go through correspondence and return emails at the staff headquarters on Walker's Point. The flow of guests both in Maine and in Texas was never ending. It was not unusual to find, say, the Oak Ridge Boys and John Major at the dining room table or out on the stone porch. Other callers and correspondents included figures from Hollywood (Chuck Norris, Brooke Shields, Kevin Costner, Teri Hatcher); country music (Reba McEntire, Vince Gill, Larry Gatlin); politics (Brian Mulroney, Helmut Kohl, Mikhail Gorbachev), and both Hollywood and politics (Arnold Schwarzenegger).

There was an annual cruise in the Greek isles with family and friends, quail hunting in rural Texas, golf and fishing in Florida, and pilgrimages to Bohemian Grove, the men's enclave in Northern California. He read fiction and nonfiction (*The Private Life of Chairman Mao* was a favorite early in his retirement), but instructed his staff not to tell anyone. "Don't want people thinking I'm an intellectual," he said, half-smiling.

Bush's understanding of life after the presidency was straightforward:

Make money in a dignified way and don't complicate your successors' lives by opining publicly. He delivered many highly paid speeches, creating enough wealth to keep the family very comfortable for the rest of his life—and beyond. A 1993 engagement for a $100,000 address to an Amway convention attracted press attention: It was thought to be the most money a former president had ever commanded for a single domestic appearance.

Though he avoided serving on corporate boards, in later years Bush accepted a position as a senior adviser for the Carlyle Group, a global private-equity firm based in Washington. (Jim Baker, former secretary of defense Frank Carlucci, and Dick Darman were also part of Carlyle.) Bush's role was to travel to Asia, Europe, and the Middle East to deliver lunch and dinner speeches before audiences of potential investors in the group's funds. As compensation, he asked that the accumulated speaking fees (roughly $100,000 per speech in the 1990s and into the 2000s) for each trip be invested in Carlyle funds, which, in turn, produced strong returns.

The first six months or so of Bill Clinton's term were difficult, with the new president distracted by the issue of whether gays could serve openly in the military, by a $200 presidential haircut on Air Force One at LAX, and by chaotic relations with Capitol Hill. In June 1993, Bush confided a skepticism to Baker. "I take no joy in the way Clinton is screwing things up—I really hope their act down there improves," Bush wrote from Maine on Wednesday, June 9, 1993.

One of Clinton's first decisions about the use of force was connected to Bush. In April, the former president had led a small delegation of family and friends to Kuwait (Baker and Sununu joined the party), where he accepted the thanks of the nation he had liberated. Bush received, as *The New York Times* put it, "a hero's welcome," taking on what the newspaper called "a rock-star aura as police officers and teachers restrained children from running out to try to touch his car."

A 175-pound car bomb was discovered and more than a dozen men were arrested for being part of a plot to kill the former president on a motorcade route. The FBI and the CIA investigated and found human and forensic evidence that Iraq's intelligence service had directed the attempted attack. "It was a big bomb," Clinton recalled. "I was furious."

He summoned Colin Powell, who was still serving as chairman of the Joint Chiefs. "This guy just tried to kill an American president," Clinton said to Powell. "I think we ought to knock the living hell out of them."

"Mr. President, the question is, 'Do you want to get in another war, or do you want to punish them?'" Powell replied. "This was a ham-handed effort with little chance of success. You need a response, but not another war. If Saddam had killed Bush or wounded him, you would have to take Saddam out," Powell said, but under the circumstances a more proportionate response was in order.

"I really wanted to make them pay," Clinton recalled. "I was so mad"— but he agreed with Powell and authorized a Tomahawk missile strike on the Iraqi intelligence headquarters. Speaking to the nation on the evening of Saturday, June 26, 1993, Clinton said: "It was an elaborate plan devised by the Iraqi government and directed against a former president of the United States because of actions he took as president. As such, the Iraqi attack against President Bush was an attack against our country and against all Americans."

The White House kept Brent Scowcroft informed about the investigation and the retaliation. Clinton called Bush at four forty on the afternoon of the U.S. response, which took place about six P.M. Washington time. "We completed our investigation," Clinton told Bush. "Both the CIA and the FBI did an excellent job. It was directed against you. I've ordered a cruise missile attack." On the phone, Bush was reserved. "Clinton closed the conversation by assuring Bush that he had done everything he could to minimize the loss of life," recalled George Stephanopoulos, the senior Clinton adviser. "Maybe that's what Bush needed to hear most; maybe his bred-in-the-bone patrician modesty made him a little embarrassed by all the trouble everyone was going to for him."

"I think he thinks we did the right thing," Clinton said to his aides. "Thought it was a tough call."

Secretary of State Warren Christopher traveled to Maine to brief the former president. The missile strike took out part of the targeted headquarters; eight people were killed when several of the Tomahawks struck a residential neighborhood. Bush maintained a dignified silence about the entire affair. "I'm not in the interview business, but thank you very much for calling," Bush told the Associated Press in Kennebunkport. In later years, when visitors would raise the subject of the attempt on his life, Bush was terse: "Glad it failed."

In September 1993, Bush returned to the White House at Clinton's invitation for the signing of an Arab-Israeli peace accord and to appeal for the passage of NAFTA. Bush was happy to make the trip; Barbara wrote that she was "just not ready to go back yet."

Bush spent the night in the Queen's Bedroom in the Residence; the Carters had the Lincoln Bedroom; the Fords chose to stay at the Willard Hotel nearby. As Clinton and Carter settled in for a long night of talk, Bush retired. "You know he's always been early to bed, early to rise," Clinton said the next day. "And he stayed up pretty late for him last night." Asked whether things were strained between the recent foes, Clinton said: "I wouldn't say it was awkward. It got more informal as it went along."

In the East Room, presidents past and present made the case for NAFTA. After listening to Clinton's eloquent pitch for the trade agreement, Bush told the audience that he now understood why Clinton was president, and he wasn't. It was, Clinton recalled, a "wittily generous" thing for Bush to say.

One February Monday after he left the White House at first seemed like any other day. Bush was in Houston, just doing what he always did—giving a speech, shaking hands, posing for photographs. He was taking questions at a parachute association annual meeting when somebody asked him to describe what had happened at Chichi-Jima. As he was telling the story, he recounted how he had "pulled the rip cord and released my chest straps too early, and how I had sunk fairly deep when I hit the water."

Then it came to him. "For some reason, I went back to a thought I had way in the back of my mind," he recalled in a letter to his children. "It has been there, sleeping like Rip Van Winkle, alive but not alive. Now it was quite clear. I want to make one more parachute jump!"

It was a piece of unfinished business for a man who liked to finish what he started. Once he started thinking about it, he could think of little else. "Why has this now become an obsession?" Bush wrote. "I have everything in life, far more than I deserve. I want to finish my life as

God would have it. I have never been happier, but I want to do this jump."

There was a sporting, teasing, self-aware tone to his preparations for the jump at age seventy-two, but there was also an undercurrent of seriousness. Thinking about Chichi-Jima on "that dreadful day," Bush remembered that he had been "scared then. Will I be scared again?" When he informed the children, he asked Doro "not to tell anyone."

"You must be kidding," she said. "Do you think I would tell anyone about *this*?" (Recording her reaction, Bush wrote: "I felt Doro was ready to support me—tentative but okay.")

The day in the Arizona desert with the U.S. Army Golden Knights went splendidly. He felt "a twinge of fear—not panic, but rather a halting feeling in the leg, groin, and gut." Then he jumped, and all was well. He would jump again on his eightieth, eighty-fifth, and ninetieth birthdays— "reveling in the freedom, enjoying the view." As he always did.

T he inveterate letter writer remained an inveterate letter writer. His notes to the outside world offered a window on an active, sympathetic, eclectic mind.

In the aftermath of the April 1995 bombing of the federal office building in Oklahoma City by right-wing extremists, the National Rifle Association attacked federal agents as "jack-booted thugs." Bush was furious and resigned as a life member of the NRA, writing that "your broadside against Federal agents deeply offends my own sense of decency and honor; and it offends my concept of service to country. It indirectly slanders a wide array of government law enforcement officials, who are out there, day and night, laying their lives on the line for all of us."

With *The Washington Post*'s Ann Devroy, a longtime antagonist who was being treated for cancer at Houston's MD Anderson, Bush rose above the old divisions. There had been a tension between the two of them, Bush wrote:

> Perhaps an inevitable tension, that clouded things between us— never a visceral dislike, but a tension. I was the out of touch President, the wimp; you were the beltway insider who thrived on who's up, who's down—who will be fired, who will win. But now I am out of it, happy in my very private life, away from the arena; and you are on leave fighting a battle that far transcends the battles of the po-

litical wars. Strangely, wonderfully, I feel close to you now. I want you to win this battle. I want that same toughness that angered me and frustrated me to a fare-thee-well at times to see you through your fight.

To parents—friends of Marvin's—who had lost a young son, Bush drew on his own pain to offer comfort.

> I expect you are now saying "Why?" Well, I can't, even now, pretend to know the real answer; but let me tell you something that might help a little bit. Only a few months after Robin died, the grief and awful aching hurt began to disappear, to give way to only happy memories of our blessed child. . . . She's never left us. The ugly bruises, trade marks of dread Leukemia, are gone now. We can't see them at all. . . . I hope you will live the rest of your lives with only happy memories of that wonderful son who is now safely tucked in, God's loving arms around him.

He tried to stay in touch with Ronald Reagan, whom he always thought of fondly. "I don't know how you feel," Bush wrote Reagan in 1995, "but I must say I do not miss politics at all; however, Barbara and I are, of course, very proud of our two sons who got into the Political arena last Fall."

The rise of the Bush sons began as George W. and Jeb started to seriously consider seeking the governorships of Texas and of Florida. Sons following a father into politics: It was a familiar Bush story.

On a long-ago summer Saturday at home in Houston in 1977, Bush had taken to his typewriter to lay out his thoughts for George W. on the son's upcoming bid for Congress. "Your father will be an issue—I hope not an albatross, though in some . . . [right-wing] groups because I served at the UN and was in Peking you could get zapped with that," Bush wrote. "I suggest that you establish very fast that you are your own man, that you agree on some issues with me and that undoubtedly there will be many where you would have voted differently. . . . I will help by coming there or by staying away."

The 1977 letter foreshadowed how George H. W. Bush would treat his political sons in later years: with deference and with the expectation that there would "undoubtedly" be differences of opinion between the generations.

Unless asked, Bush would not insert himself into his sons' political lives. In this he was doing one of the things he liked best: carrying on a sound tradition. After he had retired from the Senate, Prescott Bush had described S. P. Bush's view of fatherhood. "He did not attempt to influence me at all, in connection with my later life," Prescott Bush recalled. "I might say parenthetically that I have followed that same idea with my own five children, four of whom are sons, and while I've been ready to talk with them, as he was with me, about the various possibilities, I've never borne down on them, any more than he did with me, and said, 'What you really ought to be is a lawyer,' or what you really ought to be is this or that."

George H. W. Bush had followed the same basic code, and now, in the 1990s and beyond, stories comparing and contrasting the father and the sons were going to be endless. At first, the narrative was about how the sons were better politicians than their defeated father. (The story line would change in 2000 and beyond, when the toll of a presidential campaign and then of the presidency itself bore down on George W., and his father's historical stock began to rise.) In the 1990s Bush gave George W. and Jeb a permanent dispensation. They should say and do what they thought best:

> Your Mother tells me that both of you have mentioned to her your concerns about some of the political stories—the ones that seem to put me down and make me seem irrelevant—that contrast you favorably to a father who had no vision and who was but a place holder in the broader scheme of things. I have been reluctant to pass along advice. Both of you are charting your own course, spelling out what direction you want to take your State. . . . But the advice is this. Do not worry when you see the stories that compare you favorably to a Dad for whom English was a second language and for whom the word destiny meant nothing. . . . At some point both of you may want to say 'Well, I don't agree with my Dad on that point' or 'Frankly I think Dad was wrong on that.' Do it. Chart your own course, not just on the issues but on defining yourselves. . . . So read my lips—no more worrying.

In 1994, George W. was challenging incumbent Democratic governor Ann Richards, who seemed formidable. "George," Barbara said to her son, "you can't win." Other old Bush advisers suggested waiting out a second Richards term, but George W. felt he was ready. In Florida, Jeb would face Democratic governor Lawton Chiles.

The father's counsel to George W. from 1977 remained sound for both sons: "Do it with all you've got. Keep your cool, work like hell, don't let the meanness that will surface get you down, don't overreact, see the other guy's point of view. See his merits but convince people you are the better man—for you are."

FORTY-EIGHT

The Proudest Father in the Whole Wide World

★

If I were "The One," no one told me about it.
I didn't get the memo.
—JEB BUSH

He doesn't need a voice from the past.
—GEORGE H. W. BUSH, on George W.'s 2000 campaign for president

I N THE LARGER BUSH CIRCLE, the two eldest sons had long stood in contrast: It was Unserious George and Serious Jeb. George W. was given to streaks of sarcasm and swagger; Jeb could be sarcastic, too, but adopted a quieter, more studious mien. In the bitterness of the loss to Clinton in 1992, Chase Untermeyer, one of the most loyal of Bush devotees, mused about a restoration in the fullness of time. He predicted that Jeb, not George W., was the likelier brother to lead the way back to the White House. Jim Baker believed the same thing: "George W. was the cutup in the Bush family. . . . Jeb was always more serious. Many of us thought that maybe, just maybe, Jeb would be the one to carry on the Bush family tradition in politics."

That is not, however, the way Jeb recalled the family dynamic. "If I were 'The One,' no one told me about it," Jeb said. "I didn't get the memo. And the relationship between George and Dad is incredibly close and loving. I've always been bemused by people who state as fact that which is highly speculative, or untrue, which happens a lot. I don't think my mom and dad think that way—'He's the one, more than that one.' Literally I never had a conversation about that. Ever. I'd say in terms of topics of conversation in the Bush family: family; sports; and then . . . well, that's about it."

George W. thought the broad pro-Jeb impression was partly rooted in the brothers' different experiences as young men. Jeb had finished college in two and a half years, married Columba early, and gone to work building a life in Florida; George W., by his own account, "was viewed as a less serious person. I was seen as more like my mother than my father in many ways. I was more of a cutup, I was irreverent." He was, he recalled, "unattached," interested in girls and adventure and decidedly uninterested in putting down roots. After graduating from Harvard Business School in the 1970s, he moved to Midland "with no possessions, lived in an alley." He went to Alaska one summer just to check it out and was reluctant to buy a house in Midland until a friend talked him into it. "It's totally different from Jeb, who falls in love early and gets married in college and has babies early," George W. recalled. "He's just a different kind of person."

Put another way, Jeb, though seven years younger, grew up faster. Combined with the expectations of 1994, when Florida looked more likely than Texas to elect a Bush son governor, the image of Jeb as the favored brother took hold—hard. *Jeb was supposed to be president—not George W.* Or so the story went. "The whole idea that Jeb was the favorite one because he was more knowledgeable—that's all bullshit," George H. W. Bush recalled. "Nothing to it. I thought Jeb had a better chance to win than George when George went up against Ann Richards. Nobody thought he could win."

As Baker and others testified, it was true that Jeb had appeared most likely to succeed in the 1970s and '80s, but that was then, and 1994 was now. Soon it wouldn't much matter what the family thought. What the voters of Texas and Florida thought would be decisive.

Bush could not stay off the telephone during the campaigns, peppering both sons' headquarters with calls about how things looked. On the Sunday night before the '94 elections, the Bushes stayed at their Florida retreat in Boca Grande. Jeb walked into his parents' suite, and Bush asked what the polls showed. "Jeb said about the same as they were when GB called at 9 am in the morning!" Barbara wrote. "We are so nervous."

On election night 1994, the elder Bushes stayed in Houston, anxiously watching the returns from both states. The results: a win in Texas, a loss in Florida. In his suite at the Four Seasons in Austin,

George W. spoke with his parents from a bathroom. He thought their pain over Jeb's loss seemed to overwhelm their happiness at his victory. "Bush listened to his father's distress over his brother's defeat; when the conversation finished, he shrugged his shoulders and went back into a room awash in joy and excitement," George W.'s strategist Karl Rove recalled.

"The joy is in Texas," the forty-first president told reporters, "but our hearts are in Florida." As George W. recalled, "To some, his reaction was surprising. Not to me. It was typical of George [H. W.] Bush to focus on the person who was hurting."

In late November 1994, on the evening of the day of the ground-breaking for Bush's presidential library in College Station, Barbara and Jeb sat down for a talk over supper at the Post Oak Grill in Houston. "It kills me that he hurts so," Barbara wrote in her diary. "He worked so hard and so long. I know he was exhausted from being such a good sport and, I'm sure, seeing GWB with all the praise and state troopers must give him a twinge. He told me that the one great joy he had Election Night was that George won. At one time he asked me 'How long was it going to hurt?' That killed me." Barbara and Jeb went back to the Bushes' house to find George W., who had just finished exercising and was having a bowl of cereal. Jeb sat down, and their mother left her two eldest sons talking in the night.

Inauguration Day in Austin in January 1995 dawned with rain, but the weather cleared early on. The extended Bush family attended church services with Billy Graham. Columba and Jeb flew in from Florida. Bush gave his eldest son the cufflinks that his own parents had sent him when he got his wings at Corpus Christi during World War II. In a letter to the new governor, the former president wrote: "You have given us more than we ever could have deserved. You have sacrificed for us. You have given us your unwavering loyalty and devotion. Now it is our turn." Their son replied with a note of his own.

Dear Mom and Dad,
    This is my first letter written on my first day as your governor. What a day!
    Your letter moved me so much that I knew I could not look at

either (of you) after I was confirmed. I would have wept with love and pride to be your son.

I am where I am because of you. You should always know this.

With love,

George

In his first summer as governor, George W. traveled to Walker's Point after a meeting in Vermont. The day before he was to arrive his mother looked outside the window and saw strange men prowling around the driveway. "I asked what they were doing and was told that they were advancing GWB's expected arrival," she wrote. "How funny to have George's agents (Texas Rangers) checking on our security!!!"

It did not take long for talk of a national Bush restoration to begin. At a fiftieth birthday party for George W. at the governor's mansion in Austin in the summer of 1996, Bob Bullock, the powerful Democratic lieutenant governor whom Bush had courted, toasted George W.: "Happy birthday. You are one helluva governor. And Governor Bush, you will be the next president of the United States."

As George W. recalled it, Bullock's words "shocked" him. "Ten years earlier, I had been celebrating my fortieth birthday drunk at The Broadmoor," Bush recalled, alluding to the night of hard drinking in Colorado in 1986 that had led him to give up alcohol. "Now I was being toasted on the lawn of the Texas Governor's Mansion as the next president. This had been quite a decade." Pride in the journey he had made was an important element in George W. Bush's character. Confident in his own abilities, he thought the history of his life from the age of 40 forward offered clear evidence that he could make his way in the larger world. He would go on as he had set out: defining himself in the public eye as a loving son, but as his own man.

The 1996 Republican presidential nominee, Bob Dole, visited Walker's Point that summer, joining the senior Bushes and Laura and George W. for a conversation and lunch. They discussed possible running mates, and Dole pointed out that everybody seemed to have some problem or another. A story from the Dole selection process shed light on a new truth about the Bushes. Haley Barbour, the chairman of the

Republican National Committee, called Jim Baker to see whether the former secretary of state would be interested in talking about the vice presidential slot on the 1996 ticket. Baker telephoned Bush to ask what he thought; Bush heard Baker out and said he would call right back. Bush checked in with George W., then telephoned Baker again. "I think it's a great idea—and, more important, George does, too," Bush said. In that moment Baker realized there was a changing of the guard in the Bush universe. The former president had thought it proper to seek the governor of Texas's opinion on an important political question before offering his own.

In the wake of Clinton's defeat of Dole in November 1996, George W. felt, as he put it to *The Washington Post*'s David Broder, like a "cork in a raging river" as the 2000 campaign approached.

The 1998 allegations that President Clinton had carried on an affair with a White House intern, Monica Lewinsky, horrified the Bushes. "Can one believe that this conversation is going on about the president of the United States?" Barbara wrote. The former president was decorous in public; in private, he was troubled. On a winter 1999 visit to France—he and Scowcroft were promoting their book on foreign policy, *A World Transformed*—Bush was invited for a meeting with French president Jacques Chirac in the Elysée Palace. "We had a genuine tour d'horizon," Bush recalled in a letter to his friend Hugh Sidey of *Time* on the transatlantic flight home to Houston. Chirac's dismissive view of the Clinton scandal, however, left Bush unsettled. "I am worried," Bush wrote. "Like most world leaders I think Chirac feels we have 'lost it' over the Lewinsky matter. That was the view of everyone I talked to. Oddly, no one I talked to in France focused in on 'lack of respect for the office' [to] say nothing of lying under oath or obstruction of justice."

The scandal unfolded as speculation about George W.'s prospects for the presidency in 2000 grew. The elder Bush could not sleep on the night before the 1998 midterm elections. (He tried a Tylenol PM, but it did not work.) He worried about both of his political sons—and about what awaited George W. in the wake of reelection. "Yesterday I told him—'George, on November 4th things will be very different,'" Bush wrote Sidey. "He knew exactly what I meant. . . . He is strong though—tough enough, too, to withstand the pressure."

His view of his eldest son: "He is good, this boy of ours. He's uptight at time[s], feisty at other times—but who wouldn't be after months of grueling campaigning. He includes people. He has no sharp edges on issues. He is no ideologue, no divider. He brings people together and he knows how to get things done. He has principles to which he adheres but he knows how to give a little to get a lot. He doesn't hog the credit. He's low on ego, high on drive."

The forty-first president was watching the Florida exit polls with care. If Jeb's numbers in the gubernatorial race "look even fairly good," Bush wrote, he and Barbara were going to fly to Miami to surprise their latest governor son. "The plan is to show up at his hotel rooms unannounced, unadvanced—just a mother and dad wanting to be with their boy. I love the thought." Jeb prevailed, the trip was made, and, as Bush wrote Hugh Sidey, "there is no question in my mind that he will become a major political figure in the country. He is passionate in his caring and in his beliefs. He speaks well and at 6′4″ he is an impressive man. Take it from his proud Dad."

And the governor of Texas, safely reelected, was widely expected to join the 2000 presidential campaign, only eight years after his father's defeat.

In June 1999, George W. Bush made it official. He would be a candidate for the Republican presidential nomination. After announcing his bid in Amana Colonies, Iowa, he traveled to Kennebunkport to see his parents. The Bushes served hamburgers and hot dogs on the deck at Walker's Point before a one thirty press conference on the lawn. The senior Bush made clear that the 2000 campaign was the next generation's, not his. "He doesn't need a voice from the past," the former president said of his son that afternoon. Bush treated George W. in much the way he had treated Ronald Reagan or any other president. The candidate was the candidate, and the president was the president. The job was so tough, the critics so numerous, the second-guessing so intense, that Bush decided his best role was that of a loving, attentive father.

In a primary debate, an answer of George W.'s underscored the generational and cultural distinctions between father and son. Asked to name his favorite philosopher, George W. replied: "Christ, because he changed my heart." Calling his son afterward, Bush senior said, "Don't worry, son, I don't think the Jesus answer will hurt you very much." George W. was struck by the remark; it had never occurred to him that what he thought of as honesty about his faith *could* hurt him.

"My dad went to Greenwich Country Day School in Connecticut," the younger Bush would say, "and I went to San Jacinto Junior High in Midland." Inspired by his father's example, he also made clear that he had learned from his father's mistakes. When George W. talked about the need for a clear vision, or about keeping one's word to the base, or about projecting an unmistakable identity, it was not hard to infer that the son understood where his father had fallen short—and where he was determined to hit the mark.

The passing of the generational mantle had its awkward moments for the forty-first president. He had urged his sons to make their own way, but he could not help but occasionally feel a little left out as time marched on. Karl Rove, George W.'s chief strategist, traveled to Houston from Austin for dinner with the senior Bushes in April 2000. "He didn't mean to, but he really hurt George's feelings," Barbara wrote. "He sort of intimated that we should not come to the Convention other [than] to make the speech that a former President would normally give. He was worried about the picture. It should be the Presidential candidate and the VP and their families. We agree, but surely we would be in a box with the rest of our family to cheer him on as a mom and dad." Told later that he had upset the former president, "Poor Karl was sick." The elder Bush did attend the whole convention but declined to speak. It was George's turn, he told friends, and who wanted to hear a former president anyway? Waste of prime time.

Heading into the summer of 2000, George W.'s chief concern was who to name as his running mate. As he weighed the different options, he kept coming back to the man he had put in charge of the search process, Dick Cheney. For Karl Rove, at least, the Cheney choice seemed too retro, too much a throwback to the father's era. When George W. asked him to make the case against Cheney—with Cheney in the room— Rove argued that picking Cheney would "send the message, I feared, that the young governor was falling back on his father's administration for help."

George W. asked his father for advice on the choice; the senior Bush warmly endorsed Cheney. In July, Don Evans, the son's campaign chairman, called the Bushes to give them a heads-up that Cheney was the pick. On the telephone with Evans on the porch at Walker's Point, Bush said: "Well, that's great, and she's great, too," referring to Lynne Cheney.

At the elder Bush's request, legendary Houston heart surgeon Dr. Denton Cooley had reviewed Cheney's health records and offered the opinion that Cheney was up to the challenge of the campaign.

At the convention in Philadelphia, Jeb offered a toast to George W. during a family dinner. "I have watched you, big brother, for the last year, and about five months ago I suddenly found myself thinking: 'I am looking at a president.' I am in awe, I'm proud of you, and I love you." The family continued to be impressed by their Florida son as well as by the presidential nominee. "Jeb is a workaholic and is still in constant touch with the world through email," Barbara wrote. "He has made his email address public and gets several hundred a day, ALL of which he answers late into the night, early morning, or before lunch—just all the time."

The Bushes' minds had been taken far off politics on a Friday in May 2000. With the rector of St. Martin's, their church in Houston, they slipped away to College Station to re-inter the remains of their beloved Robin, whom they had brought from Greenwich to their future burial plot at the presidential library. "It seems funny after almost 50 years since her death how dear Robin is to our hearts," Bush wrote the rector, Larry Gipson, afterward. The former president had cried when Gipson read the prayers at the grave. "But they were not the same tears of devastation, loss, and pain that I felt when Robin died," Bush wrote. "Instead they were tears of gratitude that we had her at all and maybe even tears of joy that she was still with us." Nearly a half century earlier, Bush recalled, the parent of one of Robin's fellow leukemia patients had said, " 'Well, I guess Jesus was right when he said "Let the little children suffer so they can come unto me," ' " Bush recalled. "She got it wrong . . . but maybe she also got it right, too. Her kid and ours did suffer and indeed in their innocence they went to heaven. Of that I am certain." He was certain of something else, too. "We are very comforted to know that when we are buried," Bush wrote, "the body of our beloved little four year old will be tucked in right there beside us—right next to her parents who love her so much."

On the morning of Election Day 2000, Bush spoke to students at the Bush School of Government and Public Service in College Station before he and Barbara were driven up to Austin. On the ride Bush was attached to his mobile phone, anxious for exit polls, anecdotes, and political intelligence of any kind.

At a large private dinner at the Shoreline Grill in Austin, the elder

Bush ordered a vodka from the bartender—and drank two triples. It was a cheerful gathering, full of children and grandchildren and uncles and aunts and cousins. Then, George W. recalled, "the exit polls started coming in. The networks called Pennsylvania, Michigan, and Florida for Gore." The party seemed to freeze. A distraught Jeb walked over to George W. The two men embraced. "George W. told Laura that he'd like to watch it from home" at the governor's mansion about a mile away, Barbara recalled. George W. rounded up his mother, his father, and his mother-in-law, Jenna Welch, and they hurried back to monitor the results in more familiar surroundings. The trip to the mansion, George W. recalled, was "quiet." Believing he had lost, he was thinking of what the family code dictated in such circumstances. "There isn't much to say when you lose," George W. recalled. "I was deflated, disappointed, and a little stunned. I felt no bitterness. I was ready to accept the people's verdict and repeat Mother's words from 1992: 'It's time to move on.'"

The elder Bush was, to put it mildly, a nervous wreck. Then, as the night went on, George W. appeared to have won Florida after all, and Gore called to concede, only to have the numbers tighten again, at which point Gore retracted his concession. Even after the second call from Gore, some Bush advisers argued that George W. should declare victory to the waiting throngs in the rainy Austin night; Jeb advised against it. If Florida was in fact too close to call, George W. did not want to look presumptuous or power hungry. "He took me aside and said, 'Don't do this,'" George W. recalled. "He was right. I trusted his judgment." The elder Bushes went to bed about four A.M. not knowing whether their son had won. When they rose to drink coffee three hours later with George W. and Laura, who were reading papers in bed, the results were still unknown. The senior Bushes decided to drive home to Houston.

Back in Florida after an early flight, Jeb saw a Gore-Lieberman DC-9 on the runway. "We've been invaded," he told Karl Rove by telephone. Vice President Gore announced that former secretary of state Warren Christopher would represent his interests in the recount. Don Evans, George W.'s national chairman, took the candidate an idea of the top campaign staff's: Why not ask Jim Baker, who had spent election night in Austin with his wife, Susan, to take over operations in Florida? George W. approved, and Evans and George W. both spoke to Baker. "He didn't hesitate," George W. recalled. "He said, 'I'm gone; I'm in.'" Within hours Baker was en route to Florida.

On Thursday, November 9, 2000, the Clintons hosted a dinner in honor of the two hundredth anniversary of the White House. Given the disputed election, it was an uneasy occasion. The Bushes flew up to Washington, changed into black-tie at the Jackson Place quarters set aside for former presidents, and were received at the White House, where they joined Lady Bird Johnson, the Fords, the Carters, and the Clintons. Hillary had won a U.S. Senate seat from New York, and Chuck Robb, LBJ's son-in-law, had lost his Senate race in Virginia. "So there we were: a winner (Hil), a loser (Chuck), and Mr. and Mrs. In-between (GB and BPB)," wrote Barbara.

Barbara concealed—barely—her disdain for Clinton, who had quoted John Adams's prayer that none but "honest" men should rule under this roof. "What absolute nerve," she wrote. "He was impeached because he lied to the American public and the special prosecutor. I have come to the conclusion that he really does not know right from wrong." At the end of the evening, Bush was scheduled to fly to Spain for a previously planned hunting trip with King Juan Carlos, and Barbara returned to Houston.

Bush father and son were on the telephone constantly, exchanging quick updates and offering mutual reassurances. Both men wanted to buck up the other. On the Friday after Thanksgiving, the elder Bushes went out to Crawford for a quiet day with Laura and George W., who grilled steaks. The phone buzzed with news about Florida from Baker, Rove, and Don Evans, but still nothing definitive.

Resolution finally came on Tuesday, December 12, 2000, when the U.S. Supreme Court ruled, in effect, that Bush had won Florida and that there could be no further recounts. On the night of the decision, George W. was in bed, reading, with the television off. Rove heard the news first and called him. "Congratulations, Mr. President!" Rove said. As George W. tried to understand what was being reported on the networks—the correspondents were unsure, leading to several moments of confusion—he cut Rove off, saying, "I'm calling Baker."

Baker confirmed it. The election was over. George W. had prevailed. On Wednesday the thirteenth, Vice President Gore delivered a gracious concession. After a dinner with friends, the elder Bushes watched Gore's speech. Moved, the former president picked up the telephone. He wanted to salute Gore. "His speech was absolute perfection," Bush wrote. "He did it with grace and dignity and a genuineness that enthralled the nation. I know how difficult it was for him to do what he did."

On television Bush saw Gore climb into a limousine after the speech, and he telephoned Jean Becker, his chief of staff. "I want to call Al Gore," the former president said. "I've been where he is. I've lost, and losing hurts." Bush reached the White House switchboard and asked to be connected to the vice president. A few minutes later Gore returned the call. "I congratulated him, just one sentence or two, just a few words," Bush recalled. "I suddenly felt for him, saw him as a man whose disappointment had to be overpowering." Gore was grateful. "President Bush was very emotional, very kind," Gore recalled. Hearing Gore's voice took Bush back to 1992.

> The conversation was over in a flash, but I suddenly felt quite different about Al Gore. The anger was gone, the competitive juices stopped flowing. I thought of Algore as two words (Al Gore) not one. I thought of his long years of service and of his family. I thought back to my own feelings of years before when I lost, when I had to go out and accept my defeat. He did it better than I did, and his ordeal had to be tougher because the election was so close. True I had to actually give up the Presidency that he was now seeking, but still he had been in public life a long time and he and his family were shattered.

In Austin, the president-elect was about to address the nation from the floor of the Texas legislature. Their eldest child was the president of the United States.

It was surreal. History had now struck their family twice. "What a lovely son we were given," Barbara wrote friends. "I keep reading all sorts of things about our wanting revenge or a dynasty, etc. Baloney! We feel exactly as you would feel if one of your chicks became President. It is an awesome feeling."

Cameras captured Laura and George W. holding hands before the address. "I saw in his posture, in the way he walked, [and] in his smile the same mannerisms and expressions we have known ever since he was a little boy," Bush wrote Hugh Sidey, the longtime *Time* columnist.* After George W.'s brief speech, Bush called his son's personal aide, Logan Wal-

---

* Bush and Sidey corresponded a great deal during George W.'s presidency; the letters form a kind of diary of the elder Bush's impressions of his son's election and presidential years.

ters. "Logan, this is George Bush the elder, can you hand this phone to my boy?" The president-elect took the phone. "What did you think, Dad?"

"I told him how perfect I felt his speech was," Bush recalled. Barbara repeated how proud they were. The conversation ended, but the senior Bush kept the television on, watching the rest of the coverage. He saw the president-elect's car disappear behind a white curtain at the governor's mansion—a security precaution that he remembered well.

He closed his letter about the evening with a prayer. "May God give our son the strength he needs. May God protect the 43rd President of the United States of America." Bush signed off: "Your friend, the proudest father in the whole wide world."

FORTY-NINE

It Is Not Easy to Sit on the Sidelines

★

I'm the father, and it's his turn to make the big calls, and he should know that his father's going to either be quiet or supportive. . . . I'm not going to go back and revisit decisions and say, "Hey, he should have done this or done that." Just not going to do it.

—GEORGE H. W. BUSH, on George W. Bush's presidency

R ISING EARLY AT BLAIR HOUSE on a wet Inauguration Day 2001, the father of the next president fortified himself with coffee. After putting on a skin-toned undershirt and royal blue long leggings beneath his suit, George H. W. Bush left for services at St. John's Church. In a sermon, the president-elect's minister from Dallas, Mark Craig, alluded to the senior President Bush's 1989 inaugural prayer, quoting words that Bush had written a dozen years before. "He didn't mention my name," Bush recalled, but "I recognized the prayer and was deeply touched."

It was that kind of day, and was to be that kind of decade: George H. W. Bush onstage yet silent, regal yet restrained. The Bushes were in largely uncharted territory. No son had followed his father to the presidency since John Quincy Adams won the White House in the election of 1824, nearly a quarter of a century after John Adams left the new capital in 1801, never to return. (The elder Adams died in 1826, two years into his son's term.) The senior Bush—who sometimes referred to his son as "Quincy"—was determined to carry on in the new century as he had since 1994, when George and Jeb entered the arena: be supportive, be helpful, answer questions if asked, but stay out of what Bush called "the opining business."

After the service, the former president was driven to the Hill. In a holding room at the Capitol before the ceremony, the elder Bushes waited with George W.'s twins, Jenna and Barbara. Both grandparents marveled at the girls' "stilt-like heels."

On the platform overlooking the Mall, Bush, with Barbara on his right arm, walked to the podium. "I don't want to be a braggadocio," he wrote Hugh Sidey, "but we did receive a warm welcome from the platform guests and the huge crowd below." He took his place, standing to applaud as the Cheneys and the Clintons walked to their seats, and waited. His son was announced. "George walked down the steps—not looking overly relaxed, but straight and proper and smiling at friends," Bush recalled. "He looked good. He looked Presidential." The oath administered, the forty-third president turned to seek out the forty-first. George W. hugged his mother and cupped his father's neck in an embrace. It was the only moment, miraculously, when the elder Bush cried. "Pride of a father in a son," Bush recalled. "Why not shed some tears?"

On the drive from the Hill to the White House, where the Bushes would take in the parade from a reviewing stand, the forty-first president passed anti-Bush protestors. Jenna and Barbara, who were in the car with their grandparents, expressed concern. "I tried to assure them not to worry because this simply went with the territory, all Presidents suffer through this kind of ugliness; but they were not convinced," Bush recalled.

Inside the White House, the Bushes wandered through stacks of crates. The bright blue Clinton Oval Office carpet had been rolled up; Bush 43 would use Reagan's. Walking from the West Wing to the main house and then out the North Portico door, Bush sat on the second row of the reviewing stand. Turning to a military officer, he said, "Let me know when President Bush is arriving," taking pleasure in the phrase "President Bush." A few moments later the officer gave the word: "The president is coming, sir."

As his son entered the enclosure, the father rose in respect.

It was a long parade. Barbara, as her husband put it, "pulled the rip cord and went to the White House," but Bush wanted to wait to see the Texas A&M marching band. At last the Aggies marched into view, and the new president turned to the old to ask him to come forward. "I had been sitting right behind him, but I had not wanted to go stand next to him—did not want to 'horn in,' as mother used to say," Bush recalled. At his son's invitation, however, the father stepped up, reviewed the Aggies, and excused himself to take a warm tub back in the bathroom off the Queen's Bedroom. Bush was just beginning to relax, soaking a sore hip, when there was a knock on the door. "Mr. President," he was told, "President Bush would like you to meet him downstairs to walk over to the Oval Office." Bush moved fast, drying off, throwing on a suit, and "hustl[ing]" over to the West Wing.

Bush smiled at the sight of the new president at the big desk in the Oval Office. "Over the next eight years, I would have many memorable meetings in the Oval Office," George W. recalled. "None compared to standing in the office with my father on my first day." Father and son walked back into the adjoining suite that the elder Bush had loved so. Standing in the study, Bush felt his past was vividly present: Here was where "I did a lot of work, made a lot of phone calls, kept my computer and watched the blossoms break out each spring," he recalled. "Memories rushed back of phone calls made to world leaders, Brent Scowcroft at my side. Memories of personnel problems, of happy days and sad days too." (He dropped a heavy hint to his son about restoring the horseshoe pit that Clinton had removed, but the younger Bush was more interested in building a small T-ball field.) Their inspection done, the two men went back to the Residence together, the past and the future shoulder to shoulder.

Upstairs, the new president broke off to dress in black-tie for the evening's inaugural balls while the elder Bush joined his wife for a drink and watched an NBC profile of the family anchored by Jamie Gangel. (Laura recalled that the new president was "shocked" to learn that he now had not one but two valets. "I don't think I need a valet," George W. said to his father. "Don't worry," the elder Bush replied, "you'll get used to it.")

The elder Bush was in bed by a quarter to nine, content to read a bit of a James Patterson mystery (*Roses Are Red*) and tease Jenna and Barbara and their friends—"a whole group of University of Texas glamour girls"—as they departed for the inaugural balls. In the quiet house, he and Barbara turned out the lights and said their prayers, "asking the Lord to bless our son and to lift him up when the going gets tough."

The next morning there was a Sunday service at the National Cathedral and then a reception on the main floor of the White House. Bush was ready to go home, but took a quick moment to look at his own portrait. An impromptu receiving line formed. "I kept telling the folks lined up with cameras, 'The President is in the East Room, hustle on down and say hi,'" Bush recalled. "But no they needed a quick shot with their kids with #41 so I stood there for a long time. It was OK, a bit flattering really." There were a few instances of confusion. "Having been President before there were still moments lingering on. . . . Someone goes 'Mr. President' and I'd start to acknowledge," Bush recalled. "Or walking with George someone might say 'Hi, Mr. President!' and I'd spin around." At noon the forty-first president took his leave. He pulled George W. aside for a farewell. They looked at each other, grew teary, and the father departed.

The transition had been truncated. "George W. has been so dear about calling his dad almost daily to talk over decisions that he has made. . . . George does not suggest, but listens and then comments," Barbara wrote on Christmas Eve 2000. George W. asked his father about retaining George Tenet, the Clinton-appointed director of the CIA (the elder Bush approved) but never consulted him about the choice for secretary of defense: Donald Rumsfeld, the old man's old rival. ("Knew what the answer was," George W. recalled.) Rumsfeld had been under consideration for the CIA, but after two other possible defense secretaries—Fred Smith of FedEx and Indiana senator Dan Coats—fell by the wayside, Condi Rice suggested him for the Pentagon. Rove raised the same concern he had broached the previous summer with the Cheney nomination. "I liked Rumsfeld but told Bush that tapping him would feed the story line that Cheney was in charge," Rove recalled. "Bush dismissed the fear and told me that the old hands— Cheney, Powell, and Rumsfeld—would come to understand who was in charge if they didn't already know."

The Rumsfeld appointment was a clear sign that the second President Bush was determined to pursue his own course. Rumsfeld was an aggressive figure; he told George W. that he would be "leaning forward" at the Pentagon, which was just fine with the president-elect. The history between Rumsfeld and the elder Bush did not matter to George W. In the new president's view, he had a job to do, and Don Rumsfeld could help him do it. His mother took quiet note of the decision. "It is an interesting appointment as Rummy was never fond of GHWB," Barbara wrote in her diary on Friday, December 29, 2000. "He got the credit for suggesting GB as Director of the CIA rather than Sect. of Commerce, feeling that would keep GB from ever being President." Of the Rumsfeld appointment, Bush 41 would only say: "We were never really close. No heavy hostility—just different."

The elder Bushes spent the evening of Monday, September 10, 2001, at the White House. (George W. recalled that he "had made it clear that Mother and Dad had an open invitation to stay at the White House anytime.") On the morning of the eleventh, they kissed Laura goodbye— the president was in Florida—and boarded a private flight to St. Paul, Minnesota, where they were scheduled to deliver speeches. Barbara recalled that they were in the air, drinking coffee and reading the papers, when the copilot told them that a commercial airliner had struck one of the World Trade Center towers. Soon they were told the plane would have to land. The second tower had been hit, too. "Now we knew this was not an accident," Barbara recalled, "but a terrorist attack." The Secret Service moved the Bushes from the Milwaukee airport to a motel, where they followed the horror of the day on television. They reached the president by phone. Where are you? George W. asked. "At a motel in Brookfield, Wisconsin," Barbara replied.

"What in the world are you doing there?"

"Son," Barbara said, "you grounded our plane."

The elder Bush advised his son, who was moving from air force base to air force base, to return to the capital as soon as he safely could. ("He totally agreed with that," Bush recalled.) Watching the news, Bush's mind raced. He worried about the personal security of the president. The possibility of assassination seemed strong. He was concerned, too, about violence against innocent Muslim-Americans. Behind his self-imposed public silence Bush churned with thoughts and ideas. "What can we do about all this?" he wrote Hugh Sidey on Wednesday, September 12. He recalled his terrorism task force under Reagan, an experience, he noted, that had made him "somewhat familiar with what can and can't be done." As an old spymaster he spoke of the promise and the perils of human intelligence. "This means dealing with 'bad guys,'" Bush wrote. "Evil people. Unsavory folks who will betray their own country." Bush's old concerns about executive prerogatives were revived. "Congress with its insistence on knowing every detail under the guise of 'right to know' must be more disciplined, more leak proof."

On Friday, September 14, 2001, the former presidents were to join

George W. for a memorial service at the National Cathedral in Washington. By custom the presidents sat at such events in reverse chronological order, meaning that the Bush 43s would be next to the Clintons, followed by the Bush 41s, and so on. Before the gathering at the cathedral, the elder Bush had a request for Bill Clinton. Would Clinton mind if they broke protocol? "Today I want to sit next to my son," Bush said. Clinton agreed, and the elder Bushes were next to the younger Bushes. "War has been waged against us by stealth and deceit and murder," the forty-third president told the world from the cathedral's lectern. "This nation is peaceful, but fierce when stirred to anger. This conflict was begun on the timing and terms of others. It will end in a way, and at an hour, of our choosing." When George W. returned to his pew, he felt his father squeeze his arm.

Closing his letter to Sidey on September 12, the elder Bush had made a rare admission. "It is not easy, dear friend," Bush wrote, "to sit on the sidelines now, not easy to not make decisions or take actions."

By temperament and experience, George H. W. Bush was accustomed to deferring to the wishes and to the will of the president of the United States, be he Richard Nixon, Gerald Ford, Ronald Reagan, or, now, his own son. Hour to hour, day to day, month to month, and year to year, the reality of his son's candidacy and then presidency required the elder Bush—who always respected reality—to resist a natural inclination to express his own views. "Once you've sat at that desk" in the Oval Office, the elder Bush remarked in retirement, "it's complicated to see someone else there. When you've made the big calls, it's tough be on the sidelines—but you've got to be."

By temperament and experience, George W. Bush had the self-confidence of a man who had, in the short space of a dozen years, chosen to forgo a life as what Jim Baker jokingly described as "a juvenile delinquent, damn near" and risen to the pinnacle of American life. A shrewd student of his father's career in particular and of contemporary politics in general, the younger Bush had mined the elder Bush's public life for lessons for his own journey.

The father had sometimes seemed without convictions; the son would be a man with a clear creed. The father had lost the conservative base of the party; the son would maintain his standing with the right. The father had been attacked for appearing weak; the son would project strength at all times. They were different men, running and ruling at different times. As a legislator, diplomat, party chairman, CIA director, and vice president, the father spent eighteen years implementing or managing the visions of others. He was not expected to project his own; was, in fact, discouraged from it as a man in the service of the House leadership, Nixon, Ford, or Reagan.

As a governor and a presidential candidate, on the other hand, the son had spent six years with the expectation that he would spell out what was to be done. "The difference in some ways is that I was held to account as a chief executive," George W. recalled. "My political skills were honed on defining a vision, defending it, and then implementing it, and that's different. It's a different path. When you're the governor you have to have agendas and the agendas have to be based on principles, and legislation follows. When you're governor you don't drift." When you are in administrative jobs or the vice presidency, as George H. W. Bush had been, drift was sometimes part of the job description.

By his own account George W. Bush saw himself as a president more in the mold of a Theodore Roosevelt or of a Ronald Reagan than of a George H. W. Bush. TR and Reagan were poets of leadership; George H. W. Bush was more prosaic. "I admired presidents who used their time in office to enact transformative change," Bush wrote in his 2010 memoir, *Decision Points*. He had studied TR, he reported, and learned from Reagan, "who combined an optimistic demeanor with the moral clarity and conviction to cut taxes, strengthen the military, and face down the Soviet Union despite withering criticism throughout his presidency." George W. Bush sent the word to his team: "I decided to push for sweeping reforms, not tinker with the status quo. As I told my advisers, 'I didn't take this job to play small ball.'" One Bush 43 quotation about Bush 41's time in power seemed to sum up George W.'s apparently superior view of his own political capacities: "Never underestimate what you can learn from a failed presidency."

There were two popular, often intermingled, story lines. One was that George W. Bush was in politics to avenge his father's defeat in 1992 and restore the family to power. The other was somewhat darker: that George W. was in politics to compete with, and attempt to surpass, his father—by projecting a firm ideological identity when his father had not; by winning a second term when his father had not; and, as things developed, by removing Saddam Hussein from power when his father had not.

While it is too simplistic to say George W. Bush governed the United States of America for eight years solely in reference to his relationship with his father, it would be naïve to think that their story—like the story of most fathers and sons—was not also shaped by emotional complexity. George W. had learned from his father's victories and his father's defeats—and he was determined, in his own case, to win more than he lost. Politically, George W. saw his father in much the way many other Americans did: as a gracious and underappreciated man who had many virtues but who had failed to project enough of a distinctive identity and vision to overcome the economic challenges of 1991–92 and to win a second term. He also knew that his father had suffered from the unfair characterization of a being a "wimp"—a caricature that had been shown to be faulty, given Bush's victory in 1988 and his handling of the Gulf War but which endured, painfully, in the family imagination.

George W. argued that the biggest misconception about his relationship with his father was "that there was competition between my dad and me. That I ran for office to compete with him. Which misses the point of his unbelievable character. Why would you compete with somebody you love? Now, the psychobabblists would say, 'Because that's precisely who you want to compete with.' I view it differently. I view it that you'd want to compete with somebody who you didn't love, that you'd want to show them up. It never entered my thought process. It's hard to make people understand that he is such a good man and served as such a clear example for two sons who chose the same field that we wanted to emulate him as opposed to compete with him. And he taught us valuable life lessons—that politics wasn't dirty, necessarily; that politics was noble; that family could still matter, that I could still be a good dad when I ran. I know that sounds a little Pollyannaish to some, but nevertheless that's valid."

As president, George W. Bush faced the most complicated of tasks. As a clinical political matter it was not only in his interest but in the interests of the nation and of the world for him to do as well or better than his father had done in the White House—something the elder Bush, as a political creature, intuitively understood.

They were locked in an odd bind. George H. W. Bush had opinions but would not offer them unless asked; George W. Bush had his own worldview and preferred not to ask. "If I had asked Dad for his opinion on a policy matter, he—knowing the presidency, and knowing that the president had more access to information than anybody—would have said, 'Send your briefers,'" George W. recalled.

Still, the forty-third president protested a bit much on how little he consulted his father. A careful reading of Bush 43's memoir *Decision Points* reveals that he did reach out to his father on Iraq, on national security appointments, and on other matters. George W. disliked discussing such occasions, leading to a public impression that he may have been heedless of the old man to the point of disrespect. In truth, one suspects that George W. Bush, in his effort to make his own way, purposely downplayed his consultations with his father. Asked after he left the White House whether he may have been defensive about acknowledging that he had sought the old man's advice for fear of appearing overly dependent on the previous generation, George W. Bush allowed: "That's not a bad observation."

The elder Bush could be willful, too. The more the world pounded away at the son, saying 43 should be more like 41, the less the father wanted to hear critiques of the son, even if—perhaps especially if—the critiques cast the father in a brighter, better light. Asked in 2010 what he thought of his son politically, the elder Bush replied: "I think he's a highly successful politician, elected governor of Texas when most people didn't think he would be, elected president when a lot of people didn't think he would be. I'm very proud of him. I don't know what can be done differently to get people to see what I see, but I think he made some very tough decisions, right decisions."

One irony: many of the journalists and politicians who used George H. W. Bush as a weapon with which to bludgeon George W. Bush had long derided George H. W. Bush. The former president who once could do no right was sometimes lionized as a statesman less because of his own merits as a statesman and more because he wasn't his son.

Bush was circumspect even with his closest lieutenants, Scowcroft and Jim Baker. "Both those guys [Scowcroft and Baker] know of my affection for my son, they know of my conviction that he doesn't need his father out there opining, and they know that I'm not going to do that in any way, inadvertently or directly," Bush recalled. "So there's kind of a no-man's-land there. They'll give me an opinion, but they don't say,

'You've got to get the President to do this or you've got to talk to him about that'—they don't do that. I told them early on that he's President, I'm not. I had my chance. Now he's got to do what he thinks is right."

From Florida, Jeb watched his father and his elder brother with care and concern and was unsurprised that their dad chose to be totally supportive. "No one should expect a rational view of this," Jeb recalled. "He's your son; he's getting the crap kicked out of him; it reminds you of when you were getting the crap kicked out of you by the same people, the same institutions, so you understandably settle on saying: 'This is my son, I love him, and that's it.' You shouldn't really expect anything more, or anything different. He's your son, for God's sake."

The saga of the two George Bushes became central to the history of the modern era in the aftermath of September 11, 2001, when the Bush 43 administration turned its attention to Iraq. The distance of years has made it difficult to recall the pervasive sense of danger in the immediate post-9/11 period. Each day in the Oval Office, President Bush read intelligence reports on biological, chemical, and even nuclear threats. Striking Afghanistan was one thing, but the incumbent president believed a key lesson of what he called a "day of fire" was the elimination of threats *before* they materialized, and the possibility of a dictator like Saddam passing weapons of mass destruction to terrorists was one such threat.

A war against Saddam was a bold choice, but Bush 43 was a president with an avowed interest in being bold in ways that his father had not been. The elder Bush had built his political life on reacting, carefully and pragmatically, to a changing world. The younger Bush had defined himself as a different kind of leader, a man who preferred action to reaction. So even when George W. Bush was acting without any reference to his father, he could appear to be pursuing paths—particularly in foreign policy—as a means of rebellion against, or of competition with, his father.

The targeting of Iraq in the wake of September 11 provided an irresistible context for Shakespearean speculation about dynastic rivalries. (Maureen Dowd of *The New York Times*—George W. nicknamed her "the Cobra"—was the poet laureate of the saga of father and son.) Those who held such psychological theories about George W. Bush's mind and motives—including many mainstream journalists and opinion makers—

felt vindicated on Thursday, August 15, 2002, when Brent Scowcroft published an op-ed in *The Wall Street Journal.* The headline: "Don't Attack Saddam." Here, it seemed, it all was: The old man in Kennebunkport, worried that his heir was riding to ruin, uses a liege man to warn the new regime of the folly of their course. The headline on Maureen Dowd's column about Scowcroft's piece: "Junior Gets a Spanking."

Reading the Scowcroft article in the *Journal,* George W. was, in his own recollection, "angry" that his father's old intimate "had chosen to publish his advice in the newspaper instead of sharing it with me." Moreover, George W. recalled, "I was very unhappy about it not because he disagreed with my policy but because I knew the critics would be quoting him as someone close to Dad saying it was bad."

The president called his father. "He's now going to be in every story," George W. said to his father. "If he had a problem, he could have picked up the phone and come over."

"Brent's a good man," the elder Bush replied. "He's a friend—Brent's your friend."

Some friend, George W. thought. From the forty-third president's perspective, the damage had been done. "Some in Washington," the younger Bush recalled, "speculated that Brent's op-ed was Dad's way of sending me a message on Iraq"—a kind of Allan Shivers moment, reminiscent of the appointment the father had arranged at which the former Texas governor had told George W. that the 1978 House race was a bad idea.

Bush 43 refused to believe that his father would have chosen such a method of sending a message. "That was ridiculous," the younger Bush recalled. "Of all people, Dad understood the stakes. If he thought I was handling Iraq wrong, he damn sure would have told me himself."

Did Scowcroft tell Bush 41 he was going public with his reservations about his son's path? Yes, and the elder Bush did not try to stop him. "President Bush's view was that Brent had a right to speak out," recalled Jean Becker, Bush 41's post-presidential chief of staff. ("I think Brent had some very different opinions," George H. W. Bush recalled, noting that he and Scowcroft did not have sustained conversations about the issue—"because," Bush 41 said, "of the family stuff.") Was Bush 41 using Scowcroft to send a signal to the White House? "That's too conspiratorial," the elder Bush recalled. "We don't work that way."

So what way did they work? The son occasionally asked for counsel and, on those occasions, the father gave it—confidentially and usually in the most general of terms—and the son, like most presidents, did what he chose to do in any event. "I can't sit here and say, 'Son, you've got to move the previous question in the subcommittee,'" Bush recalled. "I don't know enough, and he doesn't need that." They spoke all the time, with the father reassuring the son and the son telling the father not to watch so much cable news. The elder Bush recalled that requests from the president for explicit counsel were "very few and far between. I don't think he did ask me a lot. We'd visit, but it usually wouldn't be, 'Dad, I've got to ask you this question.' He had his own team, his own imprimatur. And he earned it, fair and square. Governor of a huge state. People forget that. He did that on his own. He wasn't some dolt, some dummy going in there. That became kind of the common wisdom, the inside view, so much that abroad he had to kind of face up to that. He was well-educated, an achiever, and I used to get furious at that kind of thing."

In George W.'s recollection, much of their communication from 2001 to 2009 could be divided into two categories. "Half the time he'd be telling me, 'Son, you're doing fine,' which meant a lot because he'd actually been president and knew what it was like," George W. recalled, "and half the time he'd be railing about what somebody had said about me, which is precisely what I did with him when he was president. Many of the phone calls, I know, were to hear my voice."

At Christmas 2002 at Camp David, George W. sought his father's counsel on Iraq. In his memoirs, Bush 43 made as little of the moment as possible while still deeming it significant enough to report. "For the most part, I didn't seek Dad's advice on major issues," Bush 43 wrote in *Decision Points*. "He and I both understood that I had access to more and better information than he did. Most of our conversations were for me to reassure him that I was doing fine and for him to express his confidence and love."

He admitted, however, that "Iraq was one issue where I wanted to know what he thought." At the presidential retreat where his father had spent so many hours in times of peace and of war, George W. explained where things stood. "I told Dad I was praying we could deal with Saddam peacefully but was preparing for the alternative," Bush 43 recalled in his memoir. "I walked him through the diplomatic strategy . . . and my efforts to rally the Saudis, Jordanians, Turks, and others in the Middle

East." The elder Bush's reply ratified the younger Bush's course. "You know how tough war is, son," the elder Bush said, alluding to Afghanistan, "and you've got to try everything you can to avoid war. But if the man won't comply, you don't have any other choice."

With these words, the father endorsed the son's decision on Iraq—a fact that does not fit the usual narrative. It is important to recall, too, that George H. W. Bush, while celebrated in memory for his management of the 1990–91 Persian Gulf crisis, was himself willing to risk impeachment by going it alone if Congress had failed to authorize the use of force. In the 2002–03 period, at least, the assumed gap between Bush 43 and Bush 41 was likely not as wide as commonly supposed.

Still, that gap was thought wide indeed. In the spring of 2004, Bob Woodward published a book on the run-up to Iraq, *Plan of Attack*. In the course of reporting it, Woodward interviewed the president and asked if he sought his father's advice. "The discussions would be more on the tactics," Bush 43 told Woodward. "How are we doing, How are you doing with the Brits? He is following the news now. And so I am briefing him on what I see. You know, he is the wrong father to appeal to in terms of strength. There is a higher father that I appeal to."

Both Bushes said later that the remark was more theological than Freudian. "George is a religious guy," Bush 41 said. Bush 43 argued that his point was about his dependence on his Christian faith in times of trial—not about his father's personal or political characteristics. Nevertheless, the "wrong father" remark fed the popular view that the two Bushes were out of phase with each other.

It is true that Bush 41 was, as one friend put it, "anxious" about going to Baghdad. The former president understood the complexities of the undertaking better than nearly any other man alive, and he worried about war and its aftermath. This same friend, though, recalled that the elder Bush was so devoted to his son that the former president set those concerns aside and rallied to George W., putting his faith in the incumbent president's judgment.

The elder Bush had signaled some of his own thinking on Iraq— thinking more in line with his son's than not—in a little-noted but revealing speech in Houston at an Arab American community dinner in the fall of 2002. "I came to assure you that our President does not want war, does not want a conflict where innocent people lose their lives," Bush told the audience on Saturday, November 2, 2002. "What he wants is to make Iraq's brutal dictator give up his ruthless quest for weapons of mass destruction; make him honor the many agreements already made and broken; make him abide by the will of the civilized world."

He alluded to his own painful decisions: "As President I worried about the loss of innocent life; but I knew in my heart of hearts we could not let a tyrant with the 4th largest army in the world take over his neighbor by force." The bottom line, according to Bush: "So put it this way: No one wants war against Iraq, but no one wants Iraq to get more terrifying weapons of mass destruction. We must do all we can to work for peace and then, if we have to fight, to protect the lives of the innocents in Iraq." Bush also believed that September 11—an act of war on continental American soil—had presented his son with a set of circumstances and challenges that no president since Lincoln had faced, a conviction that reinforced the old man's instinct to defer to the incumbent.

The day George W. Bush issued the orders to go to war, the forty-third president—like his father had before him—walked alone on the South Lawn. Upstairs in the Treaty Room, which he also used as a study, he wrote a letter to his father.

Dear Dad, . . .

At around 9:30 A.M., I gave the order to SecDef to execute the war plan for Operation Iraqi Freedom. In spite of the fact that I had decided a few months ago to use force, if need be, to liberate Iraq and rid the country of WMD, the decision was an emotional one. . . .

I know I have taken the right action and do pray few will lose life. Iraq will be *free,* the world will be safer. . . .

I know what you went through.

Love,
George

A reply came by fax:

Dear George,

Your handwritten note, just received, touched my heart. You are doing the right thing. Your decision, just made, is the toughest decision you've had to make up until now. But you made it with strength and with compassion. It is right to worry about the loss of innocent life be it Iraqi or American. But you have done that which you had to do.

Maybe it helps a tiny bit as you face the toughest bunch of problems any President since Lincoln has faced: You carry the burden with strength and grace. . . .

Remember Robin's words 'I love you more than tongue can tell.'

Well, I do.

Devotedly,
Dad

Reading his father's words a decade later, George W. Bush choked up with emotion. Tears came to his eyes as he relived, briefly, a moment when a father's love and a predecessor's approval came in a single note to offer reassurance in a troubled hour.

After the fall of Baghdad in early April 2003, Bush emailed his son. "This is a great day for our country, indeed for the world," he told the incumbent president. "You have borne the burden with no complaining, no posturing. You have led with conviction and determination; and now the whole world sees that more clearly."

He hoped, too, that his son would be spared the difficulties of history that had complicated his own war leadership. "No doubt tough times lie ahead, but, henceforth, here and abroad, there will never be any doubts about our Commander in Chief, about his leadership, about our boy George." Bush was right about the tough times ahead. The disappearance of doubt proved another matter altogether.

After Jeb was reelected to a second term as Florida's governor in 2002, his parents traveled to Tallahassee for the swearing-in. At the ceremony, Columba, her father-in-law noted, was "looking lovely."

Columba Bush was something of an enigma within the Bush family. In a clan given to endless competition and breakneck speed—one old Texas political aide to George H. W. recalled that you "never wanted to get in the way" of a Ping-Pong ball in a Bush match "because they were like missiles"—Jeb's wife was quiet and private. What mattered most to Columba's father-in-law, though, was not whether she took part in the world of Walker's Point but whether she made his second son happy. He did not pretend to understand Jeb's marriage fully, and he worried when, in Jeb's first year as governor, Columba failed to declare the merchandise she'd bought on a Paris shopping trip at customs. (She was fined $4,100 for the omission.) But what struck the old man most through the decades, through all the vicissitudes of his second son's life and marriage, was how committed Jeb was to her, and her to him.

At the inauguration in Tallahassee, George P. the eldest son, now twenty-six, was the "amazing" master of ceremonies; Jeb Jr., who was nineteen, sat next to his grandfather. "Then came quiet, lovely, troubled Noelle looking beautiful, but obviously not totally at ease." Noelle, twenty-five years old, struggled with drug addiction and had recently been arrested for prescription-drug fraud.

In his inaugural address, Jeb alluded, implicitly, to the difficulties his family faced. "Although it is an intensely private—and, at times, painful matter—you should know I have rededicated myself to being a better father and husband," the governor said. "Looking today at the faces of my wife and children, all three of them, I realize that any sense of fulfillment I have from this event is meaningless unless they, too, can find fulfillment in their lives. They have sacrificed greatly for me, and I love them dearly."

His father, whom Jeb referred to as "now and forever my greatest hero," listened with pain and with pride, later writing:

> There Jeb stood, the most loving, caring father in the world, standing in front of his addicted daughter saying he'd do better, he'd do more. It broke my heart; and I saw out there in the crowd many other faces with tears in their eyes. Everyone knows that Jeb has given his kids, especially Noelle, his unconditional love. Her addiction has broken his heart but he will always stay at her side, loving her, caring for her and praying for her.

Ronald Reagan died on Saturday, June 5, 2004, after a decade-long struggle with Alzheimer's. Fred Ryan, a trusted Reagan aide, had a to-do list in the plans for the immediate aftermath of the fortieth president's death. "I was supposed to call the kids and then, without delay, I was supposed to call Bush 41," Ryan recalled. "Mrs. Reagan was insistent that he be told as soon as possible. It was very important to her." From the first draft of the Reagan funeral plans—a service, according to presidential custom, in the works beginning in Reagan's last months in office—Bush was always set to speak, along with the incumbent president. At first, of course, he *was* the incumbent president, but even after the 1992 election Mrs. Reagan was firm that she wanted Bush to eulogize her husband. After all the years of tension, after all the slights (real and imagined, on both sides), there was, for Mrs. Reagan, a certainty that George H. W. Bush would conduct himself with grace, say the right things, and commend his fallen chief with nobility and with generosity. "Nancy was very strong about that," recalled Fred Ryan. "The pallbearers kept dying, so that changed, and the music and the hymns were open to revision, but Bush's speaking was a constant."

When he rose to deliver his remarks at the National Cathedral, he proved more than worthy of the trust of the widow who had been unjustly skeptical of him and his wife for a quarter of a century. "Once he called America hopeful, bighearted, idealistic, daring, decent and fair," Bush said of Reagan. "That was America and, yes, our friend." His voice broke when he spoke of what Reagan had meant to him. "As his vice president for eight years, I learned more from Ronald Reagan than from anyone I encountered in all my years of public life. I learned kindness; we all did. I also learned courage; the nation did." And humor: Bush quoted Reagan's one-liner to the doctors at George Washington University Hospital after the assassination attempt in 1981: "I hope you're all Republicans."

Bush paid tribute to Nancy, reaching across the strange chasm that had separated them. "If Ronald Reagan created a better world for many millions it was because of the world someone else created for him," he said. "Nancy was there for him always. Her love for him provided much of his strength, and their love together transformed all of us. . . . So, Nancy, I want to say this to you: Today, America embraces you. We open up our arms. We seek to comfort you, to tell you of our admiration for your courage and your selfless caring."

Such charitable words about Nancy might not have come easily to a less generous man. Yet Bush rose to the occasion, and his eulogy not only to the husband but to the wife was, in a sense, George Bush's final act of service to Ronald Reagan.

The 2004 presidential campaign was stressful for Bush, who worried hour by hour about his son's chances for a second term. When he read overnight polls in the final days that showed the president's num-

bers slipping, he was bereft. "This, of course, caused my aching duode-
num to throb, to pulsate, to hurt," Bush wrote Hugh Sidey. Bush was
addicted to television coverage of the campaign. Barbara bought a set of
headphones so that she could listen to audiobooks while her husband
writhed in pundit-inflicted pain.

The Sunday before the election, Bush recalled, "was a nice quiet day
for us except I could not help but watch the darned TV. The talking
heads seemed even louder, even more obnoxious.... 'Liar' was often
used to describe the President. Hatred filled the airwaves and oozed into
the print media, too." Bush had spent some time on the campaign trail,
but his scheduled events had come to an end on Saturday, October 30,
2004. The Bushes tried to relax by going to the Texans NFL game on
Sunday, but Bush was thrilled when the reelection campaign called Jean
Becker to see if the former president had one more trip in him, this one
to Green Bay on Monday. The next morning he boarded a jet for the
two-hour, twenty-minute flight, spoke to a veterans' group in Wisconsin
for twenty minutes, shook hands, and returned to Texas. Flying home his
mind wandered, briefly, to the final flight of the 1988 campaign, when
the hour of decision was at hand in his own quest.

As ever, though, the past quickly receded for Bush, who eagerly
awaited the overnight polls on Tuesday morning. To his relief, the numbers were better, and he called Jeb, whom Bush referred to as "our realist," to get his take on Florida. "Dad, we will carry Florida," Jeb told him.
Cheered by the private polling and by his second son's reassurance, Bush
turned on the television to hear a different story, with commentators
saying that the president was "behind by a smidgen" in Florida, which
had, in the private polling, seemed safe enough. "Had they seen the
tracking polls, the 'overnights'?" Bush asked in a letter to Hugh Sidey. "I
figure they haven't seen them." Or, worse, Bush worried, perhaps the
"talking heads" were right and the "overnights" were wrong—a possibility that Bush turned over and over in his mind as he and Barbara took a
midday flight to Washington's Reagan National Airport. During the
trip, Bush's speculative fears on the ground in Houston—what if the race
was closer than the reelection campaign thought?—had become real.
The early exit polls suggested a Kerry landslide, a repudiation of the
president, another one-term Bush. "I feel like I have been hit squarely in
the gut—hard," Bush wrote.

Arriving at the White House, Bush spoke on the phone with a longtime political adviser, Ron Kaufman, who told him to wait for the next "cut" of numbers—due about four P.M.—before worrying too much. It was, however, already too late for that. The former president said hello to Bush 43, who was in exercise clothes after a workout and rubdown, and to the "serene, wonderful" Laura. He tried to take a nap but failed. Describing himself as "a total nervous wreck by then," he wandered around the West Wing in search of Karl Rove, whom he found at a computer, surrounded by the exit poll data. "I sat at his table and he explained to me in great detail why I should not be concerned about the exit polls," Bush recalled. He left Rove, returned to the Residence, tried again, unsuccessfully, to nap, watched TV (which only made things worse), and finally joined his son in the Treaty Room for the long night ahead.

His son was, by comparison, calm amid the storm. Bush 43 lit a cigar, made calls, and waited. They spoke with Jeb three different times, making sure the numbers in Florida were holding up (they were) and watched the close results coming in from Ohio. If Ohio were secure, then so was reelection; the first wave of exit polls had indeed been wrong. (So much so that Bob Shrum, Kerry's chief strategist, had addressed his candidate early in the evening as "Mr. President.") As the hour grew late, though, the Ohio election officials were reluctant to announce that Bush had won the state. "There was discussion about whether the President should just go out and declare victory," Bush recalled. "I feared that without the remaining major networks declaring that we had won Ohio, the President would be taking on not only Kerry & Co but the network anchors as well."

Bush 43 decided that to claim victory now, late in the night, would be needlessly provocative. He was going to bed. They would reassess in the morning. "I was totally in accord with that decision," the elder Bush recalled, and he and Barbara retired to the Queen's Bedroom.

Father and son awoke near dawn, and both were seeking coffee when they ran into each other at the door to the younger Bushes' bedroom. The president invited his father to come to the Oval Office, where they sat together. Bush 43 called newly elected senators and top campaign staff. In these early morning hours, there was still no sense, as Bush put it, of "if and when Kerry might 'fold 'em.'" The Oval Office conversation shifted to a new question: Should the White House—or, more specifically, the forty-first president—encourage a Democratic elder statesman to reach out to Kerry to nudge him toward concession?

The elder Bush was willing, briefly. "I felt Bob Strauss would be the ideal person to call, but none of us wanted to look like it was a White House pressure move," Bush recalled. "Strauss was totally trusted but I for one worried that some Kerry minion would find out about the call and leak it to the press as an example of unacceptable pressure and/or of trying to deny the people's right to know or right to have every vote counted." Andrew Card, Bush 43's White House chief of staff, called Jim Baker to ask him to reach out to Vernon Jordan, a Kerry adviser. Baker agreed, and he asked Jordan to get his man to stand down. Within hours, Kerry conceded.

The elder Bushes were scheduled to leave midmorning. Before they departed, both walked around to the Oval Office from the diplomatic entrance to say goodbye to their son. Bush joined the president for a moment on the putting green. (Barney, the First Family's Scottish terrier, chased the putts into the cup.)

"Dad," Bush 43 said, "do you realize that this is the first time since 1988 that a President has won with a clear majority of the vote?" It was a warm remark, a reminder that the elder Bush had been the last president to receive the affirmation of a majority of American voters. Clinton had not managed it in 1992 or in 1996; neither had the younger Bush in the contest against Gore.

Standing there with his reelected son, Bush felt more than ever as though his own hour had passed. "I wish I could help this son of ours," he wrote. "I wish I could do something to help ease the burden, a burden incidentally that he never ever complains about. But I cannot. I am an old guy. My experiences are out of date." It was time to go home to Houston.

FIFTY

The Buck Stops There

★

*He had his own empire there and marched to his own
drummer. It just showed me that you cannot do it that way.*
—GEORGE H. W. BUSH on Dick Cheney's vice presidency

I love George Bush. I do.
—BILL CLINTON

O N THE DAY AFTER CHRISTMAS, 2004, a tsunami in Southeast
Asia ravaged the region, killing nearly a quarter million people
and leaving vast destruction in its wake. To signal American
compassion and American unity, George W. Bush asked two former
presidents—his father and Bill Clinton—to raise money for relief efforts. As part of their mission, the two men traveled together to the region. Bush left Houston to meet up with Clinton in Los Angeles, and
they boarded a government plane to cross the Pacific. Clinton won
Bush's heart early by deferring to the older man, insisting that the forty-
first president take the one stateroom on the plane with a bed. (Clinton
spent most of the night playing cards and talking—always talking—in an
adjoining cabin.) And Clinton "always waited so we could go off the
plane together," Bush recalled, "giving the greeters the old familiar 'wave
from the top of the stairs.'"

The two men had spent little time together before the journey, but
soon bonded. Bush was dazzled by Clinton's gifts of gregariousness and
charisma; Clinton sought Bush's fatherly approval and, given his historical imagination, enjoyed the company of the embodiment of the fading
order of Cold War statesmanship. Clinton tended to run late; Bush
tended to run precisely on time. On one occasion, when Clinton had not
yet turned up for a reception with an embassy staff, Bush went ahead
into a ballroom to say a few words, only to have the door fly open and
"bigger than life itsownself Bill Clinton strode in," Bush wrote.

"George," Clinton said, "sorry if I'm late but I had to stop by the kitchen to say hi and thank all those good people."

Bush was bemused, not angry. "He was far more easily recognized and to be frank got a warmer reception than I did, and mine was pretty darn good," Bush wrote. "Rationalization: Not to detract from Clinton's star power with the crowds, but I have been out of office for a long, long time." Clinton's volubility was striking. "He talks *all the time*," Bush recalled, emphasizing the last three words with care. "He knows every subject. You mention Nigeria, and he'll say, 'Now let me tell you about what's happening in the northern part of the country.' I don't know how much of it's bullshit and how much of it's real, factual. We went to call on different embassies—Indonesia and Thailand. We were greeted warmly by the ambassadors. There was this painting. Clinton asks who painted it, and the ambassador told him. It was one of their famous painters, Umbuga or something like that. And when we were walking out, Clinton turned to the ambassador and said, 'That is one of the most beautiful Umbugas I have ever seen.' He's just shameless. But outgoing and gregarious. I like the man." As Bush recalled the tsunami trip, "Bill did have an opinion on everything and asked questions on a lot of things. When the questions were answered he would then opine based on some experience of his own, somewhere, sometime ago." Imagining Clinton's stream of conversation, Bush continued:

> Does this purification system use reverse osmosis? This is diesel driven isn't it? I remember the hurricane damage I saw in Xland, or this reminds me of my trip to the Sudan, or I used to love to watch the kids singing in Ulan Bator. Boy, you haven't seen a wedding til you've seen one in Swaziland. These are made up examples, but the point is on every subject at every place he went on about his own experiences. I do think people were fascinated.

At one point Bush received an email about Clinton from his sister, Nancy Ellis, who had been watching the coverage of the trip. It was short and to the point: "He's still claiming more than his fair share." As Bush explained, "In grade school they had a place on our report cards 'Claims no more than his fair share of time and attention in the class room.' Bill would have gotten a bad mark there."

In Sri Lanka, the two men agreed to wrap up a dinner with the country's president by ten P.M. Everything was moving according to plan, and they were on track to be in bed on time—until Clinton started pausing to speak with every other guest. "He stopped and chatted and explained things to official after official," Bush recalled. Clinton leaned against the wall, continuing to talk. The entourage, including Bush, tried hand signals, eye signals, shoulder signals—nothing worked.

In the car at last, Clinton said, "George, you owe me big time for getting us out of there a lot earlier than we expected." Bush surrendered. "I thanked him profusely," Bush recalled. "And I said nothing more. You cannot get mad at the guy."

Bush's reluctance to broaden his post-presidential role beyond those missions his son asked him to undertake was underscored after a trip to Germany to mark the fifteenth anniversary of reunification in the summer of 2005. Among the ceremonial trappings, three eagles were brought in to take their place on the arms of Bush, Gorbachev, and Helmut Kohl. "My eagle was the biggest—I was thinking, 'Oh great symbol of American might and pride, do not claw me, do not shit upon me,'" he wrote. "It worked out OK."

Bush enjoyed being with Gorbachev—the former Soviet's ebullience reminded Bush of those heady days when the two men worked together so closely—but was wary of Gorbachev's eagerness to convene gatherings of former leaders to call for action on different issues. "Gorbachev always wants to get us 'used-to-bes' together for one good cause or another," Bush wrote his old friend Lud Ashley. "He keeps holding yellow-pad conferences trying to save the world on the environment, human rights, health care, Africa. You name the subject—then a conference will be convened. . . . Get a cause and the Gorbachev Foundation will assemble a bunch of the 'once-was' crowd. Write a paper that will then gather moss and remain unread by the current world leaders who Gorby and others hope to enlighten."

Bush's impatience with blue-ribbon panels—or what he liked to call "yellow-pad conferences"—was also rooted in his concern for his son. "I prefer Maine or A&M—besides, if I entered in to these type of things some report would inevitably show differences between the old guys and the current administration; and I do not need to cause the President grief by my signing on to some report that is not necessarily in accord with his policies," Bush told Ashley. Why complicate the forty-third president's already complicated life?

Bush thus stayed largely offstage, quietly doing a great deal of charity work; he and Mrs. Bush raised huge amounts of money for cancer research and literacy, among other causes. Then, in the aftermath of Hurricane Katrina in 2005, Bush 43 reached out once more to his father and Bill Clinton for fundraising and relief help. George W. was being attacked personally for, as his father put it, "not giving a damn." The criticism enraged the former president, who wrote Hugh Sidey a passionate letter defending his son. He was reminded, he said, of what he himself had faced after Hurricane Andrew in 1992. "Now my own son is under this kind of blistering, mean-spirited attack," Bush wrote. "People assign to him the worst possible motives. They do not recognize how complex the recovery is. They do not want to say that it was impossible to foresee the extent or even the type of the damage. . . . The critics do not know what is in 43's heart, how deeply he feels about the hurt, the anguish, the losses affecting so many people, most of them poor."

A sign of the depth of his torment over the criticism of the White House was found in a postscript to his letter. He was writing, he noted, on September 2—the anniversary of Chichi-Jima. "Now I see some of his most nasty critics trying to shoot down my beloved son—shoot him down by mean spirited attacks," Bush wrote. "I was a scared kid back then. Now I am just an angry old man hurting for my son."

In October 2006, Bush and Clinton traveled to Philadelphia to accept an award from the National Constitution Center. "If you ever have an ego problem, don't travel with President Clinton to the Maldives Islands," Bush advised the audience. "It was like traveling with a rock star. 'Get out of the way, will ya, Clinton's coming!'" Bush acknowledged that, yes, "there may have been one or two lapses in etiquette on the 1992 campaign trail. For example I really did not think that our dog Millie knew more about foreign policy than the governor of Arkansas. But hey, we were in the heat of the battle—the elbows get sharp, you know!" Competition, Bush added, was essential to democracy. "It doesn't matter if it is Democrat versus Republican, liberal or conservative, or Coke versus Pepsi. Competition is a good thing—a needed thing—indeed the very thing on which our national progress is built."

Clinton was forthright. "I love George Bush," he said. "I do. And I think that we figured out how we're supposed to do this. I developed a good relationship with the current president. I told him: I will never ask you to change what you believe, you say what you believe. I'll say what I believe. And I'll say it with respect, whatever you want me to do to help our country in good conscience, I'll do it."

The rapprochement between the Bushes and Bill Clinton did not extend to Hillary. "I don't feel close to Hillary at all," Bush said, "but I do to Bill, and I can't read their relationship even today."

"We like her, but we don't see her," Barbara said. Unlike former president Clinton, Senator (and then Secretary of State) Clinton did not come to call at Kennebunkport. Barbara thought of the Clintons when she read Doris Kearns Goodwin's biography of Eleanor and Franklin Roosevelt, *No Ordinary Time.* "The relationship between Franklin and Eleanor sounds rather like the relationship between Bill and Hillary," Barbara wrote in her diary. "Respect for each other, but separate lives. Who knows."

As time passed and it became clear that Hillary Clinton would run for president in 2008—by making a case against the years of George W. Bush—the elder Bush wrote to his immediate successor. "The politics between now and two years from now might put pressure on our friendship," Bush told Clinton in the autumn of 2006, "but it is my view that it will survive. In any event, I have genuinely enjoyed working with you. Don't kill yourself by travel or endless rope lines."

The autumn of 2006 was fraught. The situation on the ground in Iraq had deteriorated, with continuing violence and instability. An Iraq Study Group, cochaired by Jim Baker, was seeking to offer bipartisan analysis and a possible way forward. (Members included Sandra Day O'Connor and Democrats Vernon Jordan and Leon Panetta.) The panel's report was due just after the midterm elections, which went terribly for the Republicans: President Bush referred to his party's losses as "a thumping."

Even before the votes came back, Bush 43 realized it was time for Don Rumsfeld to go, and the president consulted the elder Bush about the possibility of naming Bob Gates, the incumbent president of Texas A&M, to succeed Rumsfeld. "Do you think Gates would do it, and do you think he'd be good?" Bush 43 asked. "One, I think he'd do it," the elder Bush replied, "and second I think he'd be very good." Recalling his views at the time, Bush said: "At A&M, he had a marvelous way to get the support of his people, had a wonderful manner. Bob Gates is motivated by service. He's not trying to get a better license plate. He's down to earth, bright, really good guy." (During a two-day span over the Thanksgiving weekend in 2005, Jim Baker had gotten calls from Bush 41 and then from Bush 43 to discuss Baker's coming to Washington to replace Rumsfeld as secretary of defense. The possibility was Bush 43's idea, and he had asked his father, who liked the suggestion when he heard it, to make the initial overture to Baker. Baker believed that it was a good idea to name a new defense secretary, but at age seventy-six, he decided he had best forgo a return to the Cabinet.)

Robert Gates represented the realist tradition more commonly associated with the elder Bush, Baker, and Scowcroft. To Bush, Rumsfeld had put too much value on American unilateralism, eschewing diplomacy and consistently opposing Secretary of State Colin Powell, who had served Bush 43 from 2001 to 2005. Fairly or not, Bush thought Rumsfeld an unreflective hawk who, along with a post-9/11 Dick Cheney, had formed the core of an influential hard-right element within the administration.

Bush was relieved by the call from his son and was glad to see Rumsfeld go. "I think he served the President badly," Bush recalled of Rumsfeld after Bush 43 left the White House. "I don't like what he did, and I think it hurt the President, having his iron-ass view of everything. I've never been that close to him anyway. There's a lack of humility, a lack of seeing what the other guy thinks. He's more kick ass and take names, take numbers. I think he paid a price for that." Bush was blunt: "Rumsfeld was an arrogant fellow and self-assured, swagger." Before the end of 2006, Rumsfeld was gone.

Bush 41 had no time for the argument that the son was finishing a job in Iraq that the father should have handled in 1991. "The idea of 'doing it better than we did in '91'—I think historically that isn't going to be the case, but that's juxtaposing the father against the son, and I don't like to do that, and I don't like to talk about it," Bush 41 said. "And I don't really think it's in play here." As Bush saw it, toppling and capturing Saddam were "proud moments" in American history. For him, 1991 and 2003 were not comparable. "Different wars, different reasons," Bush recalled.

Those who thought Bush 41 was sitting around shaking his head in dismay through Bush 43's two terms were wrong. "Oh, I know that's the common wisdom," the elder Bush said, "but it's not right."

The elder Bush knew that there were "people that criticize George around martinis." If Bush heard such talk, he recalled, he would reply: "So would we be better off with Saddam Hussein in there?" Mimicking a chagrined cocktail guest, Bush went on: "'Oh no, that's not what I'm saying,' they'll say back, but that's kind of the bottom line. Saddam's gone, and with him went a lot of brutality and nastiness and awfulness."

In a series of wide-ranging interviews for this book from October 2008 through November 2010, Bush 41 said he believed that the Bush 43 White House's public tone was harsher than it should have been. Though Bush 41 was supportive of the post-9/11 war in Afghanistan and, despite private anxieties, of the 2003 invasion of Iraq, he was uncomfortable with the Bush 43 administration's cowboy image. "I do worry about some of the rhetoric that was out there—some of it his, maybe, and some of it the people around him," Bush 41 recalled. "Hot rhetoric is pretty easy to get headlines, but it doesn't necessarily solve the diplomatic problem."

What was he thinking of specifically? "You go back to the 'axis of evil' and these things, and I think that might be historically proved to be not benefiting anything," the elder Bush replied. In his 2002 State of the Union address, Bush 43 had referred to Iraq, Iran, and North Korea as an "axis of evil," arguing that the three terrorist-sponsoring nations were attempting to arm themselves with weapons of mass destruction—weapons that might one day be supplied to terrorists. The use of the phrase caused consternation in the diplomatic world. A *New York Times* piece after the State of the Union caught the moment: "Europe Seethes as the U.S. Flies Solo in World Affairs."

A key question through much of George W. Bush's presidency was whether the war on terror would widen beyond Afghanistan and Iraq—chiefly to Iran, a favorite target of "neoconservatives" who often argued for the use of American force around the world. "As long as bringing down Saddam was the goal, that didn't seem to me to be unreasonable," Bush 41 recalled. "I think the world's better off with the guy gone. But it was after that—the appearance that we're going to go in there and fight with Iran, or we're going to go in there and fight with so-and-so to get our way, I didn't like that, and I don't know that the President felt that way. But because he's President, without denouncing those around him who were putting that out, why, he gets the blame, and I think probably unfairly on that."

When talking about the substance of his son's presidency, the elder Bush tended to speak in a musing, hesitant way, at once hedging and blunt. One can hear him weighing his own views, his deference toward the presidential office, his love for his son, and his awareness that responsibility begins and ends with the man in charge. "What you really need to know, and want to, is what I thought when he did this or that," Bush said. "I just don't want to go into all that. He's my son, he did his best, and I'm for him. It's that simple an equation."

In thinking over the son's eight years in power, Bush 41 returned on several occasions to the subject of Dick Cheney, whom he believed bore a large measure of responsibility for the administration's overly hawkish image. Bush 43 was himself reluctant to intervene militarily beyond Afghanistan and Iraq, preferring a more diplomatic approach in his second term, but the Cheney wing of the administration pressed for a more vigorous reaction on issues such as Iran's developing nuclear program. Neoconservative arguments about transforming the Middle East—by force if necessary—leaked out in the press and into the political conversation and influenced even Bush 41's view of Bush 43's White House.

Cheney, Bush 41 knew, was a shrewd Washington player. As White House chief of staff at the age of thirty-four under Ford, as a member of Congress, and as secretary of defense for Bush 41, Cheney knew how to maximize his influence within the system and, as vice president, was not shy about boldly stating his own bold positions. Condi Rice, who served as national security adviser in the first term and as secretary of state in the second, believed Cheney's staff was "very much of one ultra-hawkish mind . . . determined to act as a power center of its own."

Bush 41 had no doubts about whether his son was, in George W.'s own phrase, "the Decider." The father's point was not that Cheney was the power behind the throne, but that Cheney's activist vice presidency had given the administration a harsher image than it might otherwise have had. "I think George would say that 'I was the one making these decisions. I was the one doing this,'" Bush 41 said in 2009. "But I think Cheney had a real influence, for better or for worse, depending on which period we're talking about." In Bush 41's opinion, the vice president at times appeared to have a disproportionate voice in the affairs of the son's administration—and Bush always believed in proportion. "He had his own empire there and marched to his own drummer," Bush said of his son's vice president. "It just showed me that you cannot do it that way. The President should not have that worry."

The kind of "worry" Bush 41 was talking about was on public display in 2007, when a national-security aide to Cheney speculated about the use of force against Iran. Reports of the Cheney aide's remarks prompted Mohamed ElBaradei, the head of the International Atomic Energy Agency, to warn against "new crazies" who might lead America into a war with Iran. "We fully believe that Foggy Bottom is committed to the diplomatic track," an unnamed European official told *The New York Times*—which Bush 41 read every day. "But there's some concern about the vice president's office."

In Houston or in Kennebunkport, the forty-first president would read such stories with concern and puzzlement. To Bush, the Cheney of the first decade of the new century was not the Cheney of 1989–93. Secretary of Defense Cheney had seemed reasonable and measured. Vice President Cheney appeared to be a champion for thorough-going neoconservatives who believed in projecting force to promote American security interests. An irony: The elder Bush himself had helped enable the rise of the neoconservative view of foreign policy by approving the "Team B" exercise of competitive analysis at the CIA in 1976. Many of the Cold War hawks of the 1970s and '80s became War on Terror hawks after 9/11. A further irony: Bush 41 had, in his time, cast the struggle to liberate Kuwait as one of " 'good' vs. 'evil' " and had been willing to risk impeachment to go to war against Saddam—a unilateral state of mind.

Still, to the elder Bush, the Cheney with whom he had served from 1989 to 1993 seemed a changed man. "I don't know, he just became very hard-line and very different from the Dick Cheney I knew and worked with," Bush recalled. When did Bush begin to think that this was not the same Cheney? "The reaction to [the attacks of 9/11], what to do about the Middle East," Bush recalled. "Just iron-ass. His seeming knuckling under to the real hard-charging guys who want to fight about everything, use force to get our way in the Middle East." The reference was apparently to Cheney's hard line on Iran. Describing Cheney as a kind of "Dr. Strangelove," Thomas Friedman of *The New York Times* captured the zeitgeist nicely in November 2007: "Vice President Cheney is the hawk-eating hawk, who regularly swoops down and declares that the U.S. will not permit Iran to develop a nuclear weapon. Trust me, the Iranians take his threats seriously." There was also the vice president's support for an American air strike on a North Korean–built nuclear reactor in Syria in 2007. (Bush 43 declined to take Cheney's advice. Israel attacked the reactor instead.)

What did Bush think had changed Cheney? "I don't know," Bush said. "I don't know. I don't know." One theory of his, Bush mused, was that the vice president's wife, Lynne, a conservative intellectual and historian, had influenced her husband's turn rightward. "You know, I've concluded that Lynne Cheney is a lot of the éminence grise here—iron-ass, tough as nails, driving," Bush said. "But I don't know." Bush added that the Cheneys' daughter Liz, an outspoken conservative who served in the State Department for several years in the George W. Bush administration, was also "tough" and influential with her father. The implied theory: Cheney had become ever more hawkish at least in part because of the conservative leanings of his family circle.

In Bush's view, Cheney—whom Bush called "a good man"—should have held himself in greater check as vice president. When Vice President George H. W. Bush had views, he shared them with the president exclusively. When Vice President Dick Cheney had views, he and his large staff forcefully articulated them in policy-making meetings within the White House and around the government—and, in the way of Washington, the Cheney position would become known in the press and abroad. No two men could have had more divergent views of the vice presidency, and Bush, in retirement, clearly favored his conception of the office over Cheney's. "The big mistake that was made was letting Cheney bring in kind of his own State Department," Bush said, alluding to the vice president's national security team. "I think they overdid that. But it's not Cheney's fault, it's the president's fault."

The bottom line: Bush 41 believed that Cheney and his "hard-charging" staff and allies had fueled a global impression of American inflexibility—an impression that the diplomatically inclined elder Bush thought had made the forty-third president appear less reasonable than he in fact was. Yet Bush 41 acknowledged that the president, not Cheney, was ultimately responsible not only for the administration's content but also for its tone. "The buck," Bush agreed, "stops there."

In his high-ceilinged, book-lined study in McLean, Virginia, Dick Cheney read a transcript of Bush 41's comments. A small smile came to his face as he absorbed them. "Fascinating," Cheney murmured.

"No question I was much harder-line after 9/11 than I was before, especially when we got into this whole area of terrorism, nukes, and WMD," Cheney continued. "And I find it fascinating because they clearly had very different perceptions of the role of the vice president. Ours was, I think, a relatively unique arrangement. That's what President Bush 43 wanted. He wanted me to play a significant role, and he was true to his word. And I did set up a strong organization to focus on what it was that he wanted me to focus on, which was all the national security stuff." ("I do disagree with his putting it on Lynne and Liz," he said. Mrs. Cheney and Liz Cheney declined to comment on Bush 41's remarks.)

Did the elder Bush ever signal such views during his son's years in office? "I've never heard any of this from Forty-one," Cheney replied. "He would sometimes stick his head in, and we'd talk, but he never indicated anything like this." What about Bush 41's opinion that Cheney was "very hard-line and very different" than the one he'd worked with—a view shared by Brent Scowcroft? "We were dealing with a completely different kind of a threat after 9/11," Cheney replied. "We lost three thousand people. It was worse than Pearl Harbor, here at home. And so I believed then, and still do to this day, that it was very important that we recognize that this wasn't just a terrorist act or a law-enforcement problem. It was a war, an act of war, and that we were justified in taking extraordinary measures to defend the country. We did what we believed we needed to do. W is the one who made the decisions. To the extent I was a consequential vice president is because that's what he wanted."

After reading a transcript of his father's comments about Cheney, Bush 43 replied: "He certainly never expressed that opinion to me, either during the presidency or after. I valued Dick's advice, but he was one of a number of my advisers I consulted, depending on the issue." The elder Bush, his son said, "would never say to me, 'Hey, you need to rein in Cheney. He's ruining your administration.' It would be out of character for him to do that. And in any event, I disagree with his characterization of what was going on. I made the decisions. This was my philosophy."

What about the "hot rhetoric" that his father spoke of? "It is true that my rhetoric could get pretty strong, and that may have bothered some people—obviously it did, including Dad, though he never mentioned it," Bush 43 said. He remembered that his wife, Laura, had expressed skepticism about his choice of words when he had declared that he wanted Osama Bin Laden "dead or alive" after 9/11. It may have sounded too Wild West to some ears, Bush 43 acknowledged, but one thing was clear: "They understood me in Midland," he said wryly.

As the elder Bush saw it, the "iron-ass," or uncompromising, views of Cheney and Rumsfeld had failed to serve his son well, and his son's rhetorical style had been occasionally problematic. It was hardly surprising that "Have-Half" Bush felt this way. What was more surprising was that he would say so, out loud, on the record. Yet his son's presidency was moving into the realm of history, and by the time he made the remarks Bush 41 may have felt that posterity could benefit from a reminder that diplomacy and force should be seen as complementary, not competitive. Bush 43 himself had arrived at the same position, investing time and capital in diplomacy in his second term—so much so that Cheney found himself on the losing side of foreign-policy arguments more often than he had in the first term. Though they never spoke of it, then, Bush 41 and Bush 43 may have been more in sync all along than even they knew.

On Saturday, January 10, 2009, just ten days before he left the presidency, George W. Bush commissioned the USS *George H. W. Bush,* CVN-77, the Navy's newest aircraft carrier. In an emotional ceremony on a bright winter's day in Norfolk, the forty-third president, standing near a purple-scarf-clad forty-first, paid tribute to his dad.

"Over the years, our parents have built a family bound forever by closeness, warmth, and unconditional love," George W. said. "Jeb, Neil, Marvin, and Doro and I will always feel blessed to have had the best father anyone could ever ask for. We will always be inspired by the faith, humor, patriotism, and compassion he taught us through his own example. And for as long as we live, we will carry with us Dad's other lessons: that integrity and honor are worth more than any title or treasure, and that the truest strength can come from the gentlest soul."

Turning to the business at hand, the forty-third president continued: "George H. W. Bush has the deep love of his family, the admiration of his friends, and the thanks of a grateful nation. . . . So what do you give a guy who has been blessed and has just about everything he has ever needed? Well, an aircraft carrier."

The commissioning moved Bush deeply. Doro was the ship's sponsor, and in the ensuing years he loved reading email updates about the carrier on its various missions. "The ship is so majestic, and so powerful, and so strong," Bush said of the commissioning. "The honor of it all was just overwhelming. A lot of nice things happen to you after you've been something."

The elder Bush wore that same splendid purple scarf to the Obama inauguration, and he boarded the presidential helicopter at the foot of the steps of the east front of the Capitol before Laura and George W. climbed on. It was the same route the senior Bushes had taken sixteen years before—from the Capitol to Andrews Air Force Base and home to Texas. Bush 43 seemed content and upbeat. He had finished the race and now it was time to step offstage.

Asked a month later how his son was doing, the elder Bush was happy to report that all was well. "He's fine," Bush said. "Talk to him all the time. I think he's very happy, very content. I don't think he misses anything yet—he may, down the line, but he's very reluctant to criticize Obama, to me even, and I'm glad to have him back, out of the rat race, out of the name-calling, out of the Bush bashing."

He recalled an exchange between George W. and Patrick Kennedy, a son of Ted Kennedy, who was ill. "You know, it's really hard to live up to your father," said Patrick, referring to his own dad.

"Believe me," George W. replied, "I've been living with that for a long time." Telling the story, the elder Bush added: "I thought that was very nice. George has been very generous to me in public, and in private, too. We're very close."

Bush talked to himself, sometimes, about the current state of play. When he would hear President Obama, who had control of both houses of Congress in those years, say that it was hard to get things done, Bush would mutter—inwardly—"Try this one on for size: being president with *neither* house."

He lived his final years in his usual way. In the middle of a storm on a September 2 in his retirement he was eager to take out his speedboat with some of the grandchildren. The Secret Service asked Jean Becker to stop him—it just seemed too dangerous. She made a noble effort.

"Sir, it's probably too late to go out in the boat today," Becker said.

He looked at her over a pair of reading glasses. "Here's the deal," Bush replied. "This is the day the Japanese shot me down off Chichi-Jima. I survived that. I think I can survive this."

He was tireless, too. After a long weekend of events at College Station commemorating the twenty-fifth anniversary of his inauguration as president, Bush was supposed to go home to Houston to rest. (His staff all collapsed onto sofas or beds.) Instead, the former president announced that he was going over to the closing round of the Shell Houston golf open.

After he left office, except for usual age-related issues, his health was good, though he worried about his memory from time to time. Bush continued to be treated for his thyroid condition with occasional adjusted dosages of his medicine to keep his thyroid hormone level within the normal range. Around 2006–2007, the former president began experiencing issues with his balance. "The condition progressed slowly over the years, and proved to be a Parkinson's-like disorder involving mainly his legs," said Dr. John Eckstein, one of his physicians who treated Bush from 1994 to 2009. The former president was confined to a wheelchair about 2012—and used decorative socks, always a favorite, to have the most fun with his necessarily exposed ankles.

During a 2012 hospitalization over the Christmas holidays for bronchitis—he was sick enough that nervous editors and television producers were moving into obituary mode—he was coughing so badly that he began to bleed internally. In the night at Houston's Methodist Hospital, the end seemed near. A blood clot nearly killed him, but he held on until morning, when the danger passed.

It had been the closest of calls. "Did I almost buy the farm last night?" he asked the next day, lying in his bed in a small suite at the end of a quiet hospital hallway. He spent a few hours each day in a wheelchair in the sitting room with Barbara, who needlepointed, and with Neil, who read aloud to his father, usually from an iPad. In the hospital Bush came to a resolution. "I've decided to live until ninety," he announced to friends.

No one doubted it.

Life went on. There were great-grandchildren, two of whom were named after their great-grandfather: Georgia Helena Walker Bush and Poppy Louise Hager. At ninety, Bush parachuted once more, landing, roughly, at St. Ann's near Walker's Point. One day in Houston, on learning that President Obama was coming to town, the forty-first president went out to the airport to greet the incumbent. "When the president comes to your hometown, you show up to meet him," Bush told reporters.

In the fall of 2013, the elder Bushes were invited to a same-sex wedding between two women who own a general store in Kennebunkport. After the outdoor ceremony was concluded, the couple asked the former president to sign their license as a witness, which he cheerfully did. Images from the wedding went viral, and Jean Becker recalled that Bush 41 "found his popularity on gay websites intriguing."

As a presidential candidate in 1988, Bush had once mused about how the country was not ready for "codified" gay marriages, and the issue had grown in significance through the Clinton, Bush 43, and Obama years.

In a September 2015 note to the author in response to a question about whether he had changed his mind on same-sex marriages, the forty-first president wrote: "Personally, I still believe in traditional marriage. But people should be able to do what they want to do, without discrimination. People have a right to be happy. I guess you could say I have mellowed."

I Don't Want to Miss Anything

★

> As good a measure of a president as I know is somebody who
> ultimately puts the country first, and it strikes me that through-
> out his life he did that, both before he was president and while
> he was president, and ever since.
>
> —BARACK OBAMA on George H. W. Bush

ON A RELAXED AFTERNOON three fourths of the way through his son's tumultuous presidency, sitting on the family's stone porch overlooking the Atlantic, sipping coffee and occasionally lifting a pair of binoculars to look out across the blue water, George H. W. Bush was talking reluctantly but politely about his place in history.

As he grew into old age, Bush did not see himself as a Great Man, or even as an especially interesting one. He saw himself, rather, as a forgotten figure, a one-term president overshadowed by the myth of his predecessor and by the drama of his sons' political lives. At Walker's Point, the coffee cooling, Bush let his mask fall, if only for a moment. "I feel like an asterisk," he said, and lifted the binoculars again, turning to look outward, across the sea.

And so this combat hero, war president, and emblem of the rise and reign of the most powerful nation in history lived with a kind of emptiness, a curious insecurity about the legacy of his quest for power and his decades of service. History was being kinder, he knew, but history is a fickle thing. "I am lost between the glory of Reagan—monuments everywhere, trumpets, the great hero—and the trials and tribulations of my sons," Bush said one day in Houston, riding in the backseat of an SUV en route to an Italian restaurant in a strip mall near his office. On another occasion, he worried aloud about what biographers might make of him on close inspection. "What if they just find an empty deck of cards?"

He needn't have fretted. (Though that would have been unnatural.) "How great is this country," Jeb Bush once said, "that it could elect a man as fine as our dad to be its president?" The remark so struck Laura Bush that she included the moment in the White House memoir she wrote after she and George W. left Washington in 2009.

The forty-first president represented the twilight of a tradition of public service in America—a tradition embodied by FDR, by Eisenhower, and by George H. W. Bush. "My father was the last president of a great generation," George W. Bush said in accepting the Republican presidential nomination in 2000, eight years after his father's defeat. "A generation of Americans who stormed beaches, liberated concentration camps, and delivered us from evil. Some never came home. Those who did put their medals in drawers, went to work, and built on a heroic scale . . . highways and universities, suburbs and factories, great cities and grand alliances—the strong foundations of an American Century."

He brought the Cold War to a peaceful conclusion, successfully managing the fall of the Berlin Wall, the reunification of Germany, and the end of the Soviet Union without provoking violence from Communist bitter-enders. In the first Gulf War, Bush established that, on his watch, America would not retreat from the world but would intervene, decisively, when the global balance of power was in jeopardy.

His life was spent in the service of his nation, and his spirit of conciliation, common sense, and love of country will stand him in strong stead through the ebbs and flows of posterity's judgment. On that score—that George H. W. Bush was a uniquely good man in a political universe where good men were hard to come by—there was bipartisan consensus a quarter century after his White House years.

A key to understanding Bush—like other politicians who rise to great heights in America—is the recognition that what is easily perceptible is not all there is to perceive. In 1967, when Murray Kempton, the midcentury American writer, came to review the presidential memoirs of Dwight Eisenhower, Kempton discerned at a distance what he admitted he had failed to detect during Eisenhower's active years in the arena. "He was the great tortoise upon whose back the world sat," Kempton wrote in *Esquire* magazine. "We laughed at him . . . and all the while we never knew the cunning beneath the shell."

The cunning beneath the shell: The words, too, apply to George Herbert Walker Bush. He spent his life presenting a face of grace and generosity to the world, and that face was real. He was gracious, and he was generous. Yet he was more than well mannered. Beneath the kindness lay a steely ambition, a drive to win, a persistent, unshakable sense of himself as a man whose capacities were commensurate with the challenges of command. He was personally deferential—and politically determined to take his place among the great men who shaped the fates and the futures of millions, even billions, of others.

His life was not a lesson in philosophical consistency, but then political lives rarely are. The lapses from heroic narrative in his life's journey were the prices he paid for a rise to the top that enabled him, on crucial occasions, to use his power in the service of a larger good once he reached the White House. His inconsistencies and his compromises—opposition to the Civil Rights Act of 1964 to please Texas conservatives; the reversal of his views on abortion rights and on Reaganomics to win his place on the 1980 ticket—can be explained by his twin familial mandates to serve and to win. Politics, he remarked, was not "a pure undertaking"—it was a practical one.

He accepted a fundamental irony of history: One plays by the conventions of politics in order to be in power when the hour calls for unconventional decisions. As a political aspirant, Bush adapted himself to the shifting realities of his own party in the 1960s, '70s, and '80s, inviting—and enduring—charges of opportunism and cynicism. Yet as president, Bush broke with anti-tax Republican orthodoxy to strike a deal that he believed was in the best interests of the country. As president, he withstood pressure from American conservatives who argued that Mikhail Gorbachev was a faux reformer secretly seeking to expand Soviet influence. As president, he resisted isolationist calls from the right, and led the Gulf War coalition to accomplish a clearly defined mission.

Raised to serve and to compete, he naturally gravitated to the political world of his father, as did two of his own sons. A Bush appeared on six of the nine national Republican tickets between 1980 and 2012—a remarkable feat—and Bushes governed two of the nation's largest states between 1994 and 2006. (George W. in Texas from 1994 to 2000; Jeb in Florida from 1998 to 2006.)

Why the Bushes? Why have they proven so politically durable? The family's capacity to reflect a changing country, from George H. W. Bush's postwar move to Texas as the nation's center of gravity moved south and west to Jeb Bush's embrace of his wife's Hispanic heritage, is one reason. Another is the value of the now-multigenerational Bush organization in a Republican Party where no one ideological faction is truly dominant.

When assessing what makes the Bush sons run, though, the answer is less about mechanics, however important those are, and more about the man who has always been at the center of their lives. George H. W. Bush was no patriarchal mastermind. He never sat his sons down to plot a dynastic future. His power was quieter and subtler, but undeniably real. All five of Bush's children adore him in much the way he adored his own parents. For George W. and for Jeb, the politically inclined of the brood, following their father's path into the arena was a way of honoring the most compelling man they had ever known. In a sense, then, the Bush saga flows from reverence and from love for a father—for George Herbert Walker Bush—whose own twentieth-century odyssey took him to the highest levels and which, in the twenty-first, in the intertwined lives of his family and of his nation, unfolds still.

The telephone in the Bushes' Houston house rang on Tuesday, November 16, 2010. President Obama was calling; was President Bush available? He was, and the incumbent president was on the line to ask if Bush 41 would come to Washington to accept the Presidential Medal of Freedom, the nation's highest civilian honor. Bush was delighted, not least because he had been struggling of late with a form of Parkinson's disease that made it difficult for him to walk—a depressing development for a man so devoted to constant motion. "I am not doing any travel these days," Bush told Obama in a handwritten note, "but I will be there for this one."

At the White House, President Obama paid warm tribute to Bush and his decades-long attention to duty. "We honor George Herbert Walker Bush for service to America that spanned nearly 70 years," Obama said in an East Room ceremony that also saluted John Lewis and Stan Musial.

> From a decorated Navy pilot who nearly gave his life in World War II to U.S. ambassador to the United Nations, from CIA director to U.S. envoy to China to the vice presidency, his life is a testament that public service is a noble calling.
>
> As President, he expanded America's promise to new immi-

grants and people with disabilities. He reduced nuclear weapons. He built a broad international coalition to expel a dictator from Kuwait. When democratic revolutions swept across Eastern Europe, it was the steady diplomatic hand of President Bush that made possible an achievement once thought impossible, ending the Cold War without firing a shot.

I would add that, like the remarkable Barbara Bush, his humility and his decency reflects the very best of the American spirit. Those of you who know him, this is a gentleman, inspiring citizens to become points of light in service to others, teaming up with a one-time political opponent to champion relief for the victims of the Asian tsunami, then Hurricane Katrina, and then, just to cap it off, well into [his] 80s, he decides to jump out of airplanes because, as he explains, "it feels good."

It would be difficult to imagine two more different men, in terms of background, than Barack Obama and George H. W. Bush, and yet the first African American president held the consummate WASP president in the highest regard.

Reflecting on the forty-first president in an interview with the author four years after the Medal of Freedom ceremony, Obama said that the Bush he had come to know after 2008 "was exactly the gentleman that I had perceived him to be, perhaps even more gracious and thoughtful than he came across publicly." Bush, Obama thought, was "one of our most underrated Presidents," and, in the middle of a late winter afternoon a quarter century after Bush left Washington, the incumbent president made the case for the Bush legacy.

"I would argue that he helped usher in the post–Cold War era in a way that gave the world its best opportunity for stability and peace and openness," Obama said in the telephone interview from the White House. "The template he laid in a peaceful and unified Europe and in what for at least twenty-five years was a constructive relationship with Russia and the former Soviet satellites, and the trajectory away from nuclear brinksmanship at a time when things were still up in the air, was an extraordinary legacy." As challenging as the world remained, "the one thing that we don't have right now is any serious prospect of a great power war anywhere in the world," Obama said. "Part of the reason for that is that I think George H. W. Bush did a really good job in managing that post–Cold War transition." At home, Obama cited the Americans with Disabilities Act—something, Obama said, "that it's hard to imagine a current Republican president initiating. . . . So although President Bush was sometimes mocked for talking about 'a thousand points of light,' the fact is, even in his policies, there was a genuine conservative compassion there that manifested itself in working with Republicans and Democrats on the Hill to get some big things done."

As the conversation wound down, Obama offered a benediction. "As good a measure of a president as I know is somebody who ultimately puts the country first," he said of Bush, "and it strikes me that throughout his life he did that, both before he was president and while he was president, and ever since."

I n the end, after he lies in state in the Capitol Rotunda, after the funeral service at Washington National Cathedral, after the hymns and the flags and the tributes and the tears, after the last flight home to Texas, George H. W. Bush will come to rest in a quiet graveyard tucked behind a grove of trees across a small stream from his presidential library in College Station.

There he and Barbara are to be buried next to Robin. It is a serene spot, but close enough to the world that a visitor can't help but hear the subtle rumble of traffic on the Texas highways and the occasional roar of a plane. Bush will be interred beneath an enormous iron seal of the Presidency of the United States, at peace but not far from the sounds of lives still moving, still striving.

Which is fitting, for he never really stopped, either. Once when he was nearing ninety, a hurricane was about to hit the Maine coast. As the storm came in, Walker's Point was being boarded up. The power was out and there were 50 mph winds. The rain had just stopped, briefly, when Jean Becker, the forty-first president's chief of staff, realized she did not know where Bush was. She went from room to room in the house—no Bush. Finally she peeked out the door and saw the former president of the United States on a scooter on the putting green, looking out at the stormy sea.

There he sat on the stony shoreline, near the cottage path where he had learned to walk and the rocks where he had played as a child. This was the place he had proposed marriage and raised his children and grandchildren and now great-grandchildren. This was the place he had received heads of state. This was the place he had contemplated war and peace. This was the place he always returned to, in hours of victory and of defeat, in good times and in bad.

He gazed off in the distance, his still-auburn hair riffling, his jacket pressed against his body, his eyes scanning the horizon. The winds were so strong that the Secret Service agents around Bush could barely stand, but there Bush sat, serenely. Becker struggled through the winds to his side. "President Bush, what are you doing, sir?"

He looked at her with a puzzled expression, as if the answer were obvious.

"I can't see anything from the house," he replied, just audible over the whooshing weather, "and I don't want to miss anything."

AUTHOR'S NOTE

★

My first and greatest thanks are due to George H. W. Bush, who granted me access to his diaries and sat (usually patiently, and always politely) for interviews from 2006 to 2015. The former president was generous, welcoming, gracious—and insisted that I call them as I saw them.

This book was written with the cooperation of the forty-first president and of his family and of many of his lieutenants, but it is an independent work. No one, including President Bush, had right of review or of approval. There was a single exception: Mrs. Bush allowed me to read her diaries, a private archive covering the Bushes' lives from 1948 forward. Her only condition was that I clear direct quotations from those papers with her. In the end, I sought Mrs. Bush's permission to draw from roughly ninety pages of transcripts. She granted blanket permission, withdrawing nothing that I had asked for the option to use. Mrs. Bush was unfailingly helpful, answering many questions over several years. At my request, toward the end of the project, both Mrs. Bush and George W. Bush (himself the author of a biography of his father) agreed to read selected manuscript pages in order to bring any errors of fact to my attention. For the same purpose I also asked James A. Baker III; Jean Becker, President Bush's chief of staff; and Chase Untermeyer, a longtime Bush associate, director of presidential personnel under Bush 41, and U.S. ambassador to Qatar under Bush 43, to read the manuscript. They generously did so, but none of these readers, of course, is in any way accountable for the resulting book. That responsibility is mine alone.

My aim in the book was to paint a biographical portrait of the forty-first president. This is neither a full life-and-times nor a history of the Bush family; it is, rather, an attempt to give readers a sense of a singular and complicated man whose life and career span so much of our history. Because many readers will have lived through the Bush 41 years (and the Bush 43 years) there will doubtless be those who will argue with the exclusion of this episode or that issue or with my choice of narrative emphasis. So be it: I view this book as a contribution to a burgeoning historical conversation about George H. W. Bush.

The historian Herbert S. Parmet was granted access to the Bush diaries for his *George Bush: The Life of a Lone Star Yankee*, published in 1997; President Bush and Brent Scowcroft used excerpts from them for *A World Transformed*, their 1998 account of the administration's foreign policy; and Jean Becker quoted them in *All the Best*, the 1999 book of Bush's letters. (*All the Best* was updated in 2013.) For the presidential diaries, I was allowed access to transcripts of the diary tapes prepared by the Office of George Bush. I endeavored mightily to ensure the accuracy of the transcribed quotes in this book by checking transcripts against audio. (I found the transcripts to be extremely faithful.) To be sure, though, as the historian Michael Beschloss, who has edited acclaimed volumes of the Lyndon Johnson tapes, has written, transcription is as much an art as a science. For diary quotations from the pre-1988 vice presidential years, I depended on transcripts from the Office of George Bush. Some tapes from 1981 to January 1987 were not available, chiefly those from November 4, 1986, to January 2, 1988. These tapes were transcribed in Bush's Houston office in real time by Betty Green, who, according to Bush's attorneys, "routinely erased the tapes once transcripts were prepared." The existence and timely production of the diaries to the special prosecutor became an issue during the Iran-contra investigation. Bush's attorneys turned over excerpts from the transcripts to the independent counsel, and the Office of George Bush provided the author the full transcripts.* The author plans to edit the Bush diaries, including the vice presidential years, for publication in future years.

---

* Griffin B. Bell to the Honorable Lawrence E. Walsh, January 15, 1993, details the story of the tapes. This letter and report were released publicly on that day. (Bell, a former attorney general under President Carter, was representing former President Bush in the matter.) See also chapter 28 of *The Final Report* of the Iran-contra special prosecutor.

ACKNOWLEDGMENTS

★

As noted earlier, I am most grateful to George H. W. Bush and to Barbara Bush, whose cooperation and patience made this project possible. Jean Becker, the former president's chief of staff, is a close third. Jean answered question after question after question, connected me with the far-flung Bush universe, and, like her chieftain, she expected me to reach my own conclusions about what I discovered. In his acknowledgment to her in his book *All the Best,* a collection of his letters and other writings that she compiled, President Bush wrote that he could not "properly express" his gratitude to Jean. Neither can I.

In the Office of George Bush, I am also indebted to Nancy Lisenby, Linda Poepsel, Mary Sage, Melinda Lamoreaux, Laura Pears, Catherine Branch, Evan Sisley, and George Dvorsky.

The leadership and staff of the George Bush Presidential Library and Museum in College Station, Texas, was generous, intelligent, and attentive. A biographer can ask for no more than that. Director Warren Finch and Deputy Director Dr. Robert Holzweiss welcomed me years ago. In a favorite phrase of President Bush's, they were "steady as she goes." I am especially indebted to Bob Holzweiss for his counsel and for a reading of the manuscript. Thanks as well to supervisory archivist Deborah Wheeler and textual archivists Douglas Campbell, Zachary Roberts, Chris Pembelton, John Blair, Buffie Hollis, Simon Staats, and Elizabeth Staats; to archives technicians Dr. McKenzie Morse, Rachel Medders, and Kathryn Burwitz; to audio-video archivist Mary Finch (who is also the keeper of the vast Bush Scrapbooks); and to audio-video archives technician Rebecca Passmore.

I am grateful to the forty-third president, George W. Bush, who was willing to spend as much time as I asked discussing his father's life. Jeb Bush, Marvin Bush, Neil Bush, and Doro Bush Koch were all exceptionally gracious and helpful, as were Nancy Bush Ellis, Jonathan Bush, and Bucky Bush. Bush's first cousin G. H. "Bert" Walker III and his wife, Carol, were generous hosts in St. Louis.

James A. Baker III, Henry Kissinger, Dan Quayle, Dick Cheney, Brent Scowcroft, Colin Powell, John Sununu, Boyden Gray, and Richard

Haass answered my questions with grace, as did Roger Porter, Robert Kimmitt, Andrew Card, Fred McClure, Patricia Presock, Rich Bond, Roger Ailes, Mary Matalin, Tim McBride, and Vic Gold, among many others. (A full listing of interviews for the book can be found in the bibliography.) Secretary Baker opened his Princeton papers to me without restriction, shared many recollections, and offered analytic guidance. In Baker's Houston office, John Williams went out of his way to be generous. Jonathan Darman kindly allowed me access to the papers of his late father, Richard G. Darman. Nicholas Brady, the former secretary of the Treasury, shared a memoir he wrote for his family. Drs. Burton Lee and Lawrence C. Mohr helped me understand President Bush's health issues in the White House; Dr. John Eckstein was helpful with the post-presidential years. I was privileged to speak with figures ranging from James Leonard, who ran Bush's 1964 Texas Senate race, to Michael Dukakis, who candidly discussed the 1988 campaign, to Bill Clinton, who ended the forty-first president's elective career.

At Princeton University, Daniel Linke, university archivist and curator of public policy papers, Seeley G. Mudd Manuscript Library, was very helpful with the James A. Baker III Papers. At the Library of Congress Manuscript Division, I am, as always, grateful to Jeff Flannery, head of Reference and Reader Services.

Thanks as well to Barbara Cline, archivist, the Lyndon B. Johnson Presidential Library, Austin, Texas; Valois Armstrong, archivist, and Sydney Soderberg, researcher, the Dwight D. Eisenhower Presidential Library, Abilene, Kansas; Elizabeth Druga, archivist, Gerald R. Ford Presidential Library, Ann Arbor, Michigan; Jennifer Mandel, archivist, Ronald Reagan Presidential Library, Simi Valley, California; and Debbie Hamm of the Abraham Lincoln Library, Springfield, Illinois. Archivists, librarians, and staff at Phillips Academy, Andover, Massachusetts, and at Yale University were also generous.

Kathy Evans kindly shared Walker family research with me and checked me for inaccuracies; she is the author of *A Useful Life,* a book on George Herbert Walker III and the Walker family legacy slated for private publication in 2016. James E. Steen, an assistant to Dick Cheney in the Pentagon, provided me excerpts from his extensive "Desert Storm Chronology." I am also grateful to Pat Schley of the Judge David Davis House; to Paul St. Hilaire of the George W. Bush Childhood Home; and to Valerie Simpson, Jane Knowles, Nova Seals, and Laura Hooper at the library and archives at St. George's School, Middletown, Rhode Island.

I benefited enormously from the work of many other writers and historians. Walt Harrington's "Born to Run," a 1986 profile in *The Washington Post Magazine,* is indispensable, as is Richard Ben Cramer's classic *What It Takes,* a book I devoured when it was first published and which has shaped my view of George H. W. Bush (and of Bob Dole and Joe Biden) ever since. Thorough and fair-minded, Herbert S. Parmet's 1997 *Lone Star Yankee* is a foundational work for all subsequent Bush biographers. My friend Jacob Weisberg's *The Bush Tragedy* is illuminating and challenging; I am in his debt. For family history, I learned much from Peter Schweizer and Rochelle Schweizer's *The Bushes: Portrait of a Dynasty;* Fitzhugh Green's *George Bush: An Intimate Portrait;* and Nicholas King's *George Bush.* Tom Wicker's *George Herbert Walker Bush,* published in 2004, is a predictably fine work from a great journalist whom we all miss. As Wicker noted in his book, he brought his years of reporting on Bush to bear on the task of a biography, and it shows—for the good.

Timothy Naftali's 2007 biography of Bush, written for the Times Books American Presidents Series founded by Arthur Schlesinger, Jr., and now edited by Sean Wilentz, is an essential work. Deeply researched and analytically insightful, Naftali's book informed my thinking about the subject in important ways. Wilentz's own *Age of Reagan* and James T. Patterson's *Restless Giant* provided invaluable general historical context for much of the period I covered. Barry Werth's *31 Days,* about the Nixon-Ford transition, is illuminating, and I am grateful to him for counsel. For the politics of 1988 (and beyond), John Brady's biography of Lee Atwater, *Bad Boy,* is an important work; Brady also took time to help me. The Reagan assassination attempt is wonderfully rendered in Del Quentin Wilber's *Rawhide Down,* and I am grateful to him for reviewing my account of that terrible day. Michael Duffy and Dan Goodgame's *Marching in Place* offers an essential view of the White House from 1989 to 1993. Maureen Dowd's *Bushworld* is a terrific collection, and Dowd was a fun interlocutor on the project.

The campaigns of 1988 and 1992 are brilliantly covered in the work of Jack Germond and Jules Witcover (*Whose Broad Stripes and Bright Stars?* and *Mad as Hell*). And one can do no better in the search to understand those two campaigns than to read the work of the *Newsweek* special election project teams in two books coauthored by Peter Goldman: the first, with Tom Mathews, is *The Quest for the Presidency, 1988,* the second, with Thomas M. DeFrank, Mark Miller, Andrew Murr, and Tom Mathews, is *Quest for the Presidency, 1992.* I am also grateful to Don Graham, Lally Weymouth, Rick Smith, the late Maynard Parker, Mark Whitaker, Ann McDaniel, Fareed Zakaria, Michael Elliott, and my many former colleagues at the magazine, where I worked from 1995 to 2010, for engaging years of adventure in the study of politics in general and of the Bushes in particular. At *Time,* I have been fortunate to work for John Huey, Richard Stengel, Nancy Gibbs, and Michael Duffy.

This book would not have been possible without the hard work of the journalists who covered the different eras of Bush's life. Biographers stand on the shoulders of reporters and columnists. I found the Texas newspapers of the day invaluable, and of course owe much to *The New York Times, The Washington Post, Newsweek, Time, U.S. News & World Report,* the *Los Angeles Times,* the *Chicago Tribune, The Wall Street Journal,* and the many other publications cited in the source notes.

For his grace in taking the time to read the manuscript early on, I am grateful to Michael Duffy, who covered the Bush 41 White House for *Time* and is, with Nancy Gibbs, the author of several distinguished volumes of history. Mike has an intuitive feel for the nuances and rhythms of politics and generously gave me the benefit of his counsel.

I am indebted, too, to the wonderful work of Howard Fineman, who read my manuscript and made observations that improved it greatly. A gifted writer and an excellent reporter, Howard has been my friend for two decades and has covered the Bushes for three, dating back to George H. W. Bush's first moves in 1985 toward a presidential run in 1988.

Thomas M. DeFrank gave me important guidance as well. Tom met George H. W. Bush in Beijing on the day before Thanksgiving, 1974, and has covered him ever since, first for *Newsweek* and then for the New York *Daily News* and now for *National Journal.* Tom's comments on the manuscript were incisive and useful.

David Hoffman's *Washington Post* coverage was important to this work, and David offered me generous counsel. Bob Woodward was generous with his time, and his *The Commanders, Shadow,* and his volumes on the George W. Bush years informed my thinking on sundry subjects. Craig Shirley was a generous reader: His history of the 1980 campaign, *Rendezvous with Destiny,* is indispensable.

My longtime friend and colleague Ann McDaniel, who covered the Bush beat for *Newsweek,* also gave generously of her time and insights. She is stalwart in all things, be they human or historical.

I am grateful as well to a formidable company of amazing writers, historians, and readers: David McCullough, Doris Kearns Goodwin, Walter Isaacson, Tom Brokaw, Julia Reed, Louisa Thomas, Christopher Buckley, Peter Schweizer, John Brady, Tim Naftali, Herbert Wentz, and John Cooper.

James Baker's diplomatic memoir, *The Politics of Diplomacy,* coauthored by Tom DeFrank, is, along with Bush and Scowcroft's *A World Transformed,* a wonderful record of four extraordinary years. Baker's political memoir, coauthored with Steve Fiffer, *Work Hard, Study . . . and Keep Out of Politics!,* is a spirited account of Baker's amazing political life—a subject that Peter Baker and Susan Glasser will examine in a forthcoming biography of the man who still calls Bush "Jefe." John Sununu generously shared an advance copy of his 2015 White House memoir, *The Quiet Man: The Indispensable Presidency of George H. W. Bush,* an account of the substantive successes of the administration. Sununu was always available to me to answer questions, and I am grateful to him. I learned much from Dick Cheney's *In My Time,* Donald Rumsfeld's *Known and Unknown,* Robert M. Gates's two books, *From the Shadows* and *Duty,* and from Colin Powell's *My American Journey.*

Professor Jeffrey A. Engel, the director of the Center for Presidential History at SMU, was welcoming and kind; I owe him greatly for his willingness to answer questions, assess a hypothesis or two (or three), and read and comment on the manuscript. Jeff's articles and edited volumes are invaluable, and he is at work on what will no doubt be a brilliant history of George H. W. Bush's diplomacy. Thanks as well to Brian Domitrovic of Sam Houston State University, who was helpful on economic history, and to James A. Stimson of the University of North Carolina for his work on the "Policy Mood Index."

I have been fortunate in my friends at Vanderbilt University. Chancellor Nicholas Zeppos, John Beasley, and John Geer have welcomed me into their world. The chancellor took valuable time to consult on this project. John Geer contributed his wonderful scholarship, helped in many ways, and then offered a valuable critique of the manuscript. To him and to his formidable wife, Beth, I am hugely grateful. Thanks, too, to Professors Larry Bartels, Joshua Clinton, and Bruce Oppenheimer.

At the University of the South, I am indebted to Vice Chancellor and President John M. McCardell, Jr., Provost John Swallow, Deans John Gatta and Terry Papillon, Professor Woody Register, and Vice Chancellor Emeritus Samuel R. Williamson, Jr.

For kindnesses large and small, my thanks to Beth and Charles Peters, Jonathan Alter, Joe Klein, Jan Baran, Lou Cannon, Peter Hannaford, Lawrence Noble, Wick Sollers, Trevor Potter, Nicolle Wallace, Dan Bartlett, Sofia and Herbert Wentz, Claire and John Reishman, Leslie and Dale Richardson, Chris Matthews, Jamie Gangel, Dan Silva, George Hackett, Terri Lacy, Edwin Williamson, Liz Cheney, David Hume Kennerly, Rob Pearigen, Jim McGrath, Michael Meece, Logan Dryden, Freddy Ford, Valerie Jarrett, Jennifer Friedman, Kara Ahern, Sally Quinn, Daniel Klaidman, Sam Register, Tammy Haddad, Betsy Fischer and Jonathan Martin, Lisa and Richard Plepler, Christina and Willie Geist, Gardiner and Nicholas Lapham, Anna Quindlen, Don King, the late Don Rhodes, Carol D'Ambrosia, Mike Allen, Mike Barnicle, Perri Peltz and Eric Ruttenberg, Jodi and Mark Banks, Betsy and Ridley Wills, Laura and John Cooper, Corinne and Brock Kidd, Bill Frist, Dorothy Barry, Remley Johnson, Mary Pat Decker, Harold Ford, Jr., Rob Crawford, Debbie Dingell, Elizabeth and Jeffrey Leeds, Daphne and Rawls Butler, Laura and John Chadwick, Julie and Tommy Frist, Elizabeth and Bob Dennis, the late John Seigenthaler, Tom Ingram, Mark Updegrove, John F. Harris, Charlie Rose, Yvette Vega, Susan Glasser, Katty Kay, Darren Walker, Will Byrd, Louise Kushner, Kathy Murphy, Joe Scarborough, Mika Brzezinski, Alex Korson, Kristin Koch, Ann Ungar, Joseph Jones, Bret Begun, Harlan Crowe, Leslie Bowman, Ann Patchett, Andy Brennan, Andrea Mitchell, George Stephanopoulos, Chuck Todd, Jonathan Karp, Jonathan Dwyer, Lynn Hughes, Peggy Cifrino, Bill Hagerty, Mary and John Bettis, Karl VanDevender, Hannah and John Lavey, Melissa and Jay Wellons, Kathryn and Gray Sasser, Jennifer and Billy Frist, Mary and Lee Barfield, Jack May, Natasha Duncan, Teresa Smith, Christine Mejia, Nora Frances and Vaughan McRae, Selby McRae, Mary Mack Jones, Sherry and Rick Smythe, May Smythe, Leskia Menjivar, and Barbara DiVittorio. And Jack Bales worked his usual bibliographic magic.

Thaddeus Romansky was instrumental in work undertaken at the Bush Library in College Station. With a historian's eye and a good man's patience, Thaddeus carved a path for me through the wilderness of the library's collections. My old friend Mike Hill was there for me through it all; I can't imagine writing a book without his skill, his grace, and his friendship.

Samuel Adkisson proved himself truly invaluable by undertaking several targeted research projects and then devoting himself to a scrupulous fact-check of the manuscript and the source notes—an enormous task that he performed with preternatural skill, great intelligence, and a matchless eye for detail. For other research and fact-checking assistance, I am grateful to Daniel Constantine, Riley Griffin, Kolby Yarnell, and Meade Wills.

At Random House, I continue to be dazzled by Gina Centrello, who makes all things possible. My editor, Kate Medina, is the best in the world at what she does, and as always I am indebted to Susan Kamil and Tom Perry. Porscha Burke runs my life—a thankless task if there ever were one. Will Murphy and Andy Ward took valuable time out of their hectic lives to help me, and I am in their debt. I am grateful to the Random House publishing team, one without peer: Sanyu Dillon, Leigh Marchant, Paolo Pepe, Joseph Perez, Simon Sullivan, Theresa Zoro, the still-erratic-but-ever-charming Sally Marvin, Barbara Fillon, Andrea DeWerd, Anna Pitoniak, Bill Takes, Carol Poticny, and Derrill Hagood. Benjamin Dreyer and Dennis Ambrose once again proved themselves wizards, and I can never repay them their many courtesies. Amanda Urban is the best of agents and of counselors.

Michael Beschloss continues to be the best of friends and the most reassuring of advisers. His grasp of historical detail, his excellent judgment, his infinite patience, and above all his friendship are among the great gifts in my life. I can't imagine writing a book—or doing much of anything else—without the counsel and the company of Oscie and Evan Thomas, who are terrific editors and even better friends. A master biographer, Evan has taught me more than I can say.

My family endures much so that I can spend time exploring distant days, but Keith, Mary, Maggie, and Sam are the true center of everything—past, present, and future. President Bush always liked to talk about "heartbeat." They're mine.

Homes of George H. W. Bush

1 Kennebunkport, ME (continuous)

2 Milton, MA (1924–1925)

3 Greenwich, CT (1925–1937)

4 Andover, MA (1937–1942)

5 Corpus Christi, TX (1942–1943)

6 Norfolk, VA (1943)

7 Grosse Ile, MI (1945)

8 Trenton, MI (1945)

9 New Haven, CT (1945–1948)

10 Odessa, TX (1948–1949)

11 Whittier, CA (1949)

12 Ventura, CA (1949)

13 Bakersfield, CA (1949)

14 Huntington Park, CA (1949)

15 Compton, CA (1949–1950)

16 Midland, TX (1950–1959)

17 Houston, TX
    (1959–1967, 1977–1980, 1993–present)

18 Washington, D.C. (1967–1977, 1980–1993)

19 New York, NY (1971–1973)

20 Beijing, China (1974–1975)

21 College Station, TX (1997–present)

NOTES

★

Abbreviations Used

ATB: George H. W. Bush, *All the Best, George Bush: My Life in Letters and Other Writings*

AWT: George Bush, with Brent Scowcroft, *A World Transformed*

BB: Barbara Bush, *Barbara Bush: A Memoir*

BPB: Barbara Pierce Bush

BSC: Brent Scowcroft Collection, GHWB Presidential Records, Office of the President, GBPL

DF: Daily Files, GHWB Presidential Records, Office of the President, GBPL

DMN: *The Dallas Morning News*

FITZ: FitzGerald Bemiss Collection, Donated Materials, GBPL

GBPL: George Bush Presidential Library and Museum, College Station, Texas

GHWB: George Herbert Walker Bush

GWB: George Walker Bush

JB: Jean Becker, "All the Best, George Bush" File, Post-Presidential Materials, GBPL

LAT: *Los Angeles Times*

LF: George Bush and Victor Gold, *Looking Forward*

LSY: Herbert S. Parmet, *George Bush: The Life of a Lone Star Yankee*

Naftali, GHWB: Timothy Naftali, *George H. W. Bush*

NSC: National Security Council, GHWB Presidential Records, Office of the President, GBPL

NYT: *The New York Times*

PSB, COHC: The Reminiscences of Prescott S. Bush (1966–67), in the Columbia Oral History Collection

VIC: Vic Gold Collection, Personal Papers, GBPL

Wicker, GHWB: Tom Wicker, *George Herbert Walker Bush*

WP: *The Washington Post*

ZAP: Zapata Oil File, Personal Papers, GBPL

EPIGRAPHS

ix DESTINY IS NOT Bryan, William Jennings, and Mary Baird Bryan, *Speeches of William Jennings Bryan, Revised and Arranged by Himself* (New York: Funk and Wagnall's Co., 1909), 11.

ix MOODS COME AND GO *Public Papers of the Presidents of the United States: George Bush, 1992–1993*, bk 1 (Washington, D.C.: U.S. GPO, 1993), 163.

PROLOGUE

xv IT WAS LATE   GHWB diary, November 4, 1992. He had tried to sleep but could not. "I went into bed with Bar and tears kept coming, and here I am; she is asleep, but I can't sleep," he dictated at 12:15 A.M. (Ibid.)

xv SUITE 271   Ibid. The suite number was confirmed by author interviews with David Jones, White House lead advance on the trip, and Tim McBride, Bush's longtime personal aide. See also "Suite 271, Bush's Home Away from Home," *Sun Journal,* Lewiston, ME, January 1, 1990.

xv WOOD-PANELED LIVING ROOM   For images of the suite on election night, see David Valdez, comp., *George Herbert Walker Bush: A Photographic Profile* (College Station, Tex., 1997), 136–37.

xv WEARY BUT RESTLESS   GHWB diary, November 4, 1992. "I want to sleep," he dictated. "I lie down, but I can't sleep." (Ibid.)

xv ON A SMALL SOFA   GHWB diary, November 4, 1992.

xv BABY BOOMER DEMOCRATIC GOVERNOR   Naftali, *GHWB,* 142.

xv "I ACHE AND I NOW MUST THINK"   GHWB diary, November 4, 1992.

xv HE KEPT HIS VOICE LOW   Ibid. The level of his voice is evident from the audio version of the diary.

xv ASLEEP BACK IN THE BEDROOM   Ibid.

xv "I THINK OF OUR COUNTRY"   Ibid.

xvi "HURT, HURT, HURT"   Ibid.

xvi "I DON'T LIKE TO SEE"   Ibid.

xvi CONSIDERED A "DRAFT DODGER"   Ibid., November 5, 1992.

xvi WHO HAD MANAGED TO STAY OUT OF THE ARMED FORCES   Bill Clinton, *My Life* (New York, 2004), 154–61. See also Dan Balz, "Clinton and the Draft: Anatomy of a Controversy," *WP,* September 13, 1992.

xvi HAD PARTICIPATED IN   GHWB diary, November 4, 1992. See also Gerald F. Seib, "Bush Criticizes Clinton's Role Over Vietnam," *Wall Street Journal,* October 8, 1992; Wicker, *GHWB,* 199–200, 204–5.

xvi "I GUESS IT'S LOSING"   GHWB diary, November 4, 1992.

xvi "I LIKE HIM"   Ibid.

xvi "I STILL FEEL"   Ibid., November 6, 1992.

xvii "THE PASSION AND ACTION"   Oliver Wendell Holmes, Jr., "In Our Youth Our Hearts Were Touched with Fire," Memorial Day Address, May 30, 1884, Keene, New Hampshire, http://people.virginia.edu/~mmd5f/memorial.htm.

xvii "THE BOYS"   GHWB diary, November 4, 1992.

xvii "BE STRONG"   Ibid.

xvii RETIRED FOR THE NIGHT   Ibid.

xvii "IT'LL CHANGE"   Ibid., November 8, 1992.

xvii THE FARTHER THE COUNTRY MOVED   See, for instance, Jonathan Rauch, "Father Superior: Our Greatest Modern President," *The New Republic,* May 22, 2000; Peter Baker, "Bush 41 Reunion Looks to Burnish His Legacy," *NYT,* April 3, 2014. Jeffrey M. Jones, "History Usually Kinder to Ex-Presidents," Gallup, April 25, 2013, is illuminating. (www.gallup.com/poll/162044/history-usually-kinder-presidents.aspx.)

xvii "HARD TO BELIEVE"   Author interview with GHWB.

xvii ONE OF THE GREAT AMERICAN LIVES   For my portrait of Bush in the following pages, I am particularly indebted to his own books: *All the Best,* the collection of letters; *A World Transformed,* with Brent Scowcroft, on the Bush administration's foreign policy;

and the 1987 autobiography he wrote with Victor Gold, *Looking Forward*. Mrs. Bush's two volumes of memoirs—*Barbara Bush: A Memoir* and *Reflections: Life After the White House*—were also invaluable. I am not the first and will certainly not be the last to try to capture the man and what he meant. I learned much from GWB, *41: A Portrait of My Father* (New York, 2014); Herbert S. Parmet's *George Bush: The Life of a Lone Star Yankee* (New York, 1997); Timothy Naftali, *George H. W. Bush* (New York, 2007); Tom Wicker, *George Herbert Walker Bush* (New York, 2004); Jacob Weisberg's *The Bush Tragedy* (New York, 2008); Jeffrey A. Engel's two edited volumes, *The Fall of the Berlin Wall: The Revolutionary Legacy of 1989* (New York, 2009) and *Into the Desert: Reflections on the Gulf War* (New York, 2013); Peter Schweizer and Rochelle Schweizer, *The Bushes: Portrait of a Dynasty* (New York, 2004); Michael Duffy and Dan Goodgame, *Marching in Place: The Status Quo Presidency of George Bush* (New York, 1992); Fitzhugh Green, *George Bush: An Intimate Portrait* (New York, 1989); Nicholas King, *George Bush: A Biography* (New York, 1980); Mickey Herskowitz, *Duty, Honor, Country* (Nashville, 2003). For more skeptical views of Bush and his family, see Kitty Kelley, *The Family: The Real Story of the Bush Dynasty* (New York, 2004); Russ Baker, *Family of Secrets: The Bush Dynasty, the Powerful Forces That Put It in the White House, and What Their Influence Means for America* (New York, 2009); Kevin Phillips, *American Dynasty: Aristocracy, Fortune, and the Politics of Deceit in the House of Bush* (New York, 2004).

I also learned much from the scholarly literature that is cited below. I am particularly indebted to the following volumes: Greene, *The Presidency of George Bush*; Christopher Maynard, *Out of the Shadow: George H. W. Bush and the End of the Cold War* (College Station, Tex., 2008); *The China Diary of George H. W. Bush: The Making of a Global President*, ed. Jeffrey A. Engel (Princeton, N.J., 2008); Michael Nelson and Barbara A. Perry, eds. *41: Inside the Presidency of George H. W. Bush* (Ithaca, N.Y., 2014); Richard Himelfarb and Rosanna Perotti, eds., *Principle Over Politics? The Domestic Policy of the George H. W. Bush Presidency* (Westport, Conn., 2004).

Memoirs of key players in the Bush administration were invaluable: John H. Sununu, *The Quiet Man: The Indispensable Presidency of George H. W. Bush* (New York, 2015); James A. Baker III with Thomas M. DeFrank, *The Politics of Diplomacy: Revolution, War, and Peace, 1989–1992* (New York, 1995); James A. Baker III with Steve Fiffer, *Work Hard, Study—and Keep Out of Politics! Adventures and Lessons from an Unexpected Public Life* (New York, 2006); Colin L. Powell with Joseph E. Persico, *My American Journey*; Dick Cheney with Liz Cheney, *In My Time: A Personal and Political Memoir* (New York, 2011); Richard N. Haass, *War of Necessity, War of Choice: A Memoir of Two Iraq Wars* (New York, 2009); Marlin Fitzwater, *Call the Briefing! Bush and Reagan, Sam and Helen: A Decade with Presidents and the Press* (New York, 1995); Robert M. Gates, *From the Shadows: The Ultimate Insider's Story of Five Presidents and How They Won the Cold War* (New York, 1996); Richard Darman, *Who's In Control? Polar Politics and the Sensible Center* (New York, 1996).

xviii "WAY OUT THERE"   Author interview with GHWB.

xviii "THE SCIENCE OF HUMAN RELATIONSHIPS"   Undelivered address of Franklin D. Roosevelt prepared for Jefferson Day, April 13, 1945, *Public Papers of the Presidents of the United States: Franklin D. Roosevelt, 1944–45* (New York, 1950), 615.

xix IN THE WARM DUSK OF A TEXAS AUTUMN   Author interview with GHWB.

xix "MY MOTIVATION'S ALWAYS BEEN *GOAL*"   Ibid.

xix HE FELL SILENT   Ibid.

xix "WHATEVER YOU'RE IN"   Ibid.

xix OFFERED JOBS AT BROWN BROTHERS HARRIMAN   Ibid.

xix "IT JUST WASN'T"   Ibid.

xix "Wouldn't have had"   Ibid.

xx Dorothy Walker Bush's admonitions   Author interviews with GHWB, Nancy Bush Ellis, and Jonathan Bush.

xx "Nobody likes a braggadocio"   Author interview with GHWB.

xxi "the star of the family"   Author interview with Nancy Bush Ellis.

xxi "He was meant to be saved"   Ibid.

xxi "This is my son George"   Author interview with Michael Beschloss, who was told the story by a son of the ambassador. On the eve of the 1989 presidential inauguration, Bush's brother Jonathan got a call in his Washington hotel room from a childhood friend. "Well, you were right," the friend said.

"What do you mean?" Jon Bush asked.

"Fifty years ago you told me your brother was going to be president, and tomorrow he is." (Author interview with Jonathan Bush.)

In Naftali, *GHWB,* Naftali speculated that GHWB's battle against a staph infection in his Andover years may have played into this sense of himself as well. "Surviving this ordeal, which required a lengthy stay in the hospital, may have given him a sense of mission, if not destiny." (Naftali, *GHWB,* 6.) " 'There has to be a certain ego factor to drive a person to run for the Presidency,' [Bush] told a reporter in 1979. 'I've been driven to do a lot of things in life. I was driven to be a success in business, to excel in college, to be the youngest fighter pilot. I'm confident that I'm better than those guys, but so far I haven't been able to prove it.' " (Ibid., 36.)

xxi he opposed the Civil Rights Act   *ATB,* 88.

xxi only to vote for open housing   Ibid., 107–11.

xxi "Read my lips"   "Transcript of Bush Speech Accepting Presidential Nomination," *NYT,* August 19, 1988.

xxi only to break that promise   *ATB,* 481–83.

xxii a hard-hitting presidential campaign   See, for instance, *LSY,* 334–56.

xxii a "kinder and gentler"   "Transcript of Bush Speech Accepting Presidential Nomination," *NYT,* August 19, 1988.

xxii "Tell the truth"   *ATB,* 356.

xxii "One of the criticisms"   Author interview with GHWB. Asked when he decided to seek the White House, he said there had been no single epiphany. "There wasn't a defining moment," Bush recalled. "I looked around and I said, 'Why not me?' I'd had a breadth of experience and I was driven, and I wanted to do it, and I felt I could be a good president. It was more personal. It wasn't any great demand from across the world, 'This is the guy to come in and save the nation'—there wasn't any of that. . . . There wasn't a moment where I said, 'Why not me, Lord?' " So there was no burning bush moment, no hour when the call to the highest office became clear? "No burning bush—burning desire, but no burning bush," he said. "I had no, 'Once I get there, I can solve the problem of this or that.' I just felt that I could do something about the U.S. standing in the world, and help people, and broad stuff like that. But not, 'If I get in there, I'll go pass a flat tax or I'll do this or that.' " (Ibid.)

xxiii Eisenhower said that his goal   "American President: A Reference Resource on President Dwight D. Eisenhower," Miller Center, University of Virginia, http://millercenter.org/president/eisenhower/essays/biography/4.

xxiii visiting a children's leukemia ward   GHWB diary, September 29, 1987.

xxiii "My eyes flooded"   Ibid.

xxiv dictated into a handheld   Author interview with GHWB.

xxiv sometimes carrying the device   Author interview with Tim McBride.

xxiv "THE LONELINESS OF THE JOB"   Author interview with GHWB.
xxiv "A FASCINATING TIME OF CHANGE IN THE WORLD ITSELF"   GHWB diary, May 26, 1989.

Part I: A Vanished Universe, Beginnings to 1942

1 IT WAS A BEAUTIFUL WORLD   Author interview with Nancy Bush Ellis.
1 THE END DEPENDS UPON THE BEGINNING   *Academy Hill: The Andover Campus, 1778 to Present* (Andover, Mass.: Addison Gallery of American Art, Phillips Academy, 2000), vii. See also Phillips Exeter Academy Archives website, www.andover.edu.

ONE: *The Land of the Self-Made Man*

3 IS IT NOT BY THE COURAGE   William Barrett, "James Smith Bush," in *Memoirs of Members of the Social Circle in Concord: Third Series, from 1840 to 1895,* ed. John S. Keyes, Charles E. Brown, and F. Alcott Pratt (Cambridge, Mass., 1907), 180. Barrett's memoir of James Smith Bush, found in both the GHWB papers at GBPL and in the Grace Church Archives in San Francisco, is an essential source for reconstructing the nineteenth-century Bush family universe.
3 FAILURE SEEMS TO BE   Milton Rugoff, *America's Gilded Age: Intimate Portraits from an Era of Extravagance and Change, 1850–1890* (New York, 1989), 4.
3 "BUSHY" TO HIS BELOVED FIRST WIFE, FLORA   Flora Sheldon Bush to Samuel P. Bush, undated, Samuel P. Bush Papers (VFM 2954), Ohio Historical Society, Columbus, Ohio. I am especially indebted to Weisberg, *Bush Tragedy,* and Schweizer and Schweizer, *Bushes,* for my treatment of the Bush and Walker family histories. See also Kelly, *Family,* 24–35. The documents from the GBPL, cited below, were also essential, as were interviews with GHWB, Nancy Bush Ellis, and G. H. Walker III.
3 HOTEL TRAYMORE   *Railway Age Gazette,* June 16, 1915, 1378. See also "Hotel Traymore, Atlantic City, N.J.," *Bankers' Magazine,* October 1915, 541–44.
3 "THE MOST ELEVATED POINT ON THE ATLANTIC COAST"   *Railway Age Gazette,* June 16, 1915, 1378.
3 "THE HIGHEST GOLF DRIVING CONTEST"   Ibid.
3 THE TALL, ANGULAR BUSH   "Tax 'Watchdog' Passes Up Credit in Economic Victory," undated news clipping, Samuel P. Bush [Articles and Correspondence], Post-Presidential Materials, GHWB Collection, GBPL.
3 TWO HUNDRED FEET ABOVE THE BEACH   *NYT,* June 20, 1915.
3 THE DOMED TRAYMORE HAD JUST UNDERGONE   "New Hotel Traymore, Atlantic City, New Jersey," *Bankers' Magazine,* June 1915, 844.
3 "700 ROOMS AND 700 BATHS"   Ibid.
4 FINDING HIS FUTURE AT BUCKEYE   Mansel G. Blackford, *A Portrait Cast in Steel: Buckeye International and Columbus, Ohio, 1881–1980* (Westport, Conn., 1982), 10, 48–49.
4 PRESIDENT OF BUCKEYE SINCE 1908   Ibid., 48.
4 IN A LONG-SLEEVED DRESS SHIRT AND FORMAL TROUSERS   *Railway Age Gazette,* June 16, 1915, 1378. The details are evident from a photograph of Bush taken as he hit his shot.
4 *THE NEW YORK TIMES* REPORTED BUSH'S TRIUMPH   *NYT,* June 20, 1915.
4 THEIRS IS A STORY   Weisberg, *Bush Tragedy,* 11–12, discusses the familial patterns.
4 BUSH'S ANCESTORS WERE IN AMERICA   "Walker Family Genealogy," Jan Burmeister Collection, GBPL.

4 SOME ARRIVED ON THE *MAYFLOWER*   Gary Boyd Roberts, "The *Mayflower* Descendants of President George Herbert Walker Bush, First Lady Barbara Pierce Bush, and Vice President James Danforth Quayle," *The Mayflower Descendant* (January 1991), 1, Jan Burmeister Collection, GBPL.

4 THE MASSACHUSETTS PATRIOT DR. SAMUEL PRESCOTT   Patti Hartigan of *The Boston Globe* request to GHWB, April 2, 1987; GHWB statement in response, Jan Burmeister Collection, GBPL. See also David Hackett Fischer, *Paul Revere's Ride* (New York, 1994), 129–31, 156, 203, 287, 332.

4 OBADIAH BUSH   Barrett, "James Smith Bush," *Memoirs,* 176. For more on the Bush lineage, see Jan Burmeister Collection, GBPL.

4 BECAME A SCHOOLMASTER   Barrett, "James Smith Bush," *Memoirs,* 176.

5 RECALLED AS THE "COMELY" HARRIET SMITH   Ibid.

5 WENT INTO BUSINESS IN ROCHESTER   Ibid.

5 TURNED TO SENATOR WILLIAM SEWARD   Michael J. Cuddy, Jr., "By George (Bush), Obadiah Was Here," *The Citizen-Advertiser* (Auburn, N.Y.). GHWB sent this undated newspaper clipping to his mother and two aunts with a note dated November 19, 1988. (Jan Burmeister Collection, GBPL.)

5 OBADIAH GREW OBSESSED   Barrett, "James Smith Bush," *Memoirs,* 176.

5 MINING OPPORTUNITIES   Cuddy, "By George (Bush), Obadiah Was Here."

5 DIED BEFORE HE COULD   Barrett, "James Smith Bush," *Memoirs,* 176–77.

5 "A PUNY AND SICKLY CHILD"   Ibid., 177.

5 "YOU HAD BETTER"   Ibid.

5 IN 1841, AT SIXTEEN   Ibid. See also *Obituary Record of Graduates of Yale University: Presented at the Meeting of the Alumni,* 3rd printed ser., no. 10 (New Haven, Conn., June 1890), 574.

5 WAS POPULAR AND CHARMING   Barrett, "James Smith Bush," *Memoirs,* 177.

5 "HIS CLASSMATES SPEAK"   Ibid.

5 JAMES SMITH BUSH SOUGHT PROFESSIONAL SECURITY   Ibid.

5 ON A VISIT TO SARATOGA SPRINGS   Ibid., 178.

5 "THE MOST BEAUTIFUL WOMAN"   Ibid.

5 SARAH FREEMAN BUSH DIED   Ibid.

6 INITIALLY A PRESBYTERIAN   Ibid., 177.

6 HAD BECOME AN EPISCOPALIAN   Ibid., 179.

6 WAS ORDAINED   *Obituary Record of Graduates of Yale University,* June 1890, 574.

6 SERVED AT GRACE CHURCH   Ibid.

6 HE EVENTUALLY FOUND   Barrett, "James Smith Bush," *Memoirs,* 179.

6 "BRILLIANT AND BEAUTIFUL"   Ibid.

6 "SHE POSSESSED THE FINEST MIND"   Ibid.

6 HE MARRIED HARRIET FAY   *Obituary Record of Graduates of Yale University,* June 1890, 574.

6 ON SUNDAY, OCTOBER 4, 1863, A SON   *LSY,* 18.

6 PREACHED A SERMON   "The Bible in Public Schools, Or, Christian Education: A Sermon Preached by Rev. James Smith Bush, Pastor of Grace Church, Sunday, September 24," unidentified San Francisco newspaper, Grace Church Archives, San Francisco.

6 A SUPPORTER OF THE UNION   Lillian Hillyer Marsh, *One Hundred Years of Grace: A History of Grace Episcopal Church, Orange, New Jersey, 1854–1954* (Orange, N.J., 1954), 8.

6 REPORTEDLY FLEW THE AMERICAN FLAG   Barrett, "James Smith Bush," *Memoirs,* 179.

6 WROTE A SERMON   James Smith Bush, *Death of President Lincoln: A Sermon, Preached in Grace Church, Orange, N.J., Easter, April 16, 1865* (Orange, N.J., 1865).

6 "BE ASSURED, MY BRETHREN"   Ibid., 6.

6 "The President" Ibid., 8.

6 an expedition around Cape Horn For details of the journey, see Charles E. Clark, *My Fifty Years in the Navy* (Boston, 1917), 123–66, and "The Cruise of the 'Monadnock,'" *The Overland Monthly* 3 (San Francisco, 1869), 366–72.

6 In 1867 Bush accepted a call *Obituary Record of Graduates of Yale University*, June 1890, 574.

6 returning east for good in 1872 Ibid.; Barrett, "James Smith Bush," *Memoirs*, 181.

6 The more miraculous elements Author interview with Nancy Bush Ellis.

6 "I discovered early" Barrett, "James Smith Bush," *Memoirs*, 182–83.

7 On a visit to the Ashfield Ibid., 182.

7 Curtis introduced his guest Ibid.

7 I like a church Ralph Waldo Emerson, *Collected Poems and Translations* (New York, 1994), 10–12.

7 "Why, why" Barrett, "James Smith Bush," *Memoirs*, 182.

7 Around Christmas 1883 he resigned James Smith Bush to the Wardens and Vestrymen, December 17, 1883, Archives of the Church of the Ascension, Staten Island, New York.

7 moved his family to Concord Barrett, "James Smith Bush," *Memoirs*, 183.

7 died after a heart attack Ibid., 184.

7 "interested in all public questions" Ibid., 185.

7 He was buried Ibid., 184.

7 The post–Civil War era Rugoff, *America's Gilded Age*, 333.

8 This new faith Andrew Carnegie, *The Gospel of Wealth, and Other Timely Essays* (New York, 1900), 15.

8 This, then, is held to be Ibid.

8 America, wrote the banker Henry Clews Rugoff, *America's Gilded Age*, 41.

8 was "the land of the self-made man" Ibid.

8 S.P. attended Blackford, *Portrait Cast in Steel*, 48.

8 Bush worked for a number Ibid., 48–49; LSY, 19.

8 Buckeye Malleable Iron Blackford, *Portrait Cast in Steel*, 22–23.

8 of the "highest grade" Ibid., 10.

8 Buckeye invited spectators Ibid., 21.

8 "the steel came pouring forth" Ibid.

8 "respected" Author interview with GHWB.

9 Flora Sheldon of Columbus LSY, 18.

9 "Grandfather Bush was quite severe" Author interview with Nancy Bush Ellis.

9 "a snorter . . . everyone knew" Blackford, *Portrait Cast in Steel*, 50–51.

9 There was championship level golf Author interview with GHWB.

9 the building of a great house Author interview with Nancy Bush Ellis

9 creating the Ohio State football program Author interview with GHWB.

9 the establishment of the Ohio Manufacturers' Association "S. P. Bush, Retired Business, Civic Leader, Succumbs at 84," [1947], in Book 5, Bush Family Scrapbooks, GBPL. See also LSY, 19.

9 the state's Democratic Party "Tax 'Watchdog' Passes Up Credit in Economic Victory," in Samuel P. Bush, [Articles and Correspondence], Post-Presidential Materials, GHWB Collection, GBPL. See also LSY, 19.

9 the anti-tax Ohio Tax League "S. P. Bush, Retired Business, Civic Leader, Succumbs at 84," [1947], in Book 5, Bush Family Scrapbooks, GBPL; LSY, 19.

9 of symphonies, of art galleries Blackford, *Portrait Cast in Steel*, 49–50.

9   OFTEN ASKED TO SERVE AS A DIRECTOR   Ibid., 68.

9   "I COULD BE A LOT BETTER"   Samuel P. Bush to Flora Sheldon Bush, undated, Samuel P. Bush Papers (VFM 2954), Ohio Historical Society, Columbus, Ohio.

9   FLORA, WHO WAS ENGAGED   Letters of Flora Sheldon Bush to Samuel P. Bush, undated, Samuel P. Bush Papers.

9   "LET ME KNOW DEAR"   Flora Sheldon Bush to Samuel P. Bush, undated, Samuel P. Bush Papers.

9   "YOU ARE A VERY DEAR BUSHY"   Flora Sheldon Bush to Samuel P. Bush, undated, Samuel P. Bush Papers.

9   BORN IN COLUMBUS   Herskowitz, *Duty, Honor, Country,* 27.

9   "THE CHILDREN WERE HILARIOUS"   Flora Sheldon Bush to Samuel P. Bush, June 18, 1911, Samuel P. Bush Papers.

9   "I HAVE HAD ONE NEW EXPERIENCE"   Flora Sheldon Bush to Samuel P. Bush, undated, Samuel P. Bush Papers.

10   CADDIED FOR DOUGLAS FAIRBANKS, SR.   Green, *George Bush,* 2.

10   S. P. BUSH TOOK HIS SONS   S. P. Bush to Flora Sheldon Bush, "Thanksgiving" (no year given), Samuel P. Bush Papers.

10   REPORTED THE 1908 AUTOMOBILE-ACCIDENT DEATH   Flora Sheldon Bush to S. P. Bush, undated, Samuel P. Bush Papers. See also *NYT,* August 13, 1908.

10   WERE ALWAYS ANXIOUS   Flora Sheldon Bush to S. P. Bush, undated, Samuel P. Bush Papers.

10   HIS GOOD LOOKS AND CHARM   Schweizer and Schweizer, *Bushes,* 8. "As Pres reached adolescence, he became a particular frustration for the family," Schweizer and Schweizer wrote. "Perhaps it was because of the promise that his father saw in him. The boy was attractive, charming, and intelligent. But he seemed to lack the seriousness that S. P expected from him. So the decision was made to send him away to school [at St. George's]. Flora had misgivings but agreed that it was necessary." (Ibid.)

10   A "PERNICIOUS HABIT OF FOOLING"   Harriet Bush to S. P. Bush, undated, Samuel P. Bush Papers. In her 2004 book *The Family,* Kelley refers to this observation of Harriet Bush's. (Kelley, *Family,* 2, 23.)

10   PRESCOTT HAD ENJOYED   PSB, COHC, 2.

10   A "BOY OF VERY TENDER YEARS"   Flora Sheldon Bush to S. P. Bush, undated, Samuel P. Bush Papers.

10   "SOMETIMES [HAD] A FEELING"   Ibid.

10   PRESCOTT LOVED ST. GEORGE'S   Author interview with Nancy Bush Ellis. See also Herskowitz, *Duty, Honor, Country,* 27.

10   CIVICS CLUB   PSB, COHC, 3.

10   "ARE WE FOR OR AGAINST"   Ibid. See also Schweizer and Schweizer, *Bushes,* 8, and Herskowitz, *Duty, Honor, Country,* 28.

10   THE SCHOOL PRAYER   "The School Prayer," *The Lance,* 1919 yearbook, St. George's School, Middletown, R.I., 130. http://www.e-yearbook.com/yearbooks/St_Georges _High_School_Lance_Yearbook/1919/Page_130.html.

10   HE BRIEFLY ENVISIONED   PSB, COHC, 3–4.

10   YALE WAS INEVITABLE   George Mosher Murray and James Callender Heminway, eds., *History of the Class of 1917, Yale College,* vol. I, (New Haven, Conn., 1917), 105–6.

11   CALLED "PRES" AND "DOC"   Ibid.

11   BUSH LETTERED   Ibid.

11   IN HIS FINAL YEAR, PRESCOTT PLACED HIGH   Ibid., 430–32.

11   HE CROWNED HIS CAREER   Ibid., 105.

11   IN A POLL OF THE CLASS OF 1917   Ibid., 423–41.

11 "LESS CASTE, FEWER SNOBS" Ibid., 424.

11 IT WAS ALSO A THOROUGHLY REPUBLICAN Ibid., 441.

11 BUSH JOINED A NUMBER OF HIS CLASSMATES Ibid., 401–10. See also Schweizer and Schweizer, *Bushes*, 16, and Herskowitz, *Duty, Honor, Country*, 28–29.

11 AT TOBYHANNA, PENNSYLVANIA Murray and Heminway, *History of the Class of 1917*, 401–10.

11 ON MONDAY, APRIL 2, 1917 Woodrow Wilson, "Address to a Joint Session of Congress Requesting a Declaration of War Against Germany," April 2, 1917, The American Presidency Project, http://www.presidency.ucsb.edu/ws/?pid=65366.

11 WOODROW WILSON ASKED CONGRESS Herskowitz, *Duty, Honor, Country*, 36.

11 S. P. BUSH WAS SUMMONED Schweizer and Schweizer, *Bushes*, 18–19.

11 PRESCOTT BECAME A CAPTAIN Ibid., 16.

11 BUSH LED AN EXPEDITION TO CAPTURE Ibid., 16–17.

11 HEAD OF THE BOARD'S ORDNANCE Ibid., 18–19.

11 BUCKEYE'S WARTIME PROFITS Ibid.

11 "I HAVE ALWAYS" Martin J. Gillen to S. P. Bush, December 10, 1942, Samuel P. Bush Papers.

11 PRESCOTT EMBARKED FOR FRANCE Herskowitz, *Duty, Honor, Country*, 37.

11 "WE ARE CLOSE ENOUGH" Ibid.

11 AS PART OF THE 158TH Ibid.; Schweizer and Schweizer, *Bushes*, 20.

11 PRESCOTT NEVER SPOKE Author interview with GHWB. See also Schweizer and Schweizer, *Bushes*, 23.

12 A PRANK LETTER *Ohio State Journal*, August 8, 1918.

12 "3 HIGH MILITARY HONORS" Ibid.

12 BY FRIDAY, SEPTEMBER 6 Schweizer and Schweizer, *Bushes*, 22.

12 "IF *ONLY* THE GREAT EPIC" Flora Sheldon Bush to Samuel P. Bush, "Sunday Morning," undated, Samuel P. Bush Papers.

12 PRESCOTT WAS DISCHARGED PSB, COHC, 6.

12 AT A REUNION IN NEW HAVEN IN 1919 Ibid.

12 WALLACE D. SIMMONS, YALE CLASS OF 1890 Schweizer and Schweizer, *Bushes*, 34.

12 ON TUESDAY, JULY 1, 1919, PRESCOTT BUSH REPORTED PSB, COHC, 6.

12 SCION OF A LARGE ST. LOUIS HARDWARE CONCERN *St. Louis Post-Dispatch*, February 23, 1918, and April 26, 1920.

12 AT NINTH AND SPRUCE STREETS "Simmons Co.'s New Building," *Hardware* 1, no. 4 (New York, May 25, 1895), 35.

12 WITH ST. LOUIS AS A BASE PSB, COHC, 6.

12 SOME FRIENDS DRIVING BY *WP*, September 5, 1920.

13 HERBERT DAVIS OF MYSTIC, CONNECTICUT "Criminal Negligence Caused Woman's Death, Says Coroner," *Lexington Herald*, September 15, 1920.

13 SHE DIED INSTANTLY *WP*, September 5, 1920.

TWO: *A Real Son of a Bitch*

14 I'M GOING TO THROW YOU Transcript of Beth Bush's oral history of Pitty Duval, September 1981, 6–7, in Dorothy W. Bush Book Project Files, Barbara P. Bush Collection, GBPL.

14 THE WALKER HOUSEHOLD AT 12 HORTENSE PLACE *St. Louis Post-Dispatch*, January 15, 1920; *St. Louis Republic*, April 14 and October 27, 1901. See also 1910 United States Census, Saint Louis, St. Louis City, St. Louis Ward 25, Supervisor's District 10, Enumeration District 0393, Lines 1–13. I am grateful to Kathy Evans for these details.

14 BUSH HAD GOTTEN TO KNOW   Author interview with Nancy Bush Ellis. See also Schweizer and Schweizer, *Bushes,* 34.

14 "HE DID NOT KNOW A PARTY"   Betsy [Walker] to "Dear Jody, John, et all [*sic*]," Dorothy W. Bush Book Project Files, Barbara P. Bush Collection, GBPL.

14 "SHE WAS SO BLOND"   Author interview with Nancy Bush Ellis.

14 "PRES SUBSEQUENTLY ASKED"   Betsy [Walker] to "Dear Jody, John," GBPL.

14 "HE WAS KIND OF AN UP-AND-DOWN GUY"   Author interview with GHWB.

15 "HE WAS A REAL SON OF A BITCH"   Author interview with G. H. Walker III.

15 THE WALKERS' WAS A WILD, RICH LIFE   Weisberg, *Bush Tragedy,* 9–11; Schweizer and Schweizer, *Bushes,* 25–32.

15 TOLD A NEW LINE OF FORD CARS   S. Prescott B. Clement to Barbara P. Bush, December 2, 1986, Dorothy W. Bush Book Project Files, Barbara P. Bush Collection, GBPL.

15 TEMPERAMENTAL, IMPERIOUS   Schweizer and Schweizer, *Bushes,* 26–27.

15 HE BOXED WITH HIS SONS   Author interview with G. H. Walker III.

15 URGED THEM TO SETTLE DISPUTES   Ibid.

15 "HE PULLED NO PUNCHES"   Ibid.

15 THE WALKERS WERE AS OLD A FAMILY   King, *George Bush,* 13. The Walkers included Thomas Walker, originally of England, who flourished briefly in the transatlantic slave trade in the 1780s and '90s. His youngest son, George E., was the great-great-grandfather of GHWB. (Simon Akam, "George W. Bush's Great-Great-Great-Great-Grandfather Was a Slave Trader," June 20, 2013, www.slate.com/articles/life /history_lesson/2013/06/george_w_bush_and_slavery_the_president_and_his _father_are_descendants_of.single.html. Akam noted that Thomas Walker's slave trading did not lead to "lasting prosperity" for his progeny.

15 THEY SETTLED ALONG   Willard King, *Lincoln's Manager: David Davis* (Cambridge, Mass., 1960), 1–6; Roger Hughes, "Twists, Turns, Ties: David Davis & George Bush," *The Pantagraph* (Bloomington, Ill.), November 7, 2004, and "Legacy," *Illinois Times,* April 5, 2007, illinoistimes.com/article-3993-legacy.html. Hughes did pioneering research on the Walker family origins; I am in his debt. I am also grateful to G. H. Walker III, Kathy Evans, and Pat Schley for guidance on the Walker family history, particularly on the David Davis connection.

15 SLAVE-OWNING PLANTERS   King, *Lincoln's Manager,* 3–5; Weisberg, *Bush Tragedy,* 8.

15 IN THE 1830S   Hughes, "Legacy," April 5, 2007. See also Weisberg, *Bush Tragedy,* 8.

15 FUTURE SUPREME COURT JUSTICE DAVID DAVIS   Hughes, "Twists, Turns, Ties," November 7, 2004.

15 SEEING THAT YOUNG DAVID DAVIS WALKER   Ibid. "I shall send David Walker to Beloit, to the English school to stay there a year," Davis wrote to his own son George Perrin Davis in August 1854. "I hope he will improve. He needs different influences from what he has received and needs to be among good people." (Ibid.)

15 "I'VE HAD ENOUGH"   Author interview with G. H. Walker III.

15 LIKELY CONNECTED HIM WITH   Hughes, "Twists, Turns, Ties," November 7, 2004.

15 MARRYING MARTHA BEAKY   Author interview with G. H. Walker III; "A Bit of Walker Family History as Recalled by Dorothy Walker Bush," Materials on GB's Family, Barbara P. Bush Collection, GBPL. "In the Midwest, David Walker maintained the Southern attitude about race, though with a contemporary overlay of social Darwinism," wrote Jacob Weisberg. "He was a believer in eugenics and the 'unwritten law' of lynching. In a letter to the editor of the *St. Louis Republic* published in 1914, David Walker described Negroes as a greater menace than prostitution and 'all the other evils combined.'" (Weisberg, *Bush Tragedy,* 8.)

16 IN 1875 Weisberg, *Bush Tragedy*, 8.

16 NAMED FOR THE ANGLICAN PRIEST AND POET Schweizer and Schweizer, *Bushes*, 24.

16 A GRANDDAUGHTER WHO SPENT Transcript of Beth Bush's oral history of Pitty Duval, September 1981, 2–4, Dorothy W. Bush Book Project Files, Barbara P. Bush Collection, GBPL; Flora House Fairchild, "Orchids to Dotty," 2–3, Dorothy W. Bush Book Project Files, Barbara P. Bush Collection, GBPL.

16 "OH, THAT HOUSE *MUST* BE PAINTED" Transcript of Beth Bush's oral history of Pitty Duval, September 1981, 4, Dorothy W. Bush Book Project Files, Barbara P. Bush Collection, GBPL.

16 HE ATTENDED PAROCHIAL SCHOOLS Author interviews with Nancy Bush Ellis and G. H. Walker III.

16 DISPATCHED HIM Schweizer and Schweizer, *Bushes*, 25.

16 HIS PARENTS HOPED HE WOULD RETURN Dorothy Walker Bush, "A Bit of Walker Family History as Recalled by Dorothy Walker Bush," 1, Materials on GB's Family, Barbara P. Bush Collection, GBPL.

16 "BUT AS A RESULT" Ibid., 1.

16 BERT WALKER JOINED Author interview with G. H. Walker III.

16 "HE DID NOT WANT" Ibid.

16 ONE DAY AT THE WAREHOUSE Ibid.

16 "I'M NEVER GOING BACK" Ibid.

16 THE PRICE OF THE MARRIAGE Ibid.

16 "IF YOU MARRY HER" Green, *George Bush*, 18–19. G. H. Walker and Loulie Wear were married in the Wears' house on McPherson by the (Presbyterian) Reverend John F. Cannon. (*St. Louis Post Dispatch*, January 11, 1899.) See also Weisberg, *Bush Tragedy*, 8–9.

17 AN ENCLAVE FOR YOUNG, RICH FAMILIES Dorothy Walker Bush, "A Bit of Walker Family History," 4–5, GBPL.

17 THE LAMBERTS Ibid.

17 ANOTHER WAS EUGENE CUENDET Ibid.

17 THE TIME HE SHOT Weisberg, *Bush Tragedy*, 10.

17 THE NEAR-RIOT HE INSTIGATED Schweizer and Schweizer, *Bushes*, 28–29.

17 MOTTO WAS Ibid.

17 THE DRUNKEN EVENING Ibid.

17 "GET ME WHISKEY" "Speech for Walker Cup Dinner," 1985, GB Material, Looking Forward and Miscellaneous Files, VIC.

17 HE SHARED A YACHT Author interview with Nancy Bush Ellis.

17 WON THE HEAVYWEIGHT BOXING TITLE Schweizer and Schweizer, *Bushes*, 24.

17 SERVED AS PRESIDENT *St. Louis Post-Dispatch*, January 15, 1920.

17 WINTHER OUT Robert Browning, *A History of Golf: The Royal and Ancient Game* (New York, 1955), 204.

17 DURING A TROUBLED ECONOMIC HOUR Dorothy Walker Bush, "Bit of Walker Family History," 5, GBPL.

17 HAD BOUGHT LAND TOGETHER Author interviews with GHWB and Nancy Bush Ellis.

17 ON MONDAY, JULY 1, 1901, DOROTHY WEAR WALKER WAS BORN Author interview with Nancy Bush Ellis.

17 THERE WAS A FRENCH GOVERNESS Dorothy Walker Bush, "Bit of Walker Family History," 5, GBPL.

18 DOROTHY AND HER SISTER, NANCY, ATTENDED THE MARY INSTITUTE Ibid., 5–6.

18 TAILORED BY A WOMAN Ibid.

18 WALKED TO LESSONS WITH HER PIANO TEACHER   Ibid., 6.
18 SHE WAS SENT TO MISS PORTER'S SCHOOL   Schweizer and Schweizer, *Bushes,* 34.
18 AT ST. ANN'S   Author interview with GHWB.
18 IN ST. LOUIS THEY BELONGED TO WESTMINSTER   Dorothy Walker Bush, "Bit of Walker Family History," 6, GBPL.
18 ATTENDED SERVICES AT LEAST THREE TIMES A WEEK   Ibid.
18 TO REACH THE EAST EACH SUMMER   Author interview with GHWB.
18 THE TRUNKS WERE SENT AHEAD   Pitty Duval oral history, 3, GBPL.
18 THE AUTHORS BOOTH TARKINGTON   Ibid., 5. See also Schweizer and Schweizer, *Bushes,* 25.
18 THE TOWN PLAYHOUSE   Author interviews with Nancy Bush Ellis and GHWB.
18 THERE WERE CARNIVALS   Pitty Duval oral history, 3, GBPL.
18 AT SUMMER'S END   Dorothy Walker Bush, "Bit of Walker Family History," 6, GBPL.
18 AS HIS FATHER, D. D. WALKER, GREW OLDER   Author interview with G. H. Walker III. See also "Guardian for Property of David D. Walker Asked For," *St. Louis Post-Dispatch,* January 14, 1918; "D. D. Walker Gave Away $300,000 in 4 Years, Son Says," *St. Louis Post-Dispatch,* February 19, 1918; "Gifts of About $224,000 Revealed by D. D. Walker," *St. Louis Post-Dispatch,* May 5, 1918; "D. D. Walker Cuts Off Sons in Will," *St. Louis Post-Dispatch,* October 31, 1918; "Sons Left Nothing by D. D. Walker's Will," *St. Louis Post-Dispatch,* November 1, 1918.
18 D. D. WAS SO ENRAGED   Author interview with G. H. Walker III.
18 "IF YOU CROSS THAT LINE"   Ibid.
18 WHEN THE FATHER DIED   "Probate Judge Rejects Will of D. D. Walker Sr.," *St. Louis Post-Dispatch,* November 19, 1918. D. D. Walker's estate of $750,000 was divided among five family members, including G. H. Walker. (Ibid.)
18 UNCLE WILL WALKER   Pitty Duval oral history, 6–7, GBPL.
18 "THIS IS THE WAY"   Ibid.
19 "I WAS TERRIFIED"   Ibid., 7.
19 WHEN HER BROTHER HERBIE REFUSED   Dorothy Walker Bush, "Bit of Walker Family History," 7, GBPL.
19 DOROTHY WAS AT THE PLATE   "GHWB's Recollections of Dorothy Walker Bush on the Occasion of Mother's Day," Mrs. Prescott Bush (Senior) Materials, GHWB Collection, GBPL. See also Schweizer and Schweizer, *Bushes,* 36.
19 SHE FELL AND INJURED HERSELF   "GHWB's Recollections of Dorothy Walker Bush on the Occasion of Mother's Day," Mrs. Prescott Bush (Senior) Materials, GHWB Collection, GBPL.
19 THE HARRIMAN FAMILY OF NEW YORK ASKED   Schweizer and Schweizer, *Bushes,* 33. See also "G. H. Walker to Head New Financial House," *St. Louis Post-Dispatch,* January 15, 1920; and "Form Securities Company: G. H. Walker of St. Louis Backed by N.Y. Capital Organizes Firm," *NYT,* January 15, 1920.
19 ACQUIRING A HOME IN THE CITY   Schweizer and Schweizer, *Bushes,* 39.
19 MARRIED AT ST. ANN'S   Author interview with Nancy Bush Ellis.
19 JOHN POYNTZ TYLER   *NYT,* August 7, 1921.
19 SEVERAL GUESTS ARRIVED   Author interview with Nancy Bush Ellis.
19 LIVED IN ST. LOUIS FOR A TIME   Schweizer and Schweizer, *Bushes,* 36; Betsy [Walker] to "Dear Jody, John," GBPL.
19 MOVED BRIEFLY IN KINGSPORT   *LF,* 24; Schweizer and Schweizer, *Bushes,* 36.
19 STILL WITH SIMMONS   *LF,* 24.
19 MANAGED THE SALE OF A SADDLERY PLANT   Schweizer and Schweizer, *Bushes,* 36.

Prescott Bush tells this story and details his sundry moves for his job in this period, at PSB COH, 6–8.

19 THERE WERE A NUMBER OF MOVES   Schweizer and Schweizer, *Bushes,* 36.

19 BUSH DISCOVERED A CASE   Betsy [Walker] to "Dear Jody, John," GBPL.

19 THE BUSHES RETURNED TO ST. LOUIS   Schweizer and Schweizer, *Bushes,* 36.

19 SPENT A YEAR IN COLUMBUS   Ibid., 37.

19 THAT ENDED UP BEING SOLD   PSB, COHC, 7. Prescott's father, S. P. Bush, had a "substantial investment" in the concern. (Ibid.)

19 THE BUSHES MOVED YET AGAIN   Ibid., 8.

19 THEY BOUGHT 173 ADAMS STREET   Schweizer and Schweizer, *Bushes,* 37.

19 A BIG VICTORIAN   Ibid. for the "Victorian" detail, and the size of the house is evident from photographs and from the description given by John Madden, "Former President Bush Visits His Milton Birthplace," *The Patriot Ledger* (Quincy, MA), August 13, 1997, http://www.patriotledger.com/article/19970813/NEWS/308139999.

19 NEAR THE INTERSECTION OF ADAMS AND HUTCHINSON   Madden, "Former President Bush Visits His Milton Birthplace," *The Patriot Ledger,* August 13, 1997, www.patriot ledger.com/article/19970813/NEWS/308139999.

20 THE BRIEFEST OF WALKS TO GOVERNOR HUTCHINSON'S FIELD   www.google.com /maps/dir/173+Adams+St,Milton,+MA+02186/Governor+Hutchinson's+Field,+ Milton,+MA+02186/@42.2663652,-71.0684047,17z/data=!3m1!4b1!4m14!4m13! 1m5!1m1!1s0x89e37c6e736a5fb3:0xddb9b3429eeff238!2m2!1d-71.067153!2d42 .266981!1m5!1m1!1s0x89e37c6e51f23821:0xf4be1028f0104d97!2m2! 1d-71.065043!2d42.2660453!3e2. See also www.thetrustees.org/places-to-visit /greater-boston/hutchinsons-field.html.

20 THE OLD SITE OF THE ESTATE OF THE LAST COLONIAL GOVERNOR OF MASSACHUSETTS   www.thetrustees.org/places-to-visit/greater-boston/hutchinsons-field.html.

20 DOROTHY WALKER BUSH DELIVERED HER SECOND SON   Schweizer and Schweizer, *Bushes,* 37.

20 A MIDWIFE ASSISTED   Betsy [Walker] to "Dear Jody, John," GBPL.

20 BAPTIZED GEORGE HERBERT WALKER BUSH   Green, *George Bush,* 11.

20 BECAME KNOWN AS "POPPY"   Author interviews with GHWB and Nancy Bush Ellis.

20 WHILE GEORGE'S FATHER   Green, *George Bush,* 11.

20 THE PRESCOTT BUSHES MOVED   PSB, COHC, 8.

21 "I DID HAVE A VERY WIDE"   Ibid., 9.

21 BUSH BEGAN   Ibid., 8.

21 BROWN BROTHERS WAS ALREADY A NOTABLE HOUSE   John A. Kouwenhoven, *Partners in Banking: An Historical Portrait of a Great Private Bank, Brown Brothers Harriman & Co.* (Garden City, N.Y., 1968), is a comprehensive history.

21 A LETTER OF CREDIT FROM BROWN BROTHERS   Ibid., 193.

21 THE FIRM BECAME   See, for instance, Kouwenhoven, *Partners in Banking;* Walter Isaacson and Evan Thomas, *The Wise Men: Six Friends and the World They Made* (New York, 1986), 110–18.

21 AVERELL HARRIMAN SERVED   Isaacson and Thomas, *Wise Men,* 17–18, 20, 188, 584–85.

21 ANOTHER PARTNER, ROBERT LOVETT   Ibid., 21, 555.

21 AT 59 WALL STREET   Ibid., 110–11.

21 DECISIONS WERE MADE BY CONSENSUS   PSB, COHC, 37–38; Schweizer and Schweizer, *Bushes,* 47.

21 PRESCOTT ALSO JOINED   PSB, COHC, 13–14.

21 IN JULY 1941   *New York Herald Tribune,* July 31, 1941; WP, July 31, 1941; Herskowitz,

Duty, Honor, Country, 72–73; *The Boston Globe,* April 23, 2001; *The Guardian,* September 25, 2004; *The Washington Times,* October 17, 2003. See also Schweizer and Schweizer, *Bushes,* 50–51.

22 THE GERMAN CONNECTIONS NEVER   Herskowitz, *Duty, Honor, Country,* 73.

22 IN THE WAKE OF THE MERGER   Kouwenhoven, *Partners in Banking,* 12. See also Schweizer and Schweizer, *Bushes,* 47.

22 A FELLOW BONESMAN   Weisberg, *Bush Tragedy,* 14. See also Isaacson and Thomas, *Wise Men,* 110–11.

22 WORRIED ABOUT WALKER'S "DANGEROUS DEALINGS"   Herskowitz, *Duty, Honor, Country,* 68. See also Weisberg, *Bush Tragedy,* 10–11.

22 WALKER ADMIRED PRESCOTT'S GOLF GAME   Author interviews with G. H. Walker III and Nancy Bush Ellis.

22 THE BUSH CODE OF DISGUISED AMBITION   Weisberg, *Bush Tragedy,* 3–6, 14.

22 "OTHERS WOULD CLIMB"   Author interview with GHWB.

22 WHILE PRESCOTT ADORED SINGING   Author interviews with GHWB, Nancy Bush Ellis, and Jonathan Bush. See also Naftali, *GHWB,* 5–6, for a summary of life at home.

22 "IN THE THIRTIES HE WAS WORRIED"   Author interview with Nancy Bush Ellis.

22 "I WAS TERRIFIED"   Author interview with Jonathan Bush.

23 GEORGE H. W. AND HIS OLDER BROTHER   Author interview with GHWB.

23 "HE PICKED UP A SQUASH RACQUET"   Ibid.

23 "SHE HAD FIVE OF US"   "GHWB's Recollections of Dorothy Walker Bush," GBPL.

23 "MY MOTHER'S WAS A LITTLE LIKE"   Ibid.

THREE: *He Gets So Intense Over Everything*

24 "MOTHER WAS ALWAYS GENEROUS"   Author interview with Jonathan Bush.

24 "DAD? TALL, SCARY"   Author interview with GHWB.

24 THE YARD OF THE BUSH HOUSE   "GHWB's Recollections of Dorothy Walker Bush," GBPL.

24 WERE TO BE CLIMBED   Ibid.

24 "MOTHER NEVER SEEMED AFRAID"   Ibid.

24 "OF COURSE, THERE WOULD BE"   Ibid.

25 "IN THE PLAYING-FIELDS BOYS ACQUIRE"   Charles Kingsley, *The Works of Charles Kingsley,* vol. 18, *Sanitary and Social Lectures and Essays* (London, 1880), 125.

25 "THE SUN MIGHT BE BLISTERING HOT"   "GHWB's Recollections of Dorothy Walker Bush," GBPL.

25 THERE WAS A PORTE COCHERE   "Elsie Walker Recollections of Dorothy Walker Bush," Dorothy W. Bush Book Project Files, Barbara P. Bush Collection, GBPL.

25 LINED WITH FAMILY PHOTOGRAPHS   Ibid.

25 INVITED OVER FOR "TIDDLYWINKS"   Ibid.

25 ESPECIALLY "WIDE AND COMFORTABLE"   Ibid.

25 ON SUNDAYS, IF THE WEATHER WAS GOOD   Author interview with William T. "Bucky" Bush.

25 RUBBER-SPIKED GOLF SHOES   Ibid.

25 IF IT WAS RAINING OR SNOWING   Ibid.

26 DOROTHY WOULD WORK   Ibid.

26 PRESCOTT WOULD FIGHT TO STAY AWAKE   Ibid.

26 ONE SUMMER DAY IN THE MID-1930S   Author interview with GHWB.

26 TWO INFURIATED LOBSTERMEN   Ibid.

26 "THERE ARE TWO MEN"   Ibid.

26 He returned to his meal Ibid.

26 His grandchildren recalled Ibid.

26 Even breakfast could be perilous Ibid.

26 "Lots of sports, lots of summer reading" Author interview with Nancy Bush Ellis.

26 The Bush children read Ibid.

27 Poppy and Pressy boated no matter what Ibid.

27 "Ride the surf" Ibid.

27 "Mother always stressed" Ibid.

27 Christmases were spent in South Carolina Author interviews with GHWB and Nancy Bush Ellis. Recounting his privileged childhood, GHWB joked: "Yep, we had to pull ourselves up by our bootstraps, but it all worked out." (Ibid.) At another point in a joint interview with GHWB and Mrs. Ellis, there was this exchange: "We were spared the agony of the Depression, I must say," GHWB said.

"We were," Nancy said, "but we were reminded to eat *everything* on our plate because people in the country were starving."

"That's right, but we were lucky to have something on the plate," said GHWB.

"Exactly," Nancy said. (Ibid.)

27 when they woke and summoned Hansford Author interview with Nancy Bush Ellis.

27 The dogs—pointers and spaniels Author interview with GHWB.

27 Dorothy was a terrific shot, as was Prescott Ibid.

27 dinner was black-tie Ibid.

27 Prescott could be silent Author interview with Nancy Bush Ellis. See also Schweizer and Schweizer, *Bushes,* 52.

27 "Dad was grim" Author interview with Nancy Bush Ellis. Greenwich was nervous, too, after the 1932 kidnapping and murder of Charles Lindbergh, Jr., the twenty-month-old son of the flying hero Charles Lindbergh, who lived in Hopewell, New Jersey. "I remember the Lindbergh kidnapping, and all the Rockefellers in Greenwich putting iron bars on the windows of their houses," Nancy recalled. "Only cousins of the John D. Rockefellers, but Rockefellers nevertheless." (Ibid.)

27 "Now it is required" Schweizer and Schweizer, *Bushes,* 59.

27 "For unto whomsoever" Luke 12:48 (KJV).

27 "Pretty much every day" Author interview with GHWB.

28 "She cries a lot" "GHWB's Recollections of Dorothy Walker Bush," GBPL.

28 "She's always with me" Author interview with GHWB.

28 Greenwich Country Day School Susan D. Elia, Renée F. Seblatnigg, and Val P. Storms, *Greenwich Country Day: A History, 1926–1986* (Canaan, N.H., 1988), 3–9.

28 The Bushes allowed Poppy Green, *George Bush,* 12.

28 The boys were Author interview with GHWB. See also *LSY,* 28–29.

28 black-and-orange uniform sweaters Elia, Seblatnigg, and Storms, *Greenwich Country Day,* 3–9; *LSY,* 33.

28 "anything from a mouse" Elia, Seblatnigg, and Storms, *Greenwich Country Day,* 11.

28 "It was cutthroat" Ibid.

28 The school's first headmaster, John Lynn Miner Ibid., 105.

29 included the category "Claims More Than" *ATB,* 53. See also Schweizer and Schweizer, *Bushes,* 58.

29 a measure the Bushes watched carefully *ATB,* 53. As GHWB noted: "If this was checked on our card, we were in big trouble." (Ibid.) Of his general experience at GCDS, Bush always remembered the Latin classes ("which I kind of liked, actu-

ally," he recalled), but then and later he was more engaged by team efforts, be they soccer or singing. "I loved team sports. Loved them all. Even glee club—other people singing." (Author interview with GHWB.)

29 EARNING THE NICKNAME "HAVE-HALF"   Author interviews with Nancy Bush Ellis and Jonathan Bush.

29 DURING AN INFORMAL PLAYGROUND RACE   Author interview with GHWB.

29 "I SAW HIM THERE"   Ibid.

29 "HOW WELL I CAN RECALL"   Arthur Grant to GHWB, May 31, 1985, Mrs. Prescott Bush (Senior) Files, GHWB Collection, GBPL.

29 ONE CHRISTMAS HIS BROTHER BUCKY   Author interview with William T. "Bucky" Bush.

29 "YOU KNOW, BUCK"   Ibid.

29 "WOW, POP, YOU'RE"   Ibid.

29 "OH, YEAH"   Ibid.

29 BUSH HAD SECRETLY PRACTICED   Ibid.

29 "THAT WAS POP"   Ibid.

29 BEFORE GRADUATING FROM GREENWICH COUNTRY DAY   Bush ranked in the top quarter of his class of thirteen boys academically. In the school's recommendation to Andover, the headmaster who had succeeded an ailing John Lynn Miner, George Denis Meadows (*LSY*, 33), wrote that Bush was "a boy of excellent character, conspicuously straightforward and reliable. Good all-around ability both in studies and athletics. Consistently industrious in school work." In a section entitled "Other Opinions," Meadows was terse: "Attractive personality. Will adjust socially." ("Greenwich Country Day Recommendation," undated, Bush, George, Class of 1942, Vertical Subject Files, Archives and Special Collections, Phillips Academy, Andover, Mass. Hereafter cited as Phillips Academy Files.)

29 A PARENTAL QUESTIONNAIRE   "Parents Questionnaire," undated, but most likely 1937, Phillips Academy Files.

29 THE DOCUMENT REFERS TO THEIR SECOND SON   Ibid. GHWB had no recollection of his parents ever calling him "Walker," or of their asking others to do so. (Author interview with GHWB.) Bush did, however, remember a teacher at GCDS trying to call him "Walker" and encouraging the natural lefty to write with his right hand. Neither project, Bush said, succeeded. (*ATB*, 602.)

30 "WALKER HAS ALWAYS BEEN"   "Parents Questionnaire," Phillips Academy Files.

30 THEIR SON'S "FAMILY LIFE"   Ibid.

30 THE QUESTIONNAIRE GOES ON   Ibid.

32 "HE FELT THAT EVERYBODY"   PSB, COHC, 48–49.

32 "YOU HAVE GOALS"   Author interview with GHWB.

FOUR: *Not for Self*

33 AMBITIOUS AND SELF-CONFIDENT   Richard Pieters, "Counselor's Confidential Report," June 20, 1940, Phillips Academy Files.

33 YOU ARE LEAVING ANDOVER   Henry L. Stimson address to the graduating class, 1940, *Phillips Academy Bulletin* 34, no. 4 (July 1940).

33 IT WAS A RED, WHITE, AND BLUE THING   Author interview with GHWB.

33 A COMMON ANDOVER JOKE HAD IT   Alston Hurd Chase, *Time Remembered* (San Antonio, Texas, 1994), 165.

33 "FUESS, ROOSEVELT, AND HITLER"   Ibid.

33 A DISTANT, GODLIKE FIGURE   Author interview with GHWB.

33 HE WAS NICKNAMED "IRON" *LSY,* 39.

33 "BALD DOCTOR" Green, *George Bush,* 20.

33 FOUNDED IN 1778 BY SAMUEL PHILLIPS, JR. Peter W. Cookson, Jr., and Caroline Hodges Persell, *Preparing for Power: America's Elite Boarding Schools* (New York, 1985), 38, 43.

33 "THE FALL OF MAN" Ibid., 38.

33 ANDOVER LONG PREDATED Ibid., 43.

34 E. DIGBY BALTZELL, THE UNIVERSITY OF PENNSYLVANIA SOCIOLOGIST Ibid., 42. See also *NYT,* August 20, 1996.

34 "SERVE THE SOCIOLOGICAL FUNCTION" Cookson and Persell, *Preparing for Power,* 42.

34 "YOUTH FROM EVERY QUARTER" See Phillips Academy website at www.andover.edu.

34 HIS "SEVEN DEADLY SINS" Frederick S. Allis, *Youth from Every Quarter: A Bicentennial History of Phillips Academy* (Hanover, N.H., 1979), 21.

34 WHILE GROTON AND OTHER SCHOOLS Isaacson and Thomas, *Wise Men,* 47–48.

34 GROTON'S LATIN MOTTO TRANSLATED Ibid., 48.

34 "NOT FOR SELF" See "About Phillips Academy" at www.andover.edu.

34 "NOT WELL MEASURED IN ALL RESPECTS" Frederic Stott, "Counselor's Confidential Report," June 1938, Phillips Academy Files.

34 "PARENTS OF WEALTH AND SOCIAL POSITION" GHWB report card, 1938–39, with comments by Mr. Frederic Stott, Phillips Academy Files.

34 "MARKEDLY A GENTLEMAN" GHWB report card, 1939–40, with comments on back by "Leonard '39," Phillips Academy Files.

34 CHECKED INTO THE INFIRMARY FIVE TIMES Pieters, "Counselor's Confidential Report," June 20, 1940, Phillips Academy Files.

34 TRIED TO DO TOO MUCH Ibid.

35 CONTRACTED A STAPH INFECTION Author interview with GHWB. See also *LSY,* 41.

35 TO WITHDRAW HIM FROM SCHOOL GHWB report card, 1939–40, Phillips Academy Files.

35 "NOT A STRONG BOY" GHWB report card, 1940–41, Phillips Academy Files.

35 BUSH "HAS THE TYPICAL ATTITUDE" "Barrows," "Counselor's Confidential Report," May 5, 1941, Phillips Academy Files.

35 HE USED AN ANTI-SEMITIC EPITHET Author interview with GHWB.

35 THINKING OF THE MOMENT Ibid.

35 THE STORY OF BRUCE GELB *LSY,* 40–41; *NYT,* May 23, 1988; Schweizer and Schweizer, *Bushes,* 64.

36 "HE LOVES THE SCHOOL" Pieters, "Counselor's Confidential Report," June 20, 1940, Phillips Academy Files.

36 IDEAL MODEL OF AN ANDOVER MAN Claude Fuess, *Independent Schoolmaster* (Boston, 1952), 244–50.

36 STIMSON ADDRESSED THE COMMENCEMENT EXERCISES Ibid., 248.

36 "TODAY OUR WORLD" Ibid.

37 A LEGENDARILY DIFFICULT CLASS Allis, *Youth from Every Quarter,* 463–65; *LSY,* 39.

37 HE ALWAYS POLLED HIGH Allis, *Youth from Every Quarter,* 463–65.

37 HE RECALLED DARLING'S HISTORY 4 WARMLY Author interview with GHWB.

37 DARLING, SAID ONE ANDOVER ALUMNUS Allis, *Youth from Every Quarter,* 463–65.

37 DARLING TAUGHT HIS STUDENTS Arthur B. Darling, *Our Rising Empire, 1763–1803* (New Haven, Conn., 1940), 552, captures some of this thinking.

37 "AN EXTREMELY PLEASANT" "Yale Recommendation" for GHWB, May 27, 1941, Phillips Academy Files.

37 HE IS VERY MUCH OF A GENTLEMAN Ibid.

38 OVER CIGARS, A MAN FUESS RECALLED Fuess, *Independent Schoolmaster,* 250.

38 "It would be impossible" Ibid.

38 Fuess was interrupted Ibid.

38 moved over the Associated Press wire William Manchester, *The Glory and the Dream: A Narrative History of America, 1932–1972* (Boston, 1974), 256.

38 began breaking into John Toland, *The Rising Sun: The Decline and Fall of the Japanese Empire, 1936–1945* (New York, 1970), 225.

38 Bush was walking past Author interview with GHWB.

38 "My God" Ibid.

38 "After Pearl Harbor" Ibid.

38 "Dad had served" Ibid.

39 "righteous might" *NYT,* December 9, 1941.

39 There were air-raid drills on campus "Andover Undergoes First Wartime Trial Blackout: Project Declared a Success by the School Raid Directors," *The Phillipian,* January 31, 1942.

39 "a desperate life and death struggle" "The Basis," *The Phillipian,* January 10, 1942.

39 "If the government fails" Ibid.

39 he wanted to be a pilot Author interview with GHWB.

39 a small program at Andover Allis, *Youth from Every Quarter,* 14.

39 considered enlisting in Author interview with GHWB.

39 you "could get through" Ibid.

39 On the Tuesday after Pearl Harbor "Sir Herbert Ames Talks in G.W. on the R.C.A.F.: Describes Value, Setup of Canada's Air Service," *The Phillipian,* December 10, 1941.

39 an Andover alumnus who had enlisted in the RCAF "Former Andover Undergraduate Describes Life in the R.C.A.F.," *The Phillipian,* December 10, 1941. "It amazed me to find such a number of American lads in the R.C.A.F.," Clifford wrote. "I believe nearly 10 percent of enlistments are men from the states." (Ibid.)

39 a trip to New York for Fleet Week Author interview with GHWB.

39 seeking an appointment Ibid.

39 The sight of big ships Ibid.

39 The prewar military requirement Hyams, *Flight of the Avenger,* 32. See also *LF,* 30.

40 "I knew what I wanted to do" Author interview with GHWB.

40 He grew more serious GHWB, Record of Study, Phillips Academy, Andover, Massachusetts, March 26, 1942, bk. 12, Bush Family Scrapbooks, GBPL. Hereafter cited as Bush Scrapbooks.

FIVE: *That's Barbara Pierce*

41 I have never felt *ATB,* 30.

41 "a strikingly beautiful girl" Author interview with GHWB. For accounts of the dance, see *LF,* 31; *LSY,* 43–45; Schweizer and Schweizer, *Bushes,* 66–68; *BB,* 16–17.

41 at the Greenwich Country Club Author interview with BPB.

41 the band was playing Glenn Miller *LF,* 31.

41 Turning to a fellow guest Ibid.

41 in the pretty red-and-green holiday dress Ibid.

41 "That's Barbara Pierce" Author interview with GHWB.

41 Born in New York City in 1925 *BB,* 5, 13.

41 a tall, kind man Ibid., 7.

41 BEAUTIFUL BUT OCCASIONALLY DIFFICULT   Ibid., 9. "My mother ... often talked about 'when her ship came in' she was going to do such and such or buy such and such," Barbara wrote. "She was a lucky woman who had a husband who worshiped the ground she walked on, four loving children, and a world of friends. Her ship had come in—she just didn't know it. That is so sad." (Ibid.)

41 ARCHLY MONITORING BARBARA'S INTAKE   Ibid., 6–7.

41 DID BUSH WANT TO MEET HER?   LF, 31.

41 "I TOLD HIM THAT WAS"   Ibid.

41 "TOOK ME TO MEET"   BB, 16.

41 THEY DANCED BRIEFLY   Ibid.

41 FROM A FOX-TROT TO A WALTZ   LF, 31.

41 THE CONVERSATION LASTED FIFTEEN MINUTES   BB, 16.

41 ASKED BARBARA WHAT SHE WAS PLANNING   Ibid.

41 "THE NIFTIEST GIRL"   Hyams, *Flight of the Avenger*, 25.

42 "WE ALWAYS HAD TO GO"   BB, 16.

42 "THE NICEST, CUTEST"   Ibid.

42 "BY THE TIME I GOT UP"   Ibid., 16–17.

42 BUSH CONTRIVED TO SHOW UP   Ibid., 17.

42 BARBARA'S BROTHER JIM INTERRUPTED   Author interview with BPB.

42 "ARE YOU POPPY BUSH?"   Ibid.

42 JIM PIERCE HAD AN INVITATION   BB, 17.

42 "TO MY HORROR"   Ibid.

42 AFTER RYE WON THE SCRIMMAGE   Ibid.

42 BUSH MET THE PIERCE CLAN   Ibid.

42 THE BUSH FAMILY'S OLDSMOBILE   Ibid. See also Schweizer and Schweizer, *Bushes*, 68.

42 THAT HE HAD "BEGGED"   BB, 17.

42 "FOR YEARS HE HAS"   Ibid.

42 AT SPRING VACATION   Hyams, *Flight of the Avenger*, 27.

42 THEY DOUBLE-DATED TO A MOVIE   Ibid. See also Schweizer and Schweizer, *Bushes*, 68–69.

42 "DEAR POPPY"   Barbara Pierce to GHWB, bk. 12, Bush Scrapbooks.

43 OVER THE PROM WEEKEND   BB, 17.

43 KISSED HER ON THE CHEEK "IN FRONT"   Ibid., 18.

43 "I FLOATED INTO MY ROOM"   Ibid.

43 "PRESSY AND I SHARE A VIEW"   ATB, 30–31.

44 A LIGHTHEARTED BUT FAIRLY DETAILED ACCOUNTING   GHWB letter to author, April 28, 2009.

45 FUESS AND OTHERS ARGUED   Hyams, *Flight of the Avenger*, 31.

45 A FIERY HENRY STIMSON ECHOED   Author interview with GHWB.

45 PRESCOTT BUSH RAISED THE ISSUE   Ibid. See also Schweizer and Schweizer, *Bushes*, 69, and Hyams, *Flight of the Avenger*, 32.

45 THE ANSWER WAS NO   Author interview with GHWB.

45 HE WAS "HEADSTRONG"   Ibid.

45 FROM HIS ROOMS AT DAY HALL AT ANDOVER   Lieutenant F. T. Donahue, USNR, to GHWB, Andover, Massachusetts, May 18, 1942, bk. 12, Bush Scrapbooks. This letter was in reply to Bush's of the 15th. (Ibid.)

45 WITH A FOUNTAIN PEN, PRESCOTT HAD FILLED   Enlistment papers of GHWB, USNR, May 1942, bk. 12, Bush Scrapbooks.

45 THE CHIEF OF POLICE OF GREENWICH   John M. Gleason, Chief of Police, Greenwich, Connecticut, to GHWB, May 26, 1942, bk. 12, Bush Scrapbooks.

45 "ONE OF THE ABLEST BOYS"   Claude M. Fuess, "To Whom It May Concern," May 26, 1942, bk. 12, Bush Scrapbooks.

45 AFTER THE COMMENCEMENT EXERCISES   Notes on GHWB's World War II naval service provided by the GBPL archives staff to the author.

45 HE WAS MET THERE BY WALTER LEVERING   Walter Levering, Naval Aviation Cadet Selection Board, Boston, Massachusetts, to GHWB, June 17, 1942, bk. 12, Bush Scrapbooks.

45 BARBARA WAS WORKING THAT SUMMER   BB, 18.

46 AS A FAREWELL PRESENT BUSH BOUGHT HER   Hyams, *Flight of the Avenger*, 33.

46 SHE PINNED IT ON HER DRESS   Ibid.

46 WITH A GOLD BOW SET   Ibid.

46 "I DON'T BELIEVE"   ATB, 30.

46 HIS FATHER SAW HIM OFF   Author interview with GHWB. Also see Hyams, *Flight of the Avenger*, 33.

46 "SO OFF I WENT"   Author interview with GHWB.

Part II: War and Marriage, 1942 to 1948

48 MUM, IT'S A VERY FUNNY THING   ATB, 25.

48 BAR, YOU HAVE MADE MY LIFE   Ibid., 38.

SIX: *Off I Zoomed*

51 I KNEW, OF COURSE   BB, 19.

51 MOVED INTO 317 LEWIS HALL   GHWB to Claude M. Fuess, circa September 14, 1942, Phillips Academy Files.

51 THE CURRICULUM WAS A COMBINATION   Ibid. See also Hyams, *Flight of the Avenger*, 37; and *ATB*, 24.

51 CADETS ALSO HAD TO BE ABLE   Lou Grab, "Flyboy" (unpublished manuscript, March 4, 1997), 3, Miscellaneous Navy Materials, Post-Presidential Materials, GHWB Collection, GBPL.

51 "AT SOME MEALS"   GHWB to Claude M. Fuess, circa September 14, 1942, Phillips Academy Files.

51 "FELLOWS HAVE PASSED OUT"   Ibid.

51 FROM REVEILLE AT HALF PAST FIVE   Daily Routine: Monday Through Friday, U.S. Navy Preflight School, Chapel Hill, North Carolina, June 8, 1942, in bk. 12, Bush Scrapbooks.

51 "I HAVE MAINTAINED"   GHWB to Claude M. Fuess, circa September 14, 1942, Phillips Academy Files.

51 "I HAVE NEVER APPRECIATED"   ATB, 23–24.

51 THERE WAS A FIVE-HOUR HIKE   Ibid., 24.

52 "AFTER HAVING BEEN HERE"   Ibid.

52 A WALKER IN-LAW, GEORGE H. MEAD, JR.   Ibid., 25. See also "George H. Mead, Jr.," Military Times Hall of Valor, http://projects.militarytimes.com/citations-medals-awards/recipient.php?recipientid=8212.

52 ACCORDING TO THE POSTHUMOUS CITATION   "George H. Mead, Jr.," Military Times Hall of Valor, http://projects.militarytimes.com/citations-medals-awards/recipient.php?recipientid=8212.

52 ALONE, MEAD MADE HIS WAY   Ibid.

52 "He died the way" *ATB*, 25.

52 a "grand idea" Ibid., 26.

52 He met her at the Carolina Inn Ibid., 25–26. Mrs. Bush also recalled the day in an interview with the author.

52 "She looked too cute" *ATB*, 25.

52 admitted he was "self-conscious" *LF*, 31.

52 to "stretch the calendar" Ibid.

52 They had a sandwich *ATB*, 25.

52 "We laughed at everything" Ibid., 26.

52 He reported back to training Ibid.

52 Barbara boarded a bus Ibid.

52 "If she 'fluffed me off'" Ibid., 33.

52 In the autumn Bush headed north Hyams, *Flight of the Avenger*, 38.

52 a Boeing N2S-3 Stearman (a biplane) Ibid., 41.

52 noticed that his legs *ATB*, 26.

52 Taking off in foggy weather Ibid.

53 He successfully executed Ibid.

53 Roaring off into Ibid., 26–27.

53 "pretty rough" Ibid., 27.

53 The instructor, Ensign J. A. Boyle Ibid., 26–27.

53 "For a minute I was lost" Ibid., 27.

53 "Okay, take it up yourself" Ibid.

53 The blocks ("chocks") Ibid.

53 The Stearman aircraft, painted yellow Hyams, *Flight of the Avenger*, 41.

53 nicknamed "the Yellow Peril" Ibid.

53 "the Washing Machine" Ibid.

53 "Off I zoomed" *ATB*, 27.

53 "Everything seemed so free and easy" Ibid.

53 "it was the first time" Author interview with GHWB.

53 "I have gotten to know" *ATB*, 24.

54 "Most fellows here" Ibid., 31.

54 The Bushes sent him Ibid., 29.

54 She was also knitting him socks Ibid., 28.

54 On a night flight in Minneapolis Ibid., 31–32.

54 He was coming in to land Ibid., 32.

54 when his plane's wheels scraped a tree Ibid. See also Hyams, *Flight of the Avenger*, 43. As Bush himself described it to his mother, "Suddenly I heard this scraping noise—I had hit a tree—Well you can imagine my feelings." (*ATB*, 32.)

54 "I just thanked" *ATB*, 32.

54 Next stop: the Naval Air Station at Corpus Christi Hyams, *Flight of the Avenger*, 43–44.

54 became an officer of the United States Naval Reserve Ibid., 47; notes on GHWB's World War II naval training provided to the author by the archivists at the GBPL.

54 A navy band played Grab, "Flyboy," unpublished manuscript, 5.

54 His parents sent him Author interview with GHWB.

54 the youngest flying officer in the navy *ATB*, 34.

54 His assignment Hyams, *Flight of the Avenger*, 51–53, 71–73.

54 a seventeen-day leave *BB*, 19.

54 "I guess Mrs. Bush" Ibid.

55   REFERRED TO BARBARA AS "BOBSIE"   *ATB*, 24.

55   "I DO STILL *LOVE*"   Ibid., 33.

55   A THREE-AND-A-HALF-WEEK PERIOD   Ibid., 34.

55   "SCARING ME TO DEATH"   *BB*, 19.

55   THE GATHERING OF WALKERS AND BUSHES   Ibid.

55   "THE TEASING WAS ENORMOUS"   Ibid.

55   "WHEN THEY WERE COURTING"   Author interview with Jonathan Bush.

56   BARBARA BECAME "BAR"   *BB*, 19. BPB remembered Prescott Jr. as the coiner of "Bar" (Ibid.); Jonathan thought it was George. (Author interview with Jonathan Bush.)

56   BARBARA PIERCE AND POPPY BUSH BECAME ENGAGED   Author interview with BPB. See also *BB*, 20, and *LF*, 31.

56   "SO PERFECT A GIRL"   *ATB*, 24.

56   WHEN HE READ THE NEWS   Ibid., 38–39.

56   "I LOVE YOU, PRECIOUS"   Ibid.

56   HOW OFTEN I HAVE THOUGHT   Ibid.

56   THE TBF AVENGER TORPEDO BOMBER   Grab, "Flyboy," unpublished manuscript, 6. See also *LSY*, 47–48, and Hyams, *Flight of the Avenger*, 51–53.

56   THE PLANE WAS 40 FEET LONG   Grab, "Flyboy," unpublished manuscript, 4.

56   WITH HIS TRAINING GROUP   Ibid., 6.

57   AFTER FLORIDA, BUSH LEARNED   Notes on GHWB's World War II naval service provided to the author by the archivists at the GBPL; Hyams, *Flight of the Avenger*, 53. There were additional postings at Chincoteague, Virginia; Norfolk again; Hyannis, Massachusetts; and Charlestown, Rhode Island. (Ibid.) His northeastern postings put him in tantalizing proximity to Barbara, who was enrolled at Smith College in Northampton, Massachusetts. "I miss Bar something terrific but I suppose it's only natural," Bush wrote home. "It's really agony—so close and yet so far away." (*ATB*, 39.)

57   BUSH AND HIS SQUADRON WERE ASSIGNED   Hyams, *Flight of the Avenger*, 68.

57   DOROTHY HAD A MISSION OF HER OWN   Author interview with BPB.

57   MRS. BUSH ASKED WHAT KIND OF RING   Ibid. See also Hyams, *Flight of the Avenger*, 68–69. BPB wore the sapphire for the rest of her life. Holding up the ring—still on her finger—when asked about the train episode in 2014, she said wryly: "We've never had it appraised because we don't think it's real, but we don't care. We don't care. It's supposed to be a star sapphire, but nobody has ever seen the star." (Author interview with BPB.)

57   THAT COLD, CLOUDY WEDNESDAY   *The Philadelphia Inquirer*, December 15 and 16, 1943.

57   LUNCH ON THE DAY THEY SET OUT   Grab, "Flyboy," unpublished manuscript, 13. The *San Jacinto* had sailed to Norfolk from Philadelphia; the spaghetti-and-meatballs lunch was served on the day the ship left Norfolk, bound for the Pacific. (Ibid.)

57   "WE HAD A COMPLETE PUKE-UP"   Ibid.

57   AT A STOP AT TRINIDAD   Ibid., 11.

57   THROUGH THE PANAMA CANAL   Notes on GHWB's World War II naval service provided to the GBPL archives staff to the author.

57   BUSH TOOK SOME TIME   Ibid., 13.

57   THIRTY-ONE DAYS LATER   Ibid.

SEVEN: *I Wanted to Finish My Mission*

58   MY GOD, THIS THING   Author interview with GHWB.

58   THE TARGET WAS WAKE ISLAND   Hyams, *Flight of the Avenger*, 76.

58   WAKE HAD BEEN HOME   Samuel Eliot Morison, *The Two Ocean War: A Short History of the United States Navy in the Second World War* (Boston, 1963), 137–38.

58   HIS CREWMEN WERE   Hyams, *Flight of the Avenger*, 7–9, 76.

58   "WE WERE ALL TENSE"   Ibid., 76.

58   "I DON'T THINK THERE WAS ANY TIME"   Ibid.

58   BUSH EXECUTED A DANGEROUSLY DIFFICULT   Ibid, 82–85. See also *ATB*, 44. According to information provided to the author by Robert Holzweiss at the GBPL, Bush lost three planes in his naval career. The *Bar I*, as Bush called it, crashed during training at Hyannis when the landing gear collapsed on November 1, 1943; *Bar II* was lost at sea due to combat damage in June 1944; and *Barbara III*—he expanded the name from "Bar"—was lost at Chichi-Jima. (Author correspondence with Robert Holzweiss, GBPL.)

58   HE PLAYED GAMES—USUALLY ACEY-DEUCEY   Grab, "Flyboy," unpublished manuscript, 10. See also Hyams, *Flight of the Avenger*, 93–94.

58   "GEDUNKS," THE TERM USED ON BOARD   Grab, "Flyboy," unpublished manuscript, 10.

58   HE DOLED OUT NICKNAMES   Hyams, *Flight of the Avenger*, 3.

58   HE WAS CALLED *GEORGEHERBERTWALKERBUSH*   Ibid., 96.

58   THE WIDESPREAD USE OF "POP"   GHWB to "Mom and Dad," October 11[, 1944], October 1944, World War II Correspondence, Personal Papers, GHWB Collection, GBPL.

59   IN THE WARDROOM   Grab, "Flyboy," unpublished manuscript, 10.

59   HE READ BOOKS HIS MOTHER   *ATB*, 41.

59   BECOMING "PRETTY MUCH INTERESTED IN THAT END"   Ibid.

59   PLAYED VOLLEYBALL   Hyams, *Flight of the Avenger*, 93.

59   HE BELLYACHED ABOUT THE FOOD   *ATB*, 48.

59   HE WOULD LIE IN HIS BUNK   Ibid., 41–42.

59   BUSH ALWAYS REMEMBERED THE FIRST SIGHT   Hyams, *Flight of the Avenger*, 76.

59   "IT IS QUITE A FEELING"   *ATB*, 42; Ibid., 76–77.

59   HAD DISAPPEARED WITH TWO CREWMEN   Hyams, *Flight of the Avenger*, 76; *ATB*, 47.

59   "HAD JUST BECOME A FATHER"   *ATB*, 42.

59   BUSH CRIED IN GRIEF   Hyams, *Flight of the Avenger*, 77.

59   ANOTHER PILOT, ROLAND R. "DICK" HOULE   Ibid., 98.

59   "I GET SUCH A KICK OUT OF BUCK"   *ATB*, 49.

59   A STRIKE CODE-NAMED "BAKER"   Hyams, *Flight of the Avenger*, 104. My account of Bush and Chichi-Jima is drawn from the detailed version in Hyams, *Flight of the Avenger*; *LF*, 34–40; Cramer, *What It Takes*, 80–94; GHWB's contemporaneous letters about the episode; and my interviews with GHWB, among other sources.

59   TO DESTROY A RADIO TOWER   Hyams, *Flight of the Avenger*, 1. See also *LF*, 35–36. See also Chester Hearn, *Sorties Into Hell: The Hidden War on Chichi Jima* (Westport, Conn., 2003), 10–11.

60   EACH OF THE PLANES   Hyams, *Flight of the Avenger*, 12.

60   THE SQUADRON WAS BRIEFED AGAIN   *LF*, 34.

60   A LIEUTENANT JUNIOR GRADE   *ATB*, 49–52. There are differing accounts of how Ted White came to be on Bush's plane that day. In his contemporaneous correspondence, Bush reported that he had asked White. (Ibid.) In his 1987 autobiography, Bush recalled that White had approached him about the flight, not the other way around. (*LF*, 35.) In *Flight of the Avenger*, which was heavily drawn from Bush's recollections and those of his comrades, Joe Hyams also has White asking to fly that day. (*Flight of the Avenger*, 104–5.)

60   WHITE HAD LONG HOPED TO SEE   Hyams, *Flight of the Avenger*, 105.

638   *Notes*

60 PRESCOTT BUSH KNEW WHITE'S FATHER   Author interview with GHWB. See also Hyams, *Flight of the Avenger*, 104–5, and *LF*, 35.

60 THE SQUADRON COMMANDER AGREED   *LF*, 35.

60 LEE NADEAU SURRENDERED HIS TURRET AS GUNNER   Ibid.

60 THERE WERE JOKES   *ATB*, 49–50.

60 AT A QUARTER AFTER SEVEN   *LF*, 35.

60 THE WEATHER, BUSH RECALLED, WAS CLEAR   Ibid.

60 A LITTLE MORE THAN AN HOUR   Ibid. See also Hyams, *Flight of the Avenger*, 106.

60 THE JAPANESE GUNS FILLED THE AIR   Author interview with GHWB.

60 FLYING AT A THIRTY-FIVE-DEGREE ANGLE   *LF*, 36.

60 THE PLANE WAS HIT   Ibid.

60 AS THE AVENGER JOLTED FORWARD   Ibid.

60 SMOKE FILLED THE COCKPIT   *ATB*, 50.

60 FLAMES RACED ALONG THE WINGS   Author interview with GHWB.

60 "MY GOD"   Ibid.

60 BUSH RADIOED WHITE AND DELANEY   *ATB*, 50.

60 THE AVENGER, HE KNEW, "WAS GOING DOWN"   Author interview with GHWB.

60 CHOKING ON THE SMOKE   Ibid. See also *ATB*, 50.

60 THIS TIME HE SCORED   Hyams, *Flight of the Avenger*, 107.

60 "I REALIZED I COULDN'T KEEP"   Author interview with GHWB.

60 "HIT THE SILK!"   Hyams, *Flight of the Avenger*, 107.

60 HE COULD NOT BE SURE   *ATB*, 50.

60 HE LOOKED BACK   Ibid.

60 "I TURNED THE PLANE"   Author interview with GHWB.

61 "AFTER THAT I STRAIGHTENED UP"   *ATB*, 50.

61 OTHER SQUADRON FLIERS ON THE MISSION   Hyams, *Flight of the Avenger*, 107.

61 HIS OWN PARACHUTE STRAPS FASTENED   Author interview with GHWB. See also *ATB*, 50.

61 HIS HATCH OPENED   *ATB*, 50.

61 BUSH STRUGGLED UP AND OUT OF THE COCKPIT   Ibid. "I stuck my head out first and the old wind really blew me the rest of the way out," Bush told his parents. (Ibid.) See also Hyams, *Flight of the Avenger*, 108.

61 PROPELLING HIM BACKWARD   *ATB*, 50. See also Hyams, *Flight of the Avenger*, 108.

61 GASHED HIS HEAD AND BRUISED HIS EYE   *ATB*, 50.

61 BUSH PULLED HIS RIP CORD TOO SOON   Ibid.

61 SEVERAL PANELS OF THE SILK CHUTE   Ibid.

61 AT ABOUT TWO THOUSAND FEET   Hyams, *Flight of the Avenger*, 108.

61 HE SAW HIS PLANE CRASH INTO THE OCEAN   *ATB*, 50.

61 HE UNFASTENED THE BUCKLES   Hyams, *Flight of the Avenger*, 108.

61 BUSH PLUNGED DEEP INTO THE OCEAN   *ATB*, 50. But not so deep, he noted, "to notice any pressure or anything." (Ibid.)

61 GULPING DOWN BITTER SALT WATER   *LF*, 37–38.

61 KICKING OFF HIS SHOES   Hyams, *Flight of the Avenger*, 108.

61 INFLATING HIS LIFE JACKET—WHAT NAVY MEN CALLED A "MAE WEST"   *ATB*, 51.

61 HIS KHAKI FLIGHT SUIT WAS SOAKED AND HEAVY   Hyams, *Flight of the Avenger*, 108.

61 SAW THE SQUADRON'S COMMANDER, DON MELVIN, SIGNAL THE LOCATION   *ATB*, 50–51; see also *LF*, 37. Hyams, *Flight of the Avenger*, 108–9, reports that a Hellcat first signaled the raft location, but Bush's contemporaneous correspondence credits Melvin.

61 HAD FALLEN FROM BUSH'S LIFE JACKET   *ATB*, 50.

61 BUSH SWAM THE FIFTY FEET   Hyams, *Flight of the Avenger*, 109.

61 THE WIND WAS BLOWING BACK   ATB, 50–51. Hearn, *Sorties into Hell*, is a comprehensive account of the war crimes committed on Chichi-Jima.

61 THERE WAS NO PADDLE   Hyams, *Flight of the Avenger*, 109.

61 PADDLED WITH HIS ARMS   LF, 37.

61 SUMMONED THE USS *FINBACK*   Hyams, *Flight of the Avenger*, 109.

61 WHAT WAS KNOWN AS "LIFEGUARD DUTY"   Ibid.

61 THE SUBMARINE WAS TEN MILES AWAY   Ibid.

61 STUNG BY A PORTUGUESE MAN-OF-WAR   LF, 37.

61 DOUG WEST DROPPED DOWN   Hyams, *Flight of the Avenger*, 109. See also LF, 37.

61 BUSH APPLIED MERCUROCHROME   Ibid.

61 BUSH SPRINKLED DYE MARKER   ATB, 51.

62 PROMPTING WEST TO OPEN FIRE   Hyams, *Flight of the Avenger*, 115.

62 "FOR A WHILE THERE"   Author interview with GHWB.

62 VOMIT OVER THE SIDE   LF, 37–38.

62 BUSH SENSED THAT WHITE AND DELANEY HAD NOT MADE IT   ATB, 51.

62 BUSH SAT IN THE RAFT IN TEARS   Ibid. "I'm afraid I was pretty much of a sissy about it cause I sat in my raft and sobbed for awhile," Bush wrote his parents. (Ibid.)

62 HE THOUGHT OF DELANEY AND OF WHITE, OF BARBARA   Author interview with GHWB; ATB, 52.

62 BUSH HEARD THE ZOOMING   ATB, 51.

62 TIPPING THEIR WINGS   Ibid.

62 THE *FINBACK* WAS COMMANDED   Hyams, *Flight of the Avenger*, 114–15, 121.

62 "I THOUGHT MAYBE"   Author interview with GHWB.

62 FOUR ENLISTED MEN CAME OUT   Hyams, *Flight of the Avenger*, 118.

62 CHIEF PETTY OFFICER RALPH ADAMS SWAM   Ibid.

62 "WELCOME ABOARD, SIR"   Ibid., 118–19. See also LF, 38–39. Footage of GHWB's rescue was taken by Ensign Bill Edward of the USS *Finback*.

62 IT WAS FOUR MINUTES SHY OF NOON   Hyams, *Flight of the Avenger*, 119.

62 SHOT HIS RAFT TO PIECES   Ibid.

62 BUSH'S FIRST PRIORITY   Ibid.

62 "AND BELIEVED THAT THEY HAD JUMPED"   Ibid.; ATB, 52.

63 "ALL IN ALL"   ATB, 52.

63 "MY HEART ACHES"   Ibid., 51–52.

63 HE HAD BARELY ESCAPED DEATH   LF, 32.

63 LATER LEARNED THAT CHICHI-JIMA   Ibid. See also Hearn, *Sorties into Hell*.

63 "IT WORRIES ME—IT TERRIFIES ME"   Author interview with GHWB.

63 "DID I DO ENOUGH"   Ibid. To Joe Hyams, Bush recalled: "I had this very deep and profound gratitude and a sense of wonder. Sometimes when there is a disaster, people will pray, 'Why me?' In an opposite way I had the same question: why had I been spared, and what did God have in store for me?" (Hyams, *Flight of the Avenger*, 132.)

63 "MY MOTHER AND DAD"   Author interview with GHWB.

63 "I TRY TO THINK ABOUT IT"   GHWB to "Dear Mum and Dad," September 6 [, 1944], George Bush Material, WWII Correspondence, VIC.

63 ONE OFFICER, LIEUTENANT GERALDYN REDMOND, WROTE HOME   Norman K. Toerge to Prescott S. Bush, October 11, 1944, George Bush Material, WWII Correspondence, VIC.

64 "IT WAS TRANSFORMING"   Author interview with GHWB.

64 A SUBMARINE CREATED   I am indebted to Hyams, *Flight of the Avenger*, 125–31, for details about Bush's time on the *Finback*.

64 A DIFFERENT KIND OF STRESS   GHWB to "Dear Mum and Dad," September 16, 1944, World War II Correspondence, GHWB Personal Papers, GBPL.

64 BUSH STOOD WATCHES   Ibid.

64 THE FOOD WAS EXCELLENT   Ibid.

65 HIS EYE WAS HEALED   GHWB to "Dear Mum and Dad," September 16, 1944, GHWB Personal Papers, GBPL.

65 HE PITCHED IN AS A CENSOR   Hyams, *Flight of the Avenger*, 133. Bush also scanned other men's letters on the *San Jacinto*, an experience he credited with giving him insights into the passions and problems of others, a point he made to Tom Brokaw many years later. For Bush's letter to Brokaw, see *ATB*, 611–14.

65 ON THE *FINBACK* HE READ   GHWB to "Dear Mum and Dad," September 16, 1944, GHWB Personal Papers, GBPL.

65 AFTER A MONTH'S STAY   *ATB*, 54–55.

65 "I DIDN'T WANT TO GO HOME"   Author interview with GHWB.

65 THE TEXAS FLAG WAS FLYING   "A Short History of the *San Jacinto*: May 3, 1944–September 14, 1945," George Bush WWII Binder, USS *San Jacinto*, Navy File, Don Rhodes Collection, GBPL.

65 "ALL DURING THE TIME"   GHWB to "Dear Mum and Dad," November 3[, 1944], George Bush Material, WWII Correspondence, VIC.

65 "HE OFFERED ME A JOB"   Ibid.

65 "BY THE TIME THIS GETS TO YOU"   Ibid.

65 "I AM A LITTLE ANXIOUS"   Ibid.

65 "I THINK YOU HAD BETTER NOT MENTION"   GHWB to "Dear Mum and Dad," September 27[, 1944], World War II Correspondence, GHWB Personal Papers, GBPL.

66 A LETTER ARRIVED FROM PROVIDENCE, RHODE ISLAND   Hyams, *Flight of the Avenger*, 143–44. The Bushes stayed in touch with the Delaneys through the years; in his old age, Bush said, "They still feel the horror of this." (Author interview with GHWB.)

66 "NO, NOT DREAMING"   Author interview with GHWB.

66 HE WAS AWARDED   Hyams, *Flight of the Avenger*, 137.

66 "I FINISHED THE BOMBING RUN"   Author interview with GHWB.

66 BUSH FLEW A COMBAT MISSION OVER MANILA BAY   Hyams, *Flight of the Avenger*, 144–46.

66 "WELL . . . WE MADE IT"   Ibid., 146.

66 BY LATE NOVEMBER 1944   Grab, "Flyboy," unpublished manuscript, 19.

67 FINDING TRANSPORTATION TO SAN DIEGO   Ibid.

67 HE KNEW HE SOON WOULD BE BACK IN THE PACIFIC   *LF*, 41. Bush always believed that service at sea, however difficult, was vastly preferable, on a personal basis, to service in ground forces. "This was a very easy war compared to ground combat," Bush recalled of his service. "You weren't up close and personal with the enemy. You didn't have to see them in the eyeballs before you shot him, or he shot you. It was impersonal. You'd fly, and you'd land back on the carrier and you'd go in and you'd have clean sheets and nice milkshakes, whereas the marines on these islands were slogging through the dirt. So we were better off. We had a better deal in the sense of suffering and hardship. But it's an experience that has stayed with me and will stay with me forever." (Author interview with GHWB.)

EIGHT: *Life Lay Ahead of Us*

68 V-J DAY ARRIVED   *BB*, 25.

68 I'LL ALWAYS WONDER   Author interview with GHWB.

68   ELABORATELY DECORATED FOR CHRISTMAS   Author interview with BPB.

68   WHEN THE TELEPHONE RANG   Ibid.

68   WITHIN AN HOUR   Ibid.

68   ON A COLD SATURDAY   *LSY,* 61; *BB,* 23. Barbara remembered that the day was "lovely, [and] cold." (Ibid.) For my details of the wedding, I drew on *NYT,* January 7, 1945; *LSY,* 61; *BB,* 23; author interview with BPB; Green, *George Bush,* 40; Hyams, *Flight of the Avenger,* 150–51.

68   THE FIRST PRESBYTERIAN CHURCH   *BB,* 23.

68   "A GOWN OF IVORY SATIN"   *NYT,* January 7, 1945; *LSY,* 61.

68   WORE HIS DRESS BLUE   *LSY,* 61; Green, *George Bush,* 40; Hyams, *Flight of the Avenger,* 150.

68   GEORGE'S SISTER, NANCY   *NYT,* January 7, 1945.

68   SERVED AS BEST MAN   Ibid.

68   THE PIERCES HOSTED A LARGE RECEPTION   *LSY,* 61.

68   "A PARTY OF WOMEN"   Author interview with BPB.

68   THERE THE NEWLYWEDS WATCHED   *BB,* 23.

68   TOOK A SLEEPER TRAIN DOWN THE EAST COAST   Ibid.

68   JUST ABOUT THE ONLY YOUNG COUPLE THERE   Author interview with BPB.

69   DANCE LESSONS, WHICH BORED BUSH   Ibid.

69   AS PART OF A NEW COMBAT SQUADRON   Hyams, *Flight of the Avenger,* 152. See also *BB,* 23.

69   AT NAVAL AIR STATION GROSSE ILE IN MICHIGAN   *ATB,* 57.

69   "IT IS SORT OF A"   Ibid., 58.

69   IN THE LEWISTON-AUBURN AREA   Notes on GHWB's World War II naval training provided by the GBPL archives staff to the author.

69   "I REMEMBER CRYING"   Author interview with GHWB.

69   "WE WERE SICK"   *BB,* 24.

69   BUSH WAS SCHEDULED TO REPORT   Gar Hole, Stan Butchard, Lou Grab, Jack Guy, "George Bush Was No 'Wimp,' Say His Combat Buddies," *Washington Times,* March 28, 1997, Miscellaneous Navy Materials, Post-Presidential Materials, GHWB Collection, GBPL.

69   "EVERYTHING I'D EXPERIENCED"   *LF,* 41.

69   AT TEN P.M. EASTERN TIME   *Public Papers of the Presidents of the United States: Harry S. Truman, 1945* (Washington, D.C., 1961), 254–57.

69   "WITHIN MINUTES OUR NEIGHBORHOOD"   *LF,* 41.

69   "LOUD, WILD, AND FAIRLY LIQUID"   *BB,* 25.

70   THE BUSHES SLIPPED OFF   *LF,* 41.

70   ONE IMAGE FROM THE WAR   Ibid., 34.

70   "JUST A FEW YARDS"   Ibid.

70   "I'LL ALWAYS WONDER"   Author interview with GHWB.

70   ON A SUMMER DAY IN 1945   Author interview with William T. "Bucky" Bush.

70   "VERY SKINNY"   Ibid.

70   "I THOUGHT HE'D CONQUERED"   Ibid.

70   DISCHARGED FROM ACTIVE DUTY   Notes on GHWB's World War II naval service provided by the GBPL archives staff to the author.

70   HE HAD SERVED   Ibid.; Naftali, *GHWB,* 9.

70   BUSH WAS DECORATED   Notes on military awards of GHWB provided by the GBPL archives staff to the author.

71   "WE WERE STILL YOUNG"   *LF,* 41.

71   YALE ENROLLED 8,500 MEN   Emerson Stone, "The Way We Were in 'Poppy's' Days," *Yale Alumni Magazine,* February 1989, 44.

71 WHEN BUSH MATRICULATED   Ibid.

71 HE HAD TOYED WITH THE IDEA OF SKIPPING YALE   *ATB*, 46.

71 UNCLE HERBIE WALKER   Author interview with GHWB.

71 BUSH'S FATHER, WHO STRONGLY BELIEVED   *ATB*, 48.

71 ARMY AND NAVY UNITS WERE BILLETED   Stone, "Way We Were in 'Poppy's' Days," 45.

71 ROWS OF QUONSET HUTS WERE BUILT   Ibid.

71 LATER DESCRIBED AS THE "DE RIGUEUR . . . MARK"   Ibid, 44.

71 "SOME OF US ARE TOTTERING VETERANS"   "Social History," in *1948 Class Book Yale University*, ed. Thomas Frank Strook (New Haven, Conn., 1948), 49.

72 THAT OF HIS FATHER   *LF*, 43–44.

72 THE USUAL UNDERGRADUATE GRIPES   "Social History," 49.

72 IN TWO AND A HALF YEARS   *ATB*, 61; Naftali, *GHWB*, 9–10, is a useful summary of GHWB's Yale career.

72 "I WAS MAJORING"   *LF*, 44.

72 THERE WAS F.S.C. NORTHROP   *NYT*, May 28, 1989.

72 SAMUEL HEMINGWAY IN SHAKESPEARE   Stone, "Way We Were in 'Poppy's' Days," 46.

72 PAUL HINDEMITH IN MUSIC   Ibid.

72 HISTORY OF ART 36, A CLASS IN AMERICAN FURNITURE   *NYT*, May 28, 1989; *BB*, 26.

72 BUSH TOOK FRENCH   *NYT*, May 28, 1989.

72 HE LETTERED IN SOCCER   "Biography of George Bush, Yale Class of 1948," Yale Political Union, March 24, 1980.

72 HE WAS SECRETARY OF   "Biography of George Bush, Yale Class of 1948."

72 SERVING BRIEFLY AS CHAPTER PRESIDENT   *BB*, 26.

72 HE WON A FABLED HONOR   Ibid.

72 THE "LAST MAN TAPPED"   Author interview with GHWB.

72 THE SECRET SOCIETY SKULL AND BONES   Isaacson and Thomas, *Wise Men*, 81–82. See also Alexandra Robbins, *Secrets of the Tomb: Skull and Bones, the Ivy League, and the Hidden Paths of Power* (Boston, 2002).

73 BUSH'S SUCCESS AT YALE   In an introduction to a 1968 edition of *Stover at Yale*, Owen Johnson's portrait of undergraduate life in the early years of the twentieth century, Kingman Brewster, Jr., the Yale president from 1963 to 1977, wrote that "campus success was, by and large, in fact as well as feeling, more related to effort and accomplishment and contribution to the College than it was to inherited status or to the machinations of a campus-wide political 'system.' It was a pyramid, with Skull and Bones sitting aperch the top. But it was a pyramid of merit to a remarkable extent and reward did not exclude the rebel or guarantee the legacy." (Owen Johnson, *Stover at Yale* [New York, 1968], vi.)

73 "DIDN'T CARE WHAT WAS GOING ON"   *LF*, 44.

73 WILLIAM F. BUCKLEY, JR., WAS TWO YEARS BEHIND   Ibid.

73 IN NEW HAVEN, THE BUSHES FIRST LIVED   *BB*, 26.

73 BARBARA RECALLED THAT IT TOOK   Ibid.

73 A STAY ON EDWARDS STREET   Ibid., 27.

73 THEY MOVED INTO 37 HILLHOUSE AVENUE   *LF*, 44.

73 THE HILLHOUSE ADDRESS WAS FILLED   *BB*, 27–28. See also *LF*, 43–44.

73 DURING HIS FIRST YEAR   "Biography of George Bush, Yale Class of 1948"; *BB*, 27.

74 SHE KEPT SCORE AT YALE FIELD   *BB*, 27.

74 SHE GAINED SIXTY POUNDS   Ibid.

74 "THE BABY DID NOT COME"   Ibid.

74 ETHAN ALLEN, THE YALE BASEBALL COACH   Ibid.

74 "I WAS HUGE" Ibid.

74 AT GRACE–NEW HAVEN COMMUNITY HOSPITAL Author interview with BPB.

74 BARBARA GAVE BIRTH TO THEIR FIRST CHILD *BB*, 27.

74 "GEORGE'S MOTHER FINALLY" Ibid.

74 THE YOUNG PARENTS WERE SMITTEN Ibid.

74 "LOOKED UP TO" *LF*, 44.

74 HISTORIC STREAK OF PLAYING https://espn.go.com/sportscentury/features/000142 04.html.

74 ON THE AFTERNOON OF YALE'S 1948 HOME GAME "Crowd Chokes Up as Babe Hits to the Heart at Yale Where He Smacked Longest Homer," New Haven, CT, June 5, [1948,] Bush Family Scrapbooks, GBPL.

74 AS CAPTAIN, BUSH WAS TASKED Ibid · *LF*, 44–45.

74 IT HAD RAINED ALL MORNING "Crowd Chokes Up as Babe Hits to the Heart at Yale Where He Smacked Longest Homer," New Haven, CT, June 5, [1948], Bush Family Scrapbooks, GBPL.

74 STRICKEN WITH THE CANCER *LF*, 44–45.

74 "NOTHING FLASHY" Ibid., 44.

75 "DEAR SIR" Ibid., 42–43.

75 "SWINGING DEFENSIVELY" Ibid.

75 "NO RISK, NO GAIN" Ibid.

75 BUSH WAS HITTING .280 Ibid.

75 COLLEGE WORLD SERIES Ibid., 45.

76 BUSH WEIGHED APPLYING FOR A RHODES SCHOLARSHIP Ibid., 46.

76 (THOUGH THERE WERE FAMILY MEANS) Author interviews with GHWB and BPB.

76 HE INTERVIEWED WITH A RECRUITER Author interview with BPB.

76 HE WAS OFFERED, BUT DECLINED G. V. Cowper, Jr., Advertising Manager, Bates Fabrics, Inc., New York, March 1, 1948, and March 10, 1948, Bush, Personal File: Correspondence, Miscellaneous Business (1950 [1948–50]), ZAP.

76 BARBARA AND GEORGE WERE INTRIGUED Author interview with GHWB. See also *LF*, 22.

76 THEY HAD ROMANTIC VISIONS *LF*, 22.

76 "GEORGE AND BARBARA FARMS" Ibid., 23. See also *BB*, 30.

76 IN THIS SEASON OF UNCERTAINTY *ATB*, 61–63.

76 "I CAN'T IMAGINE" Ibid., 61–62. Bush added: "I have never even thought about the cloth—only a tablecloth or a loincloth." (Ibid.)

76 HE WAS IN A CANDID, EVEN CONFESSIONAL Ibid., 62–63.

77 HE HAD THOUGHT OF TEACHING Ibid., 62.

77 "I AM NOT SURE I WANT TO CAPITALIZE" Ibid.

77 FRIEND AND ASSOCIATE HENRY NEIL MALLON *LF*, 46–47. See also *BB*, 31, and Herskowitz, *Duty, Honor, Country*, 87.

77 "UNCLE NEIL" *BB*, 31.

77 OF AVERAGE HEIGHT (FIVE FOOT NINE) Ibid.

77 HE ENDEARED HIMSELF TO THE CHILDREN Ibid.

77 "WHAT YOU NEED TO DO" *LF*, 46.

77 "TEXAS WOULD BE NEW" *ATB*, 62–63.

78 HAD "GREAT APPEAL" Ibid., 63.

78 A TWO-DOOR RED STUDEBAKER *BB*, 31.

78 THEY WOULD FOLLOW BY PLANE Ibid., 32.

Part III: *Texas and Tragedy, 1948 to 1966*

81 I HAVE SOME BAD NEWS   Author interview with GHWB.

NINE: *Who Had Ever Heard of Odessa, Texas?*

83 As far as my mother   *BB,* 32.
83 We all just wanted   *LF,* 58.
83 All Bush really knew   Author interview with GHWB.
83 from Randolph Scott movies   *LF,* 47.
83 Stopping for lunch   Ibid.
83 "Chicken-fried steak"   Ibid.
83 Ten minutes later   Ibid., 47–48.
83 Odessa a sleepy one   Ibid., 48.
83 passing derrick after derrick   Ibid.
83 the small tin-roofed Ideco store   Ibid.
83 "Ideco" was shorthand for   *LSY,* 71.
83 "You'll be an equipment clerk"   *LF,* 47; *LSY,* 73.
83 monthly salary was $375   *LSY,* 73.
83 rented half of a duplex   *BB,* 32; *LSY,* 72–73.
83 the unpaved East Seventh Street   Author interview with BPB.
84 "a whole new"   *BB,* 32.
84 "Who had ever heard"   Ibid.
84 The Bushes' fellow renters   Ibid. See also *ATB,* 63; *LSY,* 73.
84 Reading trade journals   *ATB,* 63–64, 66.
84 Bush and Hugh Evans   *LF,* 19–21.
84 "supposed to spruce up"   Ibid., 20.
84 The savvy Evans   Ibid.
84 "what the thermometer read"   Ibid.
84 "George, would you mind"   Ibid., 21.
84 "Just tell me," he said   Ibid.
84 Barbara suffered a miscarriage   *ATB,* 65.
85 Her life in particular revolved around Georgie's   BPB diary and letters, Fall 1948.
85 "coughed until his little body"   Ibid.
85 After a large shot of penicillin   *ATB,* 64–65.
85 listening to Mother Goose   BPB diary and letters, Fall 1948.
85 "Whenever I come home"   *ATB,* 64.
85 Writing her parents to thank them   BPB diary and letters, Fall 1948.
85 "G.W.B. has a wee bit"   Ibid.
85 Bush shot doves   Ibid.
85 There were football games   Ibid.
85 "She is something, Mum"   *ATB,* 65.
85 Barbara got a library card   BPB diary and letters, Fall 1948.
86 Her mother-in-law sent her   Ibid.
86 The young couple read *Time*   Ibid.
86 By Christmas, Bush had moved the family   *BB,* 35; *LSY,* 73.
86 their own bath   *BB,* 35.
86 On Christmas Eve, Bush was assigned   *LF,* 50–51.
86 "the way Barbara told the story"   Ibid., 51.

86 Bush's parents flew down   *ATB*, 66.
86 cleaning the house   Author interview with BPB.
86 "I have to get this in the mail"   BPB diary and letters, Fall 1949.
86 "The job continues"   *ATB*, 66–67.
86 "I have in the back of my mind"   Ibid., 67. The original letter is GHWB to FitzGerald Bemiss, January 11, 1949, Correspondence Between George Bush and FitzGerald Bemiss, 1943–51, FITZ.
86 In April 1949, the Bushes left Texas   *BB*, 35.
86 Bush worked   *ATB*, 68–69; *LSY*, 73.
87 "When I pick him up at work"   BPB diary and letters, 1949–52.
87 at 624 South Santa Fe in Compton   Ibid.
87 word of a terrible accident   *BB*, 36.
87 Marvin Pierce had been driving   *NYT*, September 24, 1949. My account is drawn from the *NYT*, as well as the *Chicago Daily Tribune*, September 24, 1949.
87 an English bone china cup of coffee   *NYT*, September 24, 1949.
87 Noticing that it was about to spill   Ibid.
87 swerved left and fell one hundred feet down   Ibid.
87 her father told her not to come east   *BB*, 36.
87 "He did not want"   Ibid.
87 Pauline Robinson Bush was born   Ibid., 36–37.
88 "Beautiful hazel eyes"   *LF*, 56.
88 Ideco wanted him back   Ibid. See also *BB*, 37.
88 to "learn the oil business and make money"   *LF*, 21.
88 "You've come to the wrong town"   Ibid.
88 "We all just wanted"   Ibid., 58.
88 Bush received a letter from 59 Wall Street   Tom McCance to GHWB, May 4, 1950, and June 29, 1950; and GHWB to Tom McCance, June 25, 1950, Bush, Personal File: Correspondence, Personal (General: Through December 1950), ZAP.
88 thinking of "nothing else"   *ATB*, 69.
88 Bush went to New York   Ibid.
88 It was not Prescott's first political twitch   PSB, COHC, 49–50; 53–54.
89 Samuel F. Pryor, a top Pan Am executive   See obituaries in *NYT*, September 19, 1985, and *LAT*, September 20, 1985.
89 might like to run   PSB, COHC, 53–54.
89 The partnership did not embrace   Ibid.
89 becoming the Republicans' Connecticut finance chairman   Obituary of Prescott Bush, *NYT*, October 9, 1972.
89 In the summer of 1949   PSB, COHC, 52.
89 composed a song   "Bush for Senator," Correspondence Between Prescott S. Bush and Charles M. Spofford 1950–59, and Miscellaneous Material About Prescott S. Bush, GHWB Post-Presidential Materials, GBPL.
89 On the Sunday before the election   Weisberg, *Bush Tragedy*, 20. Prescott Bush's account of the Pearson/birth control episode can be found at PSB, COHC, 62–64.
89 pamphlets appeared urging Roman Catholic voters   Herskowitz, *Duty, Honor, Country*, 80–81. See also *NYT*, November 6, 1988.
90 Bush denied being president   Herskowitz, *Duty, Honor, Country*, 81. He was, rather, the treasurer of the 1947 fund drive for the "First Nationwide Planned Parenthood Campaign—1947." His name appeared on the organization's letterhead on a January 8, 1947, announcement of the national drive signed by Margaret Sanger. See file on Prescott Bush in the Drew Pearson Papers, Lyndon B. Johnson Presidential Library.

90　ONE OF TWO STATES IN THE UNION　*NYT*, December 28, 1947, and April 12, 1951.

90　BUSH LOST, NARROWLY　Ibid., November 9, 1950.

90　"WE FELT TERRIBLY"　*ATB*, 70.

TEN: *I Push It Away, Push It Back*

91　WE CAN'T TOUCH HER　*ATB*, 82.

91　TIME AFTER TIME　*BB*, 46.

91　BUSH TOLD HIS IDECO BOSSES　GHWB to R. L. Brummage, April 22, 1950, JB.

91　AFTER STAYS AT KINGSWAY COURTS　*BB*, 37; GHWB to R. L. Brummage, May 19, 1950, JB.

91　"EASTER EGG ROW"　*LF*, 58.

91　THE PRICE WAS $7,500　Ibid.

91　IN MIDLAND THERE WERE SANDSTORMS　*LSY*, 78.

91　WHICH MEANT A LOT OF YOUNG FAMILIES　*LF*, 58–59.

92　JOHN OVERBEY, AN EASTER EGG ROW NEIGHBOR　Ibid., 60. Wicker, *GHWB*, 8–14, covers Bush's business career well.

92　"CAUGHT THE FEVER"　*LF*, 60.

92　THEY BOUGHT PERCENTAGES　Ibid., 62.

92　THEY INVESTED IN "FARM-OUTS"　Ibid., 62–63.

92　EXPLAINING THE BUSINESS, BUSH IMAGINED　Ibid., 63.

92　"IF I HIT, YOU'VE FOUND OUT"　Ibid.

92　A NERVOUS BUSH MADE THE TRIP　Ibid., 60–61.

92　"UNCLE NEIL" REMOVED HIS EYEGLASSES AND CLEANED THEM　Ibid., 61.

92　HE ROSE　Ibid.

92　"I REALLY HATE TO SEE YOU GO"　Ibid.

92　"I LEFT NEIL'S OFFICE"　*LF*, 61.

93　FAMILY'S 1,500-SQUARE-FOOT HOUSE　Author tour of George W. Bush Childhood Home, Midland, Texas.

93　THE ATTRACTION FOR INVESTORS　*LF*, 63. See also GHWB to Godfrey B. Simonds, May 23, 1951, JB.

93　BUSH HIT NEW YORK AND WASHINGTON　*LF*, 65–66; *ATB*, 72.

93　NORTH DAKOTA, COLORADO, NEBRASKA, AND WYOMING　*ATB*, 72.

93　PLAYED A VITAL ROLE　Author interviews with GHWB, BPB, Nancy Bush Ellis, and G. H. Walker III. See also Weisberg, *Bush Tragedy*, 24–29.

93　"HE ALMOST IDOLIZED"　Author interview with G. H. Walker III.

93　SIX FOOT EXACTLY　Ibid.

93　ALTERNATELY CHARMING AND COOL　Ibid.

93　"HE HAD STRONG VIEWS ON PEOPLE"　Ibid.

93　UNCLE HERBIE'S AFFECTION FOR　Ibid.

93　"'DOTTY DOESN'T DO THINGS THAT WAY'"　Ibid.

93　"HIS DEVOTION TO GEORGE"　Ibid.

94　HERBIE RAN G. H. WALKER　Ibid.

94　EUGENE MEYER, THE FINANCIER　*LF*, 65–66.

94　OVER BREAKFAST AT MEYER'S HOUSE　Ibid.

94　"WHAT I REMEMBER"　Ibid.

94　"OKAY, PUT ME DOWN"　Ibid., 66.

94　"YOU SAY THIS IS A GOOD"　Ibid.

94　VOLUNTEERING FOR IKE IN MIDLAND　Ibid., 80.

94　IN THIS SECOND BID　PSB, COHC, 189.

95 THEY PASSED ONE OF THE MANY BILLBOARDS   Ibid., 226.

95 "YOU'RE IN A JAM WITH ABRAHAM"   Ibid., 226–27.

95 "IT WAS ONE OF THOSE THINGS"   Ibid., 227.

95 "IF I'D WANTED TO BE ANTI-SEMITIC"   Ibid.

95 DURING THE '52 CAMPAIGN   James T. Patterson, *Grand Expectations: The United States, 1945–1974* (New York, 1996), 196.

95 FEATURED SPEAKER AT A RALLY   Herskowitz, *Duty, Honor, Country,* 123–124.

95 BEGINNING WITH A SPEECH AT WHEELING   Patterson, *Grand Expectations,* 196.

95 THE NUMBERS WOULD CHANGE   Ibid.

95 DROVES SHOWED UP TO HEAR HIM   Herskowitz, *Duty, Honor, Country,* 127.

95 SEATED ONSTAGE WITH MCCARTHY   Ibid.

95 WHEN BUSH'S TURN CAME   Ibid.

95 "I SAID THAT I WAS VERY GLAD"   Ibid., 127–28.

96 "BUT, I MUST SAY IN ALL CANDOR"   Ibid., 128.

96 THE CROWD TURNED   PSB, COHC, 101–2; Herskowitz, *Duty, Honor, Country,* 128.

96 EISENHOWER DEFEATED ADLAI STEVENSON   *Congress and the Nation, 1945–1964: A Review of Government and Politics in the Postwar Years.* Congressional Quarterly Service, Washington D.C., 1965, 13.

96 BUSH BESTED RIBICOFF BY THIRTY THOUSAND VOTES   Ibid., 75.

96 LEASED QUARTERS AT THE WARDMAN   PSB, COHC, 91.

96 SENATOR HARRY BYRD   Ibid.

96 THE PRESIDENT OFTEN INVITED   Author interview with GHWB; Herskowitz, *Duty, Honor, Country,* 105–106.

96 A DELEGATION OF POSTAL WORKERS   PSB, COHC, 132.

96 NEWS SOON ARRIVED FROM TEXAS   *BB,* 38.

97 BARBARA TURNED THE FAMILY'S SUNROOM   Author tour of George W. Bush's Childhood Home, Midland, Tex.

97 "LIFE," BARBARA RECALLED   *BB,* 38.

97 "I DON'T KNOW WHAT TO DO"   Ibid., 39.

97 WORRIED, BARBARA TOOK THE LITTLE GIRL   Ibid.

97 BUSH WAS AT THE ECTOR COUNTY COURTHOUSE   *LF,* 68.

97 "I HAVE SOME BAD NEWS"   Author interview with GHWB.

97 NEITHER HE NOR BARBARA   Ibid.; *BB,* 39.

97 "WHAT DO WE DO ABOUT IT?"   Author interview with GHWB.

97 "YOU HAVE TWO CHOICES"   Ibid.

97 THE BUSHES LOOKED AT EACH OTHER   Ibid.

97 "YOU DON'T HAVE A CHOICE"   Ibid. See also Wicker, *GHWB,* 10.

97 THE BUSHES DROVE HOME   *BB,* 40.

97 BUSH SAID HE NEEDED TO STOP OFF   Ibid.

97 THE NEXT MORNING, THE BUSHES LEFT GEORGIE AND JEB   Ibid.

98 SUTTON PLACE   Ibid.

98 THERE WERE BONE MARROW TESTS   Author interview with GHWB.

98 "GOD, THE POOR LITTLE GIRL"   Ibid.

98 "ROBIN DOES UNFORTUNATELY HAVE LEUKEMIA"   GHWB to Harold Dorris, August 4, 1953, JB.

98 "GAMPY WALKER WAS A SCARY OLD MAN"   *BB,* 43.

98 ROBIN AT FIRST HEARD THE NAME   Ibid.

98 ON A BRIEF VISIT TO KENNEBUNKPORT   Ibid.

98 CALLING THEM "SUPERMAN" BROTHERS   Ibid.

98 TAKE HER HOME TO MIDLAND   Ibid.

98   "Leukemia was not a well-known disease"   *BB,* 43.

98   Yet Robin could seem so bright   *LF,* 69.

98   The Bushes decided   *BB,* 44.

98   She had to watch over them   Ibid.

98   "changed her whole personality"   Author interview with GHWB.

99   When Bush was there   Ibid.

99   Bush's Yale friend Thomas W. L. "Lud" Ashley   *BB,* 42.

99   "I meet him every morning"   Ibid.

99   No tears in front of Robin   Ibid., 44.

99   "Poor George"   Ibid.

99   "We used to laugh"   Ibid.

99   Senator Bush came up from Washington   Ibid.

99   "That darling man"   Ibid.

99   "raging through her body"   GHWB to Jonathan Bush, September 21, 1953, JB.

99   "They wanted to operate again"   Author interview with GHWB.

99   Robin went into a coma   *BB,* 44.

100   "One minute she was there"   Ibid.

100   Barbara combed Robin's hair   Ibid.

100   held her a last time   Ibid.

100   a small memorial service   Ibid., 45.

100   had given her to research   Ibid.

100   buried Robin in the grave her grandfather had prepared   Ibid.

100   In the upstairs bedroom   Author interview with BPB.

100   at Christ Church   Ibid.

100   "For one who allowed"   *BB,* 45.

100   "We awakened night after night"   Ibid., 46.

100   Sam Houston Elementary School   GWB, *Decision Points,* 6.

100   were carrying a record player   Ibid.

100   "I could have sworn"   Ibid.

100   "My mom, dad, and sister are home"   *BB,* 45.

100   Reaching the Oldsmobile   GWB, *Decision Points,* 6.

100   "She died"   Ibid.

100   The ride home   Ibid.

100   It was the beginning   *BB,* 46.

100   "I hated that nobody"   Ibid.

101   "At least it wasn't your firstborn"   Ibid.

101   "George pointed out"   Ibid.

101   Bush would hold Barbara   Ibid.

101   The younger George Bush   Ibid.

101   "I bet she can see"   Ibid.

101   "That started my cure"   Ibid., 47.

101   "It taught me"   Author interview with GHWB.

101   Dorothy Bush commissioned   *ATB,* 81.

101   "selfishness takes over"   Ibid.

102   One evening he went "out on the town"   Ibid.

102   "You could well"   Ibid.

102   There is about our house a need   Ibid., 81–82.

104   Reading the letter aloud   Author interview with GHWB.

104   crying so hard   Author observation.

104   "When I read that"   Author interview with GHWB.

104 "But life goes on" Ibid.

104 She is playing next to a fountain Author interview with GHWB. The caption details about the president's keeping the image in his Oval Office desk are from Patricia Presock.

ELEVEN: *I Was Bleeding Inside*

105 I worried a lot in those days Author interview with GHWB.

105 The Liedtke brothers *LF,* 60.

105 The result was a new company Ibid., 67.

105 Hugh Liedtke had a simple rule of thumb Ibid.

105 after the Marlon Brando movie Ibid.

105 Under the Zapata name Ibid., 70–71.

105 West Jamieson field Obituary of Hugh Liedtke, *NYT,* April 1, 2003.

105 Bush struggled to build *LF,* 70; GHWB to Wayne Dean, August 4, 1958, Inter-Office Correspondence—Wayne H. Dean, 1954–59 (1), Business Correspondence File, ZAP.

105 pursuing offshore opportunities GHWB to Wayne Dean, August 4, 1958, Inter-Office Correspondence—Wayne H. Dean, 1954–59 (1), Business Correspondence File, ZAP.

105 In 1955, applying for a $25,000 loan GHWB to Kline McGee, November 14, 1955, JB.

106 When Zapata shares GHWB to Kline McGee, January 3, 1956, JB.

106 Zapata contracted with R. G. LeTourneau *LF,* 71–73; GHWB to "Gentlemen," R. G. LeTourneau, February 14, 1957; and R. L. LeTourneau, Vice President, R. G. LeTourneau, Inc., to GHWB, January 8, 1957, both in Correspondence with LeTourneau, Miscellaneous—Waiver of Option (1956–57), and Business Correspondence File, ZAP.

106 One morning in London Author interview with GHWB. See also *LSY,* 87.

106 "If we lost this" Author interview with GHWB.

106 Bush felt miserable Ibid.

107 "Don't worry, old chap" Ibid.

107 "I felt like hell" Ibid.

107 "You've got a bleeding ulcer" Ibid.

107 "I was bleeding inside" Ibid.

107 "what do you" Ibid.

107 (the litigation) Ibid.

107 Everything Bush heard from his parents *LF,* 81.

107 "Politics entered into my thinking" Ibid. Timothy Naftali put the dynamic well, referring to Prescott as a "trendsetter ... introducing the entire Bush family to politics." (Naftali, *GHWB,* 11.) G. H. "Bert" Walker III, Herbie Walker's son, once spent a summer living with Senator Bush in Washington. (Author interview with G. H. Walker III.)

107 Socially moderate (and sometimes liberal) Naftali, *GHWB,* 11. Naftali described Prescott as "a favorite with the elite of his party. He was a solid Eisenhower Republican—pragmatic, pro-business, but also pro–civil rights and socially liberal." In Herbert Parmet's view, "Prescott's Senate history showed that he was closer to the party's northeastern version, the most progressive wing of 'modern Republicanism,' which was less conservative than the [Eisenhower] administration in Washington. He really belonged to the Rockefeller wing, especially in its support for

reforms." (*LSY*, 89.) The truth probably lies in between—a precursor, perhaps, of his son's own complicated political identity.

107 "He was basically full" PSB, COHC, 149.

107 a strong advocate of the federal government's role Ibid., 164.

107 On civil rights he was a progressive Ibid., 128. See, for example, the following speeches and remarks made by Senator Prescott Bush on the floor of the Senate: "Civil Rights—The Republican Record," April 8, 1960, 86th Cong., *Congressional Record* 106: 7761–62; on integration in the public schools, March 15, 1956, 4753; 84th Cong., *Congressional Record* 102; and on the right to vote, July 31, 1957, 85th Cong., *Congressional Record* 103: 13139–41. See also articles about his work as chairman of the Republican Platform Committee at the 1956 Republican Convention and efforts to promote a civil rights plank: *NYT*, July 31, August 12, and August 14, 1956.

108 Bush again spoke out against Joe McCarthy Herskowitz, *Duty, Honor, Country*, 123–36.

108 McCarthy smeared a young lawyer Patterson, *Grand Expectations*, 268–69.

108 "Mr. President, all my life" "Resolution of Censure, Remarks of Senator Prescott Bush," December 1, 1954, 83rd Cong., 2nd sess., *Congressional Record* 100, pt. 12: 16268.

108 "has caused" Ibid.

108 "I realize that anybody" GHWB to Senator William Fulbright, September 3, 1954, JB.

109 would call with PSB, COHC, 351.

109 "talk quite informally" Ibid.

109 When Bush and Eisenhower played golf Ibid., 352.

109 "It's always helpful" Ibid., 354–55.

109 Bush was flown out Ibid., 92.

109 During the 1956 reelection campaign Ibid., 189.

109 Dorothy Bush was characteristically competitive Ibid., 189–90.

109 The two were, Bush recalled, "on the go" Ibid., 191.

109 At issue was legislation *LF*, 81.

109 the "opinion . . . of a Texan" Ibid.

109 Senator Bush would not change Ibid.

109 The calls to George H. W. Bush's Midland home Ibid.

110 "damn well better" Ibid.

110 "The head of Phillips" Ibid.

110 if the senator "doesn't vote for this bill" Ibid., 82.

110 At two o'clock one morning Ibid.

110 "That's all she wrote" Ibid.

110 "They'll never put you out of business" PSB, COHC, 293.

110 the lobbying effort *LF*, 83.

110 In August 1959, Zapata Off-Shore Ibid., 69–70. See also Weisberg, *Bush Tragedy*, 34, and Wicker, *GHWB*, 12–13.

110 It was time *LF*, 69–70.

110 ZOS, as the separate company was known Ibid.

110 Barbara was unhappy about the move *BB*, 52–53.

110 Mildred and Baine Kerr's house Ibid.

111 Bush set up offices Thomas Ludlow Ashley, M.C., to GHWB, August 30, 1960, JB.

111 Tuesday, August 18, 1959 *BB*, 53–54.

111 "enchanting" *ATB*, 85.

111 He was found *BB*, 54.

TWELVE: *Goldwater's Policies, Kennedy's Style*

112 THE SENATE IS A TERRIBLY SOUGHT-AFTER POST   PSB, COHC, 179.
112 HE RADIATED CHARM   Author interview with Peter O'Donnell.
112 THE HARRIS COUNTY REPUBLICAN CHAIRMAN   *LSY,* 94; Naftali, *GHWB,* 12–13; Wicker, *GHWB,* 14–16.
112 "JIMMY, WHEN ARE YOU"   *LSY,* 94.
112 ONE OF THE MOST POWERFUL DEMOCRATS   *LF,* 83–84.
112 "THEY MENTIONED SEVERAL POSSIBILITIES"   Ibid., 83.
112 THOUGH BUSH ADMITTED   Ibid.
112 "PRIVATELY MY OWN POLITICAL PHILOSOPHY"   Ibid., 80–81.
113 SUFFERING FROM ARTHRITIS   *LSY,* 89.
113 HE'D "BE A FOOL" TO RUN   PSB, COHC, 436.
113 "ONCE YOU'VE HAD THE EXPOSURE"   Ibid., 439.
113 THE DEMOCRATIC PARTY'S HOLD OVER TEXAS   *LF,* 84; Naftali, *GHWB,* 13; Wicker, *GHWB,* 13–14. See also John R. Knaggs, *Two-Party Texas: The John Tower Era, 1961–1984* (Austin, 1986), for a knowing exploration of the Texas political terrain. Another key moment for Texas Republicans was the election of Bruce Alger as a congressman from Dallas. (Ibid., 5.)
113 EISENHOWER CARRIED THE STATE TWICE   *LF,* 84.
113 ONLY NARROWLY DEFEATED   http://uselectionatlas.org/RESULTS/state.php?fips= 48&year=1960.
113 "THE LARGEST METROPOLITAN AREA IN THE COUNTRY"   *LF,* 84.
113 THEN CAME JOHN TOWER   Ibid., 80; Knaggs, *Two-Party Texas,* 1–2.
113 THE MAY 1961 SPECIAL ELECTION   Knaggs, *Two-Party Texas,* 1–15; *LF,* 80. The conservatives were led by former governor Allan Shivers, who had campaigned for Eisenhower; the liberals by the populist Senator Ralph Yarborough. When Johnson was elected vice president, the governor, Price Daniel, Sr., appointed a conservative from Dallas, William Blakley, to the seat. An intricate battle ensued in which liberal Texas Democrats either voted for Tower or simply chose not to show up at the polls, thus denying the Democratic nominee their votes. (This liberal tactic was known as "going fishing.") The goal: to elect a Republican and force a conservative exodus to a newly empowered GOP, creating a true two-party system that would give liberals more control within the Democratic Party. It was a complicated political moment, one that required hard-core populist liberals in the short term to support a candidate with whom they disagreed in order to achieve a long-term strategic objective. (Knaggs, *Two-Party Texas,* 10–12.)
114 "SOMETHING WAS STIRRING"   *LF,* 84.
114 JAMES BERTRON, THE COUNTY CHAIRMAN   *LSY,* 93–99.
114 JOHN BIRCH SOCIETY   Ibid., 93. For a history of Texas and extremism, see Don E. Carleton, *Red Scare! Right Wing Hysteria, Fifties Fanaticism, and Their Legacy in Texas* (Austin, 1985). See also Naftali, *GHWB,* 12, and Wicker *GHWB,* 15.
114 A SUNNY SPRINGTIME SATURDAY MORNING   *LF,* 84–85. *LSY,* 87–97, tells the Harris County story well.
114 BUSH'S CALLERS WANTED   *LF,* 85.
114 OVER LUNCH CAME THE QUESTION   Ibid.
114 "I DIDN'T REALLY NEED TIME"   Ibid.
114 BARBARA TOOK UP NEEDLEPOINTING   *LSY,* 95.
114 BUSH WAS ELECTED CHAIRMAN   Ibid. Just two weeks into his term, on Thursday, March 7, 1963, he wrote leading businessmen whom he suspected were Republicans

but who, as he put it, "have not elected to be identified with the local party. Some, of course, are conservative Democrats who vote Republican in national elections but there are many who are life-long Republicans who just have never gotten active in the Republican Party. One of my main goals . . . is to up-grade the image of our party through getting these people to identify as Republicans." (GHWB to John E. Lyons, March 7, 1963, JB.) He also contacted Albertine E. Bowie, a black Texas woman who had just been appointed to the women's division of the Republican National Committee. "The Republicans have done miserably in getting any negro votes and I am determined that we work diligently toward finding an answer," Bush wrote Bowie on Monday, March 11, 1963. (GHWB to Albertine E. Bowie, March 11, 1963, JB.)

114 "I FOUND OUT THAT JUGULAR POLITICS" *LF,* 86.

115 "YOU'RE EITHER FOR" Knaggs, *Two-Party Texas,* 8.

115 "NINETEEN SIXTY-FOUR" GHWB, "By George," Republican County Headquarters 1962, Business Alphabetical File, ZAP. For an account of the 1964 Senate campaign from the Democratic point of view, see Patrick Cox, *Ralph W. Yarborough: The People's Senator* (Austin, 2001), 214–20. See also Wicker, *GHWB,* 16–19; Naftali, *GHWB,* 13–16; *LSY,* 98–114.

115 BEEN HEARING GOOD THINGS Author interview with Peter O'Donnell.

115 STEWART THOUGHT THE TWO MEN Ibid.

116 "I THOUGHT I COULD WIN" Author interview with GHWB.

116 O'DONNELL BELIEVED BUSH'S ENERGY Author interview with Peter O'Donnell.

116 TWO PREVAILING FACTIONS See, for instance, Rick Perlstein, *Before the Storm: Barry Goldwater and the Unmaking of the American Consensus* (New York, 2001); Theodore H. White, *The Making of the President, 1964* (New York, 1965); Richard Norton Smith, *On His Own Terms: A Life of Nelson Rockefeller* (New York, 2014).

116 "EXTREMISM IN DEFENSE" Perlstein, *Before the Storm,* 391. The remark came in Goldwater's acceptance speech in San Francisco. In the convention's keynote address earlier in the week, Governor Mark O. Hatfield of Oregon had called out the farthest fringes of the right. "There are bigots in this nation who spew forth their venom of hate," Hatfield had told the delegates in a half-hour speech on Monday evening. "They parade under hundreds of labels, including the Communist party, the Ku Klux Klan and the John Birch Society. They must be overcome." (*NYT,* July 14, 1964; *Chicago Tribune,* July 14, 1964).

116 GROWN MORE CONSERVATIVE Author interview with GHWB.

117 EISENHOWER HAD FAILED Stephen E. Ambrose, *Eisenhower,* vol. 1: *Soldier, General of the Army, President-Elect 1890–1952* (New York, 1983), 563–67.

117 BUSH WOULD OPPOSE KEY ELEMENTS OF THE LANDMARK CIVIL RIGHTS ACT *DMN,* April 8, 1964; June 11, 1964. For a summary of GHWB's 1964 positions, see also Naftali, *GHWB,* 13–14, and Wicker, *GHWB,* 17.

117 BUSH OPPOSED MEDICARE *DMN,* October 20, 1964. The article noted that GHWB "favors the proposed increase in [Social Security] payments, but without the Medicare rider."

117 WAR ON POVERTY *DMN,* June 3 and 11, 1964.

117 THE ADMISSION OF Ibid., April 8, 1964. "If Red China shoots its way into the U.N., we should drop out—because this would torpedo the U.N.," Bush said in Austin. "Technically, Red China is still at war with the U.N." (Ibid.)

117 OPPOSED A NUCLEAR-TEST-BAN TREATY "Texas: Cactus-Nasty Campaign," *Time,* October 16, 1964.

117 BUSH PAID A CALL ON AUSTIN'S JOURNALISTS Knaggs, *Two-Party Texas,* 33–34.
117 YARBOROUGH, BUSH SAID, "IS DIAMETRICALLY" *DMN,* September 12, 1963.
117 A POPULIST DEMOCRAT *NYT,* January 28, 1996.
117 "THE WORST CANDIDATE I'D EVER HAD" Author interview with James Leonard.
117 "HE'D GO OVER TO THESE YOKELS" Ibid. Years later, James Baker encountered the same dissonance between the candidate's vocabulary and the voters'. "George was always saying 'My father inculcated in me a sense of public service,'" Baker recalled, "and a not inconsiderable number of folks listening were unaccustomed to hearing the word 'inculcate.' I'd ask him to stop, but it didn't do any good. He kept on saying it anyway." (Author interview with James A. Baker III.)
118 "I PUSHED HIM" Author interview with James Leonard.
118 COOKING SPAGHETTI FOR SCORES BPB diary and letters, November 2, 1963.
118 THERE WERE "TASTIN' TEAS" Ibid., November 10, 1963.
118 BARBARA PREFERRED SITTING IN AUDIENCES Ibid., October 9, 1963.
118 "THE IVY LEAGUE–YANKEE LABEL" Ibid., September 1963.
118 "GEORGE H. W. BUSH" BECAME JUST "GEORGE BUSH" Ibid.
118 SOME ALLIES THOUGHT BUSH Ibid.
118 THE NASCENT BUSH NETWORK Ibid., September 25, 1963.
118 "NO FOREIGN CAR DRIVER" Ibid., September 1963.
118 RUMORS ABOUT BUSH AND HIS EASTERN TIES BPB diary and letters, May 18, 1964.
118 A "TOOL OF THE COMMIES" Ibid.
119 ALSO PUBLISHED THE JOHN BIRCH SOCIETY'S HANDBOOK Ibid.; *BB,* 58–59.
119 A STATEWIDE *HOUSTON CHRONICLE* POLL Knaggs, *Two-Party Texas,* 35; *LSY,* 105.
119 THE *CHRONICLE* SURVEY APPEARED Ibid.
119 AT MIDDAY THE NEWS CAME OVER THE RADIO *BB,* 59.
119 AT A MEETING Author interview with GHWB.
119 "OH TEXAS—MY TEXAS" *BB,* 59.
119 BUSH CALLED BARBARA BPB diary and letters, November 22, 1963.
119 FLEW HOME TO HOUSTON *BB,* 59–60. The Bushes flew from Tyler to Fort Worth on a private plane. "We had to circle the field while the second presidential plane took off," Barbara wrote. "Immediately Pop got tickets back to Houston and here we are flying home." (Ibid.) From his Harris County post and from the road, Bush was so attuned to the right wing that, when he first heard the news, he thought he might have a lead for the FBI in the murder of the president. According to an FBI report:

> At 1:45 P.M. Mr. George H. W. Bush, President of the Zapata Off-shore Drilling Company, Houston, Texas, residence 5525 Briar, Houston, telephonically furnished the following information to writer by long distance telephone call from Tyler, Texas.
>
> BUSH stated that he wanted to be kept confidential but wanted to furnish hearsay that he recalled hearing in recent weeks, the day and source unknown. He stated that one James Parrott has been talking of killing the President when he comes to Houston.
>
> BUSH stated that Parrott is possibly a student at the University of Houston and is active in political matters in the area. He stated that he felt Mrs. Fawley, telephone number SU 2–5239, or Arlene Smith, telephone number JA 9–9194 of the Harris County Republican Party Headquarters would be able to furnish additional information regarding the identity of Parrott.

U.S. Government Memorandum, Special Agent Graham W. Kitchel to Special Agent in Charge, "Unknown Subject; Assassination of President John F. Kennedy," November 22, 1963, FBI, #62-2115-6.

119 "THE RUMORS ARE FLYING" BPB diary, 1963; *BB*, 59–60.

119 BUSH CANCELED HIS POLITICAL COMMITMENTS BPB diary, 1963.

119 THE BUSHES TOOK JEB AND DORO Ibid.

119 "POPPY SEEMS TO FEEL" Ibid. Johnson now loomed ever larger in Texas politics. "The recent tragedy has changed things somewhat since Lyndon Johnson is a Texan and this home state problem will be difficult to overcome here," Bush wrote John W. Smith of Seaboard Air Line Railroad in Richmond, Virginia, on December 9, 1963. Bush might, however, be lucky in his foe. "On the other hand my prospective opponent is Senator Ralph Yarborough," Bush wrote. "He is a liberal with a bad voting record and apparently a personality to match since, even though voting down the line with the New Frontier, he does not get appointments to committees to which his seniority would otherwise entitle him." Still, Bush appreciated the difficulties ahead. "I must overcome the label problem since voting Republican still is pretty unattractive in many sections of the State; but on the other hand Yarborough maintains a rabid position on Civil Rights and is all out in his support of the accommodations section of the Civil Rights Bill." (GHWB to John W. Smith, December 9, 1963, Correspondence Between George Bush and FitzGerald Bemiss, 1961–69, FITZ.)

   Neil Mallon had called Bush on Sunday, November 24, 1963, to report that he had heard the conservative Democratic faction was urging Congressman Joe Kilgore to challenge Yarborough in the Democratic primary. (BPB diary, 1963.) Then word came that the Kilgore maneuver was off: "Now we hear that no one will oppose R. Yarborough 'For Party Unity,'" wrote Barbara. "What stories fly!" (Ibid.)

   According to *The Texas Observer,* Johnson pledged to do "everything he can" to help Yarborough. A president from Texas could not abide an all-Republican senatorial delegation from his home state. (*The Texas Observer,* June 26, 1964.) One by one Yarborough's possible rivals chose not to make the race. Kilgore was out; Allan Shivers, a former governor, was out; and in the first week of January 1964, Lloyd Bentsen, a former congressman from the conservative wing of the party, announced that he, too, was abandoning his plans to challenge Yarborough. (*DMN,* January 4, 1964.) Bush and his fellow Republicans argued that the Johnson-engineered, conservative-free Democratic primary underscored the truth that conservatives could find a home only with the Republicans. The failure to field a candidate opposing Yarborough, said Peter O'Donnell, represented a "shellacking to conservatives in the Texas Democratic Party." (*The Texas Observer,* February 21, 1964.) Bush said that Democrats should "shake their heads in shame" at Johnson's interference. (*DMN,* February 7, 1964.)

119 "I DON'T HOLD WITH MURDER" *The Nation,* February 3, 1964.

119 IN THE MAY 1964 PRESIDENTIAL PRIMARY DMN, May 5, 1964.

120 SOUTHERN METHODIST UNIVERSITY WITHDREW *The Texas Observer,* May 15, 1964.

120 THE PRESIDENT OF TEXAS TECH IN LUBBOCK CANCELED Ibid.

120 ABILENE AND SAN ANTONIO DEBATED Ibid., June 12, 1964.

120 THE TEXAS MANUFACTURERS ASSOCIATION PRODUCED Ibid., March 6, 1964.

120 THE REAL CHOICE IN TEXAS POLITICS DMN, February 7, 1964.

120 VOTED "DOWN THE LINE" Ibid., March 22, 1964.

120 WITH ROUGHLY 44 PERCENT *The Texas Observer,* May 15, 1964.

120 THE FIRST REPUBLICAN RUNOFF IN TEXAS DMN, June 3, 1964.

120 HE RAISED FOUR TIMES Ibid., June 2, 1964.

120 NOTING THAT BUSH HAD ALREADY *The Texas Observer*, May 29, 1964.

120 BUSH STRUCK BACK *DMN*, June 4, 1964.

120 BUSH DEFEATED COX *LSY*, 107.

120 IN WASHINGTON FOUR DAYS LATER *DMN*, June 11, 1964; *The Texas Observer*, June 26, 1964.

121 BUSH SAID HE WAS "SHOCKED" Ibid.

121 VOTED FOR "A COURSE OF ACTION" *DMN*, June 11, 1964.

121 STRUGGLED TO RECONCILE Naftali, *GHWB*, 13–16.

121 "MY HEART IS HEAVY" *ATB*, 88.

121 "STATES' RIGHTS" *DMN*, June 11, 1964.

121 "THERE IS AT LEAST ONE" Ibid., July 26, 1964.

121 "HIS CAMPAIGN . . . GETS A LOT OF ENERGY" "Goldwater's Policies, Kennedy's Style," *The Texas Observer*, October 30, 1964.

121 "SIR, I'M GEORGE BUSH" Ibid.

122 JIM LEONARD ANNOUNCED *The Texas Observer*, June 26, 1964.

122 "THE MORE WIDELY" *DMN*, September 21, 1964.

122 "A LOT OF PEOPLE ARE TALKING BUSH" Ibid.

122 THE LIBERALS AT *THE TEXAS OBSERVER* *The Texas Observer*, June 12, 1964.

122 WOULD BE "ANOTHER" Ibid., October 16, 1964.

122 "R. Y. IS GETTING MEAN" *ATB*, 89.

122 CALLING BUSH "THE CONNECTICUT CANDIDATE" *DMN*, October 3, 1964.

122 THE CARPETBAGGER CHARGE Ibid., October 4, 1964.

122 DATING HIS BAPTISM Ibid.

122 "I WAS BORN OUTSIDE" Ibid., October 25, 1964.

122 A POLL OF LIKELY VOTERS PUT BUSH *DMN*, October 25, 1964.

122 ON TUESDAY, OCTOBER 27, BUSH BROADCAST Ibid., October 27, 1964.

122 THE TELECAST RAN ON MORE THAN A DOZEN Ibid.

122 ON THE SAME EVENING H. W. Brands, *Reagan: The Life* (New York, 2015), 2.

123 "LET'S SHOW THE WORLD" *Time*, October 16, 1964.

123 JOHNSON DEFEATED GOLDWATER http://www.presidency.ucsb.edu/showelection.php?year=1964.

123 THE UPI ELECTION NIGHT LEAD *Chicago Tribune*, November 4, 1964.

123 BUSH POLLED 44 PERCENT Michael J. Dubin, *United States Congressional Elections, 1788–1997* (Jefferson, N.C., 1998), 648. The precise figure for Bush is listed as 43.56 percent.

123 THE "FIERCEST" GENERAL ELECTION *DMN*, November 4, 1964.

123 "ACTUALLY WE RECEIVED" *ATB*, 89.

123 "I DON'T MEAN TO BE UNGRATEFUL" Ibid.

124 "THE FIGURES INDICATE" Ibid.

124 "BAFFLED BY THE RETURNS" Ibid.

124 HE HAD OUTSPENT HIS OPPONENT Ibid., November 17, 1964.

124 "I PLAN TO CONTINUE" Ibid., November 4, 1964.

124 "WE GOT BEAT" GHWB to FitzGerald Bemiss, November 3, 1964, Correspondence Between George Bush and FitzGerald Bemiss, 1961–69, FITZ.

124 "THE BIRCHERS ARE BAD NEWS" GHWB to FitzGerald Bemiss, November 11, 1964, Correspondence Between George Bush and FitzGerald Bemiss, 1961–69, FITZ.

124 "DID I GO TOO FAR RIGHT?" Author interview with GHWB.

124 "BUT I WAS NOT AS MODERATE A GUY" Ibid.

124 "POP WAS REALLY DEAD" BPB diary, March 18, 1965.

Part IV: *The Wars of Washington, 1966 to 1977*

127 ALTHOUGH FUNDAMENTALLY CONSERVATIVE   DMN, August 30, 1970.

127 THE RIGHT TO HOPE IS BASIC   ATB, 110.

THIRTEEN: *Without a Moment to Stop*

129 I'D LIKE TO BE PRESIDENT   BPB diary and letters, January 7, 1966.

129 FOR BUSH, POLITICS IS   DMN, August 30, 1970.

129 LEAVING HIS WIFE IN CHARGE   Author interviews with GHWB, BPB, GWB, and Jeb Bush.

129 GEORGE W.'S FIRST MEMORY   Author interview with GWB.

129 HE WOULD TAKE HIS CHILDREN   Author interview with Jeb Bush. Bush, Neil Bush recalled, was "like a whirling dervish." (Author interview with Neil Bush.)

129 JEB REMEMBERED A HUNDRED-DEGREE DOUBLEHEADER   Author interview with Jeb Bush.

129 "THEY RAN OUT"   Ibid.

130 "I HAVE ONLY ONE MEMORY"   Ibid.

130 ZAPATA'S RIG MAVERICK   ATB, 94.

130 "THIS WAS THE"   Ibid.

130 HE FLEW OVER THE GULF   Author interview with GHWB.

130 "GEORGE BUSH, HOUSTON BUSINESSMAN"   NYT, March 28, 1965.

130 THERE WAS SPECULATION   DMN, January 12, 1966.

130 A LAWSUIT BUSH HAD HELPED FILE   Ibid., January 13, June 23, and July 21, 1965. For the redistricting suit, see, for instance: *El Paso Herald-Post,* May 31, 1965; *Lubbock Avalanche Journal,* June 2, 1965; *Brownsville Herald,* June 23, 1965; *Bush v. Martin,* 224 F. Supp. 499 (1963); *Martin v. Bush,* 376 U.S. 222 (1964). (https://scholar.google.com/scholar_case?case=16751940927364620785&hl=en&as_sdt=6&as_vis=1&oi=scholarr and https://scholar.google.com/scholar_case?case=19069798681336020061&q=Bush+v.+martin&hl=en&as_sdt=8006&as_vis=1).

130 POLLING SHOWED THAT . . . FRANK BRISCOE   BPB diary and letters, January 7, 1966.

130 RUMORS THAT ROSS BAKER   Ibid.

130 "I DON'T WANT TO MOVE"   Ibid.

130 "I'D LIKE TO BE PRESIDENT"   Ibid.

130 "IT WOULD HAVE BEEN UNFAIR"   LF, 89.

131 HE SOLD HIS ZAPATA OFF-SHORE   LSY, 117; ATB, 94–95. He sold his shares of Zapata Off-Shore for $20 a share. "Three months later, the stock began a climb that carried it to $140 a share, where it split, two for one." (*Chicago Tribune,* July 27, 1969.) The Zapata sale was a key moment in his life. "He is really trying to get the Zapata thing done and then get on this," Barbara wrote of the House race in January 1966. In a letter to George W. on Tuesday, January 25, 1966, she wrote: "Our life has gotten to a really emotional cross road for Dad. If the deal goes through that he is working on, we will no longer be part of Zapata. I feel sure that at your age this does not seem as emotional an issue that it is at our age. Dad has spent a lot of time this week thinking back over his years with Zapata, all the people who have made our lives so easy etc. This is quite a move for Dad and he has thought long and hard about giving up his job." (BPB diary and letters, January 25, 1966.) On the financial side of things, Barbara recalled: "Had he waited four years, why, it would've been a gold mine. But money wasn't his thing. We've done well, don't misunderstand me. I did say to him,

'The only thing, George, is that I hope we'll be able to, when our children say we really want to go to camp, we'll be able to afford it.' In 1966 we put $50,000 in all five children's accounts. Some of them were so cheap that they made money on it eventually and some of them maxed out almost. That meant that they could go to private school, or camp, or travel. We were very lucky—most congressmen can't do that." (Author interview with BPB.) Jeb Bush used his account to buy a house after he graduated from college. (Author interview with Jeb Bush.)

131 BETWEEN $737,000   This figure was derived from G. H. Walker, Jr., to William Tyrrell, January 31, 1966, Zapata—Hall and Mize Agreements Returned, Business Alphabetical Files; telegram, GHWB to Walker, February 25, 1966, and GHWB to G. H. Walker, Jr., February 25, 1966, both in Zapata—Hall and Mize Agreements Returned, Business Alphabetical Files; GHWB to First City National Bank of Houston, September 29, 1966, Zapata—Hall and Mize: Bush Note (1), Business Alphabetical Files; GHWB to Bush Children Trust, September 1, 1966, Zapata—Hall and Mize: Bush Note (2), Business Alphabetical Files; all in ZAP, GBPL.

131 $1.1 MILLION   *Chicago Tribune,* July 27, 1969.

131 SOMEWHERE BETWEEN $5.5 MILLION AND $8 MILLION   Derived from calculations on DollarTimes.com, www.dollartimes.com/calculators/inflation.htm.

131 BUSH ANNOUNCED HIS CANDIDACY   BPB diary and letters, January 1966; *DMN,* January 17, 1966.

131 BARBARA WAS DRIVING   BPB diary and letters, January 1966.

131 IN JULY 1966, BUSH WAS TRAILING   Joe McGinniss, *The Selling of the President, 1968* (New York, 1969), 43–45. I am indebted to McGinniss's book for the Treleaven observations and the 1966 story.

131 BUSH'S ADVERTISING STRATEGY   Ibid., 45.

131 ORDINARY VOTERS   Ibid., 44.

131 "THERE'LL BE FEW OPPORTUNITIES"   Ibid., 44–45.

131 "POLITICAL CANDIDATES ARE CELEBRITIES"   Ibid., 45.

131 "WE CAN TURN THIS"   Ibid.

132 OVER AND OVER   Ibid.

132 "TOO LONG, REPUBLICANS"   *The Galveston Daily News,* November 6, 1966.

132 A "HUMAN INVESTMENT" PROGRAM   DMN, May 7, 1966.

132 "I WANT (THE REPUBLICAN PARTY'S) CONSERVATISM TO BE"   *The Wall Street Journal,* September 21, 1966.

132 BUSH WON THE GENERAL ELECTION   DMN, November 9, 1966; LSY, 121–22. Reflecting on the '66 campaign, Bush recalled, "The demographics were good, but it was an uphill fight. Briscoe was a conservative Democrat, a hardline prosecutor. But we out-hustled the other guys. I wasn't bad at it. I liked the personal interaction. I was a pretty good campaigner." (Author interview with GHWB.)

132 BRISCOE CONCEDED BY TEN P.M.   DMN, November 9, 1966.

132 IT HAD BEEN A BAD NIGHT   Jonathan Darman, *Landslide: LBJ, Reagan, and the Dawn of a New America* (New York, 2014), offers an insightful account of 1966 and its significance.

132 THEIR NEW WASHINGTON HOUSE   Author interview with BPB.

132 OUT TO A NEARBY SEARS   BPB diary, January 3, 1967.

132 BETWEEN JANUARY AND APRIL   Ibid., April 11, 1967.

133 IN HOUSE VOTES   J. Michael Sharp, ed., *Directory of Congressional Voting Scores and Interest Group Ratings,* 4th ed., vol. 1 (Washington, D.C., 2006), 223–24.

133 WHEN RICHARD NIXON BECAME PRESIDENT   Ibid.

133 "I know you are swamped" *ATB*, 97–98.

133 As the new Congress was forming *NYT*, January 26, 1967. See also *San Antonio Express and News*, January 22, 1967; *DMN*, January 26, 1967; *LSY*, 124–26.

133 "By choosing Bush" *DMN*, January 26, 1967.

133 Bush was the first freshman Ibid.

133 Prescott Bush had played a crucial role *LAT*, November 22, 1987.

133 "His father came to me" Walt Harrington, *American Profiles: Somebodies and Nobodies Who Matter* (Columbia, Mo., 1992), 158.

134 "Your dad was here last week" BPB diary, January 25, 1967.

134 "There's a lot of luck" *ATB*, 101.

134 Dorothy and Prescott Bush took over the F Street Club BPB diary, January 18 and 29, 1967.

134 Bush's legislative priorities Naftali, *GHWB*, 16–21, and *LSY*, 123–26, are illuminating overviews of GHWB's House career.

134 While he opposed *San Antonio Light*, January 28, 1967.

134 "a tax credit" Ibid.

134 The costs of the Vietnam War *DMN*, June 8, 1967.

135 "Unpopular though it may be" Ibid.

135 during a pre-wedding party BPB diary, November 8, 1967.

135 "Mr. President," Bush said Ibid.

135 "George, Mrs. Johnson and I" Ibid.

135 In the fall of 1967 Ibid., November 10, 1967.

135 "Does Pop want" Ibid., November 20, 1967.

135 Thanksgiving 1967 at Hillbrook Lane Ibid., November 27, 1967.

135 By year's end Bush had decided *ATB*, 104.

135 Bush visited Vietnam *LSY*, 128–32; BPB diary, January–February, 1967; *ATB*, 105.

136 "Tonight our nation" Lyndon B. Johnson: "Annual Message to the Congress on the State of the Union.," January 17, 1968. Online by Gerhard Peters and John T. Woolley, *The American Presidency Project*. www.presidency.ucsb.edu/ws/?pid=28738.

136 "Because when a great ship" Ibid.

136 CBS broadcast a Republican reply *Chicago Tribune*, January 24, 1968; *NYT*, January 24, 1968.

136 Eisenhower introduced the program with a prerecorded message *NYT*, January 24, 1968.

136 Bush was assigned the question *Chicago Tribune*, January 24, 1968.

137 had offered "no sense of sacrifice" *NYT*, January 24, 1968.

137 The overall reviews of the program were underwhelming *Chicago Tribune*, January 24, 1968. Referring to California senator George Murphy, as "in effect, the master of ceremonies," Gowran wrote. "He and the G.O.P. got carried away. The result was a procession of too many persons to the microphones, and the show lost effectiveness because of the parade." (Ibid.)

137 "Bush, a wholesome young man" Ibid. Bush pressed his Republican colleagues to take detailed alternative stands rather than simply opposing the president. At a dinner with Bush's sister, Nancy Bush Ellis, several other congressmen, and White House press secretary George Christian, Bush said "it was constructive for the Republicans to come up with specific cuts," Christian wrote in a memorandum LBJ later read.

"Bush's sister, incidentally, is a Democrat," Christian wrote. "She said she was for the President and wished her brother George had become a Democrat when he moved to Texas." (George Christian, "Memorandum for Barefoot Sanders," March 6, 1968, Lyndon B. Johnson Presidential Library.)

137 FAIR HOUSING ACT OF 1968   http://portal.hud.gov/hudportal/HUD?src=/program
  _offices/fair_housing_equal_opp/FHLaws/yourrights.

137 HIS MAIL ... WAS VICIOUS   *Big Spring Herald*, April 18, 1968. See also *ATB*, 107.

137 RECEIVED FIVE HUNDRED LETTERS   *ATB*, 107.

137 A BILL THAT WOULD HAVE BANNED RIOTERS   *NYT*, April 12, 1968.

137 HIS LIFE WAS THREATENED   *WP*, April 19, 1968.

137 HE DENOUNCED THE "HATRED AND VENOM"   *Big Spring Herald*, April 18, 1968.

137 "THAT ANYONE WOULD RESORT"   Ibid.

137 "THERE WAS A REALLY RICH GUY"   Author interview with GHWB.

138 "I VOTED FOR THE BILL"   *ATB*, 111.

138 CAME HOME FROM THE OFFICE WITH "TUMMY TROUBLES"   BPB diary, May 7, 1968.

138 "HE GOT INTO BED"   Ibid.

138 THE SHOWDOWN CAME IN HOUSTON   *LSY*, 132. See also *GWB*, 41, 87–89.

138 AT MEMORIAL HIGH SCHOOL   *Houston Chronicle*, April 18, 1968.

138 ATTACKED AS A "'NIGGER-LOVER'"   *ATB*, 108.

138 "WHAT THIS BILL DOES"   Ibid., 109.

138 IN VIETNAM I CHATTED   Ibid., 109–10.

138 ABOARD AN EVENING FLIGHT   Ibid., 111.

138 "I STARTED TO CRY"   Ibid.

139 HE PAID A CALL ON DEMONSTRATORS   *DMN*, May 23, 1968.

139 "I THINK IT IS IMPORTANT FOR MEMBERS OF CONGRESS"   Ibid.

139 BUSH PRAISED PASO   *DMN*, July 13, 1967.

139 BUSH TOLD PASO'S CONVENTION   Ibid.

139 A FOUR-POINT PROGRAM   *Wichita Falls Times*, March 29, 1968; *DMN*, January 30, 1968.

139 "WE MUST DEMONSTRATE"   *Wichita Falls Times*, March 29, 1968.

139 MEXICAN AMERICANS ARE "ESSENTIALLY"   *DMN*, January 30, 1968.

139 REPUBLICANS NEEDED TO PAY MORE ATTENTION   *Wichita Falls Times*, March 29, 1968.

140 "WE NEED TO MAKE"   "Bush Leads Effort for Birth Curbs," *DMN*, February 26, 1969. See also *Big Spring Daily Herald*, March 10, 1969.

140 "POPULATION CONTROL AND FAMILY PLANNING"   *Brownwood Bulletin*, September 10, 1969.

140 HE CREDITED HIS INTEREST IN THE ISSUE   Ibid.

140 PROPOSING THAT THE DEPARTMENT OF THE INTERIOR   *DMN*, October 17, 1969.

140 HIS INTEREST IN LEGISLATION   *LSY*, 133–35; Naftali, *GHWB*, 18.

140 "FAMILY-PLANNING SERVICES"   *LSY*, 134

140 LED WILBUR MILLS TO REFER TO BUSH AS "RUBBERS"   *LSY*, 134; Naftali, *GHWB*, 18.

140 ON RACE RELATIONS   *The Baytown Sun*, July 15, 1968.

140 A TASTE FOR WHITE OWL CIGARS   Marshall Frady, *Wallace* (New York, 1968), 2.

140 "THE REPUBLICAN PARTY HAS TOO MUCH MORE"   *The Galveston Daily News*, July 14, 1968.

140 SOMETHING OF A "LEFT-OF-CENTER IMAGE"   *LAT*, June 5, 1968.

140 AWAKENED AT FOUR A.M.   BPB diary, June 1968.

140 "A NIGHTMARE"   Ibid.

140 THE IDEA HAD REPORTEDLY ORIGINATED   *LAT*, June 5, 1968. See also *LSY*, 135–36.

140 (GRAHAM HAD GOTTEN TO KNOW)   Billy Graham, *Just As I Am: The Autobiography of Billy Graham* (San Francisco, 1997), 587; Nancy Gibbs and Michael Duffy, *The Presidents Club: Inside the World's Most Exclusive Fraternity* (New York, 2012), 375.

140 "This possibility is based partly"   *LAT,* June 5, 1968.

141 An unnamed "Texas industrialist"   Ibid.

141 Republican congressman Fletcher Thompson   Ibid.

141 Nixon's "weak spots"   Ibid.

141 Bush was also listed   *NYT,* June 30, 1968. Bill Steiger and Bill Liedtke also weighed in on Bush's behalf with Nixon. (Representative William A. Steiger to Richard Nixon, June 19, 1968, and William C. Liedtke, Jr., to Richard Nixon, July 16, 1968, Richard M. Nixon Presidential Library.)

141 Tom Dewey promoted   *LSY,* 135; Gibbs and Duffy, *Presidents Club,* 375–76; *The New Yorker,* October 5, 1992.

141 Reagan stopped in Texas en route   BPB diary, July 19, 1968.

141 "He has all the poise"   Ibid.

141 Congressman Bush had endorsed Nixon   *DMN,* July 9, 1968.

141 "I am expecting"   BPB diary, July 18, 1968.

141 "most attractive"   Ibid., summer 1968.

141 In Florida, the Bushes stayed   Ibid., August 3, 1968.

141 greeted by a banner   Ibid.

141 the Southern Association of Republican State Chairmen   *DMN,* August 3, 1968.

141 Any of the three   Ibid.

142 "I've never understood"   Ibid., August 4, 1968.

142 had shipped two thousand   *The Wall Street Journal,* August 7, 1968.

142 "Our phones rang off the hook"   BPB diary, summer 1968.

142 A friend of George's youngest brother   Ibid.

142 Nixon settled on   Naftali, *GHWB,* 20.

142 Bush had come up short   *ATB,* 117–18.

142 "Though we finished"   *LSY,* 135.

142 Nixon did ask Bush   *NYT,* August 17, 1968.

142 "in her reincarnation"   BPB diary, September 3, 1968.

142 At one point Barbara noticed   Ibid., January 18, 1969.

143 Bush transformed his House   Ibid., January 20, 1969.

143 They rode with Mr. and Mrs. Ross Perot   Ibid., January 20, 1969.

143 At the suggestion   Author interview with GHWB. See also *LF,* 98–99; and *WP,* January 21, 1969.

143 Bush shook Johnson's hand   *LF,* 99. The scene and its implications are also covered in *LSY,* 138; Naftali, *GHWB,* 20–21; GWB, *41,* 89.

143 The congressman recalled   *LF,* 98–99.

143 After Bush "wished him"   Ibid., 99.

143 Johnson also appreciated   LBJ to GHWB, January 31, 1969, Lyndon B. Johnson Presidential Library. See also *LSY,* 138.

143 he had asked Bush   Joe B. Frantz to LBJ, January 23, 1969, Lyndon B. Johnson Presidential Library. See also LBJ to Joe B. Frantz, January 30, 1969, Lyndon B. Johnson Presidential Library.

143 From Bush's perspective   *LSY,* 138.

143 should Bush challenge   Naftali, *GHWB,* 20–21.

143 it was just possible   *LSY,* 138.

143 "Please know that I value"   LBJ to GHWB, January 31, 1969, Correspondence of Lyndon B. Johnson and GHWB, Lyndon B. Johnson Presidential Library.

143 dwelling "in a world congested"   *ATB,* 120.

144 "He just must"   BPB diary, February 10, 1969.

144 WORTH THE RISK? Wicker, *GHWB*, 21–24; *LSY*, 137–42.

144 FLEW TO SEE THE FORMER PRESIDENT *LF*, 100–101. I also drew on the account of the visit in BPB diary, April 9, 1969. Bush's trip to the ranch at Stonewall was the subject of some speculation afterward. In a Washington press conference on May 28, 1969, Bush was asked whether he had consulted Johnson about a possible Senate race, and Bush said yes, he had. "I feel better informed about the Senate race. . . . You can't talk to a man like the President about Texas politics without being better informed. Our meeting at the ranch was very informal. I had a very nice letter from him asking me to drop in—really nothing more than that." Had Johnson mentioned Ralph Yarborough? "No," Bush replied. "He didn't say anything about him nor did he say anything about favoring either me or Senator Yarborough." ("Bush Press Conference" transcript, May 28, 1969, Lyndon B. Johnson Presidential Library.) After the press conference, Bush was concerned that he had inadvertently put Johnson in an awkward position. He called Tom Johnson, an LBJ aide, to explain what had been asked and what he had said, and then wrote LBJ a letter making the same points. (Tom Johnson to LBJ, May 28, 1969, LBJ Papers; GHWB to LBJ, May 29, 1969, Lyndon B. Johnson Presidential Library.)

144 "MR. PRESIDENT, I'VE STILL GOT" *LF*, 100–101.

144 "SON," JOHNSON SAID Ibid.; BPB diary, April 9, 1969.

144 BUSH CALLED ON PRESIDENT NIXON BPB diary, May 22, 1969.

144 "THE PRESIDENT SAID" Ibid.

144 "WE ARE MOVING INTO A NEW DECADE" *ATB*, 123. November 1969 had brought encouraging news: A Texas Republican, Marvin Collins of Austin, had successfully managed Linwood Holton's campaign to become the first Republican governor of Virginia in a century. The Virginia victory gave fresh hope to Republicans across the South, and Collins, a Bush adviser, now had firsthand experience in breaking the longtime Democratic hold on statewide offices. (*DMN*, January 5, 1970; *LSY*, 136.)

145 BAKER'S FATHER HAD BEEN AN ADMIRER Baker with Fiffer, *Work Hard*, 75.

145 "YOU RAN A GREAT RACE" James A. Baker, Jr., to GHWB, November 6, 1964, box 12/12, James A. Baker III Papers, Seeley G. Mudd Library, Princeton University. Hereafter cited as James A. Baker III Papers, Princeton.

145 THERE WERE COOKOUT LUNCHES Baker with DeFrank, *Politics of Diplomacy*, 18.

145 BUSH WAS QUICK AT THE NET Ibid. Bush called double faults "power outages." (Author interview with Jonathan Bush.)

145 TOGETHER THEY WON Baker with DeFrank, *Politics of Diplomacy*, 18.

145 AFTER LUNCH ON THANKSGIVING DAY Baker with Fiffer, *Work Hard*, 355.

145 BAKER CONSIDERED MAKING HIS OWN RUN JAB III to GHWB, July 24, 1969, box 12/10, James A. Baker III Papers, Princeton.

145 BUT BAKER COULD NOT DO IT JAB III to GHWB, August 22, 1969, box 12/13, James A. Baker III Papers, Princeton. For Bush's reply to Baker, see GHWB to JAB III, August 28, 1969, box 12/13, James A. Baker III Papers, Princeton.

145 THE BUSHES WERE THE LAST Baker with DeFrank, *Politics of Diplomacy*, 18.

145 "YOU NEED TO DO SOMETHING" Author interview with James A. Baker III.

146 A "BIG BROTHER—LITTLE BROTHER" DYNAMIC Baker with DeFrank, *Politics of Diplomacy*, 19.

146 (BAKER AFFECTIONATELY CALLED BUSH "JEFE") Author observation.

146 BUSH CALLED ON NIXON IN THE OVAL OFFICE *Time*, January 26, 1970; *DMN*, January 10, 1970; *NYT*, January 14, 1970; *WP*, January 14, 1970.

146 "I WISH YOU LUCK" *Time*, January 26, 1970.

146 A FILM CREW SHOT FOOTAGE *NYT*, April 6, 1970.

146 JOHN CONNALLY AND OTHER DEMOCRATS   *DMN,* December 19, 1969, December 31, 1969; *LSY,* 141; Naftali, *GHWB,* 22; and Wicker, *GHWB,* 22. There was also some talk that Connally himself might run. "One aim of the group seeking to persuade Connally or Bentsen to run for the Senate is to keep a strong conservative voice from Texas in the national Democratic party, partly with a view to helping return some influence [to] conservatives on national party affairs," wrote *The Dallas Morning News*'s Richard Morehead. (*DMN,* December 19, 1969.) For his part, Johnson publicly refused to be drawn into the primary race. (Memorandum of Tom Johnson to LBJ, January 13, 1970, Lyndon B. Johnson Presidential Library.) In the general election, Johnson denied a report that he had asked President Nixon to prevent the Teamsters from endorsing Bush for the Senate seat. "This is a pure lie," Johnson wrote on an internal memorandum reporting a press inquiry (from Charlie Bartlett) about the rumor. "I have never called Nixon on anything—Have never discuss[ed] Tex. Senate race or any other race with Nixon or any of his cohorts." (Handwritten notation of LBJ on Memorandum from Willie Day Taylor to LBJ, July 9, 1970, Lyndon B. Johnson Presidential Library.)

146 RIVALS IN THE TEXAS POLITICS OF THE AGE   Douglas Harlan, "The Party's Over," *Texas Monthly,* January 1982; Al Reinert, "Bob and George Go to Washington or the Post-Watergate Scramble," *Texas Monthly,* April 1974; *Chicago Tribune,* November 11, 1967.

146 CONNALLY HAD BEEN A LAWYER FOR SID RICHARDSON   *NYT,* June 16, 1993. See also *WP,* December 28, 1960.

147 TEXANS "WILL BE CONFRONTED"   *DMN,* February 6, 1970.

147 BENTSEN DEFEATED YARBOROUGH   Martin Waldron, "Conservative Beats Yarborough in Democratic Primary in Texas," *NYT,* May 3, 1970. See also Ibid., May 4, 1970.

147 REPORTED THAT BENTSEN HAD WON   *NYT,* May 3, 1970.

147 THE SOUTHERN STRATEGY WAS   Ibid., May 4, 1970; *LAT,* April 12, 1970.

147 A TROUBLING SIGN FOR ANOTHER SOUTHERN LIBERAL   *NYT,* May 6, 1970.

147 IN A PRIMARY AD FOR BENTSEN   *The Wall Street Journal,* October 15, 1970.

148 "SERVE AS THE FIRST BROAD REFERENDUM"   *Time,* January 26, 1970.

148 AN ELEVEN-PAGE MEMORANDUM   Richard Nixon, *RN: The Memoirs of Richard Nixon* (New York, 1978), 490–91.

148 BRIGHT, AGGRESSIVE, AND UNAPOLOGETICALLY CONSERVATIVE   Patrick J. Buchanan, *Right from the Start* (Boston, 1988), 13, 24, 267–93, 325; *Current Biography, 1985* (New York, 1986), 49–50.

148 THE KEY VOTER   Nixon, *RN,* 490–91.

148 "TO KNOW THAT THE LADY IN DAYTON"   Ibid., 491.

148 "IF THIS ANALYSIS"   Ibid.

149 "SCHOOL BUSING, TED KENNEDY"   Carl Freund, "Bush Blasts Against School Busing," *DMN,* September 16, 1970.

149 FAVORED MAKING POSSESSION OF MARIJUANA   Ibid., August 11, 1970.

149 HE OPPOSED FIREARM REGISTRATION   Ibid., October 23, 1970.

149 "THE WAY TO TURN THE KIDS OFF"   Rowland Evans and Robert Novak, "The GOP's Southern Star," *WP,* November 1, 1970. During the student unrest of the late 1960s, Bush had joined a group of fellow congressmen for a secret tour of college campuses organized by Bill Brock of Tennessee. Realizing they had too little firsthand knowledge of what was happening in terms of campus demonstrations, Brock asked Bush and four other GOP lawmakers to breakfast, where he proposed that they quietly lead groups of colleagues to different colleges to see what was happening. There

would be no advance publicity, just conversations. In a report to President Nixon after the visits, the Republicans struck a moderate tone, urging the White House to resist calls coming from the right to curtail federal money to institutions prone to demonstrations. (*WP*, May 29, 1969; *Chicago Tribune*, June 8, 1969; *NYT*, June 20, 1969.)

149 REHIRED AD MAN HARRY TRELEAVEN *WSJ*, October 15, 1970. See also *LSY*, 143.

149 "FOR BUSH, POLITICS IS A PERSONAL GAME" *DMN*, August 30, 1970.

149 WAS "TO MAKE GOOD THINGS HAPPEN" Ibid.

149 "PACKAGING [BUSH] LIKE A BAR OF SOAP" *DMN*, October 7, 1970. But it was, it seemed, working. "They've succeeded pretty well in painting Bentsen as the establishment guy, older and old-fashioned, and Bush as the fresh, young, new face," George Christian, a Bentsen adviser, told the *NYT*'s R. W. Apple, Jr. (*NYT*, October 30, 1970.)

149 IN ONE TRELEAVEN SPOT Norman C. Miller, "Television's Key Role in Politics Illustrated by Texas Senate Race," *The Wall Street Journal*, October 15, 1970.

149 BUSH TOSSED A FOOTBALL Ibid.

149 "DURING THE SEVENTIES" Ibid.

149 IT WAS ONE OF MORE THAN THREE DOZEN Ibid.

149 "OUR PROBLEM WAS" Ibid. Bentsen accused Bush of speaking in "glittering generalities." (*DMN*, October 7, 1970.)

150 BUSH CLAIMED HIS POLLING *WP*, October 13, 1970.

150 THE NIXON ADMINISTRATION'S POPULARITY Ibid.

150 "IN THE VIEW OF SOME" David S. Broder, "Nixon May Find '72 Mate," *WP*, October 27, 1970.

150 "SEEMS FAR FETCHED" Ibid. Bush made the expected noises when asked about it, saying: "I'm running for the Senate in Texas and for nothing else." (*DMN*, October 28, 1970; *LAT*, October 28, 1970; *WP*, October 28, 1970.) Broder's story was thought to have come from Robert Finch, a White House adviser who disliked Agnew, and it was widely seen as another attempt by the Nixon operation to bolster Bush. (James M. Naughton, "Agnew Rumor May Have Been a Trick," *NYT*, November 11, 1970.)

150 BUSH LOST TO BENTSEN "Voting and Elections Collection," CQ Press, http://library.cqpress.com/elections/.

150 RURAL TURNOUT *NYT*, November 4, 1970; *LAT*, November 22, 1970; *Chicago Tribune*, November 4, 1970; author interview with GHWB.

150 "LIKE CUSTER" *Big Spring Daily Herald*, November 4, 1970.

150 "GOD IT HURTS TO LOSE" *ATB*, 128. Bush had spent about $400,000 more than Bentsen, but the money was obviously not decisive. An unnamed "political source" in the *LAT* laid the blame squarely with the candidate and his men. "They think of the typical Texas voter as living in Dallas or Houston," the source said. "But he doesn't; he lives in the rural area. For another thing, Bush has always lived in the wealthy country club areas of cities in Texas, as in Odessa or Midland or Houston. And so he doesn't really know the electorate." (*LAT*, November 22, 1970.)

150 "I'M THE ONLY GIRL" *ATB*, 129; *DMN*, November 5, 1970.

150 "WE'RE TORN BETWEEN" *ATB*, 129. Barbara did worry about George W. "Georgie Bush campaigned for two months and hard. We were so proud of our son. People loved him all over the state. I now believe that the loss was as hard on Georgie as it was on us." (BPB diary, January 1, 1971.) Asked about his mother's concerns, George W. Bush recalled, "I took it hard. I love the guy." (Author interview with GWB.) In the White House, meanwhile, Nixon was happier with the overall midterm results

than he had expected to be. The Republicans lost only nine House seats and won two in the Senate, which was much better than midterms in times of economic stress usually were for the incumbent presidential party. (Nixon, *RN*, 494–95.)

150   "WHAT," *THE DALLAS MORNING NEWS* ASKED   *DMN*, November 6, 1970.

FOURTEEN: *A Turn on the World Stage*

151   THE FACT THAT ONE DOOR   "Remarks at the Swearing In of George Bush as United States Representative to the United Nations," February 26, 1971, *Public Papers of the Presidents of the United States: Richard Nixon, 1971* (Washington, D.C., 1972), 345–47.

151   CHARLES BARTLETT, THE KENNEDY INTIMATE   *ATB*, 133. See also Wicker, *GHWB*, 25–27.

151   "YOU'D BE AMAZED"   *ATB*, 133.

151   "TALKED ABOUT THE U.N."   Ibid.

151   LOTS OF THOSE   *LSY*, 146–47.

151   POSSIBILITY OF A POST WITH SECRETARY OF STATE WILLIAM P. ROGERS   BPB diary, November 7, 1969. Rogers had raised the possibility of Bush's coming to the State Department if the Texas race did not work out. (Ibid.)

151   COMMISSION TO REORGANIZE THE FEDERAL GOVERNMENT   James Reston, Jr., *The Lone Star: The Life of John Connally* (New York, 1989), 376–79.

151   PETER O'DONNELL WROTE PETER FLANIGAN   Ibid., 380.

151   TEXAS REPUBLICANS COULD NOT SEE   Ibid.

151   "CONNALLY IS AN IMPLACABLE ENEMY"   Ibid.

152   THE PRESIDENT NAMED CONNALLY   Ibid. As Reston wrote, Tower and Bush could not quite believe it. "As you know, John Tower and George Bush are extremely upset over the appointment of Connally" to the panel, Bill Timmons, Nixon's assistant for legislative affairs, wrote Haldeman, who replied: "This is not a major appointment and is not made to 'give recognition' to Connally. It is a bipartisan board with no visibility and P. needed a strong Democrat member for obvious reasons in connection with our foreign policy. Connally, as you know, was helpful in getting reorgan. passed on the Hill & can be very helpful in foreign policy areas of great importance." (Ibid., 649–50.) See also Naftali, *GHWB*, 23, and *LSY*, 145–47.

152   BY EARLY DECEMBER 1970 THERE WAS MUCH BIGGER NEWS   Reston, *Lone Star*, 380–81.

152   REPLACING THE BANKER DAVID KENNEDY   Ibid., 379–81. "I've never seen the President so pleased—from the personal standpoint," Haldeman wrote. (Ibid., 381.)

152   NIXON AND CONNALLY UNDERSTOOD   *ATB*, 131.

152   "CONNALLY SET"   Reston, *Lone Star*, 382.

152   BUSH HAD NOT FORGOTTEN   *ATB*, 133.

152   TRYING TO ACT AS A BROKER   BPB diary, January 1, 1971.

152   AN ANHEUSER-BUSCH HEIR   *WP*, December 22, 1969; *NYT*, August 1, 2013.

152   "I WAS ABOUT READY TO SUGGEST"   BPB diary, January 1, 1971.

152   FLANIGAN, LIEDTKE SUGGESTED   Ibid.

152   TAKING THE HINT   Ibid.

152   WOULD HE BE INTERESTED   Ibid.

152   BUSH SAID YES   Ibid.

153   "WELL, YOU KNOW, GEORGE"   Ibid.

153   ("HOW GEORGE KEPT HIS TEMPER")   Ibid.

153   BUSH REPORTED TO HALDEMAN'S WEST WING OFFICE   *ATB*, 132. See also *LSY*, 146–48.

153 BUSH MADE HIS CASE   Ibid.

153 "SPELL OUT"   Ibid.

153 NIXON HAD NOT CONSIDERED   Ibid. See also *LSY,* 147.

153 "WAIT A MINUTE, BOB"   *ATB,* 132.

153 NIXON PAUSED   Ibid., 132–33.

153 NIXON TOLD HALDEMAN TO GET BUSH   Author interview with GHWB. For the Bush U.N. appointment, see also Naftali, *GHWB,* 23, and Wicker, *GHWB,* 25–27.

153 WENT BACK TO   *ATB,* 133.

153 THOUGHT THINGS OVER   *LSY,* 147.

153 SEEMS TO HAVE DECIDED   Ibid.

153 "BUSH'S ARGUMENTS WERE WELL TAKEN"   Ibid.

154 BUSH "TAKES OUR LINE BEAUTIFULLY"   *The China Diary of George H. W. Bush. The Making of a Global President,* ed. Jeffrey A. Engel (Princeton, N.J., 2008), 411.

154 "YOU'VE SOLD THE PRESIDENT"   *ATB,* 133.

154 THE PRESIDENT SUGGESTED   BPB diary, January 1, 1971.

154 BUSH RESISTED THE IDEA   Ibid.; author interview with GHWB.

154 HE BELIEVED HIMSELF A TEXAN   Author interview with GHWB.

154 HIS OLD FRIEND LUD ASHLEY   *LSY,* 148.

154 "SEEMED AMAZED WHEN"   *ATB,* 134.

154 REACHING OUT TO OTHERS   This is a common theme in Bush's life. In terms of the new assignment, Timothy Naftali wrote: "At the United Nations Bush used his talents for listening and empathy to good effect." (Naftali, *GHWB,* 23.) See also Wicker, *GHWB,* 27.

155 BUSH INVITED HENRY KISSINGER   *ATB,* 135–36; BPB diary, January 1971.

155 TO PLAY TIDDLYWINKS   *ATB,* 135–36.

155 OVER A SUPPER OF   BPB diary, January 20, 1971.

155 "HENRY TOLD US"   Ibid. See also *ATB,* 136.

155 BORN IN GERMANY IN 1923   Walter Isaacson, *Kissinger: A Biography* (New York, 1992), 20, 27–28, 39–49, 59, 506; *Current Biography, 1972* (New York, 1972), 254–57; Henry Kissinger, "Sitting with DiMaggio and Steinbrenner," *NYT,* September 21, 2008.

156 THE BUSHES ENTERED THE STATE DINING ROOM   BPB diary, February 26, 1971.

156 "I DIDN'T GET ALL THIS ATTENTION"   Ibid.

156 HE HAD BREAKFASTED THAT MORNING   "Remarks at the Swearing In of George Bush as United States Representative to the United Nations," February 26, 1971, *Public Papers of the Presidents of the United States: Richard Nixon, 1971,* 345–47.

156 "THE FACT THAT ONE DOOR"   Ibid.

156 POTTER STEWART . . . ADMINISTERED THE OATH   BPB diary, February 26, 1971.

156 DOROTHY BUSH'S FACE   Ibid.

156 BUSH WAS EMOTIONAL   Ibid.

156 THE GEORGE BUSHES WERE IN NEW YORK   Ibid., March 2, 1971.

156 "I FIND IT VERY DIFFICULT"   *ATB,* 142.

157 BUSH HURLED HIMSELF   *ATB,* 139.

157 YAKOV MALIK   *LF,* 111–12.

158 "HE REPEATED ALL THE COLD WAR RHETORIC"   Ibid., 145–46.

158 AT A UN SECURITY COUNCIL SESSION   BPB diary, January 15, 1972.

158 HIS "MOST DIFFICULT ISSUE"   *ATB,* 140; Engel, ed., *China Diary of George H. W. Bush,* 418–24; Naftali, *GHWB,* 23–25; *LSY,* 151–53; Wicker, *GHWB,* 29.

158 THE REPUBLIC OF CHINA   *ATB,* 140.

158 HAD INSISTED ON RECOGNIZING TAIWAN   Naftali, *GHWB,* 23.

158 HELD CHINA'S SEAT   Ibid.; *ATB*, 140.

158 THE DEBATE OVER TAIWAN'S FATE   *ATB*, 140–41. See also *LF*, 114–16.

159 PRESSING AHEAD WITH DUAL REPRESENTATION   *LF*, 114. See also *ATB*, 149–54.

159 FOR BUSH, THE PROBLEM   *LF*, 116.

159 "THE BALL GAME IS OVER"   *ATB*, 149–50.

159 BECAUSE TAIWAN WAS IMPORTANT   Author correspondence with Jeffrey A. Engel. I am indebted to Engel for his guidance and analysis on these points. As he wrote: "I understand Bush's fight for Taiwan's continued representation along three levels. First, he was loyal: we had given our word to the Taiwanese—specifically, he had given his word to their U.N. ambassador—and he thought the U.S. should keep its promises to its old friends, even as it courted new friends. Second, he was following Nixon's orders and frankly was deluding himself a touch, I think, in telling himself that he worked for Nixon and not Kissinger, and thus could blame the prince for failures he'd rather not see in the king. Third and most important: he was told to win, and here the Bush competitive instinct kicked in." (Ibid.)

159 KISSINGER TRAVELED TO THE MAINLAND   Naftali, *GHWB*, 24; Wicker, *GHWB*, 29.

159 "IT WAS AN UGLINESS"   *ATB*, 154.

159 TAIWAN WAS ULTIMATELY EXPELLED   Ibid., 153.

159 "LIFE GOES ON"   Ibid., 154–55.

159 "CLEARLY HOSTILE TO THE UNITED STATES"   Ibid., 155.

159 "IF WE APPEAR TO BE PUSHED AROUND"   Ibid.

160 THE TWO MEN MET   Ibid. For analysis of Bush's view of the episode, see Naftali, *GHWB*, 24–25.

160 "HE STARTED OFF"   *ATB*, 155.

160 "I WANT TO TREAT YOU"   Ibid.

160 THE THREAT DID NOT SIT WELL   Ibid., 155–56.

160 "A VERY HEATED"   Ibid., 156.

160 "I TOLD HIM"   Ibid.

160 "REALLY COOLED DOWN"   Ibid.

160 A FAIRLY TYPICAL WEEKEND DAY   BPB diary, January 9, 1972.

160 BUSH LIKED TAKING DIFFERENT FOREIGN DIPLOMATS   Author interviews with GHWB and BPB.

160 AND EVEN AFTER THE TAIWAN DEBACLE   Engel, ed., *China Diary of George H. W. Bush*, 413; author interviews with GHWB and BPB; Naftali, *GHWB*, 25.

160 BUSH'S MOTHER CALLED   *ATB*, 159.

160 "HE SEEMS INSTANTLY OLD"   Ibid.

161 RESULTED IN COMPLICATIONS   Ibid., 160–61.

161 BUSH WAS SUMMONED FROM A DINNER   Ibid., 161.

161 "FULL OF TUBES"   Ibid.

161 "HE WAS CONSCIOUS"   Ibid.

161 "WHO PICKED UP THE TAB?"   Ibid.

161 PRESCOTT SHELDON BUSH DIED   *NYT*, October 9, 1972. See also *WP*, October 9, 1972. From Texas, Lyndon Johnson telegraphed: "Your father was one of the finest men ever to serve in the United States Senate." (LBJ to GHWB, October 9, 1972.) Bush replied. "I will never forget my Dad's telling me of his admiration for you, Mr President, the strong but *fair* way in which you ran the Senate." (GHWB to LBJ, October 12, 1972, Correspondence of Lyndon B. Johnson and GHWB, Lyndon B. Johnson Presidential Library.)

161 MOURNERS INCLUDED AVERELL HARRIMAN   *NYT*, October 11, 1972.

161 "OUR BOYS ALL CAME HOME"   BPB diary, October 23, 1972, January 9, 1973.

FIFTEEN: *This Job Is No Fun at All*

162 ONE REAL CHALLENGE *ATB*, 164.

162 RICHARD NIXON HAD BIG PLANS *LF*, 121. Bush remembered that Nixon "was relaxed—at least, more relaxed than than during the campaign." (Ibid.) For Nixon's 1972 win, subsequent plans, and Watergate, see, for instance: *ATB*, 162–97; *LF*, 120–25; Nicholas Lemann, "Bush and Dole: The Roots of a Feud," *WP*, February 28, 1988; Naftali, *GHWB*, 25–29; *LSY*, 155–67; Wicker, *GHWB*, 31–32.

162 IT WAS MONDAY, NOVEMBER 20, 1972 Notes of John Ehrlichman from meeting of President Nixon, John Ehrlichman, and GHWB, 11:15 A.M., November 20, 1972, Aspen Lodge, Camp David, Md., Richard M. Nixon Presidential Library.

162 "THIS IS AN IMPORTANT TIME" *LF*, 121. As Theodore H. White reported in *The Making of the President, 1972* (New York, 1973), 10, Nixon believed 1972 might well be an historical turning point. "Not only the South was shifting, but others—workingmen and Catholics, too," White wrote in describing Nixon's views aboard Air Force One on Election Day. "The Republican Party used to be a WASP party, he recalled, and he used to talk about it in the old days with Len Hall, who came from Nassau County. Len understood. You used to go to a Republican dinner in those days and there wouldn't be an Irishman or an Italian or a Jew there. If you could shift those allegiances permanently, then this landslide might mean something." (Ibid.)

Bush does not seem to have been told of Nixon's grandest political plan of all— one that would have put Bush out of work. In the tranquillity of Camp David the president had been mulling a revolution in party politics. The 1972 landslide had provided concrete evidence that Nixon's earlier thinking about a "New Majority" had merit—a "New Majority" formed by holding on to traditional Republicans and adding disaffected Democrats who were unhappy with the drift of their party. (Nixon, *RN*, 490–92; 769–70.) On Friday, December 1, 1972, Nixon, Haldeman, and Ehrlichman talked about jettisoning the Republican Party altogether and building a vehicle to elect John Connally as Nixon's successor. (Nixon, *RN*, 769–70; see also Reston, *Lone Star*, 443.)

162 KANSAS SENATOR BOB DOLE Lemann, "Bush and Dole," *WP*, February 28, 1988.

162 NIXON TALKED BIG Notes of John Ehrlichman from meeting of President Nixon, John Ehrlichman, and GHWB, 11:15 A.M., November 20, 1972, Aspen Lodge, Camp David, Md., Richard M. Nixon Presidential Library.

162 BUSH WAS SURPRISED *ATB*, 162–63.

162 A "LOVE AFFAIR" Ibid., 163.

162 NIXON WANTED HIM Ibid., 181–82; *LSY*, 157–59.

162 "A TOTAL NIXON MAN—FIRST" *LSY*, 157.

163 "I CAN AND WILL" *ATB*, 163.

163 "NOT ALL THAT ENTHRALLED" Notes of John Ehrlichman, November 20, 1972.

163 "SHE IS CONVINCED" *ATB*, 163–64.

163 "MY WIFE'S INITIAL REACTION" Ibid., 164.

163 THE SCANDAL THAT DESTROYED See, for instance, "Watergate: Chronology of a Crisis," *Congressional Quarterly* (Washington, D.C., 1973), 3–12; Naftali, *GHWB*, 26–30; *LSY*, 155–56, 160–67, 170–72.

164 BUSH TOOK COMMAND BPB diary, January 26, 1973.

164 BUSH COULD NOT COMPLAIN Ibid., January 24, 1973.

164 FROM JANUARY 20 THROUGH DECEMBER 23, 1973 "GB's Public Appearances," Office Memorandum, Republican National Committee, December 23, 1973, in BPB diary, 1973.

164 BACK AT THE COMMITTEE'S OFFICES   *LF,* 123. Bush hated what he saw as the arrogance of the Nixon political universe. In a small but nevertheless telling example, Mississippi Republican leader Clarke Reed recalled visiting Bush one day at the RNC offices. "Look at this," Bush said, waving a stack of Nixon political operative Jeb Stuart Magruder's parking tickets, which came to Bush's desk because Magruder had an RNC limo. "These guys just don't respect the law." As Reed recalled, "It was clear to me that Bush was irritated by the whole thing, didn't understand breaking the rules." (Author interview with Clarke Reed.)

164 HE WAS LOYAL TO THE PRESIDENT   *LF,* 123–24. See also Wicker, *GHWB,* 31–36.

164 THE "POINT MAN"   *LF,* 124; Green, *George Bush,* 134.

165 THEN A TWENTY-YEAR-OLD   Author interview with Jeb Bush.

165 "EITHER PEOPLE WERE SAYING"   Ibid.

165 "KNOWING DAD, AS YOU DID"   *ATB,* 176.

165 WORD OF THE NIXON WHITE HOUSE TAPES   Ibid., 184; Naftali, *GHWB,* 28.

165 IN THE SOUTHWEST LOBBY   *ATB,* 184.

165 "I AM SHOCKED"   Ibid.

165 TO RUN FOR GOVERNOR IN TEXAS   Ibid., 171–72.

165 "THIS ISN'T THE TIME"   Ibid.

165 RECALLED ENCOUNTERING BUSH   Wicker, *GHWB,* 33–34.

165 "TOOK ME ASIDE"   Ibid., 34.

165 "BUSH WAS TRYING HARD"   Ibid.

165 AGNEW RESIGNED   *LSY,* 162.

166 BUSH HAD BEEN MENTIONED   Potter, Lee Ann and Wynell Schamel, "Letter from House of Minority Leader Gerald R. Ford to President M. Nixon." Social Education 65, 2 (March 2001), 116–120. Potter and Schamel write that Nixon "received hundreds of letters from members of Congress listing potential nominees" for vice president. "Suggestions included Nelson Rockefeller, governor of New York; John Connally, former governor of Texas; William P. Rogers, secretary of state; George Bush, chairman of the Republican National Committee; Barry Goldwater, senator from Arizona; and Mel Laird, secretary of defense." (Ibid.)

166 AS HAD AN OLD HOUSE COLLEAGUE   Donald Rumsfeld, *Known and Unknown: A Memoir* (New York, 2011), 152–53.

166 BRIGHT, AMBITIOUS, AND SELF-CONFIDENT   Ibid., 37, 47.

166 AS A WRESTLER   Ibid., 48.

166 AFTER GRADUATING IN 1954   Ibid., 58–65, 120–122, 130, 139–40, 145.

166 BY OCTOBER 1973, NIXON WAS LOSING   See J. Anthony Lukas, *Nightmare: The Underside of the Nixon Years* (New York, 1976), 438–41; Stanley Kutler, *The Wars of Watergate: The Last Crisis of Richard Nixon* (New York, 1990), 406–11; David Broder, "Nixon Political Clout Shrinks," *WP,* October 22, 1973.

166 NIXON CLAIMED THAT   *ATB,* 172.

166 "I AM APPALLED"   Ibid.

166 "EXTREMELY COMPLICATED TIMES"   Ibid., 176.

166 A REJECTION BY THE UNIVERSITY OF TEXAS LAW SCHOOL   BPB diary, January 20, 1971.

166 LEFT HIM "IN SHOCK"   Ibid.

166 "BAINE SAYS THAT GEORGE"   Ibid., January 31, 1971.

166 "HE SAYS THAT IT IS POLITICAL"   Ibid.

167 AFTER A PENTAGON SCREENING   Ibid., January 21, 1971.

167 "PROMPTLY WANTED TO GO"   Ibid.

167 "HE IS REALLY WORRYING"   Ibid.

167 THERE WAS QUIET SPECULATION   Ibid., October 1, 1971.
167 "HE IS VERY SERIOUSLY CONSIDERING RUNNING"   Ibid.
167 HE WOULD HAVE FACED   Author interview with GWB.
167 "WE HOPE HE'LL FEEL SETTLED"   BPB diary, January 7, 1972.
167 JEB HAD SPENT SEVERAL MONTHS IN THE WINTER OF 1970–71   WP, January 22, 1989.
167 "JEBBY IS GOING TO NEED"   ATB, 143.
167 IN MEXICO, JEB MET AND FELL INSTANTLY IN LOVE   WP, January 22, 1989.
167 HIS FRIENDS THOUGHT COLUMBA MADE JEB   Ibid.
167 JEB ANNOUNCED THAT   BB, 103; BPB diary, December 26, 1973.
167 ON THE DAY AFTER CHRISTMAS, 1973   BPB diary, December 26, 1973.
167 CRASHED INTO SOME TRASH CANS   GWB, 41, 82.
167 "YOUR BEHAVIOR IS DISGRACEFUL"   Ibid.
167 "I UNDERSTAND"   Ibid.
167 HAD "DEFIANTLY CHARGED UPSTAIRS"   Ibid.
167 "YOU WANT TO GO MANO A MANO"   www.vanityfair.com/news/2000/10/bush 200010.
168 THE FATHER LOWERED THE BOOK   GWB, 41, 82.
168 THE SILENT STARE   Ibid. "I felt like a fool," George W. recalled. "I slunk out of the room, chastened by the knowledge that I had disappointed my father so deeply that he would not speak to me." (Ibid.)
168 "HE NORMALLY IS A GOOD GUY"   BPB diary, December 26, 1973.
168 "HE SAYS THAT HE DRANK SO MUCH"   Ibid.
168 (RECALLING THE "MANO A MANO" MOMENT)   Author interview with GHWB.
168 "HE DIDN'T REALLY WANT TO"   Ibid.
168 ("I WAS PROBABLY JUST LOOKING")   Author interview with GWB.
168 "HOW I WORRY"   BB, 104.
168 APPEARED TO BE "A GREAT INFLUENCE"   Ibid., 103.
168 "WE WERE NOTIFIED"   Ibid., 103–4.
168 BARBARA GAVE JEB HER GRANDMOTHER PIERCE'S WEDDING RING   Ibid., 104.
168 THE COUPLE WERE MARRIED IN AUSTIN   Ibid.
168 BUSH LONG INSISTED THAT   ATB, 177.
168 HE WAS, HOWEVER, "SICKENED"   Ibid., 177–78.
168 THE APRIL 1974 RELEASE   Ibid., 177.
168 "THE WHOLE AMORAL TONE"   Ibid., 177–78.
169 JULIE NIXON EISENHOWER   Author interview with GHWB. See also BB, 104.
169 "IT OCCURRED TO ME"   ATB, 180, 185.
169 THE SUPREME COURT RULED   Nixon, RN, 1051; ATB, 186.
169 BUSH WENT TO THE WHITE HOUSE   ATB, 186–88. Haig told Bush that there would be "more bad news including a major shock from one of the tapes." He thought, too, that Nixon would make one last stand. "If [that decision] was made," Haig said, "the President would have to take the offense, go up and testify himself, work with the Party, work with the Senators, have a very strong offense." (Ibid., 187.) The implied question was whether Bush and the Republican Party would follow Nixon into such a battle. If Nixon chose to fight, he needed all the help he could muster. He needed George Bush and the RNC. Would Bush and the party be there for the president during a Senate trial? The answer, phrased politely, was probably not. (Ibid., 186–89.)
169 "HE OUGHT TO DO IT NOW"   Ibid., 187.
169 "IF HE RESIGNED"   Ibid.
169 DEAN BURCH CALLED BUSH   Ibid., 188.

169   AN OLD GOLDWATER ADVISER   *NYT,* August 5, 1991.

169   RHODES HAD CALLED BUSH   *Time,* August 12, 1974.

169   "YOU GOT ANY"   Ibid.

170   NOW THE NEWS WAS THE IMPENDING RELEASE   *ATB,* 186.

170   HAD SPOKEN FOR AN HOUR   www.nixonlibrary.gov/forresearchers/find/tapes/water
gate/trial/exhibit_01.pdf; Transcripts of a recording of a meeting between the President and H. R. Haldeman in the Oval Office on June 23, 1972, from 10:04 to 11:39
A.M., Richard M. Nixon Presidential Library.

170   "THIS WAS PROOF THE PRESIDENT"   *ATB,* 186.

170   BUSH SPOKE OF STEPPING DOWN   Ibid., 188.

170   BURCH AND BUZHARDT ARGUED   Ibid.

170   "I DO NOT FEEL THE PRESIDENT"   Ibid., 189.

170   "I [AM] TORN"   Ibid.

170   THE PRESIDENT "FEELS I'M SOFT"   Ibid., 181–82.

170   THE "SYSTEM"   Ibid., 185.

170   "CIVILITY WILL RETURN TO WASHINGTON"   Ibid., 185.

171   NIXON WAS RUNNING LATE   Gerald R. Ford, *A Time to Heal: The Autobiography of Gerald R. Ford* (New York, 1979), 18.

171   THE SESSION WAS PUSHED BACK   Ibid.; *ATB,* 190.

171   "THE ATMOSPHERE"   *ATB,* 190.

171   WHEN NIXON FINALLY ENTERED   Nixon, *RN,* 1065.

171   "IT WAS OBVIOUS"   Ford, *Time to Heal,* 18.

171   WAS "SALLOW"   Ibid.

171   THE PRESIDENT CHECKED THE CLOCK   Ibid.

171   TURNING TO HIS NOTES   Ibid.

171   "I WOULD LIKE TO DISCUSS"   Ibid.

171   BUSH WAS MYSTIFIED   Author interview with GHWB.

171   "MY GOD!"   Ford, *Time to Heal,* 18–19.

171   NIXON TURNED TO WATERGATE   Ibid., 19–20.

171   HE KNEW, HE SAID   Ibid.

171   SO THERE IT WAS   Ibid., 20; *ATB,* 190.

171   "I VETOED $35 BILLION"   Ford, *Time to Heal,* 20.

171   AN UNCOMFORTABLE NIXON   *ATB,* 190; GHWB, August 6, 1974, Personal Notes—
Oct. 73–Aug. 74 (2), Republican National Committee, Personal Papers, GHWB
Collection, GBPL.

171   AND MOUTHED "GEORGE"   *ATB,* 190.

171   "MY HEART WENT TOTALLY"   Ibid.

171   BREAKING THE SILENCE   Ford, *Time to Heal,* 20–21.

172   "WELL, JERRY"   Ibid., 20.

172   "NO ONE REGRETS"   Ibid., 21.

172   NIXON, FORD THOUGHT, "SEEMED"   Ibid.

172   THE PRESIDENT TRIED   Ibid.

172   NEW FARM APPROPRIATIONS BILL   Nixon, *RN,* 1066.

172   "BILL, I HAVE THE ABILITY"   Ford, *Time to Heal,* 21.

172   BUSH TRIED TO GET NIXON'S ATTENTION   Nixon, *RN,* 1066.

172   SAXBE "WAS RIGHT"   GHWB, August 6, 1974, Personal Notes—Oct. 73–Aug. 74
(2), Republican National Committee, Personal Papers, GHWB Collection, GBPL.

172   BEST TO DO SO "EXPEDITIOUSLY"   Ibid. In his memoirs, Ford recalled Bush speaking up before Saxbe. (Ford, *Time to Heal,* 21.) My account—which has Bush reacting specifically to Saxbe's comments—is drawn from Bush's contemporaneous notes.

(GHWB, August 6, 1974, Personal Notes—Oct. 73–Aug. 74 (2), Republican National Committee, Personal Papers, GHWB Collections, GBPL.)

172 LISTENING TO BUSH Author interview with Henry Kissinger.

172 "WE ARE HERE" Nixon, *RN*, 1066.

172 "THE WHOLE GODDAMNED THING" GHWB, August 6, 1974, Personal Notes—Oct. 73–Aug. 74 (2), Republican National Committee, Personal Papers, GHWB Collection, GBPL.

173 BUSH HAD TO FLY GHWB, August 7 and 8, 1974, Personal Notes—Oct. 73–Aug. 74 (2), Republican National Committee, Personal Papers, GHWB Collection, GBPL.

173 IN HIS ROOM AT THE BEVERLY WILSHIRE GHWB personal memo, Los Angeles, Calif., August 7, 1974, Personal Notes—Oct. 73–Aug. 74 (3), Republican National Committee, Personal Papers, GHWB Collection, GBPL.

173 "DEAR MR. PRESIDENT" *ATB*, 193.

173 IT IS MY CONSIDERED JUDGMENT Ibid.

174 HE MET WITH FORD Ford, *Time to Heal*, 28–29.

174 AN "UNREAL" DAY *ATB*, 193.

174 FORD MADE TIME TO SEE BUSH Ibid.

174 TO HIS DIARY, BUSH DOWNPLAYED GHWB diary, August 7, 1974, Personal Notes—Oct. 73–Aug. 74 (3), Republican National Committee, Personal Papers, GHWB Collection, GBPL.

174 WHEN FORD AND BUSH SPOKE *ATB*, 193–94.

174 "I TALKED ABOUT THE WHITE HOUSE STAFF" Ibid.

174 "I THEN WENT ON TO THE NATIONAL SECURITY COUNCIL" Ibid., 193–94.

175 BUSH THOUGHT FORD NEEDED Ibid.

175 "PUT AN IMPRINT" Ibid., 194.

175 HE SAID HE WOULD RESIGN AS SOON Ibid.

175 THE WORK FOR 1976 Ibid.

175 "HE INDICATED THAT" Ibid.

175 THE BUSHES WERE IN THE EAST ROOM Ibid. For the complicated politics of August–September 1974—and beyond, see Barry Werth, *31 Days: Gerald Ford, the Nixon Pardon, and a Government in Crisis* (New York, 2006), an engaging account.

175 NIXON'S FAREWELL "Remarks on Departure from the White House," August 9, 1974, *Public Papers of the Presidents of the United States: Richard Nixon, 1973*, 630–33.

176 "WHAT KIND OF A MAN" GHWB, August 9, 1974, Personal Notes: Oct. 73–Aug. 74 (3), Republican National Committee, Personal Papers, GHWB Collection, GBPL.

176 BUSH GOT A CALL FROM BILL TIMMONS *ATB*, 195.

176 THE TWO MEN MET FOR THIRTY-ONE MINUTES IN THE OVAL OFFICE "Daily Diary of President Gerald R. Ford," August 11, 1974, Gerald R. Ford Presidential Library.

176 SITTING ACROSS FROM EACH OTHER Photograph of President Ford and GHWB, August 11, 1974, Gerald R. Ford Presidential Library.

176 BUSH ALLIES WERE RUNNING *LSY*, 169–70.

176 BUSH WALKED THROUGH HIS RÉSUMÉ GHWB, August 12, 1974, Personal Notes—Oct. 73–Aug. 74 (3), Republican National Committee, Personal Papers, GHWB Collection, GBPL.

176 "WORRIED ABOUT [THE] DIVISIONS" Ibid.

176 "I KEPT COMING DOWN ON THE MIDDLE GROUND" Ibid.

176 "MR. PRESIDENT, IT'S A FUNNY POSITION" Ibid.

176 "GEORGE, I DON'T HAVE ANY DOUBT" Ibid.

176 BRYCE HARLOW HAD BEEN TASKED Ford, *Time to Heal*, 142–43.

177 BUSH, HARLOW WROTE, WAS "STRONGEST" Ibid.

177 FOR FORD, THE CHOICE CAME DOWN TO   Author interview with Dick Cheney.

177 CITING UNNAMED SOURCES, *NEWSWEEK* REPORTED   Werth, *31 Days: The Crisis That Gave Us the Government We Have Today,* 114. See also *NYT,* August 19, 1974. "Townhouse" was typical of the Nixon era. (*NYT,* June 11, 1992.) See also "Gleason Interview Notes," box 131/3, James Baker III Papers, Princeton.

Working out of a townhouse in Washington, Republican operatives under the direction of Bob Haldeman reportedly distributed $3 million to various candidates in the 1970 cycle. As reconstructed by reporters and by Watergate special prosecutors, the operation was designed to fund the campaigns of Nixon favorites and, in the words of one of the political aides involved, "to set up possible blackmail for these candidates later on." (*NYT,* June 11, 1992. See also "Interviews of Jack A. Gleason," July 16, 1973, Files of Charles Ruff, Special Prosecutor's Office, U.S. Department of Justice, National Archives.)

It was ingenious in its way: By delivering $6,000 in cash to various campaigns, the Townhouse operatives hoped the money would give the Nixon team, in the words of special prosecutor Leon Jaworski, "leverage over these candidates by placing cash in their hands which they might not report." (Leon Jaworski to Charles Ruff, March 19, 1974, Files of Special Prosecutor's Office, U.S. Department of Justice, National Archives.) Jaworski wrote that Bush had received about $112,000 from Townhouse; Bush believed the number to be $106,000, and denied ever receiving the $6,000. The Watergate special prosecutor chose not to pursue Bush or his old 1970 campaign apparatus. "Bush is neither a target of our investigation nor a potential witness," Jaworski wrote. (Ibid.; see also *NYT,* June 11, 1992.)

In ensuing years Bush would maintain that his campaign had done nothing wrong. Though the issue was raised from time to time, it did not attract significant attention, perhaps because of the complicated details and an apparent lack of compelling documentation one way or another. Bush, like other Republicans of the time, including Lowell Weicker of Connecticut, was too close to the Nixon operation and may have failed to obey the letter of the reporting laws as they were written in pre-Watergate 1970. One unmistakable sign of Bush's discomfort with the whole topic: When he was at the RNC, he wondered aloud whether Townhouse records in the possession of the committee should be burned, which strongly suggests that he wanted the whole subject to go away—forever. ("Gleason Interview Notes," box 131/3, James A. Baker III Papers, Princeton; *NYT,* June 11, 1992; *WP,* August 9, 1988; *LSY,* 170–71.)

177 THE WATERGATE SPECIAL PROSECUTOR WOULD ULTIMATELY CLEAR BUSH   *LSY,* 171. See also Leon Jaworski to Charles Ruff, March 19, 1974, Files of Special Prosecutor's Office, U.S. Department of Justice, National Archives.

177 "COULD BE AN EMBARRASSMENT"   Memorandum of General Joulwan to General Haig, August 18, 1974, "Telephone Conversation with George Bush, August 18, 1974, Sunday, 11:40 a.m.," Papers of Alexander Haig, Library of Congress. Who leaked the Bush allegations in August 1974, when it could do maximum damage to his vice presidential prospects? As reconstructed by the writer Barry Werth in his study of the month after Ford took office, *31 Days,* Rumsfeld was a prominent suspect. James Cannon, a journalist who had become a Rockefeller adviser, thought the hit on Bush had to have come from Rumsfeld. "No doubt about it," Cannon later told Werth. "I'd bet money on it." Rumsfeld dismissed the speculation as "utter nonsense." (Author interview with Donald Rumsfeld.) Bush himself thought it might be Melvin Laird, who was in favor of Rockefeller. (Werth, *31 Days,* 116.)

177 THE WAITING ENDED   Werth, *31 Days,* 139.

177 "Yesterday was" *ATB*, 195.

177 Bush went to Washington Ibid., 196. See also *LF*, 129–30.

177 "What do you want?" *ATB*, 196.

177 Bush's first suggestion GHWB, August 22, 1974, Personal Notes—Oct. 73–Aug. 74 (3), Republican National Committee, Personal Papers, GHWB Collection, GBPL.

177 but Ford appeared uninterested Ibid.

177 Two diplomatic posts Ibid.

177 talked about Bush's becoming White House chief of staff Ibid.

177 Ford said that he was determined Ibid. "Initially, when I became President, I did not want to have a powerful chief of staff," Ford wrote in his memoirs. "Wilson had had his Colonel House, Eisenhower his Sherman Adams, Nixon his Haldeman, and I was aware of the trouble those top assistants had caused my predecessors. I was determined to be my own chief of staff and Al Haig [a Nixon holdover] was agreeable to this change. I would have five or six senior assistants with different areas of responsibility . . . and they would be able to see me at regular intervals during the day." Ford called it his "spokes of the wheel approach." Ford added: "But as I was to discover soon enough, it simply didn't work. Because power in Washington is measured by how much access a person has to the President, almost everyone wanted more access than I had access to give." (Ford, *Time to Heal*, 147.)

177 the ambassadorship to France GHWB, August 22, 1974, Personal Notes: Oct. 73–Aug. 74 (3), Republican National Committee, Personal Papers, GHWB Collection, GBPL.

177 "I told [Ford]" *ATB*, 196.

178 Ford had talked to Kissinger GHWB, August 26, 1974, Personal Notes: Oct. 73–Aug. 74 (3), Republican National Committee, Personal Papers, GHWB Collection, GBPL.

178 "the one that is the best for you" Ibid.

178 Bush agreed, but not without raising Ibid.

178 come in as Ford's White House chief of staff Ibid.

178 "He seemed to think" Ibid.

178 In memory . . . Bush cast the choice *LF*, 130.

178 "Back then we" Ibid.

178 "We now agreed" Ibid. Despite Bush's pairing of the roads to China and to Texas, the 1948 call had been much more of a shared project between Bush and Barbara than the China appointment was. In his 1987 campaign autobiography, Bush misremembered Barbara's role. In his recollection the two of them had discussed China before the meeting with Ford on August 22, 1974. (Ibid.)

Barbara's diary at the time and her subsequent memoir, however, show that she heard about the Beijing possibility only after it had been raised at the White House. "We were vacationing in Maine at the time, and when George returned, he told me he hoped I would understand, but he had turned down all the stylish embassies (including London and Paris) and asked for the post in the People's Republic of China—if I agreed," Barbara wrote in 1994. "To say that I was speechless is an understatement." (*BB*, 107.) Barbara quickly grew enthusiastic, not least because the assignment would mean that the two would spend more time together than they had since, perhaps, New Haven. "The more George talked, the more excited I got," Barbara recalled. "I missed being with George . . . and the thought of having him to myself sounded like the answer to my prayers." (*BB*, 108.)

178 After Watergate *LSY*, 172–73.

178 BROADEN HIS FOREIGN POLICY EXPERIENCE   Ibid., 173.

178 A BRIEF EXPERIMENT   Ford, *Time to Heal,* 147.

178 FORD APPOINTED DON RUMSFELD   Ibid., 185–87. Ford appointed Haig as supreme commander of NATO and persuaded Rumsfeld to take the chief of staff post. (Ibid.)

179 "THERE'LL BE SOME SUBSTANTIVE WORK"   *LF,* 138.

179 "WHAT THE HELL"   *LSY,* 173. Bush spoke with Ford briefly by phone before leaving for China in the middle of October. "I know you're busy," Bush said. "I just wanted to say goodbye." Ford replied, "We couldn't have found anyone more qualified."

     "If there is anything I can do to help you politically as '76 approaches, just let me know."

     "Thanks," Ford said. "I may try to visit you there by then." ("Memorandum of Conversation," Tuesday, October 15, 1974, Gerald R. Ford Presidential Library.)

SIXTEEN: *Am I Running Away from Something?*

180 PEOPLE STARE AT YOU   *ATB,* 201.

180 BUSH RECEIVED A MESSAGE   Ibid., 199–200.

180 "THE INCIDENT ITSELF"   Ibid., 200.

180 "IN GOING TO CHINA"   Ibid.

181 GLOBAL BALANCE-OF-POWER ISSUES   Engel, ed., *China Diary of George H. W. Bush,* 448–50.

181 IN THE CONTEXT OF THE TIME   Ibid.

181 "CHINA KEEPS WANTING US"   *ATB,* 230.

181 ONE LESSON OF HIS CHINA EXPERIENCE   Engel, ed., *China Diary of George H. W. Bush,* 397–463. My account of Bush's time in China owes much to *China Diary* editor Jeffrey Engel's analysis of this period of Bush's life.

181 ON THE BUSHES' FIRST NIGHT   *LF,* 138; *ATB,* 203.

181 HE GOT UP TO TURN OFF   *ATB,* 201.

181 "END FIRST NIGHT"   Ibid.

181 "WAS SOME LEADER"   *LF,* 132.

181 "I'VE BEEN HERE TEN YEARS"   Ibid., 136.

181 CHINESE DIPLOMATS COULD   Ibid.

181 THERE WERE, HE SAID, THREE WAYS   Ibid.

182 "I HAVEN'T GOTTEN A PHONE CALL"   *ATB,* 203.

182 WRITING JIM BAKER   GHWB to JAB III, November 17, 1974, box 12/13, James A. Baker III Papers, Princeton.

182 "MAYBE I'M BETTER OFF"   Ibid.

182 HE CHANGED MISSION POLICY   *ATB,* 204. See also *LF,* 142; and Engel, ed., *China Diary of George H. W. Bush,* 1–2.

182 "IT DOESN'T MATTER"   *LF,* 142.

182 THE BUSHES THEN STRUCK OUT   *ATB,* 204.

182 HOSTED THE BUSHES AT A BANQUET   Ibid., 205–6.

183 ESCHEWED THE CHIEF OF MISSION'S CHAUFFEURED CAR   Ibid., 214. See also *LF,* 139.

183 HE WOULD PUT ON A PEOPLE'S LIBERATION ARMY HAT   *ATB,* 214.

183 "BUSHER, WHO RIDE THE BICYCLE"   *LF,* 139.

183 (BUSH'S BIKE BORE   Engel, ed., *China Diary of George H. W. Bush,* photograph.

183 A MR. LO AT THE NEARBY COMMISSARY   *ATB,* 217.

183 "THEY ARE NOT THEMSELVES"   Ibid.

184 HE WROTE BILL STEIGER   *ATB,* 207.

184 KISSINGER ARRIVED IN   *LSY,* 173; *LF,* 134.

184 THE BUSHES JOINED THE KISSINGERS   *LF,* 134–35.

184 WHEN BARBARA WAS PREPARING TO MAIL A LETTER   Ibid., 135.

184 "KISSINGER IS BRILLIANT"   *ATB,* 209.

184 HE BELIEVED THE FIFTY-YEAR-OLD DIPLOMAT   Author interview with Henry Kissinger.

184 "HIS STAFF ARE SCARED TO DEATH"   *ATB,* 209–10.

184 "HE ASKED HOW LONG"   Ibid., 210.

184 "I TOLD HIM I HAD NO POLITICAL PLANS"   Ibid.

185 KISSINGER WAS WISE   Engel, ed., *China Diary of George H. W. Bush,* 12.

185 BARBARA WENT HOME TO WASHINGTON   *BB,* 117.

185 "GREAT TALKS WITH BAR"   *ATB,* 211.

185 "NO DRUGS, NO DOPE, NO CRIME"   Ibid., 221.

185 "IT IS RIGHT THAT BAR"   Ibid., 211.

185 "MOTHER ARRIVES TOMORROW"   Ibid., 212.

185 AFTER MRS. BUSH . . . LANDED IN BEIJING   Ibid.

185 ON THE TWENTY-FIFTH, THEY HAD   Ibid., 213; *LF,* 139–40.

185 TOUR OF "THE CAVES"   *LF,* 140–41.

185 "DIG TUNNELS DEEP"   Ibid., 140.

185 BUSH CLIMBED BACK OUT   Ibid., 140–41.

185 "HER COMMENT WAS"   Ibid., 141.

185 "BY THAT TIME . . . I'D BEEN IN CHINA"   Ibid.

186 BUSH HEARD ABOUT THE FALL OF SAIGON   Engel, ed. *China Diary of George H. W. Bush,* 272–73.

186 "RUSHED HAPPILY OUT OF THE ROOM"   Ibid., 273.

186 "IT IS IMPORTANT THAT THE U.S."   Ibid.

186 BUSH WOULD WATCH   Ibid., 253–56.

186 A "NEW ALIGNMENT"   Ibid., 253.

187 ON THE FOURTH OF JULY, 1975   Ibid., 345–47; *ATB,* 228.

187 HELD A BAPTISM FOR DORO   *LF,* 144.

187 KISSINGER RETURNED TO CHINA   Ibid., 145.

187 IN A SERIES OF SESSIONS   Ibid.

187 DENG EVEN INVOKED THE ANALOGY   Ibid., 146.

187 MAO HIMSELF WAS READY TO SEE THEM   Ibid., 146–49.

187 "YOU WILL MEET"   Ibid., 146.

187 IN THE CHAIRMAN'S VILLA   Ibid., 146–47.

187 "THIS PART WORKS WELL"   Ibid., 147.

187 BUSH SAT NEXT TO KISSINGER   Ibid., 147–48.

187 "I AM GOING TO HEAVEN SOON"   Ibid., 147.

188 "I ATTACH GREAT SIGNIFICANCE"   Ibid., 147–48.

188 THEY SPOKE OF TAIWAN   Ibid., 148.

188 "SEE TIME AND THEIR OWN"   Ibid., 148.

188 BUSH SAW MAO JUST ONCE MORE   *LF,* 156. See also "Memorandum of Conversation," December 2, 1975, Gerald R. Ford Presidential Library.

188 STARTED DRAFTING A LONG MEMORANDUM   Rumsfeld memo to Ford, July 10, 1975, Cheney Papers, Ford Library. See also Ford, *Time to Heal,* 323–30; Cheney with Cheney, *In My Time: A Personal and Political Memoir* (New York, 2011), 89–90; Rumsfeld, *Known and Unknown,* 192–95; Graham, *By His Own Rules,* 122–24.

188 THE PRESIDENT CAUGHT A COLD   Cheney with Cheney, *In My Time,* 90.

188 THE FATE OF VICE PRESIDENT ROCKEFELLER   Ibid.

189 In a mid-September 1975 Harris Poll   Ford, *Time to Heal,* 327.

189 "In his past"   Ibid., 253.

190 Ford and Rockefeller discussed the conservative rebellion   Ibid., 328.

190 "Mr. President, I'll do anything"   Ibid.

190 was only one of the decisions   Cheney with Cheney, *In My Time,* 90–92. Bush's account of the shifts is found in *LF,* 157–58.

190 A telegram from Kissinger arrived   *LF,* 153–54.

190 the Bushes were out bicycling   *BB,* 130.

190 "The President is planning"   *LF,* 153.

190 Bush was flabbergasted   *LF,* 153–54. See also *ATB,* 233–34. There had been some chatter about a return to Washington in some role. In a March 20, 1975, note to Jack Marsh, Russ Rourke wrote: "It's my impression and partial understanding that George Bush has probably had enough of egg rolls and Peking by now (and has probably gotten over his lost V.P. opportunity). He's one hell of a Presidential surrogate, and would be an outstanding spokesman for the White House between now and November '76. Don't you think he would make an outstanding candidate for Secretary of Commerce or a similar post sometime during the next six months?" (Russ Rourke to Jack Marsh, March 20, 1975, Gerald R. Ford Presidential Library.)

191 Bush handed the telegram   *LF,* 153–54.

191 "I remember Camp David"   Ibid., 154.

191 "return to Washington"   Ibid.

191 "The President asks"   Ibid.

191 He would do his duty   Author interview with GHWB.

191 "In the best of times"   *LF,* 155.

191 "You have given him a post"   Memorandum of Conversation, December 4, 1975, Gerald R. Ford Presidential Library.

191 With Rockefeller off the ticket   *LF,* 158.

192 Rogers Morton . . . believed   Ibid.

192 "I think you ought to know"   Ibid. Bush suspected his friends were right. "I have a gut feeling there were some behind the scenes politics—but now all that doesn't matter," Bush wrote Bill Steiger on November 9, 1975. (*ATB,* 240.)

192 In face-to-face meetings with Bush   Author interview with GHWB. See also *LF,* 158, for Bush's account of his meeting with Rumsfeld.

192 "I want you to understand something"   Author interview with GHWB. For the contrary case, which quotes Nelson Rockefeller, see Werth, *31 Days,* 340–41. In a letter solicited by Rumsfeld in 1989, Ford reiterated that he, not Rumsfeld, had made the decision about Bush. (Gerald R. Ford to Donald H. Rumsfeld, April 3, 1989, Archives of Donald Rumsfeld.) Rumsfeld had solicited the account after news reports had repeated the story that he had shunted Bush off to CIA for political purposes. (Donald H. Rumsfeld to Gerald R. Ford, March 28, 1989, Archives of Donald Rumsfeld.) See also Wicker, *GHWB,* 43–45.

192 "Man," Morton said   Author interview with GHWB.

192 loaned the Rumsfelds a car   Author interviews with GHWB and Donald Rumsfeld. The Rumsfelds' car was still in Brussels, where Rumsfeld had been serving as NATO ambassador. (Author interview with Donald Rumsfeld.)

193 the Ford restructuring initially called for Elliot Richardson   Author interviews with Dick Cheney. See also Naftali, *GHWB,* 30–31; *LSY,* 190–91; Rumsfeld, *Known and Unknown,* 199–201; and Graham, *By His Own Rules,* 122–24.

193 Ford personally switched   Author interviews with Dick Cheney. President Ford's insistence that Rumsfeld had "nothing to do" with the decision about Bush

supports Cheney's version of events—that Ford sent Bush to the CIA instead of Richardson in order to make the moment more congenial for Kissinger. In an interview, Kissinger agreed with the characterization of Richardson as someone with whom he had difficulty working. This had not always been the case, but Richardson had made no secret of his own ambition to be secretary of state. Kissinger said he had not, however, expressed any views to Ford on the Richardson–Bush CIA matter. (Author interview with Henry Kissinger.) Cheney, the incoming White House chief of staff, agreed, recalling that Kissinger's unhappiness with Richardson and willingness to work with Bush was simply part of the prevailing workaday atmosphere of the time. (Author interview with Dick Cheney.) See also Naftali, *GHWB*, 31, and *LSY*, 190–91.

193 FORD'S IMPRESSION OF THE SENSITIVITIES   Author interview with Dick Cheney.

193 "YOUR MESSAGE CAME AS A TOTAL"   *ATB*, 233.

193 "YOU ARE A GREAT PATRIOT"   Henry A. Kissinger to GHWB, November 2, 1975, Gerald R. Ford Presidential Library.

SEVENTEEN: *George Bush, Super Spook*

194 IT'S A TOUGH, MEAN   *BB*, 132.

194 OUR LIFE HAS CHANGED   BPB diary, February 23, 1976.

194 IN RETROSPECT, THE CIA JOB   *LSY*, 184–206; John Ranelagh, *The Agency: The Rise and Decline of the CIA* (New York, 1986), 628–33; Naftali, *GHWB*, 31–32; Wicker, *GHWB*, 44–47.

194 ELECTORAL OBLIVION   Author interview with GHWB. See also *ATB*, 238.

194 "THE PRESIDENT HAS ASKED US"   *ATB*, 235–36. See also Wicker, *GHWB*, 44.

194 "I LOOK FORWARD"   *ATB*, 236.

194 ON CAPITOL HILL   *LSY*, 190.

194 IN HIS MIND HE WAS SACRIFICING   *LF*, 159. Bush hated the emerging line of argument, and he hated that Church, the most celebrated senator on the intelligence issue, was pushing it so hard. "Perhaps you could ask him to withhold his fire until we have the hearings," Bush wrote Jack Marsh, the White House counselor who was overseeing the CIA confirmation, on Friday, November 7, 1975. "I will leave that to you. Maybe it's better to let him pop off." (*ATB*, 239.) The preemptive criticism bothered him. "In talking to the Senators you can emphasize for me my total commitment to laying politics totally aside," Bush told Marsh. "I have done it at the UN, I have done it in China, and I recognize that it is essential to do that in the new job." (Ibid.)

From China, Bush offered Marsh some more ideas for fighting back. "There are several incidents of my having to resist White House pressure during Watergate times. . . . The theme should be emphasized that Bush did withstand WH pressure, but did not do it glamorously on the front pages," Bush wrote Marsh. "I will approach my CIA job in the same way." (Ibid., 241.) He was also thinking of lines of argument to turn his opponents' charges around. "Further point should be made that someone with some feel for public opinion might better keep Agency out of illegal activities," he wrote. (Ibid.)

195 THE SEQUENCE OF EVENTS   *LF*, 162–63.

195 BUSH'S CONFIRMATION HEARINGS   *LSY*, 191–92. For Bush's notes as he prepared an opening statement, see *ATB*, 243–45.

195 "NOW, LET US ASSUME"   *LSY*, 192.

195 "I DO NOT THINK THAT IS DIFFICULT"   Ibid.

195 RETURNED TO BUSH'S POLITICAL FUTURE *LF*, 163. See also *LSY*, 189–92. For reporting on the Democrats' push to remove Bush from consideration for the vice presidential nomination in 1976 in exchange for his confirmation for CIA, see *NYT*, December 16, 17, 18, and 19, 1975; *WP*, December 16, 17, and 19, 1975.

195 "THEY WANT A BLOOD OATH" *LF*, 163; Ford, *Time to Heal*, 337–38.

196 BUSH AGREED TO A COMPROMISE *LSY*, 193; Ford, *Time to Heal*, 338.

196 THE PRESIDENT, NOT BUSH, WOULD MAKE *Time to Heal*, 337–38; *LF*, 163.

196 "I KNOW IT'S UNFAIR" Ford, *Time to Heal*, 338.

196 A LETTER PROMISING THAT BUSH WOULD NOT Ford, *Time to Heal*, 337–38; *LF*, 164; author interview with Dick Cheney.

196 SUPPORTED THE NOMINATION 12 TO 4 *LSY*, 192. See also *WP*, December 19, 1975.

196 WON CONFIRMATION 64 TO 27 *LSY*, 193. See also *NYT*, January 28, 1976.

196 AMONG THE FIRST TO CONGRATULATE *BB*, 133.

196 "I DON'T THINK THE AVERAGE AMERICAN" Ibid.

196 POTTER STEWART SWORE THE NEW DIRECTOR IN BPB diary, January 30, 1976. See also *NYT*, January 31, 1976, for an account of the swearing-in.

196 DONALD RUMSFELD AND HIS WIFE, JOYCE BPB diary, January 30, 1976.

196 A MEMORANDUM FROM FOUR SENIOR CIA OFFICERS The officers were L. C. Dirks, G. F. Donnelly, J. H. Taylor, and R. Lehman. ("George Bush: Calm Between Storms," footnote 7, CIA Center for the Study of Intelligence, www.cia.gov/library/center-for-the-study-of-intelligence/.) There were also practical concerns. "A manager who can assemble the experts he needs in five minutes can operate efficiently; one who needs an hour will gradually accumulate new experts in his immediate office." (Ibid.)

196 "GOING THROUGH" *LF*, 164–65.

196 THE DIRECTOR'S SEVENTH-FLOOR OFFICE *LF*, 169.

197 "WHAT ARE THEY TRYING" *LSY*, 194.

197 AT HOME—THE BUSHES HAD MOVED BPB diary, February 23, 1976.

197 THE CIA SENT MEN OUT Ibid.

197 THE BUSHES' MAIL WAS NO LONGER DELIVERED Ibid.

197 PACKAGES THAT ARRIVED AT THE HOUSE Ibid.

197 GEORGE W. HAD BEEN PLANNING Ibid., July 15, 1976.

197 "WE ARE SICK ABOUT IT" Ibid.

197 A CHAUFFEURED CHEVROLET *LF*, 168–69.

198 MARBLE WALLS WHERE ROWS Ibid., 169.

198 HE MET WEEKLY Ibid.

198 MANY DAYS WERE TAKEN UP Ibid.

198 (FIFTY-ONE TIMES IN HIS YEAR AS DIRECTOR) Ibid.

198 HE SPENT HIS LUNCH HOUR Ibid.

198 LATE IN THE AFTERNOONS Author interview with Henry Kissinger.

198 BY SEVEN P.M., IF THE SOCIAL *LF*, 169–70.

198 BUSH COULD NOT TALK OPENLY Ibid., 170.

198 "I CAN'T BELIEVE IT" BPB diary, February 23, 1976.

198 HER FAVORITE PART OF THE WEEK Ibid., March 1, 1976.

198 "I MUST CONFESS" Ibid., July 13, 1976.

198 "VERY DEPRESSED" *BB*, 135.

198 "BARBARA HAD DEPRESSION" Author interview with GHWB.

198 "HE WOULD SUGGEST" *BB*, 135.

199 "I ALMOST WONDER" Ibid.

199 "SOMETIMES THE PAIN WAS SO GREAT" Ibid.

199 "It seems so simple"　Ibid., 135–36.

199 The CIA post　BPB diary, March 1, 1976.

199 The range of concerns　*ATB*, 249–50.

200 In 1976, Bush was furious　*LF*, 174–75.

200 "Four Latin American countries"　Ibid., 175.

200 assassinated in Beirut　Ibid., 171 72.

200 the issue was whether　Ibid., 171.

200 In a tense meeting　Ibid.

200 was joined by Kissinger and Scowcroft　Ibid., 172.

200 They were seated　Ibid.

200 Bush was on his feet　Ibid.

200 "assassination signaled"　Ibid.

200 One thing Bush took away　Ibid., 173.

200 The respect was mutual　Author interview with Brent Scowcroft.

200 "He was genial and thoughtful"　Ibid.

200 "Kissinger frankly didn't have time"　Ibid.

201 overarching concern　For Bush's experience with Team B, I drew on, for instance, Anne Hessing Cahn and John Prados, "Team B: The Trillion Dollar Experiment," *The Bulletin of Atomic Scientists*, April 1993, 22–29; Tim Weiner, *Legacy of Ashes: The History of the CIA* (New York, 2007), 351–53; Ranelagh, *Agency*, 622–24; *LSY*, 198–201; Naftali, *GHWB*, 32–33; Wicker, *GHWB*, 45–47; James Mann, *Rise of the Vulcans: The History of Bush's War Cabinet* (New York, 2004), 74; *NYT*, March 6, 1988, as well as Garthoff below.

201 February 1960 had marked　Raymond L. Garthoff, "Estimating Soviet Military Intentions and Capabilities," CIA Center for the Study of Intelligence, www.cia.gov/library/center-for-the-study-of-intelligence/.

201 "The Soviet armed forces"　Ibid.

201 the chief of Air Force Intelligence dissented　Ibid.

201 Don Rumsfeld, was pushing　Rumsfeld, *Known and Unknown*, 222–32.

201 as was Reagan　Cahn and Prados, "Team B," 24–25.

201 the formation of a "Team B"　Ibid., 24; *LSY*, 198–200; Ranelagh, *Agency*, 622–24.

201 "Let her fly!!"　Cahn and Prados, "Team B," 24; Weiner, *Legacy of Ashes*, 352.

202 it was "a bad idea"　*NYT*, March 6, 1988.

202 It was wisest, Bush decided, to keep　Naftali, *GHWB*, 33; *LSY*, 198. As Parmet wrote, "It was, [Bush] explained, better to set it up than to say 'we are always going to have a hard-line team checking you guys." (*LSY*, 198.)

202 The results were evident　David Binder, "New C.I.A. Estimate Finds Soviets Seek Superiority in Arms," *NYT*, December 26, 1976.

202 "way more than number"　Ibid.

202 "All the evidence points"　Mann, *Rise of the Vulcans*, 74.

202 As it turned out　Weiner, *Legacy of Ashes*, 352. See also Naftali, *GHWB*, 33, and *LSY*, 199–201. "Bush did not accept these conclusions and was furious when they leaked; nevertheless, the process gave credence to a particularly dark vision of the Soviet threat that people close to the far right, led now by Ronald Reagan, would soon tout," wrote Naftali. "Among CIA professionals, however, Bush earned high praise for his handling of the Team B matter. By letting outsiders in, he had reduced pressures that might have forced a greater politicization of intelligence estimates." (Naftali, *GHWB*, 33). In a 1995 interview with Herbert Parmet, Bush said Team B "proved that intelligence is less than objective, that there's always going to be subjectivity in it when it comes to Soviet estimates." (*LSY*, 201.)

202 IN LATE JUNE, JIMMY CARTER "In-Depth Discussions with Carter," CIA Center for the Study of Intelligence, www.cia.gov.library/center-for-the-study-of-intelligence, 87.

202 BUSH MET CARTER IN HERSHEY Ibid., 87–88.

202 BUSH TRAVELED TO PLAINS Ibid., 88–89.

203 TO REPORTERS BEFOREHAND, CARTER Ibid., 89.

203 THE MEETING WITH CARTER Ibid.

203 BUSH RETURNED TO PLAINS Ibid., 92.

203 "JIMMY WAS GOING TO CLEAR" Ibid.

203 BUSH LED A CONVERSATION Ibid., 92–93.

203 "NOW I FIND MYSELF" BPB diary, October 22, 1976.

203 BUSH CALLED CARTER "In-Depth Discussions with Carter," 97. Carter had been advised by some to keep Bush on for a few months to send a bipartisan signal about leadership in the intelligence community. "Appointing a DCI along with a list of the new administration cabinet et al politicizes an office that should be above and beyond politics," Robert Amory, Jr., wrote in a pre-election memorandum. He added: "By all reports, George Bush has done a remarkable job of taking over a badly demoralized CIA, tautening the ship and renewing the confidence of its, by and large, superb professionals." (Memorandum of Robert Amory, Jr., September 13, 1976, NLC-17–108–7-2–5, Jimmy Carter Presidential Library.)

203 "EXOTIC AND VERY CLOSELY HELD" "In-Depth Discussions with Carter," 97. In preparation for the meeting with Bush, Carter was advised to make the point that, as president-elect, he was "not in a position to authorize any clandestine activities until" he became president and a review of all such operations was complete. The fear, according to a staff memo: "Transitions have been particularly risky times when authority for the conduct of clandestine activities has become blurred to the detriment of our national security." ("Memorandum for the President-elect," from Jack Watson, Stuart Eisenstadt, and David Aaron, November 18, 1976, NLC-126–1-3–1-7, Jimmy Carter Presidential Library.)

204 BUSH OFFERED TO SEND ALONG A LETTER "In-Depth Discussions with Carter," 97.

204 BUSH RETURNED TO PLAINS Ibid.

204 SITTING ON THE CARTERS' SOFA, HIS BACK TO THE BAY WINDOWS Author interview with Jimmy Carter.

204 NO INCOMING PRESIDENT "In-Depth Discussions with Carter," 92. See also Naftali, *GHWB*, 33, and *LSY*, 206.

204 AFTER RAISING THE QUESTION "In-Depth Discussions with Carter," 97–98.

204 CARTER AGREED, SAYING, "OKAY" Ibid., 98.

204 "HE HAS NEVER ENJOYED A JOB MORE" BPB diary, January 18, 1977.

204 BUSH WAS "TOO WEDDED" Author interview with Jimmy Carter. A leak to Evans and Novak calling the Bush briefing in Plains a "disaster" seems to have been overblown; Carter recalled to the author that he was always planning on naming his own CIA director. (*WP*, November 27, 1976.) See also David Aaron to the President-Elect, November 27, 1976, NLC-7–66–7-8–7, Jimmy Carter Presidential Library. Aaron worried that Bush was giving background briefings on the Carter meeting to David Binder of *The New York Times*. (Ibid.)

204 "IF I HAD ACCEDED" Author interview with Jimmy Carter.

204 BUSH BRIEFED CARTER *ATB*, 264.

204 BUSH ALSO WARNED CARTER Ibid.

205 WHEN AN ISSUE AROSE *LF*, 178–79.

205 "I don't need to worry"   Ibid., 179.
205 "You learn what"   Author interview with GHWB.
205 "I wonder . . . if George"   BPB diary, October 22, 1976.

Part V: The Age of Reagan, 1977 to 1989

207 I . . . thought that it was prudent   Ronald Reagan, *An American Life* (New York, 1990), 255.

eighteen: *A President We Won't Have to Train*

209 I'm so digging in   ATB, 282–83.
209 Bush has to be "acceptable"   Document, undated, box 20/5, James A. Baker III Papers, Princeton.
209 "I went home"   Author interview with GHWB.
209 "There [have] been"   *ATB*, 271.
209 "There is a missing"   Ibid.
209 speaking warmly of "normalcy"   Ibid., 272.
209 "somehow I will churn"   Ibid.
209 In Houston, the Bushes had bought   BPB diary, January 18, 1977.
209 First International Bank became Bush's home base   Ibid. See also *LSY*, 208.
210 joined the Trilateral Commission   BPB diary, April 5, 1977.
210 He accepted invitations   Ibid.
210 refusing a directorship   *ATB*, 270.
210 declined an offer from Ross Perot   Author interview with GHWB; *LSY*, 209.
210 "I'll pay you a lot of money"   Author interview with GHWB.
210 ("This was before Ross")   Ibid.
210 the Perots once visited Kennebunkport   Ibid.
210 When he did his due diligence   Ibid.
210 "Well, this is your big mistake"   Ibid.
210 Everything Bush was doing   *ATB*, 271.
210 It would not be easy   Author interview with Andrew Card.
210 welcome george busch   Ibid.
210 "Looks like I need"   Ibid.
210 Bush made his character   See, for instance, Naftali, *GHWB*, 35–36. Wicker, *GHWB*, 50–52 discusses the Bush résumé.
211 "A President We Won't Have to Train"   Bernard Weintraub, "Bush Gets Lessons in Performing on TV," *NYT*, January 13, 1980; Ray Coffey, "Selling of the Candidates, 1980," *Chicago Tribune*, March 16, 1980.
211 All things being equal   Author interview with GHWB.
211 He seemed moderate   Author interviews with Pete Teeley and Rich Bond. See also Naftali, *GHWB*, 35–36.
212 If Bush succeeded   *LF*, 191–93, offers his pre-1980 thinking, particularly on challenging Carter. On a practical level, Bush did not have a traditional political base, and he knew it. "What I had was a wealth of friends some of whom knew something about state politics and some of whom knew nothing about that but knew something about giving money to people they believed in," Bush recalled. "So we started by raising money unlike other candidates could do, and I felt that I could mobilize

those people, get them interested, and sure enough we did." (Author interview with GHWB.)

212 GEORGE W., NOW THIRTY-ONE   BPB diary, September 1, 1977. See also GWB, *Decision Points,* 37–41.

212 "THE PRIMARY WILL BE"   BPB diary, September 1, 1977.

212 "YOU KNOW, I WONDER IF"   Ibid.

212 "IT REMINDS ME"   Ibid.

213 BUSH NEVER WEIGHED IN DIRECTLY   Author interview with GWB.

213 HE DID, HOWEVER, ASK GEORGE W.   GWB, *Decision Points,* 38–39.

213 "SON, YOU CAN'T WIN"   Ibid.

213 "THERE WAS NO ENCOURAGEMENT"   Ibid.

213 IN THE FALL OF 1977   BPB diary, October 8, 1977.

213 LAURA WAS INTRODUCED TO THE BUSHES   Ibid., November 18, 1977.

213 ONE OF THE EARLIEST SKIRMISHES   GWB, *Decision Points,* 39–40; Craig Shirley, *Rendezvous with Destiny: Ronald Reagan and the Campaign That Changed America* (Wilmington, Del., 2009), 7. The maneuver came more from the Reaganites than from Reagan himself. Lyn Nofziger, a Reagan adviser, directed Citizens for the Republic, and it was widely believed that he had stepped into the Texas race to tweak the elder Bush. "That was pure Nofziger," recalled Craig Shirley, a conservative historian who was working for Gordon Humphrey's 1978 Senate campaign in New Hampshire. (Author interview with Craig Shirley.) The Reaganites argued that they had to support Jim Reese since they had backed him two years before, in the 1976 campaign. (Lyn Nofziger to GHWB, July 7, 1978, box 21/3, James A. Baker III Papers, Princeton.)

213 THE BUSHES BLAMED   BPB diary, May 13, 1978.

213 A "WASHINGTON WHISPERS" ITEM   Shirley, *Rendezvous with Destiny,* 7.

214 "A LARGE PART OF HIS CAMPAIGN"   BPB diary, November 12, 1978.

214 "I TOLD HIM"   GHWB to JAB III, May 29, 1975, box 16/3, James A. Baker III Papers, Princeton.

214 BAKER TOOK THE COMMERCE POST   Author interview with James A. Baker III.

214 "HE WAS RIGHT"   Ibid.

214 "LET'S GET CRACKING"   Baker with DeFrank, *Politics of Diplomacy,* 18.

214 TO PAY A COURTESY CALL   Author interviews with GHWB and James A. Baker III.

215 REAGAN HIMSELF HAD TO ADDRESS TWO BROAD QUESTIONS   See Shirley, *Rendezvous with Destiny,* 6, for a summary of the challenges facing Reagan in 1980. The story of the 1980 campaign is best told by Shirley in *Rendezvous with Destiny;* I am indebted to him for his exhaustively researched work and for his counsel on particular points.

215 "BUSH SHOULD AVOID"   Memorandum, undated, box 20/5, James A. Baker III Papers, Princeton. See also *ATB,* 278, for Bush on the "tough enough" theme.

215 "THE THINKING MAN'S CANDIDATE"   *Time,* February 5, 1979.

215 "CALL ME A CONSERVATIVE"   Ibid.

215 REAGAN WAS "A GREAT OLD DOG"   *Time,* May 14, 1979.

215 "GEORGE BUSH'S HOPE"   *NYT,* May 2, 1979. For more on the age issue, see Shirley, *Rendezvous with Destiny,* 118–19.

215 BUSH JOGGED CONSTANTLY   Shirley, *Rendezvous with Destiny,* 129.

215 "UP FOR THE '80S"   Ibid.

215 A BUSH BROCHURE   *NYT,* November 23, 1979.

215 "THE RIGHT AGE"   *Roanoke Times & World-News,* June 30, 1979.

215 "I DON'T QUESTION"   *Time,* November 26, 1979.

216 "Key to winning is" Memorandum, undated, box 12/5, James A. Baker III Papers, Princeton.

216 "Bush has to be 'acceptable'" Document, undated, box 20/5, James A. Baker III Papers, Princeton.

216 "Ladies and gentlemen" "George Bush Announcement Speech," May 1, 1979, text in BPB diary, 1979; *Time*, May 14, 1979.

216 "I am not promising" "George Bush Announcement Speech," May 1, 1979.

217 "The American people must be told" Ibid.

217 More than a quarter Ibid.

217 "This was the first time in memory" *NYT*, May 2, 1979.

217 "Our biggest opponent is us" *Time*, November 12, 1979.

218 His focus on the state paid off *NYT*, May 24, 1979.

218 "I've got a long way" Ibid.

218 The bad news came Ibid.

218 For Bush, Ford had been a factor Author interviews with GHWB and James A. Baker III. See also *NYT*, January 24, 1980.

218 Baker sought Ford's blessing *NYT*, January 24, 1980.

218 "It's going to be tough" Ibid.

218 "top Republicans expect Gerald Ford" *Time*, November 28, 1977.

218 Polls had him defeating Carter *NYT*, October 1, 1979.

218 you "never say 'never'" Ibid.

219 who had a lead over Carter Ibid.

219 "Cavalcade of Stars" Douglas E. Kneeland, "9 GOP Hopefuls Vie for Attention at an Iowa Dinner," *NYT*, October 15, 1979.

219 a "surprisingly low fourth" Ibid., October 16, 1979.

219 a Maine straw poll Ibid., November 4, 1979.

219 He had had enough Ibid. Bush described the occasion in Portland and his passionate remarks in *LF*, 193–96.

219 headed south, to the Florida *Time*, December 3, 1979.

219 There were hot-air balloon Ibid.

220 Bush's 21 percent *NYT*, November 18, 1979.

220 "the surprise of the weekend" *Time*, December 3, 1979.

220 "Count 'em again" Ibid.

220 347 days of campaigning *NYT*, November 23, 1979. Thirty-seven days were spent in New Hampshire, 34 in Florida, and 24 in Iowa. "He has plainly worked harder than his rivals have," the *Times* said. (Ibid.)

220 "hot property" *NYT*, November 23, 1979.

220 "I think Bush has a chance" *Time*, December 3, 1979.

220 "Iowa had been" *LF*, 187.

220 "We bet the whole thing" Author interview with GHWB.

NINETEEN: *We Have Done the Unthinkable*

221 The action begins in Iowa *Time*, January 21, 1980.

221 "I'm surprised my body" *ATB*, 283.

221 "He was just dropping" Ibid.

221 "I don't want to look back" Ibid.

221 The news in late 1979 James T. Patterson, *Restless Giant: The United States from Watergate to Bush v. Gore*, 109–10.

222 "I'm just so outraged"   John F. Stacks, *Watershed: The Campaign for the Presidency, 1980* (New York, 1981), 97.

222 "I see the world"   *Time,* December 3, 1979.

222 "I've been there"   *NYT,* November 23, 1979.

222 Marvin moved to Iowa   *BB,* 147; author interview with Marvin Bush.

222 Neil to New Hampshire   Author interview with Neil Bush.

222 Doro took a leave   *BB,* 147.

222 Dorothy Bush and her daughter   *St. Louis Post-Dispatch,* June 30, 1991.

222 In Iowa, Barbara was pleased   BPB diary, January 21, 1980.

222 In a blazer, Neil worked crowds   *Time,* December 3, 1979.

222 In 1978, when he and Columba   Author interview with Jeb Bush.

222 "It was a blast"   Ibid.

222 (After Iowa, he would run)   Ibid.

222 "I really wasn't"   Ibid. For GHWB's warm view of Jeb in the 1980 campaign, see *ATB,* 284.

222 "I look at Bar's schedule"   *ATB,* 284.

222 One night he encountered Barbara   Author interview with GHWB.

222 Neil was engaged   *ATB,* 284.

222 "Yet, we haven't"   Ibid.

223 "is in close, in tight"   Ibid.

223 "taking the tough road"   Ibid., 279.

223 On a commercial flight from Puerto Rico   Ibid., 285.

223 With its 2,531 precincts   *Time,* December 3, 1979.

223 moved to the state to work for Bush   Author interview with Rich Bond.

223 the core Bush group included   Ibid. See also Shirley, *Rendezvous with Destiny,* 87.

223 Every day Bond   Author interview with Rich Bond.

223 From eight in the morning until ten at night   Ibid.

224 "I'm Rich Bond"   Ibid.

224 on the way home   Ibid.

224 "The vast majority"   Ibid.

224 One right-winger mailed   Ibid.

224 Bond remembered the thrill   Ibid.

224 Bush press secretary Pete Teeley   Author interview with Pete Teeley.

224 "Yeah, it was two hours"   Ibid.

224 Bush spent twenty-seven days   *Time,* January 21, 1980.

224 one member of the Bush family   Ibid., February 4, 1980.

224 on the other hand, Reagan   Ibid.

224 Iowa polls had Reagan   Ibid., January 21, 1980.

225 Bush moved from commercial air travel   *NYT,* January 6, 1980.

225 "There are bigger shots"   Ibid.

225 "After doing well in Iowa"   *Time,* December 3, 1979.

225 David Keene estimated   Ibid.

225 to joke that his stance on abortion   Ibid.

225 Iowa Republicans turned out   Ibid., February 4, 1980.

225 "I was sitting"   Ibid.

225 Bush dropped in on one caucus   Ibid.

225 Reagan learned the news   Shirley, *Rendezvous with Destiny,* 103; Nancy Reagan, with William Novak, *My Turn: The Memoirs of Nancy Reagan* (New York, 1989), 204.

225 into a "madhouse"   BPB diary, January 22, 1980.

225 "How sweet"   Ibid.

225 HE NOW HAD THE "BIG MO" *LSY,* 226; Wicker, *GHWB,* 53–54.

225 WHICH REMINDED SOME OBSERVERS Stacks, *Watershed,* 107.

225 "IT WAS A CRUSH" BPB diary, January 22, 1980.

226 "WE HAVE DONE THE UNTHINKABLE" *Time,* February 4, 1980.

226 "THERE'S A LONG WAY TO GO" *ATB,* 287.

226 "REAGAN IS STILL TOUGH" Ibid., 284.

226 WENT TO BED ABOUT ONE THIRTY *NYT,* January 23, 1980.

226 "ON TO NEW HAMPSHIRE" BPB diary, January 22, 1980.

TWENTY: *It Hurt Like Hell*

227 REPORTER: "WHAT IS YOUR BIGGEST WORRY?" Elizabeth Drew, *Portrait of an Election: The 1980 Presidential Campaign* (New York, 1981), 95.

227 RISING AT FIVE TWENTY GHWB diary, January 28, 1980.

227 BUSH WAS GREETED BY A CROWD OF FIFTY *NYT,* January 23, 1980; *WP,* January 23, 1980.

227 "BETTER THAN YOU THINK" *NYT,* January 23, 1980.

227 HUGH GREGG, BUSH'S CAMPAIGN MANAGER *Time,* February 25, 1980. See also *NYT,* February 5, 1980.

227 CALLED HIM "AYATOLLAH" *NYT,* February 5, 1980.

227 AN ANDOVER AND YALE MAN Ibid., September 28, 2003.

227 HE ASSIGNED THE CANDIDATE TWENTY-TWO MINUTES *Time,* February 25, 1980.

227 A "HEADY" MOMENT *LF,* 197.

227 *NEWSWEEK* PUT HIM ON THE COVER Ibid.

227 IN *TIME,* THREE ANONYMOUS SOURCES *Time,* February 4, 1980.

227 "BUSH WAS LOYAL" Ibid.

228 BUSH "GAVE A GREAT DEAL" Ibid.

228 A FORMER DIRECTOR OF OPERATIONS Ibid.

228 AN ABC NEWS–HARRIS POLL Ibid. See also Shirley, *Rendezvous with Destiny,* 121.

228 A POST-IOWA *BOSTON GLOBE* POLL *Time,* February 11, 1980; Shirley, *Rendezvous with Destiny,* 120. One consequence of the Bush moment: Bob Dole was staying in the race in the event that a total Reagan collapse would give Dole a shot as an effective challenger to the new front-runner: Bush. "I think he's felt all along that Reagan wasn't going to make it," Kim Wells, a Dole aide, told reporters. "He sees Iowa as perhaps the beginning of it." (*NYT,* January 28, 1980.)

228 WITH EVERYTHING NOW IN DOUBT Lou Cannon, *Reagan* (New York, 1982), 248–49. See also Shirley, *Rendezvous with Destiny,* 122–27.

228 "BENEATH THE MEDIA GLOW" *LF,* 198.

228 A SERIES OF POLLS SUGGESTED *NYT,* February 5, 1980.

228 49 PERCENT OF WHOM Shirley, *Rendezvous with Destiny,* 120.

228 THE QUESTION OF REAGAN'S AGE Shirley, *Rendezvous with Destiny,* 120.

228 "RONNIE CAMPAIGNED HARDER" Nancy Reagan with Novak, *My Turn,* 204.

228 HE SPENT TUESDAY, FEBRUARY 5, 1980 *NYT,* February 6, 1980.

228 "COMPARED TO THE ALTERNATIVE" Ibid.

229 "IT'S OLD-SCHOOL TIE" *NYT,* February 7, 1980.

229 "MR. BUSH," LOEB SAID Ibid.

229 ASKED BY REPORTERS WHETHER HE WAS "TO THE LEFT" Ibid., February 8, 1980.

229 NO FEWER THAN NINETEEN CURRENT OR FORMER Ibid.

229 HAD LED TO A "SOFTENING OF DEFENSE" Ibid.

229 THE FIRST DEBATE *Time,* March 3, 1980; Shirley, *Rendezvous with Destiny,* 141.

229   "You don't win"   *NYT,* February 22, 1980.

230   "I kept hearing"   Ibid.

230   He went into the Manchester event   Cannon, *Reagan,* 250–51.

230   Reagan had a nearly two to one   *Newsweek,* March 10, 1980.

230   Reagan had initially agreed   *NYT,* February 22, 1980.

230   The plan in the forty-eight hours   For detailed accounts of Nashua, see Shirley, *Rendezvous with Destiny,* 142–55; Cannon, *Reagan,* 251–53; Stacks, *Watershed,* 119–21; Jack W. Germond and Jules Witcover, *Blue Smoke and Mirrors: How Reagan Won and Why Carter Lost the Election of 1980* (New York, 1981), 125–31; Jeff Greenfield, *The Real Campaign: How the Media Missed the Story of the 1980 Campaign* (New York, 1982), 45–48; Wicker, *GHWB,* 53–57.

230   the Federal Election Commission agreed   Shirley, *Rendezvous with Destiny,* 142; *NYT,* February 22, 1980.

230   In the hectic hours   Ibid.

231   the Bush campaign was uncertain   I am indebted to Shirley, *Rendezvous with Destiny,* and to my interviews with Shirley for this account of the run-up to Nashua.

231   Reagan had agreed   Shirley, *Rendezvous with Destiny,* 142; 148–49.

231   Bush replied   Ibid., 148.

231   Backstage at Nashua High School   Ibid., 150.

231   The Reagan camp decided to send   Ibid., 150–51; author interview with Craig Shirley.

231   for the sake of "party unity"   Shirley, *Rendezvous with Destiny,* 150; author interview with Craig Shirley.

231   took his seat on the stage   Shirley, *Rendezvous with Destiny,* 151–52.

231   "Mr. Bush is already on the stage"   Nancy Reagan with Novak, *My Turn,* 209.

231   "Why don't you all"   Ibid.

231   He briefly shook Bush's hand   Shirley, *Rendezvous with Destiny,* 152. See also https://www.youtube.com/watch?v=RRI6iSrSIkc.

231   Bush sat stonily   Shirley, *Rendezvous with Destiny,* 152; *Newsweek,* March 10, 1980; Naftali, *GHWB,* 37.

231   asked if he could make a statement   https://www.youtube.com/watch?v=RRI6iSrSIkc. See also Shirley, *Rendezvous with Destiny,* 152.

231   Reagan's face was flushed   https://www.youtube.com/watch?v=RRI6iSrSIkc.

231   a "little boy who thinks"   Shirley, *Rendezvous with Destiny,* 154.

231   Reagan insisted   Ibid., 152.

232   "I am paying"   Ibid.

232   "He froze"   *Newsweek,* March 10, 1980.

232   "Are you through?"   Shirley, *Rendezvous with Destiny,* 153.

232   "I'll get you someday"   Ibid., 154.

232   "Jim Baker," Dole said   Baker with Fiffer, *Work Hard,* 91.

232   "Of course, I looked terrible"   Author interview with GHWB.

232   Gordon Humphrey   Author interview with Craig Shirley; Shirley, *Rendezvous with Destiny,* 150–51; *LSY,* 229.

232   things were running late   *ATB,* 289.

232   "On the way to the stage"   Ibid.

232   "A lot of misunderstanding"   Ibid.

233   "The producer was signaling me"   Ibid., 289–90.

233   "I wish we had been in personal touch"   Ibid., 290.

233   Reagan considered the evening   *NYT,* March 6, 1988.

233   "I don't understand it"   Ibid.

233 "I looked like a fool" Author interview with GHWB.

233 carried the primary 50 percent Shirley, *Rendezvous with Destiny,* 161.

233 "Congratulations, sir" *Time,* March 10, 1980.

233 "If somebody asks" *Newsweek,* March 10, 1980.

233 Bush "is hoping" Ibid.

233 "We've got to win this primary" *NYT,* March 2, 1980.

233 "Now, Nancy, you all have to win" Author interview with Nancy Bush Ellis.

233 If Bush were to lose *NYT,* March 2, 1980.

233 Ford stood ready Ibid.

234 "A very conservative Republican" Ibid.

234 "That's right" Ibid.

234 "I wouldn't be deserving" Ibid., March 7, 1980.

234 the rest of March was a misery *LSY,* 230–32. For Reagan's wins in South Carolina, Alabama, Florida, and Illinois, see *NYT,* March 9, 12, 19, 1980. For Bush's victory in Connecticut, see *WP,* March 26, 1980. For a comprehensive guide to the primaries and caucuses, see https://presidentialcampaignselectionsreference.wordpress.com/overviews/20th-century/1980-overview/.

235 "I am not a candidate" *NYT,* March 16, 1980.

235 "It uncomplicates our life" Ibid.

235 "It's over" Ibid., March 17, 1980.

235 "I am discouraged" BPB diary, March 10–11, 1980.

235 "It is bad" Ibid., March 11, 1980.

235 "Young George called" Ibid., March 15, 1980.

235 "I feel we are very near" Ibid., April 12, 1980.

235 "George is about the most" Baker with Fiffer, *Work Hard,* 94.

235 In Pennsylvania, he attacked *LAT,* April 14, 1980. See also *LSY,* 232.

235 The phrase "voodoo economics" Author interview with Pete Teeley; Shirley, *Rendezvous with Destiny,* 259.

235 It got Teeley thinking Author interview with Pete Teeley.

236 "far from over" *NYT,* April 21, 1980.

236 Nine hundred and ninety-eight Ibid., April 23, 1980.

236 Bush ran a pricey campaign Ibid., April 27, 1980; *WP,* April 23, 1980.

236 "Last January, he cultivated" *NYT,* April 27, 1980.

236 "I hate to tempt fate" Ibid., April 23, 1980.

236 Yet when Bush turned on the news Ibid., May 22, 1980.

236 The answer, Jim Baker sadly concluded Baker with Fiffer, *Work Hard,* 94.

236 "goddamn tough" Ibid.

236 "If you can't do California" Ibid.

236 "Baker says you don't" Ibid., 95.

237 From a grim Holiday Inn Author interview with GHWB.

237 Bush was "furious" Baker with Fiffer, *Work Hard,* 95.

237 "George, I think it's time" Author interview with GHWB.

237 "No, Jimmy" Ibid.

237 "We just don't have the money" Ibid.

237 Jim Oberwetter, an old Texas political hand Author interview with James Oberwetter.

237 "I picked him up" Ibid.

237 "I will never give up" Ibid.

237 In the sunroom BPB diary, summer 1980.

237 "Look, we've got to fold" Author interview with GHWB.

237 BAKER WAS DIRECT   Baker with Fiffer, *Work Hard,* 95–96.
237 EVERY DAY BUSH STAYED   Author interview with James A. Baker III. Baker had also made this point to Bush on the call that brought Bush back to Texas. (Baker with Fiffer, *Work Hard,* 95–96.)
237 "WOULD BLOW ANY CHANCE"   Baker and Fiffer, *Work Hard,* 95.
238 IF BUSH WERE EVEN REMOTELY   Ibid., 96.
238 "I FINALLY SAID, 'OKAY'"   Author interview with GHWB.
238 "IT HURT LIKE HELL"   Ibid.
238 THE "TOUGHEST DECISION"   *NYT,* May 27, 1980.
238 "HE WAS A SUPERIOR CAMPAIGNER"   Ibid.
238 A DROP-IN TURNED INTO LUNCH   BPB diary, summer 1980.
238 BUSH TOOK OFF HIS SHOES   *NYT,* May 27, 1980.
238 BUSH . . . JOKINGLY POINTED   Ibid., May 28, 1980.
239 "I GUESS WE CAN PUT"   Ibid.
239 JIM BAKER THOUGHT   Ibid.
239 "THE DISPUTE OVER THE VICE PRESIDENCY"   Ibid.
239 HE SPENT MUCH OF HIS TIME   Author interview with GHWB.
239 "THERE AGAIN IS MY FATHER"   Ibid.
239 RICHARD WIRTHLIN WAS EXPLICIT   Campaign Planning Memos, July 9, 1980, Ed Meese Papers, Ronald Reagan Presidential Library.
239 IN JUNE, A SURVEY   *NYT,* June 23, 1980.
239 AT A $200-A-PLATE NEW YORK   Ibid., June 21, 1980.
240 POLLED EIGHTEEN POSSIBLE TICKETS   Ibid., July 1, 1980.
240 THE FORMER PRESIDENT HAD TOLD REAGAN   Germond and Witcover, *Blue Smoke and Mirrors,* 171.
240 "WANT ME TO PURSUE IT?"   Ibid.
240 "HELL, NO"   Ibid.
240 BUSH AND SEVEN OTHERS   *NYT,* July 1, 1980.
240 TWO OTHER NAMES EMERGED   Ibid., July 11, 1980.
240 A GALLUP POLL IN EARLY JULY   Ibid., July 8, 1980.
240 "IF YOU WISH"   William A. Rusher memorandum, January 14, 1980, William A. Rusher Papers, Library of Congress Manuscript Division, Washington, D.C.
240 ERNEST ANGELO, JR., A LONGTIME REAGAN SUPPORTER   Author interview with Ernest Angelo, Jr.
241 "I THOUGHT WE WERE DONE"   Author interview with GHWB.
241 "IT WOULD'VE BEEN TOUGH"   Ibid.
241 "I'D WANTED TO BE PRESIDENT"   Ibid.

TWENTY-ONE: *Is George Bush There?*

242 "I THOUGHT WE WERE DONE"   Author interview with GHWB.
242 STU SPENCER, A REAGAN ADVISER   Author interview with Stu Spencer.
242 "I STARTED OUT"   Ibid.
242 "'VOODOO ECONOMICS'"   Ibid.
242 ON THE PLANE   Author interview with Stu Spencer. See also Shirley, *Rendezvous with Destiny,* 331.
243 SPENCER TRIED AGAIN   Author interview with Stu Spencer.
243 "YOU HAVEN'T BEEN"   Ibid.
243 "NO, I FOLLOW"   Ibid.
243 REAGAN DID NOT REPLY   Ibid.

243 MOVEMENT CONSERVATIVES ARRIVING IN DETROIT *NYT*, July 14, 1980. See also Lewis L. Gould, *Grand Old Party: A History of the Republicans* (New York, 2003), 416–17, and John Herbers, "Ultraconservative Evangelicals a Surging Force in Politics," *NYT*, August 17, 1980.

243 "I FEEL THIS WHOLE ELECTION" *NYT*, July 14, 1980.

243 "THE MESSAGE WE WANT" Ibid., July 13, 1980.

243 THE NUMBERS ARGUED FOR BUSH "Vice Presidential Selection," June 25, 1980, VP Selection, Ed Meese Papers, Ronald Reagan Presidential Library.

244 THE SURVEYS FOUND, TOO Ibid.

244 BUSH HIMSELF WAS RUNNING Ibid.

244 A MEETING IN JESSE HELMS'S SUITE Author interview with Ernest Angelo, Jr.

244 PHIL CRANE WAS ALSO TRYING Ibid.

244 "IF SENATOR HELMS" Ibid.

244 "THEY NEARLY THREW ME OUT" Ibid.

244 MODERATES WERE UPSET *NYT*, July 13, 1980.

244 THE BUSHES ARRIVED IN DETROIT "George Bush Detroit Schedule," in BPB diary, summer 1980.

244 IT WAS GOING TO BE A LONG WEEK Ibid. Bush and Jim Baker ran into Henry Kissinger. The two explained their strategy for positioning Bush for the vice presidency: They were going to meet with all the Bush delegates and say all the right things about Reagan. The former would be visible evidence of Bush's vote-getting ability; the latter the price of admission to the national ticket. "They were hoping that I would be sympathetic, which I was, and that I might be supportive if the occasion arose," Kissinger recalled. (Author interview with Henry Kissinger.)

244 AS BUSH LOOKED OVER "George Bush Detroit Schedule," in BPB diary, summer 1980.

245 PRESIDENT FORD HAD "TOLD ASSOCIATES" *NYT*, July 14, 1980.

245 HOUR AFTER HOUR "George Bush Detroit Schedule," in BPB diary, summer 1980.

245 JIM BAKER CALLED A STRATEGY OF "ABB" Baker with Fiffer, *Work Hard*, 98; Shirley, *Rendezvous with Destiny*, 350.

245 THE REAGANS CALLED ON THE FORDS Germond and Witcover, *Blue Smoke and Mirrors*, 171–72.

245 (THE REAGANS WERE ON) Alan Greenspan, *The Age of Turbulence: Adventures in a New World* (New York, 2007), 89–90.

245 REAGAN BROUGHT HIS OLD RIVAL A GIFT Germond and Witcover, *Blue Smoke and Mirrors*, 172.

245 "SOME CALL ME" Ibid., 172–73.

245 REAGAN WAS STRUCK Ibid., 173.

246 BUSH WAS FINISHING A SESSION "George Bush Detroit Schedule," BPB diary, summer 1980.

246 "I KNOW WHAT I'M ASKING" Germond and Witcover, *Blue Smoke and Mirrors*, 173.

246 "I DON'T THINK" Ibid., 173–74. For one thing, Ford said, the two men were both legal residents of California, and the Twelfth Amendment to the Constitution held that presidents and vice presidents had to be from different states. According to Germond and Witcover, Reagan handed Ford a memorandum on that question; all Ford had to do to dispense with that obstacle was change his residency to either Colorado, where he had a house in Vail, or back to Michigan, which he had represented in Congress for a quarter century. (Ibid.)

246 WOULD FORD THINK ABOUT IT Ibid., 174. For the Ford drama in Detroit, see also Shirley, *Rendezvous with Destiny*, 321–69; Cannon, *Reagan*, 264–67; Stacks, *Watershed*,

185–91; and Richard V. Allen's memoir of the convention, "The Accidental Vice President," *NYT,* July 30, 2000.

246 A PRESS CONFERENCE FOR ELEVEN O'CLOCK ON THURSDAY MORNING   Shirley, *Rendezvous with Destiny,* 366.

246 FORD REMAINED OVERTLY SKEPTICAL   Germond and Witcover, *Blue Smoke and Mirrors,* 174.

246 AFTER THE MEETING WITH FORD   Hedrick Smith, "Reagan Woos Ford as Top Republicans Denounce President," *NYT,* July 16, 1980.

246 "I JUST SOUGHT"   Ibid.

246 BUSH WAS TAKING PART   "George Bush Detroit Schedule," BPB diary, summer 1980.

246 BACK AT THE DETROIT PLAZA   Germond and Witcover, *Blue Smoke and Mirrors,* 174–75.

247 LATE TUESDAY NIGHT, KISSINGER . . . MET   Ibid.

247 "THE POSSIBILITIES FOR FORD"   Ibid., 175.

247 "I KNOW IT MUST BE"   Greenfield, *Real Campaign,* 161–62.

247 ASKED WHETHER PRIDE   Germond and Witcover, *Blue Smoke and Mirrors,* 175–76.

247 FIGURING THAT OUT   Author interview with Henry Kissinger. See also Shirley, *Rendezvous with Destiny,* 354–55, and Nancy Reagan with Novak, *My Turn,* 211.

247 A KIND OF SUPER WHITE HOUSE CHIEF OF STAFF   Shirley, *Rendezvous with Destiny,* 354.

247 ANOTHER WOULD HAVE HAD FORD   Author interview with Henry Kissinger.

247 THERE WAS ALSO TALK OF A SCENARIO   Ibid. "When I found that out, I called Meese and said that under no circumstances would I accept a position as part of these negotiations," Kissinger recalled to the author. Ford kept the talks going, Kissinger recalled, out of a sense that "If it means defeating Carter, then you have a duty to do it. But I believe Ford never really wanted to do it." (Author interview with Henry Kissinger.)

247 "IT WAS MIND-BLOWING"   Author interview with Dick Cheney.

247 THE REAGAN-FORD RUMORS WERE BEING DISSECTED   Author interview with Jerry Rafshoon.

248 DESPITE THE POLLING   Ibid.

248 "WE THOUGHT THIS COULD BE A BREAK FOR US"   Ibid.

248 "THOUGHT THE WHOLE IDEA WAS RIDICULOUS"   Nancy Reagan with Novak, *My Turn,* 211.

248 "I DIDN'T SEE"   Ibid.

248 "IT CAN'T BE DONE"   Ibid.

248 AT THE PONTCHARTRAIN AFTER LUNCH, DEAN BURCH   *LF,* 9.

248 "IT'S ONLY A RUMOR"   Ibid.

248 "THIS IS CRAZY"   Author interview with GHWB.

248 BUSH BELIEVED HIS SPEECH   *LF,* 10.

248 WAS SCHEDULED FOR EIGHT P.M.   "George Bush Detroit Schedule," BPB diary, summer 1980.

248 JOGGED ON THE INDOOR TRACK   King, *George Bush,* 5–6.

248 HAD A SNACK   *LF,* 10.

248 IT WAS SEVEN P.M.   Greenfield, *Real Campaign,* 163.

248 THE TELEVISION WAS TUNED TO CBS   *LF,* 10.

249 SITTING WITH CRONKITE   Greenfield, *Real Campaign,* 163.

249 "I REALLY BELIEVE"   Germond and Witcover, *Blue Smoke and Mirrors,* 182. Reagan was startled to see Ford on television at all. (Cannon, *Reagan,* 266.)

249 IT WAS AN HONEST   Germond and Witcover, *Blue Smoke and Mirrors,* 182–83.

249 CRONKITE ASKED ABOUT   Ibid.

249 WATCHING, REAGAN SAT UP STRAIGHT   Ibid., 183. See also Shirley, *Rendezvous with Destiny*, 358.

249 "AS FAR AS RONNIE WAS CONCERNED"   Nancy Reagan with Novak, *My Turn*, 212.

249 BUSH WAS TYING HIS TIE   *LF*, 10.

249 HE WAS, HE SAID LATER, "STUNNED"   Ibid.

250 RETURNING TO THE ROOM   Ibid., 10–11.

250 "PUT IT OUT OF YOUR MIND"   Ibid., 11.

250 AS BUSH LOOKED OVER HIS SPEECH   Ibid.

250 "I'M SORRY, MR. BUSH"   Ibid. See also Shirley, *Rendezvous with Destiny*, 359–60.

250 "IF ANYONE WANTS TO KNOW"   Shirley, *Rendezvous with Destiny*, 359. See also *NYT*, July 17, 1980.

250 BUSH FOCUSED HIS FIRE   *NYT*, July 17, 1980.

250 HE, JEB, AND BUSH AIDE DAVID BATES   Author interview with Jeb Bush.

250 THERE HAD BEEN A COUPLE OF CALLS   Author interview with Pete Teeley; Shirley, *Rendezvous with Destiny*, 357–59. See also Allen, "The Accidental Vice President," *NYT*, July 30, 2000.

250 FROM THE REAGAN CAMP, RICHARD V. ALLEN   Allen, "The Accidental Vice President," *NYT*, July 30, 2000.

250 AS HE CHANGED INTO KHAKIS AND A TENNIS SHIRT   *Time*, July 28, 1980. See also Germond and Witcover, *Blue Smoke and Mirrors*, 188, and *LF*, 11.

250 HE OPENED ANOTHER BEER   *Time*, July 28, 1980.

250 JEB POUNDED HIS FIST   Author interview with GHWB.

250 "THIS ISN'T FAIR, DAD"   Ibid.

250 "WHAT ARE YOU TALKING ABOUT, FAIR?"   Ibid.

251 "NOBODY OWES US A DAMN THING"   Ibid.

251 "DO YOUR BEST"   *LF*, 11.

251 DAVID BATES HAD A BOTTLE OF SCOTCH   Author interview with Jeb Bush.

251 JEB TOLD HIS PARENTS   Ibid.

251 AS THE EVENING HAD WORN ON   Allen, "The Accidental Vice President," *NYT*, July 30, 2000.

251 "ALMOST RHETORICALLY"   Ibid.

251 "THERE'S BUSH"   Ibid.

251 "IF YOU COULD BE"   Ibid.

251 "WELL, IF YOU"   Ibid.

251 AT 8:55 P.M., ACCORDING TO ALLEN   Ibid.

251 KISSINGER "NOW TAKES HIMSELF OUT"   Ibid.

251 "I THOUGHT IT WAS ABSOLUTELY UNTENABLE"   Author interview with Henry Kissinger.

251 THE OLD ACTOR'S SENSE OF HIS AUDIENCE   Germond and Witcover, *Blue Smoke and Mirrors*, 186.

251 BY 10:45 P.M. MEESE RETURNED   Allen, "The Accidental Vice President," *NYT*, July 30, 2000.

251 "IT'S KIND OF HARD"   Ibid.

252 JIM BAKER HAD GIVEN UP   Author interview with Pete Teeley.

252 PETE TEELEY DOWN TO   Ibid.

252 IN THE REAGAN SUITE   Ibid.

252 "HOLD EVERYTHING"   *LF*, 13–14.

252 EVEN IF IT WEREN'T REAGAN-FORD   Ibid., 14.

252 STILL, BAKER HAD TEELEY   Author interview with Pete Teeley.

252 BY A QUARTER AFTER ELEVEN   Shirley, *Rendezvous with Destiny*, 363.

252 AT THE DETROIT PLAZA   Greenspan, *Age of Turbulence*, 91.

252 HE WENT DOWNSTAIRS   Allen, "The Accidental Vice President," *NYT,* July 30, 2000. See also Shirley, *Rendezvous with Destiny,* 363.

252 "RON, I'VE BELIEVED"   Germond and Witcover, *Blue Smoke and Mirrors,* 187.

252 "MR. PRESIDENT, I THINK"   Ibid.

252 PUTTING AN ARM AROUND REAGAN'S SHOULDERS   Ibid.

252 "WELL, WHAT DO WE DO NOW?"   Shirley, *Rendezvous with Destiny,* 364. This was Richard Allen's recollection of the question, based on his notes of the evening. Germond and Witcover reported a different, more specific question from Reagan: "Now where the hell's George Bush?" According to Germond and Witcover, "He had decided that afternoon, Meese said, that if something couldn't be worked out with Ford, his choice would be Bush." (Germond and Witcover, *Blue Smoke and Mirrors,* 187–88.)

252 "THERE WAS NO IMMEDIATE RESPONSE"   Allen, "The Accidental Vice President," *NYT,* July 30, 2000. See also Shirley, *Rendezvous with Destiny,* 364. Craig Shirley reports that Peter Hannaford, another Reagan adviser, suggested the call to Bush. (Shirley, *Rendezvous with Destiny,* 364.)

253 REAGAN HAD PLACED   Author interview with Stu Spencer.

253 "DO YOU STILL"   Ibid.

253 "A COMBINATION OF EBENEZER SCROOGE"   *NYT,* August 17, 1980.

253 "WELL," REAGAN SAID, "LET'S GET"   Shirley, *Rendezvous with Destiny,* 364.

253 AT 11:37 P.M., THE TELEPHONE IN ROOM 1912   Ibid., 365.

253 JIM BAKER PICKED IT UP   Ibid.

253 DREW LEWIS, A REAGAN ADVISER   Germond and Witcover, *Blue Smoke and Mirrors,* 188.

253 BUSH TOOK THE RECEIVER   Shirley, *Rendezvous with Destiny,* 365. The Bush camp had the slightest of inklings that good news might be at hand when the Secret Service, which had apparently learned the Bush news in the Reagan suite, called the Bushes' room before Reagan got through to announce that agents were "ready to occupy a room two floors below." (*LSY,* 245.)

253 "HELLO, GEORGE"   *LF,* 14.

253 ("YOU PRAY THAT GEORGE WILL SAY YES")   BPB diary, summer 1980.

253 BUSH TURNED TO THE OTHERS   Germond and Witcover, *Blue Smoke and Mirrors,* 188.

253 "I'D BE HONORED"   *LF,* 15.

253 "OUT OF A CLEAR BLUE SKY"   Author interview with GHWB.

253 "GEORGE, IS THERE ANYTHING"   *LF,* 15.

253 REAGAN MENTIONED ABORTION   Author interview with GHWB.

253 "I TOLD HIM THAT I HAD"   *LF,* 15.

254 "FINE," REAGAN SAID   Ibid.

254 WALTER CRONKITE HAD TO REGROUP   King, *George Bush,* 4.

254 "THE POLITICS OF IT ALL"   BPB diary, summer 1980.

254 BUSH TOOK A FEW QUESTIONS   *NYT,* July 17, 1980.

254 "I HAVE NO INDICATION"   Ibid.

254 AT THE HALL, REAGAN   Shirley, *Rendezvous with Destiny,* 367.

254 YES, REAGAN TOLD THE DELEGATES   *NYT,* July 17, 1980.

254 THE BUSHES MET THE REAGANS   *LF,* 15–16.

254 "NO HINT OF ANY TENSION"   Ibid., 16.

254 REAGAN AIDE MICHAEL DEAVER REMEMBERED   *NYT,* April 5, 1981.

255 AT A PRESS CONFERENCE   Ibid., July 18, 1980.

255 A REPORTER PRESSED BUSH   Ibid.

255 THEN BUSH MADE A POINT   Ibid.

255 But how, Bush was asked   Ibid.
255 "My view is that"   Ibid.
255 What about Reagan's   Ibid.
255 "Listen, let me"   Ibid.
255 There were two criteria   Ibid.
256 What about Bush's   Ibid.
256 "Can you ever imagine"   Ibid.
256 Working overnight and into Thursday   BPB diary, summer 1980.
256 "We found no bad feeling"   Ibid.
256 During an introductory film for Reagan   Ibid.
256 On Friday morning the Reagans and the Bushes   *NYT,* July 20, 1980.
256 "If Texas and California"   Ibid.
256 "He is a serious"   "Mr. Reagan's Second Choice," *NYT,* July 18, 1980.
256 "Life is now hectic"   *ATB,* 302.

TWENTY-TWO: *Well, What Do We Do Now?*

257 Call me if I can lighten   *ATB,* 303.
257 "It was a cliffhanger"   Richard Nixon to GHWB, July 19, 1980, Richard M. Nixon Presidential Library. "I am pleased to be on this ticket," Bush replied. "We can win, but I'm one who feels it will be a very tough race—Mr. Carter is a no-holds-barred guy." (GHWB to Richard Nixon, July 28, 1980, Richard M. Nixon Presidential Library.)
257 At the Commonwealth Club   BPB diary, summer 1980.
257 "lots of top Reagan people"   Ibid.
257 "George lost the election"   Ibid.
257 A trip to Japan and to China   *LSY,* 248; BPB diary, August 1980. Bush would be dogged for years by unsubstantiated rumors that he had played a role in an alleged effort by the Reagan campaign to delay the release of the American hostages in Iran until after the 1980 election. Bush was long alleged to have traveled to Paris for clandestine meetings as part of such an effort—a tale declared false in 1992 by a House task force on the so-called October Surprise. See, for instance, *NYT,* July 2, 1992.
257 Reagan's apparent suggestion   Cannon, *Reagan,* 272–73, Shirley, *Rendezvous with Destiny,* 448; *NYT,* August 17, 1980.
258 When the Bushes arrived   BPB diary, August 20, 1980.
258 One sign of how upset   Ibid., August 22, 1980.
258 met the press   *WP,* August 26, 1980.
258 "The governor is"   BPB diary, August 23, 1980.
258 In her diary, Barbara agreed   Ibid., August 23, 1980.
258 "Reagan's glitches"   Ibid., September 7, 1980.
258 Bush appeared on *Meet the Press*   *Meet the Press,* NBC, guest: George Bush, Republican vice presidential nominee. September 7, 1980. Vol. 80. Kelly Press, Inc., Betty Cole Dukert Papers, State Historical Society of Missouri.
259 Reagan's view that   Ibid.
259 "peripheral"   Ibid.
259 The Bushes flew in   BPB diary, October 28, 1980.
259 "Ronnie never wears"   Ibid.
259 A group of big-dollar Republican donors   Ibid., September 29, 1980.
259 "that if it looks like we're losing"   Ibid., September 13, 1980.

259   Presenting Reagan in a moderate light   *NYT,* November 1, 1980; *WP,* November 1, 1980.

259   On the last day of campaigning   Author interview with Stu Spencer.

259   "I'm awful"   Ibid.

259   "Then Reagan just nailed it"   Ibid.

260   "in like a burglar"   Cannon, *Reagan,* 302.

260   Sitting on the floor   Arthur Sulzberger Jr., "Bush, in Victory Talk, Says Reagan Will Lead U.S. 'Back to Greatness,'" *NYT,* November 5, 1980.

260   (Carter called Reagan to concede)   Reagan, *An American Life,* 221.

260   Reagan-Bush won the popular vote   www.uselectionatlas.org/RESULTS /national.php?year=1980.

260   "Well done, sir"   *NYT,* November 6, 1980.

260   "Well, what do"   Ibid.

260   The first order of business   Ibid., November 7, 1980.

260   "tons to do"   Ibid.

260   "going to a lot"   Ibid.

260   "I'd love to sit down"   *ATB,* 302.

260   "Please know that"   Ibid., 303.

261   the administrative details   Dean Burch to GHWB, November 21, 1980, box 66/1, James A Baker III Papers, Princeton.

261   "1) You and the President"   Ibid.

261   "I like it"   GHWB to JAB III, December 2, 1980, box 66/1, James A. Baker III Papers, Princeton.

261   "My presence [will] hopefully"   Undated notes, James A. Baker III Papers, Princeton.

261   "then why"   Chase Untermeyer, *When Things Went Right: The Dawn of the Reagan-Bush Administration* (College Station, Tex., 2013), 13.

261   "Because with a 70-year-old president"   Ibid.

twenty-three: *The Special Relationship*

262   He's hard to read   GHWB diary, April 13, 1983.

262   "Bush had a special relationship"   Martin Anderson, *Revolution* (San Diego, 1988), 312–13.

262   "deep into the inner sanctums"   Ibid., 313.

262   "I know both of them"   Author interview with Boyden Gray.

262   Bush had hardly been   Author observation.

262   "Don't upstage the President's staff"   Untermeyer, *When Things Went Right,* 17.

262   "no surprises"   Ibid.

262   He hoped to   Wicker, *GHWB,* 64.

263   "'Separate yourself from 1600'"   GHWB diary, September 13, 1981.

264   Bush developed a set of informal rules   *LF,* 227–30.

264   First, don't play   Ibid., 227–28.

264   "Be sure not to take"   Ibid., 232.

264   "The Vice President's authority"   Ibid.

265   Which is what had happened to Rockefeller   Ibid., 232–33.

265   "I spent sixteen years"   Untermeyer, *When Things Went Right,* 26.

265   "unthreatened by people"   *ATB,* 313.

265   there were weekly lunches   *LF,* 231–32.

265   (Bush added a lot of hot sauce)   GHWB diary, June 25, 1987.

265 "Before lunch every week"   Author interview with Boyden Gray.

265 "George, I've got a question"   GHWB diary, November 20, 1986.

265 "was busy and he wasn't"   Ibid., September 13, 1981.

266 Gray remembered a meeting   Author interview with Boyden Gray.

266 "That was the level of comfort"   Ibid.

266 While Reagan himself was perfectly pleasant   Author interview with GHWB. "Ronald Reagan had great affection for George Bush, and respect," recalled Frederick J. Ryan, Reagan's first post-presidential chief of staff. (Author interview with Frederick J. Ryan.)

266 rarely invited   Author interview with BPB.

266 "Right after Reagan"   Author interview with GHWB.

267 One sign of Bush's success   Reagan, *American Life*, 255.

267 The decision enraged Haig   Ibid., 255–56.

267 "the President simply feels"   *LSY*, 266.

267 the rollback of federal regulations   *LF*, 233; *LSY*, 263–65; Anderson, *Revolution*, 259–61; author interviews with GHWB and Boyden Gray. Bush was also essential on a tricky trade question with the Japanese. See Reagan, *American Life*, 253–54, 273–74.

268 According to domestic policy adviser   Anderson, *Revolution*, 260.

268 "they didn't have any time"   Ibid.

268 "Ronald Reagan delegated"   Author interview with Boyden Gray.

268 Bush took off on a four-day trip   Untermeyer, *When Things Went Right*, 34–35.

268 An odd rumor had begun   Ibid., 36. According to different versions, the alleged incident was said to have taken place either in Georgetown or on Capitol Hill. (Ibid., 35–36; see also *WP*, March 22, 1981.)

268 In Melbourne, Florida   Untermeyer, *When Things Went Right*, 35.

269 The next morning   Ibid.

269 Where had the story   Ibid., 36.

269 Shirley Green, teeley's deputy, warned   Ibid.

269 The FBI was called in   Ibid., 36–37.

269 *The Washington Post* published a piece   Ibid., 37. Janet Cooke and Benjamin Weiser shared a byline on the March 22 story. (*WP*, March 22, 1981.)

269 "We handled the whole matter"   Untermeyer, *When Things Went Right*, 37.

269 Bush attended   Ibid., 39. See also Del Quentin Wilber, *Rawhide Down: The Near Assassination of Ronald Reagan* (New York, 2011), 49; *WP*, March 30, 1981.

270 "Does he feel"   Wilber, *Rawhide Down*, 65.

270 "I just want to be sure"   Ibid.

270 "If the awful-awful"   Ibid.

TWENTY-FOUR: *The President Was Struck*

271 My every inclination   Untermeyer, *When Things Went Right*, 43.

271 Have you ever known   Ibid.

271 drizzling in Washington   Untermeyer, *When Things Went Right*, 39. My account of the Reagan assassination attempt owes much to Chase Untermeyer's *When Things Went Right* and to Del Quentin Wilber's *Rawhide Down*, an excellent narrative of the drama of the day. Bush's own recollections, both in contemporaneous notes and in *LF*, 217–25, were also valuable.

271 at 8:55 a.m.   *LF*, 218.

271 Bush had arranged for the CIA   Wilber, *Rawhide Down*, 49.

271 THEY HELICOPTERED OUT TO Untermeyer, *When Things Went Right,* 39.

271 AWAITING BUSH ABOARD THE JET Ibid., 39–40.

271 THE FLIGHT TO FORT WORTH *LF,* 218–19.

271 BUSH ASKED UNTERMEYER Untermeyer, *When Things Went Right,* 40.

271 AT ABOUT A QUARTER TO ELEVEN Ibid.

271 IN TEXAS THE WEATHER Ibid.

271 UNTERMEYER NOTED THAT Ibid.

271 BUSH'S FIRST STOP *LF,* 219–220.

271 IN THE WHITE HOUSE, REAGAN WAS HAVING Wilber, *Rawhide Down,* 58–60.

272 IN FORT WORTH, BUSH WAS DRIVEN Untermeyer, *When Things Went Right,* 40.

272 HE SPENT AN HOUR AND TWENTY MINUTES *LF,* 219.

272 JIM WRIGHT, THE HOUSE MAJORITY LEADER Untermeyer, *When Things Went Right,* 40; *LF,* 218–219.

272 AN AIR TRAFFIC CONTROLLER Wilber, *Rawhide Down,* 132.

272 "ARE YOU CONTINUING" Ibid.

272 "WE'RE HEADING TO AUSTIN" Ibid.

272 A SECRET SERVICE AGENT ON THE PLANE Ibid.

272 ACCORDING TO THIS FIRST REPORT *LF,* 219. See also Wilber, *Rawhide Down,* 132.

272 "SIR, WE'VE JUST RECEIVED WORD" Wilber, *Rawhide Down,* 132.

272 "WHERE DID IT HAPPEN?" *LF,* 219.

272 "OUTSIDE THE WASHINGTON HILTON" Ibid.

272 IN THE INTERVAL Wilber, *Rawhide Down,* 77–87, details the shooting itself.

272 GETTING OFF SIX SHOTS Ibid.

273 AT FIRST NO ONE, INCLUDING REAGAN Wilber, *Rawhide Down,* 88.

273 THE PRESIDENT COMPLAINED Ibid., 89.

273 AT THE DIRECTION OF Ibid., 91.

273 DOCTORS AT THE HOSPITAL Ibid., 11, 217.

273 AN INCH FROM HIS HEART Ibid., 139.

273 BARBARA BUSH LEARNED OF THE SHOOTING *BB,* 165.

273 JIM BAKER AND ED MEESE WERE Wilber, *Rawhide Down,* 112–13.

273 AL HAIG REACHED BAKER Ibid., 112.

273 HE WOULD CONTACT BUSH Ibid.

273 HAIG, STILL IN HIS TRENCH COAT Ibid., 131.

273 "MR. VICE PRESIDENT, THIS IS" Ibid.

273 BUSH HEARD THAT MUCH Ibid.; *LF,* 220.

273 THEN DON REGAN *LF,* 220.

273 "ANY ATTEMPT ON" Ibid.

274 "WE HAVE NO WAY" Untermeyer, *When Things Went Right,* 41.

274 HE WAS HANDED THE DECODED TELEX *LF,* 220.

274 "MR. VICE PRESIDENT" Wilber, *Rawhide Down,* 132.

274 THIS WAS THE FIRST BUSH KNEW *LF,* 220.

274 "IT HAD TO OCCUR TO ME" Ibid.

274 "THE [HOTEL TEXAS]" Ibid.

274 "EVEN THE PLANE" Ibid.

274 ON THE ROBERT MUELLER MUNICIPAL AIRPORT Ibid., 221.; Wilber, *Rawhide Down,* 177.

274 PICKED UP THE ABC NEWS COVERAGE Wilber, *Rawhide Down,* 133. See also Untermeyer, *When Things Went Right,* 41.

274 "THE CRACK OF GUNFIRE" *LF,* 220.

274   THE PLANE LANDED BRIEFLY   Ibid., 221.

274   OUTSIDE AIR FORCE TWO   Untermeyer, *When Things Went Right*, 41; *LF*, 218.

275   ON THE GROUND IN AUSTIN, BUSH CALLED   *LF*, 221.

275   "TO SAY A PRAYER"   Ibid.

275   THE PLANE WAS SOON IN THE AIR   Untermeyer, *When Things Went Right*, 41.

275   "I REALLY NEEDED"   *BB*, 165.

275   "UNTIL WE HAD MORE INFORMATION"   *LF*, 223.

275   "STAY CALM"   Ibid.

275   FRED FIELDING, WAS AT WORK   Wilber, *Rawhide Down*, 166–67, 181.

275   "THEY'RE PREPARING PAPERS"   Untermeyer, *When Things Went Right*, 42. See also Wilber, *Rawhide Down*, 166–67, 181.

275   "HE SEEMS SO CALM"   Wilber, *Rawhide Down*, 178.

275   "THERE MIGHT BE"   *LF*, 222.

276   POLLARD AND MATHENY ARGUED   Ibid., 224–225; Untermeyer, *When Things Went Right*, 41–42.

276   THE "MOST BASIC OF ALL THE RULES"   Ibid., 225.

276   "AT THIS MOMENT"   Untermeyer, *When Things Went Right*, 41.

276   "TOO SELF-IMPORTANT"   Ibid., 42.

276   THERE WAS PRECEDENT   Ibid.

276   "BUT WE HAVE TO THINK"   Ibid.

276   "BY GOING STRAIGHT"   *LF*, 224.

276   "*THE PRESIDENT IN THE HOSPITAL*"   Ibid. The italics are Bush's.

276   "WE'LL BE COMING IN"   Ibid., 224–25.

277   AT AROUND FOUR P.M.   Wilber, *Rawhide Down*, 171–73.

277   "IF THE PRESIDENT"   Ibid., 172–73.

277   "I CANNOT ANSWER"   Ibid., 173.

277   "LARRY, WHO'LL BE"   Ibid.

277   WORRIED THAT THIS SERIES   Ibid. For National Security Adviser Richard V. Allen's account of the afternoon—one based on his tapes and notes of what unfolded in the Situation Room—see "The Day Reagan Was Shot," *The Atlantic*, April 2001, http://www.theatlantic.com/magazine/archive/2001/04/the-day-reagan-was-shot/308396/.

277   HE DID NOT PAUSE   Wilber, *Rawhide Down*, 173.

277   OUT OF BREATH AND PERSPIRING   Ibid., 174.

277   "I JUST WANTED"   Ibid.

277   BILL PLANTE OF CBS   Ibid., 175.

277   "CONSTITUTIONALLY, GENTLEMEN, YOU HAVE"   Ibid.

277   "IS HE MAD?"   Ibid.

278   BUSH WATCHED HAIG'S PERFORMANCE   Untermeyer, *When Things Went Right*, 42.

278   AT TEN AFTER FIVE EASTERN TIME   Ibid.

278   "IT'S HARD TO DESCRIBE"   Ibid., 43. See also Wilber, *Rawhide Down*, 132–33.

278   "HAVING TO BE THE PERSON"   Untermeyer, *When Things Went Right*, 42–43.

278   AT 6:08 P.M.   *LF*, 223.

278   ED MEESE WAS CALLING   Untermeyer, *When Things Went Right*, 43.

278   MEESE WOULD MEET BUSH   Ibid.

278   "SEE YOU AT THE HOUSE"   Ibid.

278   LOOKING OUT THE WINDOW   Ibid.

278   THE COMBINATION OF THE SETTING SUN   Ibid.

278   THE AIRCRAFT LANDED   Ibid.

278 BARBARA, WITH MEESE Ibid.

278 UNTERMEYER AND FITZGERALD WENT Ibid.

278 "HAVE YOU EVER" Ibid.

279 "WHAT'S THE LATEST?" Wilber, *Rawhide Down,* 193. Jim Baker's return from the hospital about 6:15 P.M. had also calmed things down considerably. (Ibid., 189–90.)

279 THE CABINET MEMBERS . . . ROSE Hedrick Smith, "Starting as an Outsider, Bush Is Now a Star Among Team Players," *NYT,* April 5, 1981.

279 LATER A FEW WOULD RECALL Ibid.

279 "THE PRESIDENT IS STILL" Ibid.

279 EXCHANGED TENSE WORDS Allen, "Day Reagan Was Shot."

279 WHEN SENSITIVE NATIONAL SECURITY ISSUES Wilber, *Rawhide Down,* 193–94.

279 BY POSING IT THEY FURTHER DEFUSED Ibid., 194.

279 SHOULD BUSH MAKE A PUBLIC STATEMENT Ibid.

279 AT EIGHT P.M., BUSH CALLED AN END Ibid.

279 "DEEPLY HEARTENED" Ibid.

279 THE PRESIDENT . . . "HAS EMERGED" Ibid.

280 PILING ON THE SECRETARY OF STATE *ATB,* 311.

280 BUSH RETURNED TO HIS OFFICE Smith, "Starting as an Outsider"; *WP,* April 1, 1981; Untermeyer, *When Things Went Right,* 44.

280 DECIDING AGAINST VISITING THE PRESIDENT Untermeyer, *When Things Went Right,* 44.

280 "SHE LOOKED TINY" Ibid.

280 AT ABOUT NINE THIRTY P.M. Ibid.

280 ART WEISE OF *THE HOUSTON POST* Ibid., 44–45.

280 DID NEIL BUSH . . . KNOW JOHN HINCKLEY Ibid.

280 "THE HINCKLEYS ARE" Ibid.

280 WEISE MADE AN EXCELLENT POINT Ibid., 45.

280 "JESUS," BUSH SAID Ibid.

280 PETE TEELEY SUGGESTED A QUICK PROBE Ibid.

280 BUSH HAD THE FULLEST OF DAYS Howell Raines, "Reagan Making Good Recovery," *NYT,* April 1, 1981.

281 "NEVER FOR A MOMENT" Ibid.

281 IN AN EIGHTEEN-MINUTE APPEARANCE Ibid.

281 BUSH TOLD REPORTERS *NYT,* April 6, 1981.

281 "THAT'S THE MAIN POINT" Ibid.

281 THE USUAL 9:15 Untermeyer, *When Things Went Right,* 46.

281 PRESIDENT REAGAN RETURNED TO THE WHITE HOUSE Ibid., 48.

281 BUSH HAD SPENT PART OF THE MORNING Ibid.

282 A BRIGHT RED SWEATER Ibid.

282 "DID IT HELP ME" Author interview with GHWB.

282 "VICE PRESIDENT BUSH . . . SEEMS" *Time,* April 13, 1981.

282 "GEORGE BUSH STRUCK" William Safire, "One Fell Short," *NYT,* April 2, 1981.

282 "I HAVE NEVER BEEN" *LSY,* 271.

282 "I WORRIED ABOUT MY FRIEND" *BB,* 166.

282 OVER CLUB SANDWICHES Untermeyer, *When Things Went Right,* 55–56.

283 THE PRESIDENT SPILLED SOME WATER See video of GHWB eulogy of President Ronald Reagan at http://www.c-span.org/video/?182165-1/ronald-reagan-funeral-service.

283 CHRISTOPHER BUCKLEY LATER OBSERVED Christopher Buckley, *But Enough About You: Essays* (New York, 2014), 160.

TWENTY-FIVE: *George Did It*

284 DO YOU THINK WE FEEL   Untermeyer, *When Things Went Right*, 274.

284 THE NUTS WILL NEVER BE FOR ME   Ibid., 30.

284 AS HE RECUPERATED   Reagan, *American Life*, 269.

284 "I WANTED TO LET"   Ibid., 269–70.

284 "RESERVE UNTO THEMSELVES"   *Public Papers of the Presidents of the United States: Ronald W. Reagan, 1981* (Washington, D.C., 1982), 57.

284 NOW, AFTER HIS SHOOTING   Reagan, *American Life*, 270.

284 "MR. PRESIDENT," REAGAN WROTE   Ibid., 272–73.

284 "ICY REPLY"   Ibid., 273.

284 REAGAN WAS WILLING TO DEAL   Martin Anderson and Annelise Anderson, *Reagan's Secret War: The Untold Story of His Fight to Save the World from Nuclear Disaster* (New York, 2009), 93–131.

285 TO PROPOSE A "ZERO-ZERO OPTION"   "Remarks to Members of the National Press Club on Arms Reduction and Nuclear Weapons," *Public Papers of the Presidents of the United States: Ronald W. Reagan, 1981*, 1062–67. See also Reagan, *American Life*, 295–97.

285 IN THE COLD WAR OF THE EARLY 1980S   John Lewis Gaddis, *The Cold War: A New History* (New York, 2005), 221–28. See also Reagan, *American Life*, 294, 560–62, for Reagan's explanation of the zero-zero option.

285 "I THINK THERE [IS]"   GHWB diary, January 8, 1983.

285 THE SOVIETS REJECTED   Reagan, *American Life*, 353. See also Ernest Conine, "Alice in Missile Wonderland," *LAT*, January 31, 1983.

285 "THE AMERICAN GOVERNMENT"   "Britain Plans to Counter Disarmament Movement," *The Atlanta Constitution*, January 31, 1983.

285 REAGAN ASKED BUSH   For general background on the mission, see Untermeyer, *When Things Went Right*, 259–75.

285 "IMPRESS UPON THEM THE DEPTH"   "Bush Starts First Leg of Europe Trip," *Chicago Tribune*, January 31, 1983. See also Andrew J. Glass, "Bush in Europe," *The Atlanta Constitution*, January 30, 1983.

285 HE WAS "UP BUT EDGY"   Untermeyer, *When Things Went Right*, 266.

285 "THE VICE PRESIDENT SEEMS TO US"   "American Diplomacy on the Road," *WP*, January 30, 1983.

286 IN WEST BERLIN   Ibid., February 1, 1983.

286 BUSH SPOKE AT A DINNER   *Chicago Tribune*, February 1, 1983.

286 PULLING A PIECE OF PAPER   "Reagan's Letter to Europeans," *NYT*, February 1, 1983.

286 "POSITIVE DEVELOPMENT"   Michael Getler, "Bush Sees Positive Results from Reagan Summit Offer," *WP*, February 2, 1983.

286 (ANDROPOV REJECTED THE OVERTURE)   *NYT*, February 2, 1983.

286 BUSH LOWERED RHETORICAL TENSIONS   John Maclean, "Bush Says He Won Arms Converts," *Chicago Tribune*, February 6, 1983.

286 HE SPOKE OF KNOWING REAGAN'S "HEARTBEAT"   Ibid.

286 MARGARET THATCHER CABLED REAGAN   Jason Saltoun-Ebin & Andrea Chiampan, "The Reagan Files: The Euromissiles Crisis to the Intermediate Range Nuclear Forces Treaty, 1979–1987." (thereaganfiles.com), Oct. 17, 2011.

286 ON THE LAST DAY OF A LONG JOURNEY   Michael Getler, "Bush a Hit in Europe; Now, Does that Help?," *WP*, February 20, 1983.

286 "ONCE AGAIN I FOUND"   "NATO Is Far from a Dead Alliance, Bush Declares During London Visit," *The Atlanta Constitution*, February 10, 1983.

286 THE CIA WAS REPORTING INTERNALLY GHWB diary, February 10, 1983.

286 AT THE GUILDHALL Untermeyer, *When Things Went Right,* 274.

287 "GREAT SINCERITY AND ALMOST CHURCHILLIAN MAJESTY" Ibid.

287 "IT WAS A SUCCINCT WAY" Michael Getler, "Bush a Hit in Europe," *WP,* February 20, 1983.

287 "BUSH FACED HIS EUROPEAN CHALLENGE" Untermeyer, *When Things Went Right,* 275.

287 HE WAS CONGRATULATED IN THE HALLS GHWB diary, February 10, 1983.

287 BUSH APPEARED ON CBS'S *FACE THE NATION* Ibid., February 13, 1983.

287 "HE LISTENED CAREFULLY" "George Did It," *WP,* February 13, 1983.

287 "GEORGE DID IT" Ibid.

287 "THE NUTS WILL NEVER BE FOR ME" Untermeyer, *When Things Went Right,* 30.

288 IN MANCHESTER, NEW HAMPSHIRE GHWB diary, September 7–13, 1981.

288 "I DIDN'T WANT" Ibid.

288 "JIMMY BAKER AT YEAR END" Ibid., January 1, 1983.

288 "I DON'T THINK THE PRESIDENT WILL LET HIM GO" Ibid., January 4, 1983.

288 "HE KEEPS HIS CARDS" Ibid.

288 A FEW WEEKS LATER Ibid., January 17–18, 1983.

288 "JIMMY BAKER WAS IN" Ibid.

288 BUSH SUGGESTED Ibid., January 18, 1983.

288 "HE WAS THRILLED" Ibid.

289 "THEY TRY AND DRAG YOU" Ibid., January 26, 1983.

289 "I HAD BRIEFINGS" Ibid., January 15, 1983.

289 REAGAN, WHO DEFERRED ACTION *LSY,* 255.

289 "THE PRESIDENT IS A DARN GOOD COMPROMISER" GHWB diary, March 8, 1983.

289 "INCIDENTALLY, AT THIS MOMENT" Ibid., January 1, 1983.

289 "TODAY, WHEN HE WALKED" Ibid., January 20, 1983.

289 "LIGHT READING" GHWB to JAB III, November 17, 1983, James A. Baker III, Chief of Staff Files, Ronald Reagan Presidential Library.

290 DOROTHY BUSH "REALLY WAS WONDERFUL" BPB diary, 1983.

290 "I HATED IT" Ibid., 1984.

290 "TENSIONS ARE VERY" *ATB,* 338–39.

290 IN HIS EAGERNESS TO SHOW CONSERVATIVES *LSY,* 296.

290 "HIS APOSTASY" Ibid.

290 BUSH ENTERED A SILLY SEASON Naftali, *GHWB,* 42; Wicker, *GHWB,* 71–72. Bush himself thought the campaign "tough and sometimes bitter." (*ATB,* 338.)

290 "WHINE ON, HARVEST MOON" Text of the Bush-Ferraro Debate, *WP,* October 12, 1984.

290 "I'M FOR MR. REAGAN—BLINDLY" Dale Russakoff, "Bush Says He Supports the President 'Blindly,'" *WP,* November 2, 1984; Gerald M. Boyd, "Bush Says Exposure Hurt Intelligence Effort," *NYT,* November 2, 1984.

291 AT A RECEPTION FOR THE *TODAY* SHOW GHWB diary, February 25, 1987.

291 "IT'S FUNNY HOW" Ibid., July 15, 1984.

291 "SHE'S KIND OF MEAN" Ibid., July 22, 1984.

291 THE NIGHT BEFORE BB, 195–97, covers the episode. See also *ATB,* 340.

291 "NEEDLED THE PRESIDENT" BB, 195.

291 "NOT A NICE THING TO SAY" Ibid.

291 "SHE WAS VERY GRACIOUS" Ibid.

291 WAS "AGONY" FOR BARBARA Ibid., 196.

291 "SHE FELT HORRIBLE" *ATB,* 340.

291 "FOR SEVERAL YEARS" BB, 196.

291 Bush was with some longshoreman *ATB*, 339. For the "kick a little ass" moment, see also *LSY*, 298; Naftali, *GHWB*, 42; Wicker, *GHWB*, 72.

291 a "big mistake" *ATB*, 339.

292 (Bush had not noticed) Ibid.

292 "epaulette flexing" GHWB diary, September 3, 1984.

292 the Reagans offered Ibid., November 17, 1984.

TWENTY-SIX: *On the Eve of the Run*

293 These are serious people James Reston, "In Praise of Losers," *NYT*, December 31, 1986.

293 Bush first raised GHWB diary, December 15, 1984.

293 Bush made it clear Ibid. When Howard Baker called on Reagan to ask whether the president was going to be neutral in 1988, Reagan was "uncomfortable," Bush recalled. (Ibid.)

294 a thirty-seven-page memorandum Lee Atwater to GHWB, "Memorandum to the Vice President, December 25, 1984," Lee Atwater, Daily File/Transition File/Alpha File, Vice Presidential Files, George H. W. Bush Collection, Donated Materials, GBPL.

294 (Atwater talked out the strategy) Author interview with Jim Pinkerton.

294 In the 1979–80 period Ibid., 2.

294 "the VP [was] stereotyped" Ibid.

294 "High irony it is" Ibid.

294 Bush should court Ibid., 4–13.

294 "cosmology" Ibid., 30.

294 "with a track record of" Ibid., 33.

294 could hardly have been more different John Brady, *Bad Boy: The Life and Politics of Lee Atwater* (Reading, Mass., 1997), 130–36. My account of Atwater's life and career owes much to Brady's book, as well as to conversations with Mary Matalin and Howard Fineman.

295 Born in Atlanta in 1951 Brady, *Bad Boy*, 3–4.

295 "He came out and gave me" Ibid., 9.

295 fell under Thurmond's tutelage Ibid., 31–32.

295 A master of press manipulation Robert Shogan, "Lee Atwater, Tough Ex-Head of GOP, Dies," *LAT*, March 30, 1991; Brady, *Bad Boy*, 47, 133–34.

295 (In an oft-cited example) Ibid.

295 He had worked Brady, *Bad Boy*, 132–36.

295 believed that Bush Ibid., 134–35, 138–39.

295 The question for Ibid., 137–38; GWB, *Decision Points*, 43.

296 "If someone throws a grenade" GWB, *Decision Points*, 43. See also GWB, 41, 156.

296 "If you're so worried" GWB, 41, 156.

296 "I think George Bush coming up here" GHWB diary, November 11, 1986.

296 Another essential figure for Bush was Roger Ailes Author interview with GHWB. See also McGinniss, *Selling of the President, 1968*, 63–76.

296 "We'd all kill for" Author interview with Roger Ailes.

296 Bush loved Ailes's irreverence Author interview with GHWB.

296 "Bush was not" Author interview with Roger Ailes.

296 "You look like" Ibid.

296 Bush was philosophical GHWB diary, January 27, 1985.

296 "If you want to be" Ibid., February 3, 1985.

297   THE UGLINESS BUSH FEARED   George Will, "George Bush: The Sound of a Lapdog," *WP,* January 30, 1986.

297   "THE UNPLEASANT SOUND"   Ibid.

297   "NOT OFF ON ONE EXTREME"   GHWB diary, November 4, 1986.

297   ON ABORTION, HE HAD REVERSED HIMSELF   Author interview with Roger Ailes.

297   WAS HIS DEEP LOVE   Author interview with GHWB.

298   AND ON THE ROLE OF RELIGIOUS FAITH   George Bush with Doug Wead, *Man of Integrity* (Eugene, Ore., 1988), 34.

298   "LET'S JUST HOPE THE INNER STRENGTH"   GHWB diary, October 24, 1987.

298   "RUMSFELD—WE KEEP HEARING"   Ibid., November 11, 1986.

298   "BELIEVE ME"   Ibid., November 4, 1986.

298   "I KNOW I'VE GOT THE EXPERIENCE"   Ibid.

299   THE REPUBLICANS LOST CONTROL   Ibid., November 5, 1986.

299   IN THE FIRST WEEK OF NOVEMBER   Naftali, *GHWB,* 43–51; Wicker, *GHWB,* 73–84; Lawrence Walsh, *Iran-Contra: The Final Report* (New York, 1994), 10–24; Lawrence Walsh, *Firewall: The Iran-Contra Conspiracy and Cover-up* (New York, 1997), 4–10. See also Cramer, *What It Takes,* 112–26.

299   TO HELP FREE   *LSY,* 305; Naftali, *GHWB,* 46.

299   BUSH HIMSELF HAD CHAIRED   Walter Pincus and David Hoffman, "Bush Was 'Solid' Backer of Iran Deal, Note Says," *WP,* December 18, 1987.

299   IN JULY 1985   Walsh, *Iran-Contra: The Final Report,* 10–22.

299   THE RECORD IS CLEAR   Naftali, *GHWB,* 43–45; Walter Pincus and David Hoffman, "Bush Was 'Solid' Backer of Iran Deal, Note Says," *WP,* December 18, 1987.

299   "I'M ONE OF THE FEW PEOPLE"   GHWB diary, November 5, 1986.

300   "MOST IMPORTANTLY"   "Bush Was Solid," *WP,* December 18, 1987.

300   THE VICE PRESIDENT HAD ALSO BEEN PRESENT   George P. Shultz, *Turmoil and Triumph: My Years as Secretary of State* (New York, 1993), 803.

300   "NO ONE ELSE DID"   Ibid.

300   BUSH WAS SILENT   Lee Hamilton and Daniel Inouye, *Report of the Congressional Committees Investigating the Iran-Contra Affair* (Washington, D.C., 1987), 203; Walsh, *Iran-Contra: The Final Report,* 18.

300   IN JULY 1986   Walsh, *Iran-Contra: The Final Report,* 22. For Nir memo, see Craig Fuller Memorandum, "The Vice President's Meeting with Mr. Nir," (July 29, 1986). *The Iran-Contra Scandal: A Declassified History* (1993), ed. Peter Kornbluh and Malcolm Byrne (New York, 1993), 240–41; *LF,* 241–42.

300   THE ISRAELI BRIEFED BUSH   *LF,* 241–42.

300   ACCORDING TO A MEMORANDUM   Kornbluh and Byrne, eds., *Iran-Contra Scandal,* 240–41; Bob Woodward and David Hoffman, "Bush Told U.S. Arms Deals Were with Iran Radicals," *WP,* February 8, 1987.

300   "BUSH ON TV SAYS"   "Memorandum on the Criminal Liability of President Bush," March 21, 1991. Prepared for Judge Lawrence Walsh by Christian J. Mixter, 58. Though tape of this comment has never been found, Shultz clearly saw it, and Bush's initial instinct to deny reports of the initiative was also manifest in a statement issued by his vice presidential (and later presidential) press secretary, Marlin Fitzwater. ". . . Marlin Fitzwater, the Vice President's press secretary, reacted [in a *Chicago Tribune* article] by stating that the idea that Mr. Bush or any of his staff had arranged weapons deals for Iran was 'bizarre, outrageous, and absurd . . . not true [and] crazy.'" (Ibid., 57.) See also Naftali, *GHWB,* 46–47.

300   "VP WAS PART OF IT"   "Memorandum on the Criminal Liability of President Bush," 58.

301   SHULTZ AND HIS WIFE   Shultz, *Turmoil and Triumph,* 808–9.

301 BUSH FLARED "Memorandum on the Criminal Liability of President Bush," 58–59.

301 "CONSIDERABLE TENSION" Shultz, *Turmoil and Triumph,* 809.

301 "SHULTZ WORRIES ABOUT" GHWB diary, November 10, 1986.

301 JIM BAKER LATER TOLD SHULTZ "Memorandum on the Criminal Liability of President Bush," 59.

301 ROLE OF ISRAEL Naftali, *GHWB,* 45.

301 "THEY DON'T KNOW THAT I RAISED" GHWB diary, February 16, 1987.

302 IN A SPEECH Naftali, *GHWB,* 49.

302 "CLEARLY, MISTAKES WERE MADE" *LAT,* December 4, 1986.

302 APPROVED THE LEAKING OF THE MEMORANDUM Author interview with Boyden Gray.

302 "GREAT JOB, GREAT JOB" Ibid.

302 BUSH'S INITIAL DENIAL "Memorandum on the Criminal Liability of President Bush," 57–58.

302 SHULTZ RECALLED BEING "ASTONISHED" Shultz, *Turmoil and Triumph,* 809.

302 HE JUSTIFIED THE "NOT IN THE LOOP" *LSY,* 322. See also *Los Angeles Times,* January 31, 1988, and Naftali, *GHWB,* 50.

303 AFTER LUNCH ON MONDAY, NOVEMBER 24 GHWB diary, November 24, 1986; Walsh, *Iran-Contra: The Final Report,* 1–10; Naftali, *GHWB,* 48.

303 BUSH TOLD THE ATTORNEY GENERAL GHWB diary, November 24, 1986.

303 "I MUST CONFESS" Ibid.

303 REGAN, MEESE, AND THE PRESIDENT Ibid.

303 "I SAID I HOPED" Ibid.

303 "NO, I UNDERSTAND TOTALLY" Ibid.

303 "ONE OF THE WORST DAYS" Ibid.

303 AT DUSK, BUSH CALLED Ibid.

304 BUSH VOLUNTEERED TO TAKE A POLYGRAPH Ibid., November 25, 1986.

304 OVER THANKSGIVING AT KENNEBUNKPORT Ibid., November 25–28, 1986.

304 THE VICE PRESIDENT HAD BOUGHT WALKER'S POINT Ibid., September 7, 1981; *LSY,* 256–57. "The house is beyond our furthest dreams, wildest dreams, and it's a marvelous establishment," Bush told his diary in September 1981. "I worry a little bit about money. We've put so much into this house—so much more than we had thought—and I worry about what we'll do after we get out of this; how I would support things and family; and, yet, overriding it all, it's a great joy being there with the sea pounding into the rocks, the boat, the new court, being with Mother, seeing the Walkers and the kids, and our own grandchildren running around the place." (GHWB diary, September 7, 1981.)

304 NEITHER BUSH IDEA GHWB diary, December 1, 1986.

304 "⟨⟨⟨⟨⟨ ⟨⟨⟨⟨⟨⟨⟨⟨ ⟨⟨⟨⟨⟨" "The White House Crisis: 'We Gotta Take Our Lumps,'" *NYT,* December 4, 1986.

304 THE APPOINTMENT OF A SPECIAL PROSECUTOR *NYT,* December 20, 1986. In the run-up to the appointment of the special prosecutor, "Bush was terrified that his chance at the presidency was in mortal danger because of his heavy involvement in U.S. foreign policy," Timothy Naftali noted. "In a cold-blooded move, he turned on [George] Shultz and the one remaining man in the White House who had known as much about the Iran initiative as he had, Donald Regan. On November 25, 1986, he told the president, 'I really felt that Regan should go, Shultz should go, and that he ought to get this all behind him in the next couple of months.'" (Naftali, *GHWB,* 48.)

304 DONALD P. GREGG Donald P. Gregg, *Pot Shards: Fragments of a Life Lived in the CIA, the White House, and the Two Koreas* (Washington, D.C., 2014), 103, 244–46.

305 Oliver North recruited Rodriguez   Ibid., 244–246.
305 "There was no credible evidence"   Walsh, *Iran-Contra: The Final Report,* 502–3.
"During his trial, North alleged that Gregg was the person who introduced him to
Rodriguez and that he contacted Gregg before recruiting Rodriguez to assist him in
the contra-resupply effort. Gregg denied both assertions." According to Independent Counsel Lawrence Walsh, "The evidence suggests that Gregg's denials are correct." (Ibid., 503.)
   Walsh also reported that "A recurring problem in the investigation of the Office of
the Vice President was a conflict between contemporaneously created documents—
which apparently impute knowledge of North and Rodriguez's activities to the Office
of the Vice President—and subsequent testimony by Gregg, Watson, Rodriguez and
others which contradicted those documents." Those "contemporaneously created
documents" included an entry in Oliver North's notebook, several other notes, and a
"schedule memorandum detailing the purpose of Rodriguez's visit with the Vice President on May 1, 1986, as a discussion regarding 'resupply of the contras.'" (Ibid.)
305 After investigations   "Memorandum on the Criminal Liability of President
Bush," 76–89.
305 "My gut instinct"   GHWB diary, November 19, 1986.
305 "Bush's Achilles' heel"   Walsh, *Firewall,* 451.
306 Bush failed the president   Naftali, *GHWB,* 44–45; Wicker, *GHWB,* 77–84.
306 as Reagan's anti-terror adviser   Naftali, *GHWB,* 43–51.
306 Concerned about the hostages   *LF,* 241.
306 Scotty Reston published   Reston, "In Praise of Losers." *NYT,* December 31, 1986.
306 "January 1st, the power"   GHWB diary, January 1, 1987.
306 Bush called on Reagan in the White House Residence   Ibid., January 6, 1987.
307 Bush agreed with Nancy   Ibid., January 7, 1987.
307 "He is adamantly against it"   Ibid., December 18, 1987.
307 "Lee Atwater is all concerned"   Ibid., December 11, 1986.
307 Stu Spencer, the old Reagan adviser   Ibid., December 17, 1986.
307 Nancy pulled Bush aside   Ibid., December 18, 1986.
307 "Nancy, I've got"   Ibid.
307 "Well, I do it all the time"   Ibid.
307 "I suppose that one could say"   Ibid., December 21, 1987.
307 Don Regan had hung up on her   Ibid., January 7, 1987. See also Nancy Reagan
with Novak, *My Turn,* 326, and Donald T. Regan, *For the Record: From Wall Street to Washington* (New York, 1988), 90–91.
307 "I told her that I simply"   GHWB diary, January 7, 1987.
308 "get off my goddamn back"   Lou Cannon and David Hoffman, "GOP Senators
Ask President to Replace Regan, Casey," *WP,* December 6, 1986; David Hoffman,
"Top Aide Says Regan Should Quit," Ibid., December 18, 1986; Helen Thomas,
"First Lady: Reagan Upset Truth Withheld," Ibid. See also Nancy Reagan with
Novak, *My Turn,* 324–25.
308 "George, I'm going to have"   GHWB diary, February 23, 1987.
308 "obsessed" with the question   *WP,* February 27, 1987, is a telling example.
308 She brought in Robert Strauss   Ibid. See also Nancy Reagan with Novak, *My
Turn,* 320–22.
308 no longer speaking   Ibid., 328–29.
308 "The President wants to see you"   GHWB diary, February 23, 1987.
308 The president and the chief of staff spoke   Ibid., February 23–24, 1987.
308 Mrs. Reagan objected to the plan   Author interview with GHWB.

308 JIM BAKER THAT SHE BELIEVED   GHWB diary, February 24, 1987.

308 REGAN WAS A PROUD MAN   Regan, *For the Record,* 369.

308 "DIGNIFIED DEPARTURE"   Ibid., 368.

308 THAT WAS NOT TO BE   Ibid., 372–73.

308 "DAVID HOFFMAN [OF THE *POST*]"   GHWB diary, December 9, 1986.

308 MRS. REAGAN DENIED   Helen Thomas, "First Lady: Reagan Upset Truth Withheld," WP, December 18, 1986. See also Nancy Reagan with Novak, *My Turn,* 324–25.

309 "BEFORE THE SUNDAY SHOWS"   Author interview with GHWB; GHWB diary, February 24, 1987.

309 "THE STORIES ARE FULL OF NANCY REAGAN"   GHWB diary, March 2, 1987.

309 MRS. REAGAN CONSULTED AN ASTROLOGER   Regan, *For the Record,* 3–4.

309 "YOU DON'T KICK A MAN"   GHWB diary, March 2, 1987.

309 BUSH'S FIRST REACTION TO DUKAKIS'S RUN   GHWB diary, April 15, 1987.

309 A LONG STORY RAISING QUESTIONS   Ibid., May 5, 1987. See also Matt Bai, *All the Truth Is Out: The Week Politics Went Tabloid* (New York, 2014), for a complete account of the Hart episode and its implications.

309 "I MUST CONFESS"   GHWB diary, May 5, 1987.

309 JENNIFER FITZGERALD, A LONGTIME AIDE   LSY, 178–79; Naftali, *GHWB,* 52.

309 WHEN WORD OF A POSSIBLE NEWS STORY   Author interview with Roger Ailes.

309 IT FELL TO AILES   Ibid.

309 "MR. VICE PRESIDENT"   Ibid.

309 "THEY HAVEN'T GOT SHIT"   Ibid.

310 "AND I DON'T KNOW"   Ibid.

310 THE DIVORCED FITZGERALD   LSY, 178, 301.

310 SAID TO BE A STERN GATEKEEPER   Ibid., 178–79.

310 "I WAS VERY CLOSE TO HER"   Author interview with GHWB.

310 "NO," BUSH SAID   Ibid.

310 "IT SIMPLY DIDN'T HAPPEN"   Author interview with Jennifer Fitzgerald, July 7, 2015.

310 "FROM TIME TO TIME"   Confidential author interview.

310 "HE WOULD LET THINGS"   Ibid.

310 IN JUNE 1987, THE NEW YORK TABLOIDS   GHWB diary, June 5, 1987.

310 (ONE PROBLEM WITH THE ACCOUNT)   Ibid., and June 8, 1987.

310 "A WHOLE NEW RASH OF RUMORS"   Ibid., June 18, 1987.

310 A REPORTER CALLED IN SAYING   Ibid.

310 "IT GOES RIGHT AROUND"   Ibid.

310 BUSH WAS TOLD   Ibid.

310 "THERE ARE NO FACTS"   Ibid.

310 "I TALKED TO BAR"   Ibid., June 20, 1987.

311 ON MONDAY, JUNE 22, 1987   Ibid., June 22–23, 1987.

311 "IT'S UGLY"   Ibid., June 23, 1987.

311 BUSH BELIEVED DOLE'S AIDES   Ibid.

311 NEWS OF THE CALL LEAKED   Ibid., June 24, 1987.

311 "YOU'VE HEARD THE RUMORS"   *Newsweek,* June 29, 1987.

311 "THEY'RE JUST NOT TRUE"   Ibid.

311 "THE ANSWER TO THE BIG A"   Ibid.

311 THE SON HAD GONE PUBLIC   Author interview with GWB. Atwater had asked George W. what they should do about the rumors, and George W. took it upon himself to go to his father and then to call the magazine. "I didn't ask permission," George W. recalled. "I just did it." (Ibid.)

311 "GEORGE IS VERY NERVOUS"   GHWB diary, June 26, 1987.

311 "Rumor died down" Ibid., June 29, 1987.

312 Bush agreed to grant Author interviews with GHWB and GWB.

312 The editorial consensus Author interviews with Evan Thomas and Richard M. Smith.

312 "Bush, who formally declares" *Newsweek,* October 19, 1987.

312 The cover itself Ibid.

312 "Ugly, nasty" GHWB diary, October 12, 1987.

312 "Had to shoot down" Ibid.

TWENTY-SEVEN: *Like You've Been Hit in the Stomach*

313 It's really gloomy GHWB diary, February 9, 1988.

313 Lee Atwater had a bad feeling Jack W. Germond and Jules Witcover, *Whose Broad Stripes and Bright Stars? The Trivial Pursuit of the Presidency, 1988* (New York, 1989), 103–105.

313 Dole and Bush were old rivals See, for instance, Peter Goldman, Tom Mathews, and the *Newsweek* Special Election Team, *The Quest for the Presidency, 1988* (New York, 1989), 214–19; Cramer, *What It Takes,* 891–95; Lemann, "Bush and Dole," *WP,* February 28, 1988.

313 Dole had not been happy Howard Fineman, "Not in Kansas Any More," *Newsweek,* August 19, 1996.

313 offering "a record, not a résumé" Goldman, Mathews, et al., *Quest,* 210.

313 was "tough. I understand" Germond and Witcover, *Whose Broad Stripes,* 149.

313 "I got here the old-fashioned way" Ibid.

314 "It is almost like I don't exist" GHWB diary, August 4, 1987.

314 "there may be a fall-out plan" Ibid., June 25, 1987.

314 Dole was granted a coveted joint appearance Goldman, Mathews, et al., *Quest,* 215–16.

314 "He's what they call" GHWB diary, October 13, 1987.

314 Dole was leading Bush Ibid., November 30, 1987.

314 In mid-October the vice president Ibid., October 20, 1987.

314 The president accepted Bush's counsel Ibid.

314 "During this so-called crisis" Ibid.

315 "like Daddy's, smiling eyes" BPB diary, December 1987.

315 "The Doles were not there" Ibid.

315 "I am confident that I could" GHWB diary, December 8, 1987.

315 Bush had a long talk Ibid., December 8, 1987.

315 during a limousine ride with Gorbachev Michael R. Beschloss and Strobe Talbott, *At the Highest Levels: The Inside Story of the End of the Cold War* (Boston, 1993), 3.

315 "I told him that" GHWB diary, December 11, 1987.

315 "Dole looks pretty dangerous" Beschloss and Talbott, *At the Highest Levels,* 3.

315 "I told Gorbachev not to be concerned" *AWT,* 5.

315 Bush was telling Gorbachev Beschloss and Talbott, *At the Highest Levels,* 3–4.

316 "He should not take" *AWT,* 5.

316 The first sign of trouble Author interview with Rich Bond.

316 "There were thousands" Ibid.

316 Bond could only roll his eyes Ibid.

316 Bush finished third Ibid.

316 "It was" GHWB diary, September 13, 1987.

316 On the gloomy flight Author interview with Rich Bond.

316 Bond was called up Ibid.

316   "Immediately, Mrs. Bush"   Ibid.

316   "Pick up the pieces"   GHWB diary, September 13, 1987.

316   ran "against the grain"   *LAT,* January 2, 1988.

317   What had he advised   *Chicago Tribune,* January 8, 1988.

317   "I spend a couple"   GHWB diary, January 10, 1988.

317   a big article on Iran-contra   Ibid.

317   "Tension City"   Ibid.

317   Jim Gannon, the editor   See C-SPAN video of the January 8, 1988, Republican Presidential Debate at http://www.c-span.org/video/?64-1/republican-candidates-debate. See also *NYT,* January 10, 1988.

317   Bush assumed a stern look   See C-SPAN video.

317   "Jim, contrary to the hypothesis"   *NYT,* January 10, 1988.

317   "But what troubled me"   *LF,* 241.

317   "expressed certain reservations"   David Hoffman, "Reagan's Bush Remark Revised," *WP,* March 21, 1987.

317   President Reagan had issued a statement   Ibid.

318   "No, but I"   Author interview with GHWB.

318   Don Regan, whom Bush had treated   *WP,* January 15, 1988; *Chicago Tribune,* January 15, 1988.

318   "The moral of this"   GHWB diary, January 15, 1988.

318   Bush trailed Dole   Ibid., February 7, 1988.

318   Bush lunched with Reagan   Ibid., January 20, 1988.

318   "Reagan . . . is said"   *WP,* January 17, 1988.

318   Bush flew from New Hampshire   GHWB diary, January 25, 1988.

318   The network had set up   Author interview with Roger Ailes. See also Germond and Witcover, *Whose Broad Stripes,* 121.

318   Barbara brought a change of clothes   GHWB diary, January 26, 1988.

319   Roger Ailes met Bush   Germond and Witcover, *Whose Broad Stripes,* 120–21.

319   Though CBS had said   Ibid., 118–19.

319   Ailes . . . warned Bush   Ibid., 121.

319   "You've either got to go"   Ibid.

319   Rather ran a set-up piece   Ibid.

319   Bush refused to give   Ibid., 121–23.

319   Ailes grabbed a piece of paper   Author interview with Roger Ailes.

319   a line of attack Ailes   Ibid.

319   "I don't think it's fair"   Germond and Witcover, *Whose Broad Stripes,* 123.

319   A startled Rather   Ibid.

319   As time ran out   Ibid.

319   The interview over   Ibid., 124–24.

319   "Tell your goddamned network"   Ibid.

319   "look like a pussy"   Ibid., 124.

319   ("People were taking that")   GHWB diary, January 26, 1988.

319   "What do you think?"   Author interview with GWB.

320   "Man, you knocked it out"   Ibid.

320   Many viewers   Germond and Witcover, *Whose Broad Stripes,* 124. See also *NYT,* January 27, 1988.

320   Even Ronald Reagan approved   GHWB diary, January 26, 1988.

320   With two weeks to go   Author interview with Rich Bond.

320   "So, Rich, how are we doing?"   Ibid.

320   "It feels like you've been hit"   GHWB diary, February 9, 1988.

321 "I just go about"   Ibid.
321 "But there is always"   Ibid., February 7, 1988.

twenty-eight: *We Came Out of the Dead*

322 I desperately want to win   GHWB diary, February 15, 1988.
322 He was in his pajamas   Germond and Witcover, *Whose Broad Stripes,* 130–31.
322 Bush had declined to spend the night   Ibid., 130. He stayed at the Clarion Hotel. (Ibid.)
322 "I had my whole little speech"   Ibid.
322 Bush was interested in today   Ibid., 131.
322 "We've got eight days"   Ibid.
322 was put in charge   Author interview with Andrew Card. Card recalled, too, a confusing state of affairs in Michigan, where Pat Robertson supporters elected a rival set of delegates at the state's GOP convention. (See, for instance, James Risen, "Bush Gets Most Delegates; Robertson Forces Elect Rival Slate," *LAT,* January 31, 1988.) "So we had two strikes against us going into New Hampshire—Iowa and Michigan," Card said. (Author interview with Andrew Card.)
322 "Nobody should get off"   Ibid.
322 "Identify the vote"   Ibid.
322 John Sununu was also a critical   John Sununu interview, George H. W. Bush Oral History Project, Miller Center. See also John Sununu, *The Quiet Man: The Indispensable Presidency of George H. W. Bush* (New York, 2015).
322 Sununu arranged for Bush to shake   John Sununu interview, George H. W. Bush Oral History Project, Miller Center.
323 On New Year's Eve   Ibid.
323 The polls were bad   Germond and Witcover, *Whose Broad Stripes,* 132.
323 threw himself into the state   GHWB diary, February 1988; Germond and Witcover, *Whose Broad Stripes,* 131; John Sununu interview, George H. W. Bush Oral History Project, Miller Center.
323 "Watch and wait"   GHWB diary, February 15, 1988.
323 "If I don't make it"   Ibid., February 11, 1988.
323 Dole continued to diminish   Germond and Witcover, *Whose Broad Stripes,* 138.
323 "He takes credit"   Ibid.
323 "It's quite clear"   Ibid., 139.
323 Roger Ailes agreed   Author interview with Roger Ailes.
323 "I wanted to go negative"   Ibid.
323 He made one anyway   Ibid. See also GHWB diary, February 15, 1988.
323 In the candidate's hotel room   Author interview with Roger Ailes.
324 Bush looked at the floor   Ibid.
324 "It seemed to me too harsh"   GHWB diary, February 13, 1988.
324 the polls in New Hampshire   Author interview with Roger Ailes.
324 "We're either eight up"   Ibid.
324 Bush's advisers came back   Ibid.
324 "I simply have to"   GHWB diary, February 14, 1988.
324 Ailes and Atwater pressed   Author interview with Roger Ailes.
324 Then Barbara Bush weighed in   Germond and Witcover, *Whose Broad Stripes,* 142.
324 Bush pondered   Author interview with Roger Ailes.
324 "Are you certain"   Ibid.
324 "I take that as a yes"   Ibid.

324 HIS OLD RIVAL DONALD RUMSFELD GHWB diary, February 14, 1988.

324 BUSH SLEPT FAIRLY WELL Ibid.

324 "I DESPERATELY WANT TO WIN" Ibid., February 15, 1988.

324 ON PRIMARY DAY IN NEW HAMPSHIRE Ibid., February 16, 1988.

324 AFTER A LUNCH OF CHOWDER Ibid.

324 WITH BARBARA AND THE REST Ibid.

324 WHEN HE RETURNED Ibid.

325 "WE CAME OUT OF THE DEAD" Ibid., February 16, 1988.

325 "THE EMOTIONS ARE HIGH" Ibid., February 17, 1988.

325 BUSH DEFEATED DOLE Germond and Witcover, *Whose Broad Stripes,* 145.

325 ON TELEVISION THAT EVENING GHWB diary, February 17, 1988.

325 "I WISH HIM WELL" Ibid.

325 "YES, TELL HIM TO STOP" Ibid.

325 ON THE DAY AFTER THE PRIMARY Ibid.

325 "I NEVER TOLD YOU THIS" Ibid.

325 "I'LL SLEEP BETTER TONIGHT" Ibid., February 29, 1988.

325 BUSH ENCOUNTERED A STONY-FACED ROBERTSON BACKER Ibid., February 27, 1988.

325 "LOOK, THIS IS" Ibid., February 28, 1988.

325 STILL, THIS STARING Ibid.

326 REAGAN "MADE A COMMENT" Ibid., February 29, 1988.

326 "JACK WILL GET OUT" Ibid., March 3, 1988. Overtures along the same lines had come "from John Loeb to Dick Allen, and from Charlie Black to Lee Atwater." (Ibid.)

326 "I DON'T KNOW" Ibid.

326 DONALD TRUMP MENTIONED Ibid., April 13–15, 1988.

326 IN THE SOUTH CAROLINA PRIMARY Ibid., March 5, 1988.

326 WENT ON TO SWEEP THE Germond and Witcover, *Whose Broad Stripes,* 152.

326 (BUSH'S ONE DEFEAT) Ibid.

326 "THAT TENSION SLEEPLESSNESS" GHWB diary, March 9, 1988.

326 "HE'S A DESPERATE" Ibid., March 13, 1988.

326 SENATOR JAKE GARN OF UTAH Ibid., March 19, 1988.

326 "THE MOOD HAS CHANGED" Ibid., March 17, 1988.

326 DOLE ENDED HIS CAMPAIGN Ibid., March 29, 1988.

326 BUSH CALLED HIM Ibid.

326 THE TWO MEN MET Ibid., April 6, 1988.

327 RICHARD NIXON CAME TO DINNER Ibid., April 15, 1988.

327 NIXON LIKED HIS SWORDFISH Ibid.

327 NIXON TICKED OFF Ibid.

327 "I ASKED NICK BRADY" Ibid., April 25, 1988.

327 THE EVENING ENDED Ibid., April 15, 1988.

327 "WHAT'S WRONG WITH" Ibid.

327 MICHAEL DUKAKIS WAS Germond and Witcover, *Whose Broad Stripes,* 354–55; *NYT,* July 6, 1988.

327 HE CUT HIS OWN GRASS *NYT,* July 6, 1988.

328 "I BELIEVE WE'RE GOING" GHWB diary, April 25, 1988.

328 "A LITTLE MIDGET NERD" Ibid., May 6, 1988.

328 "THE GUT ISSUES" Ibid., April 21, 1988.

328 "A CLASSICAL LIBERAL VERSUS CONSERVATIVE" Ibid., April 27, 1988.

328 THE PRESIDENT WROTE HIS REMARKS Ibid., May 12, 1988.

328 "NOT TOO FULL OF PRAISE" Ibid.

328 THAT EVENING, AT THE WASHINGTON CONVENTION *Public Papers of the Presidents of the*

United States: Ronald Reagan, 1988, bk. 1, *January 1–July 1, 1988* (Washington, D.C., 1990), 588–90.

328 "IF I MAY" Ibid.

328 "GEORGE BOSH" *Newsweek*, March 9, 1992; *Chicago Tribune*, May 13, 1988.

329 NO MAN WHO HAS SAT Author interview with GHWB.

329 "A GIGANTIC FLAP" GHWB diary, May 12, 1988.

329 "I WAS SURPRISED" *Public Papers of the Presidents of the United States, Ronald Reagan: 1988*, bk. 1, *January 1–July 1, 1988*, 590.

329 "I STILL HAVE" GHWB diary, May 15, 1988.

TWENTY-NINE: *I'm Stronger and Tougher*

330 I HAVE NO APOLOGIES GHWB diary, November 4, 1988.

330 YOU HAVE A GARY COOPER Ibid., April 27, 1988.

330 THERE WERE "CYCLES" Arthur M. Schlesinger, Jr., *The Cycles of American History* (Boston, 1986), 23–48. For my account of the 1988 presidential campaign, I drew on, among others, Naftali, *GHWB*, 45–64; *LSY*, 321–56; Brady, *Bad Boy*; Cramer, *What It Takes*; Goldman and Mathews, *Quest for the Presidency, 1988*; Germond and Witcover, *Whose Broad Stripes*; Sidney Blumenthal, *Pledging Allegiance: The Last Campaign of the Cold War* (New York, 1990); Wicker, *GHWB*, 98–104; and sources cited below.

330 ACCORDING TO AN INTERNAL BUSH CAMPAIGN SURVEY Memorandum to George Bush for President from Frank McBride and Fred Steeper, "Survey Findings: Components of Negative Impressions of Bush," May 13, 1988, Papers of Richard G. Darman, Private Collection.

331 BUSH TRAILED DUKAKIS Germond and Witcover, *Whose Broad Stripes*, 156.

331 "WE HAD TO DEFINE DUKAKIS" Author interview with Roger Ailes.

331 THE TASK OF DEFINITION James Pinkerton interview, George H. W. Bush Oral History Project, Miller Center.

331 "ELEVEN OF THEM" *Above the Fray*, MSNBC documentary, 2015.

331 "WOW," PINKERTON RECALLED James Pinkerton interview, George H. W. Bush Oral History Project, Miller Center.

331 YES, CARD REPLIED Ibid.

331 THE CLIPS MADE FOR COMPELLING READING Ibid.

331 HORTON WAS A CONVICTED Brady, *Bad Boy*, 173–74. See also Naftali, *GHWB*, 61–62.

331 THE *EAGLE-TRIBUNE* PUBLISHED Germond and Witcover, *Whose Broad Stripes*, 11–12.

331 WHILE THE PROGRAM HAD BEEN SIGNED Brady, *Bad Boy*, 174.

331 DUKAKIS HAD VETOED Ibid.

331 "TO BE SURE, SOME IN THE BUSH CAMPAIGN" Sidney Blumenthal, "Willie Horton & the Making of an Election Issue; How the Furlough Factor Became a Stratagem of the Bush Forces," *WP*, October 28, 1988.

332 IN THE CONVERSATION WITH PINKERTON Germond and Witcover, *Whose Broad Stripes*, 12.

332 FOR THE BUSH CAMP, A PICTURE WAS FORMING *LSY*, 335.

332 BELONGED TO THE AMERICAN CIVIL LIBERTIES UNION Ibid.

332 ACCORDING TO A MEMORANDUM Lloyd Green to GHWB, "Re: American Civil Liberties Union," July 27, 1988, ACLU, Daily Files/Subject File, Vice Presidential Daily Files, GHWB Collection, GBPL.

332 CONSIDERING THE CLUSTER OF ISSUES Goldman and Mathews, *Quest for the Presidency, 1988*, 301. "The euphemism in politics for work like [Pinkerton's] was 'opposition research,' which sounded sanitary, almost academic," Goldman and Mathews wrote.

"A more apt analogy might have been dum-dum bullets, and the moderator [at the Paramus focus groups, discussed below] began firing them. Dukakis had vetoed a bill mandating the Pledge of Allegiance in public schools. He was against the death penalty, even for kingpins in the drug trade. He opposed prayer in the schools. He had stood up for his state's generous program of weekend passes for convicts, even murderers serving life sentences without hope of parole. No one shot in the volley seemed to draw much blood, but the cumulative effect was dramatic." (Ibid., 301.)

332 WHILE A "BRIGHT, HONORABLE"   Baker with Fiffer, *Work Hard*, 265.

332 THE BUSH TEAM CONDUCTED TWO FOCUS GROUPS   Germond and Witcover, *Whose Broad Stripes*, 157–59. See also Brady, *Bad Boy*, 177–78; and Goldman and Mathews, *Quest*, 299–303.

332 TOLD ABOUT THE FURLOUGHS   Germond and Witcover, *Whose Broad Stripes*, 158.

332 BUSH RECEIVED A DELEGATION   Ibid., 159–60.

332 BRIEFED ON THE FINDINGS   Author interview with Roger Ailes.

332 WOULD "LOOK DESPERATE"   Ibid.

332 "WE *ARE* DESPERATE"   Ibid.

332 BUSH HAD BEEN HERE BEFORE   Germond and Witcover, *Whose Broad Stripes*, 141–42, 159–61. The research about the country's overall mood—the Missouri survey from the Darman Papers cited above was an example—was particularly concerning to the Bush camp. As Goldman and Mathews wrote of a Bob Teeter–Fred Steeper conversation in late April: "The news in their numbers was unsettling: people were doing well enough economically, but there was an incongruous restlessness out there, Steeper thought, a sense that things were going wrong and that it was time for a change. No one issue drove them; it was instead a worry list of seven or eight things—the environment, the deficit, the homeless—and if Dukakis managed to put them all together, he could win." (Goldman and Mathews, *Quest for the Presidency, 1988,* 299.)

333 "I COULD TELL BUSH WAS THINKING"   Author interview with Roger Ailes.

333 "IT WILL BE EASY"   GHWB diary, June 12, 1988.

333 "I THINK I'M STRONGER"   Ibid., August 12, 1988.

333 A "DEFINITIVE" SPEECH   Ibid., June 9, 1988; Germond and Witcover, *Whose Broad Stripes,* 161. See also Cramer, *What It Takes,* 1010–11.

333 "WHAT IT ALL COMES DOWN TO"   *NYT,* June 10, 1988; Germond and Witcover, *Whose Broad Stripes,* 162.

333 "I AM A PRACTICAL MAN"   Ibid.

333 "MUDSLINGING AND NAME-CALLING"   Germond and Witcover, *Whose Broad Stripes,* 161–62.

333 "THE AMERICAN PEOPLE"   Ibid.

334 "HUMAN III"   Baker with Fiffer, *Work Hard,* 240–41.

334 AFTER BUSH MADE HIS CASE   Ibid.

334 NANCY REAGAN HAD JOINED   Author interview with James A. Baker III.

334 "NANCY DOES NOT LIKE BARBARA"   GHWB diary, June 12, 1988. Bush made this entry after a conversation with Tom Arnold, a friend who had spoken with Lee and Walter Annenberg, who were friendly with both the Bushes and the Reagans. (Ibid.)

334 AS A GETAWAY   Ibid., July 19, 1988.

334 "FOR EIGHT STRAIGHT YEARS"   "Transcript of the Keynote Address by Ann Richards," *NYT,* July 19, 1988.

335 "IS NOT ABOUT IDEOLOGY"   Michael S. Dukakis acceptance speech, July 21, 1988, CNN.com, www.cnn.com/ALLPOLITICS/1996/conventions/chicago/facts/famous .speeches/dukakis.88.shtml.

335 DUKAKIS LED BUSH   Goldman and Mathews, *Quest,* 420.

335 IN A "PRIVATE AND CONFIDENTIAL" MEMORANDUM   Roger Ailes to James A. Baker III, et al., August 9, 1988, Papers of Richard G. Darman, Private Collection.

335 THE CAMPAIGN POLLED   Notes of August 4, 1988, Papers of Richard G. Darman, Private Collection. According to Darman's handwritten notes, these trial tickets were polled in California. (Ibid.)

336 EASTWOOD WAS A PASSING IDEA   Ibid. See also Richard Darman, *Who's in Control? Polar Politics and the Sensible Center* (New York, 1996), 188.

336 "BUSH'S LIST"   *LSY,* 343.

336 HE WAS INTERESTED IN   Ibid.; Naftali, *GHWB,* 59; author interview with GHWB.

336 WHOM HE'D GOTTEN TO KNOW IN THE REAGAN YEARS   Author interviews with GHWB and Dan Quayle.

336 DAN QUAYLE, WHO HAD RISEN   Quayle, *Standing Firm,* 14–15; Naftali, *GHWB,* 59.

336 BIRCH BAYH, A LEGENDARY LIBERAL LAWMAKER   Quayle, *Standing Firm,* 14–15; author interview with Dan Quayle; Naftali, *GHWB,* 59. Quayle recalled that Bayh was "considered a political giant." (Quayle, *Standing Firm,* 14.)

336 QUAYLE HAD PASSED   Quayle, *Standing Firm,* 17–18.

336 HE WAS ONE OF THE FEW MEMBERS   Author interview with Roger Ailes.

336 WAS DECIDEDLY CONSERVATIVE—A MEMBER IN GOOD STANDING   Author interviews with GHWB and Nicholas F. Brady. See also Naftali, *GHWB,* 59.

336 BOB TEETER AND ROGER AILES HAD WORKED FOR QUAYLE   Author interview with Dan Quayle.

336 "HE'S KNOWLEDGEABLE ON"   GHWB diary, July 20, 1988.

337 HE HAD BRIEFLY CONSIDERED   Dan Quayle interview, George H. W. Bush Oral History Project, Miller Center.

337 "I TALKED TO MY WIFE"   Ibid.

337 "HE WOULDN'T GET INSTANT CREDIBILITY"   GHWB diary, July 27, 1988.

337 "DOLE WOULD BE MORE INSTANTLY"   Ibid., August 13, 1988.

337 QUAYLE, WHO KNEW   Author interview with Dan Quayle.

337 "HE HAD KNOWN ME"   Ibid.

337 AS HE PREPARED TO LEAVE   GHWB diary, August 16, 1988. "I got on the plane knowing that I wanted to pick Dan Quayle," Bush told his diary. (Ibid.)

337 HE HAD NOT HAD A FINAL GUT CHECK   Author interview with GHWB. "The way Bush ultimately arrived at this decision says much about his leadership style," wrote Timothy Naftali. "He made the decision alone without a family conference or a meeting of his inner circle of advisers: James Baker, Lee Atwater, Robert Teeter, and Roger Ailes." (Naftali, *GHWB,* 59.) In an interview with the author, Bush made the same point about keeping the decision from his inner circle—he wanted to do it, he said, "on my own." (Author interview with GHWB.) As Goldman and Mathews wrote, "The vice president had shut them all out—his chairman, his G-6, his own family—and had come to the point of choice his way, alone, secretive and reckless of the cost of the consequences." (Goldman and Mathews, *Quest for the Presidency, 1988,* 315.)

337 "I WANTED IT TO BE"   Author interview with GHWB.

337 DID NOT KNOW   Author interview with Robert Kimmitt.

337 (TO BE READY)   Ibid.

337 BUSH WHISPERED HIS CHOICE   Quayle, *Standing Firm,* 5. See also Germond and Witcover, *Whose Broad Stripes,* 383, and GHWB diary, August 16, 1988. Writing Reagan after the incumbent president's Monday night speech to the convention, Richard

Nixon said: "You have given George a great send off. It will be close, but if he can make *ideology* the issue it could mean 4 more years for the Reagan Revolution." (Richard Nixon to Ronald Reagan, August 16, 1988, Richard M. Nixon Library.)

337 "ONE THING IN MY HEART" GHWB diary, August 16, 1988.

338 BUSH TOLD BAKER Ibid.

338 CHECKED OUT A LAST-MINUTE CONCERN Ibid.

338 BUSH THEN TOLD HIS TEAM Ibid.

338 THE NEW PICK AND HIS WIFE Author interview with Dan Quayle. See also Quayle, *Standing Firm*, 3–9.

338 DID NOT GO WELL Quayle, *Standing Firm*, 6–9; Naftali, *GHWB*, 59–61; *LSY*, 346–47.

338 "WE NOTIFIED QUAYLE" Author interview with GHWB.

338 "WAS A MOB SCENE" Quayle, *Standing Firm*, 7.

338 (SENT A STAFFER TO A LOCAL BOOKSTORE) James Pinkerton interview, George H. W. Bush Oral History Project, Miller Center.

338 THE FIRST CALL QUAYLE RECEIVED Author interview with Dan Quayle.

338 "VICE PRESIDENT BUSH" Ibid.

338 "THE SURPRISE PLAYED" GHWB diary, August 16, 1988.

338 THERE WERE QUESTIONS Quayle, *Standing Firm*, 30–40. See also Goldman, Mathews, et al. *Quest for the Presidency, 1988,* 320–28.

338 "I DID NOT KNOW IN 1969" Quayle, *Standing Firm*, 30; Germond and Witcover, *Whose Broad Stripes,* 388.

339 "I KNEW WHAT I HAD TO DO" GHWB diary, August 21, 1988.

339 BY REAGAN SPEECHWRITER PEGGY NOONAN Naftali, *GHWB*, 60.

339 "I MAY NOT BE THE MOST ELOQUENT" WP, August 19, 1988.

339 HE SPOKE OF AMERICA Ibid.

339 "READ MY LIPS" HAD BEEN A SOURCE Author interview with Roger Ailes; Peggy Noonan, *What I Saw at the Revolution: A Political Life in the Reagan Era* (New York, 1990), 307; Naftali, *GHWB*, 60–61; Darman, *Who's in Control?,* 191–93. See also Bob Woodward, "Origin of the Tax Pledge: In '88, Bush Camp Was Split on 'Read My Lips' Vow," *WP*, October 4, 1992.

339 "WHY?" SHE RECALLED Noonan, *What I Saw at the Revolution,* 307.

339 "FOR SEVEN AND A HALF YEARS" *NYT*, August 19, 1988.

339 IT WAS A WONDERFUL Goldman, Mathews, et al., *Quest,* 316. Describing the expectations for the speech, Goldman and Mathews wrote: "His spirits seemed to his men to rise with his master's departure from the political and emotional airspace. He was his own man at last, ready, in his own mind, to define himself in words and deeds.... His acceptance speech at the close would be the credo people had been demanding of him so long, his statement, eloquent, in its plainness, of who he was and where he meant to lead the nation. The speech, happily for Bush, would prove a brilliant success—so glittering as to mitigate, for a time, the damage he had done himself with his selection of an understudy." (Ibid.)

339 "IMMEDIATELY AFTER THE SPEECH" GHWB diary, August 21, 1988.

340 "I SAY IT" WP, August 19, 1988.

340 "I WILL KEEP AMERICA" Ibid.

340 "THAT IS MY MISSION" Ibid.

340 HE REVELED IN THE POST-SPEECH OVATIONS GHWB diary, August 21, 1988.

340 THIS HAD BEEN HIS FIRST Author interview with GHWB.

340 "SOMETIMES," . . . BUSH RECALLED Ibid.

340 "THE WHOLE THING" GHWB diary, August 21, 1988.

340 THE SEVENTEEN-POINT DUKAKIS LEAD OF MIDSUMMER   Goldman and Mathews, *Quest,* 420. See also Germond and Witcover, *Whose Broad Stripes,* 362; and Naftali, *GHWB,* 61–62.

341 IT WAS A DAY   *NYT,* September 2, 1988. My account of the Willie Horton matter owes much to Brady, *Bad Boy,* 200–218; Tali Mendelberg, *The Race Card: Campaign Strategy, Implicit Messages, and the Norm of Equality* (Princeton, NJ, 2001), 169–90; Mendelberg, "Executing Hortons: Racial Crime in the 1988 Presidential Campaign," *The Public Opinion Quarterly* 61, no. 1, Special Issue on Race (Spring 1997), 134–57; John G. Geer, *In Defense of Negativity* (Chicago, 2006); and the sources below.

341 CAMPAIGNING AS A "TEDDY ROOSEVELT" REPUBLICAN   *NYT,* September 2, 1988.

341 THE DUKAKIS CAMPAIGN POINTED OUT   Ibid.

341 WHICH WAS TO BE THE SUBJECT   Geer, *In Defense of Negativity,* 125–26.

341 "AS HIS BOAT"   *NYT,* September 2, 1988.

341 "ONLY ONE, WILLIE HORTON"   Ibid. Horton's name itself became an issue. Known as William Horton, Jr., in the Lawrence *Eagle-Tribune* reporting, Horton later maintained in an interview with *The Nation* that Republicans had dubbed him "Willie" in order "to play on racial stereotypes: big, ugly, dumb, violent, black—'Willie.' I resent that." (Jeffrey M. Elliot, "The 'Willie' Horton Nobody Knows," *The Nation,* August 23/30, 1993, 201–5; Adam Zachary Newton, *Narrative Ethics* [Cambridge, MA, 1995], 324–25; Beth Schwartzapfel and Bill Keller, "Willie Horton Revisited," The Marshall Project, May 13, 2015. https://www.themarshallproject/2015/05/13/willie -horton-revisited. The name "Willie Horton" had apparently been in circulation since at least October 1987, when Horton's victims in the Maryland kidnapping and rape reportedly referred to him that way in a public hearing at the Massachusetts State House. An account of the hearing was published in a story about the furlough issue in the conservative *Washington Times* in March 1988; the *Times* piece was reprinted in the similarly conservative *Human Events. (Human Events,* March 12, 1988.) "Ask Dukakis if he wants a Willie Horton in his basement," Clifford Barnes reportedly said on October 15, 1987. "I'd like to ask him to watch how my wife carries a knife in her hand when I'm not home; how she won't enter the house without neighbors if I'm not home." (Ibid.)

341 THE VICE PRESIDENT HAD SMILED   *NYT,* September 2, 1988.

341 "A STEADY STREAM OF ONE-LINERS"   Ibid.

341 HAD BECOME EVER MORE WIDELY KNOWN   Brady, *Bad Boy,* 177, 180–81.

341 "GETTING AWAY WITH MURDER"   Ibid., 177.

341 AVAILABLE TO MANY READERS BY MID-TO-LATE JUNE   Ibid., 180–81. According to Brady, "On June 10 *Reader's Digest* shipped copies of the July issue to West Coast subscribers. Radio talk shows picked up on the prison-furlough issue immediately, and word doubled back eastward on the airwaves, just in time for the June 25 arrival of newsstand copies across the rest of the nation." (Ibid.)

341 HAD BEEN ATTACKING "UNSUPERVISED WEEKEND FURLOUGHS"   Germond and Witcover, *Whose Broad Stripes,* 162. This remark came from the June 9 speech in Texas. (Ibid.)

341 USED HORTON'S NAME   Brady, *Bad Boy,* 181. Brady noted that this was the "first time" Bush had explicitly used Horton's name. (Ibid., 181.) For the speech itself, see George Bush Vice Presidential Audiovisual Recordings, VPP8174A, Remarks of Vice President Bush During Address to the National Sheriffs Association, June 22, 1988, in Louisville, Kentucky. For coverage of the day, see David Hoffman, "Bush Hammers Dukakis on Crime," *WP,* June 23, 1988; David E. Rosenbaum, "Bush

Talks Tough on Crime, Criticizing Prisoner Furlough Program," *NYT,* June 23, 1988.

341 "VICE PRESIDENT BUSH" Hoffman, "Bush Hammers Dukakis," *WP,* June 23, 1988.

341 AD FEATURING HORTON'S IMAGE For the controversy over the NSPAC Horton ad and the controversy in general, see Brady, *Bad Boy,* 204–8; Gabriel Sherman, *The Loudest Voice in the Room* (New York, 2014), 127–28, 130, 131, 132, 143–44; Thomas Byrne Edsall with Mary D. Edsall, *Chain Reaction: The Impact of Race, Rights, and Taxes on American Politics* (New York, 1992), 19, 96, 114, 216, 222–24; Martin Schram, "The Making of Willie Horton," *New Republic,* May 28, 1990; Joe Conason, "Roger & He," *New Republic,* May 28, 1990; Stefan Forbes' 2008 documentary film *Boogie Man: The Lee Atwater Story;* Sidney Blumenthal, *Pledging Allegiance,* 224, 227–28, 264–65, 295–96, 307–9; Sidney Blumenthal, "Willie Horton & the Making of an Election Issue: How the Furlough Factor Became a Stratagem of the Bush Forces," *WP,* October 28, 1988; Stephen Engelberg, Richard L. Berke, and Michael Wines, "Bush, His Disavowed Backers and a Very Potent Attack Ad," *NYT,* November 3, 1988; Naftali, *GHWB,* 61–62; *LSY,* 335–37, 350, 351, 352, 394, 490; Wicker, *GHWB,* 101–2; Baker with Fiffer, *Work Hard,* 269–71; Goldman, Mathews, et al., *Quest,* 305, 306–7, 337, 339, 359, 397; Geer, *In Defense of Negativity,* 112, 116, 126–27. See also Kathleen Hall Jamieson, *Dirty Politics: Deception, Distraction, and Democracy* (New York, 1992). I also drew on my interviews with GHWB, James A. Baker III, Roger Ailes, Larry McCarthy, Jesse T. Raiford, Floyd Brown, and Roger Stone.

341 RAN FOR ONLY 28 DAYS ON CABLE *NYT,* November 3, 1988.

341 ENDING OCTOBER 4 Brady, *Bad Boy,* 207.

341 WAS WIDELY DISCUSSED Ibid., 189–90.

341 THE GROUP, THE NATIONAL SECURITY POLITICAL ACTION COMMITTEE Ibid., 204–10; author interviews with Larry McCarthy and Floyd Brown.

341 THE BUSH CAMPAIGN WROTE Brady, *Bad Boy,* 208.

341 JIM BAKER, THE CAMPAIGN CHAIRMAN Baker with Fiffer, *Work Hard,* 270; *WP,* October 29, 1988; author interview with James A. Baker III.

342 "JUST THREE DAYS BEFORE" *NYT,* November 3, 1988.

342 "IF THEY WERE REALLY INTERESTED" Ibid.

342 BAKER RECALLED THAT HE HAD NO IDEA Author interview with James A. Baker III.

342 "WE WROTE THE LETTER" Ibid.

342 "IF I CAN MAKE" Brady, *Bad Boy,* 218. See also *NYT,* June 8, 1989.

342 IN A SPEECH TO SOUTHERN REPUBLICANS Thomas B. Edsall, "Race: Still a Force," *WP,* July 31, 1988.

342 "THERE IS A STORY" Ibid. See also Blumenthal, "Willie Horton & the Making of an Election Issue," *WP,* October 28, 1988.

342 ROGER AILES HAD BEEN QUOTED Richard Stengel with David Beckwith, "The Man Behind the Message," *Time,* August 22, 1988.

342 "THE ONLY QUESTION IS" Ibid.

342 "I MEANT IT AS A WISE-ASS COMMENT" Author interview with Roger Ailes.

342 (THE *TIME* CORRESPONDENT WHO) Author interview with David Beckwith. The "bravado" nature of the remark was confirmed in an author interview with Richard Stengel.

342 AILES AGREED TO PUT THE QUOTE Author interview with Roger Ailes.

342 AFTER ATWATER HANDED AILES A COPY Ibid.

343 HAD "HAD A 'FIRM POLICY' " *NYT,* November 3, 1988.

343 ASKED WHETHER THE NSPAC AD Ibid.

343 HAD BEEN MADE BY LARRY MCCARTHY   Author interview with Larry McCarthy.

343 BOTH MEN SAID THAT   Author interviews with Larry McCarthy and Jesse T. Raiford.

343 AILES, ATWATER, BAKER, AND BUSH HIMSELF ALSO SAID   Author interviews with Roger Ailes, James A. Baker III, and GHWB. Atwater's denial can be found at *NYT,* November 3, 1988. The matter was the subject of a Federal Election Commission investigation, the details of which can be found in the record of MUR 3069, http://www.fec.gov/disclosure_data/mur/3069.pdf. It was also the subject of litigation brought by the Ohio Democratic Party: Branstool v. FEC, No. 92–0284 (D. D. C. Apr. 4, 1995.)

343 "I DIDN'T HAVE ANYTHING TO DO"   Barbara Demick, "Suit Seeks Probe of '88 Horton Ad," *Philadelphia Inquirer,* February 4, 1992.

343 BAKER HAS ACKNOWLEDGED THAT "SKEPTICS"   Baker with Fiffer, *Work Hard,* 270.

343 ACCORDING TO BAKER, HOWEVER   Ibid.

343 "NOTHING TO DO"   Ibid.

343 AN AD SHOWING GENERIC PRISONERS   Geer, *In Defense of Negativity,* 126.

343 BY THE TIME ANY OF THESE ADS   Goldman and Mathews, *Quest,* 420–21; Geer, *In Defense of Negativity,* 113–23.

344 FOOTAGE OF DUKAKIS RIDING IN A TANK   Geer, *In Defense of Negativity,* 127–28.

344 JESSE JACKSON CHARGED   Mendelberg, *Race Card,* 3–4.

344 SOME MAINSTREAM OPINION-MAKERS DISAGREED   Ibid., 3. In "Executing Hortons," Mendelberg wrote: "While many commentators now view the Willie Horton case as a clear racial appeal, in 1988 it was widely perceived as primarily a message about crime and misguided liberalism, not race." (Mendelberg, "Executing Hortons," *The Public Opinion Quarterly* 61, no. 1, 139.)

344 THE *WASHINGTON POST,* FOR EXAMPLE, WROTE   "A Racist Campaign?" *WP,* October 25, 1988.

344 (THE COLUMNIST MICHAEL KINSLEY)   Michael Kinsley, "Yes, a Racist Campaign," *WP,* October 27, 1988.

344 "WAS THE USE OF WILLIE HORTON RACIST?"   Author interview with Mike Dukakis.

344 BUSH HIMSELF SAID THAT   Author interviews with GHWB.

344 "I WAS ACCUSED OF"   Ibid.

344 "THE ISSUE WAS FIRST RAISED"   Ibid.

344 HORTON AND THE FURLOUGH ISSUES   Ibid.

344 SOME NFL PLAYERS HAD TOLD BUSH   GHWB diary, September 27, 1988.

344 IN A TENSE EXCHANGE   *WP,* September 26, 1988.

345 "YOU SEE, LAST YEAR"   Ibid.

345 "WELL, I HOPE THIS IS"   Ibid.

345 THE NUMBERS FOR BUSH   E. J. Dionne, Jr., "Bush Leading Dukakis in Two Polls," *NYT,* September 23, 1988.

345 REAGAN, WHO HAD CALLED BUSH   Presidential Handwriting File—Telephone Calls, File 211, Ronald Reagan Presidential Library.

345 "WELL, I KNOW WHO'S"   "Remarks at a Republican Campaign Rally in Palos Hills, Illinois," November 4, 1988, *Public Papers of the Presidents of the United States, Ronald Reagan: 1988–1989,* bk. 2, *July 2, 1988–January 19, 1989,* 1447.

345 BUSH WATCHED FROM FORT WORTH   GHWB diary, October 8, 1988.

345 "SENATOR, I SERVED"   *NYT,* October 6, 1988.

345 "I CALLED HIM"   GHWB diary, October 8, 1988.

345 BERNARD SHAW OF CNN   Germond and Witcover, *Whose Broad Stripes,* 5–9.

346 "ROGER AILES GAVE ME"   GHWB diary, October 13, 1988.

346 "Now you keep reading" Ibid., October 18, 1988.

346 The adultery allegations Eleanor Randolph, "Bush Rumor Created Dilemma for Media," *WP,* October 22, 1988; "Dukakis Aide Quits; Remarks Are Disavowed," *LAT,* October 21, 1988; *WSJ,* October 20, 1988.

346 led to a brief drop "Bush Rumor Created Dilemma," *WP,* October 22, 1988. The average fell 43 points on Wednesday, October 19, 1988, based, it was believed, on word of the rumored Bush story. (Ibid.)

346 *Post* editors denied Ibid.

346 The next day, Donna Brazile Ibid.

346 "I wasn't on the stock market" Ibid. See also "Dukakis Aide Quits; Remarks Are Disavowed," *LAT,* October 21, 1988.

346 "It was the ugliest" GHWB diary, October 23, 1988.

346 Brazile resigned *LAT,* October 21, 1988.

346 "Generally speaking" GHWB diary, October 23, 1988.

346 Arriving in Santa Clara Ibid., October 27, 1988.

346 Jim Baker worried Ibid., October 28, 1988.

346 An anxious team Ibid., October 29, 1988.

346 "red meat, outlandish" Ibid.

347 The night before Ibid., October 30, 1988.

347 On Wednesday, November 2, just to be safe Ibid., November 2, 1988.

347 "it's blurred and blended in" Ibid., November 3, 1988.

347 "There is an apprehension" Ibid., November 7, 1988.

347 "It's fitting" Ibid.

347 "I don't know" Ibid.

347 Bush won convincingly Election of 1988, The American Presidency Project, www.presidency.ucsb.edu/showelection.php?year=1988.

347 According to exit polls http://elections.nytimes.com/2008/results/president/national-exit-polls.html. There is a small discrepancy between *The New York Times*'s figures (Ibid.) and *The Washington Post* numbers. The *Post* has Bush winning 55 percent of the white vote and 11 percent of the African American. (*WP,* November 9, 1988.)

347 The country was split *WP,* November 9, 1988.

347 Bush won 92 percent Ibid.

347 Dukakis carried 93 percent Ibid.

347 "The advertising in 1988" Geer, *In Defense of Negativity,* 36, 132.

348 Moreover, Bush and Dukakis Ibid., 119.

348 "It was the news media's coverage" Ibid., 132.

349 Bush spoke to Reagan BPB diary, November 7, 1988.

349 "We went to bed" Ibid.

449 Campaigns go away GHWB diary, January 24, 1989

349 "We ask, Lord" BPB diary, November 9, 1988

349 A few hours later Bush met the press "The President-Elect's News Conference in Houston," *NYT,* November 10, 1988.

350 Around Thanksgiving *BB,* 252.

350 "I never liked dogs" Ibid.

350 "There is this feeling" GHWB diary, January 2 and 9, 1989.

350 "I'm excited for the first time" Ibid., January 4, 1989.

350 "There's no such feeling" Ibid., January 12, 1989.

350 On the personal front Ibid., January 6, 1989.

351 "The briefings on my responsibilities" Ibid., January 7, 1989.

351 "I gasp at the prices" Ibid.

351 ON THE MONDAY BEFORE   Ibid., January 16, 1989.
351 IN THE STEADILY EMPTYING HOUSE   Ibid., January 17, 1989.
351 HE THOUGHT OF THE GOOD DAYS   Ibid., January 16, 1989.
351 "MILLIE CHASES THE FOXES"   Ibid.
351 HE ASKED HIMSELF   Ibid.

Part VI: *The Awesome Responsibility, 1989 to 1993*

352 HERE I AM   GHWB diary, May 26, 1989.

THIRTY: *The Sun Started Through*

355 FOR WE ARE GIVEN POWER   Inaugural Prayer, January 20, 1989, Michael Dannen-
     hauer to Margaret Shannon, September 11, 1996, Washington National Cathedral
     Archives. I am grateful to Margaret Shannon for sharing the relevant correspon-
     dence about Bush's prayer with me.
355 "RESULTS-ORIENTED"   Author interview with Dan Quayle.
355 "UNPREDICTABLE AND FRAGILE"   Author interview with GHWB.
355 WHAT HENRY KISSINGER THOUGHT   Author interview with Henry Kissinger.
356 COLD AND CLOUDY   GHWB diary, January 21, 1989.
356 IN THE CAR ON THE WAY   Ibid.
356 "WHEN I BECAME GOVERNOR"   Ibid.
356 (HE HAD TAKEN)   Garry Wills, *Reagan's America: Innocents at Home* (Garden City, N.Y.,
     1987), 299.
356 "AND SURE ENOUGH"   GHWB diary, January 21, 1989. Bush was thinking of oth-
     ers even at the moment of his ascent to the presidency. The president-elect had
     told Tim McBride, his personal aide, not to bother with bringing his winter coat
     along: Bush was eager to take the oath and deliver his inaugural in his suit. Inside
     the Capitol, as Reagan and Bush readied themselves to go out on the podium, the
     president-elect noticed that Reagan was heavily bundled up in an overcoat and scarf.
     Not wanting to appear overly vigorous in contrast to the aging fortieth president,
     the incoming forty-first turned to McBride. "Where's my coat?" he asked, only to
     be reminded that he had instructed his aide to leave it behind at the White House.
     "But I need it," Bush said. As McBride recalled it, "He didn't think he should be
     coatless when President Reagan was in one. That would have risked showing Rea-
     gan up as old while Bush seemed younger and more vital." Bush found a diplomatic
     solution: He asked McBride if he could borrow his aide's coat. Of course, McBride
     said, and the president-elect of the United States marched down to his inauguration
     in a borrowed coat. (Author interview with Tim McBride.)
356 BUSH'S INAUGURAL ADDRESS   "Transcript of Bush's Inaugural Address," *NYT,* Janu-
     ary 21, 1989.
356 WITHDREW A SMALL SHEET OF PAPER   Michael Dannenhauer to Margaret Shannon,
     September 11, 1996, Washington National Cathedral Archives. See also "President
     George H. W. Bush 1989 Inaugural Address," https://www.youtube.com
     /watch?v=4S2ptmXsxzs.
357 "THERE HAS GROWN"   *Public Papers of the President of the United States: George Bush, 1989*
     (Washington, D.C., 1990), 1–4; "Transcript of Bush's Inaugural Address," *NYT,*
     January 21, 1989.
357 "SOME SEE LEADERSHIP"   Ibid.

357 AS BILLY GRAHAM "January 20, 1989: Inaugural Ceremonies for George H. W. Bush," https://www.youtube.com/watch?v=MW1c2PeZu9M.

357 THE BUSHES WALKED THE REAGANS Ibid.

357 JIM BAKER, WHO HAD BEEN Ibid.

357 LAMAR ALEXANDER ... WAS ALWAYS STRUCK Author interview with Lamar Alexander.

357 "NO ONE EVER THOUGHT" Author interview with James A. Baker III.

358 "THEY KEEP PLAYING IT UP" GHWB diary, May 7, 1990.

358 BRENT SCOWCROFT For a comprehensive account of Scowcroft, see Bartholomew Sparrow, *The Strategist: Brent Scowcroft and the Call of National Security* (New York, 2015). My description of Scowcroft is also drawn from Naftali, *GHWB*, 66–67, and my interviews with Scowcroft, GHWB, Richard Haass, and James A. Baker III.

358 BELIEVED THAT THE REAGAN "EVIL EMPIRE" Author interview with Brent Scowcroft.

358 BETTER TO STRIKE MODERATE TONES *AWT*, 19–20.

358 SCOWCROFT ALSO INTUITIVELY KNEW Author interview with Brent Scowcroft.

358 SCOWCROFT ... REFUSED TO SPEAK PUBLICLY Author interviews with Brent Scowcroft and James A. Baker III. Of course, there were inevitable anxieties about spheres of influence within the new administration. Bush told Baker that he "was thinking of sending Quayle to Europe" for a round of meetings. "It would be good for Quayle," Bush said. "It would be good for us to listen." Baker was reluctant, asking Bush "if there would be a conflict between this and [Bush's] pledge to have the Secretary of State talk to the foreign secretaries. And I said, 'No, we're not talking just on the Soviet Union account, we're talking on a wide array of issues. It's a listening session, it's good for us to show this early consultation, and it's good for me to have the Vice President doing substantive things.'"

Baker had another idea. "Jim suggested a tour of South America, and Quayle should go to the Venezuelan swearing-in," Bush told his diary. "I said, 'Well, that's fine, he should go to the Venezuelan swearing-in; but the foreign leaders will all be in Venezuela and he could have a series of bi-laterals.' Jim agreed with this. I sensed a little tension, but that's certainly nothing unusual, nothing that can't be managed." (GHWB diary, January 6, 1989.)

Nearly alone at the highest levels of the incoming administration, Bush was insistently supportive of Quayle. Wyoming senator and Bush friend Alan Simpson "told me he thought Quayle was going to come on fine. He liked defending Dan, and I think of the pounding Quayle has taken. I told Dan, 'Take an eraser, erase the name Quayle, write in the name Bush, change the date, and erase the "8" for 1988 and make it '87 or early '88, and you'll have the pounding for me, the same as you're getting now, Dan.' I'll stand behind this guy, and I'll stay with him." (Ibid., January 13, 1989.)

Still, Bush worried. "He does pretty well, but I think what a pounding the guy is taking," Bush told his diary. "Marilyn apparently is being a bit of a horse's ass on some things, pushing him around, leading him, and this he doesn't need. . . . I get the feedback from the Secret Service that she's a bit of a pill. It's tough, but he needs support, not controversy. . . . He's dying to do stuff. He comes up with a lot of ideas, some of which we can and can't do." (Ibid., January 17, 1989.)

Bush was somewhat wary of Marilyn Quayle after there was speculation that she might be appointed to fill out the four years remaining in Quayle's Senate term. The governor of Indiana had asked if she might be interested, but both the vice president–elect and the president-elect thought having the Second Lady as a sitting senator would create too many complications for the administration. (Author interview with Dan Quayle.)

358   John Sununu   Author interviews with John Sununu, Dan Quayle, GHWB, and GWB. See also, for instance, Sununu, *Quiet Man;* John Sununu interviews, George H. W. Bush Oral History Project, Miller Center.

358   "Sununu thinks a mile a minute"   GHWB diary, February 16, 1989.

358   "Like a good chief of staff"   Richard Nixon to GHWB, April 10, 1989, Correspondence of Richard M. Nixon and GHWB, Richard M. Nixon Presidential Library.

359   Dick Darman, who became   Darman, *Who's in Control?,* 88, 191–201.

359   after fourteen balls   GHWB diary, January 21, 1989.

359   The next morning at eight   Ibid.

359   "I went to the Oval Office"   Ibid.

359   President Reagan had left him a note   "Ron" to "Dear George," Miscellaneous Files, "My Father, My President" Files, Dorothy Bush Koch Collection, GBPL (OAID 29458).

359   Dear George   Ibid.

359   "Mother was the star"   Ibid.

359   "So far"   Author interview with Nancy Bush Ellis.

thirty-one: *If It Weren't for the Deficit . . .*

360   I cannot break   GHWB diary, April 2, 1989.

360   "George, you know"   GHWB diary, January 25, 1987.

360   Nixon's prediction had proven accurate   Tom Kenworthy, "GAO: Higher Taxes 'Probably' Unavoidable," *WP,* November 20, 1988. See also Greene, *Presidency of George Bush,* 79–81; Naftali, *GHWB,* 63–64, 72–76.

360   "based on definitive analysis"   Darman, *Who's in Control?,* 200; Greene, *Presidency of George Bush,* 79–80. See also Naftali, *GHWB,* 63.

360   "There's no way I can raise taxes"   Author interview with Mike Dukakis.

360   "It was clear to me"   Ibid.

360   Roger Porter was weighing   Author interview with Roger Porter.

360   "Getting deficits under control"   Ibid.

360   "reflected his conviction"   Ibid.

361   In 1989, Bush faced the stubborn   Greenspan, *Age of Turbulence,* 112–13; Bruce Bartlett, "A Budget Deal That Did Reduce the Deficit," *The Fiscal Times,* June 25, 2010.

361   Without lower interest rates   For the deficit and its implications, see, for instance, Sean Wilentz, *The Age of Reagan: A History, 1974–2008* (New York, 2008), 303, 307–8; *LSY,* 367; Patterson, *Restless Giant,* 246; Darman, *Who's in Control?,* 198, 200, 203; and Bruce Bartlett, "A Budget Deal That Did Reduce the Deficit," *The Fiscal Times,* June 25, 2010.

361   In the political and cultural ethos   Paul Kennedy, *The Rise and Fall of the Great Powers: Economic Change and Military Conflict from 1500 to 2000* (New York, 1987); Wilentz, *Age of Reagan,* 303–4; Patterson, *Restless Giant,* 202–3.

361   "If it weren't for the deficit"   GHWB diary, December 7, 1988.

361   Bush saw the deficit   See, for example, GHWB diary, May 14, June 5, July 23, October 24, 25, 29, and November 6, 1989.

361   The business cycle   My analysis of the economic challenges facing GHWB owes

much to David Brauer, "A Historical Perspective on the 1989–92 Slow Growth Period," *FRBNY Quarterly Review* 18, no. 2 (Summer 1993), 1–14.

361 HAD TRIPLED FROM   Patterson, *Restless Giant,* 158-59.

361 BEGINNING IN 1989, THE ECONOMY GREW   Brauer, "Historical Perspective on the 1989–1992 Slow Growth Period," 1–14. See also Brian Domitrovic, "Decision Points: George H. W. Bush Edition," *Forbes* Online, November 29, 2010, www .forbes.com/sites/briandomitrovic/2010/11/29/decision-points-george-h-w-bush -edition/2/.

361 A SERIES OF SAVINGS AND LOAN FAILURES   Darman, *Who's in Control?,* 207, 211; Wilentz, *Age of Reagan,* 307; Naftali, *GHWB,* 73–76; Wicker, *GHWB,* 107–9.

362 "I CANNOT BREAK"   GHWB diary, April 2, 1989.

362 AS HIS FIRST BUDGET TOOK SHAPE   See Darman, *Who's in Control?,* 213–19. See also "FY 1990 Budget Revisions: Presidential Briefing," February 7, 1989, DF.

362 EARLY DAYS WERE CHEERY DAYS   GHWB diary, February 16, 1989. Still, Bush was an obsessive consumer of opinion, often negative, about the administration. After a journey to Japan for the funeral of Hirohito, Bush returned home to a turn in opinion about the administration in the first week or so of March.

"I wake up to find the magazines dumping all over the Administration . . . and then a lot of these insidious inside stories," Bush remarked of *Time, Newsweek,* and *U.S. News & World Report.* According to Bush, the story line in Sunday's *Washington Post* and in the newsmagazines was "disarray, nothing happening, no appointments, no initiatives, no vision, weak President, kind of like Carter, and on and on it went." (Ibid., March 6, 1989.) Bush was resigned and realistic. "Predictions of gloom, doom, and disaster by the media Beltway hounds mean nothing," Bush told his diary. "They have their pack journalism to go about, but tomorrow it will be something else: another fight, another battle, another win, or another loss." (Ibid.) Nevertheless, his approval ratings with the public remained high.

362 AN ABC NEWS–*WASHINGTON POST* POLL   *WP,* February 17, 1989.

362 "THE HIGHEST"   GHWB diary, February 16, 1989.

362 HE CALLED ON AN OLD FRIEND, DAN ROSTENKOWSKI   Darman, *Who's in Control?,* 209. See also Greene, *Presidency of George Bush,* 80.

362 DARMAN WAS READING   Darman, *Who's in Control?,* 218.

362 AN EIGHTY-NINE-SEAT MARGIN   http://history.house.gov/Institution/Party-Divisions /Party-Divisions/.

362 A TEN-SEAT ADVANTAGE   http://www.senate.gov/history/partydiv.htm.

362 DURING THE TRANSITION   GHWB diary, January 2, 1989. Senator David Boren, Republican of Oklahoma, shared Bush's sense that outreach was critical, particularly on the budget. In a note to the president during a White House meeting on February 9, 1989, Boren wrote: "The key thing is *regular periodic consultation with* Congressional leaders so that they feel *more institutional responsibility* It won't solve all the problems—but it will make the Cong[ressional] leaders feel like *'players'* & it will help—If it's *not somewhat formal,* it won't happen—It's like family time. It must be scheduled." Bush kept a copy of the counsel. (David Boren to GHWB, February 9, 1989, DF.)

362 "TO DEMONSTRATE THAT"   GHWB diary, January 2, 1989.

362 HE FOUND CAPITOL HILL LESS ENGAGING   Author interview with GHWB; Naftali, *GHWB,* 64.

362 INVITING LAWMAKERS TO THE RESIDENCE   GHWB diary, January 25, 1989.

363 "BARBARA REMINDED ME"   Ibid.

363 BUSH TOOK PICTURES Author interviews with GHWB and BPB; Cramer, *What It Takes*, 1022–23.

363 IN THE MIDDLE OF MARCH GHWB diary, March 13, 1989.

363 HE FACED AN EARLY TEST For the Tower nomination, see John G. Tower, *Consequences: A Personal and Political Memoir* (Boston, 1991), 47–48, 159, 220, 309–10, 316–17; Greene, *Presidency of George Bush*, 54–58; Naftali, *GHWB*, 69–70; Wicker, *GHWB*, 139–45; *LSY*, 358, 360, 371–75, 379, 382, 383.

363 BESET BY RUMORS *LSY*, 372.

363 TOWER OFFERED TO REMOVED HIMSELF GHWB diary, February 8, 1989. See also Tower, *Consequences*. "Heart to heart talk with Sam Nunn and John Warner about the Tower nomination," Bush dictated on February 7. "Sam is being accused of playing a lot of politics—the staff hating Tower, etc. He made the pitch that he just was troubled by the drinking, that there was enough testimony that Tower would be 'out of it' even though he recovered easily the next morning, to concern Sam." (GHWB diary, February 7, 1989.)

363 LED BY SAM NUNN Naftali, *GHWB*, 69–70.

363 THOUGHT TO HAVE BEEN HIGH-HANDED *NYT*, April 6, 1991.

363 "PULL THE RUG OUT" GHWB diary, February 8, 1989.

363 "WAS GOING TO STAND" Ibid., February 9, 1989.

363 BUT BUSH COULD NOT PULL TOGETHER *NYT*, April 6, 1991; Naftali, *GHWB*, 70.

363 BUSH'S FIRST THOUGHT GHWB diary, March 9, 1989.

364 BUSH RULED RUMSFELD OUT Ibid., March 9, 12, 1989.

364 THREE OTHER NAMES Ibid., March 9, 1989.

364 "I WORRY [BECAUSE CHENEY]" Ibid.

364 CHENEY CALLED ON BUSH Ibid., March 12, 1989.

364 "WE WENT OVER" Ibid.

364 GINGRICH, THEN FORTY-FIVE Dale Russakoff, "He Knew What He Wanted," *WP*, December 18, 1994.

364 (WHOM HE THOUGHT OF AS "SICK") Eve Fairbanks, "Magic Words," *NYT*, April 8, 2007.

364 GINGRICH, THE STEPSON OF A MILITARY MAN Russakoff, "He Knew What He Wanted," *WP*, December 18, 1999.

364 AS A "TRANSFORMATIONAL FIGURE" Ibid.

365 "THE QUESTION IS" GHWB diary, March 22, 1989.

365 "I DON'T THINK SO" Ibid.

365 "THE PRESS TAKE THE GINGRICH ELECTION" Ibid., March 27, 1989.

365 "HITTING ME FOR BEING" Ibid.

365 FOLLOWING HIS INSTINCT Author interview with Vin Weber.

365 "MR. PRESIDENT, YOU'VE BEEN" Ibid.

365 "WELL," BUSH ANSWERED Ibid.

365 BUSH SAT IN THE TREATY ROOM GHWB diary, April 3, 1989.

366 "I'M WONDERING AT" Ibid.

THIRTY-TWO: *Victory in Europe, Terror in China*

367 THE LONGER I'M IN THIS JOB GHWB diary, November 8, 1989.

367 "COULD DO BUSINESS" Margaret Thatcher, *The Downing Street Years* (New York, 1993), 463.

367 BORN IN 1931 See biographical sketch of Mikhail Gorbachev at the Gorbachev Foundation website, http://www.gorby.ru/en/gorbachev/biography/.

367 Bush and Gorbachev had first met *AWT*, 3–4. "I made very clear to him that we want real progress," Bush wrote after that initial hour-and-twenty-five-minute conversation. "I hope he knows how true that is." GHWB, to Your Royal Highnesses Prince Sadri and Princess Catherine Sadruddin Aga Khan, Geneva, Switzerland, March 16, 1985, JB.

367 "He was different" Author interview with GHWB.

367 "Gorbachev will package" *AWT*, 4.

367 Once in power, Gorbachev unleashed For background on Gorbachev, his reforms, and their implications, see, for instance, Gaddis, *Cold War;* Beschloss and Talbott, *At the Highest Levels,* 214, 265–66; and Philip Zelikow and Condoleezza Rice, *Germany Unified and Europe Transformed: A Study in Statecraft* (Cambridge, Mass., 1994), 4–38. "When Gorbachev talked 'new thinking' in Moscow, continuing and even increased Soviet involvement in Afghanistan, Angola, and Nicaragua became the litmus test of his sincerity and credibility," wrote Robert Gates. (Gates, *From the Shadows,* 410.) Gates also detailed how these conflicts came to an end (Ibid., 427–36), concluding that when Gorbachev "finally moved to end Soviet involvement in Afghanistan and Angola more than two years after taking power, it was the final proof that, at least in foreign policy, this was a very different Soviet leader." (Ibid., 410.)

368 "Strange meeting with Gorbachev" GHWB diary, December 7, 1988. "I felt funny speaking up, and yet I knew [Gorbachev] wanted me to," Bush told his diary. "I pledged continuity." Political men, Bush and Gorbachev could be candid with each other. "I told Gorbachev, Dukakis would be sitting here if this President hadn't been out working for me, and I really think there's something to that, because if he had been laidback or did what Ike did to Nixon, I'm not sure I would have won, and I certainly wouldn't have won by the percentage that we did." (Ibid.)

368 Bush could always tell *AWT*, 7.

368 At one point in the conversation GHWB diary, December 7, 1988.

368 Bush called Gorbachev Ibid., December 8, 1988.

368 became known as his "pause" Beschloss and Talbott, *At the Highest Levels,* 28–29; Gates, *From the Shadows,* 459–61; *AWT*, 6, 37, and 40; *LSY*, 384; Naftali, *GHWB*, 68–69, 76–78. See also David E. Hoffman, *The Dead Hand: The Untold Story of the Cold War Arms Race and Its Dangerous Legacy* (New York, 2009), 315–16. The "pause" was controversial. "He paid a lasting price for the 'pause' in U.S.-Soviet relations in early 1989: when he belatedly began to engage with Gorbachev that May, he appeared to be doing so under pressure from public opinion, Congress, and his NATO allies," wrote Beschloss and Talbott in 1993. "The delay strengthened the lingering, damaging impression that this was a president who tended to follow rather than lead." (Beschloss and Talbott, *At the Highest Levels,* 469.)

There was no doubt that Bush was eager to chart his own path forward. "I'd like to come up with something dramatic—not just responding begrudgingly to [Gorbachev's] ideas—but something big, and if not with the Soviet Union, somewhere around the world: Middle East, the subcontinent, this hemisphere," Bush recalled after the meeting on Governors Island. (GHWB diary, December 8, 1988.)

368 "From the point of view" Gaddis, *Cold War,* 235.

368 in Prague, the totalitarian Czech regime Beschloss and Talbott, *At the Highest Levels,* 14.

368 playwright Vaclav Havel Ibid.

368 In April, government troops Ibid., 51.

368 Moscow also continued to support *AWT*, 134–35.

369 What was unclear See, for instance, Naftali, *GHWB*, 77–79.

369   "TO RESTORE DYNAMISM"   *AWT,* 13.

369   EVEN BUSH'S ADVISERS   Naftali, *GHWB,* 77–78.

369   MANY BELIEVED   Ibid., *AWT,* 154–55.

369   ACCORDING TO THE PREVAILING WISDOM   Beschloss and Talbott, *At the Highest Levels,* 73–74.

369   HE SPRUNG ONE ON JIM BAKER   Baker with DeFrank, *Politics of Diplomacy,* 82–83.

369   "WE ARE IN A HISTORIC POSITION"   GHWB, "Telephone Conversation with Helmut Kohl of the Federal Republic of Germany," May 5, 1989, Presidential Telcon Files, Presidential Correspondence Files, BSC. Kohl also told Bush that Kohl "could not accept letting Gorbachev set himself up as the imitator of the voice of Europe." (Ibid.) See also Baker with DeFrank, *Politics of Diplomacy,* 93.

369   "YOU NEED TO GET AHEAD"   Baker with DeFrank, *Politics of Diplomacy,* 93. On April 5, 1989, Baker had sent Bush a March 31, 1989, memorandum from Lawrence Eagleburger outlining "Ideas for the NATO Summit." (March 31, 1989, JB.) In a covering note, Baker wrote: "I am *not* seeking a decision on any of these. I do *not* feel strongly about any of them. I *do* feel *very* strongly that NATO Summit *should* be a big success for you—and may not be without some concrete initiatives—which won't come unless *you* push it thru! JAB III." (James A. Baker III to GHWB, April 5, 1989, JB.) Bush's April 9 reply: "I am glad this kind of constructive thinking is going on. . . . We must have NATO meet[ing] seen as big USA success." (GHWB to Baker, April 9, 1989, JB.)

369   THE PRESIDENT DECIDED TO USE   *AWT,* 43–44. See also Gates, *From the Shadows,* 461–63.

370   IN A FRIDAY, MAY 19, MEETING   *AWT,* 73; Baker with DeFrank, *Politics of Diplomacy,* 93–94.

370   "I THOUGHT THIS WAS LARGE ENOUGH"   *AWT,* 73.

370   THE U.S. MILITARY   Baker with DeFrank, *Politics of Diplomacy,* 93.

370   "I WANT THIS DONE"   Ibid., 94.

370   WITH THE PENTAGON'S SUPPORT, THE PRESIDENT SETTLED   *AWT,* 74. Even the military was not wild about Bush's proposal, but acceded to the pressure from the president. (Ibid.)

370   "IF THEY WERE EVER USED"   Baker with DeFrank, *Politics of Diplomacy,* 84–85.

370   IN MILITARY TERMS   Ibid., 90–91.

370   BUSH HAD SOLVED TWO PROBLEMS   Ibid., 94–96.

370   HE KEPT THE CFE PROPOSAL SECRET   *AWT,* 79–80.

371   BUSH HOSTED FRANÇOIS MITTERRAND   Ibid., 74–78. See also GHWB, "Telephone Conversation with President François Mitterrand of France," August 26, 1989, Presidential Telcon Files, Presidential Correspondence Files, BSC.

371   THE YEAR BEFORE   GHWB diary, May 29, 1989.

371   "CHIEFS OF STATE DINNER"   Ibid., May 30, 1989; *AWT,* 82.

371   "MY FIRST IMPRESSION"   GHWB diary, May 30, 1989.

371   "THAT WOMAN"   *AWT,* 77.

371   BUSH'S PROPOSAL TO REDUCE CFE   Ibid., 73–74.

371   IMPORTANT ALLIED ADVANCE   Ibid., 81–85. "The agreement was announced, and there was almost a euphoric atmosphere," Bush dictated on May 30, 1989. (GHWB diary, May 30, 1989.) In a conversation with Jacques Delors, president of the European Commission, Bush said: "The resolution of the SNF issue and the new proposal for reducing conventional forces were historic accomplishments. The conventional arms control proposal had won broad acceptance within the Alliance. U.S. generals had also certified that the proposal was militarily sound. The first tentative Soviet re-

action was fairly good and upbeat. The U.S. would push forward now, challenging the Alliance to move faster.... All the Allies had agreed that the Summit was a success." (GHWB, "Meeting with Jacques Delors, President of the European Commission," May 30, 1989, Presidential Memcons, Presidential Correspondence Files, BSC.)

372 "WE NEED INNOVATION" Baker with DeFrank, *Politics of Diplomacy*, 96.

372 THE NEWS WENT OVER BEAUTIFULLY GHWB diary, May 30, 1989. "I see now that I have to kick the bureaucracy to make something happen, because, if I hadn't done that, we wouldn't have had a deal; and, if Jim Baker hadn't worked hard in negotiations, we wouldn't have had a deal.... So, you see, the lesson was clear, if you really want something to happen, you've really got to push it, and I will do that now with more confidence." (Ibid., May 31, 1989.)

372 PRAISED "THE WILLINGNESS" *NYT*, May 31, 1989.

372 LEE ATWATER, NOW CHAIRMAN GHWB diary, May 30, 1989.

372 THE SENSE OF CHANGE In a May 28, 1989, meeting with Wilfried Martens, the prime minister of Belgium, Bush offered a candid assessment of the state of the world and particularly of East-West relations. "It should be clearly understood that [our] Administration wanted Gorbachev and perestroika to succeed," Bush said according to a memorandum of the conversation. "The West had won the battle of ideologies and the Communist model was dead. Western values were prevailing." At the same time, Bush added, "The Allies should try to capitalize on that success and reduce arms, but not be naïve or base their foreign policies on one person." (GHWB, "Meeting with Wilfred Martens, Prime Minister of Belgium," May 28, 1989, Presidential Memcons, Presidential Correspondence, BSC.)

372 "FOR 40 YEARS" *Public Papers of the Presidents of the United States: George Bush, 1989*, 650–54.

373 THE TROUBLE HAD BEGUN *AWT*, 86–88. For accounts of Tiananmen and its implications, see also Naftali, *GHWB*, 80–83, and *LSY*, 392, 398–400.

373 BUSH WAS IN KENNEBUNKPORT *AWT*, 89.

373 JIM BAKER HAD HOPED Baker with DeFrank, *Politics of Diplomacy*, 97. Robert Gates informed the president that about 8,800 Americans were in the country at the time; of those, 500 to 600 were in Beijing. About 100 were embassy personnel. (Robert M. Gates to GHWB, "Subject: China," Thursday, June 8, 1989: For the President—Action—James W. Cicconi, DF.)

373 CASUALTY FIGURES Seth Faison, "The Persistent Mystery: How Many Died?" *NYT*, June 4, 1999. "The authorities have never made public a full accounting of the dead and injured," Faison wrote, "and they have stymied outside efforts to do so with a campaign of silence." (Ibid.)

373 THE POLITICS OF CHINA IN AMERICA Baker with DeFrank, *Politics of Diplomacy*, 108.

373 "NEITHER HAS ANY RESPONSIBILITY" GHWB diary, June 3, 1989.

373 "THE CHINESE LEADERSHIP Baker with DeFrank, *Politics of Diplomacy*, 105.

374 FROM WALKER'S POINT GHWB diary, June 4, 1989.

374 AT EIGHT A.M. ON MONDAY Ibid., June 5, 1989.

374 "I WANTED A MEASURED RESPONSE" *AWT*, 89.

374 IN TERMS OF SANCTIONS Baker with DeFrank, *Politics of Diplomacy*, 105. See also *AWT*, 89.

374 BUSH WENT TO THE WHITE HOUSE BRIEFING ROOM *AWT*, 90. For Bush's notes in preparation for the June 8 press conference, see Press conference briefing notes, June 7 and 8, 1989: For the President—Action—James W. Cicconi, DF.

374 "WE HAD NO CHOICE" GHWB diary, June 10, 1989.

374 THE PRESIDENT ATTEMPTED TO TELEPHONE Ibid., June 8, 1989.

374 "I WAS A LITTLE PISSED OFF AT THAT" Ibid.

374 HE KNEW DENG   Engel, ed., *China Diary of George H. W. Bush,* 458.

374 HIS QUIET BELIEF   Ibid., 461.

374 "HAD I NOT MET THE MAN"   Ibid. Henry Kissinger agreed that Bush's personal experience was crucial in this period. "If you had been in China, the idea of Deng Xiaoping as a dictator was not accurate—he was a reformer," Henry Kissinger recalled. "Bush had been there, had lived in that world." (Author interview with Henry Kissinger.) Engel's conclusion was that Bush's friendship with Deng "prompted from [Bush] a less caustic line than another president, less intimately involved with China and its leaders, might have pursued." (Engel, ed., *China Diary of George H. W. Bush,* 461.)

374 BUSH THEREFORE WROTE TO DENG   GHWB diary, June 18, 1989. See also Naftali, *GHWB,* 81–82.

375 "I HAVE TRIED"   *AWT,* 100–2.

375 FREEDOM OF SPEECH   Ibid.

375 THE SANCTIONS HE HAD IMPOSED   Ibid.

375 WITHIN TWENTY-FOUR HOURS   Ibid., 104.

375 IN BEIJING, SCOWCROFT FOUND   Ibid., 106–7. "The reason I have chosen President Bush as my friend is because since the inception of my contact with him I found that his words are rather trustworthy," Deng told Scowcroft in a meeting in the Great Hall of the People. (Ibid.)

375 "JUST LET IT WAIT"   GHWB diary, September 9, 1989.

375 HIS REACTION TO TIANANMEN   Press conference briefing notes, June 7 and 8, 1989: For the President—Action—James W. Cicconi, DF.

375 "STEADINESS, REALISM, [AND] THE SEARCH FOR"   Ibid.

375 EXAMPLES OF HOW "THE ENCOURAGEMENT OF"   Ibid.

375 IN JUNE, HUNGARY TOOK DOWN   Gaddis, *Cold War,* 240–41; Naftali, *GHWB,* 79–80.

375 IN THE SAME MONTH, IN POLAND   Gaddis, *Cold War,* 241–42.

375 BUSH TRAVELED TO BOTH NATIONS   *AWT,* 115–31.

376 BUSH AVOIDED LARGE CROWDS   Ibid., 115–16.

376 "WE HAD STEPPED"   Ibid., 130–31.

376 HEADING HOME FROM EASTERN EUROPE   GHWB diary, July 18, 1989.

376 "I WANT TO DO IT"   *AWT,* 132.

376 GORBACHEV AGREED   Ibid., 132–33.

376 THE PRESIDENT'S VIEW OF GORBACHEV   GHWB diary, July 30, 1989.

376 "HE'S HAVING ENORMOUS"   Ibid.

376 BUSH'S FIRST THOUGHT   Ibid., July 4, 1989.

376 "HE'S STEADY"   Ibid.

376 "SOMEDAY IT SHOULD BE COLIN POWELL"   Ibid.

376 HAD SERVED AS REAGAN'S LAST NATIONAL SECURITY ADVISER   Powell with Persico, *My American Journey,* 388–89, 399.

376 "I WISH THAT COLIN HAD MORE COMMAND EXPERIENCE"   GHWB diary, August 8, 1989.

376 "SO I SAID TO DICK"   Ibid.

377 "MY WORRY HAD BEEN"   Ibid., September 29, 1989.

377 AT BUSH'S REQUEST, CHENEY ASKED POWELL   Ibid., August 10, 1989.

377 "THE POWELL DECISION"   Ibid., September 29, 1989.

377 A BEAUTIFUL NEW ENGLAND DAY   "Remarks at the Bicentennial Convocation at Phillips Academy in Andover, Massachusetts," November 5, 1989, *Public Papers of the Presidents of the United States: George Bush, 1989,* 1458–60.

377 "THE GREAT END"   Ibid.

377 IT WAS OVER THERE   Ibid.

377 HE RETURNED TO THE WHITE HOUSE   GHWB diary, November 5, 1989.

377 "HE WAS NOT EMOTIONAL"   Ibid.

377 AFTER DINNER, WITH NIXON GONE   Ibid.

378 "THE MOVES IN EAST GERMANY"   Ibid. See also Beschloss and Talbott, *At the Highest Levels,* 132–36.

378 "HE'S AMAZED AT"   GHWB diary, November 6, 1989.

378 "IF WE MISHANDLE IT"   Ibid., November 8, 1989.

THIRTY-THREE: *The Fall of the Wall*

379 IT IS THIS THAT REALLY   GHWB diary, November 11, 1989.

379 BUSH WAS AT HIS DESK   *AWT,* 148–49. See also Naftali, *GHWB,* 84–86, for Bush and the Wall. For details of the day, see "Schedule of the President," November 9, 1989, DF. Any appointments scheduled and approved in advance appeared as type-written entries on the daily schedule with a start time and duration. As a given day progressed, the president's administrative staff hand-annotated the schedule, creating a precise record of his movements and human interactions down to the minute. For scholarly appraisals of the fall of the wall, see, for instance, Jeffrey A. Engel, ed., *Fall of the Berlin Wall: The Revolutionary Legacy of 1989* (New York, 2009); and Zelikow and Rice, *Germany Unified and Europe Transformed,* 99–101. I also found Mary Elise Sarotte, *The Collapse: The Accidental Opening of the Berlin Wall* (New York: Basic Books, 2014), instructive and illuminating.

379 "THE WALL HAD BEEN OPENED"   *AWT,* 148.

379 STEPPED OUT OF THE BIG OFFICE   Ibid.

379 EAST GERMAN OFFICIALS   Zelikow and Rice, *Germany Unified and Europe Transformed,* 99–101.

379 COMMUNICATION BETWEEN DIFFERENT GOVERNMENT AGENCIES   Ibid.

379 IT WAS DAZZLING   Beschloss and Talbott, *At the Highest Levels,* 132–36; Zelikow and Rice, *Germany Unified,* 63–101; *AWT,* 148–49; Naftali, *GHWB,* 84–85. After his trip in July 1989 to Poland and to Hungary, Bush wrote friends: "I can only conclude we are living in the most exciting *and* challenging times in modern history." (GHWB to John R. Davis, American Ambassador, Warsaw, July 31, 1989, JB.)

379 IN 1983, BUSH HAD GONE   *ATB,* 326.

379 "MR. GORBACHEV, TEAR DOWN"   Reagan, *American Life,* 681–83.

379 "STANDS AS A MONUMENT"   "Remarks to the Citizens of Mainz," May 31, 1989, *Public Papers of the Presidents of the United States: George Bush, 1989,* 650–54.

379 NOW IT HAD   Naftali, *GHWB,* 85.

380 IN HIS STUDY IN THE WEST WING   *AWT,* 148–49.

380 THERE WERE SIGNS   Gaddis, *Cold War,* 243.

380 THE EAST GERMAN SECRET POLICE CHIEF   Ibid.

380 "THE HEROIC RESPONSE"   Ibid.

380 THE CIA HAD TOLD THE PRESIDENT   Engel, *Fall of the Berlin Wall,* 28.

380 "URGING THAT WE NOT OVERREACT"   GHWB diary, November 11, 1989. See also *AWT,* 150.

380 DETERMINED NOT TO "GLOAT"   *AWT,* 149.

380 RECOMMENDED AN EXCHANGE   Ibid.

380 AS THE PRESS CORPS   Ibid.

380 IN A PREPARED STATEMENT   GHWB, "Statement to the Press," November 9, 1989, DF.

380 "A POSITIVE STEP"   Ibid.

380 "THE TRAGIC SYMBOLISM"   Ibid.

380 "Of course, I was"   *AWT,* 149.

381 Lesley Stahl of CBS News   Ibid.

381 "This is a sort of"   Ibid.

381 "I'm not an emotional kind of guy"   Ibid.

381 "The press gets all over me"   GHWB diary, November 11, 1989.

381 "This is what"   Ibid.

381 From West Berlin   *AWT,* 151. See also GHWB, handwritten notes of phone call with Helmut Kohl, November 11, 1989, DF. Kohl called GHWB at 4 P.M. eastern.

381 "It is like witnessing"   *AWT,* 151.

381 Two hundred and thirty thousand   Ibid.

381 There was a solution   Ibid., 150–51.

381 Gorbachev cabled Kohl   Ibid., 149–50.

381 "unforeseen consequences"   "Verbal Message from Mikhail Gorbachev to François Mitterrand, Margaret Thatcher, and George Bush," November 10, 1989, History and Public Policy Program Digital Archive, SAPMO-BA, DY 30/IV 2/2.039/319. Translated for Cold War International History Project by Howard Sargeant. http://digitalarchive.wilsoncenter.org/document/111536.

381 Gorbachev's tone had   *AWT,* 149–50.

381 "This was the first time"   Ibid., 150.

382 George Mitchell recommended   Author interview with GHWB. See also *AWT,* 149.

382 "sticking it in Gorbachev's eye"   Author interview with GHWB.

382 Bush sent Gorbachev a message   *AWT,* 150–51.

382 reports of violence in Moldavia   GHWB diary, November 11, 1989. See also "Clashes Reported in Moldavia," *WP,* November 11, 1989, and "Clash in Moldavia Brings Crackdown," *NYT,* November 12, 1989.

382 "It is this that really concerns me"   GHWB diary, November 11, 1989.

382 "inadequate to the moment"   Beschloss and Talbott, *At the Highest Levels,* 135.

382 a "far cry from"   GHWB diary, November 12, 1989.

382 "The thing that gets me"   Ibid.

382 "It's spreading like wildfire"   Ibid., November 25, 1989. See also *AWT,* 153, and "Shake-Up in Bulgaria Brings Cautious Optimism," *NYT,* November 12, 1989.

382 One CIA paper made a particular impression   *AWT,* 154.

382 As he prepared to meet   Ibid., 154–55.

384 Bush's appetite for debate   Ibid., 154.

384 "We were getting hints"   Ibid., 155.

384 At Valletta Harbor in Malta   *AWT,* 161–74, covers the meeting.

384 "No farting, OK?"   GHWB to JAB III, November 30, 1989, box 288, James A. Baker III Papers, Princeton.

384 "How do I feel?"   GHWB diary, December 1, 1989.

384 who loved being shipboard   *AWT,* 162; GHWB diary, December 2, 1989.

384 "Gales had been"   *AWT,* 162. See also Naftali, *GHWB,* 87.

384 Greeting Gorbachev, who was dressed   GHWB diary, December 2, 1989.

384 The Soviet leader's hair   *AWT,* 162.

384 "Spot is prominent"   GHWB diary, December 2, 1989.

384 Jim Baker had had an idea   Ibid., 160.

385 Bush had seventeen   Ibid., 160, 162.

385 As Bush opened his remarks   Ibid., 162–63. For the records of the sessions, see the following memoranda of conversation. For December 2, 1989: "First Expanded Bilateral Session with Chairman Gorbachev of the Soviet Union," "First Restricted Bi-

lateral Session with Chairman Gorbachev of Soviet Union," and "Luncheon Meeting with Chairman Gorbachev." For December 3, 1989: "Second Expanded Bilateral Session." All can be found in Presidential Memcons, Presidential Correspondence, BSC.

385 "THIS IS THE END" *AWT,* 163–64.

385 "THIS HAS BEEN" Ibid., 164.

385 IN TRUTH, GORBACHEV WAS RELIEVED Naftali, *GHWB,* 87; Baker with DeFrank, *Politics of Diplomacy,* 170. And not as surprised as Scowcroft had feared: Bush had evidently sent many of these agenda items along to Gorbachev in a handwritten letter of November 22, 1989. GHWB to Mikhail Gorbachev, November 22, 1989, Gorbachev (Dobrynin) Sensitive 1989–June 1990 (1), Gorbachev Files, Special Separate USSR Notes Files, BSC.

385 "A MULTIPOLAR WORLD" *AWT,* 164.

385 "THE UNITED STATES HAS NOT" Ibid.

385 "I HOPE YOU HAVE NOTICED" Ibid., 164–65.

386 "YES, WE HAVE SEEN" Ibid., 165.

386 A SWORDFISH AND LOBSTER DINNER Ibid., 168.

386 "I WANT TO SAY TO YOU" Ibid., 169.

386 BUSH AND GORBACHEV HOSTED *Public Papers of the Presidents of the United States: George Bush, 1989,* 1635–40.

386 ACCORDING TO BUSH'S HANDWRITTEN NOTES GHWB, handwritten notes, "At NATO: Heads of State and Government," December 6, 1989, JB.

386 THE "GREATEST REVOLUTION" Ibid.

386 THANKED BUSH Ibid.

386 "WE CAME OUT OKAY" GHWB diary, December 4, 1989.

386 THE PRESIDENT ARRIVED IN WASHINGTON Ibid., December 8, 1989.

387 "THE GENERAL AFTERGLOW" Ibid.

387 BUSH HAD DECIDED *AWT,* 173–74.

387 ON HALLOWEEN 1989 JAB III to GHWB, October 31, 1989, box 288, James A. Baker III Papers, Princeton.

387 "MR. P—WE HAVE" Ibid.

387 "AT THE MOMENT" Ibid.

388 "BE QUIET AND GO TO SLEEP" GHWB diary, December 16, 1989.

388 THAT SAME NIGHT, IN PANAMA Ibid., December 17, 1989.

388 "HE WAS KICKED" Ibid.

388 THE DECEMBER ATTACKS ON AMERICANS For background on the military action in Panama, see Patterson, *Restless Giant,* 226–27, Wilentz, *Age of Reagan,* 292–94, and Naftali, *GHWB,* 88–89. Bush was criticized for failing to support a coup against Noriega earlier in 1989. For an account of this episode, see *LSY,* 411–14. Also see Crapol, *What It Takes,* 1142–44, *Oil Bush and Panama*.

388 NORIEGA WAS A DRUG TRAFFICKER Patterson, *Restless Giant,* 226–27.

388 HE STOLE A PRESIDENTIAL ELECTION Ibid.

388 NORIEGA EVEN DECLARED WAR GHWB diary, December 17, 1989. See also Naftali, *GHWB,* 88.

388 FOR BUSH, THAT DID IT GHWB diary, December 17, 1989. See also Naftali, *GHWB,* 88–89; Cramer, *What It Takes,* 1042–43; Wicker, *GHWB,* 139–45.

388 "WE'VE HAD ENOUGH" Ibid.

388 THE LARGEST PROJECTION OF AMERICAN FORCE Naftali, *GHWB,* 89; Patterson, *Restless Giant,* 227, and Wilentz, *Age of Reagan,* 293.

388 LARGER THAN REAGAN'S See, for instance, Andrew Rosenthal, "Bush Raises Force in Panama By 2,000," *NYT,* December 23, 1989.

388   ON THE NIGHT THE TROOPS WENT   GHWB diary, December 23, 1989.

388   A SMALL COUCH   Author interview with Patricia Presock.

388   THE AMERICAN FORCES—BUSH DISPATCHED   *NYT,* January 5, 1990. "Of 26,000 U.S. military personnel stationed in Panama or deployed to the country for this operation, 23 were killed in action and another 322 were wounded. The total casualties included friendly fire incidents and injuries sustained on drop zones. The Panama Defense Forces, numbering about 15,000 personnel of all ranks and duty assignments, had 314 killed in action, 124 known to have been wounded in action, and over 5,300 detained by U.S. forces. Estimates vary among sources, but it appears that 200 Panamanian civilians were killed during Operation Just Cause." R. Cody Phillips, "Operation Just Cause: The Incursion into Panama," Center of Military History, CMH Pub. No. 70-85-1, 44, http://www.history.army.mil/html/books/070/70-85-1/index.html.

388   QUICKLY DEPOSED NORIEGA   Naftali, *GHWB,* 89; *LSY,* 416–19.

389   LEE ATWATER HAD CONVENED   GHWB diary, December 24, 1989.

389   LOOKING OVER THE WHITE HOUSE NEWS SUMMARY   Ibid., January 22, 1990.

389   "I'M INCLINED TO AGREE"   Ibid.

THIRTY-FOUR: *I Want to Do the Most Good I Can*

390   GOD, THERE ARE SO MANY   GHWB diary, January 30, 1990.

390   ON THE LAST DAY OF MAY   *NYT,* June 1, 1989; *LAT,* June 1, 1989.

390   "HAS TO BE FOUGHT"   Ibid., January 27, 2012.

390   THE "MINDLESS CANNIBALISM"   *LAT,* June 1, 1989. See also John M. Barry, *The Ambition and the Power: The Fall of Jim Wright* (New York, 1992).

390   "IN SPITE OF"   *Chicago Tribune,* June 1, 1989.

391   ATTACKED FOLEY IN A RELEASE   Brady, *Bad Boy,* 241–42.

391   BUSH SENT WORD   GHWB diary, June 6, 1989; Brady, *Bad Boy,* 245. Lee Atwater swore to Bush that he himself had had nothing to do with the release. Asked about the story at a press conference, Bush said, "The matter is closed," but he worried that he might be wrong about that. "There's still going to be reverberation, but the problem is, nobody believes Lee was innocent," Bush told his diary. "I do, because he looked me in the eye and told me so. . . . But his reputation is such that people don't believe it. . . . There may be more problems later on, but we're going to stay with Lee. Of course, if it turns out that he knew about it, regrettably, he'll be history." (GHWB diary, June 10, 1989.) See also "Possible Press Conference Questions" and "Atwater/RNC Case," both in June 8, 1989: For the President—Action—James W. Cicconi, DF.

391   "FOLEY IS A DECENT GUY"   GHWB diary, June 6, 1989.

391   "I AM, OF COURSE"   *NYT,* June 8, 1989.

391   "A VERY CHEAP SMEAR"   Ibid.

391   "TOUGH"   Author interview with GHWB.

391   "UGLINESS"   Ibid.

391   "THE DEMOCRATS STRIKE BACK"   GHWB diary, June 6, 1989.

392   "I WANT TO DO THE MOST GOOD"   Author interview with John Sununu.

392   JAMES A. STIMSON'S "POLICY MOOD INDEX"   James A. Stimson, *Public Opinion in America: Moods, Cycles, and Swings,* 2nd ed. (Boulder, Colo., 1999.) See also http://stimson.web.unc.edu for background on Stimson's work.

392   THE VICTORIES, THOUGH, DID COME FIRST   Naftali, *GHWB,* 133–34, offers a strong overview of the key domestic achievements. See also Sununu, *Quiet Man.*

392   HIS REAL-TIME ACCLAIM FOR THESE ACCOMPLISHMENTS   Naftali, *GHWB,* 134. "Besides the Clean Air Amendments, Bush's major legislative achievements, the Amer-

icans with Disabilities Act and the Civil Rights Act of 1991, reflected congressional priorities more than his own," wrote Naftali. "These were significant pieces of legislation, and the ADA empowered the disabled, including those with AIDS, by lowering barriers, real and symbolic, to full participation in American society. But they garnered little public support for George Bush." (Ibid., 133–34.)

392 "GOD, THERE ARE SO MANY" GHWB diary, January 30, 1990.

392 THE PRESIDENT SOUGHT TO APPLY Naftali, *GHWB*, 97.

392 "PEOPLE ALWAYS THINK" Author interview with Andrew Card.

393 THEIR "PLACE IN THE SUN" Author interview with GHWB.

393 WAS CONSTANTLY ON THE PHONE Author interviews with John Sununu and Fred McClure.

393 "THE MOST IMPORTANT THING" Author interview with John Sununu.

393 BROUGHT HIM DOMESTIC ACHIEVEMENTS For details in this section I drew on the Miller Center's "American President: A Reference Resource" and its account of Bush's record on domestic affairs, a helpful and thorough summary. See http://millercenter.org/president/biography/bush-domestic-affairs.

393 INCREASED FUNDING AND TAX CREDITS FOR FAMILIES Patterson, *Restless Giant*, 240; Sununu, *Quiet Man*, 246.

393 ENHANCEMENTS FOR HEAD START Himelfarb and Perotti, eds., *Principle Over Politics?*, 270.

393 THE FINANCIAL INSTITUTIONS REFORM *LSY*, 395; Greene, *Presidency of George Bush*, 82–83.

393 BANNED THE IMPORTATION OF MOST SEMIAUTOMATIC RIFLES *WP*, July 1, 13, 1989. See also GHWB to John Sununu, March 24, 1990, Chief of Staff Discussion Items 1/1/90–5/19/90 (3), John H. Sununu Files, Office of the Chief of Staff to the President, GBPL.

393 ON EDUCATION, IN THE FALL OF 1989 Author interviews with John Sununu and Bill Clinton. See also Sununu, *Quiet Man*, 232–36; Wilentz, *Age of Reagan*, 304; and Patterson, *Restless Giant*, 238–39.

393 THERE HAD BEEN ONLY TWO SIMILAR GATHERINGS Author interview with Roger Porter. Porter also wrote a memorandum to the president "explaining the surprisingly sparse history of presidentially convened meetings with the nation's governors." TR's subject, as noted in the manuscript, was conservation; "FDR," Porter recalled, "listed five issues in his letter to them, agenda items typical of what a governor might want to talk about with the President. By the time of his inauguration the banking crisis had intensified and only 25 governors stayed in Washington to gather on Monday for what turned out to be a truncated meeting with FDR before they, too, quickly returned to their state capitols." (Roger Porter email to author.)

393 NATIONAL PERFORMANCE GOALS Sununu, *Quiet Man*, 232–41.

393 THE GOALS THEMSELVES Author interview with Roger Porter.

393 CLINTON AND CAMPBELL JOINED Ibid.

393 THE CLEAN AIR ACT AMENDMENTS OF 1990 William Reilly to GHWB, "Re: The Clean Air Bill," October 30, 1990, 1990 Clean Air (3 of 3) [3], John H. Sununu Files, Office of the Chief of Staff to the President, GBPL (11696); Frederick D. McClure to John Sununu, "Re: Core Group Clean Air Strategy Session," January 23, 1990, 1990 Clean Air (2 of 3) [3], John H. Sununu Files, Office of the Chief of Staff to the President, GBPL (11665); Michael Boskin to GHWB, "Re: The Clean Air Bill," October 26, 1990, 1990 Clean Air (3 of 3) [3], John H. Sununu Files, Office of the Chief of Staff to the President, GBPL (11694); "The Clean Air Negotiations," March 9, 1990, 1990 Clean Air (2 of 3) [2], John H. Sununu Files, Office of the

Chief of Staff to the President, GBPL (11659). See also Greene, *Presidency of George Bush*, 74–78; Naftali, *GHWB*, 133; George Mitchell, *The Negotiator: A Memoir* (New York, 2015), 169–93; Patterson, *Restless Giant*, 240–41. Richard E. Cohen, *Washington at Work: Back Rooms and Clean Air* (New York, 1995), is a comprehensive account.

394 MITCHELL CREDITED BUSH   Mitchell, *Negotiator*, 170–71.

394 AFTER MORE THAN 130 HOURS   Author interview with Roger Porter.

394 ESTABLISHED BOLD GOALS   Ibid.

394 AFTER READING A "REPORT CARD"   Ibid.

394 "NOT A LOT"   Ibid.

394 THE AMERICANS WITH DISABILITIES ACT   Author interviews with GHWB, John Sununu, Boyden Gray, and Tom Harkin. See also Himelfarb and Perotti, *Principle Over Politics?*, 143–79; Wilentz, *Age of Reagan*, 305–6; Patterson, *Restless Giant*, 241; Sununu, *Quiet Man*, 251–56.

394 HIS INTEREST IN THE BILL   Author interviews with GHWB, John Sununu, Boyden Gray, and Tom Harkin. See also "Questions for Disabled Media Interview," May 1, 1990, DF; William Roper to John Sununu, "Re: Your Meeting Today with Senator Kennedy and others on ADA," July 27, 1990, Disabilities (1989), Issues Files, John H. Sununu Files, Office of the Chief of Staff to the President (11461); and William Roper to John Sununu, "Re: Status of the Americans with Disabilities Act," September 1, 1989, Science and Technology (1989) [3]: Bromley, White House Offices File, John H. Sununu Files, Office of the Chief of Staff to the President, GBPL (11341). A note card from his talking points for a press conference on April 16, 1990, offers a glimpse of Bush's priorities in this season. In frenetic longhand, GHWB added notes to the typed statements about abortion that amount to the president's worldview in brief. Most important in shaping his outlook were promising economic trends and his administration's advancement of civil rights and Clean Air legislation. (April 16, 1990, DF.)

394 CHAMPIONED THE MEASURE   See, for instance, www.dolekemp96.org/agenda/issues/disabilities.htm.

394 AFTER THEIR YEARS OF COMPETITION   Author interview with GHWB.

394 THE PRESIDENT WAS GRATEFUL   Ibid.

395 THE TELEPHONE RANG   Author interview with Tom Harkin.

395 HARKIN HAPPILY ACCEPTED   Ibid. Sununu could not recall any dispute with Harkin. (Author interview with John Sununu.)

395 IN A SUNNY, SPARKLING CEREMONY   Author interview with Tom Harkin.

395 "EVEN THE STRONGEST PERSON"   "Remarks on Signing the Americans with Disabilities Act of 1990," July 26, 1990, *Public Papers of the Presidents of the United States: George Bush, 1990* (Washington, D.C., 1991), 1069; Ann Devroy, "In Emotion-Filled Ceremony, Bush Signs Rights Law for America's Disabled," *WP*, July 27, 1990.

396 "THE LOOK"   Author interviews with James A. Baker III, Boyden Gray, and Fred McClure.

THIRTY-FIVE: *A Nation Reunited and a New NATO*

397 I DON'T THINK   GHWB diary, February 26, 1990.

397 THEODORE ROOSEVELT HAD DELIGHTED   William Draper Lewis, *The Life of Theodore Roosevelt* (Philadelphia, 1919), 186–87.

397 GEORGE H. W. BUSH LOVED THE MANSION   See, for instance, GHWB diary, November 7, 1989.

397 THE BUSHES AWOKE   Details in this section about the daily routine and personal

characteristics of the president came from GHWB diary; BPB diary; *BB*; and author interviews with GHWB, BPB, Tim McBride, Patricia Presock, and other family and staff members. Some items are singled out for a particular citation below, but all the details came from, and were confirmed by, the principals, family, and staff.

397 HE CARRIED A SPECIAL HEATING STICK   Author interview with Tim McBride.

397 YOGURT AND GRANOLA   Ibid.

397 OCCASIONALLY WITH MILLIE   Associated Press, May 1, 1989. BPB revealed this detail in the spring of 1989. (Ibid.)

397 ARTHUR A. ADLER   Author interview with Tim McBride.

397 UNIRONICALLY CALLED "SHIRTINGS"   Ibid.

397 ASCOT CHANG   Ibid.

398 TO DORO'S 1992 WEDDING AT CAMP DAVID HE WORE   *BB*, 469.

398 THE PRESIDENT WORE ONE SOCK THAT SAID "MERRY"   Powell with Persico, *My American Journey*, 423–24; Cramer, *What It Takes*, 1043.

398 A HIDEAWAY DESK   Author interview with Patricia Presock.

398 A WORLD MAP HUNG ABOVE   Ibid.

398 THE TAPPING OF HIS THUMB ON HIS DESK   Author interview with Boyden Gray.

398 BRENT SCOWCROFT WOULD BE ANXIOUS   Author interview with Brent Scowcroft.

398 "A MORTAL FEAR"   Ibid.

398 IF BUSH WERE ANGRY   Author interview with Dan Quayle.

398 "IN THE TESTICLES"   GHWB diary, November 7, 1989.

398 DOMINGO QUICHO, A VETERAN   *AWT*, 29.

398 IF BUSH WERE ALONE   GHWB diary, November 7, 1989.

399 "IT'S A GREAT MIX"   *ATB*, 326–27.

399 AMONG HIS FAVORITE ARTISTS: DOLLY PARTON   *Time*, February 4, 1980; *ATB*, 326–27.

399 ANNE MURRAY   Author interview with Patricia Presock.

399 WITH PORK RINDS AND DR PEPPER   Author interview with Tim McBride.

399 LIFE "WAS NONSTOP"   Ibid.

400 ONE SUMMER WEEKEND   GHWB diary, July 30, 1989.

400 AFTER LUNCH BUSH TOOK A NAP   Ibid.

400 THE REUNIFICATION OF GERMANY   *AWT*, 188–90; Naftali, *GHWB*, 85–86, 89–96; *LSY*, 390, 408, 411, 421, 424, 437, 452. I am indebted to Jeffrey A. Engel, "Bush, Germany, and the Power of Time: How History Makes History," *Diplomatic History* 37, no. 4 (2013): 639–63, and to Gates, *From the Shadows*, 483–95, for insights about Bush and the issue of reunification. I also learned much from Zelikow and Rice, *Germany Reunited and Europe Transformed*.

400 AT YALTA IN THE WANING HOURS   See, for instance, Elizabeth Borgwardt, *A New Deal for the World* (Cambridge, Mass., 2007).

400 "GERMAN REUNIFICATION THAT"   *AWT*, 181.

400 TO BRING EAST GERMANY AND WEST GERMANY TOGETHER   Ibid.

400 RATIFYING THE MARCH OF THE FORCES OF FREEDOM   Naftali, *GHWB*, 86, notes that reunification could "bring [Germany] into NATO and end the Cold War." (Ibid.)

400 HAD BUSH NOT PRESSED   Engel, "Bush, Germany, and the Power of Time," *Diplomatic History*, 639–63. See also Jeffrey A. Engel, "A Better World . . . but Don't Get Carried Away: The Foreign Policy of George H. W. Bush Twenty Years On," *Diplomatic History* 34, no. 1 (2010): 25–46. As Engel wrote of the period, Bush "was well aware that the wrong move at every turn could snatch defeat—and anarchy—out of the jaws of potential triumph and peace." (Ibid., 27.) Engel also observed that Bush's vision for a post–Cold War Europe "mimicked the post-1945 world American leaders aspired to lead before the Cold War thwarted their internationalist plans." (Ibid., 29.)

400 THATCHER AND MITTERRAND WERE SKEPTICAL   In February 1990, Thatcher told Bush: "Everyone accepts that there will be German unification, and that it will come very fast indeed. All are worried about the consequences, and the uncertainty." (GHWB, "Telephone Conversation with Margaret Thatcher, Prime Minister of United Kingdom," February 24, 1990, Presidential Telcon Files, Presidential Correspondence Files, BSC.) Two days later, Mitterrand explained: "It is a fact of life that Europeans will always be suspicious of Germany because of the War, although the Europeans may be vague in articulating this suspicion." (GHWB, "Telephone Conversation with French President Mitterrand," February 26, 1990, Presidential Telcon Files, Presidential Correspondence Files, BSC.)

400 IF "WE ARE NOT CAREFUL"   Gaddis, *Cold War,* 250.

401 "THE PURPOSE OF NATO"   Author interview with Dan Quayle. I am grateful to Jeffrey Engel for pointing out Thatcher's debt to Lord Ismay for this description of the mission of NATO.

401 "I DON'T THINK"   GHWB diary, February 26, 1990.

401 IN FEBRUARY 1990, BUSH RECEIVED   Ibid., February 10, 1990.

401 "CHANGE—THE AMAZING CHANGE"   Ibid.

401 A QUESTION OF BALANCE AND OF ORDER   As Bush explained to Kohl prior to Malta, "We will go forward cautiously, but will be forward-leaning on arms control and other issues—as part of a strong Alliance. . . . Stability should be the by-word. We don't want inadvertently to create instability." (GHWB, "Telephone Conversation with Chancellor Helmut Kohl of the Federal Republic of Germany," November 29, 1989, Presidential Telcon Files, Presidential Correspondence Files, BSC.)

401 ON THE MORNING AFTER MALTA   *AWT,* 200.

401 "I HOLD NO RANCOR"   GHWB quoted in Engel, "Bush, Germany, and the Power of Time," 650. As Gates observed: "Alone among the leaders of the Western alliance and the Soviet Union, George Bush believed in his heart that the Germans had changed, and he was prepared to gamble a very great deal on that faith. He would cast his lot with Helmut Kohl and the German people." (Gates, *From the Shadows,* 484.)

402 "WHO'S THE ENEMY?"   GHWB diary, February 24, 1990.

402 ONGOING SUPPORT OF MIKHAIL GORBACHEV   To Mitterrand in July 1990, Bush described Gorbachev as "the best bet there is in the Soviet Union." Mitterrand replied: "We won't find another man of that caliber in Moscow. He's a very strange phenomenon to come out of the 1917 revolution." (GHWB, "Meeting with President Mitterrand of France," July 9, 1990, Houstonian Hotel, Houston, Presidential Memcons, Presidential Correspondence, BSC.)

402 "DESTABILIZE HIM AND WE LOSE"   *AWT,* 190.

402 GORBACHEV ARRIVED IN WASHINGTON   Ibid., 279. My account of the Lithuanian crisis, the Bush-Gorbachev summit in Washington, Soviet support for German reunification, and what Naftali called the "two-pronged" Bush strategy of reaching an understanding with Gorbachev over Lithuania and trade agreements (Naftali, *GHWB,* 93), is drawn from *AWT,* 279–90; Naftali, *GHWB,* 90–96; and the sources cited below.

402 THE CONVERSATION WAS WIDE RANGING   *AWT,* 279. "Since we are in a radically new phase of our relations, we need a radically different view of, and approach to, each other," Gorbachev said. "The confrontation we got into after World War II wasted our time and energy, while others—the former vanquished—were moving ahead." (GHWB, "Meeting with President Gorbachev," May 31, 1990, Oval Office, Presidential Memcons, Presidential Correspondence, BSC.) Bush also observed: "The U.S.

has not been a historic threat to the Soviet Union, nor vice versa. Problems arose only when the Cold War developed." (Ibid.) On the question of Germany, Bush said that he had "become more sensitive" on the subject of "Soviet losses in World War II." He wanted Gorbachev to know that "We are attuned to that driving point for the Soviet Union, the fact that so many lost their lives." It was important, Bush said, "to get that comment on the table before we get—inevitably—to Germany, so you would know that I am sensitive to that historical fact. We do not want winners and losers." (Ibid.)

402 THE "OLD SUSPICIONS"   *AWT,* 279.

402 LITHUANIA. ONE OF THE BALTIC STATES   Ibid., 215–29, 279–80; Naftali, *GHWB,* 91. Led by Vytautas Landsbergis, Lithuania had issued a declaration of independence in March 1990, and affirmed it in the face of Soviet demands to retract the declaration or face stiff consequences. ("Timeline: Lithuania," BBC, http://news.bbc.co.uk/2/hi/europe/country_profiles/2133386.stm.) See also Minutes, NSC Deputies Committee Teleconference, April 21, 1990, Situation in Lithuania 1990 (1), 1989–90 Subject File, Condoleezza Rice Files, NSC, GBPL (OAID CF00721-002); "West European Reaction to Soviet Pressure on Lithuania, n.d., April 21, 1990, Situation in Lithuania 1990 (1), 1989–90 Subject File, Condoleezza Rice Files, NSC (OAID CF00721-002); and a Gorbachev letter on the subject to Bush, Mikhail Gorbachev to GHWB, May 2, 1990, Situation in Lithuania 1990 [1], 1989–90 Subject File, Condoleezza Rice Files, NSC (OAID CF00721-002). In the Washington meeting, Bush told Gorbachev: "To the degree that we see a commitment to your own principles of self-determination, we can cooperate. I have tried to conduct myself in a constrained way because I know you have big problems. But I am being hit both on my left and on my right by those who say I am subordinating U.S. dedication to principle." Yet Bush also showed he appreciated Gorbachev's position. "I will be honest: some of Landsbergis' moves could look to you like putting a finger in your eye." (GHWB, "Meeting with President Gorbachev," May 31, 1990, Oval Office, Presidential Memcons, Presidential Correspondence, BSC.)

402 MOSCOW, HOWEVER, HAD CRACKED DOWN   *AWT,* 215–16.

402 INSTITUTED AN ENERGY EMBARGO   Naftali, *GHWB,* 92.

402 BUSH WAS UNDER GREAT PRESSURE   Ibid.

402 IN A LARGER MEETING   *AWT,* 281.

402 WOULD STRATEGICALLY ISOLATE THE SOVIET UNION   Ibid.

402 HE PROPOSED, INSTEAD, THAT THE NEW GERMANY   Ibid., 282.

403 BUSH INTERVENED WITH A TECHNICAL POINT   Ibid.

403 THE HELSINKI FINAL ACT, NONBINDING ACCORDS   Ibid. See also www.britannica.com/event/Helsinki-Accords.

403 "SHRUGGING," BUSH RECALLED   *AWT,* 282.

403 "YES," GORBACHEV TOLD BUSH   Ibid.

403 THE CABINET ROOM WENT QUIET   Ibid.

403 APPEARED STUNNED AND DISMAYED   Ibid.

403 THERE WAS HEATED BACK-AND-FORTH   Ibid. "By this time the dismay in the Soviet team was palpable," Bush recalled. One Soviet official's "eyes flashed angrily as he gestured to [another Soviet official]. They snapped back and forth in loud stage whispers in an agitated debate as Gorbachev spoke. It was an unbelievable scene, the likes of which none of us had ever seen before—virtually open rebellion against a Soviet leader." (Ibid., 282–83.) The scene continued, and eventually included Gorbachev. It was, Bush recalled, a "fascinating display." (Ibid., 283.)

403 GORBACHEV MAY HAVE BEEN ACCEPTING   Ibid., 283–84.

403 "BUTTONHOLED" BUSH AFTER A STATE DINNER   Ibid., 283.

403 "He told me" Ibid., 283–84.

403 Bush went upstairs but slept poorly Ibid., 284.

403 Bush took Jim Baker Ibid., 285.

403 "The deal I suggested" Ibid. For Baker's reports of earlier conversations with Gorbachev on Lithuania, see James A. Baker III to GHWB, "Memorandum for the President," Moscow, May 18, 1990, Department of State Virtual Reading Room, http://foia.state.gov/searchapp/DOCUMENTS/FOIADocs/000053DC.pdf, accessed November 24, 2014.

403 There was a further secret condition AWT, 285.

403 "We could hand" Ibid.

404 The next morning Bush and Gorbachev GHWB diary, June 2, 1990; AWT, 286.

404 Camp David was everything AWT, 286–87.

404 ("Talk about beginner's luck!") Ibid., 287.

404 "We developed a feeling" Ibid.

404 "I've heard some report" GHWB diary, June 2, 1990.

404 "Well, I don't know" Ibid.

404 The president consulted Ibid.

404 "told him" Ibid.

404 They strolled the wood-chip trails AWT, 287; GHWB diary, June 2, 1990.

404 There was a friendly supper Ibid.

405 It was a candid conversation Ibid.

405 They returned to Washington GHWB diary, June 3, 1990.

405 Bush brought Gorbachev up Ibid.

405 Bush eagerly took his guest Ibid.

405 There was good news Ibid.

405 "He was thrilled" Ibid.

405 They went downstairs Ibid.

405 "I've got to get" Ibid.

405 Barbara was enduring a generational controversy BB, 335–42.

405 "because she hasn't" GHWB diary, April 16, 1990.

406 Mrs. Bush invited Raisa Gorbachev along BB, 336–38.

406 "Maybe we should adjust" "Barbara Bush—Wellesley College Commencement," June 1, 1990. https://www.youtube.com/watch?v=hxhuPIzOIfc.

406 She received her most sustained applause Ibid.

406 "And I wish him well" Ibid.

406 Mrs. Bush was a popular figure Ann McDaniel, "Barbara Bush: The Steel Behind the Smile," Newsweek, June 22, 1992. See also LSY, 425–27.

406 When the celebrity biographer Kitty Kelley "Barbara Bush: The Steel Behind the Smile," Newsweek, June 22, 1992.

406 "a funny, sometimes acerbic woman" Ibid. McDaniel added: "The joke in Washington is that Bush selected Dan Quayle as vice president to ensure that someone at his side would provide an adoring glance." (Ibid.)

406 "She really is the leader" Author interview with GHWB.

406 "She never becomes cross" Ibid.

406 "She's very perceptive" Ibid.

407 In East Berlin AWT, 291–92; 291–301 covers much ground on reunification.

407 suprisingly hard-line set of proposals Ibid., 292.

407 Baker saw that Ibid.

407 The Soviets needed some reassurance Ibid.

407 BUSH UNDERSTOOD GORBACHEV'S POSITION   Ibid., 294. "We needed a bold proposal if it was to win over the Soviets to German membership in NATO," Bush recalled. (Ibid.)

407 WITH SCOWCROFT AND OTHERS   Ibid., 292–93. See also "NATO Military Strategy," July 1990, NATO—Strategy (8), Subject Files, Heather Wilson Files, NSC (OAID CF00293–008).

407 A JULY SUMMIT IN LONDON   For background on the summit, see GHWB to François Mitterrand, April 17, 1990, NATO Summit—June 1990, Subject Files, John A. Gordon Files, NSC (OAID CF01640–025).

407 THE KEY PROVISIONS OF BUSH'S PROPOSAL   *AWT,* 294–95.

407 FROM LONDON, THATCHER   *AWT,* 293–95. See also GHWB to Margaret Thatcher, n.d., NATO Summit—June 1990, Subject Files, John A. Gordon Files, NSC (OAID CF01640–025). Information within the letter suggests it was drafted and sent prior to June 25, 1990.

407 THATCHER WANTED TO START OVER   *AWT,* 294–95. See also "Draft Summit Declaration: London Declaration on a Transformed North Atlantic Alliance," June 21, 1990, Subject Files, John A. Gordon Files, NSC (CF01646–024).

407 "LYNDON HAS ONE THING IN COMMON"   BPB diary, June 18, 2000.

408 THE PRESIDENT MADE   *AWT,* 295.

408 GORBACHEV GOT THE MESSAGE   Ibid.

408 THE SITUATION IN LITHUANIA   Ibid.

408 GORBACHEV FACED A TUMULTUOUS   Ibid.

408 IN MID-JULY, HELMUT KOHL   Ibid., 295–96; Naftali, *GHWB,* 99–100. See also *NYT,* July 15, 1990.

408 IT WAS A DEAL GORBACHEV FELT   *AWT,* 295–96.

408 WATCHING FROM WASHINGTON   Ibid., 296–97.

408 WHO IN TURN CREDITED THE BUSH-LED COALITION   GHWB, "Telcon with President Mikhail Gorbachev of the Soviet Union," July 17, 1990, Presidential Telcon Files, Presidential Correspondence Files, BSC. Reflecting on German reunification, Gorbachev told Bush: "The results take into consideration our common interests—of Germany, yours and ours. I believe that without the meeting in Washington and at Camp David, without the results of the NATO Summit and the London Declaration, without the major work in my conversation with Kohl and your talks with Kohl, without the activities of our foreign economic agencies, without this real political action it would have been difficult to arrive at the proximity in our points of view. We achieved all this because we understood each other's position. We tried to take into account each other's views." (Ibid.)

408 IT WAS THE KIND OF MESSAGE   Engel, "A Better World . . . but Don't Get Carried Away," by Jon Engel with "Personal diplomacy mattered to George H. W. Bush, and served as one of the three fundamental pillars of his diplomatic style alongside his penchant for stability and sovereignty, and his faith in multilateral solutions to global problems." (Ibid.)

THIRTY-SIX: *I've Got to Do What I Think Is Right*

409 IF WE DIDN'T HAVE THIS   GHWB diary, July 24, 1990.

409 READ MY LIPS: I LIED   Greene, *Presidency of George Bush,* 84.

409 THE LATE SPRING NIGHTS   GHWB diary, May 13, 1990.

409 ONE OF THE FIRST SUGGESTIONS   Author interviews with Dan Quayle and John Sununu. See also Sununu, *Quiet Man,* 164–65; and Quayle, *Standing Firm,* 191–92.

409   "WE DON'T NEED"   Sununu, *Quiet Man*, 165.

409   AT THE FEDERAL RESERVE, ALAN GREENSPAN   See, for instance, Darman, *Who's in Control?*, 201–2; Himelfarb and Perotti, *Principle Over Politics?*, 55–58. See also David J. Stockton to Alan Greenspan, "The Implications for Monetary Policy of a Major Fiscal Initiative," June 4, 1990, CEA Budget Summit Agreement Spring 1990, John B. Taylor Files, Council of Economic Advisors, GBPL (Document 8709).

410   SEQUESTRATION   Darman, *Who's in Control?*, 237. See also Naftali, *GHWB*, 97.

410   "I KNOW I'M GOING TO HAVE"   GHWB diary, March 20, 1990.

410   THE SAVINGS-AND-LOAN BAILOUT   Naftali, *GHWB*, 73–75.

410   THE GENERAL ACCOUNTING OFFICE HAD SAID SO   Greene, *Presidency of George Bush*, 79–80; Darman, *Who's in Control?*, 200.

410   BUSH HAD LONG SUSPECTED   GHWB diary entries for May 14, June 8, July 23, October 24, 29, and November 6, 1989.

410   "CONSERVATIVES STRONGLY OPPOSE"   Ibid., March 20, 1990.

410   OTHER OPTIONS INCLUDED   Ibid. See also Secretary of Housing and Urban Development Jack Kemp to GHWB, "Re: Capital Gains Question," December 25, 1990, Post-Budget Summit (1), John H. Sununu Files, Office of the Chief of Staff of the President, GBPL (Document 12337).

410   "WE'RE GOING TO HAVE TO"   GHWB diary, March 20, 1990.

410   HE HAD A RESPITE . . . IN EARLY MAY   Ibid., May 1–2, 1990.

410   THE VISIT WAS SWEET BUT PAINFUL   Ibid.

411   BUSH KEPT UP HIS PERSONAL DIPLOMACY   Ibid., May 6, 1990.

411   A WHITE HOUSE LECTURE   Ibid.

411   "OH, TO BE 42"   Ibid.

411   AFTER THE LECTURE   Darman, *Who's in Control?*, 250–51; Greene, *Presidency of George Bush*, 83–84; *LSY*, 432–34.

411   THERE MUST BE, MITCHELL SAID   Darman, *Who's in Control?*, 250–51.

411   THE WHITE HOUSE AGREED   Ibid., 251.

412   NOW A POSSIBILITY   Naftali, *GHWB*, 98.

412   ON AIR FORCE ONE   Darman, *Who's in Control?*, 252–53.

412   "THE BIG SUBJECT THIS MORNING"   GHWB diary, May 10, 1990.

412   "WE'RE GETTING POUNDED"   Ibid., May 15, 1990.

412   AT A MEETING OF THE REPUBLICAN BUDGET LEADERSHIP   Darman, *Who's in Control?*, 259.

412   "IF WE CAN GET"   Ibid.

412   IN THE SAME SESSION   Ibid., 260.

412   THE ADMINISTRATION'S HOPE   Sununu, *Quiet Man*, 193, 198.

412   SIGNALED THEY COULD "LIVE WITH"   Author interview with John Sununu.

412   THE NEXT MORNING   Darman, *Who's in Control?*, 260.

413   "MY DOG WASN'T EVEN"   Ibid., 261.

413   "WHAT DO YOU PROPOSE?"   Ibid.

413   FOLEY SPOKE FOR THE GROUP   Ibid., 261–62.

413   FOLEY HAD SPOKEN "SIMPLY"   Ibid., 262.

413   "OKAY," BUSH SAID   Ibid.

413   "IT DID DESTROY ME"   Author interview with GHWB.

413   "I PAID A BIG PRICE"   Ibid.

414   HE WAS, THEREFORE, WILLING   Greene, *Presidency of George Bush*, 86–87.

414   "THE MOOD WAS GOOD"   Darman, *Who's in Control?*, 262.

414   MEMORIALIZATION OF THE AGREEMENT   Ibid., 262–64.

414   "WHERE ARE WE"   Ibid., 262.

414 INSTEAD OF KILLING THE IDEA Ibid.

414 HE WROTE A STATEMENT Ibid., 262–63.

414 WISELY, SUNUNU ADDED THE PHRASE Author interview with John Sununu.

414 SUNUNU HOPED THE ALTERATION Ibid.

415 "IT IS CLEAR TO ME" "Statement on the Federal Budget Negotiations," June 26, 1990, *Public Papers of the Presidents of the United States: George Bush, 1990,* 868.

415 NEWT GINGRICH LEARNED ABOUT THE TAXES Author interview with Newt Gingrich.

415 "IN MY MIND" Ibid.

415 WHEN GINGRICH ALLY VIN WEBER Author interview with Vin Weber.

415 "YOU'RE KIDDING" Quayle, *Standing Firm,* 192–93.

415 "YOU NEED TO ROLL THIS DAMN THING" Author interview with Dan Quayle.

416 "WE FEEL HE SAID THE RIGHT THING" *NYT,* June 27, 1990.

416 BAKER AND BUSH EXCHANGED NOTES "Exchange of Notes Between GB & JAB," June 26, 1990, box 288, James A. Baker III Papers, Princeton.

416 "YOU'RE NOT KNOWN FOR MUCH" Author interview with Roger Ailes.

416 "IT WAS TWO YEARS AGO" Ibid.

416 "I'LL LET THE STATEMENT" *NYT,* June 27, 1990.

416 THE BUSHES HOSTED A BARBECUE GHWB diary, June 26, 1990; "Remarks at a White House Barbecue for Members of Congress," June 26, 1990, *Public Papers of the Presidents of the United States: George Bush, 1990,* 872.

416 "OUR PEOPLE WERE" GHWB diary, June 26, 1990.

417 "LOOK, I KNEW" *Public Papers of the Presidents of the United States: George Bush, 1990,* 881.

417 "HE TRULY BELIEVED THAT THE COUNTRY" Author interview with Dan Quayle.

418 "EVERYONE WANTS TO PILE ON" Darman, *Who's in Control?,* 266. Nixon also reached out to try to reassure Bush. "As you know, I had to burn a lot of my own speeches and eat a lot of words when I went to China in 1972. What mattered most was not that I had changed my mind, but that I had done what I thought was best for the country and for the cause of peace in the world." (Richard Nixon to GHWB, June 29, 1990, Richard M. Nixon Library.) Bush took pains to appear strong to his old chief. "Your letter was very comforting to me," Bush replied. "The heat has been predictably intense but nothing that we can't handle in the long run." (GHWB to Richard Nixon, July 4, 1990, Richard M. Nixon Library.)

419 CONTROVERSY OVER NEIL BUSH'S INVOLVEMENT Naftali, *GHWB,* 73–75; *LSY,* 395–97. See also GHWB diary, July 11, July 14, 1990; GWB, *41,* 222–23.

419 "MR. PERFECT" Author interview with BPB.

419 "[I'M] . . . WORRIED ABOUT NEIL" GHWB diary, July 11, 1990.

419 BUSH NEVER LET NEIL KNOW Author interview with Neil Bush.

419 (THE IMPORTANT HISTORIC THOUGHTS) Author interview with GWB. See also GWB, *41,* 222–23.

419 "WE NEVER HAD" Author interview with Neil Bush.

419 BUSH MET AT THE WHITE HOUSE GHWB diary, July 22, 1990.

419 THREE NAMES WERE UNDER CONSIDERATION Ibid.

419 DAVID SOUTER, A JUDGE FROM NEW HAMPSHIRE Sununu, *Quiet Man,* 342; Naftali, *GHWB,* 134.

419 JONES WAS THE MOST INTERESTING CHOICE GHWB diary, July 22, 1990.

419 SOUTER EMERGED IN THE CONVERSATIONS Ibid., July 22, 1990. See also handwritten notes of phone calls related to the appointment of David Souter, July 24, 1990, Supreme Court—David Souter, Sarah DeCamp Files, Office of Public Liaison, GBPL (Document 4166).

419   "SEEMED TO BE RIGHT"   "GHWB Handwritten Notes of Private Meeting with David Souter," Monday, July 23, 1990, Bios. Supreme Court Nominees, DF.

419   "I DON'T WANT"   GHWB diary, July 23, 1990.

420   "A HUGE MISTAKE"   Author interview with GHWB.

420   THE FAILURE TO NOMINATE JONES   Author interview with Dan Quayle.

420   HIS DEFENSE OF LITHUANIA   Naftali, *GHWB*, 98, argues that Bush had "risked his international prestige to slow events in the Baltics long enough to permit the inclusion of a united Germany in NATO" and then "threw himself into negotiating a bipartisan compromise at home that would heal the open budget sore. In each case, Bush sacrificed short-term political gain for what he considered the national interest." (Ibid.)

420   "THE RIGHT-WINGERS"   GHWB diary, July 23, 1990.

420   HE AWOKE ON WEDNESDAY, AUGUST 1, 1990   Ibid., August 1, 1990.

420   "ALL IN ALL"   Ibid.

420   BUSH TOOK A BREAK   *AWT*, 302.

420   BUSH WAS IN A T-SHIRT   Ibid.

420   "MR. PRESIDENT, IT LOOKS VERY BAD"   Ibid.

THIRTY-SEVEN: *This Will Not Stand*

421   I FEEL TENSION   GHWB diary, August 6, 1990.

421   IF IRAQ WINS   *AWT*, 319.

421   RICHARD HAASS BRIEFED THE PRESIDENT   Ibid., 302.

421   "SO MUCH FOR CALLING"   Ibid.

421   THE INVASION HAD BEGUN   Norman Friedman, *Desert Victory: The War for Kuwait* (Annapolis, Md., 1991), 36.

421   EIGHT-TENTHS OF A MILE   Powell with Persico, *My American Journey*, 463.

421   SADDAM HUSSEIN HAD CONTROLLED IRAQ   Friedman, *Desert Victory*, 17–34. See also Patterson, *Restless Giant*, 230.

421   A JUNE 1990 COVER STORY   *U.S. News & World Report*, June 4, 1990.

421   TO AVOID HAVING TO REPAY KUWAIT   Haass, *War of Necessity*, 55.

421   ARGUMENT OVER THE RUMAILA OIL FIELDS   Friedman, *Desert Victory*, 11.

422   (THE IRAQIS ACCUSED)   Haass, *War of Necessity*, 55.

422   THE "19TH PROVINCE"   Rick Atkinson, *Crusade: The Untold Story of the Persian Gulf War* (New York, 1993), 53.

422   IF SADDAM WERE TO HOLD   Cheney with Cheney, *In My Time*, 184; Thomas Friedman, "U.S. Gulf Policy: Vague 'Vital Interests,'" *NYT*, August 12, 1990. "The oil price argument goes as follows: If Iraq is able to get away with annexing Kuwait, it will control 20 percent of the world oil reserves," Friedman wrote. "If, in turn, it could also intimidate Saudi Arabia, the Iraqis would have influence over 45 percent of the world's oil reserves." (Friedman's article is also authoritatively cited in Micah L. Sifry and Christopher Cerf, *The Gulf War: History, Documents, Opinions* [New York, 1991], 203–6.) However, Friedman also wrote: "At root, then, the vital interests to which President Bush referred are both genuine and significant, given America's current dependence on foreign oil. Laid bare, American policy in the gulf comes down to this: troops have been sent to retain control of oil in the hands of a pro-American Saudi Arabia, so prices remain low." (Ibid.)

422   AND IF HE WERE TO USE   Cheney with Cheney, *In My Time*, 184.

422   GIVEN HIS PROVEN CAPACITIES   Haass, *War of Necessity*, 48.

422   SADDAM HAD ISSUED THREATS   State Department cable, Secretary of State (James

A. Baker, III) to all Middle East diplomatic posts, July 24, 1990, Working Files Iraq Pre-8/2/90–12/90 (3), Richard Haass Files, NSC.

422 IN LATE JULY, SADDAM HAD SUMMONED   State Department cable, Embassy Baghdad (Ambassador April Glaspie) to Washington D.C., July 25, 1990, Working Files Iraq Pre-8/2/90–12/90 (2), Richard Haass Files, NSC.

422 A FULL READING OF THE RELEVANT DOCUMENTS   Ibid. See also memo for GHWB, "Points to Be Made [in a proposed telcon] with Iraqi President Saddam Hussein (Not Used)," August 1, 1990, Working Files Iraq Pre-8/2/90–12/90 (2), Richard Haass Files, NSC; Sandra Charles through Richard Haass to Brent Scowcroft, "Inter Agency Meeting on the Persian Gulf," July 27, 1990, and State Department cable, Embassy Baghdad (Ambassador April Glaspie) to Washington D.C., July 29, 1990, both in Working Files Iraq Pre-8/2/90–12/90 (3), Richard Haass Files, NSC. Jeffrey Engel, "The Gulf War at the End of the Cold War and Beyond," in *Into the Desert: Reflections on the Gulf War* (New York: Oxford University Press, 2013), 28–32, provides a comprehensive and balanced treatment of the Glaspie-Hussein meeting and its effect on the beginning of the Persian Gulf War.

422 AS EARLY AS 1943   Engel, *Into the Desert*, 36–37.

423 WHEN THE SOVIETS INVADED AFGHANISTAN   Ibid., 37.

423 THEN, IN OCTOBER 1981   Steven R. Weisman, "Reagan Says U.S. Would Bar a Takeover in Saudi Arabia That Imperiled Flow of Oil," *NYT*, October 2, 1981. See also Friedman, *Desert Victory*, 44–46.

423 THE UNITED STATES "WOULD NOT ALLOW"   *NYT*, October 2, 1981.

423 "THERE'S NO WAY"   Ibid.

423 AT TEN P.M. OR SO   *AWT*, 302–3.

423 THE PRESIDENT ASKED   Ibid., 303, "While I was prepared to deal with this crisis unilaterally if necessary," Bush recalled, "I wanted the United Nations involved as part of our first response, starting with a strong condemnation of Iraq's attack on a fellow member," Bush recalled. (Ibid.)

423 IN AN INTERAGENCY TELECONFERENCE   Ibid., 304–5.

423 BOYDEN GRAY DRAFTED   Ibid., 305.

423 BUSH ALSO ORDERED   Ibid., 314.

423 AFTER A QUICK SHOWER   Ibid.

423 "IN DISARRAY"   GHWB diary, August 2, 1990.

424 "WHAT'S HAPPENING IS"   Ibid.

424 "IT IS NOT"   Ibid.

424 ON IRAQ, BUSH HAD GOOD NEWS   Ibid.

424 THE SOVIET UNION, A LONGTIME ALLY OF IRAQ'S   *AWT*, 314; Baker with DeFrank, *Politics of Diplomacy*, 1–16.

424 BUSH SPOKE WITH DAWN   White House Telephone Memorandum, Signal Switchboard, August 2, 1990, DF.

424 AT 8:05 A.M.   *Public Papers of the Presidents of the United States, George Bush: 1990*, 1083–85. *AWT*, 315. See also Minutes of NSC/Deputies Committee Meeting, August 2, 1990, NSC Meeting—August 2, 1990 Re: Iraqi Invasion of Kuwait, Presidential Meetings Files, Richard Haass Files, NSC.

424 THE PRESS POOL WAS INVITED IN   *Public Papers of the Presidents of the United States: George Bush, 1990*, 1083–85.

424 HELEN THOMAS OF UPI   Ibid., 1084.

424 "WE'RE NOT DISCUSSING INTERVENTION"   Ibid.

424 BUSH SIGNALED THAT   *AWT*, 315. As Scowcroft recalled: "The President's comment that he was not contemplating intervention has been taken by some to indicate he

was passive or indecisive about the notion of doing anything about the Iraqi invasion until Margaret Thatcher 'put some stiffening in his spine' at their meeting later that day. Such speculation is wrong, though his choice of words was not felicitous." (Ibid.) See also Naftali, *GHWB,* 103.

424   "The truth is"   *AWT,* 315. As noted, Scowcroft believed the president's language, while "not felicitous," was "picked with two thoughts in mind: First, don't say anything at this early point which would telegraph his thinking. Second, make clear that the NSC meeting was not a decision session but a discussion of the situation and options for reacting." (Ibid.) Bush himself added: "I did know for sure that the aggression had to be stopped, and Kuwait's sovereignty restored. We had a big job ahead of us in shaping opinion at home and abroad and could little afford bellicose mistakes at that start." (Ibid.)

424   Evidence of Bush's evolution   GHWB diary, August 2–5, 1990. See also Wicker, *GHWB,* 152–61.

425   "My fear is of"   GHWB, "Telephone Call to Prime Minister Thatcher of the United Kingdom," Oval Office, August 3, 1990, Presidential Telcon Files, Presidential Correspondence Files, BSC.

425   "a bit chaotic"   *AWT,* 315.

425   It was also unwieldy   Minutes of NSC/Deputies Committee Meeting, August 2, 1990, NSC Meeting—August 2, 1990 Re: Iraqi Invasion of Kuwait, Presidential Meetings Files, Richard Haass Files, NSC.

425   "It was a big thing"   Author interview with Richard Haass.

425   Much of the talk   *AWT,* 315–18; Naftali, *GHWB,* 103–4.

425   "a fait accompli"   *AWT,* 317.

425   described himself as "appalled"   Ibid.

425   simply a "crisis du jour"   Ibid.

425   "the major crisis of our time"   Ibid.

425   "It's halfway around the world"   GHWB diary, August 3, 1990.

425   "That was one of"   Author interview with Richard Haass.

425   "I agree"   Ibid.

425   Bush's shift from   *AWT,* 318.

425   Bush left at 9:50 a.m.   Schedule of the President, August 2, 1990, DF.

426   ("I really implore you")   *AWT,* 318. For an incisive view of Bush's telephone diplomacy in the Persian Gulf crisis, see Jeffrey Crean, "War on the Line: Telephone Diplomacy in the Making and Maintenance of the Desert Storm Coalition," *Diplomacy and Statecraft,* 26, no. 1 (March 2015): 124–38. See also Wicker, *GHWB,* 152–53.

426   "George, give us"   *AWT,* 318.

426   painting a grimmer portrait   Author interview with Richard Haass.

426   "I am as aware as you are"   Haass, *War of Necessity,* 62.

426   At the Pentagon   Cheney with Cheney, *In My Time,* 186.

426   In Colorado, Bush sat down with Thatcher   *AWT,* 319. See also Naftali, *GHWB,* 104.

426   a U.S.-Soviet statement   *AWT,* 319.

426   "If Iraq wins"   Ibid., 319–20.

426   Then they met the press   "Remarks and a Question-and-Answer Session with Reporters in Aspen, Colorado, Following a Meeting with Prime Minister Margaret Thatcher of the United Kingdom" August 2, 1990, *Public Papers of the Presidents of the United States: George Bush, 1990,* 1085–88.

427   In a large tent   GHWB diary, August 3, 1990.

427   some of which had been drafted   *AWT,* 318.

427 "Even in a world" "Remarks at the Aspen Institute Symposium in Aspen, Colorado," August 2, 1990, *Public Papers of the Presidents of the United States: George Bush, 1990,* 1089–94.

427 After the speech GHWB diary, August 3, 1990.

427 Fahd was "emotional" *AWT,* 320–21.

427 "He doesn't realize" Ibid., 320.

427 Fahd asked for more time Ibid., 321.

427 He "held back" GHWB diary, August 3, 1990.

427 "King Fahd's hesitation" *AWT,* 321.

427 "a historical Arab propensity" Ibid.

428 "We couldn't have a solo" Ibid.

428 At dusk Bush headed back GHWB diary, August 3, 1990.

428 had a more definitive view Ibid.; Naftali, *GHWB,* 105.

428 "The enormity of Iraq" GHWB diary, August 3, 1990.

428 "All the intelligence shows" *AWT,* 322.

428 (In 1990 terms) For background on the world's oil supply over time, see http://www.eia.gov/cfapps/ipdbproject/iedindex3.cfm?tid=5&pid=57&aid=6&cid=regions&syid=1990&eyid=2015&unit=BB.

428 The Arab reluctance Bush had sensed GHWB diary, August 3, 1990.

428 "The Arabs don't seem" Ibid.

428 Yemen's Ali Abdullah Saleh, an ally Ibid.

428 "Saleh got me" Ibid.

428 "Fears mount that" Ibid.

429 On Saturday, August 4, 1990, Bush convened *AWT,* 327.

429 might enforce an economic embargo Ibid., 326, 328.

429 "Both of them are" GHWB diary, August 5, 1990.

429 a dodginess whose roots had become clearer *AWT,* 325.

429 A popular diplomat "Who's Who in the House of Saud," *WP,* December 22, 2002; *WP,* January 7, 1994; Atkinson, *Crusade,* 196. Bob Woodward once referred to Bandar as an "Arab Gatsby." (Woodward, *The Commanders,* 200.)

429 After laying out the threat *AWT,* 325.

429 "He seemed ill at ease" Ibid.

429 Bandar was candid Ibid.

429 called for 150,000 to 200,000 troops Cheney with Cheney, *In My Time,* 187.

429 "We're serious this time" Ibid.

430 "We didn't have time" Ibid.

430 concerns about Muslim reaction Author interview with Richard Haass. See also Wicker, *GHWB,* 155–56.

430 Iran experienced division in the U.S. *AWT,* 448.

430 "My worry is the lack of Saudi will" "Minutes of NSC Meeting on Iraqi Invasion of Kuwait," August 4, 1990, Iraq—August 2, 1990–December 1990 (8), Working Files, Richard N. Haass Files, NSC (CF01478-030).

430 Fahd agreed to receive *AWT,* 329; Cheney with Cheney, *In My Time,* 186–87. In the confusion of the time, Bush had apparently not been told that a team was being prepared to go to Saudi Arabia until he heard about it in a call with Fahd. (GHWB, "Telcon with King Fahd of Saudi Arabia," August 4, 1990, Camp David, Presidential Telcon Files, Presidential Correspondence Files, BSC.)

430 Still, the king continued to evade *AWT,* 329.

430 "We will get the team" *AWT,* 330.

430 Bandar met with Haass, *War of Necessity,* 67.

430 THE SAUDIS . . . "HAD A CHOICE" Ibid.

430 WORD REACHED THE PRESIDENT GHWB diary, August, 5, 1990.

430 "BANDAR HAS DOUBLE-DEALT US" Ibid.

431 DECIDED TO INSIST *AWT,* 330. See also Cheney with Cheney, *In My Time,* 188.

431 "A SAUDI REJECTION" *AWT,* 330.

431 MADE A CALL HOME Haass, *War of Necessity,* 67.

431 AFTER CHENEY ARRIVED IN SAUDI ARABIA Author interview with Dick Cheney.

431 ARGUED FOR WAITING Ibid.

431 FAHD BRUSHED ABDULLAH'S WORDS ASIDE Ibid.

431 "THE KUWAITIS WAITED" Ibid.

431 "OKAY, WE'LL DO IT" Ibid.

431 BUSH CANCELED A SCHEDULED SUNDAY GHWB diary, August 5, 1990.

431 THE CHINESE HAD AGREED Ibid.

431 THERE WAS AN UPCOMING VOTE Ibid.

431 "I DON'T KNOW" Ibid.

431 AS MARINE ONE FLEW Ibid.

431 "IT'S BEEN PROBABLY" Ibid.

432 "THIS IS A TERRIBLY SERIOUS PROBLEM" Ibid.

432 "IF INDEED THE IRAQIS" Ibid.

432 BUSH STEPPED OFF THE HELICOPTER *AWT,* 332; Haass, *War of Necessity,* 69.

432 A REPORT THAT INCLUDED Author interview with Richard Haass. It was, Haass recalled, "a roundup of reaction and suggested talking points. What I showed him were different comments in the Arab world—there was a kind of pattern of passivity there." As to what Bush said next, Haass recalled: "My gut is that it was an accumulated frustration. All of his frustration bubbled over on that Sunday." The key point that Bush had come to: "Better to defend Saudi Arabia than to liberate it," Haass recalled. "One way or another we weren't going to allow Saddam to have Saudi Arabia." (Ibid.)
     Bush also had a set of typewritten talking points in hand.

     —I have had a busy weekend needless to say.
     —I have spoken over the phone with Chancellor Kohl, PM Thatcher, PM Mulroney of Canada, PM Kaifu, President Mitterrand, King Fahd, and President Ozal of Turkey. I also had a chance to speak to the Amir of Kuwait.
     —I am glad to say that in every instance I encountered strong support for our basic objectives: to bring about the immediate, complete and unconditional withdrawal of all Iraqi forces from Kuwait and the restoration of the legitimate government there.
     —I have also met with my National Security Council, and I will be convening the NSC again this afternoon at 5 to review developments and to continue to consider the options.
     —Let me just add that tomorrow I plan to meet here with Mrs. Thatcher and also with NATO Secretary General Manfred Woerner. I also expect to be in touch with other leaders in order to continue to build support for the strongest possible international response to Iraqi aggression.

     On the folded paper, Bush wrote: "File: Press remarks upon arrival 3 PM helicopter." Then he added: "Not read in entirety." (GHWB, annotated talking points, Sunday, August 5, 1990, DF.)

432 SADDAM HUSSEIN HAD CHALLENGED BUSH'S UNIVERSE Naftali, *GHWB*, 105–6; Engel, "A Better World . . . but Don't Get Carried Away," *Diplomatic History*, especially 34–35. Of a post–Cold War world, Engel wrote: "Bush believed it was a president's job to shepherd this new world through its period of change, to contain the violence and instability he could not control, and to impose structure and order whenever possible. Defeating Iraq and liberating Kuwait, removing Noriega, and pushing a humanitarian solution in Somalia were more than geopolitical necessities to his mind. These were opportunities to show the world at this critical juncture in history that order itself would prevail, that the international system would indeed function to promote stability and to protect sovereignty absent the Cold War's structural impositions. . . . 'Appeasement does not work,' Bush said in response to Saddam Hussein's assault on Kuwait." (Ibid., 34–35.)

432 HE DESCRIBED, IN GENERAL TERMS "Remarks and an Exchange with Reporters on the Iraqi Invasion of Kuwait," August 5, 1990, *Public Papers of the Presidents of the United States: George Bush, 1990*, 1100–2.

432 I'M NOT GOING TO DISCUSS Ibid., 1102.

433 "I'VE GOT TO GO" Ibid.

THIRTY-EIGHT: *No Blood for Oil*

434 I CAN'T SEE HOW GHWB diary, August 22, 1990.

434 "HOW'D I DO?" Dan Quayle interview, George H. W. Bush Oral History Project, Miller Center.

434 "WHERE'D YOU GET THAT" Ibid.

434 "IT WAS A VERY" Ibid.

434 "I JUST GOT A NEW MISSION" Author interview with Colin Powell. See also Powell with Persico, *My American Journey*, 466–67.

434 "DICK, YOU ARE AUTHORIZED" "Cheney to POTUS," August 6, 1990, box 288, James A. Baker III Papers, Princeton. See also GHWB diary, August 6, 1990. Margaret Thatcher, who was still in the United States, was in the office when Bush spoke with Cheney. Bush briefed her but asked for confidentiality. (GHWB diary, August 6, 1990.)

434 "I FEEL GREAT PRESSURE" GHWB diary, August 6, 1990.

435 SADDAM'S FIRST DIRECT WORDS *AWT*, 337.

435 "CONVEY TO PRESIDENT BUSH" Ibid.

435 "IT WAS YOUR LEADERSHIP" GHWB, "Telephone Call from Prime Minister Thatcher of the United Kingdom," August 9, 1990, Presidential Telcon Files, Presidential Correspondence Files, BSC.

435 BRIAN MULRONEY OF CANADA CAME DOWN GHWB diary, August 7, 1990.

435 "I PAY THE PRICE" Ibid.

435 AROUND A QUARTER TILL THREE Ibid.

435 MANFRED WÖRNER . . . HAD WARNED BUSH Ibid.

435 "WE WILL BE THERE" Ibid.

435 "MITTERRAND SURPRISES ME" Ibid.

435 NEXT WAS A CALL TO MUBARAK Ibid.

435 "HE THOUGHT KING HUSSEIN" Ibid.

435 BUSH'S DIPLOMATIC CALLS WERE DONE Ibid.

436 "I'M SAYING TO MYSELF" Ibid.

436 "THE TROOPS ARE UNDER WAY" Ibid.

436 TO CHECK HIS NERVES Ibid., August 8, 1990.

436 "Appeasement does not work"   "Address to the Nation Announcing the Deployment of United States Armed Forces to Saudi Arabia," August 8, 1990, *Public Papers of the Presidents of the United States: George Bush, 1990*, 1107–9.

437 Thirty-five countries would join   Wilentz, *Age of Reagan*, 298.

437 Resisting advice that he remain   GHWB diary, August 11, 1990.

437 "The press are sniping"   Ibid.

437 With a large   Greene, *Presidency of George Bush*, 109.

437 Worries that he might   AWT, 307; Friedman, *Desert Victory*, 61–62; Atkinson, *Crusade*, 296.

437 "I like wrestling"   GHWB diary, August 11, 1990.

437 The busiest of days   Ibid., August 16, 1990.

437 Later that morning King Hussein of Jordan   Ibid.

437 The king pressed   Ibid.

437 "There isn't any"   Ibid.

437 "Hussein refuses to admit"   Ibid.

438 "This is not just"   Handwritten notes of meeting between GHWB and King Hussein of Jordan, August 16, 1990, Iraq—August 2, 1990—December 1990 (2), Working Files, Richard Haass Files, NSC (CF01478-024).

438 The Jordanian king left about two thirty   GHWB diary, August 16, 1990.

438 To be followed by Prince Saud   Handwritten notes of meeting between GHWB and Prince Saud, August 16, 1990, Iraq—August 2, 1990—December 1990 (2), Working Files, Richard Haass Files, NSC (CF01478-024).

438 "God knows it may"   GHWB diary, August 17, 1990.

438 The taking of American hostages   Ibid., August 16, 1990.

438 Then, at a quarter to ten   Ibid., August 17, 1990; AWT, 349–50; Naftali, *GHWB*, 107.

438 "Blatant hostage holding"   GHWB Diary, August 17, 1990.

438 Soon Bush had to make   AWT, 351–52; Naftali, *GHWB*, 108–9.

438 The president, Scowcroft, Cheney, and Bob Gates   Ibid.

438 It fell to Bush   AWT, 352.

438 "Well, all right, George"   Ibid.

438 "a marvelous expression"   GHWB diary, August 27, 1990.

438 The UN Security Council quickly passed   AWT, 352.

438 ("In the meantime")   Naftali, *GHWB*, 109.

439 "The more I think of this"   GHWB diary, August 22, 1990.

439 Bush called the Situation Room   Ibid., August 27, 1990; September 5, 1990.

439 Nevertheless, there were stories   Ibid., August 19, 1990.

439 On a fishing excursion   AWT, 353. See also Naftali, *GHWB*, 110.

439 "I asked impatiently"   AWT, 353.

439 The broader conversation   Naftali, *GHWB*, 109–10; Engel, "A Better World . . . But Don't Get Carried Away," *Diplomatic History*, January 2010, 25–46. (I am also grateful to Professor Engel for his consultation on these points.)

439 Had Franklin Roosevelt's old vision   Naftali, *GHWB*, 109–10.

439 Perhaps a "new world order" was at hand   Sparrow, *Strategist*, 479–87, discusses the "new world order" phrase and the overall conduct of Bush foreign policy.

439 The gentle Atlantic   AWT, 353.

439 Ronald Reagan, who was about to   GHWB diary, September 5, 1990.

439 "He's looking forward"   Ibid.

440 Bush himself was refreshed   Ibid., August 27, 1990.

440 "When I was younger"   Ibid.

440 WOKE TO NEWS   Ibid., August 29, 1990.

440 "THE MORE I THINK OF IT"   Ibid.

440 "IT HAS BEEN PERSONALIZED"   Ibid., September 4, 1990.

440 IN SEPTEMBER, BUSH TRAVELED TO HELSINKI   *AWT*, 361–62.

440 "I THINK IT'S IMPORTANT TO GORBY"   GHWB diary, September 9, 1990; GHWB, Helsinki, Finland, "Meeting with President Mikhail Gorbachev of the Soviet Union," Helsinki, Finland, September 9, 1990, Presidential Memcons, Presidential Correspondence, Files, BSC.

440 "ALL COUNTRIES IN THE WEST"   GHWB diary, September 9, 1990.

441 "THE HARD-HATS CHARGE"   Ibid., September 19, 1990.

441 "YOU KNOW HOW I FEEL"   Ibid., September 11, 1990.

441 "CRITICISM OF U.S. POLICY"   *NYT*, September 20, 1990.

441 ANTIWAR SENTIMENT GREW APACE   See, for instance, Stephan Chapman, "In the Persian Gulf a Great Risk for an Unworthy Cause," *Chicago Tribune*, August 23, 1990; Ford Risley, "America's Mood," Ibid., September 2, 1990; David Gonzalez, "Talk of Ground War Intensifies Mood at Antiwar Demonstration," *NYT*, February 18, 1991; Elsa Walsh, "14 Arrested in Clash Outside White House," *WP*, January 17, 1991; "More Than 400 Are Arrested in California Antiwar Protest," *WP*, January 16, 1991.

441 "JIM BAKER IS WORRIED"   GHWB diary, August 16, 1990.

441 AFTER A MEETING ON IRAQ AT CAMP DAVID   Quayle, *Standing Firm*, 208.

441 THESE DOUBTS AND CONCERNS WERE COMING   GHWB diary, September 22, 1990.

442 HE WAS CLEAR IN HIS OWN MIND   Ibid.

442 THE PRESIDENT HAD ADDRESSED CONGRESS   "Address Before a Joint Session of the Congress on the Persian Gulf Crisis and the Federal Budget Deficit," September 11, 1990, *Public Papers of the Presidents of the United States: George Bush, 1990*, 1218–22.

442 "IT IS SAID OF ME"   GHWB diary, September 11, 1990.

442 IN THE MIDST   Naftali, *GHWB*, 110–11.

THIRTY-NINE: *Read My Hips*

443 I CAN'T DO THIS   Author interview with Newt Gingrich. See also Newt Gingrich interview in "Conversations with Bill Kristol," November 21, 2014. http://conversationswithbillkristol.org/transcript/newt-gingrich-transcript/.

443 THEY CAN PONTIFICATE   GHWB diary, October 4, 1990.

443 BUSH HAD CONVENED   Darman, *Who's in Control?*, 269–72; GHWB diary, September 7, 1990; Naftali, *GHWB*, 111.

443 "I JUST HOPE"   GHWB, diary, September 7, 1990.

443 HIS MAJOR CONCERNS   *LSY*, 429, 435; Naftali, *GHWB*, 100–111, 140.

443 IT REFLECTED   See, for instance, "More Economists Predict U.S. Recession This Year," *WP*, August 25, 1990; "Greenspan Gives Even Odds That Recession Is Near," *Chicago Tribune*, September 20, 1990. Wicker, *GHWB*, 167–69, is a useful account of the economic realities of the day.

443 ALL WEAKENING THE UNITED STATES AT AN HOUR   Author interview with GWB. The forty-third president made the same point his book *41*: "He felt that he could not afford a budget crisis at home while he was managing a national security crisis abroad." (GWB, *41*, 218.)

443 "LORD, I'VE GOT TWO YEARS"   GHWB diary, August 6, 1990.

443 "I WANT TO"   "Address Before a Joint Session of the Congress on the Persian Gulf Crisis and the Federal Budget Deficit," September 11, 1990, *Public Papers of the Presidents of the United States: George Bush, 1990*, 1218–22.

444 ON SUNDAY, SEPTEMBER 30   *NYT,* October 1, 1990; GHWB diary, October 2, 1990. Darman, *Who's in Control?,* 271–72; Naftali, *GHWB,* 115.

444 THE AGREEMENT WOULD HAVE CUT   Greene, *Presidency of George Bush,* 86.

444 BUT INCREASED TAXES   *Time,* October 22, 1990.

444 THE AGREEMENT ESTABLISHED PAY-AS-YOU-GO RULES   Darman, *Who's in Control?,* 271. See also Greene, *Presidency of George Bush,* 86; Naftali, *GHWB,* 115.

444 NEWT GINGRICH COULD NOT ABIDE   Author interview with Newt Gingrich.

444 IN THE SESSION WITH BUSH   Darman, *Who's in Control?,* 273; author interview with GHWB.

444 "I CAN'T DO THIS"   Author interview with Newt Gingrich. Gingrich told the same story to Bill Kristol. (Newt Gingrich interview, "Conversations with Bill Kristol.")

444 "HAD TO GIVE HIS PITCH"   GHWB diary, October 2, 1990.

444 GINGRICH REPRESENTED A CONSERVATIVE WORLDVIEW   Author interview with Newt Gingrich.

444 BETRAYING THE TAX-CUTTING PRINCIPLES   Ibid.

444 "BUSH WAS A CONNECTICUT MODERATE"   Ibid.

444 THE SHIFTING MEANS OF POLITICS   Author interviews with Newt Gingrich and Vin Weber.

445 GINGRICH DECLINED TO JOIN   Darman, *Who's in Control?,* 273.

445 "THIS ANNOYED ME VERY MUCH"   GHWB diary, October 2, 1990.

445 THE DRIVE FOR A HOUSE MAJORITY   Author interview with Newt Gingrich; Darman, *Who's in Control?,* 279; Naftali, *GHWB,* 115–16.

445 "WHAT IS GOOD"   Darman, *Who's in Control?,* 279–80.

445 STANDING WITH THE OTHER LEADERS   *NYT,* October 1, 1990.

445 "SOMETIMES YOU DON'T GET"   Ibid.

445 AS CNN BROADCAST   Author interview with Newt Gingrich.

445 NOT A "PHONY"   *Public Papers of the Presidents of the United States, George Bush, 1990,* 1326–29.

445 HE HAD A DINNER DATE   Ibid.

446 "TOTALLY UNNECESSARY"   Author interview with Newt Gingrich.

446 "IF HE HAD JUST LOOKED THEM IN THE EYE"   Author interview with Newt Gingrich.

447 "WE WERE STRUGGLING"   GHWB diary, October 2, 1990.

447 "EACH CONGRESSMAN THINKS"   Ibid.

447 "IT'S IN TROUBLE"   GHWB, notes of phone call with Speaker of the House Tom Foley, October 3, 1990, DF.

447 ROSTENKOWSKI CALLED THE PRESIDENT   GHWB, notes of phone call with Dan Rostenkowski, Wednesday, October 3, 1990, DF.

447 "YOU'VE GOT TO GET 51 PERCENT, PAL"   Ibid.

447 "IT IS BUDGET"   GHWB diary, October 4, 1990.

447 BUSH GATHERED THE CABINET   GHWB, notes of phone call with Chancellor Helmut Kohl of the Federal Republic of Germany, October 3, 1990, DF.

447 "ARM-TWISTING" OF "DISGRUNTLED HOUSE"   *USA Today* in White House News Summary, Wednesday, October 3, 1990, DF.

447 "NEWT IS OUT THERE"   GHWB diary, October 4, 1990.

447 ON THE MORNING OF THE FOURTH   Ibid.

447 LATER FOLEY CALLED   Ibid.

447 "I AM MAKING"   Ibid.

447 HE PLACED TWENTY   Ibid. See also Fredrick D. McClure, Assistant to the President for Legislative Affairs, to GHWB, "Additional Telephone Calls re: Budget Resolution," (dated October 4, 1990), October 3, 1990, DF.

447 "SMALL TIME: ONE CONGRESSMAN DOESN'T LIKE"   GHWB diary, October 4–5, 1990.

See also Fredrick D. McClure, Assistant to the President for Legislative Affairs, to GHWB, "Additional Telephone Calls re: Budget Resolution," dated October 4, 1990, October 3, 1990, DF.

448 IN SUNUNU'S WEST WING OFFICE   Author interview with Vin Weber.

448 "DO NOT HESITATE TO DISTANCE"   Ed Rollins, with Tom DeFrank, *Bare Knuckles and Back Rooms: My Life in American Politics* (New York, 1996), 206.

448 A FURIOUS BUSH   Author interview with Vin Weber.

448 "I KNOW WHAT PEOPLE SAY"   Ibid.

448 THE GINGRICH-LED REVOLT   GHWB diary, October 4–5, 1990; John E. Yang and Tom Kenworthy, "House Rejects Deficit Reduction Agreement," *WP,* October 5, 1990.

448 "JUST STOOD ON THE FLOOR"   GHWB diary, October 5, 1990.

448 "THEY CAN PONTIFICATE"   Ibid.

448 "WE CAN'T BE VINDICTIVE"   Ibid.

448 THERE WAS A PARTIAL GOVERNMENT SHUTDOWN   Ibid., October 6, 1990; Greene, *The Presidency of George Bush,* 87.

448 "EVERY CONGRESSMAN CAN FIND"   GHWB diary, October 6, 1990.

448 WHILE JOGGING WITH JEB   Ibid., October 10, 1990; *Time,* October 22, 1990.

448 "NOBODY IS PARTICULARLY"   GHWB diary, October 17, 1990.

449 "WEAKENED POSITION"   Darman, *Who's in Control?,* 273. See also Himelfarb and Perotti, eds., *Principle Over Politics?,* 25–30.

449 THOUGH THE PRESIDENT   Darman, *Who's in Control?,* 273.

449 "I SUPPORTED HIM"   Author interview with Bill Clinton.

FORTY: *The Threat of Impeachment*

450 IF IT STARTS DRAGGING OUT   GHWB diary, November 28, 1990.

450 I HAVE A FEELING   Ibid., January 16, 1991.

450 GAZE AT THE LARGE MAPS   Valdez, *George Herbert Walker Bush,* 107.

450 A STRATEGY TO TRANSFORM   Cheney with Cheney, *In My Time,* 184–209.

450 HALF A MILLION U.S. FORCES   Haass, *War of Necessity,* 8.

450 HE HAD THOROUGHLY ABSORBED THE . . . POWELL DOCTRINE   Rick Atkinson and Bob Woodward, "Gulf Turning Points: Strategy, Diplomacy, Prolonged Buildup Reflects Doctrine of Invincible Force," *WP,* December 2, 1990. In this *Post* piece, Atkinson and Woodward wrote: "Powell's thinking on the subject . . . can be thought of as 'Weinberger plus.' As a one-time military assistant to former Defense Secretary Caspar Weinberger, Powell has been influenced by a 1984 speech entitled, 'The Uses of Military Power,' in which Weinberger laid out his criteria for deploying forces into combat." (*WP,* December 2, 1990.) See also Powell with Persico, *My American Journey,* 302–3, and Walter LaFaber, "The Rise and Fall of Colin Powell and the Powell Doctrine," *Political Science Quarterly,* Vol. 124, No. 1, Spring 2009, 73.

451 MIGHT SIGNAL WEAKNESS   Naftali, *GHWB,* 121.

451 "WORD IS STILL AROUND"   GHWB diary, October 31, 1990.

451 (CARTER LATER ANGERED)   *AWT,* 413–14.

451 "THE FINAL ANALYSIS"   GHWB diary, November 28, 1990.

451 BUSH MET WITH THE CONGRESSIONAL LEADERSHIP   *AWT,* 400–401.

451 "THERE'S GREAT CONCERN"   Ibid., 401.

451 IN BUSH'S NOTES FROM THE MEETING   GHWB, notes of meeting with members of Congress, White House, November 14, 1990, DF.

451 GIVE "SANCTIONS"   Ibid.

451   GEPHARDT BELIEVED   Ibid.

451   BOB DOLE ALONE   Ibid.

451   CONGRESS WAS AT THE CENTER   Author interview with Boyden Gray.

452   BUSH ALLUDED TO THIS POSSIBILITY   GHWB diary, December 12, 1990, January 4 (twice), 12, 13, 1991.

452   "IT IS ONLY THE UNITED STATES"   Ibid., November 28, 1990.

452   "I'M CONVINCED"   Ibid., December 12, 1990. See also Naftali, *GHWB,* 122.

452   "IF YOU'RE WRONG ABOUT THIS"   Author interview with GHWB.

452   AT A THURSDAY, DECEMBER 20, 1990, MEETING   "Notes from Meeting Between President Bush and Mitchell Delegation from Congress," December 20, 1990, Iraq [folder], Shawn Smealie Files, Office of Legislative Affairs, GBPL.

452   "WHAT DO YOU WANT"   Ibid.

452   "COME IN"   Ibid.

452   THE RESPONSE IN THE ROOM   Ibid.

453   "CONGRESS IS IN A TURMOIL"   GHWB diary, January 4, 1991.

453   IN NEW YORK AND AROUND THE WORLD, JIM BAKER   Baker with DeFrank, *Politics of Diplomacy,* 304–28; Greene, *Presidency of George Bush,* 125.

453   BUSH AND BAKER MULLED   GHWB diary, November 28, 1990.

453   "TALKED ABOUT"   Ibid.

453   SOME OF BAKER'S ADVISERS   Author interview with James A. Baker III.

453   HE CITED IT FREQUENTLY   Ibid., December 18, 1990; Naftali, *GHWB,* 113, 120.

453   THE RIGHT REVEREND EDMOND BROWNING   GHWB diary, December 20, 1990.

453   "NOW WHAT DO WE DO"   Ibid.

453   "IF I DON'T GET THE VOTES"   Author interview with Robert Gates.

453   OVER CHRISTMAS   GHWB diary, December 24, 1990.

453   "ALL OF THEM SAYING"   Ibid.

454   "I KEEP THINKING"   Ibid.

454   "THEY SAY I"   Ibid.

454   BILLY GRAHAM CALLED IN   Ibid., January 6, 1991.

454   "IT DOES HIT ME"   Ibid.

454   WROTE THE CONGRESSIONAL LEADERSHIP   *Public Papers of the Presidents of the United States: George Bush, 1991,* bk. 1 (Washington, D.C., 1992), 13–14.

454   THE MOVE WAS TRIGGERED   GHWB diary, January 8, 1991.

454   "I HOPE THAT"   Ibid.

454   "TO TAKE AN OVERFLOW"   Ibid.

454   IN GENEVA, BAKER PRESENTED   Baker with DeFrank, *Politics of Diplomacy,* 345–46.

454   BUSH TOOK THE CALL   Ibid., 363–64.

454   WENT TO THE BRIEFING ROOM   GHWB diary, January 9, 1991, describes the day. See also *Public Papers of the Presidents of the United States: George Bush, 1991* (Washington, D.C., 1992), 17–23.

455   IT WAS SNOWING IN WASHINGTON   GHWB diary, January 11, 1991.

455   LIKE MUCH OF THE COUNTRY   Ibid., January 12, 1991.

455   "FRIGHTENED THE AMERICAN PEOPLE"   Ibid.

455   THE PRESIDENT WON THE VOTE   Greene, *Presidency of George Bush,* 127; *LSY,* 475; Naftali, *GHWB,* 122.

455   AS HE WENT TO BED   GHWB diary, January 12, 1991.

455   "THE BIG BURDEN"   Ibid.

455   "I NOW HAVE"   Ibid., January 13, 1991.

455   "I DO THINK THAT WORLD WAR II"   Ibid.

456   "IT IS MY DECISION"   Ibid.

456 FOR "A HUNDRED GENERATIONS" "Address Before a Joint Session of the Congress on the Persian Gulf Crisis and the Federal Budget Deficit," September 11, 1990, *Public Papers of the Presidents of the United States: George Bush, 1990,* 1219.

456 "IT IS MY DECISION TO STAND" GHWB diary, January 13, 1991.

456 WATCHING ON THIS SUNDAY EVENING Ibid.

456 THE SON CRIED Ibid.

456 IN THE PRESIDENT'S MIND Ibid.

456 "I REMEMBERED JUST AS CLEARLY" Ibid.

456 "I HAVE A FEELING" Ibid., January 16, 1991.

456 READING DISTURBING PREDICTIONS BPB diary, January 5, 1991.

456 "I KNOW WHAT I AM DOING" Ibid.

456 UNABLE TO CONCENTRATE GHWB diary, January 14, 1991.

456 "TODAY IS ONE OF GREAT TENSION" Ibid.

457 "WAR, WAR, WAR" Ibid., January 15, 1991.

457 PROMPTING BUSH TO DIRECT DICK CHENEY Ibid.

457 GROWING UNCOMFORTABLE WITH Ibid.

457 HE TOOK THREE WALKS Ibid.

457 "PEOPLE KEEP COMING UP" Ibid., January 16, 1991.

FORTY-ONE: *Nothing Like It Since Truman*

458 I HAVE NO FEAR GHWB diary, February 4, 1991.

458 IT'S GOING VERY WELL *AWT,* 480.

458 THE BUSHES DINED WITH BILLY GRAHAM GHWB diary, January 16, 1991.

458 BUSH HAD WRITTEN MUCH OF IT Ibid.

458 "TONIGHT, THE BATTLE HAS BEEN JOINED" "Address to the Nation Announcing Allied Military Action in the Persian Gulf," January 16, 1991, *Public Papers of the Presidents of the United States: George Bush, 1991,* 42–45.

458 AFTER A LARGELY SLEEPLESS NIGHT Ibid., January 17, 1991.

458 "MR. PRESIDENT, WE HAVE SENT" Cheney with Cheney, *In My Time,* 214.

458 AMONG THE SUCCESSES Richard Stewart, *War in the Persian Gulf: Operations Desert Shield and Desert Storm, August 1990–March 1991* (Washington, D.C., 2010), 29.

459 THE PRESIDENT OF THE UNITED STATES WAS NOT SEEKING *AWT,* 488–92. See also Naftali, *GHWB,* 123.

459 BUSH WAS SO INSISTENT Brent Scowcroft to GHWB, "Restoring Liberated Kuwait," February 8, 1991, Iraq—February 1991 (2), Working Files, Richard Haass Files, NSC.

459 "BEYOND THE GULF WAR" Policy paper, "Beyond the Gulf War," Iraq—February 1991 (2), Working Files, Richard Haass Files, NSC.

459 ONE OF "EUPHORIA" GHWB diary, January 17, 1991.

459 AFTER ATTENDING A SERVICE Ibid., January 16–17, 1991.

459 THE CONGREGATION SANG Order of worship, Memorial Chapel, Fort Myer, Va., January 17, 1991, DF.

459 "WE MUST BE REALISTIC" *Public Papers of the Presidents of the United States: George Bush, 1991,* 48.

459 AS EVENING CAME IN WASHINGTON GHWB diary, January 17, 1991.

459 AT TEN AFTER EIGHT Ibid.

459 "NOW WE DON'T KNOW" Ibid.

459 "THERE'S ALL KINDS OF RUMORS" Ibid.; *AWT,* 453.

459 THERE WERE REPORTS Ibid.

460 "THE BIG PROBLEM IS"   GHWB diary, January 17, 1991.

460 ON FRIDAY, JANUARY 18, 1991   "The President's News Conference on the Persian Gulf" *Public Papers of the Presidents of the United States: George Bush, 1991,* 48.

460 "[I] PUT ON THE HARDEST SALE"   GHWB diary, January 18, 1991.

460 AT ONE THIRTY SATURDAY MORNING   Ibid., January 19, 1991.

460 IN THE DARKNESS   Ibid.

460 "THEY ARE GOING TO RETALIATE"   Ibid.

460 YET SHAMIR AGAIN ACCEDED   Ibid., *AWT,* 455–56; Naftali, *GHWB,* 123.

460 DISPATCHED A HIGH-LEVEL TEAM   *AWT,* 456; Naftali, *GHWB,* 123.

460 "WE OWN THE SKIES"   GHWB diary, January 19, 1991.

460 THE CALLS THROUGH THE NIGHT   Ibid.

460 "A MARVELOUS MADHOUSE"   Ibid.

460 HE TOOK A CALL FROM HENRY KISSINGER   Ibid.

460 "HOW ARE THE OVERNIGHTS?"   Ibid., February 4, 1991.

460 ON SUNDAY, JANUARY 20, HE MUSED   Ibid., January 20, 1991.

461 "AS I THINK ABOUT IT"   Ibid.

461 "THE BEST THING"   Ibid., January 17, 1991.

461 IN A CALL FROM CAMP DAVID   GHWB, "Telephone Conversation with President Turgut Ozal of Turkey," Camp David, January 21, 1991, Presidential Telcon Files, Presidential Correspondence Files, BSC.

461 "IT WILL DEPEND"   Ibid.

461 FELT A COLD   GHWB diary, January 22, 1991.

461 "I COULD USE A WEEK"   Ibid.

461 "I HAVE NO FEAR"   Ibid., February 4, 1991.

461 "I KNOW THAT WE'LL"   Ibid.

461 "A TARGET FOR REVENGE"   Ibid., February 6, 1991.

461 THE KEY GATHERING OF THE DAY   Ibid., February 11, 1991.

461 THE NEWS FROM THE FRONT   Ibid., February 11–12, 1991.

462 "THEY ARE VERY, VERY OPTIMISTIC"   Ibid., February 11, 1991.

462 AS HE LISTENED TO HIS COMMANDERS   Ibid., February 12, 1991.

462 "I HAVE NO QUALMS"   Ibid., February 14, 1991.

462 ON SATURDAY, FEBRUARY 16   Ibid., February 17, 1991.

462 DISCUSSED THE QUESTION OF CASUALTIES   Ibid., February 22, 1991; Cheney with Cheney, *In My Time,* 220.

462 "BETWEEN A THOUSAND"   Cheney with Cheney, *In My Time,* 220.

462 SCOWCROFT SUGGESTED THAT   GHWB diary, February 22, 1991.

462 AT MIDDAY ON FRIDAY, FEBRUARY 22   *AWT,* 475.

462 AT TEN P.M. ON SATURDAY   "Address to the Nation Announcing Allied Military Ground Action in the Persian Gulf," February 23, 1991, *Public Papers of the Presidents of the United States: George Bush, 1991,* 117.

462 "THE LIBERATION OF KUWAIT"   Ibid.

463 "I WORRY ABOUT CHEMICAL WEAPONS"   GHWB diary, February 23, 1991.

463 "WERE SADDAM HUSSEIN FOOLISH ENOUGH"   Cheney with Cheney, *In My Time,* 220–21.

463 "THE WARNING WAS QUITE SEVERE"   Ibid.

463 CHENEY QUIETLY ASKED POWELL AND THE PENTAGON PLANNERS   Author interview with Dick Cheney. Powell confirmed the episode. (Author interview with Colin Powell.)

463 "TELL ME HOW MANY TACTICAL NUKES"   Author interview with Dick Cheney.

463 "That was the question" Ibid. "In the bowels of the building," Cheney re-called, "I could just guess they were saying, 'Oh my God, he's going to use a nuke.' " (Ibid.)

463 "the answer was 'seventeen' " Ibid.

463 Powell recalled that the speculative number Author interview with Colin Powell.

463 If the Iraqi troops were thinly spread Ibid.

463 Cheney did not brief Bush Author interview with Dick Cheney.

463 "I was curious" Ibid.

463 the ground offensive began *AWT,* 479–80.

464 "Norm says it's" Ibid., 480. See also Cheney with Cheney, *In My Time,* 221.

464 Cheney and Powell briefed him *AWT,* 480; GHWB diary, February 24, 1991.

464 "I felt myself choking up" GHWB diary, February 24, 1991.

464 "It's going to be quicker" Ibid.

464 the formal military and policy structure around the president did not raise the issue Author interviews with GHWB and Dan Quayle.

464 In the sauna at the House gym GHWB diary, February 25, 1991.

464 "Our people want him gone" Ibid.

464 "I firmly believed" *AWT,* 464.

464 Our stated mission Ibid.

465 "Nobody wants to use" GHWB diary, February 25, 1991. See also Naftali, *GHWB,* 126–27.

465 "We need a surrender" Ibid., February 26, 1991.

465 "I'm not interested" Ibid., February 25, 1991.

465 Television images of *AWT,* 485.

465 Bush asked his commanders Ibid., 485–86.

465 Powell called Schwarzkopf Ibid., 485–86; Powell with Persico, *My American Journey,* 521.

465 the hundred-hour mark *AWT,* 486. On reflection, Scowcroft thought the hundred-hour decision "too cute by half." (Ibid.)

465 Bush spoke to the nation "Address to the Nation on the Suspension of Allied Offensive Combat Operations in the Persian Gulf," February 27, 1991, *Public Papers of the Presidents of the United States: George Bush, 1991,* 187–88.

465 Barbara had been scheduled BPB diary, March 1991.

466 The Iraqis lost Stewart, *War in the Persian Gulf,* 63, 67.

466 Eighty-nine percent of Americans WP, March 6, 1991; www.gallup.com /poll/116677/presidential-approval-ratings-gallup-historical-statistics-trends.aspx. See also Naftali, *GHWB,* 131.

466 In a series of telephone calls GHWB diary, February 27, 1991.

466 (Major, a Tory, had become) *NYT,* November 28, 1990.

466 Powell and Cheney had just GHWB diary, February 27, 1991.

466 "It's just dawning on me" Ibid.

466 "I wish I could freeze" BPB diary, March 2, 1991.

467 "I know that" GHWB diary, February 28, 1991.

467 By failing to force Saddam Author interview with GHWB.

467 (Bush had not insisted) Ibid. See also *AWT,* 489–90.

467 "It hasn't been clean" GHWB diary, February 28, 1991.

467 Bush had encouraged Iraqis to rise up *AWT,* 472. See also Naftali, *GHWB,* 128–29.

467   WHEN SHIITES AND KURDS   *AWT,* 488–90.

467   "[OZAL] WANTS TO HUMILIATE SADDAM"   GHWB diary, February 28, 1991.

468   "THE BASIC THING"   Ibid.

468   "I'M SO LUCKY"   Ibid.

468   "CONFESSION: I WISH"   Ibid., February 27, 1991.

469   ALAN GREENSPAN HAD ANNOUNCED   Wicker, *GHWB,* 167.

469   "THE RECESSION BEGAN"   Patterson, *Restless Giant,* 247.

469   "IT WAS THE FIRST   Ibid.

469   UNEMPLOYMENT, PARTICULARLY AMONG   Ibid.

469   "WHATEVER THE CAUSES"   Ibid.

469   "THE EUPHORIA IS UP THERE"   GHWB diary, March 18, 1991.

FORTY-TWO: *I'm Just Not Sure I Want to Run Again*

470   SOON WE'LL HAVE TO START   GHWB diary, April 10, 1991.

470   "NOTHING EXCEPT A BATTLE LOST"   Christopher Hibbert, *Wellington: A Personal History* (New York, 1999), 185. This quotation is also an epigraph for Rick Atkinson's *Crusade.*

470   TO THE J. W. MARRIOTT HOTEL   "Remarks at a Meeting of the American Society of Association Executives," February 27, 1991, *Public Papers of the Presidents of the United States: George Bush, 1991,* 184–87.

470   THE PRESIDENT USED THE FEW MOMENTS   GHWB diary, February 28, 1991.

470   TO THE AMERICAN SOCIETY OF ASSOCIATION EXECUTIVES   "Remarks at a Meeting of the American Society of Association Executives," February 27, 1991, *Public Papers of the Presidents of the United States: George Bush, 1991,* 184–87.

470   "YOU DON'T EXPECT ME"   GHWB diary, February 28, 1991.

470   "IT FELL FLAT"   Ibid., February 27, 1991.

471   "FRANKLY QUITE EMBARRASSING"   Ibid., February 28, 1991.

471   "THE BALL WILL SHIFT"   Ibid., February 27, 1991.

471   A "DOMESTIC STORM"   Darman, *Who's in Control?,* 290. See also Quayle, *Standing Firm,* 245.

471   "TRY THIS ON"   GHWB diary, March 12, 1991.

471   "[I'D] CALL A PRESS CONFERENCE"   Ibid., March 13, 1991.

471   YOU NEED SOMEONE   Ibid.

471   AT A RALLY FOR RETURNING TROOPS   "Remarks at the Community Welcome for Returning Troops in Sumter, South Carolina," March 17, 1991, *Public Papers of the Presidents of the United States: George Bush, 1991,* 280.

472   BUSH DRANK TWO MARTINIS   GHWB diary, March 17, 1991.

472   "I'M NOT IN A GOOD FRAME OF MIND"   Ibid.

472   "MY WHOLE POINT IS"   Ibid.

472   "IT'S NOT THAT I'M BIGGER"   Ibid., March 18, 1991.

472   "THE COMMON WISDOM"   Ibid.

472   "I LOVE THE JOB"   Ibid., April 22, 1991.

472   "WE'RE STILL GETTING POUNDED"   Ibid.

472   ON SATURDAY, MAY 4, 1991   Ibid., May 4, 1991; Naftali, *GHWB,* 130–31.

472   ON THE RUN THROUGH THE MARYLAND WOODS   GHWB diary, May 4, 1991; Naftali, *GHWB,* 130; *LSY,* 490–91.

472   TWICE HAD TROUBLE RUNNING   Andrew Rosenthal, "Treatment Could Require Brief Anesthesia," *NYT,* May 6, 1991.

472   (ONCE, AT FORT MCNAIR)   Ibid.

473 HE HAD ALSO LOST SEVERAL POUNDS   Lawrence K. Altman, "In Strange Twist, Bush Is Suffering from Same Gland Disease as Wife," *NYT*, May 10, 1991.

473 HIS PANTING ON THE PATHS   Andrew Rosenthal, "Treatment Could Require Brief Anesthesia," *NYT*, May 6, 1991.

473 UNSURE WHAT WAS HAPPENING   GHWB diary, May 4, 1991.

473 HE SOLDIERED ON   Ibid.

473 "THE SAME TIRED FEELING"   Ibid.

473 AN EKG CONDUCTED BY DR. MICHAEL NASH   *NYT*, May 7, 1991.

473 NASH'S FINDING   Ibid. See also Naftali, *GHWB*, 130; *LSY*, 490.

473 "YOU'RE GOING TO HAVE TO GO"   GHWB diary, May 4, 1991.

473 BUSH'S FIRST THOUGHT   Ibid.

473 WITHIN MINUTES THE BUSHES   Ibid.; Maureen Dowd, "Bush Suffers Shortness of Breath During a Jog and Is Hospitalized," *NYT*, May 5, 1991.

473 BARBARA LOOKED WORRIED   GHWB diary, May 4, 1991.

473 THE DOCTORS AT THE HOSPITAL   Ibid., May 5, 1991.

473 AT SEVEN THIRTY P.M. HE AND QUAYLE   Maureen Dowd, "Bush Suffers Shortness of Breath During a Jog and Is Hospitalized," *NYT*, May 5, 1991.

473 "THERE ARE NO INDICATIONS"   Ibid.; Ann Devroy and Dan Balz, "Bush Hospitalized with Irregular Heartbeat," *WP*, May 5, 1991.

473 BUSH WAS RESTLESS   Andrew Rosenthal, "Treatment Could Require Brief Anesthesia," *NYT*, May 6, 1991.

473 "THE PROBLEM WITH ALL OF THIS"   GHWB diary, May 5, 1991.

474 HIS DOCTORS TOLD HIM   Ibid.; Andrew Rosenthal, "Treatment Could Require Brief Anesthesia," *NYT*, May 6, 1991.

474 "SHE'S A LITTLE MORE WORRIED"   GHWB diary, May 5, 1991.

474 I JUST CAN'T BELIEVE   Ibid.

475 WITH THE DAWN CAME GOOD NEWS   Ibid., May 6–7, 1991.

475 ("I CAME TO THE OFFICE")   Ibid., May 7, 1991.

475 "BACK TO WORK"   Andrew Rosenthal, "Doctors Decide Shock Remedy Not Needed," *NYT*, May 7, 1991.

475 BUSH WAS SUFFERING FROM GRAVES' DISEASE   Lawrence K. Altman, "In Strange Twist, Bush Is Suffering from Same Gland Disease as Wife," *NYT*, May 10, 1991; *WP*, May 10, 1991. I am also indebted to Dr. Lawrence C. Mohr, who served Bush as a White House physician, for his recollections and guidance.

475 "AN OVERACTIVE THYROID"   Lawrence K. Altman, "How an Overactive Thyroid Affects Health," *NYT*, May 8, 1991.

475 HE WOULD HAVE TO FORGO ALCOHOL   Lawrence K. Altman, "Bush Begins Tests to Treat Thyroid That Disrupted Heart Rhythm," *NYT*, May 9, 1991.

475 BARBARA TOLD REPORTERS   Andrew Rosenthal, "Doctors Decide Shock Remedy Not Needed," *NYT*, May 7, 1991.

475 (FOR A TIME, DIGOXIN, WARFARIN, AND PROCAINAMIDE)   Author interviews with Dr. Burton Lee and Dr. Lawrence C. Mohr. Lee, as chief White House physician, was in charge of the president's care; Mohr was the senior military doctor on the White House staff.

475 THE ACCEPTED COURSE OF ACTION   Ibid.

475 BUSH'S DOCTORS INTRODUCED MEDICATION   Ibid.

475 (BY SEPTEMBER 1991 THE PRESIDENT WAS TAKING ONLY)   Ibid.

475 "IT WAS A DIFFICULT BALANCING ACT"   Author interview with Dr. Burton Lee. "On all the tests post-radioactive iodine therapy, he was numerically in the normal range for thyroid function, but from my point of view as his doctor, clinically treating him,

there remained the possibility that he was still clinically hypothyroid. In my mind there remains a question about whether he was adequately 'replaced' or not, despite multiple consultations with outside thyroid experts around the country." (Ibid.)

476 FOR THE MOST PART, BUSH'S DOCTORS KEPT THE PRESIDENT'S THYROID CONDITION IN CHECK   Ibid. The president was regularly found to be in the normal range on two tests: one for levels of thyroid hormone, the other for thyroid stimulating hormone, or TSH. (Ibid.)

476 CONTRIBUTED TO HIS FAILURE TO ENGAGE VIGOROUSLY   Fitzwater, *Call the Briefing!*, 293–95; also numerous author interviews.

476 "TO THOSE OF US"   Fitzwater, *Call the Briefing!*, 293.

476 THE DAY THE PRESIDENT RETURNED   *NYT*, May 8, 1991.

476 "TOO MANY OF THE PEOPLE"   Ibid.

476 JUST AFTER NINE THIRTY   "Remarks at a Memorial Service in Arlington, Virginia, for Those Who Died in the Persian Gulf," *Public Papers of the Presidents of the United States: George Bush, 1991,* 626–27.

476 "DWIGHT EISENHOWER ONCE SPOKE"   Ibid., 626.

476 FLANKED BY BAKER, CHENEY, BANDAR   C-SPAN video of GHWB's remarks and the memorial service at www.c-span.org/video/?18424-1/desert-storm-memorial-service.

477 BUSH'S VOICE BROKE   Ibid.

477 BUSH FELT HE COULD NOT   GHWB diary, June 10, 1991; C-SPAN video of GHWB's remarks.

477 "IT WAS SO SAD"   GHWB diary, June 10, 1991.

477 BUSH HAD NOTED A SONGBIRD   C-SPAN video of GHWB's remarks.

478 THE LARGEST MILITARY CELEBRATION   *NYT*, June 9, 1991.

478 THERE ON CONSTITUTION AVENUE   Ibid.; *WP*, June 10, 1991.

478 BY THE TIME THE SUN HAD SET   *LAT*, June 9, 1991.

478 "GREAT DAY"   Ibid.

478 "I FIRMLY BELIEVE"   GHWB diary, July 7, 1991.

478 WATCHING FROM THE WHITE HOUSE   Ibid.

478 AS FOR GORE HIMSELF   Ibid.

478 THE CREATION OF A NORTH AMERICAN FREE-TRADE ZONE   Baker with DeFrank, *Politics of Diplomacy,* 604–9. See also George de Lama, "Bush Asks Hemisphere-Wide Free Trade," *Chicago Tribune,* June 28, 1990.

478 REAGAN HAD SPOKEN   Baker with DeFrank, *Politics of Diplomacy,* 606, 609.

478 WHEN CONGRESS MOVED   Linda Diebel, "U.S. Vote Puts Bush Closer to 'Fast Track' on Mexican Trade Deal," *Toronto Star,* May 24, 1991.

478 "THIS IS A VERY"   Ibid.

479 FACING CONCERNS THAT   Ibid.

479 "THE WHITE HOUSE ALMOST"   Ibid.

479 A CONFIRMED FREE TRADER   Baker with DeFrank, *Politics of Diplomacy,* 608.

479 IN LATE JUNE, THURGOOD MARSHALL   GHWB diary, June 27, 1991.

479 BUSH MOVED QUICKLY   Ibid; Naftali, *GHWB,* 134–35.

479 BUSH THOUGHT OF A YOUNG FEDERAL JUDGE   GHWB diary, June 27, 1991.

479 THE SMALL AFRICAN AMERICAN REPUBLICAN WORLD   Author interview with Clarence Thomas.

479 "VERY CLOSE TO A DECISION"   GHWB diary, July 1, 1991.

479 WHEN THOMAS ARRIVED AT WALKER'S POINT   Author interview with Clarence Thomas.

479 THE STAFF SMUGGLED   Ibid.

479 "AS AN UMPIRE WOULD"   GHWB diary, July 2, 1991.

479 PROMISED NEVER TO CRITICIZE Author interview with Clarence Thomas.

479 "IF HE WAS READY FOR THE BRUISING FIGHT" Ibid.

480 THOMAS SAID YES Author interview with Clarence Thomas.

480 "IF HE RULES AGAINST" GHWB diary, July 3, 1991.

480 AFTER A JOINT PRESS CONFERENCE *NYT*, July 2, 1991; "The President's News Conference in Kennebunkport, Maine," July 1, 1991, *Public Papers of the Presidents of the United States: George Bush, 1991*, 801–12.

480 "A MAZE OF HIGHLY LEGALISTIC" Himelfarb and Perotti, *Principle Over Politics?*, 183. For an overview of the civil rights bill battles of the Bush administration, see ibid., 182–202, and Sununu, *Quiet Man*, 25–52, 256–60.

480 SUPPORTED BY DEMOCRATS "Thumbing His Nose at Congress; Mr. Bush Signs—and Undermines—the Rights Bill," *NYT*, November 22, 1991. For the controversy surrounding the bill's signing, see Andrew Rosenthal, "Reaffirming Commitment, Bush Signs Rights Bill," Ibid.

480 ON THE FIRST WEEKEND IN AUGUST Andrew Rosenthal, "Bush and Advisors Lay Groundwork for '92 Race," *NYT*, August 4, 1991.

480 A DISPIRITING PRESENTATION FROM BOB TEETER Ibid.; GHWB diary, August 4, 1991.

480 THE GROUP OF ADVISERS WAS LARGE GHWB diary, August 4, 1991; Andrew Rosenthal, "Bush and Advisors Lay Groundwork for '92 Race," *NYT*, August 4, 1991; Notes, Political Meeting at Camp David, August 3, 1991, Correspondence Files, James W. Cicconi Collection, GBPL.

480 ACCORDING TO NOTES OF THE MEETING Notes, Political meeting at Camp David, August 3, 1991, Correspondence Files, James W. Cicconi Collection, GBPL.

480 "CONCLUSION: HAVE WORK" Ibid.

480 "UNEMPLOYMENT [HAS] REPLACED" Ibid.

481 "KEY: AT EARLY STAGES" Ibid.

481 "OFF-WHITE LEATHER SHOES" Maureen Dowd, "As Golf Duo, First Family Becomes Average Family," *NYT*, August 18, 1991.

481 AT THE ANNUAL VESTRY BREAKFAST GHWB diary, August 18, 1991.

481 BUSH WENT TO BED Ibid., August 18–19, 1991.

FORTY-THREE: *A Coup in Moscow*

482 THE COMPLEXITIES OF ALL THIS GHWB diary, August 20, 1991.

482 THE CALL FROM SCOWCROFT Ibid., August 19, 1991.

482 BUSH PICKED UP THE PHONE Ibid.; Beschloss and Talbott, *At the Highest Levels*, 422.

482 BUSH HAD JUST COME GHWB, "Meeting with President Mikhail Gorbachev of the USSR," London, July 17, 1991, Memcons/Telcons (January–December) 1991 (3), Memorandum of Conversation/Telephone Conversation Files, Meetings Files, BSC (OAID 91156-008); GHWB, "Three-on-Three Meeting with President Mikhail Gorbachev," Novo-Ogarevo, USSR, July 31, 1991, Memcons/Telcons (January–December) 1991 (3), Memorandum of Conversation/Telephone Conversation Files, Meetings Files, BSC (OAID 91156-008).

482 AT ABOUT 5:30 A.M. ON MONDAY GHWB diary, August 19, 1991. See also Naftali, *GHWB*, 135–38, for an overview of the coup attempt.

482 "HAS BEEN PUT OUT" GHWB diary, August 19, 1991.

482 "BY RIGHT-WING FORCES" Nicholas Burns to Brent Scowcroft, November 13, 1991; "Chronology of the President's Warning to President Gorbachev Concerning a Possible Coup Attempt"; Mikhail Gorbachev to GHWB, August 31, 1991; Gennady

Yanayev to GHWB, August 19, 1991; all in Gorbachev—Sensitive July–December 1991 (2), Gorbachev Files, Special Separate USSR Notes Files, BSC (OAID 91130-004).

482   SOVIET COLD WARRIORS   GHWB diary, August 19, 1991.

482   GORBACHEV'S POPULARITY HAD BEEN FALLING   Maynard, *Out of the Shadow,* 93–95.

483   BEAR-LIKE AND HARD DRINKING   *WP,* August 22, 1991.

483   YELTSIN TOOK OFFICE   Maynard, *Out of the Shadow,* 99.

483   JUST AS GORBACHEV AGREED   Ibid.

483   THE DOCUMENT HAD   Ibid.; Naftali, *GHWB,* 137; Beschloss and Talbott, *At the Highest Levels,* 418–21.

483   GORBACHEV HAD BEEN VACATIONING   Mikhail Gorbachev, *The August Coup: The Truth and the Lessons* (New York, 1991), 17–19.

483   THAT "A GROUP OF PEOPLE"   Ibid., 18.

483   "I WAS NOT EXPECTING ANYBODY"   Ibid.

483   HE PICKED UP A TELEPHONE   Ibid.

483   THE LINE WAS DEAD   Ibid. "The conspirators had apparently decided in advance that they would not succeed in coming to terms with me and had prepared the alternative of isolating me," Gorbachev recalled. (Ibid.)

483   HE SHOULD DECLARE   Victoria E. Bonnell, Ann Cooper, and Gregory Freidin, eds., *Russia at the Barricades: Eyewitness Accounts of the August 1991 Coup* (Armonk, NY, 1994), 10.

483   "THINK AGAIN"   Gorbachev, *August Coup,* 23.

483   250,000 PAIRS OF HANDCUFFS   Bonnell, Cooper, and Freidin, *Russia at the Barricades,* 17.

483   TANKS BEGAN TO ROLL   Ibid., 10–11.

483   NO ONE IN THE UNITED STATES   Author interviews with GHWB and Brent Scowcroft.

483   THE GOLF WITH ROGER CLEMENS   Author interview with Tim Samway.

484   "NOT PLAYING GOLF"   Ibid.

484   THEY WERE GREETED BY BARBARA BUSH   Ibid.

484   HER HUSBAND HAD ONCE   Author interview with BPB.

484   SIGNING A BOX OF BASEBALLS   Author interview with Tim Samway.

484   AS HE APPROVED   GHWB diary, August 19, 1991.

484   "WILL THERE BE"   Ibid.

484   THERE WAS A NEW FIGUREHEAD PRESIDENT   Ibid.

484   "GRUMBLING ALL THE TIME"   Ibid.

484   BUSH SPOKE TO HIS OPPOSITE NUMBERS   Ibid.

484   "THEY AGREE WITH"   Ibid.

484   SPEAKING TO FRANÇOIS MITTERRAND   *AWT,* 520.

484   AT TEN TO EIGHT IN THE MORNING   "Remarks on the Attempted Coup in the Soviet Union and an Exchange with Reporters in Kennebunkport, Maine," August 19, 1991, *Public Papers of the Presidents of the United States, George Bush: 1991,* 1057–62; *AWT,* 521.

484   THE RAIN HAD COME   *AWT,* 521.

485   "THE WEST OBVIOUSLY"   "Statement [to the Press] Made by GB at USSS [United States Secret Service]," August 19, 1991, DF.

485   CALLING THE DEVELOPMENTS   Ibid.

485   SUBTLY DEFENDING GORBACHEV   "Remarks on the Attempted Coup in the Soviet Union and an Exchange with Reporters in Kennebunkport, Maine," August 19, 1991, *Public Papers of the Presidents of the United States, George Bush: 1991,* 1057–62. See also Naftali, *GHWB,* 137.

485   ECHOING MITTERRAND   Ibid.

485   ASKED WHAT HE THOUGHT   Ibid.

485 SHOULD THE HARD-LINERS   Ibid.

485 HIS SENSE OF PROPORTION   Ibid.

485 HAD BUSH USED   Ibid.

486 HE HAD SENT THE MESSAGE   Ibid.

486 BUSH MADE PLANS TO RETURN   GHWB diary, August 19, 1991.

486 BRIAN MULRONEY ASKED BUSH   AWT, 522-23.

486 "A DISINTEGRATION"   Gennady Yanayev to GHWB, August 19, 1991, Gorbachev—Sensitive July–December 1991 (2), Gorbachev Files, Special Separate USSR Notes Files, BSC (OAID 91130-004).

486 JOHN MAJOR SUGGESTED A NATO MINISTERIAL MEETING   GHWB diary, August 19, 1991.

486 "IT WILL MAKE IT LOOK LIKE"   Ibid.

486 YELTSIN, WHOM THE USURPERS   "White House News Summary, 8:45 A.M. News Update," August 19, 1991, DF. See also Naftali, GHWB, 137.

486 "NO TO FASCISM"   "White House News Summary, 8:45 A.M. News Update," August 19, 1991, DF.

486 "ENORMOUS GUTS"   GHWB, "Telephone Conversation with Prime Minister Brian Mulroney of Canada on August 19, 1991," USSR Chron File: August 1991 (2), Chronological Files, Nicholas Burns and Ed Hewett Files, NSC (OAID CF01407-008).

486 BUSH CALLED VACLAV HAVEL   GHWB, "Telcon with Vaclav Havel, President of Czechoslovakia," August 19, 1991, USSR—Part 1 of 4—Moscow Coup Attempt (1991) (1), USSR—1990 Moscow Coup Attempt File, White House Situation Room File, NSC (OAID CF1407-008).

487 "WE ARE AFRAID"   GHWB, "Telcon with Lech Walesa, President of Poland," August 19, 1991, USSR Chron File: August 1991 (2), Chronological Files, Nicholas Burns and Ed Hewett Files, NSC (OAID CF01407-008).

487 JUST A FEW WEEKS BEFORE   NYT, August 2, 1991. See also John-Thor Dahlburg, "Bush's 'Chicken Kiev' Talk—an Ill-Fated U.S. Policy," LAT, December 19, 1991.

487 "SOME PEOPLE HAVE"   NYT, August 2, 1991.

487 THE "CHICKEN KIEV SPEECH"   Ibid., August 29, 1991.

487 SENT THE WRONG SIGNAL   Dahlburg, "Bush's 'Chicken Kiev' Talk," LAT, December 19, 1991.

487 "THE THING IS TO BE CALM"   GHWB diary, August 19, 1991.

487 I HOPE THEY HAVE NOT MISTREATED YOU   Ibid.

488 "WHAT HAD TO HAPPEN"   Ibid.

488 BUSH SPOKE TO YELTSIN   Ibid., August 20, 1991.

488 YELTSIN'S HEADQUARTERS   Ibid.

488 "HE THINKS"   Ibid.

488 YELTSIN REPORTED THAT   Ibid. See also AWT, 317-18.

488 BUSH TOLD YELTSIN   AWT, 528.

488 "NO, ABSOLUTELY"   Ibid.

488 "DEMAND TO SPEAK ON THE PHONE"   GHWB, "Telcon with President Boris Yeltsin of the Republic of Russia, USSR," August 20, 1991, USSR Chron File: August 1991 (1),Chronological Files, Nicholas Burns and Ed Hewett Files, NSC (OAID CF01407-007).

488 ("I HOPE THAT THE LINES")   Ibid.

488 BY THE NEXT DAY   AWT, 528–29.

488 BACK IN MAINE   GHWB diary, August 21, 1991.

488 AS THE RAINS WHIPPED   Ibid.

488 WAS ATTEMPTING TO REACH GORBACHEV   Ibid.

488 "This obviously annoys"   Ibid.

489 "an important statement"   GHWB, "Telcon with President Boris Yeltsin of the Republic of Russia, USSR," August 21, 1991, USSR Chron File: August 1991 (1), Chronological Files, Nicholas Burns and Ed Hewett Files, NSC (OAID CF01407-007).

489 The weather eased   GHWB diary, August 21, 1991.

489 Back at the pier   Ibid.

489 "Who?"   Ibid.

489 Returning to his bedroom   Ibid.

489 wearing a damp windbreaker   See photo of GHWB and BPB in photo between pages 272 and 273 of *AWT*. See also C-SPAN video of GHWB briefing reporters after telephone conversation with Gorbachev at http://www.c-span.org/video/?20779-1/failed-coup-soviet-union.

489 "There is a God"   "President Bush to President Gorbachev Phone Call," August 21, 1991, Soviet Coup Aftermath, Yeltsin Files, Special Separate USSR Notes Files, BSC (OAID 91131-009).

489 "My dearest George"   Ibid.

489 "My God"   Ibid.

489 They spoke for eleven minutes   Ibid.

489 "He sounded jubilant"   GHWB diary, August 21, 1991.

489 The coup had failed   Bonnell, Cooper, and Freidin, *Russia at the Barricades,* 17–21.

489 "We could have"   GHWB diary, August 21, 1991.

489 Three days later, in Moscow   Ibid., August 24, 1991.

489 "appears to be weakened"   Ibid.

489 Bush lunched on the terrace   Ibid., September 2, 1991.

489 "So much has happened"   Ibid.

490 about the 1992 presidential campaign   Ibid.

490 A political memorandum   Clayton Yeutter, Chairman of the Republican National Committee, to GHWB, September 4, 1991, DF. Though the document is in the September 4 DF, 7 is stamped "RECEIVED" on September 2.

490 "though that could bring his personal life"   Ibid.

490 "Bill Clinton appears"   GHWB diary, September 2, 1991.

490 Bush had gotten to know Clinton   Author interviews with GHWB and Bill Clinton. See also Naftali, *GHWB,* 142.

490 "I like Bill"   GHWB diary, September 2, 1991.

490 A former subordinate of Thomas's   *Chicago Tribune,* October 12, 1991.

490 a "last-minute smear"   GHWB diary, October 8, 1991.

491 On the day after   Ibid., October 9, 1991.

491 Bush saw the matter   Ibid., October 10, 1991.

491 The president believed Thomas's   Author interview with GHWB.

491 Barbara joined Bush   GHWB diary, October 15, 1991.

491 "I am very proud of him"   Author interview with GHWB.

491 On the helicopter ride   GHWB diary, October 14, 1991.

491 "Thirty eight—it is so hard"   Ibid.

491 While monitoring the Thomas drama   Ibid.

492 the slow economy   Ibid., December 1, 1991.

492 Bush's approval numbers   Naftali, *GHWB,* 133–34.

492 Sununu was a tough   See, for instance, GWB, *41,* 225–26, and Fitzwater, *Call the Briefing!,* 175–78. The president himself had grown tired of staff conflicts about Sununu. To his diary on April 3, 1991, for instance, Bush confided: "The main problem

that worries me now is the problem with John Sununu. Brady cannot work with him; Baker refuses to even talk to him about foreign affairs; I've been told that Cheney feels even more strongly than the others; and Bob Mosbacher is sick of him. Suddenly this matter is coming to a head and I hate it. . . . I hate these kinds of problems—always have and always will—but this one I'm going to have to solve." (GHWB diary, April 3, 1991.)

492 A SERIES OF REPORTS   See, for example, Ann Devroy and Charles R. Babcock, "Review of Sununu's Travel Widens," *WP*, May 3, 1991; David Johnston, "White House Puts New Travel Curbs on Chief of Staff," *NYT*, June 23, 1991. See also Naftali, *GHWB*, 142.

492 TAKING A CAR AND DRIVER   *Newsweek*, June 24, 1991. See also Ann Devroy, "Sununu Trip Said to Anger Bush," *WP*, June 19, 1991.

492 SUNUNU MAINTAINED THAT   Sununu, *Quiet Man*, 363–66.

492 KNOWN TO STAFFERS AS "KING JOHN"   *Newsweek*, May 13, 1991.

492 WOULD GEORGE W. POLL   Author interview with GWB.

492 "IT WAS A BIG MOMENT"   Ibid.

493 OVER DINNER IN THE RESIDENCE   Ibid.

493 THE PRESIDENT SAT   Ibid.

493 FINALLY THE FATHER   Ibid.

493 "SO WHO'S BEST"   Ibid.

493 "IF YOU'D LIKE"   Ibid.

493 "SON, GOOD LUCK"   Ibid.

493 GEORGE W. HAD A CONVERSATION   Bush, *41*, 225–26.

493 AFTER THE MEETING   Author interview with GWB.

493 (AT LUNCH, FATHER AND SON)   Ibid.

493 SUNUNU MOUNTED A BRIEF CAMPAIGN   GHWB diary, December 1, 1991.

493 THE CHIEF OF STAFF EVENTUALLY RESIGNED   Quayle, *Standing Firm*, 294–95. Sununu finally resigned after a conversation with deputy White House chief of staff Andrew Card, who advised Sununu to write a letter of resignation "that you would want your grandchildren to read." Sununu did so, by hand, and submitted it to the president. (Author interview with Andrew Card.)

493 "IT'S HARD TO GET"   GHWB diary, December 17, 1991.

494 "THE LOWEST I HAVE EVER BEEN"   Ibid.

494 "I MUST ACCEPT"   Ibid.

494 "THE BIG THING IS"   GHWB diary, December 22, 1991.

494 IN 1989, WHEN YITZAK SHAMIR HAD COME   Haass, *War of Necessity*, 39–40.

494 SHAMIR GESTURED DISMISSIVELY   Ibid., 40.

494 "BUSH THOUGHT HE HAD"   Ibid.

494 IN A SERIES OF TENSE MEETINGS   Baker with DeFrank, *Politics of Diplomacy*, 443–69.

494 HOLDING UP "$10 BILLION IN LOAN GUARANTEES"   *NYT*, September 7, 1991.

494 "IT WAS HARD"   Haass, *War of Necessity*, 145.

494 ISRAEL BELIEVED BUSH LARGELY "UNFRIENDLY"   Ibid., 146. See also *NYT*, September 7, 1991.

494 THE PRESIDENT INADVERTENTLY REINFORCED THAT VIEW   Haass, *War of Necessity*, 146.

494 HE WAS "'ONE LONELY LITTLE GUY'"   Ibid.

494 HE TOLD BUSH AND SCOWCROFT   Ibid.

494 THE MADRID CONFERENCE   Ibid., 146–47; Baker with DeFrank, *Politics of Diplomacy*, 512–13; Michael B. Oren, *Power, Faith, and Fantasy: America in the Middle East 1776 to the Present* (New York, 2007), 569–71.

495 ON CHRISTMAS DAY, 1991, AT TEN IN THE MORNING   *AWT*, 559.

495   "I can assure you"   GHWB, "Telcon with President Gorbachev of the Soviet Union," December 25, 1991, Presidential Telcon Files, Presidential Correspondence Files, BSC.

495   "An end has been put"   Gaddis, *Cold War,* 257.

495   "Mikhail Gorbachev's revolutionary policies"   "Address to the Nation on the Commonwealth of Independent States," December 25, 1991, *Public Papers of the Presidents of the United States: George Bush, 1991,* 1653–55.

496   "I didn't want to get"   GHWB diary, December 25, 1991.

496   His joy was tempered   Ibid., January 5, 1992.

496   Two days after Gorbachev's announcement   Ibid., December 27, 1991.

496   "I don't think too much"   Author interview with GHWB.

FORTY-FOUR: *It Was Discouraging as Hell*

497   I just wish   GHWB diary, August 22, 1992.

497   In Tokyo for a state visit   GHWB diary, January 9, 1992.

497   "white as a sheet"   Michael Wines, "President Has Intestinal Flu," *NYT,* January 9, 1992.

497   "I remember breaking out"   GHWB diary, January 9, 1992; *ATB,* 545.

497   "Why don't you roll me"   *NYT,* January 9, 1992.

497   The president refused an ambulance   Ibid.; GHWB diary, January 9, 1992.

497   "regurgitated food"   *NYT,* January 9, 1992.

497   "I got home"   GHWB diary, January 9, 1992.

497   Bush was back on schedule   *NYT,* January 9, 1992.

497   "Mr. Bush's bout"   Anna Quindlen, "The Stomach Thing," *NYT,* January 12, 1992. There was press speculation that Bush's occasional use of Halcion, a controversial sleep aid that had just been banned in Britain, may have played a role in his collapse in Tokyo. Dr. Burton Lee, the president's physician, replied that the drug, which Bush had taken earlier in the Asia trip, could not have played a role in the episode in Tokyo but also said that he would try to avoid prescribing it to Bush in the future. As Lawrence K. Altman of the *Times* wrote in February 1992, critics had charged that Halcion was "more likely than similar drugs to cause symptoms like amnesia, paranoia, depressions, and hallucinations." (*NYT,* February 6, 1992.) Though Lee continued to prescribe Halcion for Bush on what the doctor called "rare occasions" (*NYT,* August 14, 1992), Lee believed the Halcion issue was "a complete red herring." (Author interview with Dr. Burton Lee.) He recalled giving Bush no more than five Halcion pills through the four White House years. "He certainly did not take it on a regular basis," Lee said. (Ibid.)

498   To his right stood Pat Buchanan   GHWB diary, December 8, 10, 1991. Jack Germond and Jules Witcover, *Mad as Hell: Revolt at the Ballot Box, 1992* (New York, 1993), 130–31.

498   "sniping away"   GHWB diary, January 10, 1992.

498   Buchanan's hatred of things imperial   http://articles.latimes.com/1992-03-04/news/mn-3164_1_king-george; www.nytimes.com/2011/10/16/magazine/does-anyone-have-a-grip-on-the-gop.html.

498   Richard Nixon was predicting   GHWB diary, January 10, 1992.

498   "Look, if we want to win this"   "The Limbaugh Rule Revisited," The Rush Limbaugh Show, September 16, 2010, www.rushlimbaugh.com/daily/2010/09/16/the_limbaugh_rule_revisited2. (Accessed from the show's web archive on March 31, 2015, and on July 11, 2015.)

498 "Ride to the sound of the guns" Ibid.

498 (To win Limbaugh over) Zev Chafets, *Rush Limbaugh: An Army of One* (New York, 2010), 81–82.

498 Roger Ailes had brokered Ibid., 81.

498 In a campaign memo, Alex Castellanos Alex Castellanos to Media Group, "Re: New Hampshire," January 6, 1992; "Feeding the Optimism," n.d.; and "Additional Points," n.d.; all in New Hampshire Primary (1), Ron Kaufman Files, White House Office of Political Affairs Bush Presidential Records, GBPL. (OAID 05594-004).

498 "If we could capture" Ibid.

499 he had to do something GHWB Diary, January 15, 1992.

499 took a sleeping pill Ibid.

499 The day in New Hampshire Maureen Dowd, "The 1992 Campaign: Republicans; Immersing Himself in Nitty-Gritty, Bush Barnstorms New Hampshire," *NYT*, January 16, 1992; Mary McGrory, "Romancing the Granite State," *WP*, January 16, 1992.

499 "You try to smile" GHWB diary, January 16, 1992.

499 In Orlando the week after Andrew Rosenthal, "Bush Encounters the Supermarket," *NYT*, February 5, 1992; Naftali, *GHWB*, 140.

499 Watching a live video feed Author interview with Andrew Rosenthal.

499 "amazed" Rosenthal, "Bush Encounters the Supermarket," *NYT*, February 5, 1992.

499 The White House pushed back Joel Brinkley, "On Tape, a President Intrigued By a Scanner," *NYT*, February 13, 1992. See also Ned Zeman, "Bush Was Not 'Amazed,'" *Newsweek*, February 23, 1992, www.newsweek.com/bush-was-not-amazed-200630.

499 new technology Christopher Connell, "White House Says Media's Checkout Was Faulty on Scanner Episode," Associated Press, February 11, 1992, www.apnews archive.com/1992/White-House-Says-Media-s-Checkout-Was-Faulty-on-Scanner -Episode/id-be6124e315259d11c1fd6371ba47b68f.

499 "ripped and jumbled" Ibid.

500 "media-manufactured" Ibid.

500 "All in all" GHWB diary, February 5, 1992.

500 *New York Post* had published a story GHWB diary, January 19–20, 1992.

500 Gennifer Flowers, an Arkansas woman "Clinton Denounces New Report of Affair," *NYT*, January 24, 1992; Dan Balz and Howard Kurtz, "Clinton Calls Tabloid Report of 12-Year Affair 'Not True,'" *WP*, January 24, 1992.

500 "It makes politics ugly" GHWB diary, January 24, 1992.

500 "They ought [to] leave" Ibid., January 25, 1992.

500 a letter Bill Clinton had written Ibid., February 6, 1992. See also Germond and Witcover, *Mad as Hell*; Dan Balz, "Clinton and the Draft: Anatomy of a Controversy," *WP*, September 13, 1992; Clinton, *My Life*, 154, 61, 151, 210; Naftali, *GHWB*, 142.

500 "Here's a guy who said" GHWB diary, February 6, 1992.

500 In mid-February, after a pollster for Bob Kerrey Bob Shrum, *No Excuses: Concessions of a Serial Campaigner* (New York, 2007), 218–19.

500 Bush issued a stern memorandum GHWB to Sam Skinner, Bob Mosbacher, Bob Teeter, and Fred Malek, "Re: Dirty Campaigning," February 17, 1992, Ronald Kaufman Correspondence/Miscellaneous Memoranda 3 (3), Ron Kaufman Files, White House Office of Political Affairs Bush Presidential Records, GBPL. (OAID 07888-013).

501 a view that Lee Atwater Lee Atwater with Todd Brewster, "Lee Atwater's Last Campaign," *Life*, February, 1991.

501   "In 1988, fighting Dukakis"   "Gravely Ill, Atwater Offers Apology," *NYT,* January 13, 1991.

501   "We obviously were on opposite sides"   Robert Shogan, "Lee Atwater, Tough Ex-Head of GOP, Dies," *LAT,* March 30, 1991.

501   "He suffered a lot"   GHWB diary, March 29, 1991.

501   Bush won, but Buchanan   *NYT,* February 19, 1992.

501   Newt Gingrich told *The New York Times*   Ibid.

501   Bob Teeter argued that   GHWB diary, February 24, 1992.

501   Agreeing with Quayle   Ibid.

501   his "biggest mistake"   Ann Devroy, "Breaking Tax Pledge a Mistake, Bush Says," *WP,* March 4, 1991; Naftali, *GHWB,* 140–41.

501   "It's hard to tell"   GHWB diary, March 3, 1992.

502   On Wednesday, March 18, 1992   Ibid., March 18, 1992.

502   Ailes, who had been   Author interview with Roger Ailes.

502   ("Reelections are always")   Ibid.

502   "the ugliness the Clinton people"   GHWB diary, March 18, 1992.

502   Hillary Clinton in *Vanity Fair*   Gail Sheehy, *Hillary's Choice* (New York, 1999), 204–5.

502   "Why does the press"   Ibid., 204.

502   "I'm convinced part of it"   Ibid. Mrs. Clinton cited a conversation that she had had with Anne Cox Chambers, the Atlanta newspaper owner, about Bush and Fitzgerald.

502   "Baloney," replied Barbara Bush   Donnie Radcliffe, "Granny Get Your Gun," *WP,* August 19, 1992.

502   "lower than low"   Ibid.

502   "It's just the symbol"   GHWB diary, April 7, 1992.

502   a new biography   Howard Kurtz, "Bush Angrily Denounces Report of Extramarital Affair as 'a Lie,'" *WP,* August 12, 1992. The book was by Susan B. Trento, *The Power House: Robert Keith Gray and the Selling of Access and Influence in Washington* (New York, 1992). Bush infidelity allegations were also in the air at the time after the publication of Joe Conason, "1,000 Reasons Not to Vote for George Bush," *Spy,* July/August 1992.

502   a now-dead ambassador   Kurtz, "Bush Angrily Denounces Report," *WP,* August 12, 1992. The ambassador was the late Lou Fields. According to the *Post* account, "The book quotes the late Louis Fields, former U.S. ambassador to the arms-control talks in Switzerland, as saying that in 1984 he arranged for then–Vice President Bush and Fitzgerald to use a guest house in Geneva. Fields did not say he had firsthand knowledge of an affair but said the living arrangements made him uncomfortable. The book says Fields gave the account in 1986 to former CNN investigative reporter Joe Trento, the author's husband, and later repeated it to two other people." (Ibid.)

502   The story was being promoted by Democrats   Ibid.; Fitzwater, *Call the Briefing!,* 353.

502   At a press conference   Fitzwater, *Call the Briefing!,* 352–53.

502   a furious president   Ibid., 352. "We checked our records and found that Jennifer did stay in Chateau de Bellerive, probably in their guest house; but that I stayed in the main house, and Tim McBride and others were in the house, too," Bush told his diary. (GHWB diary, August 11, 1992.) The next day Bush added: "It was just crazy. I can't remember the details, but I do know that there were a ton of people around that house, and I know others stayed there. But it doesn't matter what the fact is, it's the salacious media that go for it." (Ibid., August 12, 1992.)

Fitzgerald, who had been appointed deputy chief of protocol at the State Department, had made news on one other occasion during the presidency by failing to declare the full value of one item and another item altogether when she returned from a government trip to Argentina. (*LAT,* April 18, 1990; GHWB diary, April 24, 1990.) *The Los Angeles Times* reported: "According to the Customs Service, Fitzgerald, who had traveled to Argentina as part of an official U.S. delegation, returned with a raincoat purchased abroad, which she declared to be worth $300. She did not mention in the customs delcaration that the coat was lined with nutria fur. The customs agent appraised the coat at $1,100, and Fitzgerald was asked to pay a penalty of $440. For a fur cape worth $1,300 that she failed to disclose altogether, Fitzgerald was assessed $208." (*LAT,* April 18, 1990.) To his diary, Bush dictated: "She made a mistake and should've reported it, and now all the people who hate her are coming out of the woodwork, and the attacks are strong. . . . She writes Bar a lovely letter, but the wolves are out, and they blow the whistle on her for something that—let's face it—many people do. It's not right and they shouldn't, and Jennifer shouldn't . . . but it's a common practice when you are given custom privileges at Andrews returning on a flight. The Congressmen do it all the time." (GHWB diary, April 24, 1990.)

502 "MY MAIN WORRY" GHWB diary, August 23, 1992.
503 ROSS PEROT, WHO HAD LONG BEEN GHWB diary, March 19, 1992; David Gergen, "Outside: Can an Amateur Like Ross Perot Shake Up the Election Professionals?" *WP,* March 29, 1992; "Perot 20 Years Later," *USA Today,* December 10, 2001; www .britannica.com/biography/Ross-Perot.
503 "A BIG MASSIVE EGO TRIP" GHWB diary, March 19, 1992.
503 "HE NOW WANTS" Ibid.
503 BUSH BELIEVED PART OF PEROT'S MOTIVATION Author interview with GHWB; Naftali, *GHWB,* 143.
503 BUSH BELIEVED THE PUBLIC ROMANCE GHWB diary, March 31, 1992; Ibid., 144.
503 TO RUN HIS CAMPAIGN, PEROT HIRED Rollins with DeFrank, *Bare Knuckles,* 234–35.
503 THE ROLLINS NEWS Author interview with Sherrie Rollins Westin.
503 IN THE PRESIDENT'S STUDY Ibid.
503 SHE WAS WORRIED Ibid.
503 THE PRESIDENT WAS UNFAZED Ibid.
503 "SHERRIE, ED IS MAKING" Ibid.
504 PEROT HAD A SPECTACULAR SPRING *NYT,* June 11, 1992.
504 "OUTRAGEOUSLY ILL-SUITED" GHWB diary, June 20, 1992; Naftali, *GHWB,* 144.
504 AFTER TERRIBLE RIOTS IN LOS ANGELES Quayle, *Standing Firm,* 317–19.
504 DISCUSSED THE HIGH COSTS OF THE BREAKDOWN Ibid., 317–29.
504 QUAYLE WAS WIDELY ATTACKED Ibid., 320–23.
504 A "TOTAL PANIC" Ibid., 321.
504 THE PRESIDENT HIMSELF . . . WAS A BIT PUZZLED Ibid.
504 "WHILE THE LIBERAL COLUMNISTS" GHWB to Vice President Dan Quayle, "Re: I thought you might like to see the attached from my boy, Jeb," n.d., Ronald Kaufman Correspondence/Miscellaneous Memoranda 3 (2), Ron Kaufman Files, White House Office of Political Affairs Bush Presidential Records, GBPL. (OAID 07888-012).
504 "I BELIEVE WE ARE IN FOR A RUMBLE" Ibid.
505 "I MUST CONFESS" GHWB diary, May 25, 1992.
505 "I'VE ALWAYS THOUGHT" Ibid., July 10, 1992.
505 BUSH NOTED THAT GORE'S FAMILY LIFE Ibid.
505 *NEWSWEEK*'S PRE-CONVENTION COVER "Young Guns," *Newsweek,* July 20, 1992.
505 BUSH WAS ENDURING A SIX-HOUR MEETING GHWB diary, July 14, 1992.

505 "I'm not getting"   Ibid.

505 he needed Jim Baker   Ibid., July 16, 1992; Naftali, *GHWB*, 142–43, 146.

505 To escape the pressures   GHWB diary, July 16, 1992.

506 "He'll do what I want"   Ibid.

506 At a quarter after nine   *NYT*, July 17, 1992; Naftali, *GHWB*, 145.

506 summoning reporters   *NYT*, July 17, 1992.

506 Bush reached Perot   GHWB diary, July 16, 1992.

506 their chat was "civil"   Ibid.

506 One of Bush's first calls   Ibid.

506 "I want to talk to George"   Ibid., July 21, 1992.

506 "He's very pissed off"   Ibid.

506 Bush and Perot were supposed to meet   Ibid., July 23, 1992.

506 Perot grew difficult   Ibid., July 30, 1992.

506 "October Surprise"   Ibid., July 29, 1992.

506 After New York, Gallup had   *Chicago Tribune*, August 5, 1992; Naftali, *GHWB*, 146.

507 "I think he"   GHWB diary, July 7, 1991.

507 On CNN's *Larry King Live*   Ibid., July 24, 1992.

507 "It's all over the television"   Ibid.

507 a largely favorable   Bob Woodward and David S. Broder, *The Man Who Would Be President: Dan Quayle* (New York, 1992). See, for instance, pages 94, 99–102, 177–79, 125–28.

507 Bush's conviction that removing   Peter Goldman, Thomas M. DeFrank, Mark Miller, Andrew Murr, and Tom Mathews, *Quest for the Presidency, 1992* (College Station, Tex.), 376–81. Also see an adaption of the book at www.newsweek.com/gunning -quayle-189348.

508 "terrible.... He's not resonating"   GHWB diary, July 21, 1992.

508 George W. Bush suggested   Author interview with GWB.

508 Jeb called in from Florida   GHWB diary, July 23, 1992.

508 "When your own sons"   Ibid., July 25, 1992.

508 "I wouldn't look strong"   Ibid.

508 Peggy Noonan told Bush   Ibid.

508 Former President Ford telephoned   Ibid., July 27, 1992.

508 Jim Baker favored   Goldman, DeFrank, Miller, Murr, and Mathews, *Quest for the Presidency, 1992*, 376–81.

508 there was one dream scenario   Ibid., 377–79.

508 A Colin Powell vice presidential nomination   Ted Van Dyk, "Will Powell Run with Bush in '92?," *NYT*, September 6, 1990.

508 The problem was that Bush   Goldman et al., *Quest for the Presidency, 1992*, 381.

508 Before the summer   Author interview with William Kristol.

508 "What I hope"   Ibid.

508 promised not to "mobilize"   Ibid.

509 the Quayle operation shrewdly   GHWB diary, July 25, 1992. See also Michael Wines, "Quayle Says He Will Remain on Ticket," *NYT*, July 26, 1992.

509 "The bottom line on Quayle"   GHWB diary, July 27, 1992.

509 Now, after an early-morning jog   GHWB diary, July 24, 1992. See also Fitz- water, *Call the Briefing!*, 293–95, for an account of this episode.

509 "felt slightly dizzy"   GHWB diary, July 24, 1992.

509 "I could tell"   Ibid.

509 had recently adjusted   Author interview with Dr. Burton Lee.

509 BUSH SNAPPED Fitzwater, *Call the Briefing!*, 293. "Shut up and sit down," Bush had shouted, Fitzwater recalled. (Ibid.) GHWB diary, July 24, 1992, describes the same events. After the speech, Dr. Lee told Fitzwater: "I don't think he feels well. He had a fibrillation this morning." (Fitzwater, *Call the Briefing!*, 293.)

509 "DRENCHED WITH SWEAT" GHWB diary, July 24, 1992. See also *Fitzwater, Call the Briefing!*, 294.

510 "I GOT TO THINKING" GHWB diary, July 25, 1992.

510 "IN ANY EVENT" Ibid.

510 HIS HEARTBEAT HAD RETURNED Ibid.

510 "IF BUSH HAD ENDED UP" Author interview with Dr. Burton Lee.

510 THERE WAS TALK GHWB diary, August 13, 1992; Naftali, *GHWB*, 146.

510 BUSH ARRIVED IN HOUSTON GHWB diary, August 17, 1992.

510 AT A WELCOMING RALLY Ibid., August 18, 1992; *Public Papers of the Presidents of the United States: George Bush, 1992*, 1370.

511 "THE PRESIDENCY IS SERIOUS BUSINESS" *WP*, August 18, 1992.

511 "A LITTLE TENSE" GHWB diary, August 18, 1992.

511 THERE WAS A TROUBLING MOMENT Ibid.

511 "WAS FRANKLIN D. ROOSEVELT" Ibid.

511 "FRIENDS, THIS ELECTION IS ABOUT" www.c-span.org/video/?31255-1/republican -national-convention-address.

511 BUSH CALLED BUCHANAN Interview of Pat Buchanan by Doro Bush Koch, "My Father, My President" Files, Dorothy Bush Koch Collection, GBPL (OAID 24959).

511 "PAT BUCHANAN LAID IT" GHWB diary, August 18, 1992.

511 "MY OPPONENTS SAY" "Remarks Accepting the Presidential Nomination at the Republican National Convention," August 20, 1992, *Public Papers of the Presidents of the United States: George Bush, 1992*, 1380–86.

512 "I JUST WISH" GHWB diary, August 22, 1992.

512 HE WAS CRITICIZED Author interview with Andrew Card; Edmund L. Andrews, "Hurricane Andrew; Bush Sending Army to Florida Amid Criticism of Relief Effort," *NYT*, August 28, 1992; Naftali, *GHWB*, 147–48.

512 "HE SAID I LOOKED TIRED" GHWB diary, September 3, 1992.

512 "ONE LITTLE SIGN" Ibid.

512 READING HIS CAMPAIGN'S POLLING Ibid.; Naftali, *GHWB*, 145.

512 "DISCOURAGING AS HELL" GHWB diary, September 3, 1992.

512 A BEAUTIFUL LATE SUMMER DAY Ibid.

512 "I GUESS I'D HAVE TO SAY" Ibid.

512 "I'VE GOT A SLIGHT CONFESSION" Ibid.

512 "FOCUSED ON ECONOMIC WEAKNESS AND OPPORTUNITIES" Ewan Quill Ladd, "The 1992 Vote for President Clinton: Another Brittle Mandate?" *Political Science Quarterly* 108, no. 1 (Spring 1993): 20.

512 "THOUGH [A] RECOVERY WAS" Ibid., 20–21.

512 BUSH CAMPAIGN ADVISER MARY MATALIN Mary Matalin to "Bush-Quayle/GOP Leadership," "Subject: Media Bashing," September 1, 1992, Credenza, Bush/Quayle Presidential Campaign, 1992, GBPL (OAID 23000). The *Post* piece was Howard Kurtz, "Republicans and Some Journalists Say Media Tend to Boost Clinton, Bash Bush," *WP*, September 1, 1992.

512 *"WE ARE NOT PARANOID WHINERS"* Mary Matalin to "Bush-Quayle/GOP Leadership," "Subject: Media Bashing," September 1, 1992, Credenza, Bush/Quayle Presidential Campaign, 1992, GBPL (OAID 23000). (Emphasis in original.)

513 "I'm tired of the guy" GHWB diary, September 9, 1992.
513 "What changes in the world" Ibid., September 17, 1992.

FORTY-FIVE: *God, It Was Ghastly*

514 How can you help us "Presidential Debate in Richmond, Virginia," October 15, 1992, *Public Papers of the Presidents of the United States: George Bush, 1992,* 1834.
514 The call was unexpected GHWB diary, September 11, 1992.
514 Baker invited Perot Author interview with James A. Baker III.
514 For two hours GHWB diary, September 11, 1992.
514 Perot lectured Baker Ibid.
514 Perot theorized that a Dallas businessman Ibid.
514 "I see no reason" Ibid.
514 By the time Baker had returned Ibid.
514 Perot could help himself no longer *NYT,* October 2, 1992; Naftali, *GHWB,* 148; Wicker, *GHWB,* 196–99.
514 The only constant www.gallup.com/poll/154559/us-presidential-election-center.aspx.
515 In an interview with CNN's Larry King Andrew Rosenthal, "Bush Questions Clinton's Account of Vietnam-Era Protests and Trip," *NYT,* October 8, 1992.
515 "I bit the bullet" "Remarks Accepting the Presidential Nomination," August 20, 1992, *Public Papers of the Presidents of the United States: George Bush, 1992,* 1381; Clinton, *My Life,* 427.
515 In their first debate "Presidential Debate in St. Louis," October 11, 1992, *Public Papers of the Presidents of the United States: George Bush, 1992,* 1786–808. See also Wicker, *GHWB,* 199–204, for the debates.
515 "a dud" GHWB diary, October 12, 1992.
515 In Richmond at a town hall–style debate "Presidential Debate in Richmond, Virginia, October 15, 1992, *Public Papers of the Presidents of the United States: George Bush, 1992,* 1821–44. See also C-SPAN video of the second debate at http://www.c-span.org/video/?33137–1/presidential-candidates-debate.
515 Glancing at the watch Ibid., and "Clinton vs. Bush in 1992 Debate," https://www.youtube.com/watch?v=7ffbFvKlWqE.
515 "Well, I think" Ibid.
516 Simpson invited Clinton Ibid.
517 "I'm going negative" GHWB diary, October 16, 1992.
517 "The debates seem" Ibid., October 21, 1992.
518 *Penthouse* magazine account Ibid.
518 "What happens if" Ibid.
518 because of rumors Paul Richter and Sara Fritz, "Perot Charges Plot Forced Him Out," *LAT,* October 26, 1992; Richard L. Berke, "Perot Says He Quit in July to Thwart G.O.P. 'Dirty Tricks,'" *NYT,* October 26, 1992. See also Michael Isikoff, "Aides Struggle to Push Perot on Charges of GOP Tricks Off Center Stage," *WP,* October 27, 1992; Kevin Sack, "Perot Aides Try to End Story but President Keeps It Alive," *NYT,* October 28, 1992; Gerald Posner, *Citizen Perot: His Life and Times* (New York, 1996), 295–96, 311–12.
518 "I could not allow" Richter and Fritz, "Perot Charges Plot Forced Him Out," *LAT,* October 26, 1992.
518 a wiretapping plot Ibid.

518 "LOONY" Berke, "Perot Says He Quit in July to Thwart G.O.P. 'Dirty Tricks,'" *NYT,* October 26, 1992.

518 THE ALLEGATIONS WERE "CRAZY" Associated Press, October 27, 1992.

518 IN THE LAST DAYS OF THE RACE Author interview with James A. Baker III.

518 INDICTING FORMER SECRETARY OF DEFENSE CASPAR WEINBERGER GHWB diary, October 30 and 31, 1992; Walsh, *Iran-Contra: The Final Report,* 405–42; Naftali, *GHWB,* 148–49; Wicker, *GHWB,* 207–8.

518 "WORRIED AND PANICKED" GHWB diary, October 30, 1992.

518 "THE NATIONAL PRESS" Ibid., October 31, 1992.

518 SADDAM WAS GOING TO HOLD Ibid., November 1, 1992.

519 HE HIMSELF "WOULD VOTE FOR BILL CLINTON" Ibid.

519 (BAKER, BUSH DICTATED, "COMES IN") Ibid.

519 BUSH'S FRENZIED, LOOPY ATTACKS Greene, *Presidency of George Bush,* 177.

519 SO TIRED THAT HE COULDN'T SLEEP GHWB diary, November 2, 1992.

519 DAVID MCCULLOUGH'S BIOGRAPHY OF HARRY TRUMAN Ibid.

519 ONLY MARY MATALIN WAS CHEERFUL Ibid.

519 GEORGE W. JOINED THE PLANE Ibid.

519 ARRIVING IN AKRON Ibid.

519 BETWEEN STOPS BUSH TRIED TO NAP Ibid.

520 AT LAST HE RETURNED HOME Ibid.

520 THERE WAS A FINAL RALLY Ibid.

520 "ROCKING AND ROLLING" Ibid.

520 IT WAS NEARLY TEN P.M. "Remarks at a Rally in Houston, Texas," November 2, 1992, *Public Papers of the Presidents of the United States: George Bush, 1992,* 2148–50.

520 "YOU KNOW, I WILL READILY CONTEND" Ibid., 2150.

520 THE BUSHES WERE DRIVEN GHWB diary, November 2, 1992.

520 "I WORRY SO" Ibid.

520 HE SLEPT TERRIBLY Ibid., November 3, 1992.

520 AFTER HIS RUN Ibid.

521 "IT LOOKS LIKE A BLOWOUT" Ibid.

521 BUSH BELIEVED SO Author interview with GHWB. See also Everett Carll Ladd, "The 1992 Vote for President Clinton: Another Brittle Mandate?" *Political Science Quarterly* 108, no. 1 (Spring 1993), 1–28.

521 EXIT POLLING, HOWEVER, FOUND Ibid., 24–25. See also Wicker, *GHWB,* 208–9.

521 CLINTON HIMSELF LONG REMEMBERED Author interview with Bill Clinton.

521 WHILE IT IS IMPOSSIBLE TO KNOW Political scientists generally believe that Ross Perot did not cost Bush the 1992 election. See, for example, R. Michael Alvarez and Jonathan Nagler, "Economics, Issues and the Perot Candidacy: Voter Choice in the 1992 Presidential Election," *American Journal of Political Science* 39 no. 3 (August, 1995), 714–44; Dean Lacy and Barry Burden, "The Vote-Stealing and Turnout Effects of Ross Perot in the 1992 U.S. Presidential Election," *American Journal of Political Science,* 43 no. 1 (January, 1999), 233–55; Paul Abramson, John Aldrich, Phil Paolino, and David Rhode, "Third-Party and Independent Candidates in American Politics: Wallace, Anderson, and Perot," *Political Science Quarterly,* 110 no. 3 (Autumn, 1995), 349–67.

Perot's decision to run for president in 1992 did, however, undoubtedly impact the voter impression of the Bush administration. (Jeffrey Koch, "The Perot Candidacy and Attitudes toward Government and Politics," *Political Research Quarterly,* 51 no. 1 [March, 1998], 141–53.) In the end, Perot's exact effect on the race is impossible to measure conclusively, because Perot may have shaped "the election by reframing the choice between Clinton and Bush or by changing the issues of emphasis in the campaign" (Lacy and Burden, "The Vote-Stealing and Turnout Effects of Ross Perot," 234).

521 "AT FIRST I HAD A FEELING"   GHWB diary, November 4, 1992.

521 "TO GET VERY ACTIVE"   *NYT,* November 4, 1992.

522 HE RETURNED TO ANDREWS   Author interview with Marvin Bush.

522 "I LET EVERYBODY DOWN"   Ibid.

522 ARRIVAL AT THE WHITE HOUSE   GHWB diary, November 5, 1992.

522 ONE YOUNG SOLDIER   Ibid.

522 "IT'S ALMOST LIKE LIVING WITH"   Ibid., November 6, 1992.

522 "THE OVERSEAS CABLES ARE WONDERFUL"   Ibid., November 8, 1992.

522 BUSH REMEMBERED THE PAIN THE MOST   Author interview with GHWB.

522 "GOD, IT WAS GHASTLY"   Ibid.

FORTY-SIX: *The Closing of an Era*

523 YOU RAN THE WORST CAMPAIGN   GHWB diary, November 30, 1992; *ATB,* 578.

523 "RANGER [IS] PERKY"   GHWB diary, November 5, 1992.

523 THE RIGHT WAS CRUDE   Ibid., November 6, 1992.

523 "THAT SAME RESTLESS WONDERFUL WIFE"   Ibid.

523 "THE L-WORD"   Author interview with GHWB.

524 A DINNER WITH THE SENATE REPUBLICAN CAUCUS   GHWB diary, November 10, 1992; *ATB,* 574.

524 BUSH SAT NEXT TO REPUBLICAN SENATOR ALAN SIMPSON'S WIFE   GHWB diary, November 10, 1992.

524 "THAT I HAD LET PEOPLE DOWN"   Ibid.

524 RETURNING TO THE WHITE HOUSE   Ibid.

524 HE REMEMBERED THAT   Ibid; Naftali, *GHWB,* 150–51.

524 WOULD "LOOK LIKE"   GHWB diary, November 10, 1992.

524 REACHING THE WEST WING   Ibid.

525 BILL CLINTON CALLED   Ibid., November 18, 1992.

525 "HE'S VERY FRIENDLY"   Ibid.

525 BUSH GAVE HIS SUCCESSOR   Ibid.

525 "WOW"   Ibid.

525 AS THEY PARTED   Ibid. See also *ATB,* 576.

525 CLINTON WAS APPRECIATIVE   GHWB diary, November 18, 1992.

525 ("SPECULATION ON HILLARY")   Ibid.

525 HE HAD HAD ONLY ONE REQUEST   Author interview with Bill Clinton.

525 NEARLY FOUR YEARS BEFORE   Author interview with Gregg Petersmeyer.

526 THE ONLY STRUCTURAL CHANGE HE MADE   Ibid.

526 "ANY DEFINITION"   Ibid.

526 "BY CO-OPTING A PIECE"   Ibid.

526 THE POINTS OF LIGHT INITIATIVE   Ibid.

526 "THERE ARE NO MAGIC SOLUTIONS"   *Public Papers of the Presidents of the United States: George Bush, 1992,* 2158.

526 NANCY ELLIS TELEPHONED HER BROTHER   GHWB diary, November 18, 1992. For Mrs. Bush's death, see also *LSY,* 507–8.

526 HE AND BARBARA GOT ON   GHWB diary, November 18, 1992.

526 BUSH CONSIDERED FLYING   Ibid.

526 "I MIGHT NOT HAVE A CHANCE"   Ibid.

527 HE WOKE EARLY   Ibid., November 19, 1992.

527 BARBARA HAD TO REMAIN   *NYT,* November 20, 1992.

527 THEY FLEW ON AN AIR FORCE JET   Ibid.

527 MRS. BUSH WAS BREATHING WITH DIFFICULTY   GHWB diary, November 19, 1992; *ATB,* 576.

527 HE HELD HER HAND   GHWB diary, November 19, 1992.

527 AFTER A FEW HOURS   Ibid.

527 "I DON'T KNOW IF MUM KNOWS"   Ibid.

527 IN THE LATE AFTERNOON   Ibid.

528 "YOUR MUM HAS DIED"   Ibid.

528 NANCY ELLIS BELIEVED   Ibid.

528 "MRS. BUSH SR. WAS"   Ibid.

528 THE CALLS STARTED COMING INTO   Ibid.

528 HER FUNERAL WAS HELD   *NYT,* November 24, 1992.

528 PRESCOTT JR. READ A LETTER   Ibid.

528 MRS. BUSH'S ASHES   Ibid.

528 INCLUDING QUESTIONS ABOUT A SEARCH   See Robert Pear, "Many Questions Linger Following State Department Inquiry," *NYT,* November 20, 1992; "Continue the Passport Probe," *WP,* November 22, 1992; Bob Woodward, *Shadow: Five Presidents and the Legacy of Watergate* (New York, 1999), 198–99, 207–8, 210–13.

528 A BUSH POLITICAL APPOINTEE   Clinton, *My Life,* 432.

528 "CHASING DOWN BOGUS RUMORS"   Ibid.

528 *NEWSWEEK* HAD BROKEN   Woodward, *Shadow,* 198–99.

528 AN EMBARRASSED—AND EXHAUSTED—JIM BAKER   GHWB diary, November 20, 1992. See also Baker with Fiffer, *Work Hard,* 329.

528 IT WAS "ABSURD"   GHWB diary, November 20, 1992.

528 A "MCCARTHYITE ABUSE OF POWER"   Clinton, *My Life,* 433.

528 BUT THE FBI FOUND   Ibid., 432–33.

528 A THREE-YEAR INVESTIGATION   *NYT,* December 1, 1995; *WP,* December 1, 1995; *LAT,* December 1, 1995.

528 "SHOULD NEVER HAVE"   Associated Press, December 1, 1995.

528 "IT WAS JUST ALL PART OF THE DEAL"   Author interview with Bill Clinton.

528 BITTERSWEET ECONOMIC NEWS   GHWB diary, November 25, 1992.

529 "THIS ONE THEY CAN'T"   Ibid.

529 "I HAVEN'T FELT LIKE DICTATING"   Ibid., November 29, 1992.

529 WHEN HE WAS IN MAINE   Ibid.

529 HE HAD A FAREWELL LUNCH   Ibid., November 30, 1992.

529 "YOU RAN THE WORST"   Ibid.

529 SOMALIA, ON THE HORN OF AFRICA   Ibid.

529 "THOUSANDS OF INNOCENTS"   "'The People of Somalia . . . the Children . . . Need Our Help,'" *WP,* December 5, 1992.

529 "THERE IS A FEELING"   GHWB diary, November 30, 1992.

529 "I UNDERSTAND THE UNITED STATES"   *WP,* December 5, 1992.

529 "I EVEN TOY"   GHWB diary, December 8, 1992.

530 HEADING INTO THE HOLIDAYS   Ibid., December 9, 1992.

530 "THE KEY RHYTHMS"   Author interview with Dana Carvey.

530 WOULD SEND THE PRESIDENT   Author interview with Sig Rogich.

530 AFTER THE LOSS TO CLINTON   Author interview with Dana Carvey.

530 DID "A PRETTY GOOD JAMES CAGNEY"   Ibid.

530 WITH THE WORK ON THE START II TREATY   GHWB diary, December 23, 1992.

530 In September 1992   Author interview with Patricia Presock. An account of the story of the emergence of the diary is also told in Walsh, *Iran-Contra: The Final Report,* 474–80. Differing details in my account are based on my interviews with Presock.

530 "Boyden seemed to think"   Author interview with Patricia Presock.

531 Gray maintained that he had not known   Author interview with Boyden Gray. Asked about the call from his office in which one of the lawyers who worked for him had said "Boyden seems to think there is a diary," Gray recalled that he may have believed there were annotated calendars but was unaware of dictated diaries. (Ibid.)

531 "It was a very"   Ibid. "The Independent Counsel had suspended production of similar sensitive material until after the election," Gray recalled. "And it did not seem unreasonable to include the diaries with the production of the other material after the election." (Ibid.)

531 He recommended   Ibid.

531 Once they were handed over   Walsh, *Iran-Contra: The Final Report,* 474.

531 "to cover my own ass"   GHWB diary, December 21, 1992.

531 In a memo to the president   Ibid., December 22, 1992.

531 The family was in favor   Ibid.

531 Bush issued the pardons   *NYT,* December 25, 1992; *ATB,* 583; Naftali, *GHWB,* 153–54; *LSY,* 509–10.

531 the annual hunting trip   GHWB diary, December 29, 1992.

531 ("I slept well")   Ibid.

531 "The closing of an era"   Ibid., January 3, 1993.

532 Nancy unnecessarily complicated things   GHWB diary, January 13, 1993.

532 "friend and mentor"   "Remarks on Presenting the Presidential Medal of Freedom to President Ronald Reagan," January 13, 1993, *Public Papers of the Presidents of the United States: George Bush, 1993,* 2243.

532 "that was a tense ceremony"   GHWB diary, January 13, 1993.

532 Reagan, however, reciprocated   C-SPAN video of ceremony at www.c-span .org/video/?37025-1/presentation-presidential-medal-freedom.

532 "He seemed much older"   GHWB diary, January 13, 1993.

532 Throughout the ceremony   Ibid.

532 Apparent missile sites   Ibid., January 11, 1993.

532 "[Saddam is] pushing"   Ibid.

532 George Strait and Brian Mulroney   BPB diary, January 1993.

532 (As were Warren Christopher and Vernon Jordan)   *LSY,* 510.

532 Bush was doing   GHWB Diary, January 15, 1993.

532 Strait sang   BPB diary, January 1993.

533 On their final night   Ibid., January 1993.

533 It was a cold, clear, blue morning   GHWB diary, January 20, 1993.

533 "There was an unreal feeling"   Ibid.

533 Scowcroft and the CIA men left   Ibid.

533 Someone had mentioned the polls   Ibid.

534 "As I told Bill Clinton"   Ibid.

534 I've tried to keep it   Ibid.

534 He thought of Barbara   Ibid.

535 They had been joking   Ibid.

535 "This," he said aloud   Ibid;, *ATB,* 584.

535 "Who gives"   GHWB diary, January 24, 1993.

Part VII: In the Twilight, 1993 to 2016

537 WHEN YOU'VE MADE THE BIG CALLS Author interview with GHWB.

FORTY-SEVEN: *I'd Like to See Old George Bush*

539 I SUGGEST THAT GHWB to George W. Bush, July 16, 1977, Looking Forward and Miscellaneous Files, VIC.

539 CHART YOUR OWN COURSE *ATB*, 615–16.

539 HUGH LIEDTKE, BUSH'S OLD TEXAS BPB diary, January 29, 1993.

539 WHEN BUSH, WHO WANTED Ibid.

539 "HAVE WE MET BEFORE?" Ibid.

539 "HE IS NOT BITTER" Ibid., February 19, 1993.

539 "HE WAS DEPRESSED" Author interview with Jonathan Bush.

539 WHEN GEORGE W. CAME OVER Barbara Bush, *Reflections: Life After the White House* (New York, 2003), 6.

540 THE RESULT WAS AN UNDERCOOKED DINNER Ibid.

540 THE FORMER PRESIDENT, ALWAYS CONSCIOUS OF HIS WEIGHT Ibid.

540 INHALED THE DAILY CIA BRIEFINGS Author interview with Jean Becker.

540 "I'LL SPEND TIME" *ATB*, 564.

540 TO A REMARKABLE DEGREE Author interviews with GHWB, BPB, and Jean Becker.

540 THE FLOW OF GUESTS Ibid.

540 THERE WAS AN ANNUAL CRUISE Ibid.

540 QUAIL HUNTING Ibid.

540 PILGRIMAGES TO BOHEMIAN GROVE Ibid.

540 HE READ FICTION AND NONFICTION BPB diary.

540 "DON'T WANT PEOPLE" Author interview with Jean Becker.

541 A 1993 ENGAGEMENT "Talk's Not Cheap: Bush Reportedly Getting $100,000," *LAT*, September 4, 1993.

541 A SENIOR ADVISER FOR THE CARLYLE GROUP Author interview with David Rubenstein.

541 BUSH'S ROLE WAS Ibid.

541 AS COMPENSATION, HE ASKED Ibid.

541 "I TAKE NO JOY" GHWB to JAB III, June 9, 1993, box 288, James A. Baker III Papers, Princeton.

541 IN APRIL, THE FORMER PRESIDENT HAD LED *NYT*, April 15, 1993; Naftali, *GHWB*, 156–57.

541 A "HERO'S WELCOME" *NYT*, April 15, 1993.

541 A 175-POUND CAR BOMB *WP*, June 27, 1993.

541 MORE THAN A DOZEN Clinton, *My Life*, 525–26.

541 THE FBI AND THE CIA INVESTIGATED Ibid.; *WP*, June 27, 1993; Gibbs and Duffy, *Presidents Club*, 421–24.

541 "IT WAS A BIG BOMB" Author interview with Bill Clinton.

542 "THIS GUY JUST TRIED" Ibid.

542 "MR. PRESIDENT, THE QUESTION IS" Author interview with Colin Powell.

542 "I REALLY WANTED" Author interview with Bill Clinton.

542 "IT WAS AN ELABORATE PLAN" *NYT*, June 27, 1993.

542 KEPT BRENT SCOWCROFT INFORMED Ibid.

542 CLINTON CALLED BUSH Ibid.

542 "WE COMPLETED OUR INVESTIGATION" Gibbs and Duffy, *Presidents Club*, 423.

542 BUSH WAS RESERVED   George Stephanopoulos, *All Too Human: A Political Education* (Boston, 1999), 162–63.

542 "CLINTON CLOSED THE CONVERSATION"   Ibid.

542 "I THINK HE THINKS"   Ibid., 163.

542 WARREN CHRISTOPHER TRAVELED TO MAINE   *WP*, June 27, 1993.

542 THE MISSILE STRIKE TOOK OUT   Gibbs and Duffy, *Presidents Club*, 423–24.

542 "I'M NOT IN THE INTERVIEW BUSINESS"   *WP*, June 27, 1993.

543 "GLAD IT FAILED"   Author interview with GHWB.

543 IN SEPTEMBER 1993, BUSH RETURNED   BPB diary, September 1993; Naftali, *GHWB*, 155. See also Clinton, *My Life*, 541–47.

543 "JUST NOT READY TO GO BACK"   BPB diary, September 1993.

543 BUSH SPENT THE NIGHT   *NYT*, September 15, 1993.

543 "YOU KNOW HE'S ALWAYS"   Ibid.

543 "I WOULDN'T SAY IT WAS AWKWARD"   Ibid.

543 MADE THE CASE FOR NAFTA   Ibid.; Naftali, *GHWB*, 155.

543 BUSH TOLD THE AUDIENCE   BPB diary, September 1993.

543 A "WITTILY GENEROUS" THING   Clinton, *My Life*, 546.

543 HE WAS TAKING QUESTIONS   *ATB*, 598; Naftali, *GHWB*, 162–63.

543 "PULLED THE RIP CORD"   *ATB*, 598.

543 "FOR SOME REASON"   Ibid.

543 "WHY HAS THIS NOW BECOME AN OBSESSION?"   Ibid., 600.

544 THINKING ABOUT CHICHI-JIMA ON "THAT DREADFUL DAY"   Ibid.

544 WHEN HE INFORMED THE CHILDREN   Ibid., 601.

544 "YOU MUST BE KIDDING"   Ibid.

544 THE DAY IN THE ARIZONA DESERT   Ibid., 600–2.

544 "REVELING IN THE FREEDOM"   Ibid., 602.

544 IN THE AFTERMATH OF THE APRIL 1995 BOMBING   Ibid., 591–92.

544 BUSH WAS FURIOUS   Ibid. See also Naftali, *GHWB*, 159–60.

544 "YOUR BROADSIDE AGAINST FEDERAL AGENTS"   *ATB*, 591–92.

544 PERHAPS AN INEVITABLE TENSION   Ibid., 594.

545 TO PARENTS—FRIENDS OF MARVIN'S—WHO HAD LOST A YOUNG SON   Ibid., 592–93.

545 I EXPECT YOU ARE NOW SAYING   Ibid., 592.

545 "I DON'T KNOW HOW YOU FEEL"   Ibid., 593.

545 "YOUR FATHER WILL BE AN ISSUE"   GHWB to George W. Bush, July 16, 1977, Looking Forward and Miscellaneous Files, VIC.

546 "HE DID NOT ATTEMPT TO INFLUENCE ME AT ALL"   PSB, COHC, 4.

546 YOUR MOTHER TELLS ME   *ATB*, 615–16.

547 "GEORGE . . . YOU CAN'T WIN"   GWB, *Decision Points*, 53.

547 JEB WOULD FACE   *ATB*, 593.

547 "DO IT WITH ALL YOU'VE GOT"   GHWB to George W. Bush, July 16, 1977, Looking Forward and Miscellaneous Files, VIC.

FORTY-EIGHT: *The Proudest Father in the Whole Wide World*

548 IF I WERE "THE ONE"   Author interview with Jeb Bush.

548 HE DOESN'T NEED   Karl Rove, *Courage and Consequence: My Life as a Conservative in the Fight* (New York, 2010), 135.

548 CHASE UNTERMEYER . . . MUSED   Chase Untermeyer 1992 diary provided to author.

548 "CUTUP IN THE BUSH FAMILY"   Baker with Fiffer, *Work Hard*, 355.

548 "IF I WERE 'THE ONE'"   Author interview with Jeb Bush.

548 GEORGE W. THOUGHT   Author interview with GWB.

549 "WAS VIEWED AS A LESS SERIOUS PERSON"   Ibid.

549 HE WAS, HE RECALLED, "UNATTACHED"   Ibid.

549 "IT'S TOTALLY DIFFERENT FROM JEB"   Ibid.

549 "THE WHOLE IDEA THAT JEB"   Author interview with GHWB.

549 BUSH COULD NOT STAY OFF THE TELEPHONE   BPB diary, November 6, 1994.

549 "JEB SAID ABOUT THE SAME"   Ibid., fall 1994.

549 ON ELECTION NIGHT 1994   Author interviews with BPB and Jean Becker.

549 IN HIS SUITE   Rove, *Courage and Consequence,* 97.

550 "BUSH LISTENED TO"   Ibid.

550 "THE JOY IS IN TEXAS"   GWB, *41,* 254.

550 "TO SOME, HIS REACTION"   Ibid.

550 IT KILLS ME   BPB diary, fall 1994.

550 BARBARA AND JEB WENT BACK   Ibid.

550 INAUGURATION DAY IN AUSTIN   Ibid., January 25, 1995.

550 BUSH GAVE HIS ELDEST SON   Ibid., January 3, 1995.

550 IN A LETTER TO THE NEW GOVERNOR   GWB, *Decision Points,* 55.

550 DEAR MOM AND DAD   BPB diary, January 24, 1995.

551 "I ASKED WHAT THEY WERE DOING"   Ibid., August 1995.

551 AT A FIFTIETH BIRTHDAY PARTY FOR GEORGE W.   GWB, *Decision Points,* 58–59.

551 BULLOCK'S WORDS "SHOCKED"   Ibid., 59.

551 "TEN YEARS EARLIER"   Ibid.

551 THEY DISCUSSED POSSIBLE RUNNING MATES   BPB diary, summer 1996.

551 A STORY FROM THE DOLE SELECTION   Author interview with James A. Baker III. Baker had weighed running for president himself in 1996. According to Barbara's diary, after a round of golf with Baker and Robert Mosbacher in October 1994, Bush told Barbara that Baker was "seriously considering running for President. He thinks that there will be almost a national primary." (BPB diary, October 1994.)

552 "I THINK IT'S A GREAT IDEA"   Author interview with James A. Baker III.

552 A "CORK ON A RAGING RIVER"   GWB, *Decision Points,* 60.

552 "CAN ONE BELIEVE"   BPB diary, January 25, 1998.

552 THEIR BOOK ON FOREIGN POLICY   Naftali, *GHWB,* 163–64.

552 "WE HAD A GENUINE"   GHWB to Hugh Sidey, February 3, 1990, Office of George Bush, Private Files.

552 "I AM WORRIED"   Ibid.

552 THE ELDER BUSH COULD NOT SLEEP   ATB, 619.

552 "YESTERDAY I TOLD HIM"   Ibid., 618.

552 "HE IS GOOD, THIS BOY OF OURS"   Ibid.

553 WATCHING THE FLORIDA RETURNS   Ibid., 619.

553 "THE PLAN IS"   Ibid.

553 JEB PREVAILED, THE TRIP WAS MADE   BPB, *Reflections,* 249–50.

553 "THERE IS NO QUESTION IN MY MIND"   ATB, 618.

553 GEORGE W. BUSH MADE IT OFFICIAL   Rove, *Courage and Consequence,* 133–34.

553 THE BUSHES SERVED HAMBURGERS   BPB diary, June 1999.

553 "HE DOESN'T NEED"   Rove, *Courage and Consequence,* 134.

553 CULTURAL DISTINCTIONS   Naftali, *GHWB,* 166, is interesting on the religious issue.

553 "CHRIST, BECAUSE HE CHANGED MY HEART"   Stephen Buttry, "*Des Moines Register*: Candidates Focus on Christian Beliefs," CNN.com, December 15, 1999, www.cnn.com/1999/ALLPOLITICS/stories/12/15/religion.register/index.html?_s=PM: ALLPOLITICS.

553 "Don't worry, son"   Author interview with GWB.

553 George W. was struck by the remark   Ibid.

554 "My dad went to"   Ibid.

554 "He didn't mean to"   BPB diary, April 25, 2000.

554 It was George's turn   Author interview with Jean Becker.

554 "send the message"   Rove, *Courage and Consequence,* 170.

554 George W. asked his father   Author interview with GWB.

554 On the telephone with Evans   Author observation.

554 "Well, that's great"   Ibid.

554 At the elder Bush's request   *Houston Chronicle,* October 21, 2013. See also GWB, *Decision Points,* 70.

555 "I have watched you"   BPB diary, August 6, 2000.

555 "Jeb is a workaholic"   Ibid., July 1, 2000.

555 a Friday in May 2000   *ATB,* 633.

555 "It seems funny"   Ibid.

555 the parent of one of Robin's   Ibid.

555 "'Well, I guess Jesus'"   Ibid.

555 "We are very comforted"   Ibid., 633–34.

555 On the morning of Election Day 2000   BPB diary, November 7, 2000. See also Naftali, *GHWB,* 166–67, for an account of election night.

555 at the Shoreline Grill in Austin   GWB, *Decision Points,* 77.

555 Bush ordered a vodka   Author interview with Benjamin Taff.

555 It was a cheerful gathering   BPB diary, November 7, 2000.

556 "the exit polls started"   GWB, *Decision Points,* 77.

556 The party seemed to freeze   BPB diary, November 7, 2000, "There was a lot of excitement and a lot of noise when all of a sudden a hush came over the room because the networks announced that Florida had gone to the Vice President." (Ibid.)

556 a distraught Jeb   Ibid. According to Barbara, "Jeb was devastated. He had knocked himself out for his brother and the press had been gloating over the closeness of the race for weeks and how come Jeb couldn't win his state for George?" (Ibid.)

556 walked over   Ibid. "Jeb came over to his brother and said that he had let him down and they hugged. Such an emotional moment and so sad!" (Ibid.)

556 "George W. told Laura"   Ibid.

556 George W. rounded up his mother, his father, and his mother-in-law   BPB diary, November 7, 2000.

556 hurried back   GWB, *Decision Points,* 77. "Laura and I slipped out of the dinner without touching our food," George W. recalled. (Ibid.)

556 The trip to the mansion   Ibid.

556 "There's isn't much to say"   Ibid.

556 Then, as the night went on   Baker with Fiffer, *Work Hard,* 359–60.

556 "He took me aside"   Author interview with GWB.

556 The elder Bushes went to bed   BPB diary, November 7, 2000.

556 Back in Florida   Rove, *Courage and Consequence,* 202.

556 "We've been invaded"   Ibid.

556 Vice President Gore announced   Ibid.

556 took the candidate an idea   Author interview with Don Evans.

556 who had spent election night   Baker with Fiffer, *Work Hard,* 359–60.

556 George W. approved   Ibid.

556 "He didn't hesitate"   Author interview with GWB.

557 THE BUSHES FLEW UP BPB diary, November 8, 2000.

557 "SO THERE WE WERE" Ibid.

557 "WHAT ABSOLUTE NERVE" Ibid.

557 BUSH WAS SCHEDULED TO FLY TO SPAIN Ibid.

557 BUSH FATHER AND SON Author interviews with GHWB and GWB.

557 WENT OUT TO CRAWFORD BPB diary, November 24, 2000.

557 WAS IN BED, READING Rove, *Courage and Consequence*, 215–16. See also GWB, *Decision Points*, 81.

557 "CONGRATULATIONS, MR. PRESIDENT" Rove, *Courage and Consequence*, 215–16.

557 AFTER A DINNER ATB, 636.

557 "HIS SPEECH WAS ABSOLUTE PERFECTION" Ibid.

558 ON TELEVISION BUSH SAW Ibid.

558 "I WANT TO CALL AL GORE Author interview with Jean Becker.

558 "I CONGRATULATED HIM" ATB, 636.

558 "PRESIDENT BUSH WAS VERY EMOTIONAL" Author interview with Al Gore.

558 THE CONVERSATION WAS OVER ATB, 636.

558 "WHAT A LOVELY SON" BPB diary, December 2000–January 2001.

558 "I SAW IN HIS POSTURE" ATB, 637.

558 AFTER GEORGE W.'S BRIEF SPEECH Ibid., 637–38.

559 "YOUR FRIEND, THE PROUDEST FATHER" Ibid., 638.

FORTY-NINE: *It Is Not Easy to Sit on the Sidelines*

560 I'M THE FATHER, AND IT'S HIS TURN Author interview with GHWB.

560 RISING EARLY BPB diary, January 2001.

560 AFTER PUTTING ON Photograph, January 20, 2001, Bush Family Album, College Station Residence.

560 IN A SERMON ATB, 638.

560 "HE DIDN'T MENTION" Ibid.

560 NO SON HAD FOLLOWED Naftali, *GHWB*, 168. "The more interesting comparison was to another, more recent father-son combination from Massachusetts," wrote Naftali: Joseph P. Kennedy and John F. Kennedy. "Joseph Kennedy and his son had very different political views. The father was fiscally conservative and tended to be isolationist. Although a stroke in 1961 robbed the presidential father of any further opportunities to influence his son, there was always speculation about the father's influence in shaping the president that his son became." (Ibid.)

560 REFERRED TO HIS SON AS "QUINCY" Author interview with GHWB. George W. Bush hung a portrait of John Quincy Adams in the small dining room in the Oval Office, quite "meant inside joke with Dad." (GWB, *Decision Points*, 86.)

560 "THE OPINING BUSINESS" Author interview with GHWB.

560 AFTER THE SERVICE ATB, 638.

561 "STILT-LIKE HEELS" Ibid., 639.

561 "I DON'T WANT" Ibid.

561 "GEORGE WALKED DOWN" Ibid.

561 THE OATH ADMINISTERED Ibid., 640.

561 "PRIDE OF A FATHER" Ibid.

561 ON THE DRIVE FROM THE HILL Ibid., 640–41.

561 INSIDE THE WHITE HOUSE Ibid., 641.

561 WALKING FROM THE WEST WING Ibid.

561 A FEW MOMENTS LATER Ibid.

561 As his son entered   Ibid.

561 It was a long parade   Ibid., 641–42.

562 Bush was just beginning to relax   Ibid., 642. For the bathtub-to-Oval-Office scene, see also BPB, *Reflections,* 385; Naftali, *GHWB,* 167–68; GWB, *41,* 264.

562 Bush smiled   *ATB,* 642.

562 "Over the next eight years"   GWB, *41,* 264.

562 "I did a lot of work"   *ATB,* 642.

562 Their inspection done   Ibid., 642–43.

562 Upstairs, the new president   Ibid.

562 (Laura recalled that)   Laura Bush, *Spoken from the Heart* (New York, 2010), 175.

562 "I don't think"   Ibid.

562 The elder Bush was in bed   *ATB,* 643.

562 The next morning   Ibid.

563 There were a few instances   Ibid.

563 At noon the forty-first president   Ibid.

563 "George W. has been"   BPB diary, December 24, 2000.

563 George W. asked his father   GWB, *Decision Points,* 84.

563 never consulted him   Author interview with GWB.

563 ("Knew what the answer was")   Ibid.

563 Rumsfeld had been   Rove, *Courage and Consequence,* 220.

563 Rove raised the same concern   Ibid.

563 Rumsfeld was an aggressive figure   Rumsfeld, *Known and Unknown,* 282–83.

563 "It is an interesting appointment"   BPB diary, December 29, 2000.

564 "We were never"   Author interview with GHWB.

564 The elder Bushes spent the evening   BPB, *Reflections,* 386–87. See also GWB, *41,* 264–65, and Naftali, *GHWB,* 171–72, for the attacks and their aftermath from the elder Bushes' perspective.

564 "had made it clear"   GWB, *41,* 264.

564 The Secret Service moved the Bushes   BPB, *Reflections,* 387. See also *ATB,* 646.

564 They reached the president   GWB, *41,* 265.

564 The elder Bush advised his son   *ATB,* 646–47.

564 Bush's mind raced   Ibid., 647.

564 "What can we do"   Ibid.

564 As an old spymaster   Ibid., 648.

565 By custom the presidents   Author interview with Jean Becker.

565 "Today I want"   Ibid.

565 "War has been waged"   GWB, *41,* 265.

565 When George W. returned to his pew   Ibid., 265–66.

565 "It is not easy"   *ATB,* 648.

565 "Once you've sat"   Author interview with GHWB.

565 "a juvenile delinquent"   Author interview with James A. Baker III.

566 "The difference in some ways"   Author interview with GWB.

566 "I admired presidents"   GWB, *Decision Points,* 272.

566 "Never underestimate"   Richard L. Berke, "Bush Shapes His Presidency with Sharp Eye on Father's," *NYT,* March 28, 2001. George W.'s quote was reported as having been made in the wake of his surprising gubernatorial victory. Rather than a condemnation of his father's presidency, the *Times* wrote, it was an admission that he "blames the people around his father, as well as himself, for not working hard enough to ensure that reelection in 1992." (Ibid.)

567 George W. argued that   Author interview with GWB.

567 "THAT THERE WAS COMPETITION" Ibid.

567 BUSH HAD OPINIONS Author interview with GHWB. See also Naftali, *GHWB*, 173.

568 "IF I HAD ASKED DAD" Author interview with GWB.

568 A CAREFUL READING OF GWB, *Decision Points*, 84 and 243 are examples.

568 "THAT'S NOT A BAD OBSERVATION" Author interview with GWB.

568 "I THINK HE'S A HIGHLY SUCCESSFUL" Author interview with GHWB.

568 WAS SOMETIMES LIONIZED Naftali, *GHWB*, 174, captures this shift in opinion well: "Nostalgia for George H. W. Bush's presidency rose as his son's popularity declined." (Ibid.)

568 "BOTH THOSE GUYS" Author interview with GHWB.

569 "NO ONE SHOULD EXPECT" Author interview with Jeb Bush.

569 EACH DAY IN THE OVAL OFFICE GWB, *Decision Points*, 229.

569 A "DAY OF FIRE" *Public Papers of the Presidents of the United States: George W. Bush, 2005* (Washington, D.C., 2006), 66.

569 NICKNAMED HER "THE COBRA" Maureen Dowd, *Bushworld: Enter at Your Own Risk* (New York, 2004), 125.

570 "JUNIOR GETS A SPANKING" Ibid., 288.

570 "ANGRY" THAT HIS FATHER'S OLD INTIMATE GWB, *Decision Points*, 238.

570 "I WAS VERY UNHAPPY" Ibid.

570 "HE'S NOW GOING TO BE" Author interview with GWB.

570 "BRENT'S A GOOD MAN" Ibid.

570 "SOME IN WASHINGTON" GWB, *Decision Points*, 238.

570 "THAT WAS RIDICULOUS" Ibid.

570 DID SCOWCROFT TELL BUSH Author interview with GHWB.

570 "PRESIDENT BUSH'S VIEW" Author interview with Jean Becker.

570 ("I THINK BRENT HAD") Author interview with GHWB.

570 "THAT'S TOO CONSPIRATORIAL" Ibid.

570 THE SON OCCASIONALLY ASKED Author interviews with GWB and GHWB.

571 "I CAN'T SIT HERE" Author interview with GHWB.

571 THEY SPOKE ALL THE TIME Author interview with Nicolle Wallace.

571 "VERY FEW AND FAR BETWEEN" Author interview with GHWB.

571 "HALF THE TIME" Author interview with GWB.

571 AT CHRISTMAS 2002 AT CAMP DAVID GWB, *Decision Points*, 243.

571 HE ADMITTED, HOWEVER, THAT "IRAQ WAS ONE ISSUE" Ibid.

572 THE ELDER BUSH'S REPLY Ibid.

572 A FACT THAT DOES NOT FIT Author interview with GHWB.

572 "THE DISCUSSIONS WOULD BE" Bob Woodward, *Plan of Attack* (New York, 2004), 171.

572 "GEORGE IS A RELIGIOUS GUY" Author interview with GHWB.

572 BUSH 43 ARGUED THAT Author interview with GWB.

572 "ANXIOUS" ABOUT GOING TO BAGHDAD Confidential author interview.

572 SET THOSE CONCERNS ASIDE Ibid.

572 A LITTLE-NOTED BUT REVEALING SPEECH ATB, 659–60.

573 BUSH ALSO BELIEVED Ibid., 661.

573 THE DAY GEORGE W. BUSH ISSUED GWB, *Decision Points*, 224–25.

574 READING HIS FATHER'S WORDS Author interview with GWB; GWB, *Decision Points*, 224–25.

574 "THIS IS A GREAT DAY" ATB, 661.

574 HE HOPED, TOO Ibid., 662.

574 "No doubt tough times" Ibid.

574 his parents traveled to Tallahassee GHWB to Hugh Sidey, January 9, 2003, Office of George Bush, Private Files. For an astute profile of Jeb Bush in this season of his life, see Mark Leibovich, "The Patience of Jeb," *WP*, February 23, 2003.

574 "looking lovely" GHWB to Hugh Sidey, January 9, 2003, Office of George Bush, Private Files.

574 you "never wanted to get in the way" Author interview with James Oberwetter.

574 He did not pretend to understand Jeb's marriage fully Confidential author interviews.

574 he worried when Ibid.

575 Columba failed to declare "Bush Embarrassed by Wife's Run-in with Customs," David Cox and John Kennedy, *Sun-Sentinel* (Broward County, Fla.), June 22, 1999, http://articles.sun-sentinel.com/1999-06-22/news/9906220022_1_columba-bush-jeb-bush-governor-s-wife.

575 But what struck the old man most Confidential author interviews.

575 the "amazing" master of ceremonies GHWB to Hugh Sidey, January 9, 2003, Office of George Bush, Private Files. "'P,' as we call him, has an amazing presence," Bush wrote in his letter about the inauguration. "His remarks were scripted and put on the prompter; but the way he did, the way he looked, you felt he was in total command. He is a modest young man, a good student, and wonderful kid in every way. He likes politics. In my view this guy will go a long way if he pursues a political path." (Ibid.)

575 "Then came quiet, lovely, troubled Noelle looking beautiful" Ibid.

575 had recently been arrested for prescription-drug fraud *NYT*, January 30, 2002; Ibid., July 18, 2002.

575 "Although it is an intensely private" "Text of Gov. Jeb Bush's Inaugural Address," Associated Press, January 7, 2003, http://jacksonville.com/tu-online/apnews/stories/010703/D7ODH7682.html.

575 "now and forever my greatest hero" Ibid.

575 There Jeb stood GHWB to Hugh Sidey, January 9, 2003, Office of George Bush, Private Files.

575 Fred Ryan, a trusted Reagan aide Author interview with Fred Ryan.

575 "I was supposed" Ibid.

575 From the first draft Ibid.

576 "Nancy was very strong" Ibid.

576 "Once he called America" See C-SPAN video of GHWB's eulogy at www.c-span.org/video/?182165-1/ronald-reagan-funeral-service.

576 His voice broke Ibid.

576 Bush paid tribute to Nancy Ibid.

576 When he read overnight polls *ATB*, 667.

577 Bush was addicted Author interview with BPB.

577 The Sunday before the election *ATB*, 667.

577 The Bushes tried to relax Ibid.

577 he boarded a jet Ibid., 667–68.

577 who eagerly awaited Ibid., 668.

577 "Dad, we will carry Florida" Ibid.

577 "behind by a smidgen" Ibid.

577 During the trip Ibid.

577 "I feel like" Ibid.

578 Arriving at the White House Ibid., 668–69.

578 HIS SON WAS, BY COMPARISON, CALM Ibid., 669.
578 (SO MUCH SO THAT BOB SHRUM) Shrum, *No Excuses,* xi.
578 AS THE HOUR GREW LATE *ATB,* 669.
578 BUSH 43 DECIDED Ibid.
578 FATHER AND SON AWOKE Ibid.
579 THE ELDER BUSH WAS WILLING Ibid.
579 CALLED JIM BAKER Author interviews with James A. Baker III and Andrew Card.
579 BAKER AGREED Author interview with James A. Baker III.
579 THE ELDER BUSHES WERE SCHEDULED *ATB,* 670–71.
579 "DAD," BUSH 43 SAID, "DO YOU REALIZE" Ibid., 671.
579 STANDING THERE WITH HIS REELECTED SON Ibid.

FIFTY: *The Buck Stops There*

580 HE HAD HIS OWN EMPIRE Author interview with GHWB.
580 I LOVE GEORGE BUSH "William J. Clinton Acceptance Speech," National Constitution Center, October 5, 2006, http://constitutioncenter.org/libertymedal/recipient_2006_speechb.html.
580 A TSUNAMI IN SOUTHEAST ASIA *ATB,* 674.
580 TO SIGNAL AMERICAN COMPASSION AND UNITY GWB, 41, 270–71; Naftali, *GHWB,* 175.
580 TO RAISE MONEY FOR RELIEF EFFORTS Ibid. "The years had softened whatever anger remained between George H. W. Bush and the former rival, and following this joint mission the two former presidents became very friendly." (Naftali, *GHWB,* 175.)
580 CLINTON WON BUSH'S HEART Author interview with GHWB.
580 (CLINTON SPENT MOST OF THE NIGHT) Ibid. See also *ATB,* 673.
580 CLINTON "ALWAYS WAITED" *ATB,* 673–74.
580 WHEN CLINTON HAD NOT YET TURNED UP Ibid.
581 BUSH WAS BEMUSED Ibid.
581 "HE TALKS *ALL THE TIME*" Author interview with GHWB.
581 "BILL DID HAVE AN OPINION" *ATB,* 674–75.
581 BUSH RECEIVED AN EMAIL Ibid., 675.
582 IN SRI LANKA, THE TWO MEN Ibid., 677–78.
582 IN THE CAR AT LAST Ibid., 678.
582 BUSH'S RELUCTANCE TO BROADEN Ibid., 684.
582 BUSH ENJOYED BEING WITH GORBACHEV Author interviews with GHWB and Mikhail Gorbachev.
582 "GORBACHEV ALWAYS WANTS" *ATB,* 684.
583 "I PREFER MAINE OR A&M" Ibid.
583 QUIETLY DOING A GREAT DEAL OF CHARITY WORK Author interview with Jean Becker.
583 IN THE AFTERMATH OF HURRICANE KATRINA *ATB,* 686–87; GWB, 41, 271; Naftali, *GHWB,* 175.
583 "NOW MY OWN SON" *ATB,* 687.
583 A SIGN OF THE DEPTH Ibid., 688.
583 "IF YOU EVER HAVE" "George H. W. Bush Acceptance Speech," National Constitution Center, October 5, 2006, http://constitutioncenter.org/libertymedal/recipient_2006_speecha.html.
583 CLINTON WAS FORTHRIGHT "William J. Clinton Acceptance Speech," National Constitution Center, October 5, 2006.
584 "I DON'T FEEL CLOSE TO HILLARY" Author interview with GHWB.

584 "We like her"   Author interview with BPB.

584 Unlike former president Clinton   Author interviews with GHWB and BPB.

584 "The relationship between Franklin and Eleanor"   BPB diary, February 10, 1995.

584 "The politics between now"   *ATB*, 690.

584 The situation on the ground in Iraq   Peter Baker, *Days of Fire: Bush and Cheney in the White House* (New York, 2013), 494–97.

584 An Iraq Study Group   For the report, see James A. Baker III and Lee H. Hamilton, "The Iraq Study Group Report," http://bakerinstitute.org/media/files/news/8a41607c/iraqstudygroup_findings.pdf.

584 "a thumping"   "Bush Transcript, Part 3: Election Loss a 'Thumping,'" CNN.com, November 8, 2006, www.cnn.com/2006/POLITICS/11/08/bush.transcript3/.

584 for Don Rumsfeld to go   GWB, *Decision Points*, 92–94.

584 consulted the elder Bush   Author interview with GHWB.

584 "Do you think Gates would do it"   Ibid.

584 "One, I think he'd do it"   Ibid.

584 "At A&M, he had a marvelous way"   Ibid.

585 (During a two-day span)   Author interview with James A. Baker III. See also GWB, *Decision Points*, 92.

585 The possibility was Bush 43's idea   Author interview with GWB.

585 Baker believed that   Author interview with James A. Baker III.

585 "I think he served the President badly"   Author interview with GHWB. Rumsfeld declined to comment on Bush 41's remarks. (Author interview with Donald Rumsfeld.)

585 "The idea of 'doing it better'"   Author interview with GHWB.

585 "proud moments"   Ibid.

585 "Different wars, different reasons"   Ibid.

585 Those who thought   Ibid.

586 "Oh, I know that's"   Ibid.

586 there were "people that criticize George"   Ibid.

586 "So would we be better off"   Ibid.

586 Mimicking a chagrined cocktail guest   Ibid.

586 "'Oh no'"   Ibid.

586 In a series of wide-ranging interviews   The conversations took place in October 2008; February, April, and June 2009; and January and November 2010. Transcripts of the quoted portions from GHWB were confirmed with him in December 2014. "That's what I said," Bush said. (Ibid.)

586 despite private anxieties   Confidential author interview.

586 "I do worry about some of the rhetoric"   Author interview with GHWB.

586 "You go back to the 'axis of evil'"   Ibid.

586 In his 2002 State of the Union address   George W. Bush, "Address Before a Joint Session of the Congress on the State of the Union," January 29, 2002, The American Presidency Project, www.presidency.ucsb.edu/ws/?pid=29644.

586 The use of the phrase   *NYT*, February 23, 2002.

586 "Europe Seethes"   Ibid.

586 "neoconservatives" who often argued   See, for instance, Baker, *Days of Fire*; Mann, *Rise of the Vulcans*; Jacob Heilbrunn, *They Knew They Were Right: The Rise of the Neocons* (New York, 2008).

586 "As long as bringing down Saddam"   Author interview with GHWB.

587 "What you really need to know"   Ibid.

587 PREFERRING A MORE DIPLOMATIC APPROACH   Author interviews with GWB, Dick Cheney, Condoleezza Rice, Robert Gates, and Steve Hadley. Both GWB and Cheney discussed their second-term differences over some policies in interviews with the author.

587 PRESSED FOR A MORE VIGOROUS REACTION   See, for instance, "Why Bush Won't Attack Iran," Steven Clemons, Salon.com, September 19, 2007, www.salon.com/2007 /09/19/iran_2/.

587 NEOCONSERVATIVE ARGUMENTS ABOUT   Ibid.; *NYT,* June 2, 2007.

587 CHENEY . . . WAS A SHREWD WASHINGTON PLAYER   Barton Gellman, *Angler: The Cheney Vice Presidency* (New York, 2008), 43–44, offered this example: Along with his own access to the president, which was substantial, Cheney arranged for his vice presidential chief of staff, I. Lewis "Scooter" Libby, to be given the title of assistant to the president, a bureaucratic stroke that put Libby—and thus Cheney—squarely in the West Wing decision-making process. As Gellman reported, "No one save Cheney and Bush themselves were his superiors. Like every assistant to the president, Libby would see and have the right to challenge any speech, legislation, or executive order before it reached the Oval Office." (Ibid.)

587 "VERY MUCH OF ONE ULTRA-HAWKISH MIND"   Condoleezza Rice, *No Higher Honor: A Memoir of My Years in Washington* (New York, 2011), 17. See also Baker, *Days of Fire,* 87–88.

587 BUSH 41 HAD NO DOUBTS   Author interview with GHWB.

587 "THE DECIDER"   "Bush: 'I'm the decider' on Rumsfeld," April 18, 2006, www.cnn .com/2006/POLITICS/04/18/rumsfeld/; *NYT,* December 24, 2006.

587 "I THINK GEORGE WOULD SAY"   Author interview with GHWB.

588 "HE HAD HIS OWN EMPIRE"   Ibid.

588 A NATIONAL-SECURITY AIDE TO CHENEY   *NYT,* June 2, 2007. Steve Clemons broke this story.

588 TO WARN AGAINST "NEW CRAZIES"   Ibid.

588 "WE FULLY BELIEVE"   Ibid.

588 WHICH BUSH 41 READ EVERY DAY   Author interview with Jean Becker.

588 "BUT THERE'S SOME CONCERN"   *NYT,* June 2, 2007.

588 WITH CONCERN AND PUZZLEMENT   Author interview with GHWB.

588 APPEARED TO BE A CHAMPION   Ibid.

588 ONE OF " 'GOOD' VS. 'EVIL' "   *ATB,* 497.

588 WILLING TO RISK IMPEACHMENT   See Chapter 41 above.

588 "I DON'T KNOW, HE JUST BECAME"   Ibid. That Cheney was different than he had been in his days as secretary of defense was an argument that Brent Scowcroft often made. (Jeffrey Goldberg, "Breaking Ranks," *The New Yorker,* October 31, 2005; Sparrow, *The Strategist,* 534–35.)

588 "THE REACTION IS"   Author interview with GHWB.

588 A KIND OF "DR. STRANGELOVE"   Thomas Friedman, "Channeling Dick Cheney," *NYT,* November 18, 2007.

589 "VICE PRESIDENT CHENEY IS THE HAWK-EATING"   Ibid.

589 AN AMERICAN AIR STRIKE ON A NORTH KOREAN–BUILT NUCLEAR REACTOR   Baker, *Days of Fire,* 551–53. See also Cheney with Cheney, *In My Time,* 465–73; and GWB, *Decision Points,* 420 22.

589 "I DON'T KNOW"   Author interview with GHWB.

589 "YOU KNOW, I'VE CONCLUDED THAT LYNNE CHENEY"   Ibid.

589 BUSH ADDED THAT THE CHENEYS' DAUGHTER LIZ . . . WAS ALSO "TOUGH"   Ibid.

589 "A GOOD MAN"   Ibid.

589 "THE BIG MISTAKE THAT WAS MADE"   Ibid. The elder Bush was so convinced he was

right about Cheney's outsized influence that he advised President-elect Obama to watch out for vice presidential empire building. There should be no "separate establishment for intelligence and foreign policy," Bush told Obama. "Vice presidents can't do that. You're going to get burned if they do that." (Ibid.)

589 "THE BUCK," BUSH AGREED   Ibid.

590 "FASCINATING," CHENEY MURMURED   Author interview with Dick Cheney.

590 "NO QUESTION I WAS MUCH HARDER-LINE"   Ibid.

590 ("I DO DISAGREE")   Ibid.

590 (MRS. CHENEY AND LIZ CHENEY DECLINED)   Author interviews with Lynne Cheney and Liz Cheney.

590 "I'VE NEVER HEARD"   Ibid.

590 "WE WERE DEALING WITH"   Ibid.

590 "HE CERTAINLY NEVER"   Author interview with GWB.

590 "WOULD NEVER SAY TO ME"   Ibid.

591 "IT IS TRUE THAT MY RHETORIC COULD GET PRETTY STRONG"   Ibid.

591 HE REMEMBERED THAT   Ibid.

591 "THEY UNDERSTOOD ME IN MIDLAND"   Ibid.

591 COMMISSIONED THE USS *GEORGE H. W. BUSH*   "USS George H. W. Bush Commissioning," January 10, 2009. CSPAN video www.cspan.org/video/?283260-1/uss-george-hw-bush-commissioning.

591 A BRIGHT WINTER'S DAY   Ibid.

591 "OVER THE YEARS"   Ibid.

591 TURNING TO THE BUSINESS AT HAND   Ibid.

592 HE LOVED READING EMAIL UPDATES   Author interview with Jean Becker.

592 "THE SHIP IS SO MAJESTIC"   Author interview with GHWB.

592 WORE THAT SAME SPLENDID PURPLE SCARF   Author observation.

592 BOARDED THE PRESIDENTIAL HELICOPTER   Author interview with Jean Becker.

592 "HE'S FINE"   Author interview with GHWB.

592 HE RECALLED AN EXCHANGE   Ibid.

592 "BELIEVE ME"   Ibid.

592 "TRY THIS ONE ON FOR SIZE"   Ibid.

592 IN THE MIDDLE OF A STORM   Author interview with Jean Becker.

593 HE LOOKED AT HER   Ibid.

593 AFTER A LONG WEEKEND OF EVENTS   Ibid.

593 HIS HEALTH WAS GOOD   Author interview with Dr. John Eckstein.

593 DURING A 2012 HOSPITALIZATION   Author interview with Jean Becker.

593 "DID I ALMOST BUY"   Ibid.

593 "I'VE DECIDED TO LIVE TO NINETY"   Ibid.

594 "WHEN THE PRESIDENT COMES"   *Houston Chronicle,* April 9, 2014.

594 WERE INVITED TO A SAME-SEX WEDDING   Author interview with Jean Becker.

594 "FOUND HIS POPULARITY"   Ibid.

594 "PERSONALLY, I STILL BELIEVE"   GHWB note to author, September 8, 2015.

EPILOGUE: *I Don't Want to Miss Anything*

595 AS GOOD A MEASURE OF A PRESIDENT   Author interview with Barack Obama.

595 ON A RELAXED AFTERNOON   Author interview with GHWB.

595 "I FEEL LIKE"   Ibid.

595 "I AM LOST"   Ibid.

595 "WHAT IF THEY JUST FIND"   Ibid.

595 "How great is this country"   Bush, *Spoken from the Heart,* 126.

596 "My father was the last president"   George W. Bush, "Address Accepting the Presidential Nomination at the Republican National Convention in Philadelphia," August 3, 2000, The American Presidency Project, www.presidency.ucsb.edu/ws /?pid=25954.

596 There was bipartisan consensus   Peter Baker, "Bush 41 Reunion Seeks to Burnish His Legacy," *NYT,* April 4, 2014. "Frail from a form of Parkinson's disease, Mr. Bush, 89, has benefited from a wave of historical revisionism that has transformed him from the biggest incumbent loser since William Howard Taft to, by at least one measure, the most popular former president of the past half century," wrote Baker, who pointed out that Bush's average Gallup post-presidential approval rating had been 66 percent, "the highest of the eight most recent former presidents." (Ibid.)

596 "He was the great tortoise"   Murray Kempton, *Rebellions, Perversities, and Main Events* (New York, 1994), 446. (The *Esquire* essay is collected in this volume.) I am grateful to Michael Beschloss for pointing me to this review of Kempton's.

597 was not "a pure undertaking"   Author interview with GHWB.

598 The telephone . . . rang   Author interview with Jean Becker.

598 "I am not doing any travel"   *ATB,* 697.

598 "We honor George Herbert Walker Bush"   "Remarks on Presenting the Presidential Medal of Freedom, February 15, 2011," *Public Papers of the Presidents of the United States: Barack Obama, 2011* (Washington, D.C., 2012), 127.

598 From a decorated Navy pilot   Ibid.

599 "was exactly the gentleman"   Author interview with Barack Obama.

599 "I would argue"   Ibid.

600 "As good a measure"   Ibid.

600 It is a serene spot   Author observation.

600 Once when he was nearing ninety   Author interview with Jean Becker.

601 "I don't want"   Ibid.

BIBLIOGRAPHY

★

Manuscript Collections

SIGNIFICANT MANUSCRIPT COLLECTIONS CONSULTED AT THE GEORGE BUSH
PRESIDENTIAL LIBRARY AND MUSEUM, COLLEGE STATION, TEXAS

Jean Becker "All the Best, George Bush" File, Post-Presidential Materials, George H. W.
 Bush Collection
FitzGerald Bemiss Collection
Jan Burmeister Collection
Barbara P. Bush Collection
Dorothy W. Bush Collection
George Bush Personal and Donated Files Related to Bush and Family, Post-Presidential
 Materials, George H. W. Bush Collection
Daily Files, George H. W. Bush Presidential Records, Office of the President, Houston
 Office Files, George H. W. Bush Collection
1980 Campaign Files, George H. W. Bush Collection
Personal Correspondence Files, Post-Presidential Materials, George H. W. Bush
 Collection
Vice Presidential Daily Files, George H. W. Bush Collection
Vice Presidential Files, George H. W. Bush Collection
George Bush/Dan Quayle Presidential Campaign 1992
Prescott Bush Materials, Personal Papers, George H. W. Bush Collection
Bush Family Scrapbooks
James W. Cicconi Collection
Vic Gold Collection
David Hoffman Collection
Dorothy Bush Koch Collection
Donald R. (Rob) Quartel Collection
Don Rhodes Collection
Brent Scowcroft Collection, George H. W. Bush Presidential Records
John Maxwell (Jack) Steel Collection
Council of Economic Advisers, George H. W. Bush Presidential Records
National Security Council, George H. W. Bush Presidential Records
Miscellaneous Navy Materials, Post-Presidential Materials, George H. W. Bush Collection
Office of the Chief of Staff to the President, George H. W. Bush Presidential Records
Office of the Chief of Staff, Office of Vice President Dan Quayle
Office of Counsel to the President, George H. W. Bush Presidential Records
Office of Legislative Affairs, George H. W. Bush Presidential Records
Republican National Committee, Personal Papers, George H. W. Bush Collection
White House Office of Political Affairs, George H. W. Bush Presidential Records
White House Office of Records Management, George H. W. Bush Presidential Records
White House Office of Speechwriting, George H. W. Bush Presidential Records
World War II Correspondence, Personal Papers, George H. W. Bush Collection
Zapata Oil File, Personal Papers, George H. W. Bush Collection

OTHER MANUSCRIPT COLLECTIONS

Papers of Howard Baker, Jr., Ronald Reagan Presidential Library, Simi Valley, Calif.

Papers of James A. Baker III, Seeley G. Mudd Manuscript Library, Princeton University, Princeton, N.J.

Papers of James A. Baker III, Ronald Reagan Presidential Library, Simi Valley, Calif.

Papers of Patrick Buchanan, Ronald Reagan Presidential Library, Simi Valley, Calif.

Papers of Philip W. Buchen, Gerald R. Ford Presidential Library and Museum, Ann Arbor, Mich.

George H. W. Bush Oral History Project, Miller Center, University of Virginia, Charlottesville, Va.

George Bush Presidential Library and Museum, College Station, Tex.

George H. W. Bush Collection, Manuscripts and Archives, Sterling Library, Yale University, New Haven, Conn.

Correspondence of George H. W. Bush and Hugh Sidey, Office of George Bush, Private Files

George Bush, Class of 1942, Vertical Subject Files, Archives and Special Collections, Phillips Academy, Andover, Mass.

Prescott S. Bush Papers, Archives and Special Collections, Thomas J. Dodd Research Center, University of Connecticut Libraries, Storrs, Conn.

Samuel P. Bush Papers (VFM 2954), Ohio Historical Society, Columbus, Ohio

Papers of James M. Cannon, Gerald R. Ford Presidential Library and Museum, Ann Arbor, Mich.

Jimmy Carter Presidential Library and Museum, Atlanta, Ga.

Papers of Richard B. Cheney, Gerald R. Ford Presidential Library and Museum, Ann Arbor, Mich.

Church of the Ascension Archives, Staten Island, N.Y.

Papers of Richard G. Darman, Private Collection

Papers of Kenneth Duberstein, Ronald Reagan Presidential Library, Simi Valley, Calif.

Dwight D. Eisenhower Presidential Library, Abilene, Kan.

Gerald R. Ford Presidential Library and Museum, Ann Arbor, Mich.

President Gerald R. Ford's Daily Diary, Gerald R. Ford Presidential Library and Museum, Ann Arbor, Mich.

Grace Cathedral Archives, San Francisco

Papers of Alexander Haig, Gerald R. Ford Presidential Library and Museum, Ann Arbor, Mich.

Papers of Alexander Haig, Manuscript Division, Library of Congress, Washington, D.C.

Papers of W. Averell Harriman, Manuscript Division, Library of Congress, Washington, D.C.

Papers of Robert Hartmann, Gerald R. Ford Presidential Library and Museum, Ann Arbor, Mich.

Correspondence of Lyndon Johnson and George Herbert Walker Bush, Lyndon B. Johnson Presidential Library, Austin, Tex.

Papers of Clare Boothe Luce, Manuscript Division, Library of Congress, Washington, D.C.

Papers of Edwin Meese, Ronald Reagan Presidential Library, Simi Valley, Calif.

Papers of Daniel P. Moynihan, Manuscript Division, Library of Congress, Washington, D.C.

Papers of the National Security Council, Gerald R. Ford Presidential Library and Museum, Ann Arbor, Mich.

Correspondence of Richard Nixon and George Herbert Walker Bush, Richard Nixon Presidential Library and Museum, Yorba Linda, Calif.

Papers of Lyn Nofziger, Ronald Reagan Presidential Library, Simi Valley, Calif.

Papers of Oliver North, Ronald Reagan Presidential Library, Simi Valley, Calif.

Papers of Drew Pearson, Lyndon B. Johnson Presidential Library, Austin, Tex.

Papers of Gerald Rafshoon, Jimmy Carter Presidential Library and Museum, Atlanta, Ga.

President Ronald Reagan's Handwriting Files, Ronald Reagan Presidential Library, Simi Valley, Calif.

Papers of Donald Regan, Ronald Reagan Presidential Library, Simi Valley, Calif.

Archives of Donald Rumsfeld

Papers of William Rusher, Manuscript Division, Library of Congress, Washington, D.C.

Washington National Cathedral Archives, Washington, D.C.

Papers of the Office of the Watergate Special Prosecutor, National Archives, Washington, D.C.

Public Papers of the Presidents of the United States

The Public Papers and Addresses of Franklin D. Roosevelt. Compiled by Samuel I. Rosenman. Vol. 13, *Victory and the Threshold of Peace, 1944–45.* New York: Harper, 1950.

Public Papers of the Presidents of the United States: Barack Obama, 2011. 2 vols. Washington, D.C.: United States Government Printing Office, 2014.

Public Papers of the Presidents of the United States: George Bush, 1989–1993. 8 vols. Washington, D.C.: United States Government Printing Office, 1990–93.

Public Papers of the Presidents of the United States: George W. Bush, 2005. 2 vols. Washington, D.C.: United States Government Printing Office, 2007–09.

Public Papers of the Presidents of the United States: Harry S. Truman. Vol. I, *1945.* Washington, D.C.: United States Government Printing Office, 1961.

Public Papers of the Presidents of the United States: Richard Nixon. Vol. 1, *1969;* Vol. 3, *1971.* Washington, D.C.: United States Government Printing Office, 1971–72.

Public Papers of the Presidents of the United States: Ronald Reagan, 1981. Washington, D.C.: United States Government Printing Office, 1982.

Author Interviews

BUSH FAMILY INTERVIEWS

Barbara Pierce Bush

George Herbert Walker Bush

George W. Bush

Jeb Bush

Jonathan Bush

Laura Bush

Marvin Bush

Neil Bush

William T. "Bucky" Bush

Nancy Bush Ellis

Dorothy Bush Koch

G. H. ("Bert") Walker III

ADDITIONAL INTERVIEWS

Roger Ailes

Lamar Alexander

Ernest Angelo, Jr.

Elizabeth Bagley

James A. Baker III

Haley Barbour

Jean Becker

Rich Bond

Benjamin C. Bradlee

Nicholas F. Brady

Floyd Brown

Andrew Card

Jimmy Carter

Dana Carvey

Laura Chadwick

Dick Cheney

Liz Cheney
Bill Clinton
John C. Danforth
Christopher J. Dodd
Michael Dukakis
Dr. John Eckstein
Rahm Emanuel
Don Evans
Howard Fineman
Jennifer Fitzgerald
Marlin Fitzwater
Robert M. Gates
Newt Gingrich
Rudolph W. Giuliani
Vic Gold
Mikhail Gorbachev
Al Gore
C. Boyden Gray
Alan Greenspan
Donald P. Gregg
David Gregory
Richard N. Haass
Steve Hadley
Tom Harkin
David Jones
Ron Kaufman
Robert Kimmitt
Henry Kissinger
William Kristol
Dr. Burton Lee
James Leonard
Fred Malek
Mary Matalin
Anita McBride
Tim McBride
Larry McCarthy
Fred McClure
Jim McGrath
George Mitchell
Dr. Lawrence C. Mohr

Sam Nunn
Barack Obama
James Oberwetter
Peter O'Donnell
James Pavitt
Susie Peake
Gregg Petersmeyer
Jim Pinkerton
Roger Porter
Colin Powell
Patricia Presock
Dan Quayle
Sally Quinn
Gerald Rafshoon
Jesse Raiford
Clarke Reed
Condoleezza Rice
Sig Rogich
Andrew Rosenthal
Karl Rove
David Rubenstein
Donald Rumsfeld
Tim Samway
Jim Sasser
Brent Scowcroft
Craig Shirley
Richard M. Smith
Stu Spencer
George Stephanopoulos
Roger Stone
John Sununu
Pete Teeley
Clarence Thomas
Evan Thomas
Chase Untermeyer
Nicolle Wallace
Vin Weber
Sherrie Rollins Westin
Frank Wisner

Books Consulted

Abrams, Herbert L. *"The President Has Been Shot": Confusion, Disability, and the 25th Amendment in the Aftermath of the Attempted Assassination of Ronald Reagan.* New York: W. W. Norton, 1992.

Addison Gallery of American Art. *Academy Hill: The Andover Campus, 1778 to the Present.* New York: Princeton Architectural Press, 2000.

Adelman, Ken. *Reagan at Reykjavik: Forty-Eight Hours That Ended the Cold War.* New York: Broadside Books, 2014.

Aldrich, Nelson W., Jr. *Old Money: The Mythology of Wealth in America.* Expanded ed. New York: Allworth Press, 1996. First published in 1988 as *Old Money: The Mythology of America's Upper Class* by Alfred A. Knopf.

Allen, Steven J., and Richard A. Viguerie. *Lip Service: George Bush's 30-Year Battle with Conservatives.* Austin, Tex.: Castle Communications, 1992.

Allis, Frederick S., Jr. *Youth from Every Quarter: A Bicentennial History of Phillips Academy, Andover.* Hanover, N.H.: University Press of New England, 1979.

Ambrose, Stephen E. *Eisenhower.* 2 vols. New York: Simon and Schuster, 1983–84.

——. *Nixon.* 3 vols. New York: Simon and Schuster, 1987–91.

Anderson, Martin. *Revolution.* San Diego: Harcourt Brace Jovanovich, 1988.

——, and Annelise Anderson. *Reagan's Secret War: The Untold Story of His Fight to Save the World from Nuclear Disaster.* New York: Crown, 2009.

Ash, Timothy Garton. *In Europe's Name: Germany and the Divided Continent.* New York: Random House, 1993.

——. *The Magic Lantern: The Revolution of '89 Witnessed in Warsaw, Budapest, Berlin, and Prague.* New York: Random House, 1990.

Atkinson, Rick. *Crusade: The Untold Story of the Persian Gulf War.* Boston: Houghton Mifflin, 1993.

Auchincloss, Louis. *The Rector of Justin.* Boston: Houghton Mifflin, 1964.

——. *A Voice from Old New York: A Memoir of My Youth.* Boston: Houghton Mifflin Harcourt, 2010.

Bai, Matt. *All the Truth Is Out: The Week Politics Went Tabloid.* New York: Alfred A. Knopf, 2014.

Baker, Dean. *The United States Since 1980.* New York: Cambridge University Press, 2007.

Baker, James A., III, with Thomas M. DeFrank. *The Politics of Diplomacy: Revolution, War, and Peace, 1989–1992.* New York: Putnam, 1995.

Baker, James A., III, with Steve Fiffer. *Work Hard, Study—and Keep Out of Politics! Adventures and Lessons from an Unexpected Public Life.* New York: G. P. Putnam's Sons, 2006.

Baker, Peter. *Days of Fire: Bush and Cheney in the White House.* New York: Doubleday, 2013.

Baker, Russ. *Family of Secrets: The Bush Dynasty, the Powerful Forces That Put It in the White House, and What Their Influence Means for America.* New York: Bloomsbury Press, 2009.

Baltzell, E. Digby. *The Protestant Establishment: Aristocracy and Caste in America.* New Haven, Conn.: Yale University Press, 1987. First published in 1964 by Random House.

——. *The Protestant Establishment Revisited.* Edited by Howard G. Schneiderman. New Brunswick, N.J.: Transaction, 1991.

Barilleaux, Ryan J., and Mark J. Rozell. *Power and Prudence: The Presidency of George H. W. Bush.* The Presidency and Leadership, no. 17. College Station: Texas A&M University Press, 2004.

Barrett, Laurence I. *Gambling with History: Reagan in the White House.* Garden City, N.Y.: Doubleday 1983

Barry, John M. *The Ambition and the Power: The Fall of Jim Wright: A True Story of Washington.* New York: Viking, 1992.

Baumgartner, Jody C. *The American Vice Presidency Reconsidered.* Westport, Conn.: Praeger, 2006.

Beschloss, Michael R. "George Bush, 1989–1993." In *Character Above All: Ten Presidents from FDR to George Bush,* edited by Robert A. Wilson, 224–45. New York: Simon and Schuster, 1995.

——, and Strobe Talbott. *At the Highest Levels: The Inside Story of the End of the Cold War.* Boston: Little, Brown, 1993.

Bisnow, Mark. *Diary of a Dark Horse: The 1980 Anderson Presidential Campaign.* Carbondale: Southern Illinois University Press, 1983.

Black, Earl, and Merle Black. *The Rise of Southern Republicans.* Cambridge, Mass.: Harvard University Press, 2002.

———. *The Vital South: How Presidents Are Elected.* Cambridge, Mass.: Harvard University Press, 1992.

Blackford, Mansel G. *A Portrait Cast in Steel: Buckeye International and Columbus, Ohio, 1881–1980.* Contributions in Economics and Economic History, no. 49. Westport, Conn.: Greenwood Press, 1982.

Blumenthal, Sidney. *Pledging Allegiance: The Last Campaign of the Cold War.* New York: HarperCollins, 1990.

Bonnell, Victoria E., Ann Cooper, and Gregory Freidin, eds. *Russia at the Barricades: Eyewitness Accounts of the August 1991 Coup.* Armonk, N.Y.: M. E. Sharpe, 1994.

Bozo, Frédéric. *Mitterrand, the End of the Cold War, and German Unification.* Translated by Susan Emanuel. Berghahn Monographs in French Studies, no. 9. New York: Berghahn Books, 2009.

———, and Marie-Pierre Rey, N. Piers Ludlow, and Leopoldo Nuti, eds. *Europe and the End of the Cold War: A Reappraisal.* Cold War History Series, no. 19. New York: Routledge, 2008.

Bradley, James. *Flyboys: A True Story of Courage.* Boston: Little, Brown, 2003.

Brady, John. *Bad Boy: The Life and Politics of Lee Atwater.* Reading, Mass.: Addison-Wesley, 1997.

Brady, Nicholas F. *A Way of Going.* Privately published memoir, 2008.

Brands, H. W. *Reagan: The Life.* New York: Doubleday, 2015.

Bremer, Frances, and Emily Vogl. *Coping with His Success: A Survival Guide for Wives.* New York: Harper and Row, 1984.

Brinkley, Alan. *The Publisher: Henry Luce and His American Century.* New York: Alfred A. Knopf, 2010.

Broder, David S., and Bob Woodward. *The Man Who Would Be President: Dan Quayle.* New York: Simon and Schuster, 1992.

Brokaw, Tom. *The Greatest Generation.* New York: Random House, 1998.

Brookhiser, Richard. *The Way of the WASP: How It Made America, and How It Can Save It, So to Speak.* New York: Free Press, 1991.

Browning, Robert. *A History of Golf: The Royal and Ancient Game.* New York: Dutton, 1955.

Buckley, William F., Jr. *The Fall of the Berlin Wall.* 20th anniversary ed. Hoboken, N.J.: John Wiley and Sons, 2009.

———. *Let Us Talk of Many Things: The Collected Speeches.* Roseville, Calif.: Forum, 2000.

Busch, Andrew E. *Reagan's Victory: The Presidential Election of 1980 and the Rise of the Right.* American Presidential Elections Series. Lawrence: University Press of Kansas, 2005.

Bush, Barbara. *Barbara Bush: A Memoir.* New York: Scribner's Sons, 1994.

———. *C. Fred's Story.* Garden City, N.Y.: Doubleday, 1984.

———. *Millie's Book.* New York: William Morrow, 1990.

———. *Reflections: Life After the White House.* New York: Scribner, 2003.

Bush, George. *All the Best, George Bush: My Life in Letters and Other Writings.* Updated ed. New York: Scribner, 2013.

———. *The China Diary of George H. W. Bush: The Making of a Global President.* Edited by Jeffrey A. Engel. Princeton, N.J.: Princeton University Press, 2008.

———. *Heartbeat: George Bush in His Own Words.* Compiled and edited by Jim McGrath. New York: Scribner, 2001.

———, with Victor Gold. *Looking Forward.* Garden City, N.Y.: Doubleday, 1987.

———, and Brent Scowcroft. *A World Transformed.* New York: Alfred A. Knopf, 1998.

———, with Doug Wead. *Man of Integrity.* Eugene, Ore.: Harvest House, 1988.

Bush, George W. *A Charge to Keep.* New York: William Morrow, 1999.

———. *Decision Points.* New York: Crown, 2010.

———. *41: A Portrait of My Father.* New York: Crown, 2014.

Bush, James S. *Death of President Lincoln: A Sermon, Preached in Grace Church, Orange, N.J., Easter, April 16, 1865.* Orange, N.J.: E. Gardner, Printer, 1865.

Bush, Laura. *Spoken from the Heart.* New York: Scribner, 2010.

Cameron, Maxwell A., and Brian W. Tomlin. *The Making of NAFTA: How the Deal Was Done.* Ithaca, N.Y.: Cornell University Press, 2000.

Campbell, Colin, and Bert A. Rockman, eds. *The Bush Presidency: First Appraisals.* Chatham, N.J.: Chatham House, 1991.

Cannon, James. *Time and Chance: Gerald Ford's Appointment with History.* New York: HarperCollins, 1994.

Cannon, Lou. *President Reagan: The Role of a Lifetime.* New York: Simon and Schuster, 1991

———. *Reagan.* New York: G. P. Putnam's Sons, 1982.

Carleton, Don E. *Red Scare! Right-Wing Hysteria, Fifties Fanaticism, and Their Legacy in Texas.* Austin: Texas Monthly Press, 1985.

Carnegie, Andrew. *The Gospel of Wealth, and Other Timely Essays.* New York: Century, 1900.

Carter, Jimmy. *Keeping Faith: Memoirs of a President.* New York: Bantam Books, 1982.

Chafets, Zev. *Rush Limbaugh: An Army of One.* New York: Sentinel, 2010.

Chase, Alston Hurd. *Time Remembered.* San Antonio, Tex.: Parker Publishing, 1994.

Cheney, Dick, with Liz Cheney. *In My Time: A Personal and Political Memoir.* New York: Threshold Editions, 2011.

Chernyaev, Anatoly. *My Six Years with Gorbachev.* Translated and edited by Robert D. English and Elizabeth Tucker. University Park: Pennsylvania State University Press, 2000.

Chollet, Derek, and James Goldgeier. *America Between the Wars: From 11/9 to 9/11: The Misunderstood Years Between the Fall of the Berlin Wall and the Start of the War on Terror.* New York: BBS PublicAffairs, 2008.

Clark, Charles E. *My Fifty Years in the Navy.* Boston: Little, Brown, 1917.

Clarke, Richard A. *Against All Enemies: Inside America's War on Terror.* New York: Free Press, 2004.

Clemens, Gus. *Legacy: The Story of the Permian Basin Region of West Texas and Southeast New Mexico.* San Antonio, Tex.: Mulberry Avenue Books for the Nita Stewart Haley Memorial Library, 1983.

Clinton, Bill. *My Life.* New York: Alfred A. Knopf, 2004.

Cohen, Richard E. *Rostenkowski: The Pursuit of Power and the End of the Old Politics.* Chicago: Ivan R. Dee, 1999.

———. *Washington at Work: Back Rooms and Clean Air.* 2nd ed. Boston: Allyn and Bacon, 1994.

Cohen, William S., and George J. Mitchell. *Men of Zeal: A Candid Inside Story of the Iran-Contra Hearings.* New York: Viking, 1988.

Connally, John, with Mickey Herskowitz. *In History's Shadow: An American Odyssey.* New York: Hyperion, 1993.

Cookson, Peter W., Jr., and Caroline Hodges Persell. *Preparing for Power: America's Elite Boarding Schools.* New York: Basic Books, 1985.

Cornuelle, Richard C. *Reclaiming the American Dream.* New York: Random House, 1965.

Cox, Patrick. *Ralph W. Yarborough: The People's Senator.* Austin: University of Texas Press, 2001.

Cramer, Richard Ben. *Being Poppy: A Portrait of George Herbert Walker Bush.* New York: Simon & Schuster, 2013.

———. *What It Takes: The Way to the White House.* New York: Random House, 1992.

Crowley, Monica. *Nixon Off the Record.* New York: Random House, 1996.

Cuff, Robert D. *The War Industries Board: Business-Government Relations During World War I.* Baltimore: Johns Hopkins University Press, 1973.

Darling, Arthur B. *The Central Intelligence Agency: An Instrument of Government, to 1950.* University Park: Pennsylvania State University Press, 1990.

———. *Our Rising Empire, 1763–1803.* New Haven, Conn.: Yale University Press, 1940.

Darman, Jonathan. *Landslide: LBJ and Ronald Reagan at the Dawn of a New America.* New York: Random House, 2014.

Darman, Richard. *Who's in Control? Polar Politics and the Sensible Center.* New York: Simon and Schuster, 1996.

Dowd, Maureen. *Bushworld: Enter at Your Own Risk.* New York: G. P. Putnam's Sons, 2004.

Draper, Theodore. *A Very Thin Line: The Iran-Contra Affairs.* New York: Hill and Wang, 1991.

Drew, Elizabeth. *Portrait of an Election: The 1980 Presidential Campaign.* New York: Simon and Schuster, 1981.

Dubin, Michael J. *United States Congressional Elections, 1788–1997.* Jefferson, N.C.: McFarland, 1998.

Dueck, Colin. *Hard Line: The Republican Party and U.S. Foreign Policy since World War II.* Princeton, N.J.: Princeton University Press, 2010.

Duffy, Michael, and Dan Goodgame. *Marching in Place: The Status Quo Presidency of George Bush.* New York: Simon and Schuster, 1992.

Edsall, Thomas Byrne, with Mary D. Edsall. *Chain Reaction: The Impact of Race, Rights, and Taxes on American Politics.* New York: W. W. Norton, 1992.

Edwards, Anne. *Early Reagan.* New York: William Morrow, 1987.

Eisenhower, Dwight D. *At Ease: Stories I Tell to Friends.* Garden City, N.Y.: Doubleday, 1967.

———. *The White House Years.* 2 vols. Garden City, N.Y.: Doubleday, 1963–1965.

Elia, Susan D., Renée F. Seblatnigg, and Val P. Storms. *Greenwich Country Day: A History, 1926–1986.* Canaan, N.H.: Phoenix Publishing, 1988.

Ellis, Richard J., and Michael Nelson, eds. *Debating the Presidency: Conflicting Perspectives on the American Executive.* 2nd ed. Washington, D.C.: CQ Press, 2010.

Emerson, Ralph Waldo. *Ralph Waldo Emerson: Collected Poems and Translations.* Compiled by Harold Bloom and Paul Kane. New York: Library of America, 1994.

Engel, Jeffrey A., ed. *The Fall of the Berlin Wall: The Revolutionary Legacy of 1989.* New York: Oxford University Press, 2009.

———, ed. *Into the Desert: Reflections on the Gulf War.* New York: Oxford University Press, 2013.

Evans, Thomas W. *The Education of Ronald Reagan: The General Electric Years and the Untold Story of His Conversion to Conservatism.* Columbia Studies in Contemporary American History. New York: Columbia University Press, 2006.

Feldman, Leslie D., and Rosanna Perotti, eds. *Honor and Loyalty: Inside the Politics of the George H. W. Bush White House.* Westport, Conn.: Greenwood Press, 2002.

Feldstein, Martin, ed. *American Economic Policy in the 1980s.* A National Bureau of Economic Research Conference Report. Chicago: University of Chicago Press, 1994.

Ferguson, Thomas, and Joel Rogers, eds. *The Hidden Election: Politics and Economics in the 1980 Presidential Campaign.* New York: Pantheon Books, 1981.

Fineman, Howard. *The Thirteen American Arguments: Enduring Debates That Define and Inspire Our Country.* New York: Random House, 2008.

Fischer, David Hackett. *Paul Revere's Ride.* New York: Oxford University Press, 1994.

FitzGerald, Frances. *Way Out There in the Blue: Reagan, Star Wars, and the End of the Cold War.* New York: Simon and Schuster, 2000.

Fitzwater, Marlin. *Call the Briefing! Bush and Reagan, Sam and Helen: A Decade with Presidents and the Press.* New York: Times Books, 1995.

Ford, Gerald R. *A Time to Heal: The Autobiography of Gerald R. Ford.* New York: Harper and Row, 1979.

Frady, Marshall. *Wallace.* New York: World Publishing Co., 1968.

Friedman, Norman. *Desert Victory: The War for Kuwait.* Annapolis, Md.: Naval Institute Press, 1991.

Fuess, Claude M. *Independent Schoolmaster.* Boston: Little, Brown, 1952.

———. *An Old New England School: A History of Phillips Academy, Andover.* Boston: Houghton Mifflin, 1917.

Fukuyama, Francis. *The End of History and the Last Man.* New York: Free Press, 1992.

Gaddis, John Lewis. *The Cold War: A New History.* New York: Penguin Press, 2005.

———. *George F. Kennan: An American Life.* New York: Penguin Press, 2011.

———. *Strategies of Containment: A Critical Appraisal of Postwar American National Security Policy.* New York: Oxford University Press, 1982.

———. *We Now Know: Rethinking Cold War History.* New York: Oxford University Press, 1997.

Garthoff, Raymond L. *Détente and Confrontation: American-Soviet Relations from Nixon to Reagan.* Washington, D.C.: Brookings Institution, 1985.

Gates, Robert M. *Duty: Memoirs of a Secretary at War.* New York: Alfred A. Knopf, 2014.

———. *From the Shadows: The Ultimate Insider's Story of Five Presidents and How They Won the Cold War.* New York: Simon and Schuster, 1996.

Geer, John G. *In Defense of Negativity: Attack Ads in Presidential Campaigns.* Studies in Communication, Media, and Public Opinion. Chicago: University of Chicago Press, 2006.

Gellman, Barton. *Angler: The Cheney Vice Presidency.* New York: Penguin Press, 2008.

Germond, Jack W., and Jules Witcover. *Blue Smoke and Mirrors: How Reagan Won and Why Carter Lost the Election of 1980.* New York: Viking, 1981.

———. *Mad as Hell: Revolt at the Ballot Box, 1992.* New York: Warner Books, 1993.

———. *Wake Us When It's Over: Presidential Politics of 1984.* New York: Macmillan, 1985.

———. *Whose Broad Stripes and Bright Stars? The Trivial Pursuit of the Presidency, 1988.* New York: Warner Books, 1989.

Gibbs, Nancy, and Michael Duffy. *The Preacher and the Presidents: Billy Graham in the White House.* New York: Center Street, 2007.

———. *The Presidents Club: Inside the World's Most Exclusive Fraternity.* New York: Simon and Schuster, 2012.

Goddard, M. E., and Henry V. Partridge. *A History of Norwich, Vermont.* Hanover, N.H.: Dartmouth Press, 1905.

Goldman, Peter, Thomas M. DeFrank, Mark Miller, Andrew Murr, and Tom Mathews. *Quest for the Presidency, 1992.* College Station: Texas A&M University Press, 1994.

Goldman, Peter, and Tony Fuller. *The Quest for the Presidency, 1984.* A Newsweek Book. New York: Bantam Books, 1985.

Goldman, Peter, Tom Mathews, and the Newsweek Special Election Team. *The Quest for the Presidency, 1988.* New York: Simon and Schuster, 1989.

Goldwater, Barry M. *The Conscience of a Conservative.* Shepherdsville, Ky.: Victor, 1960.

Gorbachev, Mikhail. *The August Coup: The Truth and the Lessons.* New York: HarperCollins, 1991.

———. *Memoirs.* New York: Doubleday, 1996.

———. *On My Country and the World.* New York: Columbia University Press, 2000.

Gordon, Michael R., and Bernard E. Trainor. *The Generals' War: The Inside Story of the Conflict in the Gulf.* Boston: Little, Brown, 1995.

Gould, Lewis L. *Grand Old Party: A History of the Republicans.* New York: Random House, 2003.

Graham, Billy. *Just as I Am: The Autobiography of Billy Graham.* [San Francisco]: HarperSanFrancisco, 1997.

Graham, Bradley. *By His Own Rules: The Ambitions, Successes, and Ultimate Failures of Donald Rumsfeld.* New York: PublicAffairs, 2009.

Green, Fitzhugh. *George Bush: An Intimate Portrait.* New York: Hippocrene Books, 1989.

Green, George Norris. *The Establishment in Texas Politics: The Primitive Years, 1938–1957.* Contributions in Political Science, no. 21. Westport, Conn.: Greenwood Press, 1979.

Greene, John Robert. *The George H. W. Bush Years.* Presidential Profiles. New York: Facts on File, 2006.

———. *The Presidency of George Bush.* Lawrence: University Press of Kansas, 2000.

Greenfield, Jeff. *The Real Campaign: How the Media Missed the Story of the 1980 Campaign.* New York: Summit Books, 1982.

Greenspan, Alan. *The Age of Turbulence: Adventures in a New World.* New York: Penguin Press, 2007.

Gregg, Donald P. *Pot Shards: Fragments of a Life Lived in CIA, the White House, and the Two Koreas.* An ADST-DACOR Diplomats and Diplomacy Book. Washington, D.C.: Vellum, 2014.

Haass, Richard N. *War of Necessity, War of Choice: A Memoir of Two Iraq Wars.* New York: Simon and Schuster, 2009.

Hagstrom, Jerry. *Beyond Reagan: The New Landscape of American Politics.* New York: W. W. Norton, 1988.

Haig, Alexander M., Jr. *Caveat: Realism, Reagan, and Foreign Policy.* New York: Macmillan, 1984.

Halberstam, David. *War in a Time of Peace: Bush, Clinton, and the Generals.* New York: Scribner, 2001.

Han, Lori Cox. *A Presidency Upstaged: The Public Leadership of George H. W. Bush.* Joseph V. Hughes Jr. and Holly O. Hughes Series on the Presidency and Leadership. College Station: Texas A&M University Press, 2011.

Hargrove, Erwin C. *The Effective Presidency: Lessons on Leadership from John F. Kennedy to Barack Obama.* 2nd ed. Boulder, Colo.: Paradigm, 2014.

Harrington, Walt. *American Profiles: Somebodies and Nobodies Who Matter.* Columbia: University of Missouri Press, 1992.

Harris, John F. *The Survivor: Bill Clinton in the White House.* New York: Random House, 2005.

Hartmann, Robert T. *Palace Politics: An Inside Account of the Ford Years.* New York: McGraw-Hill, 1980.

Hayward, Steven F. *The Age of Reagan: The Fall of the Old Liberal Order, 1964–1980.* Roseville, Calif.: Forum, 2001.

Hearn, Chester. *Sorties into Hell: The Hidden War on Chichi Jima.* Westport, Conn.: Praeger, 2003.

Heilbrunn, Jacob. *They Knew They Were Right: The Rise of the Neocons.* New York: Doubleday, 2008.

Herskowitz, Mickey. *Duty, Honor, Country: The Life and Legacy of Prescott Bush.* Nashville: Rutledge Hill Press, 2003.

Hess, Gary R. *Presidential Decisions for War: Korea, Vietnam, the Persian Gulf, and Iraq.* 2nd ed. The American Moment. Baltimore: Johns Hopkins University Press, 2009.

Hibbert, Christopher. *Wellington: A Personal History.* New York: Da Capo Press, 1999.

Himelfarb, Richard, and Rosanna Perotti, eds. *Principle Over Politics? The Domestic Policy of the George H. W. Bush Presidency.* Contributions in Political Science, no. 396. Westport, Conn.: Praeger, 2004.

Hoffman, David E. *The Dead Hand: The Untold Story of the Cold War Arms Race and Its Dangerous Legacy.* New York: Doubleday, 2009.

Houghton, David Patrick. *The Decision Point: Six Cases in U.S. Foreign Policy Decision Making.* New York: Oxford University Press, 2013.

Hutchings, Robert L. *American Diplomacy and the End of the Cold War: An Insider's Account of U.S. Policy in Europe, 1989–1992.* Washington, D.C.: Woodrow Wilson Center Press, 1997.

Hyams, Joe. *Flight of the Avenger: George Bush at War.* San Diego: Harcourt Brace Jovanovich, 1991.

Hybel, Alex Roberto, and Justin Matthew Kaufman. *The Bush Administrations and Saddam Hussein: Deciding on Conflict.* Advances in Foreign Policy Analysis. New York: Palgrave Macmillan, 2006.

Isaacson, Walter, and Evan Thomas. *The Wise Men: Six Friends and the World They Made: Acheson, Bohlen, Harriman, Kennan, Lovett, McCloy.* New York: Simon and Schuster, 1986.

James, Harold, and Marla Stone, eds. *When the Wall Came Down: Reactions to German Unification.* New York: Routledge, 1992.

Jamieson, Kathleen Hall. *Dirty Politics: Deception, Distraction, and Democracy.* New York: Oxford University Press, 1992.

Johnson, Loch K. *A Season of Inquiry: The Senate Intelligence Investigation.* Lexington: University Press of Kentucky, 1985.

Johnson, Lyndon B. *Taking Charge: The Johnson White House Tapes, 1963–1964.* Edited by Michael R. Beschloss. New York: Simon and Schuster, 1997.

Johnson, Owen. *Stover at Yale.* With an introduction by Kingman Brewster, Jr. New York: Collier Books, 1968.

Kabaservice, Geoffrey. *The Guardians: Kingman Brewster, His Circle, and the Rise of the Liberal Establishment.* New York: Henry Holt, 2004.

———. *Rule and Ruin: The Downfall of Moderation and the Destruction of the Republican Party, from Eisenhower to the Tea Party.* Studies in Postwar American Political Development. New York: Oxford University Press, 2012.

Kaiser, Robert G. *Why Gorbachev Happened: His Triumphs and His Failure.* New York: Simon and Schuster, 1991.

Kaplan, David A. *The Accidental President: How 413 Lawyers, 9 Supreme Court Justices, and 5,963,110 (Give or Take a Few) Floridians Landed George W. Bush in the White House.* New York: William Morrow, 2001.

Kelley, Kitty. *The Family: The Real Story of the Bush Dynasty.* New York: Doubleday, 2004.

Kempton, Murray. *Rebellions, Perversities, and Main Events.* New York: Times Books, 1994.

Kengor, Paul. *God and George W. Bush: A Spiritual Life.* New York: ReganBooks, 2004.

Kennedy, Paul. *The Rise and Fall of the Great Powers: Economic Change and Military Conflict from 1500 to 2000.* New York: Random House, 1987.

Kenney, Padraic. *1989: Democratic Revolutions at the Cold War's End: A Brief History with Documents.* Bedford Series in History and Culture. Boston: Bedford/St. Martins, 2010.

King, Nicholas. *George Bush: A Biography.* New York: Dodd, Mead, 1980.

King, Willard L. *Lincoln's Manager, David Davis.* Cambridge, Mass.: Harvard University Press, 1960.

Kingsley, Charles. *The Works of Charles Kingsley.* Vol. 18, *Sanitary and Social Lectures and Essays.* London: Macmillan, 1880.

Kissinger, Henry. *Diplomacy.* New York: Simon and Schuster, 1994.

———. *White House Years.* Boston: Little, Brown, 1979.

———. *Years of Renewal.* New York: Simon and Schuster, 1999.

———. *Years of Upheaval.* Boston: Little, Brown, 1982.

Klein, Maury. *The Life and Legend of E. H. Harriman.* Chapel Hill: University of North Carolina Press, 2000.

Knaggs, John R. *Two-Party Texas: The John Tower Era, 1961–1984.* Austin, Tex.: Eakin Press, 1985.

Knott, Stephen F. *Rush to Judgment: George W. Bush, the War on Terror, and His Critics.* Lawrence: University Press of Kansas, 2012.

Knowles, John. *A Separate Peace.* New York: Macmillan, 1959.

Koch, Doro Bush. *My Father, My President: A Personal Account of the Life of George H. W. Bush.* New York: Warner Books, 2006.

Kotkin, Stephen, with a contribution by Jan T. Gross. *Uncivil Society: 1989 and the Implosion of the Communist Establishment.* Modern Library Chronicles, no. 32. New York: Modern Library, 2009.

Kouwenhoven, John A. *Partners in Banking: An Historical Portrait of a Great Private Bank, Brown Brothers Harriman & Co., 1818–1968.* Garden City, N.Y.: Doubleday, 1968.

Larson, Arthur. *A Republican Looks at His Party.* New York: Harper, 1956.

Lilley, James, with Jeffrey Lilley. *China Hands: Nine Decades of Adventure, Espionage, and Diplomacy in Asia.* New York: PublicAffairs, 2004.

MacDougall, Malcolm D. *We Almost Made It.* New York: Crown, 1977.

Maier, Charles S., ed. *The Cold War in Europe.* New York: Markus Wiener, 1991. Revised edition of *The Origins of the Cold War and Contemporary Europe,* published in 1978 by New Viewpoints.

———. *Dissolution: The Crisis of Communism and the End of East Germany.* Princeton, N.J.: Princeton University Press, 1997.

———. *The Unmasterable Past: History, Holocaust, and German National Identity.* Cambridge, Mass.: Harvard University Press, 1988.

Manchester, William. *The Glory and the Dream: A Narrative History of America, 1932–1972.* Boston: Little, Brown, 1974.

Mann, James. *The Rebellion of Ronald Reagan: A History of the End of the Cold War.* New York: Viking, 2009.

———. *Rise of the Vulcans: The History of Bush's War Cabinet.* New York: Viking, 2004.

Marsh, Lillian Hillyer. *One Hundred Years of Grace: A History of Grace Episcopal Church, Orange, New Jersey, 1854–1954.* Orange, N.J., 1954.

Martin, William C. *A Prophet with Honor: The Billy Graham Story.* New York: William Morrow, 1991.

Mason, Robert. *The Republican Party and American Politics from Hoover to Reagan.* New York: Cambridge University Press, 2012.

Matalin, Mary, James Carville, with Peter Knobler. *All's Fair: Love, War, and Running for President.* New York: Random House, 1994.

Matlock, Jack F., Jr. *Autopsy on an Empire: The American Ambassador's Account of the Collapse of the Soviet Union.* New York: Random House, 1995.

Maynard, Christopher. *Out of the Shadow: George H. W. Bush and the End of the Cold War.* Foreign Relations and the Presidency, no. 9. College Station: Texas A&M University Press, 2008.

McAdams, A. James. *Germany Divided: From the Wall to Reunification.* Princeton Studies in International History and Politics. Princeton, N.J.: Princeton University Press, 1993.

McGinniss, Joe. *The Selling of the President, 1968.* New York: Trident Press, 1969.

Medhurst, Martin J., ed. *The Rhetorical Presidency of George H. W. Bush.* Presidential Rhetoric Series, no. 14. College Station: Texas A&M University Press, 2006.

Memoirs of Members of the Social Circle in Concord: Third Series, from 1840 to 1895. Introduction signed by committee members John S. Keyes, Charles E. Brown, and F. Alcott Pratt. Cambridge, Mass.: Riverside Press, 1907.

Mendelberg, Tali. *The Race Card: Campaign Strategy, Implicit Messages, and the Norm of Equality.* Princeton, N.J.: Princeton University Press, 2001.

Merriner, James L. *Mr. Chairman: Power in Dan Rostenkowski's America.* Carbondale: Southern Illinois University Press, 1999.

Merry, Robert W. *Where They Stand: The American Presidents in the Eyes of Voters and Historians.* New York: Simon and Schuster, 2012.

Mervin, David. *George Bush and the Guardianship Presidency.* New York: St. Martin's Press, 1996.

Meyer, Michael. *The Year That Changed the World: The Untold Story Behind the Fall of the Berlin Wall.* New York: Scribner, 2009.

Middendorf, J. William, II. *Potomac Fever: A Memoir of Politics and Public Service.* Annapolis, Md.: Naval Institute Press, 2011.

Mitchell, George. *The Negotiator: A Memoir.* New York: Simon and Schuster, 2015.

Morison, Samuel Eliot. *The Two Ocean War: A Short History of the United States Navy in the Second World War.* Boston: Little, Brown, 1963.

Morris, Edmund. *Dutch: A Memoir of Ronald Reagan.* New York: Random House, 1999.

Morris, Sylvia Jukes. *Price of Fame: The Honorable Clare Boothe Luce.* New York: Random House, 2014.

———. *Rage for Fame: The Ascent of Clare Boothe Luce.* New York: Random House, 1997.

Moynihan, Daniel Patrick. *Daniel Patrick Moynihan: A Portrait in Letters of an American Visionary.* Edited by Steven R. Weisman. New York: PublicAffairs, 2010.

Murray, George Mosher, and James Callender Heminway, eds. *History of the Class of 1917, Yale College.* 3 vols. New Haven, Conn.. [Yale University Press], 1917–28.

Naftali, Timothy. *George H. W. Bush.* American Presidents Series, no. 41. New York: Times Books, 2007.

National Commission on Terrorist Attacks upon the United States. *The 9/11 Commission Report.* New York: W. W. Norton, 2004.

Nelson, Michael, ed. *The Evolving Presidency: Landmark Documents, 1787–2008.* 3rd ed. Washington, D.C.: CQ Press, 2008.

———, and Barbara A. Perry, eds. *41: Inside the Presidency of George H. W. Bush.* Ithaca, N.Y.: Cornell University Press, 2014.

Newton, Adam Zachary. *Narrative Ethics.* Cambridge, MA: Harvard University Press, 1997.

Nixon, Richard M. *RN: The Memoirs of Richard Nixon.* New York: Grosset and Dunlap, 1978.

Noonan, Peggy. *Life, Liberty, and the Pursuit of Happiness.* New York: Random House, 1994.

———. *What I Saw at the Revolution: A Political Life in the Reagan Era.* New York: Random House, 1990.

North, Oliver L., with William Novak. *Under Fire: An American Story.* New York: HarperCollins, 1992.

Novak, Robert D. *The Agony of the G.O.P., 1964.* New York: Macmillan, 1965.

Parmet, Herbert S. *George Bush: The Life of a Lone Star Yankee.* New York: Scribner, 1997.

Patterson, James T. *Grand Expectations: The United States, 1945–1974.* The Oxford History of the United States, vol. 10. New York: Oxford University Press, 1996.

———. *Restless Giant: The United States from Watergate to Bush v. Gore.* The Oxford History of the United States, vol. 11. New York: Oxford University Press, 2005.

Perlstein, Rick. *Before the Storm: Barry Goldwater and the Unmaking of the American Consensus.* New York: Hill and Wang, 2001.

———. *The Invisible Bridge: The Fall of Nixon and the Rise of Reagan.* New York: Simon and Schuster, 2014.

———. *Nixonland: The Rise of a President and the Fracturing of America.* New York: Scribner, 2008.

Phillips, Kevin. *American Dynasty: Aristocracy, Fortune, and the Politics of Deceit in the House of Bush.* New York. Viking, 2004.

———. *American Theocracy: The Peril and Politics of Radical Religion, Oil, and Borrowed Money in the 21st Century.* New York: Viking, 2006.

———. *The Emerging Republican Majority.* New Rochelle, N.Y.: Arlington House, 1969.

Plokhy, Serhii. *The Last Empire: The Final Days of the Soviet Union.* New York: Basic Books, 2014.

Podhoretz, John. *Hell of a Ride: Backstage at the White House Follies, 1989–1993.* New York: Simon and Schuster, 1993.

Polack, Peter. *The Last Hot Battle of the Cold War: South Africa vs. Cuba in the Angolan Civil War.* Havertown, Penn.: Casemate, 2013.

Popadiuk, Roman. *The Leadership of George Bush: An Insider's View of the Forty-First President.* Joseph V. Hughes Jr. and Holly O. Hughes Series on the Presidency and Leadership. College Station: Texas A&M University Press, 2009.

Posner, Gerald. *Citizen Perot: His Life and Times.* New York: Random House, 1996.

Powell, Colin L., with Joseph E. Persico. *My American Journey.* New York: Random House, 1995.

Price, Raymond. *With Nixon.* New York: Viking, 1977.

Quayle, Dan. *Standing Firm: A Vice-Presidential Memoir.* New York: HarperCollins, 1994.

Ranelagh, John. *The Agency: The Rise and Decline of the CIA.* New York: Simon and Schuster, 1986.

Rauch, Jonathan. *Demosclerosis: The Silent Killer of American Government.* New York: Times Books, 1994.

Reagan, Nancy, with William Novak. *My Turn: The Memoirs of Nancy Reagan.* New York: Random House, 1989.

Reagan, Ronald. *An American Life.* New York: Simon and Schuster, 1990.

——. *Reagan: A Life in Letters.* Edited by Kiron K. Skinner, Annelise Anderson, and Martin Anderson. New York: Free Press, 2003.

——. *The Reagan Diaries.* Edited by Douglas Brinkley. 2 vols. New York: HarperCollins, 2009.

Record, Jeffrey. *Making War, Thinking History: Munich, Vietnam, and Presidential Uses of Force from Korea to Kosovo.* Annapolis, Md.: Naval Institute Press, 2002.

Reeves, Richard. *President Nixon: Alone in the White House.* New York: Simon and Schuster, 2001.

——. *President Reagan: The Triumph of Imagination.* New York: Simon and Schuster, 2005.

Regan, Donald T. *For the Record: From Wall Street to Washington.* San Diego: Harcourt Brace Jovanovich, 1988.

Regnery, Alfred S. *Upstream: The Ascendance of American Conservatism.* New York: Threshold Editions, 2008.

Remnick, David. *Lenin's Tomb: The Last Days of the Soviet Empire.* New York: Random House, 1993.

Reston, James. *Deadline: A Memoir.* New York: Random House, 1991.

Reston, James, Jr. *The Lone Star: The Life of John Connally.* New York: Harper and Row, 1989.

Rice, Condoleezza. *No Higher Honor: A Memoir of My Years in Washington.* New York: Crown, 2011.

Richardson, Elliott. *Reflections of a Radical Moderate.* New York: Pantheon Books, 1996.

Robbins, Alexandra. *Secrets of the Tomb: Skull and Bones, the Ivy League, and the Hidden Paths of Power.* Boston: Little, Brown, 2002.

Rollins, Ed, with Tom DeFrank. *Bare Knuckles and Back Rooms: My Life in American Politics.* New York: Broadway Books, 1996.

Rose, Richard. *The Postmodern President: George Bush Meets the World.* Chatham, N.J.: Chatham House, 1988.

Rothkopf, David. *Running the World: The Inside Story of the National Security Council and the Architects of American Power.* New York: PublicAffairs, 2005.

Rove, Karl. *Courage and Consequence: My Life as a Conservative in the Fight.* New York: Threshold Editions, 2010.

Rugoff, Milton. *America's Gilded Age: Intimate Portraits from an Era of Extravagance and Change, 1850–1890.* New York: Henry Holt, 1989.

Rumsfeld, Donald. *Known and Unknown: A Memoir.* New York: Sentinel, 2011.

Safire, William. *Before the Fall: An Inside View of the Pre-Watergate White House.* Garden City, N.Y.: Doubleday, 1975.

Salinger, J. D. *The Catcher in the Rye.* Boston: Little, Brown, 1951.

Sarotte, Mary Elise. *The Collapse: The Accidental Opening of the Berlin Wall.* New York: Basic Books, 2014.

———. *1989: The Struggle to Create Post–Cold War Europe.* Princeton Studies in International History and Politics. Princeton, N.J.: Princeton University Press, 2009.

Schaller, Michael. *Right Turn: American Life in the Reagan-Bush Era, 1980–1992.* New York: Oxford University Press, 2007.

Schell, Orville. *Mandate of Heaven: A New Generation of Entrepreneurs, Dissidents, Bohemians, and Technocrats Lays Claim to China's Future.* New York: Simon and Schuster, 1994.

Schlesinger, Arthur M., Jr. *The Cycles of American History.* Boston: Houghton Mifflin, 1986.

———. *The Imperial Presidency.* Mariner Books ed. Boston: Houghton Mifflin, 2004.

Schmemann, Serge. *When the Wall Came Down: The Berlin Wall and the Fall of Soviet Communism.* Boston: Kingfisher, 2006.

Schneider, Gregory L., ed. *Conservatism in America Since 1930: A Reader.* New York: New York University Press, 2003.

Schweizer, Peter, and Rochelle Schweizer. *The Bushes: Portrait of a Dynasty.* New York: Doubleday, 2004.

Sennett, Richard. *The Fall of Public Man.* New York: Alfred A. Knopf, 1977.

Sheehy, Gail. *Hillary's Choice.* New York: Random House, 1999.

Sherman, Gabriel. *The Loudest Voice in the Room: How the Brilliant, Bombastic Roger Ailes Built Fox News—and Divided a Country.* New York: Random House, 2014.

Shirley, Craig. *Reagan's Revolution: The Untold Story of the Campaign That Started It All.* Nashville: Nelson Current, 2005.

———. *Rendezvous with Destiny: Ronald Reagan and the Campaign That Changed America.* Wilmington, Del.: ISI Books, 2009.

Shrum, Robert. *No Excuses: Concessions of a Serial Campaigner.* New York: Simon and Schuster, 2008.

Shultz, George P. *Turmoil and Triumph: My Years as Secretary of State.* New York: Scribner's, 1993.

Simon, Roger. *Road Show: In America, Anyone Can Become President; It's One of the Risks We Take.* New York: Farrar, Straus, Giroux, 1990.

Simpson, Alan K. *Right in the Old Gazoo: A Lifetime of Scrapping with the Press.* New York: William Morrow, 1997.

Smith, Curt. *George H. W. Bush: Character at the Core.* Lincoln, Neb.: Potomac Books, 2014.

Smith, Jean Edward. *George Bush's War.* New York: Henry Holt, 1992.

Smith, Richard Norton. *On His Own Terms: A Life of Nelson Rockefeller.* New York: Random House, 2014.

Sparrow, Bartholomew. *The Strategist: Brent Scowcroft and the Call of National Security.* New York: PublicAffairs, 2015.

Stacks, John F. *Watershed: The Campaign for the Presidency, 1980.* New York: Times Books, 1981.

Stephanopoulos, George. *All Too Human: A Political Education.* Boston: Little, Brown, 1999.

Stewart, Richard W. *War in the Persian Gulf: Operations Desert Shield and Desert Storm, August 1990–March 1991.* Washington, D.C.: Center of Military History, U.S. Army, 2010.

Stimson, James A. *Public Opinion in America: Moods, Cycles, and Swings.* 2nd ed. Boulder, Colo.: Westview Press, 1999.

Stockman, David A. *The Triumph of Politics: How the Reagan Revolution Failed.* New York: Harper and Row, 1986.

Strong, Robert A. *Decisions and Dilemmas: Case Studies in Presidential Foreign Policy Making Since 1945.* 2nd ed. Armonk, N.Y.: M. E. Sharpe, 2005.

Strook, Thomas Frank, ed. *1948 Class Book Yale University.* ed. New Haven, Conn.: [Yale University Press], 1948.

Sununu, John H. *The Quiet Man: The Indispensable Presidency of George H. W. Bush.* New York: HarperCollins, 2015.

Tarkington, Booth. *The Magnificent Ambersons.* Mineola, N.Y.: Dover, 2006. First published in 1918 by Doubleday, Page.

Taylor, Frederick. *The Berlin Wall: A World Divided, 1961–1989.* New York: HarperCollins, 2006.

Thomas, Evan. *Ike's Bluff: President Eisenhower's Secret Battle to Save the World.* New York: Little, Brown, 2012.

——. *The Man to See: Edward Bennett Williams; Ultimate Insider; Legendary Trial Lawyer.* New York: Simon and Schuster, 1991.

Thompson, Kenneth W., ed. *The Bush Presidency: Ten Intimate Perspectives of George Bush.* 2 vols. Portraits of American Presidents, vols. 10–11. Lanham, Md.: University Press of America, 1997–1998.

Toland, John. *The Rising Sun: The Decline and Fall of the Japanese Empire, 1936–1945.* New York: Random House, 1970.

Tolstoy, Leo. *War and Peace.* Translated by Constance Garnett. The Modern Library Classics. New York: Modern Library, 2004.

Tower, John G. *Consequences: A Personal and Political Memoir.* Boston: Little, Brown, 1991.

Townsend, Kim. *Manhood at Harvard: William James and Others.* New York: W. W. Norton, 1996.

Unger, Craig. *House of Bush, House of Saud: The Secret Relationship Between the World's Two Most Powerful Dynasties.* New York: Scribner, 2004.

Untermeyer, Chase. *When Things Went Right: The Dawn of the Reagan-Bush Administration.* College Station: Texas A&M University Press, 2013.

Valdez, David, comp. *George Herbert Walker Bush: A Photographic Profile.* College Station: Texas A&M University Press, 1997.

Walsh, Lawrence E. *Firewall: The Iran-Contra Conspiracy and Cover-Up.* New York: W. W. Norton, 1997.

——. *Iran-Contra: The Final Report.* New York: Times Books, 1994.

Weiner, Tim. *Legacy of Ashes: The History of the CIA.* New York: Doubleday, 2007.

Weisberg, Jacob. *The Bush Tragedy.* New York: Random House, 2008.

Welch, Robert. *The Politician.* Belmont, Mass.: Belmont, 1963.

Werth, Barry. *31 Days: The Crisis That Gave Us the Government We Have Today.* New York: Nan A. Talese/Doubleday, 2006.

Wessel, David. *Red Ink: Inside the High-Stakes Politics of the Federal Budget.* New York: Crown Business, 2012.

White, Theodore H. *America in Search of Itself: The Making of the President, 1956–1980.* New York: Harper and Row, 1982.

——. *Breach of Faith: The Fall of Richard Nixon.* New York: Atheneum, 1975.

——. *The Making of the President, 1972.* New York: Atheneum, 1973.

——. *The Making of the President, 1968.* New York: Atheneum, 1969.

——. *The Making of the President, 1964.* New York: Atheneum, 1965.

Wicker, Tom. *George Herbert Walker Bush.* A Penguin Life. New York: Lipper/Viking, 2004.

Wilber, Del Quentin. *Rawhide Down: The Near Assassination of Ronald Reagan.* New York, Henry Holt, 2011.

Wilentz, Sean. *The Age of Reagan: A History, 1974–2008.* New York: Harper, 2008.

Wills, Garry. *Confessions of a Conservative.* Garden City, N.Y.: Doubleday, 1979.

——. *Reagan's America: Innocents at Home.* Garden City, N.Y.: Doubleday, 1987.

Witcover, Jules. *Marathon: The Pursuit of the Presidency, 1972–1976.* New York: Viking, 1977.

Woodward, Bob. *Bush at War.* New York: Simon and Schuster, 2002.

——. *The Commanders.* New York: Simon and Schuster, 1991.

———. *Plan of Attack*. New York: Simon and Schuster, 2004.

———. *Shadow: Five Presidents and the Legacy of Watergate*. New York: Simon and Schuster, 1999.

———. *State of Denial*. New York: Simon and Schuster, 2006.

———. *Veil: The Secret Wars of the CIA, 1981–1987*. New York: Simon and Schuster, 1987.

Zelikow, Philip, and Condoleezza Rice. *Germany Unified and Europe Transformed: A Study in State-craft*. Cambridge, Mass.: Harvard University Press, 1995.

Zubok, Vladislav M. *A Failed Empire: The Soviet Union in the Cold War from Stalin to Gorbachev*. The New Cold War History. Chapel Hill: University of North Carolina Press, 2007.

Selected Articles Consulted

Aberbach, Joel D., and Bert A. Rockman. "The Political Views of U.S. Senior Federal Executives, 1970–1992." *Journal of Politics* 57, no. 3 (August 1995): 838–52.

Abramson, Paul R., John H. Aldrich, Phil Paolino, and David W. Rohde. "Third-Party and Independent Candidates in American Politics: Wallace, Anderson, and Perot." *Political Science Quarterly* 110, no. 3 (Autumn 1995): 349–67.

Akam, Simon. "George W. Bush's Great-Great-Great-Great-Grandfather Was a Slave Trader." Slate, June 20, 2013. Accessed June 7, 2015. http://www.slate.com/articles/life /history_lesson/2013/06/george_w_bush_and_slavery_the_president_and_his _father_are_descendants_of.html.

Allen, Richard V. "The Accidental Vice President." *New York Times Magazine,* July 30, 2000, 36–39.

———. "The Day Reagan Was Shot," *The Atlantic,* April 2001.

Alvarez, R. Michael, and Jonathan Nagler. "Economics, Issues and the Perot Candidacy: Voter Choice in the 1992 Presidential Election." *American Journal of Political Science* 39, no. 3 (August 1995): 714–44.

Bell, David S., Erwin C. Hargrove, and Kevin Theakston. "Skill in Context: A Comparison of Politicians." *Presidential Studies Quarterly* 29, no. 3 (September 1999): 528–48.

Blumenthal, Sidney, "Willie Horton & The Making of an Election Issue; How the Furlough Factor Became a Stratagem of the Bush Forces." *Washington Post,* October 28, 1988.

Bolce, Louis, Gerald De Maio, and Douglas Muzzio. "The 1992 Republican 'Tent': No Blacks Walked In." *Political Science Quarterly* 108, no. 2 (Summer 1993): 255–70.

Brands, H. W. "George Bush and the Gulf War of 1991." *Presidential Studies Quarterly* 34, no. 1 (March 2004): 113–31.

Bush, James S. "The Cruise of the 'Monadnock.'" Pts. 1–3. *Overland Monthly,* July 1869, 15–21; September 1869, 201–8; October 1869, 366–72.

Cohen, David B. "From the Fabulous Baker Boys to the Master of Disaster: The White House Chief of Staff in the Reagan and G. H. W. Bush Administrations." *Presidential Studies Quarterly* 32, no. 3 (September 2002): 463–83.

———, and George A. Krause. "Presidents, Chiefs of Staff, and White House Organizational Behavior: Survey Evidence from the Reagan and Bush Administrations." *Presidential Studies Quarterly* 30, no. 3 (September 2000): 421–42.

Conason, Joe. "1,000 Reasons Not to Vote for George Bush." *Spy,* July/August, 1992, 29–38.

———. "Roger & He." *New Republic,* May 28, 1990, 18.

Crabb, Cecil V., and Kevin V. Mulcahy. "George Bush's Management Style and Operation Desert Storm." *Presidential Studies Quarterly* 25, no. 2 (Spring 1995): 251–65.

Crean, Jeffrey. "War on the Line: Telephone Diplomacy in the Making and Maintenance of the Desert Storm Coalition." *Diplomacy and Statecraft* 26, no. 1 (March 2015): 124–38.

Crouch, Jeffrey. "The Law: Presidential Misuse of the Pardon Power." *Presidential Studies Quarterly* 38, no. 4 (December 2008): 722–34.

Deibel, Terry L. "Bush's Foreign Policy: Mastery and Inaction." *Foreign Policy* no. 84 (Autumn 1991): 3–23.

Dowd, Maureen, and Thomas L. Friedman. "The Fabulous Bush and Baker Boys." *New York Times Magazine,* May 6, 1990, 34ff.

Engel, Jeffrey A. "A Better World . . . but Don't Get Carried Away: The Foreign Policy of George H. W. Bush Twenty Years On." *Diplomatic History* 34, no. 1 (January 2010): 25–46.

———. "Bush, Germany, and the Power of Time: How History Makes History." *Diplomatic History* 37, no. 4 (September 2013): 639–63.

Fleisher, Richard, and Jon R. Bond. "Assessing Presidential Support in the House II: Lessons from George Bush." *American Journal of Political Science* 36, no. 2 (May 1992): 525–41.

Garthoff, Raymond L. "Estimating Soviet Military Intentions and Capabilities." Central Intelligence Agency, Center for the Study of Intelligence. Accessed June 7, 2015.

"George Bush: Calm Between Storms." Central Intelligence Agency, Center for the Study of Intelligence. Accessed June 7, 2015.

Goldberg, Jeffrey. "Breaking Ranks." *The New Yorker,* October 31, 2005.

Goldberger, Peter. "The Triumph of Conservatism." Review of *The Right Nation: Conservative Power in America,* by John Micklethwait and Adrian Wooldridge. *New Labor Forum* 14, no. 3 (Fall 2005): 130–35.

Hall, Wynton C. " 'Reflections of Yesterday': George H. W. Bush's Instrumental Use of Public Opinion Research in Presidential Discourse." *Presidential Studies Quarterly* 32, no. 3 (September 2002): 531–58.

Hammer, Dean C. "The Oakeshottian President: George Bush and the Politics of the Present." *Presidential Studies Quarterly* 25, no. 2 (Spring 1995): 301–13.

Heclo, Hugh. "The Mixed Legacies of Ronald Reagan." *Presidential Studies Quarterly* 38, no. 4 (December 2008): 555–74.

Hess, Gary R. "Presidents and the Congressional War Resolutions of 1991 and 2002." *Political Science Quarterly* 121, no. 1 (Spring 2006): 93–118.

Hetherington, Marc J. "The Media's Role in Forming Voters' National Economic Evaluations in 1992." *American Journal of Political Science* 40, no. 2 (May 1996): 372–95.

Hughes, Roger. "Legacy." *Illinois Times,* April 5, 2007. Accessed June 7, 2015. http://illinoistimes.com/article-3993-legacy.html.

———. "Twists, Turns, Ties: David Davis and George Bush." *The Pantagraph* (Bloomington, Ill.), November 7, 2004.

"In-Depth Discussions with Carter." Central Intelligence Agency, Center for the Study of Intelligence. Accessed June 7, 2015.

Koch, Jeffrey. "The Perot Candidacy and Attitudes toward Government and Politics." *Political Research Quarterly* 51, no. 1 (March 1998): 141–53.

Lacy, Dean, and Barry C. Burden. "The Vote-Stealing and Turnout Effects of Ross Perot in the 1992 U.S. Presidential Election." *American Journal of Political Science* 43, no. 1 (January 1999): 233–55.

Ladd, Everett Carll. "The 1992 Vote for President Clinton: Another Brittle Mandate?" *Political Science Quarterly* 108, no. 1 (Spring 1993): 1–28.

Laffin, Martin. "The President and the Subcontractors: The Role of Top Level Policy Entrepreneurs in the Bush Administration." *Presidential Studies Quarterly* 26, no. 2 (Spring 1996): 550–66.

Lemann, Nicholas. "Bush and Dole: The Roots of a Feud." *The Washington Post,* February 28, 1988.

Lewis, David A., and Roger P. Rose. "The President, the Press, and the War-Making Power: An Analysis of Media Coverage Prior to the Persian Gulf War." *Presidential Studies Quarterly* 32, no. 3 (September 2002): 559–71.

Malman, Myles H. "United States v. Manuel Noriega: Never Before, Never Again." *Litigation* 28, no. 2 (Winter 2002): 13–20.

Mandelbaum, Michael. "The Bush Foreign Policy." *Foreign Affairs* 70, no. 1 (1990/1991): 5–22.

Mayer, Kenneth R., and Kevin Price. "Unilateral Presidential Powers: Significant Executive Orders, 1949–99." *Presidential Studies Quarterly* 32, no. 2 (June 2002): 367–86.

Mayhew, David R. "Incumbency Advantage in U.S. Presidential Elections: The Historical Record." *Political Science Quarterly* 123, no. 2 (Summer 2008): 201–28.

McDaniel, Ann. "Barbara Bush: The Steel Behind the Smile." *Newsweek,* June 22, 1992, 34.

McGuinn, Patrick. "The Era of Education: Is it Beginning or Ending?" Review of *The Era of Education: The Presidents and the Schools, 1965–2001,* by Lawrence J. McAndrews. *Reviews in American History* 35, no. 1 (March 2007): 133–39.

Mendelberg, Tali. "Executing Hortons: Racial Crime in the 1988 Presidential Campaign." Special Issue on Race. *Public Opinion Quarterly* 61, no. 1 (Spring 1997): 134–57.

Michaels, Judith E. "A View from the Top: Reflections of the Bush Presidential Appointees." *Public Administration Review* 55, no. 3 (May–June, 1995): 273–83.

Miller, Eric A., and Steve A. Yetiv. "The New World Order in Theory and Practice: The Bush Administration's Worldview in Transition." *Presidential Studies Quarterly* 31, no. 1 (March 2001): 56–68.

Mullins, Kerry, and Aaron Wildavsky. "The Procedural Presidency of George Bush." *Political Science Quarterly* 107, no. 1 (Spring 1992): 31–62.

Nacos, Brigitte Lebens. "Presidential Leadership During the Persian Gulf Conflict." *Presidential Studies Quarterly* 24, no. 3 (Summer 1994): 543–61.

Natoli, Marie D. "Campaign '88: President Bush or President Dukakis?" *Presidential Studies Quarterly* 18, no. 4 (Fall 1988): 707–16.

Newmann, William. "Causes of Change in National Security Processes: Carter, Reagan, and Bush Decision Making on Arms Control." *Presidential Studies Quarterly* 31, no. 1 (March 2001): 69–103.

———. "The Structures of National Security Decision Making: Leadership, Institutions, and Politics in the Carter, Reagan, and G. H. W. Bush Years." *Presidential Studies Quarterly* 34, no. 2 (June 2004): 272–306.

Pious, Richard M. "Why Do Presidents Fail?" *Presidential Studies Quarterly* 32, no. 4 (December 2002): 724–42.

Rauch, Jonathan. "Father Superior: Our Greatest Modern President." *The New Republic,* May 22, 2000.

Remnick, David. "Why Is Lee Atwater So Hungry?" *Esquire,* December 1986.

Rodgers, Thomas E. "Billy Yank and G.I. Joe: An Exploratory Essay on the Sociopolitical Dimensions of Soldier Motivation." *Journal of Military History* 69, no. 1 (January 2005): 93–121.

Rozell, Mark J. "In Reagan's Shadow: Bush's Antirhetorical Presidency." *Presidential Studies Quarterly* 28, no. 1 (Winter 1998): 127–38.

Schram, Martin. "The Making of Willie Horton." *New Republic,* May 28, 1990, 17–18.

Sirgiovanni, George. "The 'Van Buren Jinx': Vice Presidents Need Not Beware." *Presidential Studies Quarterly* 18, no. 1 (Winter 1988): 61–76.

Skowronek, Stephen. "The Conservative Insurgency and Presidential Power: A Developmental Perspective on the Unitary Executive." *Harvard Law Review* 122, no. 8 (June 2009): 2070–103.

Smyth, David J., and Susan Washburn Taylor. "Why Do the Republicans Win the White House More Often Than the Democrats?" *Presidential Studies Quarterly* 22, no. 3 (Summer 1992): 481–91.

Stanley, Alessandra. "Presidency by Ralph Lauren." *New Republic,* December 12, 1988, 18–20.

Stark, Leonard P. "Predicting Presidential Performance from Campaign Conduct: A Character Analysis of the 1988 Election." *Presidential Studies Quarterly* 22, no. 2 (Spring 1992): 295–309.

Steger, Wayne P. "Presidential Renomination Challenges in the 20th Century." *Presidential Studies Quarterly* 33, no. 4 (December 2003): 827–52.

Stone, Emerson. "The Way We Were in 'Poppy's' Days." *Yale University Magazine,* February 1989.

Stone, Walter J., and Ronald B. Rapoport. "It's Perot Stupid! The Legacy of the 1992 Perot Movement in the Major-Party System, 1994–2000." *PS: Political Science and Politics* 34, no. 1 (March 2001): 49–58.

Timmerman, David M. "1992 Presidential Candidate Films: The Contrasting Narratives of George Bush and Bill Clinton." *Presidential Studies Quarterly* 26, no. 2 (Spring 1996): 364–73.

Waterman, Richard W. "Storm Clouds on the Political Horizon: George Bush at the Dawn of the 1992 Presidential Election." *Presidential Studies Quarterly* 26, no. 2 (Spring 1996): 337–49.

Winter, David G., Margaret G. Hermann, Walter Weintraub, and Stephen G. Walker. "The Personalities of Bush and Gorbachev Measured at a Distance: Procedures, Portraits, and Policy." *Political Psychology* 12, no. 2 (June 1991): 215–45.

Wolfowitz, Paul. "Realism." *Foreign Policy* no. 174 (September/October 2009): 66–68, 70, 72.

Dissertation

Kreidler, Tai Deckner. "The Offshore Petroleum Industry: The Formative Years, 1945–1962." PhD diss., Texas Tech University, 1997.

PERMISSION CREDITS

★

ILLUSTRATION CREDITS

★

468 BUSH WALKS THE WHITE HOUSE GROUNDS: George Bush Presidential Library and Museum
477 BUSH SPEAKS AT ARLINGTON: George Bush Presidential Library and Museum
517 1992 PRESIDENTIAL DEBATE: courtesy CNN
527 GEORGE AND BARBARA WELCOME THE CLINTONS: George Bush Presidential Library and Museum

SECTION I

All photographs courtesy of the George Bush Presidential Library and Museum except for the following:

- JAMES SMITH BUSH: Missouri History Museum, St. Louis
- S. P. BUSH: courtesy of the S. C. Williams Library, Special Collections and Archives; Stevens Institute of Technology, Hoboken, NJ
- LIBRARY AT PHILLIPS ACADEMY: Francis Cookson/Phillips Academy
- GROUNDS AT YALE UNIVERSITY: John Phillips/LIFE magazine/The LIFE Picture Collection/Getty Images
- BUSH, WITH FOOT ON DESK, SPEAKS TO STUDENTS ON CAMPAIGN TRAIL: Associated Press
- GEORGE H. W. BUSH AND GERALD FORD: David Hume Kennerly/Getty Images
- DENG XIAOPING, GEORGE H. W. BUSH, AND GERALD FORD: David Hume Kennerly/Getty Images
- MILTON PITTS CUTS BUSH'S HAIR: David Hume Kennerly/Getty Images
- CIA DIRECTOR BUSH HOLDS HIS GLASSES DURING A CRISIS IN LEBANON: David Hume Kennerly/Getty Images
- GEORGE BROWN, BRENT SCOWCROFT, GEORGE BUSH, DONALD RUMSFELD, HENRY KISSINGER, AND NELSON ROCKEFELLER IN PRESIDENT FORD'S OVAL OFFICE: David Hume Kennerly/Getty Images

SECTION II

All photographs courtesy of the George Bush Presidential Library and Museum except for the following:

- RONALD REAGAN AND BUSH WAVE TO CHEERING CROWDS AT THE RNC: Neil Leifer/Sports Illustrated/Getty Images
- REAGAN AND BUSH WALK TOGETHER ON THE WHITE HOUSE GROUNDS: David Hume Kennerly/Getty Images
- BUSH AND TIP O'NEILL TALK TOGETHER AT REAGAN'S STATE OF THE UNION: David Hume Kennerly/Getty Images (4 photographs)
- BUSH SHAKES HANDS WITH MICHAEL DUKAKIS: Associated Press/Lennox McLendon
- BUSH WITH NEWT GINGRICH: Associated Press/Joe Marquette
- PRESIDENT BUSH AND HIS TEAM BRIEF THE PRESS IN THE ROSE GARDEN ON THE EVE OF THE GULF WAR: David Hume Kennerly/Getty Images
- BARBARA BUSH READS TO A GROUP OF CHILDREN: Everett Collection
- BUSH AND TOM BROKAW RIDE TOGETHER IN BUSH'S MOTORBOAT: David Hume Kennerly/Getty Images
- PRESIDENTS GEORGE H. W. BUSH, BARACK OBAMA, GEORGE W. BUSH, BILL

INDEX

★

Graham, Katharine, 94, 134
Graham, Philip, 94
Gramm, Phil, 412
Grant, Arthur, 29
Grassley, Chuck, 339
Graves' disease, 470, 475–76, 509, 755–56n475, 755n475, 756n476, 767n509;
Gray, Boyden, 262, 265, 266, 268, 302, 395, 419, 423, 479, 531, 535, 772n531
Gray, Gordon, 134
Gray, Robert, 502
Great Depression, 27, 629n27
Green, Betty, 272
Green, Shirley, 269
Greenberg, Morris, 74–75
Greenspan, Alan, 247, 248, 250, 409–10, 469
Greenwich, CT: Christ Episcopal Church, 25, 528; GHWB raised in, home on Grove Lane, xv, xx, 24–32, 295, 519; Lindbergh kidnapping and, 629n27; photograph of Robin at Bush family home, Grove Lane, 103, 104; Prescott Bush and local government, 22; Prescott Bushes move to, 20; Prescott Bush funeral, 161
Greenwich Country Club, 41
Greenwich Country Day School, 28–29, 629–30n29, 630n29; recommendation of GHWB to Andover, 630n29
Greenwood, Lee, 520
Gregg, Donald P., 304, 704n305
Gregg, Hugh, 227, 322
Gregg, Judd, 322
Grenada, 388, 428
Gridiron Club, 269
Griscom, Tom, 314
Groton School, Groton, MA, 11, 11
Gulf War, xvi, 356, 450–57, 458–69, 468; air war, 458–61; American losses, 466; antiwar sentiment (No Blood for Oil), 441, 453; Arlington National Cemetery memorial service for fallen of, 476–78, 477; "body-bag argument," 460; Brookings Institution projection of casualties, 462; congressional opponents, 450, 452; congressional vote, 455; GHWB address to Congress (Sept. 11, 1990), 442, 443;

GHWB address to the nation (August 8, 1990), 436–37; GHWB address to the nation (February 23, 1991), 463; GHWB address to the nation (February 27, 1991), 465–66; GHWB-led coalition, 437, 442, 464–65, 466, 744n432; GHWB mistakes at end of, 467; GHWB's decision-making style and, 428–29; GHWB's mission in, 458–59, 464–65; GHWB's postwar despondency, 467–68; GHWB ultimatum to Saddam, 462; ground war, 461–63; Iraqi losses, 466; Iraqi prisoners, 466; Iraq Scud missile attacks on Israel, 459; Operation Desert Shield, 436, 450; Operation Desert Storm, 450, 464; public approval, 441, 466; returning troops, 465–66; run-up to, 421–42, 741–42n424, 741n423; U.S. planning and strategy, 450, 745n432
gun control, 393

Haass, Richard, 420, 421, 425, 426, 430, 432, 455, 494, 744n432
Hager, Poppy Louise (great-granddaughter), 594
Haig, Alexander "Al," 169, 172, 267, 298, 309, 669n169, 672n177, 673n177; Reagan assassination attempt and, 273, 274, 277–78, 279, 280, 281
Haldeman, H. R. "Bob," 152, 153, 154, 169, 170, 664n152, 667n162, 673n177; "Townhouse Operation," 672n177
Hall, Len, 667n162
Hampton, Margaret, 118
Hance, Kent, 213, 214
Harkin, Tom, 395, 478
Harlow, Bryce, 165, 176, 195–96, 262
Harriman, W. Averell, 17, 18; Brown Brothers Harriman & Company and, 21; list of achievements, 21
Harrington, Walt, 134
Harris, Robert, 376
Hart, Gary, 196, 309, 500
Hartmann, Bob, 283
Hatch, Orrin, 256
Hatcher, Teri, 540
Hatfield, Mark O., 652n116
Havel, Vaclav, 368, 486, 495, 496n

Johnson, Lyndon Baines (LBJ), 112, 113–14, 146, 238, 262, 363, 407n, 501; assassination of JFK and, 274; balanced budget and, 361; death of Prescott Bush and, 666n161; election of (1964), 123, 132; GHWB and, 135, 136–37, 143; GHWB and visit to LBJ ranch, Stonewall, TX, 144, 661n144; Great Society, 132, 134; long memory of, 143; partisanship and, 133; State of the Union address (1968), 136–37; Texas politics and, 654n119, 661n144, 662n146; Vietnam War, 132–33, 137; as VP, 671n115; withdrawal from 1968 presidential race, 137

Johnson, Owen, 642n73

Johnson, Tom, 661n144

Jones, Edith, 419

Jones, Shirley, 340

Jordan, Hamilton, 248, 503

Jordan, Vernon, 532, 584

Joulwan, Gen., 672n177

Juan Carlos, King of Spain, 557

Judd, Naomi, 520

J. Walter Thompson agency, 131

Kaufman, Ron, 578

Keene, David, 215–16, 225

Kelley, Kitty, 406

Kemp, Jack, 239, 243, 244, 269, 298, 309, 310, 325, 326, 508; on GHWB's list for VP slot, 326, 335, 336, 337; as housing and urban development secretary, 395

Kempton, Murray, 596

Kennebunkport, ME: activities and entertainment in, 18; Barbara Pierce meets the Walker-Bush clan at, 54–56; Bert Walker and, 15, 18, 26, 56; Cape Arundel golf course, 481, Dorothy Walker Bush at, 18–19, 529; Dorothy Walker Bush married at, 68; Dotty Walker Bush born at, 17; George W. at, 551; GHWB as president, Gulf War and, 437–39; GHWB as president, meetings at Walker's Point, 370, 371, 373, 437–38, 479–80, 502; GHWB at, 25, 26–27, 177, 295, 481, 483–86, 488–89, 529, 540, 542–43, 552–53, 554–55, 593, 600–601; GHWB buys Walker's Point, 304, 703n304; GHWB family at, 142;

GHWB's boat, *Fidelity*, 399, 439, 489, 593; Martha Walker and, 16; St. Ann's Episcopal Church, 18, 19, 481, 594; Walker's Point, xv, xx, 17; Walker's Point campaign strategy meeting (1988), 332–33

Kennedy, Edward "Ted," 149, 336, 471, 490, 592

Kennedy, John F., 21, 262, 337, 345, 777n560; assassination of, 119, 653–54n119; Berlin Wall and, 379; New Frontier, 115; plaque at the Hotel Texas for, 271; style of, xviii; unpopularity in Texas, 119–20, 653–54n119

Kennedy, Joseph P., 777n560

Kennedy, Patrick, 592

Kennedy, Paul, 361

Kennedy, Robert "Bobby" assassination, 140

Kent, Bruce, 286

Kerr, Baine, 106, 107, 109–11, 166

Kerr, Mildred, 109–11, 212

Kerrey, Bob, 500

Kerry, John, 577–79

Kilgore, Joe, 654n119

Kilner, Joan, 44

Kimmitt, Robert, 337, 338

Kinch, Sam, Jr., 149

King, Martin Luther, Jr., 120, 139; assassination of, 137

King, Rodney, 504

Kingsley, Charles, 25

Kingsport, TN, 19

Kinsley, Michael, 344

Kirkpatrick, Jeane, 288

Kissinger, Henry, 127, 128, 155, 169, 172, 174–75, 190, 200; Carter and, 202; China and, 158–59, 182, 183, 184–85, 187, 189n174; dinner with the Bushes, 155; Ford administration changes and, 190, 193; GHWB and, 160, 248, 460; GHWB appointed China envoy and, 178, 179; GHWB as CIA director and, 193, 198, 676–77n193; GHWB-Dukakis debate and, 346; on GHWB's term as most tumultuous since Truman's, 355; GHWB's VP hopes and, 689n244, 690n247; Reagan and, 246–47, 250, 251, 252

Kissinger, Nancy, 184